560115385601153856011

CURRENT BIOGRAPHY

CURRENT BIOGRAPHY

WHO'S NEWS AND WHY
1950

EDITED BY

Anna Rothe

ASSISTANT EDITOR

Elizabeth Prodrick

THE H. W. WILSON COMPANY
NEW YORK, N. Y.

ELEVENTH ANNUAL CUMULATION—1950

PRINTED IN THE UNITED STATES OF AMERICA

Copyright 1951
by
THE H. W. WILSON COMPANY

Preface

During 1950 CURRENT BIOGRAPHY presented an average of thirty articles monthly. Of the total of 335 biographies published in those eleven current issues and here cumulated in one alphabet, forty were about women and approximately eighty were about individuals outside the United States. Following the practice begun in 1946, this Yearbook also contains the usual "bonus" of twenty biographies of authors which were originally printed during the year in the WILSON LIBRARY BULLETIN.

CURRENT BIOGRAPHY continues to publish superseding articles about people whose biographies first appeared in the 1940 or 1941 Yearbook, the two volumes now out of print. Among the twenty-four biographees in that group are Bernard M. Baruch, Leo Durocher, Associate Justice William O. Douglas, J. Edgar Hoover, and Pope Pius XII. These as well as all other biographies published in the course of 1950 were subject to revision to provide for any major changes in an individual's position.

Another item of statistics concerns the "Cumulated Index—1940-1950," which begins on page 654. That eleven-year compilation contains some seven thousand entries for biographies, obituary notices, and "See references." In this connection it should be mentioned that the 52-page index is available for fifty cents as a separate pamphlet, which some librarians find more convenient to use than the list at the back of this volume.

The assembling of material for these biographies entails thorough-going research. Files of clippings are drawn upon when a name is selected for inclusion in CURRENT BIOGRAPHY. Indexes to magazine articles and books guide writers to a mass of information which is culled for biographical and background facts. Various "Who's Whos," encyclopedias, and other reference works contribute data. Information is also obtained from government offices and a variety of commercial and educational organizations. Whenever it is possible to get in touch with the subjects of the biographies, they are asked to confirm or correct facts; it should be pointed out, however, that these are not authorized biographies in the usual sense of that word.

A.R.

Contents

Explanations

Authorities for biographees' full names, with few exceptions, are the bibliographical publications of The Wilson Company. When a biographee prefers a certain name form, that is indicated in the heading of the article. For example, "Baruch, Bernard M(annes)" means that Baruch commonly uses only the initial of his second given name; and when a professional name like "Hutton, Betty" appears in the heading, the original name is given in the article itself.

The heading of each article includes the pronunciation of the name if it is unusual, date of birth (if obtainable), and occupation. The article is supplemented by a list of references to sources of information, in two alphabets: (1) newspapers and periodicals, (2) books. Space limitation requires that these bibliographies be confined to sources of strictly biographical nature.

References to newspapers and periodicals are listed in abbreviated form; for example, "Sat Eve Post 217:14-15 S 30 '44 por" means *Saturday Evening Post*, volume 217, pages 14-15, for September 30, 1944, with portrait. (See the section "Periodicals and Newspapers Consulted" for full names of the publications.) The books given as references are limited to those of a biographical nature, including such reference works as *Who's Who in America, Living Musicians,* etc. (See the section "Biographical References Consulted" for complete list.) The reference following each obituary notice is to the New York *Times*; these notices appear for persons whose biographies have been published in CURRENT BIOGRAPHY. When a name in the body of an article is followed by a superior reference, such as '46, the reference is to the year in which CURRENT BIOGRAPHY published an article on that person. Such references are made when the other articles have a bearing on the subject at hand.

As indicated in the table of contents, this volume contains three name indexes, the purposes of which are self-evident. The all-inclusive index—the cumulated index to the biographies and obituary notices in the eleven volumes of CURRENT BIOGRAPHY published thus far— includes references to monthly issues as well as to Yearbooks.

KEY TO PRONUNCIATION
(Based on Webster's Guide to Pronunciation*)

ā	āle	N	Not pronounced, but indicates the nasal tone of the preceding vowel, as in the French *bon* (bôN).	û	ûrn; French eu, as in *jeu* (zhû); German ö, oe, as in *schön* (shûn), *Goethe* (gû'tě).
â	câre				
ă	ădd				
ȧ	loyȧl				
ä	ärm				
à	àsk				
a	sofa			ŭ	tŭb
		ō	ōld	ü	Pronounced approximately as ē, with rounded lips: French u, as in *menu* (mē-nü'); German ü, as in *grün*.
ē	ēve	ô	ôrb		
ĕ	ĕnd	ŏ	ŏdd		
ê	makêr	oi	oil		
		o͞o	o͞oze		
g	go	o͝o	fo͝ot		
		ou	out		
ī	īce			zh	azure
ĭ	ĭll	*th*	then		
		th	thin	′ = main accent
ᴋ	German ch as in *ich* (īᴋ)	ū	cūbe	″ = secondary accent

(*Exceptions: *th* in then; main and secondary accents.)

KEY TO ABBREVIATIONS

AAA	Agricultural Adjustment Administration
A.A.A.A.	Amateur Athletic Association of America
A.A.U.	Amateur Athletic Union
ABC	American Broadcasting Company
A.C.L.U.	American Civil Liberties Union
ADA	Americans for Democratic Action
AEC	Atomic Energy Commission
AEF	American Expeditionary Force
AFL	American Federation of Labor
Ag	August
A.L.A.	American Library Association
A.M.A.	American Medical Association
AMG	Allied Military Government
Ap	April
A.P.	Associated Press
ASCAP	American Society of Composers, Authors and Publishers
ASNE	American Society of Newspaper Editors
ATC	Air Transport Command
AVC	American Veterans Committee
AWVS	American Women's Voluntary Services
b.	business address
B.A.	Bachelor of Arts
BBC	British Broadcasting Corporation
B.D.	Bachelor of Divinity
B.L.S.	Bachelor of Library Science
B.S.	Bachelor of Science
CAA	Civil Aeronautics Administration
CAB	Civil Aeronautics Board
C.B.	Companion of the Bath
C.B.E.	Commander of (the Order of) the British Empire
CBS	Columbia Broadcasting System
CCC	Civilian Conservation Corps
C.E.	Civil Engineer
CEA	Council of Economic Advisers
C.E.D.	Committee for Economic Development
CIO	Congress of Industrial Organizations
C.M.G.	Companion of (the Order of) St. Michael and St. George
Com.	Commodore
CWA	Civil Works Administration
CWS	Chemical Warfare Service
D	December
D.A.R.	Daughters of the American Revolution
D.C.L.	Doctor of Civil Law
D.D.	Doctor of Divinity
D.Eng.	Doctor of Engineering
D.F.C.	Distinguished Flying Cross
D.J.	Doctor of Jurisprudence
D.Lit.	Doctor of Literature
D.Mus.	Doctor of Music
DP	Displaced Person
D.Pol.Sc.	Doctor of Political Science
D.Sc.	Doctor of Science
D.S.C.	Distinguished Service Cross
D.S.M.	Distinguished Service Medal
D.S.O.	Distinguished Service Order
ECA	Economic Cooperation Administration
ECOSOC	Economic and Social Council
ERP	European Recovery Program
ESA	Economic Stabilization Administration
F	February
FAO	Food and Agriculture Organization
FBI	Federal Bureau of Investigation
FCA	Farm Credit Administration
FCC	Federal Communications Commission
FEPC	Fair Employment Practice Committee
FERA	Federal Emergency Relief Administration
FHA	Federal Housing Administration
FSA	Federal Security Agency
FTC	Federal Trade Commission
G.B.E.	Knight or Dame Grand Cross Order of the British Empire
G.C.B.	Knight Grand Cross of the Bath
GHQ	General Headquarters
h.	home address
H.M.	His Majesty
HOLC	Home Owners' Loan Corporation
ICC	Interstate Commerce Commission
I.F.T.U.	International Federation of Trade Unions
I.L.A.	International Longshoremen's Association
I.L.G.W.U.	International Ladies' Garment Workers' Union
I.L.O.	International Labor Office
I.L.P.	Independent Labour Party
INS	International News Service
IRO	International Refugee Organization
I.T.U.	International Typographical Union
J	Journal
Ja	January
J.C.B.	Juris Canonici Bachelor
J.D.	Doctor of Jurisprudence
Je	June
j.g.	junior grade
Jl	July
K.B.E.	Knight of (the Order of) the British Empire
K.C.	King's Counsel
K.C.B.	Knight Commander of the Bath
L.H.D.	Doctor of Humanities
Litt.D.	Doctor of Letters
LL.B.	Bachelor of Laws
LL.D.	Doctor of Laws
LL.M.	Master of Laws
M.A.	Master of Arts
M.B.A.	Master of Business Administration
MBS	Mutual Broadcasting System
M.C.	Military Cross
M.C.E.	Master of Civil Engineering
M.D.	Doctor of Medicine
M.E.	Master of Engineering
MGM	Metro-Goldwyn-Mayer
M.Lit.	Master of Literature
M.P.	Member of Parliament
M.P.P.D.A.	Motion Picture Producers and Distributors of America
Mr	March
MRP	Mouvement Républicain Populaire
M.Sc.	Master of Science
Msgr.	Monsignor, Monseigneur
MVA	Missouri Valley Authority
My	May
N	November
NAACP	National Association for the Advancement of Colored People
NAB	National Association of Broadcasters
NAM	National Association of Manufacturers
NBC	National Broadcasting Company
N.E.A.	National Education Association
NLRB	National Labor Relations Board
N.M.U.	National Maritime Union
NRA	National Recovery Administration
NRPB	National Resources Planning Board
NWLB	National War Labor Board
NYA	National Youth Administration
O	October
OCD	Office of Civilian Defense
OEEC	Organization for European Economic Cooperation
OPA	Office of Price Administration
OPM	Office of Production Management
OPRD	Office of Production Research and Development
OSRD	Office of Scientific Research and Development
OWI	Office of War Information
PAC	Political Action Committee
P.C.	Privy Councilor
PCA	Progressive Citizens of America
P.E.N.	Poets, Playwrights, Editors, Essayists and Novelists (International Association)
Ph.B.	Bachelor of Philosophy
Ph.D.	Doctor of Philosophy
por	portrait, -s
PWA	Public Works Administration
R	Review
RAF	Royal Air Force
RCA	Radio Corporation of America
REA	Rural Electrification Administration
RFC	Reconstruction Finance Corporation
RKO	Radio-Keith-Orpheum
ROTC	Reserve Officers' Training Corps
S	September
SEC	Securities and Exchange Commission
s.g.	senior grade
SHAEF	Supreme Headquarters, Allied Expeditionary Force
S.J.D.	Doctor of Juridical Science
SPA	Surplus Property Administration
SSB	Social Security Board
S.T.B.	Bachelor of Sacred Theology
S.T.D.	Doctor of Sacred Theology
S.W.O.C.	Steel Workers' Organizing Committee
T.U.C.	Trades Union Congress
TVA	Tennessee Valley Authority
TWUA	Textile Workers Union of America
U.A.W.A.	Union Auto Workers of America
UMT	Universal Military Training
U.M.W.A.	United Mine Workers of America
U.N.	United Nations
UNESCO	United Nations Educational, Scientific, and Cultural Organization
UNRRA	United Nations Relief and Rehabilitation Administration
U.P.	United Press
USO	United Service Organizations
U.S.S.R.	Union of Socialist Soviet Republics
U.S.W.A.	United Steel Workers of America
VA	Veterans Administration
V.F.W.	Veterans of Foreign Wars
WAA	War Assets Administration
W.C.T.U.	Woman's Christian Temperance Union
WFA	War Food Administration
W.F.T.U.	World Federation of Trade Unions
WHO	World Health Organization
WLB	War Labor Board
WMC	War Manpower Commission
WPA	Work Projects Administration
WPB	War Production Board

CURRENT BIOGRAPHY

1950

ALLAN, JOHN J(AMES) Mar. 24, 1887-
Religious and social welfare director
Address: b. c/o The Salvation Army, London,
England

The first citizen of the United States to be
appointed to high-ranking leadership in the international organization of the Salvation Army
is Commissioner John J. Allan. In July 1946,
after serving since his boyhood in the religious
and social welfare body, he was appointed Chief
of the Staff, his present post, in which his
superior is General Albert Orsborn [46]. As the
organization's chief executive officer, Allan is
responsible for its work in approximately one
hundred countries. A chaplain in both World
Wars, he was active in the forming of the
USO.

John James Allan, who was born in Hazel-
ton, Pennsylvania, on March 24, 1887, has
worked in the Salvation Army since his childhood days. His parents, James and Phoebe
(Strong) Allan, had come to America from
Ireland as pioneer Salvationists, and by the
time he was ten years old Allan had joined his
parents in open-air meetings, assisting principally by playing the cornet. At thirteen his
proficiency gained him the title of the best
young cornetist in the country, and for the next
three years he was known as the "boy solo
cornetist" of the Reeves American Band.

Young Allan was seventeen when, during an
evangelistic meeting, he decided to consecrate
his life to the Salvation Army. Going to New
York, he became a bookkeeper in the headquarters in that city. He also joined the eastern
territorial staff band, with which he continued
to be associated for the next twenty-six years,
first as cornetist, then as deputy bandmaster,
and lastly as executive officer. As a soloist with
the national staff band, he was to play in a
command performance before King George V
of England.

In order to become an officer in the Salvation
Army it is necessary for every candidate to
attend one of the four training schools for a
year of intensive study. Allan attended the one
located in New York City. Under a strict military and religious regimen, he took courses in
Bible history, sociology, physiology, English,
public speaking, and bookkeeping. In 1906 he
was graduated and received the commission of
probationary lieutenant. His first appointment
was to the corps in western New York State,
where he assisted in revival meetings held
throughout that area. Later he returned to headquarters in the metropolis to take the post of
Provincial Young People's Secretary. By 1909

JOHN J. ALLAN

he had been promoted to the rank of captain
and had decided on a program of assisting the
homeless men who frequented the Bowery district of the city. In order to acquaint himself
with the conditions of the men he wished to
help, he disguised himself as a Bowery "bum,"
moving with the men as they went the rounds
of employment bureaus, eating with them, and
living in Bowery hotels. For the next nine
years Allan remained in that neighborhood and
rose to the rank of adjutant. In this work he
was helped by his wife, the former Maude Eva
Parsons. They had been married in 1909, while
both were captains in the Salvation Army.

With the entrance of the United States in
World War I, Allan was chosen the first Salvation Army chaplain for the United States
Armed Forces, during 1918 serving overseas
with the Seventy-seventh Division as senior
chaplain. He conducted services at St. Omer,
Baccarat, and Ramberville, organized the Argonne Players, one of the entertainment groups
in the AEF, and assisted in removing the
wounded and dead from the battlefields of two
major engagements. Later in the war he was
given the rank of major chaplain, the highest
military rank then granted to clergymen serving
with the army, and was appointed to General
Army Headquarters to assist in organizing
the chaplains' services for the AEF. For con-

ALLAN, JOHN J.—*Continued*
spicuous bravery he was awarded the Croix de
Guerre by the French Government.

After the war Adjutant Allan returned to
the United States to resume his position as
Provincial Young People's Secretary, organizing in 1920 the Pioneer Youth Summer Music
Camp, the first of its kind in the United States.
In 1923 he was promoted to staff captain and
made divisional officer of the Northern New
Jersey command of the Salvation Army. At the
end of a two-year period he was sent to Ohio
to organize the Central Ohio Division and there
he remained for eight years. In 1933, with the
rank of brigadier, Allan was transferred to the
New York headquarters and appointed Public
Relations Secretary for the eleven Eastern
States. He directed fund-raising campaigns, enlisting the support of business and professional
men and forming a group of eight thousand to
increase public understanding of the work of
the Salvation Army. From October 1940 to
December 1941 Allan, who had retained his
rank of lieutenant colonel in the United States
Army Reserve, served on the staff of the War
Department's Chief of Chaplains. It was during this period that he worked with the heads
of various welfare agencies in a cooperative
interfaith fund-raising and welfare program for
American servicemen that was to develop into
the United Service Organizations (USO).

At the end of 1941 Allan was promoted to
the rank of lieutenant commissioner of the
Salvation Army, in charge of the Central Territory, with headquarters in Chicago. He remained here until July 1946 when, as a Commissioner (the highest rank in the Salvation
Army) he was appointed Chief of the Staff,
second in command to the general of the international organization. In his work Commissioner Allan leads the evangelical organization
in its international system of religious and social services in ninety-seven countries and colonies, in which religious meetings were held in
102 languages. Other international statistics (of
the year before Allan became Chief of the
Staff) were: almost 18,000 corps and outposts,
operated 1,812 social institutions and agencies,
more than 1,000 day schools, besides naval and
military homes, shelters, food depots, industrial
workshops for men and women, and various
other social service centers. This phase of the
Salvation Army's program, however, is considered supplementary to its spiritual purpose of
"proclaiming and exemplifying through song,
word and deed, the regenerating and revitalizing
message of the Scriptures." Among Allan's
duties, stated the *War Cry*, are presiding at
boards and meetings "of many kinds and degrees of importance," and the handling of matters of administration before they reach Orsborn's desk—"responsibilities at once numerous,
diverse, burdensome, and entirely without intermission."

Since 1946 Commissioner Allan has been stationed in London, from which he came to the
United States in October 1949 for conferences
with Government and Salvation Army officials.
In Washington he was guest of honor at a
dinner where his leadership was lauded by

Generals Omar N. Bradley and George C.
Marshall. In the course of his visit the New
York Chapter of the Kiwanis, of which Allan
is a member, presented him with a scroll for
"distinguished service to the youth of America
and of the world." His program calls for keeping the Salvation Army "humble, giving its
attention to the man in the street—the unfortunate, the sinning, those who are touched by
none else."

The Allans, who have worked together in the
Salvation Army since their marriage, have four
daughters and a son: Maud, Jean, John, Vera,
and Elizabeth, and seven grandchildren. Mrs.
Allan was active in the organization's Home
League and since 1946 has supervised the International Comforts Department and is director of International Relief to Devastated Nations and Displaced Persons. Allan has served
on the general committee of the Army and
Navy Chaplains of the Federal Council of
Churches of Christ in America and was a director of the Welfare Council of New York
City and the Greater New York Federation of
Churches. He is a trustee of the Salvation
Army, and a member of the American Association of Social Workers and a charter member
of the American Legion. Commissioner Allan,
who is of stocky build, has blue eyes; his hair
and mustache are gray.

References

War Cry p5 Ag 10 '46
Who's Who in America, 1948-49

ALLEN, BETSY *See* Cavanna, B.

ALLEN, MEL Feb. 14, 1913- Broadcaster
Address: b. c/o Yankee Stadium, River Ave.
& 161st St., New York; h. 5430 Netherlands
Ave., New York 63

Mel Allen, who began his career as a broadcaster of sports events in 1939, in 1950 covers
the games of the New York Yankees and appears weekly on two newsreel sportscasts, a
television program, and on a network program
of his own. In the eleven years of broadcasting
thus far, Allen has reported All-Star baseball
games, World Series, and the 1949 Rose Bowl
football game. His Hooper rating has varied
from 4.2 to 10, and he has won many awards
in his field.

The eldest of the three children of Julius
and Anna (Leib) Israel (both of whom are
natives of Russia), Mel Allen was born February 14, 1913, in Birmingham, Alabama. His
parents gave him the prenames Melvin Allen,
which he was to adopt as his professional
name at the suggestion of his employers when
he began to broadcast in New York, and which,
as Mel Allen he legalized in 1943 when he
entered the army. (His brother, Larry Allen,
his junior, is now employed as statistician on
his broadcasting staff; he also has a younger
married sister, Esther.) The family lived in
Johns, a small town near Birmingham, where
Julius Israel owned a general store during part
of Melvin's childhood, which was followed by

residence in other towns in that State and in Greensboro, North Carolina. Melvin graduated from grammar school at the age of eleven and from Birmingham's Phillips High School at fifteen (in 1928).

A "letter man" in high school basketball, football, and baseball, Allen says his leading enthusiasm was baseball. At the age of nine he belonged to a baseball team of older boys; and at twelve he sold soda pop at Detroit's baseball park so that he might gain admission (he was visiting relatives in the Michigan city at that time). A year later, while living in Greensboro, he worked as a bat boy for a Piedmont League team.

After entering the University of Alabama, the youth continued to play in the three games. Then, becoming sports columnist of the campus newspaper in his junior year, he gave up active sports participation. Altogether, his activities during his eight years at the University of Alabama prepared him for his career as a sportscaster, the possibility of which he had not yet realized. Majoring as an undergraduate in political science and obtaining his B.A. degree in 1932, he began the study of law; his degree in that subject was awarded in 1936. As a student he worked in a shoe store in Tuscaloosa until he won a teaching fellowship. His assignment to teach speech at the university led to his appointment as manager of the campus public address system. "From then on," as one sports writer commented, "the stage was set for the entrance of one of the best sportscasters in the field."

In 1935 Frank Thomas, Alabama's Crimson Tide grid coach, asked Melvin Israel to announce over the public address system the details of the game—"who carried the ball, who tackled the ball carrier, and the names of substitute players." This resulted in a similar position with a Birmingham radio station. Later, when Alabama played Tulane University, he was heard by an executive of the Columbia Broadcasting System, and in January 1936 he joined that network as an announcer in New York. Contrary to some accounts, Allen states, his parents did not object to his giving up law, that they had not wanted him to become a cantor, and that his mother (who aspired to the concert stage) was especially pleased when he entered radio.

The Alabamian's first assignments with CBS were disk jockeying and news broadcasting, until a feud between the sports departments of CBS and NBC brought him into the limelight. After securing rights to cover a Poughkeepsie regatta in 1939, CBS was "scooped" when an NBC announcer reported the race from a plane. "Next weekend," related Tex McCrary and Jink Falkenburg (New York *Herald Tribune* of June 16, 1950), "CBS planned a double coup—Ted Husing was to cover the Drake Relays from a church steeple, and Mel Allen was assigned to cover the Vanderbilt Cup Races from a plane." Allen, who today is not fond of air travel, was not pleased with the prospect but overcame his fears. Rain canceled the automobile race, but Allen flew over Long Island, reporting on boat races and tennis matches for about an hour of "straight ad lib." This brought

MEL ALLEN

special CBS commendation, and by 1941 he was earning $30,000 in a year. He had already begun to cover the major college basketball doubleheaders at Madison Square Garden.

Allen's first broadcast of major league baseball occurred in 1939, as assistant to Arch McDonald. In 1940 he teamed with J. C. Flippen for the Yankee games and with Joe Bolton for those of the Giants; in 1941 he did play-by-play broadcasts for both of these clubs with Connie Desmond. In 1943, when Allen entered the United States Army as a private in the infantry, he had a record of broadcasting three World Series games and was among the most popular sports announcers. During his two years in the infantry he rose to become staff sergeant; he was then transferred to the Armed Forces Radio Service and made a featured announcer on the *Army Hour* program. Upon his discharge he became the radio voice of the New York Yankees, since which he has broadcast the 1946 All-Star game, the All-Star and World Series in 1947, 1948, 1949, and 1950. It was in 1949, when Joe DiMaggio hit four home runs in three games—after a long absence because of an injured heel—that Allen shouted "How about that!" over the microphone every time the player "belted a homer." Catching the fancy of the fans, the exclamation has become so closely identified with Allen that he is known as "Mr. How-About-That."

In a February 1950 interview with Hal Boyle, Associated Press Staff writer, Allen said that the standards of sports broadcasting were getting higher. Crediting Ted Husing with setting "the modern pattern," Allen pointed out that Husing was the first to emphasize "accuracy and play-by-play accounts—as well as color." Television, Allen said, had made it necessary for an announcer to know the game as well as a coach or a player does. The New York *Herald Tribune*'s John Crosby, placing

ALLEN, MEL—*Continued*

Allen and Red Barber as the best of sports-casters, said that they had three qualities in common—"complete impartiality, a great zest for detail, and a thorough knowledge of base-ball. . . .Allen leans toward the old school of sports metaphor. 'One game away from tri-umph in the fall classic,' he is likely to say, . . . 'DiMaggio's swing is poetry in motion.'" Another distinction of the Alabamian's coverage of a baseball game is that he manages to "brief" the game so rapidly for late listeners that it does not annoy those who tune in early. Sidney Fields (New York *Daily Mirror*) at-tributes Allen's success "to the sheer delight he gets out of every event himself. Whenever there's a hot play and the fans roar, Mel roars along with them."

Allen's income, which he says is between $80,000 and $100,000 yearly, comes from his twice-weekly broadcasts with Fox-Movietone ($15,000), Dumont-Chevrolet televison weekly programs ($20,000), broadcasting regular games of New York Yankees ($35,000), Saturday night broadcasts over the Mutual network, and incidentals, as All-Star games, World Series, and other sports events. World Series baseball games are heard over some five hundred net-work stations, including Hawaii, Alaska, and Canada, with translations into French. Winner of *Sporting News* awards since 1945, in 1950 Allen received a "Michael" in the first prize-giving by the Academy of Radio and Televi-sion Best Arts and Sciences, in 1949 was put by *Motion Picture Daily* and *Radio Daily* in top place in the nation-wide poll on outstanding sports broadcasters. In 1950 he was elected president of the Sports Broadcasters Associa-tion. In an hour-long event, "Mel Allen Day," he was honored on August 27, 1950, at the Yankee Stadium; the recipient of gifts and a purse of $10,000, he turned over the fund to two universities for scholarships.

With financial success, Allen brought his parents to New York, where they live with their two sons. Six feet one and a half inches in height, Allen weighs 195 pounds; he has brown hair and hazel eyes. He says he would like to marry when he finds "the right girl." His reading is chiefly nonfiction—Churchill is his favorite author—except on air flights when he diverts his mind by reading detective sto-ries. His religious affiliation is Conservative Judaism, his charities nonsectarian. A con-tributor to the magazine *Sport*, he also has a publisher's contract for a collection of base-ball "yarns" he has gathered through the years, to be issued under the title *How A-bout That*.

References

Look 13:50 S 13 '49
N Y Daily Mirror p16 My 30 '50
N Y Herald Tribune p22 Je 16 '50
N Y World-Telegram p29 F 23 '50
PM p16 My 13 '46
Radio Mirror 34:58+ S '50

ANDERSON, MRS. (HELEN) EUGENIE (MOORE) May 26, 1909- United States Ambassador to Denmark

Address: United States Embassy, Copenhagen, Denmark; h. "Tower View," Red Wing, Min-nesota

Sworn in October 28, 1949, as United States Ambassador to Denmark, Mrs. Eugenie Ander-son of Red Wing, Minnesota, is the first woman in the history of her country to attain the high-est diplomatic rank. Mrs. Anderson, whose early ambition it was to become a concert pianist, has been active in Minnesota politics since 1944. A Democratic National Committee-woman since 1948, she campaigned extensively that year for the re-election of President Tru-man and for the successful Democratic candi-date for the United States Senate, Mayor Hu-bert H. Humphrey [49] of Minneapolis. She is the wife of John Pierce Anderson, artist and photographer.

One of the five children of the Reverend Ezekiel Arrowsmith Moore, a Methodist min-ister, and Flora Belle (McMillen) Moore (a former school teacher), Helen Eugenie Moore Anderson is of Scottish-English-Irish ancestry. She was born in Adair, Iowa, about sixty miles west of Des Moines, on May 26, 1909, and was brought up in parsonages in various Iowa com-munities ranging in size from her birthplace (with a population of less than a thousand) to Des Moines, the State capital. "Genie," as she is called by her relatives and intimates, cites her "father's and grandfather's political discus-sions" as an important early influence; her musical talent and ambition were nurtured by her mother, who "sparked her interest" with piano lessons when she was not yet six years old.

Graduated in 1925 from the high school in Clarinda, Iowa, (where her extracurricular activities included debating and school plays, as well as music), the future Ambassador taught piano in 1926 and 1927 and during the follow-ing year worked for the Northwestern Bell Telephone Company, to put herself through col-lege. She first attended Stephens (Columbia, Missouri), then Simpson (Indianola, Iowa) and lastly Carleton (Northfield, Minnesota) where she was a scholarship student majoring in music and philosophy. It was at Carleton that she met the young University of Chicago and Yale art student, John Pierce Anderson, of Red Wing, Minnesota, son of the late Dr. Alex-ander P. Anderson (of Swedish descent), in-ventor of puffed rice and puffed wheat. They were married September 9, 1930, after the end of the bride's junior academic year. Mrs. An-derson is thus the only member of her family who does not hold a college degree. (Her brother is now a physician in Oregon; of her three sisters, an English teacher and writer, an art teacher, and a writer respectively, two wear Phi Beta Kappa keys.)

For the first two years of their marriage, the young couple resided in New York City, where Mrs. Anderson, who had won a scholar-ship at the Institute of Musical Art of the Julliard School, continued her piano study, while her husband took further studies in his own field. In 1932 they returned to Red Wing to live in the family home on the Anderson 400-acre farm. There Anderson manages the portion that is farmed and engages in his professions of construction (three-dimensional) art and photography. "Tower View," the old twelve-room house, remains their permanent home, in which were reared their two children, Johanna (who is named after Johann Sebastian Bach and who inherits her mother's musical talent) and Hans Pierce (who shares his father's mechanical and artistic interests). Interested in aspects of child psychology, Mrs. Anderson took a course in that subject at the Institute of General Semantics in Chicago, and later taught in a nursery school. Her earliest public office was as the first woman member of the Red Wing school board.

A visit to Europe in 1937 strongly stimulated Mrs. Anderson's concern over world trends. Though the original objectives of the trip were to attend an exhibition of Van Gogh paintings in Holland and a series of concerts in Vienna, she also traveled through France, Czechoslovakia and Germany, and in the latter observed with alarm what she has described as "the totalitarian state in action." Returning home "deeply disturbed," she started (stated an article in *Pathfinder*) "an intensive study of international relations." She became a member of the board and of the speakers' bureau of the Minnesota League of Women Voters, for six years "lecturing [before church, farm, and trade union groups] on the United Nations, on the Baruch plan for atomic energy control, and on other aspects of American foreign policy, such as the Atlantic Pact and the Marshall Plan" (New York *Herald Tribune* report). Mrs. Anderson is still an active member of the League of Women Voters and the United Nations Committee of Minnesota.

In 1944, aroused by the isolationist record of a Republican Representative from the First Minnesota Congressional District, Mrs. Anderson entered the political field as a precinct worker for his Democratic opponent in that year's election and also placed herself at the disposal of the speakers' bureau of the Democratic National Committee. As a delegate to the Democratic State convention in the same year, she was instrumental in effecting the State-wide fusion of the Democratic and Farmer-Labor parties, and was appointed (also in 1944) Democratic-Farmer Labor party chairwoman for Goodhue County (in which Red Wing is situated), party chairman for the First Congressional District, and a member of the State central committee. An able organizer as well as a persuasive speaker ("In politics," she asserts, "to do something without strategy you're lost. . . .To grope is to fail"), she had become a figure of significant influence in her State by 1946-47, when she had a part in the expulsion of Communist elements from the combined Democratic-Farmer Labor party. By this time, too, she had become the vice-chairwoman of the central committee and a member of its Minnesota executive committee, entering both these posts in 1946. (Her several offices in the party organization she held concurrently until 1948 or 1949.) Mrs. Anderson, who was

MRS. EUGENIE ANDERSON

one of the organizers of Americans for Democratic Action, during 1947-48 was the group's Minnesota State chairman and a member of its national executive board.

Delegate-at-large for Minnesota to the Democratic National Convention at Philadelphia in July 1948, Mrs. Anderson became a Democratic National Committeewoman in the same summer, and "campaigned vigorously" not only for the re-election of President Truman but also for the election to the Senate seat (then occupied by Republican Joseph H. Ball [43]) of her ADA co-worker, Mayor Hubert H. Humphrey of Minneapolis. ("Her presence is always a signal for intelligent planning," Senator Humphrey has said of her, "Everyone respects her judgment, responds to her suggestions for action."

After election, accordingly, the newly chosen Senator from Minnesota, working with Mrs. India Edwards [49], woman's director of the Democratic National Committee, reportedly urged the appointment of Mrs. Anderson to an appropriate post; and as early as the second week in January 1949, there were rumors that she was under consideration for appointment as an envoy from the United States. Her nomination as United States Ambassador to Denmark was announced by President Truman on October 12, 1949, the appointment being confirmed by the Senate one week later. When the oath of office was administered to Mrs. Anderson at Washington on October 28, she was quoted as saying: "I feel that the biggest job facing our nation is that of developing human understanding between the people of the United States and the peoples of other countries. . . .I meet the challenge with no apprehension." Soon after her arrival in Denmark, on December 22 the envoy presented her credentials to Frederik IX [47]. She is the first American woman to receive the title of Ambassador; Ruth Bryan Rohde [44] was Minister to Denmark in 1933-36, Mrs. J. Borden Harriman [40] was Minister to Norway in 1937-41, and Mrs. Perle Mesta [49]

ANDERSON, MRS. EUGENIE—*Cont.*

went to Luxembourg as envoy of that rank in 1949.

"Mrs. Anderson was a pretty brunette as a college girl," wrote Alvin Davis in the New York *Post*, "and she's still a pretty brunette as a diplomat." She weighs 123 pounds and is five feet four inches tall; her eyes are gray and her hair is brown. Although the most widely publicized news photographs of Mrs. Anderson show her standing at a kitchen stove, she is perhaps more accurately to be pictured as a smartly dressed hostess whose living room has been described as a place "where scientists, physicians, lawyers, artists, educators and semanticists congregate" (*Pathfinder*). Aside from music, her principal "hobby," she has a deep interest in art, is an avid reader, particularly of the novels of Henry James. Her church is the Methodist.

References

Christian Sci Mon p4 O 25 '49 por;
    p1 N 2 '49
Ind Woman 29:2-4 Ja '50 por
N Y Herald Tribune p1 O 13 '49 por;
    II p3 O 16 '49
N Y Post Mag p47 O 28 '49 por
N Y Times p1 O 13 '49 por
N Y World-Telegram p11 O 17 '49 por
Newsweek 34:27 O 24 '49 por
Pathfinder 56:36 N 2 '49 por
Time 54:25 O 24 '49 por
Washington (D.C.) Post p3B O 13 '49
    por; p7D O 14 '49

ANDERSON, (HOBSON) DEWEY Jan. 14, 1897- Economist

Address: b. c/o Public Affairs Institute, 312 Pennsylvania Ave., Washington 3, D.C.; h. 601 19th St., N.W., Washington, D.C.

Dewey Anderson is the executive director of the Public Affairs Institute, of Washington, D.C., the organization he formed in December 1947 as a private research institute, "nonpartisan and independent," although supported to a large extent by both labor and liberals. He is one of a group of men who are regarded as the "working architects" of the economic Fair Deal plan of President Truman (St. Louis *Post-Dispatch*, June 19, 1949)—Anderson thinks economic restraints and supports always will be necessary to full employment. A former Stanford University professor and member of California's legislature, Anderson was also executive head of President Roosevelt's Temporary National Economic Committee of a decade ago; and for some months in 1949 he was on the Citizens Committee for the Hoover Report.

Born in Grand Forks, North Dakota, on January 14, 1897, Hobson Dewey Anderson is one of the twelve children of Hans Daniel and Amalia B. (Peterson) Anderson. His paternal grandfather was a Norwegian sea captain who sailed around Cape Horn in 1847; his maternal grandparents were also Norwegian. When Anderson's father was fourteen years old he emigrated to the United States, where, after some

years he became a homesteader in the Dakota territory. From there the family moved north to Grand Forks, Dewey's birthplace. In the West, Hans Anderson engaged in the canvas trade, and later established a grain freight business on the navigable Red River. Interested in politics, he was active in movements of both the Populist and Democratic parties and was on the committee that first nominated William Jennings Bryan for the Presidency. When the Great Northern Railroad advanced into the Red River territory, Anderson in 1900 moved his family to San Jose, California.

About his early life in California, Dewey Anderson writes: "I saw it [Santa Clara Valley] grow from a quiet cattle, grain and farming area to one of the most intensively cultivated fruit regions of the country, with fruit canning a dominant industry. Now, it has begun to pass out of that phase into a more heavily industrialized condition. . . .My father made canvas outfits for a circus that wintered in our vicinity. . . .I was fascinated by the circus, and was able to persuade my parents to let me join an acrobatic troupe of the circus. I was . . . about nine, and was made a 'top' in the troupe, doing the high casting and tumbling stunts. My circus career was cut short by a fall that gave me a compound fracture of the leg, and kept me in the hospital for almost a year. But it was a mighty lucky accident at that, as I view things now."

After finishing elementary school, Anderson entered San Jose High School where he became a member of the debating team, editor of the school annual, and excelled in gymnastics. He graduated in 1916, the same year his father retired from the canvas business. Urged by his father to carry on the firm and by a high school teacher to go on to college, Anderson withstood his parental opposition and entered Stanford University. He was there when World War I broke out. Because of poor eyesight he was not accepted for military duty, but he left Stanford to become a physical education director for the YMCA. In time this led to his being promoted to camp director of the Puget Sound Coast Defenses. In 1921 the YMCA appointed him a field staff member of its international committee to assist prisoners of war in Poland and the Baltic states. "Some of the camps," he has said, "were as big as good-sized American towns, and it was my job to run a goodly part of their lives." He held this post until 1924, when he was appointed executive secretary of the American section of the European Student Relief, an affiliate of the Hoover relief commission and largely financed by the Laura Spelman Rockefeller fund. One of Anderson's tasks was to direct the first program of curricular physical and health education established in a Russian university.

Anderson's experience in relief administration having stimulated his interest in economic problems, at the expiration of his service he returned to Stanford to study educational sociology and economics. He was inducted into Phi Beta Kappa and elected chapter president and national council delegate to the educational honor fraternity, Phi Delta Kappa. Graduated in 1927, he received his B.A. degree "with great distinction," and his M.A. the following year. While a student at Stanford, Anderson became an assistant to Professor Percy E. Davidson, with whom he was to collaborate in writing on economic conditions after his appointment to the faculty of Stanford in 1930. The same year in which Stanford awarded Anderson his Ph.D. in educational sociology (1932), the university chose him to direct an educational, economic, and social survey of the Alaskan natives. The survey was made at the request of the United States Office of Education and was supported by a grant from the Carnegie Corporation of New York. Accompanied by Mrs. Anderson, a trained psychological tester, he attempted to determine how contact with the white man had affected the Alaskans. Throughout the 20,000-mile trip by modern and primitive means of transportation, Professor and Mrs. Anderson used modern testing devices and survey techniques. As a result of his findings, he made various recommendations to the Government, a number of which have been adopted. The study was published under the title *Alaska Natives*.

In 1935 Anderson was elected to California's legislature for a two-year term. At the same time he was appointed vice-chairman of the legislative committee on the study of California's health insurance and was also chairman of the unemployment committee and of the interim committee on real property taxation. In 1936 he was appointed research director of economic problems for the John Randolph and Dora Haynes Foundation, Los Angeles. At the expiration of this directorship in 1938, he was named California's budgeteer by appointment of the Governor-elect. This post he held until the following year, when he was appointed director of the State's Relief Administration. During his terms in both these positions he was president of California's Conference on Social Work.

The economist became, in 1939, executive secretary and economic counsel of the Temporary National Economic Committee, organized in the second term of President Roosevelt's Administration. Anderson has called this post "the most important job" he ever had. The committee examined more than ninety industries in an investigation of the concentration of economic power in the United States. It is considered that its findings have had considerable influence on American business and political life and brought about revisions in the study of economic theory and practice in American colleges. The committee was disbanded in 1941. During this period (1939-1941), Anderson was also a member of the President's Conference on Care of Children in a Democracy.

Anderson was appointed Chief of the American Hemisphere Division, Board of Economic Warfare, in 1942. The following year he was commissioned a lieutenant colonel in the Army. His Army duty was deferred, so that he could accept the assignment of Chief of Supply and Transport Division in the State Department's Office of Foreign Relief and Rehabilitation Operations, the work of which was geared to making liberated areas self-supporting as quickly as possible. While serving in this post, Anderson was also appointed to the Food Ad-

Peggy Duffy

DEWEY ANDERSON

visory Committee of the War Food Administration, which included representatives from almost every Government agency concerned with food problems. He was on a subcommittee in that group which contributed to a fifty-page report sent to the Secretary of Agriculture proposing fundamental changes in the existing food program. In 1944 Anderson was named Chief of Field Operations for UNRRA. The next year he served as executive secretary and research director for Senator James Murray's Small Business Committee. As such, he aided individuals to prepare accurate attestations for presentation to the committee.

The Public Affairs Institute (in Washington) was organized by Anderson in December 1947; he is its executive director. A liberal, independent research institute, sometimes called the "Liberal Brookings," it, according to Anderson, "engages only in 'live research,' that is, work on important issues which require an assembly of the facts and their presentation to secure action." The economist says, "It works closely with members of Congress on request for expert help. It sometimes supports, sometimes criticizes the Administration and is often called upon by columnists and reporters for opinions." As of late 1949 it had issued seventeen publications dealing with problems in the five fields of resources, domestic economy, health and welfare, labor-management, and international affairs.

When the Citizens Committee was organized in mid-1949 to further the recommendations of the Hoover Commission on Organization of the Executive Branch of the Government, Anderson was made a member. In December of the same year he resigned, declaring the Citizens Committee "no place for a liberal" (New York *World-Telegram*, December 17, 1949); he saw the leaders of the committee as aiming at curtailment of the scope of Government welfare

ANDERSON, DEWEY—*Continued*

and service programs (New York *Times*, December 17, 1949). Later in the month, testifying before a Congressional committee, Dr. Anderson recommended that a national scholarship and loan program be instituted to provide educational opportunity to students from low-income families; that an employment practices commission be established to work with the problems of persons handicapped by disability or other special reason; that a welfare review board be created to study current social welfare programs and to make recommendations as to their nature and administration; and that the present social security law be substantially liberalized (New York *Times*, December 21, 1949).

Dr. Anderson has contributed to the literature of sociology and economics. His writings, commended for their value and interesting presentation, include: *Alaska Natives; A Survey of Their Sociological and Educational Status* (with Walter C. Eells, 1935); *Occupational Mobility in an American Community* (with Percy E. Davidson, 1937); *Our California State Taxes; Facts and Problems* (1937); *American Job Trends* (monograph, with Davidson, 1940); *Occupational Trends in the United States* (with Davidson, 1940); *Technology in Our Economy* (with Lewis Lorwin, John Blair, and Ruth Aull, 1941); *Report of the Executive Secretary on the Concentration of Economic Power in the United States* (1941); *California State Government* (1942); *Ballots and the Democratic Class Struggle* (with Davidson, 1943); *Recent Occupational Trends in American Labor* (with Davidson, 1945). He also contributes reviews to the *Journal of the American Statistics Association*.

Dewey Anderson is a member of the American Economic Association, of the American Political Science Association, and of the Western Public Administration Association. He says he is a "Roosevelt-brand" Democrat; his religion is the Methodist. Of medium height, he weighs 168 pounds; the color of his eyes is blue, of his hair, brown. Erma Sams, who became his wife on June 30, 1920, was an executive of the YWCA before her marriage; they have two children, Harry D. and Mrs. June Jensen. The economist and his wife number camping trips among their most satisfying recreations.

References

N Y Times p14 Jl 14 '43; p1 Ag 16 '43
Newsweek 25:62 F 26 '45; 30:63 D 22 '47
St. Louis (Mo.) Post-Dispatch II p1 Je 19 '49
Time 37:86 Ap 14 '41

Who's Who in America, 1948-49
World Biography (1948)

ANDERSON, MRS. JOHN PIERCE *See* Anderson, Mrs. H. E. M.

ANDERSON, MARIAN   Feb. 27, 190?- Singer

Address: b. c/o S. Hurok, 711 5th Ave., New York 22; h. "Marianna Farm," Danbury, Conn.

> NOTE: This biography supersedes the article which appeared in *Current Biography* in 1940.

Since December 1935, when she gave her first overwhelmingly successful recital in New York City, Marian Anderson has remained, in the judgment of many, "the world's greatest contralto." She has been applauded by audiences throughout the United States, and her tours abroad have taken her to numerous other countries of the world. In the course of a season she may give as many as sixty recitals, for which she draws upon her repertory of some two hundred songs. The recordings of the "consummate artist" include the works of Bach, Brahms, Handel, Saint-Saens, and Schubert, as well as Negro spirituals.

Marian Anderson was born on February 27 in the Negro residential section of South Philadelphia. Her parents, who had two younger daughters, were of modest means—her father was an ice and coal dealer, and her mother a school teacher. Mrs. Anderson was widowed in 1920. After attending the local grade school, Marian Anderson became a student at the South Philadelphia High School, from which she was graduated at the age of eighteen. Her chief interest from her childhood years was music. At the age of six she was a member of the junior choir of the Union Baptist Church and had sung before the congregation in a duet. Two years later, it is told, she earned her first money as a singer—the remuneration was fifty cents. Later, in the church's senior choir, which she joined at thirteen, the young girl learned how to sing several musical parts, demonstrating then the wide range of her voice for which she was later to become famous. She also sang at high school events, and it was then that John Thomas Butler, a Philadelphia actor, arranged for an interview for her with voice teacher Mary S. Patterson. From Miss Patterson Miss Anderson received her first training, gratuitously.

A benefit concert of the Philadelphia Choral Society, at which Miss Anderson was soloist, netted five hundred dollars for the young singer, money which enabled her to study for two years with Agnes Reifsneider, a leading contralto and teacher in Philadelphia. Meanwhile, Miss Anderson continued to earn small sums of money by singing at club meetings and similar events, and well-wishers made contributions toward her musical education. At the age of nineteen the singer auditioned for Giuseppe Boghetti, well-known voice teacher, who accepted her as a student. Under his tutelage she trained for a contest among unknown singers for the privilege of singing with the New York Philharmonic Orchestra at the Lewisohn Stadium in New York City. The result was that she was chosen from among three hundred competitors, and in August 1925 appeared as soloist at the outdoor concert, singing the aria

"O Mio Fernando" from the Donizetti opera *La Favorita*. She was well received and was immediately signed for an engagement with the Philadelphia Symphony Orchestra, then under the direction of Eugene Ormandy. Aside from this and invitations from various glee clubs, choirs, and Negro organizations, Miss Anderson received relatively few engagements. The next year she studied with Frank La Forge and then, on a scholarship granted by the National Association of Negro Musicians, she went to Europe for further training, particularly in languages.

In 1929 Marian Anderson returned to the United States for a recital at New York's Carnegie Hall. There she met with a moderate response, but subsequently she received a Julius Rosenwald scholarship for study abroad. In 1933 she met a German concert manager who agreed to arrange a debut for her in Berlin, at a cost of five hundred dollars to the singer. This recital a success, he then arranged a tour of the Scandinavian countries for a series of six appearances. Not only were the six recitals successful, but her engagements had increased to fourteen before she left Scandinavia. For the next two years her engagements took her through the Continent, with command performances for the kings of Sweden and of Denmark; singing for Sibelius, who honored her by dedicating the song *Solitude* to her; and concluding with an engagement at the 1935 Mozarteum, in Salzburg, Austria. It was there that Toscanini heard her and declared, "A voice like yours is heard only once in a hundred years."

That same year S. Hurok, hearing Miss Anderson at a Paris recital, signed an exclusive contract (still in effect in 1950) with her for her American appearances. It guaranteed a specified number of concerts and a specified sum for the season. On December 31, 1935, the contralto made her Town Hall debut, managing to appear in spite of a fractured foot, caused by a fall on the ship which brought her to New York. The curtain was lowered at the end of each group of songs so that the audience did not know of her injury until the intermission, when the curtain lowerings were explained. By this time the audience was completely won by her singing. The reviewers were equally enthusiastic, Howard Taubman of the New York *Times* particularly so—he described her voice as "stunning," and "transcending"; and her projection of songs as "music-making that probed too deep for words." In a second New York *Times* review Olin Downes wrote of her as a "contralto of shining range and volume, managed with suppleness and grace." Two additional concerts were given in New York City that season, both at Carnegie Hall before a capacity audience.

Thereafter Miss Anderson's reputation as an artist increased. In 1936 she toured Europe, Africa, and South America, was asked to sing at the White House, and during the 1937-38 season gave seventy recitals in the United States, described by her management as the "longest, most intensive tour in concert history for any singer." At this time she made her initial appearance in the concert halls of cities in the Southern States. The next season she gave seventy-five concerts in sixty cities. It was while arranging for an engagement in Washington, D.C., in 1939 that her manager was refused booking at Constitution Hall, the headquarters of the D.A.R. Protest against the racial discrimination came from leading musicians and public figures; and the action was climaxed by the resignation of Mrs. Eleanor Roosevelt from the D.A.R.. Within a few days Miss Anderson was offered the use of Lincoln Memorial by the Federal government. There, on Easter 1939 she sang on the steps before an audience of approximately 75,000. (A mural depicting this event has been placed on a wall in the United States Department of the Interior.)

Since that time Miss Anderson has continued to give sixty recitals each season, appearing for at least two every year at capacity-filled Carnegie Hall, at outdoor summer recitals, and in most of the cities of the United States, including those of the South. Her regular European tours were canceled during the years of World War II, but in 1949 she resumed her visits to the Continent. In 1949 she completed her fourteenth annual concert tour of the United States. The recordings made by Miss Anderson are in constant demand—250,000 copies of one of them, her Schubert "Ave Maria," have been sold, reported *Newsweek*. She has recorded many of the songs of her recital programs—of Bach, Brahms, Handel, Haydn, Schumann, Schubert; of Mendelssohn, Massenet, Saint-Saëns, Verdi, and Rachmaninoff. Her renditions of Negro spirituals are also available for the gramophone. The contralto has sung over the radio, on the *Telephone Hour*.

In general, critical opinion of Miss Anderson's artistry has not changed greatly from the reception given it in 1935, nor has she declined in popular appeal. In 1945 when she repeated at a Carnegie Hall recital the program she had sung ten years before at her Town Hall debut, she was greeted by an enthusiastic audience. Reviewers have usually reported her "superlative musicianship and understanding," the "sensitivity and finesse" with which she interprets her varied selections of songs and arias, and the "imposing volume and proclamative firmness of texture" of her upper tones. The New York *Herald Tribune* critic of her January 1950 concert at Carnegie Hall wrote that there was "innate warmth" in her higher tones, and her "personality, commanding presence and the impression she gives her listeners of being absorbed in each song were persuasive as usual." Her programs are carefully balanced, including the vocal works of Bach and Beethoven, the German *Lieder* of Schubert, Brahms, and Strauss, several arias from the Italian operatic repertory, and concluding with a group of spirituals. Her devout demeanor on the stage is commended by the reviewers, the New York *Herald Tribune* critic finding it a reflection of her "humility," her "inwardness," and her "rare artistry."

Miss Anderson has been described by Howard Taubman, writing in the New York *Times*, as a

MARIAN ANDERSON

"tall, stately woman, with an abundance of graciousness and good humor." *Time* wrote of her as a "dedicated character, devoutly simple, calm, religious"; she is reported to have said: "I do a great deal of praying." At a 1949 interview with *Newsweek* she was asked whether she had noticed any relaxing in Southern cities on the question of racial discrimination. She answered: "In some places the improvement is slower than in others, but there is evidence of a desire to take steps in the right direction." In cities where there is segregation, she demands "vertical" seating. This means that Negro ticket purchasers, though seated apart from others, must be alloted seats in every part of the auditorium.

When not on tour Miss Anderson lives on her 105-acre farm near Danbury, Connecticut, with her husband, Orpheus H. Fisher, an architect of Wilmington, Delaware, to whom she was married in July 1943. There in her studio, with the aid of a recording system and Franz Rupp, her accompanist since 1941, she prepares four or five complete programs each year. In July 1939 she was awarded the Spingarn Medal, given annually to the American Negro who "shall have made the highest achievement . . . in any honorable field of endeavor." The 1940 Bok award, given each year to an outstanding Philadelphia citizen, was presented to Miss Anderson in March 1941. Its accompanying prize of $10,000 became the basis of a Marian Anderson Award, administered by three trustees and used to help young people, without regard to race, creed, or color, to pursue an artistic career.

The Negro contralto has received honorary degrees of Doctor of Music from Howard University, Temple University, and Smith College. She is a member of Alpha Kappa Alpha. Miss Anderson's habit of referring to herself in the first person plural when speaking of her singing

has been attributed to "the humility with which she has always approached her great gift of song, and to the fact that she looks upon her accompanist as a full partner" (*Newsweek*). "There was a time when I was very much interested in applause and the lovely things they said," she says. "But now we are interested in singing so that somebody in the audience will leave feeling a little better than when he came."

References

    N Y Times VII p9 Ap 6 '41
    Newsweek 33:84-6 Ap 25 '49
    Time 48:59-60 D 30 '46

    Ewen, D. ed. Living Musicians (1940)
    Hurok, S. Impresario; a Memoir (1946)
    Thompson, O. ed. International Cyclopedia of Music and Musicians (1949)
    Who's Who in America, 1948-49
    Who's Who in Colored America, 1950
    World Biography (1948)

APPLEY, LAWRENCE A(SA) Apr. 22, 1904- Personnel and administrative executive
Address: b. c/o American Management Association, 330 W. 42d St., New York 18; h. 11 Tuxedo Rd., Glen Ridge, N.J.

Lawrence A. Appley, authority on the various aspects of business and industrial management, in 1948 became the president of the American Management Association, a nonprofit organization devoted to the practical solution of management problems and the development of the science of management. A frequent contributor to periodicals in the administrative fields, Appley is a past deputy chairman of the United States Government's War Manpower Commission and has been an executive of the Socony-Vacuum Oil Company, the Vick Chemical Company, and Montgomery Ward and Company.

The youngest of three children, Lawrence Asa Appley was born on April 22, 1904, in Nyack, New York, to Joseph Earl and Jessie (Moore) Appley. Appley's paternal grandfather had been a carpenter and shoemaker. His father was a Methodist minister whose biennial change in pastorates made it necessary for him to move frequently from one town to another. Young Appley, with his parents and two sisters, lived successively in Pittsburgh and Myersdale (Pennsylvania), and in North Tarrytown, Yonkers, Fleischmanns, Ellenville, and Kingston (New York). It was, accordingly, in the public schools of these towns that the boy received his elementary education. For his secondary education he was enrolled at Mount Hermon (Massachusetts) School for Boys, a private institution, where his extra-curricular activities included basketball, football, debating, and membership in the glee club. He also earned some money by waiting on table and doing a number of janitorial chores.

Following his graduation from Mount Hermon in 1923, Appley entered Ohio Wesleyan University. There he was freshman class president, a member of Chi Phi and of Delta Sigma Rho, the latter the honorary forensic fraternity. To pay his way through college, he held a number of part-time jobs during school years and vacations: he worked as a washing machine salesman, short-order cook, motorcycle policeman, truck driver, and high school debate coach; he also spent a summer as streetcar conductor on a Broadway line in New York City. For the year 1924-25 he withdrew from classes entirely to teach the eight grades of a one-room, 35-pupil elementary school at Mahopac Mines, New York. Appley's major course of study at Wesleyan was English. When he received his B.A. degree from the university in 1927, he had completed four years of study in three years, and had been awarded Chi Phi's 1927 Sparks Scholarship Medal. That summer he did graduate work at Ohio State University.

In preparation for a career in law, Appley had given particular study to speech and had been a member of the college debating team. As a participant in a debating match with Colgate University in his senior year he had attracted the attention of the Colgate debate coach. Through the latter an interview was arranged between Appley and the head of the Colgate English department, and as a result Appley was engaged as Colgate speech instructor and debate coach, a position which he held for three years, from 1927 to 1930.

During the summer of 1929 Appley took graduate studies in public administration at Syracuse University's Maxwell School of Citizenship. At that time, he has related, his interest was divided between business administration and political science. His ultimate choice of profession was influenced by a Syracuse professor, Dr. Herman Beyle, who discussed industrial personnel administration as a career and brought to his attention Tead and Metcalf's book on that subject. "The book," says Appley, "did the trick completely. From then on, I was determined to get into industrial personnel administration, with emphasis upon industrial education and training work."

In connection with his work as a Colgate instructor Appley met the Albany (New York) Law School debate coach, who introduced him to the late Robert Ryan, then personnel director of the Albany division of the Standard Oil Company of New York. After a series of interviews with other company executives, Appley was engaged as personnel manager of the Buffalo division of the company in August 1930; he remained in Buffalo for four years. At the end of that time, in 1934, when the Standard Oil Company of New York and the Vacuum Oil Company merged to become Socony-Vacuum Oil Company, Appley was offered the position of educational director for the firm, in both its domestic and foreign operations. The new position brought him to New York City. In the course of the next seven years he visited European and Near Eastern countries as supervisor of Socony-Vacuum's training program. While on the staff of the oil company Appley from 1938 to 1941 was adviser to the United States Civil Service Commission on administrative organization, traveling to Washington from New York every few weeks to lecture to groups of Government administrators on personnel problems.

LAWRENCE A. APPLEY

When the United States Government's National Defense Program was being launched before World War II, Appley went to Washington in March 1941 as expert consultant on civilian and personnel training to the Secretary of War. In the meantime he had left Socony-Vacuum in 1941 to become vice-president in charge of personnel and, later, a member of the board of directors of Vick Chemical Company, New York.

After the Japanese attack on Pearl Harbor in 1941, Appley obtained leave of absence from the Vick company to remain at his Washington post. This position was terminated in December 1942, vhen he was appointed director of the placement bureau of the War Manpower Commission. Within two weeks of this first association with WMC, he was named executive director of the agency. To the responsibilities of this office were later added the duties of WMC deputy chairman under Paul V. McNutt [40]. Nation's Business commented that those familiar with the WMC say "that a lot of healthy changes took place immediately after . . . Appley took hold. People began to find out what their jobs were. Jurisdictional strife began to disappear. Businessmen who had to contact War Manpower began to hope that something would be done about their problems."

Appley returned to his New York office of the Vick Chemical Company when he resigned from the WMC (for reasons of health, on July 1, 1944), but left the company in 1946 to become a vice-president and member of the board of directors of Montgomery Ward and Company, in Chicago, he was in charge of the company's personnel and public relations until his resignation two years later.

On July 1, 1948, Appley began his full-time duties as president of the American Management Association. He was appointed to succeed

APPLEY, LAWRENCE A.—*Continued*

Alvin E. Dodd [47] in the post when Dodd was elevated to the newly created position of honorary president. Appley had previously been an A.M.A. director, a member of the group's executive committee, and vice-president in charge of A.M.A.'s personnel division. As president, he guides the conferences, publications, and research of the association, which acts as a clearing house for information on business management, serving its 12,500 members (companies and individuals) through general management conferences and through its seven specialized divisions of office management, personnel, production, marketing, finance and accounts, insurance, and packaging. Among the questions discussed by six company presidents at the 1950 conference were: "How do you keep yourself informed about the activities of the various departments of your company?" and "How does a company promote 'climate' that attracts and holds individual employees?"

The precept "Do unto others as you would have them do unto you" is the basis of his theory of management, Appley wrote in *Personnel* (the association's periodical). This, he says, "is the main principle of good management." The titles of some of Appley's contributions to various professional and business magazines are indicative of his beliefs: "Management's Responsibility to its Forgotten People" (*Personnel*, No. 91, 1945); The Human Element in Personnel Management" (*Hospitals*, May 1942); "I Like to Work for That Man" (*Manufacturers' News*, May 1938); 'Employee Education and Counseling Programs" (*Personnel*, No. 35, 1938). (A 1950 list of his writings contained some forty titles.) "Managements," he declared in the February 1950 issue of *Public Relations Journal*, "are now being evaluated . . . upon the opportunity . . . they give . . . workers for getting something out of their work situation other than income. . . . Competitive survival now depends upon the skill of management to develop the finest and most productive working force of which it is capable." Appley believes that, although technological skill is essential, skill in human relations determines the capacity of a company to produce and distribute its products successfully.

The personnel and management expert received the War Department Citation for Meritorious Civilian Service in 1944 and was awarded the Presidential Medal for Merit in 1946. The honorary degree of Doctor of Laws was conferred upon him by Ohio Wesleyan in 1946. In 1948 Appley was a member of the Hoover Commission's Personnel Policy Committee. Since then he has been a member of the Personnel Advisory Committee of the Atomic Energy Commission and has served on the President's Advisory Committee on Management Improvement in the Government since 1949. From 1940 to 1945 he was a trustee of American University (Washington, D.C.). He is a member of the Society for the Advancement of Management, and of the American Society of Mechanical Engineers.

The president of the American Management Association, who lives in Glen Ridge, New Jersey, is a past member of the board of edu-

cation of that town and a former president of the Glen Ridge Battalion Forum (1945-46). He belongs to two country clubs, in Glen Ridge and Absecon (the Seaview). His church is the Congregational, his political affiliation is Republican. On September 1, 1927, three months after his graduation from Ohio Wesleyan University, Appley married Ruth G. Wilson, a fellow student; they have two children, Ruth Ann and Judith. Appley is six feet one inch in height, weighs 195 pounds, has blue eyes and gray hair. A better than average golfer, Appley lists sailing as a favorite outdoor recreation and architecture as one of his interests.

References

Bsns W p22-4 My 22 '48
N Y Times p29 My 17 '48 por
Nation's Bsns 31:26+ Mr '43
Ptr Ink 224:80+ Jl 2 '48
Who's Who in America, 1950-51
Who's Who in Commerce and Industry
(1948)

ARNOLD, HENRY H(ARLEY) June 25, 1886—Jan. 15, 1950 Commanding general of the United States Army Air Forces, World War II; graduate of United States Military Academy, West Point (1907); became pilot in 1911; with Aviation Service of the Signal Corps, World War I; was commanding officer of various air fields, 1922-36; appointed deputy chief of staff for air 1940, chief of Army Air Forces 1941, commanding general of Army Air Forces 1942; received rank of full general 1943; retired 1946; advocate of a single national defense organization. See *Current Biography, 1942.*

Obituary

N Y Times p1 Ja 16 '50 por

BARNETT, M(ARVIN) ROBERT (bär'nĕt) Oct. 31, 1916- Official of organization for the blind

Address: b. c/o American Foundation for the Blind, Inc., 15 W. 16th St., New York 11; h. Maplewood, N.J.

The executive director of the American Foundation for the Blind, M. Robert Barnett, was appointed to the office in September 1949, after serving for several years with the Florida Council for the Blind. Barnett, who was blinded at the age of fifteen, was a journalist before he entered the field of educational and vocational rehabilitation of the sightless and partially blind in 1941. At the American Foundation for the Blind he succeeded Robert B. Irwin [48], who retired after twenty-six years in the post.

Marvin Robert Barnett was born October 31, 1916, in Jacksonville, Florida, to M. Robert and Bessie (Groves) Barnett. The economic circumstances of the family (in which there were three children) were modest; his father found it necessary to work as a printer by day in order, says his son, that "he might work as an organist by night." Upon the death of his mother when he was a year old, the boy for six years was under the care of his grandmother, a teacher of the piano. Thus he and his two sisters received some musical training while they were still young. Later, because of family difficulties, he lived in a boarding home outside Jacksonville, the kind "you read about," comments Barnett. After a few years the family was reunited and the youth attended high school in Jacksonville. Realizing that he would soon need to earn his living, he studied such practical subjects as bookkeeping and the operation of business machines, worked as an apprentice in his father's shop, and, after the death of his father, in other local printing houses. He also began to develop his flair for cartooning. In sports he was too tall and thin to play on the football team, but he did play handball and swim.

In 1932, when he was fifteen, Barnett with several companions went into an orange grove near his home as a Hallowe'en prank and tried to make off with some fruit. The irate farmer fired a shotgun with the result that buckshot pierced Barnett's eyes, breaking the optic nerve of the right one and injuring the outer eye and muscle of the left one. Because of a possibility that the left eye might be restored enough to permit partial sight, it was several years before Barnett realized that he would be blind for the rest of his life. Subsequent operations have allowed Barnett to perceive what he describes as a "glow," reducing slightly the feeling of complete visual isolation.

It was not until 1935 that young Barnett agreed to the doctor's suggestion that he finish his high school education at the Florida School for the Blind at St. Augustine. Here he came under the influence of H. W. Beatty, principal of the academic department, who convinced the student that he could prepare himself for a useful career by taking a college degree. The school also provided him with his first acquaintance with other sightless individuals, some of whom, he recalls, had never had the opportunities he had had to see.

In September 1936, with funds granted by a philanthropic individual, Barnett entered Stetson University at De Land, Florida, where he was assigned two readers from the National Youth Administration. In the lecture rooms he took notes on his Braille slate, and from these notes he could prepare such complete outlines of his courses that other fellow students came to him for assistance before examinations. He was allowed to substitute elective studies for the regular laboratory science courses and did advanced work in journalism, history, and literature. In 1940 he was graduated, cum laude.

At Stetson Barnett had been active in student affairs, was chosen vice-president of his class, and served as the editor of the college literary magazine and the campus weekly newspaper. He also played the saxophone at student dances, having learned to play wind instruments when loss of sight made piano playing too difficult. Barnett feels that by playing the saxophone he gained confidence and a feeling that he "belonged" to the social group. Blind college students need only the additional assistance of readers for five to six hours a day. In American colleges in 1949 there are approximately

M. ROBERT BARNETT

five hundred sightless students, some of whom receive Government funds and assistance from the American Foundation for the Blind to pay readers.

Before he left college Barnett had begun to think of a career. His first choices—teaching, the law, or the ministry—reflect, he believes, his own limited knowledge of the occupations in which blind people can succeed. He had thought of working for the various social agencies interested in the blind, but abandoned the idea when he learned that he would first have to qualify as a professional social worker. Teaching at below-college level was closed to him because it was believed that his blindness would prevent him from maintaining the necessary discipline. Eventually, his friendship with the president of Stetson University led to his appointment as director of publicity for the school in June 1940. Subsequently, he was an instructor in journalism at the university until January 1943, when he was able to convince the editor of the Daytona Beach News-Journal that his lack of sight would not interfere with his efficiency in covering the news. He was made manager of the De Land bureau of the paper. Later he also served as correspondent for the Orlando Sentinel, the Florida Times-Union, and the Associated Press, covering stories from the county seat. With the assistance of a friend, he was able to furnish his papers with stories of the Florida hurricane. During this period he continued to give journalism courses at Stetson University, and, active in the De Land Lions Club, was its vice-president.

In 1941, when the Florida Council for the Blind was created, Barnett offered his assistance in publicity. In September 1944, feeling that he could do more significant work, he became placement officer for the council. In order to prepare himself for the task, he traveled through the United States and Canada, visiting institutions and workshops for the blind, and

BARNETT, M. ROBERT—*Continued*
took an intensive vocational course offered by
the Federal Government. As a result, Barnett
"sampled" ninety industrial occupations open
to the blind and learned the technique and experience needed by a blind person to succeed
in these occupations. In his position as placement officer and later, as supervisor of the employment department for the Florida council,
he assisted blind individuals in training for
work, found jobs in industry suited to the
abilities of the various applicants, and, in so far
as possible, convinced employers that blind
workers could be as efficient as sighted individuals. In October 1945 Barnett succeeded to
the position of executive director of the council, in Tampa. Four years later, in September
1949, he left Florida to accept the position of
executive director for the American Foundation for the Blind, Inc., becoming the youngest
official of that rank in national institutions for
the blind. Before going to New York, for a
year (1947-48) he was president of the National Council of Executives of State Agencies
for the Blind.

The American Foundation for the Blind, organized in 1923, is a nonprofit agency supported by endowments and private contributions.
It is affiliated with the National Industries for
the Blind and engages in research and the development of education and technical aids for
the blind, sponsors special legislation for the
blind, and has pioneered in the field of "talking
books," producing special long-playing records
as well as recording machines with slow-speed
motors. It is the opinion of Barnett that a blind
individual can perform any operation, industrial
or otherwise, which "does not require sight as
the final test of quality." Special educational
and technical assistance, however, is required to
rehabilitate a person after he has lost his sight.
The understanding of the general public is also
needed in order that blind persons may be extended the same employment privileges as sighted individuals. The education of children born
blind is a special problem and one which Barnett and the foundation are helping to solve
through the development of special educational
facilities so that eventually the blind child can
be integrated into the normal home and school
environment.

Barnett, who is tall and angular, has brown
eyes and brown hair. He moves and speaks
with assurance, has a sense of humor, which
he says has saved him from feeling "tragic"
many times. He has no hesitancy in speaking
of his own psychological adjustment to his blindness; nor does he hesitate, in making his daily
trip alone from his home to his office, to ask
the assistance of fellow commuters. When he
feels "frustrated" by his lack of sight he finds
relaxation in washing his car or completing
some woodworking project. In November 1941
he married Sara Ellen Buttorff, a student at
Stetson University who won the second prize
in a short-story contest which Barnett conducted while editor of the school magazine. For
a time Mrs. Barnett acted as a reader for him

and was part-time social reporter for the local
paper. They have a small son and daughter.

References

N Y Herald Tribune p20 S 15 '49
St. Augustine (Fla.) Record Jl 3 '49

BARUCH, BERNARD M(ANNES) (bär'
ōōk măn'ĕs) Aug. 19, 1870- Financier;
statesman

Address: b. 597 Madison Ave., New York 22;
h. 4 E. 66th St., New York 21

> NOTE: This biography supersedes
> the article which appeared in
> *Current Biography* in 1941.

Bernard M. Baruch, financier, whose name in
the press is frequently followed by the term
"elder statesman," was a key figure in official
and unofficial capacities on the American home
front in the two World Wars. First called to
Washington by President Wilson in 1916, he
has been adviser to both Democratic and Republican Presidents and legislators, often being
asked, or being himself moved, to give his
opinion on many topics. He remains a strong
advocate of stand-by legislation to provide for
industrial and manpower mobilization in the
event of a national emergency. Baruch had
made a fortune by his early thirties as a customers' man and speculator in Wall Street,
adding more millions through financing new
industrial enterprises.

The second of the four sons of Simon and
Belle (Wolfe) Baruch, Bernard Mannes Baruch was born August 19, 1870, in Camden,
South Carolina. Simon Baruch, a fifteen-year-
old Jewish immigrant from East Prussia in
1855, at twenty-two was a graduate of the
Medical College of Virginia, after which he
served for three years (1862-65) as a field
surgeon in the Confederate Army. The Wolfe
family, South Carolina plantation owners since
before 1800, traced its American beginnings to
the arrival, in New York in 1690, of Isaac
Rodriques Marhues, a Spanish-Portuguese Jew
"of education and means," states Harry I.
Shumway in *Bernard M. Baruch, Financial
Genius, Statesman, and Adviser to Presidents*
(1946). Baruch's middle name, Mannes, was
given to him as a tribute to Mannes Baum, the
Camden storekeeper who offered Simon Baruch
his first job in the United States and sent him
to medical school.

The Baruchs moved to New York City in
1881, where the doctor continued his career
as general practitioner, as well as specializing
in appendicitis and hydrotherapy. He also became professor in the latter at the College
of Physicians and Surgeons of Columbia University. In time, as leisure and means permitted it (recalls Bernard Baruch), his mother
became active in Jewish, Catholic, and Protestant charitable organizations, where she was
known as "La Grande Duchesse." The four
Baruch boys were sent to public schools; and
Bernard entered the College of the City of
New York in 1884. The tall, muscular, agile
youth was a star athlete—his sports were lacrosse, boxing, and baseball (there was no foot-

ball team at the college). As a result of an injury to one ear in a baseball game, his hearing became impaired to a degree which made him unacceptable physically for entry to the United States Military Academy. Baruch, whose lively interest in sports continues, for a time took boxing lessons.

The young man's first job, after receiving the B.A. degree in 1889, was with a house that dealt in druggists' glassware. Errands took him into New York's financial district, where the pace and excitement of commerce and its money-making possibilities attracted him. (He once had an unforgettable glimpse of J. P. Morgan, Sr.) As Shumway recounts it, a brief period with a small banking concern was followed by employment in the brokerage firm of A. A. Housman and Company; his salary had now risen to five dollars a week. Before this, for a few months in 1890, according to John Hersey in the *New Yorker*, twenty-year-old Baruch worked as a mucker and driller in the Colorado gold fields. There he was "hornswoggled" into buying some poor mining stock, a venture which taught him never to invest in anything he had not first thoroughly studied.

At Housman, Baruch began as an office boy. In the evenings he took courses in bookkeeping and contract law, "on his own" studied financial and commercial manuals, became known in a small way as an authority on securities. Before long he bought his first bond; he also learned that the risks he took on his gambler's instinct usually brought losses. By 1896, when he asked for a salary of fifty dollars (meanwhile, it had risen to twenty-five), Housman offered him an eighth interest in the firm. This was fortunate for both Baruch and the firm, for a large profit for Housman meant a correspondingly good commission for himself. As a customers' man he sought new clients, recommended several wise trades, received his $6,000 share of profits at the end of the first year. In 1897 his own venture in the sugar market brought a profit of nearly $40,000 on a $200 speculation. That year Baruch bought a seat on the Stock Exchange. Meanwhile, his partnership share in Housman and the firm's prestige increased as Baruch's "studiousness, astuteness, and speed" in tradings in tobacco, railroads, and copper proved highly profitable. At the age of thirty he was a millionaire. In May 1903 (a year after he netted one and a half million in a contest with Morgan) Baruch retired from the Housman firm to set up his own office in the field of industrial development.

For the next fourteen years Baruch invested for others and for himself in promising new enterprises. "The large industrial undertakings in which he was a big factor," Shumway reports, "were Texas Gulf Sulphur, Utah Copper, Intercontinental Rubber Company, and Alaska Juneau Gold Mining Company." The first pioneering effort gave the United States a continued control of the world sulphur market; the second doubled the world output of copper; the third demonstrated that rubber could be made from the guayule plant; the fourth that gold could be profitably extracted from a low-grade ore. Altogether, Baruch's twenty-two years in Wall Street (up to the

beginning of World War I) gained him the reputation of nearly always being right in his decisions. He has stressed that he was also ethically right—he did not sit on the boards of directors of the firms in which he managed investments, and that speculations in which he "cleaned up" (about which he was questioned in 1935 in Washington) were not the result of "leaks" or confidential information but the reward of reasonable and conservative thinking. He has stated that he never waited to sell stock at its highest point, nor to buy at its lowest. Once, when asked about his career as a stock trader, he said, "I make no apologies. I am a speculator. The word comes from the Latin 'speculari,' meaning 'to observe.' I observe."

The financier, a stanch Democrat, was a liberal contributor to the party's campaign funds; and when he met Woodrow Wilson (before Wilson became the Presidential nominee), he was convinced he had come to know one of the world's greatest men. Later Baruch made frequent trips to the White House. In August 1916, when the war in Europe threatened to involve the United States, President Wilson appointed Baruch a member of the Advisory Commission to the Council of National Defense, the financier's first post in the Government. (Wilson called Baruch "Dr. Facts.") By this time Baruch had liquidated his holdings, resigned from his offices in industrial concerns, and sold his Stock Exchange seat; and he was to turn more than five million dollars into Liberty Bonds.

To other posts, as chairman of the Committee on Raw Materials, Minerals and Metals, and as member of the commission in charge of purchases for the Allies, Baruch brought his knowledge of the sources, quantities, and cost of the chief materials of war. When the War Industries Board was created in March 1918, Baruch became its chairman, with "virtually dictatorial authority"; he drew up a master blueprint for industrial mobilization of materials and men on a priorities system. Shumway details some of the WIB chairman's most spectacular exploits, in which "red tape was given short shrift." The war over, Baruch resigned from the WIB in January 1919, after which he followed President Wilson to the Versailles peace conference as economic adviser, becoming a member of the Supreme Economic Council, chairman of the raw materials division, delegate to the committee on economics and reparations clauses. In October of the same year Wilson appointed him to the Conference for Capital and Labor.

For the first few years after the war, Baruch occupied himself particularly with the problems of American agriculture—he declared that farming was "out of alignment with other commercial activities because it has not followed them into the modern field of 'big business.'" In 1922 he was appointed a member of President Harding's Agricultural Conference, and he also served as adviser to the American Farm Bureau Federation and to the United States Grain Growers' Corporation; in 1925 he pledged a million and a half dollars to the rehabilitation of the South Carolina areas stricken with the boll weevil. The year before, he urged the for-

BERNARD M. BARUCH

mation of a Court of Commerce to act in business disputes. In 1928 he said he would support Al Smith for President.

Shortly before the 1929 Wall Street crash, when asked by a group of eager investors for a tip on the constantly rising market, Baruch, to their astonishment, suggested that they put all their money into four-percent bonds. After the crash (with his own fortune apparently unimpaired) he advised President Hoover on the organization of the Reconstruction Finance Corporation in which he refused a place. During Hoover's Administration he outlined a plan for removing profiteering in wartime as well as a plan for economic recovery.

With the coming of the New Deal under President Roosevelt (who offered him the post of Treasury Secretary), Baruch continued as an unofficial adviser to the President and the "Brain Trust." A post at this time (1933) was vice-chairman of the National Transportation Committee. It is told that as early as 1934 he urged the stockpiling of two important war items, rubber and tin, and in 1937 he submitted a plan for wartime mobilization to the Senate Committee on Military Affairs. In January 1941, he urged centralization of defense powers in the President, suggested that industrialists cooperating with the Government in the defense effort be exempted from the Sherman Act, and pled for more labor representation in the mobilization plan, for a system of priorities, and for ceilings on prices, rents, and wages. Through the years reports on his frequent trips abroad included mention of conversations with European statesmen.

On August 7, 1942 (the New York *Times* reported) Dr. Karl Compton [41], president of the Massachusetts Institute of Technology, Dr. James B. Conant [41], president of Harvard Uni-

versity, and Bernard M. Baruch were observed sitting together on a bench in Lafayette Square, the park across the street from the White House. (Baruch, who also likes to sit in the park near his New York home, calls the park bench his "office.") The three men comprised President Roosevelt's special committee, headed by Baruch, to survey the nation's acute rubber shortage problem. A month later the President sent to Congress with his approval the 20,000-word report of the committee, which warned the nation of the military danger inherent in the rubber shortage and suggested stringent ameliorative measures. The Presidential committee appointed March 6, 1943, to make a report on manpower again included Baruch. On June 9, 1943, James F. Byrnes [41], director of the Office of War Mobilization, announced that Baruch was to serve as his special adviser without title or salary. A short time later, November 6, 1943, OWM asked Baruch for a study of industrial adjustments in wartime and of postwar readjustment. Voluminous reports and recommendations came from the investigations: one (September 17, 1943) called for a labor priorities system, a reduction in the turnover of workers, the enlistment of all labor sources, and the curtailment of unessential activities; the other (February 18, 1944) outlined a postwar demobilization and reconversion program.

On May 31, 1945, about six weeks after the death of President Roosevelt, a memorandum from Baruch to President Truman was published, stating that the most important factor in making peace would be "the earliest definite settlement of what is to be done with Germany and Japan." A year later, March 18, 1946, Truman named Baruch as the United States representative on the United Nations Atomic Energy Commission. Baruch presented the United States plan for the control of atomic energy to the U.N. commission on June 14, 1946, and on December 30 of the same year the commission voted 10-0 (with Russia abstaining) for the Baruch proposals and the plan was submitted to the Security Council. The proposal would provide for an international atomic development authority to control, inspect, and license all atomic projects; for the renunciation of the bomb, at a time when controls and ownership were set up, after which the bombs were to be destroyed; for the punishment, without veto, of violators whose activities were potentially dangerous to world security; for violators there would be no protection in the use of the veto power, that being surrendered so far as it affects atomic energy. The following month Baruch and the other United States delegates on the commission handed in their resignations, stating that now that the plan had been formulated the problem should be handled by Warren R. Austin [44], United States delegate to the U.N.

After the completion of his work on the Atomic Energy Commission, Baruch continued to carry on "his favorite occupation of giving his country advice gratis" (in the words of the *New Yorker*). In April 1947 he warned the country that it was "on the brink of an engulfing inflation"; in January 1950 he called for legal enactment of a complete "stand-by mobilization plan," for the formation of a permanent mobilization agency and a constant inventory of national resources in relation to a possible war; in March 1950 he proposed that the National Security Council be reorganized into a "G.H.Q. for peace" under a leader "of the stature of General George C. Marshall"; and in May 1950 he reiterated his pleas for the immediate passing of "stand-by economic and mobilization laws"; when the war broke out in Korea in June 1950, he pressed for an expanded *Voice of America* to counteract Russian propaganda. According to Hersey, in 1948 seven Senators called on him separately for advice on how to vote for the Marshall Plan.

The article on inter-Allied debts in the *Encyclopædia Britannica* (1920) was written by Baruch. He has also written many reports, articles, and official memoranda, such as *American Industry in the War,* a report of the WIB of World War I, *Taking the Profit Out of War,* a memorandum submitted to a Congressional war policies commission in 1930, and *Priorities: the Synchronizing Force,* an article in the *Harvard Business Review,* March 1941. His unofficial, unpublished writings consist of innumerable letters and notes to Presidents, legislators, foreign statesmen, and other figures in public life and business.

In memory of his father, Baruch made a gift of $1,100,000 to Columbia University's College of Physicians and Surgeons, New York University's College of Medicine, the Medical College of Virginia (located at Richmond, Virginia), several other medical schools, and fellowships to advance the teaching and research in the field of physiotherapy. He has contributed as well to other organizations and causes, including the founding of a hospital in Camden, South Carolina, and the gift of $1,000,000 to various war relief agencies on December 23, 1942. A number of biographical articles mention the various occasions he has offered money to the Government and private concerns, when funds were not immediately available in emergencies. Baruch has been decorated as a Commander of the Order of Leopold (Belgium), Commander of St. Maurizio and Lazzaro (Italy), and Commander of the Legion of Honor (France). He was given the Distinguished Service Medal by President Wilson and a Medal for Services by the alumni of the College of the City of New York. More recent awards include the Freedom House Award in 1946 "for serving with vision and statesmanship in the world's quest for peace," and the 1950 Hearing Advancement Award "as the man who has done the most to help the hard of hearing." Baruch has received an honorary LL.D. degree from Williams College (1923), the University of South Carolina (1925), Johns Hopkins University (1933), Oglethorpe University (1933), the College of Charleston, South Carolina (1935), The Citadel (1937) and the College of the City of New York (1947). He also holds an honorary D. C. L. degree from Union College (1937).

In October 1897, the year he became a partner in the Housman brokerage firm, Baruch married Annie Griffen, granddaughter of an Episcopal minister, the daughter of a glass manufacturer. Their three children are Belle Wilcox, Bernard Mannes, Jr., and Renee Wilcox (Baruch) Samstag. Mrs. Baruch died in 1938. Nearly six feet four inches tall ("straight as a ramrod") and weighing two hundred and two pounds, Baruch enjoys hearty meals; he drinks rarely (the occasion may be a toast), and has not smoked since he was sixty-four. He has white hair, "sharp," blue eyes behind pince-nez, a strong "organ-like" voice. For some years he has used a hearing aid. He is revealed by John Hersey as courtly, voluble, and persuasive. In South Carolina he owns an estate ("Hobcaw Barony") of some twenty thousand acres in the coastal region, at which he and his guests rest, hunt, or fish.

References

Collier's 122:13 N 27 '48
Look 6:11 D 29 '42
New Yorker 23:28+ Ja 3 '48; 23:30+ Ja 10 '48; 23:30+ Ja 17 '48

National Cyclopædia of American Biography Current vol A (1926)
Shumway, H. I. Bernard M. Baruch (1946)
10 Eventful Years (1947)
Universal Jewish Encyclopedia (1948)
Who's Who in America, 1950-51
Who's Who in American Jewry, 1938-39
Who's Who in New York, 1947
World Biography (1948)

BASDEVANT, JULES (bà"dē-vaN' zhül) Apr. 15, 1877- President of the International Court of Justice
Address: b. Palais de la Paix, The Hague, the Netherlands; h. 1 rue Cassini, Paris, France

The President of the International Court of Justice of the United Nations is Judge Jules Basdevant of France, who holds his present office for a term of three years, beginning March 1, 1949. He had served as vice-president of the court during 1946-49. A professor in the Faculty of Law in Paris for many years, and a member of the now-dissolved Permanent Court of International Justice of the League of Nations, Basdevant has been a representative of his country at many international gatherings, including the San Francisco Conference at which the United Nations Charter was drafted. He was legal adviser to the French Ministry of Foreign Affairs from 1919 to 1941, when he resigned in protest against the policies of the Vichy Government. After the liberation, he was reinstated in his former Government and university posts.

Jules Basdevant was born April 15, 1877, in Anost, France, the son of Louis and Maria (Gauchey) Basdevant. He was educated at the College d'Autun, and then attended the Faculty of Law (Faculté de Droit) of the University of Paris, from which he received his LL.D. in 1900 and his Sc.D. in 1901. He became a lecturer in the Faculty of Law in Rennes University in 1903, and an assistant professor in 1906. The following year he was appointed professor

Official United Nations Photo.
JULES BASDEVANT

in the Faculty of Law at Grenoble University, where he remained until 1914.

Basdevant served from 1914 to 1918 in the French Army, in which he held a lieutenant's commission at time of his discharge. He was then appointed to the Faculty of Law in Paris. In 1922 he was made professor of international law and of the history of treaties at the University of Paris, and in 1924 became professor of public law. Some years later, in 1935, as professor at the Academy of International Law in The Hague, he gave a course that was regarded as one of the finest in that field of study (Jacques Arnassan in an unpublished article). In the course of his long teaching career, Dr. Basdevant has also been a professor at the Naval School and at the School of Higher Naval Studies, at the Free School of Political Science, and for a short period at the School of Political Science of the Jagellon University at Cracow. Among his former students Basdevant can count jurists in many countries of the world.

Shortly after the close of World War I, Basdevant was made legal adviser to the French Ministry of Foreign Affairs. He attended the Peace Conference in 1919 as a French delegate and legal expert; and later was named delegate to the League of Nations Assembly and the Disarmament Conference. From 1923 to 1941 he represented France at the League's Permanent Court of International Justice. He served as chairman of the Third Committee at the Conference for the Codification of International Law, and was a delegate to the Conference of Private International Law and to the London Naval Conference. He also filled the position of vice-chairman of the International Conference for the Suppression of Terrorism, and was France's representative at a number of other international arbitration meetings. In addition, he was a member of various legal

committees set up by the League of Nations, and gave his services to the International Institute for the Unification of Private Law and to the International Red Cross Committee at meetings in Brussels and London.

During the German occupation of France in World War II, Basdevant was asked to remain as legal adviser to Marshal Pétain's Government. On May 29, 1941, he resigned from this position in protest against certain policies of the Vichy Government. As a result he was suspended from the Faculty of Law in Paris, and subsequently was dismissed at the request of the German authorities. Threatened with imprisonment, Basdevant retired to Lyons for a short time, then made his way back to the capital. Unable to serve in Paris, he returned to his native village of Anost to collaborate with the local guerrilla fighters.

After the liberation of France, Basdevant was reinstated as legal adviser to the Ministry of Foreign Affairs and as professor in the Faculty of Law in Paris. He was a member of the French Delegation to the United Nations Conference on International Organization at San Francisco in 1945. He has also been France's alternate delegate to the General Assembly of the United Nations. Before the San Francisco conference, the French jurist represented his country at the April 1945 Washington conference, at which the draft statute of the International Court of Justice was prepared for the consideration by the later conference. Thus the new court, superseding the League of Nations' Permanent Court of International Justice, is the principal judicial organ of the U.N.

The first election of the court's fifteen judges was held in February 1946, at the London meeting of the U.N.'s General Assembly and Security Council. Together with Dr. José Gustavo Guerrero [47] of El Salvador, Jules Basdevant was chosen for a nine-year period. At the court's first meeting (April-May 1946, at The Hague) Guerrero was elected its president, and Basdevant its vice-president. About three years later, on March 1, 1949, Basdevant became the court's president and Guerrero its vice-president, the terms of office to be three years.

In April 1949, Basdevant read the opinion of the International Court of Justice that the United Nations is an "international person" and can bring a claim against a responsible government for reparations when one of its agents is injured in the performance of his duties; this principle, enunciated as a response to a request from the United Nations General Assembly for advisory opinion, is expected to strengthen considerably the prestige and power of the U.N. The same month the court announced its decision in its first case, assigning responsibility for an explosion following the mining of the Channel of Corfu, and later fixing the damages to be paid. "It is heartening to find the International Court of Justice handing down decisions with an authoritative voice," was the editorial comment of the Washington *Post* at the time of the announcement. The New York *Times* also acclaimed the judiciary body as "now operating as had been hoped, in the slow and painful process of building up once again a body of international law that all nations may respect." Judge Basdevant has pointed out that "the activity of the court depends upon the will of the states to appeal to it (*Christian Science Monitor*, September 30, 1949). The court, as of December 1949, had on its calendar three disputes (between Britain and Norway over fishing rights, Colombia and Peru over the right of asylum, and France and Egypt over damages to French nationals); also before the judges were requests for advisory opinions on the violation of human rights in the Balkans, the admission of new members to the United Nations, and the status of South-West Africa.

Among Jules Basdevant's writings (in French) from 1900 to 1936 are the following (their titles are rendered in English): "Relations of Church and State in Marriage Legislation"; "Hugo Grotius"; "The French Revolution and the Law of Continental Warfare"; "International Collection of Treaties of the Nineteenth Century"; "Deportations from the North of France and Belgium and International Law"; "Treaties and Conventions in Force between France and Foreign Powers"; "Italian Maritime Prize Law"; "British Maritime Prize Law"; "General Rules of International Law in Peacetime." His legal expositions have been described as "neat, precise, objective, with logical deductions, good sense, and clarity."

Jules Basdevant is one of the board of directors of the National School of Administration and the National Foundation of Political Science. He is a member of the Scientific Committee of the Dictionary of the Terminology of International Law, and of the board of the International Institute for the Unification of Private Law. An associate of the Royal Academy of Belgium, he is also a member and former vice-president of the Institut de Droit International, a member of the Association de Législation Comparée du Droit International and of the Union Juridique. He is vice-president of the United Nations League of Lawyers, an honorary member of the American Society of International Law, and an Officer of the Legion of Honor. The Institute of France has honored him by making him a member. The international jurist, who is of medium height, has white hair. On August 5, 1905, he married Renée Mallarmé; four sons (all of whom fought the Nazis) and three daughters were born to them.

References

Christian Sci Mon p10 S 30 '49
N Y Times p30 D 20 '49
U N Bul 6:271 Mr 15 '49 por
Washington (D.C.) Post p3B D 25 '49
International Who's Who, 1949
World Biography (1948)

BATTLE, JOHN S(TEWART) July 11, 1890- Governor of Virginia

Address: b. State Capitol, Richmond, Va.; h. Governor's Mansion, Richmond, Va.

After a twenty-year membership in the Virginia General Assembly, John S. Battle was in-augurated as Governor of Virginia in January 1950, as successor to William M. Tuck [46]. An attorney by training and a legislator with special experience in fiscal matters, Battle was chairman of the State Senate Finance Committee during the last years of his service in the General Assembly. Battle, who has the support of United States Senator Harry F. Byrd [42], leader of the dominant Democratic organization in the State, shares the Senator's Right-wing views on such questions as labor legislation and civil rights.

John Stewart Battle was born on July 11, 1890, in New Bern, North Carolina, the son of the Reverend Dr. Henry Wilson Battle and Margaret (Stewart) Battle. His father, who had four sons and two daughters, was a Baptist minister; his grandfather was General Cullen A. Battle of the Confederate Army. In 1893 his father became pastor of the First Baptist Church of Petersburg and moved his family to this new home. After attending public and private schools in that city John Battle studied at Wake Forest (North Carolina) College and subsequently entered the Law School of the University of Virginia. At the university, from which he was graduated in 1913 with an LL.B. degree, he became a member of Alpha Tau Omega.

Having been admitted to the Virginia State bar in 1913, John Battle began practice in Charlottesville. At first he was associated with Lemuel F. Smith, until Smith became judge of the Eighth Judicial Circuit of Virginia; Battle then joined a partnership which eventually became known as Perkins, Battle and Minor. His law practice was interrupted by a period of service as a private in the United States Army during World War I.

To represent the Charlottesville area in Virginia's General Assembly, Battle was elected to the House of Delegates in 1929, and from 1934 to 1949 he was a member of the Virginia State Senate, the upper chamber. During his terms in the General Assembly he devoted his attention chiefly to matters of taxation and the budget. He served as chairman of the Senate's Finance Committee during his last four years in the legislature, and from 1940 until the time of his election to the governorship he was a member of the Governor's Advisory Committee on the Budget. Previous to holding this post, he acted as chairman of the Virginia Advisory Legislative Council. He also served on the Senate's committees on public institutions and education, privileges and elections, and courts of justice. The measures which Battle sponsored in the General Assembly included the establishment of the unemployment compensation system in Virginia, the establishment of probation and parole system for the State's corrective institutions, and the abolition of the sheriff's fee system in counties and cities.

Inasmuch as Battle had been elected without opposition to the House of Delegates in every election since 1929, he did not conduct an actual political campaign until he entered the primary for nomination as the Democratic party's candidate for Governor in the summer of 1949. *The Commonwealth* (the magazine of the Virginia State Chamber of Commerce) quotes him as

JOHN S. BATTLE

saying, "I never have been what you would call a politician. . . .I had gone down to Richmond for years and done what had to be done, but I never thought of myself as in politics."

With the public endorsement of Senator Harry F. Byrd, Battle's nomination brought wide attention from political observers because the August primary was generally viewed as a challenge of the twenty-five-year-old supremacy of the Byrd organization in Virginia. Battle's strongest competitor was Francis Pickens Miller, a former Army officer who had the support of labor and Negro groups. Winning over the three contenders in the primary, Battle received approximately 133,200 votes out of a total of 310,000, the latter a record at the polls. Since Virginia is an overwhelmingly Democratic State, this victory was tantamount to election in the November balloting, in which his Republican opponent was Walter O. Johnson. The comment of Richard Morris of the Washington *Post* (July 24, 1949) was: "The core of Battle's power at the polls is among farmers, businessmen and white-collar workers. Its influence is felt through the support of a majority of members in the General Assembly and at least half the State's local officeholders."

Usually described as conservative in his policies, Battle based his campaign upon a defense of the record of State administration and upon a continuation of the financial program of living within the State's present income and not increasing taxes. A leading campaign statement emphasized the need for a larger appropriation for a school building program. Earlier he had attacked "interference" by national labor leaders in Virginia's State primary, and he reiterated his support of measures barring the closed shop and mass picketing. Other recommendations in his platform included improvements in the type of services performed by the

State Department of Agriculture and greater attention to problems of public health.

In the November 8, 1949, election Battle was the choice of about five times as many voters as was his leading opponent. The voters rejected "overwhelmingly" the proposal to repeal the poll tax; on this issue Battle had supported certain amendments to the repeal measure, amendments which a New York *Times* editorial felt only compromised the issue. In his inaugural address on January 18, 1950, the new Governor asked the legislature to approve an appropriation of $45,000,000 for new schools in Virginia. Among other statements (as enumerated in the Washington *Post*) Battle said he could not recommend descreased taxes but would not ask for increases; asked for "broad" peacetime powers to permit him to seize coal mines for State operation "in the event it becomes necessary"; pressed for funds to be used for improvements in the mental hospitals; advocated expansion of local health centers; proposed adoption of Tuck's budget which would increase teachers' salaries; requested a bill that would permit women to serve on juries voluntarily.

Battle's school construction program was made possible by the General Assembly's early approval of the money he had requested. A week after legislation permitted State seizure of coal mines during strike emergencies, the Governor issued a formal declaration of emergency and ordered the continuance of the Virginia Fuel Commission. While he approved of the State-wide rent decontrol bill, he gave attention to the requests for retention of controls in the communities near Washington—a proposed bill would give the Governor authority to reimpose controls in localities where an emergency existed. Not long after his inauguration Battle said he had no plans at that time for proposing repeal of the Virginia poll tax. As expressed in the New York *Herald Tribune*'s poll of Governors on issues involving relations between Federal and State governments (April 1950), Governor Battle said: "The cause of good government would be benefited by the Federal government's withdrawal from many fields of activity, leaving these to the States, which could more properly and efficiently administer them."

Battle's honorary awards include membership in Phi Beta Kappa and Omicron Delta Kappa societies. He received an honorary LL.D. from Hampden-Sydney College, Virginia, in 1950. A past president of the Virginia State Bar Association, he has also served as president of the Alumni Association of the University of Virginia, as master of a Masonic Lodge, and as president of the Charlottesville Kiwanis Club. Other organizations to which he belongs are the American Legion, the Shrine, the Elks, the Farmington Country Club in Charlottesville, the Commonwealth Club in Richmond, and the Country Club of Virginia in Richmond. He is a member of the Baptist Church.

Married on June 12, 1918, to Mary Jane Lipscomb of Charlottesville, Battle has two sons, John S. Jr., and William Cullen, both of whom are lawyers. Six feet one inch in height and 185 pounds in weight, blue-eyed and gray-haired Governor Battle is said to have a "distinguished air, characteristic of a typical Virginia gentleman." For relaxation he turns to fishing and golf.

References

Commonwealth p42 D '49
N Y Times p17 Ag 4, 49; p10 N 9 '49
Washington (D.C.) Post p8 Jl 31 '49

BAUDOUIN, PRINCE ROYAL OF BELGIUM (bō'dwăn) Sept. 7, 1930-

Address: Palace of Laeken, Brussels

On August 11, 1950, former Crown Prince Baudouin of Belgium became Prince Royal of his country, with the constitutional powers of King. This measure had been enacted by Belgium's Parliament a few days earlier, thus ending a threat of civil war that had developed upon King Leopold III's return to the throne after six years of exile. Leopold's withdrawal in favor of his son, who will become King upon reaching his majority in September 1951, was held necessary to the preservation of the monarchy as the symbol of Belgium's continuity and a united people.

Prince Baudouin, born September 7, 1930, in the Palace of Laeken on the outskirts of Brussels, the first son of the then Crown Prince Leopold and Crown Princess Astrid (niece of Gustaf V of Sweden), was named Baudouin Albert Charles Leopold Axel Marie Gustave, Duke of Hainaut and Prince of Belgium. (The name Baudouin is the French form of Baldwin, name of medieval dukes of Flanders and Hainaut.) Prince Baudouin's elder sister, Josephine Charlotte, being the first child, was given the title Princess of Belgium; his younger brother, Albert, is Prince of Liége. At the age of three Prince Baudouin became heir apparent to the throne when his grandfather, King Albert, an ardent mountain climber, was killed in a fall from a cliff; the customary title of the Belgian Crown Prince, Duke of Brabant, was then bestowed upon Baudouin. One month before his fifth birthday, the Prince lost his mother, the highly popular Queen Astrid, when she died (in August 1935) in an automobile accident in Switzerland. A Dutch governess was added to the royal household, and the prince spent several holidays in Holland.

From an early age, Prince Baudouin was trained for kingship. His schooling began when he was seven, with classes at a chateau near Laeken Palace, where he and his brother Prince Albert resided. To prepare the Prince for ruling a bilingual kingdom, half of his classes were held in French and half in Flemish, the languages of the southern and northern parts of the realm, respectively. Occasionally accompanying his father at military reviews, sports events, and other public ceremonies, as a young boy Baudouin became a familiar figure to the Belgian people.

The education and home life of Prince Baudouin were interrupted in 1940 when Belgium was invaded by Germany. The nine-year-old Prince and his sister and brother were sent

Wide World Photos

BAUDOUIN, PRINCE ROYAL OF BELGIUM

for safety to a place in the country in Belgium, then to France, and later to Portugal. A few months after the surrender of the Belgian army in 1940, the royal children returned to their country, where they remained virtual prisoners of the Nazis. With the Allied invasion of Normandy, the members of the royal family were moved to a place in Germany well behind the German lines. There they lived a life of austerity for ten months, until liberated by the United States Army in May 1945, when they went to Switzerland and took up residence there near Geneva.

The Belgian royal family was prevented from returning to Brussels upon its liberation by feelings of opposition to Leopold III which had become increasingly evident during the course of World War II. This opposition was based on allegations that the King was pro-Nazi, in support of which were cited: his unconditional surrender within eighteen days in 1940; his refusal to join the Belgian government-in-exile in England and his opposition to its formation; his appearance at Berchtesgaden as the guest of Hitler; his marriage in 1941 to Marie Liliane Baels, a commoner, daughter of the former Minister of Agriculture, a Fleming who was accused of pro-Nazi leanings. Center of the opposition was the Socialist party led by Paul-Henri Spaak [45]; return of Leopold was supported by the country's majority party, the Social Christian (Catholic). Division of opinion on the royal question generally followed ethnic lines, the Walloons in the south opposing Leopold's return, the Flemish in the north favoring it. Thus the unity of the country, established as a kingdom in the 1830's when it won its separation from Holland, was threatened.

The government of the country was meanwhile functioning under a regency established

**BAUDOUIN, PRINCE ROYAL OF BEL-
GIUM**—*Continued*

by the Belgian Parliament on September 20,
1944, with Leopold's younger brother, Prince
Charles '46, Count of Flanders, as Regent. In
answer to Leopold's express desire to resume
his throne upon his liberation, a law was passed
July 19, 1945, which provided for the King's
resumption of constitutional powers only after a
majority vote to that effect in Parliament. A
referendum on the question, held in March 1950,
gave the King 57.6 per cent of the vote. In-
terpreting this as a mandate to return, Leopold
requested the Parliament to act.

Because of the difficulties raised by the small
majority, the King proposed the compromise
that he return as King in name only, ceding his
powers to Prince Baudouin, to resume them
when, with the Government agreeing, he found
it to be in the national interest to do so; the
demand that he leave Belgium after ceding his
powers should such an arrangement be reached
was, however, refused by Leopold. Subsequently, after the rejection of the King's proposal
and failure of attempts to form a Catholic-
Liberal coalition Government to recall him, the
Social Christian (Catholic) party, which demanded the King's unconditional return, won
in the June 4, 1950, election a majority of
four in the Chamber of Representatives, of
seven in the Senate; and a Cabinet under the
leadership of Jean Duvieusart '50 recalled Leopold to his throne. His return on July 22 was
followed by sabotage, strikes, protest meetings
and demonstrations, in which the violence was
such as to amount almost to insurrection, and
security police used sabers against rioters. By
the beginning of August the unity of the country was so far imperiled that Leopold agreed to
an immediate transfer of his powers to Prince
Baudouin and to a formal abdication on the
Prince's twenty-first birthday, September 7,
1951.

After the voting (on August 9 and 10) by
both houses of Parliament of a measure transferring to Prince Baudouin the powers of Belgium's ruler and conferring on him the title
of Prince Royal (special parliamentary action
was necessary to enable Baudouin, a minor, to
exercise all the royal powers), the Prince took
the oath of office as Chief of State before a
joint session of the two houses of the legislature on August 11, 1950. Wearing the uniform of a general of the army (the customary
official dress of Belgium's ruler), Prince Baudouin swore in Flemish and in French "to
observe the constitution and the laws of the
Belgian people, to maintain the national independence and territorial integrity." In a brief
address he solicited Parliament's full support so
as to assure "concord among the Belgians."
One of his first official acts, on August 15,
was to approve the new Social Christian Cabinet formed under the Premier Joseph Pholien.

The return of Prince Baudouin from exile
had once been suggested in 1949, that he might
learn "to know his country and people." The
suggestion was not acted upon, however, because of opposition from Leopold, who considered it a step toward forcing his own abdication. Thus, the young Prince had not taken

his seat in the Belgian Senate, customarily conferred on royal princes at the age of eighteen,
nor had he had the usual military training. His
education he completed in Geneva under the
guidance of tutors at Le Reposoir, his home,
and at a boys school there. Before World War
II it had been planned that Baudouin would
attend England's Eton College, where Leopold
III had studied. Most recent of his studies
are constitutional law and intensified courses in
history. Mathematics (a favorite subject with
Leopold) is said to be the most difficult course
for the young Prince, who reportedly devoted
extra hours of study to it because of his admiration for his father. In 1948 Baudouin made
a "study voyage" of several weeks in the United
States, where he visited museums, schools, universities, public works, and industrial plants.

One of Prince Baudouin's favorite sports is
golf, which he frequently plays with Princess
de Rethy, his stepmother. He also enjoys soccer (the European version of football), swimming, and skiing. It is said he has had little
social life and prefers no more, apparently finding little pleasure in formal gatherings. Baudouin, who has worn spectacles for several
years, is a tall, lanky youth with a full shock
of black hair. He is described as "gentle and
reserved, with a diffident, shy smile."

References

Christian Sci Mon p2 Ag 1 '50
N Y Times Mag p19 My 7 '50
U S News 29:27 Ag 11 '50

BAUMGARTNER, LEONA Aug. 18, 1902-
United States Government official; physician
Address: b. c/o Children's Bureau, Federal
Security Agency, Washington, D.C.; h. 14
Washington Sq. N., New York 11

Dr. Leona Baumgartner became Associate
Chief of the Children's Bureau, Federal Security Agency, on June 2, 1949. Previously
she had served for seven years as the director of the Bureau of Child Hygiene in New
York City and for one year as Assistant Commissioner in charge of Maternal and Child
Health in that city. Public health, especially
as it affects children, has been an important
concern of hers in her medical career, which
has also included teaching and writing.

Daughter of William J. and Olga (Leisy)
Baumgartner, Leona Baumgartner was born August 18, 1902, in Chicago, Illinois. Her father,
a professor of zoology at the University of
Kansas, has contributed articles to journals in
that field and was a member of several scientific expeditions. After graduating from Lawrence (Kansas) High School in 1919, she
entered the University of Kansas, where she
majored in bacteriology and immunology. In
1923 she received her B.A. degree from that
institution, and in 1925 her M.A. degree. During the year 1928-29, as a Rockefeller research
fellow at the Kaiser Wilhelm Institute in
Munich, she did research in the effects of Vitamin D. A university fellowship brought her to
Yale in 1930, and the award of a Sterling Fellowship the following year permitted her to

continue studies there in the relationship of age to resistance. After the degree of Ph.D. had been granted her by Yale in 1932, Miss Baumgartner went on to study for the M.D. degree. In her final year as a medical student she was presented by the New England Pediatric Society with the John Lovett Morse Prize for her thesis, entitled "Age and Antibody Production," judged to be the best paper written by a fourth-year medical student in New England on a subject of scientific interest in connection with the health of children. The degree of M.D. was conferred upon her by Yale in 1934. Then followed two years of internship as assistant resident and assistant in pediatrics at the New York Hospital and Cornell University Medical College (1934-36).

Teaching has occupied a large part in Leona Baumgartner's career. Upon becoming a Bachelor of Arts she went to Colby, Kansas, as head of the biology department in its Community High School. In the years 1924-26 she was in charge of nursing education at the Kansas City (Missouri) Junior College; and from 1926 to 1928 she headed the division of bacteriology and hygiene at the University of Montana. In 1939 Dr. Baumgartner was instructor in public health and preventive medicine, and in pediatrics at Cornell University Medical College, becoming an assistant professor in the first subject in 1940 and in the second in 1944. During this period (1939-42), she also lectured in nursing education at Teachers College, Columbia University. Since 1948 she had been visiting lecturer at the department of maternal and child health of the Harvard School of Public Health.

Dr. Baumgartner's work in the field of public health began in 1936, when she was appointed acting assistant surgeon with the United States Public Health Service. The following year she joined the New York City Health Department, where she began as medical instructor in child and school hygiene, became director of public health training (1938-39), district health officer (1939-40), and then, for seven years, held the post of director of the Bureau of Child Hygiene (the first year as acting director). As head of the Bureau, Dr. Baumgartner had under her direction sixty-three child health centers and was responsible for the administration in New York City of the Federal Emergency Maternity and Infant Care program which went into effect July of 1943 as a war measure. She was especially engaged in supplying health services for boys and girls in vocational high schools. "What's the use of sending a kid on to an airplane factory if his eyes aren't good?" she asked. "We think it's more intelligent to get him into shape while he's in school" (New York *World-Telegram*, February 24, 1942). Dr. Baumgartner made an effort during her term of office to provide all mothers, even those who did not need the services of the bureau, with modern scientific health information through printed material. One booklet issued for this purpose was a *Handbook for Parents*, which made the point that every baby is different and that not all do the same things at the same age. At this time (1940-42), too, Dr. Baumgartner was

William Vandivert

LEONA BAUMGARTNER

associated with the pediatric staff of the New York Hospital, first as an assistant pediatrician (1940), then as a pediatrician (1942). In 1948 she was appointed Assistant Commissioner in charge of Maternal and Child Health for New York City.

While on the staff of the New York City Health Department, Dr. Baumgartner saw service as a delegate to the National Council of Women, International Congress of Women (1938), and as chairman of the international committee of American Women in Public Health in the same year. In 1940 she was appointed chairman of the maternal and health section of the National Health Assembly. She also served on the children's bureau advisory commitee on maternal and child health and crippled children's services and as a member of the National Commission on Children and Youth.

As Associate Chief of the Children's Bureau in Washington, (to which she was appointed June 2, 1949, succeeding Martha M. Eliot [48]) Dr. Baumgartner will have many calls made on her training and experience. According to the *Government Manual*: "The purpose of the Bureau is to investigate and report on all matters related to child life and to increase opportunity for the full development of all children by promoting their health and social welfare. . . .The Bureau makes studies in the fields of child development and services for children, compiles statistics relating to children, gives advisory service and issues publications, both technical and popular. The Bureau is providing a clearing house for research in child life to collect and distribute information regarding research studies underway in the various universities, schools, child welfare institutes, hospitals, and other public and private agencies throughout the country. . . .The Bureau administers . . . grants to State health agencies for extend-

BAUMGARTNER, LEONA—*Continued*

ing and improving health services for mothers and children . . . grants to State crippled children's agencies for extending and improving services for crippled children . . . grants to State public welfare agencies . . . to extend and strengthen . . . child welfare services for the protection and care of homeless, dependent and neglected children and children in danger of becoming delinquent. . . .The Bureau receives information and responds to requests for information and advice on services for children and youth from agencies such as United Nations agencies. . . .The Chief of the Bureau represents the United States on the executive board of the United Nations International Children's Emergency Fund and on the Council of the American International Institute for the Protection of Childhood."

The New York *Times* reported Dr. Baumgartner as declaring, in a speech before the Spokesmen for Children, Inc., that if all mothers and children had the scientific care this country knows how to give, approximately half of the lives now lost could be saved. In addition to wider application of existing scientific knowledge she urged the need for research "to discover new ways . . . of solving many of the problems that face children who live." She pointed to our willingness to legislate, give funds, accept taxation and organize our energies in wartime, as an indication of what could be done to distribute and improve health services of the nation (New York *Times,* March 21, 1946). In commenting on the relationship of the welfare of American children to that of children in the rest of the world, she said: "These children who today in Europe are cold, hungry, homeless and hopeless, are the same individuals with whom our own children will do business, exchange ideas, visit, fight or plan for peace in the future" (New York *Times,* February 7, 1946).

A bibliography of the physician's writings, which include articles in German scientific journals as well as in numerous American ones, amounts to some fifty titles. She has been a frequent contributor in particular to the *American Journal of Public Health* (she was on the editorial board in 1943-46), *Annals of Medical History, Journal of Immunology,* the *Medical Women's Journal, Bulletin of the History of Medicine, Public Health Nursing.* Articles by Dr. Baumgartner for the lay reader have appeared in *Hygeia* ("Old Dogs and New Tricks, the Story of Ivan Pavlov"), *Collier's* ("The Root of our Family Tree"), *Baby Talk* of April 1943 and November 1945 ("Dining Room Diplomacy"), *House and Garden* ("Houses are for Children Too").

Recognition for her work has been accorded to Dr. Baumgartner. In 1942 she was made a diplomate of the American Board of Pediatrics, and in 1949, a diplomate of the American Board of Preventive Medicine and Public Health. A citation for distinguished service in the fields of immunology and public health was awarded to Dr. Baumgartner by the Kansas University Alumni Association in 1947. She was given honorary membership in the Eugene Field Society in 1945 and that same year

received the *Baby Talk* award for "furthering the health and welfare of mothers and babies." For achievements in the field of child care, the American Design Award given by Lord and Taylor, New York City, was presented to her in 1946.

Dr. Baumgartner holds membership in many organizations of a general scientific and medical nature, a large number of which are societies concerned particularly with pediatrics and public health problems; there are, in addition, several societies of specialized scientific interests to which Dr. Baumgartner also belongs. She is on the advisory boards of and holds officership in the New York Academy of Medicine, American Public Health Association, Association for Aid of Crippled Children, Medical Society of the County of New York, Child Study Association, as well as the Public Education Association. Keys of a number of societies have been awarded to Dr. Baumgartner: Pi Beta Phi, Sigma Xi (science research society), Phi Beta Kappa, Phi Sigma (biological honor society) and Mortarboard (student leadership). She belongs, also, to the Cosmopolitan Club and the Women's City Club, New York City.

In 1942 Dr. Baumgartner was married to Nathaniel M. Elias, a chemical engineer. They have two children, Peter and Barbara. The physician is five feet four inches tall, weighs 135 pounds, and has brown hair and blue eyes. She is a Presbyterian. Two simple rules govern her work, Dr. Baumgartner has said: "I get loads of fun out of my job. I never take it home with me." A favorite hobby is collecting old medical works, the subject of some of her writings.

References

American Women, 1939-40
Directory of Medical Women, 1949
International Who's Who in World Medicine, 1947
Who's Who in New York, 1947

BAYAR, (MAHMUT) CELAL (bī-är′ mä-mōōt′ jä-läl′) 1884- President of Turkey

Address: Ankara, Turkey

What has been called "the first completely honest election" in the history of the Republic of Turkey, held May 14, 1950, resulted in a victory for the five-year-old Democratic party. It ended the twelve-year tenure of the presidency of General Ismet Inönü [41], and his replacement on May 22 by former Premier and Minister of National Economy, Celâl Bayar. The chief issue in the political campaign had been between the rigid and comprehensive system of state capitalism then in force, and a freer scope for private enterprise for which the Democratic party stood. The President of Turkey is elected by the membership of the Grand National Assembly, the country's unicameral parliament elected by the people. He retains office only so long as his party commands a parliamentary majority; the term is customarily four years. Bayar is Turkey's third president; his predecessors were Kemal Atatürk, who founded the modern state in 1923-24, and General Inönü.

Mahmut Celâl Bayar, son of Fehmi and Emine Bayar, was born in 1884, in Umurbey, a village near Bursa, a Turkish town on the Asiatic side of the Sea of Marmara. His father was the village teacher. Young Bayar was sent to a French school in Bursa, a provincial capital. In his first work in business he was a clerk in a German bank at Bursa. His political activity dates from 1907, the year he joined the revolutionary Party of Union and Progress (Young Turks) and was made its principal agent in the Bursa district. Promoted in the following year (1908) to the post of executive secretary of the party's organization at Izmir (formerly Smyrna) he participated in the uprising led by Mustafa Kemal Pasha (later known as Kemal Atatürk) which forced the abdication of Sultan Abdul-Hamid II in 1909 and the establishment, under his successor, Mohammed V, of a constitutional form of government in the Ottoman Empire. Subsequently, Bayar, whose rise in banking circles meanwhile had been rapid, served as a deputy from Saruhan (Manisa) in the last Ottoman parliament.

Bayar was a friend of Kemal Atatürk, when, at the conclusion of World War I, the patriots organized the Nationalist party, dedicated to the expulsion of foreign forces then occupying Turkey as a result of alignment with the Central Powers during the war. During the war against the Greeks, who had occupied Izmir, Bayar, adopting a pseudonym (in the words of a biographical note supplied by the Turkish Information Office) "was active in organizing the national forces . . . and commanded a unit of Turkish irregulars in Akhisar and Bursa."

In the Grand National Assembly which convened at Ankara in 1920 Bayar was seated as a deputy from Saruhan, and he was elected Minister of Economy. Subsequently, in 1921, he served as acting Foreign Minister and Minister of Economy. At the conclusion of the Treaty of Lausanne (1923), which established the boundaries of the country at approximately their present locations, Turkey was proclaimed a republic. The assembly elected Kemal Atatürk to the presidency, and initiated a program of modernization. Bayar was elected deputy from Izmir to the assembly, in which he was to represent the city in all subsequent sessions until 1945. He became Minister of Settlement, Construction, and Exchange of Population.

About eight years later, in 1932, in the worst period of the international depression, he was recalled to the Ministry of National Economy. During the next year (1933) the principle of state-owned factories was enunciated by Kemal Atatürk. "With capital scarce and the Turks inexperienced in ways of corporate finance" (as *Pathfinder* put it) "most large-scale projects are financed by the Government." Bayar became known as "the chief promoter of state factories" (New York *Times*). He has been credited with playing an important part in minimizing the effects of the depression and developing his country's economy. Bayar retained the portfolio of Minister of National Economy when, on September 21, 1937, it was announced that General Inönü, then Premier, had been "granted forty-five days leave of absence at his own request" by Kemal Atatürk. Five days later Bayar was appointed Acting Premier pending reconvening of the National Assembly at the beginning of November.

Inönü having formally resigned on October 25, 1937, when the Assembly met in November Bayar had been installed as Premier. He made two minor changes in the Cabinet, and none in domestic policy; his most conspicuous success was in the field of foreign affairs when (July 1938) he concluded with France an agreement under which Turkish troops were admitted to a share in the policing of the sanjak (a subdivision of a province) of Alexandretta. (This prepared the way for the eventual incorporation of the sanjak into Turkey). When, following the death of Kemal Atatürk, General Inönü was elected the second President of Turkey (November 11, 1938), Bayar was again called upon to form the Cabinet. He served as Premier under Inönü, however, only until January 25, 1939, when he resigned, to be succeeded by Dr. Refik Saydam, Minister of the Interior.

Although Celâl Bayar remained a member of the Assembly throughout the period of World War II, his name was not prominent in international news dispatches until September 30, 1945, when he resigned his Izmir seat. The resignation (stated a New York *Times* article) was "generally connected" with a "campaign in the Turkish press for a wider scope for democratic factions in the Turkish political institutions"; and on January 7, 1946, Bayar, having left the hitherto controlling Republican People's party formed by Kemal Atatürk, announced, with three colleagues, the formation of a new Democratic party, of which he became president.

In the election held July 21, 1946, (according to schedule) the new party won only sixty Assembly seats to the 396 won by the Republican People's Party; charges of ballet box "stuffing" were widespread, with Professor Fuad Koprulu, one of the Democratic party founders, claiming that if the election had been "fair," the Democrats would have won "at lease a majority" in the Assembly. Bayar contested, and won, a seat from Istanbul.

Before the arrival of the 1950 election date, the Democratic party had opportunity to make known its policies. "In foreign policy," states the *Political Handbook of the World* (1950), "[it] is in substantial agreement with the People's Party. In domestic policy it favors more rapid democratization with parallel relaxation of present controls. In economic matters it supports *étatisme* [state capitalism] but feels that administration and controls in the country's economic life can be . . . more efficiently handled." Rigid state capitalism, which had come into being during World War II, was the chief issue at the election held on May 14, 1950, with the Democrats campaigning on promises by Bayar that rigid state capitalism "would be replaced by a much greater degree of private

CELAL BAYAR

enterprise and that there would be greater civil liberties" (New York *Times*). A campaign manifesto stated: "In economic and financial fields, our aims are to speed the economic equipment of the country, to increase national production and resources, and to lift up generally the standard of living." Of foreign policy (which has been pro-Western) Bayar asserted, "Any change whatsoever in the Government is not going to change our foreign policy."

The election, which Inönü promised would be fair, resulted in a landslide for the Democrats, who won 408 Assembly seats out of 487. Upon Bayar's refusal to organize a Cabinet until the meeting of the new Assembly, the Government of Günaltay remained in office for a short time. "Few of the Democratic leaders (wrote New York *Times* correspondent Farnsworth Fowle) "envisaged coming to power so rapidly. Most would have thought they had done well if they received 40 per cent of the vote." Bayar himself has said that most of the Democrats were confident of victory. The reporter ascribed that victory to a growing belief among the electorate that "Turkey has less to fear from private business . . . than from exploitation by ambitious and frequently inefficient state enterprises," food scarcity in consequence of a poor harvest, high taxation, rankling memories of the 1946 election, and a general desire for a change. Inönü, whose presidency terminated with the fall of the Government, was praised by Turkish newspapers for "retiring from office in good spirit." The New York *Times* (May 21, 1950) stated that the transfer of power was carried out "with scrupulous correctness" and "quiet dignity."

"Celâl Bayar," stated *Time*, "did not want to be President of Turkey. He preferred to stay offstage as the boss of the Democratic party."

This preference was overruled by his own followers who nominated him, by a 341-to-35 vote, to be Inönü's successor. On May 22 he was elected the third President of Turkey by an Assembly vote of 387 to 64. Ten minutes afterward he took the oath of office, and named Adnan Menderes (who has been described as "a· wealthy landowner of Aydin") as Premier. Premier Menderes, announcing the new party program to the Assembly on May 29, promised workers the right to strike; passage of a new liberal press law; amnesty for political prisoners; drastic curtailment of Government expenditures; administrative reform; transfer of state-controlled industries to private enterprise; and an attempt to attract new foreign capital to Turkey. At the same time it was reported that Turkey was already in process of seeking new Marshall Plan aid for economic and social development, and that President Bayar might soon visit the United States to negotiate a new loan.

Bayar and Mme. Bayar have a married son and a daughter. (Another son is deceased.) The Turkish statesman, who is of medium height, has graying hair and wears glasses. Honored by his country, he is the recipient of the Medal of Independence.

References

N Y Herald Tribune II p3 My 28 '50
   por
N Y Times p12 My 17 '50
This Week p4 Jl 2 '50
Who's Who in Central and East-Europe, 1935-36
World Biography (1948)

BEARDSLEY, WILLIAM S(HANE) May 13, 1901- Governor of Iowa
Address: b. State House, Des Moines, Iowa; h. 2900 Grand Ave., Des Moines, Iowa

William S. Beardsley, the Republican Governor of Iowa, was elected November 5, 1948, for a two-year term expiring at the end of 1950. With a background of two terms as a State Senator and one as a member of the lower chamber of the Iowa legislature, Beardsley came to prominence as a leader of G.O.P. progressives when he opposed the passage of a State law to ban the closed shop. A druggist and a farmer by vocation, he is said to ·have owed his gubernatorial nomination to the first effective political alliance of agricultural and labor forces in Iowa since the early 1930's. Since becoming Governor he has been notable as an advocate of fiscal economy, an opponent of the Brannan Plan for agriculture, and one of the six signatories of the February 1950 declaration of "forward-looking" policy for the Republican party advanced by Governor James H. Duff '48 of Pennsylvania. Beardsley was re-elected in November 1950.

The son of William and Carrie (Shane) Beardsley, Iowa's chief executive is of English and Scotch-Irish extraction. (The Beardsleys settled in the Hawkeye State in 1879, the Shanes in 1865.) A native of the small mining

village of Beacon, in Mahaska County, Iowa—
he was born there May 13, 1901—William
Shane Beardsley passed most of his boyhood
in Birmingham, Van Buren County, where his
father operated a pharmacy. The younger
Beardsley attended both grammar and high
school in Birmingham, and, after graduation
from the latter in 1918, studied at the Bowen
Institute of Pharmacy and Chemistry at Brunswick, Missouri, which awarded him a diploma
in pharmacy. Following in his father's footsteps, Beardsley in 1922 established a drugstore
at New Virginia, a small farming center in
Warren County, about thirty miles south of
Des Moines. There (stated an official biographical release) he "conducted a vigorous
enterprise, won many loyal friends, and made
contacts with people generally."

A Republican since his earliest voting days,
Beardsley in November 1930, was selected to
make the keynote speech at the party's Warren
County convention. Two years later (November 1932) he was elected a State Senator from
Warren and Clarke counties, being one of the
few Republicans to survive the Democratic
landslide of that year. Re-elected for a second
four-year term in November 1936, he became
Republican floor leader when the State Senate
reconvened. In 1938 Beardsley purchased 900
acres of farm land near New Virginia, and
began to raise hogs and cattle. (He turned over
the operation of his drugstore, to which a
jewelry business had been added, to his elder
daughter Charlotte and her husband, Doyle E.
Stickel). Thus he withdrew from public life
at the end of his second senatorial term in 1939,
and remained out of politics for the next six
years.

Beardsley's return to the political arena came
about near the end of 1946, when Harold Felton of Indianola, formerly speaker of the
General Assembly, died shortly after the
November election. Beardsley was named by
Warren County Republicans to fill out Felton's
term in 1947 (the Iowa legislature meets only
in odd-numbered years). As representative of a
farming area, he found himself in major disagreement with several of the policies of
Governor Robert D. Blue '48 (then serving his
second term), regarded as representative of the
views of the Iowa Manufacturers Association.
In particular Beardsley opposed passage of the
law signed by Governor Blue in April 1948,
which made Iowa the thirteenth State to ban
the closed shop. This bill had passed the Senate
in April 1947. When it came before the General Assembly, AFL and CIO union members
joined in a one-day labor holiday and an estimated fifteen thousand workers gathered around
the State Capitol in protest. Beardsley, in the
Assembly, maintained that labor legislation
should be handled nationally. "It is simply as
illogical to have forty-eight separate labor
codes," he stated, "as it is to have forty-eight
different monetary systems." He also criticized
Blue for cutting the school appropriation.

Approach of the Iowa State primaries on
June 7, 1948, found State Representative
Beardsley a candidate for the Republican guber-
natorial nomination in opposition to Governor
Blue, who sought to become the fourth chief

Wide World Photos
WILLIAM S. BEARDSLEY

executive in the history of the State to be
elected to a third term. Beardsley was reported
to have the support of the Iowa Farm Bureau
Federation, the Iowa State Education Association and State labor organizations, though not
actual endorsement. The candidate declared:
"I am seeking the support of all the people of
Iowa. I am not representing any clique or
group." Beardsley's campaign platform called
for "adequate, legal machinery for prompt and
equitable settlement" of industrial disputes, better roads, lower real estate taxes, State support
of up to 25 per cent of public school costs, more
comprehensive soil conservation and flood control, and "more self-government and fewer State
commissions" for Iowa. He stressed the necessity for full cooperation between the executive
and legislative branches of government. When
the results of the primary were announced, it
was found that the first farmer-labor "coalition" in Iowa since the early 1930's had been
sufficiently strong to nominate Beardsley over
Blue by a decisive margin. In November
Beardsley was victorious over Democratic candidate Switzer by 553,900 votes to 434,432. (He
polled about 30,000 more votes in Iowa than
President Truman, who carried the State in the
Presidential balloting.)

Outstanding in the early months of Governor
Beardsley's administration was the adoption of
a State budget confining "government operation
and expenditures . . . within the bounds of
current income." It was not, however, Beardsley's opposition to "inflationary spending" in
State affairs so much as his attitude toward the
so-called "Brannan Plan" for agriculture which
was to bring the Iowa Governor to the front in
the Middle West. The Brannan Plan (presented by Agriculture Secretary Charles F.
Brannan '48) proposed to guarantee farm income
with low consumer costs by means of Govern-

BEARDSLEY, WILLIAM S.—*Continued*
ment subsidies to farmers rather than by the
current method of "parity" support of prices.
In June 1949, the Democrats held a farm conference at Des Moines to promote the Brannan
Plan; Republicans countered with a conference
at Sioux City in October, at which (stated
Pathfinder) "they offered no plan, but asked
the farmers to come forward and tell the party
what they wanted." Various views were expressed: the National Grange condemned the
Brannan Plan, the National Farmers Union
favored it. Beardsley's stand was unequivocal.
"Whoever the man," said the Iowa Governor,
"or whatever the party, he who would trifle
with this important business by pretending to
offer a program which promises all things to
all people at the price of regimentation and
excessive regulation, should be branded as a
self-seeking politician."

Governor Beardsley's deviation from conservative Republicanism was emphasized when,
in February 1950, he joined five other Republican Governors (Aahndahl, Adams, Duff,
Peterson and Robins) in signing a "declaration"
drafted by Governor Duff of Pennsylvania. In
it the Republican party was urged to take a
stand as "a party of service, not of privilege,"
with a twelve-point program, including a "compulsory health plan for the people without
resort to socialized medicine," an agricultural
program developed "in cooperation with leading
farm organizations" and "assumption by the
United States of affirmative world leadership."
In response to a poll of Governors taken by
the New York *Herald Tribune* on the question
of "Federal encroachment on State government," Beardsley declared that "Iowa is not
receiving its share of Federal aid" and that
"the field of gasoline taxation should be pre-
empted to the State" for highway construction.
In the November 1950 election Beardsley was
again chosen Governor for a two-year term.

The gray-haired, clean-shaven Governor of
the Hawkeye State has been married for some
thirty years to the former Charlotte E. Manning, of Birmingham, Iowa; their wedding took
place on January 29, 1919. The Beardsleys have
four children: Blaine (who now operates a
drugstore in Alaska), Charlotte (Mrs. Doyle E.
Stickel), Mary (Mrs. Henry F. Schieg of
Iowa City), and Dan. (Another son, William,
died in boyhood.) Beardsley, who attends the
Methodist church, is a 32d Degree Mason
(Member of the Consistory, Za-Ga-Zig Temple
of the Shrine), an Odd Fellow, a former
Rotarian and an honorary Lion.

References

Cedar Rapids (Iowa) Gazette IV p2 Je 6
'48 por
Who's Who in America, 1950-51

BEBLER, ALES (bĕb'lĕr ä'lĕs) June 8,
1907- Yugoslavian Government official; United
Nations delegate
Address: b. c/o United Nations, New York;
Ministry of Foreign Affairs, Belgrade, Yugo-
slavia

Permanent delegate of Yugoslavia to the
United Nations, Ales Bebler is its representative on the U.N. Security Council. A Communist party member since 1929, Bebler fought
with the International Brigade in the Spanish
Civil War and as a Yugoslav Partisan during
World War II. After the liberation, he was
Finance Minister of Slovenia and deputy to the
Constituent Assembly. He served as Deputy
Foreign Minister of Yugoslavia during 1946-49,
receiving his appointment to the Security Council in December 1949, after successfully conducting Yugoslavia's campaign for the seat
against Russia's opposition. Bebler has said
that he seeks "to contribute in a constructive
way to lessening of world tension." For the
month of November 1950 he was president of
the Security Council.

Ales Bebler was born in Idrija, a Slovene
town near Trieste, on June 8, 1907, when
Slovenia was part of Austria-Hungary. His
father, a chemical engineer, was active in the
Slovenian independence movement. In 1918,
after the collapse of the Dual Monarchy, eleven-
year-old Ales began his "intellectual, unsenti-
mental development" (*United Nations World*).
He became aware of the political problems of
his country, which was invaded by the Italians
after twelve days of independence. At fifteen
he read Tolstoy's *Confession,* deriving from it
the conviction of sacrificing everything for
one's belief. Because the Soviet Union's program provided for self-determination for small
nations, the youth was attracted to communism,
the economic tenets of which he also approved
as he matured in understanding. He attended
high school in Ljubljana, Slovenia's capital, in
which he grew up. Upon his graduation in
1925, he enrolled at the University of Paris
to study law, in which he also took courses at
the University of Ljubljana. During this period
Bebler became active in politics, joining the
Communist party in 1929.

Shortly after being awarded his doctorate in
Paris in 1930, Bebler was warned by friends
that if he returned to Yugoslavia he would be
arrested. Accordingly, the young man traveled
in Europe, working for the communist cause
and developing his knowledge of languages.
(His foreign languages are Serbo-Croat, Italian,
German, Russian, French, Spanish and English.)
On a visit to Moscow in January 1933, Bebler
was given the assignment of "making life
agreeable for foreign specialists" (he said),
particularly Americans. Other duties involved
travel in Russia as he organized libraries, radio
programs and other "cultural endeavors," and
worked with unions on housing, education, and
economic problems. While in Moscow again
in 1935, Bebler met Josip Broz, the future
Marshal Tito [43], and made plans to return to
Yugoslavia.

These plans were interrupted in 1936 by the
outbreak of civil war in Spain. Bebler joined
the International Brigade, which fought against
Franco. As a captain, while leading an attack
at Quinto near Zaragoza, he was shot in the
left leg. After being hospitalized in France,
he returned to his homeland and presented himself to the police. Charged with having or-

ganized youth against the government, Bebler
was imprisoned one year.

When the Nazis invaded Yugoslavia, Bebler
became Partisan Chief of Staff in Slovenia
with the rank of colonel and operating under
the name of "Primozh." A leader in the resistance forces in Northern Slovenia and
Gorizia, he reportedly fought with skill and
daring. It was there he met Vera Hrescak, a
law student who, after escaping from an Italian
concentration camp, was also in the Partisan
ranks. They were married in the spring of
1944. (Bebler's sister, a physician, served with
the Partisans as a lieutenant.)

In the meantime, dissension was developing
among the patriots in occupied Yugoslavia.
General Draja Mikhailovitch [42], who by July
1942 had risen to chief of staff, was strongly
opposed by the leftists under Tito. In December 1943 Tito succeeded in establishing the
Executive Committee of Liberation, which
served as a provisional government and repudiated King Peter, then in exile. The final
eclipse of Mikhailovitch came with the November 1945 elections for the Constituent Assembly, to which Bebler was sent as deputy.
Bebler was also elected to the National Assembly of the newly proclaimed (December
1945) Federative People's Republic of Yugoslavia with Marshal Tito as Prime Minister.

Bebler was appointed Deputy Foreign Minister of the new Yugoslavian Government. As
such he has represented his country at almost
every important international conference. At
the Paris Peace Conference (August 1946) in
the dispute over Trieste, Bebler's opposition to
Italian retention of the city was "relentless and
effective," wrote Herbert L. Matthews in the
New York Times. With Soviet support, under
the 1947 peace treaty, Yugoslavia was able to
secure most of Italian Istria; but it was unsuccessful in securing sovereignty over the port
of Trieste. Bebler worked closely with Soviet
delegates at the conference in August 1948 for
restoring traffic along the Danube river; and
Yugoslavia's demands for Austrian territory
and other concessions were presented by Bebler
before the conferences of the Big Four Foreign
Ministers in 1949.

Bebler was alternate representative for Yugoslavia at the General Assembly of the United
Nations in London in 1946, serving as vice-
chairman of the U.N.'s Administrative and
Budgetary Committee. He also served on the
U.N. Special Committee for Refugees and Displaced Persons. The following year he again
represented his country at the U.N. General
Assembly in New York. During discussions by
the Political and Security Committee on the
Balkan problem in 1947, Bebler denied that his
country was interfering with the Greeks but
bitterly charged the United States and Britain
with manipulating Greek politics. The committee's approval of a ban on future aid to
Greek guerrilla forces by Yugoslavia, Albania,
and Bulgaria brought from Bebler the comment that an injustice had been committed toward his people. In October 1948 Bebler
worked with Russian delegates for dissolution
of the U.N. Special Committee on the Balkans,
calling for rejection of its report, but he joined

Wide World Photos

ALES BEBLER

in a resolution for peace talks between Greece
and her three northern neighbors. In November 1949, when the U.N. voted to impose an
arms embargo on Albania and Bulgaria until
they ceased helping Greek guerrillas, Bebler
voted with Cominform delegates against the
measure, although Yugoslavia was not included
in the proposed embargo. He has, on several
occasions, urged strong U.N. action against
Franco Spain.

On June 28, 1948, the Soviet-led Cominform
denounced Tito and the Yugoslav Communist
party for inspiring a policy against the Soviet
Union and retreating from the Communist line
in foreign and domestic policies; and on September 29, 1949, the Soviet Union abrogated its
1945 treaty of friendship with Yugoslavia.
This growing rift between the two countries
was reflected in the United Nations General
Assembly in New York in September 1949,
when Bebler did not line up with the Soviet
bloc in opposing the debate on the religious
and human rights cases in Bulgaria, Rumania,
and Hungary. On September 24 Bebler charged
"the existence of a Soviet plot against the
independence of Yugoslavia," asserting that
Yugoslavia henceforth would vote according to
her independent judgment. He also stated that
Yugoslavia's foreign policy was aimed at "full
sovereignty and complete independence."

On September 25, 1949, Bebler announced
Yugoslavia's intention of contesting Czechoslovakia, the Soviet Union's candidate, for the
seat on the Security Council left vacant by the
expiration of the Ukraine's term at the end of
1949. With the support of the United States,
Yugoslavia won the seat for a two-year term
in elections held October 20. On December 3,
1949, Tito announced Ales Bebler as Yugoslavia's representative on the Council as well as
its permanent delegate to the United Nations,

BEBLER, ALES—*Continued*

to replace Dr. Joza Vilfan, who became Deputy
Foreign Minister.

Bebler in November 1949 had questioned the
authority of the Chinese Nationalist delegation
to represent that country in the United Nations
inasmuch as a Communist government had come
into power in China. At the first meeting of
the Security Council in January 1950, Bebler
was the only delegate to support Soviet Representative Jacob Malik's '49 resolution calling for
exclusion of Dr. T. F. Tsiang '48, representative
of Nationalist China and president of the
Security Council. After attempting unsuccessfully to unseat Tsiang, Bebler refused to participate in the arms-control debate. On April 1,
1950, Bebler became chairman of the Council's
Atomic Energy Commission. Following Warren R. Austin of the United States as president
of the U.N. Security Council, Bebler presided
for the month of November 1950. This office
is assigned according to the alphabetical order
of the member countries comprising the Security Council.

According to Richard Witkin, writing in
This Week (January 8, 1950), Bebler seeks to
marshal public opinion for Yugoslavia in its
quarrel with Russia, and to win economic and
political help from the West. (Yugoslavia in
September 1949 received an emergency loan of
$20,000,000 from the United States, and a
second loan in March 1950.) Witkin pointed
out that the Yugoslav could be witty and suave
or vitriolic in his speeches. John Gunther has
described Bebler as a man of "superior intelligence." Peter Kihss, writing in *United Nations World* (February 1950), stated that Bebler "epitomizes the forces that lead Yugoslavs
today." He quoted Bebler as saying that he
was "proudest of having had faith in the victory of justice for small nations," and having
always acted in accordance with that faith.

"Tito's chief diplomatic trouble-shooter" is a
lean, wiry man with dark hair. His wife is an
actress in Yugoslavia's state theater in Belgrade, where the Beblers make their home.
They have three children: Jasna, Neda, and a
one-year-old baby. Though his doctor advised
him not to smoke lest it shorten his life, Bebler
does not wish to give up that pleasure—"there
are so many more clear and present dangers."

References

N Y Herald Tribune p17 D 6 '49 por
This Week p5 Ja 8 '50 por
UN World 4:9 F '50 por
World Biography (1948)
Yearbook of the United Nations, 1947-
48

BECH, JOSEPH (bĕk) Feb. 17, 1887- Foreign Minister of the Grand Duchy of Luxembourg

Address: b. Ministry of Foreign Affairs, Luxembourg

Joseph Bech, the Minister of Foreign Affairs
of the Grand Duchy of Luxembourg, entered
that post in 1937, before which since 1926 he
had held that title concurrently with that of
Prime Minister. His public life dates from
1914, when he was elected to the Chamber of
Deputies in his twenty-seventh year. After
World War II, Luxembourg under his leadership, joined the Benelux customs union and
was a signatory to the Brussels and the North
Atlantic pacts.

Born on February 17, 1887, at Diekirch,
Luxembourg, Joseph Bech is the son of Charles
and Marie (Tschiderer) Bech. He received his
higher education in France, studying law at the
University of Paris. After being awarded his
doctorate in 1912, he was admitted to the bar.
Soon afterward he began his political career,
as a candidate for Luxembourg's parliament.
He was elected in 1914 to the Chamber of
Deputies as a member of the Christian Social
party and remained a legislator during the
occupation of his country by the Germans in
World War I.

Following the war, the constitution of Luxembourg was amended, universal suffrage and
proportional representation being introduced.
The Christian Social party remained in power,
and in 1921 Joseph Beck was made Luxembourg's Minister of Justice and of Home Affairs, in which offices he served until 1925. He
then became Prime Minister and held also the
portfolio of Minister of Foreign Affairs, occupying these posts from 1926 to 1937. During
this period the Grand Duchy enjoyed prosperity,
for under the economic union with Belgium,
negotiated in December 1921, Luxembourg had
a customs-free outlet for its metallurgic and
mining industries. Throughout these years the
Christian Social party remained in control of
the Government. In 1937 Bech resigned as
Prime Minister, but retained the office of Foreign Minister. He was Luxembourg's first delegate to the League of Nations, representing his
country from 1925 to 1939.

When, in May 1940, Luxembourg was again
invaded and occupied by the Germans, the Government left the country in order to maintain its
position from abroad. Bech accompanied the
Grand Duchess Charlotte '49 and Prime Minister Pierre Dupong first to Paris, later to London. There they established a Government-in-
exile and protested the annexation of Luxembourg to the Reich, a move proclaimed by Germany on August 30. The seat of the Government-in-exile was moved to Montreal a few
months later, but, the Luxembourg Council of
State continuing to hold its meetings in London,
Bech remained in England.

Luxembourg was liberated from the Nazis
in September 1944. In the first postwar elections, held October 21, a coalition Government
was formed under Dupong, and Bech was confirmed in the office of Foreign Minister. The
Christian Science Monitor referred to Dupong
and Bech as " a unique two-man team": "They
have served in the Cabinet for more than two
decades—something of a European record."
Bech also holds the portfolio of the Minister
of Viticulture.

In London the Luxembourg Government had,
under Bech's guidance, been a party to discussions of a postwar customs union with Belgium
and the Netherlands. In April 1946 the Benelux

agreement was signed whereby the three nations joined in an economic agreement to eliminate tariffs on shipments between them, and to establish equivalent tariffs on goods imported into the three countries from any other nation. The agreement was to become effective January 1, 1948, and full economic union was to be accomplished July 1, 1950; in October 1949, it was announced that a "restricted" union only would come into effect on the latter date, since the three signatory countries had not reached the anticipated equality in economic recovery. It was emphasized, however, that this represents a postponement and not an abandonment of the original plan.

Relinquishing its position of perpetual unarmed neutrality as set forth in the Treaty of London (1867), Luxembourg in 1948 became a country with conscription and foreign alliances. Pointing out that mutual assistance meant reciprocal military obligations, and an end of neutrality, Bech urged his countrymen to join with Britain, France, Belgium and the Netherlands in signing the Brussels Pact, under which these countries were to pledge immediate aid to each other in case of attack. On March 17, 1948, Bech signed the treaty in the name of his country. In November of the following year he joined the representatives of the other Brussels Pact countries in ratifying an agreement extending social security benefits to nationals of the signatory countries in case of sickness, death, maternity, industrial injury, and occupational disease while working in one of the other member countries. On this occasion, a special correspondent of the *Christian Science Monitor* saw these countries as "perhaps making the most important contribution to western European unity in their quiet and limited fashion."

Together with the foreign ministers of the other Brussels Pact countries, Bech was a party to the agreement, announced January 28, 1949, to organize a Council of Europe as a step toward the creation of a United States of Europe. He serves on the committee of ministers, the executive body of the council. The consultative body of the council, called the European Consultative Assembly, was convened for the first time at Strasbourg, France, in the summer of 1949.

Foreign ministers of the United States, Canada, and ten European countries signed the North Atlantic Treaty in Washington on April 4, 1949. In signing for his country, Bech said: "The North Atlantic Pact is the logical supplement to the Brussels Pact. Like the latter, its purpose is to prevent war from breaking out, by establishing a balance between the forces confronting each other, and to win any war of aggression that may be directed against one or all of the signatory states." On September 17, 1949, Bech represented Luxembourg at the first session of the North Atlantic Council established by the North Atlantic Treaty. Meeting in Washington, D. C., the council drafted a defense system in which the United States was to participate in the military plans for safeguarding Europe. Regional planning groups were established on a geographical basis, with Luxembourg in the Western European group comprising the five Brussels Pact countries.

Wide World Photos
JOSEPH BECH

Bech served as chairman of the Luxembourg delegation to the United Nations Conference on International Organization in San Francisco in April-June 1945. At that conference and at later sessions, he presented his country's claims to the cession of two strips of territory—the right bank of the Moselle River and a piece on the German side of the Our River. Bech declared that these territories were vital to a restoration of Luxembourg's economy and were equivalent to only partial compensation for war losses. Bech also sought and later obtained for his country a voice in the International Ruhr Authority on the grounds that coke from the Ruhr valley is essential for Luxembourg's steel industry, the sixth largest in the world. The Foreign Minister likewise presented Luxembourg's claims for reparations in the form of German industrial equipment (his country eventually received 0.15 per cent of such reparations available from Germany). Bech was also head of the Luxembourg delegation to the General Assembly of the United Nations in London in 1946, where he was elected vice-chairman of the Political and Security Committee, to which many of the U.N.'s important issues are referred. The following year he served as chairman of this committee. He has represented his Government at U.N. General Assemblies in 1947, 1948 and 1949.

The Foreign Minister of Luxembourg has been awarded the Grand Cross of the Luxembourg National Order, the Grand Cross of France's Legion of Honor, and the Grand Cross of the Order of Leopold of Belgium. He was married on October 3, 1918, to Georgette Delahaye. During the occupation of Luxembourg, his wife and two children lived for a time in Canada. His son, Charles, who flew with the United States Army Air Forces during the war, is an American citizen. In addition to hunting (a recreation in which he is sometimes joined

BECH, JOSEPH—*Continued*

by his daughter, Betty), Bech seeks relaxation in fishing. A portly figure with wavy gray hair, prominent eyebrows, and a mustache, the Foreign Minister of Luxembourg is described as having "a natural and pleasant manner."

References

> U N Bul 1 :24 N 25 '46 por
> International Who's Who, 1949
> Karsh, Y. Faces of Destiny (1947)
> Who's Who in America, 1948-49
> World Biography (1948)
> Yearbook of the United Nations, 1946-47

BECK, MRS. FRANCIS CARL *See* Beck, M. B.

BECK, MILDRED BUCHWALDER Mar. 31, 1914- Association director

Address: b. c/o Child Study Association of America, 132 E. 74th St., New York 21; h. 310 1st Ave., New York 9

Mrs. Mildred Buchwalder Beck on January 1, 1950, succeeded Mrs. Sidonie Matsner Gruenberg [40] in the directorship of the Child Study Association of America. Organized in 1888 for the purpose of serving parents and professional workers in promoting wholesome family life, the agency has its headquarters in New York City and contacts in every State. Mrs. Beck's plans for future expansion include making material on parent-child relationships more widely available, extension of existing services and the opening of new ones. A graduate of the New York School of Social Work, she brings to her position a varied background in psychiatric social work, including three years with the Psychiatry Department of the Yale

MILDRED BUCHWALDER BECK

University School of Medicine and three and a half years with the New York Committee on Mental Hygiene.

Born in New York City on March 31, 1914, Mildred Buchwalder Beck is the daughter of Adolf and Malvina (Gaydushek) Buchwalder, who had emigrated from their native Hungary. When Mildred was one year old, her father, an upholsterer and cabinetmaker, died, leaving his wife in straitened circumstances. Mrs. Buchwalder, who had gained practical experience in nursing while working with her uncle, a physician, solved the problem of supporting her two children (Mildred and an older son) : while remaining at home with them, she became foster mother to children placed with her. A visit to an orphanage at the age of five left a deep impression upon Mildred, and to it she attributes her early decision to become a social service worker. This ambition she determinedly followed, earning herself the money for her education. From the age of fourteen she worked in factories while attending Brooklyn's Central Evening High School from which she was graduated in 1928.

It was in 1931, shortly before Mildred Buchwalder's eighteenth birthday that she received her first position in the field of social service. A work relief project had been set up for the jobless of that depression year by President Herbert Hoover and New York City authorities. Katharine Reynolds, mother of Quentin Reynolds, the writer and radio commentator, was influential in placing the young girl in a position in the administrative office of this pre-WPA work relief program. Continuing her education, Miss Buchwalder attended evening classes in New York University, where she majored in educational sociology and educational psychology, to earn her B.S. in 1934 and and M.A. in 1938. At the university she became president of the Educational Sociology Club and a member of Alpha Kappa Delta. In 1939 she received a diploma from the New York School of Social Work, which she had attended on a fellowship from the Educational Foundation.

While still attending New York University, Miss Buchwalder filled the post of executive secretary in the placement service of the Institute for the Crippled and Disabled, a position she held from September 1937 to October 1938. In October 1939, after receiving her diploma from the New York School of Social Work, Mildred Buchwalder became a family case worker for the Jewish Social Service Association (later called the Jewish Family Service). In the course of World War II she served, from December 1942 to June 1943, as assistant field director with the American Red Cross at Halloran General Hospital, the largest receiving hospital for disabled soldiers. From there she went to the psychiatry department of the Yale University School of Medicine, where from June 1943 to May 1946 she was chief psychiatric social worker. Her work there consisted of orienting medical students in the social aspects of psychiatry.

In May 1946 Miss Buchwalder joined the staff of the State Charities Aid Association as assistant executive secretary of the organization's New York Committee on Mental Hygiene; of this committee the psychiatric social worker eventually became acting executive secretary. While in that post she acted as chairman of the Commission on Public Education in Mental Health, and edited that body's report, which was presented to the International Congress on Mental Health in London in 1948.

Announcement that Mrs. Beck (as Miss Buchwalder became in 1948) would succeed Mrs. Sidonie Matsner Gruenberg on January 1, 1950, in the directorship of the Child Study Association of America was made by the board of directors of the organization on October 27, 1949. The body, which describes itself as "a national organization with a workshop in New York," was founded in 1888 by Dr. Felix Adler and five women associates, psychiatrists and social workers. Aiming to aid parents and professional social workers in promoting wholesome family life, it carries out its functions through a program of practical lectures, discussion groups, individual counseling services for parents, and dissemination of publications carrying current findings in child development and related fields. These services are offered to the general public at a fee, and to association members at a special rate.

The association comprises a board of directors, advisory board, a staff for family counseling service, a school and camp information service, a children's books and radio service, and a speaker's bureau. Committees on special projects in the field are open to participation by members. Support for the organization comes from the fees and contributions of members, who may join on an individual or group basis. The association publishes *Child Study*, a quarterly journal of parent education, and pamphlets on such problems as "When Children Ask About Sex," and "The Meaning and Management of Aggression." Through the circulation abroad of its publications the group maintains international contacts. In addition to its local activities in New York City, the association also has national interchanges with individuals and groups in every State.

In her first press interview after the announcement of her appointment, Mrs. Beck called for closer cooperation among groups concerned with children to prevent duplication of effort. Commenting on parent-child relationships, she pointed out, "There is a parent behind every child who has problems, but the parent also has problems because he is living in a society that has many stresses." The association of which Mrs. Beck is director works for the fostering of sound personality development of the individual child to the end of building "a happier family life, a healthier and stronger world."

Describing the Child Study Association of America as "an agency with a single purpose but multiple functions," Mrs. Beck emphasized the "tremendous value" of the agency study groups and family counseling. The 1949-50 program offered discussion groups on "The Child's First Years", "Early Childhood," and "The School Years." Parents under the leader-

ship of a psychiatric social worker discussed during the series such subjects as the infant's eating, sleeping, and play routines; the child's growing awareness of his place in the family, his quest for independence yet need for guidance; school adjustment and home-school relations. The topics were considered in the light of the part the child's parents play in his development. The family counseling service, offering parents individual interviews with experienced psychiatrically trained counselors on their own and their children's daily problems, Mrs. Beck hopes to expand "with emphasis on preventive work." In an interview with Dorothy Barclay (New York *Times* April 26, 1950) the new director said: "We hope to assist . . . clinics and health and welfare agencies to broaden their scope so that they will not be restricted to therapeutic programs. . . . They are all trained for their clinical work, of course, but parent and public education requires a somewhat different approach." One of the important possibilities, she added, was a professional leadership training program for agency workers that would prepare them to work with individuals in a community before "serious trouble arose."

On September 3, 1948, Mildred Buchwalder was married to Francis Carl Beck, a psychiatric social worker, who in 1950 is on the staff of the New York Psychoanalytic Institute. Mrs. Beck is five feet six and three-quarter inches tall, weighs 142 pounds, has blue eyes and brown hair. She has been described as modest, and her voice as "softly modulated." The social worker, who is chairman of the New York District Branch of the American Association of Psychiatric Social Workers and a member of the American Orthopsychiatric Association, is the author of "Operation Cyprus," which was published in the *Journal of Psychiatric Social Work*.

References

N Y Herald Tribune p7 O 28 '49
N Y Times p11 O 28 '49
Parents Mag 25:64 Mr '50

BELL, BERT Feb. 25, 1894- Professional football commissioner

Address: b. c/o National Football League, 1518 Walnut St., Philadelphia 2, Pa.; h. 323 Haverford Ave., Narberth, Pa.

As commissioner of the National Football League, which he became in 1946, Bert Bell steered the professional football league through the rivalry with the All-America Football Conference to their merger in December 1949 as the National-American Football League. The new association, which in March 1950 resumed the name National Football League, retains Bell in the post of commissioner for a ten-year term. It comprises thirteen teams, in Eastern, Midwestern, and Pacific Coast cities. The professional football's arbiter was at various times owner of the Philadelphia Eagles and co-owner of the Pittsburgh Steelers. He played on the University of Pennsylvania teams of

BERT BELL

1916, 1917, and 1919, and was backfield coach at that university from 1920 to 1928.

The son of John Cromwell and Fleurette (de Benneville Myers) Bell, Bert Bell, who was christened de Benneville, was born February 25, 1894, in Philadelphia, Pennsylvania. His father was district attorney of Philadelphia from 1903 to 1907, and attorney general of Pennsylvania from 1911 to 1915; Bert's brother John was elected Lieutenant Governor, after which he succeeded Edward Martin as Governor when the latter was elected to the United States Senate in 1943. Football was a family interest—until his resignation in 1913, Bell's father was second in seniority on the Football Rules Committee to Walter Camp, the selector of All-America teams. At the Haverford (Pennsylvania) School young Bell played football, baseball, and basketball, and in his senior year was captain of the three teams.

Graduated from the preparatory school in 1915, Bert entered the University of Pennsylvania, where he majored in English. There he played football, for three years as quarterback on the Red and Blue team, on which Lou Little '45 played tackle. The first of these seasons (1916) was climaxed by the selection of the Penn team to play against Oregon in the Rose Bowl game, a contest the Eastern team lost. During a thirteen-month period Bell served in World War I with Base Hospital Twenty, a unit from the University of Pennsylvania Hospital, and Mobile Hospital Number Two. When he came back from France with a citation, Bell captained Penn's 1919 football team in a season of play which, it has been said, showed the influence of the rough AEF divisional football. A member of the class of 1920, Bell returned to the Red and Blue to coach the backfield for head coach John Heisman, and retained this position under Louis A. Young until 1928. During this period, stated a release from Bell's office, he developed the "hidden ball"

offense strategy. While at university Bell became a member of Phi Kappa Sigma fraternity.

Football remained Bell's main field of endeavor, an excursion into the hotel business having been of short duration. In 1930 and 1931 he coached the Temple University backfield. Two years later he and Lud Wray, an old teammate, purchased a professional football team, the Frankford Yellow Jackets, which they renamed the Philadelphia Eagles; Wray became coach. (Bell was to take over the coaching in May 1936.) This acquisition brought him into the thirteen-year-old National Football League at a time when professional football had yet to become a different game from college football. "When I owned a team," Bell has written, "a player played eleven games for from $100 to $150 a game"—a fraction of later salaries. Attendance was small: in Philadelphia's Municipal Stadium, his Eagles played before crowds of less than five thousand. (Bell admitted children for one cent when they were accompanied by adults.)

As an owner and coach Bell was known for his quick temper. An example cited tells that on one occasion when Luke Johnsos of the Chicago Bears tricked one of Bell's players into throwing him a lateral pass, Bell sprang to his feet and raced down the sidelines, keeping in step with Johnsos and berating him. In late 1939 Bell retired as coach, engaging H. J. Miller of St. Joseph's College to fill the post. By an exchange of franchises with Alexis Thompson, owner of the Pittsburgh Steelers, Bell and Art Rooney (who had just become co-owner of the Philadelpiha Eagles), took over the Pittsburgh team. For the next five years 1941-45, Bell was president and business manager of the Pittsburgh Steelers. In 1941 he coached the team the first two games of the season and then decided to devote all his time to the business interests of the team. His teams were not noted for success, frequently ending the season in last place, or next to last. When the exigencies of World War II depleted the ranks of football players, the Steelers merged with the Eagles in 1943, then with the Chicago Cardinals for the 1944 season; they resumed their separate identity in 1945.

When Elmer Layden, of Notre Dame's legendary "Four Horsemen," was chosen in February 1941 as the first commissioner of the National Football League, Bert Bell was one of the owners who objected, on the ground that they had not been consulted. In 1946, with the league battling its new rival, the All-America Football Conference, Bert Bell was elected to succeed Layden. The owners voted him a three-year contract at $20,000 a year, replaced a year later by a $30,000, five-year term. Bell then sold his share of the Pittsburgh Steelers to his partner. As commissioner, Bell was vested with broad powers: all contracts had to be approved by him to be valid, officials were chosen by him, he functioned as a court of last resort, and made decisions in matters upon which the owners could not agree. Still greater power was to be voted him later. New York *Herald Tribune* sportswriter Stanley Woodward termed the selection of Bell an "inspired" one.

In his first year in office—a season of unprecedentedly large attendance at games—Commissioner Bell presented a gold-plated pass to President Truman. On December 15, 1946, the National League was faced with a crisis when it was revealed that players Frank Filchock and Merle Hapes of the New York Giants had failed to report the offer of a bribe (illegal under New York State law) to "throw" the championship play-off of that year. Bell barred Hapes from the game (Filchock had not yet admitted having been approached with a bribe offer), later suspended both while the investigation and trials were proceeding, and finally, three months after the game, barred them indefinitely from the league for not reporting the offer, which neither of them had accepted. Bell's words, generally approved by commentators, were: "The players must be not only absolutely honest; they must be above suspicion." Thereafter the commissioner campaigned for Federal and State laws making it illegal to offer a bribe to an athlete; he reported in November 1948 that all except one of the States in which his league had teams had passed such a law. (In mid-July 1950 Bell ended the suspension of Filchock.)

The club owners in January 1947 adopted an amendment to the league's constitution, written by Bell, giving the commissioner power over all clubs in the league and empowering him to bar from all league parks anyone deemed "detrimental to the best interests of the National Football League and/or professional football." Other matters coming under the commissioner's supervision are relations with minor football leagues and with college football associations. "The commissioner's decision and his alone shall be final, binding, conclusive, and without appeal," ran the amendment, which made Bell what sportswriter Luke P. Carroll called "the most powerful figure in all sports."

Bert Bell's league refused to recognize the All-America Football Conference, which was headed by O. O. Kessing '49. As rivalry between the leagues continued and players' salaries mounted, game attendance declined—uncoordinated game scheduling often resulted in conflicting games in the same neighborhood. Finally, on December 9, 1949, it was announced that the two "warring" associations would merge into one National-American Football League. When the merger became effective December 19, the new organization comprised the original ten N.F.L. clubs (Chicago Bears, Chicago Cardinals, Detroit Lions, Green Bay Packers, Los Angeles Rams, New York Bulldogs, New York Giants, Philadelphia Eagles, Pittsburgh Steelers, Washington Redskins), and the A.A.F.C. Cleveland Browns, Baltimore Colts, and San Francisco 49ers. (The four other teams dropped out of professional football.) Bell thereupon was retained under ten-year contract as commissioner of the new National-American Football League. In March 1950 he announced the return to the name of National Football League. Its thirteen teams would function in two divisions to be called the National Conference and the American Conference, and at the end of the regular season the winners in each conference

would meet in a championship game. "This step is obviously aimed at putting pro football on the same basis as major league baseball," was the comment in an Associated Press release.

Commissioner Bell is generally credited with bringing the rival leagues together. In effecting this consolidation, Bell did an "excellent piece of work" said the owner of the Pittsburgh Steelers, who expressed the opinion that "the new arrangement will be better for all concerned—the owners, the players, the coaches and the fans." Sports columnist Arthur Daley (New York *Times*) wrote: "Only the iron-handed tactics of Bell saved the newly merged league from dying at birth. . . .He couldn't please everyone, of course, but he was so eminently fair in every ruling that even the originally suspicious All-America Conference owners became his firmest supporters. . . .He emerged with vastly increased stature and pro football reflected that gain."

Bell and Frances Upton (musical comedy actress), were married January 4, 1934; their children are Jane, John Bert, and George Upton. The sports executive is a short (five feet eight inches), heavy (220 pounds) man, with gray hair and hazel eyes. Questioned as to his hobby, he has said it is "football in all its phases."

References

N Y Herald Tribune p15 Ja 12 '46
N Y Times p16 Ja 12 '46; p32 Ja 26 '50
Washington (D.C.) Post p13 Ja 24 '50
Who's Who in America, 1950-51

BELL, DE BENNEVILLE *See* Bell, B.

BEMIS, SAMUEL FLAGG (bē'mĭs) Oct. 20, 1891- Historian; college professor
Address: b. c/o Yale University, New Haven, Conn.; h. 120 Ogden St., New Haven, Conn.

Twice a winner of the Pulitzer Prize—the first time in history, in 1927 for his *Pinckney's Treaty* (1926), and the second for biography, in 1950 for *John Quincy Adams and the Foundation of American Foreign Policy* (1949)—Professor Samuel Flagg Bemis of Yale University has been called "an historian's historian." A student of early American diplomacy and Latin American relations, he numbers among his books *Jay's Treaty* (1923), *A Diplomatic History of the United States* (1936) and *The Latin American Policy of the United States* (1942); and his shorter writings have appeared in scholarly and general periodicals since 1916, as well as in collections of essays.

Born in Worcester, Massachusetts, on October 20, 1891, Samuel Flagg Bemis is the son of Charles Harris and Flora M. (Bemis) Bemis. His father, a newspaperman, later became a news editor of the Boston *Transcript*. After attending the public schools in or near his native city, Bemis entered Clark University

Loring Studios

SAMUEL FLAGG BEMIS

(also at Worcester) ; there he received his B.A. degree in 1912 and the M.A. in the year following. (Clark was to award him the honorary D.H.L. in 1937.) Continuing his graduate work at Harvard University, Bemis was "introduced to the professional study of history" by a faculty of distinguished professors. Bemis added Harvard's Master of Arts degree to that of Clark University in 1915, and by April of the next year had "broken into" the scholarly press with a paper entitled "Relations Between the Vermont Separatists and Great Britain, 1789-91" in the *American Historical Review*.

Bemis received his Ph.D. degree in 1916, after a year of study in England and France on a fellowship, and began his teaching career in 1917 as an instructor in history at Colorado College, in Colorado Springs. A year later he was advanced to associate professor, and saw the appearance of his essay "United States and the Abortive Armed Neutrality of 1794" in the *American Historical Review*. In 1920 he was appointed professor of history at Whitman College, Walla Walla, Washington.

It was during three years at Whitman that Bemis completed the first of his works to appear in book form, *Jay's Treaty: A Study in Commerce and Diplomacy*, published 1923. The subject, the diplomatic negotiations of the United States and Great Britain from 1783 to 1795 involving "vital national and international questions," had been suggested to Bemis by Professor Edward Channing of Harvard; and the manuscript, on completion, was entered in the competition for a $3,000 prize for a work on American history conducted by the Knights of Columbus "to encourage investigation into the origins, the achievements, and the problems of the United States . . . and to exalt the American ideal." Bemis' work was awarded the prize. J. L. Heaton, reviewing it for the

New York *World*, found it "an admirable book upon this subject, quite the best available," while the New York *Times* praised its "high standard of research" and pronounced it "judicial yet vivid" and "interesting from beginning to end."

After one year (1923-24) as a research associate with the Carnegie Institution of Washington, Bemis became professor of history at George Washington University (also in that city), a position he was to occupy for the ensuing ten years. Bemis has also, at various times, been a visiting lecturer at several other universities, among them Washington, Minnesota, Stanford, Wyoming, California (UCLA), Harvard, and Johns Hopkins. It was at the last-named that the substance of his first Pulitzer Prize book (for history), *Pinckney's Treaty*, was first made public in an annual course of lectures on diplomatic history endowed by Dr. Albert Shaw. The subject had presented itself to Bemis while he was working on *Jay's Treaty*. "My researches at that time," he has said, "suggested to me the importance of the reaction of the signature of *Jay's Treaty* on the contemporary negotiations of the United States in Spain, and particularly the close relationship of the international policies of the French Revolution with those of the United States. It was apparent no investigation of these Spanish negotiations had been made outside of purely American archives." *Pinckney's Treaty: A Study of America's Advantage from Europe's Distress*, designed "to fill that gap in diplomatic history," appeared in late 1926.

The London *Times Book Supplement*, reviewing *Pinckney's Treaty*, considered that the author had succeeded in imparting to "the record of these diplomatic debates . . . something of the quality of a novel" through "vivid characterization of the leading figures." The *American Historical Review* found that this "companion volume" to *Jay's Treaty* "fully maintains" its author's "reputation for scholarly research, mastery of technic, and sprightly writing." Award of the 1926 Pulitzer Prize in Letters for "a distinguished book of the year upon the history of the United States" was announced by Columbia University on May 2, 1927. A second edition of *Pinckney's Treaty* appeared in 1941.

Following the death of Dr. Gaillard Hunt in March 1924, the editorship of the ten-volume work *The American Secretaries of State and Their Diplomacy*, projected by Dr. Hunt and James Brown Scott, Secretary of the Carnegie Endowment for International Peace, was taken over by Bemis. To the first volume, which appeared in 1927, he contributed the study of Thomas Jefferson; for the second he wrote the pages on John Jay. Also in 1927, Bemis was named director of the European mission of the Library of Congress, a two-year appointment. In 1931 his next book, *The Hussey-Cumberland Mission and American Independence* was published, to be followed four years later (1935) by *A Guide to the Diplomatic History of the United States, 1775-1921*, a Library of Congress publication composed in collaboration with Grace Gardner Griffin; and *The Diplomacy of the American Revolution*.

The latter volume was designed as the first of three in a series to be known as *Foundations of American Diplomacy, 1775-1823.*

Since 1935 Bemis has been a member of the faculty of Yale University, first as Farnam professor of diplomatic history, later as Sterling professor of diplomatic history and inter-American relations. In December 1935 Bemis followed his paper "Washington's Farewell Address: A Foreign Policy of Independence" (appearing in the *American Historical Review* early in the previous year) with an essay, "Clarifying Foreign Policy" (*Yale Review*); and in speeches delivered in both 1935 and 1936 suggested repeal of the tenth amendment to the Constitution of the United States and the substitution of another to declare that "all powers not specifically reserved to the States shall reside in the Federal government." ("George Washington, if alive today," he asserted, "would advocate repeal of the tenth amendment.")

"More than half" of Bemis' next book, *A Diplomatic History of the United States* (1936), was "devoted to a critical account, almost an indictment, of American policy since 1898," and caused divergence of opinion among reviewers. "The most striking thing about the book is that it makes judgments," declared Professor Dexter Perkins in the *Saturday Review of Literature;* while William MacDonald, writing in the New York *Times,* considered the fact that the author had "gone out of his way to turn advocate" had resulted in "an important blemish." A new edition, brought up to date, appeared in 1942.

For the academic year of 1937-38 Bemis (who speaks Spanish fluently) was on leave of absence from Yale to serve as Carnegie visiting professor to Latin American universities. His *La Política Internacional de los Estados Unidos: Interpretaciones* was published in Mexico in 1939, his *The Latin American Policy of the United States* in 1942. This work, also, was received with certain qualifications. "Altogether a fine job, but many Latin Americans . . . will be uneasy over Mr. Bemis' repeated emphasis on our 'forebearance,' " was the opinion Hubert Herring expressed in his New York *Times* review; and B. D. Wolfe thought the author had "a blind spot when it comes to appreciating the Latin American viewpoint." In 1945, the year of his appointment as Sterling professor at Yale, Bemis was in Cuba as a visiting lecturer. In the course of the 1940's the historian contributed papers to various collections of essays; the titles of two of his articles are "North and South America: Consequences of Latitude and Altitude," and "Shifting Strategy of American Defense and Diplomacy."

Bemis' second Pulitzer Prize (for biography), *John Quincy Adams and the Foundation of American Foreign Policy* (1949) evolved from his uncompleted trilogy on the foundations of American diplomacy. "A variety of circumstances," he states in the preface, "including the appearance of excellent books on the diplomatic history of the United States during the period 1783-1826 have impelled me to take the present biographical device to acquit myself of my earlier project." The result, called by Adrienne Koch (in the New York *Times*) "the work of an historian's historian,"

does not deal with Adams' post-Presidential career except where "foreign affairs are concerned"; but within its scope it is exhaustive, and draws extensively on papers in the Adams Manuscript Trust in custody of the Massachusetts Historical Society, material apparently consulted by no other biographer except the late John T. Morse, Jr. "This new material," wrote Dr. Koch (herself an Adams scholar), "decidedly increases its value both as biography and as diplomatic history." Dumas Malone, writing in the New York *Herald Tribune,* also noted that Bemis "casts fresh light on complicated matters" in what the author himself describes as "a combination of biography and diplomatic history." Announcement of the 1949 Pulitzer Prize was made on May 1, 1950.

Samuel Flagg Bemis and Ruth M. Steele were married June 20, 1919, and have one daughter, Barbara. The historian is a member of the American Historical Association, the American Antiquarian Society, the Massachusetts Historical Society, the Colonial Society of Massachusetts, La Sociedad Geográfica y Estadística (Mexico) and La Academia de la Historia (Cuba). His church is the Congregational.

References

N Y Herald Tribune p17 My 2 '50
N Y Times p6 My 3 '27; p22 My 2 '50
Kunitz, S. J. and Haycraft, H. eds. Twentieth Century Authors (1942)
Who's Who in America, 1950-51
Who's Who in the East (1948)
Who's Who in New England (1949)
World Biography (1948)

BERGGRAV, EIVIND (JOSEF), BISHOP (bâr'gräv ā'vĭn yō'sĕf) Oct. 25, 1884-

Former Bishop of Oslo and Primate of Norway

Address: Oslo, Norway

The Norwegian churchman who was called "a symbol of free Christianity in the world" because of his resistance to the Quisling Government during the Nazi occupation of his country in World War II, the Reverend Eivind Berggrav became Bishop of Oslo and Primate of Norway in 1937. Active in promoting international accord through the churches, the Bishop was elected a president of the World Council of Churches in July 1950. After approximately ten years as editor and educator, at the age of thirty-five Berggrav became a pastor of the Evangelical Lutheran Church, the national church of Norway. In October 1950 ill health obliged him to resign from the bishopric and primacy.

Eivind Joseph Berggrav was born October 25, 1884, in Stavanger, Norway, the son of Otto Jensen Berggrav, Bishop of Hamar, whose wife was the former Marena Pedersen. His forebears were peasants—Eivind Berggrav has said that he has always been "peasant-minded," has loved to live in the country among farmers. His paternal grandfather was a headmaster, his maternal grandfather the owner of a hotel in Oslo; he tells also that there is some Scottish

BISHOP EIVIND BERGGRAV

blood in his mother's family, and that the
Berggravs (the name literally means "mountain diggers"), who originally lived in Saxony,
were invited to come to Norway in 1624 to
start working the Kongsberg silver mines.
"Austerity and piety" marked the lives of Berggrav's ancestors.

Eivind Berggrav spent his early years near
Halden, the seaport on Norway's southeast
coast. Upon graduating from Stavanger *Gymnasium* in 1902, the young man became a writer
for a local newspaper. Although a career in
engineering had been planned for him, he was
drawn toward the ministry after reading the
New Testament when he was seventeen years
old. Accordingly he attended the University of
Oslo as a theological student, where, an active
member of the general student organization, he
was chairman of the Students' Christian Association; he was enthusiastic about skiing and
swimming. While he received the master's degree in theology in 1908, there was so much
doubt in his mind, that he did not enter the
ministry until 1919.

Instead, in 1909 he became headmaster of
the folk school (for adult education) in Eids-
voll, about thirty miles from Oslo. There he
taught classes in chemistry, physics, and psychology; and concurrently for a period he was
a supervisor of Holmestrand teachers college.
In 1909, too, he became the editor of the
monthly *Kirke og Kultur* ("Church and Culture"). The recipient of stipends from the
University of Oslo, he was able to go to England, for study at Cambridge and Oxford in
1914.

When Berggrav felt ready for ordination
(in this, he has said, he was influenced by a
surgeon, his best friend since 1910), he was
appointed rector of a rural congregation, in
Hurdal, approximately forty miles from Norway's capital. After five years (1919-24) in
that pulpit, he was the chaplain of Oslo prisons

for the succeeding four years (1924-28). While
in that city, he received the D.D. degree from
the university in 1925, offering "The Threshold
of Religion" as his dissertation; and during
1923-28 he lectured on the psychology of religion at that institution. The Norwegian pastor
received his first bishopric, that of Northern
Norway, in 1929. In the eight years he spent
near the Arctic Ocean, he lived among his
parishioners, the fur trappers, fishermen, and
seamen, sharing their hardships and privations.

Appointment as Bishop of Oslo and Primate
of Norway's Evangelical Lutheran Church came
to Berggrav in 1937. He thus became the leader
of his country's religious life, since that denomination is the national Church—it is endowed by the State, and its clergy are nominated by the King, and are State officials. (All
religions are tolerated in the country; non-
Lutherans in 1946 numbered 120,106 in a total
population of 3,156,950.

Three years after Bishop Berggrav assumed
the duties of head of the State Church,
in May 1940 Norway was invaded by the Nazis.
Named by Norwegian political leaders and the
Administrative Council to serve as one of three
negotiators to ascertain intentions of the German authorities, Berggrav withdrew from the
negotiations after two days, refusing to offer
a compromise to the Germans. In the ensuing
period of German occupation Berggrav and the
six other bishops (Norway is divided into seven
bishoprics) led the Church in opposition to
Nazi edicts on spiritual matters. The bishops
maintained the right of the clergy to withhold
confidential information, the Church's right to
noninterference in its spiritual province, and
the rights of Jews; they sent letters of protest
to the Government and circulated a pastoral
letter indicting the Nazis for their "systematic
rule of terror."

In a series of incidents the Church broke
completely with the State after the appointment, on February 1, 1942, of Vidkun Quisling [40] as head of the Nazi-controlled Government. On February 24 Berggrav and the six
bishops resigned their offices in protest against
a series of Government interferences, an action
in which they were followed by 701 of Norway's 740 clergy at Easter of that year. Bishop
Berggrav, who had been deprived by Quisling
of the title of Bishop of Oslo and designated
"an ordinary private person," was arrested on
April 12, on charges of "instigation to rebellion." First imprisoned in Bretvedt concentration camp, he was later placed under house
arrest at his summer home twelve miles from
Oslo, a move ordered by Hitler, it was reported, because of public unrest following the
Bishop's imprisonment.

Bishop Berggrav signed by proxy a manifesto, issued by a provisional Church council
set up by the religious leaders in secret session,
which proclaimed the intention of the Norwegian Church to continue its religious activities independently of the Quisling regime. Meetings of the underground Church were held in
Oslo, and Berggrav, in disguise, was able to
pass his guards to meet underground leaders
and to influence the Church's activities in all
Norway by means of a coded information sys-

tem. The Primate's leadership in the Church resistance was lauded at a dinner held in New York to pay tribute to the imprisoned Bishop in March 1945, when Crown Princess Martha described him as "a symbol of the Christian will to obey God rather than bow to those who have will on earth." In April 1945, after three years of imprisonment, Bishop Berggrav succeeded in escaping, with the help of "home forces," and went into hiding in Oslo. As a result of the underground activities of the religious leaders plans were ready on V-E Day in May 1945 for the re-establishment of the Church and the suspension of Quisling pastors. Under Berggrav's chairmanship a special governmental commission set up to study the reorganization of the internal administration of the Church, made recommendations providing for more active participation by laymen.

Before the outbreak of World War II, Bishop Berggrav had become active in the international church movement. In 1938 he was elected vice-president of the World Alliance for Promoting International Friendship Through the Churches, and he also heads the United Bible Societies of the World. After the war Berggrav was a member of the provisional committee of the World Council of Churches, which held its first meeting in Geneva in February 1946. With other religious leaders (among them Martin Niemoeller [43]), who had resisted the Nazis, he assisted in the drafting of the message of the council urging man to turn to God in an effort to save the world from destruction by atomic warfare. In August 1948 the World Council of Churches was officially organized at Amsterdam by church leaders from forty-four nations and representing 156 Protestant and Greek Orthodox bodies with an estimated membership of 160,000,000. The organization enables its member churches to act together in matters of common concern. Berggrav, who had had an important part in preparations for the Amsterdam assembly, was elected to the central committee of the council. There he urged a public protest against the arrest of Bishop Ordass by the Hungarian Communist Government, declaring it similar to the oppression he had undergone.

When the ninety-member central committee of the World Council of Churches met in Toronto, Canada, in July 1950, it elected the Lutheran churchman to succeed former Archbishop Erling Eidem of Sweden, who had resigned, as one of its six presidents. Berggrav, who assumed the unexpired five-year term, will serve until the council's second world assembly, which is scheduled to be held in Evanston, Illinois, in 1953. At the Toronto meeting the central committee issued a resolution on the Korean conflict, commending the United Nations for its prompt decision to meet aggression, but urging at the same time that governments press for "a just settlement by conciliation and negotiation."

The Norwegian churchman served as Bishop of Oslo and Primate of Norway for more than thirteen years. On October 5, 1950, he announced his resignation from those ecclesiastic offices because of ill health. He stated, however, that he was permitted to continue his work with the World Council of Churches.

Eivind Berggrav, who has continued to serve as the editor of *Kirke og Kultur* since 1909, has contributed many articles to newspapers and magazines, and is the author of a number of books. The latter include four which have appeared in English translations—*The Prisoner's Soul—and Our Own* (1932), which came from his work in the prisons of Oslo; *Land of Suspense* (1943), the result of his years in the Arctic region; *The Norwegian Church in its International Setting* (1946); *State and Man* (1944). Also (in Norwegian): *Krigerliv* (1915), on "soldiers and religion," his experiences as a war correspondent in World War I; *Nathan Söderblom* (1931); "With God in the Darkness" (1943), written while he was a prisoner of the Nazis; he tells of his dramatic examination by Heinrich Himmler (in 1941) in "When the Fight Came." Several of his books have been translated as well into Swedish and German. A chairman of a number of Norwegian societies, Berggrav is a member of the Royal Academy of Science of his country; he has received honorary doctorates from the universities of Lund (1923), Kiel (1929), Copenhagen (1945), and St. Andrews (1946). Norway awarded him the Grand Cross of the Order of St. Olav, and the United States the Medal of Freedom with Silver Palm.

The marriage of Eivind Berggrav and Kathrine Seip took place August 17, 1909. A schoolteacher before her marriage, his wife became his teacher, Berggrav says in tribute to her. (Mrs. Berggrav died in 1949.) Of this union were born four sons—Otto, Øivind, Jan, and Dag. The churchman has blue eyes, light hair, a height of five feet seven inches, and a weight of 150 pounds. He still finds pleasure in skiing and swimming.

References

    N Y Herald Tribune p6 Ap 18 '45
    Time 39:65 Mr 9 '42; 44:53 D 25 '44
      por
    Hvem er Hvem? (1948)
    International Who's Who, 1950
    World Biography (1948)

BERGSON, HERBERT A(UGUSTUS)
Jan. 14, 1909- Lawyer; former United States Government official
Address: h. 7908 16th St., Washington, D.C.

As Assistant Attorney General, Herbert A. Bergson headed the Antitrust Division of the United States Department of Justice for more than two years. In that office, to which he was appointed in June of 1948, he was charged with the enforcement of antitrust acts. Bergson who was regarded as the most "zealous trustbuster" since Thurman Arnold [40], prosecuted 135 antitrust cases in the course of the two and a quarter years he held that office. In September 1950 he resigned and resumed private law practice.

The son of Harry Bergson, a Boston lawyer, Herbert Augustus Bergson was born in that Massachusetts city on January 14, 1909;

Wide World Photos
HERBERT A. BERGSON

his mother was the former Augusta Cook. Following a family tradition, Herbert Bergson attended Harvard College (for four years) and Harvard Law School (for three years), receiving the degrees of Bachelor of Arts and Bachelor of Laws in 1930 and 1933, respectively. In 1933, the year he was admitted to the bar, he entered the family law firm. After a short period of practice he became one of those "brilliant young men" with Harvard law degrees who, inspired by the teachings of the future Supreme Court Justice Felix Frankfurter, were attracted to Government service in the early years of the New Deal. It was in 1934 that the young Bostonian entered the Department of Justice as a trial attorney, under Attorney General Homer S. Cummings.

Except for two World War II years as a Coast Guard lieutenant assigned to legal work in New Orleans, Herbert Bergson spent the Washington years "hardworking his way up" (as *Time* put it) in the Department of Justice under attorneys general Cummings, Jackson '40, Biddle '41, Clark '45, and McGrath '48. An early step was his assignment to the Office of the Assistant to the Attorney General, first as assistant chief of the legislative section, then as chief. Next he was made chief legal consultant to the Assistant Solicitor General. A subsequent appointment was to the Claims Division, as first assistant to the Assistant Attorney General in charge, and in October 1947 he became the acting head of the division. (The Solicitor General represents the Federal Government in courts; the Claims Division has charge of all civil suits and claims for and against the Government.)

On June 2, 1948, President Truman named Bergson Assistant Attorney General, to head the Antitrust Division. Bergson, who had been executive assistant to Attorney General Tom Clark, thus became chief of a division

which maintains a staff of more than six hundred in Washington and twelve field offices. Activities were expanded after July 1, 1948, when the division received an appropriation of $3,400,000, the largest in its history. The Antitrust Division is charged with the enforcement of the Sherman Act of 1890, which forbade "every contract, combination in the form of trust or otherwise, or conspiracy, in restraint of commerce among the several States." It was limited in 1911 by the "rule of reason," which made the Sherman Act apply "not to monopolies as such but to those which used their power for 'unreasonable' restraints of trade" (from *Dictionary of American Politics*); the act was clarified and strengthened by the Clayton Act of 1914. Answering criticism that the terminology of the act created confusion, Bergson has maintained that its language is such as to make it "as useful an instrument in the economy of 1950 as it was in the economy of 1890."

In 1948, Bergson reported, businessmen filed 1,400 complaints (nine out of ten cases originate in complaints brought by small businessmen who charge other companies with antitrust violations). The first year of Bergson's direction saw a total of 34 new cases filed and $382,000 in fines collected. In 1949 the figures rose to 57 cases filed, 58 cases concluded, of which the Government won 46 and lost 12, and more than $1,000,000 was collected. Among the major suits filed under Bergson were these: to dissolve certain A. & P. (Great Atlantic and Pacific Tea Company) subsidiaries, separating its manufacturing and processing operations from selling operations; to divorce the American Telephone and Telegraph Company from its wholly owned subsidiary, Western Electric; to split the "Big Four" meat packers into fourteen competing companies; to divest Du Pont of some of its cellophane plants. Among other organizations charged with restraint of competition were manufacturers of gloves, automobile parts, and gelatin capsules, a newspaper, several department stores, motion picture and outdoor advertising companies, an organization for prepaid medical care, theatrical producers, and ASCAP.

Commentators who speak for large concerns have criticized Bergson for striking at the basic pattern of American industry—the "giants" in each field which claim their operation make for efficiency and fair prices. To this Bergson has replied: "We have never brought a case attacking bigness, efficiency, or selling at low prices, and as long as I am Assistant Attorney General such a case never will be brought." Bergson has repeatedly stated that monopoly power, not size, is the basis of antitrust suits, and that monopoly power consists in an exemption from the pressures of normal competition, or in other words, "the power to exclude competitors from the market." "Monopoly of technology is as significant as monopoly of raw materials," in his view. "Restraints at the research level, such as division of fields of invention, must be eliminated." Other pronouncements by Bergson include his intention to have "fewer settlements by means of *nolo*" (no defense) in criminal cases, and his refusal to postpone trial during negotiations for consent decrees, or to initiate such negotiations. "The evidence in every criminal [antitrust] case is carefully studied by me," said the Assistant Attorney General. "When I sign an indictment I am convinced that the defendants named therein have wilfully violated the law." According to the New York *World-Telegram*, the Department of Justice official favored repeal of the Miller-Tydings law, which authorizes the setting up of fair trade laws by States, and of the Bulwinkle act, which exempts railroads from antitrust laws. From time to time he addressed groups such as wholesalers, retailers, and manufacturers on the functions of his division.

In mid-September 1950 it was announced that Bergson had sent in his resignation as Assistant Attorney General, which became effective September 30. As reported by the New York *Times*, he said that "his only motive was that, after fourteen years of Federal service, he felt it necessary to resume private law practice," which he carries on in Washington. Both President Truman and Attorney General McGrath accepted his resignation with much regret.

Bergson is a tall, sandy-haired, spectacled man, who is described as having little leisure for recreation, aside from his home life—the Bergsons have two sons, Richard and Paul. When Mrs. Bergson was questioned as to her husband's hobbies, she said that he used to play golf, "but hasn't had any time for it for years."

Reference

Washington (D.C.) Post p1, p2 Je 3 '48

BERNARDINO, MINERVA 1907- Minister from the Dominican Republic to the United Nations

Address: b. c/o United Nations, New York; h. 2013 New Hampshire Ave., N.W., Washington, D.C.

Señorita Minerva Bernardino, of the Dominican Republic, in January 1950 was appointed her country's Minister Plenipotentiary to the United Nations, where she had been a delegate during several conferences. The chairman of the Inter-American Commission of Women from 1944 to 1949 and one of four women to sign the charter of the United Nations, she has been called "one of the best-known feminist leaders of Latin America." In 1929 she began to fight for the rights of Dominican women, who were granted suffrage and civil rights in 1942 under constitutional amendment; she represented her native land at the Chapultepec Conference of 1945, attended the organizational conference of the United Nations at San Francisco in the same year, was a member of the first General Assembly in 1946, and became vice-chairman of the U.N. Economic and Social Council's Commission on the Status of Women.

The eldest child in a family of four girls and three boys, Minerva Bernardino was born to Alvaro and Altagracia Bernardino at Seibo, Dominican Republic, in 1907. She is a granddaughter of a provincial governor. "My mother

was very progressive, and I was reared in an atmosphere that was, at that time, most unusual in my country," she once told Ann Foster of the *Christian Science Monitor*; and her father appears to have held opinions no less liberal than those of his wife. "Go out if you like, travel if you want, and let criticize who will," he asserted when she protested against the taboo which forbade young girls to be seen unattended in public.

The Bernardino children were left orphans when Minerva was fifteen, whereupon the young girl and her eldest brother became the family breadwinners. "We both believed in equality from the beginning," she said to the *Monitor* writer, "and were determined that he should go in for law, that my sister should do as she also wished, and become a doctor, and that I should enter public life." This Miss Bernardino accordingly did, becoming head of the file office of the Dominican Republic's Department of Development and Communications in 1926, and chief of a section of the Department of Agriculture two years later. Meanwhile she studied for, and acquired, a Bachelor of Science degree.

By 1929 the young civil servant had become active in the woman's rights movement, and four years afterwards—having meanwhile held the post of chief of the statistics section of the Department of Education (1931-33)—she became the secretary of Acción Feminista Dominicana, an organization which has been given a major share of credit for the winning of civil rights and the franchise for women under the amended constitution in 1942. In 1933, also, Miss Bernardino was named supervisor of vocational schools in the district of Santo Domingo, a position she retained for approximately a year. That year marked the beginning of her association with the Inter-American Commission of Women (within the Organization of American States, of which the secretariat is the Pan American Union). She was appointed the Dominican delegate to the commission, whose purpose is "to work for the extension of civil, political, economic, and social rights" of the women of the twenty-one American republics, and "to study their problems and propose means of solving them." Since its creation in 1928 it has submitted reports and recommendations on the status of the women of the Americas to the International Conference of American States, which is held every fifth year.

Miss Bernardino attended the Montevideo conference in the year of her appointment (1933) and was rapporteur at Lima in 1938. In the fall of 1939, when Señora Ana Rosa de Martínez Guerrero of Argentina was elected chairman of the Inter-American Commission of Women, Miss Bernardino was chosen to fill the newly created office of vice-chairman. In August 1942 Miss Bernardino was instrumental in defeating an Argentine motion to transfer the headquarters of the commission to Buenos Aires, and on the following November 11 she presented, against opposition, a resolution urging the women of Argentina and Chile to call upon their governments to "sever diplomatic

United Nations Official Photo.

MINERVA BERNARDINO

relations with the aggressor nations" (i.e. Germany, Italy and Japan). When, a little less than a year afterward, Señora Martínez Guerrero fell out of favor with the Argentine government (her organization of 50,000 women, the Junta de la Victoria, was disbanded for having engaged in raising funds for the Allies) her place was taken by Señorita Angelina Fuselli as Argentine delegate to the commission. This necessitated the choice of a new chairman; and on November 3, 1943, Minerva Bernardino was elected to assume, at the beginning of the following year, the office which she was to hold for about six years.

When the Inter-American Conference on Problems of War and Peace convened at Chapultepec, Mexico, early in 1945, Miss Bernardino, as delegate-plenipotentiary of the Dominican Republic, was one of four women seated, but the only one with the power to vote. The outcome, on April 4, was the Act of Chapultepec pledging joint action by all American republics against aggression directed at any one of them. Later in the year the Dominican feminist was a full delegate from her country to the conference in San Francisco at which the United Nations was organized; and she was a delegate to the first General Assembly meeting in London in January 1946. She was one of four women to sign the United Nations charter. Appointed to membership in the U.N. Economic and Social Council's Commission on the Status of Women in March 1946, she became vice-chairman thereof in the month following. This subcommission of nine women, a part of the larger Commission on Human Rights, held nine public sessions and about twenty closed meetings, and on May 13 submitted a report recommending universal suffrage for women, equal civil rights, full equality on the labor market, and equal, free, and compulsory education; and, when the General

Assembly reconvened at New York in October 1946, for the second part of the first session, the vice-chairman strongly supported a resolution offered by Bodil Begtrup[46] of Denmark tó the effect that "the Assembly recommend that all members not already having done so grant the same political rights to women and to men." The sub-commission was continued, and in 1948-49 was at work on a study of labor laws in relation to women and children.

At the Ninth Conference of American States at Bogotá, Colombia, in May 1948 (there was no conference in 1943 because of the war), Minerva Bernardino was one of three women plenipotentiaries and the chairman of a subcommittee which acted favorably on a convention recommending that women be guaranteed equal civil and political rights with men in all the participating republics. The basic "Charter of the Americas" which evolved from the Bogotá conference recognizes that "all human beings, without distinction as to . . . sex" have equal "right to attain material well-being and spiritual growth"; the Inter-American Charter of Social Securities specifies "equal pay for equal work regardless of sex." In June 1948 Miss Bernardino was honored as the "Woman of the Americas" for her "effort to improve the status of women" and was awarded the Pan American Union's Bolívar and San Martín medal. In August 1949, when Argentina was host to the sixth assembly of the Inter-American Commission of Women meeting at Buenos Aires, Miss Bernardino recognized, as chairman, the right of unofficial observers (that is, of opponents of governments in power) to speak at the sessions, in conflict with the stand of the honorary chairman, Señora Eva Perón[49], who maintained that all "aspirations" should be communicated through the official delegations.

Miss Bernardino resigned from the chairmanship of the Inter-American Commission of Women in Buenos Aires in the summer of 1949. In reviewing the work of the commission, commentators gave special credit to her for a number of its achievements. It was under her leadership that the commission directed the founding of the Pan American Liaison Commission in 1944. In the twenty-odd years since the commission's establishment, women have won the franchise in twelve of the twenty-one Latin American countries; more women have been elected to national legislatures, state and municipal offices than ever before; and women have the same legal rights as men to exercise a profession in seventeen of those countries.

In January 1950 Miss Bernardino was named Minister Plenipotentiary to the United Nations from the Dominican Republic. (This post makes her next in rank to the Dominican Ambassador in every country.) Her U.N. appointment signifies that the demand for equal rights for women will move into the world arena.

"Small, plump, red-haired and vivacious" are adjectives employed by a writer to describe the Dominican feminist leader. She is an effective speaker and debater and the possessor of a hearty sense of humor. In Washington, D.C., she is a member of the Political Study Club and adviser to the department of international relations of the General Federation of Women's Clubs.

References

Christian Sci Mon p4 My 4 '45; p12 Je 27 '46
U N Bul 1:28 D 17 '46 por
Who's Who in America, 1948-49
World Biography (1948)
Year Book of the United Nations, 1946-47

BERNHARD, PRINCE OF THE NETHERLANDS June 29, 1911-

Address: Soestdijk Palace, Baarn, the Netherlands

Prince Bernhard of the Netherlands, the consort of Queen Juliana [44], was called upon to take a significant part in Holland's struggle against the Nazis in World War II. In the postwar years he has become known particularly for his help in cementing cordial relations between the Netherlands and other countries. Typical of that task was his good-will tour to the Western Hemisphere in early 1950. The German-born Prince Bernhard of Lippe-Biesterfeld was married to Crown Princess Juliana in 1937, eleven years before she succeeded her mother, Queen Wilhelmina [40].

Bernhard, Prince of the Netherlands, was born on June 29, 1911, in Jena, Germany, into the princely family of Lippe, which was founded in the twelfth century by the first Bernhard. The twentieth century Prince of Lippe-Biesterfeld was given the names Bernhard Leopold Friedrich Eberhard Julius Kurt Karl Gottfried Peter by his parents, Prince Bernhard and Princess Armgard of Lippe-Biesterfeld; Princess Armgard, also of German blood, is a daughter of the Von Sierstorpff-Cramm line. Bernhard spent his early boyhood at "Reckenwalde" (the family estate) with his brother, Ernst Aschwin, three years his junior. During those years they studied under tutors. (Prince Aschwin, who later specialized in Oriental studies, became associated in 1949 with the Metropolitan Museum of Art in New York.) From 1923 to 1926 Bernhard attended a boarding school at Zuellichau, and for the next three years he was a student at Arndt Gymnasium in Berlin. He commenced the study of law in 1929, for which he attended universities in Lausanne, Munich, and Berlin to specialize in the legal aspects of international trade. In 1935 he received his law degree in Berlin. That year he joined the staff of the German dye trust, I. G. Farben, and was attached to its Paris, Berlin and Amsterdam offices.

The young German was introduced to Crown Princess Juliana of the Netherlands in 1935, and the romance reportedly developed on ski jaunts in Switzerland. The betrothal of the couple was announced by Queen Wilhelmina on September 8, 1936. Although comparatively unknown in the Netherlands, Prince Bernhard was accepted by most of the Dutch, who approved of the love match. (The Socialists, according to *Time*, called him an "ex-Storm

BERNHARD, PRINCE OF THE NETHERLANDS

Trooper.") Renouncing his German affiliations, he became a Dutch subject and was given honorary naval and military ranks, including a captaincy in the Royal Dutch Huzzars. When the Nazis suggested that the wedding was an alliance between the Netherlands and Nazi Germany, Queen Wilhelmina asserted: "This is the marriage of my daughter to the man she loves. . . .This is not the marriage of the Netherlands to Germany." Bernhard refused to insist on the playing of the "Horst Wessel" song and "Deutschland über Alles" at the wedding, and swastikas were not part of the street decorations. He and Juliana were married on January 7, 1937, in a civil ceremony at The Hague, which was followed by a simple Dutch Reformed ritual in the ancient Groote Kerk. They spent their honeymoon at a Polish winter resort and in Austria and Paris.

Upon becoming the consort of Holland's Crown Princess, Bernhard received the title of his Royal Highness, Prince of the Netherlands, and a yearly allowance of about $100,000 from the Dutch Government. He also became a member of the Council of State. Juliana and Bernhard made their home in Soestdijk Palace, a wedding gift from the Queen and the Dutch people. Showing much interest in economic and social problems, they became active in relief and child welfare work. For a time Wilhelmina and certain of her subjects were critical of the Prince's propensity for fast driving, and his absences from church on Sundays. However, with increasing responsibility of family and public life came a softened attitude toward the Prince. The first royal child, Beatrix Wilhelmina Armgard, was born January 31, 1938, and a second daughter, Irene Emma Elisabeth, was born August 5, 1939.

The pleasant life in Soestdijk Palace ended in 1940, when the Nazis invaded Holland. On

**BERNHARD, PRINCE OF THE NETH-
ERLANDS**—*Continued*

the day before their country surrendered, the royal couple escaped to England with their two children. The following month—"to safeguard the future dynasty"—the Princess and her daughters left for Ottawa, Canada. In May 1940 Bernhard rejoined Dutch troops fighting in Zeeland Province, the southwestern group of Dutch islands on the North Sea coast, where resistance to the Germans was continuing; on November 20 Queen Wilhelmina appointed her son-in-law chief liaison officer between the Dutch and British armies, navies, and air forces. Though he held the honorary rank of wing commodore in the Royal Air Force, Bernhard studied for, and passed, the usual R.A.F. examination, receiving his wings in May 1941.

At a press interview in the course of a visit to Canada and the United States in June 1941, Bernhard stated that he was "100 per cent Dutch" and that he thought the old culture and learning of Germany could not be restored until the Nazis were defeated. He was honored in New York on his thirtieth birthday by Netherlanders, who praised him for the "loyalty, conviction and nobility with which he defends our cause." He and Juliana were the guests of President and Mrs. Roosevelt in 1941 and again in April 1942. At this time the Prince declared himself "all in favor" of an Allied land offensive against the German-held Continent, saying, "We don't want your pity. We want your help." After a visit to Dutch airmen in training at an army base in Mississippi, and a brief trip to the West Indies, Bernhard returned to England via Canada. He visited his wife and children again in 1943 to attend the christening of his third daughter, Princess Margriet Francisca, born in Ottawa on January 19, 1943. He was back in the United States in December 1943 and January 1944 in consultation with the War Department concerning military plans abroad.

Prince Bernhard was made a rear admiral of the Royal Netherlands Navy and lieutenant general of the army in 1944. In August of that year he visited Netherlands troops in Normandy, and in September the Supreme Headquarters of the Allied Expeditionary Force announced that Bernhard had been appointed Commander of the Netherlands Forces of the Interior under General Eisenhower. Setting up temporary quarters in Belgium to direct Dutch partisan activities, Bernhard crossed the Albert Canal on September 10 to visit Netherlands troops fighting beside the British within twelve miles of his country's frontier. Soon afterward he received the following message: "The underground fighters joyfully welcome H.R.H. Prince Bernhard as their commander in chief. They are impatiently awaiting his commands, and, under his leadership and with their standard unfurled, they hope to expel the last enemy from Dutch soil." According to *Time* (June 25, 1945), Bernhard was effective in "fusing the quarreling Dutch resistance forces into a unified group which did a notable job of preparing the ground ahead of the Canadian liberators." After the liberation he assisted in forming resistance forces into a compact, mobile army for use in liberating the Dutch East Indies from the Japanese. On August 22, 1945, Prince Bernhard was presented with the Bronze Star by General Eisenhower for contributing "immeasurably to the creation of resistance organizations of the Netherlands." He was made Inspector-General of the Royal Netherlands Army in 1945 and Inspector-General of the Royal Netherlands Navy in 1947.

With the Allied victory in Europe, Princess Juliana and the three young princesses returned to the Netherlands in July 1945. There, on February 18, 1947, another daughter, Maria Christine (called Marijke by her family), was born. At the time the Dutch press commented that perhaps the "obscure voice of nature" was exercising good judgment in keeping royal authority in the Netherlands in feminine hands. Not long afterward, from mid-October to December 1, Princess Juliana was Regent of the Netherlands, the Queen having become ill. In the meantime, Wilhelmina, who was entering the fiftieth year of her reign, had expressed a wish to abdicate. Accordingly, on May 1948 Juliana was again installed as Regent, the title she bore until she took the oath as sovereign on September 6, 1948. Wilhelmina, who had previously announced that Bernhard would still be known as the Prince of the Netherlands (not designated as Prince Consort of the new Queen), publicly expressed her thanks to her son-in-law for the services he had rendered to the country "before, during, and after the war."

The Prince's duties continue to take him abroad from time to time. From January to March 1950, he made a good-will tour of the Dutch colonies in the Caribbean, coupled with official visits to Brazil, Venezuela, Mexico, and Canada, with unofficial stopovers at Los Angeles, Fort Worth (Texas), and Washington, D.C., where he visited President Truman. Interviewed in New York, Bernhard said that the Dutch had no desire to be neutral in the cold war, that the Marshall Plan was an indispensable support to the Dutch economy, and that "the Dutch want to earn their dollars, not just receive them—that is why they are focusing their energies on export to the United States." He stated that the object of his trip was to explore possibilities of emigration for the Dutch people, to restore contacts between Holland and her overseas territories, and, in the United States, to observe the latest developments in aviation. In line with encouraging the purchase of Dutch commodities by Americans, Bernhard in May 1950 opened an exhibition of his country's arts, crafts, cultural output, and industrial products in Philadelphia.

Prince Bernhard piloted his own plane to America, where he left it for installation of the latest flying aids—"I do considerable flying in Europe," he said, "and as you know, I always fly the Queen." A number of magazine and newspaper articles describe the Prince as a lively conversationalist, and the royal family as living in unpretentious domesticity. As does

Queen Juliana, Bernhard enjoys skiing, skating, and yachting.

References

N Y Sun p16 Ja 10 '44
Time 34:22+ N 27 '39 por

International Who's Who, 1949
10 Eventful Years (1947)
World Biography (1948)

BERRYMAN, JAMES THOMAS June 8, 1902- Cartoonist
Address: c/o Washington Evening Star, 11th & Pennsylvania Ave., N.W., Washington 4, D.C.; h. 6633 32d Pl., Washington 15, D.C.

On May 1, 1950, it was announced that the annual award of $500 established by the late Joseph Pulitzer for "a distinguished example of a cartoonist's work during the year" (1949) had gone to James Thomas Berryman of the Washington (D.C.) *Evening Star*. Jim Berryman (as he signs his drawings and the name by which he likes to be called) received the award for the cartoon which appeared in the *Star* on July 23, 1949, captioned "All Set for a Super-Secret Session in Washington." The cartoonist has been with that newspaper (with which his father was political cartoonist for many years) since 1924.

One of the two children of Clifford Kennedy and Kate Gaddis (Durfee) Berryman—his sister, Florence Seville Berryman is the art critic of the Washington *Evening Star* and a lecturer and magazine writer on the fine arts—James Thomas Berryman was born in Washington, D.C., on June 8, 1902. His father's people—Scotch-Irish-French—had settled in Virginia in the eighteenth century and later moved to Kentucky; his mother's—Scotch-French—have been Virginians since the early 1700's. Thus his forebears fought in the American Revolution and in the Union and Confederate armies in the Civil War. As a student at Central High School in Washington, Jim Berryman was a member of the cadet corps, worked on student publications, and was on the track team. At George Washington University, which he entered in 1920 (the year of his graduation from high school), he majored in journalism, was active on undergraduate publications, became a member of the student council; his college sports were baseball and track. During 1921 and 1922 he studied at the Corcoran School of Art.

After two and a half years at the university, Berryman left in 1923 for Albuquerque, New Mexico. There, he says, he had "a short, very mediocre reporting career" on the *New Mexico State Tribune*, then "drifted into cartooning." He joined the Washington *Evening Star* in 1924 as a staff artist, and has been with that politically independent newspaper (1949 circulation approximately 215,000) ever since. By 1931 he had become an editorial illustrator, and three years later he was sports cartoonist for the *Evening Star* and the *Sporting News*. Also in 1934 (September) it was disclosed that

JAMES THOMAS BERRYMAN

Berryman was the artist who composed, for the Department of Justice, his conception of the mysterious "John" who collected the ransom for the Lindbergh baby; the drawings showed a marked resemblance to photographs of the man later convicted as the kidnaper-murderer. During 1936 Berryman added magazine illustration to his other work, and in the year 1937-38 taught graphic arts at Southeastern (Washington, D.C.) University.

In 1941 Jim Berryman's signature began to appear on political cartoons on the editorial page of the *Star*, where his father's "Teddy bear" signature had been familiar for many years. While reducing his output, the senior Berryman continued to contribute until his death in 1949, winning the Pulitzer Prize for 1944 with his cartoon "Where Is the Boat Going?" In style, the work of father and son is said to be similar, though Jim Berryman varies his cartoons with crayon, pencil and brush work, whereas his father relied entirely on pen and ink work (according to an article in *Newsweek*). An editorial in the Washington *Post* commented: "At . . . times it has seemed to us that the satiric thrust of the younger Berryman was slightly but perceptibly more acidulous." Both political cartoonists, father and son, were critical of the New and Fair Deals, and supported Thomas E. Dewey for president in 1944 and 1948. Jim Berryman is, however, a long way from being a "party man." Described in the *Star* as "a man of pointed wit, who does not willingly suffer fools, or foolishness, in public life," he asserts his political independence. Asked if there are facts about him that are incorrect, he replied: "Yes; I am *not* a Republican. I am *anti*-F.D.R., *anti*-Truman. I support the *Man*, not the *Party*!"

The Pulitzer Prize-winning cartoon for 1949, as announced May 1, 1950, was the Berryman drawing entitled "All Set for a Super-Secret Session in Washington," published July 23, 1949, in the Washington *Evening Star*. It de-

BERRYMAN, JAMES THOMAS—*Cont.*

picts a conference room bare of human figures, but fully equipped with newsreel and TV cameras, four radio microphones, and a table for the press. The *Star's* article stated that Berryman originally "wanted to have the seats occupied by some legislators whose faces were well known," but that an editor had suggested that it would "be better" if the seats were empty. "The artist accepted the suggestion and drew the picture," continued the *Star* account. "The result was startling. It was cynical but traduced the motive of no individual." Berryman is reported to have been surprised by its choice for the Pulitzer Prize; of the cartoons he submitted to the committee, he himself considered "Northern Hospitality" the most effective. "In that one," stated the *Star,* "Harold McGrath, then chairman of the Democratic National Committee, was kicking the Dixiecrats out of the party, and the old Republican elephant, looking on hopefully, was singing the Bing Crosby hit, 'Going My Way?'" James Berryman's winning of the 1949 Pulitzer Prize for cartooning marked the first time a son had followed his father in receiving that honor.

In addition to his work for the Washington newspaper, Berryman has been, since 1944, a cartoonist for King Features, and is cartoonist for the Association of American Railroads. He is the author of ten or more magazine articles on hunting in the Southwest, among them "Wind in the West Again" (*American Rifleman,* September 1948), on antelope hunting, and the two-part "Happy Hunting Ground" (*American Rifleman,* October and November, 1949), on game opportunities and regulations in Arizona and New Mexico. A listing of publications in which Berryman cartoons and illustrations have appeared includes *Time, Quick, Newsweek, National Aeronautics, American Rifleman,* American Railroad Association publications, and various Sunday newspaper supplements.

During World War II Berryman worked with civilian defense agencies and wrote and illustrated features on the Navy. He turned his talent to entertaining hospitalized veterans by drawing their portraits. In recognition of his services he has received awards from the war bond committee of the United States Treasury and the American Red Cross. Other organizations which have honored him are the Infantile Paralysis Foundation, the New York World's Fair, and Central High School Alumni Association (Washington). In 1949 he received the Freedom Foundation Award, and in 1950 the American Legion's Distinguished Service Medal "for outstanding Americanism."

The Washington cartoonist belongs to the Sons of the American Revolution, is a director of the American Red Cross and of the American Automobile Association. He holds memberships, as well, in the National Rifle Association, the Outdoor Writers Association of America, and the National Society of Cartoonists. His clubs are the Gridiron (he is a vice-president), the National Press, the University and the Chevy Chase; his fraternity is the Delta Tau Delta. He is a Presbyterian. Mrs. Berryman's maiden name was Louise Marble Rhees; the Berrymans, married October 23, 1926, have one son, Rhys Morgan. The five-foot-ten-inch cartoonist weighs 167 pounds; the color of his eyes is blue, of his hair, "sandy-gray." Travel, golf, and riding are three of his recreations; fond of shooting, he also collects modern sporting rifles. To this list he adds cookery: "I am interested in unusual foods—I try to get their recipes and cook them at home."

References

N Y Herald Tribune p7 My 2 '50
N Y Times p22 My 2 '50 por
Newsweek 51:56 N 29 '48
Washington (D.C.) Star My 2 '50
Who's Who in America, 1950-51
Who's Who in the East (1948)

BERRYMAN, JIM *See* Berryman, J. T.

BETHE, HANS A(LBRECHT) (bā'tē)
July 2, 1906- Physicist

Address: b. c/o Laboratory of Nuclear Studies, Cornell University, Ithaca, N.Y.; h. 209 White Park Rd., Ithaca, N.Y.

NOTE: This biography supersedes the article which appeared in *Current Biography* in 1940.

"One of Nazi Germany's greatest gifts to the United States" is an expression *Time* once applied to Professor Hans A. Bethe of Cornell University's Laboratory of Nuclear Studies. A key figure in the development of the atomic bomb as chief of the theoretical physics division of Los Alamos, Bethe is perhaps best known for discovering "what makes the sun shine." The Bethe carbon cycle, a series of six linked transformations which require 5,000,000 years to complete, was the first and only explanation of solar and stellar energy which met all the known facts. Another main problem that has occupied him since 1930 is the passage of fast particles through matter.

Born July 2, 1906, in Strasbourg, Alsace-Lorraine, Hans Albrecht Bethe is the only child of Albrecht Theodore Julius and Anna (Kuhn) Bethe. For generations there have been university professors in the family. His mother and grandmother were daughters of professors, and his father—an eminent German physiologist who has written much on the nervous system—was properly styled Doktor Doktor Professor Bethe, having both the M.D. and Ph.D. degrees. Young Bethe attended the Goethe *Gymnasium* in Frankfurt-am-Main and the University of Frankfurt, and received his Ph.D. in 1928 at the University of Munich. He was one of the first to apply the new system of quantum mechanics, simultaneously proposed in different forms by the Austrian physicist Erwin Schrödinger and the German physicist Werner Heisenberg in 1926, to the solution of hitherto baffling problems. In 1927, when this new system of physics was still little understood, the Ph.D. candidate used it to explain the Davisson effect (of electron diffraction and refraction in crystals) which was to win Clinton J. Davisson the 1937 Nobel Prize. Bethe's first papers, "Scattering of Electrons by Crystals" and "Theory of the Diffraction of Electrons by Crystals" appeared, respectively, in *Naturwissenschaften* in 1927, and *Annalen der Physik* in 1928.

Having received his doctorate, Bethe returned to Frankfurt as an instructor in physics, and in 1929 moved to Stuttgart to fill a similar post. A paper of his on energy levels of atoms and crystals—a subject Bethe does not list among his major fields of interest—introduced mathematical methods widely used since then by researchers in molecular structure. During the next few years (1930-32), while holding the title of lecturer at the University of Munich, he worked under Sir Ernest Rutherford at Cambridge and Enrico Fermi [45] in Rome, on a fellowship from the Rockefeller International Education Board—his "Reciprocal Action of Two Electrons," written with Fermi, was published in 1932 in *Zeitschrift für Physik.* This fellowship brought Bethe into contact also with another Nobel Prize winner, Niels Bohr [45], called "the founder of modern atomic theory." Bethe was a contributor to the *Handbuch der Physik* (1933). It was in the 1930's that he became interested in the passage of fast particles through matter. That was the subject of a paper he wrote in 1930, which was to lead to a lectureship at the University of Munich. "I have returned to this problem ever since," said Bethe in 1950, the year he wrote an article on that subject for a work (edited by Emilio Segrè) on experimental nuclear physics.

When Hitler came to power, Bethe was an assistant professor at the University of Tübingen and was lecturing also at Munich as a *Privatdozent.* Bethe, whose mother was Jewish, was one of many scientists who left Germany at that time. In 1933-34 he was at the University of Manchester as a lecturer, in 1934-35 at Bristol as a fellow, and in 1935 he went to the United States to become an assistant professor at Cornell. (He has been a full professor since 1937.) Not long thereafter he was chosen one of the assistant editors of the American Physical Society's journal, for a three-year term. What amounted to a 487-page textbook of nuclear physics by Bethe appeared in *Reviews of Modern Physics*: all except twenty-six pages of the April 1936 issue were devoted to "Nuclear Physics: A. Stationary States of Nuclei" by Bethe and Robert F. Bacher [45], and the issues of April and July 1937, respectively, were given over to his "B. Nuclear Dynamics, Theoretical" and to "C. Nuclear Dynamics, Experimental," by M. Stanley Livingston and Bethe. Often used as a textbook, these three issues have been reprinted a dozen times.

Other papers came from Bethe's study. He has listed his major professional interests as "quantum theory of atoms, theory of metals, quantum theory of collisions, theory of atomic nuclei, energy production in stars, quantum electrodynamics, shock wave theory and micro-

Wide World Photos

HANS A. BETHE

waves." One of his most important treatises is "Energy Production in Stars," the first two sections of which, appearing in 1938, won him the New York Academy of Sciences' $500 A. Cressy Morrison Prize (the third section appeared four years later). The star with which he was particularly concerned was the sun. As Bethe's colleague George Gamow (professor of physics at the George Washington University) tells in *The Birth and Death of the Sun* (1940), Bethe first learned about the importance of thermoneuclear reactions in producing the sun's energy, at the 1938 Washington Conference on Theoretical Physics. The problem then was: knowing the proportion of hydrogen (about 35 per cent) in the sun, determine the other elements which could react with it in such a way as to account for the sun's radiation, size, age, and other known characteristics. His solution, which he reached in six weeks (separately and simultaneously proposed in Germany by Carl von Weizsäcker) was a six-step reaction cycle, in which carbon and nitrogen act as catalysts, transforming four hydrogen nuclei (protons) into one helium nucleus (alpha particle); the atomic weight lost (.0286 units) becomes energy, in accordance with Einstein's [40] formula. "Accepting the figure of 1 per cent of carbon as given by astrophysical evidence, Bethe was able to show that the energy liberation of his reaction chain at 20,000,000 degrees Centigrade exactly coincides with the actual amount of energy radiated by our sun." Bethe is quoted by *Time*: "At the rate of one cent per kilowatt hour, we should have to pay a billion billion dollars to keep the sun going for a single second." After this had been worked out and accepted in pure theory, Bethe and co-workers reproduced five of the steps at Cornell (the sixth was reproduced by two Cambridge physicists); results checked exactly, except that the length of time required

BETHE, HANS A.—*Continued*

for the cycle, originally calculated at 52,000,000 years, was set at one-tenth that figure.

Professor Bethe reported these results in the spring of 1940. That January he had made headlines with the first mathematical confirmation that the newly discovered particle, the meson, holds matter together; it "transmits the energy inside the nucleus from one particle to another," he reported. Calculations from this confirmed Nobel Prize-winner Rabi's [48] experimental findings of the football shape of the deuteron. When war came, the Cornell physicist (who had become a naturalized citizen of the United States in 1941) devoted himself to work which is still largely secret, as a member of OSRD, in 1942-43 as a member of the staff of the M.I.T. Radiation Laboratory, and in 1943-46 as chief of the Theoretical Physics Division of the atomic bomb laboratory at Los Alamos. The War Department's official Smyth [45] report mentions "two considerations that give unusual importance to the work of the Theoretical Physics Division under H. Bethe. The first of these was the necessity for effecting simultaneous development of everything from the fundamental materials to the necessary methods of putting them to use—all despite the virtual unavailability of the principal materials (U-235 and plutonium) and the complete novelty of the process." The second was the impossibility of creating a small explosion to study. In Smyth's words: "Thus it was necessary to proceed from data obtained by experiments on infinitesimal quantities of material and to combine it with the available theory . . . in order to make estimates as to what would happen in the bomb." Among other questions, Bethe's group had to work out the critical size of the fissionable mass—that is, the point at which it would explode—and had to decide in advance what the chances were of a continuing chain reaction which might destroy the world. The work of all other divisions was grounded upon the predictions supplied by Bethe's division.

After the war Bethe, like others who aided in developing the A-bomb, found himself a public figure, called upon to make speeches to laymen. He was one of the nine-man Emergency Committee of Atomic Scientists, headed by Einstein, which in November 1946 opened a campaign for a million dollars to spend in educating the public to the facts of atomic energy. In 1947 Bethe again became a member of the American Physical Society's board of editors, and in June 1948 was appointed visiting professor at Columbia University, as he had been in 1940-41. He is, as well, a consultant to the AEC. Deploring what he considers overemphasis on complicated nuclei and on fission—"it is, after all, only a very special phenomenon in nuclear physics"—he omitted these from the twenty-lecture course he gave at the General Electric Research Laboratories. (Notes taken by three auditors were published as *Elementary Nuclear Theory* in 1947.)

When the possibility of a hydrogen bomb (which would reproduce the sun's action, in that atomic energy would be liberated in transforming hydrogen into helium) was broached publicly in early 1950, Bethe served as spokesman for a group of twelve top researchers in the field who spoke as "worried citizens," asking that the United States resolve never to use it first, but saying, "until we have international control, we cannot afford not to have the hydrogen bomb." Eight days later Bethe presented this view on the first of Eleanor Roosevelt's television programs, and two weeks after that, he appeared on a *Round Table* broadcast on which he and professors Leo Szilard [47], Harrison Brown, and Frederick Seitz warned that radioactive H-bomb clouds could annihilate life on earth. Said Bethe, "I believe that the time to discuss this bomb is now. . . .The A-bomb now could hardly be eliminated from our armament, because most of our strategic plans are based on it. I would not like to see the same thing happen for the H-bomb."

Hans Bethe was honored by the New York Academy of Sciences with a second Morrison Prize for 1940, and the Henry Draper Medal for 1947. He is described as a modest man. Gamow has referred to "Dr. Hans Bethe's famous appetite." In 1939 the scientist married Rose Ewald, daughter of the Nazi-exiled German theoretical physicist, now physics professor at Brooklyn Polytechnic Institute; the Bethes have two children. In 1940 *Time* wrote, "Hans Albrecht Bethe likes skiing, economics, and riding on trains, but spends most of his time mulling over theoretical physics. . . . He does most of his work in an easy chair in the living room." In 1950 Bethe said he also likes mountain climbing and has come to prefer travel for pleasure rather than for business.

References

N Y Times p24 Ja 14 '40
Time 35:42 Ja 29 '40

American Men of Science (1949)
Who's Who in America, 1950-51
Who's Who in the East (1948)

BEVIS, HOWARD L(ANDIS) (bē'vĭs)
Nov. 19, 1885- University president

Address: b. Administration Building, Ohio State University, Columbus 10, Ohio; h. President's Residence, Ohio State University, Columbus 10, Ohio

> NOTE: This biography supersedes the article which appeared in *Current Biography* in 1940.

The seventh president of Ohio State University, Howard L. Bevis in 1950 is observing his tenth year as chief administrator of that institution. He came to the post in 1940, after having been a professor of law at the University of Cincinnati and later professor of law and government at Harvard University's Graduate School of Business Administration and the Graduate School of Public Administration. Also active in State affairs, he has twice served as State director of finance and for two years was an associate justice of the Ohio Supreme Court. The university that he now heads was listed by *School and Society*, in 1949, as the eighth largest in the United States.

Born on a farm at Bevis in Hamilton County, Ohio, on November 19, 1885, Howard Landis Bevis is the son of Edgar M. and Cara E. (Corson) Bevis. His father, a farmer, was a descendant of Thomas Bevis, who came from Devonshire, England, in 1720, and settled in New Jersey. After attending Colerain Township High School in Groesbeck, Howard Bevis continued his secondary education at the Cincinnati Technical School, where he was captain of the baseball team and commencement orator in 1904. Encouraged by his mother to go on to college, he entered the University of Cincinnati and there majored in economics. As an undergraduate, he served as business manager and later as editor of the *University Weekly News*, the college newspaper, and as assistant editor of the *Cincinnatian*, the yearbook. He was also president of the Economics Club and Debating Association; vice-president of the Speakers' Club; junior class orator; and a member of language, literary, scientific, and other student organizations. Receiving his Bachelor of Arts degree in 1908, he studied law at the same institution and obtained his Bachelor of Laws degree two years later.

Bevis was admitted to the Ohio bar in 1910 and began the practice of law in the Cincinnati office of Judge Stanley Struble. During 1911-12 he was a partner in the law firm of Isaacs and Bevis, after which he continued in practice alone. With American participation in World War I, he entered Government service in 1918. He first served as a civilian in the Ordnance Department, codifying the voluminous rules and orders that the Department was accumulating during the war. Later he was placed at the head of the legal section of the Finance Division of the United States Air Service. After the end of the war he attended Harvard Law School for a year as a graduate student, being awarded the degree of Doctor of Juridical Science in 1920; his dissertation was on procedure in administrative commissions.

In 1921 Bevis was made professor of law at the University of Cincinnati, where he taught courses on conflict of laws, torts, mortgages, bankruptcy, civil practice, and administrative law. During the next ten years, having become interested in the political problems of Cincinnati, he took part in the practical work of organization politics as a Democratic ward executive. Through his efforts he succeeded in getting a woman elected to the city's school board for the first time, and in 1926, as secretary of the Charter Amendment Commission, with Robert A. Taft and two other commissioners, he helped to draft a new city-manager charter. In 1931 Governor George White appointed him Director of Finance for Ohio. In this post he was faced with a difficult task, for the funds of the State were dangerously low and revenues were falling. He effected drastic economies by cutting Ohio's budget from $81,000,000 to $47,-000,000. At the same time he served as a member of the State Relief Commission (1932-33), the State board of deposits, the board of control, the board of sundry claims, and the State emergency board.

In 1933 Governor White named Bevis to fill out an unexpired term as Associate Justice of the Ohio Supreme Court. Although supported by nearly all the newspapers in the State, Bevis, according to the New York *Herald Tribune* (January 9, 1940), had "little taste for popularizing himself with the voters en masse," and lost out in the next election. However, at the request of the then Governor Martin L. Davey, he agreed to resume his former post as Director of Finance in 1935 for the few months remaining of the then current session of the State legislature. That year he was called to the William Ziegler professorship of law and government at the Graduate School of Business Administration at Harvard University, where he was also on the faculty of the Graduate School of Public Administration.

When George Washington Rightmire retired as president of Ohio State University (in Columbus) in 1938, *Time* reported that the faculty, confidentially polled, proposed as his successor, James Lewis Morrill, then vice-president of the university, and named Bevis as its second choice. "The trustees, unable to agree on Morrill or Bevis, considered more than a score of outsiders," but after eighteen months of deliberation unanimously elected Bevis as president on January 8, 1940. Assuming his new duties on February 1, Bevis was formally inducted on October 26 of that same year. In his inaugural address he declared that the university's task was to fit to each student's needs such a selection of school pursuits as would enable him to build a cultural and educational background for his intended life work. With a great array of courses already available as the raw material for this task, he continued, the university still needed to know much more about the requirements and opportunities in the various walks of life and to know how better to help the student select his studies.

The university which Bevis heads is a land-grant, State-controlled, co-educational institution, chartered in 1870 as the Ohio Agricultural and Mechanical College. With a faculty of seven teachers, this "College in the Cornfield," as it was then popularly called, opened its doors in 1873 to seventeen students. It received its present name in 1878, when the first class graduated. Since that time Ohio State University has grown rapidly until, in 1949-50, there were 20,730 full-time students (22,538 students in all) and 2,049 teachers. The university was in 1949-50 comprised of 88 departments of instruction, divided among ten colleges, a graduate school, and nine special schools. The ten colleges are: Agriculture, Arts and Sciences, Commerce and Administration, Dentistry, Education, Engineering, Law, Medicine, Pharmacy, and Veterinary Medicine. The special schools include those of Home Economics, Journalism, Nursing, Optometry, Social Administration, Aviation, Music, Fine and Applied Arts, and Mineral Industries.

The ten years that Bevis has served as president of Ohio State University have witnessed the introduction of new courses, the setting up of various new departments, and the establishment, in 1942, of the School of Aviation (including a 383-acre University Airport), and the Twilight School, for the benefit of persons

HOWARD L. BEVIS

occupied during the day; the School of Fine and Applied Arts in 1944; and the School of Music in 1945. Throughout the academic year of 1948-49 the university celebrated its seventy-fifth anniversary and conferred its 75,000th degree. In the commencement address delivered on June 9, 1950, Bevis stated that during the previous four years the university had attained its largest growth (the peak enrollment was 25,403 students in the fall of 1947) ; shown the greatest increase in research; enjoyed the largest legislative appropriations in all its history (in 1949-50 its endowment was $2,909,908) ; and seen its greatest period of building construction (28 projects, adding about 40 per cent to the total cubage of the campus, at a total cost of over $30,000,000—more than the cost of all the previous buildings combined). Among the new buildings just completed or under construction are an $8,000,000 Medical Center, a $2,500,000 addition to the library, and a $5,000,-000 Student Union. In 1950 the value of the university's properties, including over 2,000 acres of land, some 100 permanent buildings and equipment, was approximately $43,000,000.

The college president is chairman of the board of the Federal Home Loan Bank of Cincinnati. During 1942-45 he was the chairman of the Franklin County War Finance Committee, and in 1947 he was named vice-chairman of the Labor Legislative Commission. He holds membership in the American Academy of Arts and Sciences, the Ohio and Cincinnati bar associations, American Law Institute, Association of American Law Schools, Order of Coif, Phi Beta Kappa, Omicron Delta Kappa, Phi Alpha Delta, Newcomen Society, Sons of the American Revolution, Ohio Society, and the Masonic Order. His clubs include the Torch, Kit-Kat, Rotary, Crichton, Columbus, and Faculty, all of Columbus. Honorary doctorates in law have been bestowed upon him by the University of Cincinnati and Western Reserve University (1940), Kent State University (1942), Toledo University and Baldwin-Wallace College (1945), University of New Mexico (1946), and the University of Hawaii (1947).

A frequent contributor to various legal, business, and educational periodicals, Bevis is the author of *Cochran's Law Lexicon* (1924) ; *Bevis' Ohio Law Quizzer* (1926) ; *Public Law* (in the "National Law Library," 1939) ; and co-author of *Private and International Law in Ohio Jurisprudence* (1933). On June 30, 1914, he married Alma Darst Murray, of Cincinnati; they have one son, Murray Bevis. Mrs. Bevis, who was a teacher both before and after her marriage, wrote *Diets and Riots: An Interpretation of the History of Harvard University* (1936). Nicknamed "Stick" because of his physical appearance, the Ohio administrator stands six feet tall and weighs 175 pounds; his eyes are blue, and his brown hair is graying. He lists himself as a Methodist. The recreations he enjoys are reading, fishing, and hunting.

References

N Y Herald Tribune p16 Ja 9 '40
Time 35 :74-5 Ja 22 '40
Directory of American Scholars, 1942
Leaders in Education (1948)
National Cyclopædia of American Biography Current vol F, 1939-42
Who's Who in America, 1950-51
Who's Who in Law, 1937
Who's Who in the Midwest (1949)
World Biography (1948)

BHUMIBOL ADULYADEJ *See* Rama IX, King of Thailand

BIGGS, E(DWARD GEORGE) POWER
Mar. 29, 1906- Concert organist
Address: b. c/o Mercury Music Corp., 47 W. 63d St., New York 23; h. 53 Highland St., Cambridge 38, Mass.

A foremost interpreter of Bach's works for the organ, E. Power Biggs has devoted his efforts to bringing the great organ music of the past out of the confines of the cathedral into the concert hall and, through records and the radio, into the listener's living room. His success in helping to revive public interest in serious organ music has, in turn, stimulated contemporary composers to write organ works for him in the modern idiom. Official organist of the Boston Symphony Orchestra, Biggs is also known for his broadcasts, concert tours, recordings, and guest appearances with major symphony orchestras and at special music festivals. The series of weekly organ recitals he gives over Columbia Broadcasting System's coast-to-coast network began its ninth consecutive year in September 1950.

Edward George Power-Biggs (who no longer uses the hyphen in his name) was born in Westcliff, England, on March 29, 1906, the son of Clarence and Alice Maud (Tredgett) Power-Biggs. Educated at Hurstpierpoint College, in Sussex, he studied electrical engineering for two years before he decided upon a career in music. Winning the Thomas Threlfall Organ Scholarship to the Royal Academy of Music in London, he studied under conductor Sir Henry Wood and organist George D. Cunningham. Upon his graduation in 1929 he was awarded the Hubert Kiver Organ Prize and won highest honors in organ, harmony and counterpoint, and piano. His concert career began rather unexpectedly when Sir Henry Wood requested him to prepare, on two days' notice, a program for presentation in Queen's Hall in London. This was followed by recitals in a number of England's historic cathedrals and leading concert halls.

In the fall of 1929 Biggs went to the United States and Canada with a Welsh singer and the latter's accompanist. In a tour lasting about six months he was heard in 197 concerts. The organist returned to the United States in 1932 to make his formal New York debut at the Wanamaker Auditorium on March 31. Later that year he was appointed organist and choirmaster of Christ Church in Cambridge, Massachusetts, and his recital at the 1932 annual convention of the National Association of Organists, in Rochester, New York, "aroused the audience to sustained applause" and bravos for his playing (*The Diapason*, August 1932). Subsequently he was engaged to give a series of recitals at Harvard Memorial Church, after which he toured the United States and Canada. He was named organist and music director of the Harvard Church in Brookline, and began teaching a master class in organ at the Longy School of Music in Cambridge, (affiliated with Harvard and Radcliffe), positions he held for a number of years. In 1937 he became an American citizen.

Since 1937 the name of E. Power Biggs has been closely associated with his favorite instrument, the famous Baroque Organ in the Germanic Museum of Harvard University. Designed to approximate as closely as possible the sound produced by the great organs of the eighteenth century, this instrument is almost identical with the one that Bach played in Weimar, except for the electrical action controlling wind pressure and stops mechanism. The first of its kind in the United States, the Germanic Museum's organ (designed by G. Donald Harrison, and also known as the Harrison organ) has two manuals, 25 stops, and 1,582 pipes. Unlike the "shouting and strident" modern symphonic organ designed for large halls, it is voiced on low wind pressure and has a limpid and mellow quality of tone. It has no swell box (to increase or diminish the volume of tone), tremolos, or so-called "solo" stops, and its pipes are not enclosed.

Biggs, who believes that "authenticity is best in both organ and performance," has explained that the construction of the Germanic Museum organ was an attempt to recapture the almost lost art of "voicing," the regulation of the tone of organ pipes to secure proper power, pitch, and quality, made possible by the eighteenth century organ builders, whose achievement he has compared to that of the master violin makers Stradivarius and Guarnerius. Reviewing the musician's first performance on the new

CBS Photo.
E. POWER BIGGS

organ in April 1937, a critic for *The Diapason* wrote that Biggs "more than justified his reputation in the manner in which he sensed the possibilities of the instrument. His playing was marked by beautifully defined rhythm and brilliant and clear rendition of the larger numbers, coupled with a real appreciation of the traditional manner of playing such music." During the winter and spring of 1937-38 he attracted large audiences to the Germanic Museum when he played the complete organ works of Johann Sebastian Bach in a series of twelve recitals, an accomplishment called by the Boston press "unique for our day and age." He repeated the cycle in 1940 at St. Paul's Chapel, Columbia University.

During his annual concerts at the Germanic Museum, Biggs has often been assisted by members of the Stradivarius Quartet and Arthur Fiedler's Sinfonietta. At the suggestion of Sir Henry Wood, Biggs asked Leo Sowerby, the American composer, to write a concerto for organ and full orchestra. This was given its first performance in 1938, with Biggs as soloist with the Boston Symphony Orchestra, conducted by Serge Koussevitzky. Later he repeated the rendition with the Chicago and Cincinnati symphony orchestras, and in 1950 he gave its English première at a London Promenade Concert in Royal Albert Hall. Since dedicating the Baroque Organ at the Tanglewood Music Shed, near Lenox, Massachusetts, in 1940, the organist has frequently appeared on the programs of the Berkshire Music Festival and has taught classes in organ at the Berkshire Music Center. In the fall of 1949 he dedicated the new organ commissioned by the trustees of the Boston Symphony Orchestra to celebrate the fiftieth anniversary of Symphony Hall. Besides his almost annual concert tours of the United States and Canada, Biggs has served as soloist at the Elizabeth Sprague Coolidge [41] chamber music

BIGGS, E. POWER—Continued

festivals at the Library of Congress, Washington, and he has taken part in numerous Bach festivals, particularly those at Bethlehem (Pennsylvania) and Toronto (Canada).

Dissatisfied with the average organ program —consisting largely of church selections, transcriptions, and "show" pieces calculated to display various stop effects—Biggs felt that the musical appreciation of the American public had reached a point where the finest organ music would have widespread appeal. This appreciation has been developed by the radio, which he considers the ideal medium for the organ. Accordingly, as an experiment, he broached his plan to Mrs. Coolidge, who arranged for ten organ recitals originating from the Germanic Museum to be broadcast over CBS as a gift to Harvard University. The initial program took place on September 20, 1942. The response from coast to coast was so enthusiastic that Biggs's series of Sunday half-hour morning recitals has been continued as a regular weekly feature of the CBS network. The organist has received "fan mail" from points as far distant as Germany, Australia, South America, Alaska, and the Yukon.

During 1945-46 Biggs presented for the first time on the air the entire organ works of Bach, which he repeated throughout 1949-50 in honor of the bicentenary of Bach's death. Other features of his radio series have been Bach's *The Art of the Fugue*, in Biggs's arrangement for organ, and the complete organ literature of Wilhelm Friedrich Bach, Handel, Mozart, Mendelssohn, Brahms, and Hindemith. In 1950 he played Antonio Soler's Concerto in G for Two Organs by recording the first organ part prior to the broadcast and having this recording superimposed on his "live" performance of the second organ part. Biggs has invited other contemporary composers to write for the organ— he has found that his radio programs require the maintenance of a large and constantly changing repertoire. As a result he has broadcast the world premières of organ works by Walter Piston '48, Roy Harris '40, Howard Hanson '41, Quincy Porter, Alec Templeton '40, Benjamin Britten '42, as well as Sowerby and others. Both music editors and the public have rated Biggs's program as first in its class in *Musical America*'s annual radio polls since 1946.

In the opinion of the New York *Times* critic, Biggs "has, in no small way, created a kind of musical renaissance of that great instrument— the organ." Other judgments were: "He produced one of the most transparent and startlingly effective realizations of Handel's organ music that it has been my privilege to hear" (Cleveland *Plain Dealer*). "He can unerringly establish a mood, as in Franck's *Pastorale*, which breathed peace and serenity under his fingers, or paint a tone picture, as in Sowerby's Fantasy" (Washington *Star*). "He has again proved that an organ recital need not be a bore or a rite, but can be a stimulating experience" (Boston *Transcript*).

Most of the organist's earlier (78 rpm) recordings, for Victor, are now "out of print." Since 1947 he has recorded exclusively for Columbia, including Mendelssohn's Sixth Organ Sonata; an album of French organ music (Widor, Gigout, Boellmann, Dupré, Alain, and Vierne); music by Franck and Poulenc; the "Westminster Suite" (English music); and three albums of Bach's works.

The organist is also a well-known music scholar, having edited Brahms's organ works, the Mozart organ sonatas, Daquin's Noels, and other music from his repertoire. An associate of the Royal College of Organists and a member of the Lotos Club in New York City, Biggs was elected a fellow of the Royal Academy of Music and of the American Academy of Arts and Sciences. He married the Boston pianist, Colette Josephine Lionne, in 1933; his second wife is the former Margaret Allen. Blackhaired, with the "square-cut jaw of a boxer," Biggs has been described as "a tall, well-built man with a quietly genial manner." Travel and gardening are among his recreations.

References

Newsweek 17:16 Ap 22 '46
Time 31:12 Mr 21 '38
Who's Who in Music, 1949-50

BING, RUDOLF Jan. 9, 1902- Operatic impresario

Address: b. c/o Metropolitan Opera Association, Broadway & 39th St., New York 18

The managerial direction of the Metropolitan Opera of New York passed on June 1, 1950, to Rudolf Bing, Austrian-born impresario, when he succeeded Edward Johnson '43, who filled the post for fifteen years. Bing comes to the Metropolitan Opera Association with a background of service as assistant manager in various operatic organization in Europe. He was also director of the well-known Edinburgh International Festival of Music and Drama.

Rudolf Bing was born in Vienna, Austria, on January 9, 1902, one of the four children of Ernest Bing, an industrialist, and the former Stefanie Hoenigsvald. The household in which he grew up was musical—there were chamber music concerts at home and regular attendance at the opera—but he was the first member of his family to consider making a career of music. He received a liberal arts education, with emphasis on painting and music, and at a relatively early age began taking vocal lessons with the intention of appearing on the concert stage. World War I and the consequent economic collapse of Austria, however, made it necessary for him to find immediately rewarding employment. He therefore decided to enter the publishing field, where he felt he would find at least some measure of artistic satisfaction.

The firm which Bing entered at this time— he was about twenty—was a leading Vienna bookshop, which also operated a concert agency. Within a year Bing transferred from the bookshop to the concert agency and was presently placed in charge of that division; there he instituted a special opera department. This brought him into association with important artists of the day, especially those of the Vienna State Opera, and determined the direction of his future career. He remained with the Vienna agency until 1927, then accepted a post with one of the largest theatrical agencies in Berlin, from which some eighty opera houses throughout Germany drew singers and other members of their staffs. The position required his visiting a number of cities, he told an interviewer, and gave him an insight into operatic management and experience in choosing singers to meet various requirements.

In the latter part of 1928 the young music agent was engaged by the general manager of the Darmstadt State Theatre, Carl Ebert (of British Glyndebourne fame and now on the faculty of the University of Southern California), as Leiter des Betriebsbureaus. This office, the title of which is not easily translatable into English, has been described by Ebert as comparable to that of an artistic secretary of New York's Metropolitan Opera and by Bing himself as similar to the position occupied under Edward Johnson by Frank St. Leger, whose duties include casting and general artistic supervision of the many performances. When, two years later, Ebert was called to head the Municipal Opera of Charlottenberg, a suburb of Berlin, he took Bing with him to serve in the same capacity at that theater. In these positions both remained until they left the country soon after Hitler came to power in 1933.

Bing and Ebert were associated again, for more than a decade, in the Glyndebourne Opera Company. This company was founded by John Christie, a wealthy Englishman, for the production of Mozart's operas. Christie built on his estate in Sussex an operatic theater especially designed for Mozart productions, and engaged as his musical director and conductor Fritz Busch '46 (now on the Metropolitan roster) and Carl Ebert as the artistic and stage director. Bing helped to bring together singers from many countries for the initial season of 1934. The Glyndebourne festivals, as the spring seasons of opera came to be known, were a success from the first with recordings made during actual performances given in 1934, 1935, and 1936. The productions have been called "jewels of perfection."

In 1935 Bing was appointed the company's general manager, and from the third season through 1939 he served it in this capacity. When, in 1946, the company resumed production after being interrupted by World War II, Bing again became general manager, in which position he remained until he accepted the Metropolitan appointment in New York.

During the war years Bing was temporarily associated with the John Lewis department store in London, first as a clerk and then as a junior executive. When he returned to the operatic field in 1945, it was with ideas for a new and broader festival which would encompass drama, ballet, opera, symphony, chamber music and solo performances, a British equivalent of the Salzburg Festival. Bing may not have been the only proponent of the plan, but authorities agree that it was his persistence which in 1947 brought into being the Edinburgh International Festival of Music and Drama, sponsored jointly by the Arts Council of Great Britain and the City of Edinburgh.

Underwood & Underwood

RUDOLF BING

Initial skepticism concerning the success of the festival in the midst of the war's economic disruption was strong. Bing overcame most of this, as told in a biographical article in *Opera News*: he asked Bruno Walter '42 if he would consent to come if he, Bing, could secure sufficient funds and the services of the Vienna Philharmonic Orchestra. To those conditions Walter agreed, and his interest, made public, immediately kindled the enthusiasm of the other groups whose cooperation Bing was trying to enlist. He secured the Vienna Philharmonic, the Liverpool and Halle orchestras, L'Orchestre Colonne from France, London's Old Vic theater, the Sadler's Wells Ballet, soloists Artur Schnabel '42, Joseph Szigeti '40, Pierre Fournier, Lotte Lehmann '41, Kathleen Ferrier, and others, and the Glyndebourne Opera; the festival was regarded in its first year as having established itself as a worthy counterpart of the Salzburg event to which it is most often compared. Bing was its artistic director from the incorporation of the Edinburgh Festival Society in 1946 until his release by the society in 1949 from a contract extending through 1951. He was given the post of artistic adviser.

The appointment of Bing as managerial director of the Metropolitan Opera Association of New York, succeeding general manager Edward Johnson, was made by unanimous vote of its board of directors on May 25, 1949, and announced to the public on June 1. It was an unexpected appointment, Bing having been little known in the United States before that time, and the offer is said to have come as a surprise to Bing himself. The announcement stated that he would take office in June 1950, upon Edward Johnson's retirement at the end of the 1949-50 season. In November 1949 Bing arrived in New York for a period of observation in preparation for assuming the post. "I must learn about the Metropolitan and its ways before I start put-

BING, RUDOLF—*Continued*

ting into practice plans of my own," he said. "After three months' study, when I know something about conditions there, I shall start formulating my plans." An editorial in the New York *Herald Tribune* commented on Bing's appointment: "Consistently on the side of quality as well as of the artistically advanced, he is eminently prepared to guide . . . international-repertory opera. . . .It is doubtful whether his match could be found today among opera impresarios for taste and vision."

In the first week of February 1950 the new general manager of the Metropolitan made public the basic changes in policy: the next season would consist of eighteen operas in a season of twenty weeks (instead of twenty-five or thirty offerings in eighteen weeks); and there would be two subscription periods (instead of the single season-length subscription). The reduced repertory will permit more full rehearsals—"big-name" artists have been known to absent themselves from rehearsals. Another innovation will be the reauditioning of all singers. There was much comment on the roster of singers Bing was selecting for the 1950-51 season, the most notable return being that of Kirsten Flagstad '47. Among Bing's most often quoted statements were: "I will attempt to run this house—unmoved by promises or threats—on the principle of quality only." "I am moved only by artistic, not by racial or political considerations." "We want an ensemble of stars—not of comets."

In 1929 Rudolf Bing married Nina Schelemskaya, a Russian-born dancer then living in Vienna—her family had fled from Russia at the time of the revolution, in 1917. The impresario is a tall, thin man whose speech has a slight Austrian accent with British intonations. He has been described as businesslike, considerate, and modest; and anecdotes about him indicate that he has a sense of humor.

References

Mus Am 69:3+ Je '49 por
N Y Herald Tribune p1+ Je 2 '49 por;
   p22 Je 7 '49; p21 Je 29 '49
N Y Times p1+ Je 2 '49 por; II p5
   Jl 3 '49
Newsweek 33:77-8 Je 13 '49 por
Opera News 14:4-6 O 10 '49 por
Pathfinder 56:38-9 N 16 '49 por
Time 53:66-7 Je 13 '49 por

BLACK, EUGENE R(OBERT) May 1, 1898- World Bank official; financier

Address: b. c/o International Bank for Reconstruction and Development, 1818 H St., Washington, D.C.; h. Princeton, N.J.

Eugene R. Black is the president of the International Bank for Reconstruction and Development, which was established by the Bretton Woods conference of 1944. Black had become United States executive director of the International Bank (also known as the "World Bank") early in 1947 and its third president in May 1949, succeeding John J. McCloy '47, who

was appointed United States High Commissioner for Germany. The official is a former senior vice-president of the Chase National Bank of New York City.

Eldest of the three children of the late Eugene Robert and Gussie King (Grady) Black, Eugene Robert Black was born in Atlanta, Georgia, on May 1, 1898. His father, after a successful career as a lawyer, became the president of the Atlanta Trust Company and subsequently governor of the Federal Reserve Board in Atlanta and in Washington; his mother was the daughter of the Southern orator and journalist, Henry Woodfin Grady, founder of the Atlanta *Herald* and later part-owner of the Atlanta *Constitution*. A graduate of the University of Georgia, Atlanta, where he took the Bachelor of Arts degree *cum laude* in 1918, the future head of the International Bank served as an ensign in the United States Navy during World War I.

Attached to the Atlanta office of the New York investment house of Harris, Forbes and Company in 1918, Black quickly (states *Business Week*) "showed a real knack for selling"; and in the following year when the firm became the Chase-Harris-Forbes Corporation, he was appointed the district manager for Atlanta. Later he was also in charge of branches in New Orleans, Dallas, and Houston, and by 1933, when the corporation was dissolved, had risen to an assistant vice-presidency.

After considering joining certain other former Harris-Forbes executives in the new firm of Starkweather and Company, Black decided to associate himself with the Chase National Bank of New York. Appointed (in June 1933) a second vice-president in charge of contacts in eight Southern states, he at first had headquarters in Atlanta, but in the year following he moved to New York, where he became widely known in financial circles as an expert on the bond market; and in February 1936, was offered (and accepted) appointment as Under-Secretary of the Treasury. "The Administration," stated the New York *Times*, "was anxious to obtain his services in connection with the financing that must be done to pay the soldiers' bonus." Black found, however, that the change would entail a financial sacrifice he felt at the time unable to make, and was released from his acceptance. Remaining with the Chase National Bank, he was promoted to a senior vice-presidency in 1937. During the War Loan drive of April 1943 Black served in an executive capacity with the New York Victory Bond Committee; and during the following June was appointed director of the Banking and Investment Division of the War Finance Committee of New York State. As World War II drew to a close, he became increasingly active in the international work of the Chase National Bank, and in the period 1945-47 made a number of trips to Europe in connection with foreign credits.

Black's appointment as United States executive director of the International Bank for Reconstruction and Development was announced by President Truman on February 28, 1947. The bank had begun operations in June of the previous year, after the necessary twenty-eight of the member governments in the United Nations had ratified articles of agreement formulated at the July 1944 monetary conference at Bretton Woods, New Hampshire. But although as yet active for only seven months, the World Bank (the primary purpose of which is officially defined as "to make available from its own resources, or by other means, international investment capital for productive purposes") was already encountering major financing difficulties. The bank's first president, Eugene Meyer [41], and more especially the first United States executive director, John G. Collado, former State Department economic adviser, favored what the *United States News* has characterized as "a more liberal loan policy" than was "thought wise" by the New York financial community. Meyer resigned as president and was succeeded February 28, 1947, by John J. McCloy, former Assistant Secretary of War, who, however, made his acceptance of the post conditional on the direction of the bank being "placed in the hands of persons who could be depended upon to pursue sound, non-political lending policies" (in the words of the New York *Times*). He insisted that Black be named executive director for the United States, and Collado accordingly resigned.

"All powers of the Bank," states the *United States Government Organization Manual* of 1949, "are vested in the Board of Governors, which comprises one representative of each member country. The Board of Governors has delegated most of its authority to the Executive Directors, who are in continuous session at the Bank's headquarters in Washington, D.C. They are now 14 in number, 5 appointed by the countries having the largest capital subscriptions, 9 elected by the Governors of the remaining members. Voting power of the member countries is roughly proportionate to their capital subscriptions." The bank as of May 15, 1949, is capitalized at around $8,348,500,000, but of this sum only 20 per cent is "paid in" by the member countries (in 1949 numbering forty-eight), and of that amount all but 2 per cent "can be used for lending only with the permission of the country concerned." Thus, as only the United States has been in a position to allow full use of its quota, and as a large proportion of the bank's lending funds must be raised through the sale of its own bonds, the key nature of the United States executive director's position becomes obvious.

The appointment of Black reassured the New York banks, which very shortly absorbed around $250,000,000 in bonds; and by the middle of August 1947, loans had already been made to five nations (207 millions to the Netherlands, 40 millions to Denmark, 250 millions to France, 16 millions to Belgium, and 12 millions to Luxembourg). Subsequent loans to Chile, Mexico and Brazil raised the disbursements to a total of $508,342,928 by May 15, 1949, three days before President McCloy, named to fill the new post of United States High Commissioner for Germany, resigned as head of the International Bank and was succeeded by Black who, at the same time, gave up his position as a senior vice-president of Chase National. (The president's term is for five years.) Earlier loans by the

Wide World Photos
EUGENE R. BLACK

World Bank had been for rehabilitation and reconstruction needs in war-impaired areas; but with the implementation of the Marshall Plan, the bank was to a large extent relieved of the need to devote its resources primarily to this end, and the Latin American loans already mentioned had been for purposes of industrial, agricultural and power development.

This policy was continued under Black's presidency. Thus, on July 17, 1949, announcement was made that a loan of two million dollars would be made to Yugoslavia for timber development; on August 1, twelve and a half millions was allotted to Finland for the development of her wood-products and other industries; and on August 18, thirty-four millions were granted to India for the development of her railway system. In September Black recommended that European countries experiencing economic difficulties should revalue their currencies, since their "most urgent requirement is obviously to sell more of their production abroad, and particularly in dollar markets." His recommendation is believed to have been a major factor in bringing about the devaluation of the pound sterling. Black also felt that the cost of social welfare programs should be reduced in countries which could not afford them. In December of 1949 the World Bank's president announced that the entire $100,000,000 issue of the bank's 2¼ per cent bonds, which are due for payment in mid-1957, would be paid off at the call price of 101 early in January 1950. In the years immediately ahead he anticipates that the institution will be lending between 200 and 250 million dollars annually. On October 14, 1949, he had announced that three hundred million dollars of uninvested money was available, and that no more bonds would be sold until well into 1950. In a statement in the *United Nations Bulletin*, Black

BLACK, EUGENE R.—*Continued*

wrote, "We have made some progress. We will make more."

The bank official was married January 25, 1930, to Suzette Heath of Atlanta; he has three children: Mrs. Betty Campbell, Eugene Robert, Jr. (by a previous marriage), and William Heath. "Tall, bald, informal and pleasantly approachable," is the verbal "snapshot" of President Black supplied by the *United States News*; while an interviewer for *Business Week* noted also that the financier is "soft-spoken" as well as "keen-minded," and "enjoys a reputation for being studious but not stuffy." Now a resident of Princeton, New Jersey, Black may find relaxation in bridge, which he reportedly plays excellently; and he is "a southpaw golfer who shoots in the high seventies."

References

    Bsns W p6 Je 4 '49 por
    Com and Fin Chronicle 165:1279 Mar 6
      '47
    U S News 26:36+ My 27 '49 por
    International Who's Who, 1949
    Who's Who in America, 1948-49
    Who's Who in Commerce and Industry
      (1948)
    Who's Who in the East (1948)
    World Biography (1948)

BLAKELY, MRS. HENRY LOWING-TON *See* Brooks, G.

BLALOCK, MRS. RICHARD W(ATTS)

Aug. 1, 1905- Girls organization official

Address: b. c/o Camp Fire Girls, Inc., 16 E. 48th St., New York 17; h. 305 Perry Dr., Marshall, Tex.

Mrs. Richard W. Blalock was chosen president of the national council of Camp Fire Girls, Inc., at the October 1949 convention of the girls organization, to succeed Mrs. John C. Parker '[47]. A native and resident of the Southwest, Mrs. Blalock had been president of the Marshall (Texas) Council of Camp Fire Girls from 1942 to 1946. She served on the national board of the organization during 1946-47 and was the vice-president of the national council for two terms thereafter. During the period of World War II the youth leader was active in the work of the Red Cross and participated in the various War Bond drives and United War Chest campaigns. Mrs. Blalock was re-elected president of the Camp Fire Girls in October 1950.

The youngest of eight children (five girls and three boys), Mrs. Richard Blalock was born August 1, 1905, in Chickasha, Oklahoma. She was given the name of Ruby by her parents, Richard Kelly and Effie Dalton (Scales) Wootten. Both her father, who had come to Oklahoma (then a Territory) from Mississippi, and her mother, who was born in North Carolina, were descended from early settlers in America. Richard Kelly Wootten is listed in Rex Harlow's *Successful Oklahomans*

Gittings

MRS. RICHARD W. BLALOCK

as "one of the foremost financiers in the Southwest." He was important in the development of the cotton oil business, the owner and president of a chain of banks, and was known for his philanthropies—"generous toward all worthy causes . . . one of the most enthusiastic supporters of education [he contributed to endowments for Oklahoma City University and Oklahoma College for Women] . . . has sent scores of young men and women through university."

Ruby Wootten attended the Chickasha High School, from which she was graduated in 1922, and then studied at Ward-Belmont College in Nashville, Tennessee, until 1924, the year she entered the University of Oklahoma to major in history and sociology. Her B.A. degree, from that university, is dated 1926. At Ward-Belmont she was president of the senior class, manager and treasurer of the athletic association, a member of the glee club and of the cabinet of the YWCA. At the university she became a member of Kappa Kappa Gamma, social sorority, and of Phi Mu Gamma, the dramatic sorority. She was chosen May Queen, served as secretary of the junior class, and was on the board of Stadium Union. Before her marriage on February 27, 1929, to Richard Watts Blalock, a Texas attorney, the young woman took postgraduate work at the University of Oklahoma.

The Blalocks went to live in Marshall, Texas. There, after the birth of her daughter (Anne Wootten) in 1934, Mrs. Blalock began to participate in civic groups. She is a past president of Marshall's Federation of Women's Clubs, for two years she was president of the South Marshall Parent-Teachers Association, she has served on local and county chapters of the American Red Cross, and for three years during World War II was chairman of the War Fund Drive of the American Red Cross.

It was in 1942, when her daughter joined the junior organization (Blue Birds) of the Camp

Fire Girls, that Mrs. Blalock began her association with this youth organization. From 1942 to 1946 she was president of the Marshall Council of the Camp Fire Girls. In 1945 she became secretary for Region IV, filling that post for a year, and in 1946 was elected a member of the national board of the Camp Fire Girls, Inc. From 1947 to 1949 she was vice-president of the national council, and in October 1949, at the triennial conference she was elected unanimously by the national council to serve as president of Camp Fire Girls, for the 1950 term of office.

The organization which Mrs. Blalock heads was founded in 1910 as an outgrowth of the progressive education movement. Among its sponsors were Dr. Luther H. Gulick '45 (founder and first president), Ernest Thompson Seton '43, John Collier '41, Dr. Mary Schenck Woolman (professor of household arts at Teachers College and founder of the Manhattan Trade School for Girls, who helped compile the first *Book of the Camp Fire Girls*), and Dr. James West, chief executive of the Boy Scouts of America. The purpose of the organization is to provide the constructive leisure-time activities for young girls which will "perpetuate the spiritual ideals of the home" and "stimulate and aid in the formation of habits making for health and character." Its tenets are: "Worship God, seek beauty, give service, pursue knowledge, be trustworthy, hold on to health, glorify work, and be happy." The insigne of the Camp Fire Girls shows crossed logs and a flame, symbolizing the hearth fire of the home and the campfire of the outdoors. "Wohelo," watchword of the group, is composed of the first two letters of the words "Work," "Health," "Love."

The program of the organization's activities is divided into seven crafts—home, outdoors, creative arts, frontiers, business, sports and games, and citizenship. Since its inception, more than 2,500,000 girls, ranging in age from seven to eighteen, have been members of the three divisions: Blue Birds (girls seven to ten years old), Camp Fire Girls (ten through fourteen years) and Horizon Clubs. In 1950 there are more than 360,000 girls who belong to approximately 260 local councils throughout the United States. In addition to providing year-round camping activities, instruction in various skills, and help in the development of personality, the organization presents training in citizenship and international understanding. Members of the local councils send gift packages to children overseas, cooperate in Community Chest drives, contribute time to children's hospitals, and help to make clothes for infants of indigent families.

On the occasion of her election to the national office Mrs. Blalock spoke on the obligation of adults to young people. Adults, she said, "must make more of an investment in our youth, our greatest asset and our most challenging responsibility. . . . Together we can give our girls those everlasting values which nothing can tear down or destroy. I like to think that you and I, united in service for Camp Fire, can indeed be worthy of our generation." The observance of the fortieth anniversary of Camp Fire

Girls, Inc., in 1950, evoked editorial comment on the significance of the organization. At its annual conference on October 27, 1950, Mrs. Blalock was re-elected to the presidency.

Mrs. Blalock is a member of the Texas Committee for Children and Youth, and represented that organization in the 1950 White House Conference Planning Committee. She is also a member of the Citizen's Committee of Texas on Mental Health and of the Texas branch of the Save the Children Federation. Her other civic activities include membership on the boards of trustees of the Kahn Memorial Hospital and of the Texas Society for Mental Hygiene. For her "outstanding service to the community" Mrs. Blalock in 1946 was granted the Gulick Award from the Camp Fire Girls. In November 1949 the Marshall Chamber of Commerce honored her with a testimonial dinner at which she was presented with a plaque as a token of "appreciation and highest public esteem." From the American Red Cross she has received a Certificate of Recognition for Service, and from the United War Chest of Texas, of which she was chairman in 1914, the Award of Recognition.

Described by her associates in the Camp Fire Girls as "a dynamo with a Texas drawl," Mrs. Blalock is of small stature (five feet in height and 110 pounds in weight), has blue eyes and brown hair. Her political affiliations are with the Democratic party and her church is the Methodist. She lists square dancing, photography, gardening, and collections of all kinds as her recreational interests.

Reference

Marshall (Tex.) News Messenger O 30 '49

BLALOCK, RUBY WOOTTEN *See* Blalock, Mrs. R. W.

BLOUGH, ROY (blou) Aug. 21, 1901-
United States Government official; economist
Address: c/o Council of Economic Advisers, Executive Office Bldg., Washington, D.C.

President Truman's nomination of Dr. Roy Blough on May 10, 1950, to the three-man Council of Economic Advisers filled the vacancy left by the resignation of Dr. Edwin G. Nourse '46 on November 1, 1949. Blough, an economist, has held professorships in five universities and positions of authority in State and Federal tax and treasury offices, and has gained "a national reputation as a tax expert" (*Time*, May 22, 1950). He has been described as taking a position "on the moderate edge of the Fair Deal" (New York *Herald Tribune*, May 11, 1950). Other Federal posts he had held were part-time consultant to the Social Security Board and tax adviser and assistant to the Secretary of the Treasury of the United States.

Roy Blough, a native of Pittsburgh, Pennsylvania, is the son of the Reverend Silas S. Blough (a minister in the Church of the

ROY BLOUGH

Brethren) and of Mary Alice (Wertz) Blough. His birth date is August 21, 1901. Young Blough went to Manchester College, North Manchester, Indiana, for his university studies, and was graduated with the B.A. degree in 1921. After receiving his Master's degree from the University of Wisconsin the following year, he returned to Manchester to become assistant professor of history and economics. Upon completion of his first year of teaching, he was advanced to the status of associate professor, his title from 1923 to 1925. In 1925 he returned to the University of Wisconsin to continue his graduate study, and while there, until 1927, was an assistant in economics. In the latter year he became statistician for the Wisconsin Tax Commission. While in this post, he did graduate work at the University of Wisconsin, and earned his Ph.D. degree in 1929.

The following year (1930) Blough was promoted by the Wisconsin Tax Commission to chief statistician in charge of research and statistics; he continued in this work until 1932. At that time he returned to the teaching profession as associate professor of economics in the Graduate School of Public Administration at the University of Cincinnati, where he was a fellow in the Graduate School during 1937-38. (During the summer of 1936 he taught, with the rank of professor, at Columbia University in New York City.) While on staff at Cincinnati, Blough acted as director of research and statistics in State and city finances for the Federal Emergency Relief Administration (July 1933 to February 1934); as consultant to the Social Security Board (1937 and 1938); as a member of the United States Treasury Department (summer of 1937). He was an associate director on the committee on

taxation which prepared *Facing the Tax Problem,* a survey of taxation in the United States with a program for the future, published in 1936 by the Twentieth Century Fund.

In June 1938 Blough joined the United States Treasury Department as director of tax research and in December 1944 became assistant to the Secretary of the Treasury. He remained with the Treasury until September 1946. A year later he was called to testify before the Senate Finance Committee in connection with an accusation that had been made that corporations had accumulated "carry back" credits under the excess-profits tax, and that they had a pool of 30 billion dollars in reserves upon which they could draw. Blough, as a tax expert, stated that corporations could demand this amount in refunds or tax credits—but only if they lost a great deal more than 30 billion dollars in operations during the next year.

In the fall of 1946 Blough joined the faculty of the University of Chicago as professor of economics and political science. In 1947 he appeared with Beardsley Ruml [43], chairman of the board of R. H. Macy and Company, and Senator Robert A. Taft [48] of Ohio, in a discussion of national tax reduction on a University of Chicago Round Table broadcast. Ruml and Taft favored a tax cut, but disagreed as to the means and amount. Blough opposed any cut in tax rates at that time, maintaining that "surpluses of receipts over expenditures in prosperous times should be applied to the debt rather than to tax reductions" (New York *Times,* March 10, 1947).

Announcement of President Truman's nomination of Dr. Roy Blough to fill the post formerly held by Dr. Edwin G. Nourse on the three-man Council of Economic Advisers was made May 10, 1950. At the same time Leon H. Keyserling [47] was appointed chairman (he had been acting chairman since Nourse's resignation) and Dr. John D. Clark [47] was named vice-chairman. Upon announcement of Blough's nomination, Senator Taft observed, "The President now has three left fielders on the team to advise him on economic affairs" (*Herald Tribune,* May 12, 1950). The consensus, however, according to *Time* (May 22, 1950) was that Blough "plays a mite closer to center field." Before the Senate Banking Committee, which was considering his nomination to the council, Blough stated he opposed deficit spending as a "continuing policy" because of its "inflationary effects." Though "perturbed" by the size of the national debt, he said he felt it would not be wise to reduce it at that juncture as such a move would tend to curb production, employment, and the national income generally. The New York *Times* (May 11, 1950) pointed out that the members of the council in its new setup have different fortes in economics: Keyserling is a specialist on housing, public works, social security, banking, and credit; Clark, who has been a businessman, banker, and professor, is a leading adviser on Federal anti-trust policy; Blough is a tax and fiscal expert.

The Council of Economic Advisers was established in the Executive Office of the President by the Employment Act of 1946 to keep the President posted on economic trends, to appraise the activities of the Federal Government in their effect on the national economy, and to recommend policies fostering free enterprise. It is directed to assist the President in the preparation of his Annual Economic Report to Congress and is charged with advising measures necessary to maintaining full employment, production, and purchasing power. Each member receives a yearly salary of $16,000 and serves "without term"—that is, as long as the President approves and the member is willing. Originally, the council's sights were on the achievement of stability; more recently they have seemed to be trained on the target of a constantly expanding economy (New York *World-Telegram and Sun*, May 24, 1950.) The council has been a leader in promoting extension of social security and enlargement of the housing program, and has done much of the research for President Truman's recent small-business recommendations to Congress. Chief among the CEA difficulties in the past has been failure to achieve harmonious working relations with the Joint Congressional Committee on the Economic Report. Deficiencies were also felt in the field of general tax reform.

On the question of whether the CEA members should act as confidential advisers to the Chief Executive or publicize their findings and promote Administration economic programs, Blough has indicated that he believes council members should feel free to testify before Congressional committees and make public appearances, and that the council should work for Congressional action on the measures it advocates. (This was the issue over which Nourse resigned, he having favored the first view while his colleagues held to the latter.) Editorial comment in the *Christian Science Monitor*, commending the latitude allowed the council by the President, advocated as a solution of the policy controversy that the CEA be given a more independent status and its members be constituted "technical counselors" to the Congressional Joint Committee on the Economic Report as well as to the President. The achievements of the CEA were analyzed by Washington correspondent Peter Edson to have been largely educational or inspirational: he cited the fact that at least 10,000 copies of every report have been ordered by college economics departments and university business schools. "The influence here and on the real thinking business leaders probably has been greater than it has on Congress," he concluded.

Contributions by Dr. Blough in the fields of public finance economics, government, and business have appeared in the *Proceedings of the American Philosophical Society*, the *Tax Law Review*, the *American Economic Review*, and the *Congressional Digest*. He has been editor of the *National Tax Journal*. For a book prepared by the Tax Institute, *Curbing Inflation Through Taxation*, Blough wrote "Individual Income Tax as a Method of Inflation Control," and "Postwar Tax Structure" for *Economic Reconstruction*, a symposium published in 1945. The tax expert holds membership in the American Economic Association, the National Tax Association, the American Society for Public Administration, Midwest Economic

Association (president 1947-48), American Political Science Association, and Econometric Society. He is a member of the Church of the Brethren. By his marriage to Marie Goshorn on May 19, 1923, he has three sons—Richard, William, and Donald. The economist, who has been described as "boyish faced," has thick, wavy hair, and wears glasses.

References

N Y Herald Tribune p40 My 11 '50 por
N Y Times p24 My 11 '50 por
N Y World-Telegram and Sun p30 My 24 '50
Time 55:22 My 22 '50 por
Washington (D.C.) Post p2 My 11 '50 por
Directory of the American Political Science Association, 1948
Who's Who in America, 1950-51
Who's Who in Government, 1932-33
Who's Who in the Midwest (1949)

BLUM, LEON (bloom lä"ôn') Apr. 9, 1872—Mar. 30, 1950 French political leader; chairman of the Socialist party executive board in 1919; elected to the Chamber from a Paris district in 1919; leader of the Socialist party, then of the Popular Front, a group of leftist, labor, and middle-of-the-road parties; Premier of France June 4, 1936-June 21, 1937, and briefly for two periods in 1938 and 1946; carried through radical reforms affecting labor, banking, and agriculture; arrested by the Vichy Government after the defeat of France in 1940; transferred to prison in Germany in 1943; released in 1944; lawyer, journalist, and man of letters; founder of *Le Populaire*, Socialist newspaper. See *Current Biography*, 1940.

Obituary

N Y Times p31 Mr 31 '50 por

BONNER, MARY GRAHAM Sept. 5, 1895- Author
Address: h. 706 Riverside Dr., New York 31

Reprinted from the *Wilson Library Bulletin*, May 1950.

It may come as somewhat of a shock to boy readers, but the M. G. Bonner who writes so authoritatively on baseball is a woman. Mary Graham Bonner keeps her baseball personality rigidly separated from her everyday one, doubting that the young correspondents who write her to settle sports arguments would concede that "a woman can recognize a squeeze play when she sees one."

Miss Bonner's interest in the game may be an environmental one, for she and baseball share a common birthplace, Cooperstown, New York. Daughter of George William Graham Bonner, a Scot, and Margaret Cary (Worthington) Bonner, an American, she was born September 5, 1895. The family left Cooperstown when she was still an infant, settling in Halifax, Nova Scotia, where her father was a bank manager. Miss Bonner has dual citizenship, since her

MARY GRAHAM BONNER

birth makes her an American, and British law, a Canadian. She was educated at Halifax Ladies' College and the Halifax Conservatory of Music. In school she played basketball, hockey, and rounders, the British version of baseball. She won cups for swimming and high diving, and became expert at skating, ice boating, and camping.

Her early ambition was to become a pianist, but by the time she finished her musical training she had fallen in love with writing as a career. Hers has been the unusual experience of having all her written work accepted, with none of the discouraging rejections familiar to most beginners. She estimates that she has published "thousands" of reviews, articles, and stories. She wrote a daily story for the Associated Press for ten years. Her books in 1950 number thirty-three. Most of the earlier ones were collections of bedtime stories, or small volumes for the very young. A good example is *Mrs. Cucumber Green* (1927), of which the *Saturday Review* said: "The imaginings are the same definite, rambling inventions of a happy child in an old-fashioned household. Townspeople wander pleasantly in and out, and all the toys, especially a favorite doll, take on real personality." Of *Miss Angelina Adorable* (1928) the New York *Times* wrote, "Little girls of five or six or seven years, and doubtless little boys of similar ages . . . will think Miss Bonner's new story very charming indeed."

The Big Baseball Book for Boys (1931) was a history of the sport and a digest of the rules. The Boston *Transcript* thought it "rather sketchy in its treatment. . . .So far as it goes, the volume is readable in a limited way." The Springfield *Republican*, however, said, "The book abounds in useful information concerning the national pastime as well as much highly entertaining matter. . . .Instruction on the arts of pitching, batting, and base running is made read-

able and convincing." *Canada and Her Story* (1942) is a factual book covering history, geography, and daily life. May Lamberton Becker said, "Welcome for the history of Canada it provides children of the United States to whom it will come as news, this admirable book is even more welcome for the blend of history and present-day life it affords." *Horn Book* called it "an inviting book of information which fills a need." *Made in Canada*, a survey of Canada's arts and crafts, followed in 1943. E. L. Buell said in the *Times*, "Although it is loosely organized, the book is full of interesting facts, and it will serve as a stimulating introduction to the subject for readers of from ten to fifteen."

Courier of the Sky (1944), a book about pigeons, was called "a splendid informative and enlightening book for those interested in raising pigeons for pleasure or profit" by *Library Journal*. *Surprise Place* (1945) and *Something Always Happens* (1946) were easy-reading stories for third and fourth grades. In *Out to Win* (1947) Miss Bonner tells a baseball story that both *Horn Book* and Virginia Kirkus describe as "excellent.' *The Hidden Village Mystery* (1948) and *The Mysterious Caboose* (1949) were juvenile mystery stories. Of the second of these, the New York *Times* said, "a suspenseful . . . story filled with action and excitement." *Winning Dive* is scheduled for 1950 publication.

Miss Bonner, winner of the Women's National Book Association's Constance Lindsay Skinner award, is an attractive person, tall and slender, with brown hair and blue-gray eyes. She lives in New York City, in an apartment overlooking the Hudson. She retains her interest in music and sports. Her writing ideal is to "give the youngsters an idea of democracy with a small 'd.' None of the blatant kind of propaganda . . . but the real feeling of understanding."

BOOTH, EVANGELINE (CORY) Dec. 25, 1865—July 17, 1950 Daughter of the founder of the Salvation Army; a leader in that religious body's work in England; credited with effecting Parliament's repeal of the by-laws forbidding open-air preaching; in 1888 appointed commander of all Salvation Army operations in London, and principal of the International Training College; served during 1893-1904 as commissioner in command of the Army in Canada; became commander (1904) of the organization in the United States; in 1934 elected general of the international movement; retired in 1939; noted for her eloquence; composer of Salvation Army hymns and author of several books. See *Current Biography*, 1941.

Obituary

N Y Times p29 Jl 18 '50

BOWMAN, ISAIAH Dec. 26, 1878—Jan. 6, 1950 Leading American geographer and educator; member of faculty of Yale University, 1909-15; director of the American Geographical Society, 1915-35; elected president of Johns

Hopkins University 1935, retired at the end of 1948; led geographical expeditions in South America (1907, 1911, 1913); geographer for the Peace Conference, Paris, following World War I; adviser to the State Department World War II, and in postwar period; author of geographical and educational works. See *Current Biography*, 1945.

Obituary

N Y Times p17 Ja 7 '50

BOWRON, FLETCHER (bou'rŭn) Aug. 13, 1887- Mayor of Los Angeles
Address: b. City Hall, Los Angeles 12, Calif., h. 2158 Rockledge Rd., Los Angeles 28, Calif.

Fletcher Bowron, who was chosen Mayor of Los Angeles on May 31, 1949, for the fourth time, had first come into that office in 1938 on a nonpartisan reform ticket in a recall election which, said *Time*, deposed the "corrupt machine which functioned during the regime of his predecessor." Bowron, a Republican, had begun his career as a reporter in San Francisco; later he practiced law in Los Angeles, and for twelve years he served as a jurist with a county Superior Court. During his administration Los Angeles had a period of quick growth: Bowron states it is the third largest city in the United States in terms of population; it is the world's largest in metropolitan area, covering 452 square miles. As a result of the November 1950 recall election, which followed a strong movement to oust him, Bowron was retained in office.

Born on August 13, 1887, in Poway, San Diego County, California, Fletcher Bowron is the son of Samuel and Martha (Hershey) Bowron, to whom two other sons and a daughter were born. His mother was of Dutch-Irish stock, his father of English-Irish. " 'De Bolrun,' the original spelling of the family name," reports Mayor Bowron, "indicates the family came to England from Normandy with William the Conqueror." In 1280, the date of the first family record, the name was changed to "Bolron" and in the sixteenth century to "Bowron." His great-grandfather came to America from England and settled in the northern part of New York in 1791; in 1885 his parents migrated to California. Fletcher Bowron spent his childhood on his father's fruit ranch near Poway. He attended near-by rural and town schools until 1902; in that year his father moved to Los Angeles, where he became a building contractor. Thus Fletcher completed his secondary education at the Los Angeles High School in 1906. During those years he held a number of odd jobs.

In 1907 young Bowron entered the University of California, at Berkeley; and in 1909 he began the study of law at the University of Southern California, which he left in 1911 without obtaining a degree. For the next six years he worked as a reporter, first with the San Francisco *Sun* and *Chronicle* and later with the Los Angeles *Record and Examiner*. Having studied law in his free hours, in 1917

Wide World Photos
FLETCHER BOWRON

he was admitted to the California bar. Shortly afterward he entered the wartime United States Army; at first assigned to the 144th Field Artillery, he later became a member of the Army Intelligence Division of the General Staff with the rank of second lieutenant.

In 1919 Bowron formed a law partnership with Z. B. West in Los Angeles. He continued to practice his profession until 1923, when he was appointed a deputy State corporation commissioner. In this post he came to the attention of Friend William Richardson, then the Governor of California. Two years later (1925), the Governor made Bowron his executive secretary, and after one year, impressed with his thoroughness, appointed him to a vacancy on the bench of the Superior Court of Los Angeles County. Bowron during his twelve years with the court (elected in 1929 and re-elected in 1935), served in every department and during 1937-38 acted as presiding judge. He counts among his most successful achievements a calendar system he established, which has proved helpful in court procedure. It was at this time, according to the city's reference library biography, that his activities against municipal corruption brought him into the limelight.

Under the mayoralty of Frank L. Shaw, Los Angeles was noted for its "underworld of organized crime and vice rackets, condoned by corrupt city officials and members of the police department" (*Time*, July 4, 1949). In 1938, upon the implication of various police officers in an attempted murder, an aroused public secured a special election on the question of the recall of Mayor Shaw. Remembered for his efforts to combat civic crime and corruption in 1934, Republican Judge Bowron was drafted as a candidate on a fusion ballot. On September 16, 1938, in a recall election, he was chosen Mayor by a two-to-one vote. His four sub-

BOWRON, FLETCHER—*Continued*

sequent re-elections occurred in 1941, 1945, 1949, and 1950.

In an article for the *American Magazine* (July 1946), Mayor Bowron explained the difficulties he encountered in his reform efforts. "Actually, in many ways a mayor's power and authority are very limited. In Los Angeles the mayor can hire and fire just one employee, his secretary. All others are under civil service. After I took office I found it particularly difficult to get rid of police officers with itchy palms." In the course of seven months (after he first took office) he secured the resignation of twenty-three high-ranking officers. In 1949 Colonel Frank M. Kreml of the International Association of Police Chiefs pronounced the Los Angeles police department to be "outstanding" among those of large cities. *Time* has reported that in accomplishing these reforms, Bowron "made scores of enemies," but that his reputation for being "fiercely honest" and for cleaning up Los Angeles had continued to win his re-election.

A fresh outbreak of scandal in the city police department in the summer of 1949 brought about the filing of a petition for the Mayor's recall, a demand the Mayor's supporters attribute to machinations of his political opponents. In March of 1949 Governor Earl Warren's special civic study commission on organized crime stated that Mayor Bowron and Governor Warren were named by national slot machine kings as "the two persons most important to remove from California public affairs" (*Christian Science Monitor*, March 15, 1949). The report also supported Mayor Bowron's frequent assertions that strong pressure was being brought to bear to make Los Angeles a "wide-open town." In response to a request from the Washington *Post* for comment on a forthcoming national crime conference, Mayor Bowron said he recommended "a Federal antiracketeering law" and advocated that "the transportation of money or credits across State lines for financing local political campaigns for the purpose of establishing illicit operations be made a Federal offense."

In the summer of 1949 a movement to recall Bowron from his municipal office was started, and by mid-October of 1950 it took definite form as seven aspirants qualified as candidates for his position. The recall election, which was held November 7, resulted in a victory for the Mayor—approximately 388,000 votes favored his retention, about 245,000 his recall. This vindication of Bowron's administration, commented the *Christian Science Monitor*, "can be interpreted as a rebuke to underworld pretensions and to the opportunistic hope of pro-Communists that they could capture this city's highest office. . . .Mayor Bowron himself attributed the recall effort to underworld gambling and vice interests."

The rapid growth of Los Angeles' population—from 1,504,277 (1940) to 2,039,623 (1949) —has given the office of its mayor a multiplicity of problems. Bowron has likened his task to the management of a corporation with a capital investment of more than a billion dollars. The operating expenses of Los Angeles were over $170,000,000 yearly in 1946 and have increased since then. During Bowron's administration thirty-four schools were built in ten years; gas and water mains, sewerage system and electric lines were provided for the 240,000 new homes built during the past eight years. In 1949 Bowron and the city council, taking advantage of the new Federal Housing Act, signed a cooperative agreement with the local housing authority for the spending of $100,000,000 in Government funds for the construction of 10,000 housing units.

Bowron during 1947-48 was president of the American Municipal Association, an organization, representing some 9,500 cities in forty-odd States. He is also a member of the board of directors of the League of California Cities. During his presidency of the municipal association, he was prominent in a drive for payments from the Federal Government to offset the loss of tax revenue on city property owned by the Federal government. In an article, "How Uncle Sam Mooches on Your City," published in the *American Magazine* (1946), Bowron pointed out that city taxes were high because the Federal Government, "reaching into our pockets," was taking several potential sources of city revenue, such as excise taxes on night clubs, theaters, telephone service, and many retail commodities. Other articles by Bowron on city government problems have appeared in *American City* (1947), and the *Southern California Social Science Review* (February 1949). During World War II, the Mayor served as United States Coordinator of Civilian Defense for the Los Angeles Metropolitan Area (1942-45) and was a member of the Secretary of Defense's Joint Orientation Conference; he is in 1950 a member of the Pacific Coast Board of Intergovernmental Relations.

The California Mayor belongs to the Jonathan and Kiwanis Clubs (Los Angeles), and is a member of the American Legion, the Masons, Delta Chi, and of the Native Sons of the Golden West. He is a Methodist. Six foreign decorations he has received are: Knight of the Royal Norwegian Order of St. Olav (1940), the Legion of Merit (Chile), Commander in the Order of Orange-Nassau (the Netherlands), the Mexican Order of the Aztec Eagle, the Médaille de la Reconnaissance Nationale Verneuil (France), and Commander of the Crown of Oak (Luxembourg). On September 16, 1922, Fletcher Bowron married Irene Martin, a Canadian. The couple have one adopted son, Barrett. Living in a hilltop house overlooking the Hollywood Bowl, Bowron likes to work in the terraced garden. Five feet seven and a half inches tall, he weighs 185 pounds, has blue eyes and gray hair. The *Christian Science Monitor* commented on his penchant for blunt speaking.

References

Am Mag 142:32-3+ Jl '46
Collier's 104:12-13+ S 2 '39 por
Time 54:8-15 Jl 4 '49

Who's Who in America, 1948-49
Who's Who in the West (1949)
World Biography (1948)

BOYD, BILL   June 5, 1898-   Actor

Address: b. Hopalong Cassidy Productions, Hollywood, Calif.

Bill Boyd is often called "Hopalong Cassidy," the cowboy character he has played exclusively since 1934 in motion pictures, on a radio program, and in television releases. In 1943 he became vice-president and executive producer of the Hopalong Cassidy Productions; after acquiring the radio, television, commercial, and all other rights to the character in 1948, he consolidated the various enterprises presenting Hopalong into a highly profitable business. He had entered the films as an extra in 1919, became a Cecil B. De Mille "discovery," in 1926 was promoted to leading romantic roles, then to stardom. Boyd was first cast as Hopalong in 1934; he has since made it the longest sustained characterization in film history.

Born on June 5, 1898, in Cambridge, Ohio, Bill (William) Boyd is one of five children of William Boyd, a laborer. Before he reached the age of seven the family had moved to Tulsa, Oklahoma. There he attended school until he was thirteen: his father was killed while rescuing fellow workers who had been trapped by an explosion on a construction job, and young Boyd went to work to help support the family. He held various jobs—as tool dresser, surveyor, and automobile salesman—before setting out, at the age of twenty, for California. When his funds were gone by the time he reached Globe, Arizona, by sawing wood in a lumber camp he earned enough money to take him as far as Orange, some thirty miles from Hollywood. After deciding to try his luck as a motion picture actor, Boyd obtained a suitable wardrobe for that project by first working as an orange packer and an oil driller.

Boyd's rugged physique, photogenic features, and prematurely gray hair won him a place as an extra in *Why Change Your Wife?* (1919) and attracted the attention of Cecil De Mille, its director. Boyd was placed by Famous Players-Lasky under a seven-year contract at a weekly salary of twenty-five dollars for the first year. In 1922, related a *Photoplay* article of March 1934, he left Famous Players to appear in westerns on the Fox lot. A broken ankle ended this contract. His big opportunity came when De Mille cast him as the lead in *The Volga Boatman*, a 1926 release, which brought the twenty-eight-year-old actor good notices. *King of Kings* (1927), *Two Arabian Knights* (1928), and *Beyond Victory* followed. When the "movies" became the "talkies" the motion picture actor became known for his good speaking voice. In 1932 the Pathe Studios gave Boyd a contract calling for $2,500 weekly, with star ranking. He appeared in *Skyscraper, The Leatherneck, Officer O'Brien,* and *The Painted Desert* before this contract was terminated. Then followed a period in which he was cast in lesser roles.

"The sun was rapidly sinking on Bill Boyd," wrote Collie Small in a 1947 *Saturday Evening Post* article, "when he discovered Hopalong." Producer Harry Sherman in 1934 bought the

BILL BOYD

screen rights to six of Clarence E. Mulford's books about the cowpuncher, Hopalong Cassidy. Boyd, who had been playing "heavies," was chosen for the villain of two productions. The actor, however, not only succeeded in being cast in the sympathetic Hopalong role but won a contract for the series of six pictures at a blanket salary of $30,000. His success as the western hero led to the continuation of the "Hoppy" films on a six-a-year basis. Hopalong's creator, Mulford, was a Brooklyn license clerk who had never been west of Chicago until he had written twenty-eight books around the cowboy character. Sherman, after exhausting the Mulford stories, bought the motion picture rights to the character and employed film writers to create new stories. Hopalong, a Western cowboy Robin Hood, never has a love interest in the stories. He wears a black cowboy outfit, which contrasts with his white horse, Topper.

By 1938, Boyd's salary had risen to $100,000 a year. Managerial disputes began (according to the *Saturday Evening Post* article) when Boyd, believing it good business to improve the pictures, returned to Sherman $40,000 of his year's salary for the employment of better writing and other production talents. According to Small, Boyd, charging Sherman with employing "more geniuses" than necessary, "walked out" in 1943. Paramount, the distributors of the Hopalong films, refused to accept a substitute for the man who had made the role popular. After eighteen months of negotiation, Sherman turned over to the actor a ten-year lease on a sub-royalty basis of $25,000 a year for the motion picture rights to the character. Boyd then formed with Benedict Bogeaus and Lewis Rachmil the Hopalong Cassidy Productions, which from 1946 have been released through United Artists.

Each production was budgeted at $10,000 and a ninety-hour shooting schedule. These

BOYD, BILL—*Continued*

limitations, said *Variety* "in no way reflect on the first-rate photography, excellent locations, and unusually good musical backgrounds." *The Devil's Playground*, the first picture made under the new production setup, when presented in 1946, was pronounced by the theatrical weekly to have "an edge on the average western." *Bar 20* (1943), *Texas Masquerade* (1944), *Riders of the Deadline* (1944) are among the fifty-four pictures made under the Sherman management. *Fool's Gold, Unexpected Guest, Lost Canyon, Border Vigilantes,* and *Stick to Your Guns* are regarded outstanding among the Hopalong releases of the new producers. The yearly series of six was made during four consecutive months, leaving Boyd free from acting and production work during eight months of the year. Early in 1950 it was reported that Boyd, after not having made a film for several years, had signed a contract to make six pictures for Paramount, in the first of which he would co-star with Bing Crosby.

In 1948, Boyd, in addition to his ten-year motion picture lease on the character, bought from Mulford all other rights. Through this transaction, the actor "has compounded what appears to be a magic formula for extracting a maximum of profit from a minimum of outlay," as Small expressed it in the *Saturday Evening Post*. In 1949, when fifty-four of the Hopalong films became eligible for television (films must be seven years old before television rights can be exercised), NBC paid Boyd a quarter of a million dollars for the weekly video presentation of a Hopalong Cassidy script. Televised in thirty-nine cities, the Hopalong programs are rated high in popularity with audiences ranging in age from "six to sixty"; it is also reported that attendance at theaters showing his revived films has increased.

Hopalong made two debuts in January 1950—on the radio and in a comic strip. The Sunday afternoon broadcast over the Mutual network can be heard on a total of 496 stations by an audience estimated at about twenty-five million. The comic strip (syndicated by the Los Angeles *Mirror*) was bought at the outset by some fifty newspapers. Hopalong also reaches the public in comic books (15,000,000 distributed in 1949), records (50,000 of the first issue sold in a month), and fifty novelties, such as juvenile cowboy regalia (manufactured by thirty-five concerns paying 5 per cent royalty for the brand name). And Boyd himself makes personal appearances—in a 1949-50 coast-to-coast tour of twenty-six cities he was greeted by more than a million fans. His interests are said to yield a multi-million-dollar income for the actor. A New York *Sunday News* article of January 8, 1950, reported that Boyd has consolidated his five Hollywood offices into two —one for his merchandising exploitation, the other for a clearing house of his other projects. He has a backlog of twelve movies (said the article), which as they reach the required age will be televised, thus assuring him of a considerable sum from that source alone.

Since 1937 the actor has been married to Grace Bradley of Brooklyn, an actress who has played in Broadway musicals and a number of Hollywood films. (He was formerly married to Elinor Fair and Dorothy Sebastian, motion picture actresses.) The Boyds have a California ranch, which they call "Boyd's Nest." During World War II they lived in Los Angeles so that he might take part in the Armed Forces Radio Service Shows (he performed in 125) and make transcriptions for the occupation forces (which he is still doing). The physical statistics of "Hopalong Cassidy" are five feet eleven inches height, 180 pounds weight, blue eyes, and white hair. Writer Sidney Skolsky tells that Boyd will not say, "I am going on tour," but, "Hoppy is going on tour."

References

Life 27:151 S 12 '49
N Y Herald Tribune p23 O 4 '49
N Y Post Mag p13 Mr 5 '50
N Y Sunday News p90 Ja 8 '50
N Y Times X p5 Mr 16 '41
Photoplay p31 O '32; p54 Mr '34
Sat Eve Post 219:20 Je 14 '47

International Motion Picture Almanac, 1947-48

BOYD, WILLIAM *See* Boyd, B.

BOYLAN, ROBERT P(ETER) Oct. 29, 1891- Stock exchange executive
Address: b. c/o New York Stock Exchange, 11 Wall St., New York 5; h. Biltmore Hotel, New York 17

While serving his third successive term as chairman of the New York Stock Exchange's board of governors, Robert P. Boylan on January 12, 1950, was made president pro tem of the Exchange. Formerly the president of the Chicago Board of Trade, in 1936 Boylan bought a seat on the New York Stock Exchange and in 1938 was elected to membership on its board of governors. He became chairman of that body in 1947. In February 1950 Chairman Boylan went on record before a Senate Banking subcommittee as favoring the Frear bill, legislation which proposes to extend the protection of the Securities Exchange Act of 1934 to investors in some 1,118 companies not yet covered by the Act.

Robert Peter Boylan, born on October 29, 1891, in Cincinnati, Ohio, is the son of Robert Hughes and Mary (Murphy) Boylan. Young Boylan attended Our Lady of Sorrows Parochial School and St. Phillip's High School in Chicago until the age of fourteen, when he became a clerk in one of Chicago's grain brokerage firms. Seven years later (1912) he acquired partnership in Edward S. Adams & Company, a connection he continued until 1918. In that year he began operating under his own name in Chicago as a broker in grains and stocks. Boylan became a member of the Chicago Board of Trade in 1915, and, after having served as a director and vice-president, in January 1935 was chosen as its president, which office he held until August 1936.

In 1936 Boylan moved his interests to New York, there acquiring a seat on the New York Stock Exchange. He was elected to membership on its board of governors two years later. During 1940-41 he was vice-chairman of that body and was a member of a special committee which in 1941 recommended amendments to the constitution of the exchange. In April 1947 he succeeded John A. Coleman as chairman. In the absence of President Emil Schram [41] (because of illness) from his duties as president of the exchange, Boylan was appointed president pro tem on January 12, 1950. In addition to his other posts, he serves as chairman of the boards of directors for the allied exchange corporations, the New York Stock Exchange Building Company, and the New York Quotation Company and Stock Clearing Corporation. On assuming the chairmanship of the board of governors, Boylan expressed the opinion that the exchange had been "a vital force in the development of this country" by channeling savings into mass production and mass distribution; and that it was now organized and operated "on a basis which assures more competent service than ever before in its history."

Tradition has it that the New York Stock Exchange, market house for the sale of stocks, bonds, and other securities, had its first meeting under a buttonwood tree on Wall Street in 1792, a few blocks from its present site in Wall Street. Government of the organization is vested in a governing committee, consisting of a president, treasurer, and twenty-five governors. A committee on constitution (limited to five members) studies all proposed changes to its constitution and reports its findings to the governing committee. The membership of the exchange is limited to 1,375, the majority of the members being partners in some six hundred New York brokerage and investment firms. An applicant may acquire membership only through the purchase of a seat from a retiring member and after approval by the board of governors. The organization operates as an auction market, the highest or lowest bid having "the floor." Through the auction of securities or bonds, corporations obtain funds to finance their operations. "Thus, surplus funds of the people," states an exchange brochure, "are converted into real savings—factories and other durable wealth."

Changes in the constitution of the exchange, affecting the board of governors primarily. were suggested in two petitions in October and December 1949. (The second petition was a modification of the first.) Earlier changes had reduced the number of governors from fifty to thirty-two in 1938 and to twenty-five at a later date. The 1949 petition requested an increase in the board membership and revision of the allocation of seats on the ground that the administrative setup as constituted was inefficient and gave inadequate representation to active floor members. (On March 12, 1950, the board of governors declared itself opposed to the petition.) Procedure requires that the petition be voted on by the general membership of the exchange.

In October 1949, Boylan, as chairman of the board of governors, addressed the Association

ROBERT P. BOYLAN

of Stock Exchange Firms, and referred to the possibility indicated by the present Administration and the preceding one of "a more abundant life," involving an expansion of the American economy by 1960 to an annual income of $300,-000,000,000 and a domestic market in which consumers spend $160,000,000,000. To serve such a market, he pointed out, business would have to expand at the rate of $8,000,000,000 a year for the next ten years. "If it cannot get [the investment capital] from private investors, it will have to get it from the Government which, of course," continued Boylan, "would mean that eventually private capital would be eliminated from our enterprises." Among devices advocated by the exchange to stimulate investment capital, said Boylan, is the promotion of stock ownership plans and stock bonuses for employees in industry.

As temporary president, Boylan in the New York Stock Exchange's annual report for 1949 (released in February 1950) attributed the lower 1949 volume of trading (272,203,402 shares as compared with 302,218,965 in 1948) to "a desire on the part of the public for security rather than for gain; the payment by corporations of cash dividends that are conservative in relation to earnings, and a lack of knowledge of stock investment." Boylan advocated a re-examination of the tax structure with a view to eliminating double taxation of dividends. The report pointed out that the latter part of 1949 showed a promising revival in market interest. This, Boylan said, had been augmented by the exchange's public relations program, which among other things, had included distribution of the brochure, *Investment Facts*, and of more than thirty prints of a documentary film *Money at Work*.

In a speech to the Association of Stock Exchange Firms early in 1950, the exchange official told his audience that the tax policy of the country was "eating away its strength" by

BOYLAN, ROBERT P.—*Continued*

discouraging incentive. The evidence of "under-investment" on the part of individuals and business, he mentioned as being particularly alarming "when we consider that it takes about $5,000,000,000 annually in new investment to create some 700,000 new jobs for young people entering the labor force each year." As other forces militating against incentive, Boylan listed the expansion of the Federal establishment and public indifference to its size and cost, unfair competition and loss of tax revenue due to operations of tax-free organizations and government assumption of lending functions.

In endorsing the Frear bill before the Senate Banking and Currency subcommittee, Boylan said that the board of governors of the New York Stock Exchange favored the proposed legislation "because we believe it is in the interest of investors generally." The bill proposes that corporations having assets of $3,000,-000 or more and having at least 300 stockholders should be made to register with the Securities and Exchange Commission, file periodic reports, including financial statements, and make available to their stockholders all proxy-solicitation material. Officers and directors of these companies, reported the New York *Times* (February 9, 1950) "would be subject to Section 16 [of the Securities Exchange Act of 1934], which is designed to prevent 'insiders' of a company from taking advantage of inside information." The New York *World-Telegram and Sun*'s financial editor, Ralph Hendershot, regarded Boylan's support of the proposal as a justifiable expediency measure—to gain more listings of stocks on the Stock Exchange and more commissions for brokers.

Robert Peter Boylan married Julia M. Bagley on June 24, 1913. The couple has two children, Robert Peter, Jr., and Patricia Ann. He is a Roman Catholic. A member of the National Golf Club of America (Southampton, Long Island), the Manhattan Club (New York), and the Garden City (Long Island) Golf Club, he belongs also to the Chicago Athletic Association, the Attic Club, and was president of the Edgewater (Chicago) Golf Club during 1931-33. His political party is the Democratic.

> *References*
>
> Who's Who in America, 1950-51
> Who's Who in Chicago and Illinois (1945)
> Who's Who in Commerce and Industry (1948)
> World Biography (1948)

BREEN, JOSEPH I(GNATIUS) Oct. 14, 1890- Motion picture production code administrator

Address: b. c/o Production Code Administration, Motion Picture Association of America, Inc., 5504 Hollywood Blvd., Hollywood, Calif.

The Production Code Administration of the Motion Picture Association of America, Inc., through which the studios are guided by self-imposed standards for their product, is di-

rected by Joseph I. Breen. Breen became head of the industry's self-regulatory "censorship" in 1931, when the advent of the talking picture increased the responsibility of that entertainment "for spiritual or moral progress, for higher types of social life, and for much correct thinking" (from the preamble to the production code). Except for one year, when he was general manager of the RKO studios, Breen's service in the film code administration has been continuous. (Until 1945 the M.P.A.A. was the Motion Picture Producers and Distributors of America; its first president was Will H. Hays '43, its present head is Eric A. Johnston '43.)

Joseph Ignatius Breen was born October 14, 1890, in Philadelphia, Pennsylvania. (He has two sisters; his two brothers, one of whom was a Roman Catholic priest, the other a lawyer, are deceased.) Following his graduation from St. Joseph's College in his home city, Breen worked for a few years as a reporter on Philadelphia newspapers. He left this occupation to enter the United States consular service, in which he remained for four years, serving in the consulates in Kingston, Jamaica (British West Indies) and in Toronto, Canada. For the next two years he was employed in the bureau of immigration of the National Catholic Welfare Conference, and in 1926 directed the publicity for the International Eucharistic Congress held in Chicago. It was while he was the press agent for the Peabody Coal Company of Chicago some years earlier that he met Will H. Hays, at that time lawyer for the coal company, who was to become the first president of the Motion Picture Producers and Distributors of America.

The code of the motion picture industry was adopted in 1930 by the M.P.P.D.A., an organization of leading producers formed some years previously to act as a board of arbitration for labor disputes in the industry, with the added function of a public relations committee. The industry in 1922 engaged Hays as "independent public relations counsel." Later, under Hays (who had become president) the producers, with the coming of talking pictures, adopted a system of voluntary censorship as part of their "cleanup" campaign, but it was not until 1930 that code of standards was formulated.

The preamble to the Production Code states the producers acknowledge their moral obligation to the public in respect to the motion picture, "the universal form of entertainment," because of "the high trust and confidence which have been placed in them by the people of the world." The three general principles on which the code is based are: "(1) No picture shall be produced which will lower the moral standard of those who see it. Hence the sympathy of the audience shall never be thrown to the side of crime, wrong-doing, evil, or sin. (2) Correct standards of life, subject only to the requirements of drama and entertainment, shall be presented. (3) Law, natural or human, shall not be ridiculed, nor shall sympathy be created for its violation." The code's twelve particular applications are to crimes, sex, vulgarity, obscenity, profanity, costume, dances, religion, locations, national feelings, titles, and repellent subjects.

Implementation of the code is administered by a department set up within the association and known as the Production Code Administration; the department, with headquarters in Hollywood, maintains a New York office. In 1931 Breen was appointed director of this administrative department. As a result of increased pressure from outside the industry, largely stemming from the Legion of Decency, inaugurated by the Catholic Church to issue a "moral evaluation" of every motion picture released, the Production Code Administration was reconstituted and a "resolution for uniform interpretation" was adopted by the M.P.P.D.A. on June 13, 1934.

The new regulations included provision for a $25,000 fine to be levied against "recalcitrants" and a stipulation that only pictures having the stamp of approval of the code office could be distributed through M.P.P.D.A.-affiliated theaters. (The latter account for a high percentage of the gross box-office receipts of the motion picture industry in the United States.) While these regulations gave much power to the Code Administration, *Variety* (January 1, 1935) commented that "the belief that Hollywood would only be allowed to make namby-pamby stories hasn't materialized." The New York *Times* in May of the same year observed that "the hostility toward the cleanup" which had prevailed immediately following the reorganization had changed to "enthusiastic cooperation on the part of recalcitrant studios." The foreword to the code pointed out in 1949: "No one is compelled to produce motion pictures in accordance with the Code regulations. No attempt is made to force producers to accept the service of the Production Code Administration. As a result, however, of almost eighteen years of day-by-day operations . . . there is evident on all sides a ready disposition to conform to the regulations of the Code and to be guided in large measure by the judgment and experience of its administrators."

Breen continued in "the industry's most controversial and thankless job" (*Newsweek*) until May 1, 1941, when, quoted as saying he was "punch-drunk" from work, he declined a new five-year contract offered him by Hays, and resigned. *Newsweek*, speculating on possible reasons for his leaving, mentioned "a growing tendency among producers to ignore Breen's pre-filming suggestions," a controversy over Breen's refusal to grant Howard Hughes' *The Outlaw* a seal of approval, and protests by the sweater industry over the Breen criticism of "sweater girls" on the screen.

"A few hours after his resignation" (according to the New York *Times*), RKO officials renewed efforts to induce Breen to take an executive position in the production end of the business. He agreed, and after a short vacation assumed the office of general manager of that studio. At his first press conference in his new capacity, Breen declared that in his opinion the production code was a "liberal document," and that "any subject in the world" could be treated "in an adult fashion" under it. He also announced plans to put emphasis on

JOSEPH I. BREEN

stories rather than on stars in future RKO productions, said he believed thoroughly in both escapist dramas and "adult films," and declared that too many pictures were being made, and that too few of them possessed entertainment value (New York *Times*, June 29, 1941).

A year later Breen returned to his former post in the Production Code Administration. In May 1943 he was elected president of the Motion Picture Society for the Americas. By resolution of the board of directors of M.P.P.D.A. he served as vice-president of that organization; in 1945, shortly after Eric A Johnston replaced Hays as president, Breen was elected "vice-president in charge of self-regulation." (That year the association changed its name to the Motion Picture Association of America, Inc.)

In July 1946, at the invitation of the British Film Producers Association, Breen visited England to discuss the requirements of the American production code. He stated that by doing so he "hoped to save the British industry thousands of pounds annually in anticipating scenes" not acceptable to the American Code Authority. Shortly after this trip, Bosley Crowther, writing in the New York *Times*, noted that there had recently been "several brushes of new films with the Production Code," and suggested that increased vigilance on the part of Breen's office might have reflected the industry's "fear of organized opposition from militant moral forces outside." Such outside forces, in addition to the Legion of Decency and the Protestant Film Commission, which was organized in 1948, include censorship bodies established by law in eight States and sixty cities of the United States.

The code director answered what *Variety* called "a growing chorus of complaint" against the regulations of the M.P.A.A. office in an interview published in the New York *Herald*

BREEN, JOSEPH I.—*Continued*

Tribune in July 1949. Breen declared, "We have a grave responsibility because of the peculiar nature of this mass entertainment movement . . . we try to be all things to all men—youngsters, adolescents, and adults. If pictures would cost less to make and were aimed at specialized audiences, that would be a solution." One hundred and twelve (1949 figure) producers regularly submit their products to the code office for approval. According to Breen, 99 per cent of the films shown in the United States have the code seal of approval. In 1949, 363 domestic feature films, 58 foreign films, and 501 short subjects were approved by the code administration. In addition, the administrator and his staff analyzed and appraised 2,145 books, plays, synopses, and scripts before they were put into production. Breen was asked in 1950 by the American Television Society for advice on possible self-regulatory measures for that industry.

Breen is married to the Philadelphia girl who was a childhood playmate, said a *Saturday Evening Post* writer. They are the parents of six children. In 1938 Breen, who is of the Roman Catholic faith, was made a Knight of St. Gregory by the Pope. A "big, florid, hearty" man, Breen, in commenting on a somewhat unfriendly reception he received from the British press, said the newsmen may have been disappointed by his appearance: "I appeared miscast to them as a bluenose. . . .I am too fat and too genial."

References

Sat Eve Post 211:8 D 24 '38

American Catholic Who's Who, 1950-51
International Motion Picture Almanac, 1948-49

BRIDGES, HARRY (RENTON) July 28, 1901- Labor leader

Address: b. c/o International Longshoremen's and Warehousemen's Union, 604 Montgomery St., San Francisco, Calif.

> NOTE: This biography supersedes the article which appeared in *Current Biography* in 1940.

Recognized early as a powerful labor leader in America's maritime industry, Harry Bridges became the president of the International Longshoremen's and Warehousemen's Union in 1937, at the time of its organization. This followed upon fifteen years as longshoreman and labor leader; in 1934 he emerged as a strong leader on the West Coast water front. Demands for his deportation as a Communist were investigated and invalidated several times, before, in 1950, he was convicted of perjury in denying at his 1945 citizenship hearing that he had ever been a Communist.

Harry Renton Bridges (whose first name originated in the nickname he was given by American sailors) was born Alfred Bryant Renton Bridges on July 28, 1901, in a "comfortable" suburb of Melbourne, at that time the capital of Australia. His parents are Al-

fred Earnest and Julia (Dorgan) Bridges. Mrs. Bridges came of a family active in the struggle for Irish independence. Politics was a frequent subject of debate in the Bridges household—the boy's father, a prosperous real estate man, was "a real British Tory," and two uncles were Laborites. One of them, Charles Bridges, was to be elected in 1936 to the state legislature on the Labor ticket. Young Alfred entered a public elementary school before he was five, graduated at twelve, and went on to St. Brendan's parochial school, an institution conducted by the Christian Brothers (the boy was reared in the Catholic faith). He "showed himself well above average as a student," reported Matthew Josephson in his *Collier's* article "Red Skies Over the Water Front." Unintentionally his father brought him into contact with the depressed classes by introducing him to the real estate business. Harry Bridges has said that no person with any sensitivity could have collected rents from poverty-stricken people in Melbourne and not have had his opinions colored by the experience (this is reported in Minton and Stuart's *Men Who Lead Labor*).

After completing his secondary education in 1917, young Bridges became a clerk in a retail stationery store. According to the *Collier's* article, he was paid well and was promised rapid advancement. However, the books of Jack London had filled him with a desire to go to sea, and for the next five years he shipped on sailing vessels touching many ports of the world. He was in two shipwrecks; in one, his father has said, "Alf went overboard with my mandolin and kept afloat on it until he was picked up." In 1920 the young Australian entered the United States, when the barkentine *Ysabel*, from the South Seas, came to California. There he drifted from San Francisco to Mexico, working in the oil fields with explosives and as a rigger. Bridges once told Theodore Dreiser that it was Mexico's strong laws protecting labor which "opened his eyes" (in *Friday* of October 4, 1940).

For two years Bridges worked on American vessels plying the Pacific Coast. In 1921 his ship steamed into New Orleans during a maritime strike, the next day he reported for picket duty, and by the end of the strike he was in charge of a picket squad. He was arrested once and held overnight, but released without a hearing. Afterward, believing that "the A. F. of L. sold out the strike," he joined the Industrial Workers of the World and served as an organizer. (In 1921 and again in 1928, the Australian filed applications for citizenship, but allowed them to lapse because, he once testified, he did not have the necessary fees.) For a time during this period Bridges was in the service of the Coast and Geodetic Survey, as quartermaster on the *Lydonia*.

In October 1922 Harry Bridges became a longshoreman in San Francisco. For nine months he managed to dodge membership in the company union, but eventually joined in order to obtain work. Bridges had a personal grievance about not receiving full pay for time worked on the Luckenbach Steamship Company dock. In 1924 he was one of a group of militants who tried to set up an International Longshoremen's Association local, to replace the company union, but this ended after a few months when an organizer embezzled the funds. Despite the blacklisting of union-minded workers, Bridges was usually able to get jobs because his skill and all-round experience qualified him for a "star gang." As such, he often worked twenty-four to thirty-six hours at a stretch, earned about $60 a week, and paid the usual graft to do so, said Josephson. Then, in late 1932 a group which included Bridges took over a mimeographed bulletin, *The Waterfront Worker*, which had been published by the Communist-backed union, and made it a "rank and file paper," with Bridges as editor from 1933 to 1936.

Bridges' organizing campaign began in July 1933, and within six weeks most longshoremen had joined the new San Francisco local of the I.L.A., which was an AFL union. In February 1934 the new union demanded coast-wide recognition, wages higher than the prevailing $10.45 a week, and a thirty-hour week. On May 9, 1934, after unsuccessful efforts at mediation by the Regional Labor Board and a special board appointed by President Roosevelt, the longshoremen struck, demanding in addition a closed shop and union hiring halls. Teamsters and ship crews struck in sympathy, later presenting demands of their own; Bridges was elected chairman of the Joint Maritime Strike Committee. Minton and Stuart say that this was the "first time in many years the rank and file fully controlled the conduct of a major strike." I.L.A.'s international president Joseph P. Ryan[49] failed in an attempt to end the strike. On July 5, 1934 ("Bloody Thursday"), police charged the long picket line, in which two were killed and a hundred injured. Governor Merriam declared martial law along the Embarcadero (the city's waterfront) and sent in the militia. This resulted in a general strike in San Francisco: nearly 150,000 workers walked out, and all industry ceased except gas, electricity, telephone, and newspapers. After three days the general strike collapsed, and the marine strike went to arbitration, in which the longshoremen won substantially all their demands. During the strike Bridges had given up his $40-a-week union salary and lived for six weeks on relief.

The next year (1935) Bridges organized the Maritime Federation of the Pacific, seven unions strong, and began his campaign to unionize the unorganized, sending organizers as far as Hawaii. "The racketeers took flight from the San Francisco docks," wrote Matthew Josephson, "terrorized, it has been reported, by Harry Bridges' 'Red Guards.'" Bridges failed in his attempt to have the 1935 international convention oust Ryan. In 1936, when Ryan cut off Bridges' weekly $75 salary as president of the I.L.A. West Coast district, the autonomous district continued to pay him from its own treasury. After the 1934 arbitration award lapsed in September 1936, Bridges directed a Maritime Federation strike in which 40,000 men stopped work simultaneously, and all shipping was tied up until February 1937. After this successful strike,

Bridges led all the I.L.A.'s Pacific locals (except 200 men in Puget Sound ports) into John L. Lewis'[42] new CIO, reorganizing them as the International Longshoremen's and Warehousemen's Union. Bridges, its president, became CIO regional director for the Pacific Coast and a member of the CIO executive board.

Among the practices which made Bridges' union powerful was the "quickie strike," by which any working group would down tools to protest any action which they considered to violate the union's contract. It was then remarked that Bridges' stand was similar to that of the leftist groups. The C. P. newspaper, the *Western Worker*, gave full reports of the 1934 strike; Bridges backed the Farmer-Labor Party and the Commonwealth Federation; his men refused to load war materials for Nazi Germany and Fascist Italy and scrap metal for Japan. He supported Roosevelt (though he was against NRA) in 1934-37, and approved international "collective security" against the Axis until the signing of the Nazi-Soviet pact in August 1939; he opposed Roosevelt, the Allies, and the "imperialist war" with Nazism until the German attack on Russia in June 1941, after which he worked for national defense.

10 Eventful Years says of Harry Bridges, "His tremendous influence . . . aroused the antagonism of business groups, who launched a campaign (which soon became nation-wide) denouncing the Australian-born labor leader as a Communist and demanding his deportation." This movement, which came to include the Dies Committee, reached such a pitch that in February 1938 Bridges asked Secretary of Labor Frances Perkins for a ruling on his status. The Secretary issued a warrant for his deportation; and in July 1939 Special Examiner James M. Landis[42], dean of the Harvard Law School, opened a nine-week 1,600,000-word hearing of the case. Landis' finding was that Bridges was "energetically radical" but "there was no evidence that he tried to realize those aims by unconstitutional or undemocratic methods." In 1940 the House of Representatives, by a 330-to-42 vote passed a bill for the deportation of Bridges, but this, regarded as unconstitutional, died in the Senate Immigration Committee. When the statute was changed to make "affiliation" with a revolutionary organization grounds for deportation, FBI director J. Edgar Hoover[50] directed an investigation which led to the second Bridges hearing. After eleven weeks of testimony beginning in March 1941, Judge Charles B. Sears ruled for deportation, a decision overruled by a board of review, which was in turn overruled by Attorney General Biddle in May 1942. Thereupon Bridges telegraphed WPB head Donald M. Nelson, "I will do all possible to offset any effect this might have on the production program and labor-management unity." *Time* reported "When Army-Navy bickerings caused topheavy loading . . . he [Bridges] wangled appointment to a labor-management board, got a Navy tribute for record ship loading." While his deportation case was on appeal to higher Federal courts, Bridges, reported *Fortune*, prefaced all contracts with a no-strike pledge

HARRY BRIDGES

"for the duration of the war and beyond," provided the employer maintained union security. In June 1945, by a 5-3 decision, the Supreme Court invalidated the deportation order, stating, in a decision written by Justice Douglas, "Inference must be piled on inference to impute belief in Harry Bridges of the revolutionary aims of the groups whose aid and assistance be tolerated." That September (1945) the labor leader became a citizen of the United States. (In that month he served as joint chairman of the labor-management panel of the San Francisco *Chronicle* Forum.)

In the postwar years Bridges' power increased. In 1946 he shut down Pacific shipping, concurrent with an eleven-week strike of Hawaii sugar workers—I.L.W.U. had already doubled their former 26c-an-hour wages, won them housing and medical care. Other strikes alienated the public, especially a ninety-five-day maritime strike in 1946, and a 178-day Hawaiian strike in 1949, and national CIO officials were angered by his criticism and by his union's opposition to official CIO policy. In May 1949 a Federal grand jury indicted Bridges and his two naturalization witnesses for perjury in swearing at his citizenship hearing that he was not a Communist. In November began a four-and-a-half-month trial (eighty court days). Ten Government witnesses included former chairmen of Bridges defense committees and some ex-Communists who testified that Bridges joined the Communist party in 1933 and rose in its ranks to the Central Committee in 1936.

On April 4, 1950, after testimony of two million words had been heard, Bridges was found guilty of swearing falsely at the naturalization hearings in 1945 that he was not a Communist. In his charge to the jury, Federal Judge George B. Harris emphasized that the issue was solely perjury, not communism.

Bridges received a five-year sentence on the perjury charge and a two-year sentence for conspiracy to obstruct and defeat the naturalization laws, the two sentences to run concurrently. Together with two codefendants, he planned to appeal; the bail set for each defendant was $5,000. Bridges, who was on the stand ten days, vigorously denied the charge of membership in the Communist party, stating that Government witnesses were motivated by personal hatred toward him and by rivalry in union affairs.

Considered "his own best witness," Harry Bridges is noted for his quickness, shrewdness, and sardonic humor—in 1940 and 1941 he enjoyed confusing FBI investigators by "planting" meaningless evidence in his wastebasket. He is a short, lean man with bony features. His first marriage, in December 1923, was to Agnes Brown, of Scottish parentage; they have one daughter. In September 1946, after a divorce, Bridges married New York dancer Nancy Fenton Berdecio; there are two children in the family. The labor leader has contributed the column *On the Beam* in I.L.W.U.'s official paper.

References

Collier's 118:17+ O 5 '46
Fortune 16:123 S '37
Forum 101:195 Ap '39 por
Friday 1:1 O 4 '40
Life 28:8 Ap 17 '50
N Y Herald Tribune II p3 Je 24 '45;
  Ap 5 '50
San Francisco (Calif.) Examiner p8 Ap
  5 '50
Sat Eve Post 210:25 My 14 '38
Time 34:15 Ag 14 '39 por
Gunther, J. Inside U.S.A. (1947)
Minton, B. and Stuart, J. Men Who
  Lead Labor (1937)
10 Eventful Years (1947)
Ward, E. E. Harry Bridges On Trial
  (1940)
Who's Who in America, 1950-51
Who's Who in Australia, 1947
Who's Who in Labor (1946)
Who's Who in the West (1949)

BROKENSHIRE, NORMAN (ERNEST)
June 10, 1898- Radio announcer
Address: b. 30 Rockefeller Plaza, New York 20; h. 272 W. 84th St., New York 24

"Pioneer announcer" Norman Brokenshire is heard on the network programs of *Theatre Guild of the Air* (NBC) and *Inner Sanctum* (CBS). Brokenshire, who began his radio career as an announcer in 1924, is credited with many radio "firsts," including big-news and special events broadcasts, "soap operas," and celebrity interviews. In 1932 he was chosen "King of the Announcers" in a New York *Mirror* radio personality poll and, at another time was awarded second place in a *Radio Digest* contest. In 1950 he also has two weekday disk-jockey programs.

Born in Murcheson, Canada, a small town in the Province of Ontario, on June 10, 1898,

Norman Ernest Brokenshire is one of four sons of William Henry and Georgina (Jones) Brokenshire; he also has one sister. His father, of Scottish descent, was a minister, serving Presbyterian, Congregational or Methodist churches. In Murcheson the boy was often left with his grandparents because his father's circuit included three other towns. Of his childhood Brokenshire has said it was a "typical minister's family existence, a maximum of three years in any one town, living in many communities in Eastern Canada and the United States." After his father became pastor of the Wood Memorial Congregational Church, in Cambridge, Massachusetts, Brokenshire attended Harvard Grammar School and, upon graduating, entered Rindge Manual Training School.

During his free time young Brokenshire had a miscellany of jobs: he was a bellhop, a truck driver, a secretary, inspector in a shoe factory. He completed his secondary schooling at Arlington High School, in Boston, in 1915. Following a summer as head of the garage of a White Mountains hostelry and two years as apprentice draftsman at the Schenectady plant of General Electric, in 1918 he enlisted in the United States Infantry. (Meanwhile, World War I had scattered his family—his father became a teacher in the Army of Occupation, his mother went to London, where one of his brothers was a war casualty.) After the Armistice, Corporal Brokenshire became a YMCA Secretary at Fort Totten, New York. With the aid of YMCA scholarships he was able to enter Syracuse University in 1920. There he started to major in forestry, but later transferred to the School of Liberal Arts to major in English. He supported himself by working as a night engineer for a hotel and as an organizer for the Near East Relief, and for his extracurricular activities chose the glee club and crew. Upon his graduation in 1924 he was employed for a time by the Inter-Church World Movement.

It was while Brokenshire was in New York, later in 1924 that he answered a "blind" advertisement for "a college man with knowledge of musical terminology." From among four hundred applicants the radio station (WJZ) chose Brokenshire and three others. "I didn't know music terms," Brokenshire has said, "but even for those crude 'mikes' my voice was perfect. I could vary the tone, the speed, the expression; the engineer's control needle would scarcely waver." For a weekly sixty dollars he announced, directed, produced, created and wrote new shows, secured free talent, acted as guide to station visitors.

Brokenshire, whose informal style, the New York *Sun* reported, "attracted wide attention in those early days of broadcasting," was the first announcer to identify himself by name on a program instead of by initials. By adding an emphasized "How *do* you *do!*" to the "How-do-you-do, ladies and gentlemen," with which most announcers opened programs, he evolved his radio trademark in 1924. In the fall of that year the announcer began his list of "firsts on the air" by broadcasting the Democratic National Convention from New York's Madison Square Garden. In the first "airing" of a **Presidential inauguration** (that of Calvin

NBC Photo.
NORMAN BROKENSHIRE

Coolidge, March 4, 1925) Brokenshire, chief commentator of WJZ, had as competitor the late Graham McNamee. Both men went on the air two and a half hours before the ceremony started and "ad-libbed" the entire time; in this Brokenshire developed such facility that he has been described as "one whose gift of ad-libbing of news features is excelled only by his reading of studio continuity" (*Journal-American*). He has covered every Presidential inauguration since that time. His claim to two other "firsts" in radio are a special event broadcast (he held the microphone out of a studio window to pick up street sounds while he described the scene) and for the conception of "soap operas" (he cut short a human interest story one day, which brought thousands of letters and telephone calls demanding to know the ending).

Among the historical events which the commentator has "put on the air" were the memorial services for Woodrow Wilson (February 1924), funeral services for William Jennings Bryan (July 1925), and New York's reception for Charles A. Lindbergh (June 1927). On August 4, 1929, he was one of several radio and newspapermen who, as guests of Bell Telephone Laboratories, met the dirigible *Graf Zeppelin* on its second trip in a plane which was equipped to permit an interview with the airship's commander to be broadcast from the air for the first time.

In the autumn of 1926 Brokenshire, deciding that "as time goes on the announcer's role will become less and less important," invested his savings in an amusement company. When it failed, he was employed by Atlantic City (where he had broadcast the first beauty contest to go on the air) as the "highest paid city press agent in America" (*Time*). Following a world cruise as lecturer (1928), he was briefly affiliated with Station WCAU (Philadelphia),

BROKENSHIRE, NORMAN—*Continued*

then was heard over the Columbia Broadcasting System (organized in 1927) as a free-lance announcer. As such he headed the radio department of the New York advertising firm of Kastor & Sons. In 1932, Brokenshire became announcer for *The Chesterfield Hour.* Eddie Cantor's *Radio Follies*, Major Bowes's *Amateur Hour*, the *Good Gulf Program* and the *Children's Hour* were other of his well-known programs. In a New York *Daily Mirror* radio popularity contest held in 1932, Brokenshire headed the poll for announcers, and in a *Radio Digest* contest for announcers (1934), he was second.

Brokenshire's radio work during eight or nine years was desultory. During part of that period he was an inebriate, a condition from which he was to recover after he was brought into Alcoholics Anonymous. The New York *World-Telegram* reported his getting "still another chance in radio" presiding over a WOR Sunday afternoon musical (February 1937), and with a WABC serial from Chicago (March 1938). The commentator did the narrative accompaniment of a film, *Soviet Russia Through the Eyes of an American* (September 1935), and of other motion pictures and newsreels. In July 1936 the New York *American* reported him as master of ceremonies at a "local night club." A vaudeville tour with Hawaiian entertainers (1938) and transcribed programs (*Memories*, WOR, 1940) followed. He was also employed during these years as office clerk, carpenter, house painter, elevator operator, and a cruise lecturer. In 1943, while working as a plane inspector in a Farmingdale (Long Island) war plant Brokenshire was offered a disk-jockey job on WWDC, a Washington, D.C., station. A year later he found a similar position on WBYN, Brooklyn (1944); his show, a reviewer said, was "different from the usual record-playing program."

In September 1945, a New York *World-Telegram* review of United States Steel's new program *Theatre Guild of the Air* over ABC reported that the announcer was "Norman Brokenshire, long absent from big-time radio. . . .He still has a fine, easy way of announcing, mercifully lacking in the phoney exuberance we have too much with us these days." Two years later he gave WNBC (1947) its first disk-jockey show, called *Take It Easy Time.* His income increased: in 1948 a New York *Mirror* reporter said, "He earns $60,000 yearly," while a *Time* account (November 1949) gave his income as "about $100,000." On June 22, 1949, the announcer marked the twenty-fifth year after he had entered radio by a show at which Niles Trammell, Bruce Barton, Milton Cross, and Ezra MacIntosh were guests. He is reported to have been "feted by congratulatory messages via transcription." Brokenshire in 1950 is announcer for two shows on WNBC, both of 1947 origin, and is the announcer for *Inner Sanctum* on CBS network and for *Theatre Guild of the Air* on NBC. In May 1950 it was announced that Brokenshire was one of the narrators in Warner Brothers' feature-length newsreel compilation, *Fifty Years Before Your Eyes.*

The announcer is a member of the National Republican Club, the International Lions Club, the American Legion; he serves on the board of directors of the Guide Dog Foundation for the Blind (Long Island). His church is the Episcopal. In December 1927 Brokenshire married Eunice Yvonne Schmidt, who was associated with WJZ and who later became a food consultant. They maintain a home in Manhattan and a country place. The radio announcer has a height of six feet one inch, a weight of 207 pounds, and blue eyes and black hair. His friendliness is a trait frequently mentioned by commentators. Chief among his recreations are deep-sea fishing and cabinet making, a hobby he has had since his high school days.

References

N Y Daily Mirror D 8 '48
N Y Herald Tribune D 12 '27
Syracuse University Alumni N S '31
Time 54:66 N 14 '49 por
Who's Who in America, 1950-51

BROOKS, GWENDOLYN June 7, 1917-
Poet

Address: h. 9134 Wentworth Ave., Chicago, Ill.

The recipient of the Pulitzer Prize in poetry for 1949, Gwendolyn Brooks won the award in 1950 for her second volume of verse, *Annie Allen*, published the preceding year. The publication of her first collection of poetry, *A Street in Bronzeville*, in 1945, was followed by the award of two Guggenheim Fellowships in succeeding years and a grant from the American Academy of Arts and Letters and the National Institute of Arts and Letters. The poet, who is the first Negro woman to win a Pulitzer Prize, was named one of the Ten Women of 1945 by *Mademoiselle.*

Gwendolyn Brooks was born June 7, 1917, in Topeka, Kansas, to David Anderson and Keziah Corinne (Wims) Brooks. When she was one month old the Brooks family moved to Chicago. There the girl grew up and received her education. After completing her secondary schooling at Englewood High School in 1934, she entered Wilson Junior College to major in literature, and was graduated in 1936. Miss Brooks was encouraged to write poetry by her teachers; when she was fourteen, one of her poems appeared in *American Childhood.* Miss Brooks was reared in a family of artistic inclinations: her mother composes music, her father is employed by a music house, and her brother, Raymond, is an artist. By encouraging her to "read and think," her parents were a formative influence in her interest in literature, the poet has said; to them she dedicated her first volume of verse.

Upon leaving college, Miss Brooks engaged in newspaper, magazine, and general office work. She became actively associated with the South Side Community Art Center in Chicago, where, she has said, she "learned a lot about technique" from Inez Boulton, who conducted a poetry class for Negroes there in 1941. Recognition for the quality of her verse came in 1943 and 1944, when she was presented with the Poetry Workshop Award at the summer Midwestern Writers' Conference held at Northwestern University. In 1944 the poet also won the prize of the annual Writers' Conference in Chicago. It was in the latter year that Miss Brooks's work was published in *Poetry*; it has since appeared in *Common Ground, Negro Story, Harper's Magazine, Yale Review, Saturday Review of Literature*, and other publications. The anthologies *The Poetry of the Negro* (1949) and *Cross-Section 1945* contain some of her poems.

In 1945 the first collection of Miss Brooks's poetry was published. The volume, *A Street in Bronzeville*, was well received by the critics. Rolfe Humphries in the New York *Times* acclaimed it "a good book" and its author "a real poet." "Gifted, passionate and authentic," were terms applied to the work by Virginia Kirkus. The *New Yorker* commented: "She writes with style, sincerity, and a minimum of sentimentality. Her city-folk poetry is particularly fresh." A. N. Wilder in *Poetry*, while remarking an unevenness in the quality of the verse not unusual in a first collection, pointed to "considerable resources evidenced for future work."

To advance the cause of such future work, Miss Brooks in 1946 and 1947 was presented with a Guggenheim Fellowship for creative writing. She was also the recipient of a $1,000 award from the American Academy of Arts and Letters and the National Institute of Arts and Letters in 1946. In naming the poet one of the Ten Women of 1945, *Mademoiselle* magazine in its January 1946 issue said: "One collected impression of everyday life establishes her as indelibly realistic, original."

In 1949 appeared Miss Brooks's second volume of verse, which won that year's Pulitzer Prize for poetry (announced in May 1950). Entitled *Annie Allen*, the collection of poems reflects the feelings of a woman as daughter, wife, and mother. The New York *Herald Tribune* critic, in writing of the poems as a portrayal of experiences in "the life of one woman, whose environment is also Bronzeville," felt that the experiences were "not merely personal or racial but universal in their implications." When Miss Brooks essayed social criticism, as in "I love those little booths at Benvenuti's," her work tended to be "clever if somewhat trite," in the opinion of Phyllis McGinley (New York *Times*), who preferred the verse of lyric intent. The final poem in the volume, "Men of careful turns, haters of forks in the road," was adjudged by the Chicago *Sun* critic to be "a sober, magnificent speech against the racial inequality which is bondage with politeness."

While the content of *Annie Allen*, in presenting impressions of the Northern urban milieu, resembled that of *A Street in Bronzeville*, the style was generally judged to differ. "Miss Brooks has turned from her earlier poetic realism to a strain of lyric emotion. She has turned, too, to elaboration and experiment in language," noted the *United States Quarterly Booklist*. Ruth Lechlitner in the

Wayne Miller

GWENDOLYN BROOKS

New York *Herald Tribune Weekly Book Review* analyzed the elements of the poet's style as an "individual staccato manner—the partial statement, the deliberately broken scansion, the startling, particularized image." The poems on the childhood and early girlhood were cited by Miss Lechlitner as particularly successful. The first of these, "The birth in a narrow room," opens with the following lines:

Weeps out of western country something
*   new.*
Blurred and stupendous. Wanted and un-
*   planned.*
*   Winks. Twines, and weakly winks*
Upon the milk-glass fruit bowl, iron pot,
The bashful china child tipping forever
Yellow apron and spilling pretty cherries.

The freshness and vitality of Miss Brooks's writing were widely acclaimed and her assured sense of form praised, the sonnets being mentioned as especially felicitous. Commending the poet's "sophistication of thought and phrase," Miss McGinley singled out "The Anniad," writing of it, "Full of insight and wisdom and pity, technically dazzling, it is a surprising accomplishment in combining storytelling with lyric elegance." In illustration of the qualities of the poem, the critic quoted lines describing Annie with:

All her harvest buttoned in,
All her ornaments untried;
Waiting for the paladin
Prosperous and ocean-eyed
Who shall rub her secrets out
And behold the hinted bride.

In an article in the *Saturday Review of Literature* it was stated that Miss Brooks is particularly interested in the modern poets, whose work she describes as "more relaxed and daring"; she especially admires the style of T. S.

BROOKS, GWENDOLYN—*Continued*

Eliot and of Elinor Wylie. The article reported the Chicago poet to be at work on a book of about seventy-five fiction pieces (of which she says, "I do not call these short stories") and on a novel in verse form.

Miss Brooks on September 17, 1939, was married to Henry Lowington Blakely; One son, Henry Lowington 3d, has been born to the couple. The family lives in Chicago, where Blakely is a garage operator. The poet is a member of the board of directors of the South Side Community Center.

References

> N Y Times p22 My 2 '50 por
> Sat R Lit 33:23 My 20 '50 por
> Who's Who in the Midwest (1949)

BROWN, DAVID M. Mar. 21, 1890- Veterans organization official

Address: b c/o Disabled American Veterans, Cincinnati, Ohio; Brown Coal Company, 86 Spring St., Akron, Ohio; h. 638 Sunset View Dr., Akron, Ohio

After being nominated by General Jonathan M. Wainwright '42 as national commander of the Disabled American Veterans, David M. Brown was unanimously elected to that office for 1949-50 at the organization's twenty-eighth annual convention, held in Cleveland, Ohio, in August 1949. The hero of Bataan was the retiring commander, while Brown moved up from the second office of command—that of national senior vice-commander, a position which he had held for two terms. Brown, who lives in Akron, Ohio, is a coal dealer.

A native of Pennsylvania, where he lived until 1918, David M. Brown was born March 21, 1890, in Baileyville, to Ira Fuller and Annie

Special Correspondents

DAVID M. BROWN

Knox (Lutz) Brown. Ira Brown, whose Irish forebears came to America three hundred years ago, was a Methodist minister. Mrs. Brown was of Scottish and German descent. In the Brown family there were six other children, of whom five were girls. David Brown was reared on a farm near Smithmill and was sent to Ramey for his secondary education. Upon graduating from high school, the student entered Lock Haven State Normal School, which awarded him the teacher's diploma in 1911. At the latter institution his sports were baseball and basketball.

Brown taught school for a year, then became a mine superintendent. He entered the World War I army on April 14, 1918. While attached to the Quartermaster Corps, he served overseas for twelve months. As a result of a truck accident, he was hospitalized for eleven months with serious knee and back injuries. His discharge is dated August 29, 1919. Back in the United States, he settled in Akron, Ohio, his home since then. His first employment was with the Goodrich Rubber Company, which was followed four years later by two public offices. He served as superintendent of sanitation for the City of Akron and subsequently as deputy sheriff of Summit County for two years. In the early 1930's he entered the coal business, in which field he has been the owner of a retail coal company since 1933.

When Brown joined the Disabled American Veterans in 1935, the organization was approximately fifteen years old. Originally known as the Disabled American Veterans of the World War, it came into being shortly after the close of World War I, being chartered by Congress and holding its first convention in 1920. The name was later shortened to designate that membership was open to all disabled servicemen in the United States. The purpose of the D.A.V. is to render free aid to men and women who have received honorable disabilities in the service of their country; this is done through hospitalization, legislation, liaison, insurance, claims, and other phases. In the course of twenty-five years it has handled more than one million claims, obtained nearly 190,000 medical examinations and hospitalizations, and established disability compensations of $125,000,000. One of the most important services it renders is the rehabilitation of the disabled through securing work; this calls for job analysis, worker appraisal, counseling, training, supervision, etc. All of the service workers of the organization (which has a membership of four million) are disabled veterans. Since the D.A.V. is dependent upon the public for support, it makes annual fund drives; its monies and other property are managed by the Disabled American Veterans Service Foundation, the incorporated trustee for the D.A.V. It issues a semi-monthly newspaper.

Since Brown became a member of the D.A.V. he has held many elective chapter, department, and national offices. He was first the commander of his local chapter for two years, then commander of the Department of Ohio, later national executive committeeman of the Seventh District. By 1947 he had become national senior vice-commander, a post he held for two years (1947-48 and 1948-49) before his election as national commander at the August 1949 convention held in Cleveland. The year before, when he was a candidate for the top office, he withdrew from the contest when he learned that General Jonathan M. Wainwright was willing to run for that office. Thus he succeeded Wainwright, who had placed Brown's name in nomination at the Cleveland convention. Brown was opposed by one candidate, who withdrew after Brown polled 475 of the 574 delegates' votes, making the choice unanimous.

At his first appearance as D.A.V.'s 1949-50 commander, Brown outlined the year's program. He said he would seek to accomplish four benefits for his organization: "First, the restoration of the 16,000 beds which have been cut from the Veterans Administration hospital bed program. It is imperative that all disabled veterans obtain proper medical and hospital treatment. Second, housing for disabled veterans. And by that I mean that low-cost housing should be available for all veterans with special preference for the handicapped. Third, I will fight for civil preference for our disabled veterans. Certainly our government should lead the way in employing those whose health and well-being has been impaired in our defense. And, fourth, I shall strive to make the D.A.V. strong in membership. We must be united now more than ever before to fight the battle of the disabled veteran." Brown travels much in carrying out his duties, one of which was to participate in a series of transcribed programs of five-minute stories about the return of disabled men to normal civilian life.

The D.A.V. leader maintains membership in two other veterans groups, the American Legion and Veterans of Foreign Wars. His lodges are the Moose, Eagles, and the Masonic—he is a 32d Degree Mason and a Shriner. He is a Republican voter, a Methodist in religious affiliation, and belongs to the local chamber of commerce. He and Mrs. Brown (Bessie Olive), who were married in October 1924, have two children, Anna Frances and David Milton. Brown has a height of five feet nine inches, a weight of 198 pounds; the color of his eyes is gray, of his hair, brown. As a spectator of sports he lists baseball, football, and basketball His D.A.V. associates describe him as genial.

BRYAN, ERNEST ROWLETT Aug. 14, 1906- Religious leader; United States Government official

Address: b. c/o International Society of Christian Endeavor, 1201 E. Broad St., Columbus 5, Ohio; c/o Motion Picture Branch, United States Naval Photographic Center, Anacostia, D.C.; h. 5203 Massachusetts Ave., N.W., Washington 16, D.C.

Dr. Ernest Rowlett Bryan was elected president of the International Society of Christian Endeavor at that organization's convention in Toronto, Canada, in July 1949. He succeeded Dr. Daniel A. Poling '43, who has called him "the Field Marshal of Christian Endeavor's Forward Movement," an interdenominatonal, international, and interracial organization whose aim is to "promote an earnest Christian life among its members." Associated with the movement from his youth, Bryan has been editor of the *Christian Endeavor World* since 1947. An official of the World Peace Foundation, Bryan has also been a director of publications for the United States Public Health Service and the National Archives Establishment. In March 1950 he was appointed assistant head of the Motion Picture Branch of the United States Naval Photographic Center at Anacostia, D.C.

One of the four children of Daniel Beach Bryan, a banker, and Anna Rowlett (Aulls) Bryan, Ernest Rowlett Bryan was born in Bath, in southern New York, on August 14, 1906. His grandfather, Daniel Barnes Bryan, was a member of the New York State Assembly. (His brothers are Dr. Leslie Aulls Bryan, director of the Institute of Aviation at the University of Illinois, and Leland Beach Bryan, president and trust officer of the First National Bank and Trust Company at Corning, New York; Mrs. Herbert L. Hedges, Jr., of Syracuse, New York, is his sister.) At Haverling High School in Bath, from which he was graduated in 1925, Ernest Bryan took part in track and public-speaking contests, was class secretary and prophet, played in the school orchestra, was elected president of the Hi-Y Club, and participated in student dramatics. The high school student became active in the Christian Endeavor movement, at sixteen years of age being named president of the local Steuben County (New York) Christian Endeavor Union. At Syracuse (New York) University, where he majored in political science and helped to pay his expenses by working as advertising manager of the Drumlins Country Club, he won the Judge Shove Scholarship in Liberal Arts and the Public Speaking Prize; he was also editor of the campus newspaper, the *Syracuse Daily Orange*, a member of the student senate, and the president of his class.

In June 1929, after receiving the B.A. degree from Syracuse, Bryan secured employment in New York as a salesman of chemicals for the Solvay Sales Division of the Allied Chemical and Dye Corporation. After three months he left the position upon being appointed field secretary of the World Peace Foundation, in Boston, Massachusetts. During 1930 he took courses at near-by Harvard University, and was a delegate to the World's Christian Endeavor Conference in Berlin, Germany. In March 1931, Bryan was appointed assistant publications director of the National Education Association in Washington, D.C. While in this position he attended both American University (where he was the first holder of the Alfred P. Sloan research fellowship in economics) and George Washington University, where he took the Master of Arts degree in government in 1933. (His thesis subject was "Humanitarian Activities of the League of Nations"; he was later to serve in the publications department of the League's Secretariat at Geneva, Switzerland, on several temporary assignments.) Bryan returned to the World Peace Foundation as educational secretary in April 1934. Part of his work in this capacity was in New York

ERNEST ROWLETT BRYAN

City, a circumstance which enabled him to do additional postgraduate study at New York University. At this time, too, he became citizenship superintendent of the New York State Christian Endeavor Union.

Bryan entered the service of the Federal Government in August 1936, as a lecturer and forum leader for the United States Office of Education, with a territory covering seven States. For thirteen months (June 1937-July 1938) he was executive secretary of the National Council for Adult Civic Education; he was then appointed chief of the motion picture, radio and publications section of the United States Public Health Service. The author of *America Turns to Social Security* (1938), he has since contributed to various publications; among his articles are: "And Out Comes a Film", "We'll Find Out—About Films," and "Civilization at the   Crossroads." In March 1942, Bryan became chief of the information and publications division of the National Archives Establishment and, during the same year, was a lecturer on public relations at American University.

A lieutenant (junior grade) in the United States Naval Reserve, Bryan was called into active service in April 1943. Assigned as project supervisor for training films, he subsequently saw 119 days of sea duty, mostly in the Pacific area, and was promoted to full lieutenant in 1944 and to lieutenant commander in January 1946. From July 1946 Bryan served the Navy Department in a civilian capacity as project head and supervisor of training films production; he later also became a member of the guided missiles testing and training group of the Research and Development Board of the Department of Defense. In March 1950 he was appointed assistant head of the Motion Picture Branch of the United States Naval Photographic Center at Anacostia, D.C.

Bryan's association with the International Society of Christian Endeavor has been uninterrupted since his youth. Christian Endeavor was founded in 1881 by the Reverend Francis E. Clark of Portland, Maine, to "promote an earnest Christian life among its members [young people], to increase their mutual acquaintance, to train them for work in the Church, and in every way to make them useful in the service of God and their fellow men." It comprises in 1950 (one year before it marks its seventieth anniversary) some 80,000 unions. The motto of the movement, which includes almost all non-Catholic Christian denominations except the Episcopalian, the Methodist and the Baptist (which have their own societies) is "For God and the Church." The society is described in the *Encyclopedia Americana* as "a bureau of information with international scope" which publishes religious literature, including the monthly magazine, *Christian Endeavor World*. The International Society of Christian Endeavor consists of young people's societies in the United States and Canada; the World's Christian Endeavor Union is composed of organizations representing forty-odd nations.

In 1947 the headquarters of the International Society of Christian Endeavor was transferred from Boston to Columbus, Ohio, and an expansion drive was prepared. Bryan, then serving as president of the Maryland Christian Endeavor Union, was made acting general secretary of the society on January 30 and took over from President Daniel A. Poling the editorship of the *Christian Endeavor World* commencing with the June issue. The following year (1948) he was a prominent figure in the World's Christian Endeavor Conference for Europe, Africa and the Near East, held at Bournemouth, England. Under his secretaryship the international society's membership has increased to approximately one million. Bryan, who is an ordained minister of the Christian (Disciples of Christ) Church, in July 1949 was named president of the International Society of Christian Endeavor to succeed Dr. Poling, who retired from the office at that year's convention (the forty-first) of the organization.

The Christian Endeavor leader received an honorary Litt.D. from Whitworth College, Spokane, Washington, in 1949. He is six feet tall, weighs 182 pounds, and has hazel eyes and brown hair. Mrs. Bryan is the former Mildred Seymour Gott of Washington, D.C., who both before and after marriage has practiced law. The Bryans were married on September 15, 1932, and have one daughter, Carol Norris. Bryan, who is a trustee of the International Society of Christian Endeavor as well as its president, is also a life member of the National Education Association, a member of the Association for Education by Radio (charter member and first president, Washington, D.C. Chapter) and an American Legionnaire. He is a member of the board of directors of Pierce, Hedrick & Sherwood, Inc., financial counselors, New York City. Fraternities and college societies to which he belongs include the Zeta Psi, Pi Delta Epsilon, Janus, Phi Kappa Alpha,

Pi Gamma Mu and Monx Head; his clubs are the National Press in Washington, the Town Hall in New York, and the Boston City in the Massachussets city. He lists himself as an Independent Republican.

References

> Christian Endeavor World 62:3 Mr '47
> Washington (D.C.) Post Jl 7 '49
> Who's Who in America, 1950-51
> Who's Who in the East (1948)

BUCK, FRANK Mar. 17, 1884—Mar. 25, 1950 Animal entrepreneur and showman; was co-author of *Bring 'Em Back Alive*, a book on his adventures in capturing live animals, whose title became a frequent appendage of his name; co-author of books on his exploits, several of which were made into motion pictures in which he appeared; platform and radio lecturer. See *Current Biography, 1943.*

Obituary

> N Y Times p92 Mr 26 '50 por

BUTLER, HUGH (ALFRED) Feb. 28, 1878- United States Senator from Nebraska

Address: b. Senate Office Bldg., Washington, D.C.; h. The Omaha Club, Omaha, Neb.

Hugh Butler, Republican United States Senator from Nebraska, in 1950 is serving his second term in the Senate. His nomination as candidate for that term in 1946 by a two-to-one vote over Governor Dwight Griswold ", was regarded as a "victory for Middle Western isolationism." Butler's principal interests during his incumbency have been the foreign policy of the United States and the affairs of the Territories of Alaska and Hawaii. Beginning his career as a technical man with a railroad construction crew, he went into the grain business in Omaha in 1908. He entered public life in 1934.

Born February 28, 1878, in Missouri Valley, Iowa, the son of Harvey Gibson and Ida (Wills) Butler, Hugh Alfred Butler as descended from farmers who had come to the West from the South and the North, his father's family through Kentucky, his mother's from New England. The Butler family in 1883 staked a claim to a homestead near Cambridge, Nebraska; there the boy attended the local schools. Finding farming unprofitable, the family moved into town, where Butler's father secured work in a local flour mill. Upon graduation from the Cambridge High School in 1895, young Butler entered Doane College (then Academy) in Crete, Nebraska. He had won a four-year tuition scholarship to the college by selling subscriptions to a church paper; and he earned money for his other expenses by clerking in a store, working as a janitor, and ringing the college bell.

Upon his graduation in 1900 with the degree of Bachelor of Science, Butler began work with a construction crew of the Chicago, Burlington and Quincy Railroad. He became, successively, an instrument man, chief of a survey party, and finally construction engineer, living much of the time in a tar-paper shack in Wyoming. In 1908 he bought a grain elevator and flour mill in Curtis, Nebraska, and in 1913 he became manager of the Crete Mills, which were owned in part by his wife's father. In 1918 Butler, as senior partner with Roy Welsh, organized the Butler-Welsh Company in Omaha, a concern that eventually developed into "one of the outstanding grain firms in the Middle West," reported a United Press release. Butler was later chosen a director of the Nebraska Consolidated Mills and of the Sheridan (Wyoming) Flour Mills, Inc.

Butler's first political office was the chairmanship of the Republican central committee in Nebraska's Douglas County, to which he was elected in 1934. Two years later he became a member of the Republican National Committee. In 1940 he was elected to the United States Senate, defeating his Democratic opponent, Governor Roy L. Cochran, by 93,000 votes. When he took his seat in the first session of the Seventy-seventh Congress, he was assigned to five committees—Post Offices and Post Roads, Education and Labor, Irrigation and Reclamation, Privileges and Elections, and Public Buildings and Grounds.

In the summer of 1943 the Senator made a sixty-day, 20,000-mile tour of twenty Central and South American countries. As a result, on November 26, 1943 he submitted his 176-page report to the Senate (a condensed version was concurrently published in *Reader's Digest*): it criticized the United States policy of aid to Latin American countries as "naively conceived and badly coordinated boondoggling," on which "at least" $6,000,000,000 had been wasted. A Senatorial controversy arose over the report, several of his colleagues questioning his facts and figures. On January 20 Butler presented to the Senate a "certified and documented account" of the expenditures by the United States in Latin America, which he declared showed his first report to be "95.5 per cent right" (one critic had said his figures were "95 per cent wrong").

In 1944 Butler unsuccessfully demanded an inquiry into the CIO Political Action Committee. Later he sought an explanation of the Administration's "secrecy" on foreign policy, particularly in reference to the Yalta conference. During this first term in the Senate, Butler opposed Lend-Lease, extension of the draft act, repeal of the Neutrality Act, UNRRA, the Bretton Woods Agreement, extension of the reciprocal trade agreements, and the loan to Britain.

Upon his return to the Senate in 1946 Butler voted for the entrance of the United States into membership in the United Nations. He opposed the Marshall Plan and the Truman proposal of aid to Turkey and Greece, calling the latter a return to the basic philosophy of the New Deal—"the way to meet any problem is to spend Government money." As chairman of the Senate Committee on Public Lands, Butler made a trip to Alaska in 1947 and also visited the Virgin Islands and Hawaii. Following his Alaska visit Butler recommended the transfer by the Department of the Interior to

HUGH BUTLER

Alaska itself of authority over its Indian lands and administration of laws relating to the Indians. Critics of the bills contended such measures would open up Indian territory to private exploitation and place responsibility for the welfare of Indians on the Territorial Government which could not economically support such a burden. When the question of Hawaiian statehood was raised in Congress in 1947, Butler succeeded in postponing action on it for two years. At one time he proposed that Hawaii be declared a county of California. In June 1949 he recommended to the Interior and Insular Affairs Committee that "statehood be deferred until communism in Hawaii is under control."

One of the Nebraska Senator's primary interests has been the foreign trade policy and the tariff. In December 1946, when sugar control became a Congressional issue, Butler called for "a plain, old-fashioned tariff to protect this important industry." He also proposed that all economic negotiations with other countries be postponed until the new Congress wrote a new trade policy. When debate was begun on the Administration's reciprocal trade agreements program, Butler attacked it as "a gigantic hoax on the American people" and as intended "to destroy our system of tariff protection." During his second term he opposed Federal aid to education, the long-range housing program, and extension of the ECA; he has supported local option on rent control, no surplus buying abroad, and 5 per cent cuts in labor, harbor-river, and farm appropriations.

With Senator Harry F. Byrd [42] Butler introduced a resolution in 1947 to reform the Congressional method of budgeting appropriations by establishing one "omnibus" appropriations bill, or a "legislative budget." In December 1946, during the coal strike, Butler had urged a strike-curb bill with "teeth in it," which led him in the next few months to support and help pass the Taft-Hartley Act. In June 1949 he urged an extension of this act to all United States possessions and territories, a proposal that was rejected. The Midwesterner voted in favor of the ratification of the North Atlantic Treaty in July 1949, having previously supported restrictive amendments offered by opponents of the treaty. On July 15, 1949, the Senator demanded a Congressional investigation of former officials of Government agencies who, following severance, accepted large legal fees for representing clients before those same agencies. On January 3, 1950, he declared that the Democratic majority in the Senate was "loading" the Senate Finance Committee "in order to force through a program of unsound finances."

In his home State, Senator Butler has been active in a number of organizations. In civic affairs, he has served on the board of the Community Chest and of the Omaha Board of Education; and he was a member of the YMCA board and of the Salvation Army advisory board. He is chairman of the board of trustees of Doane College, from which he received the honorary degree of LL.D. in 1940. A Rotarian, he was Nebraska district governor in Rotary International (1932-33) and served on the international board (1934-35). His business associations are the Omaha Chamber of Commerce, and for two terms each he was president of the Omaha Grain Exchange and of the Grain and Feed Dealers National Association. His lodges are the Masons, the Odd Fellows, and the Modern Woodmen of America; his clubs are the Omaha Club and the country and athletic clubs in the same city.

The Nebraskan is a member of the Congregational Church, and was State moderator of Nebraska Congregational churches during 1937-38. Married on February 5, 1903, to Fay Johnson, he had two children, Lawrence Hugh and Robert Johnson. (His wife and sons are deceased.) The Senator has been described as a "peppery" man, "white-haired and handsome."

References

N Y Sun p17 N 29 '43; p16 Mr 6 '45
Congressional Directory (1st ed., 1949)
Who's Who in America, 1948-49
Who's Who in the Midwest (1949)

BUTTENWIESER, BENJAMIN J(OSEPH) (bŭt'ĕn-wē-sĕr) Oct. 22, 1900- United States Government official; banker
Address: 52 William St., New York 5; h. 17 E. 73d St., New York 21

The United States Assistant High Commissioner for Germany, adviser to High Commissioner John J. McCloy [47], is the former banker, Benjamin J. Buttenwieser. Appointed to that post in Germany on September 19, 1949, Buttenwieser resigned from his partnership in the firm of Kuhn, Loeb and Company, which he had held since the beginning of 1932.

Fourth of the five children of Joseph Leon and Caroline (Weil) Buttenwieser, Benjamin Joseph Buttenwieser was born October 22,

1900, in New York City, where his father was prominent in the real estate business. (Two of his sisters and his brother survive.) The future banker was reared in the city of his birth. He is a graduate (1916) of the Townsend Harris Hall Preparatory High School; his university is Columbia, where he majored in English and history and took his B.A. degree as of the class of 1919, though he had completed the requirements a year earlier. He is a member of the Zeta Beta Tau fraternity.

"I began my career," Buttenwieser relates, "as a clerk [in 1918] with the investment banking firm of Kuhn, Loeb and Company, New York City. This was the only business affiliation I ever had." The young man's advancement was rapid: by 1925, when the firm began the marketing, over a period of four years, of some ninety million dollars worth of Chilean bonds, he had risen to a position of responsibility—he was later to spend a day testifying before a United States Senate banking subcommittee on the history of these transactions. (This was in June 1933, when the Senate was conducting an investigation into "the general activities and methods of operation" of private banks.) Buttenwieser held Kuhn, Loeb's joint power of attorney as early as 1928 and became a partner in the firm on January 1, 1932.

During 1937 Buttenwieser appeared twice before Senate banking subcommittees: one time in relation to railroad financing; another (as chairman of the Investment Bankers Association's trust indenture committee) on the pending Barkley trust indenture bill. This measure was designed to "increase the responsibility of trustees for security issues" by forbidding them to have "any conflicting interests in the firms floating the bonds," and by other restrictions. Buttenwieser saw merit in parts of the proposed legislation as "decidedly constructive and sound," but felt that other sections conferred too much ill-defined power on the Securities and Exchange Commission. Formerly Democratic in his political inclination, Buttenwieser had become critical of Roosevelt policies. "My greatest criticism of the New Deal," he said in 1938, "is that for the first time in our history, as a national administration, it has sought to array class against class." During the 1940 pre-election months, he accepted responsibilities as a vice-chairman of the Wendell Willkie Manhattan Campaign Committee; and since that time has been a Republican. From February 1942 to November 1945 Buttenwieser served in the United States Navy, and is today a commander in the Naval Reserve.

"Men should go into public service during their careers, not after them. I've made enough money out of this country; it's time I gave something back in return. And I want to get into Government while I'm still young enough to be of some use." This was Buttenwieser's remark to Sylvia F. Porter of the New York *Post* in the summer of 1947. His opportunity came two years later when, by Executive orders issued in June 1949, the United States High Commission of Germany was created to serve as "supreme United States Authority in Germany, exercising all governmental functions of the United States, including . . . representa-

BENJAMIN J. BUTTENWIESER

tion in Germany with respect to all matters of concern to the Economic Cooperation Administration" (*United States Government Organization Manual*). John J. McCloy was designated High Commissioner, and at Frankfort, Germany, on September 19, 1949, he announced appointment of Buttenwieser as his Assistant High Commissioner with duties as "general adviser." Buttenwieser resigned his Kuhn, Loeb partnership to accept the post. In a McCloy-and State Department-approved speech on the topic "The Reorientation of Germany" (delivered before the Foreign Policy Association in May 1950) Buttenwieser reported on the progress of de-Nazification in Germany. The official was seen as doing "an excellent job" in that country (New York *Times*). (The speech was to have been given before a convention of the Anti-Defamation League of B'Nai B'rith, which, however, found it unacceptable because that organization regarded the speech as "an apologia for the limited job that has been done" and as a comfort to former Nazi party members.)

In 1932, in a summary of Buttenwieser's career, the New York *Times* reported that he had for several years been interested in furthering settlement work and in other philanthropies. He was at that time a director of the Federation for the Support of Jewish Philanthropic Societies in New York City. He was also a trustee of the Baron de Hirsch Fund, and president of Stuyvesant Neighborhood House. Buttenwieser's charitable activities were to widen throughout his subsequent seventeen and a half years as a Kuhn, Loeb partner. In October 1933 he served as co-chairman of the annual New York City drive of the Federation for the Support of Jewish Philanthropic Societies. At about this time he was listed as a trustee of the Jewish Welfare Board and as a member of the Hebrew Sheltering Guardian Society.

BUTTENWIESER, BENJAMIN J.—*Cont.*

In October 1938, after having served as chairman of the commerce section of the Greater New York Fund, he was elected president of the Federation for the Support of Jewish Philanthropic Societies; he was re-elected in 1940. He was active in the annual drive (1947) of the United Jewish Appeal, and also assumed the presidency of the Henry Meinhard Memorial Health Center, and became a trustee of Dalton Schools, Inc., the Graduate Faculty for the Political and Social Services of the New School for Social Research, and of the Greater New York Fund. He is as well a trustee of the American Jewish Committee, the National Urban League, the 110th Street Community Center and the Lenox Hill Hospital.

Brown-haired and brown-eyed Buttenwieser is five feet six and a half inches in height and weighs about 150 pounds. He enjoys skiing and playing tennis and squash. Mrs. Buttenwieser is the former Helen Lehman, daughter of the late Arthur Lehman and a niece of United States Senator Herbert H. Lehman; a social worker before her marriage, she later took a law degree at New York University and practiced law for more than fourteen years. The Buttenwiesers were married on October 3, 1929, and have four children: Lawrence Benjamin, Carol Helen, Peter Lehman, and Paul Arthur. Buttenwieser, whose clubs are the Midday, Harmonie, Century, and Country, is a member of the Congregation Shearith Israel.

References

America's Young Men, 1934-35
Who's Who in America, 1950-51
Who's Who in Commerce and Industry (1948)
Who's Who in the East (1948)
Who's Who in New York, 1947

CARMONA, ANTONIO OSCAR DE FRAGOSO (kĕr-mō′nȧ aʌn-tô′nyōō ôshkȧr′ dĕ frȧ-gō′zōō) Nov. 24, 1869- President of Portugal

Address: Lisbon, Portugal

Portugal's President for almost a quarter of a century has been Marshal António Oscar de Fragoso Carmona, who came into power through a military coup in 1926 and served as Provisional President until 1928, when he was elected to the Presidency. Re-elected for seven-year terms in 1935, 1942 and 1949, Carmona has kept as his Prime Minister since 1932 Dr. Antonio de Oliveira Salazar ⁴¹, considered to be the country's most powerful figure. Early in 1950 Portugal received its first aid under the Marshall Plan. In 1949 it signed the North Atlantic Pact.

António Oscar de Fragoso Carmona was born in Lisbon, Portugal, on November 24, 1869, the son of General Inácio Maria Morais Carmona and Dona Maria Inês de Melo Fragoso Carmona. In keeping with the tradition of his family, he entered the Royal Military Academy in 1882, which schooling he completed in 1888. That year he was enrolled in the School of

the Army, and in 1892 became a cavalry ensign and in 1894 a second lieutenant of cavalry.

Carmona's first post was that of mathematics instructor in the College of St. Joaquim in Chaves; later he taught at the Escola Prática de Cavalaria, Vila Viçosa. Meanwhile he continued to rise in military rank, being promoted to lieutenant in 1899 and to captain in 1907. In his next teaching position he was professor at the Escola Prática of cavalry of Torres Novas. In addition to his other duties at that time, he worked with the commission for the reorganization of the Army under the direction of General Morais Sarmento.

During the first and second decades of the 1900's Portugal passed through a turbulent period of internal disturbances, between 1910 and 1926 experiencing sixteen revolutions and forty-three changes in Cabinets. A revolution in 1910 resulted in the abolition of the monarchy and the adoption of a republican constitution; the republic, proclaimed October 5, 1910, was recognized 1911 by the powers. In the reorganization of the army Carmona was named to represent the cavalry branch. Carmona, who was made a major in 1913, taught at the Escola Central for officers in Mafra and then served for a time as secretary to the Minister of War. In 1916 Carmona was promoted to the rank of lieutenant colonel and named commander of the Second Cavalry (Lisbon), a regiment that was to see some action on the Allies side in World War I. He was also made commander of the Escola Prática of cavalry of Torres Novas. In 1919 he was commissioned a colonel, and in 1922 he was promoted to the rank of general. Carmona was put in command of the Fourth Military Division in 1922, and was appointed military prosecutor in the military tribunal which tried the men accused of instigating the October 1921 assassination of high government officials. The following year (1923) he held the portfolio of Minister of War. Not long afterward, however, a Navy-civilian revolt overthrew the Cabinet, and General Carmona returned to military life as commanding general of the Fourth Division at Elvas.

As military prosecutor at the special tribunal trying the cases of the revolutionists of April 18, 1925, Carmona in speaking of the military leaders General Sinel de Cordes, Commander Filomeno de Câmara, and Colonel Raúl Esteves, said: "If men of such civic valor as these are brought here as criminals while men of ill will can walk freely in the land, then our country has really fallen into evil ways." The tribunal acquitted Cordes and his colleagues, as a result of which Carmona was removed from his military command at Elvas.

In 1926 another insurgent movement, begun in the north by Marshal Gomes da Costa, was joined by General Carmona. The revolutionists entered Lisbon on June 3 and seized the Government, setting up a Cabinet headed by Mendes Cabeçadas, with Costa as War Minister and Carmona as Minister for Foreign Affairs. Costa assumed the Premiership on June 17, deposing Cabeçadas; three weeks later, on July 9, 1926, Costa was replaced by Carmona, who became President of the Council (or Prime

Minister and Minister of War. In November of the same year he assumed the duties of Chief of State (then the provisional President) in addition to the premiership. He was elected President of Portugal in March 1928, at which time he ceased being Prime Minister.

Portugal's constitution of 1933 established it as a corporate republic, with a President elected by direct suffrage for a seven-year term, a Privy Council of ten members to assist the President, and a National Assembly (one chamber) of 120 deputies elected for a four-year term. Carmona has held the post of President since 1928, being returned in the elections of 1935, 1942, and 1949. "Though he ruled chiefly through others," states *Columbia Encyclopedia*, "the guiding hand was his." Dr. Antonio de Oliveira Salazar, appointed Minister of Finance in 1928 and Prime Minister in 1932, became virtual dictator.

Carmona made a state visit to Spain in 1929 at the request of King Alfonzo XIII. As part of Portugal's program to strengthen her colonial bonds, Carmona paid official visits in 1938 to Madeira, São Tomé, Principe, and to Angola, where he inaugurated a trade exhibition. In 1939 he continued his good-will tour with visits to Cape Verde and Mozambique, also making a state visit to the Union of South Africa at the invitation of King George VI of England. In June 1940 he presided over Portugal's festival which celebrated her eight hundred years of existence as a nation and the tercentenary of the restoration of independence after sixty years under Spanish rule. He made an official visit to all the islands of the Azores in 1941.

Portugal maintained its neutrality throughout World War II. In November 1942 Carmona sent thanks to President Roosevelt for his assurances that the Allied North African campaign was not a threat to Portugal or its possessions. Implementing a 570-year-old treaty with England, Portugal in 1943 permitted establishment, for war-duration use, of British air bases in Terceira and gave the United States an air base on Santa Maria, both in the Azores. Portugal signed the North Atlantic Pact in April 1949, making the reservation that no use of bases would be granted in time of peace and urging inclusion of Spain in the treaty. During February 1950 the Government of Salazar and Carmona received its first monetary aid from the United States under the Marshall Plan. (Portugal is not a member of the United Nations.)

For the first time since he took office, Carmona in 1949 faced an opponent for the presidency, General Norton de Mattos. Backed by Liberal, Democratic and Communist supporters (though he himself has an anti-Communist record), Mattos conducted a heated campaign that brought threats of Army intervention from Salazar. Mattos offered a rallying point for critics of the regime who charged that it had favored the upper classes, that prices were high while wages remained low, that there was widespread economic distress, and that the country was being governed undemocratically. On February 11 Mattos withdrew his candidacy on the grounds that the Government had given

Casa de Portugal
ANTONIO OSCAR DE FRAGOSO CARMONA

no guaranty that the elections would be free. Re-elected to his fourth term on February 13, 1949, and inaugurated on April 20, 1949, Carmona asked Salazar to form a Government.

President Carmona was given the rank of marshal by the Supreme Army Council in May 1947. He is a General of the Honorary Division of the Brazilian Army. Besides being the inventor of a telemeter which was used in the Army and bears his name, he was the first to have aërial photographs of Portugal made for military purposes, and for this was made honorary member of the Aero Club of Portugal. The universities of Spain have given Carmona honorary doctorates. He is a member of the Spanish College of Doctors, and is honorary president of the Portuguese Academy of History as well as of numerous other cultural organizations. Carmona is Grand Master of the Military Orders of Torre e Espada, of Christo, of Aviz, and of Santiago de Espada. He has been awarded the Order of Merit in Agriculture and Industry, the Order of Public Education, the Order of Meritorious Service, and the Order of the Imperial Portuguese Colonies. Among the countries which have decorated him are Britain, Norway, the Netherlands, Poland, Spain, Italy, Czechoslovakia, Rumania, Hungary, Chile, and Peru.

The wife of the President of Portugal is Dona Maria de Carmo Ferreira da Silva Carmona. For many years the Carmonas made their home in Chaves, and there their three children were born. The elder daughter is Dona Cesaltina Amélia da Silva Carmona e Costa; the younger is Dona Maria Inês da Silva Carmona Santos, wife of the Minister of Portugal in Rome; the son, António Adérito da Silva Carmona, served for a time as consul of Portugal in Casablanca. Carmona has

CARMONA, ANTONIO OSCAR DE FRAGOSO—*Continued*

been described as a man of wit and culture, a student of world history. He admires particularly the work of the sixteenth century poet Luiz Vaz de Camoens.

References

International Who's Who, 1950
Quem é Alguém (1947)
World Biography (1948)

CASALS, PABLO (kä-säls' pä'blō) Dec. 29, 1876- Violoncellist; conductor; composer
Address: h. Prades, Pyrénées-Orientales, France

Of the numerous musical events held in 1950 to commemorate the two hundredth anniversary of the death of Johann Sebastian Bach, the one that aroused widest international interest took place in June in the little French village of Prades. It marked the reappearance in public of Pablo Casals, who is generally considered the world's greatest living violoncellist and the most renowned modern interpreter of Bach's music. To play and conduct Bach in the town where he lives in self-imposed exile from his native Spain, Casals came out of retirement for the first time since 1947, the year he vowed, as a moral protest, never again to play in public so long as Spain was under the rule of Generalissimo Francisco Franco.

Born in Vendrell, which is about forty miles from Barcelona, Spain, on December 29, 1876, Pablo (or Pau in Catalan) Carlos Salvador Defilló de Casals is the second of the eleven children—nine boys and two girls—of Carles and Pilar Defilló de Casals. Of pure Catalan ancestry, his father's family is traceable back to the sixteenth century; his mother, born in Puerto Rico of Catalonian parents, had one German grandparent. Carles Casals, who was organist of the parish church in Vendrell, gave his son his first musical instruction. At the age of four Pablo joined the church choir; by the time he was six, he was learning to play the piano and had begun to write and transpose music; at seven, he started to study the violin. His father also gave him lessons on the organ, and within a year the boy could substitute at church services when the elder Casals was ill. After hearing the violoncello for the first time, Pablo expressed a desire to master that instrument and accordingly received his first lessons from his father.

When he was eleven years old, Pablo Casals was sent to Barcelona to study the cello with José García at the Municipal School, where he also took lessons in harmony and counterpoint with José Roadereda, and continued his piano studies. To earn money, he formed and played in a cafe trio. It was in this period that he first discovered Bach's unaccompanied suites for the cello, which he was to study and practice for twelve years before playing them in public. After three years in Barcelona, he went to Madrid in 1892, where he found a patron in the Count of Morphy, who was adviser to the Queen Mother and Regent, María Cristina. The Queen took an interest in the young cellist,

inviting him to give concerts at the Royal Palace and often playing piano duets with him. Meanwhile, for two and a half years, Casals studied chamber music with the violinist, Jesús de Monasterio, and composition and counterpoint with Tomás Bretón at the Royal Conservatory of Music. After a brief and disheartening stay in Paris, when he earned his living by playing in a vaudeville theater, Casals returned to Barcelona in 1897 and succeeded García as professor of cello at the Municipal School. He also played the cello in several churches; became first cellist of the Liceo (opera) Orchestra; formed his own string quartet with the Belgian violinist, Mathieu Crickboom; and assisted the noted Spanish composer, Enrique Granados, at his Conservatory and in various chamber music concerts.

Casals' career as a virtuoso may be said to date from October 1899, when he made his professional debut in Paris, playing Lalo's Cello Concerto with the Lamoureux Orchestra. His success was immediate, and engagements soon followed in the capitals of Europe. He made his home in Paris, where in 1905 he formed a trio with the French artists, Jacques Thibaud, violinist, and Alfred Cortot, pianist. Another musician with whom he was heard for many years was Harold Bauer, the English pianist: they gave sonata recitals throughout Europe, the United States, and South America. Each spring upon his return from concert tours, Casals held classes as professor of cello at the Ecole Normale de Musique in Paris, where he had many distinguished pupils. In 1901 he came to the United States to appear in a series of concerts with the singer, Emma Nevada; he returned in 1904 to make his New York debut, playing Saint-Saëns' Cello Concerto with the Metropolitan Opera Orchestra. On his third visit, in 1915, Fritz Kreisler exclaimed that the "King of the Bow has arrived." From 1915 until his last New York recital in 1928 Casals gave concerts almost every year in the United States.

According to his American biographer, Lillian Littlehales, Casals "felt that the cello did not give him his truest way of expressing himself." Since the beginning of his artistic career, he maintained that conducting was the real work of his life, and the orchestra "the grandest instrument of them all." At the conclusion of World War I he returned to find Barcelona a city which could not support a permanent symphony orchestra. Taking matters into his own hands, he gathered together the best players available and began rehearsals. After numerous difficulties, the Orquestra Pau Casals gave its first concert on October 13, 1920. Public response was apathetic at first, but by rigorous training, innumerable rehearsals, and defraying expenses from his own pocket, Casals succeeded in knitting together a superior orchestra, which presented annual spring and fall seasons and eventually became self-supporting. Feeling strongly that the working class of the city should also have the opportunity of hearing good music, he helped to establish a musical organization for workingmen, the Associació Obrera de Concerts, in 1925. By paying dues of about a dollar a year, members of this association were entitled to attend several musical events, including concerts by Casals' orchestra. He also served as guest conductor of the New York Symphony Vienna Philharmonic, Lamoureux and Colonne orchestras in Paris, London Symphony, as well as orchestras in Rome, Berlin, Prague, Zurich, Buenos Aires, Mexico City, and Havana.

Since the Spanish Republic, which was established in 1931, granted autonomy to his native Catalonia and made efforts to foster education and culture, Casals collaborated wholeheartedly with the new regime. He became a member of the Junta de Musica formed within the Council of Culture of the Generalitat de Cataluyna, the government of autonomous Catalonia. The city of Barcelona made him an honorary citizen, named a street after him, and paid him tribute in 1934, and Madrid did likewise in 1936; he was elected a member of honor of the Spanish Academy in 1935. On July 18, 1936, the day after the outbreak of the Spanish Civil War, Casals conducted his orchestra for the last time. Identifying himself with the Republican cause, he toured as soloist in 1937 and 1938 to raise money to feed Catalan children, and returned to Barcelona each year to play in hospitals while the city was under bombardment. In January 1939, shortly before the final defeat of the Loyalists by Franco's forces, Casals sought shelter in France. Later that year he settled in Prades, a French-Catalonian town of 4,400 inhabitants, near the Spanish border, where he could devote all his efforts to aiding the Spanish refugees held in French detention camps. After the fall of France in World War II (1940) he lived in seclusion in Prades. The Nazis offered him rewards if he would play in Germany, but he emphatically refused.

Casals' first major reappearance after the end of the war in Europe took place in London, where, on June 27, 1945, he played as soloist with the British Broadcasting Orchestra. The London critic of *Musical America* reported that "from the first notes it was clear that none of the magic of his playing has been lost." However, late in November of that same year, Casals reached the decision not to perform again in England or the United States as a protest, "moral rather than political," against the continued recognition or tacit approval of Franco's regime by these two countries. Later this self-imposed exile was extended: he refused to play anywhere in public again until Franco should be ousted. His last public appearance took place at the University of Montpellier, in France, on March 10, 1947. Writing in the New York *Times* (May 28, 1950), Howard Taubman explained that Casals does not belong to any political party. "Since he is not a politician, he feels that he must take his stand through his role as a musician." The government of Czechoslovakia recently offered him a home, money, and official position, but he declined to live in a Communist-dominated country. The Franco government has even indicated that he would be welcomed back to Spain, where his two remaining brothers, Enric, a violinist, and Lluís, a farmer, live unmolested. Casals still retains his Spanish passport and

Paul Senn—Black Star

PABLO CASALS

citizenship. When asked why he didn't give them up, he replied: "It is my country. Let Franco give up his passport!"

The idea of the Prades Festival was conceived by one of Casals' pupils, the American violinist, Alexander Schneider, both to celebrate the Bach bicentenary and to give musicians an opportunity "to pay personal tribute to Casals as a man of moral force and integrity." Such distinguished soloists as Rudolf Serkin, Joseph Szigeti, Isaac Stern, Eugene Istomin, and others, volunteered their services. Under the musical direction of Casals, the festival was held from June 1 to 20, 1950. Its twelve concerts, each attended by over a thousand persons, were given in the Eglise de Saint-Pierre.

Of Casals' achievement as a cellist, Grove's *Dictionary of Music and Musicians* states that he inaugurated a new era in the playing of the violoncello. Whereas, at the beginning of the twentieth century, opera fantasias and other little pieces comprised the repertory of the solo cellist, Casals made Bach's unaccompanied suites for cello, formerly regarded as works of only academic interest, admired and understood; revived the important cello concertos of the eighteenth and nineteenth centuries; and inspired contemporary composers to write new works for the instrument. By working out new methods of fingering and various bow techniques, he "greatly widened the resources of the cello as a medium of artistic interpretation." "Technically he is a master of the instrument," wrote Taubman; "his tone is pure gold, mellow, resonant, infinitely flexible. . . .But these accomplishments are means to an end—to serve the music as devotedly as he can." When Casals appeared in London both as conductor and soloist in 1927, Arthur Fox-Strangways, of the *London Observer*, wrote: "Whether with the bow or the stick, he plays as if he held a responsible trust, determined that at all costs the purity of the faith shall not suffer at his

CASALS, PABLO—*Continued*

hands. He refrains from anything histrionic or ephemeral; he wants the truth of it. . . .In whatever he does, he seems to aim at some invisible ideal, and if some part of that is reached, immediately to set the standard higher.

As a composer, Casals is less well known. His compositions include two oratorios, *La Visión de Fray Martín*, and *La Crêche*; several Masses; a *Miserere, Ave Maria*, and other choral works; two symphonies; two *sardanas* (the national Catalonian dance); eight string quartets; and pieces for violin and piano, cello and piano, and cello solo; as well as many songs. Under the Victor label he has recorded the Boccherini, Dvořák, and Elgar cello concertos; the six unaccompanied suites of Bach; Beethoven's Cello Sonatas Nos. 1, 3, 4. Together with Thibaud and Cortot, he has also recorded trios by Beethoven, Haydn, Mendelssohn, Schumann, and Schubert, and the Brahms' Double Concerto (with Cortot conducting the Orquestra Pau Casals). Records of Casals own conducting include Beethoven's Symphonies Nos. 1 and 4, *Ruins of Athens*, and *Coriolanus* overtures. In 1950 he signed up with Columbia Records, which helped to finance and recorded the major events of the Prades Festival.

A grand officer of the French Legion of Honor and a member of many distinguished European musical societies, Casals has received orders and decorations from Spain, Austria, Rumania, and Portugal, and honorary degrees from the universities of Edinburgh, Barcelona, and Montpellier. He has been married twice: in 1906, to his pupil, Guilhermina Suggia, the Portuguese cellist; and in 1914, to the American singer, Susan Metcalfe. whom he used to accompany in *Lieder* recitals, revealing his considerable powers as a pianist. Physically the cellist has been described as "stout, vigorous, indefatigable." At Prades, where he lives in a gardener's cottage on the estate of a Frenchman, he plays on his Gofriller cello every day and receives his pupils. One of his pupils has said: "A lesson from him is not a lesson; it is a great musical experience."

References

Life 28:152-8+ My '50
N Y Times II p7 D 29 '46; II p9 Ja 8 '50
N Y Times Mag p14 My 28 '50 por
Archives Internationales (1950)
Baker's Biographical Dictionary of Musicians (1940)
Ewen, D. ed. Living Musicians (1940); Men and Women Who Make Music (1949)
Grove, G. Dictionary of Music and Musicians (1927)
International Who's Who, 1949
Littlehales, L. Pablo Casals (Rev. and enl. ed. 1948)
Riemann, H. Das Neue Musiklexikon (1926)
Thompson, O. ed. International Cyclopedia of Music and Musicians (1949)
Tobel, R. von Pablo Casals (1945)
Who's Who, 1950
World Biography (1948)

CASTRO, MORRIS F(IDANQUE) DE
See De Castro, M. F.

CATES, CLIFTON B(LEDSOE) Aug. 31, 1893- United States Marine Corps Commandant

Address: b. United States Marine Corps Headquarters, Arlington Annex, Navy Department, Washington, D.C.; h. Commandant's House, Marine Barracks, 8th & I Sts., S.E., Washington, D.C.

The Commandant of the Marine Corps of the United States is General Clifton B. Cates, who entered the Corps in 1917, reached the rank of general in 1948. Distinguished combat records in World Wars I and II have earned him many high honors. A veteran of major campaigns in France in 1918 and of battles for the islands of the Pacific in World War II, Cates has in the course of his career commanded all units under fire—a platoon, company, battalion, regiment, and division. He was appointed to the command of the USMC on January 1, 1948.

Clifton Bledsoe Cates was born in Tiptonville, Tennessee, on August 31, 1893, the son of Willis Jones and Martha (Bledsoe) Cates. He studied law at the University of Tennessee, receiving the LL.B. degree in 1916. He entered the Marine Corps as second lieutenant (reserve) on June 13, 1917, and was assigned to the Marine Barracks at Parris Island, South Carolina.

As a member of the Sixth Marine Regiment, Cates sailed in January 1918 for France, where he participated in the Aisne-Marne defensive at Chateau Thierry, the Aisne-Marne offensive at Soissons, the St. Mihiel offensive, the Meuse-Argonne offensive at Champagne, and the Meuse-Argonne offensive in the Argonne Forest. He was gassed and wounded a number of times; he also escaped so many "close calls" that his fellow officers nicknamed him "Lucky." The Marine officer was awarded the Navy Cross and Distinguished Service Cross with Oak Leaf Cluster for bravery in the Aisne-Marne defensive—he had led his command to an objective "despite the fact that he was rendered temporarily unconscious by a bullet striking his helmet. Exposing himself to extreme hazard, he reorganized his position with but a handful of men" (quoted from the citation).

Cates remained in Germany with the Army of Occupation until September 1919. Between World Wars I and II he rose to the rank of colonel. For two years he served, successively, as aide-de-camp to the Corps commandant, White House aide to President Woodrow Wilson, and aide to the Commanding General, Department of the Pacific, at San Francisco. As commanding officer of a Marine detachment he spent two years at sea aboard the U.S.S. *Cali-*

fornia in 1923. For the next two years he was assigned to recruiting duty at Spokane, Washington, and at Omaha, Nebraska, followed by a year in Washington, D.C., where he served on the American Battle Monuments Commission. After two terms of foreign shore duty in Shanghai (in 1929-32 with the Fourth Regiment and again in 1937-39 as commanding officer of the Second Battalion of the Sixth Regiment) and three training courses (at the Army Industrial College in Washington, 1932, the Marine Corps School at Quantico, Virginia, 1934, and the Army War College at Washington, 1939), he was appointed director of the Basic School at the Marine Barracks in Philadelphia, Pennsylvania.

Cates's service in World War II, with the exception of a period as commandant of the Marine Corps School at Quantico, was entirely in the Pacific. As Commanding Officer of the First Marine Regiment, he participated in the Guadalcanal campaign from the first landing (August 7, 1942) until mid-December. In July 1944 (the year he became a major general) he was attached to the Fourth Marine Division as observer in the final battle of Saipan. He took command of the division at the end of the campaign, just prior to the Tinian operation, which was regarded as the model amphibious operation of the war. The Marine commander flew on reconnaissance flights over the island, and following the successful landing of the Fourth Division, the commander visited the front lines almost daily to "study terrain and boost morale." The Iwo Jima campaign (February-March 1945) in which Cates's Fourth Marine Division took part with the Third and Fifth Divisions, was called "by far the bloodiest in the history of the Marine Corps."

For his achievements prior to and during the Iwo Jima operation, from February 10 to March 20, 1945, General Cates was awarded a Gold Star in lieu of a second Distinguished Service Medal (he received the first in World War I). His citation read, in part: "He landed his force . . . against heavy enemy resistance and, defying the terrific, continuous bombardment . . . pushed his relentless advance. Repeatedly disregarding his own personal safety, Major General Cates traversed his own front lines daily to rally his tired, depleted units by his undaunted valor."

Returning to the United States in November of 1945, General Cates served briefly as president of the Marine Corps Equipment Board before he was assigned as commanding general of the Marine Barracks at Quantico in June 1946. On January 1, 1948, he was advanced to the rank of general and was appointed Commandant of the Marine Corps by President Truman.

The United States Marine Corps had its beginnings in the Continental Marines, organized in 1775; the present Corps was established by act of Congress in 1798. By the National Security Act of 1947 and amendments of 1949 (the "unification act"), the Corps, as an integral part of the Department of the Navy, was incorporated in the Department of Defense. While the Corps operates as a part of

U. S. Navy

GEN. CLIFTON B. CATES

the Navy, its headquarters organization (states the *United States Government Organization Manual*) "is a complete operating organization in itself and is self-contained." Cates, as Commandant, "is charged with and is responsible for the procurement, discharge, education, training, discipline, and distribution of officers and enlisted personnel of the Marine Corps, including the Reserve." In the words of the *United States News*, the Corps is "essentially a selected force of shock troops, adept at amphibious operations and guerrilla warfare, constantly hard trained and ready for embarkation to distant trouble spots."

In October 1949 General Cates expressed his apprehension about the reduction of the Marine Corps before the House Armed Services Committee, stating that there was widespread fear that the functions assigned the Corps by law were being "usurped by others." About a year later (September 1950) legislation was introduced in the House and Senate to raise the manpower of the Marine Corps to a minimum of 300,000 men, to create an Assistant Secretary of the Navy for the Marine Corps, and to make General Cates a member of the Joint Chiefs of Staff. (It was President Truman's objection to these proposals that brought forth his harsh words about the Marine Corps, words for which he later apologized.) Fears that the "Leathernecks" would be eliminated by military unification were somewhat relieved in mid-1950 when marines were in Korea and their record was lauded anew. Cates himself was in Korea in October 1950, to inspect the units which had participated in the recapture of Seoul, the South Korean capital.

The USMC Commandant has received many decorations in addition to those already mentioned. Among them, in World War I, are the Legion of Merit, Croix de Guerre with Palms and Gold Star, Silver Star with Oak

CATES, CLIFTON B.—*Continued*

Leaf Cluster, Purple Heart with Oak Leaf Cluster, Army of Occupation Medal, Legion of Honor and the Fourragère (France); several medals for his peacetime service in China; in World War II: citations and medals for his achievements in Guadalcanal (1942) Tinian (1944), Iwo Jima (1945), Asiatic-Pacific Campaign Medal with five Bronze Stars, World War II Victory Medal. He was made a commander in the Order of Orange-Nassau by the Netherlands in 1943.

The Marine officer and Mrs. Cates (he married Jane Virginia McIlhenny on October 7, 1920) have two children, Lieutenant Commander Clifton Bledsoe Cates, Jr., of USN, and Ann Willis Cates. The Commandant has been described as a "quick-talking, alert, vigorous" man who takes special pleasure in hunting and fishing.

References

Sat Eve Post 221:20 F 5 '49
U S News 29:33 Ag 18 '50
Who's Who in America, 1950-51

CAUDILL, REBECCA (cô'd'l) 1899- Author

Address: h. 501 Iowa St., Urbana, Ill.

Reprinted from the *Wilson Library Bulletin*, May 1950.

"Many children's book have been written about orphans who have had to make their way alone. I like to write about families that are intact. I guess I have a soft spot for fathers and mothers." There, in her own words, is the key to the unique quality of Rebecca Caudill's work. Her child characters are not isolated individuals, but integrated units in a family group. The result is a complete, full-rounded picture

REBECCA CAUDILL

of childhood, which after all must contain some adults. Miss Caudill's grownups are as real and as lovable as her youngsters.

No doubt her attitude toward the family circle was conditioned by her own experience. Born in Harlan County, Kentucky, in 1899, Rebecca Caudill was one of ten children. Her parents, George W. and Susan (Smith) Caudill, were both teachers who made their home an informal schoolroom. The children attended the one-room district school, its term often as short as three months, but their real education came at home, through reading together and through family discussions. When young Rebecca was four the Caudills moved to a farm in Tennessee. She attended public school and Sumner County High School at Portland, Tennessee, and went to Wesleyan College at Macon, Georgia. There she had the distinction of being the first student to work her way through, earning her expenses by assisting in the bursar's office. She found time to edit a student publication and serve as president of the college YWCA. She did postgraduate work at Vanderbilt University, Nashville, taking her M.A. in 1922. For the following two years she taught English in a girls' school at Rio de Janeiro. On her return she became editor of a Methodist church paper in Nashville. In 1931 she married James Sterling Ayars, also an editor.

At her husband's urging she began writing short stories and, later, books for children. The first one, *Barrie & Daughter*, appeared in 1943. For it she drew upon the memory of her Kentucky childhood, modeling the Barrie of the title after her own father. Margaret McElderry in *Christian Science Monitor* called it "a book of very real values, written with sensitive understanding of people, young and old, with a sense of the mountain country, and ways of life there at the turn of the century." A. M. Jordan, in *Horn Book*: "The story has to do with real people and keenly invigorating situations. It has lasting value, especially for older girls and also for adult readers, who will be interested in the social life of the region." This book was a Junior Literary Guild selection, as were the three that followed it. *Happy Little Family* (1947), for a younger age group, was made up of little stories of old-time family life. Virginia Kirkus: "Each chapter is a lively portrait in action full of amusing details and honest-to-goodness child talk. It's worth all the rereadings which you'll be implored to give it."

Tree of Freedom (1949), a junior historical novel for twelve and upward, ran second in the vote for the current Newbery Award. Louise Seaman Bechtel wrote of it in the New York *Herald Tribune*, "In the mass of historical fiction for young readers this story of pioneers in Kentucky shines out with rare individuality and with moving beauty. The writer has become so imaginatively a part of her period that the extraordinary details carefully collected, the old phrases, the old-time language, flow together in a truly living stream." Ellen Buell in the New York *Times* said: "It is doubtful that Stephanie was quite as farseeing about the issues of the Revolution as the author makes her. But otherwise the story is sound, rich in perspective, a rewarding one for thoughtful readers." Reviewing *Schoolhouse in the Woods* (1949) the *Horn Book* said, "The author gives real character to each child in a large family as it prepares . . . for Monday morning. Children just beginning school will love Bonnie and share her feelings."

Miss Caudill, Mrs. James Ayars in private life, lives with her husband and two children in Urbana, Illinois, home of Illinois University. Blue-eyed and brown-haired, with a warm sympathetic smile, she considers her chief occupation homemaking, her chief interest, sharing in her children's "growing pains." She does, however, engage in many activities outside the home. Besides her writing schedule, which will produce *Up and Down the River* for 1950 publication, she does able work in the League of Women Voters, the Chicago Children's Reading Round Table, and the Parent-Teacher Association. She sponsored the first interracial, interfaith house for girls on the Illinois University campus, and organized and managed Urbana's first Book Fair.

CAVANNA, BETTY (kȧ-văn'ȧ) June 24, 1909- Author

Address: h. Radnor Rd., R.D. #1, Wayne, Pa.

Reprinted from the *Wilson Library Bulletin*, June 1950.

Elizabeth Cavanna Headley (who also writes under the names of Betty Cavanna and Betsy Allen) looks very much like one of her own heroines out of a high school romance, a smiling, slender brown-eyed girl, with the added charm of a maturer wisdom and the poise won by her experience and accomplishment. Girls, dogs, careers, horses, the arts, modern life situations set to a teen-age tempo, the joys and aches of growing-up—from this potpourri this deservedly popular author has created a proud list of books in her as yet brief professional career.

Born in Camden, New Jersey, June 24, 1909, Betty Cavanna is the daughter of the late Walter Cavanna and of Emily (Allen) Cavanna. She knew early that she wanted to be a writer. The seeds of this knowledge were planted long before her birth, and one must go back to those old French and Irish and English roots in her ancestry, the Gallic love of words, the Irish wit and tenderness, and the Anglo-Saxon adventuring, for the explanation. These combined in the little schoolgirl to give her an awareness long before the desire to write became an active thought. Her memories of emotions are still more vivid than those of place and face. Now that awareness of feeling has been transmuted for the girls of the present generation "to live and grow thereby." They have welcomed this author with lively enthusiasm because her books for them are mirrors in which they see themselves reflected, or the pattern of girls they would like to become.

School activities and early career all pointed one way for Betty Cavanna. She had a place on the yearbook staff and the managing editorship of *Campus News* during her journalism

BETTY CAVANNA

major at New Jersey College for Women, which granted her B.A. in 1929 and honorary Phi Beta Kappa in 1949. Later there were editorial work on newspapers, an advertising job, a post as art director for a publishing house, which led to radio scripts and short stories. A season of travel rounded it well. The whole has become a structure fitly fashioned upon the foundations of that early ancestral bequest. It shows in the sparkle of the brown eyes, and in the continuing warm understanding of girlhood's calamities and joys, and the flashing words which express that clear perception.

Whether she is reviewed as Betty Cavanna, Elizabeth Headley, or Betsy Allen, critics have been almost uniformly commending, though of course several of her books have won higher praise than others. Each succeeding title has made its own place on library shelves since the publication of *Puppy Stakes* in 1943, the first book length after a number of short stories in juvenile publications. Then came *The Black Spaniel Mystery* in 1945, and four later ones, each chosen for the Junior Literary Guild: *Going On Sixteen* (1946), reviewed as "a valid story . . . good storytelling, sound characterization . . . contemporary," and "a warm convincing story of a girl growing up"; *Spurs for Suzanna* (1947), "an unpretentious but wise story of young people with a healthy balance of work and fun"; *A Girl Can Dream* (1948) with an aviation background which the author took care to learn at first hand; and then *Paintbox Summer* (1949) with Peter Hunt's Peasant village at Cape Cod as the identified locale. Miss Cavanna hopes that "through Kate, girls may get a little perspective on their own problems and their own romances." A critic wrote of it, "The author has mixed her people and her backgrounds with the ingenuity of the artist. . . . This is an important book for teenage girls . . . as neat as a still life of the

CAVANNA, BETTY—*Continued*

Dutch school and as gay is its Peter Hunt decorations."

There have been a series of mysteries, still going on, written as Betsy Allen; and a group of three stories, so far, for the younger teens: *A Date for Diane*; *Take a Call, Topsy*; and *She's My Girl*. *Secret Passage* (1947), a mystery story set apart from the others by its tone and its historical significance, the scene in Haddonfield, New Jersey, and Virginia a few years before the Civil War, was an honor book in the *Herald Tribune* Spring Festival.

The Headleys, Betty, Edward T. (they were married in 1940), who does sales research, and young Stephen, aged seven, live in Wayne, Pennsylvania, not far from Philadelphia. There, between books, the writer becomes domestic and gardens with the same force that drives her pen. She confesses to a passion for the antiques which beckon from hundreds of wayside shops in Pennsylvania. There has been time, too, since her marriage to raise a few of the cockers which have gone into several of her sixteen books. Not a professional kennel idea, the author insists, but just a few pups because they happened along to a family pet. She admits to using Stephen for a prototype once when he was three, and she occasionally dips into the memories of her sister, who is her junior and therefore a quite reliable consultant. Farther than that Miss Cavanna has not committed herself, but a little of biography and a little of the locale of her childhood home town (Haddonfield) are recognizable as one reads.

There is in preparation for the fall of 1950 another horse story, but we are sure it will not be any of the "mixture as before." The many facets in Betty Cavanna's life have contributed to the distinction of dissimilarity in her work except at the point of quality.

CHADWICK, FLORENCE (MAY) Nov. 9, 1918- Swimmer

Address: h. 2120 Warrington St., San Diego, Calif.

On August 8, 1950, Florence Chadwick established a new record for women swimming the English Channel, breaking the 1926 record of Gertrude Ederle. A Californian, Miss Chadwick has been swimming since she was six years old, and at ten was the first child to swim the San Diego Bay Channel. Two years ago (1948) she left Southern California to take an office position in Saudi Arabia, where she trained for the channel swim in the Persian Gulf.

Florence May Chadwick was born November 9, 1918, in San Diego. Her father, Richard William Chadwick, whose ancestry is English, French, and Irish, served for twenty-three years in that city's Police Department as a detective and narcotic agent. Her mother is Mary Chadwick, of Austrian descent. Since her father's retirement from the police force, the Chadwicks have operated a restaurant. A brother, Richard William Chadwick, Jr., also lives in San Diego.

Acme Photo

FLORENCE CHADWICK

Miss Chadwick learned to swim in early childhood. She has attributed her interest in aquatics to an uncle, Mike Lacko. "He entered me in a race, which I lost," she has related. "I was six years old, but I decided to work harder and prove somehow that his confidence was not misplaced." When she was ten she succeeded in swimming the channel at the mouth of San Diego Bay, the first child to do so. During the next eighteen years she was ten times the winner of the annual two-and-a-half mile race at La Jolla.

At Point Loma Junior and Senior High School in San Diego, Florence engaged in competitive swimming, was a member of the Girl Reserves (junior branch of the YWCA), and was president of the high school Associated Student Body. She graduated in 1936. High school was followed by a year at San Diego State College, a year at the Southwestern University of Law at Los Angeles, and a year at the Balboa Law School in San Diego. At this point Miss Chadwick abandoned the study of law and spent a year and a half at the Dickenson Business College in her home town, before a period of training at the comptometer school of the Felt and Tarrant Manufacturing Company.

During World War II the young swimmer directed and produced aquatic shows for various military service groups and for veterans hospitals. In 1945, after nineteen years of swimming, she relinquished her amateur standing when she went to Hollywood to appear in an MGM motion picture starring Esther Williams. Upon completion of the film she worked as a professional swimming instructor at the La Jolla Beach and Tennis Club.

Miss Chadwick's mother has been quoted as saying that her daughter's "one ambition" was to swim the English Channel. In June 1948, partly in order to raise money for the venture, the swimmer went to Saudi Arabia to work as a comptometer operator in the office of the

Arabian-American Oil Company. Here she began training in earnest, first in the 150-foot pool at Dhahran and later, when she was transferred to an office at Ras Al Mishab, in the rough waters of the Persian Gulf, where she swam before and after work and on her free days, on the latter as many as ten hours in a day. She terminated her employment with the oil company in June 1950 and went to Wissant on the French coast to prepare for the Channel attempt.

The speed record of 14 hours and 31 minutes set by Gertrude Ederle when, in 1926, she was the first woman to swim the 19-mile channel, had remained unbroken, although eleven women had succeeded in completing the cross-channel swim. On August 8, 1950, Miss Chadwick, the thirty-second person to complete the crossing, set a new record of 13 hours and 20 minutes (about two hours longer than the men's record). She had applied for entry into a contest held by the London *Daily Mail*, but was not accepted as a contestant. In July she made a practice swim (not an attempt) in the English Channel. At 2:37 A.M., August 8, she left Cape Gris Nez on the French coast, accompanied by a party of fifteen in an escorting fishing boat. (The group was composed of her father, officials, crew, and friends from Saudi Arabia.) She started at 60 strokes a minute until she had negotiated the strong inshore currents. The rest of the course was swum at a rate of 48 strokes. Miss Chadwick's nourishment during the swim was lumps of sugar. It took four hours to cross the ebb-tide encountered in the last three miles before she reached Dover. British artillery practice fire had been suspended as she entered the area about six miles offshore. When Miss Chadwick was met by newsmen as she reached land, her comment was, "I feel fine. I am quite prepared to swim back."

Asked about his daughter's future plans, Miss Chadwick's father is quoted as saying, "We're through with channel swimming. We did it, and that was all we wanted." It was pointed out that the several thousand dollars needed for expenses were the Chadwicks' own funds. Upon her return to the United States Miss Chadwick spent a few days in New York, during which she appeared on several radio and television programs. In San Diego she was accorded a homecoming welcome which included a ticker-tape parade and a public luncheon in her honor. In recognition of her achievement she was awarded the Helms Athletic Foundation Award as the athlete of the month for August 1950.

The swimmer is five feet six inches tall. Weighing 141 pounds at the start of the channel swim, she lost five pounds during the time she was in the water. Her eyes are brown, her hair is dark brown. She is a Catholic; her political stand she designates as "nonpartisan." After swimming, Miss Chadwick says, her chief interest is "to encourage the youth of America to further their own interests in their favorite sports."

Reference

Washington (D.C.) Post p5C Ag 13 '50

CHAUVEL, JEAN (MICHEL HENRI)
(shō″vĕl′ zhäɴ mē″shĕl′ äɴ″rē′) Apr. 16, 1897- United Nations delegate
Address: b. c/o United Nations, New York

The head of the French delegation to the United Nations, Jean Chauvel is his country's permanent representative in the Security Council. Appointed to his present post on February 2, 1949, to succeed Alexandre Parodi [46], Chauvel had for the four preceding years served as Secretary General of the French Foreign Office. He officiated as president of the Security Council through the month of May 1950.

The son of a Breton surgeon and his half-English wife, Jean Michel Henri Chauvel was born April 16, 1897, in Paris, but passed most of his childhood in the ancient Brittany town of Quimper. Prepared in a Catholic school for matriculation at the University of Paris, he received the degree of *docteur en droit* (Doctor of Jurisprudence) from the latter's law school in 1921. On October 7 of 1921 he embarked on what (except for a short period during World War II) has amounted to nearly thirty years of continuous service to his country in various diplomatic capacities.

After a preliminary assignment as attaché to the Cabinet of Raymond Poincaré, Chauvel received his first foreign appointment that year, when he was sent to Peking as third secretary in the French Embassy at what was then the capital of China. Subsequently he served as secretary general of the French High Commissariat in Syria and Lebanon. In 1938 he was appointed consul general at Vienna, but later in the same year was recalled to Paris to become subdirector for Asia-Oceania at the Quai d'Orsay. He was in occupancy of this important Foreign Office post when the Germans overran northern France in the summer of 1940.

After the surrender at Compiègne, Chauvel accompanied the Pétain Government to Vichy, where he became chief of the Far Eastern division of the Foreign Ministry of Unoccupied France. In this capacity (stated a dispatch to the New York *Times*) he "worked closely with American diplomats" both "before and after Pearl Harbor." On November 11, 1942, when the Nazis took over Vichy territory, he resigned and "went underground" with the resistance movement; it was then that he organized a committee called *Bureau d'études clandestines des Affaires Etrangères*. ("I always managed to keep a step ahead of the Nazis," he was to tell Arthur Massolo of the New York *Post* about six years later. "I never slept in the same bed more than twice.") He escaped in the spring of 1944 to Algiers, where he became secretary-general of the Commissariat of Foreign Affairs of the Committee of National Liberation.

At the beginning of January 1945, after the liberation of France, Jean Chauvel was named secretary-general of the Ministry of Foreign Affairs in the provisional government of General de Gaulle, and on the eighteenth of the same month was promoted to the rank of Ambassador. This post, which is permanent and nonpartisan in character and has been compared with that of the Under Secretary of

Official United Nations Photo.

JEAN CHAUVEL

State in the United States, he was to hold continuously under successive Premiers until his appointment as permanent French delegate to the United Nations. As Foreign Office secretary-general, Chauvel participated in high-level talks in London (June 1948) on the six-power accord on Germany, and also (stated Massolo) "helped to write the Anglo-French accord, the Brussels treaty, the Western Union, the North Atlantic Pact, and other agreements cementing the world against the Soviet bloc."

Chauvel's appointment as head of the French delegation to the United Nations and permanent representative of France to the Security Council was announced in Paris on February 2, 1949; he exhanged places with Ambassador Alexandre Parodi, who succeeded him at the Quai d'Orsay. The appointment took Chauvel for the first time to the United States where, at Security Council sessions at Lake Success, he acquired the reputation of a "scholarly diplomat who gives tightly reasoned arguments replete with detail and documentation" and also upon occasion with "Latin adages and other classical material." (The quoted words are William Frye's, in the *Christian Science Monitor*.) One such argument was that which he voiced on April 7, 1949, when he urged that administration of the former Italian colonies of Tripolitania, Somaliland, and a part of Eritrea, be entrusted to the new Italian republic; and on April 19, in connection with the trials of Cardinal Mindszenty in Hungary and fifteen Protestant leaders in Bulgaria, he stressed that the concern of his government was "not limited to the particular fate of some ecclesiastical dignitaries" but went rather to "the fundamental question of human rights." At approximately the same time he was a participant, with Sir Alexander Cadogan [44] of Great Britain, in the conferences between Philip Jessup [48] of the United States and Jacob Malik [49] of the

U.S.S.R. which resulted in the announcement, on May 5, of the end of the Berlin blockade.

In the middle of October 1949 the French diplomat met a Soviet proposal that the Security Council "call for information from the fifty-nine members of the United Nations on atomic as well as other armaments" by insisting on the need of inspection as provided in the plan of control adopted by the General Assembly in the previous Assembly; and in mid-November, in a lengthy address, he assailed the U.S.S.R. suggestion that international differences be examined by a Council of Five comprising only the permanent members of the Security Council. In January 1950, when Malik "walked out" of the Council after it had declined to unseat the delegate of Nationalist China and substitute a Communist representative, he criticized the Soviet delegate's action as "tending to weaken the prestige of the United Nations."

In accordance with an alphabetic system of rotation, the presidency of the Security Council went to France for the month of May 1950; Chauvel took over the chair from Mahmoud Fawzi Bey of Egypt and yielded it at the beginning of June to Sir Benegal Rama Rau of India. Immediately after the termination of his presidency, Chauvel went to Paris for regular policy consultations; and while there he issued what the New York *Times* described as a "carefully guarded" statement supporting Secretary-General Trygve Lie's repeated contention that "the issue of the representation of China" must be settled before the convening of the next General Assembly in September. "There is at present a doubt as to the validity of the Chinese representation," Chauvel declared, "and that doubt must somehow be cleared." This was interpreted as a hint that France was contemplating recognition of the Chinese Communist regime.

On June 27, 1950, Chauvel gave his "unreserved support" to the American resolution recommending that the United Nations use armed force in repelling the North Koreans' attack on South Korea, and cast his vote for it on the following day; and on July 7, he himself was cosponsor, with Cadogan, of the resolution which, when adopted by the Security Council by a vote of 7 to 1, created a unified command of United Nations armed forces in Korea. On August 2, the day after Malik came back into the Security Council to take over the presidency for the month, Chauvel supported the American contention that the withdrawal of the Communists from South Korea must precede any discussion of the question of the Chinese representation; but the following day added that "the French government wishes to reserve its position for the moment" on the latter issue. In a subsequent long speech Chauvel disputed the Soviet assertion that the United States had been the aggressor in the Korean war and that United Nations action on Korea had been illegal because of the absence of the U.S.S.R. from the Security Council.

The French diplomat is a commander of the Legion of Honor and was awarded the United States Medal of Freedom with Silver Palm in recognition of his services to the Allied cause during the war. In the Chauvel family (Mme. Chauvel, who was LeMaire de Warzac d'Hermalle, is the daughter of a former Belgian Minister to China) there are two sons (Jean and Allen) and two daughters (Patricia and Beatrice). An amateur painter and a poet in his leisure moments, Chauvel published two limited-edition volumes of free verse entitled *Préludes* (1946) and *D'Une Eau Profonde* (1947). In his reading, stated Massolo, the United Nations delegate from France has been "rediscovering" Hemingway, Faulkner, and Saroyan. He is described by that writer as "a quiet man, not given to the pomp and ceremony attendant to the traditions of his office."

References

N Y Post May p37 Je 7 '49 por
U N Bul 6:330 Ap 1 '49
International Who's Who, 1950
World Biography (1948)

CHUTE, (BEATRICE) JOY (choōt) Jan. 3, 1913- Author

Address: b. and h. 450 E. 63d St., New York 21

JOY CHUTE

Reprinted from the *Wilson Library Bulletin*, Sept. 1950.

Boys who revel in the slangy, regular-fellow realism of the camp and sports stories, adults who feel that the novel's sensitive handling of a husband's reactions can only be autobiographical—these readers will be thunderstruck to learn that B. J. Chute (as her name appears on some of her writings) is a pretty girl named Joy. Her mastery of the masculine viewpoint is her own trade secret, and one she reserves for her trade. At home she is as charmingly feminine as her real name would indicate.

Beatrice Joy Chute, who dislikes her first name and never uses it, is the younger sister of Marchette Chute, author of *Shakespeare of London.* Joy was born January 3, 1913, to William Young and Edith Mary (Pickburn) Chute, at the family home near Minneapolis. Of her early childhood she says, "I can't remember not writing. My sisters and I played endless writing games, and I suppose that kind of background would be bound to influence a writer." With her sisters she shared the services of a devoted tutor who gave especial attention to the technique of English composition. She attended the Minneapolis public schools, graduating from West High School in 1929. This was followed by extension work at the University of Minnesota. She did secretarial work for her father, and later for the Property Owners' Association and the Minneapolis Better Housing Committee. Upon the father's death in 1939 the girls and their mother spent a year in California and then settled in New York City, where they now live.

Joy Chute's first appearance in print came in 1931, with a juvenile short story. She has continued to write short stories for *Boys' Life* and *Boys' Own Paper* (England), but nowadays the bulk of her short story writing is for adult readers. She is a frequent contributor to *Collier's, Saturday Evening Post, Good Housekeeping, Today's Woman, Cosmopolitan,* and

Fight Stories. She is represented in numerous anthologies. A *Collier's* story won both the quarterly and the annual award of the Bureau for Intercultural Education in 1947.

Miss Chute's first book, a juvenile, appeared in 1939. Sonja Wennerblad in *Library Journal* said, "*Blocking Back,* written in modern slang prose of today without being cheap, will be popular with boys of sixth to eighth grades." Next came *Shattuck Cadet* (1940). Anne Eaton wrote in the New York *Times:* "Attention is entirely on personal relations of a few students rather than the background of military school life, but a wholesome attitude toward sportsmanship is developed, which partly makes up for lack of atmosphere. . . .Better than the usual run of school and sports stories in which pranks predominate and personal rivalries are melodramatically intense." Of *Camp Hero* (1942) the *Christian Science Monitor* said, "A good story of camp life, with special emphasis upon sports, and importance of cooperation." *Shifts to the Right* (1944) and *Teen Age Parade* (1949) were collections of sports stories. Of the first one Mary G. Davis said in *Saturday Review of Literature,* "The boys who take part are natural, likable, and humorous. This should have wide reading."

The Fields Are White, published early in 1950, has had unusually good reviews for a first adult novel. Virginia Kirkus called it, "An often amusing, sometimes wise, novel of marriage and maturity . . . has manners as well as social graces." Anne Whitmore in *Library Journal:* "A thoroughly adult, cleverly written novel. . . .A seductive siren, an understanding, gracious wife, amusing conversation, a touch of satire, and the author's sure sense of detail, all keep the reader from becoming even slightly bored. This is a fine story of a modern marriage. Recommended." Vivian Wolfert in the New York *Times:* "Miss Chute is not the first one to say life begins at forty. But she is probably the

CHUTE, JOY—*Continued*

first to make it seem so easy." In spite of her novel's success, Miss Chute is not planning to desert the short story field. She is now working on a new one.

Joy and Marchette Chute, with their mother, have an apartment on New York's upper East Side. A third sister, also a writer, lives in Greenwich Village with her husband and two children. Joy Chute, devoted to her little niece and nephew, has a warm spot in her heart for all children. She gives two afternoons a week to the Police Athletic League, designed to provide recreation for New York's underprivileged youngsters, and she does volunteer work at the McMahon Memorial Center in Spanish Harlem, where temporarily homeless children are cared for. She made herself responsible for three war orphans under the Foster Parents' Plan for War Children. Aside from her writing and her volunteer social service work, she finds her chief interest in reading, cooking, and photography. It is difficult for her to name a favorite author, but she says, "If I were cast away on a desert island, I would probably want Shakespeare's works most."

CHUTE, MARCHETTE (GAYLORD) (chōōt mär-shĕt′) Aug. 16, 1909- Author *Address*: b. and h. 450 E. 63d St., New York 21

Reprinted from the *Wilson Library Bulletin*, Sept. 1950.

Scholarly biographies and commentaries on Shakespeare crowd our library shelves. The most impressive thing about many of them is the string of degrees attached to the authors' names. It remained for a young woman from Minnesota, with an unpretentious B.A. from her State university, to tackle the oft-tackled problem from a refreshingly new angle. Dis-

MARCHETTE CHUTE

carding three hundred years' accretion of academic retelling and interpretation, she went straight back to Shakespeare and his world as recorded by the men who shared that world with him. The biography she produced from those contemporary sources has created a literary sensation.

Marchette Chute's practical approach to history is characteristic, for the Chutes are a practical family. The three children, all girls, decided early in life that they would grow up into professional writers. All three of them did exactly that. Marchette is the middle sister, born August 16, 1909, to William Young and Edith Mary (Pickburn) Chute. The mother is English. The paternal grandfather went to pioneer Minnesota from New England. The father of the writing Chute sisters was a real estate man who played an important part in the growth of Minneapolis. The girls grew up at Hazelwood, a large country home eight miles outside the city. They had an excellent tutor who gave them a good grounding in grammar, and encouraged the ambition to write. Marchette was graduated from Central High School, Minneapolis, in 1925, and from the University of Minnesota in 1930. At college she received an award for an essay from Lambda Alpha Psi, and another for verse from *Minnesota Quarterly*.

Two years after graduation Miss Chute published her first book of verse for children. *Rhymes about Ourselves* (1932) was the first of a series of juveniles, usually verse, and illustrated by the author. *Rhymes about the Country* (1941) was followed by *Rhymes about the City* (1946), which Phyllis Whitney in *Book Week* considered "a volume to set beside Stevenson and Milne." Lois Palmer in *Library Journal* called it, "A charming collection of verse for very small children, illustrated by the author in perky and amusing silhouettes." *The Innocent Wayfaring* (1943) was prose, a romantic story of Chaucer's England. Ellen Buell said of it in the New York *Times Book Review*, "The whole is as light and enchanting as a midsummer song, yet somehow the aspects of fourteenth century life stay vividly in the mind. . . . Older girls who appreciate the compliment of good writing and mature humor will thoroughly enjoy Anne's attempt to live dangerously."

Miss Chute's first published work for adults was *The Search for God* (1941), an examination of the Scriptures for enduring values pertinent to modern living. The book received mixed reviews in the religious press. *Christian Century* said, "The findings of her intelligent mind are more enlightening than one might expect, though not strikingly original." From *Christian Science Monitor*: "No one can peruse this book without gaining a clearer understanding of the ceaseless search for God made by humanity, and the reward in the revelation of Christ Jesus."

In 1946 came the biography, *Geoffrey Chaucer of England*. W. W. Watt in *New Republic* reported, "This book is neither a typical popular biography nor an addition to Chaucerian scholarship. Miss Chute has written instead an informal, witty survey of Chaucer for literate adults who do not happen to be Chaucerians.

...The facts about Chaucer are pleasantly presented against a series of well-painted fourteenth century backdrops." The *New Yorker*: "Popular writing at its best, a fine introduction to the man and his time. The analyses of his major works . . . are a pleasure in themselves."

Shakespeare of London (1950), a Book-of-the-Month Club dual selection had an instantaneous success. Miss Chute's unique approach, her determination to strip away the mass of accumulated speculations and return to rock-bottom facts, seems as satisfactory to readers as it must have been to the author. Oscar James Campbell concludes a lengthy article in *Saturray Review of Literature* with these words: "The truth is that in *Shakespeare of London* Marchette Chute succeeds brilliantly in the task she set for herself. She has written a learned, wise, and vastly entertaining book about the colorful life of Shakespeare's world. The volume should become the cherished possession of everyone who takes delight in the works of our greatest poet." Harry Levin wrote in the New York *Times*: "Miss Chute has had the happy idea of basing her life-sized portrait entirely on contemporary evidence. From the facts as we know them . . . she has pieced together a readable and credible presentation of the man in his time."

Miss Chute, slim, hazel-eyed, brown-haired, crisply smart in dress, relaxed and pleasant in manner, takes her laurels lightly. She now lives in New York with her mother and her sister Joy. She belongs to the Royal Society of Arts, Phi Beta Kappa, and the P.E.N. Club. Her recreations are reading, the theater, and going for walks. She is presently engaged in completing a juvenile book on Shakespeare.

CLAYTON, MRS. JOSEPH E. *See* Sampson, Mrs. E. S.

COCHRAN, H(ORACE) MERLE July 6, 1892- United States Ambassador to the Republic of Indonesia

Address: b. United States Embassy, Djakarta, Java

When the United States of Indonesia—comprising the greater part of what was the Dutch East Indies—joined the company of sovereign nations on December 27, 1949, the Government of the young republic departed from usual diplomatic procedure by directly requesting that H. Merle Cochran be named as the first United States Ambassador to its capital, Djakarta (formerly Batavia). Cochran, a foreign service career man and financial expert for more than thirty years, was regarded as one of the strongest influences in the mediation which resulted in recognition by the Netherlands of Indonesian independence and cosovereignty in what is formally known as the union between the Kingdom of the Netherlands and the Republic of the United States of Indonesia. (In August 1950 its new name, the Republic of Indonesia was proclaimed.)

A native of Crawfordsville, Indiana, Horace Merle Cochran was born July 6, 1892, the son of Lewis W. and Martha Frances (Hutton) Cochran. He completed his education at the University of Arizona, where he received the B.S. degree in 1913 and the M.S. degree in the year following. He began the career in the foreign service of his country which—with one short interruption—has covered a span of more than thirty years.

His first appointment (in June 1914) was as United States vice- and deputy consul at Mannheim, Germany; by December he had been transferred to Nogales, Mexico, where he became vice-consul under the Act of Congress approved February 5, 1915. In 1916 he was detailed to Guatemala. In August of that year he resigned that post, after which he engaged in ranching for a year and a half in Mexico. Cochran re-entered the service of the State Department in February, 1918. He was assigned as clerk to the American Legation at Berne, Switzerland; in October he became United States vice-consul at Lugano, Italy; and from April 1919 until the end of the year he was stationed at Kingston, Jamaica. Sent to Port-au-Prince, Haiti, in February 1920, he was reassigned later in the year to Montreal, Canada, to serve as vice-consul until 1923.

Four years in the State Department at Washington followed, where he was concerned with many trade and financial problems. His next appointment (in 1927) kept him in Paris for three years as the United States consul. There, it is reported, he handled the consular commercial business with such marked competence that in 1930 he was transferred to the Bank for International Settlements, in its headquarters in Basel, Switzerland. In 1932 he was assigned to the American Embassy at Paris as foreign service officer (later ranking first secretary) and put in charge of the Treasury Department's negotiations with the French Government—the New York *Times* stated that he "played an important role in completing the French-British-United States tripartite monetary agreement" signed in 1936. (A full account of these negotiations may be found in an Alsop and Kintner article in the *Saturday Evening Post* for April 8, 1939, wherein Cochran is described as "actually . . . the No. 1 dollar man in Europe, who secretly played America's hand in the great money game.") The agreement concluded, Cochran took a brief vacation in Spain, where, caught by the outbreak of the Spanish Revolution, he was one of the first eleven foreigners to be safely evacuated. Upon returning to duty at Paris, Cochran was in 1937 attached to the League of Nations Committee for the Study of International Loan contracts for its second session.

On August 8, 1939, announcement was made that Cochran was being recalled to Washington to take charge of the Treasury Department's Stabilization Fund; one of its functions is the handling of international loans. Cochran occupied this post until the late summer of 1941, when he was sent on a special mission as financial adviser to the Chinese Nationalist Government at Chungking to help adjust the confused currency situation. Another special mission, this time to Argentina, followed in 1942. In December of the latter year Cochran em-

Wide World Photos

H. MERLE COCHRAN

barked on a new phase of his career when he
was appointed a foreign service inspector. "A
foreign service inspector," explained Mary
Van Rensselaer Thayer in the Washington
Post, "is a glorified policeman, accountant and
public relations expert rolled into one. He enjoys the closest approach to *carte blanche* of
any member of the Foreign Service.") In
the ensuing five or six years, Cochran visited,
with few exceptions, all of the United States
consular and diplomatic posts in the Central
and South Americas, Africa, Asia, and Europe.

Cochran was, in 1948, on an inspection visit
to the United States Embassy in Moscow when
he was recalled by the State Department to
become the American member of the three-man
Good Offices Committee of the United Nations.
The commission had been appointed in 1947 to
mediate differences between the Government of
the Netherlands and the Indonesian leaders in the
former Dutch East Indies. On the failure of
Dutch attempts to restore by force their sovereignty over these regions after World War
II, negotiations had been entered into with the
thought of establishing an Indonesian republic
within a Netherlands-Indies union under the
Netherlands Crown. The first agreement to this
end was terminated by the resumption of open
warfare in July 1947. Thereupon the United
Nations Security Council issued a cease-fire order
to both sides, and on the acceptance of its proposal to mediate, set up a three-man commission for that purpose. Renewed negotiations,
under the auspices of this commission, resulted
in the signature of the Renville agreement on
January 17, 1948. In October of that year,
however, a Communist uprising in the Indonesian Republic led to "police action" by the
Dutch. Protests in the United Nations were

vehement. Cochran, now (in 1948) chairman of
the U.N. commission, had meanwhile flown to
Batavia, and shortly he gave an interim report severely critical of the Netherlands. Later
in December the U.N. Security Council, "having taken note of" the Cochran report, called
upon both parties to "cease hostilities forth-
with" and on the Dutch to release their political prisoners.

On February 17, 1949, President Truman
nominated Cochran to be the first American
ambassador to Pakistan; the appointee, however, never assumed the duties of this post, because of the resumption of the Dutch-Indonesian
peace talks in which he had become an important figure. By May 1949, he and his associates had secured release of the Indonesian
leaders and restoration of the Republic's authority; and by late August a final conference
opened at The Hague. Negotiations, nevertheless, had almost foundered on the question of
the size of the Indonesian debt to the Netherlands, but the dispute was eventually settled on
the basis of a compromise worked out by a
special group of which Cochran was a member.
The Hague conference then concluded (November 2, 1949) with the proclamation of the United
States of Indonesia as an equal partner in a
new Netherlands-Indonesian Union resembling
the British Commonwealth of Nations, bound
by common loyalty to the Dutch Crown. On
December 27, Queen Juliana of the Netherlands
signed the act of transfer of authority, and
Indonesia became a nation, with Soekarno [47] as
its first president, and Mohammed Hatta [49] as
Premier. The next day the United States of
America extended formal *de jure* recognition to
the new Republic, and at the same time President Truman nominated Cochran as Ambassador
to Djakarta. Nomination of Cochran to
Djakarta, where he presented his credentials
on December 30, was at the specific request of
the Indonesians who, it is said, had come to
regard him "almost as a deliverer." On February 1, 1950, the Senate approved Truman's appointment of Cochran.

The marriage of Cochran to Barbara Parnell
occurred October 17, 1917. He belongs to the
American Club and Union Inter-Aliée in Paris,
and is a member of the Phi Delta Theta fraternity. Organizations to which he belongs
include the American Foreign Service Association and the American Academy of Political
Science. America's first envoy to Djakarta is
bald, clean-shaven and portly. He weighs no
less than 260 pounds—a story is told (in the
Washington *Post*) that when the Indonesians
expressed a desire to erect a statue of him,
"they desisted only when Mr. Cochran . . .
asked them to defer the honor on the grounds
that the work would cost them too much so
long as he retained his present girth."

References
    N Y Times p5 Ag 9 '39
    Washington (D.C.) Post p5B D 30 '49
    Who's Who in America, 1948-49
    Who's Who in Government, 1932-33

COOKE, MORRIS LLEWELLYN May 11, 1872- Consulting engineer in management; United States Government official

Address: b. c/o Water Resources Policy Commission, Washington 25, D.C.

The name of Morris ·Llewellyn Cooke, who was appointed January 3, 1950, by President Truman to head the Water Resources Policy Commission, is familiar to students of the American economic and political scene of the New Deal era. Cooke, an engineer, was director of the Water Resources Section of the National Resources Board in 1934, administrator of the Rural Electrification Administration from 1935 to 1937, and chairman of the Great Plains Commission in 1936-37. From 1928 to 1933 he was a trustee of the Power Authority of the State of New York.

Morris Llewellyn Cooke was born May 11, 1872, in Carlisle, Pennsylvania, one of the six sons in the family of William Harvey and Elizabeth Richmond (Marsden) Cooke (who also had two daughters). His father was a physician; a grandfather was a physician and clergyman, who, with his parents, influenced young Cooke greatly. His antecedents were Quakers and Presbyterians. While he was still young, the family moved to Bethlehem, in the same State—it was there he was principally reared. There was a family rule that the children take turns in bringing to the dinner table a subject of general conversational interest gleaned from the daily newspaper or other source. Cooke believes this was one of the factors which directed himself and three of his brothers toward public life.

After graduating in 1889 from Ulrich's, a private secondary school in Bethlehem, Cooke enrolled as a mechanical engineering student at Lehigh University, also in that town. At the end of his freshman year his course was interrupted by an official suspension for "some harmless daylight hazing." He thereupon turned to newspaper work, becoming a reporter for the Philadelphia *Press.* Later readmitted to Lehigh, he resumed newspaper work when his funds were exhausted in the middle of his junior year: he was first a reporter on the Denver *News* and then financial editor of the New York *Evening Telegram.* As a student he became a member of the Delta Phi fraternity and was manager of both the athletic and dramatic societies at the university. His degree of mechanical engineering was conferred upon him by the university in 1895.

Cooke's first job after graduating from college was as an apprentice machinist in Cramp's Shipyard in Philadelphia. Some months later he moved up to the position of journeyman machinist in the Southwark Foundry, a Philadelphia engine building plant. There, according to an article in the *New Republic* of February 12, 1945, his interest in scientific management began and he started a movement to reform inefficient practices in the shop. Eventually he formed a friendship with Frederick Taylor, the engineer known as the father of scientific management. Cooke accepted Taylor's theories with some reservations, maintaining that there is a human factor which

MORRIS LLEWELLYN COOKE

transcends mechanical efficiency. (Cooke joined the Taylor Society and was its president in 1927.) From his foundry job Cooke went to the Acetylene Company in Washington, D.C., as an engineer. During the Spanish-American War of 1899 he was an assistant engineer with the United States Navy.

After he left the Navy, Cooke began his career as a free-lance consultant. From 1899 to 1905 he was engaged in commercial organization work and from 1905 to 1911 he was a consulting engineer. Indicative of one kind of project he carried out during these years is the study of collegiate administrative methods in the United States and Canada he made in 1910 for the Carnegie Foundation for the Advancement of Teaching.

In 1911, evincing a strong interest in the problems of municipal government, he accepted the post of director of the Department of Public Works of Philadelphia, which he held until 1916. His jurisdiction comprised public utility regulation as well as the municipality's construction and repair program. In a court action which became widely known because it was the first such attempt in Pennsylvania, Cooke's office forced a substantial reduction in the rates charged by the Philadelphia Electric Company, especially to rural users. Cooke's pamphlet *Snapping Cords* (1915), on the "changing attitudes of American cities toward the utility problem," is also regarded as a landmark in the history of cheap power. During World War I, Cooke was at first chairman of the storage section of the War Industries Board of the Council for National Defense and a member of the Depot Board of the United States Army; and later he was executive assistant to the chairman of the United States Shipping Board.

Other articles by Cooke appeared in technical journals. He also edited several volumes, in-

COOKE, MORRIS LLEWELLYN—*Cont.*
cluding *Public Utility Regulation* (1922). Thus
in the forefront of the electrification movement, he became the choice of Governor Gif-
ford Pinchot of Pennsylvania to head his Giant
Power Survey in 1923. Its purpose was to
study the means by which cheap electric power
could be obtained for both home and industrial
use and the feasibility of using generating stations to obtain such power at the coal mines.
Cooke, who was occupied with it for the next
two years, regards it as having been the second
step on the road to the Federal rural electrification program. (The Philadelphia Electric
case he considers the first step.) The report
he issued proposed a central authority to plan
the State's future utilization of electric power
on an over-all basis (such as the later-developed
TVA). This report he supplemented in 1925
by his editorship of *Giant Power, Large Scale
Electrical Development as a Social Factor*
(*Annals of the American Academy of Political and Social Science,* Vol. 118).

Governor Franklin D. Roosevelt of New
York, on the suggestion of Governor Pinchot,
chose Cooke as a trustee of the Power Authority he established to consider the marketing of power from the St. Lawrence River to
small consumers. Shortly after he became
President of the United States, Roosevelt called
upon Cooke to fill the chairmanship of the Mississippi Valley Committee, a temporary agency
of the Public Works Administration created to
survey the economic realities and possibilities
of that valley's terrain. The recommendations
of the committee, incorporated in a document
known as the Mississippi Valley Report, dealt
with flood control, agriculture, power development, reforestation, navigation, and the elimination of pollution of the waters, outlining in
a twenty-year program the measures essential
to preservation of a vital economy in the region
under study. They set forth Cooke's belief that
the problems of an entire drainage basin should
be considered as one project; that flood control should begin where soil erosion starts—in
improper methods of cultivation; and that
dams should be built with water needs (electrical and recreational) as well as flood control needs always in mind.

The Mississippi Valley Report was later
amplified by the report of the Water Resources
Committee of the National Resources Board,
which drew up a series of public works projects
designed to achieve the same objectives on a
national scale. Cooke was director of this
Water Resources Committee in 1934. In 1935
by executive order the Rural Electrification
Administration was created. This body was designed to finance the construction of electricity
distribution systems in rural areas lacking
them, with loans authorized for farmer cooperative associations, municipalities, and private utility companies. From the institution of
the program in May 1935 until early 1937
Cooke was its administrator.

While still with REA, Cooke was appointed
to the leadership of the Great Plains Committee, set up after the drought of the summer of 1936. The report submitted by the
committee recommended that for administrative

purposes the drought area be divided into sub-
areas, within which farming and grazing methods should be adapted to the nature of the soil,
and that the authorities take into consideration
land and water conservation needs when making
or revising land tenure, tax, health, and relief
laws, all having a bearing on agricultural practices.

During 1940-41 Cooke was a technical consultant in the labor division of the Office
of Production Management, where he initiated
the program of subcontracting military orders
to small business in order to speed up defense
production and to revive the economies of
"ghost towns" which developed from the concentration of defense orders in the hands of
large manufacturers. In 1942 he was sent on
two foreign missions, one to Mexico to ad-
judicate the conflicting claims of the American
oil companies and the Mexican Government
arising from Mexico's expropriation of foreign
oil properties in 1938; the other to Brazil as
head of the American Technical Mission to determine how Brazil could increase her contribution to the hemisphere defense effort. Out of
the latter grew his book *Brazil on the March*
(1944), which indicates economic progress possible to that country through development of
her communications system, electric power and
mineral wealth with the aid of American technical assistance and investment capital. Cooke
was chairman of the War Labor Board's panel
mediating an anthracite coal miners' strike in
1943, and in 1946-47 he was a member of a
committee appointed to survey the patent
system.

In January 1950 Cooke was appointed by
President Truman to the chairmanship of the
Water Resources Policy Commission, a temporary seven-man committee set up to consider
Federal participation in water resources projects and to make recommendations for a coordinated long-term policy. Stressing the need
for comprehensive and consistent policies, the
President requested the commission to complete its study by December 1, 1950, and to
submit interim recommendations on urgent issues in time for action by Congress in 1950.
Chairman Cooke stated in a press release that
the commission would hold a series of public
hearings across the country, concentrating on
nation-wide problems such as the economic
changes entailed in water resource development;
the relationship among water conservation, irrigation, and public and private power development; relation between use of surface water for
irrigation and storage of water underground;
costs of water development in relation to potential benefits.

The consulting engineer in the decade of the
1940's campaigned to stir professional men to
their responsibilities as leaders in public affairs. He has expressed the conviction that it
is more important to be a good citizen than
a good engineer, and he has defined politics as
"just one name for those efforts, good or bad,
by which individuals or groups persuade the
community to undertake any kind of organized
activity by means of government." This is a
theme which has appeared with increasing frequency in the many articles he has written

over the years for professional periodicals and general magazines. Among his books not mentioned earlier are *Our Cities Awake* (1918) and, in collaboration with Philip Murray '49, *Organized Labor and Production* (1940). He also edited several volumes of the *Annals of the American Academy of Political and Social Science.*

Cooke, who is a fellow of the American Association for the Advancement of Science and of the American Society of Mechanical Engineers, holds an honorary D.Sc. from Lehigh University, and has been decorated with the Czechoslovak Order of the White Lion and the Mexican Order of the Aztec Eagle. He is a member of the Franklin Institute and of the Masaryk Academy (Prague), and is an honorary member of Sigma Xi. His clubs are the University and Engineers, both in Philadelphia, the Engineers in New York, and the Cosmos in Washington. In politics he is a Democrat, and he calls himself a "nomad Episcopalian." He married Eleanor Bushnell Davis in 1900; Mrs. Cooke shares her husband's interests, and also his dislike of airplanes. Five feet nine inches in height, the engineer weighs 170 pounds; he has brown eyes, and his white hair formerly was black. Tennis and squash have been his sports for most of his life. He has indicated that he has gone to the "deep woods" one year in three, and has made several trips to Europe. Cooke has been described as giving an impression of sternness and aloofness until he begins to talk about the project he has in hand.

References

Am Pol Sci R 42:431-47 Je '48
Bsns W p22-3 Je 8 '35 por
New Repub 112:220-3 F 12 '45 por
PM p9 Mr 5 '41 por
Scholastic 29:25 S 26 '36 por
Survey G 26:145-9 Mr '37
Time 40:90 D 7 '42 por
International Who's Who, 1949
Who's Who in America, 1950-51
Who's Who in Engineering, 1948
Who's Who in the East (1948)

COOPER, JOHN SHERMAN Aug. 23, 1901- United States Government official

Address: b. c/o Department of State, Washington 25, D.C.; c/o Gardner, Morrison, and Rogers, Woodward Bldg., Washington, D.C.; h. 524 N. Main St., Somerset, Ky.

After representing Kentucky for approximately two years in the United States Senate, lawyer-administrator John Sherman Cooper, Republican, was appointed a delegate to the United Nations in September 1949. Six months later President Truman strengthened bipartisan support of his foreign policy by naming Republican Cooper consultant to the Secretary of State for the meetings of the North Atlantic Pact nations and the Foreign Ministers' Council held in May of that year. Following the cessation of World War II, in which he had served with General Patton's Third Army,

Cooper was legal adviser on the repatriation of displaced persons in the Third Army Zone.

John Sherman Cooper was born August 23, 1901, in Somerset, Pulaski County, in the mountainous part of Kentucky. His parents were John Sherman and Helen Gertrude (Tartar) Cooper. Educated in public schools, the youth attended Kentucky's Centre College at Danville in 1918-19, and received his B.A. from Yale in 1923. During the terms 1923-25 he studied at Harvard Law School, and in 1928 was admitted to the bar.

In 1928 Cooper was elected to the lower house of the Kentucky legislature. At the expiration of this term in 1930, the Republican began eight years of service as county judge of Pulaski County—an office which, like that once occupied by President Truman in Missouri, was administrative rather than judicial, corresponding to a district supervisor or county commissioner. While filling this position Cooper was made a trustee of the University of Kentucky in 1935; he remained on that board until 1946.

After an unsuccessful campaign for the governorship of Kentucky in 1939, Cooper resumed the practice of law in his home town, a community with a population of 6,154 in the 1940 census. The forty-one-year-old lawyer enlisted in the Army as a private in 1942, went through Officer Candidate School, and received a commission as second lieutenant at Fort Custer, Michigan, in 1943. He served overseas twenty months with General Patton's '43 Third Army, taking part in five major campaigns, as it fought its way across France, Luxembourg, and Germany. He had attained the rank of captain. After hostilities ended, he was legal adviser on the repatriation of displaced persons in the Third Army Zone. Later Cooper was put in charge of reorganizing the German judicial system in Bavaria. Meanwhile, in 1945, he was elected circuit judge of the Twenty-Eighth Judicial District of Kentucky, *in absentia.* Cooper remained in Germany until early in the following year.

According to reporter Carroll Kilpatrick, (San Francisco *Chronicle*), John Sherman Cooper "has been crusading for a vigorous foreign policy ever since he marched across France and Germany." A few months after taking up his judicial duties in 1946, the war veteran resigned to run for election to fill the unexpired term of Democratic Senator A. B. ("Happy") Chandler '43, who had resigned to become Baseball Commissioner. Republican Cooper was elected with 53 per cent of the vote—a 41,823-vote margin over his Democratic opponent—at a time when his party also gained two House seats, and already held the governorship of his State. Thus Cooper became the third Republican Senator in Kentucky's history, the first in twenty-two years.

Entering the Senate in January 1947 when the Republicans, for the first time in sixteen years, were the majority party, Cooper soon proved himself an independent in his votes. The first test placed him in the Morse-Aiken-Tobey-Langer liberal wing of the party, in opposition to the conservative leadership of

JOHN SHERMAN COOPER

Senator Taft '48. In what the New York *Times* described as "one of the most complicated legislative achievements of the Eightieth Congress"—the bill extending the President's full wartime control over exports and certain imports—was brought through the Senate without a record vote by the new Senator from Kentucky in July 1947. Altogether, Cooper acquired a name as "an able and vigorous supporter of the bipartisan foreign policy." May and June 1947 he bolted his party by voting against cutting taxes. "I have become convinced," he told the Senate, "that there will be no final peace, there will be no restoration of the world's economy, until we exercise the full leadership we have assumed. It is idle to talk of peace, and our adherence to a world order, unless we are willing this year to make some sacrifices in terms of money to support it." Cooper had previously charged the Truman Administration with contributing to inflationary trends by "resistance to reduction of expenditures" and "failure to provide for proper debt management."

In the first and second sessions of the Eightieth Congress (which first convened in January 1947) Senator Cooper was a member of the District of Columbia, Public Works, and Judiciary committees. His votes on international measures were as follows: in favor of the Greek-Turkish aid bill, emergency relief to France, Italy, and Austria (both in 1947), the Marshall Plan, and admittance of displaced persons (both in 1948). On labor issues: for outlawing portal-to-portal pay suits, against curbs on industry-wide bargaining, for the Taft-Hartley bill (1947). He was against reimposing the excess-profits tax, for overriding the 1948 tax-cut veto (1947). In August 1948 he voted against a compromise housing bill, containing no subsidies for low-rent and slum-

clearance projects. That year (April) he voted for Federal aid to education, but was against earmarking a portion for private and church schools. He was in favor of the Republican anti-inflation bill, against the confirmation of Lililenthal to the AEC, against the second Truman reorganization plan for the government (all in 1947).

In October 1948 Joseph Alsop in the New York *Herald Tribune* described Cooper as "the sole modern-minded Republican Senator up for re-election." He was also the only candidate on whom Presidential nominee Dewey '44 "really heaped laudations" on his Southern tour, reported Ernest K. Lindley (*Newsweek*), and he was backed by the Louisville *Courier-Journal*. At the election, however, Cooper lost the election to Virgil Chapman, for twenty-two years a Representative, in the Democrats' conservative ranks. "It was a matter of general regret," wrote the New York *World-Telegram*, "that a most promising career was terminated by his (Cooper's) defeat." Cooper remained in Washington to practice law—he became a partner in the law firm of Gardner, Morrison, and Rogers.

"Hailed by Democrats and Republicans alike," according to the New York *Herald Tribune* correspondent, was President Truman's appointment in September 1949 of ex-Senator Cooper to the United States delegation to the fourth session of the U.N. General Assembly, along with Warren R. Austin '44, Ambassador-at-large Philip C. Jessup '48, and Eleanor Roosevelt '49. (John Foster Dulles '44, whom Cooper succeeded, had resigned to serve as Senator from New York.) The choice was "certain to be universally applauded," commented the Washington *Post*, which described Cooper as "a member of conspicuous ability and integrity." The new delegate's first policy statement was a speech to the U.N. administrative and budgetary committee in which he said, "There have been substantial improvements in economic conditions claimed by many states which are not reflected in the scale of contributions"; he urged that revisions be made accordingly which would lower his country's contribution quota from 39.79 per cent of the U.N.'s $44,315,000 budget to one third. "His service as a United States delegate," reported the New York *Herald Tribune*, "was recognized as a task expertly fulfilled."

It was announced in March 1950 that Cooper would be an adviser to Secretary of State Acheson '49, to help prepare for, and to be a consultant at, the London meetings of the North Atlantic Council and the conferences with British and French leaders that May. Editorial comment in the *Herald Tribune* lauded the appointment as an effort on the part of the Administration "to repair the breaches that have been made in bipartisanship." On being sworn in on April 3, 1950, the Kentuckian said, "It is proposed that the Democratic and Republican parties shall make in the national interest a continuous good-faith effort to reach the greatest possible measure of agreement by consultation and debate before action is taken. Such an effort requires initiative on both sides." In urging national backing for the Secretary of

State, Cooper declared, "Bipartisan foreign policy does not preclude disagreement and debate, but does mean a true interchange of information and a good-faith effort to agree on matters affecting the security of the country."

Expressing disagreement with the proposal of former President Hoover that the United Nations be reorganized to exclude the Communist nations, Cooper stated: "To do what he suggested would take away all hope of peace and lead to a freezing of the present situation. . . . Finally, it would mean the United States would not be living up to its commitments in the United Nations Charter." In a press interview before his departure for the London conference, the Republican adviser warned that the decisive hour in the "cold war" was at hand. To build strength against communism he recommended: closer political organization of Europe, including Germany, with North America; a speeding-up of the defensive strength of Europe and the United States on a mutual defense rather than a nationalistic basis; the adoption of a European payments union, early removal of trade barriers, the relaxing of controls on Germany together with promotion of her industry and trade, increase in United States imports, and post-Marshall Aid planning. Emphasizing his conviction that Germany should not be rearmed, Cooper expressed the opinion that there could be no effective economic reorganization or security without that country.

John Sherman Cooper has been described as "handsome, modest, self-effacing." He has a hesitant manner of speaking. For his war service he was awarded the Bronze Star. Cooper's wife, whom he married in March 1944, is the former Evelyn Pfaff. Since his return from World War II Cooper has been a director of the Citizens National Bank in his home town, and of the Centre College Alumni Association. His church is the Baptist. He is a member of the Kentucky State Bar Commission and has joined Rotary International, the American Legion, and the Veterans of Foreign Wars. His fraternity is Beta Theta Pi.

References

N Y Herald Tribune X p57 O 30 '49
N Y Times p1 Mr 29 '50
San Francisco (Cal.) Chronicle p1 My 7 '50
U S News 21:70 N 15 '46
Washington (D.C.) Post p1 S 15 '49
Congressional Directory (2nd ed. 1948)
Who's Who in America, 1950-51
World Biography (1948)

COOPER, LOUISE FIELD Mar. 8, 1905-
Author

Address: h. Woodbridge, Conn.

Reprinted from the *Wilson Library Bulletin*, Dec. 1950.

"I have been lucky," said Louise Field Cooper, author of *The Boys from Sharon*, the April 1950 Book-of-the-Month Club selection. "Time and money have never been important to my writing. I have always been able to find time for fiction—and I have never had to depend in any way upon the money I earned by writing. I know I would not be able to complete my novels without the assistance I have at home." She has never attempted to paint herself as a typical housewife developing her gifts despite a daily humdrum round.

Blue-eyed, with light hair and a slight figure, Mrs. Cooper is the daughter of Francis Elliott Field and Anna (Dunning) Field. She was born in Hartford, Connecticut, March 8, 1905, of English and French Huguenot extraction. Hers was a family following the classic New England pattern, including sea captains engaged for generations in the China trade. When she had finished at Miss Porter's boarding school in Farmington, she took the usual trip to France and Italy with a school roommate. Then for a year she worked as society staff member on the Hartford *Times*. This job, she has observed, received no supervision from her parents; the *Times*, a Democratic paper, never entered the Field home.

Later Louise Field sold books in Brentano's Hartford shop and then married James Wayne Cooper, an attorney now associated with a New Haven law firm. The Coopers live in a rambling brick house on twenty hillside acres just above the Litchfield Turnpike in Woodbridge, Connecticut. There they have raised three children of their own: Field, a nineteen-year-old sophomore at Radcliffe; James Nicoll, fifteen, at Westminster School in Simsbury; and Peter Brintnal, ten.

Included also in the household is Jackie Fu, a Chinese boy of fourteen, whose father is head of Formosa University. Jackie's family paid a visit to Yale two years ago, and when they went home he stayed on with the Coopers to finish his schooling. He also is a Westminster pupil. "And he is by far the most modern-minded member of the family," Mrs. Cooper commented in an interview with the New Haven *Register*. "He is our authority on movies, pin-ups, comic books, and fast automobiles—a splendid addition to a New England household."

About fifteen years ago (1935) Mrs. Cooper submitted her first short story manuscript to the *New Yorker*. It was accepted and she has contributed with some regularity ever since. The magazine now has first call on all her short stories. Her first novel, *The Lighted Box*, appeared during the war. It was followed in 1943 by *The Deer on the Stairs* (highly praised generally by reviewers) and in 1947 by *Summer Stranger*, called by E. C. Benet, "an excellent study of summer resort life, done with meticulous detail, unexpected depth, and a surprise in the way of a grim ending."

A collection of her short stories has been published under the title, *Love and Admiration*. Mrs. Cooper herself is dissatisfied with *The Deer on the Stairs*, which was in print only about a year after her first novel. She feels that for proper regeneration of creative and critical abilities she must wait at least three years between publication of novels.

Working three hours each morning in a small studio shed (a routine interrupted only by the children's holidays), she writes with what critics have called "fine, sensitive skill" and "a keen,

LOUISE FIELD COOPER

cool eye for the workings of many minds." Because all her work reflects the life she knows, the Cooper characters are upper middle-class people, enjoying comfortable lives and struggling, for the most part, through only minor tempests and she portrays her fiction so deftly that most acquaintances are convinced, despite her denials, that they can identify almost every character in her books.

"All I write about," Mrs. Cooper has volunteered, "are the things I know myself—and I've never had very much happen to me. Besides, I believe political or moral purpose, regardless of how sincere, makes a poor basis for fiction." It would be presumptuous of her, she feels, to write on the grand scale or to attempt to solve the world's problems.

Because she depicts social satire of a most delicate and subtle order, Mrs. Cooper has a greater natural kinship with such British novelists as Virginia Woolf, Henry Green, Evelyn Waugh, and Gilbert White than with most modern American writers. She does admire William Faulkner and Eudora Welty for their perceptiveness and John Hersey's talents as displayed in *The Wall*; the Danish woman, Isak Dinesen, and Marcel Proust are also favorites.

The miasma in which the reading public finds itself plunged by both authors and publishers could be lessened, she has said, if publishers would select fewer and better manuscripts. "There is no balance and often no discrimination in what is passed on to the public."

Since *The Boys from Sharon* was a Book-of-the-Month selection, Mrs. Cooper has been in increased demand for radio programs, publishers' meetings, etc., but she has made it a rule to let nothing interfere with her writing. As hobbies, she enjoys gardening, preferably of the indoor kind, and traveling. Since her household includes a Great Dane, several cats, some domesticated mallard ducks, "and a chicken or two," it may be assumed that life on the

twenty acres in Woodbridge is far from routine, dull, or monotonous. After a summer trip to England in 1950 she is working on another novel.

CORDIER, ANDREW W(ELLINGTON)
(côr-dēr)   Mar. 3, 1901-   United Nations official

Address: b. Executive Office of the Secretary General, United Nations, New York; h. 6 Merrivale Rd., Great Neck, N.Y.

The executive assistant to Secretary General Trygve Lie of the U.N., Andrew W. Cordier has been on the U.N. Secretariat since 1946. While holding a position as expert on international security for the United States Department of State (1944-46), he became technical expert and United States delegate to UNCIO in 1945, that same year receiving the titles of chief of section and adviser to the executive-secretary of the Preparatory Commission. Previously he had been a member of the faculty of Manchester College in Indiana, and of Indiana University.

Andrew Wellington Cordier is a native of Canton, Ohio. He was born March 3, 1901, to Wellington J. and Ida Mae (Anstine) Cordier. (Their other son is Ralph Waldo.) Young Cordier went to high school in the Ohio town of Hartville, from which he was graduated at the age of seventeen as valedictorian of his class; in high school football he had been quarterback. In 1918 he enrolled at Manchester College, Indiana. After one year of study there Cordier for two years taught at Greentown (Ohio) High School: he was instructor in Latin, history, and mathematics, and football and dramatics coach. At the same time he continued his college studies and was graduated from Manchester with the B.A. degree in 1922.

To obtain his M.A. degree in 1923 and his Ph.D. in 1926, Cordier went to the University of Chicago, where he was a teaching fellow in 1924-25. The subject of his Ph.D. thesis was the *Reconstruction of Southern France after the Abigensian Crusades.* Having returned to Manchester College in 1923, he remained a member of its faculty until 1944, first as associate professor of history until 1927, then as chairman of the department of history and political science.

His teaching career was not confined to the Manchester campus; he was also lecturer on the social sciences for Indiana University from 1929 to 1944. During 1937-38 he was forum leader of the Federal adult education program and in 1942 regional educational director of the OPA. During his chairmanship of the Republican Committee of Wabash County, Indiana, from 1932 to 1936, he had the satisfaction of seeing the Republicans win every office in the county, even though Democrats were victorious in many normally Republican sections of the State at that time. Most of Cordier's activities required speech-making—he is said to have delivered as many as three hundred lectures on various subjects in a single year. Cordier conducted his campaign on a platform based upon "an objective approach" to all county, State, and national issues, and urged his Democratic rivals to do the same. Arguing that the electorate should have the opportunity to choose between two well-conceived programs, he opposed partisan politics based upon "the empty practices of defense and attack."

Further studies took Cordier abroad, to the Graduate Institute of International Studies in Geneva, Switzerland, during 1930-31. Traveling in Europe in 1928, 1938 and 1939, and in South America in 1941, he made surveys in the Sudetenland, Danzig, and the Chaco country. In 1944 he accepted a post on the staff of the United States Department of State as adviser on international security. In this capacity he was technical expert on the United States delegation to the United Nations Conference on International Organization at San Francisco in 1945. The same year saw him a section chief on the Preparatory Commission for the United Nations, in London; on that commission he became adviser to the executive secretary. Cordier performed the same service for the president of the first session of the General Assembly held in the English capital in 1946. In March of that year he assumed the post of executive assistant to the Secretary General of the United Nations, Trygve Lie, having joined the staff of the Secretariat at Lie's request.

Sometimes designated as "The Man on the Left of the President" (*United Nations World,* November 1948) as compared with Lie, who always sits on the president's right at Assembly Sessions, Cordier acts as "middleman and peacemaker, trying to bring together countries bitterly at odds over a tough issue," in the words of the New York *Herald Tribune* (January 2, 1948). Besides acting as mediator among the delegates to the United Nations to facilitate smooth operation of the Assembly, he charts the meetings, outlines the programs, and supervises the U.N. staff, which consists of approximately 3,200 persons drawn from the member nations. His immediate staff comprises fifty men and women. Six aides or lieutenants, the secretaries of the Assembly Committees, meet with Cordier each afternoon to plan the next day's work and to adjust any difficulties which may have arisen.

As chief coordinator of U.N. activities, Cordier is responsible for the coordination of the entire program of the Secretariat and for the maintenance of liaison with the fifty-nine member nations. He organizes and directs the General Assembly on the Secretariat level and coordinates the implementation of decisions and recommendations of U.N. organs. In the field of external coordination, among other tasks, he is responsible for the coordination of all political missions, which include U.N. activities in Korea, Indonesia, India, Pakistan, the Balkans, Palestine, and the Italian colonies. In his capacity as coordinator he is also chairman of the U.N. publications board, which controls the great volume of printed literature of the organization.

He also serves as principal secretary to the "Little Assembly" or Interim Committee. He must have a command of the rules of procedure of the General Assembly and their possible

United Nations Official Photo.
ANDREW W. CORDIER

interpretations as well as the terms of the U.N. Charter and previously passed resolutions which may relate to topics under discussion. But, Cordier has remarked, "Remembering things has always been easy for me" (*PM,* September 7, 1947.) His co-workers "regard him as a demon parliamentarian," according to the *United Nations World.* It is told that a dispute once arose in the Assembly at a time when Cordier, then ill, was at home; when a delegate called him on the telephone for information, Cordier thought for a moment, then quoted the exact number of the applicable rule.

Cordier said (in September 1947) that the United Nations was wasting more than one-fourth its time wrangling over matters of procedure (the New York *Times*). It is his duty to try to locate the crux of such troubles, and to create a means of eliminating them. Numerous resolutions await the executive assistant when he returns to his desk after the close of a session.

No regular office hours are possible for the executive assistant, for his duties extend beyond a routine schedule. He must, for example, greet visiting celebrities, regardless of the hour of their arrival; he attends important luncheons and other social functions and accompanies Trygve Lie on his travels preparatory to U.N. General Assembly meetings. With the launching of NBC's weekly radio program *Your United Nations* from June 18 through September 10, 1949, Cordier accepted the role of commentator, it being his expressed belief that "the principles of the United Nations Charter can best be realized if they are supported by an informed people."

Cordier's faith in the work of the U.N. has been given frequent expression. He thinks the organization is succeeding "far better than most people of the world know but perhaps not as well as the peoples of the world suffering from

CORDIER, ANDREW W.—*Continued*

two wars deserve" (New York *Times,* September 26, 1949). The executive assistant has also said, "I don't believe in the inevitability of any given course of human conduct. It is possible to shape our own ends, and we must do so through the United Nations. Given faith, time, patience, intelligence, and energy, we can get results" (New York *Post,* April 21, 1947). It is his conviction that "the hundred million dollars spent so far in the creation of this organization are the best investment humanity has made" (*PM,* September 7, 1947).

Organizations in which Cordier holds membership include the American Political Science Association, American Historical Association, and the American Association of the United Nations—he is a member of the board of directors of the latter body. In 1946 the LL.D. degree was conferred on him by his alma mater, Manchester College. He met his wife, the former Dorothy Elizabeth Butterbaugh, while she was a student at Manchester College. They were married May 23, 1924, and have two children, Lowell Eugene and Louise Lanette. Cordier, who enjoys travel, would like to visit Asia. Among his recreations are listening to symphonic music and reading historical novels. A golfer himself, he is a football and baseball fan. An interviewer once described him as a "cheerful, blue-eyed man," of massive build.

References

N Y Herald Tribune p8 Ja 2 '48 por
N Y Post Mag p27 Ap 21 '47 por
PM Mag p3 S 7 '47 por
U N Bul 1:5 D 24 '46; 2:23 Ja 14 '47
U N World 2:62-3 N '48 por

Who's Who in America, 1948-49
Who's Who in the East (1948)
Yearbook of the United Nations, 1947-48

CRAIG, GEORGE N(ORTH) Aug. 6, 1909- Veterans organization official; lawyer
Address: c/o American Legion, 777 N. Meridian St., Indianapolis 6, Ind.; h. 810 S. Walnut St., Brazil, Ind.

When the American Legion, at its thirty-first national convention in September 1949, elected George N. Craig as national commander for 1949-50, it broke precedent in placing a veteran of World War II in that office. An Indiana lawyer, Craig was discharged from the United States Army in 1946, after nearly four years of active combat service, in which his rank had advanced to lieutenant colonel of infantry.

Born in Brazil, Indiana, on August 6, 1909, George North Craig is the only son (he has two sisters) of Bernard C. and Clo (Branson) Craig. His ancestry is Scotch-Irish; he traces his American lineage back several generations, the family having settled first in Virginia, then moved to Kentucky, Missouri, and Indiana. His father is an attorney. While attending Brazil High School, young Craig enrolled at the Culver Military Academy for three summer sessions (1923-25). In 1928 he graduated from high school (where his chief extracurricular activities were wrestling and crew) and entered

the University of Arizona for a year of prelaw study. His legal education was received at Indiana University, where his other major courses were in political science and history. Outside the classroom, he played football, served on the inter-fraternity council, and was elected president of the Delta Chi fraternity and of Delta Theta Phi, honorary law fraternity. One of his law professors was Paul V. McNutt [40], who years later was to nominate him for his present office in the American Legion. Craig was graduated from the university in 1932 with a degree of LL.B.

Admitted to the Indiana bar immediately after obtaining his degree, Craig began to practice in his home town of Brazil. Exclusive of his war service years, as of 1950 he has spent fifteen years at law practice—he has called himself a "plain old country lawyer." The young attorney entered the United States Army Reserve Corps simultaneously with beginning his law practice in June 1932; ten years later, on March 12, 1942, he was called into active service in World War II.

Entering the Army as first lieutenant in the 318th Infantry, Craig became successively platoon leader; battalion executive officer; battalion command, assistant G3, Eightieth Division; G3 air, assistant, Twentieth Corps. He was sent to Fort Benning, Georgia, where he graduated from the basic and advanced infantry schools; he then went on to courses at the Command and General Staff School at Fort Leavenworth, Kansas, and subsequently to the Assault School at Fort Belvoir, Virginia. With the Eightieth Division Craig was ordered overseas in July 1944. For the remainder of the war that division was attached to General Patton's Third Army. Landing on Omaha Beach on August 6, 1944, Craig saw action in Northern France, the Rhineland, the Ardennes, and in Germany. Speaking of his division's record, Craig has said, "The Eightieth Division was in constant contact with the enemy from the sixth day of August 1944 until May 7, 1945, during which period they captured approximately 175,000 German prisoners." The infantry officer was discharged from the army on January 17, 1946, with the rank of lieutenant colonel; he had won four campaign star decorations, including the Bronze Star and Oak Leaf Cluster, and the Croix de Guerre from France.

Returning to his law office in Brazil, the veteran joined Clay County Post 2 of the American Legion and became active in local service programs projected by the organization. He was elected commander of his post, southern vice-commander for the department of Indiana; and as Indiana's representative on the national executive committee of the Legion, he acted as liaison chairman between that group and the Legion's national rehabilitation commission. According to the public relations division of the Legion, Craig first attracted nation-wide American Legion attention when in 1947-48 he led the protest in the discrimination against veterans in the sale of homes in the Federal housing project in Knox, an Indiana town. In the course of this campaign he authored a resolution (adopted by the national executive committee) condemning the failure of public housing officials to provide housing for veterans, and testified before Congressional committees and in the Federal court.

In the course of his campaign for the office of national commander, Craig visited local Legion posts in thirty-three states, traveling 108,000 miles in ten months. His three competitors were also World War II veterans. Nominated by McNutt at the Legion's "most orderly" convention, held in Philadelphia from August 29 to September 1, 1949, Craig's victory became apparent in the first ballot, whereupon, following a motion, he was declared unanimously elected. (His annual salary as national commander is $15,000, with $35,000 for expenses.) Commenting editorially on "the changing of the guard" in the Legion, the New York *Herald Tribune* expressed the possibility that "under new management the Legion will put the responsibilities of veterans as citizens first, and give their whole thought, in the words of their new commander, to 'promoting and safeguarding those principles necessary for our continued strength and prosperity as a nation'."

More than one hundred resolutions were adopted by the Legion at the Philadelphia convention, which was attended by 3,344 accredited delegates. Among the resolutions were opposition to more lenient immigration laws, and to payment of veterans' benefits to former members of the merchant marine and the Red Cross; approval of a civilian defense and disaster service plan, of keeping the atomic energy program under civilian control, and of a national veterans pension bill. They also advocated aid to the Chinese Nationalist army, the outlawing of the Communist party in the United States, and the establishment of a national air academy.

The new Legion head began his term of office by pledging, as quoted by the *Christian Science Monitor*, that he accepted the responsibility of "making the Legion an important voice in the nation's political and social life." At one of his first public functions as national commander, Craig described the major activity program adopted by the organization for 1950. This is a national campaign for self-initiated and self-supported community development programs "designed to bring back to modern America the pioneer virtues of hard work and thrift." To test the possibilities of the program, it was tried in Burnet, Texas, a town with a population of 2,500. In twenty months, through individual and community action "sparked by the local American Legion post," fifty-nine new businesses were established and 325 new jobs created. Craig emphasized that this was achieved without Federal aid or advice, and declared that the Legion's aim was to help the American people "retain their powers of self-government rooted in the soil of industrial freedom."

On the same occasion Craig was quoted by the *Christian Science Monitor* as saying that the American Legion "does not countenance violence in any situation short of war," and would not give its "sanction to counterdemonstrations" against "pro-Communist demonstrations." The Legion, Craig was quoted as adding, "does not propose to make martyrs of the

Noble Bretzman

GEORGE N. CRAIG

subversive elements in this country." Speaking at the American Federation of Labor convention in St. Paul on October 7, Craig was reported by the New York *Times* as having injected a note of controversy into the convention when he declared that the American Legion wanted a state of welfare in America, but not a "Welfare State," and that too many demands were being made upon the Government for "services for which it was never designed."

Among other American Legion policies on which Craig has given public expression since his election are opposition to national health insurance, the support of universal military training in place of continuation of the peacetime draft laws, and opposition to recommendations for reorganizing the Veterans Administration contained in the Hoover Commission Report. When American Consul General Angus Ward was held by Chinese Communists in November 1949, Craig issued a statement criticizing the State Department's handling of the case, demanding that United States troops be sent to rescue Ward, and protesting "contemplated recognition of the Chinese Communist regime." On Christmas Day he launched the Legion's "Tide of Toys" campaign, designed to send millions of American toys as gifts from the children of this country to the children of Europe. Projected by Craig in October 1949 was a new Legion program, a two-day "All-American Conference" which was held January 28-29, 1950, in New York, and at which representatives of fifty-eight national organizations met and voted to establish a "permanent organization to combat Communism in the United States."

Craig is a member of the B.P.O.E., the Masons, the Eagles, and the Brazil Chamber of Commerce; he "enrolls" annually in Red Cross and the Salvation Army. In his political allegiance he is Republican, in his church mem-

CRAIG, GEORGE N.—*Continued*

bership a Methodist. Mrs. Craig is the former Kathryn L. Heiliger; married on August 29, 1931, they have two children, John David and Margery Ellen. The Legionnaire's favorite recreations are fishing and hunting. Five feet, eleven inches tall, and weighing 185 pounds, with brown hair and eyes, he has been called "second only to Mr. McNutt as being the handsomest national commander."

Reference

N Y World-Telegram p12 O 8 '49

CRANSTON, ALAN (MACGREGOR)
June 19, 1914- Executive of world federation organization
Address: b. c/o United World Federalists, Inc., 7 E. 12th St., New York 3; h. Los Altos, Calif.

Elected the second president of the United World Federalists, Inc., Alan Cranston took office October 1, 1949, as the successor to Cord Meyer, Jr. '48, the founder of the organization. The new president was a director of the executive committee of Americans United for World Government, one of the six groups that merged to form the United World Federalists. A writer, Cranston was present at the Dublin (New Hampshire) Conference on World Government in 1945, which gave impetus to the movement that eventually resulted in the establishment of the U.W.F. early in 1947. Cranston was re-elected to the U.W.F. presidency in October 1950.

An only son, Alan MacGregor Cranston was born on June 19, 1914, in Palo Alto, California, to William MacGregor and Carol (Dixon) Cranston. He has one sister, Eleanor. Of his father (a realtor) and his mother Alan Cranston has said: "I think they've been unusual in

Editta Sherman
ALAN CRANSTON

that fairly early they started giving me advice, but leaving decisions up to me. No doubt they were often appalled at my decisions but they went on the theory that you learn best from experience and that this practice would develop resourcefulness."

Cranston spent his boyhood in Los Altos, California, which is still his home. He attended Mountain View Union High School, where he was on track and football teams, edited the annual, and wrote a column for the school paper. A year (1932-33) at Pomona College, in Claremont, was followed by a summer term at the University of Mexico, and enrollment in the autumn of 1933 at Stanford University. From the latter he received the B.A. degree in 1936. In college he engaged in track sports and joined Sigma Nu. Discussions with campus friends of phenomena of the period, such as the depression, the beginning of the Roosevelt era, and the rise of Hitler, played a large part in the formation of his ideas. Having majored in English, he worked as a reporter for small-town papers during college vacations. He says that writing, sports, and "riding freight trains" were his hobbies in those days.

The friendship of Cranston's father with the late Fremont Older, (the famous editor of the old San Francisco *Bulletin*), and his own association with newspapermen were partly responsible for his entering journalism. Joining the staff of the International News Service, he spent the years of 1936-38 as foreign correspondent in England, Italy, and Ethiopia. Upon his return to the United States he lived during 1939 and part of 1940 in New York, lecturing and contributing articles to papers and magazines; among the latter were *American Mercury* and the New York *Times Book Review*. His subjects were the imminence of war, fascism, and the dangers of American isolationism. With Lee Falk he collaborated on a play. He also published a popular ten-cent anti-Nazi brochure composed of replies to segments of *Mein Kampf*; the lively sale of this publication (500,000 copies) was cut short by court action banning it as an infringement on Hitler's copyright.

Cranston's next position was in Washington, D.C., (1939-41) as representative for the Common Council for American Unity, which worked against discriminatory legislation. He is said to have been partly responsible for Italian aliens being removed from the "enemy alien" classification, thereby disposing the people of Italy to be friendly to American troops. When the United States entered World War II Cranston went to Washington, to become the chief of the foreign language division of the Office of War Information, a post which he held until he enlisted in the Army as a private in 1944. To him is credited (in *World Government News*) the idea of the christening of Lidice, Illinois, after the Czechoslovakian town of that name was destroyed by the Nazis.

By the end of the war Cranston, a sergeant, had been editor of *Army Talk* and co-author of a pamphlet, *Fascism*. It was Karl Schriftgiesser's *The Gentleman from Massachusetts: Henry Cabot Lodge* (1944), says Cranston, which led him to the determination to help build a world organization (Lodge had an important part in keeping the United States from entering the League of Nations). Cranston's account of American isolationism after World War I is contained in *The Killing of the Peace*, which appeared in 1945. In his foreword Cranston describes his book as the "story of how a handful of men caused us to withdraw from the world; the story of how we lost World War I . . . [told] in the hope that the telling will help us win lasting victory in World War II." The book found favor with most reviewers, who thought well of Cranston's interpretation and documentation; the *Christian Science Monitor* critic felt it suffered from "a measure of one-sidedness"; the *New York Times* named it one of the ten best books of the year.

The Killing of the Peace brought to Cranston an invitation to join some thirty prominent workers for permanent peace—editors, writers, educators, lawyers, and other influential citizens—at the Dublin (New Hampshire) Conference on World Government in the fall of 1945. There began his friendship with Grenville Clark, a New York attorney who is credited by *Fortune* with having "played one of the most important . . . roles in the United States during the period of the world wars," and who, Cranston reports, had a "profound influence" on his interest in world government. To Cranston the conference assigned the carrying of its "Dublin Declaration" to United Nations delegates meeting in London in February 1946. This declaration took the form of a proposal to lay plans for converting the United Nations Assembly into a world legislature with "limited but definite and adequate power for the prevention of war."

After serving as chairman of a world government conference at Princeton, New Jersey, and as executive director of the Council for American-Italian Affairs (1946), the Californian returned to the West early in 1947, where he became a partner of his father, a realtor and builder. Continuing his work for world government, he headed the San Francisco chapter of United World Federalists, later being made chairman of the Northern California branch.

Unanimously elected to the presidency of United World Federalists by the national executive council on July 16, 1949, Cranston has dedicated himself to work "for world federal government with powers limited but adequate to assure peace." The incorporated organization was formed in February 1947 by the merging of six American world government groups; it is a member of the International Movement for Federal World Government. A statement of its beliefs, purposes, and policies, adopted in October 1949, reads, in part, as follows: "World peace can be created and maintained only under a world federal government, universal and strong enough to prevent armed conflict between nations, and having direct jurisdiction over the individual in those matters within its authority." While endorsing the efforts of the United Nations in furthering world peace, the U.W.F. works for the establishment of world government "by urging use of the amendment proc-

esses of the United Nations to transform it into such a world federal government; by participating in unofficial international conferences . . . seeking to produce draft constitutions for consideration and possible adoption by the United Nations or by national governments; by pursuing any other reasonable and lawful means to achieve world federation." Cranston has named 1955 as "the outside date for a conference revising the U.N. Charter toward limited world government" (the Charter provides for automatic consideration of revision of the U.N. on its tenth anniversary). When the U.W.F. convened in October 1950 Cranston was re-elected its president.

In the fall of 1949 Cranston appeared before the House Foreign Affairs Committee to urge support of a House-Senate resolution seeking development of the United Nations into a world federation with powers to enact, interpret, and enforce world law in a limited area. The economy of world peace through world government is one of the points Cranston emphasizes: "Eighty per cent of our taxes are now going to pay off past and future wars. The cost of world government would be infinitesimal in comparison."

Cranston is a member of the Overseas Press Club, the San Francisco Committee on Foreign Relations, and the American Veterans Committee. He and Geneva McMath, who were married on November 6, 1940, have a son, Robin. Mrs. Cranston aids her husband in his cause—she accompanied him to London in 1946 and is "an occasional lobbyist," he says. In commenting on his recreational interests, she has called him "an almanac of sports statistics"; and to this hobby he has added motion pictures, the comic strip *Blondie*, and political anecdotes. The tall (six feet two inches is his height), brown-eyed, brown-haired Cranston is considered a forceful speaker.

Reference

World Government News Ag '49

CRAWFORD, BRODERICK Dec. 9, 1911-
Actor

Address: b. c/o Columbia Pictures Corp., 729 7th Ave., New York 19; h. Encino, Calif.

For his portrayal of the character Willie Stark, the politician, in the film version of Robert Penn Warren's Pulitzer-prize novel, *All the King's Men*, Broderick Crawford was awarded the 1949 "Oscar" as the best male actor of the year. This award is given annually by the Academy of Motion Picture Arts and Sciences. Although he had appeared in more than twenty motion pictures since he first began to work in Hollywood in 1937, Crawford had not played a starring role before. On Broadway, however, in 1937 he had won high praise from the critics for his creation of Lennie, the "big, lumbering half-wit" in the stage production of John Steinbeck's *Of Mice and Men*. Before that, he had played minor roles in London, New York, and summer stock.

The theater is a traditional occupation of the members of Crawford's family. His maternal

BRODERICK CRAWFORD

grandfather, William Broderick, was a baritone in light opera; his maternal grandmother, Emma Kraus, was a popular opera singer; his mother, Helen Broderick, is well known for her appearances in Broadway musicals and before the camera; and his father, Lester Crawford, had a long career in vaudeville. William Broderick Crawford was born in Philadelphia, Pennsylvania, his mother's native city, on December 9, 1911. Since his parents at that time were appearing together in vaudeville acts, the young boy accompanied them on their tours; and as he became older, he occasionally appeared on the stage with them. The actor recalls that when he was on one such vaudeville tour, the comedian Harry Breen paid him a dollar a week for running in from the wings to speak one line—"Tag, you're it." Since he had attended grammar school sporadically and his parents wanted him to have a good education, he was enrolled in Dean Academy in Franklin, Massachusetts. There he spent his high school years. In athletics he won letters in football and baseball and served as captain of the swimming team. Crawford graduated from the academy when he was seventeen, in 1928.

At that time vaudeville was still popular. The youth therefore joined his parents in a Max Gordon vaudeville unit, then touring the country. He played three or four minor parts in several sketches, including an abridged version of *The Trial of Mary Dugan*. His salary was fifty dollars a week. The next year, with the decline in vaudeville, his parents left the field, his mother joining a musical comedy production. At the insistence of his parents, Crawford was registered at Harvard University, but within three weeks, realizing that he was not suited to academic studies, he left Cambridge for New York City. For a period he worked as a stevedore on the city's waterfront, then signed as an able-bodied seaman on a tanker. He remained in the maritime service for about seven months and once more returned to New York City. In

the course of the next four years the actor appeared occasionally on radio programs. He had a role in Warden Lawes's show, *Twenty Thousand Years in Sing Sing,* and for thirteen weeks played a "stooge" for the Marx Brothers radio show.

Broderick Crawford's first opportunity to play in a stage production came in the early part of 1934 when Howard Lindsay chose him for the part of the football player in the London production of *She Loves Me Not.* The play, which opened in April 1934, closed after three weeks. Broderick, however, had met Alfred Lunt and Lynn Fontanne in London and had been admired by Noel Coward for his performance. Thus he was chosen by the playwright for the role of the American in the 1935 production of *Point Valaine,* starring Lunt and Fontanne. The show ran for twenty weeks on Broadway, with Crawford's small part in it well received by the critics. He next appeared in *Punches and Judy* and *Sweet Mystery of Life,* both of which were unsuccessful. Then followed several seasons in stock companies and summer theaters. Eventually, in June 1937 he signed a contract with Metro-Goldwyn-Mayer for the part of a comic butler in *Woman Chases Man.* Although it was a fairly important role, Crawford's performance of it was not noted by the critics. He returned to New York in the fall of 1937.

En route to the East the actor read Steinbeck's novel, *Of Mice and Men,* and immediately recognized a good role for himself in the character of Lennie, the moron who kills the things he loves, and in the end is killed by his friend. George Kaufman, who was then casting for the play version of the novel and who had met Crawford some time before, thought he might be suitable for the role. According to an account in the New York *Herald Tribune* for November 28, 1937, Crawford read the lines "so definitely authentic the first time" that he was engaged immediately—Kaufman considered Crawford the "inevitable actor" for the part. When the play opened on November 23, 1937, the critics agreed with Kaufman's choice. The play, "a singular tragedy in the comradeship of two foot-loose men," won the New York Drama Critics Circle award for that year. Crawford's creation of Lennie was described by the New York *Times* as a "perfect counterpart in uncomprehending earnestness and good will," played with "compassion" and "meticulously and affectionately modulated."

Crawford, who did not play the role in the film version of the play, next appeared on the screen in *The Woman's Touch* (1938). He then was engaged by several studios, including Warner Brothers and Paramount, for roles in Class-B pictures. Among these were *Submarine D-1, Ambush, Undercover Doctor, The Real Glory,* and *Eternally Yours,* in which characterizations were either comic or melodramatic. His first featured performance was in *Slightly Honorable,* released in 1940 and noted with approval by the critics. Subsequently, for some time Crawford was to be cast in westerns, one of which, *When the Daltons Rode,* was described by the New York *Herald Tribune* reviewer as "the latest of the historical horse operas" with

Crawford playing the "desperado role with proper vigor."

In 1942 Crawford entered the United States Army, in which he served as a sergeant in the air force during World War II. Overseas for eighteen months, he fought in the Battle of the Bulge. Upon his discharge in 1945 he returned to Hollywood to play the parts of policemen and detectives in several Class-B pictures, including *Sin Town* and *The Flame*. His next camera assignment, *The Runaround* (released in 1946), was judged by the New York *World-Telegram* critic a "very agreeable movie," with Crawford giving the audiences "a vigorous time with his role of the rival specialist in rough and tumble methods." That same year Crawford played the detective in the mystery melodrama, *The Black Angel*, and the next year appeared in *Slave Girl*, a "harem-scarum farce." In 1948 he had a featured role in the film, *Time of Your Life*; in the characterization of a policeman who "grows skeptical of his calling," he received approving comments from the New York reviewers.

Broderick Crawford was not a box-office star when he was chosen by director-producer Robert Rossen to create the role of Willie Stark in the Columbia picture *All the King's Men*. This suited Rossen's idea of having comparative unknowns portray the story of one man's impact on the political life of a State. When the picture was released in November 1949, the critics agreed that Crawford was excellently cast. The New York *Times* reviewer wrote: "Crawford concentrates tremendous energy into every delineation he plays. . . .He draws a compelling portrait, in two dimensions, of an egomaniac." The critic for the New York *Herald Tribune* found the actor "exceedingly resourceful in creating a fully dimensioned portrait of a man on horseback." From the New York *World-Telegram* came this praise: "For once the full force of this magnetic and dominant actor is allowed to sweep unchecked and the result is a memorable performance." *Life* mentioned the "excellent acting" when the editors judged *All the King's Men* the "most exciting film to come out of Hollywood this year."

Since its release, *All the King's Men*, the principal actors, and the writer-director-producer have received about thirty awards, the most significant being the choice of the film as the best of the year by the Academy of Motion Picture Arts and Sciences and the choice by the same group of Crawford as the best male actor of 1949. The New York Film Critics' Award for the best acting of 1949 also went to Crawford; he was similarly chosen by a poll of eighty Hollywood correspondents and by the editors of *Look*.

In March 1949 Crawford had signed a term contract with Columbia Pictures. His next important role will be that of the junk dealer in the cinema version of the long-run Broadway show, *Born Yesterday*. During 1950 he will also be seen in featured roles in *Anna Lucasta* and *Cargo to Capetown*.

Of a powerful build, the actor stands more than six feet, weighs 210 pounds; he has brown hair and blue eyes. Crawford's sport is golf;

he also enjoys cards, particularly poker and gin rummy, and is known for his cooking. Married in 1940 to actress Kay Griffith, he has a son, Kim. Their home is a ranch in Encino, California. According to Sidney Skolsky, writing in the New York *Post*, Crawford (who is "Brod" to his friends) "never forgets a face, is a favorite with stage crews."

References

N Y Herald Tribune N 28 '37
N Y Post Mr 26 '50

International Motion Picture Almanac, 1949-50

CUNEO, JOHN F. (kū'nē-ō) Dec. 24, 1885- Printer; binder

Address: The Cuneo Press, Inc., 2242 S. Grove St., Chicago 16, Ill.; h. Hawthorn Farms, Libertyville, Ill.

The man whose commercial printing establishment Wall Street has called the largest of its kind, John F. Cuneo of Chicago is the president of the Cuneo Press, Inc. His plants, which are located in five cities in the United States, are equipped to handle any sized job of printing, binding, and mailing or shipping. A good number of his customers are publishers of magazines with circulations in the millions, book publishers, and firms requiring large production of printed matter.

John F. Cuneo was born in Chicago, Illinois, on December 24, 1885, to Frank and Amelia (Gondolfo) Cuneo. Chicago is also the birthplace of his father, whose parents had come from Italy in 1857 to that city, there to open a grocery store and run a small farm near by. A wholesale fruit dealer and investor in real estate, Frank Cuneo became a wealthy man. His son was sent to the Chicago Latin School and the University School for his pre-college education. Upon graduating from the latter John Cuneo enrolled at Yale University, which he attended for two years (1904-06). As told in *Inland Printer* ("The Amazing Mr. Cuneo") by A. G. Fegert, young Cuneo declined to return to the Eastern college after his second year. Instead, he found a job in a bookbindery, where he gained his first experience with the tools and processes of the craft.

Within a year, in 1907, Frank Cuneo made a loan of $10,000 to his son, with which to buy a bookbinding shop. Of that amount, $6,600 was spent for the tangible assets of the business. The young man became the president of the new business, the John F. Cuneo Company, which is still the name of the hard-bindery division of the Cuneo Press, Inc. (Fegert pointed out that that fund was the only one Cuneo has borrowed from an individual, all subsequent financing of his enterprises being made through profits, sales of stocks and bonds, and bank loans.) Since a bindery thrives on print, and printers and publishers need paper, Cuneo early developed into a buyer of paper for the concerns for which he did binding, and so became known among paper mill owners. For about ten years the John F. Cuneo Company contracted for all the binding of a number

JOHN F. CUNEO

of Chicago printers; among them was the large W. F. Hall Printing Company, from which Cuneo had rented space. In this period, too, he served during World War I as associate chief of the poster division of the information and educational service, United States Department of Labor.

The year 1919 saw the expansion of Cuneo's interests into printing. The Henneberry Company, printers, which had suffered reverses during the war, found itself with liabilities of more than half a million dollars. These debts Cuneo took over, and by means of reorganization, sound financing, and increased sales, was able to pay creditors an acceptable percentage. The reorganized firm, the Cuneo-Henneberry Company, became the Cuneo Press, Inc., a few years later when president Cuneo acquired full control.

Some of the largest printing contracts Cuneo obtained when publishers found it too costly to operate their own printing plants and Cuneo convinced them substantial savings could be effected by turning over the printing to his establishment. In some instances he purchased or leased the plants and acquired long-term contracts at the same time. Among the biggest printing contracts acquired were Hearst's *Cosmopolitan* (in 1921), Sears, Roebuck and Company catalog (1922), and *McCall's Magazine* (in 1923) for the seven months while its publisher was in the process of moving the McCall plant to Dayton, Ohio. An important selling point of Cuneo's was the advantage the publishers would gain by having the printing and mailing done in centrally located Chicago, from which the zoned postal rates are lower in supplying western subscribers and dealers. Other well-known periodicals that came or still come from the Cuneo presses are *Time, Saturday Evening Post, American Legion, American Home, Christian Science Monitor,* and *Etude. Liberty,* another national-circulation magazine,

became the property of Cuneo in the early 1940's in lieu of paying its indebtedness to the Cuneo Press; while the latter sold it in 1945, it still prints the magazine. In addition, Cuneo prints fifty-some pulp magazines, syndicate newspaper sections, telephone books, mail-order catalogs, calendars, labels, boxes, and printed matter for automobile manufacturers, department stores, and railroads. He also prints and binds the output of a book company he owns. Often the contracts are for five years or more, with provision for adjustment in the event of changes in the price of raw materials and in labor costs. Some contracts amount to $250,000 annually.

Beginning in 1926, John Cuneo acquired plants in other cities. That year two were combined in Milwaukee to form the Wisconsin Cuneo Press. In 1927 the Neo Gravure Company was purchased in New York, and two similar affiliates were soon established to handle rotogravure reproduction in Chicago and San Francisco. The large Butterick plant, in New York, came into the Cuneo domain in 1932; as the Eastern Cuneo Press, Inc., it later was moved to Philadelphia, where satisfactory collective bargaining contracts were effected. (The *Annalist* reported that Cuneo holds contracts with the major unions in the various crafts employed in his plants, which have been "remarkably free of labor trouble.") Altogether, Cuneo has nine plants in five cities; five of the plants are in Chicago. As of 1946, the total floor area measured more than one and a half million square feet, there were 130 high-speed rotary presses, 148 one- and two-color cylinder presses; 31 carloads of paper were required for one day's printing; total number of employees, 10,000; evaluation, $17,000,000. When the Cuneo Press, Inc., was a newcomer in the New York Stock Exchange (in 1940), the *Magazine of Wall Street* reported that "in a business notorious for fluctuation," Cuneo had not shown a loss in thirteen years.

The Chicago printer is able to supply his printing presses with some of the "raw material" from his own factories—he owns a printing ink factory and a paper mill. In the mid-1920's he acquired large real estate holdings in Chicago. As one of the chief stockholders in the National Tea Company, in 1945 he inquired into the reason for low net profits from high gross sales figures. After an analysis (under Cuneo's direction) of all phases of that chain-store system, drastic changes brought improved business to National Tea Company, of which Cuneo became executive committee chairman. The printing tycoon is also the proprietor of the Hawthorn-Mellody Farms Dairy—he is the owner of the 2,100-acre Hawthorn Farms, which daily sends 400,000 pounds of milk to Chicago. He is a director of the Continental Illinois National Bank and Trust Company, Chicago. During World War II he was a member of the National War Labor Board.

The list of Cuneo's clubs consists of The Cloud, Yale, Wykagyl Country, Recess, and Bankers, in New York; Chicago Athletic Association, South Shore Country, Chicago Golf, The Tavern, in Chicago. Another interest of

Cuneo's outside of printing is the Frank Cuneo Memorial Hospital for Women and Children, which is managed by a religious order—Cuneo is of the Catholic faith. Five feet eight inches in height, he weighs 170 pounds; his eyes are blue, his hair is brown. At Hawthorn Farms, where he maintains a large stable, he raises hackney ponies and likes to take friends on drives in his tallyho. He is a familiar figure at the annual Chicago Horse Show (in which he also has a financial interest), when he may drive a four-in-hand. Cuneo is frequently described as a man of "tremendous energy."

References

Inland Ptr. 117:43-8 My '46
Time 45:77-8 Mr 5 '45
Who's Who in America, 1950-51
World Biography (1948)

CURZON, CLIFFORD (kûr'zŏn) May 18, 1907- Pianist
Address: b. c/o Columbia Artists Management, 113 W. 57th St., New York 19; h. "The White House," Millfield Place, London, N.6, England

Clifford Curzon, English pianist who was already internationally known when he gave his first recital in America in 1939 and whose second appearance there was postponed eight years by war, has been acclaimed by critics as one of the greatest pianists of the day. His distinction, according to many music critics, is his refusal to use his prodigious technical accomplishment as a means of dazzling his listeners with his own virtuosity, preferring instead to devote himself to an interpretation of the composer—bringing the music not the performer to the fore. His repertory, which includes fifty-three concertos, ranges from the early classics to contemporary compositions. Critic Virgil Thomson considers him "the most satisfactory interpreter . . . of pianoforte's Romantic repertory. . . .Certainly no one brings to life [Schubert and Schumann] with quite the delicacy and the grandeur of Mr. Curzon."

Clifford Curzon was born in London on May 18, 1907. His parents, Michael Curzon, a dealer in antiques, and Constance (Young) Curzon, were music lovers. Young Clifford began the study of the violin when he was five years old, but at six turned to the piano, because, he said, "you can be alone with a piano." At twelve he entered the Royal Academy of Music, which offers a three-year course in every branch of music, and at thirteen he began study with the man he names as his first important teacher, Professor Charles Reddie, who had been a pupil of Stavenhagen, one of Liszt's best pupils. The boy also studied with Katherine Goodson and Tobias Matthay. At the academy he won two scholarships, and all the prizes open to pianists, including the McFarren Gold Medal for Pianoforte.

Sixteen-year-old Curzon made his first public appearance in London, when he played Bach's Triple Concerto at a Queen's Hall Promenade Concert. The conductor was the late Sir Henry Wood, Curzon's early great sponsor. The following season (1924) Curzon gave the first performance in England of Germaine Tailleferre's Ballade in the same auditorium. In the two years after his debut he played widely in England, at the same time teaching at the Royal Academy as a subprofessor until 1926, when, aged nineteen, he was old enough to be a full professor. He was later elected an associate, and in 1937, five years after he resigned his professorship to devote himself to concert work, he became a fellow of the academy of music.

Curzon experienced at eighteen what he called a revelation, an entirely new vision of what a pianist could be, when he heard Artur Schnabel play a Schubert sonata. A few years later, in 1928, he decided to leave the concert stage in order to study with Schnabel in Berlin for two years. (During his first year in Berlin a fellow student was Lucille Wallace, a Chicagoan who had gone to Europe to study the history of early music, and who shared his interest in the harpsichord. Three years later, on July 16, 1931, in Paris, she became his wife.) Later in Paris young Curzon studied with the great harpsichordist Wanda Landowska [45], and worked at "just music" with the composer and conductor, Nadia Boulanger, who has taught many noted young composers.

In 1930 Curzon resumed his concert career. He toured the Continent, appearing with leading orchestras such as the Colonne Orchestra and the Société Philharmonique in Paris. In England he played at leading music festivals, in the Royal Philharmonic Society's concerts and with the British Broadcasting Corporation's symphony orchestra; with the latter he went to Paris in 1937 for a performance of Constant Lambert's *Rio Grande*. In 1936 he was chosen to tour Europe with Lionel Tertis in sonata recitals for viola and piano on the first Continental tour of British musicians organized by the British Council, and in 1938 again toured Europe under the auspices of the Council.

Clifford Curzon first came to the United States early in 1939. According to *Newsweek*, he rented two halls for two recitals without engaging a manager. His American debut took place in New York's Town Hall on February 26, 1939, and shortly afterward, on March 10, he played three concertos with the New York Philharmonic Symphony Orchestra under Alexander Smallens at Carnegie Hall. Critical enthusiasm for his "superior musicianship, polished technique, and sure grasp of style" (New York *Times*) was echoed by manager Arthur Judson, who offered the pianist a contract for a tour of the United States the following year. But Curzon's return to America was to be postponed eight years by World War II. During the war years Curzon, as did other English artists, played "day and night" throughout England; he recalls that during the worst of the blitz it was no uncommon experience for him to hear a near-by building collapse while he was in the midst of a performance.

Returning to the United States in late 1947, Curzon appeared for the second time with the New York Philharmonic Symphony at Carnegie Hall on November 30, to play the

Blank & Stoller

CLIFFORD CURZON

Tchaikovsky Concerto in B-Flat Minor, under the baton of Dimitri Mitropoulos. On December 20 he gave a recital at Town Hall, a program of Schubert, Beethoven, Brahms, and Liszt. It was this performance that brought from Noel Strauss (New York *Times*) the tribute: "Curzon must be reckoned among the greatest keyboard artists of the time. . . .An unexcelled technician and interpreter." Jerome D. Bohn of the *Herald Tribune* used almost the same words—"One of the greatest pianists of the time."

After that success the English pianist signed with concert manager Arthur Judson, who arranged a 1948-49 concert tour—forty-five appearances with orchestras and in recitals in the United States and Canada, including two *Telephone Hour* radio guest appearances. The tour was sold out almost as soon as it was announced, and Curzon's appearances were a succession of critical triumphs, from "one of the best Mozart readings of recent seasons" (New York *World-Telegram*) with the Little Orchestra Society at Town Hall in November 1948, to three appearances in March 1949 in the New York Philharmonic Symphony Beethoven Cycle under Bruno Walter. Of the January 8, 1949, recital Strauss wrote that Curzon "again impressed as one of the most poetic, sensitive, and refined keyboard artists of the day. . . .[a] fine exhibition of bravura playing at its most meaningful . . . brought his splendid recital to a brilliant and memorable close." His February appearance with the Philadelphia Orchestra at Carnegie Hall in Rachmaninoff's Second Piano Concerto, brought from Olin Downes (New York *Times*) the accolade, "One of the outstanding performances by a pianist in many years." His playing, said Downes, was "a renaissance" of the concerto. With these and similar notices behind him Curzon sailed for England on March 18, to a

full schedule of engagements in that country, France, and Belgium. In one he played (with his wife at the harpsichord) C.P.E. Bach's Concerto for Piano and Harpsichord with the Boyd Neal Orchestra under Nadia Boulanger. The following November he returned to the United States for a sold-out 1949-50 itinerary of coast-to-coast appearances.

The pianist again drew high praise from the music critics. Of his February 14, 1950, performance of Beethoven's Fourth Piano Concerto (with the Cleveland Orchestra under George Szell) Virgil Thomson said that Curzon's "tender grace and grand perspective of expression all made his rendering both a message and a monument." It was agreed by critics that the Englishman's technical virtuosity was matched by musical intellect and imagination "of the loftiest order."

Curzon has particularly impressed listeners with his "completely graduated range of dynamics" (*Musical America*, January 15, 1949), ranging from "the most gossamer of pianissimos" to "thunderous fortissimos" with the graduations between completely distinct from one another. Noting that this dynamic range is wider "than is at all common," Virgil Thomson has commented: "Particularly in his soft playing is it noticeable that no element of shading is absent, that the musical effect is as full and alive as that of any orchestral pianissimo. Very loud effects being, by the nature of the piano's limitations, impossible to execute with much variety of tonal color, he employs them sparingly, saves them for climatic moments." Thomson also has emphasized Curzon's "thoroughly modern, thoroughly musical and thoroughly intelligent approach" to nineteenth century piano music, which the pianist "reconstitutes" by using modern technique. Olin Downes has ascribed his "sense of style" partly to an "intuition" of "penetrating truthfulness," and has termed him "an artist of true humbleness and a consecrated devotion to his task." This is echoed by the *Musical America* critic, who found him "an artist who is more concerned with essences than with surfaces."

Often lauded for his command of differing styles, Curzon discussed that quality with Quaintance Eaton (*Musical America*, March 15, 1948). "One should try to be a good student of the history of the times in which the music was written. To learn, for example, what was possible on certain instruments of the time. Only up to a point is music 'music,' without relation to its period." Curzon also pointed out to Miss Eaton that he had preferred to establish himself in the classic and romantic schools in America before venturing into the music of impressionists or moderns; among his contemporaries he has performed in particular the compositions of Benjamin Britten and Lenox Berkely. The English pianist practices for a minimum of four hours daily, eight when he can. He makes constant use of a dummy keyboard while he is traveling. He has explained: "I practice and practice, and work and work. I dare not take anything for granted." Curzon's recordings for Decca in the United States include: Brahm's Concerto for Piano and Orchestra in D Minor, Opus 15;

Mozart's Concerto for Piano and Orchestra No. 23 in A Major, K 448; several of Britten's compositions; De Falla's *Nights in the Gardens of Spain.* A recent recording with a London imprint is Beethoven's Concerto No. 5 in E-Flat Major ("The Emperor Concerto"), with the London Philharmonic Orchestra.

Curzon and his wife, whom he considers the world's second greatest claveciniste (surpassed only by Wanda Landowska), enjoy playing duets; they have given historical recital series, playing such instruments as Elizabethan virginals and harpsichords. The Curzons once debated the subject of harpsichord versus piano over the B.B.C., Mrs. Curzon defending the piano and her husband arguing for her harpsichord. The Curzons have two houses in England, "The White House" in the north of London, where Curzon tends the garden as a hobby, and a stone farmhouse in Cumberland in the north lake country, which Curzon has called his "escape." "There are no 'conveniences' and it is perfectly quiet." Other of his hobbies are swimming and motoring. The pianist, who has been judged "a small man" from a critic's seat, is actually six feet tall and weighs 154 pounds. His eyes are green, his hair is brown, and he wears spectacles. Miss Eaton has described him thus: "The smile is sweet but diffident, under a nose of prominence. His manner is eager, urbane and friendly."

References

Mus Am 68:8 Mr 15 '48; 69:18 Ja 15 '49 por
Newsweek 32:84-5 N 8 '48 por
Grove, G. Dictionary of Music and Musicians Suppl vol (1940)
Thompson, O. ed. International Cyclopedia of Music and Musicians (1949)
Who's Who, 1949

DAVIES, CLEMENT (EDWARD) Feb. 19, 1884- British political leader
Address: Liberal Party Central Office, 58 Victoria St., London, S.W. 1; h. 31 Evelyn Mansions, Carlisle Pl., London, S.W.1; Plas Dyffryn, Meifod, Montgomeryshire, Wales

The Right Honorable Clement Davies, Liberal Member of Parliament for Montgomeryshire, Wales, was first elected to that seat in 1929, and has been returned by his constituency in each succeeding election for twenty-one years. A prominent barrister (he was made a King's Counsel in 1926) and businessman, he has since 1939 devoted himself entirely to the political sphere. Since being officially named leader of the British Liberal party in 1945, he has been outspoken in affirming that body's determination to remain an independent force in British politics despite the decline its parliamentary representation has suffered since World War I. Speaking at the annual party meeting in May 1950, after the election of that year in which nine Liberal candidates had been successful while the party polled about one-ninth of the total votes, Davies said: "I want to make it clear beyond a doubt, beyond a

British Inf. Services
CLEMENT DAVIES

peradventure, that the Liberal party lives on as an independent party."

Clement Edward Davies was born February 19, 1884, the youngest of the seven children of Alderman M. Davies and Laura (Jones) Davies. His birthplace is Llanfyllin, Montgomeryshire, Wales, where his father was also an auctioneer and appraiser. Reared there, young Davies became bilingual in English and Welsh. As a schoolboy he sometimes worked on his father's farm in his free time. After passing the London Matriculation Examination held under the auspices of a Welsh board, he entered Trinity Hall, Cambridge, in 1904 to read law. Two of his brothers and a sister had preceded him to the universities of Edinburgh, London, and Wales; and he was also encouraged and aided financially by his brother David, who had entered law and later headed Land Evaluation for Wales. Clement Davies won a Senior Foundation Scholarship which maintained him through his law studies, and took a double first in the Law Tripos (honor school) in 1906 and 1907. A law studentship for the period 1907-11 was granted him by his college.

In the session 1908-09 Davies was a lecturer in law at the University College of Wales, Aberystwyth; meanwhile he read for the bar. In 1909 he was called by Lincoln's Inn, taking a first class in all bar examinations, gaining a certificate of honor in his final, and winning prizes for criminal law, constitutional law, and the law of real property. He at once began to practice in the courts, on the North Wales circuit in 1909-10, then transferred to the Northern circuit, and finally to London in 1913, where he worked in the King's Bench division and specialized in the commercial and admiralty courts. He was secretary to the president of the Probate, Divorce and Admiralty Division, in 1918-19, and to the Master of the Rolls dur-

DAVIES, CLEMENT—*Continued*
ing 1919-23. A junior counsel to the Treasury
from 1919 to 1925, he reached the highest rank
of barrister in 1926, when he was made a
King's Counsel. In 1931 he accepted a directorship in Lever Brothers, the soap corporation,
giving up his legal practice; he remained in
commerce until the fall of 1939, when he resigned to devote his time entirely to politics.

In 1929 Davies was nominated as Liberal
candidate for Montgomeryshire, a division
which had voted Liberal for seventy years
(Wales and Cornwall are generally considered
traditional Liberal strongholds), and was
elected to Parliament. His party, "lineal successor to the historic Whig party" in the words
of the *Encyclopædia Britannica* (1947), was in
a period of decline which had become evident
with its defeat in 1922 following a lengthy
period in which it had held political power,
either as the majority party or as leader in a
coalition. During its term of office it had introduced a number of social insurance benefits
and measures for the progressive taxation of
the rich. Defining British Liberalism's policy,
Britannica states: "Its aims are compatible
with a very active policy of social reorganization, involving a great enlargement of the
functions of the State. They are not compatible with Socialism . . . strictly interpreted."
The same source points out that as a movement
it has been particularly subject to dissensions
within its ranks. Such dissensions in the postwar years caused a weakening of the party
structure and in subsequent elections a series
of reverses drastically reduced the number of
Liberal Members—156 were elected in 1923,
59 in 1929, 21 in 1935, 12 in 1945, 9 in 1950,
in a House of 640 seats. Actual ballots cast
for the Liberals amounted to roughly one-ninth
of the total vote, a situation not reflected in
the party's parliamentary representation; Liberals have been advocating examination of the
prevailing electoral system of single-member
constituencies.

In the economic crisis of 1931 Davies, re-
elected that year, joined a group of Liberals
headed by Sir John Simon [40] which gave its
support to the MacDonald Government composed of men from the three principal parties
(Labor, Conservative, Liberal). From that time
until 1942 Davies sat in Parliament as a Liberal National, supporting National Governments under Conservatives. He officially
rejoined the Liberal party in 1942, having become increasingly out of sympathy with the
Chamberlain Government, particularly with
reference to the initial prosecution of World
War II. In this connection he refused the
Government Whip (i.e. voting summons) because he felt the Government was not taking
the necessary measures in the war, stated a
British Information Services release. The same
source related that he had been prominent in
the movement which resulted in the resignation of Chamberlain and the formation of the
Coalition Government under Churchill in 1940.
Upon rejoining the Liberal party, Davies became a leader in its Radical Action Group, one
of the three broad divisions of the party.

Davies was named official leader of the Par-

liamentary Liberal Party in 1945; he succeeded
Sir Archibald Sinclair [40], who had been defeated in that year's general election. In his
new capacity Davies stressed the autonomy of
the Liberal party (reduced to twelve Members
in Parliament), issuing warnings against Conservative overtures and making clear his party's
disagreement with Labor policies and measures.
His subsequent speeches were to accuse the
Government of over-legislation; to condemn
conscription; and to express fears of a coal
shortage and doubts about excessive trade union
influence and the burden of food subsidies.
Voicing his party's view of England's position under Labor policy, he said: "We are
breaking almost every practical common-sense
rule of business which was observed by the
men who built up the great industrial strength
of the country. Politically, we are losing day
by day the ordinary freedoms which we have
cherished."

Under Davies the Liberal party has consistently voted according to its principles,
whether voting with the Government, with the
Opposition, or abstaining. In November 1948
Davies expressed Liberal opposition to the iron
and steel nationalization bill and made known
that he would oppose future nationalization
measures. In 1950 he joined with the leader
of the Conservatives in a motion (rejected by
the House) that Britain participate in the
Paris conference on the proposed European
coal-steel pool. He assured the Government of
his party's support of its stand in the Korea
conflict; because of that war, he later joined
Winston Churchill [42] in a request to Prime
Minister Attlee [47] (refused) that the British
Parliament be reconvened at an earlier date
than the one set by the Labor Government.

Davies, who has a reputation for skill in
drafting Parliamentary reports, has served on
a number of commissions and committees, legal
and miscellaneous. Notable among these were
the Royal Commission on the Despatch of
Business at Common Law (1934-35); Committee of Enquiry into Broadcasting (1935); Parliamentary Charity Commission (1936-37);
Committee on Third Party Insurance (1936-
37); Committee on the Incidence of Tuberculosis in Wales (chairman, 1937-38); Joint Committee of both Houses on Consolidation of Bills
(1936-39); Committee on Colonial Empire Marketing (since 1937); West African Commission
(1938-39). In 1945-46 he was chairman of the
Advisory Committee on Greater London Planning and of the committee on the method of
carrying out the Plan for Greater London. The
all-party British delegation to the conference of
the Inter-Parliamentary Union in Stockholm in
September 1949 had Davies as its leader. Always maintaining his interest in the affairs of
his native Wales, he founded the Montgomeryshire Society in London, and was its president
in 1929-32. In 1937 he introduced a bill proposing a Secretary of State for Wales. He
was a president of the Royal National Eisteddfod (national arts festival) in 1938-39 and
of the Powys Eisteddfod, 1924-39. During
1945-48 he was president of the Welsh Liberal
Federation, and has been president of the Ap-

proved Societies (social insurance groups) of Wales since 1945.

During his twenty-three years in the law Davies wrote a number of legal treatises: *Agricultural Law* (1910; 2d ed., 1919); *The New Land Valuation Under the Finance Act, 1910*; *An Epitome of Agricultural Law* (with Ernest Evans, 1911); *The Agricultural Holdings Act* (1912; 4th ed., 1949); *Finance (1909-10) Act* (1910, 3 vols., 1913-14); *Law of Auctions and Auctioneers*, 1913. Throughout his political life he has preserved a link with the law as chairman of the Montgomeryshire Quarter Sessions (court for minor criminal cases), a post which he has held since 1935. For his political and public services the Liberal leader was created a Privy Councilor in the New Year's Honors List of 1947. He was chosen president of the Law Society of Trinity Hall, Cambridge, in 1950, and was awarded an honorary fellowship by that college.

On September 20, 1913, Davies married Jano Elizabeth, eldest daughter of the late Morgan Davies, M.D., F.R.C.S., a well-known physician and surgeon. Mrs. Davies during World War II was representative for Wales of the Women's Voluntary Service; she was High Sheriff for Montgomeryshire in 1947-48. Of their family of three sons and one daughter, only the youngest son survives. Davies' club is the Reform.

References

Everybody's S 6 '47 por
Liberal Party Leaflets N '48; My '49
International Who's Who, 1950
Who's Who, 1950
World Biography (1948)

DEAN, GORDON (EVANS) Dec. 28, 1905- United States Government official; lawyer

Address: b. c/o United States Atomic Energy Commission, 19th St. & Constitution Ave., N.W., Washington 25, D.C.; h. 3804 East-West Highway, Chevy Chase, Md.; Alta Vista Dr., Vista, Calif.

The new chairman of the United States Atomic Energy Commission, successor to David E. Lilienthal [44], is Gordon Dean of California. First named to the commission in 1949 to fill out the unexpired term of a member who had resigned, Dean was confirmed for a full three-year term at the end of June 1950. He was appointed chairman on July 11 of that year. A lawyer, and an authority on Federal and State cooperation in crime enforcement, Dean was in 1946 an assistant to Justice Robert H. Jackson [40], chief United States counsel at the Nuremberg war crimes trials. He is on leave from the faculty of the University of Southern California Law School for the term of his assignment to the Atomic Energy Commission.

The son of the Reverend John Marvin and Beatrice Alice (Fisken) Dean, Gordon Evans Dean was born December 28, 1905, in Seattle, Washington, where his father was pastor of the Tabernacle (Baptist) Church. The elder Dean, a native of New York State, came of forebears dating back in America to pre-

Revolutionary days; his wife, whose birthplace was a Scottish town, migrated with her parents and ten brothers and sisters to the Pacific Northwest to live in Vancouver and Seattle. Young Gordon Dean passed his boyhood, successively, in Seattle, San Jose (California), Chicago, New York City, and Pasadena (California), attended his first grammar school in Chicago, and completed his secondary education in Pasadena. He then entered the University of Redlands for the prelegal course, working during summers as a reporter on the Pasadena *Evening Post* and *Star News*, and took his B.A. degree in 1927. During the ensuing year he was employed as a law clerk in the offices of Meserve, Mumper, Hughes and Robertson in Los Angeles. He was admitted to the California bar in 1930, the year in which he acquired the Doctor of Jurisprudence degree from the University of Southern California.

In 1930, when Justin Miller, dean of the University of Southern California Law School, went to Duke University (Durham, North Carolina) to reorganize its Law School faculty, he took along Dean as an instructor and assistant dean. The latter was admitted to the North Carolina bar in the following year. and gave his services as an attorney to the Duke Legal Clinic. In 1932 he received Duke University's Master of Laws degree, offering "Organized Crime and Our Changing Criminal Law" as his thesis.

In the course of Dean's fourth year as an instructor at Duke, he met the United States Assistant Attorney General in charge of the Criminal Division, Joseph B. Keenan [46], who was then conducting an investigation of crime legislation. According to Harlan Trott (in the *Christian Science Monitor*), Keenan was responsible for the offer of a post in the Department of Justice being sent to Dean. Before the end of 1934, accordingly, Dean joined the staff as an attorney in the Criminal Division; in that capacity he assisted in the preparation of laws to extend Federal power in the prosecution of crimes. He was admitted to practice before the United States Supreme Court in 1935, and in the next year became Chief of the Appellate Section of the Justice Department's Criminal Division, in which capacity he prepared and argued in the United States Supreme Court many criminal cases. It was, however, his "able job in the backstage management of the First National Crime Conference" (according to Harlan Trott) which brought about his appointment, on March 18, 1937, as Special Executive Assistant to the Attorney General in charge of public relations. This post he retained until June 1940. Also, in 1937, Dean became a special lecturer at American University, in the capital, on the American legal system.

Among the notable cases prepared by Dean while a trial lawyer with the Department of Justice was that against P. D. Peacher, an Arkansas town marshal, who in 1936 was tried and convicted, under Title 18 of the United States Code, for "causing Negroes to be held as slaves" on a cotton plantation. (This was the first case to be tried under the slavery statute.) In this Dean was associated with

GORDON DEAN

Brien McMahon '45, Assistant United States Attorney General (since 1945 United States Senator from Connecticut). A friendship resulted, and in June 1940 Dean retired to private law practice as a partner in the firm of McMahon, Dean and Gallagher. Later in 1940 Dean was appointed by the United States Supreme Court to sit on its advisory committee to draft rules of criminal procedure for the United States District Courts; he served on this body until the rules were adopted by the Congress and the Supreme Court in 1944.

Meanwhile, the United States had become a belligerent in World War II, and in 1943 Dean was commissioned a lieutenant, senior grade, in the Navy. Assigned to the Intelligence Branch, he later "managed to swap his desk for a ship in the shooting navy" (*Christian Science Monitor*). He was demobilized in September 1945. While still in the armed service, on May 16, 1945, Dean was appointed Assistant to Justice Robert H. Jackson, United States Chief Counsel for prosecution of the major Nazi war criminals. (Jackson had begun his term as United States Attorney General in 1940 when Dean was on the Justice Department staff.) Dean was put in charge of public relations at the Nuremberg trials. He also served in London and Berlin.

On his return to the United States, Dean went to California, where he accepted a post as professor of law at the University of Southern California, resumed his law practice, and purchased and operated a citrus and avocado farm at Vista, near San Diego. In February 1949 he was appointed a member of the Western States Loyalty Board. A few months later (May 9, 1949) his appointment to the Atomic Energy Commission was announced to fill out the unexpired term of William W. Waymack '47. *United States News & World Report* stated that Dean then "undertook a rigorous indoc-

trination. He spent hours studying the intricate scientific principles involved." In public statements Dean made in January and May 1950, he emphasized the possible relaxing of Government monopoly in the atomic field (when weapon production reached a "saturation point") so that industry and science might benefit by the development of peacetime use of the atom.

The Atomic Energy Commission was created by the Atomic Energy Act to take over (as of December 31, 1946) "certain interests, property and facilities of the Manhattan Engineer district" in order to "effectuate the declared policy of the people of the United States that, subject at all times to the paramount objective of assuring the common defense and security, the development and utilization of atomic energy shall, so far as practicable, be directed toward improving the public welfare, increasing the standard of living, strengthening free competition in private enterprise, and promoting world peace" (*United States Government Organization Manual*). Its major programs in the interests of scientific progress, are to assist and foster private research in atomic energy, to control scientific and technical information, to permit the sharing of knowledge of practical industrial application of atomic energy; to carry on a program of Government-conducted research, and of production to assure the common defense and security (from the *Government Manual*).

When David E. Lilienthal resigned from the chairmanship of the AEC in February 1950, Sumner T. Pike '47 was named acting chairman. Pike, however, was opposed in Congress for the chairman's post, although his reappointment in July 1950 to a four-year term received approval. In the meantime, Dean's reappointment (together with H. D. Smyth's '48 and Thomas E. Murray's '50) was confirmed on June 30, 1950. About ten days later, on July 11, Gordon Dean was appointed permanent chairman by President Truman. (The fifth member, T. Keith Glennan, was named in August—Lewis Strauss '47 and Robert Bacher '47 also having resigned.) Senate approval of Chairman Dean, already confirmed as member, was not required.

In assuming the chairmanship of the AEC, Dean succeeded Lilienthal, who had been under sharp attack by legislators in the capital; and the resignation of Carroll Wilson '47 as AEC's general manager was regarded as the final departure of the "Lilienthal influence." Wilson himself was critical of Dean, while other (the Joint Congressional Committee on Atomic Energy, headed by McMahon, and the editorial columns of the New York *Times*) expressed confidence in Dean. An early statement by the new chairman was: "During the past few months we've had the best teamwork I've observed since I've been on the commission." His annual salary is $17,500.

Dean was awarded the honorary Doctor of Laws degree by the University of Redlands in April 1950. His contributions to various legal publications include "Liability of Physicians for Sterilization Operations," written in collaboration with Justin Miller (American Bar Association *Journal*, March 1930); "Bar Associations and the Law School Student Body" (*American Law School Review*, December 1931); "Interstate Compacts and Crime Control" (American Bar Association *Journal*, February 1935). He is a member of the American Bar Association; the Kappa Sigma Sigma, Phi Delta Phi, and Pi Kappa Delta fraternities; the Order of the Coif. In his political affiliations Dean is a Democrat; his church is the Baptist. His clubs are the Kiwanis International, the Athletic in Los Angeles, and the National Press in Washington, D.C.

Mrs. Dean, the former Adelaide Williamson of Palo Alto, California, was a fellow student of Dean's at Redlands; they were married August 9, 1930, and have two children, Martha and Franklin Evans. Dean, who is five feet nine inches in height and about 168 pounds in weight, has brown eyes. "His receding dark hair," wrote Charles Van Devander in the New York *Post,* "is brushed almost straight back from a high forehead. Dean wears rimless spectacles and has a friendly confident smile." Van Devander adds that Dean dresses conservatively, avoids cocktail parties, but "confesses to a regular highball before dinner" and "consumes over a pack of cigarettes a day." Hunting, fishing and golf are the recreations he prefers.

References

        Christian Sci Mon p3 Ag 2 '50 por
        N Y Herald Tribune p1 Jl 12 '50 por
        N Y Post Mag p18 Jl 30 '50 por
        N Y Times p1 Jl 12 '50 por
        U S News 29:32 Ag 25 '50

        American Men in Government (1949)
        America's Young Men, 1936-37
        Who's Who in America, 1950-51
        Who's Who in Law, 1937

DE CASTRO, MORRIS F(IDANQUE)

(dä käs'trō) Feb. 5, 1902- Governor of the Virgin Islands

Address: b. and h. Government House, Charlotte Amalie, St. Thomas, Virgin Islands

The first Virgin Islander to become Governor of that United States West Indian possession, Morris F. de Castro took office on March 24, 1950. A career Government official, his years of service have been spent entirely in the administration of the Islands. The economic development and the financial autonomy of the Islands are the main points of his program. The nomination of De Castro was hailed as an example of the United States policy to increase the self-government of American territories and possessions.

The son of David M. de Castro and the former Ada H. Fidanque, Morris Fidanque de Castro was born in Panama on February 5, 1902. His father, a commission merchant in the Virgin Islands, was working at the time of the boy's birth in the Canal Zone in Panama. In 1906 he returned to St. Thomas to serve as consul for several Central American republics. The boy attended the Roman Catholic School in St. Thomas, from which he was graduated

in 1916; he had studied stenography and typewriting after school hours.

In the year of De Castro's graduation, the United States bought for $25,000,000 from Denmark, after half a century of negotiation, the three main islands, one of them St. Thomas. Their administration was put into the hands of the United States Navy, since they are of strategic significance for the protection of the eastern entrance of the Panama Canal.

The American authorities took formal possession of the Islands in 1917, and the following year Morris F. de Castro, then sixteen years old, began his career in the service of the Government as a clerk in the sanitation service. In 1920 he was posted as a secretary for one year to the naval station in St. Thomas, and in 1921 was made chief clerk in the offices of the Governor and of the Government Secretary. This post was held by De Castro until 1931, when a civil Government was established for the Islands and the city of St. Thomas on the island of the same name was designated to be the capital; in 1937 the name of the city was changed to Charlotte Amalie.

The posts of Assistant Government Secretary and Assistant Commissioner of Finance were assigned to De Castro in 1931. These he filled until 1934, when he became Commissioner of Finance, a position he held for ten years. In 1944 he was made Administrative Assistant to the Governor, and the following year Government Secretary for the Virgin Islands, an office in which he remained until he became Governor on March 24, 1950, after serving upon occasion as Acting Governor.

During World War II he was Coordinator for Civilian Defense in the Virgin Islands, was first a member and later chairman of the Public Utilities Commission, served as Deputy State Director of Selective Service, and worked on the Price Control Board. His record in the last two capacities earned for him the Office of Price Administration Award and, in 1947, the Selective Service Medal.

The Virgin Islands, discovered by Columbus in 1493, are owned only in part by the United States. Belonging to the Lesser Antilles and situated east of Puerto Rico, they number about one hundred, cover an area of nearly 465 square miles, and are mostly uninhabited. The westernmost islands, with an area of 133 square miles, are United States possessions, while the remainder are British. With a population of almost 25,000 (1940), 79½ per cent of whom are of Negro descent (8 per cent are white, 12½ per cent mixed, mainly Puerto Rican), the American possessions essentially comprise the three main islands of St. Croix, St. John and St. Thomas, the last with an excellent harbor. English is universally spoken. Sugar and rum and bay rum are the main products but far from being economically self-sufficient, the islands are largely dependent upon Federal assistance.

In 1927 the inhabitants of the Islands became citizens of the United States, and ten years later the Roosevelt Administration replaced the old colonial councils by a Legislative Assembly, composed of the elected municipal councils of St. Croix and St. Thomas, whose council

MORRIS F. DE CASTRO

also includes representatives from St. John. Universal suffrage for all able to read and write English went into effect in 1938. The United States Department of the Interior has jurisdiction over the Islands; the Governor, appointed by the President of the United States, holds certain veto powers.

In his first message to Congress in 1946 President Truman recommended "an increasing measure of self-government" for the Virgin Islands; in May of the same year William H. Hastie '[44] a Negro lawyer and educator was inaugurated as the fourth civilian Governor of the Islands. When in October 1949 Hastie was nominated judge of the Third District Court of Appeals (the first Negro ever appointed to a United States Circuit Court of Appeals), the Legislative Assembly of the Virgin Islands urged President Truman to nominate Acting Governor de Castro. This recommendation of the Legislative Assembly reflected strong feeling on the part of the Islanders that their next Governor should be one of their own people.

De Castro's nomination, announced on February 28, 1950, by Truman, was widely acclaimed. His inauguration on March 24 was marked by general rejoicing, and was greeted enthusiastically in press editorials in the United States, the New York *Times* commenting, "It is a symbol of right thinking in the field of political relationships and of movement in the proper direction." In his inaugural address De Castro strongly emphasized "the importance of self-support and self-dependence" for the Islands, pointing to limited economic resources as a source of great difficulty to be overcome in this respect. In appointing a native Governor, President Truman, he said, had "honored the Virgin Islands by recognizing our ability to govern ourselves."

De Castro's plans for the Islands center upon a gradual reduction of Federal aid and include the establishment of a Resident Commissionership in Washington, the refund of Internal Revenue taxes to the Islands, and eligibility for social security, educational, health and welfare grants. These public measures are to be supplemented by stimulation of the tourist trade and attempts to attract small industries such as hosiery and leather goods manufactures. For this purpose an eight-year property tax exemption is offered to manufacturers as well as to hotel owners.

De Castro belongs to the Jewish faith, and is a member of the Ancient Free and Accepted Masons of England. On January 31, 1923, he married Gladys Robles. They have one son, Morris Raymond. Five feet eleven and one-half inches tall, De Castro weighs 150 pounds, has black eyes and black hair. At the time of his inauguration as Governor, the *Washington Post* pointed to his "outstanding record for loyal hard work and integrity" as well as to his "modesty and high ethical standards."

References

Christian Sci Mon p3 Mr 13 '50
N Y Times p2 Mr 25 '50
N Y World-Telegram p13 N 8 '49
Scholastic 56:23 Mr 15 '50 por
Washington (D.C.) Post p49 Mr 26 '50

DE LUCA, GIUSEPPE (dā loō'kä joō-zĕp'pä) Dec. 25, 1876—Aug. 26, 1950 Operatic and concert baritone famed in the art of *bel canto*; as a boy sang in St. Peter's (Rome) and before Pope Leo XIII; studied with Persichini; made his operatic debut in 1897; career in Italy included period with Milan's La Scala; with the Metropolitan Opera Company in New York 1915-35; of approximately one hundred French and Italian roles in his repertoire, was best known for Figaro and Rigoletto; sang on concert stage and on radio. See *Current Biography*, 1947.

Obituary

N Y Times p17 Ag 28 '50

DENNY, GEORGE V(ERNON), JR. Aug. 29, 1899- Forum executive

Address: b. c/o The Town Hall, Inc., 123 W. 43d St., New York 18

> NOTE: This biography supersedes the article which appeared in *Current Biography* in 1940.

Of the radio forum program and panel discussions that have been launched since the advent of that medium, *America's Town Meeting of the Air*, which was founded in 1935 by George V. Denny, Jr., is considered to be the most significant. It has been estimated that the program (which observed its fifteenth year in May 1950) has reached a radio audience of approximately ten million. Denny, who is president of The Town Hall, Inc., is the moderator of *America's Town Meeting*, to which he brings spokesmen for opposing sides of current issues for debate, followed by questioning in the assembly. Town Hall states it was the first radio forum to have such audience participation.

Washington, a North Carolina county seat, is the place of birth of George Vernon Denny, Jr., who was born August 29, 1899. He is the son of George Vernon and Carrie Ricks (Cobb) Denny. During his boyhood he earned money by working on an uncle's tobacco and cotton farm, and after entering the University of North Carolina, he was able to pay his college expenses by various means, for a time managing a student boarding house and selling clothes on commission. In his freshman year (1918) he was in the Students Army Training Corps (he is now a first lieutenant in the Reserve), and in the following year he came under the influence of Professor Frederick H. Koch. Koch was the founder of the well-known Carolina Playmakers, a student acting troupe which sought to develop a regional drama. Denny, who took his B.S. degree in commerce in 1922, was a member of the troupe and, subsequently, its company manager at a salary of fifty dollars a month.

In 1924 Denny began a two-year period as instructor in dramatic production under Koch. Later the casting of Paul Green's Pulitzer Prize drama *In Abraham's Bosom*, at a Greenwich Village playhouse brought him to New York as an actor. Other engagements followed, but the plays were not successful. Denny, a family man by this time, realized that he must have financial security. Thus, after a year on the stage, he became the manager of W. B. Feakins, Inc., lecture bureau. This was to prove a turning point in his career: he attracted the attention of certain people at Columbia University, who in 1928 (according to Frederick L. Collins in a *Liberty* article on Denny) were looking for someone with lecture bureau experience to manage the program of lectures and concerts offered by its Institute of Arts and Sciences to the general public at the university's McMillin Academic Theater. In the performance of his duties (which included the engaging of lecturers), Denny (according to *Current History*) began to formulate principles he was to follow in *America's Town Meeting of the Air* some years later. "I saw," Denny said, "that whatever the subject might be, people could be attracted only by one of two devices—the presentation of a personality or the putting on of a show."

After two years at Columbia, Denny was appointed in 1930 the associate director of the League for Political Education, with headquarters at the ten-year-old Town Hall on 43d Street near Broadway in New York City. The league was established in 1894 by six prominent New York women pioneers in the suffrage movement: in the interests of general enlightenment it offered a program of lectures and discussions on public affairs. Since 1900 it had been under the direction of Robert Erskine Ely, who was by now approaching seventy and looking for a young assistant director. Denny was the choice. "At Town Hall," stated *Current History*, "he found the Economic Club and noticed that its members liked to ask questions of speakers who appeared before them. Radio was becoming more and more of a force

GEORGE V. DENNY, JR.

just then; Denny noticed that the Foreign Policy Association had begun to broadcast its meetings." Denny considered putting Town Hall speakers on the air, and the idea simmered until late in 1934 when, at his home in suburban Scarsdale, New York, he heard of a neighbor who said he "wouldn't for worlds be caught listening to a radio broadcast by President Roosevelt." Shocked at this unwillingness to accept the first essential of democracy, he saw the necessity of furthering free speech and free discussions by bringing eminent speakers before a real audience for the discussion of controversial issues in a program to be broadcast to an unseen audience of millions.

This was the "immediate genesis" (the phrase is Denny's) of *America's Town Meeting*. Through Mrs. Richard C. Patterson, Jr., a league director and the wife of a vice-president of the National Broadcasting Company, he succeeded in interesting NBC in putting on six experimental programs over the "Blue" network (which became the American Broadcasting Company), beginning May 30, 1935, with Denny as director and moderator. The initial topic was "Which Way America—Fascism, Communism, Socialism, or Democracy?" with Lawrence Dennis, A. J. Muste, Norman Thomas, and Raymond Moley as the panel. The response was of totally unforeseen volume: more than three thousand letters were received, and subsequent programs, on which former Ambassador James W. Gerard, Senator Alben Barkley, and the late Ogden Mills were among the speakers, were received with the same enthusiasm. From the start, much of the appeal of *America's Town Meeting* was due to Denny's use of such devices as the phrase "Town Meetin' Tonight," the crier's bell, and his own "folksy" greeting of "Good evening, neighbors." After the experimental broadcast, which ended July 5, *America's Town Meeting* was instituted

DENNY, GEORGE V., JR.—*Continued*
as a seasonal weekly program of an hour's
length.

On March 27, 1937, the announcement was
made that Dr. Ely would retire as director
of the League for Political Education on May
1, and would be succeeded by George V. Denny.
When the latter took office the name of the
organization was changed to The Town Hall,
Inc., and the title of its chief officer to president. In his first annual report as such (January 4, 1938) Denny announced the plans to
"make Town Hall a sort of people's university,"
in which *America's Town Meeting of the Air*
was assigned a conspicuous part. A few days
later (January 8) in what Denny himself considers (according to the *Atlantic Monthly*)
one of the most important broadcasts, Wendell
L. Willkie (later Presidential candidate) and
Robert H. Jackson (the Assistant Attorney
General of the United States) debated the topic
"How Can Business and Government Work
Together?" From all the programs on political,
sociological, or economic questions, *Good Evening Neighbors!* (a large pamphlet issued by
Town Hall to mark its fifteenth year) selected
others as outstanding examples: "Are Parents
or Society Responsible for Juvenile Crime?"
(February 1946); "Is a Hitler Defeat Essential
to the United States?" (January 1941);
"What's Wrong With the Comics?" (March
1948); "Do We Have a Free Press?" (Jan-
uary 1939); "How Can We Find a Basis for
Industrial Peace?" (November 1945); "How
Can We Improve Race and Religious Relations?" (October 1947); "Should the Com-
munist Party be Outlawed?" (April 1947).
Among the spokesmen for opposing sides of
these issues were Dorothy Thompson, Father
Flanagan, Dean Acheson, Verne Marshall, John
Mason Brown, Al Capp, Frank E. Gannett,
Harold L. Ickes, Ira Mosher, William L.
Green, Charles P. Taft, Walter White, Joseph
R. McCarthy, Ellis Arnall. Altogether, 1,403
speakers have appeared in the 614 broadcasts
of fifteen years, in 1950 on 274 ABC stations.

In the course of years, the format, time,
length, and place of origin of *America's Town
Meeting of the Air* have varied (in 1950 the
programs run 30 minutes, in 1951 they will be
45); underlying principles have not changed.
These, says Denny, are three in number: (1)
Conflict ("We try to avoid the old-fashioned
debate technique"); (2) Suspense ("Anything
may happen at these meetings, and often does");
and (3) Fair play ("If we ever attempted to
'load the dice' in favor of a conclusion . . . the
days of our usefulness would be over"). Until
1941 all broadcasts originated in Town Hall;
then a policy of touring the country during
part of the year was instituted, and today about
half the programs emanate from points outside
New York, for which there are 53 local sponsors. Denny was also responsible for the program originating simultaneously in New York
and London, and for arranging for broadcasts
and assemblies in Japan and other countries.
From June 26 to September 7, 1949, *Round-
the-World Town Meeting*, consisting of Moderator Denny and a "seminar" of about forty
representatives of twenty-eight national organ-

izations, held forums in fourteen cities in Europe, the Near East, and the Orient. The
editor of *Faith for Today*, a collection of
statements of creeds by prominent clergymen
and laymen, Denny has also contributed to
magazines.

The production assistant of *America's Town
Meeting* is Mrs. Denny, the former Jeanne
Sarasy, to whom Denny was married on April
2, 1944. By his first marriage, to Mary Traill
Yellott in 1924, he has three children, Mildred
Nelson and the twins George Vernon 3d and
Mary Virginia; the marriage was terminated
by divorce in 1943. Of average height, with
white hair and blue eyes, Denny has been described as an energetic, affable man. Because
of the need to maintain his reputation for impartiality, he is not a "joiner," limiting his club
membership to the Town Hall Club; his fraternity is Pi Kappa Phi. The theater remains
among his chief "outside" interests, and his
favorite sports are tennis and golf.

References

Christian Sci Mon Mag p2 D 6 '47 por
Cue 10:18 Ap 19 '41 por; 19:18-19 My
    27 '50 por
Cur Hist 51:33-5+ F '40 por
Liberty 16:41-5 D 9 '39 por
N Y Times Mag p16+ Je 6 '43 por
America's Young Men, 1938-39
Overstreet, H. A. and B. W. Town
    Meeting Comes to Town (1938)
Who's Who in America, 1950-51
Who's Who in New York, 1947
Who's Who in the East (1948)
World Biography (1948)

DEPINET, NED E(VERETT) (dĕp'ĭ-nā")
Sept. 9, 1890- Motion picture executive

Address: b. c/o Radio-Keith-Orpheum Corp.,
1270 6th Ave., New York 20; h. 1085 Park
Ave., New York

Ned E. Depinet, the president of Radio-
Keith-Orpheum (RKO) Corporation, the parent
body of several subsidiaries in motion picture
production, distribution, and exhibition, and in
television, assumed that office in September 1948.
The executive's entire career has been in the
film industry, which he entered at the age of
seventeen when he began work as a ticket taker
in the New Orleans theater his father managed.
As head of RKO, he holds similar posts or
chairmanships in the subsidiary units of RKO.

Ned Everett Depinet was born September 9,
1890, in Erie, Pennsylvania. His father, John
Depinet, held several public offices, as register
and recorder of Erie county for two terms,
and as mayor of the city of Erie. He was the
owner of the Chicago & Erie Stove Works and
of the Erie baseball team for a period while
it was still in the Eastern League. Mrs. Depinet
was the former Jessie Densmore, daughter of
the proprietor of the Central Market House
and the Densmore Flour Mill in Erie. Ned
Depinet grew up in Erie and attended its public
schools, including two years at Erie High
School, where he was enrolled in the class of
1909. As a high school student he was able to

earn some money by collecting bills for the Erie Businessmen's Association. His secondary schooling ended in 1907—he obtained a full-time job as ticket taker at the Dreamland motion picture theater in New Orleans, Louisiana, to which the family had moved when his father became manager of the movie house.

The next year, 1908, Depinet became a film salesman with the Imported Film and Supply Company of New Orleans; and in 1909 and 1910 he was a film salesman for the Pearce Exchange in the same city. In 1911 he advanced another step, to southern district sales manager for the Universal Film Company. This took him to Dallas, Texas, where that district office was located. About thirteen years later (in 1924) he was transferred by the company to its home office in New York as one of three general sales managers in what was called its "sales cabinet." However, before the year was out he was back in Dallas, as southern division manager for First National Pictures. This time he stayed only about a year. In 1925 Warner Brothers was arranging to purchase First National Pictures, and in the new concern, First National Pictures, Inc., Depinet became vice-president and the general sales manager, with an office again in New York. He remained with that corporation until 1931.

The Radio-Keith-Orpheum Corporation (RKO), of which Ned E. Depinet was to become president in 1948, has the most complex history in the industry, says the *International Motion Picture Almanac*. It and its various subsidiaries originated in several enterprises begun more than forty years ago—a nickelodeon in Milwaukee, the Keith vaudeville organization, and the Martin Beck Orpheums. Through a number of reorganizations (one of them, Mutual Film Corporation, was the first to employ a high-salaried actor, Charles Chaplin), Radio-Keith-Orpheum Corporation was formed in 1928, and RKO Radio Pictures in 1931, a producing and distributing unit of the parent RKO. In January 1931 RKO took over various elements of the Pathe Exchange, and two months later Depinet entered the organization to become vice-president and general manager of RKO-Pathe, and vice-president of RKO Distributing Company; of the latter he became president in 1934. Another office, that of vice-president of RKO Radio Pictures-Pathe, came to him in 1937.

After RKO Corporation went into equity receivership in January 1933, a reorganization (retaining that name) was completed in January 1940. Of this Depinet became vice-president and director. As a result of Federal anti-trust action RKO's production and exhibition activities (as well as those of other motion picture corporations) were separated. RKO voluntarily agreed to divest itself of its interests in theaters now wholly owned by it. (The consent decree was handed down in November 1948.) Meanwhile, Depinet in 1942 had become president of RKO Radio Pictures, in 1946 vice-chairman of the board and executive vice-president of RKO Corporation, the parent body. The date of his election to the presidency

NED E. DEPINET

of RKO is September 8, 1948. Aside from his continuing presidency of RKO Radio Pictures, the offices Depinet holds in other RKO subsidiaries are the presidency of RKO Television Corporation, board chairmanship of RKO Theaters, Inc. RKO, which grossed $123,109,000 in 1947, showed a net profit of more than $5,000,000 that year. Some of the famous motion pictures it has produced or distributed are *Fantasia*, *Notorious*, *Best Years of Our Lives* (all in 1946), and more recently or projected, *The Outlaw*, *My Foolish Heart*, *The Man on the Eiffel Tower*, *Cinderella*, *Joan of Arc*, *Stromboli*, *White Tower*, *Treasure Island*.

In February 1949 Depinet was honored, together with Irene Dunne, Richard Rodgers, and Oscar Hammerstein 2d, by the National Conference of Christians and Jews for his work as a chairman and representative of the motion picture industry on the committee for Brotherhood Week. He has written a number of articles about the motion picture industry. Chairman of the community and exhibitor relations of the Motion Picture Association of America, he is a member of the Motion Picture Pioneers. Other organizations to which he belongs are the Variety Clubs, the Masons (32d Degree, Knight Templar, Shriner), the Elks, and the Westchester Country Club. He is a Republican. Mrs. Depinet is the former Alida Livingston Cammack, to whom he was married in 1914. A tall man, he stands one inch over six feet, and weighs 175 pounds; the color of his eyes and hair is gray. For recreation he turns to swimming and golf, and enjoys watching football games and racing.

References

International Motion Picture Almanac, 1947-48
Who's Who in America, 1950-51
World Biography (1948)

DE SYLVA, BUDDY Jan. 27, 1896—July 11, 1950 Theatrical and motion picture producer and song writer; began career as ukelele player and singer of ballads; among the best-known of some 500 songs which he composed or on which he collaborated are "Somebody Loves Me", "A Kiss in the Dark", "Sonny Boy"; librettos include *Ziegfeld Follies of 1921*, six editions of *George White's Scandals*; produced five Shirley Temple motion picture successes and film versions of musical comedies *Du Barry Was a Lady, Louisiana Purchase, Panama Hattie*, which he had produced on Broadway. See *Current Biography*, 1943.

Obituary

N Y Times p29 Jl 12 '50

DE SYLVA, GEORGE GARD *See* De Sylva, B.

DICKINSON, ROBERT L(ATOU) (lä-tŏŏ) Feb. 21, 1861—Nov. 29, 1950 Physician; educator

Bulletin: Robert L. Dickinson
died on November 29, 1950.

From March 1950 issue:

A retired physician and surgeon and a pioneer in the furthering of birth control and sex education, Dr. Robert L. Dickinson was first elected president of the Euthanasia Society of America in 1946. It is the aim of the society to have made legal the practice of euthanasia (the painless putting to death of sufferers from distressing and incurable diseases) when it is desired by the patient and authorized and supervised by a committee of physicians and laymen appointed by a court. Dr. Dickinson is also known for his work in the field of medical art, particularly for his sculptures which are used in instructing the student of medicine and the general public.

Robert Latou Dickinson was born in Jersey City, New Jersey, on February 21, 1861, to Horace and Jeannette (Latou) Dickinson. The family home was in Brooklyn, New York, the city in which he was reared and in which he lived for some sixty years. At the age of ten he was injured in a boating accident, an experience, he has said, that made him decide to become a surgeon. After attending the Brooklyn Polytechnic Institute, he went to Europe—to Switzerland and Germany—for four years of study. The Doctor of Medicine degree was awarded to him in 1882 by the Long Island College Hospital. The year before, he had interned at Brooklyn's Williamsburg Hospital.

The doctor was to spend his years of active medical and surgical practice in Brooklyn. Specializing in obstetrics and gynecology, he became the senior doctor in those branches at Brooklyn Hospital and a professor at Long Island College Hospital. He was also on the staffs of the Methodist Episcopal and Kings County hospitals. In 1917 he was called to Washington for service in World War I, to be appointed assistant chief of the medical sec-

tion of the National Council of Defense. With the rank of lieutenant colonel, he was medical adviser on the General Staff during 1918-19. This was followed by missions to China (1919) and to the Near East (1926) for the United States Public Health Service.

In his sixtieth year Dickinson retired from practice to devote most of his time to the cause of birth control, one of the several controversial issues he was to support. He was one of the first leading physicians to support Margaret Sanger [44] in her early crusade, which took him on research travels in the United States, Europe, and Asia. Since 1939 the senior vice-president of Planned Parenthood Federation of America and the senior consultant of the Margaret Sanger Research Bureau, Dr. Dickinson is the author of several books on the subject. (One of his textbooks, first published in 1941, appeared in revised edition in 1950.) Dickinson has also been active in the promotion of sterilization in cases where it is medically or socially desirable. In the spheres of maternal health, sex education and practice, and marriage counseling he is regarded as an authority.

The Euthanasia Society of America—founded in 1938, it has a membership of 590 members in 1950—elected Dr. Dickinson its president in 1946, and has re-elected him to that office at its subsequent annual meetings. One of the earliest discussions of voluntary euthanasia appeared in *Literary Digest* twenty-five years ago, since which it has been explained, defended, and sharply attacked in newspaper editorials, letters to editors, magazine articles, petitions, and from the pulpit and platform; it is the subject of medical and social texts and the theme of novels. Public interest in the issue, pro and con, is heightened when a person who has been moved to "kill for mercy" is brought to trial on the charge of murder.

Since the Euthanasia Society does not condone illegal "mercy killings," it seeks to legalize the practice by bringing the debate to the floors of State legislatures, submitting petitions signed by physicians, Protestant ministers, rabbis, and other people of influence. It has also addressed a petition to the United Nations for amendment of the Declaration of Human Rights to include the right to voluntary euthanasia.

The bill proposed by the society provides that: "(1) Any one person over twenty-one years of age, 'suffering from severe physical pain caused by a disease for which no remedy affording lasting relief or recovery is at the time known to medical science,' may address to a Court of Record a signed and attested petition for euthanasia, accompanied by an affidavit from his attending physician that the disease is, in his opinion, incurable. (2) The Court shall appoint a commission of three persons, at least two of them physicians, to investigate all the factors involved and report to the Court whether the patient understands the purpose of the petition and comes within the provisions of the act. (3) Upon a favorable report by the commission, the Court shall grant the petition, and euthanasia, if still requested by the patient, may be administered by a physician or any other person chosen by the patient or the commission." Dickinson, who is a charter member of the Euthanasia Society, aided in the drafting of the proposed bill, which was defeated in the Nebraska legislature, and is seeking introduction in New York and Connecticut.

As a young physician Dr. Dickinson was dissatisfied with the inadequacy of the illustrations in medical books. Training himself in that art form, he did the drawings for the first medical book a long-established medical publishing house brought out. He has illustrated his own books, notably his several atlases of anatomy; these and models (figures and plaques) of his designing are used for teaching purposes. A sculptured model, "Birth Series" (created by Dickinson and Abram Belskie), was an exhibit at the New York World's Fair. Dickinson's medical art is also often on view at medical conventions, where (reported *Time*) he is sought by exhibitors when displays need "a few finishing touches from the Dickinson palette and brush."

In 1895 Dickinson was co-editor of *American Text Book of Obstetrics*; and a number of his important books have been written after his seventieth year. He began to gather material for *A Thousand Marriages* (1931, since reprinted) in 1890. His volumes on sex education and practices are the result of many years of investigation, which has also gone into some two hundred reports on obstetrics, gynecology, and hospital organization. Dickinson has initiated or improved several surgical techniques.

The physician's achievements in his various fields have been recognized by a number of honors—from Long Island Medical College Alumni Association (1944), the American Physical Education Association (1945), and the Albert and Mary Lasker Foundation. The citation of the latter's award in planned parenthood (given annually) reads in part: "Dr. Robert L. Dickinson, gynecologist, anatomist, educator, scholar, artist. For more than a quarter of a century he has devoted the major part of his time to furthering knowledge about human fertility and its control. . . .With exceptional literary and artistic skill, he has illuminated many unknown fields of human anatomy and physiology. A medical historian, he has himself made history in his chosen field." (Dickinson is the sculptor of the Lasker Award.)

The professional organizations to which Dickinson belongs are the American College of Surgeons (fellow and director); American Gynecological Society (ex-president), Obstetrical Society (ex-president), and various local societies in that specialty; American Gynecological Travel Club (ex-president; formed for purpose of observing operations in American and European clinics); American Medical Association (past chairman of the section of obstetrics), New York Academy of Medicine; National Committee on Maternal Health, which he helped to found (secretary, 1923-27; honorary chairman since 1937); American Association of Marriage Counselors. He belongs, too, to the National Sculpture Society, the Authors League of America, and the American Geographical Society; his clubs are the Cen-

Camera Associates

ROBERT L. DICKINSON

tury, Hamilton, Cosmos, Town Hall. He is a former vestryman of the Holy Trinity Church, in Brooklyn. In politics he is a Democrat.

Dickinson and Sarah Truslow, who were married May 7, 1890, had three daughters. Now a widower, his immediate family consists of two daughters (Dorothy, Mrs. George B. Barbour; Jean, Mrs. T. S. Potter) and six grandchildren. The octogenarian lists clinical travels, sculpture, drawing, and reading of English, French, and German literature among his recreations, which also include map making, sailing, and forestry. A veteran hiker, he has explored the Palisades and New York City—he is accounted an authority on trails: he is the author and illustrator of the American Geographical Society's *Palisades Guide* (1921), and the co-author and illustrator of *The New York Walk Book* (1923 and 1939). A man of "whimsical humor," he is described by associates as "the warmest of people, outgoing, helpful."

References

N Y Post Mag p45 F 6 '46
Time 37:46 Je 16 '41; 48:70 N 18 '46
Who Knows—And What (1949)
Who's Who in America, 1948-49
Who's Who in New York, 1947

DOHERTY, ROBERT E(RNEST) Jan. 22, 1885—Oct. 19, 1950 President of Carnegie Institute of Technology, Pittsburgh, Pennsylvania; for more than twenty years (1909-31) electrical engineer with General Electric Company; designing engineer, 1910-18; assistant to Charles Steinmetz, 1918-23; construction engineer, 1923-31; professor of electrical engineering at Yale University, 1931-33; dean of its School of Engineering, 1933-36; served in advisory capacity to the United States Government during World War II; known for his ex-

DOHERTY, ROBERT E.—*Continued*
tension of theory of alternating current in machinery and for skill in applying to practice. See *Current Biography*, 1949.

Obituary

N Y Times p31 O 20 '50

DOUGLAS, ARTHUR F(ISKE) Oct. 14, 1902- Hotel corporation executive; lawyer
Address: c/o Hotels Statler Company, Inc., Hotel Statler, New York 1; h. 44 Masterton Rd., Bronxville, N.Y.

One of the leaders in the field of modern American hotel construction and operation is Arthur F. Douglas, president of Hotels Statler Company, Inc., the oldest of the three largest hotel chains in the United States. A lawyer by profession and for nine years a specialist in the corporate reorganization of hotels and other realty, he joined the Statler company in 1937

Fabian Bachrach
ARTHUR F. DOUGLAS

as secretary-treasurer. Later, as executive vice-president, he was credited with being "one of the principal motivating forces" in bringing about the erection of the Washington (D.C.) Statler hotel in 1943, and as president since 1945 he is identified with a "major expansion program" which includes the erection of new Statler hotels in Los Angeles (California) and Dallas (Texas).

Arthur Fiske Douglas is the son of the Reverend William Douglas, a Presbyterian pastor, a native of Nova Scotia; his mother, nee Julia Bickford Fiske, came from a small town in Minnesota. Born October 14, 1902, at Estrella, near San Luis Obispo in California, Arthur Douglas grew up in Yakima, Washington, where his family had moved in 1904, the year his father died. Arthur Douglas, his elder brother

William '50 (now an Associate Justice of the United States Supreme Court), and their sister Martha (who is now a department store executive in Chicago) all contributed to the family finances while attending the Yakima public schools, the two boys picking fruit in the orchards of central Washington, or working in canneries. On completing high school, the three young Douglases attended Whitman College at Walla Walla. (Arthur worked in a jewelry store to defray his educational expenses.) After graduation from Whitman with the B.A. degree in 1924, Arthur entered the Law School of Columbia University in New York City; while there he met tuition and living costs by tutoring. In 1927 he qualified for his LL.B.

In September 1927 Arthur Douglas entered the offices of the New York City firm of Root, Clark, Buckner and Ballantine, corporate attorneys. Admitted to the New York bar in 1928, he specialized for the subsequent nine years in corporate reorganization, involving hotels, office buildings, and other real estate. "He was active," stated the New York *Times*, "in the management of more than 130 hotels and institutions." "This experience" (according to an official biographical statement) "resulted in his being offered a connection with Hotels Statler Company, Inc., as secretary-treasurer in July 1937." Appointed a director on January 30, 1938, he was made executive vice-president the following year, continuing as treasurer as well as vice-president. Douglas was elected president of the company on August 29, 1945, succeeding Frank A. McKowne, who had resigned; he assumed the office on October 1, 1945.

The first hotel in what was to be the Statler chain was built in 1904 by Ellsworth M. Statler in Buffalo, New York. It introduced a new era in the theory of construction and operation: it was the first hostelry in the United States to provide running ice water and a private bath with every room, and the first to function under the now famous slogan: "The guest is always right." Since that time Statler hotels have become known for scientific organization of layout and standardization of servicing details. Rufus Jarman, writing in the *Saturday Evening Post* of October 7, 1950, described them as "noted for being clean, attractive, efficient, as generally satisfactory and as typically American as well-kept plumbing is." Other links in the chain were the hotels in St. Louis, Cleveland and Detroit; and in 1949 the new Hotel Pennsylvania in New York City, owned by the Pennsylvania Railroad, was placed under Statler management. The Boston Statler, opened in 1927, was the last to be added during Statler's lifetime. (He died in the following year, and the enterprise was carried on by Hotels Statler Company, Inc., under the board chairmanship of his widow.) Since that time the company has taken over the William Penn in Pittsburgh, and has built the Statler in the nation's capital. The erection in 1943 of the latter, described as a "streamlined, contemporary-type edifice," is said to be largely the result of the initiative of Douglas as vice-president of the chain. (Jarman described the negotiations for this project in his *Saturday Evening Post* account.)

On August 10, 1948, the Hotels Statler Company purchased from the Pennsylvania Railroad for a reported $13,500,000 the Hotel Pennsylvania in New York City, which Statler Management, Inc., (of which Douglas is the head) had operated for twenty-nine years. The name of the 2,200-room hotel was changed to Statler as of January 1, 1949. Meanwhile (stated *Time*), "to the hotel 'firsts' of Founder Ellsworth Statler . . . Douglas added some 'firsts' of his own, e.g., television sets in hotel rooms. He also increased the income of the chain by renting wasted ground-floor space to shops." In April 1950, president Douglas was able to inform Hotels Statler stockholders that during 1949 the corporation's net earnings had risen to a record $4,134,717 (as against $3,-810,889 for 1948) due to "a greater volume of group business, expense control and earnings from the New York Statler."

At the same time it was announced that the company would proceed on "a major expansion program," to include the building of "Statler Center," a 23-million-dollar Los Angeles project, and an 800-room hotel in Dallas, Texas. The thirteen-story Los Angeles hotel, the first Statler in the Pacific Coast area, will be operated by the Statler California Corporation (Douglas is president). Its features are to include an outdoor swimming pool, complete air conditioning, 500-car garage, 75,000 square feet of space for shops, and outside exposures for every guest room. Ground was broken for the Los Angeles Statler, and for an adjacent 13-story office building, containing 150,000 square feet of space, on July 5, 1950; completion of the hotel is expected by 1952.

In 1944 Whitman College conferred an honorary LL.D. degree on Douglas. Mrs. Douglas is the former Florence Noble Peebles. The couple, who were married January 5, 1927, have three daughters—Florence Noble, Nancy Archibald, and Mary Alexander. The hotelman's other executive positions and directorships include the presidency of Trylon Studios, Inc., secretary-treasurership of the Buffalo Jenny Company, Inc., a trusteeship in the Dollar Savings Bank, and membership on the board of Sydney Blumenthal, Inc. He is six feet tall, slow-spoken, and "quiet and reserved" in manner. His relaxations are squash, tennis, and trout fishing, and he enjoys the life of a dairy farmer at his summer home in Ira, Vermont. His winter home is in Bronxville, New York, where he attends the Dutch Reformed Church. Douglas' social clubs are the Bronxville Field (of which he is a past president) and the University in New York City; his Greek letter societies are the Beta Theta Pi and the Phi Delta Phi.

References

Time 55:85 Je 19 '50 por
Who's Who in America, 1950-51
Who's Who in Commerce and Industry (1948)
Who's Who in New York, 1947
Who's Who in the East (1948)
World Biography (1948)

DOUGLAS, DONALD W(ILLS) Apr. 6, 1892- Airplane manufacturer

Address: c/o Douglas Aircraft Company, Inc., Santa Monica, Calif.; h. 1433 San Vicente Blvd., Santa Monica, Calif.

> NOTE: This biography supersedes the article which appeared in *Current Biography* in 1941.

One of the leading figures in the American aviation industry is Donald W. Douglas, president of the Douglas Aircraft Company and its board chairman. Designer of the Army planes which accomplished the first successful around-the-world flight in 1924, Douglas and his company were responsible for the manufacture of one-sixth of the aircraft produced in the United States during World War II. A pioneer in the commercial aviation field, his name is associated with the well-known DC-3 and DC-6 air transports.

Donald Wills Douglas, the second son of William Edward and Dorothy (Locker) Douglas, was born April 6, 1892, in Brooklyn, New York; he is of Scottish descent on his father's side—his great-grandfather, John Duncan Douglas, came to America from Glasgow and later settled in Albany, New York, in 1813; on his mother's side, his forebears were German and Scandinavian. After attending a Brooklyn grammar school, Douglas was prepared for college at the Trinity Chapel (Episcopal) School in Manhattan, where he edited the student magazine and won a number of prizes, including a five-dollar gold piece for an essay on Trinity Church. His boyhood enthusiasm is said to have been about equally divided between sailing (his father, a banker, was a member of the New York Yacht Club) and reading, particularly of anything pertaining to the early flying experiments of Langley, Santos-Dumont, and Wilbur and Orville Wright.

In 1909, on graduation from Trinity Chapel, he was appointed to the United States Naval Academy, to which his elder brother, Harold, had preceded him two years earlier. In the summer of his appointment, but before beginning his midshipman's course, Douglas went to Fort Myer, Virginia, to see the Wright brothers' demonstration of their biplane to the Army. This experience was to determine his future. He became increasingly absorbed in the potentialities of aircraft and increasingly irked by what a biographical release described as failure to "interest his officers in the airplane as a naval weapon." Accordingly he resigned from Annapolis (where his grades were high) in 1912 and entered the Massachusetts Institute of Technology.

On being graduated from M.I.T. in 1914 with a B.S. degree in civil engineering Douglas was appointed an assistant to Professor Jerome C. Hunsaker of the school's aerodynamics department. With Hunsaker he worked for one year on the designs for the first wind tunnel, a development credited with "taking the guesswork out of airplane performance," and was co-author with H. E. Rossell of the chapter entitled "Adjustment of Velocity Gradient Across a Section of the Wind Tunnel" in the Hunsaker report (Smithsonian Institution,

DONALD W. DOUGLAS

1916). In 1915 he worked briefly at the Connecticut Aircraft Company plant in New London on the construction of the D-1, the Navy's first dirigible. Later in the year, on the recommendation of Professor Hunsaker, he was engaged by the Glenn L. Martin Company of Los Angeles, as chief engineer, and subsequently he contributed much to the design of the first Martin bomber. For approximately one year, beginning in 1916, Douglas served as chief civilian aeronautical engineer for the United States Army Signal Corps. He rejoined the Martin company in 1917 as chief engineer, this time at the Cleveland factory; he remained there until 1920, rising to a vice-presidency.

"At twenty-eight, already an outstanding authority on aeronautics," stated Frank J. Taylor in a New York *Herald Tribune* article (June 8, 1941), "Douglas decided to strike out for himself as a builder of aircraft. His dream, at the time, was a completely streamlined plane with engines and other obstructions completely concealed in the teardrop fuselage." With $600 as his total assets, stated a company release, he returned in 1920 to California, where he succeeded in interesting David R. Davis, a wealthy Los Angeles sportsman who was anxious to be the first man to make a nonstop flight across the continent. A partnership, the Davis-Douglas Company, was formed; and, with an office at the rear of a barber shop in Santa Monica, and space rented on the second floor of a planing mill, work on the first Douglas "Cloudster," a single-bay biplane, was begun. The following June the plane started on its flight, but was grounded in Texas by engine trouble. Davis thereupon turned over to Douglas his half interest, for a promissory note of $2,500. With the plans of the Cloudster (it was the first effectively streamlined plane, the first with gas-dumping valves, and the first with an efficient instrument panel), Douglas went to Washington, where he convinced the Navy

Department that the model could be adapted to torpedo-bombing. "The result," stated the biographical release, "was an order to build three for $120,000 to be paid at progressive stages of the work. But Douglas had no money. His confidence and ability, however, persuaded fifteen businessmen of Los Angeles to lend him $1,000 each." In July 1921, accordingly, the Douglas Company, with Douglas continuing as president, was incorporated as successor to the Davis-Douglas concern, a former motion picture studio at Santa Monica was secured as a plant, and there the three Navy planes were constructed.

Other Government contracts followed, among the first being a 1923 order for a plane capable of flying around the world. The DWC was evolved, and April 6, 1924, four Army planes of this model took off from Seattle, Washington, on the first successful globe-circling flight, which was completed by two of the planes. Foreign orders resulted—the first from the Government of Norway—and a year later, when the United States Post Office Department began air mail service, Douglas planes were used. Operations had shown a profit from the start, and by 1928 Douglas had paid off his debts and was in a position to acquire the assets of the Douglas Company, which was reincorporated under the laws of Delaware as the Douglas Aircraft Company. The president of the new company since its establishment, Douglas is now also the chairman of its board of directors.

Four years later (1932), when the Northrop Corporation was organized to manufacture aircraft, Douglas acquired a controlling share of the stock; at approximately the same time he signed a contract with Transcontinental and Western Airlines for the development of a new twin-motored, all-metal commercial transport. Thus the well-known DC (Douglas Commercial) types were initiated. The DC-1 (the prototype) began flying in 1932; it was later modified as the DC-2, and in 1936 as the DC-3, the first sleeper-transport plane. (It was claimed in 1947 that of eleven thousand DC-3's built up to that time, a high percentage were still in service). The Douglas and Northrop companies were merged in 1937, and in the following year the DC-4, the largest land transport yet built, was completed. Douglas was the recipient of the Collier Award for 1936 for the "outstanding twin-engine transport plane," and in 1940 won the Daniel Guggenheim Gold Medal for his contributions to transport engine development.

As war became imminent the designer-manufacturer again turned his attention to military craft, and in 1939 produced the A-20 (Havoc) light bomber for the Army and the SBD (Dauntless) dive bomber for the Navy. (At that time the Douglas Aircraft Company employed about 8,000 workers at Santa Monica and at a secondary plant at El Segundo.) The B-19, described as the biggest land plane yet built, and designed as a "flying laboratory" for the Army, made its first flight in July 1941. With the entrance of the United States into World War II the Douglas organization expanded greatly. New plants were opened at

Long Beach (California), Tulsa and Oklahoma City (Oklahoma), and Chicago, and personnel increased to a peak of 160,000 in 1944. Meanwhile, the DC-3 had been adapted to military use as the famous C-47 (ten thousand of these had been completed by the end of the war in Europe); in March 1942, the C-54 (military version of the DC-4) was ready. The Douglas company also developed the A-26 (Invader), fastest attack bomber of the Army, and under a pooling arrangement with Boeing and Consolidated, shared in the manufacture of the B-17 (Flying Fortress) and B-24 (Liberator) heavy bombers. The *World Aviation Annual* credits the Douglas company with producing a total of 29,385 aircraft during the war years, or 14 per cent by weight of all planes turned out in the United States during the period of hostilities.

"Where there is no work in a shop, you have to shut it up. My theory is that when the time comes, contracts should be tapered off and employees gradually reduced." So wrote Douglas in the magazine *Aviation* in January 1944, when he was looking ahead to the end of the war and of emergency plane construction. In the postwar retrenchment the Douglas employment roster shrank to about 25,000, and all except the Santa Monica, El Segundo, and Long Beach plants closed down. Before the close of the war, production of the C-74 (Globemaster), a large four-engine transport with a range of 7,800 miles, was begun; and the company was at work on the B-42, described as "a radically new bomber, utilizing liquid-cooled engines mounted in the fuselage to activate counter-rotating." The D-558, a jet-propelled, experimental transonic Navy fighter, twice broke the world's speed record in August of 1947; and early in the following year the DC-6 super airliner entered service. In November 1949 improved DC-6A and DC-6B models were shown, and a new Super DC-3 made its first flight on the New York-Montreal route. By the end of the year (according to Selig Altschul in *Aviation Week*) the Douglas company had "the strongest financial position of any major aircraft builder." A company report released in October 1950 revealed a working capital of $55,888,414 as of August 31 and an increase of $7,000,000 in sales and billing over the previous year's. The increase was atttributable largely to military orders made necessary by the Korean crisis, and in some degree to an increase in commercial orders.

An honorary fellow of the Institute of Aeronautical Sciences (president in 1935), a member of the Aircraft Industries Association, and a former chairman of the board of governors of the Aeronautical Chamber of Commerce, Douglas in World War II organized the Aircraft War Production Council and was several times its president. He is a director of the Farmers and Merchants National Bank of Los Angeles. His clubs are the Los Angeles Yacht, the Los Angeles Athletic, the Santa Monica Athletic, the Pacific Coast, the California Yacht, and the Brentwood Country. In his political allegiance he is a Republican, in his church membership an Episcopalian. On June 5, 1916, Charlotte Marguerite Ogg of Marion,

Indiana, became Mrs. Douglas; they have four sons, Donald Wills, Jr., William Edward, Malcolm Angus, and James Sholto, and one daughter, Barbara Jean. "A tall, good-looking, brown-eyed, brown-tweedy sort of man" (in the words of *Time*), Douglas seems to prefer an evening at home with a pipe and a book, or perhaps a week end on his yacht, to social activities. A musical liking of his is said to be the bagpipe of his paternal forebears.

References

Collier's 98:20+ Jl 4 '36 por
Forbes Mag 47:20+ Je 15 '41 por
N Y Herald Tribune X p4 Je 8 '41 por
Nation's Bus 25:26-9+ Mr '37 por
Pop Sci 137:126-7 D '40 por; 140:52-8 Mr '42 por
Sat Eve Post 216:9-11+ N 27 '43; 216:22+ D 4 '43 pors
Time 31:33-4+ My 23 '38 por; 42:77-80+ N 22 '43 por
Blue Book of American Aviation (1942)
Cunningham, F. Sky Master, the Story of Donald Douglas (1943)
Forbes, B. C. ed. America's Fifty Foremost Business Leaders (1948)
National Cyclopædia of American Biography, Current vol F (1939-42)
Who's Who in America, 1950-51
Who's Who in Aviation, 1942-43
World Biography (1948)

DOUGLAS, WILLIAM O(RVILLE) Oct. 16, 1898- Associate Justice of the Supreme Court of the United States
Address: b. c/o United States Supreme Court, Washington, D.C.; h. 2029 Connecticut Ave., N.W., Washington, D.C.

> NOTE: This biography supersedes the article which appeared in *Current Biography* in 1941.

An Associate Justice of the Supreme Court of the United States, to which he was appointed in 1939, William O. Douglas has shown himself a liberal in his voting, and has become known for his pronouncements on civil liberties. While a professor at Yale University Law School he made a name for himself in studies of the legal aspects of bankruptcy proceedings, and was appointed to aid investigations in that field on New York City and Federal committees. From 1934 he served on the Securities and Exchange Commission, first as a member and then as chairman until his appointment to the country's highest court. Douglas is a Democrat.

The second of the three children of William and Julia Bickford (Fiske) Douglas, William Orville Douglas was born October 16, 1898, in Maine, Minnesota. His father, a Presbyterian home missionary, who had come from Nova Scotia, Canada, was taken to the West Coast by his calling, and William thus spent his early years in a succession of small towns in California and Washington. When Douglas senior died in 1904, Mrs. Douglas settled with her children in Yakima, Washington, where she had

WILLIAM O. DOUGLAS

relatives. There William Orville, his sister Martha (now a department store executive in Chicago), and his brother Arthur '50 (now president of the Hotels Statler Company, Inc.) were reared; all contributed to the family finances, earning money outside school hours in odd jobs about the town and helping harvest the crops in the orchards of the district (later William worked in fields with itinerant labor). Graduated from Yakima High School, where he was class valedictorian, with a tuition scholarship, William Douglas proceeded to Whitman College in Walla Walla. There his school record included presidency of the student body, membership on the debating team, and election to Phi Beta Kappa. In 1920 he received the B.A. degree and took a teaching position. (The summer and fall of 1918 he had spent as a private in the United States Army and in an officers training camp.)

After two years of teaching English and Latin in the Yakima High School, where he also coached the debating team and taught public speaking, in 1922 Douglas set out for New York to enroll in Columbia University Law School, undertaking to "herd" a carload of sheep bound for Chicago to pay his fare. While studying at Columbia he paid his way by tutoring and supplying cases to illustrate a law textbook for a correspondence course school. He was graduated in 1925, second in his class and one of the editors of the *Law Review.* At law school he had been particularly interested in the study of the relation between law and business (states Max Lerner in a study of Douglas in the book *Ideas Are Weapons*), and on graduating he joined the Wall Street firm of Cravath, DeGersdorff, Swaine and Wood "like an anthropologist" to "study the facts of law and life among the natives." There he had a chance to learn the intricacies of corporation finance under conditions of a boom market. The

same commentator points to Thorstein Veblen's *Absentee Ownership* and Louis D. Brandeis' *Other People's Money* as formulative influences on the young lawyer's thinking. He was admitted to the bar in 1926.

A lecturer at Columbia Law School from the time of his graduation, Douglas in 1927 left Wall Street to become assistant professor of law at Columbia. One year later he resigned, when President Butler appointed a dean for the Law School without consulting the faculty. A chance meeting with Robert Maynard Hutchins, then dean of law at Yale University, resulted in the offer of an assistant professorship there, which Douglas accepted. Within a year he had been raised to associate professor; in 1931 he was made a professor, and in 1932 was appointed to the chair of Sterling Professor of Law. (Hutchins, when President of the University of Chicago, was to call Douglas "the outstanding professor of law in the nation.")

During his years at Yale Douglas became known for his studies in bankruptcy. In 1929 he was special adviser to William J. Donovan in a bankruptcy investigation in New York City, and during the next four years carried on, in association with the United States Department of Commerce, bankruptcy studies for the Yale Institute of Human Relations. In addition to the findings published by the institute, Douglas' studies in that period provided material for articles in law journals, and several case books, four written with C. M. Shanks, and one with Charles Edward Clark.

The Yale professor was also called upon, in the years 1930-32, to be secretary to the committee on the study of business of the Federal courts, an investigation undertaken for the National Commission on Law Observance and Law Enforcement. (A two-volume work entitled *Business of the Federal Courts* embodies the findings of the committee.) In 1934 Douglas was asked to direct a study of protective committees to be carried out by the Securities and Exchange Commission. From that year (1934) until 1936, he held hearings, examined records, investigating those committees which are formed when businesses fail; his eight-volume report criticized the performance of bankers as bond trustees, and pointed out abuses on the part of protective and reorganization committees.

In 1936 Douglas was appointed a member of the Securites and Exchange Commission, and in 1937 its chairman. In the introduction to *Democracy and Finance*, a collection of Douglas' addresses and statements as chairman of the SEC published in 1940, James Allen says, "If the administration of William O. Douglas were to be characterized in a single word, the word would be action." Emphasizing the desirability of "simple honesty" and "social responsibility," Douglas conducted conferences and studies which led to a reorganization of the Stock Exchange. His contention throughout had been that the Exchange could and should formulate the plan for its own reorganization, and this it eventually did, voting in March 1938 for reorganization along lines approved by Douglas. In his work with SEC he "succeeded in establishing many protections for the small investor," stated Jack Alexander in a *Saturday Evening Post* article, "Washington's Angry Scotsman."

President Roosevelt in March 1939 nominated Douglas an Associate Justice of the Supreme Court to succeed Louis D. Brandeis, who had retired the previous month. With Senate confirmation, Douglas took his seat on the bench on April 17, 1939. (It is reported that Brandeis said to Douglas on his appointment, "I wanted you to be here in my place"—*Fortune*, January 1947, "The Supreme Court: 1947" by Arthur M. Schlesinger, Jr.) Since coming to the Supreme Court Douglas has written many of its opinions in financial cases; his style was characterized by Jack Alexander as "distinguished for blunt clarity."

The majority decision of May 16, 1949, ruling that free speech must be guaranteed even to a speaker who "stirs the public to anger, invites disputes, brings about . . . unrest or creates a disturbance," was written by Justice Douglas. In this connection the jurist stated that free speech might well serve its purpose when creating such conditions. (The decision roused much controversy and called forth a vigorous dissent from Justice Jackson '50.) Another majority opinion written by Douglas which has attracted considerable attention is that of June 5, 1950 (which the court refused to reconsider on October 16, 1950), ruling in two tidelands oil cases, involving large sums of money and constitutional relations between States and the Federal Government, that the latter has "paramount rights" to oil-rich areas off the coasts of Texas and Louisiana.

In 1947, in what has been termed "an indignant dissent," Douglas (with Justices Black, Rutledge, and Murphy) differed from the court's rejection of a Justice Department charge that purchase of the Columbia Steel Company by the Consolidated Steel Corporation, a United States Steel subsidiary, violated antitrust laws; he called it the most important antitrust case before the court in years, one revealing "the way of growth of monopoly power." Delivering a nonvoting opinion on a decision (rendered June 13, 1949) invalidating Standard Oil of California's "exclusive dealer" contracts, Douglas declared the ruling suggested a "formula" which would enable the oil companies to build "service station empires of their own." The opinion developed into an attack on the Supreme Court's basic stand on monopoly, in which Douglas stated: "The economic theories which the court has read into the antitrust laws have favored rather than discouraged monopoly," and, "the court approves what the antitrust laws were designed to prevent. It helps remake America in the image of the cartel." In a June 20, 1949, dissent Douglas held that an 1886 ruling according to which corporations were "persons" entitled to protection under the Fourteenth Amendment should be reversed.

An analysis of the Supreme Court voting record in nonunanimous decisions during 1937-47 (*The Roosevelt Court* by C. Herman Pritchett) placed Douglas in the liberal bloc of the court and showed a high rate of agreement between his voting and that of Justice Black.

Schlesinger attributed to Douglas and to Black a belief "that the Supreme Court can play an affirmative role in promoting social welfare" and a tendency "to settle the particular case in what they regard as the spirit of the American democratic tradition" rather than on legal merits.

Statistics in the Pritchett study (as summarized by Arthur Krock in a New York *Times* article) showed that in the period 1939-46 Justice Douglas upheld administrative acts sixteen times, while rejecting them once; voted against acts of the Interstate Commerce Commission five times, and for them once; found against business in the three cases in which it was charged under the Sherman Act; voted for labor in related causes eight times in ten; sustained the taxpayer as against the Federal Government five times out of nine, and the State Government against the taxpayer three times out of three; upheld the States against the Federal Government four times out of eight; sustained eminent domain against individuals three times out of four. Since that time his opinions on some of the other outstanding cases have been as follows: March 1947 voted with the majority in ruling John L. Lewis and the U.M.W.A. in civil and criminal contempt of court in strikes at Government-operated coal mines in November 1946; was with the majority in finding the Norris-La Guardia Act barring antistrike injunctions not applicable to the Federal Government; dissented from a majority ruling that antitrust consent decree barring Ford from owning or advocating the use of a particular finance company (imposed by the United States District Court for North Indiana) should be lifted; dissented (February 28, 1949) from a decision upholding a Wisconsin labor board ban on frequent union meetings of AFL United Auto Workers at Briggs and Stratton Corporation plants as a "slowdown" device in a wage dispute; dissented (June 20, 1949) from a ruling that the FPC has no control over a natural gas company's disposal of its gas reserves; voted (June 5, 1950) to declare unconstitutional the Taft-Hartley law "non-Communist affidavit."

Among cases rejected for review but which Douglas favored reviewing were: the appeal of the RD-DR motion picture corporation, in a case based on censorship of a film—the movie concern sought classification for the industry as "press," with freedom guaranteed in the Constitution; the appeal from contempt conviction of Hollywood writers John Howard Lawson and Dalton Trumbo for refusing to reveal to a Congressional committee whether or not they were Communists; appeal from a New York State Court of Appeals ruling upholding exclusion of Negroes from an insurance company public housing project; the appeal from the $1,420,000 contempt-of-court fine imposed on John L. Lewis and the U.M.W.A. for failure to curtail a strike in 1948.

"The recurrent Douglas boom whenever a vacancy occurs in a top Government job is a familiar feature of the Washington landscape," wrote Schlesinger in 1947. Named with Truman by Roosevelt in 1944 as persons acceptable to him as Vice-Presidential candidate should

DOUGLAS, WILLIAM O.—*Continued*

Wallace be refused the nomination, Douglas in 1948 found himself boomed for the White House, but discouraged the movement, announcing July 10 that he had no intention of running. On July 12 he refused President Truman's invitation to run for Vice-President.

Excerpts from some of Douglas' speeches were published in 1948 under the title *Being An American*; its contents included a passage from the eulogy he delivered when unveiling the Roosevelt plaque at Hyde Park in 1948. *Commonweal* in reviewing the book, stated: "Mr. Douglas reveals himself as a phrasemaker with eloquent and optimistic devotion to civil rights and the well-being of the common man." A number of his addresses have also been printed in *Vital Speeches,* and he has contributed to various popular magazines as well as to professional journals. At a 1949 rally of United World Federalists, Inc. (of which he was elected vice-president in 1950) Douglas said that the Western nations could find "new hope and promise for peace" in a world federation, even if the Soviet Union refused to participate.

In *Of Men and Mountains,* published in 1950, the jurist tells of his experiences as a mountaineer in the Cascade and Wallowa Mountains of the Pacific coast. (After an accident while riding on one such expedition in October 1949, Douglas was hospitalized for six weeks with broken ribs suffered when his horse rolled on him.) He emphasizes the strengthening of physical and moral fiber the experiences have brought him, from the time of his early climbs as a boy seeking to strengthen his legs after having overcome infantile paralysis. Reviewing the book, N. F. Morse of the Chicago *Sun* wrote: "Justice Douglas writes with disarming simplicity. . . . His trout fishing forays are an armchair adventurer's delight to read . . . small classics of their kind." Orville Prescott pointed out in the New York *Times*: "Its quality lies in the character of its author, the warmth, friendliness, humanity, and bedrock idealism."

An honorary M.A. degree was conferred upon the jurist in 1932 by Yale University; honorary LL.D. degrees followed: from Whitman College (1938), Wesleyan University (1940), Washington and Jefferson College (1942), College of William and Mary (1943), Rollins College (1947). In 1950 he was named to be recipient of the annual Morris Morgenstern Award of Yeshiva (New York) University. He is a member of Beta Theta Pi, Phi Alpha Delta, and Delta Sigma Rho fraternities, and is a Mason. His religious faith is the Presbyterian. On August 16, 1923, while a student at Columbia law school, Douglas married Mildred Riddle, a fellow teacher with him when he was on the Yakima High School staff. Their children are Mildred Riddle and William. (Douglas was named Father of the Year by the National Father's Day Committee in New York in May 1950.) The Associate Justice is a little under six feet tall, has sandy hair and blue eyes; he is known for informality of dress and bearing—descriptions frequently refer to his hair as tousled. His qualities have been summed up by Schlesinger as "executive vigor, intelligence, simplicity, and considerable charm." It has been his habit to spend his summer vacations in a cabin in the Wallowa Mountains of Oregon, where he can fish and climb mountains—the latter interest has taken him abroad. In his Washington chambers he keeps a collection of mountain flora.

References

Am Mag 127:20-1 My '39 por
Collier's 97:9 My 9 '36 por; 101:12-13 Ja 29 '38
Fortune 35:73-9 Ja '47
Holiday 7:82 F '50
Lit Digest 125:12-13 Ja 29 '38 por
N Y Post My 7 '48; Je 15-20 '48
Read Digest 34:58-60 Je '39
Sat Eve Post 215:9-10 O 17 '42
Lerner, M. Ideas Are Weapons (1939)
National Cyclopædia of American Biography Current vol F, 1939-42
10 Eventful Years (1947)
Who's Who, 1950
Who's Who in America, 1950-51
Who's Who in the East (1948)
Who's Who in United States Politics (1950)
World Biography (1948)

DREW, CHARLES R(ICHARD) June 3, 1904—Apr. 1, 1950 Negro scientist and surgeon; authority on blood plasma; director of the first plasma division of the Blood Transfusion Association, supplying blood plasma to the British 1940-41; first director of the American Red Cross Blood Bank, supplying plasma to the United States armed forces, February-May 1941; professor of surgery and head of the department at Howard University's College of Medicine since 1941; chief surgeon and chief of staff at Freedman's Hospital (Washington, D.C.) and medical director there since 1946. See *Current Biography,* 1944.

Obituary

N Y Times p76 Ap 2 '50

DUROCHER, LEO (ERNEST) (dū-rŏch'ĕr) July 27, 1906- Baseball club manager

Address: b. c/o New York Giants Baseball Club, 100 W. 42d St., New York 18

NOTE: This biography supersedes the article which appeared in *Current Biography* in 1940.

The manager of the Brooklyn Dodgers in 1939-46 and 1948, Leo Durocher became the manager of the New York Giants in 1948. He had first become famous in baseball in the early 1930's, when he was fielding shortstop on the St. Louis Cardinals team. As the Dodgers' manager for nine years he saw them win their first pennant in twenty-one years and led them to third place or better in seven of those seasons. While Durocher's Giants finished in fifth place in 1949 and did not distinguish themselves during the first half of the 1950 season, Durocher's management has reportedly led to a "faster, tighter type of team," with emphasis on speed, youth and "hustle." Durocher's contract as manager of the Giants, renewed in May 1949, extends through the 1951 baseball season.

Leo Ernest Durocher was born July 27, 1906, in West Springfield, Massachusetts, where his father, George J. Durocher, worked for the Boston and Albany Railroad. Both of Durocher's parents were of French stock—the family attended St. Louis' Catholic Church, which had a congregation almost entirely of French extraction. According to Stanley Woodward ("That Guy Durocher," *Saturday Evening Post,* June 3, 1950) Durocher received his schooling at Main Street and Park Avenue grammar schools in West Springfield, and played on the baseball team of the Immaculate Conception Church of the Catholic Junior League. Taking a job as a mechanic, he worked for the Wico Electric Company, Gilbert and Barker, and the Boston and Albany Railroad.

Durocher's first chance in professional baseball came when he played for the Merrick team against the Liberty Braves in an important local series. It was then, when the playing of the eighteen-year-old youth was reportedly a "sensation," that he was engaged by a baseball scout for the Hartford team of the old Eastern League. Sold to the New York Yankees in 1925, he played a year each in Atlanta and St. Paul before going to New York in 1928 to join the Yankees' home team.

From his first day with the Yankees, Durocher was "the cockiest player in the training field," and his teammates promptly named him "Lippy." Durocher was the Yankee's second base in the 1928 World Series, when his fielding average was 1.000 in the four games he played. By 1929, however, his fielding seemed less spectacular than before, and his batting, which had not been too good, seemed less so. He was then sold to the last-place Cincinnati Reds (he had now entered the National League) in February 1930, for whom he alternated between second base and shortstop during the seasons of 1930, 1931, and 1932. The team finished seventh in 1930, and eighth during the next two seasons.

At the end of three years with the Cincinnati Club, Durocher was traded to the St. Louis Cardinals. It was with the latter team (with which he remained five years) that he became a star as a shortstop in the memorable 1934 World Series between the Cardinals and the Detroit Tigers. When the series was over, the Cardinals had beaten Detroit in seven games, and Durocher, now "at the top of his game," was recognized as the best fielding shortstop in baseball. Durocher's record in that series was: at bat, 27 times; 4 runs; 7 hits; a fielding average of 1.000 and a batting average of .259. In 1935 Durocher was made captain of the Cardinals and in 1936 and 1938 he played shortstop in the two All Star Games of the National League. His total for both games was 6 times at bat, batting average .333, 1 run, 2 hits, put-

LEO DUROCHER

outs 4, assists 3, fielding average 1.000. The outstanding performances of his career as a player were the two doubles he made in one inning in the first game on August 25, 1936; and in 1933, 1936, and 1938 he led National League shortstops in the field.

After four years as "keyman" of the Cardinals, Durocher was traded in October 1937 to the Brooklyn Dodgers in exchange for four players. Because by that time Durocher had developed a reputation for truculence and was no longer a young player, the baseball world thought the trade might turn out to be a bad one for Brooklyn. Durocher, however, proved his worth. He became the Dodgers' captain in 1938, the year in which he was named manager of the team. The Dodgers' standing was then seventh; and in 1939, when the team traveled West under Durocher, it received six straight defeats. Durocher, using strong language to his players, both collectively and individually, threatened them with dismissal unless their record improved. Within two weeks the Dodgers were in third place, and at the end of the season Durocher was presented with the *Sporting News* award as the "Manager of the Year."

In his nine seasons as their manager the Dodgers won their first pennant (in 1941) in twenty-one years, winning 100 games and losing 54. (In the World Series that year they won 1 game, lost 4.) In the three years they held second place in the National League, games won and lost were as follows: 1940—88, 65; 1942—104, 50; 1946—96, 60. In the three years they held third place, the record was: 1939—84, 69; 1943—81, 72; 1945—87, 67. In fifth place in 1948, games won were 36, games lost, 37. In the two seasons they lost more games than they won: 1944, seventh place, won 63, lost 91; 1948, fifth place, won 36, lost 37. Durocher himself did not play in 1942, 1944, or after 1945; in 1938-40 he played many games,

DUROCHER, LEO—*Continued*

in 1941 in 18 (shortstop and second base), in 1943 in 6 as shortstop, and in 1945 in 2 games.

For one year—1947—Leo Durocher was not the Dodgers' manager. In "the most drastic action ever taken against a major league baseball pilot" (New York *Times*), on April 9, 1947, Durocher was suspended for a season by Commissioner Chandler. The disciplinary action came after Durocher had accused Yankee team president Larry MacPhail [45] of having gamblers in his box at an exhibition game between the Dodgers and Yankees at Havana in March 1947. There had also been bickering between the two men and criticism of MacPhail in Durocher's ghost-written column in the Brooklyn *Eagle*. Chandler fined the two clubs because (according to the official report) "they engaged in a public controversy detrimental to baseball"; and Durocher was suspended for "not measuring up to the standards expected or required of managers" and because of "cumulated unpleasant incidents." Aside from the Havana incident, sportswriters were not certain as to what specific incidents Chandler referred to, and they felt that Durocher had been dealt with more harshly than he deserved. In his last season (1948) in Brooklyn the team passed into the second division, in fifth place.

In a mid-season change, on July 18, 1948, Durocher succeeded Mel Ott as manager of the New York Giants Baseball Club. In fourth place at that time, it finished the season in fifth. This, coupled with a suspension of a few days following an assault charge by a fan against the manager (in which he was later exonerated by Chandler), "put Durocher on the spot." However, in what the New York *Times* called a "surprise move," the Giants directors gave the manager "a vote of confidence" by announcing on May 13, 1949, that a new contract, extending through the 1951 season, had been signed. (The annual salary is estimated to exceed $60,000.) During Durocher's second season—his first full season—with the Giants, the team won 73 games, lost 81, placing fifth at the close. The highest winning score was 15 games against the Cincinnati Reds, and it lost the greatest number of games (also 15) to the St. Louis Cardinals. In the 1950 season, when the Giants seemed to be making a better showing, on June 30 it was in sixth place, had won 31 games, had lost the same number, was behind 5 games.

"Durocher," said *Time* (April 14, 1947), "has immense ability. . . . As a tactician he is unsurpassed. . . . He has an instinct for knowing just what his players can do in any situation. He yanks pitchers quicker than any other manager and the results usually bear out his judgment. . . . Says Leo, 'I play hunches. . . . Maybe other managers are afraid to take chances.'" "Lippy" Durocher is famous for his arguments with umpires as well as with fans. "It is a slow season," commented *Time*, "when The Lip gets less than five notices from National League headquarters. Sample: 'For prolonged argument, delaying the game, use of violent, profane language, you are fined $100.'" When questioned by a reporter of the New

York *Sunday News* as to why he argued with umpires when he knew they could not change their decisions, Durocher replied that a challenge makes an umpire more alert the next time; that if a player thinks the umpire is wrong, it is mandatory that his manager support his man—"Wouldn't I be a heck of a manager if I didn't?"

Mrs. Durocher is Laraine Day, motion picture actress. They were married in January 1947, after she had obtained a divorce in Mexico; they went through a second ceremony in February 1948 after her California divorce became final. (Durocher's two previous marriages, to Ruby Hartles in 1930, and to Grace Dozier in 1934, were terminated by divorce.) The Durochers have two adopted children, Christopher and Michele. Five feet nine inches in height, the baseball club manager weighs 175 pounds; he has blue eyes and brown hair. He is said to be a speaker who feels at ease before any kind of crowd. In earlier years he was an expert at pool, and excelled in games of all kinds so that those who knew him well learned never to "try to beat him at anything for money." His hobby, he says, is golf; and bridge is reportedly his only poor game. The *Saturday Evening Post* writer said that Durocher has "a passion for racy autos, fancy ties, and $175 suits."

References

Collier's 112:24+ S 11 '43
Life 22:37+ F 3 '47 por
N Y Herald Tribune p1 Ap 10 '47
N Y Post p15 Ap 11 '42
N Y Times p50 My 10 '49; p16 My 14 '49
PM p22 Ap 10 '47
Sat Eve Post 222:25+ Je 3 '50
Time 49:56+ Ap 14 '47

DUVIEUSART, JEAN (dü"vyû"sär' zhäɴ) Apr. 10, 1900- Belgian political leader

Address: h. 24, Boulevard de l'Athénée, Charleroi, Belgium

In June 1950 Jean Duvieusart became head of the first one-party Cabinet to govern Belgium in thirty-six years. As leader of the Social Christian (Catholic) party, he pledged his Government to bring exiled King Leopold III [44] back to the throne. In the face of threatened violence by Socialists and other groups representing about half the population, Duvieusart arranged for the King's return to Brussels on July 22. As riotous opposition to Leopold developed, bringing the country to the brink of civil war, Duvieusart urged the King's withdrawal in favor of Crown Prince Baudouin [50]. This accomplished on August 11, Duvieusart and his Cabinet resigned, to be superseded by another Social Christian Government. The Premier had been Minister of Economics in the Cabinets of Paul-Henri Spaak [45] and Gaston Eyskens [49].

Born on April 10, 1900, in Frasnes-lez-Gosselies in the province of Hainaut, Belgium, Jean Duvieusart is the son of Léopold and Marie (Boval) Duvieusart. He was educated at the

College of the Jesuit Fathers (in Charleroi) and at the University of Louvain. From the latter he received his LL.D. in 1922, when he began to practice law. Having entered politics, at the age of twenty-seven he became Mayor of his native town, an office he was to fill for nineteen years. During the 1933-36 period he was a member of the Provisional Council of the province of Hainaut.

Jean Duvieusart entered the national political scene in Belgium in 1944 when he was elected a member of the Chamber of Representatives, the lower house. Re-elected in 1946, he became vice-president of the Social Christian group in the Chamber. On March 19, 1947, Duvieusart was appointed Minister of Economic Affairs in the Cabinet of Spaak. During that year Belgium, the Netherlands, and Luxembourg agreed on a customs union to become effective January 1, 1948. The union, to be known as Benelux, in the fall of 1947 reached an accord with France and Italy on the free exchange of currencies. Another treaty with which the Minister of Economic Affairs was concerned was the fifty-year defense, economic, and social and cultural treaty signed in Brussels March 17, 1948, by Benelux, Britain, and France, the step toward the Union of Western Europe. In the meantime, the Marshall Plan was being implemented through the European Recovery Program.

While Belgium was rebuilding its postwar economy, its political climate was disturbed by the issue of King Leopold III's return to the throne. The King's brother, Prince Charles '46, had been made Regent in 1944, and Leopold had been barred from his country by parliamentary decree in 1945 because he had surrendered the Belgian armies to the Germans in 1940. Nevertheless, Leopold commanded strong supporters at home, particularly among the Flemish and from the Social Christian (Catholic) party. Most of the French-speaking Walloons, the Socialists, Liberals, and Communists opposed the King's return.

In the elections of June 26, 1949, the Social Christians won a majority in the Senate and lacked only two votes to hold a majority in the Chamber of Representatives. As a consequence, Spaak's Coalition Cabinet of Socialists and Social Christians gave way to a Cabinet of Social Christians and Liberals. In this new Cabinet, formed by Eyskens on August 10, 1949, Duvieusart retained his post as Minister of Economic Affairs.

An advisory referendum held on March 12, 1950, showed that 57.6 per cent of the Belgian voters favored the King's return. Socialists and trade union members, however, particularly in Brussels and in French-speaking Walloon areas, voiced strong opposition. On March 18 the Eyskens Cabinet resigned after the Liberal party had decided that Leopold had failed to win a convincing majority in the plebiscite. Eyskens remained as Acting Premier while three other leaders made unsuccessful attempts to form a Cabinet. On April 15 Leopold offered to allow his nineteen-year-old son, Prince Baudouin '50, to assume the throne "temporarily." This offer was tentatively accepted by most on April 20, and the country seemed near the

R. Martin, Brussels
JEAN DUVIEUSART

end of its Cabinet crisis. However, the agreement came to an end April 25, by Leopold's rejection of a Socialist demand that he agree to remain out of the country after abdicating in favor of Prince Baudouin.

Prince Regent Charles dissolved Belgium's Parliament April 29, 1950, calling for new elections to be held June 4. In these elections, the Social Christians, who demanded Leopold's immediate and unconditional return, won 108 seats in the Chamber (a majority of four) as well as a majority of seven in the Senate. On June 7 Prince Regent Charles named Jean Duvieusart Premier. The *Christian Science Monitor*'s correspondent commented: "M. Duvieusart, a French-speaking Walloon, apparently was chosen by this [Social Christian] party as chief of the bring-back-Leopold government because he may help to allay Walloon opposition and because of his reputation as a moderate." Thus, the new, all-Social Christian Cabinet (the first one-party government in thirty-six years, and the first in Belgian history in which Flemings outnumbered Walloons) sworn in the following day, was pledged to call a joint meeting of the Parliament to repeal the law of July 19, 1945, which had set up the regency.

After conferring with Leopold in Geneva, Duvieusart told newspapermen there was no doubt the King would return to Belgium in the near future, adding that he hoped partisans of the ruler would welcome him with extreme discretion while those opposed to the monarch would accept the decision of Parliament. "It is possible that the King's offer to delegate his powers to Prince Baudouin will form the basis of future negotiations after the sovereign's return to Belgium," Duvieusart pointed out.

Meanwhile, important matters of an economic nature required action by Duvieusart's Government. On June 21, 1950, it ratified the revised European Payments Union plan, a system aimed

DUVIEUSART, JEAN—*Continued*

at removing obstacles to multilateral European trade. The Premier on June 28 pledged to continue Belgium's postwar foreign policy which, he said, "has been and still is to help maintain peace and develop material prosperity." He declared that his Government would favor larger freedom in trade relationships and planned "a maximum effort to fulfill its national defense obligations as outlined by the five-power Brussels pact and the North Atlantic treaty." The Government also drew up plans for a ten-year project for the Belgian Congo, intended to enlarge the transport and electrical power system, aid agriculture, and improve living conditions and public services.

Duvieusart's Government on June 30, 1950, received a vote of confidence in the Chamber of Representatives, 108 deputies voting for it, 100 against, and one abstaining. On July 4 the Senate gave it a vote of confidence of 90 to 83 after a thirteen-hour debate. Both houses convened in joint session on July 6 to take up the issue of the King's return, and violent opposition in the Parliament delayed the vote for two weeks, during which there were widespread protest strikes and a number of mass anti-Leopold meetings. On July 20 the joint session of Parliament voted 198-0 to welcome back the King; this represented the full strength of the Social Christian party plus one Liberal, the Socialists, Communists and other Liberals having walked out. The next day Duvieusart and the Presidents of the House and Senate flew to Switzerland to accompany the King on his return on July 22.

The King's return was met with serious disturbances—strikes, sabotage, riotous demonstrations, threats of secession by Wallonia—all pointing to civil war. The result was that Duvieusart came out in favor of Leopold's retirement and the delegation of ruling powers to Prince Baudouin, which was effected August 11, 1950, after obtaining Leopold's agreement and Parliament passed the empowering bill. In this the Premier was supported by the Socialists, the Liberals, but not all of his own Social Christian (Catholic) party members, some of them remaining uncompromisingly pro-Leopold. The day Prince Royal Baudouin became the new Chief of State, Duvieusart and his Cabinet resigned. His successor, Joseph Pholien (a Social Christian) also chose a one-party Cabinet, which, apart from the now settled Leopold issue, is regarded as committed to the policies of Duvieusart's Government.

Jean Duvieusart is an officer in the Infantry Reserve Regiment of the Belgian Army. By his marriage to Blanche Dijon, which took place July 8, 1930, he has four children.

Reference

World Biography (1948)

DWORSHAK, HENRY C(LARENCE)
(dwôr-shäk) Aug. 29, 1894- United States Senator from Idaho

Address: b. Senate Office Bldg., Washington, D.C.; h. Burley, Idaho

Shortly before the end of the first session of the Eighty-first Congress in October 1949, a change occurred in the membership of the United States Senate. The junior Senator from Idaho, Democrat Bert H. Miller had died earlier that month, and was replaced, through interim appointment by Republican Governor C. A. Robins, by the predecessor Miller had defeated in the November 1948 election—Henry C. Dworshak. As United States Representative, Dworshak, a newspaper publisher, had sat in Congress for four terms, beginning in 1939, before being elected in 1946 to fill out the remaining two years of the Senatorial term of the late John Thomas. Dworshak, who served on the Appropriations Committees of both the House and Senate, belongs to that wing of the Republican party which has been conspicuous for opposition to free Federal spending and for its isolationist viewpoint on foreign policy. A Senatorial candidate again in election year 1950, the Idaho Republican was returned to Washington for four years.

Henry Clarence Dworshak was born in Duluth, Minnesota, on August 29, 1894. The son of Henry and Julia (Ohotto) Dworshak, he attended the public schools of his native city until his fifteenth year. He then left in 1909 to learn the printing trade and subsequently worked in the mechanical and editorial departments of several newspapers. Dworshak is a veteran of World War I, his service with the army (1918-19) having included six months overseas with the American Expeditionary Force. Some few months after his discharge he was engaged in 1920 as the manager of a printers supply business in Duluth, and was so occupied until 1924, when he became publisher and editor of the weekly Burley *Bulletin*. (Burley, in Cassia county, about 40 miles east of Twin Falls, is described in the Idaho volume of the *American Guide Series* as "one of the two most thriving centers" in that part of the State, with large-capacity alfalfa meal and beet sugar mills and the biggest potato flour mill in the world.) Dworshak was quick to make the impress of his small town and rural paper (circulation about 3,000) felt, and by 1931 he had been elected president of the Idaho Editorial Association. He also became active in the local Rotary Club and, later, in Rotary International, attending the convention in France in 1937 for installation as governor for the Idaho-Utah district.

Known as "an aggressive champion of conservation, irrigation and Government economy," he was elected to the United States House of Representatives with ease on the Republican ticket in November 1938, to represent the Second Idaho District (embracing twenty-five southern counties with a population of about 255,000) in the Seventy-sixth Congress. He was later re-elected to the Seventy-seventh, Seventy-eighth, and Seventy-ninth Congresses, despite the country-wide Democratic trend in the greater part of the period.

Throughout his eight years in the House of Representatives, Dworshak (reported the *United States News*) was "closely associated with the conservative party leadership, both in matters of legislation and of national politics." He also reflected with regularity the pre-Pearl Harbor isolationism of his area, and as early as March 25, 1939, sponsored a bill of his own designed to "take the profits out of war" by imposing 75 to 90 per cent taxes on certain classes of income above $50,000. In the same year he cast his "Aye" for the mandatory arms embargo in the Neutrality Act, and in 1940 and 1941, respectively, voted against the introduction of conscription and Lend-Lease.

Early assigned to the House Appropriations Committee, Representative Dworshak quickly underscored his views on the desirability of curbing Governmental expenditures by voting against authorization of an additional one hundred million dollars for work relief in 1939 and the granting of an additional fifty millions to the Civilian Conservation Corps in 1940. He went on record in his opposition to the policy of farm parity payments as early as his first year in Congress, and throughout his career as a legislator has voted against extension of the Reciprocal Trade Agreements Act. With a like consistency he fought against Federal regulation of prices, and what he regarded as Governmental intrusion into the field of private enterprise, casting votes against the creation of OPA in 1941, increased funds for rural electrification in 1943, and the public housing features of the Emergency Housing Bill of 1946. To the right of center on labor questions, Dworshak endorsed the Smith antistrike bill in 1941 and the Case bill five years later.

In the matter of foreign relations and postwar foreign aid, the Representative from Idaho remained economy-minded and generally isolationist; for although he supported the Fulbright world organization resolution in 1943, he voted against authorization of UNRRA in 1944 and against its continuation in the year following, and opposed authorization of the loan to Great Britain in 1946. During the latter year, also, he strongly fought the transfer of atomic energy control from military to civilian hands and the creation of the Atomic Energy Commission. (In 1947 he was to vote against the confirmation of David E. Lilienthal [44] as chairman of the AEC.)

Other demands upon his time caused Dworshak to dispose of his Burley *Bulletin* in 1944, but not before demonstrating that he had not forgotten his early training as a working printer by "putting in a shift of more than seventeen hours" setting type for his paper in an emergency during a Congressional recess. In November 1944, Idaho went Democratic and elected Glen H. Taylor [47] (later the candidate for the Vice-Presidency as Wallace's running mate) to the United States Senate. In another two years, however, the political trend had reversed, and Representative Dworshak, seeking election to the Senate to fill out the unexpired term (ending January 3, 1949) of the late John Thomas, was successful. (Dworshak succeeded Charles C. Gossett, a temporary Democratic gubernatorial appointee.) The only important local issue of the campaign (according to C. P. Trussell of the New York *Times*) was "the question of the Columbia River Power Authority, with the Republicans favoring the

HENRY C. DWORSHAK

status quo, and the Democrats plugging for a Columbia River TVA."

Sworn into the Republican-controlled Eightieth Congress in January 1947, the new junior Senator from Idaho was assigned to the Appropriations and Public Lands Committees; and in March he was one of two "freshmen" named to sit with his party's Senate Policy Committee, following the forceful suggestion by Raymond Baldwin [46] of Connecticut that the sixteen Republican newcomers to the upper chamber be given a greater voice in shaping party procedure. Dworshak supported both the Republican income tax reduction bills of 1947, while among the economies he proposed—though unsuccessfully—as an Appropriations committeeman was to trim $100,000,000 from the War Department civil functions bill. The Senator was one of a Public Lands subcommittee of three which made an on-the-spot investigation of the Centralia (Illinois) mine disaster of March 25, 1947, and reported on June 5 that "almost everyone concerned was guilty of negligence in one degree or another," including the United Mine Workers. Later in June he voted for the Taft [48]-Hartley [47] bill, both on its original passage through the Senate and on reconsideration after the Presidential veto.

His stand on Soviet Russia, American foreign policy in general, and European relief was in line with his House record. One of those who had voted in the lower chamber to make the House Un-American Activities Committee permanent, Dworshak in the Senate demanded (April 19, 1947) to know whether "the President and the State Department are intent upon building Russia into a still greater military power" when the unblocking of $17,000,000 in Lend-Lease equipment was requested. He opposed passage of the Greek-Turkish Aid bill and ratification of the Italian peace treaty in May and June 1947, respectively, and the Euro-

DWORSHAK, HENRY C.—*Continued*
pean Recovery (Marshall Plan) Act in 1948.
Also, in the second session of the Eightieth
Congress he favored striking out the public
housing features from the Taft-Ellender [46] bill,
but supported the principle of Federal aid to
education. On the issue of universal military
training, Dworshak said he was against that
measure, but would support the draft if the need
was "as acute as represented"; he voted for
the temporary draft.

In the Democratic victory of November 3,
1948, Dworshak was defeated for a new full
term in the Senate by Idaho Supreme Court
Justice Bert H. Miller of Boise. The Governorship of the State was not, however, in contest, Republican C. A. Robins having been elected in 1946 for a four-year term. Thus, when
Senator Miller died suddenly on October 8,
1949, Governor Robins named Dworshak to fill
the vacancy so created until the next State-wide
election in November 1950. Dworshak was
sworn into the Senate for the second time on
October 14, just before adjournment, in time to
participate in a majority vote to send back to
committee the House-approved bill to increase
by 134,000 the number of European refugees
eligible to enter the United States.

The Idaho Republican sought election to his
seat to complete the Senatorial term. In the
November 1950 contest his Democratic opponent was Claude J. Burtenshaw, a newcomer to
the political scene. While labor was reported
to be "going all out to try to accomplish the
defeat of Senator Dworshak" (New York
Times), the Senator was the victor at the polls
on November 7. Accordingly he was returned
to Washington for four years; when he took
his oath November 28, he was sworn in as a
member of Congress for the seventh time.

Senator Dworshak, who as Idaho State
commander of the American Legion in 1932,
is a Thirty-third Degree Mason, an Elk, and
an Odd Fellow. Married December 31, 1917,
to Georgia Belle Lowe, he is the father of
four sons, Henry Irving, Charles Lowe, Ward
Winston, and Calvin George.

References

U S News 21:72 N 15 '46 por
Congressional Directory (1st ed., 1949)
Who's Who in America, 1948-49
World Biography (1948)

DYKSTRA, CLARENCE A(DDISON)
(dīk'strá) Feb. 25, 1883—May 6, 1950 Professor of political science; public administrator; president of the University of Wisconsin
(1937-45), provost of the Los Angeles branch
of the University of California, 1945-50; commissioner of the Department of Water and
Power of the city of Los Angeles from 1922
to 1930, city manager of Cincinnati for the
years 1930-37; member of the President's Committee on Fiscal Relations between the Federal Government and the District of Columbia,
member of the Advisory Committee on Education, Recreation and Welfare to the Army and
Navy, chairman of the National Defense Medi-

ation Board (1941), first National Director of
Selective Service (1940-41); writer in the fields
of education and government. See *Current
Biography,* 1941.

Obituary

N Y Times p106 My 7 '50 por

EISENDRATH, MAURICE N(ATHAN)
July 10, 1902- Religious leader
Address: b. c/o Union of American Hebrew
Congregations, 3 E. 65th St., New York 21;
h. 440 E. 23d St., New York 10

"The high order of religious statesmanship"
Rabbi Maurice N. Eisendrath gave to his work
as director of the Union of American Hebrew
Congregations during 1943-46 won him the
presidency of that organization, a post he entered upon in 1946. He has served as a rabbi
of several Reform synagogues and is the author
of numerous articles published in *Liberal Judaism, The Jewish Layman,* and other religious
periodicals. In 1939 a collection of his sermons
and addresses was published in book form
under the title *The Never Failing Stream.* The
Union of American Hebrew Congregations is
the central body of Reform Judaism.

Born in Chicago on July 10, 1902, Maurice
Nathan Eisendrath is the son of Nathan Julius
and Clara (Oesterreicher) Eisendrath. His
education was obtained in Cincinnati schools; in
1921 he was graduated from Hughes High
School and in 1925 received his B.A. degree
from the University of Cincinnati, where he
had majored in philosophy. He was elected to
Phi Beta Kappa fraternity. After studies at
Cincinnati's Hebrew Union College (founded in
1875 by the Reform group of Judaism), Eisendrath won the Fleisher Prize and in 1926 was
given the title of Rabbi. His first appointment
as a rabbi was with the Virginia Street Temple
in Charleston, West Virginia (1926-29).

In 1929 Eisendrath was called to Toronto to
be rabbi of the Holy Blossom Temple there.
During his fourteen-year tenure the congregation grew into Canada's largest gathering of
Reform Jews; its rabbi became outstanding as
a promoter of good will and interfaith cooperation. After its reorganization in 1934, Eisendrath was actively associated with the Canadian
Jewish Congress as a member of the executive
board of its national body and chairman of the
public relations committee of its central division. In the latter capacity he was prominent
in Jewish-Gentile relations in Canada's most
heavily populated area. With the Reverend Dr.
C. E. Silcox, an Anglican clergyman, Eisendrath in 1938 made a tour of Ontario "to ex-
pound interfaith cooperation." The rabbi became noted for a weekly radio forum he conducted, and for his addresses over the Canadian
Broadcasting Corporation's Dominion-wide network. His book *The Never Failing Stream*
(1939), containing his radio addresses, was
well received by reviewers; other of his writings appeared in the *Canadian Jewish Review.*
A vice-president of the Canadian Conference
of Social Workers, he was also among the
speakers at Hart House debates in the Uni-

versity of Toronto. During World War II Rabbi Eisendrath was associated with the Wartime Information Board of Canada.

In recognition of his achievements in the Union of American Hebrew Congregations, in 1943 Eisendrath was made its director, in its headquarters in Cincinnati. Three years later he became its president, which took him to New York. In 1950 the organization represented the lay members of some 400 Reform congregations, located in 325 communities in the United States and Canada. When founded in 1873, its objectives were stated as: (1) to establish and maintain institutions in the higher branches of Hebrew literature and Jewish theology with necessary preparatory schools; (2) to provide means for relief of Jews suffering from political oppression; (3) to promote religious instruction. The policy-making body of the union is the board, composed primarily of lay members. *Liberal Judaism*, a pocket-size pictorial monthly, is its official organ. Eisendrath, a regular contributor to the magazine, has written some of its "most forceful editorials" and articles on current subjects. In February 1950 the Union of American Hebrew Congregations announced the proposed erection of a national center of Reform Judaism to be built in New York City and to be called Moritz and Josephine Berg Memorial House of Living Judaism.

The Reform movement in Judaism had its American origin in 1824 at Charleston, South Carolina. At the first conference of Reform Rabbis (1889), the Declaration of Principles was formulated—monotheism, immortality, and good will toward all men as children of God. All Mosaic law or legislation "not adapted to the views and habits of modern civilization" was rejected, as was the tenet that Eden and Gehenna are abodes for everlasting reward or punishment.

In a New York *Times* interview (May 4, 1945) Eisendrath is quoted as saying "forms and expression" of the Jewish religion in the United States had been so affected by events of the war years that he believed a new pattern of American Judaism might emerge. Though the Reform adherents represented only about 10 per cent of American Jews, he pointed out that of the 271 Jewish chaplains in the armed forces, 132 were from Reform synagogues. This had resulted in a synthesized service which, he believed, might influence future worship. He also noted the change in attitude of the members of the Central Branch of American Rabbis (the rabbinical organization of the Reform Jews), who in 1945 "veered definitely from their former anti-Zionist position" to at least a more sympathetic one. In 1949 Eisendrath was quoted (New York *Times*, May 20, 1949) as saying that while he approved of the continuation of overseas philanthropy and the support of Israel, he deplored the fact that "overzealous philanthropic leaders" were in danger of making the European emergency "self-perpetuating and eternal." The allocation to religious, cultural, and educational purposes of only four-tenths of 1 per cent of the money raised by the American Jewish Welfare Funds

MAURICE N. EISENDRATH

during 1948 he considered inadequate to meet the needs. He declared that unless a more rational distribution of the funds were made American Jewry might be destroyed in the process of saving Jews elsewhere (New York *Times*).

At San Francisco in 1945 Rabbi Eisendrath served as an American Jewish Conference consultant at the United Nations Conference on International Organization. In 1945 he received from the Hebrew Union College the degree of Doctor of Divinity. He has been representative of the Union of American Hebrew Congregations to the Synagogue Council of America. The rabbi is a member of the board of governors of Hebrew Union College-Jewish Institute of Religion, a member of the executive board of the Central Conference of American Rabbis; he is national co-chairman of commissions on religious organizations of the National Conference of Christians and Jews. Other organizations he has served include the National Community Relations Advisory Council, the National Jewish Welfare Board, American Association for the International Office of Education (member of the theologian's committee), and World Union for Progressive Judaism (vice-president). His clubs are the Harmonie (New York) and Standard (Chicago).

On November 24, 1926, Maurice Nathan Eisendrath married Rosa Brown, a pianist. The Eisendraths live in New York City's Peter Cooper Village, in an apartment overlooking the East River. The rabbi, who stands about five feet eleven inches and weighs 175 pounds, has blue eyes and brown hair. He has been described as a man of tremendous energy.

References

Universal Jewish Encyclopedia (1948)
Who's Who in America, 1950-51
Who's Who in American Jewry, 1938-39

ELIAS, LEONA BAUMGARTNER *See* Baumgartner, L.

ELIAS, MRS. NATHANIEL M. *See* Baumgartner, L.

EMBREE, EDWIN R(OGERS) (ĕm'brē) July 31, 1883—Feb. 21, 1950 American sociologist and administrator; from 1907 to 1917 at Yale University as administrative officer; in 1917 joined the Rockefeller Foundation to be successively secretary, director of the division of studies and vice-president; president of the Julius Rosenwald Fund from 1928 to 1948; president of the Liberian Foundation since 1948; author of books, monographs, and articles in the field of sociology. See *Current Biography,* 1948.

Obituary

N Y Times p29 F 22 '50

ENCKELL, CARL J(OHAN) A(LEXIS) June 7, 1876- Finnish statesman

Address: h. Korkeavuorenkatu 1, Helsinki, Finland

Carl J. A. Enckell has frequently been associated with Finland's foreign policy since 1917, when he served as his country's first Minister to the Soviet Government. During 1918-19, 1922, and 1924 he was Minister of Foreign Affairs, serving also as delegate to the League of Nations during 1920-26 and as Minister to France during 1919-27. An engineer by training, he held managerial positions in that field before 1917; after 1927 he became associated with various banks, insurance companies, and other commercial enterprises. Re-entering the

Wide World Photos
CARL J. A. ENCKELL

political field in 1944, he was appointed Foreign Minister under President Baron Carl von Mannerheim [40], and participated in important conferences with the U.S.S.R. to draw up armistice and peace terms following the Russo-Finnish war. He served as Foreign Minister under five different Prime Ministers until March 1950, when he was replaced by Ake Gartz in the Cabinet of Dr. Urho Kekkonen.

Born on June 7, 1876, in St. Petersburg, Russia, Carl Johan Alexis Enckell is the son of General Carl and Helena (Bronikowsky) Enckell. There have been clergymen and officers in his family, whose history is traceable for more than two hundred years. The youth was educated at the Finnish Cadet Corps Academy in Hamina, from which he graduated in 1896. After serving for three years as a second lieutenant in the Ismailov Guard, he studied engineering at the Technical University of Dresden, receiving his engineering diploma in 1902. From 1903 to 1905 he worked as an engineer with the Kuusankoski Paper Mills. He subsequently became engineer and later managing director in various shipyards and metal works plants, one a machine and bridge manufacturing plant, where he held the position of manager during the years from 1911 to 1917.

Following the Russian Revolution of 1917, Finland, which had been ruled by Czarist Russia as a semi-autonomous duchy, declared its independence on December 6, 1917. That year Enckell began his diplomatic career, when he was sent as the first Finnish Minister to Russia. On January 4, 1918, Finnish independence was recognized by the Bolsheviks, and the treaty of Brest-Litovsk (March 3, 1918) confirmed Finland's new status. In 1918, Enckell, continuing as Minister to Russia, was also appointed Minister of Foreign Affairs. During 1918-19 there was civil war in Finland between the "Red Guard" of Russian sympathizers and the "White Guard" of Finnish Nationalists led by Baron von Mannerheim. This resulted in a victory for the latter. When a peace treaty with the U.S.S.R. was signed at Dorpat on October 14, 1920, Enckell was a member of Finland's delegation headed by Juho K. Paasikivi [44]. Under the terms of the treaty, Petsamo was ceded to Finland, providing the country with an Arctic port.

In 1919 Enckell went to Paris as chairman of the Finnish delegation to the Peace Conference. He had his headquarters in the French capital for eight years, serving as his country's Minister to France and holding also the position of Foreign Minister during 1922 and 1924. When Finland was admitted to the League of Nations on December 16, 1920, Enckell was appointed delegate. He presented Finland's claims to sovereignty over the Aaland Islands, which had been disputed by Sweden, before the Council of the League during 1920-21. In June 1921, the League of Nations decided in favor of Finland. In 1922 Enckell was assigned to Moscow as chairman of the Finnish delegation to the Disarmament Conference. His appointment as delegate to the League of Nations terminated in 1926 and the following year he completed his term as Finland's Minister to France.

Carl Enckell returned to the world of commerce in 1928 when he accepted a position in the banking field as assistant manager of Unionbanken. Four years later, in 1931, he became director of the Helsingfors Aktiebank, remaining in that post for five years. In 1936 he was appointed board chairman and manager of the Finnish Industries Mutual Fire Insurance Company, a position he held until 1946. Enckell has also been associated with several other commercial organizations. In 1929 he became chairman of the Finnish section of the International Chamber of Commerce; and in 1938 was named chairman of the board of the Finnish subsidiary of the International Business Machines Corporation.

The U.S.S.R. attacked Finland in November 1939 to enforce territorial demands. After withstanding the assault for 105 days, the Finns surrendered, ceding to Russia a tenth of their country's area, including the Karelian isthmus. During 1941-44, under German pressure, the Finns joined the Nazis against Russia and were again defeated. Paasikivi, accompanied by Enckell, who was reported to be "one of Mannerheim's personal representatives," went to Moscow in March 1944 to discuss peace terms. The terms they secured were not accepted by the Finnish Government, which had been led since 1940 by pro-German President Risto Ryti '41. When Russian troops entered Finland again in June 1944, demands for peace forced Ryti to resign on August 1, 1944, and Baron von Mannerheim was appointed President by special parliamentary decree. A "peace Cabinet" under Antti Hackzell as Prime Minister was formed on August 4, with Enckell as Minister of Foreign Affairs.

Under the truce signed by the new Government with Russia on September 3, 1944, Finland agreed to announce publicly her break with Germany. All German troops were to be evacuated by September 15, and any remaining were to be disarmed and turned over to the Allies. Enckell replaced Hackzell as head of the Finnish delegation in Moscow to discuss the armistice terms when sudden illness incapacitated the latter. (Enckell's brother, Lieutenant General Oscar Enckell, also served on the delegation.) The terms, announced September 19, repeated the truce provision concerning German troops, imposed reparations of $300,000,000, gave Russia Karelia and Petsamo, placed the merchant fleet, airdrome and military equipment at the disposal of the Allies, and reduced Finland's military force to its peacetime basis.

Carl Enckell retained his post as Foreign Minister in the Cabinet of Urho Castrén, who replaced Hackzell in September 1944. On November 11, Castrén resigned and Paasikivi became Premier. He at that time retained Enckell as Foreign Minister, reappointing him also in March 1945 after the general elections. Finland formally declared war on Germany on March 3, 1945. On August 7, 1945, the Soviet Government announced that normal diplomatic relations had been resumed with Finland.

When Paasikivi was elected to the Presidency on March 4, 1946, to fill the unexpired term of Mannerheim, who had resigned, Mauno Pekkala of the Socialist Unity party, formed a Cabinet regarded "as being committed to Paasikivi's policy of sincere and friendly cooperation with the Soviet Union." In this Cabinet, also, Enckell (an Independent) remained as Foreign Minister.

Pekkala, Enckell, and Yrjo Leino (of the Finnish Communist party) arrived in Paris in August 1946 to present the cause of Finland at the Peace Conference. Paasikivi was reported as favoring the acceptance of the draft peace treaty without question; Enckell was reported as favoring an attempt to obtain better terms in Paris, at risk of incurring Soviet displeasure, and Pekkala as steering a middle course. When Enckell in his address to the Conference on August 15 suggested "it would be well" if Finland's burden of reparations were reduced by $100,000,000, he was rebuked by Soviet Foreign Minister Molotov '40 who refused to grant Finland alleviation of the terms of their armistice. The Finnish delegation asked for no territorial concessions, but did ask for a doubling of the air and naval forces proposed in the draft treaty. The Allied Committee on Finland, however, approved the principal articles of the draft treaty which in general followed the 1944 Russian armistice provisions. The draft treaty was approved by the Peace Conference on October 14, signed in Paris on February 10, 1947, and ratified in Finland on April 18. Early in 1948 Enckell took part in discussions in Moscow on Soviet proposals for a Mutual Assistance pact (Finland in 1947 had refused to join Marshall Plan discussions) which came into effect May 31. As a consequence, the U.S.S.R. reduced Finnish reparations by $70,000,000 (in round figures) and granted Finland credit of $5,000,000.

Following the general elections of July 1948 Pekkala resigned as Prime Minister, and Karl August Fagerholm '48 formed a Social Democratic Cabinet in which Enckell was once again appointed Foreign Minister. The Government stated its foreign policy as being one of "orientation toward the East" but of developing "contacts with the West . . . as a free country." Paasikivi, who had been re-elected President in February 1950, with the support of the Social Democrats, Conservatives, Liberals and the Swedish People's party, in his inaugural address on March 1, promised to work for "good and trustful relations, especially between Finland and Russia." In the coalition Government formed in March 1950 composed of ten Agrarians, three Swedish People's party members, one Liberal and one nonparty expert, Enckell was not reappointed as Foreign Minister, the post going to Ake Gartz of the Swedish People's party.

The Finnish statesman has written articles on economic and political questions. His decorations include the following: Grand Cross of Finnish Order of White Rose with diamonds; First Class Grand Star, Finnish Order of Cross of Liberty; Grand Cross Royal Sweden Wasa Order; Grand Cross Royal Danish Dannebrog Order; Grand Cross Polonia Restituta; Grand Cross Royal Belgian Order of Crown; Grand Cross of Annamite Dragon; Grand Cross, Icelandic Order of Falcon; Grand Officer in the Legion of Honor, and Est Order of Lib-

ENCKELL, CARL J. A.—*Continued*

erty, first class. Since 1927 he has been chairman of the Finnish Cadet Club.

In 1903 Enckell married Lucy Ponsonby-Lyons, who died in 1945. Their four children are Maritta, Ralph, Estelle, and Bernard.

References

International Who's Who, 1949
Who's Who in Central and East-Europe, 1935-36
World Biography (1948)

ENTEZAM, NASROLLAH (ĕn-tĕ-zàm nàs-rō-lá) Feb. 16, 1900- United Nations delegate; Ambassador from Iran to the United States

Address: b. c/o United Nations, New York; Embassy of Iran, 3303 Massachusetts Ave., Washington, D.C.

The fifth United Nations General Assembly, which convened in September 1950, chose as its president 50-year-old Nasrollah Entezam, the representative of Iran to the U.N. and Iran's Ambassador to the United States. A career

NASROLLAH ENTEZAM

diplomat, Entezam had served "with distinction" as chairman of the Assembly's special political committee in 1949. His nation, known as Persia before 1935, is politically important on the world scene chiefly because of its rich oil deposits.

Born in Teheran, the capital of Iran, on February 16, 1900, Nasrollah Entezam was the third of five children. "My father was a man exactly like me," he was later to tell an interviewer for the New York *Post.* "Perhaps I am too proud in saying so because he was a good man and unselfish." Young Entezam received his degree in law and political science

from the universities of his country and of Paris. Following family tradition (his father, as his grandfather, was a career diplomat), he entered Government service, beginning in the Ministry of Foreign Affairs in Iran in 1918 at the age of eighteen. He was secretary to the Iranian Legation in Paris in 1926, in Warsaw in 1928, and in London in 1928-29. From 1929 to 1938 he was the Iranian representative at the League of Nations. During that period, in 1933 he represented Iran at the World Economic Conference in London, and was from 1934 to 1938 chargé d'affaires at Berne, Switzerland.

On his return to Iran in 1938 Entezam was appointed director of the political department of the Ministry of Foreign Affairs. Four years later he was appointed Grand Master of Ceremonies at the Imperial Palace of the Shah, Mohammed Riza Pahlevi [50]. The next year (1943) he held several Cabinet offices, becoming, in turn, Minister of Public Health, Minister of Posts and Telegraph, and Minister of Communications. It was in December of that year that Prime Minister Churchill of Great Britain, President Roosevelt of the United States, and Premier Stalin of the Soviet Union, meeting in what was to become known as the Teheran Conference, issued the Declaration of the Three Powers Concerning Iran. That document pledged respect for the independence and territorial integrity of Iran, and promised her economic assistance after World War II. (British and Russian troops had occupied Iran in August 1941 and were still there.)

In 1944 Entezam was named Minister of State for Foreign Affairs. (The Cabinet in Iran, which is a constitutional monarchy, exercises executive power and is responsible to the Majlis, or National Assembly.) Sent in 1945 to San Francisco to represent his Government at the conference which established the United Nations, Entezem subsequently attended the first session of the General Assembly. Meanwhile, in 1945 a movement in the Iranian province of Azerbaijan, reportedly under Russian influence, demanded autonomy. These events claimed the U.N.'s attention in early 1946, when the Iranian delegation protested that Russian troops had remained past the treaty evacuation date of March 2, 1946. The U.S.S.R. withdrew its troops May 6, after it had obtained promises of oil concessions in the north of Iran. Entezam, who had been with Iran's United Nations delegation during this period, was made his nation's permanent representative to the U.N. in 1947.

The Iranian diplomat served on the United Nations Special Committee on Palestine, traveling with that body on a fact-finding mission to Jerusalem in mid-1947. When the committee gave its final recommendations to the U.N Assembly in September Iran was with the dissenting minority of three (India, Yugoslavia, and Iran) which recommended a federal government for Palestine with equal representation in a lower house for Jews and Arabs, an upper house reflecting the Arab majority, and with local affairs to be left to the control of the states. (The seven-nation majority proposal was for separate Jewish and Arab states.)

At the third session of the General Assembly Entezam was chairman of the Fourth (Trusteeship) Committee and of the Special Committee on Methods and Procedures. It was as chairman of the Ad Hoc Political Committee of the fourth session of the Assembly that he earned a reputation as an efficient and (as *Look* magazine described him) "soothing" chairman. The New York *Times* later commented that he had distinguished himself as chairman of a committee which "handled some of the most controversial issues" (these included such problems as atomic weapon control and the partition of Palestine).

In September 1950 Entezam presented his credentials to President Truman as Ambassador Extraordinary and Minister Plenipotentiary of Iran to the United States, succeeding Ambassador Hussein Ala. The new Ambassador told news reporters that one of his missions was to negotiate an economic assistance program with the United States. Earlier that month the State Department had announced that the United States was planning to grant one or more loans to Iran.

At the 1949 session of the United Nations General Assembly Entezam had been a candidate for president, but had withdrawn, according to the New York *Times* "in the interests of Asian unity, making possible the election of Brigadier General Carlos P. Romulo of the Philippines by an overwhelming majority." Entezam was again a candidate in September 1950; his strongest opponent was Sir Mohammed Zafrullah Khan [47], Foreign Minister of Pakistan. Some delegates were said to be considering whether Iran's position of exposure to possible Soviet pressure might not make the election of another candidate more desirable. The United States held that either Entezam or Sir Zafrullah would be a good choice; France supported Entezam, and Great Britain preferred Sir Zafrullah. That the post should go to a representative of a Middle-Eastern nation was generally conceded. Entezam was elected on September 19 by a vote of 32 to 22 (30 votes would have given him a legal majority); the five other votes went to Polish and Czech candidates. After his election in a brief speech delivered in French, Entezam pledged himself to be an impartial chairman.

During the opening days of its fifth session, the General Assembly empowered Entezam to set up a special committee to study the problem of the admission of Communist China, by acclamation voted Indonesia into the United Nations (bringing the number of U.N members to sixty), and passed a resolution guaranteeing freedom, unity, and independence to Korea after the U.N. war to halt North Korean aggression was won. Entezam's argument that, since there had been no new developments on atomic control, no purpose would be served by renewed debate in the Political and Security Committee, put that issue on the agenda for Assembly debate in plenary session. Commenting on his "competence" in getting through Assembly business, Fern Marja of the New York *Post* reported, "At the initial meeting of the powerful, conflict-ridden steering committee, he drove his colleagues through the provisional agenda in a record-shattering eighty-five minutes."

In an address welcoming President Truman before the United Nations on October 24, 1950, President Entezam referred to U.N. action in Korea as reason for hope for world peace. "For the first time the world organization has, in common interest, met force with force," he said. "The future of peace will largely depend on the outcome of this experience." He predicted that the 1950 session might come to be known as "the Assembly of Collective Security."

The Iranian diplomat has dark hair, a mustache, and has been described as slight, with a narrow face. He is unmarried. United Nations observers have commented on his "mild" manner and "graciousness." (A stickler for niceties, Entezam has said that personal attacks were not in keeping with the dignity of the United Nations.) While in New York with the Assembly he misses the opportunity for riding and skiing, but continues his "omnivorous" reading in French, English, and Persian—among his favorite non-Persian authors are Maurois, Zweig, and Maugham.

References

Look 14.172 O 24 '50
N Y Herald Tribune p1 S 20 '50
N Y Post Mag p2 O 22 '50 por
N Y Times p8 S 20 '50 por
Time 56:20 O 2 '50
U N Bul 9:283 O 1 '50

World Biography (1948)
Yearbook of the United Nations, 1947-48

ERHARD, LUDWIG (är'härt lōōt'vĭk) Feb. 4, 1897- Economic Minister of the Federal Republic of Germany
Address: Bonn, Germany

In the thirteen-man Cabinet formed by Chancellor Konrad Adenauer [49] of the new Federal Republic of Germany in September of 1949, Dr. Ludwig Erhard, a Christian Democrat, was named Minister of Economics. This appointment was considered highly significant in that Erhard, as director of the Economic Council of Bizonal Germany during 1948-49, had maintained his strong stand of governmental noninterference in the free enterprise system—a policy also regarded as important to the Western world, said *Fortune* in the article "New Chance in Germany." A former professor of economics at Munich and Nuremberg, Erhard served as economic counselor to the American Military Government after the capitulation of Germany.

Ludwig Erhard was born in Fürth, Bavaria, on February 4, 1897. He was educated in Nuremberg, studying political science and economics at the Handelsschule (school of commerce). His education was interrupted by World War I, in which he was seriously wounded. After the war he entered the University of Frankfurt, where he studied until 1924 for his doctorate in economics and political science under Franz Oppenheimer. He soon acquired a reputation as an outstanding economist, one of the school of thought that sup-

LUDWIG ERHARD

ports the free enterprise system and is opposed to doctrinaire socialism and regulation by the state. Erhard became an assistant at the Institute of Economic Studies in Nuremberg in 1926, and director of the institute four years later, a position he held until 1942. He then entered the field of industry during the Nazi regime.

Specializing in the field of production, he served as a counselor and was subsequently appointed an adviser in economic affairs. With funds provided by German industry, he founded the Institute for Industrial Research. In 1943 he was attached to the staff of the *Gauleiter* of Alsace-Lorraine to advise on matters relating to the manufacture of glass. He became Minister of Economic Affairs in Bavaria in April 1945 and served in that office until September 1947. During this period he also acted as economic counselor to the American Military Government. In 1947 Erhard was named professor of economic sciences at the Faculty of Political Science in Munich. He was cofounder of the Society of Political Economy, which was established in 1947; and in that year he was placed in charge of money and credit in Bizonia (the British and American zones of Germany). On March 3, 1948, he was elected director of the Economic Council for that area.

Having "preached the gospel of free enterprise" for twenty years, said *Time*, Professor Erhard was given "his historic chance to put his faith into practice" in the spring of 1948. The long-projected currency reforms for Germany were made in June 1948. In the Western Zone, the new German mark replaced the Reichsmark on June 20; the reform was favorable for wage earners but the opposite for pensioners and people with savings. At the same time, Erhard's Economic Administrative Office abolished all price controls except for basic foods, coal, iron, and steel. Wages, too, re-

mained frozen. As a result of this action, goods that had been hoarded appeared in shops, and black market prices dropped to 10 per cent of their previous levels. In the months that followed, however, prices of industrial articles rose, even though Erhard tried to check them by publishing "price mirrors" or lists of reasonable prices, and by securing passage of a profiteer law. Refusing in spite of pressure to bring back price controls, he announced his "Everyman" plan in October 1948 for production of utility wares. In protest against the high prices the trade unions of Württemberg-Baden organized demonstrations on October 28, which resulted in rioting. The discontent of the trade unions with "Erhardism" was again expressed in a twenty-four-hour token general strike which took place in the bizone on November 12. Erhard remained firm in his policy, insisting that if the experiment were continued a little longer, supply and demand would meet. By late 1948, prices had leveled off, output of workers in all industries except coal had risen, absenteeism in factories had practically disappeared, and foreign trade figures for the bizone showed considerable improvement over the preceding year (*Fortune*).

"The structure of German economy under Nazism was completely wrong," Erhard stated in an interview with C. L. Sulzberger of the New York *Times* in July 1949. "It was not governed by rules of competition." Reviewing the economic situation, he stated that a balanced economy had been reached by the end of 1948, and that during 1949 prices had fallen, the quality of goods had improved, and wages which had been raised earlier in the year, had been stabilized. Though the standard of living was still low, it had "improved immeasurably." Erhard declared that more than twelve million persons were employed in the bizone, and about one and a fifth million were unemployed. Industrial production had doubled since 1948 and was 90 per cent of the West German output in 1936, the last prewar year before armament production distorted the economic picture.

Pointing out that lack of capital prevented construction and modernization, Erhard expressed the hope that the Economic Cooperation Administration of the United States would allow "the German counterpart fund to be made available for fixed capital investment." He has also expressed his belief that over the next few years Germany should reduce its dependence on the United States, and that more normal processes of private capital investment should be resumed.

Dr. Erhard's economic policy was considered a decisive factor in the victory of the Christian Democrats in the first national postwar German elections, held in August 1949. The Christian Democratic Union and its counterpart in Bavaria, the Christian Social Union, together won 139 of the Bundestag's 402 seats. Next strongest were the Social Democrats with 131 seats. (Erhard, a Christian Democrat, was elected to the Bundestag at Ulm.) Before the elections, the Social Democrats campaigned specifically against Erhard and his free enterprise program in the Bizonal Economic Council. Kurt Schumacher [48], Socialist leader, at one point let it be known that he was not basically opposed to a Socialist coalition with the Christian Democrats, provided Erhard were not named Minister of Economics.

After the elections, Dr. Konrad Adenauer, Christian Democratic Chancellor of the newly established Federal Republic of Germany at Bonn, formed a Cabinet composed of eight Christian Democrats, three Free Democrats, and two members of the German party. He announced that the new West German Government would follow an economic policy of free enterprise, regarding the election results as a victory for this form of economy over the planned-economy policies of the Socialists. On September 20, 1949, he presented his first Cabinet to the Bundestag; as expected, Erhard was made Economics Minister.

In September 1949 the West German mark was devalued to conform with the devaluation of the English pound. Though in favor of devaluation in view of the British action, Erhard criticized the latter as "a mere palliative, not a solution. It does not solve the fundamental problem. The only true solution is more work, better work, more productive work." The first trade negotiations between the Cabinets of France and Western Germany were held in November 1949, when Erhard conferred with Maurice Petsche [49], French Finance Minister, on a French-German commercial treaty. "We Germans understand France's desire for security and are ready to guarantee it even in an economic way," Erhard stated, pointing out that Germans would welcome investment of French capital in their industries, thereby sharing the responsibility of Germany's industrial expansion in the postwar years. He also discussed the possibility of the German Federal Republic entering the proposed economic and financial collaboration plan for France, Italy, the Netherlands, Belgium and Luxembourg.

The German Cabinet Minister has been described by Wolfgang Peifer of the University of Marburg as having "exceptional energy and force of personality." Another writer sees him as "a man of iron nerves," with a sense of humor. He is stocky in build, has graying hair and a light complexion, and is given to smoking big black cigars.

References

Fortune 40:72-6 O '49 por
La Documentation Française-Chroniques Etrangères 61:21 O 25 '49
Politique Internationale 6:193 N '49 por

EVANS, HUGH IVAN, REV. May 6, 1887- Religious organization president: clergyman

Address: c/o The Presbyterian Church in the United States of America, Office of the General Assembly, Witherspoon Bldg., Philadelphia 7, Pa.; 125 N. Wilkinson St., Dayton 2, Ohio; h. 14 E. Schantz Ave., Dayton 9, Ohio

The leader of the Presbyterian Church in the United States of America—that country's largest Presbyterian body, with a membership of well over two millions and headquarters at Philadelphia—is, for the term 1950-51, the Rev-

erend Dr. Hugh Ivan Evans. He gains this distinction by reason of his election, on May 18, 1950, as Moderator of that church at its 162d General Assembly held in Cincinnati, Ohio. A native of the Middle West, Dr. Evans has been pastor of the Westminster Church in Dayton, Ohio, since 1923.

Hugh Ivan Evans, son of James and Mary Ella (Boyce) Evans, was born May 6, 1887, in Delaware, Ohio, a town not far from Columbus. His parents, farmers (his mother was a teacher before her marriage), lived with their seven sons and one daughter in a log house in Paulding County. Reared there, Ivan Hugh attended local schools, and graduated (1904) from the high school of the near-by community of Scott. After a supplementary year at Wooster (Ohio) Academy, he entered Wooster College (a liberal arts institution, chartered by Presbyterians in 1866), where he majored in English, and took the B.A. degree in 1909. While at college he served as manager of the weekly magazine *The Wooster Voice*. The youth was strongly influenced by his parents (his father was a Presbyterian elder; two of his brothers became ministers), his pastor, and the faculty, as well as by his own inclination, to prepare for the ministry. Accordingly he proceeded to Princeton (New Jersey) Theological Seminary, and there in 1912 he received the S.T.B. degree in systematic theology in addition to the regular B.D. diploma. The Doctor of Divinity degree was conferred on him by Wooster College in 1924.

All four of the pastorates held by the Reverend Evans have been in Ohio. On his ordination in 1912 he was called to the Presbyterian Church at Gallipolis, and automatically became a member of the local presbytery. (A presbytery, which is above the session and below the synod in authority, is composed of the minister and one or more elders from each church in a certain district.) After four years at Gallipolis, Evans went in 1916 to the Presbyteran Church at Marysville; and five years later (1921) to the Second Presbyterian Church of Portsmouth.

Dr. Evans was called to the Westminster Presbyterian Church in Dayton in 1923, the pulpit he has filled since that time. "Under his leadership," stated an official biographical release, "two former Dayton churches have been merged into one unified congregation; a cathedral-like edifice erected; and the debt liquidated. The church membership has grown from 1,400 to more than 2,700. The church supports three missionaries—in Alaska, Brazil and India—and is contributing generously to the erection of two new Presbyterian churches in Dayton."

In 1930-31 Dr. Evans was moderator of the Presbyterian Synod of Ohio. The synods, whose boundaries in the United States are ordinarily the State lines, have jurisdiction over the presbyteries. The moderator, chosen by the membership, is the presiding officer or chairman; Evans had been moderator of each of the four presbyteries to which he had belonged. Two years later (1933-34) the Dayton minister was president of the Ohio Pastors' Convention, and in 1934 he became a member of American Seminar in Europe. In 1936 he was elected to

REV. HUGH IVAN EVANS

the Presbyterian Board of National Missions, which has headquarters in New York City. He subsequently represented the board in a survey of the Presbyterian Hospital at San Juan, Puerto Rico, and is one of the institution's trustees. His duties took him to visit mission fields throughout the country and to speak for the board in synod meetings of Washington, Oregon, California, New Mexico, and Arizona.

At the 162d General Assembly of the Presbyterian Church in the United States of America, meeting in Cincinnati, Ohio, on May 18, 1950, Dr. Evans, who had been endorsed for moderator by the Dayton presbytery, was proposed and elected moderator of the church by a vote of 449 to 405. The General Assembly (or General Synod) is the body of the Presbyterian Church in which supreme authority on church policy is vested. Composed of approximately 850 members (ministers and elders in equal numbers) chosen by the presbyteries, its decisions are final and binding. It holds annual sessions at which one of its ministerial members is elected for the year. He takes precedence over all members, and is recognized as the official head of the church during his term of office. "His position is one of great honor and influence, but he remains a simple presbyter, without any special rule or jurisdiction," (in the words of the *Encyclopædia Britannica*). Inducted as moderator (and presented with the Celtic cross symbolic of office), Dr. Evans exhorted the Assembly with the words: "I summon you to a year of spiritual daring." He continued: "I summon your wills to an extension of Christianity . . . at home and abroad, through interdenominational cooperation."

At the Cincinnati meeting, a membership gain in 1949 of 71,713 was announced, bringing the total to 2,402,849. The Assembly voted to participate in the work of the Conference on Church Union, an organization that is working for "the organic union of the evangel-

ical Protestant churches in the United States." It also heard a report on the status of the discussions of unity with the Presbyterian Church in the United States (Southern), which had split away at the time of the Civil War; organization and dogma of both bodies are similar, but differences in viewpoint on certain issues, for example, racial segregation, exist, and the Southern church has deferred action on the union question for five years. On May 22, by a unanimous vote, the Assembly adopted a resolution declaring that "in no circumstances should a member of this church give any understanding, as a condition of marriage, that the children should be brought up in the practice of another communion." The session was ended on May 24, after adoption of resolutions favoring Federal aid to education (without subsidies to private or parochial schools); opposing racial segregation, regimentation, gambling and betting, and liquor advertising; calling for "immediate cessation" of the manufacture of hydrogen bombs and "all other weapons of mass destruction"; and urging the President and the Secretary of State to "uphold the principle of separation of church and state" by "scrupulously avoiding any official relations with the Vatican."

Foreign lands visited by the Dayton pastor in the course of extensive traveling have included Palestine, the Soviet Union, most European countries, and the South American republics. He has helped to set up and promote the "three-year plan" of evangelism of his church body's "New Life" committee; is a member of the boards of the Princeton and Lane theological seminaries and the McCormick Theological Seminary; a trustee of Wooster College and of Ohio Presbyterian Homes. Postwar religious duties took him abroad to Geneva in 1948 as the official delegate of the Presbyterian Church in the United States of America to the World Alliance of Reformed Churches; and in the same year he was an accredited visitor to the World Council of Churches at Amsterdam, Holland. In the fall of 1950 he began a tour of the United States, during which he will preach in many churches. Dr. Evans was one of the church leaders present at the ceremony at which the National Council of the Churches of Christ in the United States of America was officially constituted—on November 29, 1950, twenty-nine Protestant denominations and four Eastern Orthodox bodies united in forming the council.

Dr. Evans has been prominent in Dayton civic affairs. In 1942 he was chairman of the local fund drive, and in 1943 became general chairman of the first Dayton War Chest Campaign, which raised more than a million dollars. For two years beginning in 1945 he was president of the Dayton Community Chest and he also served as vice-chairman of the National War Fund Campaign for Ohio. He is a trustee of the Miami Valley Hospital; a member of the Dayton Metropolitan Housing Authority, Civic Committee to Study Juvenile Delinquency, Urban League and Mayor's Committee on Race Relations; and a director of both the Salvation Army and Goodwill Industries. During 1920-22 he was a member of the Ohio National Guard.

Hugh Ivan Evans and Edith Bean were married June 30, 1914; they have one son, the Reverend Hugh Bean Evans, and one daughter, Edith Mabel (Mrs. Wallace Macgregor). Dr. Evans is five feet eleven and a half inches in height, weighs slightly over 190 pounds, and has brown hair, hazel eyes. He is a 33d Degree Mason (Knights Templar), a Republican in his political views. His clubs are the Rotary, Discussion, Executives and Dayton Country.

References

Religious Leaders of America, 1941-42
Who's Who in America, 1950-51

FEIKEMA, FEIKE (FREDERICK) (fī'-kĕmá fī'ká) Jan. 6, 1912- Author
Address: Route 4, Minneapolis 9, Minn.

Reprinted from the *Wilson Library Bulletin*, Nov. 1950.

In a bare half-dozen years, Feike Feikema, a new agrarian novelist, has published a body of work which has given rise to inevitable comparisons with Thomas Wolfe. Viewing Feikema and learning some details of his family history, one finds the phrase most likely to rise to the lips is "Giants in the Earth."

Feike Frederick Feikema was born January 6, 1912, on a farm near Rock Rapids, Iowa, a few miles from the Minnesota and South Dakota borders, in a district called Siouxland in his novels. He is the oldest, tallest (six feet nine inches) and heaviest (270 pounds) of the six sons born to Feike Frank and Aeltje (von Engen) Feikema. The elder Feikema is of West Frisian descent (Franeker, the Netherlands); his wife's racial strain was East Frisian and Saxon (northwest Germany). Their son remained on the family farm till he was eighteen, graduating from Hull Academy, a Calvinistic parochial school, at sixteen; and from Calvin College, Grand Rapids, Michigan, with a B.A. degree and a never-used teacher's life certificate, at twenty-two, in spite of being obliged to stay out for weeks at a time to work on the farm. At college he played basketball and helped edit the *Calvin Chimes*. From 1934 to 1937 Feikema "bummed the country" from Atlantic to Pacific, working as factory hand, filling station attendant, bus boy, driver, painter, carpenter, and harvest hand.

In May 1937 Feikema landed a job as reporter on the Minneapolis *Journal* and held it until he was "fired for incompetence" in January 1939. In spare hours he had begun writing novels, and continued "enormous and voracious" reading in economics, philosophy, science, and literature. Social service work and public opinion surveys kept him going awhile, but overwork and malnutrition sent him to a tuberculosis sanatorium in 1940 for two years. Leaving there 105 pounds heavier, Feikema took a job on the staff of *Modern Medicine* at Minneapolis, and a wife in the person of Maryanna Shorba. The Feikemas have two daughters, Freya and Marya.

In June 1943 Feikema "quit all work and decided it was now or never as a writer." His

FEIKE FEIKEMA

first novel, *The Golden Bowl*, was written on a University of Minnesota fellowship and published in St. Paul in 1944. Praised by the New York *Times* for its "lean prodding prose" and "knowing feel of the land," its story of a roving young Oklahoma bindle stiff was largely autobiographical, as was its successor, *Boy Almighty* (1946), which drew on his experiences in the sanatorium. The *Saturday Review of Literature* called this "a thoughtful novel written in a mixture of crudest realism and sensitive poetry."

Next came *This Is the Year* (1947), about an ignorant Frisian farmer who wrecks his farm through disregard for soil conservation. Its "relentless realism" bothered some urban reviewers; so did the earthiness of *The Chokecherry Tree* (1948), described by Virginia Kirkus with a refined shudder as "indelicate, distasteful." Its hero is Elof Lofblom, an Iowa farm boy with a theological training and an inferiority complex, who makes a fortunate marriage. Paul Corey objected in the *Weekly Book Review* to the book's use of "costume jewelry" words, but thought it an improvement over its predecessors. The New York *Times* called it "direct, swift, and fresh."

The Primitive (1949) is the first volume of a trilogy, *World's Wanderer*, and was called a "successful beginning" by the New York *Times* reviewer. A college novel, it deals with Thurs Wraldson, an enormous, ungainly young fellow who comes from Siouxland for an education. *The Brother*, next in the series, is in process of publication, and will be followed by *The Giant*. Feikema writes at Macalester College, St. Paul, Minnesota, where he conducts a seminar in creative writing.

Apart from his own adult life, influences in Feikema's writing have been his grandfather, "a brilliant man, a Socialist and an agnostic

FEIKEMA, FEIKE—*Continued*

during the first world war"; his Aunt Kathryn, who read him fairy tales; and his mother, "who was a Christian who believed in love." The American Academy of Arts and Letters awarded him a grant-in-aid in 1945, and he has received fellowships from the Field and the Andreas Foundations. He is vice-president of the Society of Midland Authors.

Feikema has performed physical feats consonant with his size, once scoring 57 points in a basketball game, lifting a thousand pounds, and hitting a home run that measured 470 feet on the fly. He enjoys gardening and traveling in the Rockies; would like to travel "over the whole world," including Frisia. His most favored reading is Charles Montagu Doughty, Chaucer, Spenser, the Bible in Frisian, Melville, and Whitman, in that order, with a long list of second favorites. Among younger and less-known authors he mentions Virgil Scott, J. F. Powers, and Sheila Alexander. "An original, a primitive himself," concludes E. A. Laycock, Feike Feikema is "a regional writer whose work transcends its regionalism."

FERNANDES, L(UIS) ESTEVES (fĕr-năɴn'dĕsh loo-ĕsh' ĕs-tăv'ĕsh) July 6, 1897- Portuguese Ambassador to the United States

Address: Embassy of Portugal, 2125 Kalorama Rd., N.W., Washington, D.C.

The Ambassador from Portugal to the United States, L. Esteves Fernandes, took over his duties in Washington in June 1950. This followed upon his service during 1946-49 as director general of the economic division of the Portuguese Ministry of Foreign Affairs in Lisbon. In the course of thirty years in the diplomatic service, Fernandes has been stationed in Peking, Paris, London, Pretoria, and Madrid.

He was also Portugal's permanent delegate to the League of Nations from 1937 to 1939, and for six years during World War II was Minister to Japan.

Luis Esteves Fernandes was born in Lisbon, Portugal, on July 6, 1897, the son of Joaquim A. Fernandes and the former Dona Virginia de Lemos Esteves. He was educated in his country's capital, where he studied at the Faculty of Law in the University of Lisbon and received the Master of Laws degree in 1919. After passing the examinations for diplomatic and consular service in 1920, he began his career as third official at the Ministry of Foreign Affairs in Lisbon.

The young man's first foreign post was in China, where he took over the duties of secretary of the Portuguese Legation in Peking in 1924. The following year he was made chargé d'affaires in Peking; he remained in this position for six years. In 1925 he served as secretary of the Portuguese delegation to a special conference on customs and tariffs, and in 1926 he was his country's delegate to the international commission on extraterritorial affairs. At the funeral ceremonies (in 1929) of Dr. Sun Yat Sen, first President of the Chinese Republic, Fernandes was the special representative of his Government.

Transferred to Paris in 1931, Fernandes spent two years in France as secretary of the Portuguese Legation. In 1933 he returned to Lisbon for a year, to hold the post of first secretary of the Foreign Office. His next assignment was to London, where he served in 1934 as first secretary and in 1935 as chargé d'affaires of his country's Embassy. His transfer to Pretoria, Union of South Africa, took place in 1935; there he was chargé d'affaires of the Legation for two years.

Fernandes, who had been a permanent delegate to the League of Nations since 1926, was appointed chargé d'affaires for Portugal with that organization in 1937, and took up residence in Geneva, Switzerland. During 1937-39, he was Portugal's delegate to the International Conference of Labor and secretary-general of the Portuguese delegation to the League of Nations. He also served as a delegate to the league's commission for formulating a convention relating to German refugees, to a conference preparing for the restriction of the cultivation of poppies for opium, to the consultative commission and the permanent committee on opium.

The diplomat's next assignment was to the Portuguese Embassy in Spain in 1939, as counselor. (It was in March 1939 that Spain and Portugal concluded a treaty of nonaggression and friendship, followed in December by a trade agreement.) That same year he was appointed Minister in the Portuguese Legation in Tokyo, where he remained during the years of World War II. Portugal maintained a position of neutrality throughout the war, thus continuing relations with Japan during that period.

Fernandes returned for duty in Portugal in 1946, when he was made Minister Plenipotentiary, First Class, and director-general of economic affairs of the Foreign Office in Lisbon, of particular significance in the ERP. Though Portugal itself is only 34,240 square miles in area, its colonial empire is twenty-three times as great, the third largest in the world. The country's strategic location near the Atlantic approaches to Gibraltar, its Azores possessions in the mid-Atlantic, its Cape Verde islands off West Africa, its colonies in Southwest Africa and East Africa, and its possessions in the Pacific area, have given it importance in the postwar realignment of nations. Though Soviet opposition has barred Portugal from the United Nations, the country's Government has become associated with the countries of Western Europe. Portugal has been a partner in the European Recovery Program from the beginning, and in April 1949, after consultations with Spain, joined the North Atlantic Pact. During the second half of 1949, the OEEC announced an appropriation for Portugal for 1949-50 of $31,000,000 in direct aid and $26,000,000 drawing rights. W. Averell Harriman, conferring with Premier Salazar '41 in Lisbon in November 1949, declared that Portugal was "loyally cooperating" in the Marshall Plan, and in February 1950 Portugal received its first aid grant of $1,930,000 under that plan, to be used to buy recovery commodities in the United States and Canada.

The appointment of Luis Esteves Fernandes as Ambassador to the United States was announced in March 1950, and on June 23 he presented his credentials to President Truman. The Portuguese Ambassador is the author of a book on travels in China. He holds the Grand Cross of the Order of Christ, is a Commander of the Order of the Spanish Republic and of the Order of Merit of Chile, Knight of the Order of Civil Merit of Spain, and Knight of the Order of St. Olav of Norway. He was also presented with the Medal of the Jubilee of George V of England.

Fernandes, who is of the Roman Catholic faith, claims no political affiliation. By his marriage in 1933 to Dona Helena Saboia de Medeiros, a Brazilian lady, he has one son, Roberto. A man of cosmopolitan tastes, the Portuguese Ambassador collects Chinese antiques and paintings by modern European artists. He enjoys the theater, and lists tennis as his favorite sport.

References

Washington (D.C.) Post p33 My 30 '50
Quem é Alguém (1947)

FISHER, WALTER C. July 10, 1906-
Service organization official

Address: b. c/o International Association of Lions Clubs, 332 S. Michigan Ave., Chicago 4, Ill.; h. Dulverton Fruit Farm, Queenston, Ontario, Canada

At its thirty-second annual convention, held in New York City in 1949, the International Association of Lions Clubs elected Walter C. Fisher president of the service organization for the 1949-50 term. Fisher, a fruit farm operator in Queenston, Ontario, Canada, has been successively third, second, and first vice-presi-

WALTER C. FISHER

dent of the international association, as well as an international director; he has also held executive positions in his local club and the national organization in Canada, serving as president of the latter during 1943-44.

Walter C. Fisher is the son of C. Howard Fisher, operator of the Dulverton Fruit Farm at Queenston, in the rich fruit-growing Niagara Peninsula of Ontario. His mother was Emelie Boynton. Born (July 10, 1906) and reared on the farm, Fisher got his elementary education in the Queenston public schools; later, for his secondary schooling he attended the Niagara Falls (Ontario) Collegiate Institute. He then proceeded to the Ontario Agricultural College at Guelph (an institution affiliated with the University of Toronto), to earn the Bachelor of Scientific Agriculture degree, granted him by the college in 1926. He returned to assist in the operation of the fruit farm, C. Howard Fisher & Sons, Ltd., which has been the property of the Fisher family since 1882; it is the oldest commercial peach orchard in Ontario, some portions of it having produced peaches continually since 1815. Eventually Walter Fisher became secretary-treasurer of the company.

The fruit farmer's association with the Lions Clubs began in 1933, when he became a member of the Lions Club of St. Catharines, a near-by community, the center of the fruit-growing district. His activities with the local club have included chairmanship of various committees and membership on the board of directors. He was elected club president for the fiscal year 1941-42. During the following year Fisher was deputy district governor of Zone 5, District A, during 1943-44 district governor of District A-2 and chairman of the board of governors of District A. That same year he served as president of the International Association of Lions

FISHER, WALTER C.—*Continued*

Clubs of Canada. His service with the over-all International Association included terms as third, second, and first vice-president, and as an international director. In 1947 he represented Lions International at a special conference of nongovernmental agencies which was called at Lake Success to formulate plans for the dissemination of educational material concerning the United Nations.

The International Association of Lions Clubs is a fraternal service organization founded in 1917 by Melvin Jones. The first aim of the Lions, states Fisher, is "to create and foster a spirit of generous consideration among the peoples of the world through a study of the problems of international relationships," as well as "to unite members thereof in the closest bonds of good fellowship; to encourage active participation in all things that have to do with commercial and civic betterment; to uphold the principles of good government; and to bring about a better understanding among men." Membership, as of 1949, stood at 381,426 members in 7,427 clubs located in twenty-six countries.

The international association's July 1949 convention (its thirty-second annual meeting) unanimously elected Walter C. Fisher president for the 1949-50 term, to succeed Eugene S. Briggs '48. (Fisher had held the post of first vice-president during the preceding term.) The convention adopted a resolution stressing the importance of the United Nations as the framework within which to build world peace, and calling for sponsorship by Lions clubs of forums, essay contests, and other measures to promote an awareness of U.N. aims and influence among adults and young people. A resolution endorsing the voluntary enlistment program of the United States was also adopted. Convention delegates were informed that the Lions International board had approved the long-term project of a "Lions International City," to be built thirty miles south of Chicago, Illinois, on 370 acres of property acquired near Matteson and Olympic Fields on the Lincoln Highway. (The present headquarters of the association is in Chicago.) The project is expected to include homes for the organization's staff, a large printing plant, hotel, library, museum, colleges, interdenominational house of worship, and homes for Lions who may wish to settle in the fraternal community. In recognition of the services of the association in selling United States Savings Bonds, the Lions were presented with a citation by the Assistant Secretary of the Treasury.

A New York *Herald Tribune* editorial welcoming the Lions to the city stated: "The Lions are a service organization devoted to improving community, national, and international relations, and they operate on the personal, not the theoretical level." President Fisher emphasized this quality in the association's work when he pointed out that the clubs could "set a pattern for public opinion" such as would "insure a spirit of generous consideration among the peoples of the world." Urging the Lions to be "intelligently realistic," the new president warned: "The only safe course to pursue is to be eternally alert and take intelligent action to make the moral and spiritual fiber of our countries so vibrantly strong that we will be immune to the consuming disease of despotism."

The orchard operator is a past vice-president of the Niagara Peninsula Fruit Growers Association, a past director of the Ontario Fruit Growers Association, and is a member of the Agricultural Institute of Canada. He is a director of the Premier Trust Company of Toronto. Prominent in numerous community affairs in Queenston and St. Catherines, Fisher was for many years a member of the Queenston School Board. His religious affiliation is with the United Church of Canada, of whose local Sunday school he has served as superintendent for some twenty years. In 1929 Fisher married Alice Petrie of Hamilton, Ontario; they have three children, Carolyn, Cathie, and Walter, Jr. Hunting and fishing are his favorite sports, and color photography is a hobby. He is a man of solid build, has graying hair, and wears glasses.

FOLSOM, MARION B(AYARD) Nov. 23, 1893- Corporation executive

Address: b. c/o Committee for Economic Development, 444 Madison Ave., New York 22; c/o Eastman Kodak Co., Rochester, N.Y.; h. 106 Oak Lane, Rochester, N.Y.

The research and policy committee of the Committee for Economic Development—a private research organization formed in 1942 for the purpose of studying and attempting to solve current and future economic problems—is under the chairmanship of Marion B. Folsom. The executive is the treasurer and a director of the Eastman Kodak Company. Long known as an authority on matters relating to social security and old age pension systems, and a past member of several important State and Federal economic bodies, Folsom succeeded Philip D. Reed '49 as head of the C.E.D. research and policy unit in August 1949. The C.E.D., which is supported by contributions from individuals and corporations, is governed by a board of trustees including prominent figures in the industrial world.

A native of McRae, Georgia, a small town about sixty miles southeast of Macon, Marion Bayard Folsom is the son of William Bryant and Margaret Jane (McRae) Folsom. He was born November 23, 1893. His undergraduate years were spent at the University of Georgia (in Athens), from which he received the B.A. degree in 1912. He then entered Harvard's School of Business Administration, which awarded him the Master's degree with distinction two years later. Joining the Eastman Kodak Company at Rochester, New York, in 1914, he has remained with that organization ever since, except for the period of World War I. (A member of the First Officers Training Camp, he was commissioned a second lieutenant in the Army; he advanced to a captaincy and was overseas with the Twenty-sixth Division.) In 1921 Folsom was appointed assistant to George Eastman, the company's president; in 1930 he became assistant treasurer;

and in 1935 he was appointed treasurer of the company.

Folsom was chief proponent of the thirteen-month year system adopted by Eastman in 1928 for bookkeeping and operational purposes. (In a symposium conducted by the *Congressional Digest* in April 1929, he was to argue in favor of the adoption of a universal thirteen-month calendar.) Folsom, further, took a lead in working out the old-age pension plan adopted for Eastman employees, as described in his article "Old Age on the Balance Sheet" in the *Atlantic Monthly* for September 1929. "Good management cannot keep employees on the force when they are no longer needed," he observes. "The solution lies in the inauguration of a sound and adequate pension plan."

Following the stock market crash of 1929 and the beginning of the depression, Folsom made a study of the problem of stabilizing production and employment, with concrete results embodied in what has come to be known as the "Rochester Unemployment Plan." The wide interest this program attracted led to Folsom's appointment (for 1934-35) to President Roosevelt's Advisory Council on Economic Security, and to his assignment as delegate to the International Labor Conference at Geneva, Switzerland, in 1936. In 1937-38 the Eastman treasurer was a member of the Federal Advisory Council on Social Security, and from June 1940 to January 1941 he served as a division executive of the National Advisory Defense Commission. He was a member of the Regional War Manpower Commission from 1942 to 1945.

When the Committee for Economic Development, officially described as "a private, non-profit, nonpolitical association under a board of trustees composed of some of the nation's leading businessmen," was organized in September 1942 under Paul G. Hoffman [46] (later administrator of the Marshall Plan), Folsom was one of the original trustees. The announced objectives: (1) to help businessmen plan for quick reconversion and expanded production, distribution and employment after the war; (2) to help determine through objective research those economic policies that would encourage both the attainment and maintenance of high production and employment. Achievement of the first objective was the task of a field development division, which set up approximately 2,900 local committees with 60,000 volunteer workers to maintain contacts with 2,000,000 employers about jobs and opportunities in the postwar period. Folsom was chairman of the C.E.D. field development division from its organization in 1942 until March 1944, when he resigned to become staff director of the House of Representatives Special Committee on Postwar Economic Policy and Planning (the Colmer Committee). He served in this capacity through the Seventy-eighth and Seventy-ninth Congresses, until the committee completed its work in 1946. Its eleven reports formed the basis for legislation concerning postwar problems.

When, in 1946, the objectives of the C.E.D. field development division had been largely attained, it was decided to wind up its work. This decision was coupled with a resolution to concentrate on C.E.D.'s second

MARION B. FOLSOM

aim of formulating forward-looking economic policies. The board of trustees was enlarged (Folsom became one of six vice-chairmen), and an information committee was appointed. It was unanimously agreed that the program of the research division (headed by Ralph E. Flanders [48] of Vermont, who held this post until January 1947, when he became a United States Senator) should be "intensified and accelerated." A two-year research plan was then mapped out, to be carried on by four groups; (1) a research and policy committee composed entirely of businessmen selected from the board of trustees and charged with over-all direction as well as sole responsibility for the committee's "Statements on National Policy," a series of brochure-length publications on current problems; (2) a research advisory board composed of economists and social scientists, with Professor Sumner H. Slichter [47] of Harvard as chairman; (3) a research director and his staff; and (4) research experts selected by the research director to prepare reports in the fields of their specialized knowledge. These reports, which are signed and are of book format, have included such titles as *International Trade and Domestic Employment*, *Agriculture in an Unstable Economy*, and *Small Business: Its Place and Problems*. Folsom appears to have been prominent in the research and policy committee between the retirement of Senator Flanders and the appointment of Philip D. Reed of the General Electric Company as chairman in 1948.

Folsom has been a member of the Business Advisory Council of the Department of Commerce since 1936 and has served for several years as vice-chairman. He also served as a director of the Chamber of Commerce of the United States from 1942 to 1948. During this period he was as well a member of the New York Advisory Council on Unemployment Insurance; and in March 1947 he was appointed by President Truman to the new Advisory

FOLSOM, MARION B.—*Continued*
Committee on the Merchant Marine, of which
he became vice-chairman. The executive was a
member of the Advisory Council on Social Security appointed by the Committee on Finance
of the United States Senate in 1947. In 1948
he became a member of the Advisory Council
of the School of Industrial and Labor Relations of Cornell University. In 1949 he was
elected a director of the Federal Reserve Bank
of New York.

In 1948-49 Folsom, as vice-chairman to Reed,
supervised the issuance of various C.E.D.
national policy reports, including *Tax and Expenditure Policy for 1949*, *The International
Trade Organization and the Reconstruction of
World Trade*, and *The Uses and Dangers of
Direct Controls in Peacetime*. His election as
chairman of the research and policy committee,
following Reed's resignation on accepting the
presidency of the International Chamber of
Commerce, was announced by C.E.D. Chairman
W. Walter Williams '48 on August 9, 1949. In
an interview on November 3, Folsom announced
that an economic education program instituted
by the C.E.D. at twelve colleges would be
greatly expanded, and disclosed that the 1950
research program would cover such subjects
as "freedom and national security, how to raise
'real' wages, tax and expenditure policy, facilitating equity financing, international economic
reconstruction, and agricultural policy" (from
the New York *Times*). From time to time
Folsom has contributed articles on social insurance, industrial relations, and business subjects to other periodicals, among them *Review
of Reviews*, *Nation's Business*, and the *Annals
of the American Academy of Political and Social Science*. He has also appeared on the
speakers' platform before such organizations
as the National Industrial Conference Board.

Folsom, who was the recipient of an honorary LL.D. degree from the University of
Rochester (1945), has been associated with
local enterprises and movements. He is a director of the Lincoln-Alliance Bank and Trust
Company and of the Buffalo branch of the
Federal Reserve Bank of New York, and is a
trustee of the Rochester Savings Bank and the
Rochester Bureau of Municipal Research. A
past president of the Rochester Chamber of
Commerce, he is also a trustee of the Allendale
School and a director of the Rochester YMCA
and Community Chest. National organizations
in which he is active include the United States
council of the International Chamber of Com-
merce, the American Economic Association, and
the American Statistical Association. His clubs
are the University, Rochester Country, Genesee
Valley, and Pundit in Rochester, the Harvard
in New York City, and the Metropolitan in
Washington; his fraternities are the Phi Beta
Kappa and the Sigma Nu. Marion Folsom and
Mary Davenport were married on November 16,
1918; three children have been born to them,
Jane McRae (deceased), Marion Bayard, and
Frances. Folsom's church is the Presbyterian.
Five feet ten and one-half inches in height,
the business executive weighs 155 pounds; the

color of his eyes is blue, of his hair, brown.
His outdoor recreations are golf and fishing.

References

Who's Who in America, 1948-49
Who's Who in Commerce and Industry
(1948)
Who's Who in New York, 1947
Who's Who in the East (1948)
World Biography (1948)

FOOT, MICHAEL July 23, 1913- Member
of British Parliament; journalist
Address: b. House of Commons, London;
c/o Tribune Publications, Ltd., 222 Strand,
London, W. C. 2; h. 62 Park St., London, W. 1.

Labor Member of the British Parliament
since 1945, Michael Foot has come into prominence as a Left-wing journalist and co-author
of *Guilty Men* (1940) and *Keep Left* (1947).
For a time a writer for the Beaverbrook press,
he has been a political journalist on the Labor
Daily Herald since 1944, and co-editor of the
Tribune, Labor weekly, since 1948. Reflecting
the views held by Aneurin Bevan '43, left of
center, he came forward as a castigator of
Conservative policies between the two wars.
In November 1950 he again expressed his Left-
wing opposition to the foreign policy of the
Labor Government, when, as a member of the
party's national executive committee, he submitted two resolutions challenging the party
leadership.

Michael Foot was born July 23, 1913, in
Plymouth, England, the third son of Isaac Foot,
lawyer and Member of Parliament, and Eva
(Mackintosh) Foot. Isaac Foot, a Liberal, sat
in the House of Commons in 1922-24 and
1929-35, and became Secretary of Mines in the
first National Government, of James Ramsay
MacDonald. An outstanding political figure,
he was president of the Liberal organization in
1947. Michael Foot's brothers have also been
in politics, Dingle as Liberal M.P. for Dundee
(1931-45), John as an unsuccessful candidate.
Receiving his earlier education at Forres School
and Leighton Park School, Michael Foot entered Wadham College, Oxford, where he was
a scholarship student. He was president of the
Union (the student debating group which is
often a training ground for well-known political figures) in 1933 and toured the United
States as its representative. In 1933 he was
described by *Isis*, a students' magazine, as "the
most brilliant postwar figure in Oxford politics . . . the youngest president the Union has
ever had." Prominent among the Liberals, he
set forth his convictions in "Why I am a Liberal," an article that appeared in the *News
Chronicle* on April 4, 1935. He was graduated
from Oxford in July 1934 with honors.

In March 1935 Foot joined the Labor party.
The family's reaction to that was expressed
by his mother, speaking to the Truro Women's
Liberal Association: "I think he is grievously
mistaken, but I believe he is entirely honest
and sincere." In October 1935 he was accepted
as the Labor candidate for Monmouth, but
was defeated in that year's election; and in

with the newspaper field: until 1942 he wrote a syndicated daily column of commentary on business and finance for Hearst and other newspapers. These columns were once described as being "as easy to read and digest as a summer novel." Before the launching of *Forbes*, its publisher became a naturalized citizen of the United States.

In Forbes's own words, his publication came into being because of his feeling "that business and industry were run too harshly, that employees were not given enough consideration, that, looking ahead, it was imperative that more humantarianism be introduced." His first editorial (in the first issue of the magazine) opened with the sentence, "Business was originated to produce happiness, not to pile up millions." This outlook Forbes amplified by means of nation-wide speaking and observation tours for his own publication and the King Features Syndicate.

The publisher and writer has specialized in life stories of businessmen, of which more than five hundred have appeared in the pages of his magazine or in his daily columns. In an early issue *Forbes* carried the names of fifty men named by the editor as the nation's business leaders of the day. The thirtieth anniversary issue, November 1947, gave a new list of that date's fifty foremost industrial leaders, with Forbes noting a shift from the rugged individualist or "empire builder" like Andrew Carnegie to the salaried man risen from the ranks, or "employee-manager."

Today, with a circulation of more than 100,000, *Forbes* is staffed by a group of editors—specialists in labor, finance, economics and industry—posted throughout the country. B. C. Forbes remains personally at the head, writing his own editorial column, forecasting trends, interspersing the content of the magazine with maxims and proverbs, which also characterize his books, speeches, and conversation. Forbes, a Republican, was opposed to President Roosevelt's New Deal, putting his opinions strongly in writings against planned economy. He had also opposed the use, in local public schools, of Harold Rugg's social science textbooks on the ground that they were "subversive and un-American."

The Forbes company announced in the fall of 1948 a new publishing project, a bimonthly magazine with the name *Nation's Heritage,* to be sold at an annual subscription of $150. In its depiction of facets of the American scene and civilization, illustrations, many of them colored plates, were a prominent feature. Before it ceased publication at the end of 1949, Forbes was the recipient of one of the first annual awards given by Freedoms Foundation to individuals and organizations judged to have contributed "most during the last two years to the American way of life."

Giving up the writing of his daily syndicated column in 1942, Forbes formed, in collaboration with B. A. Javits, an organization called the Investors League, Inc., in which he held the post of president. Designed to represent the interests of stock- and insurance policyholders and other property owners, the league's announced purpose was to unite these segments

Editta Sherman

B. C. FORBES

of the economic population into a group to influence national policy in financial matters. At the 1947 annual meeting of the association, as reported in *Forbes* (November 15, 1947), it was announced that the league had attained national recognition. President of the body since its formation, Forbes resigned in 1949 and was elected to the position of chairman of the board, from which post he called on members of the board to resign in order to facilitate executive reorganization at that time, following what has been described as a "turbulent" period. A few months later (March 1950) Forbes retired from the chairmanship.

Forbes's books are *Finance, Business and the Business of Life,* 1915; *Men Who Are Making America,* 1917; *Forbes Epigrams,* 1922; *Men Who Are Making the West,* 1923; *Automotive Giants of America,* 1925; *How to Get the Most Out of Business,* 1927; *Little Bits About Big Men,* 1940; *499 Scottish Stories,* 1945. He also was editor in 1948 of *America's Fifty Foremost Business Leaders.*

The publisher's clubs are the Knickerbocker Country, New York Athletic, and National Republican of New York. He has memberships in the Saint Andrew's and Burns Societies; Metropolitan Museum of Art, Academy of Political Science, and Institute of Journalists (London). He received an honorary Litt.D. degree from the University of Southern California in 1935.

B. C. Forbes married on April 20, 1915, Adelaide Stevenson. Their four sons are Bruce Charles, Malcolm Stevenson, Gordon Buchan, and Wallace Federate. (Another son, Duncan, is deceased.) Forbes, who has black eyes and gray-black hair, stands five feet seven inches and weighs 185 pounds. He is a Presbyterian in his church affiliation. Annually he supplies funds for Christmas treats and picnics for the

FORBES, B. C.—*Continued*

children and families of the Scottish communities where he attended school and church as a boy. His favorite forms of diversion are golf, fishing, and gardening.

References

Forbes 60:180 N 17 '47
Time 36:37 D '40; 50:91 N 17 '47 por
Who's Who in America, 1948-49

FOSTER, WILLIAM C(HAPMAN) Apr. 27, 1897- United States Government official

Address: b. c/o Economic Cooperation Administration, 800 Connecticut Ave., N.W., Washington, D.C.; h. 1411 34th St., Washington, D.C.; 25 Kensington Rd., Scarsdale, N.Y.

The successor to Paul G. Hoffman '46 as head of the Economic Cooperation Administration is William C. Foster, formerly ECA Deputy Administrator and Under Secretary of Com-

Wide World Photos
WILLIAM C. FOSTER

merce. The new director of the Marshall Plan had been closely associated with Hoffman, and with W. Averell Harriman '46 while the latter was the United States Special Representative in Europe. Foster took the oath of office as ECA head on October 2, 1950.

William Chapman Foster, son of Jed Smith and Anna Louise (Chapman) Foster, was born in Westfield, New Jersey, on April 27, 1897; the elder Foster is a mechanical engineer. The boy was prepared for college at the private Kingsley School at Essex Fells, from which he was graduated in 1914. He then entered the Massachusetts Institute of Technology, but left at the end of his junior year to serve (1917-18) as a second lieutenant and military aviator in World War I.

One of those to receive in 1918 a wartime degree from M.I.T., Foster worked after demobilization for both the Packard Motor Company and the Public Service Corporation of New Jersey. In 1922 he became sales engineer at the Pressed and Welded Steel Products Company, Long Island City, New York; its secretary-treasurer in 1925, and sixteen years later, in 1941, its vice-president, continuing as treasurer. In 1946 Foster became his company's president. For about two years (1944-46) he had also served as secretary and a director of the Wegner Machinery Corporation of Long Island City.

Although the Pressed and Welded Steel Products Company is a relatively small manufacturing concern (at the peak of production during World War II it employed about three hundred persons) it fell definitely into the "essential industry" classification, and Foster's national service in the 1941-45 conflict was accordingly performed on the home front. During 1942 he was named to the advisory board of the New York Ordnance District; he also became a member, and later chairman, of the board of governors of Region II of the Smaller War Plants Corporation, and was considered for the chairmanship of the entire Smaller War Plants Corporation. (Largely for political reasons, said *Business Week*, the post was given to former Representative Maury Maverick '44 of Texas.) Foster was appointed assistant director of the purchases division of the Army Service Forces in 1944, later becoming deputy director and finally director. Also, in 1944, he was chosen for the chairmanship, which he was to hold for the next two years, of the subcommittee on small business of CED's research and policy committee.

Foster's wartime record—in recognition of which he was given the United States Medal for Merit and the War Department's Commendation for "exceptional civilian services"—included also duties as special representative of the Under Secretary of War on procurement for the Army Air Forces. Early in 1946 he was named to the War Department's Policy Committee on Labor-Management Relations. ("He was No. 2 man in setting up the Army's smooth contract-settlement procedures, and later was head of the Contract Settlement Board," stated *Business Week*). In the same year Foster became a member of the United States Department of Commerce's Advisory Committee on Small Business as well as of the Mayor's Postwar Industrial Committee in New York City, and was "on Commerce Secretary Wallace's slate . . . for head of the Office of Small Business, which would have become an assistant secretaryship if Congress had consented to the plan" (*Business Week*).

On November 29, 1946, about two months after W. Averell Harriman had succeeded Henry A. Wallace as Secretary of Commerce, the White House announced the appointment of Foster as Under Secretary to succeed Alfred Schindler. Foster's nomination was the first of major importance to be made by President Truman after the Democratic losses in that year's elections; and the revelation that the new Under Secretary was a Republican, as well as "a widely known small businessman," w. s found very interesting by political commentators and the press. The appointment was interpreted on the one hand as a gesture of cooperation toward the majority party in the incoming Congress, and on the other as "motivated in part by desire to balance off the business connections (railroads and banking) of Secretary Averell Harriman," who recommended Foster for the post (New York *Herald Tribune*).

As Under Secretary of Commerce, Foster's special function (according to *United States News*) was "general supervision of the Department's many programs of statistics and assistance to American businessmen"; and after being sworn in on December 6 he soon enhanced his reputation as "a competent executive and administrator . . . not inclined to get excited over arising issues." Confirmed by the Senate on January 27, 1947 (his had been a recess appointment), Foster urged changes in tax laws to permit small businesses "to carry forward their losses from current operations to apply against subsequent earnings for a period of years" (New York *World-Telegram*, February 19, 1947). In March he joined Secretary Harriman in expressing, to the Department's Business Advisory Council, the thought that "certain prices are too high, and that a review of factors which determine price levels might show the need for readjustment." He believed that "the United States . . . must increase the volume of its imports to enable other nations to pay for the goods and credits they receive"; and in July 1947, as a witness before a House of Representatives committee investigating the possibility of a domestic oil shortage, Foster strongly opposed "drastically curtailing" the export of petroleum products on the ground that to do so would "upset the world system of distribution."

When the Cabinet Air Coordinating Committee was transferred from the Department of State to the Department of Commerce on January 3, 1948, Foster became the new chairman. According to a White House statement, the problems before the committee that year would for the most part be related to the condition of the aircraft industry, navigational aids, joint support of international facilities, and the coordination of research and development in civil air transport. On April 24, in accordance with President Truman's order of March 13 that "no files of investigations of Government employees' loyalty be turned over to Congress for reasons of security," Foster refused to provide the House Committee on Un-American Activities with the Federal Bureau of Investigation report on the Director of the National Bureau of Standards, Dr. Edward U. Condon[46].

When Congress adopted the Marshall Plan in April 1948, Harriman resigned as Secretary of Commerce to become "Ambassador at large to Western Europe" for the newly authorized Economic Cooperation Administration headed by Paul G. Hoffman. Harriman appointed Foster as his General Deputy in charge of Paris headquarters, and the latter accordingly resigned from the Commerce Department as of May 31. In his new post Foster was regarded as Har-

riman's "chief trouble-shooter . . . more concerned with action than elaborate programming," and is credited with successfully "working Greece into the Marshall Plan framework" (*Business Week*). A release from the ECA Washington office stated that "an atmosphere of perpetual crisis existed in the summer of 1948 as the European governments wrestled with the problems of setting up the OEEC in Paris," to correlate their requests for help from the ECA. By the fall of that year "the ECA staff in Paris had combined Europe's procurement plans into a single package for presentation to Congress." President Truman conferred on Foster the rank of Ambassador Extraordinary and Plenipotentiary in December of that year.

Foster was called back to Washington in June 1949 to succeed Howard Bruce[48] as the ECA Deputy Administrator, the appointment having been confirmed by the Senate without objection. In a speech before the Women's National Republican Club in New York in January 1950, Deputy Administrator Foster, pointing out that the Marshall Plan (which is due to end on June 30, 1952) was at a midway point, voiced the belief that "the task in the second half of the plan" would require "reducing trade barriers, adjusting exchange rates, coordinating monetary policies," with the object of creating a single market for all western Europe. "We must do more," he added. "We must be willing to face competition from increased imports."

That address and one entitled "Business and the National Interest" delivered at the University of Washington in Seattle in June, are regarded as doing much to prepare the way for the generally favorable reception of Foster's elevation to the post of ECA Administrator when Paul Hoffman's resignation became effective September 30, 1950. (Because of Hoffman's illness preceding his resignation, Foster was for two months the Acting Administrator.) "The change in the headship of the Economic Cooperation Administration will not alter its direction," predicted the Washington *Post*. "Mr. Foster has long had the reputation as the best administrator in Washington." Hoffman himself called his successor "as able an administrator" as he had "ever known," while the New York *Times* was of the belief that, while Foster could not "at the beginning speak with the same authority" as his predecessor, he was well able to handle his new responsibilities. Foster took the oath of office as ECA Administrator on October 2, 1950. On December 7 the Senate Foreign Relations Committee approved his appointment.

The general functions of ECA Administrator Foster are to: "(1) review and appraise the requirements of participating countries for assistance; (2) formulate programs of United States assistance . . .; (3) provide for the efficient execution of any such program; and (4) terminate provision of assistance or take other remedial action as he deems necessary" (*United States Government Organization Manual*). The course of action Foster advocates in the present world crisis is "to strengthen the material and moral resources of the free world, so that the free countries to-

FOSTER, WILLIAM C.—*Continued*

gether can deter future aggression." In this
the Marshall Plan is both "a practical development program" and a means by which the
United States can demonstrate an understanding
of other countries' problems. The staff which
carries out the ECA plan comprises four thousand persons in the United States and abroad.

Foster and the former Beulah Robinson—
they were married in May 1925—have one son,
Seymour Robinson. A resident of Scarsdale,
New York, for many years, he is a past chairman of the local Community Service Council
and a former trustee of the Hitchcock Memorial (Presbyterian) Church. Finding his relaxation chiefly in golf and yachting, he is a
member of a number of country and yacht clubs,
in several of which he has served as secretary
or president; he also belongs to the Chevy
Chase Club (near Washington) and the University Club (New York City). He is a
Legionnaire. In a brief description of him the
United States News wrote "tall, spare, genial,
and approachable."

References

> Bsns W p5 D 7 '46 por
> N Y Herald Tribune p4 D 2 '46 por;
>   II pl O 1 '50 por
> N Y Times p24 S 26 '50
> U S News 21:73-4 D 13 '46 por
> American Men in Government (1949)
> International Who's Who, 1950
> Who's Who in America, 1950-51
> Who's Who in Commerce and Industry
>   (1948)
> Who's Who in New York, 1947
> Who's Who in the East (1948)
> World Biography (1948)

FRANKLIN,   WALTER   S(IMONDS)
May 24, 1884- Railroad president

Address: b. c/o Pennsylvania Railroad, Broad
Street Station Bldg., Philadelphia, Pa.; h. Old
Gulph Rd., Ardmore, Pa.

On June 16, 1949, Walter S. Franklin became the president of the Pennsylvania Railroad upon the elevation of Martin W. Clement [46] to chairman of the board. This advancement to the highest executive post in the
Pennsylvania Railroad came to Franklin after thirty-four years in transportation, most
of which he served with the 103-year-old
Pennsylvania Railroad or its subsidiaries. The
two-and-a-third-billion-dollar system owns about
6 per cent of the railway trackage in the United
States.

Walter Simonds Franklin, the son of Walter
Simonds and Mary Campbell (Small) Franklin,
was born "within a stone's throw of the Pennsylvania tracks" in Ashland, Maryland, on May
24, 1884. His father, who commanded a regiment of volunteers in the Union Army during
the Civil War, began the long association of
the Franklin family with "Pennsy" by going to
work for it upon his graduation from Harvard
in 1857, when the road was ten years old. He
became head of the Ashland Iron Works and
the Maryland Steel Company (later incor-

porated into the Bethlehem Steel Company)
and president of the Baltimore City Passenger
Railway, the city's transit system. Of his four
sons, two were to become heads of transportation companies. Walter Franklin attended the
Marston School in Baltimore and then went
on to Harvard University, from which he graduated in 1906 with the degree of Bachelor of
Arts. That same year, on October 1, he entered
the employ of the Pennsylvania Railroad.

After a brief period of work on the freight
platform at Dock Street Station in Philadelphia,
Franklin was advanced to clerical duties in the
overcharge claim bureau and the freight rate
bureau in the Philadelphia office of the general
freight agent. After performing similar duties in
the office of the superintendent of the Northern
Central Railway at Baltimore, in 1908 he was appointed assistant to the freight agent at York,
Pennsylvania. In the course of the next six years
he was freight solicitor in Baltimore (1909), in
New Haven, Connecticut (1911-12), in Toronto,
Canada (1912), and in Pittsburgh, Pennsylvania
(1912-14). After a year as Southern freight
agent at Atlanta, Georgia, he went to Baltimore
in December 1915 as division freight agent.
This early concentration of Franklin on the
problems of freight movement and freight rates
laid the basis for his present reputation (as
reported in the New York *Times*, June 19,
1949) as the best-informed railroad executive
in the United States on the subject of rail
transportation rates.

The Pennsylvania Railroad granted Franklin
leave from July 1 to September 18, 1916, for
service in the United States Army, with the
Maryland Field Artillery, during the trouble on
the Mexican border. He was also to serve in
World War I: on May 31, 1917, he entered the
army as a captain in the Quartermaster Corps
at the Schuylkill Arsenal at Philadelphia, where
he was in charge of transportation details. Assigned to the Transportation Corps, he was
promoted to major, then to lieutenant colonel;
it was his duty to supervise the movement of
all troops of the American Expeditionary Force
through England to their embarkation for
France. Following the Armistice he was kept
overseas for the supervision of the homeward
movement of American troops from England
and France, and for the procurement of additional foreign ships required for this purpose.
In recognition of Franklin's skill in the solution
of complex transportational problems, he was
awarded the American Distinguished Service
Medal and the British Distinguished Service
Order and was made a Chevalier of the French
Legion of Honor.

On November 15, 1917, while still on war
duty in Europe, Franklin was appointed assistant general freight agent of the Pennsylvania Railroad in Philadelphia, and upon his
return to the United States he served the railroad in that capacity until August 31, 1919. At
that time he resigned to become vice-president
and later the president of the American Trading Company, an export-import firm of New
York, where, according to an article in the
Girard Trust Company's magazine, he "acquired a shipper's viewpoint," knowledge of
value in his later work in transportation. In

1928 he returned to the Pennsylvania, in the general freight office in New York City. After a period as general agent at Detroit, to which he was assigned on July 1, 1928, Franklin in June 1929 was appointed general superintendent of the Northwest division of the road, with headquarters in Chicago; he remained there for about a month.

For the next two years (1929-31) Franklin was the president of the Detroit, Toledo and Ironton Railroad Company, an affiliate of the Pennsylvania. From January to October of 1931 he was again associated with the Pennsylvania as assistant to the vice-president in charge of operation. Then, in October he joined the Wabash Railway Company and the Ann Arbor Railroad, a subsidiary of the Wabash, as their president. When the Wabash went into receivership at the end of that year, he was named coreceiver. He continued in that office until the fall of 1933, which marked his return to the Pennsylvania Railroad. With the reorganization of the Wabash line he was named one of its directors in January 1942. The Philadelphia *Inquirer* (June 13, 1949) quoted the railroad man as reminding reporters, after his election as president of the Pennsylvania, that he had twice previously been president of railroads. "They might have been smaller than the Pennsylvania," he said, "but they were railroads."

Since his return to the Pennsylvania Railroad on October 16, 1933, as the vice-president in charge of traffic, Franklin's service with that company has been uninterrupted. His election to the road's board of directors took place in December 1938, and his advancement to the executive vice-president's office in April 1947. The president of the Pennsylvania at that time, Martin W. Clement, had already passed the voluntary retirement age of sixty-five by one year; and it was logical, said commentators, that Franklin, who was called by *Business Week* "the driving force behind the giant Pennsy's postwar improvement and modernization program," should be considered for the presidency. In June 1949 Clement became the chairman of the board, and Franklin was appointed to the presidency.

The president of the Pennsylvania Railroad has appeared before the Interstate Commerce Commission and before various State commissions as spokesman for the carriers in several hearings on petition for rate and fare changes. In a statement released on January 3, 1950, he declared that the Pennsylvania and other roads had "made notable progress in modernizing and improving" their services by the expenditure of "large sums, mostly borrowed," and had "substantially scaled down expenses in proportion to reduced revenues." He emphasized that further satisfactory service depends "not only on the efforts of railway management, but on fair and equitable treatment in the matter of subsidized competition, the assurance of a reasonably free hand in conducting business, and the reasonableness of labor in its future demands." As reported by the Philadel-

Fabian Bachrach

WALTER S. FRANKLIN

phia *Inquirer*, Franklin is of the opinion that "carriers must have rate relief if they are to be able to maintain their properties in good condition and carry through their modernization and improvement programs to effect operating economies and permit the lowering of rates later." In a statement Franklin made in late December 1949, the net 1949 income would approximate nineteen million dollars; the outlook for 1950 was declared as even better.

Active in the Eastern Railroad Presidents Conference and a member of the board of directors of the Association of American Railroads, Franklin is a director of the Norfolk and Western Railway Company, of the Railway Express Agency, Inc., of the Bell Telephone Company of Pennsylvania, and of the Guaranty Trust Company of New York; he is also a member of the board of managers of the Western Savings Fund Society and of the Girard Trust Company of Philadelphia. His clubs are the University, Harvard, and Recess in New York, and the Gulph Mills Golf, the Racquet, the Merion Cricket, the Philadelphia, and the Harvard in Philadelphia. The railroad president belongs, too, to the Pennsylvania Society in New York, the Newcomen Society of England (American branch), and the Society of the Cincinnati. He is a Presbyterian.

Married on December 6, 1919, to Cassandra Morris Small, Franklin has two children, William Buell and Cassandra Small (Mrs. Caspar W. Morris, Jr.) The chief recreations of Franklin (who is six and a half feet tall and weighs 205 pounds) are walking, playing tennis, and sailing. He has been described as having an "affable manner and quiet speech"; another comment is that he makes hard work his hobby.

(Continued next page)

FRANKLIN, WALTER S.—*Continued*

References

N Y Times III p3 Je 19 '49
Philadelphia (Pa.) Inquirer Je 13 '49
Time 53:80 Je 20 '49

National Cyclopædia of American Biography Current vol D (1934)
Who's Who in America, 1948-49
World Biography (1948)

FRED, E(DWIN) B(ROUN) Mar. 22, 1887- University president; bacteriologist

Address: b. c/o University of Wisconsin, Madison 6, Wis.; h. 10 Babcock Dr., Madison 6, Wis.

E. B. Fred, twelfth president of the University of Wisconsin, the eighth largest school in the United States, had been a member of its faculty for thirty-two years when he was appointed president in February 1945. A noted bacteriologist, he had been dean of the Graduate School and of the College of Agriculture. During World War II he directed the United States Government's program of research in bacteriological warfare.

Descended from Quaker ancestors, one of whom (John Fred) came from Ireland to settle in Pennsylvania in 1713, Edwin Broun Fred was born on the family farm in Virginia, near the town of Middleburg, on March 22, 1887. He is one of the four children (three boys and a girl) of Samuel Rogers and Catherine Conway (Broun) Fred, who was of English descent. With one brother and a sister E. B. Fred still owns and operates the 2,000-acre Virginia dairy farm. Young Fred was reared in an atmosphere of Confederate tradition; his farm

Fred Dierksmeier
E. B. FRED

home was in the country that had seen much of the fighting in the Civil War. (Fred likes to tell how his maternal grandfather raised Traveler, General Robert E. Lee's horse.)

In 1902-3 Fred attended the Randolph Macon Academy at Front Royal, Virginia, preparatory to entering Virginia Polytechnic Institute. At the latter he earned his B.S. degree in 1907, and, after a year as an assistant in bacteriology, his M.S. in 1908. He proceeded for further study to Germany, where in 1911 he was awarded the Ph.D. degree for work in bacteriology at the University of Göttingen. He then returned to the Virginia Polytechnic Institute, to remain for one year (1912-13) as an assistant professor of bacteriology.

Dr. Fred began his association with the University of Wisconsin in 1913 as assistant professor in the department of agricultural bacteriology; the next year he was advanced to associate professor, and in 1918 to full professor. In 1918, too, with the entry of the United States into World War I, he was commissioned a first lieutenant in the Chemical Warfare Service of the United States Army. In the years following the war Fred became known as a leading bacteriologist. His work, as summarized in *American Men of Science*, had to do with fermentation products of the growth of micro-organisms and root nodule bacteria. In 1923 he collaborated with F. Löhnis on *Textbook of Agricultural Bacteriology*, and in 1928 with S. A. Waksman [46] on *Laboratory Manual of Microbiology. Root Nodule Bacteria and Leguminous Plants*, which he wrote with his University of Wisconsin colleagues Ira L. Baldwin and Elizabeth McCoy, was published in 1932 as one of the university's "Studies in Science' series. In 1934, the president of the university appointed Fred the dean of the Graduate School.

In 1941 the Wisconsin bacteriologist was asked by the Secretary of War to head the committee on biological warfare of the National Academy of Sciences. After six months of investigation Fred reported that, although the value of biological warfare would remain "debatable" until proven by experience, there was "but one logical course" for the Government—"to study the possibilities of such warfare from every angle, making every preparation for reducing its effectiveness and thereby reducing the likelihood of its use." This recommendation led to the establishment of research activity under the Federal Security Agency, to initiate and direct research in biological warfare; Fred was appointed director of the service. Experimental work in university and institutional laboratories was organized, and, to facilitate more intensive research, a central "germ warfare" installation was established at Camp Detrick, Maryland. In 1944, when the War and Navy Departments assumed germ warfare research, Fred continued as a special consultant to the Secretary of War. His war work brought him the nation's highest civilian award, the Medal for Merit.

In 1943 Dr. Fred had returned to Wisconsin's College of Agriculture to be dean of the college and director of its Agricultural Experiment

Station, which conducts research in the natural and social sciences as they relate to agriculture and homemaking. "The Agriculture College," stated *Life*, "is the school that has made the university famous." Discoveries made in its laboratories include the Babcock butter-fat test; the drug dicumarol (preventative of blood clotting), developed in collaboration with the Medical School; an oat variety, Vicland, which is credited with increasing the State's farm income by several million dollars a year.

On February 15, 1945, Dr. Fred became president of the University, elected by the State Board of Regents to succeed Clarence A. Dykstra '41, who had resigned. Fred's name was one of three suggested by the faculty of the University, which has a reputation for the academic freedom accorded its staff and students. Having come to his post after thirty-two years as scholar, teacher, and administrator, Fred has been called a "professor's president." The University of Wisconsin, frequently called one of the most beautifully located in the United States, includes on one campus in Madison, the Colleges of Letters and Science, Engineering, and Agriculture, as well as the Schools of Law, Medicine, Nursing, Education and Commerce, the Graduate School, and Departments of Physical Education, Military Science, and Naval Science. About 18,000 students attend classes on the campus, and 5,000 in its Milwaukee Extension Division. The university offers 450 correspondence courses and conducts extension classes in ten other Wisconsin towns. "The roots of the university are deep and widespread in the soil of the State. Of this fact we are justly proud," president Fred said at the 1946 dedication of the Racine Extension Center.

President Fred has said that he is not "alarmed" at the growth of the University of Wisconsin: "Bigness is not evil in itself. . . . A State university's doors should be open on easy financial terms to all who possess sufficient intellectual endowment to gain by what it can offer." But he includes in this philosophy the warning that the university, if compelled to grow, should remain "a human institution where the individual is important." To the university regents he once outlined the purposes of the university: (1) to accumulate knowledge, (2) to disseminate knowledge in order that people may better adapt themselves to their environment, and (3) to prepare young people in the art of discovering, using, and disseminating knowledge. On the occasion of Fred's second anniversary as president, the Board of Regents passed a resolution commending him for having "exhibited great leadership" during the "crucial" period after World War II when the university was "faced with the most difficult problems of enrollment and staff, and with the need for expansion of facilities and services."

Articles by Dr. Fred have appeared in the *Journal of Bacteriology* and *Soil Science*; he was consulting editor of the latter as well as of *Archiv für Mikrobiologie*), and other scientific periodicals. Soil bacteriology, nitrogen-fixing bacteria, and fermentation were among the subjects of his research. A member of the Society of American Bacteriologists, he was the group's president in 1932. His other scientific member-

ships include the National Academy of Sciences (he is a member of its biological warfare committee), the American Association for the Advancement of Science (fellow), and the American Philosophical Society. Since 1945 he has been a member of the National Advisory Health Council and a trustee of the Nutrition Foundation, since 1946 a member of the board of trustees of the Carnegie Foundation for the Advancement of Teaching, and since January 1949 on the United States Advisory Commission on Educational Exchange. In December 1950 he was elected vice-chairman of the National Science Board, under the National Science Foundation; the latter was created by Congress to promote the progress of science for national welfare and defense. He received membership in the Newcomen Society of Britain, and also belongs to Alpha Sigma Epsilon, Phi Kappa Phi, Sigma Xi, Gamma Alpha, Phi Sigma, Epsilon Sigma Phi, and Phi Beta Kappa. His six honorary degrees comprise an LL.D. from Northwestern University (1947) and a D.Sc. from the University of North Carolina (1946), Lawrence College and Marquette University (1945), and Northland College (1946).

Described as a "modest and pleasant Virginian" who is "popular with students and faculty" (*Newsweek*, October 11, 1948), Fred begins his day at 7:30 A.M. and is usually at work until 10 P.M. This schedule he is able to maintain, "thanks to his splendid physical condition," stated the editor of the *Wisconsin Alumnus*. The president and his family do not live in the president's residence, preferring to remain in another house on the campus. Mrs. Fred is the former Rosa Helen Parrott, daughter of a professor at the Virginia Polytechnic Institute, where Fred studied and taught; they were married June 21, 1913. Their two daughters are Ann Conway Fred and Mrs. Thomas Moffatt (Rosalie Broun). Dr. Fred is a Democrat.

References

Look 12:27 Ag 17 '48 por
N Y Times p34 Ja 26 '45
Newsweek 32:88 O 11 '48 por
American Men of Science (1949)
Leaders in Education (1948)
National Cyclopædia of American Biography Current vol F, 1939-42
Who's Who in America, 1950-51
Who's Who in the Midwest (1949)

FROST, FRANCES MARY Aug. 3, 1905-
Author

Address: b. and h. 79 Horatio St., New York 14

Reprinted from the *Wilson Library Bulletin*, Oct. 1950.

The quixotic fairy who hands out gifts at our birth must have felt completely relaxed and genial on that third day of August 1905 in St. Albans, Vermont, when she bestowed versatility on Frances Mary Frost.

(Continued next page)

FRANCES MARY FROST

In addition to nonstop writing practically ever since she was in the eighth grade, Miss Frost has found time to travel widely, to marry twice, to teach creative poetry at the University of Vermont, to work on newspapers and in stores, to raise two children, to drive a taxi and do defense work during the second world war. Yet she entered under "Occupations other than writing," when asked what her activities had been, the terse word "None." We do not know, in this connection, why we are always surprised to learn a writer knows how to do something besides wear out typewriters.

The parents of Frances Mary Frost, Amos L. and Susan (Keefe) Frost, combined Scotch-English and Irish in their ancestry, which accounts for the lyric quality of their daughter's prose and the glowing lines of her poetry. She was an only child, too, which may have something to do with the wistful reality of the large-family life depicted in two of her books for children, *Windy Foot at the County Fair* and *Sleigh Bells for Windy Foot*. The second is also a Christmas story. In fact, Christmas appears so often as a theme throughout her writing and is handled with such sentiment that one suspects those childhood Christmases of hers in Vermont were remembered as perfect.

Frances Frost had published a number of short stories before she began doing verse. Now there are eight volumes of poetry for adults and a great many single poems which have appeared in magazines such as the *New Yorker, Coronet, Saturday Review of Literature, Atlantic, Harper's*, the editorial page of the New York *Times*, and the poetry page of the New

York *Herald Tribune*. There have been five adult novels, since 1943 five books for children, with a sixth, "Then Came Timothy," to be published in September 1950.

After graduation from Middlebury College in Vermont, the author took a Ph.D. degree in 1931 from the University of Vermont. The record shows that she had the normal extracurricular campus activities during her college years, with club and sorority memberships, and that she was writing as well during that time for the Burlington (Vermont) *Daily News*.

It is as a poet, however, that most people think of Frances Frost. Hers is the sort of poetry that expresses the thoughts everyday people have, who would set them down as she does if they could. The country poems in *Mid-Century* are so real one feels as if he were looking in at the people in them through a window. One critic says, "Frances Frost is a poet who has something to say and says it."

Reviewers have not been uniform in praise of the work of this author. That would be true of any writer as forthright as she is. In 1942, when *Village of Glass*, a novel, was published, a *Saturday Review of Literature* critic said: "She has written a beautifully planned study in balance . . . of horror with beauty, evil with good, pain with peace, death with birth." Yet another called it "an inept and ridiculous novel."

The same divergence of opinion occured when *American Caravan* came out in 1944. This was a story for children which told in rhyme the adventures of an American family traveling through the forty-eight States via car and trailer. Small pictures were substituted in several places for words. Virginia Kirkus was indignant, not seeing any reason for such a novelty and adding that as verse it was negligible. A little later the *New Yorker* pointed out that "children have fun with rebuses and this is a good rattling rhymed verse."

The Little Whistler was her first book of verse for children; it was selected as one of the best ten books of the year for young readers by the New York *Times*, and was included in the New York Public Library's 1949 Christmas list of best books. And there was this review for *Windy Foot at the County Fair* (1947) in the *Atlantic*: "The plot is skillfully handled with a mounting almost unbearable suspense, and there is not one detail in it which could fail to delight a child."

There have been deserved honors along the way: the Shelley Memorial Award; Golden Rose of the New England Poetry Club; Poet Laureate of New York State; Mary R. Cromwell Traveling Fellowship, through the Mac-Dowell Colony, Peterborough, New Hampshire; membership in the MacDowell Colony for seven years, and in Pen and Brush of New York, also.

Miss Frost is modest, apparently keeping no scrapbook of her many publicity clips. In person she is petite, five feet high and slight in build, with black hair and "eyes that change color with the weather." And in her spare time she raises cats.

FULLER, ALFRED C(ARL) Jan. 13, 1885- Manufacturer

Address: b. c/o Fuller Brush Company, Hartford 2, Conn.; h. 32 Colony Rd., West Hartford 7, Conn.

The "Fuller Brush Man," hero of a motion picture and the subject of cartoons and quips, is one of about 7,600 independent dealers selling from door to door the 135 products of the Fuller Brush Company. The founder of the company and chairman of its board, Alfred C. Fuller made a brush in a new way and developed the distinctive method of retailing the products of his company. These range from his three "top sellers," hairbrushes, toothbrushes, and wet mops, to waxes and polishes, and industrial brushes for various uses. More than 20,000,000 families in the United States and Canada buy Fuller brushes, stated John Bainbridge in the *New Yorker*.

Alfred Carl Fuller was born in Kings County, Nova Scotia, January 13, 1885, the eleventh of twelve children. His parents were Leander Joseph and Phebe Jane (Collins) Fuller. Two of his forebears had come from England on the *Mayflower* to settle in the Connecticut River Valley. From there in 1761 his great-great-great-grandfather moved to Nova Scotia to accept a 100-acre Crown grant of land. That farm, eventually inherited by his father, was Alfred Fuller's birthplace. There he was reared, attending a country schoolhouse through the grammar grades.

When Alfred Fuller was eighteen (1903) he left home for Boston, where two of his brothers and two sisters were living. His first job was as a conductor for the Boston Elevated Railway Company. For a period (as told in the *New Yorker*) he worked as a gardener-handyman on a suburban estate, and later as an express wagon driver. Then, on January 7, 1905, young Fuller took a position as salesman in near-by Somerville, with the Somerville Brush and Mop Company. Successful as a salesman and foreseeing the possibilities of his commodity, at the end of a year (when he had saved $375), twenty-three-year-old Fuller resigned, spent $80 on equipment and materials, and set up a workshop in the basement of his sister's home. For making the twisted-wire brushes he designed a small hand-operated wire-twisting machine. Spending the evenings in making brushes for clothes, the hands, the floor, and other uses, he sold his products during the day from house to house.

After a selling trip to Hartford, Connecticut, in 1906 Fuller decided to move to that city. There he rented a shed for $11 a month, hired an assistant, and formed the Capitol Brush Company; upon learning that there already was a Capitol Brush Company, he changed the name to the Fuller Brush Company in 1910. By that time he had twenty-five men selling for him and six factory workers. He had recruited his salesmen while on selling trips through New England, New York, and Pennsylvania by advertising in local newspapers. In 1911, after he placed a small advertisement in a national magazine, he was deluged with replies. Within three months he added almost

ALFRED C. FULLER

a hundred salesmen throughout the United States. "That little ad changed the whole thing from a one-man effort to a company operating nation-wide," he has said. In 1913, when he was twenty-eight, Fuller incorporated his business, becoming president, treasurer, and a director. He estimated the value of the firm as $50,000, of which $30,000 was considered good will.

By 1920 (according to the *National Cyclopædia of American Biography*) the company's sales were $5,000,000 yearly, and by 1924, they had reached $12,000,000. Fuller salesmen after 1929 were called "dealers" to make clear their status as independent businessmen who bought brushes wholesale and sold them retail (making an average 30 per cent profit) rather than a commission or salary. Fuller's only deficit came in 1932. The company thereupon cut prices to improve sales, and by 1938 *Fortune* magazine reported that in the preceding year Fuller had sold brushes amounting to $10,000,000 and yielding a net profit of $208,000 to the company. Ten years later the company was said to gross $30,000,000 a year. Fuller himself once pointed out (reported in *Newsweek*, May 10, 1948) that the advertising value of jokes about the Fuller brush man enabled his company to get along with the low advertising budget of $50,000 annually.

With the outbreak of World War II the company decreased its output of civilian products to make brushes for cleaning guns. Fuller himself served as a member of the Committee on Purchases in the Procurement Division of the War Department, and as a member of the Connecticut State War Council (1942-46). In 1943 his son Alfred Howard took over a major share of responsibility as president of the company, while Fuller himself assumed the chairmanship of the board of directors. During the 1940's the company became outstanding in the manufacture of brush-making machinery, and developed new industrial brushes. In 1948

FULLER, ALFRED C.—*Continued*
women "Fullerettes" appeared when the company added "Debutante Cosmetics" (manufactured by Daggett and Ramsdell, Inc.) to its line and young women to its organization to sell the new products from house to house. By that time, according to the *New Yorker,* Fuller's 7,600 dealers were making approximately 50,-000,000 calls yearly to do a business of $25,000,-000 in Fuller's products. Another $5,000,000 came from sales of the products of the company's industrial division, which manufactured 90 per cent of the brushes used in American-made vacuum cleaners, and 700 other types of industrial brushes, as well as brush-making equipment, textile-making machinery, and nuts and bolts manufactured in Fuller's machine shop.

Each Fuller dealer has an exclusive territory of about 2,000 homes or about 10,000 persons. According to *Time* (July 12, 1948), he averages a profit of $70 a week. A high turnover causes Fuller to recruit over 5,000 new men a year; only two out of seven find themselves well enough suited to the work to make it a career. Those who remain with the firm may advance to field manager (he receives a 2 per cent commission on sales in his area), to branch manager (salary plus percentage on sales), and to district supervisor (salary plus bonus). Factory employees of the company in Hartford have membership in the Fuller Club and use of Fuller Park, a clubhouse with twenty-two acres of grounds for recreation.

Fuller, who became an American citizen in 1918, is a Republican voter. He is a Christian Scientist and a Thirty-second Degree Mason, a Knight Templar and Shriner. His clubs are the Hartford, Rotary, Hartford Golf, Shelter Harbor Golf, Congressional Country (Washington, D.C.), and Indian Hill Country Club; in 1948 he was initiated into the Circus Saints and Sinners Club of New York. A member of the American Society of Sales Executives, he has been a director of the National Better Business Bureau, president of the Connecticut Manufacturers Association (1942 to 1947), vice-president and a director of the Hartford Chamber of Commerce, and a member of the National Association of Manufacturers. The brown-eyed, dark-haired manufacturer has been described as "kindly" and "dignified" by *Time.* John Bainbridge has called him "an even-tempered, agreeable, outsize man [he is six feet one inch tall, weighs 215 pounds] of metaphysical inclinations"—he has remarked that his biggest interest outside his business is Christian Science. Fuller married a Nova Scotian, Evelyn W. Ells, on April 8, 1908. Their two children are executives in the company, Alfred Howard as president, and Avard Ells, the second son, in charge of sales. Fuller's second wife is the former Mary Primrose Pelton, whom he married October 21, 1932. The brush manufacturer lists travel and golf as his chief recreations.

References

Fortune 18:68-73+ O '38
N Y Herald Tribune p21 Mr 15 '50
New Yorker 24:36-8+ N 13 '48

Business Executives of America (1950)
National Cyclopædia of American Biography, Current vol A (1926)
Who's Who in America, 1950-51
Who's Who in Commerce and Industry (1948)
Who's Who in the East (1948)
Who's Who in New England (1949)
World Biography (1948)

FUREY, WARREN W(ILLIAM) Jan. 8, 1898- Physician; radiologist
Address: b. 104 S. Michigan Ave., Chicago 3, Ill.; h. 7144 Jeffery Ave., Chicago 49, Ill.

The president of the Radiological Society of North America, Dr. Warren W. Furey, assumed that office on December 8, 1949, during one of the sessions of the annual meeting of the society. A native of Chicago, the physician has practiced in or near that city, where he is radiologist at the Mercy Hospital, and consulting radiologist at the Lewis Memorial Maternity Hospital and at the Municipal Tuberculosis Sanitarium. He is past president of the Chicago Roentgen Society and of the Chicago Medical Society, and is on the board of directors of the Tuberculosis Institute of Chicago.

Warren William Furey was born on January 8, 1898, one of four sons of Warren William and Alice Gertrude (Cavanaugh) Furey. He was reared in Chicago, where he was a student at St. James High School; the year of his graduation was 1915. His premedical college work was taken at the University of Illinois, which he attended from 1915 to 1918. In the latter year (in World War I) he was a member of the Students' Army Training Corps. He then entered the Medical School of Northwestern University and in June 1923 received the M.D. degree from that institution. While at Northwestern his sports had been baseball and track, and he had become a member of Phi Kappa, Theta Nu Epsilon, Phi Rho Sigma (medical fraternity), and of the medical honorary societies of Phi Kappa Epsilon and Alpha Omega Alpha.

Furey spent his internship at Chicago's Mercy Hospital, on the staff of which he continues to serve in 1950. Upon receiving his medical degree he went to Everett, Washington, to work as an assistant in the Quigley Clinic for one year. He then returned to Chicago, where he maintained a general practice as physician and surgeon until 1930. For the nine years from 1924 to 1933 he was associated with the X-ray department of Mercy Hospital. During and after that period he also engaged in radiological work at various other hospitals in or near Chicago: the Jackson Park (1927-37), the Little Company of Mary, at Evergreen Park (since 1930), St. Joseph's Mercy, of Aurora (1932-37), South Shore (since 1939), and the St. Francis, at Blue Island (since 1937). He has been on the staff of Mercy Hospital since 1944, and is consultant in radiology at the Lewis Memorial Maternity Hospital and the Municipal Tuberculosis Sanitarium of Chicago. He was an instructor in roentgenology

Joseph Merante

WARREN W. FUREY

at Northwestern University until 1939, associate at Loyola University (Chicago) from 1939 to 1942, and has been assistant professor there since the latter date.

One of the oldest associations in the field of radiology, the Radiological Society of North America was founded in 1915. According to the bylaws of the society its purpose is "to promote the study and practical application of radiology in all of its aspects . . . [and] . . . to create a closer fellowship among radiologists and closer cooperation between [them] and the members of other branches of medicine and the allied sciences." The society publishes a monthly journal, *Radiology*, maintains a library and a museum, and provides meetings "for the reading and discussion of papers and the dissemination of knowledge." Prerequisites for joining the society are membership in the American Medical Association or its equivalent, at least three years practice in radiology, and engagement in such practice at the time of application for membership. The use of the science of radiology in the diagnosis and treatment of disease dates from the discovery of X rays. Highly significant developments in the field came with the discovery of radioactive isotopes and the invention of the betatron.

At the 1949 annual meeting of the Radiological Society of North America, held in Cleveland, Ohio, on December 4-9, Furey was installed as president—he had been chosen in 1948—for a year. Active in the society since 1933, he had served on many of its committees, and has been a member of its board of directors since 1945. Dr. Furey has contributed articles to several scientific journals, including the *American Journal of Roentgenology*, and *Radiology*. He is the author of an article on the tumor clinic of the Little Company of Mary Hospital printed in the *Hospital*

Council Bulletin. In 1944 a paper by him, "X-Ray Findings of the Acute Abdomen," was included in the *Proceedings* of the International Assembly of the Inter-State Postgraduate Medical Association of North America.

Furey is a member of the Chicago Medical Society, of which he was secretary from 1944 to 1946 and president in 1947-48, the Chicago Roentgen Society, of which he was president from 1942 to 1944, the American Roentgen Ray Society, the American Radium Society, the Illinois State Medical Society, and the Mississippi Valley Medical Society. He is a fellow of the American College of Radiology (treasurer since 1946), of the Institute of Medicine of Chicago, the International College of Surgeons, the American Medical Association. His clubs are the South Shore Country Club and the Illinois Athletic Club. He holds the Selective Service Medal.

The radiologist married, on October 22, 1924, Veronica A. Lindstrom, who had been a nurse prior to her marriage. Their four children are Rosemary Kathleen, Virginia Alice, Warren William 3d, and Edward Charles. Furey is "independent" in politics; he is a member of the Roman Catholic Church. Six feet tall and weighing 160 pounds, he has blue eyes and black hair. He lists golf and bowling as his favorite recreations.

References

Directory of Medical Specialists (1949)
Who's Who in Chicago and Illinois (1945)

GAITHER, FRANCES 1889- Author
Address: h. 460 W. 24th St., New York 11

Reprinted from the *Wilson Library Bulletin*, March 1950.

Frances Gaither, Southerner, lives quietly in New York City because her life is wrapped up in her writings and her husband. Her writing requires a large and adequate public library; her husband works on the New York *Times*. She loves New York's concerts, operas, plays, and happy shopping marts on Ninth Avenue as much as she does the State of Maine, where her maternal grandfather was born and where she and Rice, her husband, spend summer vacations on Bailey Island. Mrs. Gaither's paternal grandfather was a cotton planter and slave owner in Tennessee. She has suggested that perhaps it was due to these grandfathers arguing inside of her that the lot of Negroes always has affected her poignantly.

Born in Somerville, Tennessee, in 1889, Frances Gaither is the daughter of Annie Walker (Smith) and Paul Tudor Jones. Her father was a medical man with additional manufacturing interests in Corinth, Mississippi. The family moved to Corinth in Frances' early childhood, and it was there that she graduated from high school. A B.A. degree was achieved

FRANCES GAITHER

at the Mississippi State College for Women in Columbus in 1909.

Author of *Double Muscadine*, a recent Book-of-the-Month Club selection, as well as countless short stories, masques, pageants and six novels (her first story had been sold in 1918 to a magazine called *All Story*), Mrs. Gaither doesn't believe she is writing historical novels. "I don't base characters on actual personages. What I try to do in dealing with the past is to create an illusion of the present. I work terribly hard to get my characters to think and feel and speak as if they were living now, in this moment. My books, I like to think, are bare of costume and trappings, of set stage and stock actions. The important thing for me in research is to absorb the period so completely that I am able to give out what I believe are its realities." For *Double Muscadine* she had to learn the laws about slavery. Law books being completely incomprehensible, Mrs. Gaither hired a young law student as tutor. The result was that the reviews of the novel invariably praised the "taut, expert" courtroom scenes.

Frances Gaither's novel writing started with juveniles, a field where storytelling and graceful style are essential. Her children's books, all dealing with Southern history, still sell regularly. They are *The Painted Arrow* (1931), *The Scarlet Coat* (1934), and *Little Miss Cappo* (1937). *Double Muscadine* is her fourth adult book. Earlier ones are *The Red Cock Crows* (1944), *Follow the Drinking Gourd* (1940), and *The Fatal River: The Life and Death of La Salle* (1931). At present she is writing a new novel.

Although writing is a hard job to Mrs. Gaither, she works at it all day every day and finds it her greatest joy. After she has gotten her husband's breakfast and sent him off to work, she dispenses such necessary duties of household and business as telephoning and then settles down, usually not later than 9:30, to

writing. She does not agonize. Some days a whole chapter will come out with the ease of a dream. At other times she labors long over a single passage. When the writing bogs down, there are always research, editing, and cutting to afford mental relaxation and outlets for creative energies. A novel usually has been worked out in general outline in her mind and in the large collection of notes amassed before the actual writing starts. Changes do occur, however, as the story develops. No one sees the novel or hears a word about it until it is entirely finished, but then her husband is the first critic. Because Rice Gaither is an experienced writer and editor, the fortunate publisher need do nothing but read and publish the submitted manuscript.

Reading aloud to her husband at the end of a long day's work is her happiest recreation. Classics, such as *Anna Karenina, Jean Christophe, Middlemarch,* and *Maurice Guest* are preferred by both. Her favorite contemporary Southern writer is William Faulkner. She has admiration as well for Eudora Welty, Ellen Glasgow, Elizabeth Maddox Roberts, and DuBose Heyward. In a biographical sketch entitled "Frances Gaither Speaks," Harvey Breit wrote in the New York *Times,* "Literature is, as it should be with a serious-minded writer, both her work and her ease, the goal of her ambitious striving and the comfort of her leisure." In addition to reading aloud, Mrs. Gaither has listed her favorite recreations as swimming and pastel-sketching.

A person who suggests the tending of flower gardens rather than the tendering of deep-grained novels on the deep South, Frances Gaither has blue eyes, light-brown hair, and weighs considerably under 120 pounds.

GAITSKELL, HUGH (TODD NAYLOR)
Apr. 9, 1906- British Cabinet member
Address: Cabinet Offices, Great George St., London, S.W. 1

On October 25, 1950, Hugh Gaitskell was installed in the British Cabinet as Chancellor of the Exchequer. Eight months before, he had been appointed Minister of State for Economic Affairs, an office not actually a Cabinet post but described as "of Cabinet rank." Gaitskell, a trained economist of the intellectual wing of the Labor party, had previously been Minister of Fuel and Power. Employed in the Ministry of Economic Warfare and later in the Board of Trade during the years of World War II, Hugh Gaitskell was first elected to Parliament in the Labor party victory of 1945. In the 1950 general election he was re-elected to represent the constituency of Leeds South.

Born April 9, 1906, Hugh Todd Naylor Gaitskell is the son of Arthur and Adelaide Mary (Jamieson) Gaitskell. Arthur Gaitskell, of a Cumbrian family, was a member of the Indian Civil Service; the Scottish father of Mrs. Gaitskell was a consul general in Shanghai. First sent to Winchester College, Hugh Gaitskell then entered New College, Oxford. There he read "Modern Greats" (philosophy, politics and economics). In the mid-twenties young Oxford was turning leftward, and Gaitskell, who had already founded a branch of the League of Nations Union at Winchester, joined the Labor party in 1926, the year of the general strike. While many young men of Gaitskell's social class were driving autobuses for the public, he drove a car for the strikers and distributed copies of the *British Worker*. He was graduated B.A. with first-class honors in 1927.

Gaitskell's first employment was with the Workers' Educational Association, as tutor in the department of adult education at University College, Nottingham, during the 1927-28 session. In the autumn of 1928 he moved to University College, London, as lecturer in economics. His connection with London University continued until 1939, by which time he was reader in political economy and head of the department of economics there (appointed in 1938). During 1931-33 he was honorary assistant secretary of the New Fabian Research Bureau. In the session of 1933-34 he was a Rockefeller research fellow, studying in Vienna —he was in that city at the time of the bombardment of the Socialists' apartment houses and the assassination of Dollfuss. Returning to England in late 1934, Gaitskell served on a Labor party committee set up to investigate social credit and was joint author of an adverse report on that economic doctrine. In the summer of 1935 he acted as discussion leader at a privately arranged summer school convened at Geneva for thirty selected young members of the Labor movement.

Gaitskell made some speeches in the political campaigns of 1929 and 1931, and in 1932 was adopted as prospective Labor candidate for Chatham, Kentish naval dockyard town. In the general election of 1935 he was not elected, however, and, there being no general election because of the war, ten years were to pass before he was seated in Parliament (having been adopted for Leeds South in February 1938). In September 1939, having entered the Civil Service, he was asked to join the newly created Ministry of Economic Warfare, was named principal private secretary to the Minister, and assigned to the German Intelligence Branch. There he remained until 1942, the year he was appointed to the Board of Trade, where his title was principal assistant secretary. He became adviser to Hugh Dalton [45]. Before he left the Board of Trade in 1945, he had been assigned as head of the department concerned with price control, retail trade, films, and the disposal of surplus Government stores. He also participated in the planning of the Beveridge [43] rationing system. While Gaitskell was with the Board of Trade, one of his major responsibilities was in the field of the fuel and power department (later to become a Ministry).

Just before the election of 1945 Gaitskell was offered a senior appointment in UNRRA, with the prospect of a high place in the Civil Service hierarchy. "The question was," said the London *News Chronicle*, "whether to take it or go out on to the hustings. Dalton urged him to stick to politics. They sat through the night discussing it. And at 3 A.M. the decision

HUGH GAITSKELL

was taken." Gaitskell stood for Leeds South and was returned with a 10,000 majority. In the King's birthday honors of the same year he was created Commander of the Order of the British Empire (C.B.E.).

On May 10, 1946, a junior office came to Gaitskell, as Parliamentary Secretary to the Ministry of Fuel and Power. Ten days later he was the member to move the third reading of the coal industry nationalization bill. The following October, speaking in Parliament on coal mining, he said: "A deeper cause affecting manpower in the mines is that of status. We are encouraging a 'white collar snobbery,' and there will have to be a revolution in our attitude in that matter." Gaitskell, who is called " a hard hitter" in debate, won Prime Minister Attlee's congratulations by his speech in which he moved the second reading of the electricity bill, to be carried by 340 votes to 165 on February 4, 1947, against the bitter opposition of the Conservatives. "In a hectic forty-five minutes," reported the London *Daily Mail*, "while Mr. Gaitskell wisecracked and Mr. Attlee and Mr. Shinwell rocked with laughter, the howls, jeers, and cheers from all sides of the House reached a wild crescendo."

On October 7, 1947, Prime Minister Attlee appointed Gaitskell Minister of Fuel and Power to succeed E. Shinwell [43] (who moved to the War Office). The new Minister inherited a critical situation, for Britain at that time was suffering from its worst winter in fifty years, in a time of severe fuel stringencies. Speaking at the Mansion House on October 13, Gaitskell said: "If this winter domestic consumers 'go crazy' and there is a runaway expansion of the electricity demand, that will constitute the gravest threat that I can see to our whole national recovery." It was found necessary to impose restrictions on the use of electric power —factories and office buildings were assigned a

GAITSKELL, HUGH—*Continued*

day a week on which they were to operate on reduced power. In his task of defending fuel restrictions of many kinds Gaitskell exhorted the public, on the one hand, to consume less, and the miners, on the other, to produce more. In December 1947 he announced for 1948 a coal production objective of 300,000 tons a week for exports and shipping needs. In June of the following year he warned that production was running 100,000 tons a week short of the quota, and spoke of a "critical situation." At the annual conference of the National Union of Mine-workers, in July, he told the delegates that while the miners were getting a "square deal" the public was not. He specifically cited low output, poor quality fuel, bad financial results, rising prices, low manpower, and high absenteeism.

In spite of coke cuts, power cuts, gasoline rations, coal rations and the like, the British public did, on the whole, receive some alleviation of its lot during the Gaitskell term in the Ministry. A small "basic" gasoline ration for private motoring was allocated on June 1, 1948; work on nineteen power stations went forward; from April 2, 1949 electric signs and shopfront lighting were again permitted. Gaitskell shepherded the gas bill (for the nationalization of coal-gas) through the House in 1948. Nationalization, said Gaitskell in April 1949, is not an end in itself, but a means to the achievement of the primary aims of Socialist policy.

In the general election of February 23, 1950, Gaitskell was re-elected for Leeds South with a majority of 15,359. Prime Minister Attlee, in announcing his Cabinet for the new Parliament on February 28, 1950, made known the revival of the post of Minister of State for Economic Affairs. (Sir Stafford Cripps '48, appointed Minister for Economic Affairs in September 1947, had retained the position when he became Chancellor of the Exchequer two months later.) The duty of the new Minister was announced to be (in the words of the London *Daily Telegraph*) "to give some relief to the Chancellor [of the Exchequer] from growing pressure in the dual function of finance and economics." To fill this post Attlee named Gaitskell, promoting him to a position which, though not actually in the Cabinet, is described as "of Cabinet rank."

On October 19, 1950, Sir Stafford Cripps resigned as Britain's Chancellor of the Exchequer—ill health had forced him to retire from politics for at least a year. Appointed to the Cabinet post, Hugh Gaitskell received the seal of the office on October 25, upon his return from conferences in Canada and the United States. That Gaitskell would continue the economic and financial policies of his predecessor was expected. Early in November, in his maiden speech as Chancellor of the Exchequer, Gaitskell warned his country of new austerities. He foresaw retail-price increases and, if shortages developed, reimposed controls to "insure that defense needs, exports, and essentials for the British home market were provided" (in the words of the New York *Times*).

Gaitskell is the author of the book *Chartism*, published in 1929. There followed chapters in three composite works: "Economics," in Victor Gollancz's *Outline of Knowledge for Boys and Girls* (1932); "Four Monetary Heretics," in G. D. H. Cole's *What Everybody Wants to Know about Money* (1933); "Financial Policy in the Transition Period," in G. E. Catlin's *New Trends in Socialism* (1935). In 1939 Gaitskell's *Money and Everyday Life* appeared. The new Chancellor of the Exchequer is said to be a mild-mannered man who remains unperturbed in the face of difficulties. By his marriage to Anna Dora Creditor he has two daughters, Julia and Cressida. He finds pleasure in walking and gardening.

References

N Y Times p23 Je 15 '48; p6 Jl 9 '48
News Chronicle (London) O 8 '47; O 9 '47
Sunday Chronicle (London) O 12 '47
World Report 3:30 O 28 '47
Who's Who, 1949

GAMBLING, JOHN B(RADLEY) Apr. 9, 1897- Radio broadcaster

Address: b. c/o WOR, 1440 Broadway, New York 18

Known as the "Human Alarm Clock," John B. Gambling celebrated, on March 8, 1950, the completion of twenty-five years of early morning broadcasting from Station WOR, New York. *Gambling's Musical Clock*, a mixture of banter, news and other announcements, and light musical selections heard each weekday morning from 7.15 to 8, Eastern Standard Time, developed from a calisthenics program for which Gambling became the announcer in 1925. *Rambling with Gambling*, which comes on the air an hour earlier, was begun in 1942 as an afternoon program.

A guest at the anniversary observance was the broadcaster's octogenarian father, John Gambling of Cambridge, England; his mother, nee Alice Symonds, was in less robust health and was not permitted to make the air trip across the Atlantic. John Bradley Gambling himself was born in Norwich, England, on April 9, 1897, but was reared in Cambridge, where his father became a civil engineer to the municipality; he attended the Cambridge County School for Boys until 1910, serving in the school's Officers Corps and winning the school prize for horticulture. "I left school at thirteen, to learn horticulture," he writes. "Father had built a nursery for me to take over at twenty-one." Gardening and flower-raising were, however, destined to be his avocation instead of his vocation.

"I had always wanted to go to sea," Gambling has told, "and the sinking of the *Titanic* fired me with the ambition to become a wireless operator." Accordingly he entered the British College of Wireless Telegraphy at Clapham, London, and completed its one-year course in eight months. This was in 1914, the year of the outbreak of World War I; Gambling, though actually only seventeen at the time, gave his age as eighteen, the minimum enlistment age in the Royal Navy. For the first three of the four and a half years of the war he served as a wireless operator aboard the 70-foot trawler *Xylopia*, which had been converted into a mine sweeper for duty at the mouth of the Thames and along the coast of Belgium; later he was chief petty officer aboard H.M.S. *Lunka*, a former merchantman patrolling the East African shore. The war over, he was radio operator on various tankers, freighters, and passenger ships until 1925, for the latter part of that period working on vessels of United States registry.

Gambling's marriage to Rita Graubart of Albany (New York), whom he had met as a passenger aboard the Morgan liner *Creole*, took place on February 25, 1925. A week and a half later Gambling applied for a job at WOR, and was taken on as a probationary engineer at thirty dollars a week. The station (a subsidiary corporation of the department stores of R. H. Macy of New York and L. Bamberger of Newark, New Jersey) was then about three years old, and had recently opened a New York studio. In those early days of broadcasting, an engineer was expected not only to be a general mechanical handyman but to be able, in emergency, to "fill in" with songs or glib patter. It so happened on March 8, 1925, when the announcer for the 6.30 A.M. setting-up exercises (conducted by Bernarr Macfadden, physical culturist) failed to appear at the studio, that Gambling found himself at the microphone, "ad-libbing" his way through an hour-long program. This he did with such effect that he was given the position. Six months later, when Macfadden withdrew, Gambling took over as calisthenics instructor also, and continued as such until 1934. At that time a survey revealed that the physical culture "craze" was all but over, and the setting-up exercises were gradually abandoned.

Meanwhile, during the late 1920's, Vincent Sorey's three-piece orchestra (later augmented by another player) had been added to the program, which became known as *Gambling's Musical Clock* and was moved to the 7:15 to 8 A.M. Eastern broadcast time. The program's pattern was then established, not to be greatly varied since. The *Rambling With Gambling* program, originally on afternoons when it was begun in 1942, was moved in 1948 to the 6-to-7 A.M. hour. In this program the music is recorded, in the *Musical Clock* Sorey's "live" orchestra plays; the selections are what Gambling calls "middlebrow music, no boogie-woogie, and no opera either." On both programs the music is interspersed with impromptu anecdotes, jokes, time signals, news bulletins, and weather reports. In the earlier program, short commercial announcements advertise a number of products; for the later, there is one advertising sponsor. Gambling, who likes puns, says, "WOR has two morning vices, Bier and Gambling," referring to Joe Bier, a fellow announcer; while of his show in general he declares that it is "the corniest on the air."

Gambling's listeners (he calls them "the most loyal audience in radio") have been found to resent change in the format of their first program of the day. One innovation, introduced in the winter of 1939, found instant favor,

JOHN B. GAMBLING

however. This originated one icy morning when a New Jersey school principal telephoned in the request that Gambling announce on the *Musical Clock* that there would be no school in that locality. Gambling did so, the idea spread, and at the present time more than six hundred schools in New York, New Jersey, and Pennsylvania use his "school-closed" service. He accompanies his announcements with the ringing of an old-fashioned bell presented to him by a New Jersey State Education Commissioner, and has worked out with principals a private code system to guard against school-boy pranks. Gambling has had other programs, too. In 1940, when he celebrated the completion of his first fifteen years on the air with the first of a succession of gala anniversary broadcasts, he was also announcing a commercially sponsored hour four days weekly, and was conducting the Mutual Airplane Club hour on Saturday mornings.

Rejected for military service in World War II ("I hope it's nothing mental," he remarked to the examining doctor), Gambling has since continued his early morning program without interruption (except for brief vacations), winning citations from the Army, Navy, Red Cross and other such official or semi-official services for radio assistance during the war. Gambling celebrated the completion of twenty years of broadcasting on March 8, 1945, when he was congratulated by Mayor La Guardia of New York City. Gambling was master of ceremonies at WOR's special twenty-fifth anniversary program on February 22, 1947. Since that time the chief additions to his radio work have been the *Gardening with Gambling* fifteen minutes on Saturday mornings, and a Wednesday evening television show inaugurated over WOR-TV in October 1949.

"Enormous changes have taken place in Gambling's quarter-century on the air," wrote John Crosby in the New York *Herald Tribune*

GAMBLING, JOHN B.—*Continued*

early in 1950, "but he remains as persistently horse-and-buggy, as old-fashioned as a cigar store Indian. . . .Gambling admits that his program is not exciting, but he feels that in a period of enormous change his timeless, quiet chatter is reassuring." Among "fans" are such men as Governor Alfred E. Driscoll of New Jersey and Borough President Robert F. Wagner, Jr., of Manhattan, both of whom were participants in the Gambling jubilee broadcast from the stage of a New York City theater on the morning of March 8, 1950. At that time the staff of Station WOR estimated that *Gambling's Musical Clock* was heard by more than a million persons daily, from Maine to the Potomac and in the western areas of the Eastern States.

During winter months Gambling occupies a New York City apartment, rises at 4.30, breakfasts and listens to the news, then drives to the studio, arriving at 5.15, in time for *Rambling with Gambling* hour. Except for Wednesdays and Saturdays, his broadcasting duties are over by 8 o'clock, but not his working day; he has, among other things, "fan" mail to acknowledge. (In this he may be assisted by his wife, who was a secretary before her marriage.) Gambling makes a point of taking a short afternoon nap, and is usually in bed by 10 at night. Summers and week ends he spends at the nine-room home which he and Mrs. Gambling maintain at Massapequa, Long Island, where he may find diversion in reading, gardening, or cruising in his 25-foot boat. Gambling became a United States citizen well over twenty years ago, and votes Republican; he attends the Episcopal Church. Gray-eyed and gray-haired, five feet eight inches in height and weighing about 190 pounds, Gambling speaks with what Richard D. Leahy of the New York *World-Telegram* has described as a "dry and quizzical" voice; there is only a faint trace of British accent in his speech. The broadcaster's club is the Radio Pioneers of America. The Gamblings have one son, John Alfred, a student at Dartmouth College, where he is manager of the campus radio station.

References

N Y Herald Tribune p7 F 27 '50; p8 F 28 '50
N Y World-Telegram p3 Ap 19 '41 por; p18 F 27 '45
N Y World-Telegram and Sun p13 Mr 4 '50 por
Nassau (L.I., N.Y.) Review-Star Ag 30 '46 por
Newsweek 15:36 Mr 18 '40 por
Time 35:36 Mr 18 '40 por

GARREAU, ROGER (gàr″rō′ rô″zhā′) May 31, 1891- United Nations official; diplomat

Address: b. c/o United Nations, New York; h. 8 Elmridge Rd., King's Point, N.Y.

The president of the Trusteeship Council of the United Nations for the 1949-50 term is Roger Garreau, French career diplomat. His country's Ambassador to Poland from 1945 to 1947, he was for more than thirty years before that appointment a consular or foreign service officer. He has been France's permanent representative on the Trusteeship Council since 1947, and is author of the so-called "Garreau Plan" (1950) for the administration of Jerusalem.

A native of Dôle, a town in the Jura Department of Eastern France, Roger Garreau was born May 31, 1891, to Henry and Beatrice (Nicolet) Garreau. He completed his education at the Ecole Nationale des Langues Orientales Vivantes at Paris, there receiving diplomas for mastery of the Russian, Chinese, Siamese and Malay tongues. Subsequently he took the degree of Doctor of Laws.

Entering his country's foreign service in 1913, Garreau was first assigned to Bangkok as an interpreter and French consular agent at the Court of Siam. Approximately three years later he returned to Europe for military duty in World War I, in which he served on the western front until the signing of the Armistice in November 1918. Early in 1919 he was appointed attaché on the staff of the Minister of Foreign Affairs in Paris. There he remained until the beginning of 1922, when he was assigned as second secretary to the French Embassy at Peking (Peiping), then the capital of the Chinese Republic. Three years later (1925) he was named first secretary of his country's embassy at Moscow.

Garreau's skill in what the New York *Herald Tribune* describes as "negotiating difficult agreements for France" was demonstrated in 1927-28, during the period he was attached to the Indo-Chinese colonial government as a political expert, assuming a prominent role in the conferences which resulted in the conclusion of the Franco-Siamese convention of the latter year. From that time until 1932, when he helped to negotiate the Franco-Chinese treaty of that date, his duties kept him in Paris, first as a Foreign Ministry political expert and later as director of the press and information services.

In 1933 Garreau was sent to Zagreb, Albania, as acting consul (subsequently he was appointed consul general); and in 1935 he was assigned to Cairo, where he assumed the duties, first, of secretary and, later, of counselor of the French Embassy in the Egyptian capital. Garreau was a representative of France at the conference held in Montreux, Switzerland, in 1937, for the abolition of the Egyptian capitulatory regime. His next appointment, the same year, was to the staff of the French High Commissioner of Syria, a League of Nations mandate. As commissioner of the sanjak of Alexandretta (a subdivision of a province) on the Turkish border, he was successful in replacing an arrangement whereby Syria was responsible for the foreign policy of Alexandretta with one by which the sanjak was incorporated into Turkey on June 23, 1939. Appointed consul-general at Hamburg, Germany, Garreau had served there only briefly when World War II broke out and he was transferred to Lausanne, Switzerland, late in 1939, and to Zurich in 1940. He was again detailed to Bangkok toward the end of the latter year, this time as his country's Minister to the Imperial Court of what is now known as Thailand.

After the capitulation of the Pétain [40] Government in September 1941, Garreau was identified with the Free French movement, joining General Charles de Gaulle [49] in London; he headed the Free French mission to the Soviet Union in 1942-43 and was French Committee of National Liberation delegate to the U.S.S.R. in 1943-44. Following the liberation of Warsaw by Soviet forces in 1945, Garreau was sent to the Polish capital to arrange for the repatriation of French military personnel, and while there was appointed Ambassador to the revived Polish state. He remained at Warsaw for approximately two years. In the course of his ambassadorship to Poland, he participated in the first session of the United Nations General Assembly and was French alternate at the session of the Council of Foreign Ministers held at Moscow in December 1946.

Garreau was relieved of his Warsaw duties to become permanent French alternate in the General Assembly of the United Nations and representative of France on the Trusteeship Council. The latter council was set up by the General Assembly in New York on December 14, 1946, in accordance with Chapters XII and XIII of the United Nations charter. The statement of its purpose indicated that it was "to safeguard the interests and welfare of non-self-governing peoples in territories held either under League of Nations mandates or detached from enemy countries under World War II or whose populations voluntarily wish to place themselves under the Council." The membership of the Council was to be equally divided between "those members administering trust territories" (permanent members) and others elected for three-year terms from among the nations not administering such territories.

The Council commenced to function, under the chairmanship of Francis B. Sayre [40] of the United States, in March 1947. On April 21, Garreau vigorously though unsuccessfully challenged the right of the Council to hear petitions from enemy aliens. (The petitioners were German internees in Tanganyika Territory (East Africa), of which Great Britain was the administering authority by the terms of a World War I mandate.) Later, in an article entitled "The Spirit of the Trusteeship System," which he contributed to the *United Nations Bulletin,* Garreau was to characterize the hearing of petitions as an "interesting innovation" and to assert that the "system of visits to Trust Territories" was "perhaps the most original and valuable aspect of the trusteeship system."

The Trusteeship Council, which has a present membership of twelve, holds two regular sessions each year, in summer and winter, the president being chosen annually at the beginning of the summer session. When the Council convened in June 1949, for its fifth regular session, Garreau was elected president for the ensuing twelve months. In November 1949, following the apointment two months earlier of a Council commission to investigate conditions in French Cameroons and British Togoland, the Trusteeship Committee of the General Assembly ap-

United Nations Official Photo.
ROGER GARREAU

proved a joint United States-Mexican resolution calling for a U. N. investigation of educational conditions among the 200,000,000 inhabitants of various dependencies.

In December 1949, Garreau was responsible for expressing, both in the Council and the Assembly, his nation's objections to an Assembly ruling that colonial powers provide the United Nations with data on political rights in their dependencies. The French representative, together with the British Minister of State, Hector McNeil [46], voiced the opinion that the resolution calling for political information was a violation of the U. N. charter ("So flagrant that it is difficult to consider it accidental," said Garreau), since the charter specified only provision of information on social and economic conditions; the delegates announced that their Governments would refuse, therefore, to comply with the resolution.

A resolution passed by the General Assembly on December 9, 1949, decreed that "Jerusalem should be placed under a special international regime to be administered by the United Nations as a *corpus separatum,* which would envisage appropriate guarantees for the protection of the Holy Places, both within and without Jerusalem"; it called on the Trusteeship Council "to discharge the responsibilities of the Administering Authority," to prepare and approve a Statute of Jerusalem, and "proceed immediately with its implementation" (*United Nations Bulletin,* January 15, 1950). The problem was complicated by the fact that Israel had declared the intention to transfer her capital from Tel Aviv to Jerusalem and had already moved certain government offices to the latter city. On December 20, by a 5-to-0 vote (with seven members abstaining), the Trusteeship Council instructed its president to "invite" Israel to remove her government departments from Jerusalem, an invitation not acted on; and shortly afterward the Council adjourned,

GARREAU, ROGER—*Continued*

meanwhile entrusting the president, Garreau, with "the preparation of a working paper on the Statute of Jerusalem" for action by the Council at its sixth session beginning January 19, 1950, at Geneva, Switzerland.

When the Council convened in Geneva early in 1950, Garreau presented the tentative plan he had evolved. He proposed the division of the disputed city into three parts, one to be under Israeli authority, a second to be controlled by Hashemite Jordan, the third, taking in "all Holy Places covered by the Status Quo of 1757," to be administered by a United Nations governor and to have its own police force and courts. The proposal was rejected as exceeding the powers delegated to the Council by the Assembly. It was seen (primarily by representatives of the Arab world) as presenting "a new solution" in its suggestions of modified internationalization; Garreau maintained that it was not a plan or "new solution," but a suggestion of interpretations the Council might place on the Assembly's resolution of December 9, 1949. The interpretations were adjudged too liberal by Council members, and a resolution was adopted calling for the immediate completion of a Statute for the City of Jerusalem. Acting on a further resolution, the Council issued Israel and Jordan invitations to send qualified representatives to advise the Council on the views of their Governments on the question of a revision of the draft Statute for Jerusalem; the invitations were accepted. (The Governments of both Israel and Jordan had declared themselves opposed to the suggestions made in the Garreau paper.)

Honors and decorations which the French diplomat has received include the Legion of Honor, the Médaille de Résistance, the Norwegian Medal of Liberty, and the Grand Cross of leading orders in Belgium, Luxembourg and the Netherlands. Garreau married Yvonne Jacques-Chur on November 23, 1930. They have two sons.

References

N Y Herald Tribune II p3 F 5 '50 por
U N Bul 2:436 Ap 22 '47 por; 7:27 Jl 1 '49 por
International Who's Who, 1949
World Biography (1948)
Yearbook of the United Nations, 1947-48

GIANNINI, L(AWRENCE) M(ARIO) (jä-nē'nē) Nov. 25, 1894- Banker

Address: b. c/o Bank of America, 300 Montgomery St., San Francisco 20, Calif.; h. 945 Green St., San Francisco, Calif.; 29 Atherton Ave., Atherton, Calif.

The president of Bank of America National Trust and Savings Association, L. M. Giannini was elected to that office in 1936. The bank, which his father had founded, by 1945 was considered the largest private commercial bank in the world and in January 1950 had total resources of more than $6,000,000,000. Giannini, who has been associated with the bank for

thirty-two years, also serves as president of Bank of America (International), established in 1949, and is a director of the Transamerica Corporation. A director of a number of other banking and insurance firms, Giannini became a member of President Truman's Committee for Financing Foreign Trade in 1946 and has served on the Committee on International Economic Policy since 1947.

Lawrence Mario Giannini was born in San Francisco on November 25, 1894. His father was the "fabulous" Amadeo Pietro Giannini [47], who, once a San Francisco commission merchant, rose to become the founder and chairman of the Bank of America and the Transamerica Corporation. His mother was Clorinda Agnes (Cuneo) Giannini. Giannini was reared "in a closely knit family group in which every waking thought turned on banking," stated a Bank of America biographical release. He was about ten years old when his father went into the banking business, opening a small private bank which he called the Bank of Italy. The boy was fascinated by the growing business and spent much of his time there, profiting by his opportunities to "understudy" clerks, tellers, and minor executives of the bank, working part time during school years and full time during his vacations. He graduated from the Union High School, San Mateo, California, in 1916, and in 1920 he received the LL.B. degree from the University of California's Hastings College of the Law. He was admitted to the California State bar in 1922, and later (in 1939) was admitted to practice before the Supreme Court of the United States.

Between 1918 and 1922 Giannini held various clerical positions in the Bank of Italy, his first official post being that of clearings clerk. During the next ten years, as personnel director he sponsored the Bankamerica Club for employees' social and athletic activities and the Bankamerican Family Estate, a benefits project. In 1928 he was appointed vice-chairman of the board of directors and became a member of the bank's general executive committee. The Bank of Italy became the Bank of America in 1930. In the same year, Giannini succeeded his father as president of Transamerica Corporation, which had been formed in 1928 as a holding company for Giannini enterprises, including industrial and insurance organizations, as well as the Bank of America and other banks. When Eastern interests with stock ownership in Transamerica sought to deviate from Giannini functioning principles, L. M. Giannini resigned the presidency of the holding company, called his father back from semiretirement, and together they launched and won a "proxy fight," obtaining 63 per cent of the corporation's proxies and "routing" the Eastern interests.

Following this victory, L. M. Giannini was, on February 15, 1932, appointed senior vice-president of the Bank of America National Trust and Savings Association. In January 1936 he was elected president of the bank and chairman of its executive committee. Under the leadership of Giannini, the institution continued to follow the policy of branch banking established by the senior Giannini; it is the firm's contention that the branch banking system makes possible service to both small and big depositors, that it results in a diversity and flexibility of great advantage in weathering economic storms. By 1945 the Bank of America stated that in deposits and total resources it had become the world's largest private bank; in 1949 resources totaled $6,250,402,000. The bank, which has several hundred branches in California, and branches in London, Manila, Tokyo, Yokohama, Kobe, and Shanghai, announced in June 1950 that a $70,000,000 Bank of America N.T. and S.A. offering of common stock to its shareholders (described as the largest offering of stock in banking history) had been substantially oversubscribed. In November 1949, a new corporation, a wholly owned subsidiary called Bank of America, was formed, with Giannini as its president, to engage in international activities. An article in *Fortune* (July 1947) had attributed to Giannini a "capacity for compromise that has advanced the bank's fortunes without modifying its principles." In 1947 he had been selected as one of the nation's fifty foremost business leaders in a *Forbes* magazine poll.

In addition to his Bank of America duties, Giannini holds the position of a director of the Transamerica Corporation. In course of 1950 Senate banking subcommittee hearings on legislation to subject bank holding companies to strict Federal Reserve Board regulations, it was stated by the treasurer of Transamerica that the corporation does not in any way control the Bank of America—the latter ceased to be a subsidiary of the former in 1937; the institutions have no senior officer in common: L. M. Giannini has never been president of both at the same time, as his father had been. In 1948 the Federal Reserve Board charged Transamerica with building a credit monopoly in the West by gaining control over 600 bank offices in five States, including the branch offices of the Bank of America. In regard to relations between the two institutions, testimony was given at October 1950 hearings (reported in the New York *Times*) to the effect that the holding company at that time owned 11.1 per cent of the stock of the Bank of America. Giannini stated that his family's shares amounted to two-tenths of 1 per cent of Bank of America stock, and three-tenths of 1 per cent of Transamerica stock.

On the death of his father in 1949, Giannini was joined on Bank of America's board of directors by his sister, Claire Giannini Hoffman. Giannini is chairman of the board of the Occidental Life Insurance Company and acts as a director of the Merchants National Realty Corporation, the Fireman's Fund Insurance Company, Pacific National Fire Insurance Company, the National City Bank of New York, and the City Bank Farmers Trust Company of New York. He is also a director of the Inter-America Corporation, and the Capital Company; is president-director of the Corporation of America, and serves on the advisory council of United States Associates. Since 1946 he has served on President Truman's Committee for Financing Foreign Trade and he has been a

L. M. GIANNINI

member since 1947 of the Committee on International Economic Policy.

Bank president Giannini is also chairman of the board of associates of San Francisco State College's School of World Business. He served as campaign chairman for California March of Dimes 1950, and is regional chairman of the Crusade for Freedom movement conducted under the auspices of the National Committee for a Free Europe. He is a member of the California and San Francisco bar associations. In 1950, he was given a special award for outstanding public service by the Southern California Financial Writers Association. For his contribution to the reconstruction of Italy, he was awarded Italy's highest civilian honor, the Order Stella della Solidarietta, Italiana, first class, in 1949.

Giannini is a director of Californians, Inc., of the San Francisco Civic Ballet Association, and a sponsor of San Francisco's Building for Youth. He is associated in an advisory capacity with the Salesian Boys Club and is a committee member of the Crusade for Children in San Francisco. A member of the Knights of Columbus, the Benevolent Protective Order of Elks, the Native Sons of the Golden West, Giannini lists among his clubs the Bohemian, Olympic, Commercial, Commonwealth in San Francisco, and Los Angeles' Athletic, and Jonathan. His other clubs include the Menlo Circus in Menlo Park, the Gymkhana in San Mateo, and the Tennis and Racquet, Palm Springs, all in California.

Giannini married Anna Mercedes Collins on April 7, 1929. They have two daughters, Anne and Virginia. Giannini, who is a Roman Catholic, is politically an independent. For recreation he chooses swimming and "long-distance" automobile driving. He is five feet four inches in height and weighs 160 pounds. By *Fortune*

GIANNINI, L. M.—*Continued*

and *Time* he has been called analytical, shrewd, cool, and able.

References

American Catholic Who's Who, 1950-51
Business Executives of America (1950)
Who's Who in America, 1950-51
Who's Who in Commerce and Industry, (1948)
Who's Who in the West (1949)
World Biography (1948)

GIAUQUE, WILLIAM F(RANCIS) (jē-ōk) May 12, 1895- Nobel prize winner; chemist

Address: b. University of California, Berkeley, Calif.; h. 2643 Benvenue Ave., Berkeley, Calif.

The 1949 Nobel prize for chemistry was awarded to Dr. William F. Giauque "for his contribution to chemical thermodynamics, especially for his investigations of the properties of substances at extremely low temperatures." Giauque has been associated with the Univer-

Wide World Photos
WILLIAM F. GIAUQUE

sity of California for more than thirty years, as student, instructor, and professor of chemistry. In 1928 he discovered, with a colleague, the existence of two hitherto unknown isotopes of oxygen, a discovery which necessitated the establishment of two scales of atomic weights. The chemist's primary interest has been in cryogenics, "the study of what happens to matter as the temperature is reduced to a small fraction of a degree above absolute zero." His researches, according to a University of California report, "has been enormously important to industry in many ways."

William Francis Giauque was born May 12, 1895, in the Canadian town of Niagara Falls, Ontario. His parents, William Tecumseh Sher-

man and Isabella Jane (Duncan) Giauque, were American citizens. After graduating from high school and working at the Hooker Electro-mechanical Company, in Niagara Falls, for two years, Giauque went to Berkeley, California, to enroll at the University of California. He was influenced in his choice of schools, he has said, by its low tuition fees and the presence there of great men in chemistry. His B.S. degree was conferred in 1920 and his Ph.D. in 1922, whereupon he joined the faculty. His titles were, successively, instructor (1922-27), assistant professor (1927-30), associate professor (1930-34); his full professorship dates from 1934.

Giauque has specialized throughout his entire career in studies of the properties of matter at the lowest attainable temperatures. Since Fahrenheit's experiments in 1714, scientists have been attempting to reach the lowest temperature possible in nature; by the 1920's a group of Dutch chemists had reached one degree from what has been generally accepted as absolute zero—459.688 degrees below zero Fahrenheit, a fraction of one degree above absolute zero. Since the magnetizing of matter raises its temperature, Giauque proposed to reduce magnetized substance to the lowest temperature possible by means of the Dutch method, and then, by demagnetizing it, to reduce it still further. It required eight years for the chemist and his associates to build the equipment necessary to carry out an experiment based on that theory. In 1933, working with Duncan Mac-Dougall, he succeeded in establishing a temperature of 459.544 degrees below zero. By using Giauque's method, the Dutch group has since reached 459.681 degrees. "At the University of California," Giauque has said, "we could go lower than we've gone, but that hasn't been our prime objective."

The principal value of these achievements has been in the ability to measure the entropy ("the degree of disorder in matter") of various compounds. As temperature is reduced, the amount of energy (heat) in molecules is reduced, and at a fraction of a degree above absolute zero the molecules are in relatively simple and orderly relationship to each other. In this state, subtle properties of matter not otherwise observable can be studied. By measuring the types of motion brought about by the application of small amounts of heat (as little as one thousandth of a calorie at a time), Giauque has been able to determine the entropies and heats of formation of various compounds, which in turn "furnish the key to whether chemical reactions can take place or not."

While Giauque's interest in low temperature experiments may be regarded as pure science, his work has had significant time- and money-saving effects in the industrial world. Principally, his methods have been applied in the designing of chemical processes and plants, and in determining without elaborate trial and error experiments whether certain chemical reactions are possible. It has been said that, among the results of Giauque's experiments, are "better gasoline, stronger steel, longer-wearing rubber, better glass, and cheaper fertilizer" (*Saturday Evening Post*).

The discovery of two unknown isotopes of oxygen (17 and 18) came about as the result of an experiment which Professor Giauque conducted with Herrick Johnston (then a graduate student at California, now professor of chemistry at Ohio State University), to calculate the entropy of the oxygen molecule. As a result of the discovery, the same method was applied by other scientists to other elements, leading eventually to the finding of the hydrogen 2 isotope, known as deuterium, a component of "heavy water," important in atomic research. Another specific result of Giauque's low temperature research was his demonstration that there are two forms of the hydrogen molecule, the "ortho" and the "para" forms.

Many of the experiments in Giauque's field are long and demand constant attention; in the early days of his low temperature research he and his assistants sometimes worked for as many as forty to sixty hours without sleep. Most of the authorities in his field in the United States have been trained in his laboratory. In addition to his research, the scientist continues to teach general chemistry to freshmen, to hold undergraduate classes in thermodynamics and advanced physical chemistry, and to supervise the research of graduate students.

In contrast to many of the elaborate industrial laboratories which his own research has made possible, Giauque's experiments have been carried on for thirty years in two small rooms, where $50,000 worth of equipment presents "an alarming maze of glass pipes . . . clacking motors and whirring compressors." Five hundred thousand dollars has recently been allocated by the university for a laboratory in which Giauque will install equipment designed to create "magnetic fields more powerful than any in the world—if I can build them that way," he has said.

The only interruption in Giauque's career on the Berkeley campus was during World War II. According to Milton Silverman, writing in the *Saturday Evening Post*, top Government officials "made an exception" in the chemist's case by exempting him from writing the "customary biweekly and time-consuming 'progress reports.'" One of his achievements was the designing of a mobile unit for the production of liquid oxygen; much of his work during the war is still classified as secret.

On November 3, 1949, the Royal Swedish Academy of Science announced the award of the Nobel prize for chemistry to Dr. Giauque, in recognition of his achievements. Giauque remarked at the time to a *Christian Science Monitor* interviewer, "I certainly didn't expect it," adding, "I'll take good care of it"—the prize money, which amounts to approximately $30,000. The award was bestowed on the chemist in Stockholm on December 10; two days later he delivered, before four hundred professors and students, his Nobel lecture, "Some Consequences of Low Temperature Research in Chemical Thermodynamics." (Hideki Yukawa [50], Japanese physicist, was another Nobel prize winner who spoke on this occasion.)

"If I take time to write about my work," the California scientist has said, "then I have less time to do any." He has, however, published some seventy papers in scientific journals. In 1929 the Pacific Division Prize of the American Association for the Advancement of Science was awarded to Giauque and H. L. Johnston for their discovery of the oxygen isotopes. In 1936 Giauque was lecturer and medalist of the Charles Frederick Chandler Foundation at Columbia University, which awarded him the honorary D.Sc. degree; the lecture was published by the Chandler Foundation under the title of "Temperatures Below 1° Absolute." In 1937 he was given the Elliott Cresson Medal of the Franklin Institute. Both of the latter honors were awarded to the chemist for his discovery of the "adiabatic demagnetizing" method of reducing temperature. He was invited to contribute a paper on his work at the Seventh International Congress on Refrigeration at The Hague, also in 1936. From 1936 to 1938 he was a member of the National Research Council Committee on Low Temperature Scales, and in the earlier year he was elected a member of the National Academy of Sciences. A committee of Giauque's fellow faculty members at California chose him as the Faculty Research Lecturer for 1947-48. The chemist, who calls himself "a chronic non-attender of meetings," is a fellow of the American Physical Society, a member of the American Chemical Society, the Institut International du Froid, the American Philosophical Society, and Sigma Xi, national honorary scientific fraternity. He belongs to the Faculty Club of Berkeley.

On July 19, 1932, Giauque married Muriel Frances Ashley, who holds a B.S. and a Ph.D. from the University of California. She is a physicist, now engaged in botanical research on "the initial growth period of ferns." Their two early teen-age sons, William Francis Ashley and Robert David Ashley attend Berkeley schools. "Science is Giauque's hobby, his avocation, his profession," stated a press release from his university. During the academic year he spends most of his time in the classroom or the laboratory. (His associates have described him as "a bear for work.") He does not smoke, drink, play cards, or drive a car. He does admit, however, that his sons see to it that he seldom misses a football game. (*Newsweek* has said that "Giauque, if he were younger, might be taken for a fullback on California's football team.") The six-foot one-inch scientist weighs 200 pounds (although he "gives the appearance of slenderness"), has hazel eyes and iron-gray hair. He takes an annual six-week vacation with his family "where there's swimming." His hobby, says Giauque, is in his laboratory— "I am one of those fortunate people who get a kick out of their work."

References

Christian Sci Mon p2 N 12 '49 por
N Y Times p1 N 4 '49
N Y World-Telegram p4 N 3 '49 por
Sat Eve Post 222:38 D 10 '49 por
American Men of Science (1949)
International Who's Who, 1949
Who's Who in America, 1948-49

GIMBEL, BERNARD F(EUSTMAN)
Apr. 10, 1885- Merchant

Address: b. c/o Gimbel Brothers, Inc., Broadway & 33rd St., New York; h. "Chieftans," Upper King St., Greenwich, Conn.

The head of one of the largest retail organizations in the United States is Bernard F. Gimbel, president of Gimbel Brothers, Inc. President of the firm since 1927, he has directed much of its growth since 1909, when he be-

BERNARD F. GIMBEL

came a vice-president—its fifteen department stores are located in New York and other large cities of the country. For his contribution "in the field of human relations," he has been honored by the National Conference of Christians and Jews. Active in local affairs, he was made chairman of the Madison Square Garden Corporation board of directors in 1947, and in 1948 president of the New York Convention and Visitors' Bureau.

Bernard Feustman Gimbel was born April 10, 1885, in Vincennes, Indiana, the town in which his grandfather, Adam Gimbel, an early immigrant, had founded a retail establishment in 1842, seven years after his emigration from Bavaria. Called the Palace of Trade, it was unique in being a set-price store at a time when customers were used to bargaining rather than being charged uniform prices. Bernard Gimbel is the son of Adam's second son, Isaac, and of the former Rachel Feustman. Isaac and his six brothers (there were originally fourteen children, ten of them boys, but not all lived to maturity) were taught the retail business "from the ground up" by their father. In 1887, the seven brothers moved to Milwaukee to open a store known as Gimbel Brothers.

When Bernard was nine, Isaac and his brothers established a second store, in Philadelphia, to which the family then moved. The

boy received his elementary and secondary education at the William Penn Charter School there, where he was outstanding in the sports of football and boxing. He entered the Wharton School of Finance and Commerce of the University of Pennsylvania and was graduated with a B.S. degree in 1907. He continued to play football and to box, becoming the boxing champion at the university, where he also played water polo and earned the title of wrestling champion. Throughout his youth Bernard Gimbel retained boxing as an activity; his friendship with Gene Tunney is well known, and he has sparred with other prize-fighting champions.

As had his father and his uncles, young Gimbel learned the retail business from the bottom. His first job, the year he graduated, was in the Philadelphia Gimbel's, on the receiving platform. After working brief periods in the selling and nonselling departments of the store he became a vice-president in 1907. Upon his father's retirement from the presidency in 1927, Bernard Gimbel was elected to the post. (Isaac Gimbel served as chairman of the board of directors until his death in 1931.)

In 1910 Gimbel Brothers moved into the highly competitive New York market (where Macy's store had been established fifty-two years earlier) and began the famed rivalry, reportedly relished by the presidents of the two organizations. There Gimbel rented a site on Broadway and Thirty-third Street, which was considered strategically located (a site serviced in 1950 by several railways, four subways, and four bus lines); Gimbel Brothers later bought the property from the railway. Flourishing in the new venture, the firm was able to help in the financing of the Fifth Avenue store for the Saks Company (a Herald Square neighbor), and by a stock transfer arrangement, the latter became a subsidiary of Gimbel Brothers. (In 1929 a Chicago branch of Saks Fifth Avenue was established; it moved into larger quarters there in 1936.) Pittsburgh became the location of a store belonging to the company when Kaufmann & Baer of that city sold out to it in 1925 (the name of the store became Gimbel Brothers in 1928) and in 1940 Gimbel's bought site and building. By 1944 the company was leading its field of retailing in the volume of goods sold. "Bernard Gimbel," stated *Fortune*, "has become the top merchant of the U.S." In the year 1950 Gimbel Brothers has fifteen stores, including ones in New York, Philadelphia, Milwaukee, Chicago, Detroit (another Saks Fifth Avenue branch), and Beverly Hills, California. Employees numbered some twenty thousand. It is Gimbel policy to encourage the executives of each store to operate it in the way they consider is best suited to its particular community.

From his earliest years in the business, Bernard Gimbel has made contributions to the store's growth and policy. It was due to his urging, and to his calling on the opinion of his father's friends Julius Rosenwald (of Sears, Roebuck) and Louis Horowitz (of Thompson-Starrett), that the brothers decided to buy (for nine million dollars) the site their New York store occupies. It is said that it was due largely to him that the company became a corporation with a public stock offering in 1922. (In 1950 the immediate Gimbel family owned 20 per cent of the stock.) He is given the credit, also, for launching the firm in the field of quality merchandising by closing the Saks transaction with his friend, Horace Saks. (Saks died in 1925, the year after the Fifth Avenue shop was opened, and Adam Gimbel, a first cousin, became head of the store.)

Bernard Gimbel has been reported as saying, "I'm not a great merchandiser like my father." But several of his policies have made merchandising history. At the start of World War II, (after borrowing twenty million, said *Life*) he ordered his buyers to purchase as much as they could—he rented warehouses to hold goods when the regular warehouses were filled. During the years of the war, Gimbel's was therefore able to advertise scarce items and thus draw increasing numbers of customers. In 1945 he began to buy war surplus supplies, and to turn this Army material into saleable consumer goods. *Life* wrote, "For years he calculatedly kept the twenty-eight acres of his New York emporium as dowdy as was decent, on the shrewd theory that lack of fancy frills would encourage bargain hunters." In 1949 the department store was refurbished, with Raymond Loewy [*] as designer.

The president of Gimbel Brothers (who is also the chief stockholder), besides giving his attention to decisions in matters of real estate, finance and major corporate policy, maintains a close watch on public taste and on retailing trends. He rarely interferes with the affairs of store management, although he makes numerous suggestions, the results of frequent walks through his own and neighboring stores and of subway rides. He studies the advertising of other establishments across the country (as well as that of Gimbel stores) and takes part in promotions planned by the firm's advertising department. The company encourages its branch stores to support local projects; it has sponsored art contests in Pennsylvania and Wisconsin, and the University of Pittsburgh's Graduate School of Retailing.

In 1943 the merchant was awarded a silver plaque by executives of the company to mark completion of the firm's hundredth year in business. It was headed: "To Bernard F. Gimbel, Organizer, Merchant, Leader, Comrade" and cited his possession of "the ability of the business organizer, the acumen of the merchant, and the quality of leadership that knits men together in successful enterprise." The preceding year, when the centennial of the founding of the Palace of Trade was observed, Vincennes University conferred on the merchandising executive an honorary LL.D. degree. A scroll for "distinguished service in the field of human relations" was presented to him in 1949 by the National Conference of Christians and Jews. Of that honor, the New York *Herald Tribune* commented editorially: "It would be a safe wager that Mr. Gimbel not only has more real friends than any other New Yorker but has them among the widest array of groups and classes."

Gimbel in 1947 was made chairman of the Madison Square Garden Corporation board of directors, of which he had been a member for sixteen years, and became president of the New York Convention and Visitors' Bureau in 1948 (he had been a director since 1929). He is also a member of the Retail Dry Goods Association of New York. The president of Gimbel's is chairman of the board of Saks & Company and a member of the board of directors of the Coca-Cola Company. His clubs include the Advertising, the Madison Square Garden, and the Century Country. He was a director of the New York World's Fair (1939). From New York University he received the honorary degree of Doctor of Commercial Science. A Democrat, he is reported to have voted four times for Franklin D. Roosevelt.

Mrs. Bernard Gimbel—the former Alva Bernheimer, whom he married on April 4, 1912—is prominent in civic activities. Their Greenwich (Connecticut) home, "Chieftans," a 200-acre estate, has a stable of thoroughbred hunters and jumpers. His daughter Hope is the wife of David Solinger and his daughter Caral, of Hank Greenberg, of baseball fame. (The daughters are twins.) There are three sons—Bruce and identical twins, Peter Robin and David Alva. Gimbel is six feet tall, weighs 210 pounds. He rides, golfs, fishes, and gambles moderately at golf, races, and cards. He is a regular first nighter.

References

Fortune 32:124+ Jl '45 pors
Life 27:100+ D 12 '49 pors
New York Post Mag p 27 Jl 2 '47 por
International Who's Who, 1949
National Cyclopædia of American Biography Current vol E, 1937-38
Who's Who in America, 1948-49
Who's Who in American Jewry, 1938-39
Who's Who in Commerce and Industry (1948)
Who's Who in the East (1948)
World Biography (1948)

GLENNAN, T(HOMAS) KEITH Sept. 8, 1905- United States Government official; college president

Address: b. c/o United States Atomic Energy Commission, 19th St. & Constitution Ave., N.W., Washington 25, D.C.; c/o Case Institute of Technology, 10900 Euclid Ave., Cleveland 6, Ohio; h. 2530 Fairmount Blvd., Cleveland 6, Ohio

T. Keith Glennan, electrical engineer, business executive, and president of the Case Institute of Technology, was appointed to the United States Atomic Energy Commission in August 1950. The administrator, who was one of the first technologists to work in the field of talking motion pictures, was awarded the Medal for Merit for his service in directing the development of submarine detection devices during World War II. His term on the AEC is for five years, during which he is on leave of

Harry A. Cole

T. KEITH GLENNAN

absence from Case Institute. On October 2, 1950, he was sworn in as the AEC member.

Enderlin, a town in the southeast part of North Dakota, is the birthplace of Thomas Keith Glennan; the date of his birth is September 8, 1905. Son of Richard Henry and Margaret Laing (Pauline) Glennan, he passed most of his boyhood in Eau Claire, Wisconsin, and is a graduate (1922) of that town's high school. At the Sheffield Scientific School of Yale University he majored in electrical engineering, held the Lord Strathmore scholarship in his junior and senior years with a stipend of $600, and took the Bachelor of Science degree in electrical engineering, *cum laude*, in 1927. This was somewhat less than one year after the first public demonstration of talking pictures.

In August 1927 Glennan entered the employ of Electrical Research Products, Inc., a subsidiary of Western Electric in Chicago and Seattle. During the ensuing twelve months the engineer was responsible for the installation of the first sound reproduction apparatus in Philadelphia and converted motion picture theaters in Chicago, Seattle, and Los Angeles for use of sound equipment. In August 1928 he was sent to England as installation manager, and for about eighteen months superintended the work of about eighty-five American and two hundred British engineers and technicians. Appointed assistant continental manager in March 1930, he set up operating companies in ten European countries before returning to America, where he was employed by Electrical Research Products, successively, as assistant general service superintendent in New York City, operating manager of the Southeast division, and assistant manager of an educational picture project.

In the spring of 1932 Glennan became the general manager of Audio Cinema, the original Edison studio in New York City's borough of

The Bronx. A year later he went to Long Island City, New York, as vice-president of Eastern Studios (which provided operating facilities and services to talking-picture managers); and in March 1944 he moved to California, to become vice-president and general manager of the General Service Studios of Hollywood. In August 1935 Glennan was appointed operations manager of Paramount Pictures, Inc., and four years later (1939) was made studio manager. As such, his responsibility covered the budgeting of production costs, lighting, sound, set production, the wardrobe and art departments, and the film processing laboratory. In September 1941, after a brief period (in August) with the Vega Airplane Corporation in a general administrative capacity, Glennan joined the Samuel Goldwyn Studios in Hollywood as studio manager.

Glennan was called upon to contribute his service in World War II. In June 1942 he was appointed administrator of the United States Navy Underwater Sound Laboratory at New London, Connecticut, which was operated for the Office of Scientific Research and Development by Columbia University's Division of War Research, under the direction of T. E. Shea, on leave from the vice-presidency of Electrical Research Products. In December Glennan succeeded Shea as director, and from that time until June of 1945 he guided the activities of a large corps of engineers, scientists, and naval personnel in the research, development, and testing of submarine detection and location. One device evolved was the expendable radio sonobuoy which (stated *Nature*, the science weekly) "led to the destruction of a large number of German submarines and played an important part in the Battle of the Atlantic." For his work at the New London submarine base, Glennan received the Medal for Merit, the Government's highest civilian award; later on he was to serve as a deputy committee chairman with the Ordnance, Research and Development Board of the National Military Establishment.

Following the end of the war in Europe, Glennan joined the Ansco Division of the General Aniline and Film Corporation, located at Binghamton, New York. From assistant production manager he advanced in January 1946 to manager of administrative services; his province was general direction of engineering, production planning, purchasing, personnel, industrial and public relations, and office services. His success as an administrator attracted the interest of the trustees of the sixty-seven-year-old Case School of Applied Science, in Cleveland, Ohio, who were seeking a businessman to succeed their third president, Dr. William E. Wickenden, whose retirement after eighteen years as head of the school was to take effect September 1, 1947.

Appointment of Glennan to head the school was announced in June 1947, and on July 1 the name was changed to Case Institute of Technology. "A major step of the Glennan regime," stated *Business Week* at the time, "will be to make Case a national institution." That magazine added that the school, which had an endowment of six million dollars, received $250,-000 to $400,000 a year from companies who bring in scientific puzzles for practical solution, the backers of research projects including the Lubricol Corporation, the Paint and Varnish Association, the Firestone Tire and Rubber Company and the Air Material Command of the United States Army. On October 17, 1947, about six weeks after assuming his new duties, Glennan received from Clarkson College at Potsdam, New York, the honorary degree of Doctor of Science.

In Cleveland the new president of Case became prominent in civic and local business affairs, joining the Chamber of Commerce and becoming a director of the Equity Savings and Loan Company and the Cleveland Electric Illuminating Company, a trustee of the Cleveland Clinic Foundation and the Council on World Affairs, and a member of the Community Relations Board. (He resigned his directorship after confirmation for the Atomic Energy Commission.) Glennan has spoken before industrial and scientific bodies. Addressing the American Foundation for High Blood Pressure at its Cleveland meeting in April 1949, he urged increased industrial support of medical research; before the Akron chapter of the Society of Metals in February 1950, under the title of "Private Responsibility" he outlined a seven-point program for individual effort "to protect our democratic system against attack from within"; and in an address ("Accent the Positive") delivered to the Builders Exchange at Cleveland in the following April he urged "greater production through new incentives" as "a constructive alternative to the handout state." Glennan received a second honorary Doctor of Science degree, from Oberlin (Ohio) College on June 12, 1950.

The choice of T. Keith Glennan to fill the vacancy on the five-man Atomic Energy Commission which had been created by the resignation of Lewis L. Strauss[47] in April 1950 was made known on August 11, 1950, by President Truman. "My interests have been in administration and in people," the Case president (now on leave of absence) has been quoted as saying, while disclaiming any special knowledge of atomic energy. In the statement, the comment is made, may be found the reason for the appointment. In approximately three and a half years of existence the AEC had been under repeated attack in certain Congressional quarters for alleged "mismanagement" as well as alleged laxness in the maintenance of security; its original chairman, David E. Lilienthal[44], had resigned in February and had been succeeded in July by Gordon Dean[50], one-time law partner of Senator Brien McMahon[45], the chairman of the Congressional Joint Atomic Energy Committee. It was seen as a prime objective to introduce additional and proven executive ability and understanding of personnel into a body charged by law with the operation of such production and research plants as those at Oak Ridge in Tennessee, Los Alamos in New Mexico, and Brookhaven on Long Island. The choice of Glennan was endorsed by Senator McMahon, and his nomination was unanimously approved by the Joint Committee on August 16, and likewise confirmed by the Senate on August 22. Glennan's term is for five

years, and his post commands a salary of $15,000 per annum. The other AEC members, in addition to Chairman Dean, are Sumner T. Pike[47], Thomas E. Murray[50], and Dr. Henry DeWolf Smyth[48]. Glennan was sworn in October 2, 1950.

Mrs. Glennan is the former Ruth Haslup Adams of New Haven, Connecticut; the Glennans were married June 20, 1931, and have one son, Thomas Keith, Jr., and three daughters, Catherine, Pauline and Sarah. Brown-eyed, brown-haired Glennan lists woodworking, tennis, squash, and golf as his favorite forms of relaxation or exercise. His church is the Presbyterian; a member of the Newcomen Society of England, he belongs to the Union, University and Philosophical Clubs in Cleveland, and the Yale Club in New York City.

References

N Y Herald Tribune p3 Ag 12 '50
N Y Times pl Ag 11 '50 por
Nature 161:83 Jl 19 '47

Leaders in Education (1948)
Who's Who in America, 1950-51
Who's Who in Engineering, 1948
Who's Who in the Midwest (1949)

GOLDMAN, MRS. MARCUS SELDEN
See Goldman, Mrs. O. R.

GOLDMAN, MRS. OLIVE REMINGTON
United Nations official

Address: b. c/o United States Mission to the United Nations, 2 Park Ave., New York 16; Chief of Public Education, Illinois Division of Vocational Rehabilitation, 700 East Adams St., Springfield, Ill.; h. 203 Michigan Ave., Urbana, Ill.

Mrs. Olive Remington Goldman was appointed by President Truman in January 1950 to the post of United States Representative to the United Nations Commission on the Status of Women. In this office she succeeded Judge Dorothy Kenyon[47] of New York. Mrs. Goldman is also Chief of Public Education in the Illinois Division of Vocational Rehabilitation; she previously served as consultant in the Department of the Interior, Washington, D.C., on problems concerning the Pacific territories, and has twice been the Democratic candidate for Congress from the Twenty-second District of Illinois, in 1946 and 1948.

Born in Newark, New Jersey, and reared there and in Montclair, Mrs. Olive Remington Goldman is the only child of Mortimer and Blanche Campbell (Mulliken) Remington. Her parents were of Scottish, Irish, and English descent, tracing their ancestry to early settlers in America; several of the family fought in the Revolutionary War. In later history of the Mulliken family, Olive Remington's maternal grandfather fought as a commander in the Union Army during the Civil War. Mortimer Remington, Olive's father, was on the staff of one of the largest advertising agencies in New

MRS. OLIVE REMINGTON GOLDMAN

York. Her mother is a graduate of the New England Conservatory of Music.

From kindergarten through high school, where she was editor of the student paper and which she completed in 1916, Olive Remington attended Miss Craven's School in Newark, a participant in dramatics and athletics. At Vassar she majored in psychology and English, winning the Dana prize for a play in her senior year and obtaining her B.A. degree in 1919. During the course of her college years she took part in dramatics, was chairman of the sophomore musical comedy, and edited the college literary magazine. Active also in athletics, she became captain of the basketball team. Miss Remington was chairman of Class Day and of Commencement Week. Upon graduating from Vassar, she became a case worker for the home service division of the American Red Cross in New York City. In 1921 she returned to her studies, taking postgraduate work in playwriting in Professor George Pierce Baker's famous "47 Workshop" at Harvard; and she spent the summer of 1922 at the Mac-Dowell Colony in Peterboro, New Hampshire, when one of her plays was produced.

The following year Miss Remington traveled in France and Italy, where she witnessed the disturbances at the time of the rise of Mussolini. During this period she was writing plays on international and sociological topics. One of these, entitled "The Braveness of Him," won first prize in a contest for one-act plays in Paris. At that time the drama and fine arts critic for the New York *Herald*'s Paris edition was Marcus Selden Goldman, whom she met when he interviewed her as the winner of the drama prize. Their wedding took place September 1, 1925, in Newark, New Jersey, after which they went to Harvard; there Goldman completed his graduate studies. When he joined the staff of the English Department of the University of Illinois in 1926, the young couple moved to Urbana, where they have lived ever since, and where their four children were born. (An associate professor, Goldman in 1950 has military leave of absence to serve on the faculty of the Command and General Staff College, Fort Leavenworth, Kansas, with the rank of colonel.) There Mrs. Goldman continued her drama activities, serving as director and playwriter for church and benefit pageants and plays. For ten years she was lecturer on religious drama for Midwestern Episcopal Conferences.

In discussing influences in her life, Mrs. Goldman has stated that a strong sense of social responsibility had been an attribute of her parents and some of her favorite teachers. Her conviction of the need for developing human understanding and cooperation upon a local, national, and international plane to work for the growth of democracy and peace was stimulated by her father's World War I service, and by her husband's service in World Wars I and II and his interest in world events and the work of the Episcopal Church.

As her four children became older, she began to find broader scope for expression of her interests. Resuming her postgraduate studies, she obtained her Master's degree at the University of Illinois in 1941; her thesis was "Religious Drama in Twentieth Century England." She began teaching in the speech department at that university when her husband went on active duty in the Army in 1941, and taught winter and summer terms until his return in October 1946. For three years during the war Mrs. Goldman conducted weekly radio programs on foreign policy and served as local chairman of foreign policy for the League of Women Voters and American Association of University Women. In 1945 she worked with the Committee for the Win-the-Peace-Now Resolution, which was proposed in the Senate by four members of the Truman Committee. Her wartime activities included service on the William Allen White Committee and on Defend America by Aiding the Allies, and work for British war relief.

Nominated Democratic candidate for Congress from the Nineteenth District of Illinois (later the Twenty-second District), Mrs. Goldman was defeated in 1946 and in 1948 in the traditionally Republican district. (In 1948 the candidate won 20,000 more votes than in 1946.) Between the two elections, in 1947 Mrs. Goldman served as assistant to the director of the Stimson Committee for the Marshall Plan, contacting national non-Governmental organizations publicizing the project. During this period she made speeches on the Marshall Plan before many audiences; an advocate of the North Atlantic Pact, Mrs. Goldman also spoke frequently in support of closer cooperation between the United States and the democratic nations of Western Europe.

From March until September 1949 Mrs. Goldman held a position with the Department of the Interior, Division of Territories and Island Possessions, as consultant on statehood for Alaska and Hawaii. In October of that year Mrs. Goldman returned to Illinois as Chief of

Public Education of the Illinois Division of Vocational Rehabilitation, a State-Federal program; her duties in this connection require her to travel throughout the State. This post Mrs. Goldman continues to maintain since her appointment to a United Nations position, securing leave of absence from Illinois for the weeks of the meetings of her commission.

Nominated by President Truman on January 10, 1950, to serve a three-year term as the United States Representative to the United Nations Commission on the Status of Women, a division of the Economic and Social Council, Mrs. Goldman was confirmed in the post by the Senate on February 3, 1950. For this post she was recommended to the President by Mrs. India Edwards [49], head of the women's division of the Democratic National Committee. Mrs. Goldman had been prominent in national work on the status of women, speaking on this subject in 1949 before numerous national women's groups.

At the time of her nomination to the U.N. office Mrs. Goldman stated: "The goal of the commission is concerned with the political and economic rights and general welfare of the women of the world. It is a question, for instance, of the right of married women to keep a nationality of their own. Health and legal rights for women and the question of equal pay for equal work also are of great concern." Emphasizing the need for women to assume their responsibilities, the woman's leader, in an interview with V. Y. Dallman, editor of the *Illinois State Register*, advocated willingness to serve in humble jobs, adding, "I encourage women to serve as precinct workers as well as to be candidates for high office and to be business executives or supervisors. The new representative to the U.N. commission stressed the necessity of practical and professional training for young women to enable them to make use of "the opportunities which greater leisure and increased ability of maturity provide after the children are grown."

Referring to Mrs. Goldman as the "second most important American woman representative at the United Nations, next to Mrs. Roosevelt," the *Christian Science Monitor* of May 15, 1950, commented that Mrs. Goldman caused a few "raised eyebrows" on the Women's Commission when, in making her opening address, she suggested that they might do well with a few male members. "I'd like to see men on this commission," she said, "just as I would like to see discrimination against women abolished on other commissions." The May 1950 session of the fourteen-member commission, its fourth since its establishment in 1946, was marked by the absence of Mme. Popova, Russian delegate, in protest against participation by a Chinese Nationalist delegate; in this connection Mrs. Goldman commented before the commission: "I hope the women of the Soviet Union know that they are being deprived of their voice in our commission and an opportunity to collaborate with us for their own and all women's benefit."

Among the publications in which articles by Mrs. Goldman have appeared are the *American Association of University Women Quarterly* and the *Democratic National Digest*. She has translated, with her husband, seven French miracle plays by contemporary authors, to be published in 1950 as a collection under the title *St. Anne and the Gouty Rector and Other Plays*. A number of her dramas, including *Tobruk Time Table* and *Light Shining in Darkness*, have been produced at the University of Illinois and on other campuses. Clubs and organizations to which Mrs. Goldman belongs include the American Association of University Women, the League of Women Voters, National Federation of Business and Professional Women's Clubs, women's auxiliaries of the American Legion and the Veterans of Foreign Wars, alumnae of Vassar and Radcliffe colleges and of the University of Illinois, the Associates of Sisters of St. Mary. She has been chairman of the residential campaign of the Community Chest, is a founder of the Children's Theater of Urbana, and a member of the Faculty Players of the University of Illinois.

At home in Urbana the Goldmans are members of the Episcopal Chapel of St. John the Divine at the university (Mrs. Goldman is a member of its women's auxiliary). Their children are: Agnes (Mrs. John Francis Burke), Marcia Elizabeth, Charles Remington, and Olive Mary Louise Goldman. The family, which Mrs. Goldman describes as "a closeknit one whose members enjoy being together," has a summer cottage in Canada. The U. N. representative has brown eyes, graying brown hair, a height of five feet four and a half inches. and a weight of 140 pounds. Among her favorite sports are fishing and swimming; and she names her other interests as "an aquarium of native Illinois water life, the theater—and hats."

References

Christian Sci Mon p14 Ja 14 '50
Ind Woman 29:92 Mr '50
N Y Herald Tribune p16 My 15 '50
N Y Times p61 Ja 15 '50

GOLDMARK, PETER C(ARL) Dec. 2, 1906- Television engineer; broadcasting company executive

Address: b. c/o Columbia Broadcasting System, 485 Madison Ave., New York 22; h. New Canaan, Conn.

NOTE: This biography supersedes the article which appeared in *Current Biography* in 1940.

In October 1950, ten years after its demonstration in the first known color television broadcast in history, Dr. Peter C. Goldmark's field sequential system of color television was approved by the Federal Communications Commission. Accordingly, the Columbia Broadcasting System, for which Goldmark invented and developed the method, was authorized to begin commercial transmissions in color. Associated with the research laboratories of CBS since 1936, Goldmark was appointed vice-president of the organization in September 1950, in charge of the engineering research and development. The owner of many patents in the field of television and radio, Goldmark is best known for

CBS Photo.

PETER C. GOLDMARK

his development of an ultra-high frequency, full-color system for transmitting and receiving color television and for the long-playing phonograph record which he developed for Columbia Records, Inc., in 1948.

Born in Budapest, Hungary, on December 2, 1906, Peter Carl Goldmark is the son of Alexander and Emmy Goldmark. His profession as a scientist and his enthusiasm for music were part of a family tradition. One of his granduncles, Joseph Goldmark, a chemist who came to America, discovered red phosphorus and invented the percussion cap for rifles, a device used for the first time in the Civil War by the Union troops; a granduncle, Carl Goldmark, was a Viennese composer of operatic, orchestral, and chamber works. As a boy, Peter Goldmark studied the piano and the cello, and, early interested in science, crowded the family bathroom with his laboratory equipment. Later he built his own radio set.

Goldmark began his advanced studies at the University of Berlin, after which, in 1925, he began to study at the University of Vienna, where he majored in physics. From the latter he received a B.S. degree and, in 1931, the Ph.D. degree. While still a graduate student in Vienna (as told in the New York Post) he and a friend constructed equipment which could receive television pictures transmitted from London. For his doctoral thesis he wrote "A New Method for Determining the Velocity of Ions," which was read before the Academy of Science in Vienna and which led to television research as the chief pursuit of his life.

From Vienna Dr. Goldmark moved to Cambridge, England, where he worked as a physicist for Pye Radio, Ltd., organizing a television section. After coming to the United States in 1933, for about three years he was consulting engineer to several television and radio companies. His association with the Co-

lumbia Broadcasting System began in January 1936, when he was employed to work in the research laboratory. There his title later became chief television engineer. In 1944 he was appointed CBS's director of engineering research and development, and in September 1950 he was named vice-president in charge of that activity. During the period of World War II the scientist interrupted his research programs for CBS to carry out special assignments for the Government in the field of electronic research. This work, chiefly in radar, took him to the radio research laboratory of Harvard University, to England, and to the South Pacific.

During the years that Goldmark has been directing research for CBS he has been responsible for two major developments: a method and equipment for transmitting and receiving color television and the long-playing microgroove phonograph record. The first development was the result of a chance visit to a motion picture house in Canada in 1940 where he saw the Technicolor film *Gone with the Wind*. He was so impressed with the color on the screen that he developed (as he told in an interview with the New York *World-Telegram*) "an inferiority feeling about television in black and white." With his associates in the CBS laboratories, he began to work out a method of transmitting color in television. Three months later, in August 1940, he demonstrated the invention when he transmitted motion pictures of flowers and marine scenes.

The development of color transmission was delayed until after the war, when in 1945, Goldmark again continued his research for CBS. By March 1946 he was able to give another demonstration, this time of an improved ultra-high frequency, full-color system. Later that year the invention was considered sufficiently perfected for CBS to apply to the Federal Communications Commission for a commercial license to broadcast color television. Since the FCC is the authority for assigning channels for nation-wide civilian and military radio communications and must set engineering standards for all television, including color, it was necessary for FCC to carry on extensive hearings on standards for color television, as well as to render judgment as to whether Goldmark's system was ready to be commercialized. These hearings were begun in the latter part of 1946. The FCC decision was complicated by the announcement of an all-electronic color system from the laboratories of the Radio Corporation of America, and, later, by the introduction of another system, developed by Color Television, Inc. During the course of the 1949 hearings, the FCC withheld permits on all new applications for television channels.

In February 1950 the FCC reopened its hearings, permitting each of the three organizations involved to demonstrate its color system and to listen to the position of manufacturers of television receiving equipment, represented by the Radio-Television Manufacturers Association. In September 1950 the FCC issued a report declaring that the CBS system of color television, a field sequential technique in which the picture is photographed through a spinning three-color disk, transmitted, and then viewed through a similar synchronized disk, was the best and cheapest offered thus far. However, since the pictures could not be received without special adapters on the television sets already in use throughout the country, the FCC withheld its final approval until manufacturers could voice their willingness or unwillingness to construct sets capable of receiving both standard and CBS color transmissions. On October 11, after many manufacturers had refused to produce the desired equipment, the FCC gave approval to the CBS color system by permitting it to begin color transmissions on a commercial basis, to begin November 20, 1950. The controversy over the "incompatibility" of the CBS device with the present black-and-white sets, which received much attention in the press, left television owners somewhat puzzled as to what the FCC approval of Goldmark's development would entail on their part. That color televison was highly pleasing to the eye was evident at the first demonstration to the public on November 14, 1950.

Previous to the FCC approval, Goldmark's color system had been utilized in the building of equipment which enables physicians to see medical and surgical procedures on color television. The first surgical operation to be televised in color was held in May 1949 at the University of Pennsylvania. Since that time the equipment has been used in cities throughout the country for instructional purposes. In March 1950 Goldmark was appointed Visiting Professor of Medical Electronics in the University of Pennsylvania's School of Medicine. One of his first assignments will be the supervision of the installation of color television in the university's new medical center. *Pathfinder* commented that he may also be expected to make contributions in radiology and isotope research.

The second development for which Dr. Goldmark received nation-wide attention was the long-playing phonograph record, described by *Life* (July 26, 1948) as the "most revolutionary development to hit the recording industry since the invention of the automatic changer." The record was the direct result of the engineer's enthusiasm for recorded music and his exasperation with the necessary interruptions in listening to lengthy works on the standard disks of 78 revolutions per minute. Using the research facilities of Columbia Records, Inc., an affiliate of CBS, he developed in June 1948 a record for commercial distribution which makes possible 45 minutes of music by playing both sides of one 12-inch record. The system has since been adapted by other record manufacturing companies in the United States and England.

While he was developing his color television system, Peter Goldmark made reports in technical papers before various engineering societies and in 1945 received his first award for his discoveries from the Television Broadcasters Association. In January 1946 his work in television won for him the Morris Liebmann Memorial Prize, granted by the Institute of Radio Engineers. He is a fellow of that institute, the Society of Motion Picture Engineers, and of the British Television Society. Among the articles Goldmark has written for the general public was "Big Things Ahead" (*American Magazine*, October 1948), on the importance of science to the development of consumer conveniences.

Goldmark, who became a citizen of the United States in 1937, married Frances Charlotte Trainer on January 12, 1940, and has two children, Frances and Peter Carl. He is described as a man of quiet mien, with the habit of saying "we" when describing the research carried on at the CBS laboratories. His outdoor recreations are tennis and skiing. Continuing his proficiency on the piano and the cello, he invites his friends to join him in the evenings in playing chamber music.

References

N Y Post Mag p43 Mr 21 '46 por
N Y World-Telegram p17 Ja 5 '45 por
Pathfinder 57:44 Ap 19 '50
Variety Radio Directory, 1940-41
Who's Who in America, 1950-51
Who's Who in Engineering, 1948
World Biography (1948)

GOMEZ, LAUREANO (gō'mās) Feb. 20, 1889-   President of Colombia
Address: Presidential Palace, Bogotá, Colombia, S. A.

On November 27, 1949, Laureano Gómez, the unopposed Conservative candidate for the presidency of Colombia, was elected in what *Time* called "as bitter a campaign as any in modern times." He succeeded President Ospina Pérez '50 (also a Conservative) August 7, 1950, for a four-year term. Gómez, editor of the Bogotá newspaper *El Siglo*, has long been a leading figure in Colombia's Conservative party. He first entered the country's politics as a national deputy in 1911; in 1931 he was elected a Senator. Minister of Public Works (1925) and Foreign Minister (1946-48), he has represented his country in Argentina and in Germany.

Laureano Gómez was born to Laureano Gómez and Dolores Castro de Gómez on February 20, 1889, in the Colombian capital, Bogotá. He received his education in his native city, obtaining the Bachelor's degree from the Colegio de San Bartolomé and the degree of engineer from the National University in 1909. In that year he founded *La Unidad*, which remained under his direction until 1918.

Gómez first entered public life as a national deputy, in which elective office he served from 1911 to 1918 and from 1921 to 1923. When the Fifth Pan-American Conference met in 1923 in Santiago, Chile, Gómez attended as a delegate. The following year he was named Minister Plenipotentiary to Argentina. Then, during 1925-26 he was Minister of Public Works. Four years later he went abroad as Minister Plenipotentiary to Germany, and upon his return in 1931 he was elected a Senator.

Wide World Photos

LAUREANO GOMEZ

The Conservative party, losing power in Colombia in 1930, remained out of office until 1946. Gómez, who was regarded as the Conservative party's "unchallenged boss" for eighteen years (*Time*, October 24, 1949), is said to have aided the Liberal President, Alfonso López, in campaigns against the Conservatives. (According to *Time*, the Conservative leader is credited with deposing three Presidents, two Conservatives and one Liberal.) In 1939, when violent opposition between the two parties resulted in nine persons being killed and seventeen wounded, Gómez charged the police with responsibility for it; and he was instrumental in the Conservative party's issuance of a declaration stating that its members should arm for self-defense, a declaration condemned by some Conservatives, as well as by Liberal President Santos.

As a member of the Colombian Senate, in the course of its 1939 discussions of the Good Neighbor Policy, Gómez emphasized the "conflict of cultures between the United States and South America," and recommended a "Catholic Spanish Empire" to embrace areas with "elements . . . susceptible of an imperial conception." Later (October 21, 1949), he was to speak of the United States as "a happy land" where people "have always followed the admonition that honesty is the best policy" (*Christian Science Monitor*).

Gómez was prominent in Conservative opposition to the Liberal Administration of López (who had been elected President for the second time in 1942). In 1944 in connection with anti-Government agitation, the Conservative Senator was imprisoned for a short period. After an abortive attempt at revolution in July 1944, Gómez took refuge in Quito, Ecuador, under protection of the Brazilian embassy; he returned to Colombia in December of the same year.

During World War II the cordiality of Gómez' newspaper, *El Siglo*, toward the Franco regime is said to have attracted the support of Falangist elements to the Conservative party. John Gunther, who was then a United States correspondent, cited Gómez' efforts as being of use to the Nazis. When the Falangists among the Conservatives grew powerful enough to move to create their own party, Gómez was primarily responsible for preventing the schism, according to the *Christian Science Monitor*, November 28, 1949. That element is considered by some observers to be one of his strongest sources of support.

Choice of the Conservative candidate for the 1946 Presidential elections (in which the Conservatives won their first triumph in sixteen years) has been attributed to Gómez. Conservative Mariano Ospina Pérez, opposed by two Liberal candidates, polled a majority over the leading Liberal, though not over the total Liberal vote. In his Cabinet, posts were divided equally among Conservatives and Liberals until March 1948, when the Liberal ministers resigned and Ospina Pérez appointed an all-Conservative Cabinet, naming Gómez to the post of Foreign Minister.

As Foreign Minster, Gómez presided over the Ninth Inter-American Conference in Bogotá in 1948 until its disruption by the rioting following the assassination of Jorge Eliécer Gaitán, Liberal leader. The Conservative Foreign Minister, known for his anti-Liberalism, resigned his post the day after the assassination and went abroad. His house and the plant of *El Siglo* were burned by rioters. He returned from Spain, where he had taken refuge, to be nominated Conservative candidate on October 12, 1949, for the Presidential elections scheduled for November of that year. Gómez gave as his first aim in the event of election, elimination of "the disease of playing politics."

The 1949 election was held under conditions of martial law, a state of siege having been declared November 9 by President Ospina Pérez to quell pre-election disturbances. Upon the withdrawal of Darío Echandía, the Liberal candidate, his party announced a boycott of the election, contending that the voting would be held under conditions of "coercive violence." (Eduardo Zuleta Angel, Colombian Ambassador to the United States, in a letter to the New York *Times* on November 23, stated that this would not be the first Colombian election held under a state of siege, nor the first in which only one candidate would present himself; he pointed to the 1934 and 1938 elections in which, he recalled, the successful Liberal candidates had no Conservative opposition, the latter abstaining on grounds that there were inadequate guarantees.) The Liberal party called a general strike, which met with but moderate success, hampering bus and train service and ending the day after the election. The polls, guarded by troops, were reported as quiet on election day. Gómez received more than 956,000 votes, a majority which *El Siglo* claimed to be the greatest in the history of Colombia. His inauguration for a four-year term took place on August 7, 1950.

In his inaugural address President Gómez emphasized his wish to strengthen the bonds between Colombia and the United States; referring to Korea, he stated that his country was on the side of the South Koreans. About Colombia itself he was quoted as saying, "We are all convinced that we belong to a nation backward in many aspects of civil and economic organization" (New York *Times*); he invited a change, one mark of which would be honesty in the Government's administration.

The President of Colombia, who has been charged with being Fascist and Falangist, maintains he is neither, attributing such allegations to political maneuverings by his enemies. His *El Cuadrilátero*, published in 1936, is in the opinion of Luis Gonzalez Barros, former Colombian U.N. Security Council delegate, "the only serious book against totalitarianism and Hitler written by a Colombian."

In a statement on his policy, Gómez told the press that his Administration will encourage investment of foreign capital in Colombia, granting it proper safeguards and endeavoring to adjust the constitutional question of expropriation without prior indemnification. With respect to the United Nations and the Organization of American States (Pan American Union), the Colombian leader said his policy would be to "invigorate and strengthen them," (in the words of the New York *Times*).

A contributor to foremost publications in Colombia and Argentina, the editor and cofounder of *El Siglo* has written several books on Colombian affairs and figures. He is married to the former Maria Hurtado. "Highly cultured, intensely Catholic" is *Newsweek's* comment on Gómez, whose hobbies are sculpture and painting.

References

Christian Sci Mon N 28 '49 por
Time 54:43 O 24 '49 por
Who's Who in Latin America (1940)

GONZALEZ VIDELA, GABRIEL (gôn-sä′läs vē-dä′lä gä″brē-ĕl′) Nov. 23, 1898- President of Chile

Address: b. and h. Palacio de la Moneda, Santiago, Chile; h. Viña del Mar, Chile

Gabriel González Videla was elected President of the Republic of Chile in the fall of 1946 for a term of six years. His political activity began in his school days, when he joined the local club of the Radical party. Member of the Chilean Congress for many years, envoy to European and South American countries, he was a signatory to the United Nations charter in 1945 as a member of the Chilean delegation to the San Francisco conference. A partisan of close cooperation with the United States, he paid a state visit to that country in April 1950.

The son of Gabriel González, a grocery store owner, and Teresa Videla, Gabriel González Videla was born November 23, 1898, in La Serena, capital of the northern Chilean province of Coquimbo, where the Chilean Declaration of Independence had been proclaimed in

César González

GABRIEL GONZALEZ VIDELA

1818. The eldest son in a large family of children (of whom eleven survive), González Videla became head of the family at the age of fifteen upon the death of his father. After a public school education in his home town, he entered the Law School of the University of Chile in Santiago, where he wrote a thesis on statistics. He was graduated in 1922, the year he opened a law office in La Serena. There he remained until 1930, when as a Radical party candidate he was first elected a deputy to the Chamber of Deputies of the National Congress. Several times president of the Radical party, he has also served as president of the Chamber.

In the course of his political career González Videla has often become involved in situations that demanded quick solution. He has risen to such situations, say biographers, because he has a gift for oratory, a quick emotional reaction, and inexhaustible energy. "In politics," he once stated, "I only obey my intuition, and it has never proved wrong." His first arrest occurred in 1925, when he had introduced a resolution against the Chilean dictator Ibañez in the town assembly of La Serena. On the way to the police station he managed to escape to the near-by clubhouse of his party.

During the nine years he served as national legislator, González Videla was one of the foremost leaders in the fight against the reactionary forces, which eventually lost control of the government. In 1938, when President Alessandri attempted to suppress gatherings of the Radical party, González Videla organized socalled "lightning meetings" in Santiago, and was wounded several times in clashes with the police. Badly beaten when the police cleared the Congress in May 1938, it is said he had enough presence of mind to signal the press photographer the best moment for taking a

GONZALEZ VIDELA, GABRIEL—*Cont.*

picture. In the same year González Videla organized the Popular Front of Radicals, Socialists, and Communists for the presidential election, a course he had followed in the congressional election in 1937. While the Popular Front did not obtain the majority in Congress, it succeeded in having its candidate Pedro Aguirre Cerda [41] elected.

In 1939 the Chilean was the leader of his country's delegation to the International Confederation of Democracies of America (held in Montevideo), of which he was vice-president. That year he left his legislative seat to become Chile's Minister to France, in which appointment his duties as envoy also extended to Belgium and Luxembourg. It was while he was in Paris that the former Foreign Minister of Republican Spain, Julio Alvarez del Vayo (then a refugee from the Franco regime) was ordered by the French authorities to leave the city at the outbreak of World War II. Upon hearing that, the Chilean Minister offered him asylum in the legation. The latter reported that other exiled Loyalists were also befriended by González Videla. The Chilean envoy remained in France until he was named Ambassador to Portugal in 1941. This appointment was followed by an ambassadorship to Brazil in 1942. Elected to Chile's Senate in 1945 to represent the provinces of Tarapacá and Antofagasta, he was also that year a member of the Chilean delegation to the United Nations Conference on International Organization in San Francisco and thus signed the charter of the United Nations.

When the Presidential election was held September 4, 1946, González Videla was the candidate of the Radical party and had the support of the Communists as well. Since his plurality was not sufficiently large, Congress was called to elect the chief executive on October 24, which resulted in a victory for González Videla in a 138-46 vote. The new President's inauguration on November 3, 1946, was witnessed by missions from the United States, a number of the Latin American countries, Russia, the Vatican, as well as a Spanish Loyalist delegation. González Videla's Cabinet was a coalition of Radicals, Liberals, and Communists. The Communists, to whom he owed his plurality in the popular election, received three seats, thus becoming the first of that party to be included in any American Government.

From the outset President González Videla faced serious economic problems, particularly those of rising living costs and an unbalanced budget. The disturbed economy was caused by a drop in the price of copper and nitrate after World War II, an unfortunate turn of events for a country which has the largest copper reserve in the world and the only known natural nitrate resources. (As a by-product of nitrate Chile produces 60 per cent of the world's iodine.) To stabilize the strike-torn country, the new President announced a long-range program of anti-inflationary measures, industrialization, and raising of the economic and cultural level of the people. At the same time he rejected any trend towards socialization. Under-

scoring that he owed his election to a national program, he refused to adopt the program of any one party. A few days after he took office the President himself became head of a council of national economy (in which the state, capital, and labor received equal representation) for the purpose of organizing and planning the country's economy. The chief emergency measure was designed to curb Chile's inflation by suppressing speculation, hoarding, and profiteering.

In carrying out his program, González Videla re-formed the Cabinet several times, his own Radical party continuing in most of the ministries. In the meantime, changes of far-reaching importance affected the Communists. When the 1947 and 1948 strikes (particularly in the coal mines) brought serious consequences, the Communists were accused of fomenting unrest. A Presidential decree placed the capital under military control, and the Chamber of Deputies authorized the suspension of individual liberties in the crisis. Communists were arrested, and diplomatic relations with Yugoslavia, Czechoslovakia, and the Soviet Union were broken off in the fall of 1947. Within another year (September 3, 1948), González Videla signed a bill outlawing the Communist party in Chile. With the disfranchisement of some 25,000 Communists, a number of them fled the country. Another charge against the Communists was that they had planned to kidnap the President, his family, Cabinet Ministers, and other prominent anti-Communists.

Before the March 1949 Congressional elections, the Communists attempted to make a "behind-the-scenes" comeback, but the vote gave González Videla's forces a two-thirds majority in both houses. With the spread of strikes in other fields (banks, railways, newspapers), martial law was instituted in August, and troops were sent to occupy copper and coal mines. A return to normalcy seemed probable with the settlement, in early February 1950, of the wave of strikes (a bill passed by Congress required all Chilean firms to distribute 25 per cent of their annual earnings to employees). On February 27, 1950, González Videla appointed a new Cabinet. Drawn largely from four major parties and excluding the Communists, it is composed of Radicals, Conservatives, Independents, Democrats, and Falangists.

In the furtherance of his programs the President of Chile undertakes trips throughout his own country, the frequency of which have earned for him the nickname of "Don Gavion" (formed from the first letter of his name and the Spanish word for airplane). State visits have also taken him to Brazil and Argentina, and in February 1948 to Antarctica to lay claim to a large area for Chile, a point of dispute with Great Britain. From April 12 to May 4, 1950, he visited the United States at the invitation of President Truman. The Chilean guest declared that he did not come for a loan, but it was reported that he was anxious to discuss the vital question of the United States tariff exemption for Chilean copper which expires June 30. During his trip he visited Washington, New York, Hyde Park, Lake Success, the TVA, oil fields in Louisiana, and ranches in Texas. Besides being honored at official and social events, González Videla met with representatives of the AFL and CIO and made several addresses in which he emphasized international cooperation. (Two of these were before the National Press Club in Washington, and the Chamber of Commerce of the State of New York.) In an unexpected speech before the United States Senate he expressed the hope that one day "all the countries of this hemisphere [will] give to their democratic structures a certain uniformity of understanding of representative democracy."

President Truman presented his guest with a gold medal struck for the occasion, and Fordham University conferred the honorary degree of Doctor of Laws on him. The Chilean President is also the recipient of honors from Portugal (Order of Christ) and France (The Legion of Honor). He is honorary president of the Sociedad de Amigos de America, a Brazilian organization; in that country, too, he is an honorary member of the Lawyers Institute of Rio de Janeiro. In his own country he serves on the board of directors of two newspapers—*La Hora* (in Santiago) and *El Chileno* (in La Serena). While he was a law student González Videla met Rosa Marckmann, whom he married in 1923. Honorary president of the Chilean Federation of Women's Clubs, the President's wife conducts an office, with two women lawyers, which is devoted to all affairs concerning the women of Chile, who have recently been granted the suffrage. The couple's two daughters, Silvia and Rosita, are married, both to members of the Liberal party—one a legislator, the other a lawyer.

Comments on the personality of Chile's President frequently include mention of his high spirits, hot temper, and boundless energy. The day he returned to Chile from the United States, a newspaper account reported that he spoke to the welcoming crowd for two hours, held a reception for another two hours, and followed these with a press conference lasting almost as long. He receives the public every Wednesday, listening to each petition and assigning it to one of fifteen aides from the various government departments. According to *The Lutheran,* no legal arguments are permitted; fines may be forgiven—or increased; lost jobs restored; unions defended or reprimanded; inequities passed to the proper department for adjudication. González Videla (who is of medium height) does not smoke, drinks beer moderately. Favoring outdoor sports, he enjoys swimming, canoeing, horseback riding, and tennis; and a former student of the piano, he names Brahms as one of the composers he likes best. He is very fond of his native town, where his mother and two of his sisters have a shop carrying women's wear and accessories. "When I leave the presidency," he once said, "I would like to spend the rest of my life as Mayor of La Serena."

References

Bul Pan Am Union 81:8-9 Ja '47
Chilean Gazette p3 1st quarter '47

Life 28:126+ My 1 '50 pors
N Y Herald Tribune II p3 Ap 16 '50 por
N Y Sunday News p94+ Ap 23 '50 pors
N Y World-Telegram and Sun p15 Ap 15 '50 por
Nation 163:467 O 26 '46
Newsweek 35:21-22 Ap 24 '50
U N World 4:46 My '50
Who's Who in America, 1950-51
Who's Who in Latin America (1947)

GORDON, DONALD Dec. 11, 1901- Railroad president; banker
Address: b. c/o Canadian National Railways, 360 McGill St., Montreal, P.Q., Canada

The president of the Government-operated Canadian National Railways, Donald Gordon, who entered that post January 1, 1950, was one of Canada's leading bankers and the director of his country's wartime price-control system. In his banking career he was associated first with the Bank of Nova Scotia and then with the Bank of Canada, the country's central bank. He became secretary of the latter institution at the time of its establishment in 1935, and its deputy governor in 1938, a post he held until his appointment to the presidency and chairmanship of the Canadian National Railways.

Donald Gordon was born December 11, 1901, in Old Meldrum, thirty miles from Aberdeen, Scotland. His parents were John and Margaret L. (Watt) Gordon; the father, who was town clerk, was a watchmaker by profession. In 1914, when Donald was thirteen, the family emigrated to Canada, and settled in Toronto, Ontario, where John Gordon opened a watch repair shop. The boy did odd jobs about the shop and sold newspapers while continuing his schooling until he was fifteen years of age. In 1916 he joined the staff of the Bank of Nova Scotia in Toronto as a junior clerk. Through the educational system operated by the Canadian banks Gordon took first the associate correspondence course and then a fellowship course established by Queens University (Kingston, Ontario), to earn the equivalent of a university degree in economics. Three years after joining the bank Gordon became an accountant.

In 1920 Gordon went to the head office of the Bank of Nova Scotia (in Toronto). As a member of the inspection staff he traveled to all parts of the country in 1924 and 1925. After a period as secretary to the general manager he became assistant chief accountant at the head office in 1927. In 1930 he was made assistant manager of its main Toronto branch. He was in this position in 1935 when the Dominion Government established the central Bank of Canada under Graham Towers as Governor. Towers, as assistant general manager of the Royal Bank of Canada, had become acquainted with Gordon on various interbank committees, and he now selected Gordon as secretary of the new central bank at Ottawa (February

DONALD GORDON

1935). In this position Gordon had supervision of organizing the bank's facilities, including such physical aspects as the actual construction, furnishing and opening of its headquarters in the capital city. In 1938 he was appointed the Bank of Canada's deputy governor. At the beginning of World War II Gordon was given much of the responsibility of organizing Canada's Foreign Exchange Control Board, of which he became alternating chairman.

After the first two years of the war the Canadian Government, alarmed by the steady rise in prices, established a nation-wide economic control organization, called the Wartime Prices and Trade Board (WPTB). In November 1941 Gordon was appointed chairman of the WPTB, to administer the pivotal machinery of this control. Commenting on the appointment, the New York *Times* correspondent remarked that Gordon was "the most dynamic man the Government could find for the job." The board was given extensive powers to control all retail prices, to demand severe penalties for infraction of its regulations, and to advise on tariffs and subsidies to offset the effect on Canadian prices of uncontrolled economies in the United States and elsewhere. A ceiling on prices went into effect on December 1, 1941, following the decision to act quickly and thus avoid a gradual item-by-item control. "You cannot compromise with inflation," Gordon stated.

At the end of the first year of price control Gordon was able to announce that Canada's cost-of-living index had remained virtually stationary during that period. In making the controls effective, Gordon emphasized reliance on public acceptance and the voluntary technique, paraphrasing Abraham Lincoln, in one speech, to say, "Let it be regimentation of the people, by the people, and for the people." The

WPTB administrator laid stress upon the employment of representative businessmen in the various areas of WPTB control, on the theory that this would be a means of minimizing bureaucratic tendencies. Described (by Leslie Roberts in *Collier's,* July 1, 1950) as a man with "a natural instinct for public relations," Gordon made many radio addresses explaining and asking cooperation for the control program, in what Roberts called "blunt but homey phrases."

When the United States set up its price-control machinery, Gordon was invited to confer with Leon Henderson [40] of OPA and other American officials: it was felt that Canadian experience could be adapted to the United States. Gordon's attitude, as evidenced in such remarks as "You can never make a thing like this work in a democratic society if you load it with snafu," and "If you want the cooperation of business, you have to let business name its own policemen," appealed to Americans (*Collier's*). The continuing close relationship between Gordon and Henderson has been described by the former as one of the "happiest explosive relationships" he has ever had.

As the war drew to a close Gordon warned that it would be disastrous to end controls until the period of shortages was over. The rise in the Canadian cost of living up to the end of the war had been held to less than 18 per cent, most of it coming before the establishment of the WPTB. The controls entered a period of gradual elimination in September of 1945, with Gordon stating, "The Board must assume that expansion of civilian output will take place within the framework of a system that relies mainly upon private enterprise."

Gordon began to take up more actively the duties he had nominally retained throughout the war period as deputy governor of the Bank of Canada; and, in April of 1947, when the bank's governor was named Canadian executive director of the International Bank for Reconstruction and Development, Gordon returned to full-time work as deputy governor. In 1947 he was appointed a director of the Central Mortgage and Housing Corporation, a Government agency, and in 1948 executive director of the International Bank for Reconstruction and Development.

Addressing the thirty-sixth National Foreign Trade Convention in New York (November 1949) on the subject "The World Trade Challenge to North America," Gordon expressed the view that the "dollar problem" required "that North America now replace Europe as the dynamic center and chief support of the world trade structure" (*Christian Science Monitor,* November 1, 1949). The same theme was presented in an article in the *United Nations World* (December 1949). His thesis was that the temporary expedient of loans to Europe has distracted attention from the fact that in the interests of a more stable prosperous world trade the American export surplus must be eliminated or greatly reduced by increased imports into North America. The Canadian banker suggested that both the Canadian and American tariffs tend to protect uneconomic industries and stated: "When action of this kind comes from North America, the home of free enterprise, that surely is an extraordinary state of affairs and suggests that economic thinking has not kept pace with economic change."

On January 1, 1950, Gordon went to the Canadian National Railways as president and chairman. In this position he is chief of Canada's largest employer (112,000 personnel) and biggest income-earner (about $500,000,000 in 1949). The C.N.R. has a coast-to-coast network of 24,179 miles of trackage, 3,318 of which traverse eleven American States. It also operates three steamship lines, twelve large hotels (including the Chateau Laurier in Ottawa), an express company, and a nation-wide telegraph system. Its total capital is one and a third billion dollars. The system originated at the end of World War I when the Canadian Government bought out several private trunk-line railways on the verge of financial collapse and amalgamated them with the Government-owned Intercolonial. The Canadian National Railways, as the new system was named, has had to make large fixed interest payments on the debt assumed by the Government to the original private owners, with the result that interpretation of its financial position is confused, and is a matter under consideration by the Royal Commission on Transportation.

One of Gordon's first acts in his new position was to request the Government to scale down the C.N.R.'s capital structure. Claiming that Canada's transportation needs are exceptional he has said: "The main trouble is that communications have moved so fast that we haven't had a chance to digest them. What is clear, however, is that the mode of transport required anywhere is the one that will give the best kind of service to the most people and, in Canada's case, open up the country. The essence of this business is providing transportation that makes economic sense, from trains to ships and from pipe lines to airplanes" (from the *Collier's* article). On his first day in office Gordon made a broadcast to the railroad's employees and the country at large, calling for a greater consciousness of Canada's growing achievement and the part played by her transportation systems; the country, he said, had been "built around her railways."

In 1926 Gordon married Maisie Barter, of St. John's, Newfoundland. Mrs. Gordon, who was widely known for her war service, died in 1950, leaving two sons, Donald Ramsay and Michael Huntley. Gordon is a Presbyterian. Proud of his Scottish birth, he has a repertoire of Scottish songs, which he accompanies on the accordion. The executive, who weighs 240 pounds and stands six feet four inches, has been described by the press as a "big, black, broad-shouldered Highlander." His hair and mustache are dark; he wears glasses. Gordon finds recreation in fishing, for which purpose he has built a cottage on Lustre Lake, north of Ottawa. In recognition of his wartime services he was made, in 1944, a Companion of the Order of St. Michael and St. George. He has received also an honorary LL.D. from Queens University. His clubs are the St. James's and Mount Royal (in Montreal), the Rideau (in Ottawa), and the Toronto.

References

Canadian Banker Spring '50
Canadian National Mag D '49
Christian Sci Mon p5 Ja 12 '42; p2 Mr 22 '47
Collier's 125:21 Jul 1 '50 por
N Y Times p39 O 13 '49
Newsweek 34:69 O 24 '49
Time 39:30 Mr 30 '42; 54:43 O 24 '49 por
Toronto Daily Star N 22 '41
Toronto Globe and Mail D 15 '41; Ja 3 '50
Toronto Star Weekly p2 Ap 25 '42
International Who's Who, 1949
Who's Who, 1950
Who's Who in America, 1950-51
Who's Who in Canada, 1947-48
World Biography (1948)

GOSHORN, CLARENCE B(AKER) (gŏs'hôrn) May 12, 1893—Dec. 10, 1950 Advertising executive

Bulletin: Clarence B. Goshorn died on December 10, 1950.

From March 1950 issue:

Clarence B. Goshorn, president of Benton & Bowles, Inc., advertising agency, in April 1949 became the chairman of the American Association of Advertising Agencies. His own firm annually places $39,000,000's worth of advertising in all media and employs approximately 440 people in its five offices in the United States and Canada. His term as A.A.A.A. chairman expired in April 1950.

Born May 12, 1893, in Saugatuck, Michigan, Clarence Baker Goshorn is the son of William Seward and Ida M. (Baker) Goshorn. The boy was graduated from the Central High School in Grand Rapids in 1911, and subsequently entered the University of Michigan, from which he received the B.A. degree with the Phi Beta Kappa honor in 1915. He was teaching history and rhetoric (after taking graduate studies in American history at that university in 1915-16) when the United States entered World War I. He joined the Army and served during 1917-18 as an instructor in bombing and bayonet tactics, with the rank of second lieutenant.

When the war ended Goshorn sought employment that would be more remunerative than teaching—he was now a family man, having been married on July 30, 1917, to Gladys Musselwhite, a newspaper writer who was also a University of Michigan graduate. The couple in 1919 went to Philadelphia where Goshorn took a post with the Curtis Publishing Company. As manager of its subscription department Goshorn directed the operations of a hundred subscription agencies which sold the Curtis magazines, *Country Gentleman, Ladies' Home Journal,* and *Saturday Evening Post.* It was Goshorn's special task to supervise the writing of sales letters and advertisements for the agencies.

After eleven years in the employ of the Curtis company, Goshorn left the publishing firm in

CLARENCE B. GOSHORN

1930. Following negotiations with Arthur Kudner, at that time the president of Erwin, Wasey & Company, he joined that New York advertising firm as an account executive. In this position he handled the accounts of Koppers Coke, Macfadden Publications, and Procter & Gamble; he also wrote some of the promotion material for General Foods products. Four years later (1934), Kudner resigned to form his own agency; Goshorn went with him. According to *Advertising Age*, Goshorn helped the new agency, Arthur Kudner, Inc., to obtain and develop the account of the Association of American Railroads, and worked on the accounts of United States Tobacco, Quaker Oats, the Anchor Steamship Line, and Koppers Coke.

In 1937 Goshorn joined the staff of Benton [45] and Bowles [43] Inc., as vice-president and account executive on Best Foods. Five years later (1942), when Chester Bowles was called to Washington to take the post of administrator of the Office of Price Administration, Goshorn was elected president of the advertising agency. (William Benton, who later became Assistant Secretary of State, in 1949 went to the United States Senate from Connecticut; and Bowles became Governor of that State.) Neither of the founders have been active for some years in the agency, which is owned by fifty active members of the firm. In its offices in New York, Cincinnati, Hollywood, Lakeland (Florida), and Toronto, Benton & Bowles employes some 550 people; its gross profits are approximately 15 per cent of the $39,000,000 its accounts expend for advertising in the various media—newspapers, magazines, radio, television, etc.

The advertising executive, who had been active for some years in committee work within the American Association of Advertising Agencies, in 1947 became its secretary-treas-

urer, in 1948 its vice-chairman in charge of its "area of ethics." His election to the chairmanship (of which the term is for a year) took place in April 1949. The organization, known as the "Four-A's," has a membership of more than two hundred advertising agencies (maintaining four hundred offices), which are admitted upon presentation of qualifications as to "experience, ability, character, ethical and business standards and financial responsibility." The three main aims of the association are: "to protect, strengthen, and improve the advertising agency business; to advance the cause of advertising as a whole; to give service to members." Its four major areas of activity for improvement are personnel, research, advertising content, and public relations.

In four speeches (at the 1949 convention) described by *Printers' Ink* as "well larded with infectious humor, and. . .delivered as though he really enjoyed sharing his fun and philosophy with the audience," Goshorn emphasized maintaining public esteem for advertising in a changing situation which saw the return of a buyer's market. "Advertising was made for a buyer's market—for a time when goods and services need to be sold," he said in part. "We have earned confidence by good performance when we didn't have much chance to be bad. Let's not lose it by reckless behavior when we have everything to gain by being good." He pointed to growth and "progressive adulthood" in the advertising of the past ten years.

Goshorn has laid special emphasis on the danger of keener competition developing into "a drug to conscience." To an *Advertising Age* reporter he commented that there was "a suspicious trickle of little things" not altogether ethical that might presage the "bursting of the dam"—the dam is the standards of practice laid down by the Four-A's.

Goshorn has helped raise funds for the Girl Scouts, the Metropolitan Museum of Art, and the Red Cross (he has been chairman of the publishers and advertisers division of the Red Cross campaign for Greater New York). One son, Robert, is head of research on *Country Gentleman*; the other son, William, is a metallurgist. Mrs. Goshorn, the author of the books *Do You Know Your Garden?* and *Plant Ecology*, lectures on that subject. The advertising executive shares his wife's interest in gardening, Chinese porcelains, and travel in Central America, to which they have made annual trips. In his reading, he may often turn to Shakespeare. Goshorn has been described as having something of a "collegiate air." He is five feet ten and a half inches tall, weighs 175 pounds, has blue eyes and gray hair. His bow tie, his habit of not wearing a hat, and his "relaxed" manner have been commented upon.

References

Adv Age p42-3 Ap 11 '49
Ed & Pub 82:5 Ap 9 '49
Ptr Ink 227:80 Ap 15 '49
Who's Who in America, 1948-49

GOSS, ALBERT S. Oct. 14, 1882—Oct. 25, 1950 Master of the National Grange, farmers' organization, since 1941; began as a bookkeeper in 1901, later engaged in cereal and flour milling, in operating a country store, and in telephone business; became a farmer about 1914; first identified with Grange affairs in 1920; master of the Washington State Grange from 1922 to 1933; director (1928-33) of the Federal Land Bank in Spokane; commissioner of the Federal Land Bank of the Farm Credit Administration, 1933-40; served as chairman of the executive committee of the National Grange, 1924-33; member of President's Committee on Mobilization at time of death; opposed Government's subsidy policy. See *Current Biography*, 1945.

Obituary

N Y Times p28 O 26 '50

GRACE, ALONZO G(ASKELL) Aug. 14, 1896- Educator

Address: h. Coventry, Conn.

A well-known educator in the United States, Alonzo G. Grace has served in several important administrative posts. For ten years he was Connecticut's Commissioner of Education, after which he became director of the Educational and Cultural Relations Division of the American Military Government in Germany. Upon his resignation in October 1949, Grace joined the faculty of University of Chicago's Department of Education. In December 1950 it was stated he would head the new Division of Advanced Study in the School of Education, New York University, in January 1951.

Alonzo Gaskell Grace was born August 14, 1896, in Morris, Minnesota, to Richard H. and Sarah Elizabeth (Murphy) Grace. His mother's ancestors came to the New World from Durham, England in 1687, settling in New Castle County, Delaware, and subsequently migrating to Illinois; while his father's family left Europe early in the nineteenth century. Both of his parents, who were born near Springfield, Illinois, moved to Minnesota in the early 1890's. After receiving his elementary education in a one-teacher rural school and graduating from a small village high school, Alonzo Grace entered the University of Minnesota to major in sociology and anthropology. He received his B.A. degree in 1917.

Upon his graduation (when the United States had entered World War I) Grace enlisted in the United States Army. From private he advanced to a second lieutenant in the 135th Infantry and the 76th Field Artillery. In 1919 he was assigned to Europe with the Army of Occupation, as leader of the 76th Field Artillery Band, having studied music in his earlier years. While in Europe he was granted a diploma from the American Musicians School in Chaumont, France, in 1919.

Returning to civilian life, young Grace obtained his M.A. from the University of Minnesota in the department of anthropology in 1920. After an additional year's graduate study in government, anthropology, and sociology (he

Wide World Photos

ALONZO G. GRACE

received a scholarship in 1919 and a fellowship in 1920), he served as instructor of anthropology at the university for the academic year 1921-22. The following year Grace left the university to teach social studies in rural schools, and from 1923 to 1925 he gave courses in the same subject at State Teachers College in Aberdeen, South Dakota.

In 1925 the educator went to Cleveland, Ohio, where for five years he was chairman of the adult education department of the Cleveland School of Education and, successively, assistant supervisor, supervisor, assistant director, and director of adult education on that board. In the latter capacity he made a survey of reading interests, adult abilities and aptitudes in the city, a study published in the *Journal of Educational Research* and the *Guidance Journal* (1929). In 1930 he joined the faculty of the University of Rochester, where for eight years he served as assistant and later as associate professor of administration in the department of education, and as assistant director of extension courses and director of summer sessions. It was in the field of administration that he received a Ph.D. degree from Western Reserve University, in Cleveland.

As Commissioner of Education for the State of Connecticut, a post which Grace held from 1938 to 1948, he applied theories of education which were later to have greater extension in his educational program for Germany. Summarizing his aims in an article in *School Management* (January 1948), the commissioner placed emphasis on the "movement to improve and strengthen local initiative and responsibility." The principles upon which such a movement must be based he outlined as the desirability of "growth from the bottom up" rather than "domination from the top down"; the concept of the local community as the democratic "cell" of our constitutional government; recognition of the

GRACE, ALONZO G.—*Continued*

responsibility of local boards of education, with the function of a State department remaining that of leadership, service and planning; and, in general, the need for democratizing and humanizing the administrative processes in education. In applying these principles to the school system of Connecticut, Grace made use of regional citizens' councils on educational problems, of research resources in such existing organizations as the American Association of University Women and the Parent-Teacher Association, and of advisory committees on specific problems. Albert I. Prince, member of the Connecticut Board of Education, speaking at a dinner given in honor of Grace on June 17, 1948, said: "Our Connecticut Regional Citizens' Councils and other groups by which public education gets closer to the people, to the grass roots of sympathy and support, is a pattern that the army hopes can be followed in Germany."

Preceding and during the decade of his work in Connecticut, Grace took part in several survey and research projects, including a study of the schools of Buffalo, New York, by the United States Office of Education (1932); a New York Regents' inquiry into the character and cost of education (1936-37); a survey of the educational system of the State of Washington by the State Planning Council, which Grace directed (1937-38); and a survey of the New Orleans public schools made by the Citizens' Committee for Public Education (1937-8). In 1939 he was a consultant for the Nebraska State Planning Council, the Citizens' Committee on Public Education of Rochester, the National Youth Administration, and other bodies. In the same year he was a member of the staff surveying the work of the Lincoln and Horace Mann schools in New York for Columbia University. Of his work as director of the Study of Armed Services Training and Education Programs and Implications for Civilian Schools and Colleges, completed in 1948, George F. Zook '46, president of the American Council on Education, said, "The volumes resulting from this study will be a lasting testimony to his planning and careful attention in a very important area of American education."

The office of director of the Education and Cultural Relations Division of the American Military Government in Germany was accepted by Grace in February 1948. At a conference of all professional personnel of the division held at Berchtesgaden October 7-12, 1948, the director stated his belief that "to establish a firm foundation for sound progress, the most important single step must be education at the grass roots level." Heading a staff of about 150 American educators, Grace attacked three immediate and specific tasks—the retraining of teachers, rewriting of textbooks, and revision of curricula. He emphasized in a booklet published by the Commission on the Occupied Areas of the American Council on Education (entitled *Basic Elements of Educational Reconstruction in Germany*) that his policy placed primary emphasis "on moral and spiritual matters, attitudes, cultural exchange, informal education activities,

education of teachers, machinery to establish democratic practices, rather than on the structure and organization of formal education."

At a conference held at Bad Nauheim in May 1949 Grace stressed the need for reforms, on the university level, of education in Germany, and outlined an expanded program of cultural exchange of teachers, administrators, professional men, and technical experts between Germany and the United States. He also urged the adoption of an "educational Marshall Plan," by means of which all nations involved in the European Recovery Program would "pool their educational resources . . . and, in general, cooperate to put education on a strong basis."

Dr. Grace resigned from his post in Germany in October 1949, by which time the Military Government had been superseded by the High Commissioner. The educator reportedly resigned "in disillusioned protest" (*Washington Post*) over the omission of an adequate educational program for the occupied country. In December, at the National Conference on the Occupied Countries (held in Washington and sponsored by the American Council on Education, assisted by the Department of State), when concern was voiced over evidence of revived nationalism in Germany, Grace was to say: "Had such a conference been held four years ago, I feel quite certain that a much more secure program would now prevail in Germany." In the fall of 1949 Grace had been appointed to the faculty of the Department of Education, University of Chicago, where he remained through the year 1950. Beginning January 1, 1951, he will head the new Division of Advanced Study in the School of Education, New York University.

Results of four of the surveys conducted by Dr. Grace have been published in book form: *State Aid and School Costs* (1939), *Educational Lessons from Wartime Training* (1948), *Tomorrow's Citizens* (1939), and *Education in the State of Washington*. Among his monographs, published by the Connecticut Department of Education, are *Living and Making a Living, Redirection of Education,* and *Learning to Make a Living.* Approximately one hundred articles by Grace have appeared in such educational journals as *School Executive, Education, School and Society,* and *The American School Board Journal,* as well as in the *Harvard Educational Review, Survey* and *State Government.*

The administrator is a member of the staff of the National Advisory Committee on Education. He served as director of field operations for pre-induction training in World War II (1942-44), and as a consultant to the War Department in 1945; he became consultant to the advisory commission of the Council of National Defense in 1940. Among other activities are membership on the board of directors of the Rochester School for the Deaf (1936), the Rochester Museum of Natural History (1936-38), the Monroe County (New York) Charter Commission, the Connecticut Teachers' Retirement Board (1938-48), the board of directors of the Town and County Officers Training School of New York (1936-46), and chairmanship of the Connecticut Public Library Committee (1939-48). He was a member of the Problems and Plans Committee of the American Council on Education from 1940 to 1944, was president of the Harvard Teachers' Association (1946-48), and has been on the Educational Policies Commission since 1948.

An instructor on the Yale faculty since 1940, Grace has lectured at Western Reserve University, Columbia, Harvard, Johns Hopkins, and the Universities of Chicago, Pittsburgh, and New York. In 1946 he was awarded an Sc.D. degree by Boston University. He belongs to the American Association of University Professors, the American Academy of Political and Social Science, the American Association for the Advancement of Science, the American Association of School Administrators, the National Education Association, the American Vocational Association, the American Society of Public Administration, and Phi Kappa Sigma. His clubs are the Hartford and the Yale Faculty Club. Married on June 18, 1921 to Jeannette Meland, Grace is the father of three sons, Alonzo Gaskell, Richard Simmons, and David Harlan. His church is the Congregational.

References

    Directory of American Scholars, 1942
    Leaders in Education (1948)
    Who's Who in America, 1948-1949
    Who's Who in New England (1949)
    Who's Who in the East (1948)
    World Biography (1948)

GRAHAM, CLARENCE R(EGINALD)
Feb. 28, 1907- Librarian; library association president

Address: b. c/o Louisville Free Public Library, Library Pl., Louisville 3, Ky.; h. 145 N. Crestmoor St., Louisville 6, Ky.

Clarence R. Graham, president of the American Library Association for the term 1950-51, assumed that office in July 1950, at the seventy-fourth convention of the association, held in Cleveland, Ohio. A member of the association since 1936, Graham has served on several of its committees, two of which he chaired. He was president of the Kentucky Library Association during 1946-47, and of the Southeastern Library Association during 1948-50. Since 1942 Graham, as chief librarian of the Louisville Free Public Library, has become known for the use he has made of the most modern audio-visual equipment in widening library service.

Of Scottish and Irish ancestry, Clarence Reginald Graham (who prefers the nickname "Skip," by which he is usually called) was born February 28, 1907, to Samuel J. and Lillian Ellen (Paris) Graham. His father was a lumber manufacturer (this had also been the business of Mrs. Graham's father) in Louisville, Kentucky; and it was there that the boy was born and that he and his only sister were reared. Graham has said that everyone in his father's family taught school sometime and that his sister became a teacher. He attended the R. J. Reynolds High School in Winston

Salem, North Carolina, until 1924, and while there was business manager for the high school yearbook. From 1924 to 1927 he studied at the University of North Carolina, where he was student assistant in the university library. Graham has indicated that his contact with Dr. Louis R. Wilson, who was the university's librarian, and with Charles M. Baker, assistant librarian, was of influence in his choice of the same profession. During his last two years at the university the student was field representative for the North Carolina State Department of Health.

Returning to Louisville, Graham worked in the department of statistics of the Brown and Williamson Tobacco Company during 1929-30. In the latter year he entered the library field, to serve until 1934 as librarian of the Parkland Junior High Schol in that city. At the same time attending the University of Louisville, he received the B.A. degree in 1934, then proceeded to the School of Library Science of Western Reserve University in Cleveland, Ohio, to earn the B.S. in 1935. The next year he spent as assistant to the librarian of the Louisville Free Public Library.

In 1936 Graham was appointed director of the library of the National College of Education, located in Evanston, Illinois. He remained in this post until 1942, in which year he was appointed chief librarian of the Louisville Free Public Library. (While in Evanston, he took postgraduate work at Northwestern University, during the year 1937-38.) In 1946 the librarian assumed the duties of instructor in library science at the University of Louisville. Two years later he was cofounder, with the university, of "Neighborhood Colleges," a system of college courses given by University of Louisville faculty members to classes held in library branches, using such library facilities as free books and audio-visual equipment.

As Louisville's chief librarian, Graham has made a name for himself as a progressive by working to put into effect his definition of a library, (as reported in "People Listen to 'Skip' Graham," *Library Journal*, October 1949): "A library is a collection of materials organized for use. By materials I mean everything from a book to a museum piece, or from a television set to a microcard reader. By organized for use I mean using all the techniques from cataloging to the latest commercial advertising methods taking library materials to the public quickly, effectively, and simply." Innovations introduced in Louisville under Graham's leadership include: linking by wire of the central library and the university with ten branches, sixteen high schools, and several hospital wards for the transmission of music and educational matter (the library-university link is 2-way); lecture series on the classics, with discussion periods; "Introduction to Music," a series of lectures on the practice and history of music, with the Louisville Philharmonic Orchestra participating; the "Neighborhood Colleges"; an audio-visual department, which supplies films, transcriptions of educational programs, records, a microcard service, etc.; television receivers installed in the main library and all branches (book circulation is

CLARENCE R. GRAHAM

reported to have increased appreciably since TV was installed); a 250-watt frequency-modulation broadcasting station operated by the library, carrying educational and cultural programs (WFPL—the first library-operated FM radio station in the United States.)

Graham has explained that the emphasis on facilities for adult education is deliberate, while pointing out that at the same time work with children is receiving due attention. The library's services represent "a unique enterprise in adult education," Graham is quoted as saying in an article in the Louisville *Courier-Journal* (July 18, 1948), which mentioned that the library had been given $50,000 by the city to help expand the audio-visual program. Some day Graham hopes to see the library housed in a skyscraper building, "paying its way" by renting out the lower floors. Tribute was paid to the librarian's contribution to the functioning of the library in the community by the publisher of the Louisville *Times* and *Courier-Journal* when he said: "Skip has made the library a living reality instead of a depository of books" (*Library Journal*).

The new A.L.A. president's participation in American Library Association activities dates from 1936, when he became a member. Within that organization he has been Kentucky State chairman of the membership committee (1948); program consultant of the public libraries division (1948); chairman of the committee on radio and television (1949). In 1949, at a special session of the council (by petition of twelve council members) Graham's nomination for the post of A.L.A. first vice-president and president-elect was added to the official ballot drawn up by the nominations committee. The announcement that the Louisville librarian had been elected to the office was made August 22, 1949,

at the Far West Regional Conference (of A.L.A.) in Vancouver, British Columbia; he took office as first vice-president on November 23, 1949. In the presidency he succeeded Milton Lord '⁵⁰, his installation taking place at the July 1950 conference of the association. Since he is president for the 1950-51 term, he will preside at the observance of the seventy-fifth anniversary of the association, to be held at Chicago in 1951.

The American Library Association, founded in Philadelphia in 1876, is an organization of some 19,000 librarians, libraries, library trustees, and other friends of libraries, primarily of the United States and Canada. Following the concept that "libraries exist to make books useful to people," the organization has stressed library participation in adult education, and advocated State aid to libraries and the establishment of county and regional libraries to increase the efficiency of service to the rural population. The association, whose headquarters are in Chicago, maintains an office in Washington "to facilitate participation in programs relative to library service." Publications with the A.L.A. imprint include numerous books and pamphlets as well as several periodicals.

Prior to becoming A.L.A. president, Graham was president of the Southeastern Library Association during 1948-50, president of the Kentucky Library Association, 1946-47. He is a member of the Kentucky State Board of Certification of Librarians. Articles by him on library science and educational films have appeared in various books and periodicals. For the year 1948-49 he was president of the Louisville Library Club. Other community projects in which Graham has participated include: the war recreation committee of the Louisville Defense Council (chairman); the Louisville Family Service Organization; the Community Chest; the Louisville Area Veterans Clearing House Association; the health and welfare division of the council of social agencies of the Louisville Urban League. A strong supporter of harmonious relations among all cultural organizations, he is a member of the citizens advisory committee of the College of Arts and Sciences of the University of Louisville. In 1949 he became a member of the Newcomen Society of England. He belongs to the Filson, Arts, and Quindecim clubs.

Graham married Esther Charlotte Lothman, a librarian, on February 28, 1930; they have one daughter, Carolyn. In political affiliation he is a Democrat, and his church is the Presbyterian. Of large stature, he has a height of five feet eleven inches, a weight of 195 pounds; his hair is brown, his eyes are gray-blue. The librarian is a man of lively temperament.

References

Am Lib Assn Bul 43:263 S '49
Library J 74:1405 O '49
Newsweek 35:79 Mr 6 '50 por

Leaders in Education (1948)
Who's Who in America, 1950-51
Who's Who in Library Service (1943)

GRAHAM, HARRY CHRYSOSTOM, REV. Sept. 4, 1901- Roman Catholic priest; organization director

Address: b. and h. c/o Holy Name Society, 141 E. 65th St., New York 21

The Very Reverend Harry Chrysostom Graham, O.P., (within the Dominican Order, of the Order of Preachers devoted to preaching, literary and scientific pursuits) is the national director of the Holy Name Society. This Roman Catholic organization, which in 1950 comprises an estimated three and one half to four million men in the United States, Canada, and the Philippines, is dedicated to "personal sanctification, the public manifestation of faith, and the promotion of reverence for the person and name of Jesus Christ, the Savior." In its social and educational program it works with boys in study groups, social action clubs, in music, dramatics, and other activities. Father Graham came to his post in 1939 after seven years as a teacher, including four years as professor of education at the De Paul University in Chicago.

One of three sons, Harry Chrysostom Graham was born September 4, 1901, in New Haven, Connecticut, which was his childhood home. His father, John Henry Graham, a post office employee, was born in Edinburgh, Scotland, of Irish parents en route to America; his mother was the former Mary Gertrude McAllister. The family history shows many examples of lives devoted to the work of the Church: John Graham had a cousin and nephew who were priests, three cousins who were monks; Mrs. Graham's sister and aunt were nuns, a brother was a priest. Thus the thought of being a priest was always more or less in the background of his thinking, Father Graham has said.

The boy was sent to a boarding school, Aquinas College High School in Columbus, Ohio, a Dominican preparatory school. There his extracurricular interests included football and baseball, and the school dramatics society. Graduated in 1921, he went to Providence (Rhode Island) College from which college he received the B.A. degree in 1925. His major study was philosophy, his club a dramatics group, and his athletic interests football and baseball. After his graduation he began his years of preparation for the priesthood at Catholic University of America, (Washington, D.C.). In 1930 at the age of twenty-nine he was ordained a member of the Order of Preachers of the Dominican Order at St. Dominic's Church, Washington. In 1932 Catholic University awarded him the Master of Arts degree in the philosophy and psychology of education.

The priest's first post was as teacher of mathematics and vocational director in a Dominican school in a suburb of Chicago, the Fenwick High School in Oak Park. This post he filled for seven years, in the meantime continuing his studies in education: at the University of Pennsylvania in 1933 he studied teaching methods in secondary schools, and at the University of Wisconsin (1934) principles of vocational guidance. For four of those years

REV. HARRY CHRYSOSTOM GRAHAM

(1934-38) he was a professor of education in the graduate school of De Paul University, giving courses in the history, psychology, and principles of education. He also gave week-end courses to teachers at Aquinas College High School.

In January 1939 the Very Reverend Harry C. Graham was called to New York to be named the fifth national director of the Holy Name Society. The group traces its origin to 1274 when Pope Gregory X entrusted to the Dominican Order the duties the society still fulfills under Dominican leadership. As stated in the *Catholic Encyclopedia*, "The primary objective of the society is to beget due love and reverence for the Holy Name of God and Jesus Christ." Another of its objectives is to suppress blasphemy, perjury, profanity, improper language, and, as far as the members can, to prevent such offenses in others. Members are granted special indulgences, and are required to receive Holy Communion in a body at least once a month. The society was organized on a national scale in the United States in 1909, with headquarters in New York, and in 1910 had 500,000 members; in forty years the organization has increased its membership sevenfold. When Father Graham assumed the directorship, the society used the services of three lay persons and two priests; in 1950 seven priests, in addition to Father Graham, and sixteen lay persons conduct the headquarters work of the organization.

As director of the Holy Name Society, Father Graham has established Holy Name Unions, centralized organizations of the society, in the archdioceses and dioceses of the nation. From approximately nine thousand units in 1939, the national director has seen the society grow to 14,100 parish units. Holy Name officers training groups were promoted under his guidance, and handbooks published for both officers and spiritual directors. Before the Japanese attack on Pearl Harbor the priest had founded the

GRAHAM, HARRY CHRYSOSTOM, REV.—*Continued*

first military unit of the Holy Name at the Marine Corps base in Quantico, Virginia, in December 1940. When the United States entered the war, Father Graham, working with military chaplains, supervised from his office the establishment of 732 Holy Name units at bases and on ships where American Armed Forces were stationed all over the world. Father Graham was also responsible for supplying servicemen with prayer books and other literature, and with religious articles such as rosaries and Holy Name medals.

The priest is also editor of the *Holy Name Journal*, subtitled "A National Magazine for Men." Published since 1907, the periodical has a circulation of 43,000. The March 1950 issue carried, in his monthly column (*News and Views*), Father Graham's description of his first trip abroad, in January 1950, to Fátima in Portugal, and to Rome, where he had a private audience with Pope Pius XII '50. During this visit he arranged an audience with the Pope for an expected 2,000 Holy Name pilgrims to Rome during the 1950 Holy Year. (The all-expense tours arranged by the society provide for a visit to Rome and shrines elsewhere in Europe.) Two of the magazine's departments are given over to notes on the current scene and on labor-management relations.

Other literature published by the Holy Name Society under Father Graham's direction includes the "Theology for the Layman" series, a pamphlet course presenting the *Summa Theologica* of St. Thomas Aquinas in popular form. Of the projected 138 pamphlets, thirty-three were available in March 1950. Over one million copies of the pamphlets *The Rosary Crusade* and *Rosaries for Russia* were published in connection with the society's "crusade of prayer for the conversion of Communistic Russia." It has also issued short articles on John of Vercelli, the father of the Holy Name movement. (The Society has awarded since 1947 an annual Vercelli medal, its highest honor, for service to the organization.)

The "public demonstrations of faith" by the members of the society include annual processions, rallies, and outdoor Holy Name Hours. At the fourth national Holy Name convention in Boston in October 1947, 130,000 men assembled for the parade closing the convention; the business sessions and faith demonstrations of the convention constituted what the society has called "one of the largest religious undertakings seen in this country." Father Graham has recalled how he twice marched the parade route and then reviewed the men marching eighteen abreast for nine hours.

In 1947 Rome conferred on Father Graham the Cross of the Knights of Malta. A member of the Catholic War Veterans, he was awarded that group's Order of St. Sebastian in 1944. He also has membership in the Knights of Columbus. The blue-eyed, red-haired priest is one inch under six feet in height, 215 pounds in weight. He retains his interest in sports.

Reference

Who's Who in America, 1950-51

GRANVILLE, WILLIAM SPENCER LEVESON-GOWER, 4TH EARL (lōō's'n-gōr) July 11, 1880- Governor of Northern Ireland

Address: Government House, Hillsborough, County Down, Northern Ireland; Stone Park, Staffordshire, England

William Spencer Leveson-Gower, fourth Earl Granville, is the Governor of Northern Ireland, the post to which he was appointed in 1945 after seven years as Lieutenant Governor of the Isle of Man. That had followed upon nearly forty years as officer in the Royal Navy, from which he retired in 1935 in the rank of vice-admiral.

William Spencer Leveson-Gower was born July 11, 1880, younger son of Granville George, the second Earl (a statesman who filled several ministerial posts) by his second wife, Castalia Rosalind, youngest daughter of Walter Frederick Campbell, of the Isle of Islay, Scotland. The Leveson-Gowers (some branches use a hyphen, others not), a distinguished English family, have contributed notable names to the Army, the Navy, and the Government. The Granville peerage dates from 1815 as a viscounty and from 1833 as an earldom. In 1939, on the death without issue of his elder brother, Granville George, third Earl, William Spencer succeeded as fourth Earl, with the subsidiary titles of Viscount Granville and Baron Leveson, of Stone. Countess Granville, whom he had married in 1916, is the former Lady Rose Constance Bowes-Lyon, second daughter of the 14th Earl of Strathmore and Kinghorne; she is thus a sister of the Queen of England, who was Lady Elizabeth Bowes-Lyon. Their son, Granville James, Lord Leveson, in 1950 is a major in the Coldstream Guards. There is also a daughter, Lady Mary Cecilia Leveson-Gower.

Leveson-Gower entered the Royal Navy as a cadet on board H.M.S. *Britannia* at the age of fourteen, and received the education and training of a naval officer. From his training ship he passed out as a midshipman in 1896, and served for three years on the China station in H.M.S. *Narcissus*. In 1899 he joined the *Cleopatra*, and took part in the last cruise of the "Mast and Yard" training squadron, which was paid off at the outbreak of the South African War. He was promoted to the rank of sub-lieutenant in April 1900, and of lieutenant in June 1902, having served in the destroyers *Sylvia* and *Star*. The naval officer then spent nearly six years in the northeastern and southern seas off Africa. During 1902 and 1903 he was in the Red Sea, in operations against slave traders and piracy. Toward the end of this period he made a journey through the Yemen. From 1904 to 1907 he was on the Cape station in the first-class cruiser, *Crescent*.

Then came a stretch of seventeen years' service in destroyers and destroyer leaders. During World War I, having become commander in June 1913, Leveson-Gower served with the Grand Fleet Flotillas, commanding destroyer divisions successively in the *Comet*, the *Marmion* and the *Scott*. April 22 and 23, 1918, brought the raid on Zeebrugge harbor under Sir Roger

Keyes, and Leveson-Gower was in one of the destroyers taking part. He was promoted to a captaincy in June 1918. A few months later (in August) he narrowly escaped death when his ship, the *Scott*, blew up. After becoming destroyer captain in the Grand Fleet, he was assigned to peacetime duty, from January 1919 to 1921 in the Mediterranean being chiefly employed in operations against the Bolsheviks in the Black Sea. The war brought him the Distinguished Service Order (1919), the Order of the Redeemer, of Greece, and the Russian Order of St. Anne. From 1922 to 1924 he was destroyer captain at Devonport.

There followed three years, 1924-27, on a home station as Chief of Staff and Maintenance Captain to the Commander-in-Chief, The Nore; then two years on the China station commanding the new eight-inch gun cruiser, *Cornwall*. In 1929 Leveson-Gower served as a naval aide-de-camp to King George V, and was promoted to be Rear Admiral. From 1931 to 1933 he was Rear Admiral Commanding, Coast of Scotland. He was made Companion of the Bath (Military) in 1932. In May 1935 he received the rank of Vice-Admiral, and the same year retired from the Navy.

Following a tradition of Government service common among distinguished British soldiers and sailors, Leveson-Gower accepted in July 1937 the office of Lieutenant Governor of the Isle of Man. This small island of 221 square miles' area lies in the Irish Sea off the northwest coast of England. It runs its own budget, levies its own taxes, and is largely autonomous, being governed in accordance with its own laws by an assembly called the Court of Tynwald, on whose Legislative Council the Governor sits. Leveson-Gower's term of office was extended a year from September 1944. In July 1945 King George VI visited the island to preside over a session of Tynwald (being the first British monarch to do so). During his visit he knighted Granville (as he had now become) as K.C.V.O. (Knight Commander of the Victorian Order) and honored his lady similarly as D.C.V.O. (Dame Commander).

In July 1945 Granville was appointed Governor of Northern Ireland, and assumed the duties of this viceregal post (salaried at £8,000 annually) on September 7 of that year. By the Government of Ireland Act, 1920, as amended by the Irish Free State Act, 1922, provision was made for the setting up of a separate parliament and executive government for Northern Ireland within the United Kingdom. (The term "Ulster" was not used officially, though it is often heard unofficially, because three counties of the old Province of Ulster, Donegal, Cavan, and Monaghan, became part of the Irish Free State.) The six parliamentary counties composing Northern Ireland, Antrim, Armagh, Down, Fermanagh, Londonderry and Tyrone, and the county boroughs of Belfast and Londonderry have continued to return a majority of Unionist (pro-British) party members to the Parliament. In the 1949 election that party won 37 of the 48 seats, the remaining 11 being occupied by the Nationalists, who

Wide World Photos
THE EARL GRANVILLE

oppose the division of the island into Northern Ireland and the Republic of Ireland. The bill on Ireland, passed in London on May 17, 1949, recognizing the Republic of Ireland as an independent country outside the Commonwealth, provided for Northern Ireland to remain in the United Kingdom until its own Parliament should decide otherwise. Since the constitution reserves certain legislative and fiscal powers to the United Kingdom parliament, twelve Northern Irish members are returned to the latter. The legislative power of Northern Ireland resides in a parliament consisting of the Sovereign, represented by the Governor, a Senate, and a House of Commons. Vested with executive power, on the advice of Ministers responsible to Parliament, the Governor summons, prorogues, and dissolves Parliament in His Majesty's name and gives or withholds the Royal Assent to bills passed by both Houses. His term of office is six years.

Earl Granville has been awarded an honorary LL.D. degree by Queen's University, Belfast, and was made honorary colonel of the Fifteenth Light Anti-Aircraft Regiment in 1939. He is chairman of the board of the Lilleshall Company. His club is the United Service. Described by an official who knows him as dignified yet friendly in manner, he is a man of few words, always to the point. In moments of relaxation, when he often smokes a pipe, he enjoys telling and listening to good stories. The tall and powerfully built Governor of Northern Ireland is keenly interested in boxing and fencing: president of the British Amateur Fencing Association and of the All England Fencing Club, he was Scottish international for sabre and épée from 1931 to 1939 and British international for sabre in 1937. He is fond of shooting, fishing, gardening, and golf.

(Continued next page)

GRANVILLE, WILLIAM SPENCER LEVESON-GOWER, 4TH EARL—*Cont.*

References

Belfast News-Letter Jl 3 '45
The Times (London) F 25 '31
Burke's Peerage (1949)
Debrett's Peerage (1945)
Who's Who, 1950

GREGG, ALAN *See* Mallette, G. E.

GREEN, MARTYN Apr. 22, 1899- Singer; actor

Address: b. c/o D'Oyly Carte Opera Company, London; h. Savage Club, 1 Carlton House Terrace, London, S.W.1.

A leading performer in London's D'Oyly Carte Opera Company, which presented the favorite Gilbert and Sullivan operettas in its first postwar tour in America in the 1947-48 season, Martyn Green has scored a success that is considered the more remarkable in that he succeeded to the roles of a famous man. Sir Henry Alfred Lytton, a mainstay of the D'Oyly Carte Company, gave his last performance at Dublin's Gaiety Theatre in June 1934, and thereafter Green was given all his parts. The latter had played minor roles when the company toured the United States in 1928-29; he was an important member of the cast in its 1934, 1936, and 1939 seasons in that country. In 1947-48, when the company spent seventeen weeks in New York, Green received a particularly enthusiastic press for his renderings in *H. M. S. Pinafore, Iolanthe, The Yeomen of the Guard, The Mikado,* and other Gilbert and Sullivan roles.

Born in London, April 22, 1899, and christened William Martyn, Green is the son of William Green, a well-known concert tenor, and Sarah Ann (Martin) Green. He was educated at Latymer Upper School, Hammersmith, London. "I have a vague idea that my father knew Sullivan," he told a *New Yorker* interviewer in January 1948. "I have an equally hazy idea that I once sat on Gilbert's knee." Singing was definitely "in the family." Green's father had studied under Manuel García (who had taught Jenny Lind) and more extensively under his son, Gustave, who was also to teach Martyn.

In April 1915, when he was nearly sixteen years old, young Green, falsifying his age, joined the British army. After a few months the deception was discovered and the boy was discharged; but a clerical error on his discharge papers gave his age as eighteen, so he was able to enlist again in September, and was duly trained and ordered to France. In 1918 he was in the Monchy sector as a lance corporal in the Royal Fusiliers when he was badly wounded by a shellburst. The whole of his left side was badly lacerated and his left knee shattered. He spent many months on crutches and for some time it seemed that he might always have to use two canes. However, by 1921 he had regained full use of his wounded

leg, though retaining a degree of weakness in it which precludes his putting his whole weight on it; to this disability is ascribed certain of the eccentricities which characterize his style of dancing in Gilbert and Sullivan roles.

After demobilization, in February 1919 Green, persuading Robert Evett, a theatrical manager, to give him a "walk-on" part, made his first stage appearance at the Theatre Royal, Nottingham, in the chorus of a musical called *A Southern Maid.* He won a scholarship to the Royal College of Music, and studied there (under Gustave García) from 1919 to 1921. His first appearance in London took place September 1921 at the Palladium in a sketch, *Thirty Minutes of Melody.* In November 1922 began his long connection (broken only by World War II) with the D'Oyly Carte Opera Company. "I just walked into the London offices," he told the *New Yorker,* "and got a job, which is something very few people could do now."

The world-famous D'Oyly Carte Opera Company maintains the tradition of the old forms and procedures in its presentation of Gilbert and Sullivan operettas, the original manuscript orchestrations of which are in its possession, together with Gilbert's notes on accompanying stage business. Every member of the cast is required to undergo rigorous training in the chorus, whether or not he or she is understudying leading roles. Founded in 1876 as the Comedy Opera Company by Richard D'Oyly Carte, concert and lecture manager responsible for bringing together Gilbert and Sullivan, the company was formed for the express purpose of continuing the collaboration of the librettist and composer, and the production of their works under D'Oyly Carte's management. So successful were the productions, that in 1881 the manager was able to build the Savoy Theatre in London especially for the presentation of Gilbert and Sullivan comic operas. From this association, the latter came to be kown as the Savoy operas, and their admirers as Savoyards. (Richard's son, Rupert D'Oyly Carte [45], was the company's proprietor from 1913 until his death.)

Engaged in 1922 as a member of the chorus and understudy, Martyn Green later advanced to play Luiz, in *The Gondoliers,* and other small parts. In 1923, while playing in a second company at Westcliff-on-Sea, he got his first chance in a major part. At the end of the first act of *The Mikado* the performer playing the role of Ko-Ko fell ill, and Green took over for the rest of the performance. During the 1926 season at Prince's Theatre, in London, he appeared as Major Murgatroyd in *Patience;* the Associate, in *Trial by Jury;* and Cox in the F.C. Burnand-Arthur Sullivan opera, *Cox and Box.* A Canadian tour was made in 1927 by the first company, of which Green was now a member, and during 1928-29 he played with it in various towns in Canada and the Western United States, returning in November 1929 to the Savoy Theatre in London, where he again played Murgatroyd, and became understudy for Sir Henry Lytton.

On September 26, 1932, at the Savoy, came a real "trial by jury," (in the words of the London *News Chronicle*), when Green took over from Lytton a major role. "No singer or actor ever made a more difficult debut," said that paper, "than Mr. Martyn Green, appearing as Major General Stanley in *The Pirates of Penzance* last night. Not only was his great predecessor, Sir Henry Lytton, watching the performance, but the audience contained many people who knew every word and note of the opera, and every gesture and feature of Lytton's interpretation of the role. . . .The verdict was favorable to Mr. Green." The London *Times*: "Mr. Martyn Green showed that he had learnt every tradition of the part and could rattle off the famous patter-song like a machine-gun."

Green succeeded to all the Lytton parts in the autumn of 1934, and at a New York season beginning in September of that year at the Martin Beck Theatre, played the Duke of Plaza-Toro, in *The Gondoliers*; the Lord Chancellor, in *Iolanthe*; Ko-Ko, in *The Mikado*; Sir Joshua Porter, in *H.M.S. Pinafore*; and sundry other of the major roles. Early in March 1935 he was interviewed by the Washington correspondent of the London *Morning Post* on what impressed him most about a highly successful season. "We are getting Gilbert's humor across the footlights to our American audiences," said Green. "Gilbert's jokes came to them fresh and to the point, and were laughed at as jokes—the laughter was not part of the traditional ceremonial practised by all Gilbert and Sullivan devotees."

Until the company was disbanded in September 1939 because of the imminence of World War II, Green continued to perform leading roles with it, and was a member of the cast which played in the United States earlier that year. In 1938 he made his only screen appearance as of 1950 as Ko-Ko in *The Mikado*. February 1940 found him in a show called *Lights Up*, playing at the Savoy Theatre. On its conclusion, Green, then forty-one, joined the Royal Air Force. Too old for operational duty, he served as an administrative officer, lecturing on airmanship and discipline. In 1944 he produced and acted in *Charley's Aunt* in India, as a British troop entertainment. He had joined as a pilot officer (the lowest commissioned rank, not necessarily connoting any piloting). In due course he learned to fly, and emerged from the service as squadron leader (equivalent to army major). He took a year's vacation before returning to the stage.

The D'Oyly Carte company returned to New York in December 1947, with Green in its ranks, and so great was the success of the Savoyard season that it was extended by seven weeks. While by tradition the Gilbert and Sullivan company is regarded as a unit, with individual members of the cast forbidden to acknowledge any applause as personal, reviewers did not subject themselves to this strict code, but were enthusiastic in their praise of the leading performers, frequently devoting a large part of their reviews to Green's work. After the opening performance of the season, *The Mikado*, William Hawkins in the New York *World-Telegram* commented on Green's playing: "He has control over his body in comic

Valentine, London

MARTYN GREEN

pantomime that is as deft as a card sharp's over his fingers. He can roll on the floor, or climb up the scenery with such aplomb that he is startlingly funny. He has a sense of timing that often makes his silent movement seem strictly orchestrated." "Stars or no stars," declared Howard Barnes (*Herald Tribune*), Martyn Green is the wheel-horse of the company. . . .His agility is pronounced, but it is in perfect keeping with the nature of his assignments. His patter songs are virtually a trademark of D'Oyly Carte presentations. His acting has an extraordinary range, as he can turn from the sheer clowning of *The Mikado* to the poignant miming of Jack Point in the final scenes of *The Yeomen of the Guard*. It would be hard to find a substitute for Green."

Martyn Green has a light baritone voice, which has been found eminently adapted to the rendering of Gilbertian roles; he is not, however, known as an outstanding solo singer. A few have found him "entirely too frisky." In this connection Green told Russell Rhodes of the New York *Herald Tribune*: "Gilbert wanted, above all, a lively show. Gilbert also wanted personality. He must have taken into consideration the player's intelligence and met him half way on whatever business was introduced into the pieces. This has been passed along by word of mouth down the years. It cannot be unalterable, but it must seem in tradition, according to our best understanding of how it was done in Gilbert's own day and, at the same time, preserve the illusion of freshness." In a comment on the D'Oyly Carte recordings of the operettas, Howard Taubman of the New York *Times* wrote of the singers: "They convey, even on records, their delight in

GREEN, MARTYN—*Continued*

the repertory that amounts to a career for them."

Green married Joyce Mary Fentem on November 30, 1933, with Sir Henry Lytton as a witness. His club is the Savage (reputed to be the most pleasantly informal of London's clubs), frequented largely by authors, actors, painters, and scientists. Riding and golf provide his recreation.

References

N Y Herald Tribune V p1 Ja 4 '48
New Yorker 23:16 Ja 31 '48
Who's Who in the Theatre (1947)

GREEN, THEODORE FRANCIS Oct. 2, 1867- United States Senator from Rhode Island

Address: b. Senate Office Bldg., Washington 25, D.C. and 32 Westminster St., Providence 3, R.I.; h. University Club, Washington 6, D.C.; 14 John St., Providence 6, R.I.

Theodore Francis Green, Democrat, who in 1950 is serving his third term as United States Senator from Rhode Island, was elected to Congress after he had been Governor of his State for two terms (1932-36). In Washington his record has been that of a strong supporter of the Administrations of President Roosevelt and President Truman, in both their domestic and foreign policies.

Of Colonial ancestry, Theodore Francis Green was born October 2, 1867, in Providence, Rhode Island, the son of Arnold and Cornelia Abby (Burges) Green. The eldest of six children who lived to maturity, he was tutored at home for some years—as a child he suffered from a respiratory illness and malarial fever. In due course Green was graduated from the Providence High School in 1883, whereupon he entered Brown University to major in mathematics and Greek. Graduating in 1887 with the degree of Bachelor of Arts, he received the Master of Arts degree from the same university a year later. He attended Harvard Law School from 1888 to 1890, which was followed by study in Germany at the Universities of Bonn and Berlin from 1890 to 1892.

Green was admitted to the Rhode Island bar in 1892, in keeping with the family tradition in which the eldest son for four generations had become a lawyer. Two years later he was admitted to the United States Circuit Court and also joined his father's law office. From 1894 to 1897 he taught Roman law at Brown University. In the Spanish-American War, Green was commissioned a first lieutenant and commanded a provisional company of infantry. Following his father's death in 1903, he continued practice alone, and in 1905 was admitted to the United States Supreme Court bar. Next year (1906) he became senior member of the firm Green, Hinckley and Allen, and, subsequently, in 1923 of Green, Curran and Hart. When the latter was dissolved in 1926 Green again resumed practice alone.

The attorney began his political career in the Rhode Island House of Representatives, to

which he was elected for the term of 1907-8. There he advocated the abolition of the personal property qualification required of voters, and drafted and procured the passage of a bill punishing bribery of voters. Green was the Democratic candidate for Governor of the State in 1912, the year he was a delegate to the Democratic national convention (in Baltimore) which nominated Woodrow Wilson for President (he subsequently was sent as delegate to all the Democratic conventions) and was also a Presidential elector. He was chairman of the Democratic State Convention in 1914, and was chairman of the Democratic State Central Committee in 1929 and 1930, since which year he has been a member of the executive committee.

During World War I Green was active in war effort, serving on the Rhode Island Council of Defense, with the "Four-Minute Men," and the Rhode Island War Service Committee of the American Library Association. He was, too, chairman of the American Citizenship Campaign, director of War Savings for Rhode Island, commander in the Providence Special Constabulary, and a member in various Brown University programs concerned with the national emergency.

Green was an unsuccessful candidate for the United States Congress in 1920 and for Governor of Rhode Island in 1928 and 1930. Successful in his third attempt to win the governorship, in 1932, Green gave unemployment relief precedence over other legislation. He was also at this time serving as president and director of the Rhode Island Emergency Public Works Corporation (1932-36). In the fall of 1934 he conferred with President Roosevelt on the textile strike crisis at Saylesville and Woonsocket that had forced the Governor to call out the State militia. During his second term (1935-36) Green approved an old age pension bill for those over sixty-five and completed the reorganization of the State government.

Green, who has been a member of the Democratic National Committee since 1936, has been elected to the United States Senate for three terms, in 1936, 1942, and 1948. From the first Green gave vigorous support to the New Deal measures of President Roosevelt, and later to the Truman Administration. Among the domestic issues he favored were the Supreme Court retirement bill, the wages and hours bill, and the Wagner low-cost housing bill in 1937. An advocate of farm and work relief measures, Green voted for continuing appropriations for relief (1939), the Public Works Administration (1939), the Civilian Conservation Corps (1940), the National Youth Administration (1943), and for the Farm Security Administration (1943).

Consistently casting his "aye" for national defense legislation, Green backed expansion of naval power and of the armed forces from as early as 1937. In 1943 he assailed former President Hoover's suggestion that the potential size of the army be reduced by making one million more workers available for farms, mines, and oil production; and the March 17 Senate roll call recorded the Senator's stand against blanket deferment for farm labor. In

July of the same year a bill introduced by Green providing for the release of Government-owned silver for war purposes became a law. With Senator Scott W. Lucas [47] of Illinois, in October Green offered a Federal ballot bill to facilitate servicemen's voting, an Administration-sanctioned measure. Precipitating a bitter and extended controversy over States' rights, the bill was amended to the extent that Green dropped his support and President Roosevelt allowed it to become a law without his signature in March 1944. In August an amendment proposed by Green and Lucas that would liberalize political propaganda restrictions of the Servicemen's Voting Act won Senate approval.

The Rhode Island legislator, while serving as chairman of the Senate Committee on Campaign Expenditures during 1944 and 1945, was called upon to investigate complaints of violations of the Hatch Act, which limited campaign contributions. In May 1944 he heard charges against the Political Action Committee of the CIO, and alleged gifts to a W. Lee O'Daniel [47] publication at Fort Worth, Texas (an anti-Roosevelt newspaper) were investigated in October. In its report in 1945, the committee, noting evasion on a national scale, labeled the Hatch Act "unrealistic," and urged its repeal. "Publicity and public opinion," Green felt, would be better restraints than arbitrary limits. As chairman of the Committee on Privileges and Elections in 1946, Green investigated the nature of Senator Theodore G. Bilbo's primary campaign in Mississippi. In response to President Truman's request for a law placing the Speaker of the House second in line for the Presidency, Green sponsored a proposal to set up a joint Congressional committee to study such a measure; however, he voted against the bill as it was finally revised (1947).

During his second term in Washington Senator Green continued in his support of social legislation. In 1945 he offered a social security extension bill; joined the fight for Federal aid to education with the introduction of a bill in January 1947 proposing a subsidy supplementing public school teachers' salaries; supported rent control extension in 1947, 1948, and 1949; opposed the Taft-Hartley Labor Act of 1947 and the income tax reduction bills of that year; favored raising personal exemptions. In the Eighty-first Congress, beginning his third term, Green voted for the long-range housing bill and was one of the sponsors of the proposal to increase the minimum hourly wage to seventy-five cents. In June 1949, as a member of the Senate Public Works Committee, he introduced a bill authorizing loans to public agencies to provide for advance planning of public works; Green was numbered as one of the eighteen Senate sponsors of the economic expansion bill of 1949, introduced July 15.

As a new Senator in 1937 Green had seen the approaching war in Europe. At a New York City mass meeting in December 1938 he scored Nazi political and racial persecution. Expressing fear that the United States would enter the European war, he supported national defense legislation and aid to nations combatting aggression. Green voted with the Administration

Harris & Ewing

THEODORE FRANCIS GREEN

on the questions of continuing the arms embargo (October 27, 1939), the Selective Service Act (August 28, 1940), Lend-Lease (March 8, 1941), the extension of military service for eighteen months (August 7, 1941), and keeping the combat zone bans of the Neutrality Act (November 7, 1941). A strong believer in international cooperation, Green has voted consistently from 1937 to 1949 for the extension of reciprocal trade act agreements, for the Connally [49] Resolution on World Organization (1943), the authorization of UNRRA (1944), participation in the United Nations and the Bretton Woods Agreement (1945). In June 1946 Green was a member of the Congressional delegation to the Empire Parliamentary Association Conference in Bermuda, which agreed on the need for the United Nations and for the use of force to carry out its decisions. The Greek-Turkish aid bill and the ratification of the Italian Peace Treaty (1947), the European recovery bill and the displaced persons bill (1948), and the North Atlantic Security Pact (1949) received Green's "aye" in the Senate roll calls.

The Senator's committee assignments in 1950 include the Rules and Administration Committee, the Foreign Relations Committee, and the Joint Committee on the Library. As chairman of the last-named Green announced in August 1949 that the Library of Congress would no longer award prizes in literature, music, and art, in view of the protests following the award to Ezra Pound of the Bollinger Foundation Prize in 1948.

Green has been associated with numerous civic, commercial, and cultural enterprises. Among some thirty listed in *Who's Who in America* are: the Butler Hospital (trustee 1900-19); the Rhode Island Civic Committee (president, 1923-31); the J. & P. Coats Company (president, 1912-23); the Providence & Danielson Railway Company (vice-president,

GREEN, THEODORE FRANCIS—*Cont.*
1914-20) ; the Netop Land Company (president since 1921) ; the John Thayer Company (president since 1924) ; the Bankers Security Life Insurance Society, New York (director since 1923) ; the Rhode Island School of Design (trustee in 1900, vice-president, 1907-39) ; Brown University (trustee, 1900-29 and fellow since the latter year). A trustee of the Providence Public Library since 1903 (secretary since 1908), he observed in 1933 that "the library . . . has become more than ever a great public school." He is a member of the Rhode Island Historical Society and of the American Federation of Arts and a fellow of the American Academy of Arts and Sciences (Boston). His professional societies are the Rhode Island and American bar associations, the Harvard Law School Association, and the American Law Institute; he holds membership in Phi Beta Kappa, Psi Upsilon fraternity, the Society of the Cincinnati and the Rheno-Colonia zu Bonn. Among his clubs are: the University and the National Press (Washington); University and Brown (New York); Hope, Economic, University, Agawam Hunt, Psi Upsilon (Providence). Honorary degrees have been awarded him by Rhode Island State College (LL.D., 1935) and Providence College (LL.D., 1935).

The bachelor Senator, who has gray hair and gray eyes, is about five feet ten inches in height, and has a weight of 149 pounds. His outdoor recreations are mountain climbing, tennis playing, and swimming; and he is a collector of Chinese paintings.

References

N Y Post Mag p7 O 21 '44
Congressional Directory (1st ed., 1949)
International Who's Who, 1948
National Cyclopædia of American Biography Vol 18 (1922)
Who's Who in America, 1948-49
World Biography (1948)

GRIFFITH, CLARK (CALVIN) Nov. 20, 1869- Baseball club president
Address: b. c/o Washington American League Baseball Club, 7th & Florida Ave., N.W., Washington, D.C.; h. 4720 16th St., N.W., Washington, D.C.

In November 1949 Clark Griffith observed his eightieth birthday, his sixty-first year in professional baseball, and his thirtieth year as president and co-owner of the Washington Senators. Griffith is the only major league owner to have come up through the ranks— from bat boy to semi-pro, to minor leaguer, to big leaguer, to manager, to president. During the 1890's he earned the title of "The Old Fox" for his skill and cunning as a pitcher. At the turn of the century he played a leading role in the formation of the American League. Often referred to by sportswriters as "the true father" of the New York Yankees, Griffith set up, during the next decade, the first American League team in that city. Since 1912 he has made baseball history by guiding the Washington Senators

to win the American League pennant three times and the world championship in 1924.

Clark Calvin Griffith was born in a log cabin in Clear Creek, Vernon County, Missouri, on November 20, 1869, the son of Isaiah and Sarah Ann (Wright) Griffith. His parents were pioneers who had settled there two years before. Shortly after Clark's birth, his father was killed in a hunting accident; his mother continued to work the farm with the assistance of her children. Griffith has said: "I never thought of anything from the time I was seven years old except playing baseball." His first baseball job, at the age of eleven, was as bat boy for a group of Civil War veterans who played on the Stringtown (Missouri) team. Later his mother moved the family to Normal, Illinois, where young Griffith attended high school. He made his first money in baseball during the summer of 1887 by pitching for the Hoopeston (Illinois) team for ten dollars.

In 1888 Griffith entered organized baseball as a pitcher with the Bloomington (Illinois) club, of the old Inter-State League. Because his mother did not approve of his becoming a baseball player, for a time he attended Illinois Wesleyan University at Bloomington. Later, when she learned he was receiving "the incredible, fabulous sum of fifty dollars a month" for playing ball, she changed her mind. He lost his first game to Decatur and made five errors; by midseason, however, he was leading the league with 13 wins and 2 losses. As told by Considine and Povich in the *Saturday Evening Post*, when he beat a strong minor league Milwaukee team in an exhibition game, he was immediately signed by Jimmy Hart, the Milwaukee manager, at $225 a month. In 1889 he became the leading pitcher on the Milwaukee team, and the next year was again out in front with 25 victories. He "jumped" his contract in 1890 to join the St. Louis Browns, of the American Association, a major league, where he was a team-mate of Charles A. Comiskey. Later he was traded to Boston, of the same league. When the circuit collapsed, he returned to the minors and signed up with Tacoma, of the Northern Pacific League. After the league disbanded, Griffith persuaded the players of the Tacoma team to go as a body to the Missoula team, Montana State League. He next pitched for the Oakland club, of the Pacific Coast League. After the management missed five paydays, he led the club to file suit against the owners for back pay. That suit, Griffith has said, may have contributed to the disbandment of the league.

By August 1893 Griffith had saved enough money to go to Chicago, where Jimmy Hart, then president of the Chicago Colts, of the National League, hired him. Between the years of 1894 and 1900 he made his reputation as a big league pitcher with Cap Anson's famous Chicago Nationals. He was thin and under-sized for a pitcher, but what he lacked in speed he more than made up in tricky right-hand delivery. From this period dates a legend that he never threw the ball over the heart of the plate, reported the *Post* writers. It was a clash between Griffith and his special opponent, John McGraw, of the Baltimore Orioles, that led to the present rule making the first two fouls count as strikes. In none of his six years with the Colts did he win less than 20 games a season and in two of them he won 25. Twice in Chicago he pitched more than 400 innings in a single season, and his lifetime record added up to 236 wins against 139 losses for a good average of .629.

At the peak of his career as a pitcher, Griffith began to make plans for a bigger future. Together with Ban Johnson, president of the Western League, the principal minor circuit, and Comiskey, then managing St. Paul, Griffith in 1900 projected a new major league to challenge the National League's supremacy in Eastern cities. As vice-president of the Ballplayers Protective Association, he had spent much of the 1900 season getting National League players to promise not to renew their contracts in 1901 unless the maximum wage was raised to $3,000 a year. When the National League refused his demands, Griffith wired Johnson from New York: "Ban, there's going to be a new major league, if you can get the financial backing! I can get the players." Money was obtained from the wealthy Charles Somers, and the American League entered the field in 1901 with Johnson as its president. Griffith was the first big league star to join the new organization, but he soon added to it 39 National League players. Comiskey set himself up as owner of the Chicago White Sox, and at the beginning of the 1901 season Griffith became the team's manager and piloted it to win the American League pennant in that year.

The American League was determined to prove its power by invading New York City, "the richest major league territory extant," and transferred the Baltimore franchise to that city in 1903. Griffith was selected to manage the new American League team, which was christened the Highlanders (later to be known as the Yankees), because its ball park was on one of the highest points in Manhattan. At that time New York was the stronghold of the Giants, who were managed by Griffith's old rival, John McGraw. While the Highlanders faced an unfriendly press and were boycotted in the beginning, in 1904 Griffith was able to put together a team which almost won the American League pennant. His own pitching days ended in 1907, although he made his last mound appearance at the age of forty-five in 1914. By the time he left the Highlanders in 1908, because of disagreements with its owners, the American League was firmly entrenched in New York. "With a twinge of conscience," Griffith went back to the National League as manager of the Cincinnati Reds until 1911.

At the close of the 1911 season Griffith had the opportunity of buying a 10 per cent interest in the Washington American League Club. This made him the largest single stockholder and gave him the right to manage the Senators as he saw fit. The team had never finished higher than sixth place in the previous eleven years. Griffith made many changes in the line-up, and during his first season as manager spurred his players to finish second behind the

CLARK GRIFFITH

Boston Red Sox in the race for the pennant. It was in this year (1912) that he also helped to certify baseball as the national sport by persuading President Taft to throw out the first ball at the opening game of Washington's season. This has become accepted as a ceremonial "must" on the part of all Presidents. Griffith has paid thirty-seven visits to the White House to present the Chief Executive and the First Lady with season passes.

In 1913 the Senators again finished in second place, and Walter Johnson, the biggest star on the team, enjoyed the best year of his long career as a pitcher. Johnson signed the next year with the newly formed Federal League. It was then that Griffith "pulled a master stroke of baseball diplomacy" by convincing Johnson that it was his duty to return to the Washington team. After the United States entered World War I, Griffith used all his influence in the capital to speak up for the game and its right to continue. He founded the Bat and Ball Fund, which supplied over $100,000's worth of baseball equipment to American soldiers then in camp. By the end of the war it was apparent that the Washington club needed money to buy talent if it was ever going to make progress in the American League. In 1919 Griffith found a backer in William Richardson, a Philadelphia grain dealer and exporter, who was willing to put up the same amount as Griffith would. They were able to buy 80 per cent of the stock, which they divided equally between them. Griffith was given full authority over all matters of policy. He was made the club's president in 1919, and the next year relinquished management of the team.

Often called "the shrewdest player-trader of them all," Griffith had already begun to assemble what is generally regarded in baseball

GRIFFITH, CLARK—*Continued*

circles as the cheapest championship team in the modern history of the game. In 1924 he appointed the 28-year-old second baseman, Bucky Harris [48], as manager of the team, which by that time included such stars as Johnson, Goose Goslin, Joe Judge, Ossie Bluege, and Sam Rice. This team clinched its first American League pennant in that year from the Yankees, and went on to defeat John McGraw's Giants, 4 to 3, in a sensational World Series. The Senators again won the pennant in 1925, but lost the series in a close race with the Pittsburgh Pirates. During the following years, Griffith's winning team broke up, but in 1933 he made another comeback. He made shortstop Joe Cronin his manager, and organized in a short time a team that won the pennant from the rich and powerful Yankees. However, the Senators were defeated in the World Series by the Giants in five games.

Since the year he took over the Senators, Griffith said in July 1950, the team finished in the first division twenty times and in the second division eighteen times. Before World War II Griffith began scouring Latin America for low-priced players who might be "draft-proof." Having once fought every move to introduce night baseball into the major leagues, he became a leading advocate of after-dark games during the war and practically discontinued day baseball in Washington. He is opposed to unionizing professional baseball players, and in 1946 the American Baseball League, an independent union, filed charges against him and his club for unfair labor practices. Griffith vigorously denied having influenced his players against joining the union. In December 1949 the Richardson estate sold its 40 per cent holdings in the Washington club for $550,000 to John James Jachym, backed by millionaire Hugh A. Grant; but minor stockholders, who held the deciding balance of the shares, unanimously re-elected Griffith president in January 1950.

In 1900 Griffith married Ann Robertson, the sister of his old ball-playing friend, Jimmy Robertson. After Robertson's death, Griffith and his wife looked after his family, supporting the widow and five of the children (one of whom died later) and adopting Thelma and Calvin (the latter has been vice-president of the Senators since 1943). Five feet eight inches tall, Griffith weighs 160 pounds; his hair is white and his eyes are brown. While he has few interests other than baseball, he occasionally plays golf and enjoys a game of pinochle. Washington's stadium bears his name. In 1946 he was elected to Baseball's Hall of Fame, in Cooperstown, New York.

References

Newsweek 2:22 S 30 '33
Sat Eve Post 212:17 Ap 13 '40; 212:18 Ap 20 '40 pors
Smith, K. Baseball's Hall of Fame (1947)
Who's Who in America, 1950-51

GRISWOLD, A(LFRED) WHITNEY

Oct. 27, 1906- University president; historian
Address: b. c/o Yale University, New Haven, Conn.

A. Whitney Griswold, a member of the history faculty of Yale University, was chosen the sixteenth president of that institution in January 1950. On July 1, 1950, he succeeded Charles Seymour [41], who retired after thirteen years as president of the third oldest university in the United States—Yale was founded in 1701. The new president, a Yale graduate (class of 1929), has been on the faculty of the university since a few months after his graduation. His writings—books and articles—are in the fields of political science and American foreign policy. Griffith was formally installed as Yale's president on October 6, 1950.

A native of Morristown, New Jersey, Alfred Whitney Griswold was born October 27, 1906, the son of Harold Ely and Elsie Montgomery (Whitney) Griswold. Among his ancestors were six Colonial Governors of what was to become the State of Connecticut; through his mother he is a collateral descendant of Eli Whitney (Yale 1792), the inventor of the cotton gin. Young Griswold attended the Peck School in Morristown and the Hotchkiss School in Lakeville, Connecticut. As an undergraduate at Yale he wrote for the *Yale Daily News* and was managing editor and acting chairman of the college humor magazine, *Yale Record.* He was elected to the Pundits, the Psi Upsilon fraternity, the Elizabethan Club, and Wolf's Head (senior society); his fellow students named him the "wittiest" and "most original" member of the class. He received his B.A. degree in 1929.

During the summer months of the year of his graduation, Griswold worked in a brokerage office in New York. Returning to Yale in the fall, he was an instructor in Freshman English for one year. The summer of 1930 was spent in study in Germany. In the fall of that year he enrolled in the graduate school of Yale, changing his major from English to history. Upon receiving his Ph.D. degree in 1933, he became an instructor in the history department. In the course of nine years he was appointed, successively, research assistant in international relations (1936), assistant professor in government and international relations (1938), and associate professor (1942). Since 1947 he has held a full professorship in history. He is a fellow of Timothy Dwight College (of Yale).

Griswold was one of the founders of the Yale Political Union, a student forum on public affairs established in 1934. More recently he was active in formulating a plan to bring Yale's alumni into closer association with the university. The result was the creation of the University Council, composed of alumni representatives from all parts of the country, whose purpose, as enunciated by President Seymour, is "to study the major constituent parts and activities of the university at close range, to offer recommendations for their improvement, and develop plans for their support."

During World War II Griswold held two governmental posts, as director of the Foreign

Area and Language Curriculum of the Army Specialized Training Program, and as director of the Civil Affairs Training School held at Yale for the Army. In the first capacity he organized courses in Oriental and Western European languages, and in the latter he supervised classes in the cultures, economics, and politics of various areas. President Seymour has observed that in these posts Griswold "demonstrated his executive ability under difficult conditions."

The election of Griswold as President Seymour's successor was made public by the Yale Corporation on February 12, 1950. In making the announcement the outgoing president declared that Griswold "is admirably equipped to direct the policy of a privately endowed university in modern society at a time when it is facing critical decisions." The New York *Times* observed: "On the record he has qualities which should make him a constructive force, not only for one university but for higher education." The New York *Herald Tribune's* comment was that, while other colleges had appointed men prominent in one or another field of public life to their presidencies, Yale "has placed the primary emphasis upon familiarity with the world of scholarship, and has put its trust in the zeal, the clearsightedness, and the energy of youth."

As reported in the New York *Times Magazine*, Griswold has given his views on the important role of education in the world situation, and has said he feels that the character of "political and social institutions" will reflect the character of schools and universities. He is outspoken on the subject of full academic freedom of thought and opinion. "If the spirit of free inquiry dries up at the source—the universities—where can it live?" he remarked to Charles Poore in an interview. Asked for a definition of democracy, the educator said he believed it to be "a political society in which the greatest possible measure of justice implicit in the phrase 'equal opportunity' is combined with the greatest possible measure of freedom and encouragement for the individual to develop his own talent, initiative and moral responsibility." "Education," he has said, "is a part of the process of government."

On leave of absence from Yale until he became president on July 1, 1950, Griswold visited other universities in the United States and abroad "seeing how universities can work together," in line with Yale's policy of "sharing fields of learning"; this, according to Seymour, is increasingly replacing the older interuniversity competition. Seymour has called Griswold "university-minded"—he not only knows his own department thoroughly, but has studied the problems of each of the schools of which the university is composed (the Law School, the Medical School, the Divinity School, the School of Music, the School of Social Sciences), and believes they must work with their equivalents in other universities. The inaugural ceremonies at which Griswold was formally installed as president of Yale University were held on October 6, 1950.

A. WHITNEY GRISWOLD

The historian has been a frequent contributor to a number of publications, among them *Yale Review, Virginia Quarterly Review, Atlantic Monthly, New England Quarterly, Annals of the American Academy, American Journal of Sociology, Foreign Affairs, Asia, Harper's*, the *American Political Science Review*, and *Life*. The subject matter of several of these articles has been Germany's role in World War II. Writing in *Atlantic* in 1941 in an article entitled "Paving the Way for Hitler," he discussed the geopoliticians who, by their philosophy of *Lebensraum*, laid the ideological groundwork for Nazism. A large part of Griswold's published work has been on a subject in which he has become a specialist, the foreign policy of the United States in the Far East and Europe.

Griswold's first book, published in 1938, is *The Far Eastern Policy of the United States*, in which he traced that policy through the preceding forty years "with emphasis on the changes behind the diplomatic notes." In the opinion of E. O. Hauser (*Survey Graphic*), an "extremely dynamic language and the author's keen sense for the dramatic element in history make the volume stimulating and interesting even to the nonspecialized reader." The New York *Times* reviewer, historian Allan Nevins, declared it the "most thorough and authentic treatment in print" of its subject; he found it "a bold and acute interpretation." Regarding the element of Griswold's "interpretation" of American Far Eastern diplomacy, A. N. Holcombe in the Boston *Transcript*, calling the book "indispensable reading for all Americans concerned about the future relations between their country and those of the Far East," added, "In the light of all the available evidence, the author's main conclusions must be pronounced unproved."

(Continued next page)

GRISWOLD, A. WHITNEY—*Continued*

Farming and Democracy, published in 1948, was the result of a study of 150 years of farming and the democratic processes in Britain, France and the United States, a study begun in 1943 on a Guggenheim Fellowship. The preface states, "This is a book about an idea—that farming as a family enterprise is the 'backbone of democracy.'" In his volume Professor Griswold advocated a realistic replanning of American farming to adapt it to twentieth century democracy. It was called a "solid, brilliant book" by the New York *Times* and "interesting . . . thought-provoking" by the *Annals of the American Academy.* John M. Gaus of Harvard characterized it as "the best kind of book on public policy—informative, provocative, not too long. . . . The account of the evolution of government agricultural policy and administration in the United States and of agricultural pressure groups and programs is excellent."

Speaking before a joint meeting of the Rural Sociological Society, the American Sociological Society, and the American Farm Economics Association, Griswold called for improved educational facilities for farm children. "A family farm is no more democratic than the family that occupies it," he said, "and if that family is to be democratic it must be able to refresh its mind and its spirit from the wellsprings of democracy." The Yale University News Bureau has announced that Griswold is in 1950 at work on a third book, describing Federalism as a product of democracy.

The Yale historian is a member of the American Political Science Association; an alumni trustee of Hotchkiss School from 1943 to 1947, he has been a trustee since 1948. Griswold married Mary Morgan Brooks of Scranton, Pennsylvania, on June 10, 1930. Their four children are Sarah Brooks, Mary Brooks, Susanna Whitney and Alfred Whitney, Jr. The university administrator is described in the *Times Magazine* as "a wiry, sandy-haired historian who . . . talks with a blazing passion that suddenly breaks down into a colloquial epigram and a grin."

References

> Life 28:45 F 27 '50
> N Y Herald Tribune p1 F 13 '50 por;
>   II p3 F 19 '50 por
> N Y Times p1 F 13 '50 por; p13 F 26
>   '50 por
> Directory of the American Political Science Association, 1948
> Who's Who in America, 1950-51
> Who's Who in New England (1949)
> Who's Who in the East (1948)

GROTEWOHL, OTTO (grō'tĕ-vŏl ōt'ō) Mar. 11, 1894- Premier of the German Democratic Republic

Address: b. Lothringerstrasse 1, Berlin, Germany

In October 1949 the Soviet-sponsored German Democratic Republic was established with Otto Grotewohl as its first Premier. During the Weimar Republic he had been a leader of the Social Democratic party and after World War II he became chairman of the central committee of the reconstituted Social Democrats in Berlin. He was the key figure in the 1946 merger of the Left-wing Social Democrats and the German Communists to form the Socialist Unity party (SED), the strongest political party in the Russian Occupation Zone. Together with the Communist leader, Wilhelm Pieck '49, President of the East German state, Grotewohl served as co-chairman of the Socialist Unity party from its formation until the new republic was proclaimed.

Born in Brunswick, Germany, on March 11, 1894, Otto Grotewohl was educated at the Leibniz Academy in Hanover and the Institute of Politics in Berlin. He began his career as a printer (states *Wer ist Wer?*), later worked as a health insurance official, and for a time was president of the Brunswick State Social Insurance Institute. After World War I he became prominent both in the city and the state of Brunswick as a Social Democratic (Socialist) party leader, serving as chairman of the party in that area until 1933. A member of the City Council, he was sent to the State Parliament in 1920 and held the posts of State Minister of Interior and Popular Education (1921-22) and State Minister of Justice (1923-24). He was elected to the Reichstag in 1925, and during the following years contributed numerous articles on political, social, and trade union topics to newspapers and periodicals. At this early period he had advocated a single Marxist Labor party in Brunswick.

Reports vary as to Grotewohl's activities after the Nazis seized dictatorial powers in 1933. Joachim Joesten (in *Germany: What Now?*) says Grotewohl was arrested in March 1933, and spent long periods in concentration camps before he was released when Allied troops captured Dachau in April 1945. According to *Wer ist Wer?* he was imprisoned as the result of a "fixed" trial, but later was released and became a businessman in Hamburg and Berlin. Because of his anti-Hitler activities and trips abroad in connection with the Social Democratic underground (continues the German source), he was imprisoned for seven months during 1938 and 1939 and then tried for high treason before the People's Court. He was arrested again after the attempt to kill Hitler in Munich in November 1939. Warned in time that he would be included in the wave of arrests after the unsuccessful *Putsch* of July 20, 1944, when another attempt was made on Hitler's life in East Prussia, Grotewohl went into hiding and continued to work with the German underground movement.

After the defeat of the Third Reich, the Social Democratic party (Sozialdemokratische Partei Deutschlands, the SPD) was re-established in Berlin on June 17, 1945, when Grotewohl was elected chairman of its central committee. At this time there was a strong feeling among Social Democrats and Communists for close collaboration, since both groups realized that the split between them after World War I had weakened the working class and enabled

Hitler to come to power. Grotewohl received an ovation in Berlin when he called on the SPD and the German Communist party to form "a united working class front" and revealed that a fusion of the central committees of the two parties had already begun. However, a large majority of the Social Democrats in the American and British zones were reported as being against the merger.

In early 1946 Grotewohl proposed to Kurt Schumacher '⁴⁸, leader of the Social Democrats in Western Germany, that a national party congress be called to decide the issue, but Schumacher (who, it has been said, feared that the congress would not be permitted by the occupation authorities), refused to agree until the zones were abolished. Grotewohl accordingly called a meeting of the SPD central committee at which a proposal for immediate merger was approved. When, however, the merger resolution was brought before a meeting of 2,500 Berlin Social Democrats on March 31, 1946, he was shouted down by the assembly, which demanded that the question be put to a secret vote of all party members in the Soviet zone and in all Berlin. A referendum in West Berlin showed that 82 per cent of the party membership in the Western sectors of Berlin were against "immediate merger" with the Communists, according to Russell Hill in *The Struggle for Germany*. No vote was taken in the Soviet sector. A week later the anti-fusionist members of the SPD in Berlin voted to expel Grotewohl and the central committee. At a joint meeting on April 21, 1946, the German Communists and the section of the Social Democrats headed by Grotewohl formally merged into a new organization, the Socialist Unity Party (Sozialistische Einheits Partei, the SED), and Pieck and Grotewohl were elected co-chairmen of its executive committee. The SED was estimated to have about 1,121,000 members, divided evenly between the two parties.

The new Socialist Unity party gained practically undisputed control of the political life in the Soviet zone. It has supported the objectives of Moscow's policy, the foremost being the political union of Germany. When Pieck and Grotewohl toured the British and American zones in 1946 and 1947, they called for a strong, centralized German government and criticized the Western powers for their support of a divided Germany. In a Frankfurt political rally, Grotewohl declared: "No one but the Germans can solve their problems" and "Germany must not suffer just because the Allied occupying powers cannot agree among themselves" (New York *Herald Tribune*, March 9, 1947). He announced a two-year plan in 1948 to increase industrial production in the Soviet zone, which, he said, must be exclusively "oriented toward the Soviet Union." Later he demanded a purge of "diversionist and obstructionist elements" in Eastern Germany and began to transform the SED along Soviet lines into an elite cadre of highly trained political workers (New York *Times*, August 1, 1948).

Wide World Photos

OTTO GROTEWOHL

In the spring of 1949 the Communistic People's Congress and its superior body, the 400-member People's Council (called by Grotewohl "the only legitimate representative of the German people") approved a constitution for the new state in East Germany. On October 7 of that same year, the German Democratic Republic was proclaimed in the Russian sector of Berlin, its capital, by the People's Council, which became a provisional legislative body, the People's Chamber, and declared the constitution in effect. The People's Chamber then elected Pieck as President and Grotewohl as Premier (he is known also as the Minister-President) and the new government was formally inaugurated on October 11, 1949. The next day Grotewohl took office and introduced his Cabinet, in which Communists held eight key posts. Outlining his policy, he stressed friendship with the Soviet Union, increased trade with Eastern Europe and Communist China, the payment of reparations to Russia, the end of food rationing within a year, the granting of citizenship to ex-Nazis who were not directly guilty of war crimes, and the recognition of the Oder-Neisse line as the final peace frontier between Poland and Germany.

When Premier Grotewohl was hospitalized with influenza and pneumonia in December 1949, a number of reasons were advanced in the Western press for what appeared to be withdrawal from public life. After three weeks, reported the New York *Times*, he left for a six-week convalescent stay in Russia. When he returned to Berlin to assume his duties in February 1950, he called for a list of candidates to support the National Front in the October 1950 East German elections.

Grotewohl has been described as a "quiet, rather philosophic type of politician." In 1946 the SED was reported to have presented Grotewohl and Pieck each a life gift of a castle

GROTEWOHL, OTTO—*Continued*

near Berlin. It was recently disclosed that Grotewohl and his first wife had been divorced and that in June 1949 he had remarried.

References

Time 54:22 D 19 '50
International Who's Who, 1949
Wer ist Wer (1948)

GRUENTHER, ALFRED M(AXIMIL-IAN) Mar. 3, 1899- United States Army officer

Address: b. c/o Department of the Army, The Pentagon, Washington 25, D.C.

Lieutenant General Alfred M. Gruenther, who in September 1949 was appointed Deputy Chief of Staff for Plans, in December 1950 was chosen by General Eisenhower (Supreme Commander of Western Europe's armed forces) as Chief of Staff in that North Atlantic Treaty defense command. Gruenther (called

U. S. Army
LIEUT. GEN. ALFRED M. GRUENTHER

the "Brain of the Army") had been Eisenhower's Chief of Staff in World War II.

Alfred Maximilian Gruenther was born March 3, 1899, in Platte Center, Nebraska. His father, Christian M. Gruenther, "widely known in Nebraska politics," was the editor of the weekly Platte Center *Signal*; his mother was the former Mary Shea. As a youth Alfred Gruenther used to edit the paper in his father's absence. According to a *Collier's* article by Pat Frank, on one occasion the teen-age boy wrote an editorial excoriating Congress for spending on military appropriations millions of dollars which he thought might better be used for libraries and community services, a point of view not shared by his father. Gruenther has

said that he entered West Point two years later to make his father happy.

Although "not a bookworm," Gruenther, one of the younger cadets, ranked fourth in a class of 277. He was a member of West Point's "joker" class which was graduated from the Military Academy twice. The first time, on June 14, 1917, they received their B.S. degrees, but were not commissioned. Having an oversupply of second lieutenants at the time, the Army sent the new graduates back to West Point for another term. Graduated again on November 1, 1918, nineteen-year-old Gruenther was commissioned a second lieutenant in the Field Artillery. His military education includes graduation from the Field Artillery School (1920), the Chemical Warfare School, and later the Command and General Staff School in 1937 and the Army War College in 1939. Throughout the 1920's and 1930's Gruenther had routine peacetime assignments. His promotion to the captaincy came on May 1, 1935, and he was made a major on July 1, 1940. For eight of those years he was instructor and assistant professor of mathematics and electricity at West Point.

During the Louisiana maneuvers of September 1941—the first large-scale war games in years—Army Ground Forces commander Lieutenant General Lesley J. McNair [42] is said to have remarked that young Major Gruenther was "capable of a much higher command." On September 15, 1941, Gruenther was given the temporary rank of lieutenant colonel, and that October he was appointed deputy chief of staff of Lieutenant General Walter Krueger's [43] Third Army, of which the chief of staff was Brigadier General Dwight D. Eisenhower [48]. After Pearl Harbor Gruenther succeeded Eisenhower as Krueger's staff chief and, according to the citation accompanying the Legion of Merit awarded him two years later, "developed an efficient operating staff." Then, on August 1, 1942, he was sent to London to serve, again, as a deputy chief of staff, this time at Allied Force Headquarters with Eisenhower the commanding general. Later the headquarters moved to Algiers for the campaign against Marshal Rommel's [42] forces. On December 11, 1942, he received the permanent rank of lieutenant colonel.

"From the initial planning of the landings in North Africa," according to the citation which accompanied Gruenther's D.S.M., "he displayed ability to cope with great masses of detail and preserved an unruffled calm in the face of exceptional difficulties, lifting those associated with him above themselves." According to reports, Eisenhower referred to Colonel Gruenther as his "right arm" and "when Lieutenant General Mark W. Clark [42] formed the Fifth Army no one else was considered for the chief of staff." Gruenther worked with Clark throughout the North African, Sicilian, and Italian campaigns; and when Clark became the youngest full general in the Army of the United States, his forty-three-year-old chief of staff became the youngest major general, a temporary rank which was later made permanent in August 1944.

A chief of staff normally takes care of all the routine tasks of running an army, supervises the assembling of the information upon which the commanding general's decisions are based, and gives the many detailed orders necessary to put those decisions into action. As chief of staff of the Fifth Army, Alfred Gruenther met problems of "territorial and political responsibility in French Morocco, a comprehensive training program for troops in North Africa, the planning and execution of a mass amphibious assault on the shores of Italy, and the subsequent campaign up the Italian peninsula through the German Gothic Line in the northern Apennines" (from a citation). In December 1944 Clark became commanding general of the Fifteenth Army Group, the over-all field command of Allied troops in Italy, composed also of British, French, Polish, New Zealand, and Italian units. His chief of staff was "faced with the problem of readjusting a predominately British staff to the requirements of an American commander" for the campaign which led to the surrender, on May 2, 1945, of the German forces in Italy and western Austria.

After V-E Day, when Clark became commander of the United States forces in Austria, Gruenther served as his deputy. He led the American mission to Vienna to make the arrangements, and it was he who arranged the first meeting of the American-British-French-Russian Allied Council there in August. His next assignment, back in Washington, was as deputy commandant of the former Army War College, which had become the National War College.

In October 1947 Gruenther assumed duty in the newly created post of Director of the Joint Staff of one hundred officers who served as a planning staff for the Joint Chiefs of Staff. He and his opposite numbers in the Navy and Air Force formed the "Little Chiefs," who themselves settled the noncontroversial problems; and Gruenther's unofficial position as adviser to the Secretary of Defense was formalized a year later (September 1948). In September 1949, when Gruenther was named Deputy Chief of Staff for Plans, the Washington Post commented editorially on the "consummate skill" with which Gruenther (now lieutenant general) had organized the Joint Staff, and remarked, "The Joint Staff . . . has toiled virtually twenty-four hours a day. . . . General Gruenther has had to be not only a workhorse and strategist of the broadest concepts, but also a leader and diplomat. Withal he has managed to keep an affability back of what is perhaps the most incisive mind in the military establishment." As Deputy Chief of Staff for Plans his responsibility was the coordinated preparation of Army plans and programs.

On December 20, 1950, it was announced that General Dwight E. Eisenhower had chosen Gruenther as his Chief of Staff in the Western European command, of which integrated Atlantic Pact forces Eisenhower is Supreme Commander, with headquarters in Paris.

In addition to the decorations already mentioned, General Gruenther received the United States Bronze Star Medal and has been awarded the following foreign decorations: Companion of the Bath (British); Legion of Honor, degree of Officer, and Croix de Guerre with Palm (French); Grand Cross of the Crown of Italy and Silver Medal for Military Valor (Italy); Silver Cross of Virtuti Militari (Poland); Order of the Military Cross (Czechoslovakia); Ouissam Alaouite, Grand Officer (French Morocco); Cavaliere Magistrale of the Order of Malta; Order of Military Merit, degree of Commander (Brazil).

In 1920, while attending the Field Artillery School at Fort Knox, Kentucky, Lieutenant Gruenther learned to play the new game of contract bridge, at which he became expert because of a "fantastic" memory. Gruenther obtained leave to watch the Eastern championship play in New York City in 1928. On an impulse he entered the amateur pairs event, in which he and his partner came out fourth. Although impressed by the high standard of play, the officer was dismayed at the lack of punctuality and of discipline. Later, having invited a team from New York's Knickerbocker Whist Club to West Point (where he was then an instructor) to play an Army foursome, Gruenther directed the match with such dignity and precision that he was invited to serve as section director at a Knickerbocker event. Proving "a squabble-settler par excellence," he was soon in demand to manage all the large Eastern tournaments, the best known of which was the Lenz-Culbertson "classic" of 1931. For his services as the "Judge Landis of contract bridge" he was paid $100 a night. After the tournament, Gruenther wrote The Referee's Analysis of the Decisive Hands of the Lenz-Culbertson Match. His 328-page Duplicate Contract Complete—A Guide to Playing In and Conducting All Duplicate Bridge Contests, published in 1933, "is still considered the standard work on the subject," said the New Yorker ten years later. At the time of Pearl Harbor Gruenther was secretary of the Vanderbilt Cup Committee.

A lean, wiry man of average height with a "booming" voice, Alfred Maximilian Gruenther "pours every ounce of his energy into every job and expects those around him to do the same." Gruenther married on August 22, 1922, Grace Elizabeth Crum, then secretary of the Fort Knox officers' club, and also a bridge player; both their sons, Donald Alfred and Richard Louis, are Army officers. While much in demand at the bridge table, the General also enjoys tennis. He is a nonsmoker and seldom uses alcohol. In Washington he is a member of the Army and Navy Club.

References

Collier's 126:15 Ag 26 '50
N Y Herald Tribune II p3 S 19 '43
N Y Sun p17 N 17 '42; p15 S 16 '43
N Y Times p17 S 7 '49
New Yorker 19:18 O 2 '43
Newsweek 15:48 Ap 22 '40
Time 41:62 F 22 '43
Who's Who in America, 1950-51

GUINNESS, ALEC Apr. 2, 1914- Actor
Address: h. 7 St. Peter's Sq., London, W. 6.

The British actor Alec Guinness, who starred on Broadway in *The Cocktail Party*, the verse drama by T. S. Eliot, in the 1949-50 season, is also known to English and American audiences for his roles in motion pictures, among which have been *Great Expectations* and *Kind Hearts and Coronets*. His stage debut was made in 1934, his screen debut in 1946. For his performance in *The Cocktail Party* he was hailed by New York critics as a great actor. The American National Theater and Academy presented him with its scroll for his excellence in that role and eight portrayals in the motion picture *Kind Hearts and Coronets*.

Wide World Photos
ALEC GUINNESS

Alec Guinness (who is not connected with the family which brews the famous Guinness stout) was born April 2, 1914, in Marylebone, London. For his education he attended Pembroke Lodge, in Southbourne, and Roxborough School, in Eastbourne. At the age of eighteen he entered the employ of an advertising firm, for which he became a copywriter. However, with the theater as his goal, he left that position after eighteen months, to take lessons in acting from Martita Hunt, who thought he showed little promise. At the end of his second lesson she said, "You've got no talent at all," and wanted to return his fee. Young Guinness did not lose heart, but insisted that they continue, and in due course won a scholarship to the Fay Compton Studio of Dramatic Art. During his training there, it is told, he lived a meager existence in an attic, with meals consisting of apples, buns, and milk, and walking four miles every Friday night to sit in the gallery of the Old Vic theater.

His dramatic course completed, Guinness spent fruitless months looking for an engagement. Early in 1934 he secured a walk-on part in *Libel!* Then, in September he was given

a minor part in *Queer Cargo*; and in November he made his first Shakespearean appearance as Osric and the Third Player in *Hamlet*. The following year (1935) he played the wolf in *Noah* and Sampson and the Apothecary in *Romeo and Juliet*, and in 1936 The Workman and later Yakov in *The Sea Gull*. From September 1936 to April 1937 he had an Old Vic season as Boyet in *Love's Labour's Lost*, then as Aguecheek in *Twelfth Night* and Exeter in *Henry V*. That summer he played Osric, Reynaldo, and the Player Queen in his company's presentation of *Hamlet* at Elsinore, the Danish castle in which Shakespeare set the play.

In the fall of 1937 Guinness joined John Gielgud's company at the New Theatre, appearing in *Richard II*, *The School for Scandal*, *The Three Sisters*, and *The Merchant of Venice*. Back at the Old Vic in the autumn of 1938, he was the lead in a modern dress performance of *Hamlet*, played Bob Acres in *The Rivals* and Arthur Gower in *Trelawney of the Wells*, toured the Continent and Egypt with the company, and, among other roles, was Michael Ransom in *The Ascent of F.6*. July 1939 brought him the major part of Romeo, at the Scottish Theatre Festival, at Perth. By the end of the year his own adaptation of Dickens' *Great Expectations* was produced, with himself as Herbert Pocket. He remained on the stage throughout 1940, playing Richard Meilhac in *Cousin Muriel*, and later in the year, at the Old Vic, Ferdinand in *The Tempest*; he also toured that year as Charleston in *Thunder Rock*.

Between 1941 and 1945 Guinness was on war service with the Royal Naval Volunteer Reserve; he joined as an ordinary seaman and was commissioned a lieutenant in 1942. Most of this period he spent in the Mediterranean. Of his naval service he remarked to a *New Yorker* interviewer: "My nautical methods were by guess and by God, and I was certainly glad to return to the theater." He had a brief re-, turn from December 23, 1942, to January 3, 1943, while his ship was under repair, when on special leave he played the flight lieutenant in Terence Rattigan's *Flare Path* at Henry Miller's Theatre in New York. The New York *World-Telegram* gave him "highest honors" for his American debut, while the *Times* described him as "bringing a nervous energy and bounce to the part, but seeming realistic only part of the time." Near the close of the war, in April 1945, the actor played Lord Nelson in London in the pageant, *Hearts of Oak*.

Guinness, who returned to civilian life later in 1945, appeared in his own stage adaptation of *The Brothers Karamazov*, as Mitya, in June 1946. The play, he told the *New Yorker* "was what might be called an artistic success, although it was nothing much commercially." The year 1947 saw the actor on the London stage as the Dauphin in Shaw's *St. Joan*. Critical opinions of his performance in the title role of *Richard II* in April 1947 were mixed. One, in London *Sunday Express* was: "Mr. Guinness is slight, with an interesting angular face and a clear, flexible voice. He has dignity, but no majesty; he has range and control, but no surprises. He is intensely good without being great—yet. His future may bring that." When Guinness directed *Twelfth Night* in a 1948 presentation (in which he did not act), he transposed the first two scenes, thus making the part of Feste the "most arresting" character in the production. Of Guinness' interpretation of the play, Harold Hobson wrote from London that he found it curious, "but no one can deny its interest, nor even its beauty."

With his appearance as Sir Henry Harcourt-Reilly, the metaphysical psychiatrist in T. S. Eliot's verse drama, *The Cocktail Party*, in New York (January-June 1950), Guinness was judged to have achieved new heights of serious, intellectual stage presentation. The play had been briefly given previously at Edinburgh Festival and at Brighton, when Harold Hobson, writing in the *Sunday Times* (London) declared: "Mr. Guinness is going to be one of our greatest actors. The triangle of Gielgud Olivier, and Richardson is visibly changing into a quadrilateral." The New York *Journal-American* found the presentation "by far the worthiest performance by an actor, imported or domestic, on Broadway today." "Not only is his playing brilliant in range, variety, and power," said the New York *Post*'s critic, "but he acts a complex role without seeming to touch more than a fraction of his potentialities . . . it is quite possible that he is the most accomplished actor extant."

Guinness left the cast of *The Cocktail Party* in June 1950 to work in London on a Twentieth Century-Fox film, *The Mudlark*, in which he was given the role of Disraeli opposite Irene Dunne's Queen Victoria. His first work in motion pictures had come in 1945, when he adapted *Great Expectations* for the screen and in it played the role of Herbert Pocket. (His old teacher, Martita Hunt, was Miss Havisham.) The production won uniformly high praise, the New York *Herald Tribune* describing it as "the most authentic reproduction of Dickens yet screened." Among the adjectives applied to his Pocket were "wonderful" and "tremendously comic." In 1949 another Dickensian role was "wonderfully subtle," that of Fagin in *Oliver Twist*, a film not shown in the United States because of protests that it would stir up anti-Semitism.

The British actor's next cinema appearance was in the witty, satiric *Kind Hearts and Coronets*, in which he played the eight heirs to a dukedom who, standing in the way of an aspiring kinsman, are murdered or die natural deaths. Guinness' portrayals, which included characters as distinct as a duke, a banker, a clergyman, a general, and a suffragette, were felt by Archer Winsten in the New York *Post* to be "one of the treasures of the cinema, a classic of incredible virtuosity." Praising the actor's "astonishing range," John Mason Brown wrote in the *Saturday Review of Literature*: "He goes far beyond quick impressions or superficial details to create individualized characters rather than types. . . .He is an all-star cast in his own person." The actor told the London *Picturegoer* that he enjoyed the role of the frail old clergyman more than any of the others: "It's a wittily written part, and the character itself is the most sympathetic of them all."

Guinness was also seen in the light comedy picture, *A Run for Your Money*, in the part of the garden editor. "A delightfully clever job, sketching a brilliant little portrait of a harassed and wretched Fleet Street snob," was the opinion of the reviewer for the New York *Times*.

In recognition of his performances in *The Cocktail Party* and in *Kind Hearts and Coronets* Guinness was presented with a scroll by the American National Theater and Academy; and he was chosen the best actor of the 1949-50 Broadway season in *Variety*'s annual poll of New York drama critics. The *New Yorker* described the English actor as "middle-sized, slightly prognathic, rather shy, completely ingratiating . . . and much impressed by Mr. Eliot's approach to the theater." His eyes are blue, his face rather long and pale. *Time* related that he met his actress wife, Merula Salaman, in 1937, when both were playing animals in *Noah*, a children's play. They have a son, Matthew, whom Guinness would like to be an actor, but not to begin his professional training until he is about eighteen. "Time permitting," reported London's *Leader Magazine*, "Guinness likes painting and reading Dickens and Dostoevsky, making toys for his small son, and, just to prove what an unusual man he is, he likes letterwriting."

References

Leader Magazine (London) Je 18 '49
N Y Sunday News II p2 Je 11 '50
N Y Times II p3 F 26 '50
New Yorker 25:25-6 F 4 '50
Picturegoer (London) Je 18 '49
Time 49:55 My 12 '47
British Film Annual, 1949
Who's Who, 1950
Who's Who in the Theatre (1947)

GURNEY, (JOHN) CHAN(DLER) May 21, 1896- United States Senator from South Dakota

Address: b. c/o Senate Office Bldg., Washington 25, D.C.; h. Yankton, S. D.

As Senator from South Dakota, Chan Gurney became known as a sponsor of legislation on military measures, including service unification, the draft, and universal military training. He was first elected to the Senate in 1938, thus being seated in the Seventy-six Congress in 1939. In the Eightieth Congress he was chairman of the Armed Services Committee, and in the Eighty-first its second-ranking Republican member. A businessman in his home State, he was treasurer of the House of Gurney, Inc., a seed and nursery business, and president of the Chan Gurney Oil Company, of Sioux Falls.

John Chandler Gurney was born to Deloss Butler and Henrietta (Klopping) Gurney on May 21, 1896. His birthplace is Yankton, the South Dakota town where his pioneer forebears had established a seed and nursery-stock business which made the Gurney name a well-known one among the farmers of the State. After graduating from the local high school in 1914, the youth entered the family business.

CHAN GURNEY

In World War I he served overseas for nineteen months with Company A of the Thirty-fourth Engineers. Although he did not see combat, he "was impressed with how arrogant and unbeaten the German prisoners were, even behind barbed wire," he said later in life, attributing his anti-isolationism and interest in military preparedness to this experience.

After the war Gurney became secretary and treasurer of the House of Gurney, Inc., the family business. Ten years later, in 1928, while retaining this position, Gurney established the first radio station in South Dakota, and for years was his own news commentator and sportscaster. He branched out into the oil business in 1933, as president of the Chan Gurney Oil Company, of Sioux Falls.

Entering politics, Gurney became Republican candidate for United States Senator in 1936, but was defeated; he succeeded on his second attempt in 1938, on a strong anti-New Deal platform, and was re-elected in 1944. Like other Midwestern Congressmen, he was to be found taking the regular Republican stand on most domestic issues; but unlike most of them, he supported the Roosevelt foreign policy "virtually 100 per cent," reported *Time*. In October 1941, when the Senate was debating the bill to arm merchant ships, Gurney denounced it as a halfway measure and fought for outright repeal of the Neutrality Act; he also voted for Lend-Lease. Gurney offered the amendment setting the deferment age for military inductees at twenty-eight (rather than at an age to be set at the discretion of the President) and introduced the Administration bill lowering the draft age to eighteen. He and Democrats Barkley, Reynolds, Lucas, and Thomas were the only Senators opposing a restriction which would have prevented the services from sending eighteen-year-olds into combat.

During his first term Senator Gurney's recorded votes on foreign policy included those for the Connally resolution in favor of international organization, and for the UNRRA appropriation. Unlike the majority of his party, in a June 1, 1943 vote he opposed weakening the Reciprocal Trade Agreements Act. In his second term, 1945 through 1950, Gurney supported the proposals for aid to foreign countries, but voted against the 1945 Bretton Woods Agreement, which established the World Bank and World Fund, against extending the Reciprocal Trade Agreements Act for three years, and in favor of retaining the provisions of the DP Admission Act.

Since the Military Affairs Committee chairman, Senator Thomas '42 of Utah, was an opponent of draft extension, Gurney, a minority member, became prominent when he introduced and led the fight for measures sought by the Army and by the President. His were the bills for "unabridged" extension of the draft, for raising servicemen's pay, for universal military training, for terminating inductions at such time as voluntary enlistments should fill the needs of the services. In January 1947, with his party in the majority for the first time in his Senate career, Gurney became the chairman of the important Armed Services Committee, —under the Legislative Reorganization Act of 1946, the Naval Affairs Committee was included in it. Soon he opposed his own party's budget cuts, objecting that the proposed slashes would "hamstring national security" and produce "disarmament by an insidious deterioration"; and he was the only Republican member of the budget subcommittee who did not vote for them (he abstained from voting).

He was also chairman of the military appropriations subcommittee of the Appropriations Committee. After eleven weeks of committee hearings on a problem which had been studied for thirty-five years, Gurney introduced the bill to unify the armed forces in July 7, 1947. A year later came the bill to re-establish Selective Service in peacetime; Gurney's committee had begun study of this two hours after President Truman's March 1948 warning that voluntary enlistments were inadequate. In 1950 military legislation Gurney introduced a bill to draft medical specialists up to the age of forty-five, and recommended that application of the proposed universal military training measure be automatic rather than at Presidential discretion.

On domestic questions Gurney voted in his first term against the Federal soldier's vote provision, against appropriating funds for the National Resources Planning Board, for requiring consumer cooperatives and labor unions to file income-tax returns, and repeatedly against subsidizing wartime price controls on food. On farm questions the South Dakotan departed from the Republican party line by supporting a hundred-million-dollar increase in funds for soil conservation, and for continuing the FSA's power to make loans to small farmers. In March 1943, he stood, with nine other Republicans and fifteen Democratic Senators, against the bill which gave blanket deferment from the draft to all men who "had or could obtain . . .

substantially full-time employment in agriculture."

In his second term, which began in 1945, he went on record for overriding the veto of the Taft-Hartley Act, to forbid portal-to-portal pay suits, to limit Social Security coverage, to end public housing, to exempt railroads from the antitrust laws, and to override the President's tax-cut veto. He was against the Administration's anti-inflation program, except for his February 2, 1948, vote against weakening rent control. On educational questions, Gurney voted against the proposal for segregated Southern regional colleges for Negroes, and he was one of the twelve Senators (five Democrats and seven Republicans) who went on record against allocating a proposed $300,000 a year for aid to public schools.

Other committees on which the Senator from South Dakota served during his two terms in office (he was defeated in the 1950 primaries by Representative Francis Case [46]) included: Interstate Commerce, Irrigation and Reclamation, Public Lands and Surveys, Special Committee to Investigate Production, Transportation, and Marketing of Wool, Special Committee to Investigate Petroleum Resources; he was on the Board of Visitors to the Military Academy and to the Naval Academy, and on the Goethals Memorial Commission. Among other pronouncements which drew attention to him were his call for the reimposition of export controls on petroleum, which was in short supply, and his vote in late 1947 for the Democratic resolution authorizing Secretary of Agriculture Anderson [45] to release the names of commodity speculators. In the spring of 1948 Gurney called the largest rivers-and-harbors bill ever introduced "a stupendous pork barrel . . . but it will put pork chops and roast pork and bacon on millions of tables." Later that year, on his return from an official trip through Europe and the Near East, the Senator urged an immediate military alliance with Franco Spain, in contradiction to State Department and U.N. policy. Also noteworthy was his opposition to the erection of power plants by the Rural Electrification Commission "except where the agency could prove that sufficient current was not available at reasonable rates." In 1949, too, he "discounted the urgency of state enabling legislation for public power districts."

Described as calm, quiet, and pleasant, Chan Gurney is short and stocky—he stands five feet six and one-half inches and weighs, he says, "too darn much" (about 180 pounds). He is a member of the VFW, a past State commander of the American Legion, an Elk, an Odd Fellow, and holds the Masonic title of Knight Commander of the Court of Honor. By his marriage to Evelyn Bordeno on July 4, 1917, Gurney has three children, John Bordeno, Deloss Braddock, both of whom served in the war Air Forces, and Ida Elaine (Mrs. Morgan T. Smith). He is of the Protestant faith. Fond of fishing, he is also reportedly a dead shot when pheasant hunting.

References

N Y Sun p28 D 5 '46
Time 40:18 S 14 '42
U S News 22:54 F 21 '47
Washington (D.C.) Post p2 Mr 23 '48
Congressional Directory (1950)
International Who's Who, 1950
Who's Who in America, 1950-51
World Biography (1948)

GUSTAF V, KING OF SWEDEN (goo' stäv) June 16, 1858—Oct. 29, 1950 Succeeded his father, Oscar II, in December 1907; educated at Uppsala University; became general in both Swedish and Norwegian armies in 1898; was considered largely responsible for keeping Sweden neutral in World War I and World War II; the first sovereign in Europe to recognize a labor government which made Sweden an example of "middle-way" democracy; an avid tennis player on the Riviera, when he used the name "Mr. G." See *Current Biography*, 1942.

Obituary

N Y Times p1 O 29 '50

GUSTAF VI, KING OF SWEDEN (goo' stäv) Nov. 11, 1882-
Address: Royal Palace, Stockholm

When Gustaf V [42], King of Sweden since 1907, died at the age of ninety-two on October 29, 1950, his son Crown Prince Gustaf Adolf, came to the throne of the constitutional monarchy as Gustaf VI Adolf (the formal nomenclature, since he is the sixth Gustaf, but not the sixth Adolf). The forty-three years he has been Crown Prince were a continuous preparation for the task of wearing the crown. By serving as Regent during his father's illnesses and vacations abroad, he gained a practical knowledge of a sovereign's manifold duties. An archaeologist of distinction, an interest which has taken him on a number of expeditions, he has also twice visited the United States.

King Gustaf VI Adolf is the sixth sovereign of the Royal House of Bernadotte de Ponte Corvo. His father was a great-grandson of the dynasty's founder, Jean Baptiste Bernadotte, the son of a French lawyer who became one of Napoleon's marshals, the heir apparent to the crown of Sweden in 1810, and succeeded to the throne in 1818 as Karl XIV Johan. Through his mother, the late Queen Victoria, daughter of Friedrich, Grand Duke of Baden, Sweden's new ruler is descended from the Royal House of Vasa, originally a branch of the Swedish nobility, which in the sixteenth and seventeenth centuries gave Sweden some of its great kings and military leaders. Gustaf VI Adolf is the first monarch with Vasa blood in his veins to reign in Sweden since 1818.

The new King was born in the Royal Palace at Stockholm on November 11, 1882, at which time his grandfather, Oscar II, occupied the throne. Christened Oscar Fredrik Wilhelm Olaf Gustaf Adolf, he was given the title of

Pressens Bild, Stockholm

GUSTAF VI, KING OF SWEDEN

Duke of Skåne. He had two younger brothers: Prince Wilhelm, Duke of Södermanland, who is a poet, novelist, and dramatist; and Prince Erik, Duke of Västmanland, who died in 1918. As the prospective heir to the throne, the young Prince received a rigorous as well as democratic education in the Palace schoolroom. After passing examinations in 1900, he entered the University of Uppsala, where he studied political economy, civil government, statistics, civil law, and archeology. Until 1905 Norway was still united with Sweden, and since Gustaf Adolf was also a Prince of Norway, tradition required that he should spend a part of his time at the University of Christiania (Oslo). Completing his college studies, he began a practical training in the details of civil administration by serving as a clerk in nearly every major government department.

Meanwhile, a part of each year he had to devote to his military education. He started as a cadet in the Svea Life Guards and the Crown Prince's Regiment of Hussars, with special orders that he was to receive no favors. During military maneuvers he "roughed it," sleeping in hay lofts or under the open sky. He passed his officer's examination in 1902 and the next year became a lieutenant in both his regiment and in the Norwegian Jaegerkorps. After attending the War College in Stockholm, he was promoted to be a captain in 1909, a major in 1913, and a lieutenant colonel in 1916. While World War I was raging in other European countries, he served with the staff of the Fourth Army Division (August 1914-May 1915), the General Staff (October 1915-May 1916), and the Naval Staff (November 1917-May 1918). In the latter year he was made a colonel, rose to major general in 1923, to lieutenant general in 1928, and to a full general in both the infantry and cavalry in 1932.

It was while traveling in Egypt during the winter of 1904-5 that the Prince first met Princess Margaret of Connaught, elder daughter of Prince Arthur of Great Britain, Duke of Connaught, who was the third son of Queen Victoria. Their marriage at Windsor Castle on July 15, 1905, marked the first union between the British and Swedish royal houses since 1406. They became Crown Prince and Princess of Sweden when Gustaf V succeeded to the throne on December 8, 1907, upon the death of his father, King Oscar II. Four sons and a daughter were born to the royal couple: Prince Gustaf Adolf, Prince Sigvard, Princess Ingrid, Prince Bertil, and Prince Carl Johan. Crown Princess Margaret died May 1, 1920. Gustaf VI's second and present wife is also British-born. The former Lady Louise Mountbatten, she is a sister of Louis, Earl Mountbatten of Burma and a great-granddaughter of Queen Victoria. Their marriage took place in London on November 3, 1923. She shares her husband's interests in social welfare, the arts, and travel.

During the years that followed, the Crown Prince took on an increasingly important part of his father's duties, substituting for him at public observances, traveling abroad in official capacities, and acting as Regent when the King was ill or was vacationing on the Riviera. Together with Crown Princess Louise, he made his first visit to the United States for two months during the summer of 1926. In Washington, where they were entertained at the White House by President Calvin Coolidge, the Prince dedicated a memorial in Potomac Park to John Ericsson, the Swedish-born engineer who built the famous Union ironclad, the *Monitor*. After a cross-country tour of various Swedish-American communities, the royal couple sailed from San Francisco to continue their nine-month journey around the world by way of Hawaii, Japan, China, and India. In 1934-35 they traveled through Greece, the Near and Middle East, and Egypt and Ethiopia. Their second American visit, for twenty-six days in the summer of 1938, was made in connection with the tercentenary celebration of the arrival of the first Swedish settlers. In the course of his two trips to the United States, the Crown Prince was awarded honorary doctorates from Princeton, Yale, Clark, and Chicago universities (1926) and from Harvard, Pennsylvania, and Lafayette (1938). He also holds honorary degrees from the Universities of Lund (Sweden, 1918), Cambridge (1929), Dorpat (1932), and the Royal Institute of Technology in Stockholm (1944).

When King Gustaf succumbed to a chronic bronchial condition October 29, 1950, Crown Prince Gustaf Adolf immediately became King Gustaf VI Adolf. Following the precedent set by his father, he dispensed with the coronation rites and was sworn in at a simple state ceremony which took place in the Royal Palace the next day. At this time he took the royal oath, pledging to uphold the constitution and to rule "as a righteous King and gracious father of the Swedish people by a legal, just, and mild government." The oath was administered by Premier Tage Erlander, in the presence of the Cabinet and two princes of the royal house, who immediately thereafter gave their pledge of allegiance. According to the tradition, the Premier then formally tendered his Government's resignation and the King, in turn, requested the Cabinet to remain in office. At a subsequent throne room ceremony, during which he received oaths of loyalty from the assembled heads of the armed forces, state administration, and judiciary, the King announced that his motto would be "Duty Above All." The King and his consort then appeared on the Palace balcony where they were greeted with a tremendous ovation.

Since the new King's eldest son, Prince Gustaf Adolf, was killed in an airplane crash at Copenhagen in 1947, the heir apparent to the throne is the late Prince's only son, Carl Gustaf, Duke of Jämtland, born nine months before the air tragedy. The new ruler's second and fourth sons, Sigvard and Carl Johan, forfeited their rights to the throne as well as their titles by marrying commoners. His daughter, Princess Ingrid, married Crown Prince Frederik '47 of Denmark and became Queen of that country when her husband ascended the throne in 1947. His third son, bachelor Prince Bertil, Duke of Halland, is second in the line of succession to the throne of Sweden.

Sweden's new King has inherited his family's intellectual and artistic gifts. As a student at Uppsala University, he became intensely interested in archaeology, conducted excavations of ancient Swedish monuments, and published papers on his findings. He has initiated and sponsored large-scale Swedish archaeological expeditions to China (which in 1926 unearthed remnants of the so-called Peking Man); to Greece (at Aisne, in Argolis, where he dug with pick and spade for six weeks in 1922) to Cyprus, Egypt, and the Near East. During his travels he has personally investigated the results of these researches. He has also presided over the Swedish Oriental Society and China Committee, which have supported the explorations in China, and under his chairmanship the Swedish Archaeological Institute was founded in Rome in 1926. Through his studies of antiquity, the King early acquired a taste for the fine arts. Considered an authority on Chinese ceramics, he owns one of the largest private collections of Asiatic pottery in the world, as well as an extensive collection of modern Swedish art and handicrafts. A patron of the arts, he has been active for many years as chairman of the Friends of the National Museum in Stockholm, and lent his support to the establishment of Far Eastern and Egyptian museums in the capital.

An outstanding athlete in his youth, the King has served as chairman of the Swedish National Association for Athletics and Sports (1903-32), the Central Union for the Promotion of Sports (1908-32), the Military Athletic Association, and the Skiing Association. As chairman of the Swedish Olympic Committee, he helped organize the Fifth Olympic Games, held in Stockholm in 1912. His personal liking for a wide variety of sports led to the establishment of tests in all-athletic ability, which **were** conducted on a national basis to confer

on all who passed the gold insignia of "athlete." At the age of thirty-four he participated in the first tests and won an insignia for himself. As late as World War II he took part in an open walking competition. His own favorite sports are skiing, golf, and tennis.

While he was Crown Prince, Gustaf Adolf and the Princess divided their time between an apartment in the Royal Palace in Stockholm, a suburban chateau at Ulriksdal, near the capital, and a summer home, "Sofiero," in Skåne (in south Sweden), where they enjoyed their mutual hobby of gardening. Reporters who interviewed the Crown Prince on his arrival in the United States commented on his serious and scholarly appearance, but in conversation (he speaks English fluently) found he was "animated, with a quick, engaging smile" (New York *Times*). Over six feet in height, with a robust physique, he has gray-brown hair and wears thick-lensed glasses. He does not drink nor smoke. Descriptions of his personality stress his "personal modesty and simplicity of manner."

References

American-Scandinavian R 14:5 My '26
Christian Sci Mon p4 O 30 '50
Forum and Century 75 :870-6 Je '26
Independent 116 :606-7 My 22 '26
Literary Digest 89 :40-6 My 22 '26
N Y Herald Tribune p3 O 30 '50
N Y Times IV p7 My 16 '26 por
Outlook 143 :141-2 My 26 '26
Time 41 :26 My 31 '43
Svenska Män och Kvinnor (1948)

GUTHMAN, EDWIN O(TTO) Aug. 11, 1919- Journalist

Address: b. c/o Seattle Times, Seattle 11, Wash.; h. 800 McGilvra Blvd., Seattle, Wash.

Winner of the Pulitzer Prize for distinguished reporting on national affairs in 1949, Edwin O. Guthman of the Seattle *Times* received the award on the basis of articles clearing a University of Washington professor of charges of communism leveled at him before the Washington State Legislature's Un-American Activities Committee. When the Pulitzer award was made, in May 1950, Guthman had been attached to the Seattle *Times* as a reporter on general assignments and at the State Legislature for a little less than two years. Earlier he had been on the staff of the Seattle *Star*; and previous to that, he had served for four and a third years in the United States Army in World War II.

Born in Seattle, Washington, on August 11, 1919, Edwin Otto Guthman is the son of Otto and Hilda (Leiser) Guthman. His father, now deceased, was vice-president and sales manager of a Seattle wholesale grocery firm, The National Grocery Company. The families of Guthman's parents came originally from Germany. Guthman's maternal grandfather, Simon Leiser, was a pioneer settler of Victoria, B. C. Guthman himself was the youngest of four children and the only boy in his family. "We were a middle class family living in a middle class neighborhood," he says, "and my childhood was

EDWIN O. GUTHMAN

uneventful. I began dreaming about being a newspaperman when I was ten. In fact, I have never wanted to be anything else." At Seattle's Broadway High School, from which he was graduated in 1937, he was the editor of the school paper and on the track team.

Following his bent, Guthman enrolled at the University of Washington (in Seattle) to major in journalism. He became the editor of the university daily and a member of Sigma Delta Chi, journalism honorary fraternity. During his summer vacations he held odd jobs; in two of these he worked in a warehouse and in a ladies' wholesale ready-to-wear establishment. In the summer of 1940, as one of fifty-six students from leading American colleges and universities, he represented Washington at the American-Japanese Student Conference in Japan. His professional journalistic experience began with work (1940 and 1941) as a part-time sports reporter on the Seattle *Star* while he was still a student at Washington.

Directly upon his graduation from the university with a B.S. degree in journalism in 1941, the year of the United States entry into World War II, Guthman was drafted into the Army, to serve as a private in the infantry until December 1942. Having attended an Officer Candidate School, he became a reconnaissance platoon leader of the 339th Infantry Regiment, 85th Division. Wounded in action in Italy, he was awarded the Purple Heart and the Silver Star. When he was discharged from the armed services in November 1945, Guthman had served for four years and four months and had achieved the rank of captain.

The year 1946 found him working as a general assignment reporter for the now defunct Seattle *Star*, the paper for which he had worked as a part-time sportswriter during his college days. He became assistant city editor of the *Star* in 1947, but in August of the same year he was engaged as general assignment and

State Legislature reporter by the "conservative . . . successful . . . Seattle *Times*, circulation 208,442" (*Time*, November 7, 1949).

Guthman's Pulitzer Prize was awarded to him on the basis of the articles he wrote for the Seattle *Times* in 1949. In it he cleared a University of Washington professor of a charge of communism made by the Washington State Legislature's Un-American Activities Committee. The professor, Dr. Melvin R. Rader, denied the charges and instituted perjury proceedings against his accuser (ex-Communist George Hewitt). However, Hewitt had meanwhile flown to New York, where a court judge refused to allow his extradition to face the perjury charge in Seattle. The *Times* did not become actively interested in the case until after the action of the New York judge, whose decision had left the Rader-Hewitt dispute unsettled. The newspaper's managing and city editors, Guthman recalls, "felt that the question of who told the truth was of great . . . importance to the people of Seattle. Not only was the reputation of a university professor in doubt, but the reputations of the committee and Hewitt—who had figured as an important witness for the government in immigration cases—also were at stake."

When Guthman was given his long-term assignment to determine the truth of the matter, he had been covering hearings of the State's Un-American Activities Committee for two years. His research and subsequent news stories on the Rader case disproved Hewitt's testimony, led to Rader's exoneration by the president of the University of Washington, and indicated that evidence favorable to the professor had been suppressed during the committee's investigation (*Time*, November 7, 1949). The story of Guthman's "detective work," together with the statement of the university president, was headlined on page one of the Seattle *Times* on October 21, 1949. The Pulitzer Prize awarded to Guthman for his work was the first such award to be bestowed on a citizen of his State, where he was also honored by the Washington State Press Club's 1949 award for distinguished reporting.

Edwin O. Guthman married Jo Ann Cheim on July 6, 1947; they have a son, named Lester. The journalist lists his religious faith as Jewish, his political classification as independent. He is a member of Seattle's Glendale Golf Club and the Country Club. Of large stature, he is five feet eleven inches tall, weighs 180 pounds; he has brown hair and blue eyes. For recreation he turns to golf, gardening, and a game of cards—"particularly poker."

References

N Y Herald Tribune p17 My 2 '50
N Y Times p1, 22 My 2 '50 por
Time 54:63 N 7 '49 por

GUTHRIE, A(LFRED) B(ERTRAM), JR. Jan. 13, 1901- Author; teacher
Address: h. 246 Tahoma Rd., Lexington, Ky.

A. B. Guthrie, Jr., the winner of the 1949 Pulitzer Prize for fiction, received that award for *The Way West.* His earlier novel, *The Big Sky* (1947), had also achieved distinction as a widely praised, best-selling book. Before devoting his full time to authorship, Guthrie for some twenty years had been engaged in newspaper work in Lexington, Kentucky.

Scottish-Irish descended Alfred Bertram Guthrie, was born in Bedford, Indiana, on January 13, 1901. His father, for whom he was named, was an educator and country newspaper editor; Mrs. Guthrie was the former June Thomas. When the junior Guthrie was six months old, the family (in which there were several other children—a brother and a sister are living) moved to Choteau, Montana, a little town on the eastern slope of the Rockies, where the elder Guthrie had been appointed the first principal of the newly established Teton County High School. Reared in Choteau (near which he now owns a summer home), Guthrie attended the county high school and graduated in 1919. After school hours he worked as a printer's devil on the Choteau *Acantha*, of which his father earlier had been editor and publisher.

It was during these years that his father's interest in newspaper-making and Western history became the greatest single influence on young Guthrie, whose ambition it was to be a newspaperman. After his freshman year at the University of Washington, he transferred to Montana State University, where he majored in journalism. While at college he was a student assistant, contributed articles to a little regional magazine, *The Frontier*, spent one summer working in the Lewis and Clark National Forest in Montana, and other summers on ranches in Montana.

Graduated with honors in 1923, Guthrie and a fellow student bought an old Model-T Ford with which they went to the Yaqui Valley in Mexico to work for five months on an irrigation project. From there Guthrie went to California with the intention of starting his newspaper career, but conditions there were unfavorable. He was next employed at the Western Electric plant in Emoryville, became a clerk in a chain grocery, and in the fall of 1924 went home to take a Federal agricultural census, for which he traveled about in a Ford or on horseback. The census finished, Guthrie entered the advertising and selling department of a flour and feed mill, which a relative of his ran in Attica, New York. This employment ended when the mill burned down in 1926.

At this point Guthrie, while visiting in Kentucky, got his first opportunity in journalism. The editor of the Lexington *Leader* engaged him as a reporter, and three years later in 1929 he was advanced to the post of city editor. In the course of the twenty-one years he was with the *Leader* he became an editorial writer and finally its executive editor. "My newspaper stories I am proudest of," he has said, "are those that brought results in terms of social welfare."

In 1939, at the age of thirty-eight, the newspaperman made his first attempt at writing fiction, something he had wanted to do before, but for which he had never had the time. That year, while he was visiting his ill mother

Erich Hartmann

A. B. GUTHRIE, JR.

in a Rochester (Minnesota) hospital, he had much time for reading, and turned to Westerns and detective stories. Feeling that he might do as well as those authors, he began to write a mystery story with a Western background. When he ran into difficulties, he considered it "a matter of self-discipline" to see if he could finish the book, a task he worked at for four years. In 1943 it was published under the title *Murders at Moon Dance*, and was also brought out in England and Argentina. Today its author considers that first book "a trashy piece of work."

The journalist, on leave from his Lexington paper, in 1944-45 attended Harvard University on a Nieman fellowship, which provides working newspapermen with a year's unrestricted study. Two of the courses Guthrie took were on international relations and creative writing, the latter a seminar under Theodore Morrison. He now wrote a portion of the book *The Big Sky.* From Harvard Guthrie returned to his Kentucky newspaper, where he remained until February 1947, shortly before the publication of *The Big Sky.* The novel received much favorable attention from reviewers, one of whom, Allan Nevins (in the *Saturday Review of Literature*) described it as "skillfully planned and beautifully finished." In his story of the primitive life of the frontier during the opening of the American West, the author was highly successful "in evoking a time, a land, and a people," commented Bruce Lancaster (in the *Atlantic*), remarking that his style contained "passages of sheer poetry that suggest Carl Sandburg, while remaining entirely Guthrie." The book's "skillful balance between sentiment and realism" was commended by the *United States Quarterly Booklist.*

Guthrie's next book, *The Way West*, which became the Book-of-the-Month Club selection

GUTHRIE, A. B., JR.—*Continued*

for October 1949, was awarded the Pulitzer Prize for fiction in May 1950. It is a story of an emigrant trek from Missouri to Oregon in the 1840's, in which one of the characters in *The Big Sky* reappears. Of it, E. B. Davis wrote in the *Herald Tribune*: "If it is not as big a book as *The Big Sky*, it is a better novel. Its pattern of character is more various, more human, and warmer." A *Time* reviewer, while praising the book's "fictional fidelity to time and place," criticized the author's "overripe" prose, a point of style remarked upon by other critics. Walter Van Tilburg Clark, stressing what he considered the author's "superior achievement in structure," estimated Guthrie's second novel to be "in both conception and manner, a better book than *The Big Sky*" (*Saturday Review of Literature,* October 8, 1949).

The Big Sky and *The Way West* form the first half of a panel on the West which Guthrie wants to complete with one novel on the gold-mining camp and cattle days, and another one dealing with the Northwest from 1900 to the present. In the meantime he is at work on a book (in 1950) about the Yellowstone River for the "Rivers of America" series. In May 1950 he made a 1,400-mile journey on the Missouri River with Bernard De Voto and Commander William J. Lederer of the United States Navy, retracing the Oregon trail and touring the Army Engineers' flood control projects from Montana to St. Louis. Guthrie, who has written numerous short stories and articles, also gives a winter course on creative writing at the University of Kentucky.

The Montana State University awarded Guthrie an honorary doctorate in literature in 1949. With respect to clubs or organizations Guthrie describes himself as "not much of a joiner"; but he did found in Lexington (about 1940) the still existing Speakeasy Club for timid speakers, "which", he says, "God knows I am." He conducted, however, a publicity campaign for the revision of the State constitution of Kentucky in 1949. Politically he qualifies himself as a "maverick."

In June 1931 Guthrie married Harriet Helen Larson, of Choteau, whom he had known since childhood and courted for nine years "long distance," as he once said. They have a son, Alfred Bertram 3d, and a daughter, Helen Larson. Fairly tall (five feet ten inches), Guthrie weighs 170 pounds. His eyes are blue, his hair is brown. His favorite recreations are woodworking, fishing, following old trails and "soaking up summer atmosphere in Montana," to which the Guthries go to spend vacation months at their small lodge. For more than twenty years the writer has collected Western Americana, especially old books and early firearms. A short biographical piece in the *Saturday Review of Literature* described him as easygoing and popular, "probably because other people's anecdotes interest him as much as his own."

References

Ed & Pub 82:26 O 22 '49
N Y Herald Tribune p17 My 2 '50; II p3 My 7 '50
N Y Times p22 My 2 '50
Sat Eve Post 220:10 Ag 16 '47
Sat R Lit 30:9 My 3 '47; 31:10 F 14 '48

GUY, RAYMOND F(REDERICK) July 4, 1899- Radio engineer; radio association official

Address: b. c/o Institute of Radio Engineers, 1 E. 79th St., New York 21; c/o National Broadcasting Co., 30 Rockefeller Plaza, New York 20; h. 370 Tryon Ave., Englewood, N.J.

During the term of 1950 the president of the Institute of Radio Engineers, which is international in scope, is Raymond F. Guy. For over twenty years Guy has been the manager of the radio and allocations engineering division of the National Broadcasting Company. He is the author of numerous papers on aspects of radio broadcasting and engineering in trade journals and professional reviews.

Born in Hartford, Connecticut, on July 4, 1899, Raymond Frederick Guy is the only son of George E. and Mary (Stevens) Guy, both of English descent. (He has one sister, now Mrs. Helen Winget.) The father of the future radio engineer was a machine designer. A series of "early radio books naming Marconi, Fessenden and others" aroused the boy's interest in the new medium of communication, in which (he declares) he has been "absorbed . . . since twelve years of age," when he became an amateur wireless operator.

Upon his graduation from high school in 1916, young Guy entered the professional ranks when he became a ship's radio officer. As a radio inspector he was employed at intervals by the Marconi Wireless Telegraph Company, the Independent Wireless Telegraph Company, and the Shipowners Radio Service. In 1918, the United States having become a belligerent in World War I, he enlisted; in the Signal Corps, he served through the closing engagements in France. On receiving his discharge he entered Pratt Institute, Brooklyn, New York, where he majored in electrical engineering and was awarded that engineering degree in 1921.

"Mr. Guy," stated a biographical release, "is a pioneer in radio broadcasting, having been on the original staff . . . at WJZ when it started operation in 1921 in a tiny shack on the roof of the Westinghouse factory building in Newark, New Jersey. The audience consisted of only a few amateurs, commercial broadcasting was unknown, and practically all operating methods and techniques had to be originated by trial and error." Among his radio "firsts" as engineer-announcer in 1921-23 were a World Series game and broadcasts of theatrical productions, concerts, sports events, and speeches. Guy remained at WJZ, which was the world's second licensed broadcasting station, for somewhat less than three years, during which period (according to an article in

Electronics) he "was the chief engineer, station manager, part-time announcer, chief wrangler of the Edison phonograph, and stand-by listener for SOS calls." For another year, after the Newark station was dismantled, he was director of the field activities of the new WJZ and WJY stations in the Aeolian Building in New York. In 1924 he joined the engineering staff of the Radio Corporation of America's Research Laboratories, and in the course of the next five years directed the engineering, development and construction of standard and shortwave broadcasting apparatus, stations and systems and participated in RCA's earliest television development.

During this period Guy took an active part in pioneering network broadcasting, designing and building repeating apparatus for Western Union and Postal Telegraph used to create a network from Washington to Schenectady. He also took part in effecting (in 1925) the first transatlantic broadcast, when 2LO in London was received in Belfast, Maine, for retransmission; he aided in the development of short wave relaying. In 1925 he directed the design and construction of one of the world's first high-powered international broadcasting stations, taking a leading part in gaining an important position for the United States in that field.

In 1925 Guy became an associate member of the Institute of Radio Engineers. This body, established in 1912 to promote high standards in "the theory and practice of radio, and allied branches of engineering and of the related arts and sciences," had a charter membership of about seventy. After the termination of World War II the enrollment was approximately 16,000, and by the end of 1949 the figure was 28,000. In its early days the institute through its committee on stabilization, was largely responsible for the application of accurate measurement and sound engineering principles to the infant science of radio; and today its monthly magazine, *Proceedings of the I.R.E.*, is considered the most authoritative medium for the presentation of the latest advances in radio and television.

Guy in 1931 was admitted to full membership in the I.R.E., and was elected a fellow in 1939. He has served on a large number of the organization's committees, functioning as chairman of the standards, public relations, founders, transmitters, membership and office practices committees, and vice-chairman of the building fund and executive committee. Elected to the board of directors in 1943, he served thereon until 1948, was treasurer for one term, and has represented the Institute in the activities of the American Standards Association. On November 18, 1949, announcement was made that he had been elected president of the Institute of Radio Engineers for the year 1950, succeeding Stuart L. Bailey of Washington, D.C. (The new vice-president of the I.R.E., elected at the same time, is Sir Robert Watson-Watt [45], who has been described as England's outstanding radar authority.) The new president was installed on March 7 at the institute's 1950 convention.

Famous Studio

RAYMOND F. GUY

In 1929, when the National Broadcasting Company's facilities group of six research engineers was formed, Guy was placed at its head and, as manager of radio and allocations engineering, has since directed the company's frequency allocations engineering and the planning, design, and construction of all NBC transmitting facilities. He was largely responsible for the course of NBC's experiments with frequency modulation. In 1937 Guy was admitted to practice as a professional engineer in New York and New Jersey. The engineer is principal author of "Rules and Standards for Broadcasting Stations" which appeared in *Electronics* for August 1939 and may also be found in *Radio Digest*.

The radio engineer supervised the moving of Station WEAF to Port Washington, Long Island, and was responsible for the design and construction of the WNBT television station, the WNBC-FM station in the Empire State Building, New York City, and six international broadcasting stations at Bound Brook, New Jersey. He has given a comprehensive account of FM development in a series of papers entitled *The Why and How of Frequency Modulation* which appeared in the *A.T.E. Journal*, *Radiocraft*, and the *Broadcast Engineers Journal* between September 1940 and September 1941.

During World War II the radio engineer served as a consultant to the Coordinator of International Affairs, assisted on an Office of Strategic Services project, and participated in the work of the Office of War Information. Since the end of the war he has taken part in international conferences on radio in Havana, Mexico City, Montreal, and Washington.

Guy has served on the Radio Technical Planning Board, and is engineering chairman of the Television Broadcasters Association. The first of some forty articles and technical papers he

GUY, RAYMOND F.—*Continued*

has contributed to special journals and reviews appeared in *Popular Radio* in 1927 under the title "The Fight Against Distortion." Since that date his writings have been published in *Electronics, The A.T.E. Journal, Radiocraft, Scientific American, Broadcast Engineers Journal*, and other radio and electronics magazines; he is the author of the article on network broadcasting in *Nelson's Encyclopedia* (1946). From time to time Guy speaks before professional and laymen groups.

A fellow of the Radio Club of America, life member of the Veteran Wireless Operators' Association and a charter member of the Radio Pioneers Club, the radio expert is also a member of the Radio Executives Club and of the Society of Professional Engineers. Raymond Guy and Myrtle Bennett were married in August 1922; their daughter is Mrs. Betty Guy Hanson. They make their home in Englewood, New Jersey, where the I.R.E. president may find relaxation at golf or his hobby of color portraiture. The gray-eyed engineer, who is five feet eleven and one-half inches tall and weighs 210 pounds, attends the Methodist church and is a Republican in political affiliation.

References

Bergen (N.J.) Evening Record p25 D 28 '49
N Y Times p8 N 19 '49 por
Proceedings of the I. R. E. 38:2 Ja '50 por
Tele-Tech p37 D '49 por

HAIG-BROWN, RODERICK (LANGMERE) Feb. 21, 1908- Author

Address: b. Campbell River, British Columbia, Can.

Reprinted from the *Wilson Library Bulletin*, March 1950.

The fish of British Columbia have a tireless defender and an equally relentless pursuer in Roderick Haig-Brown, who began fishing as a boy between the chalk hills of Dorset in England, and eventually brought his family to live at Campbell River, a village about two hundred miles north of Victoria, British Columbia. Writing of *A River Never Sleeps* (1946), Orville Prescott remarked in the New York *Times*: "Fishing, to Mr. Haig-Brown, is not the lazy or contemplative man's relaxation. It is infinitely more than a mere sport, partaking of many of the solemn rites of a religious cult, the etiquette, tradition, and stern discipline of an art like the ballet, and the brotherhood and mystic union of a lodge or fraternity."

Roderick Langmere Haig-Brown was born February 21, 1908, in Lancing, Sussex, England, the grandson of Dr. William Haig-Brown, headmaster and second founder of Charterhouse School, and son of Lieutenant Colonel A. H. Haig-Brown, D.S.O., and Violet Mary (Pope) Haig-Brown. He has two younger sisters, Joan and Valerie. Their father was killed in action at Bapaume in 1918. (He had published three books, *Sporting Sonnets, My Game Book*, and *O.T.C. in the Great War*.)

RODERICK HAIG-BROWN

The boy was raised at the Victorian home of his maternal grandfather, Alfred Pope of Wrackelford, Dorset, who owned plenty of land for fishing and shooting. At Charterhouse young Haig-Brown went in for general athletics. Graduating in 1925, he studied history for a year with a tutor before quitting England in search of "broken country," found in a logging camp in the State of Washington.

Moving up to British Columbia in 1927, he worked as second loader, rigger, timber cruiser, and surveyor, and as a guide on the Nimpkish River conducting hunting and fishing trips. At the end of 1929 he returned to England for a year or so, where he settled in the Chelsea district of London and wrote his first book, *Silver* (1931), the story of an Atlantic salmon. (He had already published several articles in British sporting magazines, the first at fifteen.) Here he also drafted *Pool and Rapid* (1935), dealing with his favorite river country.

After his return to Canada Haig-Brown married Ann Elmore, of Seattle, Washington, in 1934, and moved that year from the Nimpkish country on Vancouver Island, which had no highway connection with the rest of the world, to Campbell River, which did. The Haig-Browns have four children, Valerie, Mary, Alan, and Celia. They moved to their present home, "Above Tide," a house on the bank of the Campbell River with twenty acres of land, in 1936.

Ki-Yu (1935), written in Canada, was a story for young readers about a blackstreak Vancouver Island panther. His next book, *Western Angler* (1939), writes the author, "kept the family broke, because I took so long writing it. Largely scientific, it concerns British Columbia game fishing and is in two volumes. Definitely a 'prestige' book in publishing circles, it took four years to write." It was reissued in revised form in 1947.

Return to the River (1941), written to recoup the family finances, was an almost sensational success. After finishing the first two chapters, Haig-Brown sent them to his agent to get sufficient money to make a research trip to the Columbia River to finish this life story of a salmon. In a front-page review in *Books*, J. R. de la Torre Bueno called it "nothing less than a masterpiece," whose author "feels as a humane and broad-minded man and writes like an angel." *Timber, a Novel of Pacific Coast Loggers* (1942) seemed to the *New Yorker* "a technically expert, colloquial and likable story."

Starbuck Valley Winter (1943), a book for boys about an American boy trapping on Vancouver Island, received the Canadian Library Association award as the best Canadian juvenile of the year. At that time Haig-Brown (as he still is) stipendiary magistrate and judge of the juvenile court for the area north of Sayward, and chief A.R.P. warden for the same district. The New York *Times* found "dramatic and plausible" another boys' book, *Saltwater Summer* (1948), which won the Governor-General's citation as the best Canadian juvenile published that year.

In praising *A River Never Sleeps* (1946), an autobiographical fishing record, Orville Prescott noted that "few men today write about nature with such a felicitous combination of exact observation and literary charm." He portrays nature better than man, according to critics of *On the Highest Hill* (1949), a tragic novel about an introverted Canadian. Haig-Brown has another autobiographical book in progress under the working title of "No Want of Wonder."

Major Haig-Brown, a six-footer with brown hair and brown eyes, weighs 160 pounds; his favorite recreations are "fishing and not going anywhere." He has no political affiliations ("None, definitely!") and is a member of the Church of England. His favorite author is Henry Fielding, another magistrate. He says, "I have a great reputation as a conservationist . . . based chiefly on the fact that I have worked and written at various times in favor of such unexceptionable objects," but he adds that he has "rarely been successful in achieving anything except a reputation by these activities."

HALPRIN, ROSE LURIA *See* Halprin, Mrs. S. W.

HALPRIN, MRS. SAMUEL W. Zionist organization official

Address: b. c/o Hadassah, 1819 Broadway, New York 23; h. 225 E. 74th St., New York 21

The president of the Women's Zionist Organization of America, Hadassah, is Mrs. Samuel W. Halprin, who has long been active in Zionist circles. For five years she lived in Palestine, working there as liaison officer between the Hadassah groups in the United States and in Palestine. She is the only American woman member of the executive of the Jewish Agency for Palestine. Mrs. Halprin was first elected president of Hadassah in 1932, and was re-elected the following year. In 1947 she again was chosen for the presidency, in which she serves her fourth consecutive term after her re-election in August 1950.

Mrs. Samuel W. Halprin was born Rose Luria, in New York's Lower East Side, to Philip and Rebecca (Isaacson) Luria. "I was the first-born, and I was supposed to be a boy," she has related, "so I got a better Jewish education than my brothers." Reared in the district of her birth, for her early religious education she attended a neighborhood Hebrew school, where she was the only girl. At the age of ten she joined a children's Zionist organization, and by the time she was twelve had delivered her first speech on the subject of the Jewish national home in Palestine; and before she was much older she taught Hebrew at the Educational Alliance. For her secular education she attended Washington Irving High School. Shortly after her graduation from that institution she was married to Samuel W. Halprin, a cousin, on April 26, 1914.

Mrs. Halprin then attended Hunter College and afterward took French, German, and philosophy courses at Columbia University. She thus developed into a linguist with a ready command of Hebrew, French, and German. During her college years she had been active in Hadassah, the Women's Zionist Organization of America, and in 1932 she became the youngest president in its history. She was re-elected the following year. In 1934 she went to Jerusalem with her husband and for five years remained there as liaison officer between the national board of Hadassah in the United States and the Hadassah Medical Organization in Palestine. In 1938 she became a member of the legislative council for Zionist affairs between Zionist congresses.

In 1942 Mrs. Halprin (who had returned to the United States in 1939) became a member of the American section of the Jewish Agency for Palestine, to serve as vice-president of the section until 1946, when she was elected to the executive body of the agency proper. The Jewish Agency for Palestine, consisting of Zionists and non-Zionists, comprises representatives from all Zionists groups throughout the world. It is recognized as "an agency for the Jewish people in all matters pertaining to the upbuilding of the Jewish National Home" (in the words of the *Statesman's Yearbook*). Thus, acting as a "quasi-government" of the Jewish people, it was responsible for a large part of the political work which led to the proclamation of Israel's independence on May 14, 1948, and represented the nascent state at the U.N. sessions on the Palestine problem. Mrs. Halprin, who is the only American woman member of the organization's executive, was a delegate at the Paris Conference of the policy-making group. Her work with the agency has entailed several trips to Palestine.

Mrs. Halprin was a representative to Hadassah's actions committee from 1939 to 1946; from 1939 to 1941 she was chairman of the Palestine committee ,and from 1941 to 1947 of the political committee. Since 1942 she has been a representative to the American Zionist

Tesslère

MRS. SAMUEL W. HALPRIN

Emergency Council (treasurer in 1942; a vice-chairman 1945-47). In 1946 she was a delegate to the Twenty-second Zionist Congress, and a member of the American committee of eight of the World Zionist Organization. The Secretariat for the Organization of an American Jewish Conference acquired Mrs. Halprin's services in 1946; she subsequently became a member of its interim committee, of its executive committee, and chairman of its Palestine committee. Mrs. Halprin was vice-chairman for America of the World Confederation of General Zionists.

In 1947 the Zionist leader was once again elected national president of Hadassah, the office to which she was re-elected in 1948 and 1949. The Women's Zionist Organization of America, Hadassah (the Hebrew for Esther), was founded in 1912 by Henrietta Szold [40], who at that time established a clinic in Palestine for the treatment of trachoma. The purpose of the organization (as stated in the American Jewish Yearbook) is: "To foster Zionist ideals in the United States and conduct health, medical, and social service activities in Palestine." Two publications, *Hadassah Newsletter* and *Hadassah Headlines*, are issued by the group. Its membership, by the end of 1949, amounted to some 270,000 women in the United States and Puerto Rico. (This figure does not include the membership of Junior Hadassah, a youth group.) Particularly concerned with improving medical facilities in Palestine, the organization established several clinics and hospitals and founded the Hadassah-Hebrew University Medical Center, the development of which Mrs. Halprin helped to supervise during her five years in Jerusalem. Attached to the center was a research center, a nurse's training school, and a postgraduate medical school. During 1946-48 Hadassah, in conjunction with the American Friends of the Hebrew University, carried on a campaign for funds with which to finance

the addition of an undergraduate medical school. The organization has also undertaken recreation projects, vocational education, youth refugee and land work, public health and feeding problems in Palestine.

Hadassah has been one of the groups most actively working for the establishment of the Jewish state. It accepted the partition proposal reluctantly "as a heavy sacrifice in the hope that it will speedily end the homelessness of the Jewish people." Of the new state, Mrs. Halprin once said, "It couldn't ever be a military state with a great army or navy and we see no danger of its evolving into a communist state, though some enemies of independence have advanced that objection. Palestine is, and doubtless always will be liberal and progressive in educational and cultural fields but advocates of communism are so few as to be almost nil."

Discussing the question of Jewish-American political allegiance in the light of the establishment of the new state of Israel, Mrs. Halprin declared: "Our political allegiance is to the United States, the land of our birth and our citizenship. It is because Jews . . . understand the transcendent value of the liberties we enjoy here, that we are eager to foster a movement designed to bring the same benefits to the people of Israel." With reference to Hadassah's work in Palestine, its president said, "We have given Israel a medical standard and a pattern. Now we have begun to turn over our functions to the community." The organization, however, plans to continue its work in the new nation, and a budget of $5,935,000 was voted for the year 1949. Included in its plans are a land purchase project and continued health work.

Mr. and Mrs. Halprin have an apartment in New York City, where the husband is in the export-import business. Among their interests are books and pictures, and a collection of rare metal and pottery gathered in Palestine. The Halprins have two children: Larry, a landscape architect, and Rose, a sculptress. The Zionist leader is described as "tiny, pink-cheeked" and "brown-haired, merry-eyed." She does not consider herself domestically inclined. "I make good chicken en casserole, brisket and broiled chicken—and everyone who has been to my house has eaten them twenty-seven times."

References

N Y Post Mag p39 D 22 '48 por
Who's Who in America, 1950-51

HAND, LEARNED (lûr'nĕd) Jan. 27, 1872- Judge
Address: b. United States Court House, New York 7; h. 142 E. 65th St., New York 21

By the end of 1949 Judge Learned Hand had completed forty years on the Federal bench—from 1909 to 1924 as a judge in the United States District Court for Southern New York, since 1924 in the United States Circuit Court of Appeals for the Second Judicial Circuit, on which he has sat as senior judge since 1939. During those years he has rendered approximately 1,800 decisions which Justice Frankfurter has described as "an enduring source of truth-seeking and illumination."

An ancestor of Judge Hand's came to America in 1644 as one of the nine original settlers of Easthampton, Long Island. His grandfather, Augustus Hand, attended the first law school in the United States and eventually became a justice of the New York State Supreme Court. A leading New York lawyer, his father, Samuel Hand, had the reputation of having argued more cases before the New York Court of Appeals than any other lawyer of his time. His two uncles, Clifford and Richard Hand, were also prominent in the legal profession. His cousin, Augustus N. Hand, has been a United States District Judge and since 1927 a member of the same Circuit Court as himself—the two cousins often serve on the same judicial panel. Learned Hand, who has not used his first given name (Billings) since he was thirty, was born in Albany, New York, on January 27, 1872. His mother was the former Lydia Colt Learned.

When he was eighteen years old, Hand entered Harvard University, where, under the guidance of Professors Santayana, Royce, and William James, he majored in philosophy. He was graduated with highest honors and a Phi Beta Kappa key in 1893. As an undergraduate he acquired the nickname of "Ancient Mongolian" because of the mustache and beard he then affected. His interest in writing, which later manifested itself in judicial opinions notable for their stylistic brilliance, was evident during his Harvard years, when he served as editor of the *Harvard Advocate*. He was the class day orator at his graduating ceremonies. Completing graduate studies in philosophy in a year, he was granted a Master's degree in 1894. Then, according to an article on the jurist ("The Great Judge," by Philip Hamburger in the November 4, 1946, issue of *Life*), he decided to enter Harvard Law School. "There were so many lawyers in the family," he said, "so I went too." Young Hand became editor of the *Harvard Law Review* and was granted his LL.B. degree with honors in 1896.

In 1897 Hand, who was admitted to the New York State bar, began his career as a law clerk for Marcus T. Hun in Albany. Two years later he became a member of the firm of Hun, Johnson and Hand. In 1902, dissatisfied with the routine of mortgage claims and small civil suits, he left Albany for New York City, where his first position was as managing clerk for the Wall Street firm of Zabriskie, Burrill and Murray. Subsequently, in 1904, he became a member of the law firm of Gould and Wilkie, with which he remained until 1909. The American Bar Association *Journal* of September 1947 described Hand during this period as a "doughty opponent in civil cases as well as a trusted adviser of business concerns." His handling of cases also demonstrated his particular judicial talents, and in 1909 he was appointed by President Taft to serve as a judge for the Southern District of New York. It was a few years later that Hand took an active part in politics, in the Progressive (Bull Moose) party Presiden-

LEARNED HAND

tial campaign of Theodore Roosevelt in 1912; he was in the year following an unsuccessful candidate for the chief judgeship of the New York State Court of Appeals.

The United States District Courts are the principal Federal trial courts of original jurisdiction—they hear most of the cases within Federal jurisdiction and make final disposition of the majority of them. During the fifteen years from 1909 to 1924 in which Hand served in the Court for the Southern District of New York, he rendered 637 opinions, touching on all phases of the law. Of the many cases he decided, two have often been referred to in law journals. The first, at the time of World War I, concerned the issuance of a magazine, *The Masses*, which took an antiwar stand. The Postmaster General decided the paper was nonmailable because it violated the recently passed Espionage Act of 1917. In a *Harvard Law Review* article for February 1947, Hand's ruling in favor of the magazine and against the Government action as a threat to free speech was described as "a notable example of fairness and self-restraint" which tended to "discourage hotheads and to reassure objectors who are really conscientious." The second case dealt with the application of the Prohibition Act and Eighteenth Amendment to United States vessels on the high seas and to ships of foreign registry coming within the three-mile limit of the United States. In an analysis of the case, *Current History* for December 1922 wrote that Hand had "pronounced a very able opinion sustaining the contention of the Government that in both instances the law applied." After his interpretation of the legislators' intention in passing that amendment, Hand in his opinion wrote: "Naturally, I have nothing to say about the wisdom of the amendment or the law, but wise or not, one thing is clear, that a drink of whiskey is as hurtful to

HAND, LEARNED—*Continued*
health and morals outside as inside Ambrose light."

In December 1924 Learned Hand was named by President Coolidge to the bench of the United States Circuit Court of Appeals for the Second Judicial Circuit, a life appointment. These courts, created by Congress in 1891, do not have original jurisdiction, but hear many of the appellate cases formerly assigned to the United States Supreme Court. Decrees of these courts are final unless reviewed by the highest court. The jurisdiction of Judge Hand's court covers Vermont, Connecticut, and the districts of New York. As the senior judge of that court since 1939, Judge Hand annually discusses with the Chief Justice of the United States conditions in the Second Circuit.

A count made in September 1947 revealed that Judge Hand had filed 1,192 opinions during his years thus far on the bench of the Circuit Court of Appeals. A compilation covering the years from 1909 to 1946 showed that the cases he had heard had been concerned with more than twenty branches of law, ranging from administrative law to cases of war powers and emergency legislation, and from copyrights to taxation.

A notable copyright case was *Sheldon v. Metro-Goldwyn Pictures*, (1936) which involved a novel, a play, and a film based on an actual incident. It was necessary to decide whether the film was based on the facts of the incident known to all, or on the novel and play written by Sheldon. In his opinion, which required a critical study of parallelism in creative expression, Hand found the motion picture company had made unfair use of the novelist's copyright. Among members of the legal profession his opinion in this case ranks as "a model of judicial style."

Another decree involved the Associated Press, which the Federal Government charged was monopolistic in its distribution of news. Considered "one of the most important legal cases in the history of the American press," it came before Judge Hand's court in 1943. After a year of study, he wrote the opinion that it was a by-law of the association, permitting members to veto admission of competing papers, which constituted a monopolistic practice under provisions of the Sherman antitrust law. A second important case of monopoly was the Government suit against the Aluminum Company of America; it came before him in 1945 after a District Court had dismissed the Government's complaint. Hand again wrote the opinion of the court, reversing the lower court by holding that the aluminum company was a "concentration of producing power . . . which was to be regarded as within the prohibition of the statute." The opinion he wrote is considered characteristic of his "approach to problems of statutory interpretation and illustrative of his power of effective statement." Previously, antitrust prosecution had (according to *Fortune*, July 1948) been concerned with "snipping at abuses," whereas Hand's opinion was concentrated on "what makes abuses possible." In the case of the Aluminum company it was market control of virgin aluminum by a single company which created a monopoly. Subsequent antitrust cases have been modeled on Hand's analysis and opinion in the 1945 suit.

According to an article in the *Harvard Law Review* (February 1947), Judge Hand's interpretation of constitutional law has been that the "Federal judiciary is the umpire between the nation and the States." The jurist himself has described the Constitution as "primarily an instrument to distribute political power; and so far as it is, it is hard to escape the necessity of some tribunal with authority to declare when the prescribed distribution has been disturbed." He has written that the provisions of the Bill of Rights are not "eternal verities," since they "are emptied of the vital occasions which gave them birth, and become moral adjurations, the more imperious because inscrutable." Rebelling against the literalism used by some to interpret the Constitution, Hand has written that the "colloquial words of a statute have not the fixed and artificial content of scientific symbols; they have a penumbra, a dim fringe, a connotation for they express an attitude of will, into which it is our duty [as judge] to penetrate." In order to analyze this legislative will, Judge Hand often refers to the history of a legislative act in order to clarify some ambiguous provision or phrase.

As the principal speaker at the May 1944 "I Am An American Day" celebration, Judge Hand described liberty as something in "the hearts of men and women; when it dies there, no constitution, no law, no court can help it." He said, too, that liberty was not the "ruthless, the unbridled will," but a spirit "which is not too sure that it is right; the spirit of liberty is the spirit which seeks to understand the minds of other men and women." Reprinted in magazines and newspapers, his remarks are considered "the finest definition of liberty uttered by a living American." On another occasion he spoke of liberty as "an essence so volatile that it will escape any vial, however corked." The *Life* article quoted Hand's concept of justice as "the tolerable accommodation of the conflicting interests of society; and I don't believe there is any royal road to attain such accommodations concretely." Although he considered each case a "new intellectual pursuit of freedom," his manner in the courtroom is described as "formidable," particularly when a counsel enters what the judge has called "the meadows of easy assumptions."

As a tribute to the Judge on his seventy-fifth birthday, the February 1947 issue of the *Harvard Law Review* was devoted to articles (written by eminent members of the legal profession) on Hand's contributions to public, criminal and constitutional law; on the unique lucidity and brilliance of his opinions; and on the quality of his judicial thinking. Justice Frankfurter wrote that Hand's many opinions would be referred to because of their "insights, the morality of the mind which respects these insights, and the beauty with which they are expressed," mentioning the "enduring language" of the opinions, illumined with "occasional flashes of sardonic humor and dissolving wit." Another commentator described the "great personal charm, keenness of perception, ready appreciation of the other man's point of view, and hearty dislike of affectation and sham" revealed in Hand's courtroom manner and final opinions. In cases dealing with copyright, monopoly, and constitutional law, Hand has been, as one commentator phrased it, "particularly happy."

Judge Hand has received honorary doctorates in law from several colleges and universities: Columbia (1930), Yale (1931), Pennsylvania (1933), Harvard (1939), Princeton (1947), and Amherst and Dartmouth (1938). In May 1947, Judge Hand's law clerks and the Harvard Law School Association honored him by placing a bust of him in the Harvard Law School Library. He is a member of the Association of the Bar of the City of New York and of the American Bar Association. His clubs are the Century and Harvard. In February 1923 he became a member of the American Law Institute, the organization which he helped to found. On the institute's executive committee, he is also a member of its council, which passes on the institute's publications dealing with fundamental questions of common law. He assisted in preparing A.L.I.'s *Model Code of Evidence, Restatement of Torts,* and *Restatement of Conflict of Law.*

Since his marriage, in 1902, to Frances Amelia Fincke, a Bryn Mawr graduate, Hand has occupied the brownstone New York City residence he purchased at that time. He has three daughters, Mary Deshon, Frances Lydia, and Constance; and four grandsons and three granddaughters. When court is in session the robust, stocky jurist usually walks the four miles from his home to his office every morning. Formerly his summer holidays were spent in Europe, but in recent years he has retired to his summer home in New Hampshire, where he enjoys reading and tramping through the woods. "Hand loves talk, morning, and night," is Charles C. Burlingham's comment on the conversational powers of the Judge, whose humor shows itself in mimicry and stories—"the delight of his friends."

References

Am Bar Assn J 33:869-72 S '47
Harvard Law R 60:3 F '47
Life 21:116-18 N 4 '46
Who's Who in America, 1950-51
Who's Who in Law, 1937

HARBACH, OTTO A(BELS) Aug. 18, 1873-   Librettist; song lyric writer

Address: b. c/o American Society of Composers, Authors and Publishers, 30 Rockefeller Plaza, New York 20; h. 125 E. 84th St., New York 28; 631 Orienta Ave., Mamaroneck, N.Y.

Otto A. Harbach, one of the most successful American librettists and writers of song lyrics, became president of the American Society of Composers, Authors and Publishers (ASCAP) in May 1950. Originally a professor of English, later a newspaper and advertising man, he had his first success on Broadway with the production *The Three Twins,* a musical comedy

of which he was librettist, in 1907. Since then he has written many famous librettos, among them *The Firefly, No, No, Nanette, Rose Marie, The Desert Song* and *Roberta.* The lyrics for more than a thousand songs, including "The Night Was Made For Love", "Sympathy", "Who", "Giannina Mia", "Indian Love Call", "The Touch of Your Hand," are by Harbach.

A son of Adolph Julius Hauerbach, a watchmaker and jeweler, and Hansina (Olsen) Hauerbach, Otto Abels Harbach (he shortened his name before 1920) was born in Salt Lake City, Utah, on August 18, 1873. His father, a native of Denmark, had emigrated to the United States ten years before and had driven an ox team to Salt Lake City. Hauerbach had a family of seven sons and one daughter. Otto attended the Salt Lake Collegiate Institute, from which he graduated in 1891. In his free time he delivered papers and groceries, and shined shoes in a barber shop. Harbach has said that during these years he was influenced mainly by the principal of the Collegiate Institute, Robert Caskey. Later, at Knox College, Galesburg, Illinois, its president, the educator and editor John Huston Finley, was his mentor. As Finley had done, Harbach worked his way through college and won the annual interstate prize for oratory in 1895, the year he received his B.A. degree. Three years later Harbach was given the M.A. degree in English by Knox, where he belonged to the fraternity Phi Gamma Delta.

After the completion of his studies Harbach became teacher of English and public speaking at Whitman College, Walla Walla, Washington. In 1901 he went to New York in order to study for the doctorate at Columbia University. Finding his five-hundred-dollar scholarship insufficient, he left Columbia after a brief stay to become a reporter for the New York *Daily News* in 1901. In 1903 he joined the George Batten Advertising Agency as a copywriter. He was to remain with that firm until 1910.

During his first years with the advertising agency, Harbach made attempts to write drama —he has related that, using a Western theme, he wrote and rewrote for eight years the scenes for a play which never reached production. Harbach, one of whose maxims is that no honest effort is ever wasted, cites in proof the experience he gained from these attempts. His first writing assignment, the rewriting of *Tom, Dick and Harry,* was offered him by a producer who had read his play. Taking part in college dramatics at Whitman and playing the violin in a Salt Lake City theater orchestra are also considered by the librettist as early experiences which contributed to his later successes. He has made a practice of trying out melodies on the violin when working for the lyrics for a musical show.

In 1907 Harbach and composer Karl Hoschna, with whom he had been collaborating, found a backer for the musical comedy, *The Three Twins,* for which Harbach had written the lyrics. Produced on Broadway that year, it was an immediate success and established Harbach's name as a librettist—one of the show's songs,

Moss Photo.
OTTO A. HARBACH

"Cuddle Up a Little Closer," became particularly popular. This collaboration with Hoschna continued until the latter's death in 1911. In 1908 they wrote *Bright Eyes,* the following year *Madame Sherry,* and in 1910 three musicals: *Girl of My Dreams, The Fascinating Widow* and *Dr. De Luxe.* In 1910 Harbach felt himself firmly enough established as a librettist to leave the advertising business so as to devote his time entirely to writing.

The list of librettos (original books and musical versions of plays and stories) which Harbach wrote, or to which he contributed, grew longer with *Girl of My Dreams* (1909), *The Firefly* (1912), *High Jinks* (1913), *Crinoline Girl* (1914), *Katinka* (1915), *Kitty Darlin'* (1917), *Up in Mabel's Room* (1919), *Mary* (1921), *Jimmie* (1920), *The O'Brien Girl* (1921), *June Love* (1921), *The Blue Kitten* (1921), *Molly Darling* (1922), *Jack and Jill* (1923), *Kid Boots* (1923), *Oh! Oh! Madeleine* (1924), *Rose Marie* (1924), *No, No, Nanette* (1924), *Sunny* (1925), *The Song of the Flame* (1925). In the 1926 season Harbach set a record with five different works in production, namely *Kitty's Kisses, Wild Rose, Criss Cross, The Desert Song* and *Oh! Please.* For several years he was librettist for as many as four productions in a season, including such successes as *Nina Rosa* (1929), *The Cat and the Fiddle* (1931), and *Roberta* (1933). Performances of his works had numbered more than twelve thousand by 1950. *The Silent Witness* (1915), a drama, and *Men in the Sky,* a motion picture, are examples of Harbach's work in fields other than musical comedy. Many of Harbach's best-known songs come from his musical plays: "Giannina Mia" from *The Firefly;* the title song and the "Indian Love Call" from *Rose Marie;* "One Alone" from *The Desert Song;* "She Didn't Say Yes, She Didn't

Say No" from *The Cat and the Fiddle;* "Smoke Gets In Your Eyes" from *Roberta,* and "Learn to Smile" from *The O'Brien Girl.*

Other composers (besides Friml and Hoschna) who were Harbach's collaborators were Louis Hirsch, Sigmund Romberg, Jerome Kern, and Peter de Rose. Among the productions for which Friml wrote the music were *The Firefly, High Jinks, Katinka, Rose Marie;* Hirsch composed *Mary* and *The O'Brien Girl;* Kern composed *Sunny, The Cat and the Fiddle,* and *Roberta;* and Romberg wrote the music for *The Desert Song* and *Nina Rosa.* Some outstanding successes were achieved with composers with whom Harbach collaborated but once, as in the cases of *No, No, Nanette,* composed by Vincent Youmans, and *The Song of the Flame,* composed by George Gershwin. Not all the librettos and lyrics were written by Harbach alone; one of several writers with whom he collaborated was Oscar Hammerstein 2d, who worked with Harbach and Herbert Stothart on *Wildflower* (1923), and who subsequently was a collaborator with Harbach on *Rose Marie, Sunny, Song of the Flame, Desert Song,* among others. Frank Mandel also collaborated on the book of *Desert Song,* and on *Mary, Jimmie, The O'Brien Girl,* and *No, No, Nanette.*

It is Harbach's belief (according to an article in the Salt Lake City *Deseret News*), that a musical play should not be merely a collection of pretty girls, catchy tunes, and lively lines, but that the music, the songs in particular, should form an integral part of a logical plot with human interest. Among his own works he considers *The Cat and the Fiddle* the best example of integrated construction. According to the *National Cyclopædia of American Biography,* Oscar Hammerstein 2d has said that Harbach, more than any other librettist, has evolved the integrated formula for the successful musical comedy, and that Harbach has had more successes than "any living writer for the light musical stage." Jerome Kern considered him "second to no American dramatic author in his understanding of musical values." Harbach does his writing in his country home, but he has also expressed the opinion that a playwright should keep in close contact with the theatrical atmosphere of Broadway.

When, in 1914, composer Victor Herbert and eight associates founded the American Society of Composers, Authors and Publishers (ASCAP), Harbach became one of its 192 charter members, and since its foundation has been prominent in the organization. In 1920 he was elected to its board of directors and from 1936 to 1942 he served as one of its two vice-presidents. He again held this office in 1949 and in May 1950 was elected to succeed Fred E. Ahlert as president of the society.

ASCAP is an organization for the protection of the copyrights of its members; membership (which is voluntary) is open only to those who have demonstrated the ability to create or to publish successful music, the kind and quality of the music being no criterion so far as membership is concerned. The entire field of creative music is reflected in the membership (preface to *ASCAP Biographical Dictionary*), which in 1950 stood at 2,521. The association, together with affiliated societies in other countries, besides protecting copyrights, collects fees for public performances of the works of members. Royalties continue to accrue and copyright protection to be maintained even after the death of the creator since membership privileges may be assumed by his heirs for his work. ASCAP is of value to commercial users of copyright music in that it relieves them of the legal responsibility of obtaining permission for each commercial use.

In recognition of his work as librettist and dramatist Knox College presented Harbach with an honorary degree of Doctor of Literature in 1934. He belongs to the Society of American Dramatists and Composers. President of the Knox Alumni Club of New York for many years, Harbach is also a member of the Green Room, Friars, The Players, and The Lambs. On December 4, 1918, Harbach married the former Eloise Smith; two sons were born to them, William Otto and Robert Abels; and the immediate family consists also of Mrs. Harbach's children by her first marriage, Bernard and Virginia. With a height of five feet eleven inches, Harbach has a weight of 170 pounds; his eyes are hazel, his hair is white, and his complexion is ruddy. He lists his political allegiance as Republican, his church as Presbyterian. Horseback riding, golf, and yachting provide him with outdoor recreation.

References

Deseret (Salt Lake City) News Mag D 4 '49
ASCAP Biographical Dictionary of Composers, Authors, and Publishers (1948)
International Motion Picture Almanac, 1947-48
National Cyclopædia of American Biography Current vol E, 1937-38
Who's Who in America, 1950-51
Who's Who in the Theatre (1947)

HASLETT, DAME CAROLINE Aug. 17, 1895- British engineer; international women's organization officer

Address: b. c/o Electrical Association for Women, 35 Grosvenor Pl., London, S.W.1.

A member of the British Electricity Authority, which governs the nationalized industry, and director of the Electrical Association for Women, Inc., Dame Caroline Haslett is a women's leader who has been largely responsible for the opening of the light engineering industry to women in England. Herself an engineer, she is a Companion of the Institution of Electrical Engineers and a Member of the Royal Institution. During World War II she was adviser on women's training for industry to the Minister of Labor. In 1950 Dame Caroline Haslett, president of the British Federation of Business and Professional Women, was named president of the International Federation of Business and Professional Women, a body of

which she had previously been a vice-president.

Born August 17, 1895, in Sussex, England, Caroline Haslett is the eldest daughter of Robert Haslett, railroad engineer, and his wife, Caroline Sarah (Holmes) Haslett. Her home circumstances were modest, the family was nonconformist in religion, the atmosphere a progressive one. She was educated locally, at Haywards Heath High School, which she left at the outbreak of World War I, when war exigencies were opening up new job opportunities for women. Employed in a clerical post with the Cochran Boiler Company, Miss Haslett, who felt an interest in what engineering could develop for the home, decided to become an engineer and asked for a transfer from the office to the plant. For five years she worked in London and at Annan, qualifying first in general, and then in electrical, engineering.

In 1919 Miss Haslett accepted the secretaryship of the newly formed Women's Engineering Society, founded to work for the "establishment of highly trained women in engineering." For many years she edited the Society's journal, *The Woman Engineer*, which she founded. She directed her efforts to persuading employers that women had special aptitudes for light engineering work and to showing the various engineering institutions that the time had come to admit women to their membership. (In 1943 the Amalgamated Engineering Union, the chief trade union of skilled workers in that industry, decided to accept women members.) Active in the movement for woman suffrage, Miss Haslett worked for the application of electrical devices to domestic uses in order to give women more time for civic activities.

In November 1924 Miss Haslett became director of the Electrical Association for Women, founded by the Women's Engineering Society to further the training of girls in that branch of technology, to educate housewives in the advantages of using electrical devices, and to encourage manufacturers to produce for home needs. Meeting Sir Andrew Duncan, chairman of the Central Electricity Board, a body formed to administer the new nation-wide electricity distribution, she persuaded him that the program would be incomplete without a campaign to inform housewives as to the availability and advantages of electrical household aids. Duncan asked for a detailed plan, approved it, and arranged for the association to receive a grant of £10,000 (then roughly $50,000 at par) for its work. In a quarter of a century the Electrical Association for Women has grown from a one-room-office body to an organization numbering over ninety branches and 10,000 members. To provide scholarships and traveling fellowships for teachers of domestic science, the association has endowed a £2,000-a-year trust, which it has named the Caroline Haslett Trust in honor of the woman engineer who has been director of the association since its founding.

Through her activities in the Electrical Association for Women and other organizations— she became a member of the Council of the Industrial Welfare Society, of the National Industrial Alliance, chairman of the home safety committee of the National Safety-First

British Inf. Service

DAME CAROLINE HASLETT

Association—Miss Haslett gained a reputation as an engineer, executive, and organizer. In 1930 she was the only woman delegate to a conference on power in Berlin; in 1936 at the Washington World Power Conference she was one of two women delegates. The woman engineer was made a Companion of the Institution of Electrical Engineers in 1934, the first woman to be admitted to that body. (She was to become a member of its postwar planning committee.) Recognized as an expert on the training of women for engineering, she was asked to organize a simplified course in engineering and electricity for the Home Office and the Board of Education.

In World War II the British Ministry of Labor made Miss Haslett adviser on women's training for industry. "She tramped through factories all over the country," said Margaret Culkin Banning, in *Independent Woman*, "talking to employers about their reaction to women in their plants, analyzing part-time work, putting up a fight for actual equal pay for equal work." In an address to the Royal Society of Arts in January 1941 the English engineer spoke of the admission of women, by consent of the Engineering Employers' Federation and the trade unions, to factory training on an equal basis with men, and pleaded that a field of opportunity should be left open to women after the war. In November of the same year she was in New York for a two-month visit to study the participation of American women in industry. On that occasion she told the New York *Herald Tribune* how even the older women in Britain were adapting themselves to factory work and were not content to remain units of the assembly line. "In one big factory women are in charge of the toolroom," she said. "For women to be in the toolroom at all is remarkable, but for women to run it!" At the end of the war the Board of Trade nomi-

nated Caroline Haslett to be chairman of the Hosiery Working Party, one of several fact-finding commissions set up to study various industries. In 1947 she was appointed a part-time member of the board formed to manage the nationalized electrical industry, the British Electricity Authority. The same year Dame Caroline (she now received that honor) was made a member of the Crawley-Three Bridges New Town Development Corporation, a body established by the Labor Government with authority to plan and build a model town as part of a program to create satellite towns to act as a corrective for overcrowding of big cities. Other Government bodies on which she has served include a committee of the Ministry of Works dealing with housing problems, and a committee, which she chaired, of the Ministry of Fuel and Power.

President of the British Federation of Business and Professional Women for several years, the English engineer visited America in the summer of 1944, in response to an invitation from the Canadian and the National (United States) Federations of Business and Professional Women. Among ideas she was taking back to England for postwar use she named: "Shelves that do not bump the head, less noisy vacuum cleaners and thermostats, more effective uses of plastics, glass, and nylon, and the Tennessee Valley Authority," which she termed "the greatest piece of social engineering in the world." Defining her idea of the role of women in the postwar world, the British women's leader wrote in *Independent Woman* that they should share as technical experts the work of international committees and conferences such as UNRRA, the ILO, the Monetary Conference, and should be heard at the peace table. Stating that she thought there was little difference in the natural abilities of men and women, Dame Caroline expressed a belief that there was a difference in psychological approach, and affirmed her conviction that both approaches were needed to solve postwar problems. In 1945 she visited Sweden and Finland; addressing a university audience in Helsinki, she again emphasized the necessity of women's taking their full share in the postwar world.

At the eighth biennial congress of the International Federation of Business and Professional Women (with which the national groups are affiliated) held in London in August 1950, Dame Caroline Haslett was elected president of the association. Succeeding Sally Butler[46] in the post, Dame Caroline became the international body's third president, the first British subject to be named head of the organization since its inception in 1930. (She had previously been a vice-president.) Among the international organization's postwar projects have been financial aid for the re-establishment of business and professional women's federations in wartorn European countries, and presentation before the U.N. of the case for the removal of discrimination against women.

The educational aspect of Dame Caroline's career is emphasized by her membership on governing bodies of colleges. She is a governor of the London School of Economics and Political Science and of Bedford College for

Women (both branches of the University of London); council member of King's College of Household and Social Science; member of the court of governors of the Administrative Staff College; member of the Comité International de l'Organisation Scientifique. Other activities include: membership on the women's consultative committee of Labor; on the correspondence committee on women's work of the International Labor Office; on the advisory council of the Institute of House-Workers; on the council of the British Institute of Management; on the Institution of Electrical Engineers Codes of Practice Committee for the Electrical Equipment of Buildings; vice-presidency of the British Electrical Development Association. She is a past president of the Women's Engineering Society, Inc., and a member of the council of the Royal Society of Arts.

A contributor of papers and articles to engineering and industrial journals, Caroline Haslett founded and edited *The Electrical Age*, and was editor of *The Electrical Handbook for Women* (fifth edition, 1950), *Household Electricity, Munitions Girl, Problems Have No Sex.* In 1931 the British Government made her a Companion of the British Empire, and in 1947 a Dame of that order. In 1950 Dame Caroline was named a Justice of the Peace for the County of London. Her club is the Forum. She was described by Helen Worden in the New York *World-Telegram* as "tall and capable, with frank eyes and friendly manner." In *Who Runs Britain?*, a symposium of "portraits" of leaders of fourteen aspects of British life, Dame Caroline, the only woman included, is said to be "not only a first-class organizer of other people's activities but—a much rarer accomplishment—conspicuously skillful in organising her own." Her relaxations are golf, motoring, and gardening.

References

Ind Woman 29:98-100
N Y Sun p33 N 10 '41
New Zealand Herald N 21 '35
Reynolds News (London) N 24 '40
Times (London) Ja 16 '41
Burke's Peerage (1949)
Who Runs Britain? (Contact Book No. 16) S '49 pors
Who's Who, 1950

HAWORTH, LELAND J(OHN) (hä' wûrth) July 11, 1904- Physicist

Address: b. c/o Brookhaven National Laboratory, Upton, N.Y.; h. Suydam Lane, Bayport, N.Y.

The director of the Brookhaven National Laboratory—operated by nine Eastern universities under contract with the United States Atomic Energy Commission as a center of experimentation in nuclear energy for peacetime application—is Dr. Leland J. Haworth, previously a professor of physics at the University of Illinois. He succeeded Dr. Philip M. Morse '48, the first director, in October 1948, after the latter had resigned. Haworth, who is a specialist in nuclear physics and electronics,

did research work in radar development during World War II, and is a holder of the Certificate of Merit.

The eldest of the three children of Paul Leland and Martha (Ackerman) Haworth, Leland John Haworth was born July 11, 1904, in Flint, Michigan, the girlhood home of his mother. (He had two sisters, of whom one is deceased.) The elder Haworth was of English descent from early Quaker immigrants, his mother of German-English. The boy was reared in what he describes as "rural surroundings" at West Newton, near Indianapolis, Indiana, where his father found relaxation from his academic duties (as professor of history at Indiana University and at Butler University) on a large fruit farm.

At the West Newton High School Leland Haworth was a member of the baseball team; graduated in 1921, he entered Indiana University, where he majored in physics. Again he played baseball, making the varsity team both in that sport and in tennis. He received his B.A. diploma in 1925, then worked as a teaching assistant at that university while qualifying for the M.A. degree, conferred on him in 1926. During his undergraduate days, Haworth became a member of the Lambda Chi Alpha fraternity; later he was elected to the Phi Beta Kappa, Sigma Xi, and Gamma Alpha societies.

On leaving Indiana University, Haworth taught physics for two years at the Arsenal Technical High School in Indianapolis, and also, during the summer of 1927, did technical work for the Indianapolis Power and Light Company. In 1928 he obtained a scholarship in physics at the University of Wisconsin, and in the following year was granted a fellowship. Appointed an instructor in physics at Wisconsin in 1930, he received the Ph.D. degree in 1931, and remained to teach at the same university for the next six years, until he was named to the Lalor fellowship in physical chemistry at the Massachusetts Institute of Technology in 1937. After a year of research work at M.I.T. Haworth was appointed in 1938 an associate in physics at the University of Illinois. Promotion to an assistant professorship came in the following year. The author of numerous articles for scientific journals, he continued research and experiments, his interests (as listed in *American Men of Science*) being emission of electrons, the Joule Thompson effect at very low temperatures, neutron physics, nuclear excitations and general nuclear design, and high energy accelerator design. *Who Knows —And What* credits him with "various inventions in electronic circuitry."

Haworth in 1941 obtained a leave of absence from the University of Illinois to join the staff of the Radiation Laboratory of the Massachusetts Institute of Technology. There he engaged in work on radar development, and became group leader early in 1942. In 1943 the physicist was appointed division head; he remained in that post until 1946, when he returned to the University of Illinois to take up the duties of the full professorship to which he had been promoted two years earlier. The nature of Haworth's wartime experiments is reflected in the chapters he contributed to the

LELAND J. HAWORTH

"Radiation Laboratory Technical Series," which reported developments at the Massachusetts Institute of Technology project.

On April 15, 1947, Dr. Haworth was called in as a consultant to the Brookhaven National Laboratory. This organization, which occupies the site of the United States Army's former reception center of Camp Upton, Long Island, is an outgrowth of the famous Manhattan Project of the World War II years. Owned and supported by the Government, it is under the jurisdiction of the Atomic Energy Commission. It is jointly operated under contract by nine Eastern universities—Columbia, Cornell, Harvard, Johns Hopkins, the Massachusetts Institute of Technology, Pennsylvania, Princeton, Rochester, and Yale—as a center for scientists to "cooperate in pure research" in the field of atomic energy. "In all of that pure research," stated Professor Philip M. Morse of the Massachusetts Institute of Technology shortly after his appointment as the first director of Brookhaven in August 1946, "we will have in mind the peacetime applications of our work to the medical and industrial fields."

In August 1947 Haworth joined the permanent executive staff of the laboratory as assistant director in charge of special projects. As such he assisted in the planning and erection of Brookhaven's $25,000,000 nuclear reactor (which began operation in August 1950), and the designing of what is expected to be the world's largest accelerator (capable of accelerating heavy particles of matter to 500,000,000 volts), completion of which is expected early in 1951. When Dr. Morse resigned on July 17, 1948, to resume his professorship at M.I.T. Haworth became acting director of the Brookhaven project. Announcement of his appointment as permanent director was made by the trustees of Associated Universities, Inc. (the supervising body of the nine operating institu-

tions) on the following October 14. On May 11, 1950, as director of Brookhaven, he accepted on behalf of the Laboratory the National Safety Council's award for distinguished service to safety. "The award," the New York *Herald Tribune* reported, "was based on the laboratory's average of one fourth as many disabling injuries and one twenty-second as many resulting days lost a year in 1948 as the average for all industries reporting to the council."

Haworth was honored in 1948 by President Truman with the Certificate of Merit in recognition of his wartime and other services. Professional and other bodies to which the physicist belongs include the American Physical Society (of which he is a fellow) and the Lions Club. In religious affiliation he is a member of the Society of Friends; he is an independent in political affiliation. Mrs. Haworth, the former Barbara Mottier, was a secretary before their marriage on July 2, 1927. The Haworths have one daughter, Barbara Jane, and one son, John Paul. The scientist stands six feet one inch, weighs 193 pounds, has brown hair and brown eyes. His favorite recreations are tennis and sailing.

References

N Y Times p6 O 15 '48 por
American Men of Science (1949)
Who Knows—And What (1949)

HEADLEY, ELIZABETH CAVANNA
See Cavanna B.

HEARNE, JOHN J(OSEPH) Nov. 4, 1893- Ambassador from Ireland to the United States
Address: b. c/o Irish Embassy, 2234 Massachusetts Ave., Washington 8, D.C.; h. 2339 S St., Washington, D.C.

The first Ambassador to be sent by Ireland to the United States—appointed after the American and Irish Governments had mutually agreed in February 1950 to raise the status of their respective legations in Washington and Dublin—is the Honorable John J. Hearne, S. C. Ambassador Hearne, a member of the Irish Senior Bar, had, at the time of this appointment, been his country's High Commissioner in Canada for about ten years. Prior to that he had served the Irish Department of External Affairs as legal adviser for twelve years and, as such, took a major part in the composition of the constitution of Ireland, which was adopted in 1937. He presented his credentials to President Truman on April 17, 1950.

John Joseph Hearne was born November 4, 1893, the son of Richard and Alice Mary (Power) Hearne. His birthplace is the South of Ireland seaport of Waterford, where his father established the first boot and shoe factory in that country, a family enterprise the envoy's brother carries on. John Hearne received his secondary education from the Irish Christian Brothers at Waterpark College, Waterford, then matriculated at the National University in Dublin, where he majored in law. Graduated, he entered King's Inns, Dublin, for advanced legal training, in the fall term of 1916, a few months after the suppression by the British of the "Easter Week" rebellion led by the Sinn Fein party, an uprising now viewed as the real beginning of Ireland's "War of Independence." Hearne was still in attendance at that school of law when, following their election to the House of Commons in London in 1918, seventy-three Sinn Feiners refused to take their seats, gathered instead in Dublin, proclaimed themselves an Irish parliament, and issued a declaration of independence.

Called to the Irish Bar as a junior counsel in 1919, Hearne began his career as a barrister when the Black and Tans were active. That effort of a British military constabulary to suppress the Irish nationalists lasted from January of that year until May 1921, when it ceased, pending negotiation of a treaty finally ratified in the following December, whereby Ireland (exclusive of the six Ulster counties) acquired dominion status within the British Empire. William T. Cosgrave, leader of the so-called "Right wing" of Sinn Fein, became in 1922 the first president of the new Irish Free State ("President of the Free State Executive Council" was his precise title) ; and it was in his Government during the ensuing year that Hearne assumed the duties of Judge Advocate General in the Department of Defense. In 1925 Hearne was appointed Assistant Attorney General, and in the following year accompanied the Attorney General, John A. Costello [48] (later Premier of Ireland), to the Imperial Conference in London. In 1926, too, he took his seat in the Assembly of the League of Nations at Geneva, Switzerland, as a delegate of the Irish Free State. He also at various times lectured on law, Ireland, and other subjects, at the University of Dublin, New College in Oxford, the Institute of International Relations at Geneva, and elsewhere.

Hearne's next appointment, in 1927, was as legal adviser to the Department of External Affairs. Five years later (1932) the Fianna Fáil party of Éamon de Valera [40] won control of the Irish parliament. While Costello left the Government, the change did not affect Hearne, who accompanied De Valera to Geneva in 1934 to the League of Nations. Hearne attended every assembly of the League until 1939. He remained in his legal post with the External Affairs Department until the same year.

As legal adviser in the External Affairs Department, Hearne was in an influential position when the abdication (1936) of King Edward VIII [44] opened the way for De Valera to realize the aim of ending all British control over Ireland's domestic affairs. At a special session of the Dail Eireann (Irish Parliament) summoned December 10, 1936, to accept the abdication, bills were introduced to remove the name of the King from the Free State constitution and to abolish the office of Governor General. Adoption of these bills on the next day was followed by passage of another ac-

JOHN J. HEARNE

knowledging the accession of George VI [42] but authorizing him to act for the Free State "in external matters only" (External Relations Act). A new constitution was then drafted, supplanting the Governor General by a President elected for a seven-year term, establishing a bicameral legislature, changing the name of the Free State to "Republic of Eire," and declaring "the right of the Irish people to . . . determine its relation with other powers." It also included what Hearne has called "the most comprehensive code of Christian democratic social doctrines and principles ever enacted in a national constitution." The new constitution, "overwhelmingly adopted" in a plebiscite on July 1, 1937, went into effect on December 29, with the late Dr. Douglas Hyde becoming the first President, and De Valera the Premier. Hearne has commented on what was considered an important part in the authorship of that document. "I shall always be proud, sir," he told Mark Hatch of the Boston *Post* (March 19, 1950), "that I had some little part in the formulation of that unique instrument."

In the late spring of 1939 Hearne accompanied Deputy Premier (now President) Sean T. O'Kelly [48] to New York City to dedicate the Irish pavilion at the World's Fair; and on return to Dublin in June he received the high legal honor of admission to the Senior Bar. (This entitles him to append the letters "S. C." —standing for "senior counsel"—to his name, and to wear the shoulder-length wig in court). On the sixteenth of the same month his appointment as the first High Commissioner of Ireland in Canada was announced. He arrived in Ottawa in August, just before the outbreak of World War II, and, remaining there for a few months less than eleven years, represented Irish interests in Canada, both in the period

HEARNE, JOHN J.—*Continued*

of Irish neutrality in World War II and in the postwar years.

Hearne's appointment as the first Irish Ambassador to the United States was announced February 24, 1950, and he presented his credentials to President Truman on April 17, 1950. Hearne, en route to the capital, held a press conference in New York City. "The partition of Ireland," he declared, "is a long-standing problem which I hope will be settled within the period in which I am Irish Ambassador to this country. . . . It is a crime against the whole principle of democratic government." In the capital, on the following day, he told newsmen that he would welcome discussions with the United States of the possibility of his country's membership in the North Atlantic alliance, but that Ireland would not join so long as the six northern counties remained separated from her. Some weeks later, at Boston, Massachusetts, he suggested that the future of Ulster be determined by a plebiscite covering all of Ireland, south as well as north.

Ambassador Hearne's height is five feet five inches, his weight about 123 pounds; he has "bright alert," gray eyes. Mrs. Hearne, the former Monica Mary Martin, is the daughter of a retired sea captain. The Hearnes were married in June 1930, and have four children: Maurice Isadore, John Justin, David Anselm and Mary Elizabeth. The ambassador's faith is the Roman Catholic. "After a decade in Canada," Hearne told an interviewer, "my chief avocation is ice hockey."

Reference

Boston (Mass.) Sunday Post A-p3 Mr 19 '50 por

HELPMANN, ROBERT   Apr. 9, 1909-
Dancer; choreographer

Address: b. c/o Sadler's Wells Ballet, Royal Opera House, Covent Garden, London; h. 3 Trevor Place, Knightsbridge, London.

The leading male dancer and choreographer of the Sadler's Wells Ballet is Robert Helpmann, who in the fall of 1949 made his American debut as dancer with the Government-sponsored British dance company. Motion picture audiences in America, however, had seen him previously—in 1944 as an actor in *Henry V*, and in 1948 as a dancer in *The Red Shoes*, for which he designed the choreography. Helpmann joined the Sadler's Wells Ballet in 1933, before which he appeared as solo dancer and actor in various theatrical productions in Australia. In 1941, after rising to the position of premier dancer with the English company, he turned his talents to the field of choreography. By the end of 1949 he had created five ballets, two of which were included in the repertory of the Sadler's Wells Ballet on its first American tour. As an actor he has appeared in several of Shakespeare's plays, including the title role in the 1944 production of *Hamlet* by the Old Vic Company.

Robert Murray Helpmann was born April 9, 1909, in Mount Gambier, Australia one of the

two children of James Murray and Mary (Gardiner) Helpmann. His father was considered one of the leading judges of wool, and his mother, who had wanted to go on the stage, was an amateur actress of some distinction. Helpmann's sister has become one of Australia's leading actresses. His childhood in Australia was characterized by "dramatic flights of fancy," by poor adjustment to school regulations, and by regular attendance at the Saturday matinees of the local theaters. Later, as a student of Prince Alfred's College, in Adelaide, he began to develop himself as a dancer, taking lessons in "fancy dancing" every Saturday. In 1923, at the Theatre Royal, in Adelaide, he made his first appearance as a solo dancer, in the musical comedy *Fraquita*. According to Caryl Brahms, in *Robert Helpmann: Choreographer*, this early performance was "madly passionate and very energetic." Three years later he joined the Australian touring company, owned and directed by J. C. Williamson, and for the next five years was a dancing actor and mime.

In 1929 Helpmann saw Anna Pavlova, the Russian ballerina, at a dance recital. So deeply impressed was he by her performance that he gave up his connection with the Williamson company and for the next eighteen months toured Australia and New Zealand with the Pavlova company, not as a member of the troupe, but as a student of the dancing of Novikov, her partner. In those months Helpmann is said never to have missed a performance. In 1931 he met Margaret Rawlings, the English actress, who suggested that he study dancing with Ninette de Valois.[49] Miss de Valois had just inaugurated the ballet school and dance group that was to develop into the Sadler's Wells Ballet. In 1932 Helpmann went to England and presented himself at Miss de Valois' studio. In a foreword contributed by Miss de Valois to a book of photographic studies by Gordon Anthony, she recalls Helpmann appearing at the school making a "discreet and well-timed" entrance, and showing himself to be "polite but quite self-assured." He impressed her as a "young man with a strange sense of power." Accordingly, he was accepted as a student and for the next six months received his first rigorous training in the ballet technique. By 1933 he had become a member of the corps de ballet and appeared with the company in its gala performance of that year. The performance also marked Helpmann's acceptance as a permanent member of the company.

In the autumn of 1933 the dancer appeared in his first principal role with the company—as Satan in Miss de Valois' ballet *Job*. His next role was Hilarion in *Giselle*, with Markova[43] and Dolin[46] as the soloists. (In recent years he has danced the part of Albrecht.) In the spring of 1934 he made his first appearance in a role created especially for him, that of the Master of Tregennis in *The Haunted Ballroom*. In this interpretation he proved, "according to Miss de Valois, "that a young English male dancer of considerable dramatic scope had been discovered." The next year he studied all the principal male roles in the classic ballets and was partner to Markova. In 1936, when Margot Fonteyn [49] became prima ballerina, he became her regular partner, an association which continues in 1949. Since that time, Helpmann has remained with the Sadler's Wells, participating in the prewar European tours, the performances throughout the English provinces during the period of World War II, and the 1949 debut of the group in the principal cities of Eastern United States and Canada. For a brief period in 1935 he was the leading dancer in the revue, *Stop Press*, produced at the Adelphi Theatre in London.

Helpmann has made several ventures in the field of acting—both on the stage and in motion pictures. While still in Australia he had appeared in 1929 in *This Year of Grace* and later in *The Barretts of Wimpole Street*. During the 1937-38 season of the Old Vic Company, he played Oberon in *Midsummer Night's Dream* and in 1939 he was Gremio and Nicholas in *The Taming of the Shrew*. In 1944 he appeared in the title role of the "gorgeous and rather over-elaborate production" of *Hamlet* given by the Old Vic. The London critic for the New York *Times* felt that Helpmann's performance showed an "intellectual and emotional grasp of the character," while lacking the "tragic stature, princeliness, magnificence and sonority" demanded by the role. In 1947 he appeared at the Duchess Theatre in John Webster's *The White Devil*, with the *Christian Science Monitor* critic finding the "grave beauty" of his voice suited to the speaking of verse and his training as a dancer making it possible for him to be "fluent in gesture and in movement." That same year he played in *He Who Gets Slapped* and the next year participated in the Shakespearean productions at Stratford-on-Avon.

His work before the camera began in 1944, when, after playing in the documentary *One of Our Aircraft is Missing*, he appeared in the film production of *Henry V*, playing the role of the Bishop of Ely. · In 1946 he portrayed Wyecroft in *Caravan*, and in 1948 he was chosen the choreographer and premier danseur for the film *The Red Shoes*. He designed for the screen both the fifteen-minute ballet of the Hans Christian Andersen story of the magic dancing slippers and the sequences from several classical ballets included in that film. Both his choreography and dancing were considered "effective" by the reviewers. Helpmann is enthusiastic about the filming of ballet, believing that the medium will help to increase public interest in this art form.

Since 1941 Helpmann has produced five ballets. His first, *Comus*, taken from Milton's poem, delineates the masque in a series of tableaux, with the principal dancer (in all cases it has been Helpmann) declaiming the lines. It was well received by the critics as a "notable early work by a man with a great instinct for the theater." Several months later, while touring with Sadler's Wells, he created *Hamlet*, a ballet based on the soliloquy in the Shakespeare play describing the dreams Hamlet may have had. In 1942, when it was produced by the company, with Helpmann in the title role, it was received with strong feelings fa-

ROBERT HELPMANN

vorable and unfavorable: some critics thought it outside the proper realm of the dance, others considered it "a first-rate piece of imaginative theater, excitingly assembled, brilliantly decorated, and appropriately tuned." When the ballet was performed in the 1949 season in the United States, the critic for the New York *Herald Tribune* wished that Helpmann "had chosen to convey the emotional crises . . . in dance movement rather than in highly exaggerated pantomime." Martin of the New York *Times* on the other hand judged *Hamlet* "a marvel of dramatic composition." Similar debate occurred with the production in 1944 of Helpmann's third ballet, *Miracle in the Gorbals*, a modern parable, laid in Glasgow. Some critics held that the work was more appropriate for the legitimate stage, whereas others, such as A. H. Franks writing in *Approach to the Ballet*, were of the opinion that it could not be played as legitimate drama, using, as it does, considerable dancing to develop the mood.

New York reviewers were also divided in their views of *Miracle in the Gorbals*—the New York *Times* critic finding it "banal in the extreme and by no means innocent of bathos." However, Terry in the New York *Herald Tribune* considered it a "work of remarkable integrity, both in its conveyance of emotions and in the simplicity of its movement details." Miss de Valois considers Helpmann a choreographer who "says all in direct terms of the theater, a theater seen fearlessly and aggressively." Helpmann himself has defended his use of the ballet for dramatic purposes in a speech before the Royal Academy of Dancing: "A ballet, like a play, is an elastic medium which must be used by each creator in an individual way. . . .Mime is as legitimate a medium in the element of ballet as dancing." Three other choreographic works of Helpmann, not in-

HELPMANN, ROBERT—*Continued*

cluded in the American tour of Sadler's Wells, are *The Birds, Adam Zero,* and *Corroboree.*

Helpmann has been admired for his "positive genius for both make-up and characterization," for "his sense of situation expressed in line," and for his "gallant and mimetically impressive" creation of the Prince in *The Sleeping Beauty.* New York critics particularly appreciated his impersonation of one of the ugly sisters in *Cinderella.*

The dancer-choreographer is a "small, slim man, wonderfully expressive both in gesture and in facial movement." A writer for the New York *Sun* described him as "svelte, dark, handsome." His speech off the stage is "quick" and his face so "mobile" that "one can almost read his thoughts." His great interest is playgoing (while in New York he saw five Broadway plays), his other diversions are swimming, riding, and tennis.

References

> Anthony, G. Robert Helpmann (1946)
> Brahms, C. Robert Helpmann: Choreographer (1943)
> Chujoy, A. Dance Encyclopedia (1949)
> International Motion Picture Almanac, 1947-48
> Who's Who, 1949
> Who's Who in the Theatre (1947)
> World Biography (1948)

HENCH, PHILIP S(HOWALTER) Feb. 28, 1896- Physician

Address: b. c/o Mayo Clinic, Rochester, Minn.; h. 517 4th St., S.W., Rochester, Minn.

For discoveries in the hormones of the adrenal cortex, their structure and biological effects, Drs. Philip S. Hench and Edward C. Kendall [50] of the United States and Prof. Tadeus Reichstein of Switzerland were jointly awarded the Nobel Prize in medicine in 1950. Dr. Hench, specialist in arthritic diseases at the Mayo Clinic, initiated the treatment of rheumatoid arthritis with injections of the suprarenal cortex hormone, which has been named cortisone. His co-sharers (who are chemists) in the Nobel award are credited with achieving the isolation and synthesis of that and other hormones, of which ACTH has also been used in arthritis with spectacular results. Associated with the Mayo Clinic since 1923, Hench became head of its Department of Rheumatic Diseases three years later. He is also professor of medicine at the Mayo Foundation of the University of Minnesota.

The son of Jacob Bixler and Clara John (Showalter) Hench, Philip Showalter Hench was born in Pittsburgh, Pennsylvania, on February 28, 1896. In 1916, after obtaining his B.A. degree from Lafayette College, he entered the University of Pittsburgh School of Medicine, from which he received the M.D. degree in 1920. The following year he became a fellow of the Mayo Foundation (in Rochester, Minnesota), the graduate school of the University of Minnesota's Department of Medi-

cine. He entered the Mayo Clinic in 1923 as a first assistant in medicine, and successively rose to become an associate in the division of medicine in 1925, and in 1926 to his present posts, staff consultant and head of the Department of Rheumatic Diseases. In 1928-29 he studied in Germany, at Freiburg University and at Munich's Von Mueller Clinic. In 1931 he received the M.Sc. in internal medicine from the University of Minnesota. He served as an instructor in medicine at the Mayo Foundation (1928-32), assistant professor (1932-35), associate professor (1935-47), and since 1947 as a full professor. He has also been a consultant at Rochester's St. Mary's Hospital.

Various forms of arthritis, "one of the most baffling of human ills," affect some seven million people in the United States alone. Until the discovery of cortisone and its "sister substance," ACTH, there was no effective remedy for the disease. Steven M. Spencer in a *Saturday Evening Post* article (June 23, 1949) told that Hench is known among his colleagues for "an uncanny skill in recognizing slight suggestions of cause and effect" and of pursuing them "relentlessly." On April 1, 1929, three years after he became head of the Mayo Clinic's Department of Rheumatic Diseases, related Spencer, Hench was impressed with the experience of a sixty-five-year-old physician who came to his office complaining of jaundice. Four years a victim of arthritis, after an attack of jaundice the patient noticed that the pain and swelling in his joints disappeared. Repeatedly in his practice Hench observed the favorable effect of jaundice on arthritis as well as pains of fibrositis and sciatica. The same effect on arthritis was noticed in pregnancy, in instances when anesthesia was given, and in periods of "starvation" diet. Following this clue (stated Paul de Kruif in *Reader's Digest,* November 1950), Hench deduced that since the blood of such patients is high in steroids the unknown antirheumatic substance would be one of the steroid group.

During 1930-38, at the Mayo Foundation, Dr. Edward C. Kendall, one of the foremost steroid chemists in the world (who was to share with Hench the 1950 Nobel Prize) had crystalized six steroids he isolated from the cortex (outer layer) of the adrenal gland. These were designated Compounds A to F. For some years Hench and Kendall "tossed ideas back and forth" in numerous discussions. Hench at one time experimented with Compound A on arthritic patients without obtaining benvolent results. In 1941 he and Kendall decided to try Compound E, later to be named cortisone.

Seven and a half years elapsed between this decision and its execution. First, there was not enough Compound E available for experiments except for a few small animals. Though Kendall had worked out the steps in its synthesis, the process was not perfected until undertaken by Merck and Company, who found it to be a most complex and costly procedure. Delay was also caused by World War II, when Hench was commissioned a lieutenant colonel in the

United States Army Medical Corps. His work in directing the Army's rheumatism center won recognition, and for outstanding researches he was awarded in 1942 the medal of, and made an honorary member of, the Heberden Society of London. Discharged from the Army in January 1946 with the rank of colonel, the physician returned to his duties at Mayo.

Two and a half years later, September 21, 1948, he and two associates, Drs. Charles H. Slocumb and Howard F. Polley, began tests at the Mayo Clinic on fourteen bedridden arthritic patients. Seven months later (April 20, 1949) Drs. Hench and Kendall read reports on the results of the tests, and in motion pictures showed formerly incapacitated patients running.

Two of the patients Hench had treated with ACTH, a hormone produced by the pituitary gland which stimulates the adrenal gland, and which had been synthesized at the Armour and Company laboratory at about the same time that cortisone was synthesized. The two hormones were equally effective, but neither proved to be a cure. The *Saturday Evening Post* article quoted Hench as saying: "Cortisone is the fireman who puts out the fire, it is not the carpenter who rebuilds the damaged house." Further details were given in a 120-page report by Hench and Kendall and in the *Archives of Internal Medicine*, which emphasized that more study was needed. That constant medication is necessary (as in the use of insulin in diabetes) means that a great many doses are required, and that at tremendous cost since ox bile obtained from 14,600 head of cattle supply dosages for only one patient for one year. According to William L. Laurence of the New York *Times*, the seed of an African plant, which yields a substance similar to the animal product, may solve that problem. Cortisone has been effective in certain cases of burns, asthma and other allergic conditions, skin conditions and eye inflammations. It has a less striking effect on certain other conditions, among them leukemia. The hormones' undesirable reactions are also being studied.

On October 26, 1950, the announcement came from Stockholm that the Swedish Caroline Institute of Medicine had awarded the Nobel Prize in medicine to Drs. Hench, Kendall, and Reichstein for their research in the field of suprarenal cortex hormones. Hench, who was in Ireland at that time, stated that he would share his part of the award (the whole amount is approximately $31,000) with Drs. Slocumb and Polley, his associates at Mayo.

Other awards received by Hench include the Passano Foundation ($5,000), the Lasker Award of the American Public Health Association, and Page One of the Newspaper Guild. In 1940 he was given honorary Doctor of Science degrees by Lafayette and by Washington and Jefferson college. He is a fellow of the American Medical Association, of the American College of Physicians; a member of the Association of Military Surgeons, the American Committee for Control of Rheumatism (secre-

Harris & Ewing

PHILIP S. HENCH

tary, 1931-38), the American Rheumatism Association (executive councilor, 1933-41, president, 1939), American Society for Clinical Investigation, Central Society for Clinical Research, Minnesota Society of Internal Medicine. Active in foreign and international medical societies, he is an honorary member of the Royal Society of Medicine and of the Heberden Society (both of London), is chairman of the American Committee of the Ligue Internationale contre le Rheumatisme, is an honorary member of Argentinian, Brazilian, Danish, and Canadian societies in the same field. His Greek letter societies are Sigma Xi, Sigma Alpha Epsilon, Alpha Omega Alpha, Nu Sigma Nu. Since 1946 he has been expert civilian consultant to the Surgeon General, United States Army; is vice-president of the board of managers of the Walter Reed Memorial Association. Hench has contributed articles to *Hygeia*, the *Annals of Rheumatic Diseases*, and other medical periodicals. He has served as chief editor of the *Annual Rheumatism Review* and as associate editor of the *Annals of Rheumatic Diseases*, the journal of the Empire Rheumatism Council (London).

Philip Showalter Hench married Mary Genevieve Kahler on July 14, 1927; their four children are Mary Showalter, Philip Kahler, Susan Kahler, and John Bixler. Described as young-looking for his years, the physician has a "crew" haircut, is tall and "husky." He is a Republican and a Presbyterian.

References
N Y Times p1+ O 27 '50
Sat Eve Post 222:28+ Jl 23 '49
American Men of Science (1949)
Who's Who in America, 1950-51
World Biography (1948)

HENDERSON, E(LMER) L(EE) Mar. 23, 1885- Surgeon; medical association officer
Address: b. 606 S. 4th St., Louisville, Ky.; h. 87 Valley Rd., Louisville, Ky.

Chosen president-elect of the American Medical Association in June 1949, Dr. E. L. Henderson assumed the presidency in June 1950. A surgeon in Louisville, Kentucky, since 1911, Henderson is active in the leadership of county, State, national, and international medical and

Joseph Merante

E. L. HENDERSON

surgical societies. As president of A.M.A. for the year 1950-51 he continues to voice that body's opposition to Government-planned compulsory health insurance and to further prepaid hospital- and medical-care plans.

Elmer Lee Henderson was born to Jonas and Henrietta (Lewis) Henderson on March 23, 1885, on a Kentucky hill farm, near Garnettsville. After his elementary and secondary education in local schools, in 1909 he received his M.D. degree from the University of Louisville Medical School. He had worked those years in order to pay the expenses of his medical education. Then followed internship in the University and Louisville City hospitals. Beginning practice as a family doctor, he made his calls on a bicycle. "He was bitten by more dogs than any other man in the country," his wife says today (Reader's Digest). Since 1911 he has been practicing general surgery in Louisville, where he is a member of the staffs of the Kentucky Baptist Hospital and the St. Joseph Infirmary. He is on the consultant staff of Sts. Mary and Elizabeth Hospital, is on the courtesy staff of other private hospitals in Louisville, and is a member of the board of governors of the Kosair Crippled Children's Hospital.

During the first World War Dr. Henderson served as a lieutenant, captain, and major in the Medical Corps, with nine months' service with the AEF. After that war ended he held the rank of lieutenant colonel in the Medical Reserve Corps (1919-20). In World War II he was chairman of the Fifth Service Command Committee, Procurement and Assignment Service for Physicians, Dentists and Veterinarians (1942-47) and since 1942 has been surgical consultant to the Air Surgeon's office.

Henderson's leadership in medical associations dates from 1918, when he was president of the Jefferson County Medical Society (of which he is still a member). Since then his activity in medical organizations has been unbroken. He is a member of the Southeastern Surgical Congress (he was its president in 1946-47 and since 1947 has been a member of the executive committee); member of the Southern Medical Association, which he served as councilor from Kentucky during 1938-42 as chairman of its surgical section in 1942-44, as president in 1946-47, and of which he is now trustee; diplomate of the American Board of Surgery; fellow of the American College of Surgeons; member of the Kentucky State Medical Association, serving as its president in 1941-42.

A member of the Kentucky State and his county medical associations, Henderson has long been affiliated with the A.M.A. He became a member of the house of delegates in 1937, in 1939 he was made a member of the board of trustees, and since 1947 has served as chairman of the board. He was also chairman of the coordinating committee for its national education campaign. In 1949 he was elected to the office of president-elect, and in June 1950 succeeded Dr. Ernest E. Irons '49 to the presidency.

In 1950 in its one hundred and third year, the A.M.A. has a membership of 143,000, who for the first time in its history (as voted in December 1949) pay annual dues of twenty-five dollars. (Formerly, membership in State and county organizations made one eligible to membership in A.M.A. without further assessments.) Of the money so collected, reported the New York Times, about half would be spent to promote voluntary health insurance and half to defeat the compulsory plan authored by Oscar R. Ewing '48 and sponsored by the Truman Administration.

A.M.A.'s new head has long been a vigorous opponent of compulsory national health insurance. He was a member of the A.M.A. group which in August 1949 "took to the road" in a new country-wide campaign against the government's plan. At that time he said (as reported in the New York Post), "No Federal legislation of any sort is needed except to provide financial aid to medical schools. . . .The A.M.A. is preparing a report on the nation's health in order to correct 'misrepresentation.'" The Christian Science Monitor in April 1949 quoted another of his statements: "The inevitable deterioration in the quality of care which would result from government herding of patients and doctors into assembly-line medical mills would lower the standards of healthy

America to those of sick, regimented Europe. . . .There is neither hope nor promise of progress in this system of regimented medical care. It is the discredited system of decadent nations which are now living off the bounty of the American people, and if adopted here it would not only jeopardize the health of our people but would gravely endanger our freedom. It is one of the final, irrevocable steps toward state socialism, and every American should be alerted to the danger." On another occasion, reported *Time*, Henderson "sounded the war cry: Let's face our battle of Armageddon. . . .No other profession, in this country, has been brought under such violent attack by those ambitious for political power over it." In his "Here's Health—the Voluntary Way" (*Reader's Digest*, May 1950) he set forth A.M.A.'s stand on socialized medicine versus voluntary measures.

In 1947 Henderson was a delegate from the American Medical Association to the London conference, at which the World Medical Association was organized. He was a delegate from the same body to the new organization at its first general assembly in September 1947 in Paris, and to the meeting the following year in Geneva. The *Journal of the American Medical Association* stated that Dr. Henderson's "skill in diplomatic negotiation has been evidenced by his activities in W.M.A.," in which he has held a number of board and committee posts, both in the United States group and the parent body. At the third annual convention of the W.M.A. in London in October 1949, the American surgeon was chosen president-elect by the delegates from thirty countries. He assumed the presidency of the international organization in October 1950, succeeding Dr. Charles Hill of the British Medical Association.

Henderson's professional interests have also taken him to the Orient. He was a member of the mission (in 1948) to Japan to survey and make recommendations on social security, medical education, medical service, and public health; and he became honorary fellow of the recently organized Japanese Medical Association. A member of the International College of Surgeons, he belongs as well to the Società Piedmontese di Chirurgia. He is the author of many papers on various aspects of surgery.

E. L. Henderson and Laura Bell Owen were married April 4, 1911. They live in Louisville and have two children, a son, William Owen, and a daughter, Henrietta Marie. The surgeon is a member of the Alumni Association of the University of Louisville (he was its president 1938-41), Honorary Alpha Omega Alpha, and the American Legion. He is a Baptist. A Mason ((33d Degree) he belongs to the Scottish Rite and is a Shriner. His Louisville clubs are the Pendennis, Filson, and the Big Spring Golf Club. The surgeon's "iron routine" has been described by Paul de Kruif in *Reader's Digest* (May 1950). He may operate as early as 7:45 A.M, which is followed by a full day of office and hospital calls and reading of professional literature in the evening. Another phrase applied to Dr. Henderson is "A drayhorse for work."

References

J Am Med Assn 140:7 Je 18 '49
American College of Surgeons, 1947-49
Directory of Medical Specialists (1949)
Who's Who Among Physicians and Surgeons, 1938
Who's Who in America, 1950-51

HERRING, (EDWARD) PENDLETON

Oct. 27, 1903- Educational organization executive; political scientist

Address: b. c/o Social Science Research Council, 230 Park Ave., New York 17; h. 219 Rockingstone Ave., Larchmont, N.Y.

Pendleton Herring in June 1948 was named president of the Social Science Research Council, an organization devoted to the advancement of research in the social sciences. Composed of representatives from the fields of anthropology, economics, history, political science, psychology, sociology, statistics, and related fields, the council plans programs of research into social processes and human relationships and administers funds for research purposes and fellowships for advanced study. Prior to this appointment, Herring, a specialist in public administration, taught at Harvard University for eighteen years; held research posts with various Government agencies during World War II; and for a year was director of the Atomic Energy Commission's Group of the United Nations.

One of the five children (of whom four are sons) of Arthur Pendleton and Agnes (Kinney) Herring, Edward Pendleton Herring was born in Baltimore, Maryland, on October 27, 1903. His father was a physician, who for a time held the position of Commissioner of Mental Hygiene for the State of Maryland. After graduating from Baltimore City College in 1921, young Herring entered Johns Hopkins University, where he majored in English literature. As an undergraduate he won Woodyear scholarships, joined Delta Phi fraternity, and served as art editor of *The Blue Jay*, the college humor magazine, and of the college annual. He received his Bachelor of Arts degree in 1925. Continuing his studies at Johns Hopkins, he obtained his Doctor of Philosophy degree in political science three years later. He began his career in 1928 as an instructor in government at Harvard University. Nine years later he rose to the rank of assistant professor and was appointed secretary of the Harvard Graduate School of Public Administration. In 1939 he was made a lecturer in government at Harvard, and was promoted to associate professor in 1943. He introduced a case method of instruction in public administration that has been developed further at Harvard and elsewhere.

In the fall of 1941 Herring became a consultant to the United States Bureau of the Budget of the Executive Office of the President. At the suggestion of President Franklin D. Roosevelt, the director of the Bureau of the Budget in March 1942 appointed a seven-man Committee on Records of War Administration to provide guidance and support in the assem-

PENDLETON HERRING

bly and analysis of material on the administration of the nation's war effort. Herring was made executive secretary of the committee at that time, and three years later succeeded Waldo Leland as its chairman. The committee supervised the preparation of a volume entitled *The United States at War* (1946), an account of the Federal Government's role in the mobilization of the nation's human and material resources for World War II. Named a member of the Advisory Committee on Military History of the Department of the Army in 1942, Herring joined the Advisory Panel on Human Relations of the Department of the Navy in 1945, both of which posts he still held in 1950. From June to September 1945 he worked on the report to the Secretary of the Navy, James V. Forrestal '48, on the unification of the Army, Navy, and Air Forces as the National Military Establishment.

Herring left Harvard in 1946 to become an executive associate of the Carnegie Corporation of New York, where he was in charge of work associated with public administration and international relations. United Nations Secretary-General Trygve Lie '46 in June of that same year appointed him the director of the U.N. Atomic Energy Commission Group, a position he held until March 1947. In this capacity he served as secretary of the United Nations Atomic Energy Commission, then holding its first meetings.

From 1942 to 1945 Herring had served as vice-chairman of the committee on public administration of the Social Science Research Council, and in 1946 he joined its board of directors. On June 15, 1948, he became president of the council. As the first step in his new appointment (which had been made in mid-April) he surveyed research in England, France, and other Western European countries. Established in 1923, the Social Science Research

Council fosters scientific inquiry in the social fields through all phases of research—by developing personnel, improving techniques, mapping opportunities and needs, designing projects, assuring the existence of proper materials, encouraging the investment of funds in research, and bettering the total circumstances under which research is conducted. In his annual report for 1948-49, Herring summarized the situation confronting social science research as follows: "There is need for a much broader operating basis so that social scientists may respond to the demands for the application of their knowledge by government and industry. This means the improvement of research training and a larger supply of competent practitioners as well as men with essentially research orientation. It means the strengthening of the research institutes already in existence in many of our major universities, and involves a more effective utilization of specialists whether in the colleges or in departments that have no formal research organization." During that fiscal year the council was the recipient of a total of $432,000 in new grants from the Carnegie Corporation of New York, the Rockefeller Foundation, and the American Philosophical Society, and disbursed $570,901 for fellowships and grant-in-aid programs, specific projects, and the basic program of research planning.

Since 1949 Herring has also been a member of the Advisory Research Council of the Human Resources Research Institute, United States Air Force; consultant, Operations Research Office, Department of the Army; consultant to the Committee on Human Resources of the Research and Development Board of the National Military Establishment; and a member of the Program Committee of the United States Commission for the United Nations Educational, Scientific, and Cultural Organization (UNESCO). In May 1950 he was appointed to the board of directors of the Woodrow Wilson Foundation in New York City. During May and June of that year he attended the UNESCO General Conference at Florence, Italy, as an adviser to the United States delegation.

Herring is the author of *Group Representation Before Congress* (1929), survey of lobbying; *Public Administration and the Public Interest* (1936), which describes the functioning of the administrative agencies of the Federal Government and the influences exerted by special interest organizations; and *Federal Commissioners: A Study of Their Careers and Qualifications* (1936), "an attempt to determine the elements of training, character, and experience that should be sought in choosing members for the regulatory commissions." Probably his best-known work is *The Politics of Democracy* (1940), which, according to the foreword, analyzes "the politics of democracy in order to show the nature of our party system and its relations to other social processes." Allan Nevins, writing in the New York *Times*, praised the exposition as "really simple, concrete, shrewd, and founded both upon wide reading and catholic observation." That year also saw the publication of a monograph, *Presi-*

dential Leadership: The Political Relations of Congress and the Chief Executive. In 1941 *The Impact of War* appeared. This book was regarded by Louis Hacker of the New York *Herald Tribune* as "one of the most significant analyses produced by the current emergency." Herring has also edited *Civil Military Relations* (1940). Articles by him appeared in the *Harvard Business Review, Yale Law Journal, George Washington Law Review, North American Review, Current History, Annals of the American Academy of Political and Social Science, Southwestern Social Science Quarterly, Public Utilities Fortnightly, Social Forces, Virginia Quarterly Review,* and the *Pennsylvania Magazine of History and Biography.* He served as editor in chief of the *Public Administration Review* (1945-47) and was on the editorial boards of the *American Political Science Review* (1943-45) and the *Public Opinion Quarterly* (1937-44).

The executive holds membership in the American Political Science Association, American Historical Society, American Philosophical Society, American Society for Public Administration, and the Council on Foreign Relations. His clubs include the Century and the Harvard in New York City and the Cosmos in Washington, D.C. An honorary Master of Arts degree was conferred on him by Harvard in 1944, and for his war work he received a Navy Citation and Distinguished Civilian Service Award in 1946. On June 21, 1933, he married Katharine Sedgwick Channing; they have two sons, James Hugh and Thomas Sedgwick. With a height of five feet seven inches, he weighs 170 pounds; the color of his eyes is gray, of his hair, brown. He lists himself as a Republican and an Episcopalian. A favorite recreation of his is gardening.

References

Directory of the American Political Science Association, 1948
Who's Who in America, 1950-51

HICKERSON, JOHN D(EWEY) Jan. 26. 1898- United States Assistant Secretary of State

Address: b. c/o Department of State, Washington, D.C.; h. 3314 Ross Pl., N.W., Washington, D.C.

A veteran of twenty-nine years in the United States diplomatic service, John D. Hickerson was named head of United Nations Affairs for the Department of State on May 26, 1949. After seven years in consular service he had entered the State Department in 1927, where he became Director of the Office of European Affairs in 1947. He represented the United States on the Permanent Joint Board of Defense for the United States and Canada from 1940 to 1946, and was adviser to the United States delegation at the United Nations Conference on International Organization in 1945.

John Dewey Hickerson, son of Alva James and Mary (Hill) Hickerson, was born in Crawford, Texas, on January 26, 1898, and received his schooling in that State. At the time

of World War I, in 1918, he interrupted his studies to serve in the United States Army. In 1920 he was graduated with the B.A. degree from the University of Texas. The year of his graduation Hickerson entered the consular service of the United States, in September 1920 being assigned as vice-consul at Tampico, Mexico, where he remained for two years. With an elevation in rank, he was transferred to Rio de Janeiro on July 15, 1922, at which office in the following year he received appointment to the rank of consul.

The year 1924 saw Hickerson appointed a Foreign Service Officer, class 8, and detailed for duty in Para, Brazil. In 1925 he went to Ottawa, Canada. While in that post (1925-27) the Foreign Service officer advanced to Class 7 (August 31, 1925) and to Class 6 (June 30, 1927). With the latter rank he entered the Department of State on August 18, 1927, where he progressed to Class 5 on May 23, 1929.

In the Department of State Hickerson in mid-1930 became Assistant Chief of the Division of Western European Affairs and of the Division of European Affairs. The British Commonwealth Division of the Office of European Affairs received him as its chief in January 1944; of the latter he became deputy director in December of that year. With the institution of defense plans by the United States before the attack on Pearl Harbor, in August 1940 Hickerson was appointed to the Permanent Joint Board of Defense for the United States and Canada; he served on that board for the duration of World War II. As adviser to the United States delegation at the United Nations Conference on International Organization in San Francisco in April 1945, he assisted in drawing up plans for the Security Council. His appointment as director of the Office of European Affairs took place in 1947, after which he was political adviser for the Council of Foreign Ministers in London that year. Later he was to be one of the architects of the North Atlantic Treaty.

On May 26, 1949, in the reorganization of the State Department, President Truman announced the appointment of five new Assistant Secretaries of State, naming Hickerson to be Assistant Secretary for United Nations Affairs. His appointment confirmed by the Senate, the new Secretary entered upon the duties of his post on July 8, 1949.

Shortly after assuming his new position, Hickerson was designated to represent the United States in discussions of the Big Five powers (the United States, Great Britain, Russia, France and China) and Canada, aimed at finding a solution to the disagreement on atomic energy control. The U. N. Atomic Energy Commission, deadlocked in its discussions of the majority plan for atomic control adopted by the General Assembly, suspended its work during the six-power consultations. The majority plan advocated supervision of the processing of ores and keeping account of the consumption of nuclear fuels in non-military activities, that is, complete control of uranium and thorium from the time of their extraction to the time

Wide World Photos

JOHN D. HICKERSON

of their final consumption. The basic dispute, as defined in the New York *Herald Tribune* of July 29, 1949, was over "whether control should be via actual international operation of dangerous atomic activities, as favored by forty-six nations during 1948 Assembly meetings, or by periodic inspection of national operations, subject to Security Council veto, as demanded by the Soviet Union."

In its meetings the commission had arrived at an impasse on the issue, and it was felt that the United States, in appointing Hickerson to the new consultations, was testing the effect of a new negotiator, who, while maintaining the same stand as his counterpart in the commission, would introduce representation on a higher diplomatic level. In an effort to encourage the free exchange of opinions, Hickerson was responsible for instituting the practice of holding meetings of the six-power group in closed session. The desired effect was not attained, the Russians labeling the action an aspect of a plot on the part of Wall Street to obtain control of the world's supply of uranium and a negation of freedom of the press. On January 19, 1950, the Russian representative withdrew from the consultations, after fourteen fruitless meetings. Hickerson saw this as an indication that Russia was ignoring the desires of the General Assembly to see a sincere effort to reach atomic agreement, according to the New York *Times* of January 20, 1949, which quoted him as saying: "The difference is not among the five countries. The Soviet Union and the Soviet Union alone is standing in the way of effective agreement."

In meetings of the Special Political Committee of the United Nations, the Assistant Secretary of State for U. N. Affairs spoke (November 9, 1949) in opposition to the Russian proposal of a simultaneous prohibition of atomic weapons and adoption of an international con-

trol plan, asserting it was essentially the same plan turned down by the Assembly in 1948. In response to a declaration by the Soviet that it was applying atomic energy on a large scale to peace uses, Hickerson on November 11 countered with a query as to what the U.S.S.R. was doing to share that knowledge. His reaction to Herbert Hoover's proposal that Russia be ousted from the U.N. was that the United States would strengthen the world organization by encouraging all other nations to participate fully.

When discussions in the Special Political Committee on the question of control of conventional (non-atomic) armaments seemed in danger of breaking down, Hickerson stated there was "little hope of any real progress until some constructive change takes place in the attitude of the Soviet Union." The committee subsequently, (November 19, 1949) approved a proposal calling for a world-wide census of such armaments and military personnel potential, with the Assistant Secretary of State emphasizing that atomic energy control should be rigorously dissociated from the proposed census (in opposition to a Soviet motion), since complete abolition of weapons based on nuclear fission was the aim of the majority report of the U. N. Atomic Energy Commission. (The census plan cannot go into effect since the Soviet Union had already vetoed it in the Security Council.) Interviewed by Richard H. Rovere, writer for the *New Yorker* (February 11, 1950), Hickerson said: "Taxpayer Hickerson would demand the head of State Department Hickerson if State Department Hickerson left so much as a pebble unturned in trying to solve this thing."

When a group of seven resolutions, including proposals for world federation, Atlantic Union, and other plans for a new world peace organization was brought before the Senate Foreign Relations subcommittee on February 15, 1950, Hickerson approved only one, which urged President Truman to seek agreement in the Security Council on limiting the use of the veto and other changes in current procedures. The other resolutions, he felt, would be ventures in foreign relations beyond the existing U.N. machinery.

Tribute was paid Hickerson by Arthur Krock in his column *In the Nation* (New York *Times*, December 13, 1949) as one of the comparative "unknowns" who have been elevated to positions of high command in the State Department and who is "serving with competence and distinction." Krock called the Department's action "a worthy disregard of mere 'name chasing.'" At the Harvard Law School the Department of State official has acted as a member of the advisory committee on research in international law and he has been a regular lecturer in the School of Foreign Service at Georgetown University (Washington) since 1928. Hickerson in 1922 married Vida Corbin, and is the father of one son, John Hightower. He has a "deferential" manner of speaking, according to the *New Yorker*, which also noted that "he can be very firm." Assistant Secretary Hickerson belongs to the Metropolitan and Chevy Chase clubs in Washington, D.C.

References
Who's Who in America, 1950-51
Who's Who in Government, 1932-33
Who's Who in the East (1948)

HIGGINS, DANIEL PAUL Sept. 12, 1886-
Architect

Address: c/o Eggers and Higgins, 100 E. 42d St., New York 17; h. 19 E. 88th St., New York 12

Partner in the architectural firm of Eggers and Higgins, Daniel Paul Higgins has "drawn plans for billions of dollars worth of buildings representing the 'Who's Who' of construction," stated a New York *Times* writer. A number of commissions have come to Higgins from the United States Government, notably for the Jefferson Memorial and the National Gallery of Art. Hospitals, schools, churches, residences, and housing projects are among the other achievements of the architect.

Daniel Paul Higgins, born in Elizabeth, New Jersey, on September 12, 1886, is the son of Patrick and Mary (Dowd) Higgins. He attended that town's public schools and business college, took various extension courses in business and architecture at New York University, Alexander Hamilton Institute, and elsewhere. In 1905 he was engaged by the architectural firm of John Russell Pope. In 1922, having risen to be an associate of the firm, he received a partnership. After Pope's death fifteen years later, in 1937 Higgins joined Otto Eggers in the formation of another architectural firm, Eggers and Higgins, which completed a number of the commissions assigned to Pope.

While associated with Pope, Higgins had worked on a number of residences for wealthy Americans, one of whom was Mrs. Graham Fair Vanderbilt. It was this experience in residential design that led Higgins, when queried by the directors of the Syracuse Memorial Hospital about the firm's capability in hospital construction, to reply: "We make the finest homes in America, and your hospital should be a secondary home." The more than forty hospitals the firm has designed include Triboro Hospital for Tuberculosis on Long Island, and the Alfred E. Smith Memorial at Saint Vincent's Hospital in New York City. The general plan of the almost entirely self-contained Triboro Hospital, stated *Architectural Forum* upon the project's completion in 1941, is the result of "a compromise between an awkward site which faced west and the needed length, and a desirable southerly orientation of the wards." Modifications of Saint Vincent's Hospital, begun in 1947 as a part of the $7,000,000 Alfred E. Smith Memorial, included a ten-story new addition, and a two-story kitchen and laundry unit to be constructed in the courtyard of the existing building.

To house the headquarters of private organizations, Higgins' firm designed the Junior League Building in New York City, Constitution Hall for the Daughters of the American Revolution in Washington, D.C., and the American Red Cross Building, also in the nation's capital. The "secondary home" principle he enunciated in Syracuse has also been the guiding element in the designs for the interior of the S.S. *America*, of the United States Lines, and for the interiors planned for four ships of the Grace Line. An 18th century-inspired design of Higgins' firm provides the background for the French masterpieces in New York's Frick Collection. In the field of industrial building, they have projected the plans for the Union Gas and Electric Building in Cincinnati, Ohio, and, in collaboration with the firm of Cross and Cross, for the Aetna Life Insurance Company in New York. The latter building was distinguished by the use of glass brick for the admission of more light and the exclusion of noise and dirt. Another solution of an architectural problem evolved by Eggers and Higgins was the circular plan for the Schaefer Center at the New York World's Fair in 1939, which permitted access to the building from all sides.

Robert H. Fetridge (writing in the New York *Times*) termed the Higgins firm the architects for "colleges and schools that represent a cross section of educational institutions in the country." These are the Syracuse Medical College, the Indiana University Music Hall, the Spence School in New York, the projected law center for New York University, the Yale Gymnasium, and Silliman College at Yale. The last-named, built around a central quadrangle, has been described by *Architectural Record* as "closely following the Colonial idiom . . . the new building group carries on a still vigorous tradition." In New York Higgins' firm has participated in the designs for the Cardinal Hayes Memorial High School and the Archbishop Stepinac High School. Appointed in 1937 to the New York City Board of Education as chairman of the board's committee on buildings and sites, the architect was reappointed to that post in 1944 for another term by the late Mayor Fiorello H. La Guardia, to draw up postwar construction plans. Higgins' achievements in this position were cited by the American Institute of Architects at the time of his nomination to a fellowship in the institute in 1949: "He guided the school problem of New York toward structures of individuality and usefulness." He is also a member of the board of design for the Gateway Project of Pittsburgh, Pennsylvania, a plan comprising eight buildings.

A number of architectural commissions have come to Eggers and Higgins from the United States Government. The structures designed by them, outside Washington, D.C., are the Bainbridge Naval Training Station in Maryland, the Air Support and Ferry Command Base in Memphis, Tennessee, and the Elmira Holding and Reconsignment Point in Horseheads, New York. For Washington Eggers and Higgins designed the Senate Office Building, the Jeffer-

Samuel H. Gottscho

DANIEL PAUL HIGGINS

son Memorial, and the National Gallery of Art. As successors to the firm of John Russell Pope, they constructed the controversial Jefferson Memorial for which Congress had appropriated an initial $500,000 in 1938, although the design had not yet been approved by the Federal Commission of Fine Arts. The fifteen-million dollar National Gallery aroused varying reactions among architectural critics.

In the offices of Eggers and Higgins specialists are assigned to various phases of construction problems—a former athlete to gymnasium design, a former chemist to laboratories—in a manner first suggested by Higgins in his 1932 article, "Firm Specifications," for *Architectural Record.* The architect has also written for the *American Institute of Architects Journal, American Architect, Empire State Architect,* and *Modern Hospital.* He contributed the introduction to *Houses of Character,* by Marcia Mead (1926).

The New York architect has been the recipient of the medal of honor of the New York Chapter of the American Institute of Architects, the gold medal of the Architectural League, and has won the *Christian Herald* church building competition. He was treasurer of the American Institute of Architects from 1932 to 1936 and of the Architectural League of New York from 1931 to 1933. In 1944 Higgins was chairman of a committee of leading architects who took part in the Greater New York Fund drive. He belongs to the New York Building Congress. Higgins also holds membership in the board of real estate and mortgage management department of the Manufacturers Trust Company of New York. Another New York bank with which he is associated is the Emigrant Industrial Savings, as a trustee and member of the executive committee.

As a prominent Roman Catholic layman, Daniel Higgins has served as president of the Catholic Youth Organization, of which in 1948 he was chairman of the board. He was a member of the wartime board of directors of the National Catholic Community service, and is a member of the Association of Master Knights of the Sovereign Order of Malta in the United States. In 1948 he received the Club of Champions award of the Archdiocese of New York. For the University of Notre Dame he serves on the advisory council of the School of Commerce.

Daniel Higgins, who has "served on the board of so many youth movements that he can't remember all the names," is a recipient of the thirty-five-year medal, for youth works, of the Boys' Clubs of America; he received as well the exposition work medal, in which all the boys' clubs of the country participated. As a member of the boards of directors he is associated with the Boys' Clubs of America, the Police Athletic League (PAL), the Madison Square Boys' Club, and the Boy Scouts of America. Other forms of community service with which the architect is identified are the Greater New York Fund (of which he is a member of the board of directors), the National Institute of Social Sciences (vice-president), and the New York Tuberculosis and Health Association (member of the executive committee). He was a member of the board of trustees of the Museum of the City of New York. The clubs of which Higgins is a member are the New York Yacht, the New York Athletic, the National Horse Show Association, and the Dutchess Valley Rod and Gun; he also belongs to the Coffee House, the Metropolitan, the Cornell, Gipsy Trail, and Engineer clubs, the Circus Saints and Sinners, and India House.

On October 6, 1909, Higgins married Anna Dorothea Boll; their children are Daniel Paul and Patricia Dorothea. The black-haired, blue-eyed architect has a height of five feet five inches and a weight of 150 pounds. His preferred sports are boxing, tennis, squash, horseback riding, and hunting.

References

N Y Times III p3 Ag 6 '50
American Catholic Who's Who, 1950-51
Business Executives of America (1950)
Who's Who in America, 1950-51

HILL, HARRY W(ILBUR) Apr. 7, 1890-
United States Naval officer

Address: United States Naval Academy, Annapolis, Md.

Vice-Admiral Harry W. Hill, superintendent of the United States Naval Academy at Annapolis, was appointed to that post in April 1950. During World War II he commanded amphibious forces which aided in the capture of Tarawa, Eniwetok, Tinian, Okinawa, and other islands in the Pacific.

Harry Wilbur Hill is a Californian, born in Oakland, on April 7, 1890, to John Clayton and Ida Belle (Miller) Hill. The boy attended public grade and high schools in the city of his birth, then took a competitive examination for appointment to Annapolis by Congressman J. R. Knowland. In July 1907 Hill entered the United States Naval Academy. "Outstanding in athletics," he was a member of the first varsity basketball and lacrosse teams to be organized at Annapolis, and became captain of the latter. At his graduation in 1911, Hill stood twenty-third scholastically in a class of 193.

The first eight years of the naval officer's career were spent in battleships and destroyers in the Atlantic and Pacific; from this period date his Second Nicaraguan and Mexican campaign ribbons. During World War I he served with the British Grand Fleet in the battleship *Texas*; as navigator in the battleship *Wyoming* he witnessed the surrender of the German Fleet in November 1918. After the end of the war came several tours of shore duty, first as aide to the Chief of Naval Operations, then assignment at the Norfolk (Virginia) Naval Operating Base. There followed duty at Annapolis, and then in the Navy Department in Washington. In 1923 Hill studied at the Army Chemical Warfare School.

Back at sea for three years as gunnery officer of the light cruiser *Concord*, Hill was commended by the Secretary of the Navy for winning the Gunnery Trophy, and was made gunnery officer of the battleship *Maryland* for another three years. After receiving a second Gunnery Trophy, in 1933 the Californian was ordered to a similar post on the staff of the Pacific Fleet Battle Force. In 1934 came his first command, the U.S.S. *Dewey*, the first of a new type of destroyer to be added to the fleet. It was he who placed the ship in commission.

On June 23, 1938, Harry Hill was given the permanent rank of captain, the year he received the service's most advanced training at the Naval War College. He was next ordered to the Pacific Fleet as war plans officer on the staff of the commander in chief. Captain Hill's subsequent assignment was to the War Plans Division of the Office of the Chief of Naval Operations, in 1940. As part of this work he served in 1940-42 as an American member of the United States-Canadian Permanent Joint Board on Defense.

The month after Pearl Harbor, Hill went to sea in command of the heavy cruiser *Wichita*. Once again he operated with the British Home Fleet, in the North Atlantic, in Scapa Flow, and on Russian convoy duty. The Soviet Order of Kutuzov, 2d class, was awarded to Hill for outstanding service in protecting Russian-bound convoys between Iceland and North Russian ports. Promoted to rear admiral (temporary) in September 1942, the fifty-two-year-old naval officer was assigned to the battleship *Maryland* (where he had once been gunnery officer) as Commander of Battleship Division Four. In November 1942 Hill joined the battle for Guadalcanal in the South Pacific.

Commander of the first task force to comprise battleships and escort carriers ("baby flattops"), Admiral Hill served in this capacity until September 1943, when Admiral Richmond Kelly Turner[44] chose him as the first am-

VICE-ADM. HARRY W. HILL

phibious group commander. (The number of amphibious group commanders was to grow to fourteen.) Hill's first task as commander of Amphibious Group Two was the capture of Tarawa. Located between Hawaii and New Guinea, near the junction of the international date line and the equator, Betio Island in Tarawa Atoll had been built up by the Japanese as one of the world's strongest bastions. Hill called it "the hardest nut any naval or military commander has ever been ordered to crack," and the three-day invasion battle in November 1943 has been described as "the fiercest, bloodiest, and most ruthless in the Pacific war." British correspondent Henry Keys reported, "We won by the narrowest of margins," and quoted Admiral Hill as saying that if the enemy had been able to sink even one of the American transports, the invasion forces might have been defeated.

In the Tarawa battle Hill directed the capture of Apamama Atoll. Rear Admiral Hill's name appeared in a communiqué on February 18, 1944, in connection with the capture of Eniwetok Atoll; meanwhile, he had commanded the forces occupying Majuro Atoll in the Marshall Islands, where on January 31, 1944, the first American flag was hoisted over Japanese territory. "To supervise the Eniwetok amphibious operation," reported *Time*, "Rear Admiral Richmond Kelly Turner sent one of his most trusted deputies. . . .Harry Hill's ground forces were fewer than had been used on either Tarawa or Kwajalein—less than two regiments." About seven hours after the Marines had landed on Engebi Island, following a thousand-ton naval bombardment, the island was theirs, and the Marines joined the infantry in cleaning up the rest of the atoll. This was the deepest westward penetration into the Japanese defenses

HILL, HARRY W.—*Continued*

up to that time, and gave the Americans a valuable naval and air base.

From June 15 to July 9, 1944, Hill was second in command of the assault force of Marines and Army elements which captured Saipan, and fifteen days later he directed the same troops' invasion of Tinian. That operation began when Hill tricked the enemy commander by a feint off Tinian Town and sent Marines ashore at the opposite end of the island, within range of American artillery based on Saipan. The shore-based artillery joined with naval guns and plane bombardment to harass the defenders day and night, while the landing troops killed nearly all the counterattacking force of 1,200. From that time, reported an Associated Press, the sweep down Tinian was "the most rapid of any in the Marianas campaign, averaging a mile daily." American casualties were particularly low, the number of dead, wounded, and missing coming to about one-third of the toll of the Japanese dead alone.

In the Iwo Jima battle of February 19 to March 15, 1945, Admiral Hill took part as deputy commander of the attack force. A month later he was advanced to the temporary rank of vice-admiral, and on May 17 he relieved Admiral Turner (who had been promoted) as commander of the Fifth Amphibious Force at Okinawa, directing the amphibious and support operations until the island was secured on July first. After V-J Day, Hill's amphibious force landed the Sixth Army in southwestern Japan for occupation duty.

Back from the Pacific, Hill joined the staff of the Chief of Naval Operations, and was serving there when the President made his rank of vice-admiral permanent. In November 1945 Hill took up his duties as commandant of the former Army War College, which was renamed the Army and Navy Staff College and later redesignated the National War College (the next April). The Unification Act having become law, the Admiral had as his deputy an Army general, as his second deputy an Air Force general, and as his third deputy, a State Department official. They called upon leading American educators for aid in planning a course to teach diplomats about war and the military about peace, foreign policy, and the economics, geography, and psychology of their own and other countries. Planned for the most promising colonels, Navy captains (with twenty years of service), and diplomats of equivalent rank and service, this new ten-month course opened September 3, 1946, with an enrollment of one hundred. After three years in this post, in July 1949 Vice-Admiral Hill was ordered to duty as chairman of the Navy Department's General Board. In April 1950 he was appointed to the United States Naval Academy to succeed retiring superintendent James L Holloway, Jr. '47.

The Distinguished Service Medal was first awarded Admiral Hill for "brilliant initiative, sound judgment and forceful leadership" in the operations for the capture of Tarawa, Eniwetok, Apamama and Majuro; a gold star in

lieu of a second D.S.M. for "exceptionally meritorious service" at Saipan and Tinian, with a second gold star for his services at Iwo Jima and Okinawa. He is also entitled to wear the American Medal, the European Campaign Medal with one star, the Pacific Campaign Medal with five stars, and the American Defense ribbon. He has been awarded the British Distinguished Service Order, and was made a Companion of the Order of the Bath, for service while commanding the National War College.

Hill's church is the Episcopal; he follows service tradition in expressing no political preference. On October 8, 1913, the naval officer married Margaret Harwood Hall of Annapolis. Their daughter, Elizabeth Stockett, was sent to England and France on OWI assignments, and their son, John Clayton 2d, who graduated from Annapolis at the time of Pearl Harbor, served in the Pacific and reached the rank of lieutenant commander. The Admiral, who is described as "handsome, gray, genial," is an expert pistol shot. Something of an antiquarian, he is the author of *Maryland's Colonial Charm Portrayed in Silver*. His clubs are the Army and Navy Club of Washington, and the Chevy Chase (Maryland) Club.

References

Who's Who in America, 1950-51
World Biography (1948)

HILLENKOETTER, ROSCOE H(ENRY) (hĭl′lĕn-kŏt″tēr) May 8, 1897- United States Naval officer

Address: b. c/o Department of the Navy, Washington, D.C.; h. 4147 Green Lea Pl., St. Louis, Mo.

Rear Admiral Roscoe H. Hillenkoetter was from May of 1947 to September of 1950 the director of the Central Intelligence Agency, the first permanent intelligence office to be organized in peacetime by the United States Government. It is under the National Security Council, which is one of the divisions of the Executive Office of the President. The Rear Admiral's appointment was announced on May 1, 1947, when he was called from the post of naval attaché at the American Embassy in Paris, to which he had once been assigned as assistant attaché in 1933. That intelligence service, together with his record in the setting up of the wartime intelligence network in the Pacific, was the basis of his selection as the director of the CIA upon its establishment in 1947. In August 1950 it was announced that Hillenkoetter would be succeeded as CIA director by Walter Bedell Smith '44; and in November the Rear Admiral returned to sea duty when he took command of the Seventh Task Force, which is stationed near Formosa.

Roscoe Henry Hillenkoetter, son of Alexander and Olinda (Deuker) Hillenkoetter, was born in St. Louis, Missouri, on May 8, 1897. Appointed to the Naval Academy at Annapolis, Maryland, from the Twelfth District of Missouri in 1916, he graduated with distinction and received his ensign's commission in June 1919; he was twentieth in the class of four hundred and sixty-seven. He was training as a midshipman in the U.S.S. *Minnesota* while it operated with the Atlantic Fleet during World War I in the summer of 1918.

Hillenkoetter served in a submarine from July to September 1920; in the gunboat U.S.S. *Paducah* from September 1920 to September 1921; and in the U.S.S. *Israel* of the Atlantic Fleet's mine force from October 1921 to July 1922. After a brief period of instruction at the submarine base at New London, Connecticut, he served for a year with the submarine 0-2, from which he proceeded, in December 1923, for duty with the Fifteenth Naval District at Balboa, Canal Zone. From February 1925 until October 1925 he was attached to that Naval District as aide to the commandant. His next assignment, as aide on the staff of the commander, destroyer squadrons, scouting fleet, was completed in July 1927, when he was assigned as aide and flag lieutenant on the staff of the commander, special service squadron. A two-year shore duty was spent as an instructor in the department of modern languages at the Naval Academy, followed by service at sea again, in 1931 on the U.S.S. *Memphis* and in 1932 on the U.S.S. *Bainbridge*. After duty with an electoral mission to Nicaragua from March to December 1932, he proceeded to the Canal Zone to serve both as aide and flag lieutenant (January to May 1933) and aide and flag secretary (May to October 1933) on the staff of the commander.

The naval officer was ordered to Europe in the fall of 1933, where for about two years he was assistant naval attaché at the American Embassy in Paris. Then followed service in the U.S.S. *Maryland* (October 1935 to February 1938) and two months in the Office of the Chief of Naval Operations, in Washington. Returning to France, he resumed his duties there, with additional assignment as assistant naval attaché in Madrid and Lisbon. He was designated naval attaché and naval attaché for air (in Paris) in April 1940, and, relieved of his duties in Spain and Portugal, was assigned additional duty in the same capacities at the American Embassy in Vichy, France. Thus, as assistant and full attaché, the naval officer spent those years in the intelligence branch of the service; and the Vichy assignment entailed intimate work with the French underground, "gathering information and helping hunted men escape the Nazis," reported the *United States News*.

On November 19, 1941, Hillenkoetter was again assigned to sea duty as executive officer in the U.S.S. *West Virginia*. Wounded when the *West Virginia* was sunk at her berth during the Japanese attack on Pearl Harbor, Hillenkoetter was transferred, with the same title, to the U.S.S. *Maryland*, which had survived the attack (with some damage) and was returned, after repairs, to duty in the South Pacific. In July 1942 Captain Hillenkoetter (he had advanced to that grade in June) was called to Washington for brief duty in the

U. S. Navy
REAR ADM. ROSCOE H. HILLENKOETTER

Office of the Chief of Naval Operations, from which he was assigned for service as officer in charge of intelligence on staff of Commander in Chief Nimitz'[42], Pacific area, from September 1942 until March 1943. His next post was to the command of the U.S.S. *Dixie*, with additional duty in the South Pacific, which terminated in February 1944. For his meritorious services while in command of the *Dixie*, during operations against the enemy in the Solomon Islands and New Hebrides he was awarded the Bronze Star Medal. For the remainder of the war the officer was on shore duty, as assistant director of training, later as director of planning and control in the Bureau of Naval Personnel, Navy Department, Washington (August 1944 to September 1945). His Legion of Merit award was given for his services in the last-named post.

With the fall of Japan, Hillenkoetter was given command of the U.S.S. *Missouri*, which he took on its postwar cruise on diplomatic missions to Turkey, Greece, Italy, and North Africa. He spoke of this assignment as "a stroke of luck—like holding the winning ticket in a lottery." When the cruise was completed on May 9, 1946, he was ordered to report to the American Embassy in Paris as naval attaché. He declared that he liked this post so much that he was reluctant to change it when, on April 7, 1947, he was assigned to the Office of the Secretary of the Navy in Washington. (Before this, his advancement to the grade of Rear Admiral had been approved by President Truman in November 1946, to date from March 4, 1944.) The President's appoinment of the Rear Admiral as director of the Central Intelligence Agency followed quickly, on May 1, 1947.

The CIA, as a peacetime successor to the wartime Office of Strategic Services, was es-

HILLENKOETTER, ROSCOE H.—*Cont.*
tablished under the National Security Council by the National Security Act of 1947. Its director is appointed by the President with the advice and consent of the United States Senate. The *United States Government Organization Manual* describes the purpose of the CIA as "the coordination of the intelligence activities of the several Government departments and agencies in the interest of national security." The law specifically provides, states the *Congressional Directory*, "that the Agency shall have no police, subpoena or law-enforcement powers, or internal-security functions. However, the director is responsible for protecting intelligence sources and methods from unauthorized disclosure." The Army and Navy intelligence and the State Department are now required to channel their intelligence data through the CIA for analysis and interpretation, stated Ronald Robinson in his *Saturday Evening Post* article, "They Fight the Cold War Under Cover." The Federal Bureau of Investigation relinquished its wartime Latin American network to the CIA and, in the field of international intelligence, the FBI is now responsible only for counterespionage activities within the United States and its possessions.

While Hillenkoetter was the first director of the CIA as such, his predecessors in central intelligence work were Lieutenant General Hoyt S. Vandenberg '45 and Rear Admiral Sidney W. Souers '49, who is Executive Secretary of the National Security Council. These shifts in command have been seen by the *United States News* as one of the obstacles that Hillenkoetter had to face to make the CIA fully effective. Other obstacles, according to the same periodical, were "the squabble between the Army's G-2, Naval Intelligence, and the State Department as to CIA's exact function," and the apprehensiveness of Congressmen "at the idea of the United States indulging in international espionage."

The disturbances in Colombia during the first week of the Inter-American Conference which convened in Bogotá on March 30, 1948, precipitated the first public investigation of the work of the CIA. Hillenkoetter was called before the House Executive Expenditures subcommittee on April 15 to testify on charges that the CIA had failed to warn the State Department of any possible violence. Hillenkoetter declared that the CIA "did know of unrest in Colombia" and that a CIA dispatch from Bogotá, dated March 23, revealed that "advance delegate [of the State Department] O. J. Libert . . . does not consider it advisable to notify the State Department of this situation, since he feels adequate protection will be given by police and does not want to alarm delegates unduly."

Subsequent to the Bogotá incident two surveys of the CIA were conducted, one by the Hoover Commission, the other by a group appointed by the President and headed by Allen Dulles '49. Clarke Beach, Washington correspondent of the New York *Herald Tribune*, stated that the "Hoover Commission indicated

that on the whole it felt CIA had made a good start." Admiral Leahy, who reportedly was responsible for Hillenkoetter's appointment to the CIA, has said that "no man in the country has a better grasp of the mechanics of foreign intelligence than Hillenkoetter" (Robinson's words), and is said to give him personal credit for virtually all of CIA's accomplishments. According to Robinson, its director receives an annual salary of $14,000.

In June 1950, a few days after the outbreak of the Korean war, several Congressmen demanded an explanation of what they regarded as CIA inefficiency, the United States having apparently been surprised by the North Koreans' invasion of South Korea. Appearing before the Senate Appropriations Committee, Hillenkoetter stated that the attack had been expected for the past year—concentrations of Communist forces were known to have taken place—but that it was not possible to predict the "zero hour." Committee members, reported newspapers, were satisfied by the CIA director's explanation. On August 18 the White House announced that General Walter Bedell Smith, commander of the First Army and ex-Ambassador to Moscow, would succeed Hillenkoetter as CIA director at the end of September. Hillenkoetter, who had previously requested return to sea duty, in early November took command of the Navy's Seventh Task Force, which is assigned to the protection of Formosa.

The Navy man has been awarded (in addition to the two decorations mentioned) the Purple Heart Medal, the Victory Medal, the Atlantic Fleet Clasp, (U.S.S. *Minnesota*), and is entitled to wear the American Defense Service Medal, the Asiatic-Pacific Campaign Medal, the American Campaign Medal, and the World War II Victory Medal. He was awarded the Order of the Phoenix, degree of Commander, by the government of Greece; the Order of Saint Maurice and Saint Lazarus, degree of Commander, by Italy; the Legion of Honor, rank of Officer, and the Order of Maritime Merit, by France; and the Medal of Merit by Nicaragua.

Hillenkoetter is a tall man, with closely cropped hair. He married Jane E. Clark, daughter of a Navy doctor, on November 21, 1933; they have one daughter, Jane. It is reported by his friends that he only broke his routine of twelve to fourteen hours of work a day in the guarded offices of the CIA for an occasional afternoon of golf, which he shoots in the low nineties. According to the *Saturday Evening Post* article, Hillenkoetter's "chief recreation is the reading of history, and he is said to be an expert on the writings of Marx, Lenin and Stalin, quoting at length from them to prove a point."

References

N Y Times VI p11 S 21 '47 por
Sat Eve Post 221:30 N 20 '48 por
U S News 22:70-1 My 16 '47
Who's Who in America, 1948-49
World Biography (1948)

HIRSCHFELDER, JOSEPH O(AK-
LAND) May 27, 1911- Physical chemist;
educator
Address: b. c/o University of Wisconsin Naval
Research Laboratory, 422 Farm Pl., Madison,
Wis.; h. University Houses, Eagle Hgts., Madi-
son, Wis.

Professor of chemistry at the University of
Wisconsin and the director of that institution's
Naval Research Laboratory, Dr. Joseph O.
Hirschfelder has been judged by fellow scientists to be "one of the ten ablest physical chemists in the United States." An authority on
nuclear energy, he participated in the development of the atomic bomb at Los Alamos, New
Mexico, during World War II, and was chief
phenomenologist at the first of the Bikini Atoll
underwater explosion tests. More recently
(1948-50) he was chairman of the board of
editors for the Government-sponsored symposium, *The Effects of Atomic Weapons*, the
guide for the organization of civilian defense
against a possible attack.

Son of the late Dr. Arthur Douglass Hirschfelder and May Rosalie (Straus) Hirschfelder,
the physicist and chemist is the third of his
family to attain professional distinction. The
paternal grandfather whose full name he bears,
and who was the first white child to be born
in Oakland, California, became the first professor of clinical medicine at Leland Stanford
University. Arthur Hirschfelder, a heart specialist, was the author of the textbook *Diseases of the Heart and Aorta*, published in
1910, when he was an associate in medicine at
Johns Hopkins University. Joseph Oakland
Hirschfelder, born in Baltimore, Maryland, on
May 27, 1911, was reared in Minneapolis, where
his father had accepted the professorship of
pharmacology at the University of Minnesota,
a position he was to fill until his death in 1942.
("My father," the scientist recently stated, "has
been my inspiration.")

A graduate (1927) of the West High School
in Minneapolis, where tennis was his principal
extracurricular activity, Hirschfelder spent two
years (1927-29) at the University of Minnesota, majoring in chemistry and playing freshman tennis and football. He then entered Yale
University to take the Bachelor of Science degree in 1931. His postgraduate work was done
at Princeton. It was in the course of this
work that, in collaboration with Dr. Eugen
Paul Wigner, he first contributed to the scientific press, with a paper, "Separation of Rota-
tional Coördinates from the Schrödinger Equa-
tion for *N* Particles," which appeared in the
proceedings of the National Academy of Sciences for February 1935. In the same year
Hirschfelder was appointed a research associate in the Princeton Chemistry Department.
He received his Ph.D. in physics and chemistry
from that university in 1936.

For one year after acquiring the doctoral
degree, Hirschfelder continued postgraduate
work at Princeton as a fellow of the Institute
of Advanced Studies. In 1937 he became a research associate of the Wisconsin Alumni Research Foundation, Chemistry Department, Uni-

versity of Wisconsin; and in 1940 he was appointed an instructor in the university's chemistry and physics departments. He was promoted to an assistant professorship in chemistry
one year later. While at Princeton Hirschfelder worked with Professors Henry Eyring
and Hugh S. Taylor in developing "the theory
of absolute reaction rates, liquid structure,
chemical reactions produced by ionizing radiation." At Wisconsin his research concerned
"determination of intermolecular forces, gas
imperfections, molecular quantum mechanics,
semiempirical theory of activation energies." He
has contributed to a number of publications,
including the *Journal of Chemical Education*,
Journal of Chemical Physics, and *Physical Review*, his articles being on such subjects as
quantum mechanics, statistical mechanics, the
theory of reaction rates, properties of liquids
and gases, penetration of gamma rays and the
theory of flames.

After the United States became a combatant
in World War II Hirschfelder was granted
leave of absence from Wisconsin to join the
National Defense Research Committee as a
consultant on interior ballistics of guns, rockets,
and recoilless guns, and group leader of the
geophysics laboratory, working on the thermodynamics of powder gases and their products.
In 1943 he was appointed group leader of theoretical physics and ordnance at the Los Alamos
Atomic Bomb Laboratory, Los Alamos, New
Mexico, and in 1945 became head of the theoretical physics division of the Naval Ordnance
Test Station at Inyokern and Pasadena, California. As chief phenomenologist he was present at the 1946 Bikini atom bomb test, and was
named special adviser to the Radiological Safety
Committee. Since the same year, when he returned to the University of Wisconsin to become both a full professor of chemistry and
the director of the university's Naval Research
Laboratory, he has served the Army, Navy,
Atomic Energy Commission, and National Advisory Committee for Aeronautics as a consultant, and has been a panel member of the National Research Council.

When a panel of the Atomic Energy Commission in 1948 suggested that a handbook
should be prepared on the effects of atomic
bomb attack, the project was placed under the
direction of the Los Alamos Scientific Laboratory, and Hirschfelder, a consultant of that
organization, was chosen to head the board of
editors. Some forty scientists were selected to
do the actual writing of the book, to be sponsored jointly by the AEC and the Department
of Defense. The work took about two years to
complete, a year longer than anticipated. Among
the difficulties encountered were considerations
of accuracy, style, and what Hirschfelder stated
(New York *Times*, August 13, 1950) was "lack
of active support" from the AEC; that he was
"discouraged from bringing together groups of
chapter authors with technical experts." Strong
feeling over the respective prerogatives of the
central offices of the AEC and the laboratories
retarded work on the handbook, Hirschfelder

JOSEPH O. HIRSCHFELDER

added, criticizing also the commission's "extreme compartmentalization."

The Effects of Atomic Weapons was issued August 12, 1950, and the original edition was exhausted at the Government Printing Office two hours after it went on sale. W. L. Laurence [45] of the New York *Times*, in a news story on its content and conclusions, called it "the most comprehensive report made public so far on the various effects of atomic explosions." As a guide to the organization of civilian defense against A-bomb attack, it is written with municipal officials, boards of health, engineers primarily in mind, and stresses the need for a "well-disciplined population" to resist panic. Practical suggestions for the treatment of the aftereffects of contamination are given and steps to be taken in long-range planning are recommended.

A fellow of the American Physical Society and the American Association for the Advancement of Science, and a member of the American Chemical Society (president of the Wisconsin section) and the American Acoustical Society, Hirschfelder has been listed by the Chicago section of the American Chemical Society as "one of the ten ablest physical chemists in the United States." The scientist, who has brown hair and hazel eyes, stands five feet ten inches, and weighs 185 pounds; he lists tennis and flying as his favorite recreations. His clubs are the University in Madison and the Cosmos in Washington; his fraternities are the Alpha Xi Sigma, Sigma Xi, Gamma Alpha and Phi Lambda Upsilon. He is not married.

References

Newsweek 36:56 Ag 21 '50 por
American Men of Science (1949)
Who Knows—And What (1949)
Who's Who in America, 1950-51

HOEY, JANE M(ARGUERETTA) (hoi) Jan. 15, 1892- United States Government official; social work executive

Address: b. c/o Bureau of Public Assistance, Social Security Administration, Washington 25, D.C.; h. 1200 16th St., N.W., Washington 6, D.C.; 135 Central Park West, New York 23

Jane M. Hoey is director of the Bureau of the United States Social Security Administration, for the relief of the needy aged, the blind, and dependent children. After a score of years as an executive in public and private social work, Miss Hoey was called upon to organize the new bureau in 1936. She is one of the 1 per cent of key Federal executives who are women, a group of which *American Men in Government* says, "Despite the dearth of women in top Government jobs, those who are in the Federal service occupy very important posts and have generally achieved wide recognition in their fields." During the 1940-41 term Miss Hoey was president of the National Conference of Social Work.

One of the youngest of the nine children of John and Catherine (Mullen) Hoey, who had emigrated from Ireland, Jane Margueretta Hoey was born January 15, 1892, in Greeley County, Nebraska. When she was about six years old, her father, a rancher and contractor, took his family to New York City, where the Hoeys had lived before Jane's birth; she was consequently reared in the Eastern metropolis. Miss Hoey has told that her mother, who "had a deep concern for people, especially those in trouble," introduced her at a very early age "to service to neighbors and to old people in institutions." Her life was influenced, too, by the fact that during her childhood a brother served in the State legislature, as a result of which she came to know many of his fellow Democratic legislators, among them Al Smith, Robert Wagner, and Franklin D. Roosevelt. "My brothers and sisters," Miss Hoey says, "made it possible for me to secure college and professional education, to travel widely, and to know intimately a wide variety of people of different racial, economic, and cultural backgrounds."

Graduated in 1910 from Wadleigh High School, where she was active in athletics and sang in the glee club, Jane Hoey entered Hunter College. Later she attended Trinity College in Washington, D.C., from which she received her B.A. degree in 1914. A history and political science major, she credits two professors, the Reverend Dr. William J. Kerby and the Reverend Dr. John A. Ryan, with stimulating her concern about economic and social conditions and imbuing her with a desire to help the underprivileged through social work. At college she participated in athletics, and in her senior year she was president of the student government. After graduation Miss Hoey returned to New York to begin a course of study which led to a Master's degree in political science from Columbia University, and a diploma from the Columbia-affiliated New York School of Social Work, both awarded in 1916.

Shortly after completing her studies, Miss Hoey was in a supervisory position. From April 1916 to December 1917, as assistant secretary of the Board of Child Welfare, New York City, she supervised the work of investigators. From January 1918 to June 1921 she was in charge of organizing home service sections in local chapters of the American Red Cross to care for the families of men in the armed services; she also supervised and prepared material for the use of the staff. Her title was field secretary and director of field service organization and supervisor of field staff for home service, Atlantic division, American Red Cross. In September 1921 the National Information Bureau appointed Miss Hoey and two faculty members of the New York School of Social Work to make a study of the work of local units of national organizations. In that task, for approximately two years Miss Hoey was assistant director of the project, which made a survey of forty-six national agencies (ranging from the Boy Scouts to the W.C.T.U.) in fourteen communities, twelve cities and two rural counties, in various parts of the United States. The 157-page report was published in 1926.

Meanwhile, in July 1923 Jane Hoey began three years' service as secretary of the New York Tuberculosis and Health Association's Bronx division, a post in which she supervised the tuberculosis clinic, directed the sending of children to camps, and organized programs to make the public aware of the division's work. In April 1926—the year she was awarded an honorary LL.D. by Holy Cross College—the social worker joined the Welfare Council, a newly formed "clearinghouse" for the leading social agencies of New York City. Her position was that of assistant director and secretary of the health division. In this capacity, for ten years Miss Hoey supervised the work of divisional secretaries and the central services of the council's social service exchange, by means of which the data of all member agencies is made available to any of them.

The Welfare Council executive served on State commissions in the administrations of Alfred E. Smith and his successors, Governors Roosevelt and Lehman. In April 1926 she was appointed to the New York State Crime Commission, which was organizing and supervising studies of the causes of crime, investigating situations, helping legislators frame new laws. Her work with the commission continued for four years. From May 1926 to January 1936 Miss Hoey served on the New York State Correction Commission, which supervised State prisons and county jails, with the object of raising standards of care and promoting the rehabilitation of inmates. During the last three years of this period she was also a member of the Commission of Education of Inmates of Penal Institutions. Miss Hoey served, too, on the planning committee for Governor Lehman's 1935 Conference on Crime—the Criminal and Society.

In August 1935 the United States Social Security Act was approved and in February 1936 *Survey* reported that the new Social Security Board had "snatched" three valued staff members of the Welfare Council, chief among them

Harris & Ewing

JANE M. HOEY

Jane M. Hoey. Council director Robert P. Lane was quoted as saying, "It will take two or three good ones to replace her." The post to which Miss Hoey was appointed was that of director of the Bureau of Public Assistance, to administer the Federal Government's part in the joint Federal-State program of financial aid to the needy aged, the blind, and dependent children. Taking office at the time of the depression of the 1930's, she had much of the responsibility of organizing the unprecedentedly large program then instituted. It is the task of her bureau to determine whether individual State programs meet Federal standards and to allot Federal funds to those approved. Miss Hoey's bureau makes available more than a billion dollars a year in Federal grants-in-aid. Under the Social Security Act, the Federal contribution to the programs, which are State-initiated and State-administered, is more than one-half and may be as much as three-fourths of the State's assistance payments, the amount being set by the average of the payments made by the State. The bureau functions through regional representatives and a central staff. Compared with general relief and unemployment insurance, aid to the needy aged, blind, and dependent children was little affected by wartime prosperity, since many of the recipients were physically unable to take war jobs—the average age in the first-named category, Miss Hoey reported in 1943, was over seventy. Youthful marriages during wartime and illegitimate births resulted in an increase in dependent children, while many self-supporting families suffered hardships as a result of shortages of materials, which led to the closing of businesses.

"One does not run for the office of president of the National Conference of Social Work. It is conferred by the profession for distinguished achievement," wrote *Survey* in reporting the coming of Jane M. Hoey to that office in

HOEY, JANE M.—*Continued*

1940 (for the term 1940-41). Her presidential address at the 1941 conference in Atlantic City included some points which she is still stressing in 1950, such as the hardship wrought upon many dependent persons by rigid State residence laws: she cited one case, of three aged sisters who wished to live together but could not because they were in different States, which they could not leave without losing their old-age pensions. As chairman of an interdepartmental committee on the aged, Miss Hoey pointed out in May 1950 that the United States has eleven million persons over the age of sixty-five and that fifteen million could be expected by 1960. "We do not believe it wise," she said, "to have that large group go unproductive." An alternate representative to the sixth session of the United Nations Economic and Social Council's Social Commission, Miss Hoey expected helpful data from U.N. research on the problem.

Among Miss Hoey's honors are the Sienna Medal for achievement in social work, presented to her in 1940 by Theta Phi Alpha, and a second honorary degree, the D.Sc., awarded by her alma mater in November 1949. In the course of her work, she has made many public speeches, appeared before legislative committees, written numerous articles for professional journals. She is president of the William J. Kerby Foundation and contributed the chapter, "Social Work, Democracy, and the Human Personality" to *Democracy: Should It Survive?*, published by the foundation in 1943 (Spanish translation 1949). Miss Hoey serves on the executive committee of the National Social Welfare Assembly, the study committee of the National Council on Social Work Education (both in New York City), is a member of the board and the executive committee of Washington's United Community Services. She belongs to eighteen other organizations concerned with social work, education, group health, child labor, race relations, Catholic culture, and the interests of consumers, migrants, women workers, and American Indians. Miss Hoey is auburn haired and blue eyed; she stands five feet five inches and weighs 153 pounds. In religion she is a Roman Catholic, in politics a Democrat (her voting residence is New York). She has mentioned as her favorite occupations "reading, music, travel, participation in civic affairs, and . . . professional social work."

References

American Catholic Who's Who, 1950-51
American Men in Government (1949)
Who's Who in America, 1950-51
Who's Who in the East (1948)

HOFFMAN, JOHANNES 1890-   Prime Minister of the Saar

Address: Saarbrücken, Saarland

Elected the first Prime Minister of the Saar Government in December 1947, Johannes Hoffman has pressed for the political autonomy of his country and for the integration of its economy with that of France. In February 1950 he was head of a delegation to Paris to complete arrangements for the economic union of the Saar with France under which France was granted a fifty-year lease of Saar coal mines. Before World War II Hoffman held journalistic positions in Berlin, Saarbrücken and Luxembourg. He is the founder and leader of the Christian People's party, the strongest political party in the Saar, and served as president of the Saar Constitutional Commission in 1947.

Johannes Hoffman was born in 1890. He was educated at the university of Innsbrück and Freiburg, and completed his studies at the University of Berlin, receiving his doctorate degree from that institution. During 1914-18 he served in the German Army. After the end of World War I he entered the journalistic field: he was reporter and editor in Berlin and in 1929 became editor of the Saar paper *Saarbrücker Landeszeitung*.

The Saar, an industrial and mining region on the Franco-German frontier, was administered from 1920 to 1935 by an Interim Governing Commission responsible to the League of Nations. In the period preceding the plebiscite scheduled to be held in 1935 to determine whether the Saar should be returned to Germany, united with France, or still administered by the League, Hoffman opposed the territory's return to Germany. His policy caused the Nazi Government in Berlin to bring about his dismissal from the editorship of the *Saarbrücker Landeszeitung* in 1934. To campaign for his beliefs, Hoffman founded and edited the *Neue Saarpost* in December 1934. In the plebiscite held on January 13, 1935, nearly 98 per cent of all qualified voters went to the polls, and 90.3 per cent declared for reunion with Germany. Undue interference on the part of Germany has been alleged. When the Saar was returned to Germany on March 1, 1935, Hoffman moved to Luxembourg, where he worked on the *Luxemburger Wort* during 1935-40. Upon the Nazi invasion of Luxembourg in 1940, he fled first to France and then to Brazil, returning to the Saar only after the liberation.

After the conclusion of World War II, the Allies gave France provisional control of the Saar, with final decision on its status reserved, pending the signing of a German peace treaty. The territory, 738 square miles in area with 926,000 inhabitants, is German in population. It is economically important as a producer of coal and steel—products which France needs to compete with German output and as "security guarantees against any future German aggression" (in the words of the *Christian Science Monitor*). When Hoffman returned to the Saar in 1945 he set about founding the Christian People's party (C.V.P.). In May 1947 he was made president of the Saar Constitutional Commission created by the French Military Government and composed of twenty members representing the four main Saar parties—Christian People's, Social Democrats, Democrats, and Communists. A constitution, opposed by the Communists, was issued on September 28, 1947, in which the Saar was defined as "an autonomous, democratic country, economically linked to France." It further stated that the Saar was politically independent of Germany and gave responsibility for its defense and foreign policy to France. The constitution guaranteed full democratic and human rights to the people of the Saar.

In the elections held on October 5, 1947, Hoffman's party won 51.2 per cent of the votes and 28 of the 50 seats in the Saar Landtag (Parliament). The Social Democrats won 32.8 per cent of the vote and 17 seats; the Democrats won 3 seats, the Communists 2. A Coalition Cabinet of Christian Populists and Social Democrats was formed on December 18, 1947, with Dr. Johannes Hoffman as Prime Minister. He was also named Minister of the Interior and Reconstruction. Upon taking office Hoffman stated that he hoped the Council of Foreign Ministers would accede to the economic union of the Saar with France with as little delay as possible.

During January and February of 1948 discussions between French, British and American officials were held in Berlin; these resulted in a tripartite agreement signed February 20. The French Assembly on February 26 passed a bill authorizing the President of France to ratify the convention, which provided for the economic incorporation of the Saar into the economy of France. Under the terms of the union, which came into effect on April 1, France appointed a High Commissioner to the Saar with legislative powers in the economic sphere. France assumed responsibility for the defense and foreign representation of the Saar, and made French fiscal and customs regulations applicable there. On December 15, 1948, another agreement was signed to establish the region's first university with both French and German professors and to provide for the teaching of French courses in the schools.

On September 2, 1949, French Foreign Minister Robert Schuman [48] declared that his Government would propose and support the candidacy of the Saar for membership in the Council of Europe. It would have the status of an "associate member" with representation in the European Consultative Assembly but not in the Council of Ministers. In December 1949 Prime Minister Hoffman was invited to participate in the discussion of new agreements on the economy and autonomy of the Saar, to be held in France in February 1950.

The Federal Republic of Germany in Bonn expressed such alarm at these developments that shortly before Schuman was scheduled to leave for Bonn in January 1950 to discuss a trade agreement, Hoffman made a trip to Paris to confer with the French Foreign Minister and to obtain assurance that the plans for the Saar would not be changed at Germany's demand. When West German Chancellor Konrad Adenauer [49] made it clear to Schuman that the Germans considered the Saar "historically and ethnically" German and would oppose any one-sided change in its status before a peace treaty had been made with Germany, Schuman restated his determination to carry out French plans to integrate the Saar more closely into the French economy. (His position was supported by a statement from United States Secretary of State Dean Acheson [49].)

Wide World Photos
JOHANNES HOFFMAN

As Schuman and Adenauer met in Bonn, Hoffman in Saarbrücken declared that he considered a plebiscite (which the Germans were demanding) "quite superfluous" inasmuch as the Saar population had already indicated its approval of the present Government's policies in all elections since 1945. He accused the West German Government of "deliberate attempts to stir up trouble" and of sending in a "wave of propaganda" similar to the Nazi propaganda directed at Saarlanders in 1935. To counteract it, he announced the immediate introduction in the Saar Landtag of emergency legislation "for the protection of the democratic order of the Saar state." In newspaper interviews Hoffman pointed out that by integrating economically with the French the Saarlanders would avoid having to pay the reparations demanded of German industry and would not be subject to the Potsdam agreement which fixes the level of total German steel production (and of other German industry). He also observed that the Saar was seeking to establish ownership of its own industries, which formerly were owned or controlled from the Ruhr or Berlin.

In February 1950 Hoffman in Paris headed a delegation of forty-nine members in discussions with the French Foreign Minister and his delegation. The consultations, lasting three weeks, were under continuous attack by the Bonn Government, which contended that even provisional long-term arrangements would be difficult to change when eventual peace negotiations should take place. On March 3 a convention was signed in Paris by Schuman and Hoffman under which France secured the lease of the coal mines of the Saar territory for fifty years, and agreed to support the Saar's claims

HOFFMAN, JOHANNES—*Continued*

to ownership of the mines in any negotiations for a German-Allies peace treaty. Other agreements signed at that time defined the economic union of the Saar with France, and made provisions for greater independence for the Saar Government, including the replacement of the French High Commissioner by an official with diplomatic status. France retained control of the defense and foreign policy of the Saar, but granted some diplomatic privileges to Saar officials. The right of nationals of each country to circulate freely and set up residence or business in the other country was also guaranteed. The Saar railroads, which the French had thought to incorporate into the French national system, were instead to be administered by a joint Franco-Saar council responsible to the Saar Minister of Transport.

After the conventions were signed, the West German Government issued a White Paper proposing international administration of the Saar along the lines of the seven-nation authority which now controls the industrial Ruhr. The White Paper met with sharp criticism and refutation of its objections by the French Foreign Ministry. Hoffman said he was unable to understand the "excitement outside the Saar" since whatever agreements had been made would have to be sanctioned by the peace treaty. At the end of 1950 it was announced that the Saar would become an "independent" nation on January 1, 1951. Ratification of the agreement gives the region its limited freedom, under French control—"at least," said a United Press dispatch, "until the Big Four powers can agree on a peace treaty for Germany."

Johannes Hoffman has stated: "We shall never be French. We are Germans. But we are also Saarlanders." When asked whether at some future time the Saar might change its course, Hoffman said: "No one can tell. But if Europe is united, there will be no problem of the Saar." The Saar statesman's religion is the Roman Catholic, which is the major religious faith in the Saar. In appearance he is rotund and bald; he wears spectacles. The New York *Times* mentioned that he is "more or less affectionately" known by the first syllables of his name—"Yo-Ho."

Reference

International Who's Who, 1949

HOLLAND, SIDNEY G(EORGE) Oct. 18, 1893- Prime Minister of New Zealand

Address: b. Parliament Buildings, Wellington, N.Z.; h. 74 Derby St., Christchurch, N.Z.

As a result of the November 1949 New Zealand election, the National party, headed by Sidney G. Holland, defeated the Labor party and achieved a majority position in the Commonwealth's Government. In December Holland was named Prime Minister, as well as Minister of Finance. He had served as a Member of Parliament since 1935, and since 1940 had been leader of His Majesty's Opposition and head of New Zealand's National party, which was formed by a coalition of Liberals

and Conservatives. A businessman and industrialist, Holland in 1950 is a director of five commercial enterprises.

Sidney George Holland is one of eight children born into a New Zealand pioneering family. His father, Henry Holland, was a native of Yorkshire, England, and his mother, Jane (Eastwood) Holland, had come to New Zealand from Lancashire. (Both of his parents received the decoration of the Order of the British Empire.) When Sidney Holland was born, on October 18, 1893, the family was living in Greendale, a small town approximately thirty miles from Christchurch, one of the larger cities of New Zealand. The family moved to the latter place when Sidney Holland was five years old in order that his father might take over the firm of W. A. McLaren and Company, Ltd., a haulage business. At Christchurch Holland attended the primary school and subsequently was a student at the West Christchurch High School. It was at school that Holland began to play hockey, a sport that continued to be a major interest of his. In 1919 he served as captain of the Canterbury Hockey team and later served as chairman of the Canterbury Hockey Association. In 1932 he was manager of the unbeaten New Zealand Hockey Team, which toured Australia. He founded and edited the *New Zealand Hockey Bulletin*.

Holland left school at the age of fifteen to work in a hardware store, and at nineteen he joined the father's haulage company when the elder Holland was elected Mayor of Christchurch and needed his son's assistance in the directing of the family business. At the same time the young man enrolled as a night student at the Christchurch Technical School. After the outbreak of World War I he volunteered for active military service in 1915, receiving a commission as second lieutenant with the Seventeenth Reinforcement Division, which was sent to France. He returned to New Zealand in 1918 as the recipient of a Coronation Medal for his war services.

Back in Christchurch Holland resumed his directorship of the McLaren Company; at the same time he organized, with one of his brothers, the Midland Engineering Company and bought a small factory, the Christchurch Mechanical Works, which was later to have the name of S. G. Holland, Ltd. The two companies were associated in the manufacture and distribution of agricultural implements and machines. During the first years of the enterprises, Holland was the chief salesman, canvassing the farm regions of New Zealand. Some commentators have attributed his fluency and ease in speaking to farmers and businessmen to this early selling experience. It was some time before the two companies succeeded; when they did, a program of profit-sharing among the employees was instituted. Meanwhile, his father had become a Member of Parliament, representing the district of Christchurch North. During the election campaigns Holland had been his father's organizer and secretary. Thus he was ready to become a candidate himself in the 1935 elections when an injury prevented his father from running for re-election. Holland won the seat in the House of Representatives by a majority of 917 votes.

This was the election in which conservative groups, which had held a majority in the New Zealand Government since 1931, were swept out of power by the Labor party. In that election Holland was one of the two new nonlabor members to enter the Parliament. He was returned to the legislature in 1938 and with each subsequent election his majority votes increased, in 1946 to 3,004 votes. From 1935 until its strong majority began to decline in 1946, the Labor party instituted various measures to end a severe economic depression in New Zealand and then to embark on what has been described as "an unprecedented expansion of social services." The program began with the Social Security Act of 1938, which extended to all citizens a system of pensions and of medical and health benefits. State housing was also introduced during the Labor party regime, as well as nationalization of the Reserve Bank, the Mortgage Corporation, the major industrial utilities. and the airways system. As a member of the National party, which had been formed in 1931 by a merging of the Conservative and Liberal parties, Holland opposed these measures. By 1940 he was elected leader of both the National party and the opposition groups. During World War II an attempt was made to give the opposition a wider participation in the Government. The War Cabinet was enlarged in June 1942 to include Holland. But in October of that year, Holland and three of his colleagues resigned from the Government in protest against the handling of a strike at the Waikato coal fields. Holland continued to head the opposition and worked to increase membership in the National party, finding his support among the rural groups and the industrial leaders.

By the 1943 elections the National party had won thirty-four of the eighty seats in the House of Representatives and by 1946 its number of seats had increased to thirty-eight. In the 1949 elections the Labor party, which had held control for fourteen years, lost eight Parliamentary seats, with the National party thus coming into control of the Government with forty-six seats. New Zealand political commentators agreed that the party had been able to increase its following through Holland's personal efforts as shown in "political astuteness, in debating powers, and in leadership." His practical experience in both the manufacturing and distributing industries was also recognized as a basis for his following among voters. Campaigning on a program to reduce Government expenses and consequently taxes, and to ease the import licensing procedure that has kept automobiles, nylon hosiery, and other consumer goods out of the country, Holland won not only the expected rural vote but gained followers from among industrial workers who were interested in removing the import restrictions. The question of "Welfare State" (which dates back to 1898, when New Zealand was the first country to institute old-age pensions), was not involved in the election debates—Holland promised to continue security benefits and the national health program. Nor did he propose to undo the legislation which nationalized many

SIDNEY G. HOLLAND

industries. He did, however, cite the losses in the state-owned railroads, coal mines, and airways, and proposed that the airways be returned to private ownership and that other measures be taken to permit private enterprise to compete with the government.

The Nationals' platform, as summarized by *Life*, was "a social policy divested of socialism. . . .The party had succeeded in implanting in the minds of the people the ideal of personal freedom. Social and economic security was there in the background—but as a line of defense, not an ultimate objective." With this platform the National party defeated the Labor party, and in December 1949 Holland became Prime Minister as well as Minister of Finance. Immediately the opposition groups in Australia, where an election was to be held several weeks later, and in England, where elections will be held during 1950, saw New Zealand's swing from the Labor party as indicative of a similar trend in the other countries. (The Australian election resulted in a victory for Robert Gordon Menzies '50, the leader of the opposition.) The New York *Times* pointed out that the proportion of New Zealand voters who had turned to the right was only about 7½ per cent; and the New York *Post* described the National party as being "left of the Fair Deal in its social welfare program. New Zealand is not seeking conservatism, but only moderation."

Commenting on the victory of his party, Holland said that he did not intend to make any revolutionary changes in the Government, admitting that the Labor party had left behind "much that will endure." In a report carried by the *Christian Science Monitor* he said of his election: "We have only one aim and desire—to maintain prosperity and production at the highest level so that people of all classes will enjoy those advantages." He also stressed his desire to continue New Zealand's record

HOLLAND, SIDNEY G.—*Continued*
of close cooperation with the other countries within the British Commonwealth.

In addition to serving as director of the two firms with which he began his business career, Holland is a director of several insurance companies and of the association of Engineers and Motor Trades. He is a past president of the Canterbury Employers Association and a past vice-president of the Canterbury Chamber of Commerce; he is a member of the Returned Soldiers Association of New Zealand. Holland, who has been described as an "affable man" with a "common touch," is said to have an "excellent" radio voice and a good platform manner He is still an active sportsman, enjoying tennis, fishing, and golfing. Since 1939 he has owned a sheep station in North Canterbury and here he may do his own gardening. On May 20, 1920, he married Florence Beatrice Drayton, a resident of Christchurch. The couple has two sons and two daughters, who are named Eric, Geoffrey, Jocelyn, and Lois. New Zealand's Prime Minister attends the Methodist Church.

References

Christchurch (N.Z.) Press S 21 '49
Wellington (N.Z.) Dominion D 1 '49
International Press Who's Who, N.Z., 1938
International Who's Who, 1949
Who's Who in New Zealand (1941)
World Biography (1948)

HOLLAND, SPESSARD L(INDSEY)
July 10, 1892- United States Senator from Florida
Address: b. Senate Office Bldg., Washington, D.C.; c/o Holland, Bevis & McRae, Bartow, Fla.; h. 1005 S. Broadway, Bartow, Fla.

Although a comparative newcomer to the United States Senate, the junior Senator from Florida, Spessard L. Holland, is regarded as one of the ablest strategists in the Southern Democratic bloc which has opposed some of the Administration's measures. He thus is considered to represent that body of Florida opinion which does not find its spokesman in his senior colleague, Senator Claude Pepper[41]. Holland, who took his seat in the Senate in September 1946, had been Governor of his State during the greater part of World War II.

A native of Florida, Spessard Lindsey Holland was born in Bartow, Polk County, on July 10, 1892. He is one of the three children (two boys and a girl) of Benjamin Franklin Holland, a schoolteacher, farmer, and owner of a title company, and of the former Fanny Virginia Spessard, who, before her marriage, also taught school. The Hollands, who came originally from England, settled in America in early Colonial times; the Spessards and Lindseys on the maternal side are of German and Scotch-Irish extraction, respectively, dating, in America, from pre-Revolutionary days.

After attending the local grammar school and Summerlin Institute at Bartow—he was graduated from the latter in 1909—the future

Senator entered Emory College (subsequently Emory University) at Oxford, Georgia, where his record, both academic and extracurricular, was outstanding. He was a member of the debating team, the literary editor of the college magazine, and the winner of the D.A.R. history medal as a sophomore, and of the mathematics medal as a senior. In the field of athletics he was a member of the baseball, football, basketball and track teams. Upon his graduation in 1912 he received the Ph.B. degree, *magna cum laude*. In May 1942 he was made a member of Phi Beta Kappa at Emory University, which honor fraternity came to Emory after Holland graduated therefrom.

By the year 1912, parental encouragement, Holland's inclination, and his aptitude in debate had already determined him on a legal career. Thus, after two years (1912-14) as a teacher in the high school at Warrenton, Georgia, Holland began regular attendance at the Law College of the University of Florida, where he met expenses by teaching in the University's subfreshman department. Here again his record was considered out of the ordinary, winning, as he did, both the Board of Control Oratory Medal and the Practice Court Law Prize, and election to the Phi Kappa Phi honorary fraternity.

Receiving his LL.B. degree in 1916 and admission to the Florida bar in the same year, Holland became junior partner in the law firm of Huffaker and Holland in his home town of Bartow. He had engaged in his profession for less than a year when the United States became a combatant in World War I. As an officer in the Coast Artillery Corps, Holland served in France first as a brigade judge advocate and assistant adjutant, then at his own request was transferred to the Air Service and assigned to the Twenty-fourth Aero Squadron as an aerial observer. (He was never a pilot, as has sometimes erroneously been stated.) He flew on four fronts, was awarded the Distinguished Service Cross in October 1918, and in July 1919 was demobilized with the rank of captain.

Upon his return to civilian life Holland became prosecuting attorney for Polk County in the fall of the same year, and in 1920 was elected a county judge. This position he retained for the next eight years. At the beginning of 1929 he established in Bartow the law firm of Holland and Bevis (later Holland, Bevis and Hughes, and still later Holland, Bevis and McRae). Elected to the Florida State Senate in November 1931, Holland served two four-year terms. Among the legislative measures he pushed were the Florida State code for schools (1939), which he helped to draft and sponsored, and a measure increasing old-age pension funds by two million dollars. Holland was commended as "a friend of labor" in the periodical reports of trade unions (*National Cyclopædia of American Biography*). When he entered the State Democratic primaries in May 1940, as a candidate for the gubernatorial nomination, Holland defeated his closest challenger, Francis P. Whitehair of De Land. He was unopposed in the November election.

As Florida's Governor from January 1941 to January 1945, Holland approved numerous fiscal measures, among them the revision of the assessment and collection of real estate taxes, and refunding of the Everglades drainage bond debt. One of his major financial measures was the sponsorship of a gas tax amendment to the constitution under which a greatly reduced interest rate became available on county and district road bonds, and by which a larger part of the gas tax was used for road construction. Early Holland put pressure on the sheriffs of Dade and Broward counties to oust racketeers and gamblers from the Miami and other resort areas. In June 1943, he incurred a loss of popularity in some quarters by approving a law placing labor unions under State regulation. He called for more liberal gasoline rations for Florida and, at the Conference of Governors held in Denver, in 1943, was a leading figure in the Southern bloc fighting for the revision of railroad freight rates then favoring the North and East. In the last year of his administration, Governor Holland negotiated the deeding by Florida to the United States of some thousands of acres of marsh or submerged land, so that the Federal Fish and Wild Life Service could establish protective patrols as a preliminary step toward the establishment of the Everglades National Park. He opposed portions of the New Deal (as reported by the New York *World-Telegram*, April 24, 1943), believing of government that, "the further off it gets, the less economical it is, the more wasteful, the more bureaucratic. . . .Some of our reformists in Washington have seized upon wartime as a time to further their political ideas."

The governorship of Florida is limited to a single term. In January 1945, accordingly, Holland turned over the gubernatorial duties to his successor, Millard F. Caldwell '48, and resumed law practice at Bartow. Early in 1946, however, the State's junior United States senator, Charles O. Andrews, whose term would expire with the then current Congress, announced that his health would not permit him to seek re-election. Holland entered the May primaries and won the Democratic Senatorial nomination in a landslide. On September 18, Senator Andrews died, and one week later, after his widow had declined the honor of filling out the unexpired term, Governor Caldwell named Holland in her place. Actually, the appointment was merely a fulfillment of constitutional requirements, as the Seventy-ninth Congress was in adjournment from August to the beginning of the new year, and Holland's election in November was a foregone conclusion; thus when the Eightieth Congress convened in January 1947, the new Senator's credentials as interim appointee were presented "for the record" simultaneously with his seating for his full elective term expiring January 1953.

Assigned to the Senate's District of Columbia and Rules and Administration Committees, Holland served also on the joint committee on the Library of Congress, the special Committee to Study Problems of Small American Business, and, subsequently, the National Capital Sesquicentennial Commission. A majority of Hol-

Virgil R. Boozer Studios

SPESSARD L. HOLLAND

land's early ballots were cast in support of the Truman Administration. He voted to confirm David E. Lilienthal as head of the Atomic Energy Commission, opposed limiting the Presidency to two terms, supported the President's 1947 budget, and favored the Greek-Turkish aid bill. He parted company with the Fair Dealers, however, on the Taft-Hartley labor law, which he strongly supported. Later in May 1947 he attracted much attention by a long speech against the Republican tax-reduction measure, which he criticized as giving "too much relief to high-income groups and not enough to the small taxpayer," because it included the so-called "community property" principle and allowed increased personal exemptions and credits for dependents. He did support the 1948 Republican tax-reduction bill. Other votes he cast during the second session of the Eightieth Congress included approval of the Marshall Plan, of repeal of federal taxes on oleomargarine, of Federal aid to education, of extension of the Reciprocal Trade Agreements Act.

When the Eighty-first Congress met in January 1949 Senator Holland—whose principal assignments now were to the Agriculture and Forestry and Public Works Committees—took immediate prominence. On March 3, in the course of the Southern fight to prevent the Truman civil rights legislation from reaching the Senate floor, he spoke for five and a half hours, one of the longer addresses delivered during that successful filibuster. Later in the same month he voted to return rent controls to State and local authorities, and in April to eliminate the antisegregation provisions from the Administration's public housing bill. During the final week of June, when the Administration attempted unsuccessfully to replace the Taft-Hartley Act with a revised measure more favorable to organized labor,

HOLLAND, SPESSARD L.—*Continued*

Senator Holland authored an amendment, supported by Senator Taft, which (in the words of Phelps Adams of the New York *Sun*) would have empowered the President "to obtain sixty-day injunctions against 'national emergency' strikes, but which would bar plant seizures." (This amendment was defeated by 54 to 37.)

On August 30, 1949, when raising of the national minimum hourly wage from forty to seventy-five cents under the Fair Labor Standards Act was in debate, Holland offered an amendment exempting most retail and service establishments from its provisions, which amendment was adopted by a vote of 50 to 23. Previously (July 21) Holland supported the party leadership by voting for ratification of the North Atlantic Pact, and opposed (August 8) forbidding use of Marshall Plan funds for the nationalization of industry. He supported the Foreign Military Aid bill (September 22). On October 7 he was recorded against extending 90 per cent of parity farm price supports indefinitely.

The recipient in 1941 of honorary LL.D. degrees from Rollins College and Florida Southern College, and in 1943 from Emory University, Holland has served three years each on the boards of trustees of the two last-named institutions. Brown-eyed, with gray hair that was originally black, the Senator is six feet tall, weighs 180 pounds. He finds recreation in hunting, fishing, tennis, and collecting Floridiana. A Mason (Shriner) and an Elk, he is also a member of the American Legion, the Veterans of Foreign Wars, and the Kiwanis Club; his social fraternity is the Alpha Tau Omega, while professional bodies to which he belongs include the Bartow, Florida State and American bar associations. He is a Methodist. Mrs. Holland is the former Mary Agnes Groover. The Hollands, who were married February 8, 1919, have four children—Spessard Lindsey, Jr., Mary Groover (now Mrs. Jeff D. Lewis), William Benjamin, and Ivanhoe Elizabeth.

References

> Congressional Directory (1st ed., 1949)
> International Who's Who, 1949
> National Cyclopædia of American Biography Current vol F, 1939-42
> Who's Who in America, 1948-49
> Who's Who in Law, 1937
> World Biography (1948)

HOLTZ, JACKSON J(ACOB)　Oct. 10, 1907-　Veterans organization official; lawyer

Address: b. 85 Devonshire St., Boston 9, Mass.; h. 419 Washington St., Brookline, Mass.

A Boston lawyer who had served in his State legislature and for nine years as a Government attorney, Jackson J. Holtz was chosen the 1949-50 national commander of the Jewish War Veterans of the United States. Organized in 1896 by Jewish Civil War veterans, in 1950 it has a membership of approximately 100,000 veterans and a ladies auxiliary of 45,000. Holtz is the first veteran of World War II (who had not also fought in World War I) to become its head.

Born in Boston, October 10, 1907, Jackson Jacob Holtz is the son of Nathan and Fanny (Sternberg) Holtz. He attended the Boston English High School, graduating in 1923. In 1927 he was granted the Bachelor's degree by the Boston University College of Business Administration, and two years later he received the LL.B. from the university's School of Law. That he was an unusually articulate young man is indicated by his extracurricular successes— he was captain of a college debating team which won an intercollegiate championship, and he was elected to the honorary debating fraternity Delta Sigma Rho. On the editorial staffs of the college and law school periodicals, he wrote for the *B.U. News*, the *B.U. Bean-pot*, and the *B.U. Law School Brief*; he also worked in the university's publicity office.

After admission to the Massachusetts bar in 1929 Holtz began law practice in Boston. Five years later, in 1934, he formed a partnership with David A. Rose (since 1935 associate justice of the Municipal Court of the Dorchester district), and has since practiced law as a partner in the firm Holtz and Rose. In September 1937 Holtz was appointed Assistant United States Attorney. The previous year he sought elective office, and won a seat in the Massachusetts House of Representatives by the largest plurality ever cast in the Dorchester district. A member of the State legislature for one year, during that time he served on a Massachusetts Legislative Recess Commission for the Investigation of Un-American Activities. Meanwhile he continued as a Government attorney except for the period from 1942 to 1946, for which he took a leave to serve on active military duty as an officer in the Ordnance Corps. He left the army in the rank of major, with a Certificate and Ribbon of Commendation for "outstanding performance of duty" (1945).

The Jewish War Veterans, which represents 647 posts in thirty-three States and the District of Columbia, elected Holtz national commander by acclamation on October 23, 1949 for a one-year term. (He succeeds Myer Dorfman of St. Paul, Minnesota.) Holtz had previously served as a J.W.V. national executive committee member, and as a department commander. As Holtz explained it to Lawrence R. Goldberg, an interviewer for the Boston *Post*, the principal purpose for which the J.W.V. was organized, was "to confront anti-Semites and allied bigots with a living refutation of slanders against the patriotism of their targets."

As J.W.V. national commander (the post he holds till October 1950) Holtz is centering his program of action in early 1950 on seven campaigns, according to reporter Goldberg. The J.W.V. is opposing budget cuts in the Veterans Administration and other agencies, economies based on the Hoover Report which would limit veterans' studies under the G.I. Bill of Rights and reduce the number of veterans' hospital beds. (In an interview with President Truman, January 24, 1950, Commander Holtz charged that the Hoover Commission recommendations, while promising "theoretical benefits" would result in giving the veterans "the same run-around as after World War I.") The J.W.V. also opposes legislation to modify the laws which give to veterans preference in Federal positions, opposes political selection for appli-cants to United States naval, military, and coast guard academies, and fights discrimi-nation in employment, education, housing. At the same time the organization emphasizes the importance of national defense and supports President Truman's plan for an expanded pro-gram of guidance for young men in the armed forces, designed to return the men to civilian life "aware of their rights and responsibilities under a democratic form of government." Holtz's group also is working to have Febru-ary 3 designated "Four Chaplains Day" in com-memoration of the four World War II chap-lains of Protestant, Catholic, and Jewish faiths who gave their lifebelts to others and went down with their ship on that day in 1943.

In the carrying out of his duties Holtz travels frequently. Shortly after his election he went to Washington to join in urging Amer-ican protest of the treatment of the Jewish minority in Iraq. On Armistice Day (1949) he participated in ceremonies at the tomb of the Unknown Soldier. At the time of his call on the President in January 1950 he expressed "appreciation for his [Truman's] tenacity with reference to civil rights," and he pledged J.W.V. support of the President's programs for middle-income housing, liberalization of the displaced persons law, and continuation of foreign economic aid. As a speaker, Holtz has visited cities and towns through the United States as well as Havana. The Goldberg article stated that he is "in demand as a counselor, guest of honor, chief speaker and advocate, day after day." Communism and other forms of totalitarianism are said to rouse the ire of the normally "quiet" veterans' leader: "The Jewish War Veterans," he asserted, "'are opposed to communism not only because it represents the No. 1 threat to the preservation of the United States, but because communism is an enemy of Judaism. A man cannot be a good Jew and a communist at the same time."

Other Jewish organizations to which Holtz belongs are: B'nai B'rith (he is a former president of Amos Lodge); the Jewish Big Brother Association (past president); the Temple Israel Brotherhood in Boston; the Zionist Organization of America (former secre-tary N.E. Zionist Region, former president Dorchester Zionist District). His other asso-ciations include the American Red Cross (a member of the Speakers Bureau), Children's Hospital, Brookline Community Forum (a moderator), Knights of Pythias (Common-wealth Lodge), Masons (Moses Michael Hays Lodge), Phi Sigma Pi and Tau Delta Phi.

The lawyer is a member of the Massachu-setts and Federal bars, the United States Tax Court and the United States Court of Claims, the American and Federal bar associations, and the Law Society of Massachusetts. He is the author of several legal treatises: "The Doctrine of *Stare Decisis* in Massachusetts

Bill Kobrin
JACKSON J. HOLTZ

(1935), "Here and There Among the Opin-ions" (1930), both published in the *Massachu-setts Law Society Journal*, "Legislation As It Affects Defense Contracts." He is a former instructor in Federal law at the Massachusetts State Police Academy. Honors which have come to him are awards from B'nai B'rith (1946 and 1947) and from Tau Delta Phi Fraternity (1949).

The veterans' leader married Edith Wein-stein, also of Boston, on July 7, 1937; their two daughters are Jane and Ellen May. Holtz attends the Temple Israel in Boston, and he is a Democrat. He has a height of five feet ten and a half inches, a weight of 165 pounds, gray-green eyes, and light-brown hair. The Boston *Post* interviewer described him as a man of "graceful qualities of mind, quiet and courteous."

References

Boston (Mass.) Post Ja 1 '50
Who's Who in American Jewry, 1938-39
Who's Who in Massachusetts, 1942-43
Who's Who in New England (1949)
Who's Who in the East (1948)

HOOVER, J(OHN) EDGAR Jan. 1, 1895- United States Government official; crimin-ologist

Address: b. c/o Federal Bureau of Investiga-tion, United States Department of Justice, Washington, D.C.; h.

NOTE: This biography supersedes the article which appeared in *Current Biography* in 1940.

The director of the Federal Bureau of In-vestigation of the Department of Justice, J. Edgar Hoover, looked forward in the early

J. EDGAR HOOVER

months of 1950 to the completion, on May 10 of that year, of twenty-six years of continuous occupancy of his post. He was appointed thereto in 1924, after three years as assistant director, and two years of experience in the prosecution of alien agitators following World War I. To Hoover is given the credit of building the FBI into one of the most efficient and respected law enforcement agencies. With his G-men he was responsible during World War II for the prevention of sabotage, and is today charged with the duty of investigating, in such instances as may be required, the loyalty of Federal employees as well as the enforcement of about 120 major Federal laws.

John Edgar Hoover, one of four children of Dickerson Naylor and Annie Marie (Scheitlin) Hoover, was born January 1, 1895, in Washington, D.C. His father, who died in 1921, was a government employee who became superintendent of engraving and printing in the United States Coast and Geodetic Survey; he was the descendant of a Swiss pioneer who had settled in Pennsylvania in colonial times. Mrs. Hoover, who survived her husband by seventeen years, counted among her forebears Switzerland's first consul general in the United States; she has been described as "a strong-willed woman with firm belief in the stern principles of Calvinism." Her son's boyhood ambition was to be a minister. "My imagination was captured by a young Presbyterian preacher, Dr. Donald Campbell MacLeod, who . . . symbolized the supremacy of fair play and good sportsmanship," Hoover has said, "If ministers were like Dr. MacLeod, I wanted to be one." He taught a class of young people at the Old First Presbyterian Church in Washington, and joined the church. (Earlier, at the Church of the Reformation, he had sung in the choir.) At Washington's Central High School where, although only 110 pounds in weight, he rose to be captain of cadets and earned the nickname

of "Speed," he "chastened" his contemporaries with his "morality." By the time of his graduation—as valedictorian of the class of 1913—Hoover had, however, determined on a legal career.

The young man got a job as messenger in the Library of Congress, studied law at night, and in 1916 acquired the LL.B. degree from George Washington University. The LL.M. degree followed in 1917; and Hoover (who is now admitted to practice before the United States District Court of the District of Columbia, the United States Court of Claims, and the Supreme Court) entered the employ of the Department of Justice as a file reviewer. In 1919 he was appointed special assistant to Attorney General A. Mitchell Palmer and assigned to handling deportation proceedings against alien agitators. It was a period of "mass hysteria in high places" and one on which Hoover is said to look back "with considerable distaste" (*Time*).

The Bureau of Investigation of the Department of Justice, as the FBI was originally called, had been established in 1908 by order of Attorney General Charles J. Bonaparte for the "investigation of violation of the laws of the United States, collecting evidence in cases in which the United States is or may become a party, and performing other duties imposed . . . by law." Its power was actually much more circumscribed than this would suggest, since the Treasury and Post Office Departments maintained, as they do now, their own investigating organizations. The Bureau was mainly concerned before World War I with violations of neutrality, bankruptcy, and antitrust laws and the white slave traffic. During the war years its special agents, under the direction of A. Bruce Bielaski, investigated sabotage, espionage, and subversive activities.

In 1921, when William J. Burns, the famous detective, was the director, Hoover was named assistant director. He was appointed acting director of the Bureau of Investigation by Attorney General Harlan Stone on May 10, 1924, with the assurance that there would be "no politics, no outside influence." With this guarantee Hoover (who was confirmed as director seven months later) overhauled the Bureau, returning to the policy of employing lawyers and public accountants as special agents. Another of his early measures was to establish the central fingerprint bureau, expanding an initial file of 810,000 prints assembled from various sources in 1924 to 114,000,000 in 1950. New methods in training were also introduced, and new scientific methods of detection studied. On June 11, 1930, Congress passed an Act authorizing the Bureau to collect, compile and publish crime statistics from police agencies throughout the nation; and two years later the present FBI laboratory "to carry out the scientific studies of evidence," and accessible to all law enforcement agencies, was instituted.

Elevation of the G-man to the role of national hero may be said to date from 1932, when a rising tide of gangsterism in general and kidnaping cases in particular, aroused Congress to new preventive action. The National Kidnaping Act, making it a Federal offense to transport kidnaped persons across State lines, was passed. This was followed by the National Extortion Act and the Bank Robbery Act, which enabled Federal agents to take action where national banks, and member banks in the Federal Reserve system, had been robbed. By 1934 the Bureau had been specifically authorized by Congress to "blot out the wave of lawlessness," and its agents, now armed and empowered to make arrests, proceeded with dispatch to round up notorious "public enemies." This was not done without considerable criticism, however, the charge being brought at times that the raids on gangsters were not legal in all aspects, that the G-men were addicted to needless shooting, and that there was insufficient cooperation with local authorities.

Hoover made a generally successful effort to meet the latter accusation, losing no opportunity to address State and municipal law enforcement groups; and in 1935 (the year in which the name Federal Bureau of Investigation was adopted) established the FBI Academy at Quantico, Virginia, which trains "selected police officers from every State in the Union and many foreign countries" in up-to-date methods. Hoover did not participate personally in the early raids on gangsters, but when in 1936 Senator Kenneth McKellar of Tennessee inquired why the FBI chief "was not sticking out his own neck," Hoover went out and himself captured the notorious Alvin Karpis. At about the same period Hoover decided, "If there is going to be publicity, let it be on the side of law and order," and led an organized campaign to acquaint the country with the work of the FBI. This resulted in the only book on which his name appears as author, *Persons in Hiding* (1938); he has written forewords to several other books as well as numerous articles for newspapers and general and special magazines. A recent piece is "Hoover Answers Ten Questions on the F.B.I." (the New York *Times Magazine*, April 16, 1950).

In September 1939, when President Roosevelt declared a national emergency in view of the war in Europe, the FBI was directed to "coordinate" all matters relating to "espionage, sabotage, and violations of the neutrality regulations." A plant-protection survey was made and registration of aliens ordered, with the result that twenty-four hours after the Pearl Harbor attack, 1,771 enemy aliens were in custody. The number of FBI agents was increased from 600 to a wartime peak of 5,000; and the fact that "no major instance of foreign-directed sabotage succeeded" was due in part at least to their vigilance.

Hoover, who held the rank of lieutenant colonel in the Officers Reserve Corps, before resigning because of his active civilian work, was the recipient in 1946 of the Medal for Merit in recognition of his wartime achievement, and in the same year received the United States Selective Service Medal and the Order of Honor and Merit of the Cuban Red Cross. He is an honorary Knight Commander of the Most Excellent Order of the British Empire.

Postwar years were to put the FBI to new tests. Early in 1947 Hoover, in his annual report, revealed that crime had increased 7.6 per cent in 1946 "to a ten-year peak." He ascribed this state of affairs in some measure to a "gradual breakdown of the American home" and the fact that "juvenile delinquents of the war years are graduating from petty thieves to armed robbers." Also, under the postwar Atomic Energy Act of 1946 the Bureau was required to "investigate all violations"; and in March 1947, President Truman assigned the FBI what *Time* has called its "toughest, most controversial assignment"—namely, to check the loyalty of more than 2,800,000 Federal employees.

On May 10, 1949, Hoover saw the completion of a quarter of a century as head of the FBI. (At that time the FBI was employing about 4,000 agents in the enforcement of some 120 major Federal laws, and claimed that in approximately 9,000 cases during 1949 it had obtained 97.2 per cent convictions.) Editorially the New York *Times* stated: "Postwar, a paramount FBI concern—indeed, a world concern—has been to track the progress of Communist infiltration and proceed against it wherever the law allows."

In the April 16, 1950, New York *Times*, Hoover made a statement on FBI wire tapping: "Wire tapping is employed only in matters involving internal security or when human lives might be in jeopardy. Information secured as a result of wire tapping is not used as evidence, and is not divulged publicly by the FBI except under force of judicial compunction, over the objection of the Government." He further pointed out that the FBI does not undertake investigations except at the specific request of responsible authorities, and has no power to prosecute. When during the winter and the spring of 1949-50 Senator Joseph R. McCarthy brought charges of widespread Communist infiltration in the State Department, Hoover opposed (March 27) giving the subcommittee access to FBI files, asserting not only that "the disclosure . . . would reveal confidential procedures and techniques" but also that inasmuch as "the files do not consist of proved information alone" the effect might well be to "smear the innocent" in many instances.

FBI Director Hoover has been awarded many honorary academic degrees. Among these have been an LL.D. from George Washington University, in 1935; the LL.D. degree from the Pennsylvania Military College as well as from New York University (both in 1936), Westminster College (1937), Oklahoma Baptist University (1938), Georgetown University (1939), Drake University (1940), Notre Dame University (1942), the Law School of St. John's University (1942), Rutgers University (1943), the University of Arkansas (1943), and Holy Cross College and Seton Hall College (1944); the D.Sc. from Kalamazoo College in 1937; and the D.C.L. from the University of the South (1941). Among other awards have been the distinguished service medal of the Boys' Clubs of America (1936); the *Liberty* gold medal for good citizenship; and the alumni achievement award of George

HOOVER, J. EDGAR—*Continued*

Washington University; he has also been recognized by the National Institute of Social Sciences, the American Legion, the Veterans of Foreign Wars, by the National Academy of Sciences (the latter for application of science to public welfare). Hoover has been a member of the board of the Boys' Club of America since 1943 and is a member-at-large of the national council of the Boy Scouts of America, and a member of the advisory council of the Girl Scouts. He is a life member of the International Association of Chiefs of Police, an honorary life member of the International Association for Identification and of the Chief Constables Association of Canada, and an honorary member of many other law enforcement bodies. A trustee of George Washington University and of the National Presbyterian Church in Washington, he is also a member of the board of directors of the Central Dispensary and Emergency Hospital in the capital city.

Until the death of his mother in 1938 Hoover made his home in the house in which he was born. He has remained a bachelor. Frederick L. Collins has described him as having an "alert face below . . . close-cropped, slightly curling, thick black hair," and a "compact body, with shoulders of a light heavyweight boxer and waist of a tennis player." (Tennis is one of Hoover's principal recreations: others are baseball, football, boxing, and "browsing for antiques, particularly bronzes"). A Mason (K.T., Shriner), and a member of the Kappa Alpha, Omicron Delta Kappa, Delta Theta Phi, Alpha Phi Omega and Zeta Sigma Pi fraternities, he may find social diversion at the Columbia Country and Metropolitan Clubs in Washington. A life-long resident of the unfranchised capital, he lists no political affiliation.

References

American Weekly p15 Jl 20 '47
Liberty 17:7-10 Mr 10 '40 por; 37-40
    Mr 23 '40 por
N Y Post p16 Ja 20 '40 por
New Yorker 13:20-5 S 25 '37; 21-6
    O 2 '37; 22-7 O 9 '37
Reader's Digest 31:42-45 D '37; 52:107-
    10 Ap '48 por
Time 54:12-15 Ag 8 '49 por
U S News 26:40-1 Je 24 '49 por
Washington Post p4 Ap 20 '47
American Men in Government (1949)
Collins. F. L. The FBI in Peace and
    War (1943)
Cooper, C. R. Foreword to "Men in
    Hiding," by J. E. Hoover (1938)
Encyclopedia Americana (1949)
Karsh, Y. Faces of Destiny (1947)
Look, Editors of. The Story of the
    FBI (1947)
National Cyclopædia of American Biography Current vol F, 1939-42
Who Knows—And What (1949)
Who's Who, 1949
Who's Who in America, 1950-51
World Biography (1948)

HOPKINS, ARTHUR (MELANCTHON)
Oct. 4, 1878—Mar. 22, 1950 Theatrical producer in New York since 1912; first successful with *The Poor Little Rich Girl*; introduced plays by Eugene O'Neill, Philip Barry, Maxwell Anderson; produced revivals of Ibsen and Shakespeare; discovered Katharine Hepburn; presented John Barrymore in *Redemption, The Jest* (with Lionel Barrymore also), *Richard III* and *Hamlet*; author and co-author of several plays, author of three books. See *Current Biography*, 1947.

Obituary

N Y Times p29 Mr 23 '50 por

HOPPER, EDWARD July 22, 1882-
Painter; etcher
Address: b. c/o Frank K. M. Rehn, Inc., 683 5th Ave., New York 22; h. 3 Washington Sq. N., New York 3

Credited with being the first painter to record the "American provincial scene," Edward Hopper is in 1950 placed in the foremost rank of American artists. Undeviating in his devotion to realistic painting, the artist has declared: "My aim in painting has always been the most exact transcription possible of my most intimate impressions of nature."

Descended from English, Welsh, and Dutch forebears, Edward Hopper was born to Garrett Henry and Elizabeth Griffiths (Smith) Hopper on July 22, 1882. As a child he was sent to a private day school in his native town of Nyack, New York, on the Hudson River. This proximity to the river provided young Hopper with access to the one sport which early interested him, sailing; his free days were passed at the Nyack shipyards. After attending the local high school, in 1899-1900 he decided to study art.

Shortly thereafter Edward Hopper enrolled at the New York School of Art, in a student group which then included George Bellows, Guy Pène du Bois, Eugene Speicher, Rockwell Kent. For five years Hopper worked under the tutelage of Kenneth Hayes Miller and Robert Henri. During three different periods of several months each, in the years between 1906 and 1910, Hopper painted in Europe, chiefly in France, where he was little known to other American painters and had but slight contact with the modernists. Some of his time was also spent in Spain. The pre-1910 paintings, artist Charles Burchfield has stated, show an impasto finish applied with an Impressionistic touch. Some of these were contributed by Hopper to a group showing at the old Harmonie Club in New York in 1908. Hopper's Paris-inspired work included *Valley of the Seine*, *The Wine Shop*, and *Le Quai des Grands Augustins*. For the summer of 1912 Hopper was at Gloucester, Massachusetts. Consistently rejected by the Academy jury, Hopper took the opportunity to exhibit at the Armory Show of 1913, and there he made his first sale, of a canvas entitled *The Sailboat*. After working on several paintings in Maine during the summers of 1914 and 1915, Hopper ceased painting in oils—he was to return to the use of that medium only in 1924. The Whitney Studio Club gave a one-man show of his work in 1919.

For a number of years Hopper worked as an illustrator—in 1950 he recalled for a *Time* magazine interviewer that he had been mediocre in that field. In the year 1915 he had commenced to study the technique of etching under Martin Lewis, and it was this form of the graphic arts which was his chief concern for about a decade. Of the twenty plates which the artist produced, Virgil Barker declared (*The Arts*, June 1924): "When an artist masters a technique which requires . . . accuracy . . . that is almost mathematical in its severity and which yet remains largely unpredictable in its means of materializing the conception, it is only just to admire his skill. But when he does all this and thereby perpetuates conceptions as strong and convincing as those of Edward Hopper, it is time to acknowledge with gratitude the addition of something genuine and lasting to American art." Childe Reece, in a study of Hopper's etchings written for the *Magazine of Art*, observed that his works in this medium had "an importance far greater than their limited number would indicate." In such studies as *The Railroad* and *American Landscape*, declared Reece, "he plucks mystery from the commonplace." In 1923 Hopper's etchings were recognized with two awards: the W. A. Bryan prize for etching at the International Print Makers Exhibition in Los Angeles, and the Logan prize of the Chicago Society of Etchers.

Some of Hopper's Paris caricatures were shown at the Whitney Studio Club in 1922, and two years later an exhibition of his water colors at the Rehn Galleries in New York. Encouraged by the success of this latter exhibition, the artist resumed his work in oil, producing among other canvases one which he sent to the Pennsylvania Academy's 1925 annual. What was to be the distinctive subject matter of his painting began to emerge: "the dignity and vigor" of the American Victorian scene, recorded in an increasingly unobtrusive brushwork. The Rehn Galleries in New York showed several of his water colors and four oils in 1927, and two years later, twelve of his oils. Commenting on the mental "growth and amplitude" evident in this group, the *Arts* reviewer said of Hopper: "The quality and scope of the works there shown place him in the very forefront of American painters." In *Creative Art*, some little time afterward, Guy Pène du Bois defined Hopper's work: "There is a definite static quality in his better things, a stillness which has its counterpart in the calm preceding a storm." When in 1932, Hopper's *Hills, South Truro* was purchased by the Cleveland Museum after the Eleventh Annual Exhibition of Contemporary American oils, the same observer felt that it was "one of the purest pieces of landscape painting that has been done here in years."

Major recognition came to Hopper (who until that time had sold two canvases) in 1933, when New York's Museum of Modern Art accorded him a one-man retrospective exhibition.

Berenice Abbott. Courtesy Art News
EDWARD HOPPER

Among the oils shown were *Houses by the Railroad, Sunday, Manhattan Bridge Loop*, and *Room in Brooklyn*; among the water colors, *Le Concierge, Roofs of Washington Square*, and *Cold Storage Plant*; and among the etchings, *Cat Boat, Lonely House*, and *Girl on Bridge*. In Hopper's style, Horace Gregory pointed out in the *New Republic*, it could be seen that "his relationship with his immediate contemporaries" was "of the most superficial order." The American quality of his work was referred to by Helen Appleton Read in *Parnassus* and by Mary Morsell in *Art News*. The former declared: "He brought a point of view that is so essentially American, a combination of Puritan austerity and nothing excess with Yankee impatience of 'side' and 'bunk,' that his work has become synonymous with racial quality in contemporary American painting." The latter critic also mentioned the element of Puritanism, but in another context: "His major weakness seems to arise from a certain Puritan disdain of the more sensual aspects of painting—beauty and texture and charm of color." As had other critics, she noted the frequent use made by this "true and powerful interpreter of the American scene" of long horizontals at the base of many of his paintings.

Hopper, who had shown at the Carnegie International in 1928, was invited to give a one-man show at the Carnegie Institute in 1937. To it he sent thirty-two oils, fifty-four water colors, and eleven etchings. Ernest Brace, in the *Magazine of Art*, wrote: "Each of Hopper's canvases is an integration of long, ordered experience by which salient characteristics and kaleidoscopic sensations are digested into permanent and architectural form." Early paintings of Hopper's were shown at the Rehn Galleries in 1941. He next exhibited, the following year, at the Fifty-third Annual Exhibi-

HOPPER, EDWARD—*Continued*

tion of American Paintings and Sculpture at the Art Institute of Chicago, where he was awarded the Ada S. Garrett $750 prize for the canvas *Night Hawks*. With other American realists, including Charles Sheeler '50, Hopper was represented in the 1943 American Realists and Magic Realists show at the Museum of Modern Art, which later that year purchased his *Gas*. In December of 1943 the Rehn Galleries showed water colors done by the painter in Mexico, the Far West, and on Cape Cod. "He stands," judged *Art News*, "among the half-dozen supreme water colorists in American art." The succeeding October Hopper's *Six-Day Bicycle Rider* was displayed at the Sport in American Art Exhibition at the Boston Museum. In company with other artists and composers "whose artistic works are considered to have outlasted temporary appeal," Hopper in December 1944 was elected to life membership in the National Institute of Arts and Letters. His induction took place the following May, when several of his paintings were hung in a group show at the institute.

Hopper's *Office at Night* received a $1,000 prize at the May 1945 anniversary exhibition held at New York's Salmagundi Club. This painting was characterized by Edward Alden Jewell of the New York *Times* as "a triumph of abstract architectonic design over what may appear, on the surface, to be mere photographic realism." What the New York *Sun* considered a "static study" by Hopper, *August in the City*, was exhibited by the Rehn Galleries in May 1946. Two years elapsed before Hopper again was shown, this time in an exhibition devoted entirely to his work, at the Rehn Galleries. Emily Genauer of the New York *World-Telegram* felt he painted with "a hard, matter-of-factness which made no concessions to decorative charm." Judith Kaye Reed at *Art Digest* discerned, however, that his realism was "tempered by a poet's sense of mood." The *New Yorker*'s Robert M. Coates declared: "I feel that the source of his extraordinary evocativeness lies in the balance he has achieved between the rigidity and monumentality of abstraction and the immediacy and particularity of realism." *Time*, in a January 1948 biographical piece on Hopper, said: "His work has the strange clarity of something seen for an instant by a passing driver. It is familiar vision without any of the dullness familiarity brings."

The year 1950 saw another retrospective exhibition devoted to Hopper, at New York's Whitney Museum. The increasing maturity of his work, said the New York *Herald Tribune*'s Carlyle Burrows, showed him to be "worthy of a lasting appreciation." Howard Devree of the New York *Times* remarked, "He is fascinated by obsolete architecture, but he records rather than comments." *Time* conjectured that the "qualities that seem to move him most are loneliness and a bittersweet mixture of beauty with man-made ugliness." Robert M. Coates's summation was: "In the main his view of life is searching, compassionate, and profound. At his best he can invest the simplest subjects with a magic and mystery it would be hard to duplicate." (A number of the paintings in the Whitney retrospective were reproduced in the April 17, 1950, issue of *Life*.)

Among the prizes awarded to Hopper are the Baltimore Museum of Art award (1931), the Temple gold medal of the Pennsylvania Academy of Fine Arts (1935), the Worcester Museum purchase prize, (1935), the first W. A. Clark award and gold medal of the Corcoran Gallery (1937), and the Mr. and Mrs. Frank G. Logan prize and medal of the Chicago Art Institute (1945). In 1950 he was awarded the honorary degree of Doctor of Fine Arts by the Art Institute of Chicago. His work is in the major museums of the United States and England, among them being the British Museum, the Victoria and Albert Museum, the Phillips Memorial Gallery, the museums of Brooklyn, Cleveland, Indianapolis, Toledo, Boston, Hartford (Connecticut), and Worcester (Massachusetts). Private collectors who have acquired his paintings include the late Mrs. John D. Rockefeller, Jr., Helen Hayes, and Edward G. Robinson. Articles by Hopper have appeared in the art magazines.

Hopper usually produces three paintings a year, working either at his New York apartment or at his summer home in Truro, Massachusetts. Etchings are occasionally lent to exhibitions from the collection of his wife, the former Josephine Verstille Nivison, who is a painter. (They were married July 9, 1924.) Hopper sometimes lists himself as a Republican. The artist, who is six feet four inches tall, has been described in *Life* as having a "frank and quietly brooding face."

References

Art N 49:14 Mr '50 por
Carnegie Mag 24:351 My '50
Christian Sci Mon Mag p12 F 25 '50
Life 28:100 Ap 17 '50
New Yorker 23:56 Ja 17 '48
Time 51:59 Ja 19 '48

American Artists Group. Edward Hopper (1945)
Du Bois, G. P. Edward Hopper (1931)
Who's Who in America, 1950-51
Who's Who in American Art (1940-47)
Who's Who in the East (1948)
World Biography (1948)

HOSKINS, LEWIS M(ALONEY) Feb. 23, 1916- Social service organization official
Address: b. c/o American Friends Service Committee, 20 South 12th St., Philadelphia 7, Pa.; h. Gwynedd, Pa.

The American Friends Service Committee, which (in the words of *Time*) "has come to symbolize Quakerism to many non-Quakers," is an organization carrying on the work of the Religious Society of Friends in the social service field, both in the United States and abroad; in recognition of its efforts, the service committee in 1947 was awarded the Nobel Peace Prize. The new executive secretary of the committee, appointed in 1950, is Lewis M. Hoskins, who was previously its personnel secretary. Before that he had worked with the

Friends Service Unit in China and had been a college professor and dean.

Lewis Maloney Hoskins' middle name was his mother's maiden name—she was Louise Maloney until she was married to Hervey M. Hoskins, a banker and later a county judge in Newberg, Oregon. Their only son was born on February 23, 1916, in McMinnville, in that State. Lewis and his sister were reared in Newberg, a community founded by Friends, where he attended Union High School. After his graduation in 1934, young Hoskins, a member of the Oregon Yearly Meeting of the Religious Society of Friends, enrolled at Pacific College (renamed George Fox College for the founder of the Quakers in England), also in Newberg. A debater and an athlete in high school, Hoskins continued those activities in college. He also took part in dramatics and journalism. In his studies he concentrated on German, English, and mathematics as major subjects, and in 1938 received his Bachelor of Arts degree from Pacific.

Having chosen history as his field of graduate study, Hoskins attended Haverford (Pennsylvania) College (the first college established by the Society of Friends in the United States) for his Master of Arts degree, which he received in 1939. He then embarked on a teaching career, which was interspersed with various jobs on small-town newspapers, on farms, and as a salesman. His first teaching position was that of an instructor in history at Friends University in Wichita, Kansas, where he taught for the school year 1939-40. In September 1941 he entered the University of Michigan as teaching fellow and spent three years there. From that institution he received his Ph.D. in history in 1946, after writing the thesis, "Class and Clash in Seventeenth Century Mexico." In 1943 he had gone to his alma mater, Pacific College, to serve as a history professor and dean of the faculty.

An interest in sociology prompted Hoskins to volunteer for service in work camps operated by the American Friends Service Committee. This organization is an incorporated body under the laws of the State of Pennsylvania, formed in 1917 by members of the Society of Friends in America who wanted to make a "constructive and nonmilitary contribution to the world." The declaration of purpose enunciated at the group's first meeting reads: "We are united in expressing our love for our country and our desire to serve her loyally. We offer ourselves to the Government of the United States in any constructive work in which we can conscientiously serve humanity." The organization's symbol is a red and black star.

Based on the fundamental tenets of the Quaker religion, which stresses the value and dignity of the individual life and is opposed to all forms of violence and coercion, the work of the American Friends Service Committee has been directed to relieving distress involving problems of human conflict. Thus it works in the fields of war relief and rehabilitation, employment of conscientious objectors, peace education, interracial fellowship, aid to the victims of industrial dislocation. Seeking practical so-

Milton R. Holmes

LEWIS M. HOSKINS

lutions to such problems, the organization headed by Hoskins has established Quaker international centers in many cities of the world, instituted "peace caravans" to disseminate information and institutes of international relations where members of various nations meet and discuss problems, as well as relief centers and work camps. Aiming at spiritual ministry and emphasizing the benefits of practical work and cooperation in constructive projects, the committee has promoted self-help programs by distributing seeds, farm equipment and animals, and other such necessities of human rehabilitation, as well as relief goods.

For purposes of administration, the American Friends Service Committee, which represents most of the twenty-nine American Yearly Meetings of the Religious Society of Friends, is organized in two sections, the Foreign Service Section and the American Section; these function through the Service Committee's executive board and administrative staff. Hoskins' staff in 1950 numbered 492; its budget for that year was set at $3,000,000, with $950,000 devoted to projects in the United States, the rest to programs in Europe and the Orient, where the committee is making an attempt to maintain "bases of neutrality in areas of conflict." The committee supports the efforts of the United Nations, and accepted from that body the responsibility for the administration of the relief program in Southwest Palestine. In 1947 the committee received the Nobel Peace Prize.

After his service with the work camps Hoskins in 1945 became a volunteer in the American Friends Service Committee as a member of its staff in China. There his first assignment was that of business manager of a hospital in Honan Province. Then he went to Shanghai as agent for the Friends Ambulance Unit and the American Friends Service Committee.

HOSKINS, LEWIS M.—*Continued*

While in Shanghai he taught at National Fuh Tan University and St. John's University. In February 1947 he became executive secretary of the China unit and in March 1948 he was named its chairman. The Friends Service Unit in China was formed in 1947 as successor to the Friends Ambulance Unit. It is an international organization, functioning autonomously but responsible to the American Friends Service Committee, the Friends Service Council in London, the Canadian Friends Service Committee and the New Zealand Friends Service Committee. Not controlled by political currents, the unit maintained relief services in both Nationalist and Communist territories. It was part of Hoskins' responsibility as chairman of the unit to negotiate with Communist authorities in respect to the work of the group in China. For this purpose he spent five months in Communist territory, and was successful in obtaining two documents of identification and approval for the unit's medical-relief program in disputed areas.

In March 1949 Hoskins returned to the United States to become acting executive secretary for the Oregon regional office of the American Friends Service Committee, located in Portland. In July he went to the main offices in Philadelphia to serve as personnel secretary. Upon the retirement of Clarence Pickett [45] who became honorary secretary, Hoskins was appointed executive secretary of the committee, and assumed that office February 1, 1950.

Mrs. Hoskins, the former Lois Roberts, was a public school teacher before her marriage to Hoskins on September 2, 1941; she shared his work in China. They have three daughters, Theresa Ann, Laurel Page, and Adrienne Ruth. Hoskins' hobbies tend to keep him outdoors: he is an amateur photographer, studies birds, plays tennis, and likes to work in wood. An associate of his has described him as "a small [he is five feet nine inches in height], trim person, slight of build [he weighs 145 pounds]." Hoskins has brown hair and brown eyes and wears rimless glasses.

HOUGHTON, MRS. HIRAM COLE (hō't'n) Mar. 11, 1890- Women's organization executive

Address: b. c/o General Federation of Women's Clubs, 1734 N St., N.W., Washington 6, D.C.; h. Red Oak, Iowa

On June 3, 1950, Mrs. Hiram Cole Houghton succeeded Mrs. J. L. Blair Buck [47] as president of the General Federation of Women's Clubs, which has an international membership of some 10,000,000 women. The new president's major plans for her three-year tenure of office include a program to attract membership from among women in industry, to study business and investments, old-age problems of women, the opening of a radio program, and, as a world-peace means, exchange visits by women of the United States and other countries. Mrs. Houghton, whose first club leadership was as president of the Women's Club in her home town in Iowa, has been active in the educational affairs of her State.

Mrs. Houghton was born Dorothy Deemer on March 11, 1890, in Red Oak (an Iowa town with a population of 6,000), where she was reared and still makes her home. Her father was Judge Horace Emerson Deemer, a justice of the Iowa Supreme Court from 1889 until his death, in 1917. From her mother, Jeannette (Gibson) Deemer, she inherited her liking for club activities. After graduation from Red Oak High School in 1908, Dorothy Deemer entered Wellesley College to major in English and history. She participated in student affairs and became a member of the Shakespeare Society. In 1912 she received the B.A. degree.

On December 18, 1912, Dorothy Deemer was married to Hiram Cole Houghton, Jr. (in 1950 he is president of the Houghton State Bank in Red Oak and executive of other banking houses in Iowa). Mrs. Houghton was the first woman to serve on the Iowa State Board of Conservation, receiving appointment to it in 1916. Following her presidency of the Red Oak Woman's Club, she became the recording secretary of the Iowa Federation of Women's Clubs, then second vice-president, and in 1927 first vice-president. After holding the presidency of the State body from 1935 to 1937, Mrs. Houghton in 1938 assumed executive duties in the national body, the General Federation of Women's Clubs. In it she served from 1938 to 1940 as a director, from 1940 to 1944 as education chairman, from 1944 to 1947 as second vice-president, and from 1947 to 1950 as first vice-president. She also served as chairman of its "Build a Better Community" contest. An unopposed candidate for the presidency, she was installed in that office on June 3, 1950, for a three-year term, during the fifty-ninth annual convention held in Boston. The convention was attended by 2,500 delegates and guests, representing 17,000 clubs with a total membership of some 5,000,000 in the United States and approximately the same number in the affiliated clubs of thirty-five other countries.

Indicative of the federation's interests are some of its achievements during the years 1947-50 (as outlined by the retiring president, Mrs. J. L. Blair Buck). Through the Council of International Clubs, 23,422 American clubwomen corresponded with women overseas, and sent abroad clothing, food, and medical supplies valued at approximately $629,000. Through its youth conservation program, the federation gave $625,369 in scholarship aid, $64,376 of which was allotted to foreign students from thirty-two countries. The federation has announced its support of the Marshall Plan, the North Atlantic Pact, the Reciprocal Trade Agreements Act, the International Trade Organization, United States membership in the World Health Organization, the liberalizing of the Displaced Persons Act, and adequate appropriation for the United States educational and cultural exchange program.

Mrs. Houghton, in addressing the convention, gave a four-point program for maintaining "the American way of life" and for the realization of "everlasting peace," which was summed up by Doris Greenberg in the New York *Times* (May 31, 1950) as follows: "Maintenance of powerful defense forces; limitation of Government spending to make the United States 'financially solvent'; extension of efforts to 'sell' Americanism; and rededication of the nation 'to the Christian way of life.'" Under Mrs. Houghton's leadership the convention "overwhelmingly endorsed" President Truman's Point Four program calling for technical aid to undeveloped areas of the world.

In her first press conference (June 19, 1950), Mrs. Houghton announced her plans for new lines of activity the federation will institute in the course of her presidency. To enlist members from industrial fields, the industrial division was set up within the federation's public affairs department to study the needs of factory workers and to determine what assistance can be given them by the federation. The division of gerontology (also referred to as the "living the later years" program) of the welfare department will seek "more useful ways to spend old age," and possibly aid in the establishment of an institution for such a study at the University of Michigan. The exchanging of women between the United States clubs and clubs abroad will be done through "organized hospitality." Mrs. Houghton has expressed the belief that such visits will make for better understanding and so be a means of promoting world peace. Because, she pointed out, women control 85 per cent of the wealth in the United States, a study of banks, insurance companies, and investment companies is another new project. To prepare members for platform appearances, Mrs. Houghton announced the appointment of a public speaking consultant to the federation.

In August 1950 she asked the federation's membership to support the no-hoarding movement, launched to combat "panic buying" which had begun shortly after the war in Korea. That month Mrs. Houghton was appointed by Herbert Hoover to the citizens' advisory committee of the Health Information Foundation; the committee will suggest ways to serve the health needs of the public. With a group of thirty-eight representatives of the G.F.W.C., Mrs. Houghton left in September for a seven-week good-will tour of northern and western Europe. When the federation took steps (in October 1950) to form a national clearing house to get women into top-level national defense positions—to aide in military, economic, and spiritual defense—Mrs. Houghton was chosen chairman of the clearing house plan.

In the capacity of vice-president of the federation, Mrs. Houghton addressed club groups in almost every State of the union and in Cuba, and in the summer of 1949 attended the Pan Pacific Women's Association conference at Honolulu. During her three-year term as president she will live in Washington where she and her husband have taken an apartment. The Houghtons have four children, Deemer, Cole Hayward, Joan, and Hiram Clark; the three sons are veterans of World War II. There are six grandchildren.

Mrs. Houghton's other activities include acting as curator and director of the Iowa Historical Society (she is a life member) from 1928 to 1940 and serving on the Iowa State Board of Education for two six-year terms

MRS. HIRAM COLE HOUGHTON

(in 1950 she is in her second term). She is a board member of the National Society for Crippled Children and Adults. In 1939 she was on the advisory committee of Iowa's 100 Women on the New York World's Fair. During the early 1940's, while acting as president of the Iowa Library Association, Mrs. Houghton was a contributor of articles on the problems of libraries to periodicals in that field. She is a member also of the Daughters of the American Revolution, the American Association of University Women, Pen Women of America, National Safety Council, Delta Kappa Gamma, Zeta Phi Eta, Pi Beta Phi. Two honorary degrees have been conferred on her: Doctor of Laws from Coe College (Iowa) in 1942 and Doctor of Humanities from Tarkio (Missouri) College in 1949. She was made particularly happy, she says, when she was named as the "Iowa Mother of 1948." A Washington *Post* article described Mrs. Houghton as a person of much charm, "generous with her spontaneous, throaty laugh"; she is short and "plump," has red hair. A Republican, she won the 1946 "distinguished public service" award given by the Iowa Council of Republican Women. Her church is the Congregational.

References

Washington (D.C.) Post p5B Je 20 '50
American Women, 1939-40

HOUSTON, CHARLES H(AMILTON) (hūs′tŭn) Sept. 3, 1895—Apr. 22, 1950 Negro lawyer and champion of minority rights; at Howard University as instructor in law (1924-29), associate professor and vice-dean of the School of Law (1929-35); special counsel to the National Association for the Advancement of Colored People in 1935, member of the association's national legal committee since 1940; general counsel for the Association of

HOUSTON, CHARLES H.—*Continued*

Colored Railway Trainmen and Locomotive Firemen, and the International Association of Railway Employees; vice-president of the American Council on Race Relations in 1944; a member of the President's Committee on Fair Employment Practice. See *Current Biography*, 1948.

Obituary

N Y Times p29 Ap 26 '50

HOWELL, WALLACE E(GBERT) Sept. 14, 1914- Meteorologist

Address: b. 2 Divinity Ave., Cambridge 38, Mass.; h. 35 Moon Hill Rd., Lexington 73, Mass.

The City of New York in March 1950 engaged Wallace E. Howell as consulting meteorologist to head its Rain-Stimulation Project, an undertaking designed to replenish the city's dangerously depleted reservoirs. This, prob-

Wide World Photos

WALLACE E. HOWELL

ably the biggest "order" of its kind thus far, is being watched with much interest by scientists, local officials, and the general public in other parts of the country. A specialist in the physics of clouds and the growth of cloud droplets, "Rainmaker" Howell is director of the Mount Washington (New Hampshire) Observatory, research meteorologist at Harvard's Blue Hill Observatory in Massachusetts, and a member of the subcommittee on icing problems of the National Advisory Committee for Aeronautics.

Born in Central Valley, New York, on September 14, 1914, Wallace Egbert Howell is the son of James Cox and Alice Edith (Egbert) Howell. When he was six months old, the family went to live in Salisbury, Connecticut.

His father (in real estate) and his mother (a former teacher and once a member of the Connecticut State Board of Education) now live near New Haven. (Howell has two sisters, the elder of whom is affiliated with the U.N. World Health Organization in Geneva, Switzerland, and one brother, who is a social economist.) After graduating from Tabor Academy in Marion, Massachusetts, in 1932, Howell entered Harvard College to major in physics. "I didn't find the theoretical side too inviting at the time," he is quoted as saying (New York *Herald Tribune*), "so I went into the applied fields—meteorology, radio communication, and the like." He thought meteorology, in particular, "would lead to interesting scientific work in the outdoors." While an undergraduate, he was coxswain of a second-string freshman crew, and a member of the Mountaineering Club, the Glee Club, and the varsity swimming team. He received his Bachelor of Arts degree from Harvard in 1937.

That same year Howell began his career in Kansas City by organizing the weather department of the Mid-Continent Airlines as its first and chief meteorologist. He returned to Boston in 1939 to join the Yankee Network Weather Service as associate meteorologist, where he prepared a fifteen-minute daily weather forecasting program. He was made assistant regional forecaster for the United States Weather Bureau in East Boston the next year; and in 1941 obtained his Master of Science degree from Massachusetts Institute of Technology, with a thesis on the history of the international cloud classification system. In the course of five years' military service (1941-46), he served with the Army Air Force Weather Service in various technical capacities, rising from private to lieutenant colonel. He was overseas in 1945 as an operational long-range forecaster for the Fifteenth Air Force in Italy. After his discharge in 1946, he became acting director of the Harvard-Mount Washington Icing Research Project and Abbott Lawrence Rotch research fellow at the Blue Hill Observatory (of Harvard) in Milton, Massachusetts. He took his Doctor of Science degree at M.I.T. in 1948 with a dissertation on the growth of cloud drops in uniformly lifted air. Appointed acting director of the Mount Washington Observatory that same year, he has also held the post of research meteorologist at the Blue Hill weather station since 1949.

While working at the Mount Washington Observatory, Howell became acquainted with Dr. Vincent J. Schaefer '48, who had long been associated with Dr. Irving Langmuir '50 at the General Electric Research Laboratories, where they investigated weather control for the Army-Navy-Air Forces' "Project Cirrus." Schaefer and Langmuir had discovered that the formation of rain in a cloud requires the presence of "sublimation nuclei," or tiny particles around which the moisture vapor can form ice crystals; these ice crystals, in turn, may grow in size until they are large enough to fall to the earth as rain. Schaefer and Langmuir found that when other conditions are favorable they could "trigger" clouds into rain by supplying artificial nuclei, either by dry-ice pellets, which chill parts of the cloud to the point where ice-crystal seeds are formed spontaneously, or by vaporized silver iodide, which forms an invisible stream of sub-microscopic particles that act as nuclei. Together with Schaefer, Howell carried on some informal seeding tests from the summit of Mount Washington. By sowing the clouds with dry ice, they were able to create several snow flurries in the vicinity.

During the winter of 1949-50, the City of New York was faced with a grave water shortage, due to abnormally low precipitation over the watershed area since the drought of the previous summer. When substantial water savings had not been effected by such measures as weekly twenty-four-hour "water holidays" as well as a strict curtailment in the use of city water for such purposes as street sprinkling and car washing, city officials investigated the possibilities of inducing rainfall to relieve the critical situation. They consulted Dr. Langmuir, who felt that the results of previous tests were conclusive enough to warrant the experiment, and recommended that Howell be put in charge of the city's rain-making project.

Accordingly, on February 20, 1950, Mayor William O'Dwyer [47] asked Howell to make a preliminary estimate of the manpower, equipment, and money needed to carry out the experiments. Howell's report received unanimous approval from the Mayor's six-man Advisory Committee of Scientists, and on March 14, the city's Board of Estimate appropriated $50,000 for a Rain-Stimulation Project to last for six months (which was renewed upon its expiration). This sum covered expenses for two Police Department planes equipped with chutes for dropping dry-ice pellets, two light trucks fitted with silver iodide ejectors, and mobile radar equipment used in spotting rain-laden clouds. At the same time Howell was officially engaged as the city's consultant meteorologist at a fee of $100 a day. He made it clear that no single rain-making attempt could be considered in terms of success or failure, since there was no positive method of distinguishing between artificial and natural rain on any given occasion. Statistics on rainfall in the target area would have to be compared with data on precipitation in immediately surrounding areas over a minimum six-month period, he warned, before any definite conclusions could be drawn from the tests. He stated, however, that the chances of increasing rainfall over the city's watershed were "good enough to justify a concerted and sustained attempt." New York City's goal was to fill its reservoirs, then at 51 per cent of capacity, by June 1, in order to meet summer demands.

Howell concentrated his rain-making activities in the Catskill system (about a hundred miles from the metropolis), where the mountains offered more favorable cloud-seeding situations than in the flatter and more heavily populated Croton area (less than fifty miles distant). The first two flights were unproductive because of bad weather and heavy static;

further flights were postponed on several occasions by melting snows in the watershed area, which caused one reservoir to overflow and created the danger of floods. The first actual seeding experiment took place on April 13, when 100 pounds of dry ice were sprinkled into the clouds near the Ashokan Reservoir. The next day ground battalions sprayed the clouds with silver iodide smoke, and New York City was blanketed with a one-inch fall of snow, bringing the temperature down to 25 degrees, a record low for that date. Howell said: "It is impossible to tell whether we caused any of the snow flurries." Later that month, ground crews twice released silver iodide from a spot in Eastern Pennsylvania, and heavy rainfalls followed in the watershed area after both attempts. Howell again disclaimed direct credit and termed the results inconclusive.

Criticism of Howell's rain-making project came from certain New York, Connecticut, and New Jersey officials. Albany's Mayor expressed fear that the experiments might adversely affect Albany's watershed. A bill was introduced into the (New York) State Legislature to give the State complete control over all artificial rain-making by its individual cities. Owners of a hotel in Ulster County sought a permanent injunction against the New York rain-makers, but it was rejected by the State Supreme Court, which held that clubhouse owners "clearly have no vested property rights in the clouds or the moisture therein." To numerous complaints about the cold, misty, and foggy weather that prevailed during the latter part of April and the first half of May, Howell replied that the bad weather was of normal origin, and the effects, if any, of cloud-seeding were restricted to the Catskill area and did not affect New York City. Whatever the cause of the increased precipitation, the city's water supply continued to rise until June 1 found its reservoirs filled to 91 per cent of capacity. Rainfall in the watershed area was estimated on June 20 to have been 4 per cent above average. As of June 13, the record of Howell's Rain-Stimulation Project totaled four cloud-seeding flights by plane and twelve cloud-spraying tours from the ground, three of these being combined operations.

The author of various Army training publications, Howell has also contributed some technical articles to several scientific periodicals. He is a member of the American Meteorological Society and the American Geophysical Union. He also belongs to the Appalachian Mountain Club—as a young man he spent several summers climbing in the Alps; amateur photography is one of his recreations. He helped to finish the modern house (of which Walter Gropius was one of the designers) in Lexington, Massachusetts, where he lives with his wife, who was Christine Gallagher (they married on December 30, 1942), and their three children, Stephen Barnard, Jeremy, and Holly Catherine. Described as a "slight, wiry man," Howell is five feet nine inches tall and weighs 140 pounds; his eyes and his hair are brown.

HOWELL, WALLACE E.—*Continued*

References

N Y Herald Tribune II p1 Mr 26 '50
    por
New Yorker 26:26-7 Ap 8 '50
American Men of Science (1949)
Who's Who in New England (1949)

HOXHA, ENVER (hôd-jä ĕn-vĕr') 1908-
Prime Minister of Albania
Address: Tirana, Albania

The Premier of the republic of Albania, Enver Hoxha, had been a leader of the resistance against the Italians and Germans, who had successively held the country during World War II. The leader of the Albanian Communist party and head of the National Liberation Front, which established the Provincial Government in 1944, he was elected Prime Minister of the new republic, a state proclaimed in January 1946, after the general election held a month earlier. Hoxha soon indicated that his Government looked to Soviet Russia rather than to the Western Powers for political, economic, and military support. When the U.S.S.R. quarreled with Tito of Yugoslavia in June 1948, Hoxha was among the first of the leaders in Soviet-satellite countries to break off trade relations with that country. He is carrying out a two-year plan for the economic and industrial development of Albania, designed to transform his agricultural country into a modern industrialized state.

Enver Hoxha was born in 1908 in Gjinokaster, Albania, the son of a Moslem cloth merchant. In his early childhood the boy is said to have known misery and hunger. Educated on a scholarship at the French *lycée* at Koritza, young Hoxha is also reported to have attended the American Technical School in Tirana. In 1930, at the age of twenty-two, he left Albania for France to study natural science at Montpellier University. When the Albanian Government canceled his scholarship a year later, reported *Contemporary Review* (August 1949), Hoxha proceeded to Paris, where he met Paul Vaillant-Couturier, editor in chief of the Communist newspaper *L'Humanité*; the result was that Hoxha wrote a series of articles on Albania for the paper. In 1934 he was appointed secretary to the Albanian consulate general in Brussels. Concurrently, Hoxha took a law course at Brussels University and continued to contribute articles to *L'Humanité*. Inasmuch as these articles were critical of his Government's administration, the discovery by home authorities of Hoxha's writing activities resulted in the termination of his consulate appointment in 1936. Recalled to Albania, Hoxha took a position as professor of French at the Koritza *lycée*. Because of his continued political agitation, he was arrested in January 1939 on a charge of conspiracy, for which he served a brief term in prison.

On April 7, 1939, Mussolini's troops invaded Albania. King Zog I ['44], who had ruled since 1925, fled the country, and a puppet government was established, a regime which was to last

five years. At the time of the invasion Hoxha was again teaching at the *lycée* and working secretly against King Zog's rule. When the new Italian educational authorities dismissed Hoxha for his anti-Fascist views, he made his way to Tirana and began organizing underground resistance to the Fascists. As a shield for his activities he opened a tobacco shop, with the anti-Fascist headquarters in its back room. Founder of the Albanian Communist party in 1941, Hoxha became its political secretary and chief editor of its paper, *Zeri I Popullit* ("The Voice of the People"). When his activities became known to the Italians, he was sentenced to death *in absentia*, and a price placed on his head.

According to *Contemporary Review's* writer, three main resistance groups were formed during the occupation period: the Nationalist Balli Kombetar, the Royalist Legality Movement, and the Communistic National Liberation Front, or F.N.C. (Fronti Nacional Clirimtare), of which Hoxha was one of the principal organizers. In September 1942 a convention of patriots met at Peza to coordinate the activities of all resistance groups. The following July (1943), Hoxha was appointed military and political head of the F.N.C. and established secret military headquarters for his general staff in the mountains near Elbasan. Aided by Soviet army officers who had parachuted into Albania, as well as by British and United States liaison officers, he directed intensive warfare against the Italians, and, after the Germans took over Albania in September 1943, against the Nazis. Other Albanian resistance groups gave their support to Hoxha's F.N.C., and as military unification was achieved a civil and political organization took form which provided the framework for Albania's postwar administration. In October 1944, when the Provisional Government was established, Hoxha was elected its Premier and Commander in Chief with the rank of full general. (His army had grown to number 70,000 trained fighters.) A month later the Government was moved to Tirana, and on December 4 Hoxha announced that the Germans had been completely driven out of Albania.

Nearly a year later, on November 10, 1945, Hoxha's Provisional Government was recognized by Britain, the United States, Russia, and France, with the understanding that free elections would be held. In the general election of December 2, 1945, the F.N.C. secured an overwhelming majority. According to Allen Raymond in the New York *Herald Tribune* (December 3, 1945), "it was a rather primitive but absolutely fair and secret ballot," the most enthusiastic voters being women, who voted for the first time. Opposition leaders, however, declared that they had canceled plans to distribute leaflets criticizing the elections because of a threat that such action would result in "slaughter." Recognition by the Big Four powers followed on January 5, 1946. Six days later Albania was proclaimed a People's Democracy by the Constituent Assembly, and Hoxha was elected President and Prime Minister. He also continued as Commander in Chief of the

Albanian armed forces, with the rank of colonel general.

Albania, which has an area of 10,629 square miles and a population of about 1,300,000, suffered whole or partial destruction of 1,600 of its villages; and 28,000 of its people killed. In its reconstruction program Hoxha's Government nationalized the mines, industries and factories, partitioned the great estates of absentee landlords, giving the land to the peasants, began an anti-illiteracy drive, and started building roads, bridges and public utilities. Bounded on the north and east by Yugoslavia, Albania on November 27, 1946, entered a twenty-year economic treaty with its neighbor. Relations with its southern neighbor, Greece, however, became increasingly unfriendly during 1946, due to border disputes and to Greek's claim to Northern Epirus. In August 1946 Hoxha flew to Paris to present his country's case before the Peace Conference. In a fiery address he asked for reparations for his country from Italy and refuted the Greek claim to Northern Epirus. He again asked admission of Albania to membership in the United Nations (his first request in 1945 had been rejected), but on August 29, 1946, the U.N. Security Council voted down his request, the United States and Great Britain having been against it, and Greece having formally objected to it. On September 16, 1946, Hoxha left Paris, after denouncing the Conference and affirming Albania's determination to keep its frontiers with Greece unaltered. He made another unsuccessful plea for admission to the U.N. in October 1946. (As of January 1950 Albania was not in the U.N.)

During 1946 relations between Albania and Great Britain were broken off. In April of 1946, Britain recalled its military mission, revoked a decision to send an envoy to Albania, and refused to accept an Albanian envoy. The break became complete on October 22, 1946, when two British destroyers struck mines in the Corfu Channel. Britain brought the matter before the U.N. Security Council which recommended over Hoxha's protests, to submit the case to The Hague International Court. On April 9, 1949, the Court decided that Albania was responsible for the mines. Meanwhile, the United States in November 1946 decided not to recognize the Albanian Government and to recall the diplomatic mission at Tirana. Turning to the U.S.S.R. for assistance, Hoxha in July 1947 received "a small credit" (New York *Times*) for his country for the purchase of industrial and agricultural machinery. Tito was also reported to be sending wheat and other supplies from Yugoslavia.

When, in June 1948, the Cominform attacked the nationalism of Yugoslavia's leaders, Hoxha's Albanian Communist party was among the first to endorse the denunciation. At the end of June, Hoxha's Government canceled its standing agreements with Yugoslavia, including the twenty-year economic treaty ratified in 1946. In speaking of his country's economic position on July 24, 1948, Hoxha said: "We are not as isolated as our enemies make out," and later announced that both industrial and consumer goods would soon be arriving from Soviet

Wide World Photos

ENVER HOXHA

Russia, Czechoslovakia, and Bulgaria. In the fall of 1948, the Hoxha regime moved against Albanian Communist leaders friendly to Tito, among them the Albanian Communist Koci Xoxe, former Vice-Premier and Minister of the Interior, who was arrested, tried, and in 1949 was executed.

Throughout 1948, relations between Albania and Greece continued to be strained. In August the U.N. Special Commission on the Balkans decided that Albania had given aid and sanctuary to the Greek rebel forces. Notes of protest from Britain, the United States, and France suggested that observers from the U.N. Commission be permitted to operate in Albania. Hoxha's reply forbade this and accused the three Western powers of interfering in Albania's affairs. During 1948, reported the *Britannica Book of the Year* of 1949, there were acts of suppression directed largely against the Catholic Church: Catholic schools were closed and in April and May five church dignitaries were executed, the prosecution stating they had collaborated with anti-Government sympathizers.

Working toward completion of his two-year plan, Hoxha in 1949 has arranged with the U.S.S.R., Poland, Czechoslovakia, Rumania, and Bulgaria for shipments of industrial equipment and other supplies needed to help transform Albania into an industrialized state. Provision for national education has also been promoted by Hoxha, 109,000 persons having been taught to read and write by 1949. His Government has also fostered the trade union movement which had 25,000 members in 1945 and 51,000 in 1948.

In the biography of Hoxha in the *Contemporary Review* for August 1949, David Ingber reported that the Prime Minister is "flamboyant, self-assertive," but "no mere poseur"; he is "a resourceful organizer who can think

HOXHA, ENVER—*Continued*

in terms of planning and development. He owes his success to an acute grasp of realities as well as to excellent insight into the nature of his fellow-man." Admired by his followers for his "courageous leadership in battle and his fine oratory," Hoxha's manner has been described as "easy" and "sure" with "absolute dignity." While heading the Albanian Army of liberation, Hoxha met a young schoolteacher, a leader of the resistance among women and girls, who was to become his wife. The Albanian leader, who is more than six feet tall, is described as impressive in appearance.

References

Contemp R 176:86-93 Ag '49
N Y Herald Tribune p22 D 7 '45
N Y Post p16 D 7 '45
World Rep 1:34 D 3 '46

Gunther, J. Behind the Iron Curtain (1949)
International Who's Who, 1949
10 Eventful Years (1947)

HUGHES, R(OY) O(RLO) Sept. 24, 1887-
Labor union official

Address: b. c/o Order of Railway Conductors, Cedar Rapids, Iowa; h. 3291 N. 46th St., Milwaukee 16, Wis.

R. O. Hughes assumed the office of president of the independent Order of Railway Conductors on August 1, 1950. A railroad worker since 1907, he had held important offices in the O.R.C. since 1929; and while serving as vice-president during the years 1940-50, he had negotiated and won a number of wage increases for his union. The joint strike called by Hughes' union and the Brotherhood of Railroad Trainmen for August 28, 1950, resulted in President Truman's order to the United States Army to seize and operate the roads.

Burke & Dean

R. O. HUGHES

Born on September 24, 1887, in Portland, North Dakota, Roy Orlo Hughes is one of five children (four boys and a girl) of Elijah and Maria Madeline (Olson) Hughes. The father, a blacksmith, was of Irish stock, and the mother's family was Norwegian. Reared in Portland and in Mora, Minnesota, young Roy attended school until 1906. He had reached the last year in Mora High School when he left: money intended for his college education was used for the purchase of an unimproved farm in 1907. The high cost of improvements and the need for working capital made young Hughes start work, as a machinist's helper with the Great Northern Railway Company at Superior, Wisconsin.

During the following twenty-one years (1907-28) Hughes was both a farmer and a railroad worker. As a farmer he raised pure-bred Guernseys, made official dairy records in butterfat and in other farm products at national farm shows. As a railway employee, after a short period with the Great Northern, Hughes joined the Northern Pacific at Duluth as a brakeman, and by 1912 had become a conductor. In the same capacity he was employed by the Chicago, Milwaukee, St. Paul & Pacific at Duluth in 1925. When this railroad transferred him in 1928 to St. Paul, Minnesota, he gave up farming.

On April 23, 1916, Hughes became a member of the Order of Railway Conductors, entering the independent union's Division 336. After serving the division as legislative chairman and local chairman of adjustment (first for the Northern Pacific and later for the C. M. St. P. & P.) his union duties broadened. In 1929 he was elected secretary to the Milwaukee general committee of the latter railroad, an office he held until 1932, when he was made general chairman of the committee of adjustment. In 1940, after administering that post for eight years and three months, he was appointed Grand trustee (International) of the Order of Railway Conductors, and in the same year (1940) was elected vice-president. *The Railway Conductor* stated in its June 1950 issue that Brother Hughes had won the respect of his fellow union members by the way he had handled major problems of the union on a national level: "Among these were the joint wage-rules movements of the Five Brotherhoods in 1941, 1945, and 1947. He was negotiator of the 1948 wage movement and 1948 vacation agreement and displayed his full powers of bargaining and leadership in the joint ORC-BRT rules program taken under advisement by the presidential emergency board during the 1950 Grand Division meeting."

R. O. Hughes succeeded to the presidency of his union on August 1, 1950. (Fred H. Nemitz had acted as an interim head after the death of President H. W. Fraser on May 13, 1950.) Hughes was elected to the office during the forty-fourth grand division session of the union, May 9-12, 1950. In his acceptance speech he promised to devote himself to preserving "the high standard of leadership set by his predecessors." He pointed out that O.R.C. had "a splendid record as a cooperating organization and in gaining objectives that form a substantial bridgehead for obtaining new members." In 1950 the Order of Railway Conductors had a membership of 37,000; the Brotherhood of Railroad Trainmen, 210,000. (The B.R.T., of which William P. Kennedy [50] is president, is also an independent union.)

The Government's seizure of the railroads in August 1950 was the fifth in thirty-two years. Threatened strikes over wage disputes was the cause in 1943, 1946, and 1948. A general breakdown in railway transportation facilities prompted President Woodrow Wilson on January 1, 1918 (during World War I) to place the roads under Government management. This, the longest period of such operation, lasted until March 15, 1920. The 1950 seizure came after a wage dispute between workers and owners (which began in February 1949) reached a deadlock. The demands of the O.R.C. were a reduction (for roadmen) of working day from 150 to 100 miles (beyond which overtime would be paid) and wages on sliding scale based on engine weight. The B.R.T. asked (for yardmen) a 40-hour week in place of existing 48-hour schedule, and an hourly increase of thirty-one cents to compensate for work-week reduction. A fact-finding board under Roger McDonough on June 15, 1950, refused requests of the O.R.C. for raises and replacement of the existing scale. For the B.R.T. the Government board proposed a 40-hour week with an 18-cent raise. Railroad management accepted the fact-finding proposal of June 15 and on August 19 offered a compromise.

In the early part of August the two unions had begun a series of "token," or five-day local strikes as well as strikes involving railway terminals in Louisville, Cleveland, and St. Paul. Both Hughes and Kennedy urged President Truman to seize the nation's roads to prevent a nation-wide strike, which he refused to do at that time. On August 23 the two unions ordered a strike to begin five days later. To avert the stoppage of all rail transportation in the country President Truman directed the United States Army to seize and operate the roads. Hughes and Kennedy immediately instructed the members of their two unions to cooperate with the Government. The threatened walkout was postponed indefinitely or pending settlement of the dispute through mediation.

The Army took over the roads on August 27, 1950. Editorial comment in the *Christian Science Monitor* (August 17, 1950) was that apparently the concrete objective of the striking unions was "Government seizure of the roads as a means of bringing their bargaining position more nearly in balance. They complain bitterly that 'the railroads are taking advantage of the international situation.'" The New York *Herald Tribune* called the tactics of the two unions "reckless and irresponsible." J. A. Livingston, Washington *Post* columnist analyzed the reasons of the unions—"who for years have been the most stable, most mature group among organized American workers"— as prompted by causes "far below the economic

surface." Pointing out that the railroad industry has not kept pace with the automobile, oil and other industries, in its earnings, he said that the railroads can no longer "afford to match wage rises with faster growing industries."

Roy Orlo Hughes was married to Mary Ellen Penrod, a former accountant, on November 26, 1912. Mrs. Hughes is a past president of the Ladies Auxiliary of the Order of Railway Conductors, Howard Division 139 of Milwaukee, Wisconsin. There are three daughters in the family: Margery Elizabeth (Hughes) Rittmann, Helen Rosemary, and Barbara Lois. A Mason, in 1912 Hughes belonged to the Master Mason Ionic Lodge in Duluth; he is a Charter member of the Trinity Lodge, Number 282, Duluth, and at present is a member of the Wisconsin Consistory, Scottish Rite (Milwaukee) and the Masonic Tripoli Shrine, also of Milwaukee. His church affiliation is Presbyterian and he votes independently. The five-foot-nine-inch union leader weighs 180 pounds, has brown eyes, and gray hair. Once a semi-professional baseball player, he names it his favorite spectator sport.

References

Railway Conductor p170 Je '50
Who's Who in Labor (1946)

HUGHES, SARAH T(ILGHMAN) Aug. 2, 1896- Women's organization official; district judge

Address: b. c/o National Federation of Business and Professional Women's Clubs, Inc., 1819 Broadway, New York 23; c/o Texas 14th District Court, Dallas 2, Tex.; h. 3816 Normandy, Dallas, Tex.

Sarah T. Hughes, district judge of Dallas, Texas, succeeded Dr. K. Frances Scott [48] as president of the National Federation of Business and Professional Women's Clubs, Inc., at the July 1950 convention in San Francisco. Judge Hughes, who practiced law in Dallas from 1922 until her appointment to the bench in 1935, in 1937 was admitted to practice before the Supreme Court of the United States. While serving in the Texas legislature (1931-35), she framed and helped to pass one of the State's divorce laws. She is the author of many articles on judicial and juvenile delinquency subjects. For her distinguished work in county affairs she was honored in 1941 by the East Texas Chamber of Commerce and in 1946 was the recipient of the Zonta (Dallas) Service award.

Born on August 2, 1896, in Baltimore, Maryland, Sarah Tilghman Hughes is one of two children of James Cook and Elizabeth (Haughton) Tilghman. Originally English, the first members of the Tilghman family in America settled in 1660 in Maryland's eastern shore of the Chesapeake Bay. Among Sarah Tilghman Hughes's direct ancestors were a justice of the Provincial Court and James Tilghman, the first Attorney General of Maryland and judge of the Court of Appeals. (Richard H. Tilghman,

SARAH T. HUGHES

Judge Hughes's only brother, is an engineer in San Francisco.) Reared in Baltimore, Miss Tilghman attended its Western High School and was graduated in 1913. While there she was a member of the basketball team, a class officer, and the winner of a four-year scholarship to Baltimore's Goucher College.

At Goucher the student majored in biology, played on the basketball and hockey teams, had a post on the business staff of the campus weekly newspaper, monthly magazine, and annual, became president of her sophomore class, and joined Delta Gamma. She held also an official position in an athletic association, another in the YWCA, and during summer vacations worked as a playground instructor. After obtaining her B.A. degree (1917) from Goucher College, Miss Tilghman taught science until 1919 at Salem (Winston-Salem, North Carolina) College. Then, joining the Washington (District of Columbia) Metropolitan police as a policewoman in 1919, she worked chiefly with women and children. While holding this post she studied law at the George Washington University and in 1922 obtained her LL.B. and was admitted to the District of Columbia bar. Her marriage to George E. Hughes, fellow law student and a Texan, on March 13, 1922, took her to Dallas, where both she and her husband began the practice of law—she was admitted to the Texas bar in October 1922.

In 1931 Mrs. Hughes was elected to the Texas Legislature as a representative from Dallas County. Re-elected in 1933 and in 1935, during her three terms she was voted one of the most valuable members of the legislature. In a New York *Times* interview (August 24, 1943) Judge Hughes said the divorce law she had helped to pass "was working particularly well under war conditions." The law, which permits support while a decree is pending, prohibits alimony after a decree has been granted.

It provides, however, support of minor children from either or both parents: when a wife was employed in a war plant and earning more money than her husband did in an armed service, the law was considered most just. In commenting on the 25 per cent increase in divorce suits during a seven-month period in 1943, Judge Hughes stated it was the result of "furlough marriages." A 40 per cent increase in juvenile delinquency cases in Dallas County during a four-month period in 1943, she attributed to war conditions—"the breaking of homes by war or war work preventing parents from giving children proper supervision."

In 1935 Governor James V. Allred appointed Mrs. Hughes the judge of the 14th District Court, of Dallas County, Texas, to a two-year term. She was subsequently elected to this judgeship in four successive elections, running on an unopposed ticket in 1940 and in 1948. "Courts are very informal [in Texas]," she told Jessie Ash Arndt of the *Christian Science Monitor*, in an interview (July 15, 1948). She, the only woman on a Texas bench, wore neither the conventional judicial black robe nor a black dress and during summer months neither men lawyers nor men jurors wore coats. Emphasizing that Texas does not permit women to serve on juries, Judge Hughes said that she, as a member of the National Federation of Business and Professional Women's Clubs, was working with the association for the inclusion of women to Texas juries.

During World War II Judge Hughes was active in civilian defense and USO, and served on the board which selected the first WAC officer candidates. She was also a member of the Governor's Committee on Economy in Government and on the Governor's Committee on Mental Hygiene. A zealous worker in the Business and Professional Women's Clubs, she has been president of the Dallas branch and of the Texas federation, and from 1948 to 1950 vice-president of the National Federation.

For its tenth biennial convention—the largest to date—the National Federation of Business and Professional Women's Clubs met in San Francisco during July 3-7, 1950; of the total registration of nearly three thousand, 1,315 were delegates representing some 158,000 women. While an unopposed candidate for the presidential office, Judge Hughes received only 871 votes, reflecting (reported the New York *Times* correspondent) criticism of her affiliation with the United World Federalists, the organization which favors transforming the United Nations into a world federal government. (The federation is a strong supporter of the U.N. as it is now constituted.) Mrs. Hughes declared her federation duties "would come first."

In her acceptance speech, the new president in pointing out the responsibility which rested on the federation as the largest organization of business and professional women in the world, said, "United, we can be a greater force in directing human events than women have ever been. . . Let us assume our responsibility." In an interview given to the *Christian Science Monitor* on July 8, 1950, she urged women to "attach themselves to the [political] party of their choice, go into precinct meetings, and run for office." This she considered a moral obligation because of the difficulty of finding qualified women willing to be candidates. Judge Hughes was widely quoted in October when she made the statement, "If it [war] comes, women should be drafted for civil defense, production, and the three services. They have the rights and privileges of government, they should take the responsibilities, too." The theme of the federation's twenty-third observance of National Business Women's Week that month was "Measure Up for Full Partnership."

Among the resolutions adopted at the convention were approval of President Truman's action on the Korean crisis; pressing for implementation of the Government reorganization as recommended by the Hoover report; disapproval of "any curriculum which discriminates against women in equal educational opportunities"; broadening of the federation's support of "adequate appropriations for the Women's Bureau of the United States Department of Labor"; continued work for the passage of the proposed equal rights amendment to the Constitution.

Judge Hughes's other club memberships include the Texas State, Dallas, and American bar associations, National Association of Women Lawyers, American Judicature Society, Democratic Women of Dallas County, the Zonta Club, and the American Association of University Women. She has served as president of the Dallas Zonta Club, District and Appellate Judges Association, and as first vice-president of the Council of Social Agencies. Other offices she holds are Council membership in the Dallas United World Federalists, and in the Civic Federation (Dallas). In June 1950 Goucher College awarded her an honorary LL.D., in 1937 the George Washington University gave her its Alumni Achievement award. She belongs to the honorary fraternities of Phi Beta Kappa, Delta Kappa Gamma (honorary educational fraternity), and Delta Sigma Rho, honorary debating fraternity. During 1942-43 she was instructor in law at Southern Methodist University, in Dallas. Her political party affiliation is the Democratic, her church membership Episcopal.

Sarah T. Hughes is five feet one, weighs 117 pounds, and has gray eyes and brown hair. Her personality is described as "genial." Both she and her husband enjoy horseback riding, square dancing, and their vegetable garden.

References

Christian Sci Mon p6 Jl 15 '48
Dallas (Texas) News My 29 '49
Ind Woman 29:75 Mr '50
American Women, 1939-40
Texian Who's Who (1937)
Who's Who in Law, 1937

HUSTON, WALTER (hŭs'tŭn) Apr. 6, 1884—Apr. 7, 1950 Stage, screen, and radio actor; for fifteen years in vaudeville (1909-24); first stage success in title role of *Mr. Pitt* in 1924; subsequently in *Desire Under the Elms*

(1924), *Elmer the Great* (1928), *Dodsworth* (1934), *Knickerbocker Holiday* (1939), *Apple of His Eye* (1946), among others; starred in many motion pictures, including *Abraham Lincoln* (1930), *Dodsworth* (1936), *All That Money Can Buy* (1941), and *the Treasure of Sierra Madre* (1948). See *Current Biography*, 1949.

Obituary

N Y Times p13 Ap 8 '50 por

HUTTON, BETTY Feb. 26, 1921- Actress
Address: b. c/o Paramount Pictures, Inc., Hollywood 38, Calif.

The starring role in the motion picture version of the Broadway musical *Annie Get Your Gun* is played by Betty Hutton, who is known for her ebullience. Miss Hutton has been quoted as saying, "I shoved and clawed my way up, through vaudeville, night clubs, movie show houses and contests into pictures." During her ten years in Hollywood (as of 1950) she has appeared in sixteen films. *Time* has estimated her present income as $260,000 a year, and the success of *Annie Get Your Gun* has prompted the prediction that she "looks certain to be 1950's top box-office attraction."

Betty Hutton was born Betty June Thornburg on February 26, 1921, in Battle Creek, Michigan. Her father, Percy Thornburg, was a railroad brakeman. When Betty was two years old and her sister, Marion, was four, their mother, Mabel (Lum) Thornburg, became the sole support of her children, working in the upholstery division of an automobile factory. The family lived for a few years in Lansing and, when Betty was eight, moved to Detroit. To augment the family income Betty took care of babies and did cooking and housework when she was ten and eleven, while Marion worked at the soda fountain of a Detroit drugstore. Mrs. Thornburg, who played the piano and the guitar, had taught her little girls to sing popular songs—there were only two ways to "lick poverty," she said: be educated or have talent. Accordingly, as earnings became smaller in the depression period, Betty turned her talent to account by singing on street corners and in neighborhood beer gardens for the coins that were tossed her way.

At the age of thirteen, Betty, who was then in the first year of high school (she had been "double promoted" three times), left school to sing with a high school band directed by Harry Winegar. After a summer at a resort near Lansing and a year of touring Michigan and neighboring States, the young girl and three members of the band, with a capital of $200, went to New York and "hit Broadway with a thud." A music publisher advised the young singer to return to her home, supplying her with funds for the fare. Back in Detroit, she was singing in a local night club when Vincent Lopez heard her and engaged her at $65 a week to sing with his orchestra. She has often been quoted as saying that she had never eaten steak until the day Lopez employed her, when

BETTY HUTTON

she celebrated by eating steak for breakfast, lunch, dinner, and supper.

The Hutton "rough-and-ready" technique of song delivery is attributed by the actress to the fact that her sister was the beauty in the family. Dan Fowler, writing in *Look*, has told that when the girls sang on street corners, Betty, "shrewd from being scrawny, freckled, hungry and desperate," discovered that if she "sang louder than sister Marion and threw in pratfalls, cartwheels and bloodcurdling yells," she received more attention than her prettier sister. While her career with the Lopez orchestra began with a more conventional type of singing, when a member of the band informed her that she was going to be dismissed, she sang her next number with the famous "whoop-and-holler" technique. The result was that Lopez signed her to a five-year contract. Changing the singer's name to Hutton after consulting a numerologist, he developed a new style for his band to match hers. A successful tour followed, culminating in a twenty-one-week engagement at Billy Rose's night club, the Casa Mañana, in New York. (Miss Hutton's sister, who became a singer with Glenn Miller's orchestra, is now Mrs. John Thomas Philbin 3d.)

In 1939 Miss Hutton left the Lopez organization for the musical stage. She made her first Broadway appearance early in 1940 in the musical revue *Two For the Show*. *Vogue* called her "the most supercharged" member of the cast, adding that she looked "like an adorable Easter chicken with a fluff of yellow hair." Miss Hutton's next "break" in the theater came when she consulted a theatrical lawyer, A. L. Berman, about a breach-of-contract suit brought against her by Lopez. It so happened that producer B. G. De Sylva telephoned Berman from Hollywood to find someone for a comedy role in the Broadway musical comedy *Panama Hattie*, of which Ethel Merman was the star. Miss Hutton was given the part.

In 1941 De Sylva, then executive producer at the Paramount studios, brought Miss Hutton to Hollywood on a picture contract to play in *The Fleet's In*. Her rendition of "Arthur Murray Taught Me Dancing in a Hurry" in that picture, according to *Look*, "made her a star overnight." This was followed by parts in *Star Spangled Rhythm*, *Let's Face It*, and *Happy Go Lucky*. With the release (in January 1944) of *The Miracle of Morgan's Creek* came praise for Miss Hutton in her first acting role. John McManus of *PM* called the picture "a masterwork of fine casting, excellent characterization and a rare sense of satire, invention, and emotion." Miss Hutton's performance was received by the critics with such comments as "Betty Hutton carved a brand-new career for herself," and "the fiery little song bombshell . . . plays a straight light comedy role and does it exceptionally well. She's real star material." Other assignments followed in *Here Come The Waves*, *And The Angels Sing*, and *The Stork Club*.

The actress' second dramatic part was in *Incendiary Blonde*, made in 1943 and released two years later. Based on the life of Texas Guinan, it received mixed reviews, ranging from "a sound musical drama" to "a very tasteless and pointless production, lacking any values at all except Betty Hutton's eager talent and personality." Most critics agreed that Miss Hutton's portrayal of the night club queen of the 1920's "entrenches her firmly as an actress of ability."

Miss Hutton's first return to the stage after her film commitments was in a series of personal appearances in the summer and fall of 1944. As "master" of ceremonies for a forty-minute variety show, she often appeared seven times a day. In three Midwestern cities in which the company played attendance records were broken. In January 1945 Miss Hutton traveled with a USO unit to entertain troops in the Pacific area. "We did a 50,000-mile tour in eight weeks," the actress told an interviewer. "At Saipan they were still shooting. We moved around with thirty marines as a bodyguard." After making *Duffy's Tavern* upon her return to pictures, she made a six-week USO tour of European army camps, before ill health cut short her activity and brought her back to the United States in August.

During the following year (1946) the actress appeared in two motion pictures: *Cross My Heart*, and a second re-creation of an earlier day, *Perils of Pauline*, in which she played the role of death-challenging serial star Pearl White. Reviewers generally agreed that the picture was not "a valid reflection of the days of early movie-making, which it loosely pretends to be," but that it was "a free-swinging comedy with no holds barred." The New York *Sun* critic noted that "Miss Hutton grabs hold of the picture and squeezes all possible entertainment out of it."

The role of Annie Oakley in the Irving Berlin musical *Annie Get Your Gun* was a part to which Miss Hutton has said she aspired ever since she saw Ethel Merman in the Broadway production. "I connived and begged for that part," she has said. "And then I prayed for it.

And I got it." *Time* wrote of her performance, "She lacks Ethel Merman's craftiness with comedy, but along with her unbridled vitality, she gives the role something that brassy Ethel Merman never attempted; she kindles the love story into poignancy." Several critics, remarking that Miss Hutton's "frenetic" style had not been popular with them in the past, expressed admiration for her "great triumph," her "quite captivating portrayal of Annie," and her "rare blend of singing and acting talent." The picture itself was called "show business at its bright, gay, glossy, glittering best."

Still to be released in 1950 is *Let's Dance*, in which Miss Hutton co-stars with Fred Astaire. A period of ballet training and study with Astaire, and eight weeks of rehearsal of dance routines, preceded work before the camera. Miss Hutton has said that this is the first picture in which she has a chance to "dance like a lady." Other films planned for the star are *The Keystone Girl*, based on the life of Mabel Normand. Miss Hutton has been under contract to Paramount during her Hollywood career thus far, but under the terms of her present contract she is permitted to act in one film a year for another studio. The New York *Times* has reported that as a result of the agreement under which she appeared in *Annie Get Your Gun*, produced by Metro-Goldwyn-Mayer, she has agreed to star in two more films for that studio.

Honors won by the Hollywood actress have included designation as one of the "Stars of Tomorrow" in a poll held by the *Motion Picture Herald* in 1941, and *Look*'s Film Achievement Award for 1944. In 1945 she was voted "The Most Cooperative Actress of the Year" by the Hollywood Women's Press Club, and in the same year received a "Gizmo" from the editors of the Marine Corps magazine, *The Leatherneck*. *Cosmopolitan* in July 1947 chose Miss Hutton's performance in *The Perils of Pauline* for its citation for the best musical-comedy performance of the month. Another facet of her career has been recording, with Capital Records and, since 1946, with RCA-Victor.

The actress was married September 2, 1945, to Theodore S. Briskin, president of the Revere Camera Company. Their two daughters are Lindsay Diane and Candice. Miss Hutton was granted an interlocutory divorce decree in 1950. She is brown-eyed, five feet four inches tall and weighs about 112 pounds. Generally as volatile and energetic in real life as she appears before audiences, she is at times "quiet, moody, tortured by self-doubt" (*Time*). Among her recreation interests are bicycle riding, bowling, swimming, golf, and deep-sea fishing.

References

Collier's 110:14 O 31 '42
Liberty 21:44 Ap 1 '44
Look 7:40 Jl 27 '43; 14:48 Ja 3 '50
PM Mag Ap 29 '45
Quick 2:48 My 15 '50
Sat Eve Post 216:27 Je 10 '44
Time 55:66 Ap 24 '50

International Motion Picture Almanac,
    1950-51

IGLEHEART, AUSTIN S(MITH) (ī'g'l-härt) Oct. 25, 1889- Food corporation executive

Address: b. c/o General Foods Corporation, 250 Park Ave., New York 17, N.Y.; h. Round Hill Road, Greenwich, Conn.

Austin S. Igleheart is the president of the General Foods Corporation, "the largest processor of packaged foods in the United States" (in the words of *Barron's* magazine). Manufacturing over 250 branded products, ranging in variety from breakfast cereals, desserts, and beverages to ingredients, frozen foods, and laundry aids, General Foods operates 142 plants, warehouses, and sales offices in the United States, as well as ten plants in Canada, England, Mexico, and the Philippines. Igleheart has spent his entire business career in the packaged food business, beginning in 1912 with the family milling firm of Igleheart Brothers, and after 1929 holding various executive posts with General Foods Corporation, where he assumed the post of president in 1943.

Born in Evansville, Indiana, on October 25, 1889, Austin Smith Igleheart is the son of John L. and Belle (Smith) Igleheart. Of German descent, the Igleheart (or Iglehart as the name is variously spelled) family can be traced back to Prince Georges County in southern Maryland, at the beginning of the eighteenth century. Reared in Evansville, young Igleheart entered the family milling firm there in 1912 after graduating from the University of Wisconsin. He saw service with the Navy in World War I.

The company of Igleheart Brothers, incorporated in 1882, had its origin in a small grist mill built on the outskirts of Evansville in 1856 by Austin's grandfather, Levi Igleheart, in partnership with his two brothers. By the time of the Civil War the mill was producing 100 hundredweights of flour a day, as well as feeds, brans, and middlings. Within three years after joining the firm, Austin Igleheart became the manager of the department then producing Swans Down Cake Flour, first milled by the company in 1894. Concerned with advertising and sales promotional activities until 1926, he helped build up a national demand for cake flour by extending Swans Down advertising.

In January 1926 Igleheart Brothers was acquired by the Postum Cereal Company, parent organization of the General Foods Corporation. Founded in 1895 by Charles William Post, the Postum firm was originally built around three cereal products developed through Post's experiments. In 1924, when Colby M. Chester, Jr., became president of the firm, the Postum Cereal Company began to expand and broaden its line through a series of "circular mergers," acquiring lines of noncompeting packaged foods with long-established and well-advertised brand names, whose sales would counterbalance each other seasonally. In 1925 it purchased Jell-O; in 1926, Swans Down Cake Flour and Minute Tapioca; in 1927, Walter Baker's Chocolate, Franklin Baker's Coconut, and Log Cabin Syrup; in 1928, Maxwell House Coffee, Calumet Baking Powder, and La France Laundry

Fabian Bachrach

AUSTIN S. IGLEHEART

Aids; in 1929, Certo Fruit Pectin, North Atlantic Fisheries, Diamond Crystal Salt, and the patents and equipment of Clarence Birdseye [46] for the quick-freezing of perishable foods. The firm's name was changed in July 1929 to the General Foods Corporation, a title more adequately describing its extended field of operations.

Igleheart was elected a director and vice-president in charge of General Foods manufacturing and transportation in 1929. According to an article in *Fortune*, G.F.'s manufacturing operations are largely concerned with keeping the "continuous, automatic, conveyor-belt" system of production running smoothly. In 1935 Igleheart was made vice-president in charge of sales and general merchandising and automatically became president of the General Foods Sales Company, its marketing subsidiary. G.F. does not, in any large measure, rely on the activities of individual salesmen in selling goods to individual grocers, but sells primarily to corporate chain stores and jobbers. Three years later (1938) Igleheart was appointed to the post of executive vice-president of the firm, and on November 17, 1943, succeeded Clarence Francis [48] as president of the corporation.

In recent years the firm of which Igleheart is president has been concentrating on the introduction of new products and the opening up of new markets rather than on new acquisitions, although Sanka Coffee, Gaines Animal Foods, Bireley's Soft Drinks, Colonial Salt, and Snider's Canned Foods have been added to its list. Since 1939 it has spent about $13,000,000 developing new foods and improving old ones in its numerous research laboratories and test kitchens throughout the United States. Inasmuch as the food industry is highly competitive, G.F. must spend large sums each year to keep its brands before the public. In 1948 advertising expenditures totaled $29,000,000 (New York

Times), a large portion of which was devoted to buying radio and television time for the many programs it sponsors. G.F.'s gross sales in 1949 reached an all-time high of $509,000,000; net sales totaled $475,000,000, the sixteenth consecutive year in which they have surpassed any previous year; and in the net earnings added up to $27,000,000, the best in the firm's history. The corporation is owned by some 67,000 stockholders, about two-thirds of whom own fewer than twenty shares each. (Those statistics are from the company's 1949 annual report.) In 1947, according to the SEC, Igleheart received a salary of $115,000.

The War Food Administration issued a complaint against the General Foods Corporation in 1945, alleging that it had been a party to an attempt "to corner" the rye market in May 1944, and "to manipulate" prices of that grain, contrary to the provisions of the Commodity Exchange Act. Francis and Igleheart issued a statement to G.F.'s stockholders and employees denying these charges and explaining that they had bought rye—the one grain on which there were no price ceilings—as a means of guarding against possible reduction of profit in the manufacture and sale of wheat and corn products, "where a combination of price ceilings on products . . . and advancing prices in these grains . . . threatened the company with a squeeze." In 1948 the United States Court of Appeals cleared G.F. of the charges, stating: "Self-preservation has oftentimes been referred to as the first law of nature, and we suppose it applies to traders as well as others."

In an address given before the Traffic Club of New York in 1948, Igleheart stressed the need for management to explain the benefits of the profit-and-loss, free enterprise system to its employees and to the general public. "Management has left open a wide hole," he remarked, "through which its adversaries are driving half truths and falsehoods." He estimated that 35,000,000 people in the United States are still unconvinced of the merits of this system, and that only one worker in five receives any information about profits, wages, and his employer's financial condition. He said further: "We are neither noblemen nor frock-coated fat cats. We are just human beings, with worries and problems like other human beings. We make mistakes, but our intentions toward other people are generally good." Later that year he told a meeting of the National Association of Food Chains that it was imperative to counter the belief of the "average consumer" that the food industry is monopoly-controlled; he stated that G.F. does less than 2 per cent of the total volume of the packaged food business in the United States. In August 1949 he received for his company the third annual Distinguished Service Award of the Special Devices Association (a group composed of naval reserve officers who have served or are serving in the Special Devices Center of the Office of Naval Research). The award certificate cited G.F.'s "intelligent personnel administration" of its 19,000 employees, and "the progressive use of the best training methods and devices" in both its sales and plant training programs.

Since 1947 Igleheart has served as a member of the Department of Commerce's Business Advisory Council; he is a member of the National Industrial Conference Board. The executive is also a director of the Grocery Manufacturers of America, the National Association of Manufacturers, the Chicago and Eastern Illinois Railroad, the Chase National Bank, and the Commercial Solvents Corporation. His clubs, in New York and Connecticut, are the Racquet and Tennis, Clove Valley Rod and Gun, Union League, and the Round Hill. On November 2, 1915, he married Suzanne Bridwell: their four children are named Austin S., James B., John David, and Evaline (Mrs. Wesley D. Hamilton). He has made his home in the East since he moved from Evansville in 1929. Hunting is his favorite relaxation.

References

Business Executives of America (1950)
Who's Who in America, 1950-51
Who's Who in Commerce and Industry (1948)
World Biography (1948)

ROBERT H. JACKSON

JACKSON, ROBERT H(OUGHWOUT)

(hou′ŭt) Feb. 13, 1892- Associate Justice of the Supreme Court of the United States
Address: b. c/o United States Supreme Court, Washington, D.C.; h. McLean, Va.

> NOTE: This biography supersedes the article which appeared in *Current Biography* in 1940.

Robert H. Jackson, Associate Justice of the United States Supreme Court, who was chief prosecutor for the United States at the international trial of Nazi war criminals, was appointed to the bench in 1941. After beginning his legal career as an attorney in Jamestown, New York, he entered Government service in 1934, and held a succession of Federal posts, including those of United States Solicitor General (1938-39) and United States Attorney General (1940-41).

Robert Houghwout Jackson was born February 13, 1892, in Spring Creek Township, Pennsylvania, on a farm his great-grandfather, Elijah Jackson, had cleared when he moved there from Litchfield, Connecticut, in 1797. He is the son of William Eldred and Angelina (Houghwout) Jackson. His father, a breeder of horses, was of English descent; his mother's ancestors were Hollanders, who settled in America in the seventeenth century. Believing western New York a better region than Pennsylvania for breeding horses, William Jackson moved to Jamestown, New York, to operate a livery stable and hostelry. Robert received his grammar school education in Spring Creek and finished high school in Jamestown. Having entered Albany Law School (Union University) while in his middle teens, he completed a two-year course in one year.

The young man returned to Jamestown to practice law, and was admitted to the New York bar in 1913, the year he attained the age of twenty-one. (It is related that he had to get court permission to plead his first case, since he was still a minor at that time.) Studying at the Chautauqua Institute while carrying on his practice, Jackson earned the B.A. degree. In 1918 he became corporation counsel for the city of Jamestown. Jackson also became vice-president and general counsel of the Jamestown Street Railway Company, the Jamestown, Westfield, and Northwestern Railroad, and the Jamestown Telephone Company. After the 1929 stock market crash the lawyer directed the merging of the three Jamestown banks and became a director of the consolidated institution.

While serving on a State commission investigating courts Jackson came to the notice of Governor Franklin D. Roosevelt, and after Roosevelt became President of the United States he was called into Federal service with appointment to the post of general counsel for the Bureau of Internal Revenue in 1934. In this capacity Jackson began an investigation of the Mellon oil and aluminum empire, and won a $750,000 tax suit against it. As special counsel for the Securities and Exchange Commission (which he was appointed in 1935) Jackson investigated the Electric Bond and Share case, in which the holding company law was put to the test. In 1936 he went to the Department of Justice, first to the Tax Division, later as Assistant Attorney General to head the Antitrust Division. In the latter capacity he prosecuted an antitrust case against the Aluminum Company of America, and during a two-year period, cases against big oil companies and automobile finance firms in the course of extensive Federal investigations of monopolies. Jackson was considered a prospect for the New York governorship in 1937, but was not supported by the State's Democratic leaders.

In 1938 Jackson was appointed United States Solicitor General. During the year he filled

JACKSON, ROBERT H.—*Continued*

that post (1938-39) he won in the Supreme Court thirty-eight of forty-four cases, a high proportion of which involved the constitutionality of New Deal legislation. In a study entitled "Robert Jackson, New Deal's Lawyer" (*Christian Science Monitor*, July 13, 1940), Richard Lee Strout credited Jackson's work with being "an indispensable factor" in the adoption of much New Deal legislation. "He was the legal buttress of the New Deal," stated Strout. Analyzing Jackson's point of view the *Monitor* article quoted from his speeches: "We must fight radicalism by removing its provocation"; and, "They [New Deal social measures] must go on, the cost of them far more than offset by the terrible cost of not having them." The New Deal judicial crisis was treated by Jackson in a book entitled *The Struggle for Judicial Supremacy*, published in 1941. Of it, C. B. Swisher wrote (in the *American Historical Review*, January 1942) : "Mr. Jackson's [book] is a particularly stimulating study of the judicial process, written with a background of sound knowledge of the entire history of the struggle for judicial supremacy, even though with an obvious bias in favor of the New Deal."

Appointment to the post of Attorney General of the United States came to Jackson in January 1940. He was in that office when the transfer of the Immigration and Naturalization Service from the Department of Labor to the Department of Justice gave the latter the responsibility of investigating fifth column activities with the attendant task of safeguarding the civil liberties guaranteed by the Bill of Rights. Another question arising out of World War II was the exchange of fifty old United States destroyers for air and naval bases on British possessions in the Western Hemisphere; this was negotiated with Jackson as adviser.

Jackson was named an Associate Justice of the Supreme Court of the United States in June 1941, and he took the oath of office on July 11. On that body his dissenting and separate concurring opinions have earned him the reputation of a "maverick who does not fear to make the Court feuds public" (in the words of Max Lerner, writing in *Holiday*, February 1950). Attributing to the Associate Justice the conviction that the members of the bench were obligated to exclude their own views from their work, the same commentator analyzed Jackson's attitude as a "fight against the judicial activism" of some of his colleagues. In a separate concurring opinion on a Supreme Court ruling in a wage-hour dispute in February 1947, Justice Jackson criticized the basis of the decision and of two earlier ones in the same field in that they took "no account of contract or custom," having recourse rather to legalistic interpretations of the Wage-Hour Act. His dissenting opinion on a ruling upholding the right of a township to levy a fee on a redistributing coal storage warehouse stated, "If this is not the sort of burden and barrier to a nation's free trade that our commerce clause was designed to end, I should think one would be hard put to find an example. This decision represents a trend that seems to me quite out of the spirit of our history." A dissenting opinion on a Supreme

Court reversal of findings by Illinois courts upholding a "breach of the peace" judgment attracted much attention by the sharpness of its wording and the nature of the question involved. After outlining the circumstances of the incident which gave rise to the case, the justice concluded his fifteen-page opinion with an accusation that the Court decision in effect sanctioned the position "that all local attempts to maintain order are impairments of the liberty of the citizen," and the statement: "The choice is . . . between liberty with order and anarchy without either. There is danger that, if the court does not temper its doctrinaire logic with a little practical wisdom, it will convert the Constitutional Bill of Rights into a suicide pact."

In an examination of the position of the Communist party in the United States which attracted wide attention (excerpts were printed in the New York *Times* Magazine of May 21, 1950) Jackson outlined the characteristics of the party which, in his opinion distinguished it from any other substantial party and made it liable to treatment in law different from that constitutional in respect to other parties. The study formed part of an opinion on a case involving the section of the Taft-Hartley Act requiring officers of unions to take an oath of nonmembership in the Communist party; in respect to the case the Justice concluded that Congress was competent to enact an oath requiring disclosure of "overt acts of affiliation or membership in the Communist party," but that a clause calling for disclosure of belief "unconnected with any overt act" was beyond its power to enact. In the case of ten Communists convicted, in the lower courts, of conspiracy to teach and advocate forcible overthrow of the Government, whose bail had been revoked pending final appeal, Justice Jackson on September 25, 1950 (as Circuit Justice of the Second Judicial Circuit) overturned the revocation. He stated that disregard of their rights before the law would "cast aside protection for the liberties of more worthy critics who may be in opposition to the Government of some future day."

Many of the majority opinions of the Supreme Court have been written by Jackson, among them the 5-4 ruling in favor of the American Can Company in collecting a contract debt, which the debtor had tried to void by claiming the company had violated the Patman Act (decision rendered April 7, 1947); the 6-3 decision rejecting the right of the New York State Labor Relations Board to recognize unionization of foremen, reserving that power to the National Labor Relations Board since the foremen were employees of companies engaged in interstate commerce (decision rendered April 7, 1947); the 5-4 opinion (rendered April 26, 1948) that the Supreme Court should not "readily" upset its previous rulings on the grounds that Congress could make the necessary alterations in questions "of statutory construction, not of constitutional import."

An interlude in Jackson's Supreme Court duties occurred when he served as chief prosecutor for the United States in the trials of European Axis war criminals at Nuremberg, Germany. Appointed by President Truman on May 2, 1945, to the War Crimes Commission and to be chief United States prosecutor in the projected trials, Jackson took a prominent part in the conference in London which reached an agreement (announced August 8, 1945) creating an International Military Tribunal. The conference agreed on a definition of war criminals, a codification of crimes against international order, and a trial procedure acceptable to the legal experts of the four powers (the United States, Great Britain, Russia, and France). Justice Jackson, who had an important part in drawing up the indictments against twenty-four war criminals and six Nazi organizations, at the opening of the trials made a "masterly" presentation of the charges.

The trials began November 20, 1945, lasted ten and one-half months. Jackson, as chief counsel for the United States, was in charge of presenting what Victor H. Bernstein, writing in *PM*, called "the core" of the indictment—the count charging the defendants, as individuals, with conspiracy to wage a war of aggression; he conducted the prosecution of the twenty leading Nazis including Goering, Von Ribbentrop, Von Papen, Keitel, Streicher, and Jodl. Upon completion of the trials, Justice Jackson in October 1946 resigned from the International Military Tribunal. In 1947 he received the Medal for Merit for his "oustanding services" to the United States in the Nuremberg trials in a presentation which also cited his role in the establishment of the tribunal's charter. He was also the recipient of high honors from French and Belgian law societies.

Two documentary books prepared by Jackson, and published in 1946 and 1947, presented aspects of the trials. *The Case Against the Nazi War Criminals* (1946) comprised the text of Jackson's opening statement and of other documents, including the agreements that formed the legal basis for the trials and of the indictment itself. Reviewing it in the *Survey Graphic* (May 1946) M. C. Bernays wrote: "Justice Jackson's opening statement should be 'must' reading for every literate citizen. It is a document of majestic force and inexorable conviction." *The Nürnberg Case* (1947), containing the opening and closing statements of the chief United States prosecutor, excerpts from the cross-examination of prominent Nazis, and other official records, was described as "a valuable adjunct to the author's earlier book on the trials, and indispensable reading for an adequate understanding of the first international criminal prosecution" (W. M. Kunstler in the *Columbia Law Review*, April 1947). Surveying the achievements of the tribunal in an address to the Association of American Law Schools in 1948, the Justice stated, "The demonstration that an international criminal trial can be successfully conducted and that the nations can reconcile their procedures in this most delicate kind of trial may have more importance than any other feature of the Nuremberg experience."

Justice Jackson has been awarded the honorary LL.D. degree by the University of Brussels, the University of Warsaw, Dartmouth College, Syracuse University, the University of Buffalo (1946) and Western Maryland College (1946). A number of his addresses (he is a frequent guest speaker) have been printed in *Vital Speeches of the Day*. In 1944 he delivered the annual Benjamin N. Cardozo lecture entitled *Full Faith and Credit—the Lawyer's Clause of the Constitution* (published in 1945). A member of the New York State and American Bar associations, Jackson was president of the Federation of Bar Associations of Western New York during 1928-32, and chairman in 1934 of the National Conference of Bar Association Delegates; he is an honorary member of the Canadian Bar Association. In 1946 he was honored in England by election to the Honorable Society of the Middle Temple, London. He is a Mason; his clubs are the Congressional Country, the National Press and University in Washington, and the Athletic in Buffalo, New York.

Justice Jackson and Mrs. Jackson, the former Irene Gerhardt, whose marriage took place April 24, 1916, have a son, William, and a daughter, Mary Margaret. The jurist's church is the Episcopal, his political affiliation, Democratic. An enthusiastic rider, his chief hobby is raising horses; he also enjoys working in his garden. Max Lerner described Jackson as of "massive frame" with a "squarish face."

References

Christian Sci Mon Mag p6 Jl 13 '40 por
Holiday 7:82+ F '50
Look 4:10-13 Mr 12 '40 pors
N Y Herald Tribune II p3 Mr 24 '46 por
N Y Times Mag p13 Je 24 '45
P M p22 Ag 10 '45 por
America's Young Men, 1936-37
International Who's Who, 1950
National Cyclopædia of American Biography Current vol G, 1943-46
10 Eventful Years (1947)
Who's Who in America, 1950-51
Who's Who in Law, 1937
Who's Who in New York, 1947
Who's Who in the East (1948)
World Biography (1948)

JANAS, SIGMUND (jăn'ǎs) Nov. 23, 1899-
Airline executive

Address: c/o Colonial Airlines, Inc., 230 Park Ave., New York 17; h. 277 Park Ave., New York

Colonial Airlines, Inc., whose planes ply between New York, Montreal, Ottawa, Washington, and Bermuda (as well as smaller cities in New York and Pennsylvania) is headed by Sigmund Janas. The executive became Colonial's president in 1938, when he and a group of associates acquired the company. In 1949—the beginning of its twentieth year of operation—Colonial Airlines announced that it had set a new record in safety, without fatality or serious injury to a passenger or crew member

SIGMUND JANAS

in nineteen years. Janas originated the slogan "Safety Is No Accident."

A Californian by birth and upbringing, Sigmund Janas was born to Joseph and Mary Clara (Ellett) Janas on November 23, 1899, in Lake County, California. As a boy he had been thrilled by the achievements of the Wright brothers and other pioneers of aviation; and by the end of 1914, when he was a high school student at the Sacramento (California) Institute, he had made several flights with Lincoln Beacy, a California flier. (Janas himself was to become a licensed pilot.)

When America entered World War I young Janas enlisted in the Army, at the age of eighteen . He served as a private with an infantry division, and was later commissioned a second lieutenant. Demobilized with the rank of first lieutenant, he entered the University of California at Berkeley, where he majored in money and banking and received the B.A. degree. He later took courses at the University of San Francisco Law School and the American Institute of Banking. On completing his studies Janas became a police reporter on the Sacramento *Union,* advancing to the handling of feature assignments and special coverage of the State legislature. Moving to San Francisco, he became commercial and assistant financial editor of that city's *Chronicle.*

Subsequently Janas was employed in the banking field when he became assistant cashier in the California National Bank and later received appointment as chief deputy for the Superintendent of Banks for the State of California. Other California concerns with which Janas has been associated are the Richfield Oil Company, where he was assistant to the president, and the Petrol Corporation of California (treasurer). He has been president of the North American Oil and Refining Company and also of the Silver Peak Mining Company.

Janas entered aviation in its pioneer days as assistant to Harris Hanshue, president of Western Air Express. He resigned from that position in 1933 to become associated with American Airlines, Inc., taking charge of their Washington, D.C., office. Subsequently he became assistant to the president of the corporation, C. R. Smith [45]. During this association Janas purchased control of the bankrupt Central Airlines and became chairman of its board. After fifteen months that company was sold to Pennsylvania Airlines, to be merged into what is now known as Capital Airlines, at a price upward of a million dollars.

In 1938, with a group of associates, Janas purchased control of the Canadian Colonial Airways from the Aviation Corporation of America, a holding company. Canadian Colonial, which operated a New York-Montreal service had its origin in Colonial Air Transport, a company organized in 1923 to provide a service from Newark, New Jersey, to Boston, Massachusetts. The latter had obtained the first United States Air Mail contract in 1924; on March 6, 1928, the New York-Montreal route had been added and the company had been awarded the first American Foreign Air Mail contract: after 1930, when the holding company assumed control, the Newark-Boston service was merged into American Airlines, and the New York-Montreal run was maintained on a minimum schedule only, and that largely for the sake of the air mail subsidy. Thus, through an eight-year period, no new equipment had been acquired, no effort to expand had been made, and when Janas and his associates bought the company, its fleet had been reduced to two fourteen-passenger DC-2's.

In 1938, when Janas became president, he inaugurated a program of expansion. New DC-3 airplanes were acquired, an advertising campaign was launched, and airway beacons were set up to make night flying possible along the company's single route. In 1939 (when the New York-Montreal night service was inaugurated) the number of passengers carried totaled 15,898—the 1937 total had been 3,295. The right to make intermediate stops at Glen Falls, New York, and Burlington, Vermont, was obtained in 1941, and subsequently other calling points, such as Poughkeepsie, Albany, Lake Placid, Rutland and Plattsburg were added. The name of the line was shortened to Colonial Airways, Inc., in 1942.

Expansion plans were halted by war conditions in 1942. Four of the six DC-3's and the two DC-2's which the company was then operating were turned over to the Army Transport Corps, and from June of that year until the summer of 1944 Colonial was engaged in operating a cargo service between Chicago, New York and points in New England. It also conducted a transitional training school for pilots for the Army Air Forces. With the end of World War II, expansion was resumed; routes from New York to Ottawa and Washington to Ottawa, with intermediate stops, were authorized and flights inaugurated in 1945. The next year, New York-Bermuda and Washington-Bermuda services (with Foreign Air Mail contract No. 33) were begun. (An effort was also made to start a service between New York and Lewiston, Maine, with stops at various New England cities, and one from New York to Newport, Rhode Island, with an intermediate stop at Southampton, Long Island, but these plans were blocked by the Port of New York Authority.) Later applications were filed with the Civil Aeronautics Board for routes extending south to the Bahamas, west to Chicago, and north to Quebec.

In the summer of 1949 Colonial's monopoly on the Montreal-New York service (source of 60 per cent of its profits, Colonial claimed) was threatened when an "executive agreement" was concluded between the United States and Canada, whereby, in return for the right to the use of the Canadian airport of Gander, Newfoundland, by American overseas lines, the United States granted Canada, among other concessions, the right to operate a Montreal-New York service. Colonial brought suit against the Civil Aeronautics Board, charging that the "agreement" was in reality a treaty which should have been, but was not, submitted to the Senate for ratification. In February 1950, Colonial announced that it was withdrawing a Supreme Court appeal it had made on the suit, after its rejection by a lower court. Janas stated the withdrawal was being made because, in view of "the increasing gravity of the international situation," it was not in the public interest to question the constitutionality of executive agreements. Janas pointed out that the American-Canadian agreement gave the Civil Aeronautics Board and the President (by whom all international air agreements must be ratified) "ample power" to grant "route compensation to Colonial." This was taken to mean that the company hoped for favorable action on its pending application for permission to operate on additional routes. Meanwhile, the Canadian Air Transport Board (which had started proceedings to bar Colonial) suspended proceedings.

Colonial Airlines on April 19, 1949, commenced its twentieth year without a fatality or serious injury to passenger or crew—this, the company states, is a world record. (Colonial has publicized the slogan "Safety Is No Accident," a phrase coined by Janas.) As of early 1950, milage covered by the Colonial route system stood at 3,182 as against an original 334. The younger of Janas' two sons is district traffic manager for the airway company.

A believer in the cultivation of good public relations (he is said to give much credit to his early training as a newspaperman), the president of Colonial Airlines stresses the fact that the visitor "does not have to face a battery of secretaries" to reach his door. Janas is a Roman Catholic. He is married and the father of twin sons, George Radcliff and Sigmund, Jr. His clubs are the River and Canadian in New York City. As his sports he names fishing, sailing, and golf.

Reference

Who's Who in the East (1948)

JEWETT, FRANK B(ALDWIN) Sept. 5, 1879—Nov. 18, 1949 American physicist and electrical researcher of international repute; contributed to advancements in the fields of communications and transportation; for forty years an executive engineer with the American Telephone and Telegraph Company (1904-44); chief organizer and president of the Bell Telephone Laboratories, and chairman of the board of directors; advised on development of technical apparatus for armed forces, World Wars I and II; favored complete freedom for experimentation in scientific research as well as national and international exchange of scientific information. See *Current Biography*, 1946.

Obituary

N Y Times p17 N 19 '49

JOHNSON, HOLGAR J(OSEPH) Aug. 4, 1896- Life insurance executive
Address: b. c/o Institute of Life Insurance, 488 Madison Ave., New York 22; h. Lake Ave., Greenwich, Conn.

At the 1949 annual meeting of the Institute of Life Insurance, a public relations association formed in 1938, Holgar J. Johnson was reelected to the presidency, a position he had held for ten years. Johnson has been in the life insurance field throughout his career, starting as an agent shortly after leaving college, and advancing through the years to the presidency of the National Association of Life Underwriters, which was the position he held before the creation of the institute.

Holgar Joseph Johnson was born August 4, 1896, in Middletown, Connecticut, where his father and mother, Joseph and Hannah (Erickson) Johnson, had settled as immigrants from Sweden at the ages of twenty-one and seventeen, respectively. Four sons were born of this union. Holgar was eleven years old when his father died, and thereafter he helped in the support of the family, which in the meantime had moved to New Britain, Connecticut. Young Holgar attended the New Britain High School and Mt. Hermon School (Massachusetts), then went on to the University of Pittsburgh (Pennsylvania), earning the necessary funds by working in the YMCA.

After an interruption in his studies by service with the United States Naval Reserve Force in World War I, with overseas duty on the U.S.S. *Moccasin*, Johnson returned to the University of Pittsburgh. He received the Bachelor of Arts degree in 1922, with history as his major. Johnson had participated as a high school student in football and debating, and in college had become president of the sophomore class, student counselor, member of the YMCA board, and assistant director of boys' work at the Sarah Heinz Community House.

After graduating, Johnson sold insurance for the Connecticut Mutual Life Insurance Company in Pittsburgh from 1922 until 1926, when he was advanced to the position of assistant superintendent of agencies at the company's office in Hartford, Connecticut. In 1928 he returned to Pittsburgh, where for ten years he

Harris & Ewing

HOLGAR J. JOHNSON

maintained his own agency for the Penn Mutual Life Insurance Company. In this period Johnson served as president of the Sales Managers Club of Pittsburgh, the Pittsburgh Life Underwriters Association, the Pennsylvania State Association of Life Underwriters, and as vice-president (1937) and president (1938) of the National Association of Life Underwriters. He became a trustee of the University of Pittsburgh, and in 1937 he was vice-chairman of the city's Community Fund.

In 1938, at the mid-year meeting of the National Association of Life Underwriters, a resolution was adopted calling for a permanent public relations organization to speak for the insurance field as a whole. This resulted in the establishment of the Institute of Life Insurance, with headquarters in New York City, and the selection of Holgar Johnson as its first president. The institute was organized for the dual objective of "(1) providing the public with a clearer concept of life insurance and what it means to the individual and to the social and economic development of the nation; and (2) translating public viewpoints to the life insurance business, thereby enabling it to render constantly broadening and more effective service" (*The Journal of The American Society of Chartered Life Underwriters*, September 1949). At the time of its formation in 1938, the institute represented seventy-six American and Canadian legal reserve life insurance companies; after ten years of Johnson's guidance it was supported by 160 companies, representing 90 per cent of all life insurance in the United States and including the Canadian companies which maintain American offices.

President Johnson's first concern was to make the institute a storehouse of life insurance information. He then initiated a coast-to-coast news service with three departments:

the first for life insurance news only, the second for general economic news, the third devoted primarily to the economic interests of women. Johnson's emphasis on this categorized news service arose from his conviction that "this nation is not just 150 million people—it is a combination of many publics, each with individual special interests." With the advent of World War II, the president of the institute directed its public relations projects to making known the contribution insurance was making to the war effort through the investment of premiums in Government securities and through the check to inflationary tendencies provided by the diversion of public funds from consumer markets to premium payments. For this wartime service as president of the institute, Johnson was selected in 1945 by the editors of *The Insurance Field* to receive its annual award to the man making the greatest contribution to the insurance industry.

In 1946, with life insurance ownership in the United States at an all-time high of $174,000,-000,000 (*Christian Science Monitor*, January 2, 1947), Johnson announced to the press that the insurance companies, in the face of the postwar housing shortage, had at that time contracted for the building of $150,000,000 worth of rental housing for an estimated 75,000 people. From this practical concern with housing, the insurance companies, through the institute, placed a new emphasis on the American family unit as the basis for their entire public relations program. The institute prepares an annual *Life Insurance Fact Book* which is circulated to more than 100,000 librarians, editors, writers, and researchers. For the insurance field itself, the association issues a monthly publication, *Life Insurance and the American Public*. In May 1949 Johnson presented to the public the institute's fourth film, *For Some Must Watch*, a documentary based on the part a life insurance agent had in assisting a town and its people in solving certain problems.

In a speech to the Des Moines (Iowa) Kiwanis Club Johnson stated that "the greatest research project of all time is the composite research now being undertaken by business as a whole into the broad subject of product, productivity, distribution, living standards, health and other aspects of the social-economic structure" (New York *World-Telegram*, April 9, 1947). As a recognized voice for this point of view, the president of the institute was one of fifty United States business leaders to attend the eighth International Management Congress at Stockholm, Sweden, July 3 through July 8, 1947 (the first postwar conference). The American delegation pledged itself to "giving Europe new incentive for a speedy return to productive democracy." Johnson was chairman of the commerce and industry commission of the congress.

Johnson was awarded the Delaware Medal by the King of Sweden in 1938; was given the honorary degree of LL.D by Bethany College, Bethany, West Virginia, in 1940; and in 1947 was selected by the National Association of Life Underwriters for the John Newton Russell Memorial Award as the "spokesman for life insurance and its representatives at the court of public opinion." (He has written articles on life insurance, economics, and related social subjects.) At the 1949 annual meeting of the institute, Leroy A. Lincoln '46, president of the Metropolitan Life Insurance Company, presented Johnson with an expression of the membership's appreciation of his services.

The executive has membership in the National Association of Life Underwriters, the Penn Mutual Agency Association (past president), the American Legion, and of the American Academy of Political and Social Science. He is a member of the board of the Insurance Federation and the Insurance Society of New York City, and the American Council of Public Relations. He is a charter member of Phi Alpha Theta, honor society in history, and also belongs to Omicron Delta Kappa, honor society in leadership, and to Sigma Alpha Epsilon fraternity. His clubs are the Duquesne and the University in Pittsburgh; the Round Hill and the Greenwich Country (Greenwich, Connecticut); and the Uptown and the Economic in New York City. He is on the board of directors of the Greenwich Academy and formerly served on the board of the Greenwich Community Chest and Council. Serving as a director of the YMCA of New York City, Johnson is also chairman of the Army and Navy Committee of the YMCA National Council. He is a former vice-president of the USO. Johnson married Muriel Sinclair Cole on April 25, 1925; their two children are Nancy Carol and Joan Sinclair. He lists himself as a Republican and an Episcopalian. Five feet ten and one-half inches in height, he weighs 175 pounds; he has blue eyes and black hair. His favorite recreation is golf.

References

Who's Who in America, 1948-49
Who's Who in Commerce and Industry (1948)
Who's Who in Insurance (1948)
Who's Who in the East (1948)

JOHNSON, JOSEPH E(SREY) Apr. 30, 1906- Peace organization official; former college professor
Address: b. c/o Carnegie Endowment for International Peace, 405 W. 117th St., New York 27; h. Buxton, Northwest Hill Rd., Williamstown, Mass.

A professor of history at Massachusetts' Williams College who had spent four years as a State Department officer, Joseph E. Johnson was in May 1950 elected president of the Carnegie Endowment for International Peace by its trustees. That organization, established in 1910 by Andrew Carnegie, seeks to promote international peace largely through its publications and other forms of education. Since the establishment of the United Nations it has done much to support the efforts of that body. Johnson's work for the State Department had taken him to the San Francisco conference at which the U.N. was organized, and to early meetings of the Assembly and Security Council as an adviser to the United States delegation.

Joseph Esrey Johnson was born in Longdale, Virginia, on April 30, 1906. He was named after his late father, who was a mining and metallurgical engineer, a Pennsylvanian of Scotch-Irish descent; his mother, the former Margaret Hilles (herself a member of the Society of Friends) is descended from Pennsylvania and New Jersey Quakers. Because the senior Johnson's work entailed frequent changes of location, his son lived his early years in a number of States, Virginia, Alabama, Wisconsin, and New Jersey. By 1918 the family, in which he was the only child, had settled in Scarsdale, New York, and there the boy attended the town's high school during 1918-20. He next went to the Milton (Massachusetts) Academy for two years. At Harvard University, where he majored in history and literature, he was awarded the B.S. degree in 1927. Intending to become a metallurgist, he studied briefly at Carnegie Institute of Technology, in Pittsburgh, and worked in a steel mill. Illness, however, forced him to reconsider his choice of career, and he returned to Harvard to specialize in American history. It was from Harvard he received the M.A. degree in 1932, and the Ph.D. in 1943; his doctoral dissertation was a study of James Logan, a Pennsylvania colonial leader.

Johnson's first position was as an instructor in history at Bowdoin College, in Brunswick, Maine. He taught there in 1934-35. Then, after a year of work on his dissertation, he took an instructorship at Williams College, in Williamstown, Massachusetts. Two years later (1938) he was advanced to the rank of assistant professor in history, and in 1947 to professor. With the entry of the United States into World War II Johnson sought to join the armed forces, but was unsuccessful. In 1942 he accepted a position as an officer with the Department of State, obtaining a leave of absence from Williams to enable him to do so.

Johnson's first post with the State Department, that of an administrative assistant in the Division of American Republics, brought him into contact with the work of the Pan American Union. In September-October 1944 he served as an area adviser on Latin American affairs during the last two weeks of the Dumbarton Oaks Conference. It was partly this experience in the problems of world organization that brought him the post of acting chief in 1944-45 and chief in 1945-47 of the Division of International Security Affairs in the Office of Special Political Affairs of the State Department (now known as the Bureau of United Nations Affairs). His division was concerned with political and security activities in the United Nations Security Council and in the Assembly, among them matters relating to the veto, atomic energy, and armaments; in late 1945 it was given "working level" or drafting responsibility for United States proposals, for submission to U.N., of the problem of atomic energy control. Early in 1945 Johnson attended the Inter-American Conference on Problems of War and Peace in Mexico City, and later that year was adviser to the United

JOSEPH E. JOHNSON

States Delegation to the Conference on International Organization held in San Francisco, out of which came the United Nations.

Johnson acted as adviser to the United States delegation at 1946 meetings of the United Nations Security Council. During the second part of the first session (also in 1946) of the General Assembly, held in New York, Johnson, though not a permanent member of the United States mission to the U.N., was "on detail" from the State Department as an adviser, and occasionally sat as the United States representative in committee meetings having to do with security. He thus participated in the work of a subcommittee on the regulation of armaments, and represented the United States on a fourteen-nation subcommittee of the Political and Security Committee of the Assembly. In meetings of the latter group in December 1946 Johnson exchanged arguments with Andrei Y. Vishinsky [44] of the Soviet Union in debates on an Australian resolution objecting to what Australia considered the misuse of Big Power veto rights.

In the spring of 1947 Johnson, who had decided to return to teaching that fall, was asked to be a member of a new State Department policy planning staff, which was formed in May to assist Secretary of State Marshall. Its purpose, reported James Reston (New York *Times*) was "to make long-range plans in the field of foreign policy." During the time that Johnson was a member, the group gave its attention to the Marshall Plan, proposed by the Secretary of State in a talk at Harvard in June of that year. In the autumn Johnson returned to Williams College as a professor of history, to remain there until 1950. For the summer of 1948 a Presidential appointment made him deputy United States representative on the Interim Committee of the U.N. General Assembly (the so-called "Little Assembly").

In an address at Ohio State University in 1947 Johnson discussed the efforts of the United Nations Military Staff Committee to set up armed forces for the United Nations, commenting that the work had been delayed by the Soviet representatives. His discussion of the root of Russian-American misunderstanding appeared in the October 11, 1947, issue of *Nation* under the title "What Keeps Them Apart?" Johnson cited the difficulties of what he called "fish-bowl diplomacy," the inexperience of both the United States and Russia as world leaders, and the "nonfriendly" attitude of Russian diplomats to all nations not within the Soviet orbit, which he said made it impossible to build up a "bank of good will" such as existed with other nations.

In May 1950 Professor Johnson accepted the post of president of the Carnegie Endowment for International Peace, to which he had been elected by its trustees. This office, he felt, was a natural continuation of the work he had done in the State Department and the United Nations. On July 1 he took over his new post, succeeding Dr. James T. Shotwell [44], who became president emeritus. The peace organization was established in December 1910 by Andrew Carnegie, with a fund of ten million dollars, "the revenue of which is to be administered . . . to hasten the abolition of international war, foulest blot upon our civilization." Among the purposes listed in the act of incorporation of the foundation were: "To hasten the renunciation of war as an instrument of national policy; to encourage and promote methods for the peaceful settlement of international differences and for the increase of international understanding and concord; and to aid in the development of international law and the acceptance by all nations of the principles underlying such law."

As one of its 1950 projects to improve international relations, the Carnegie Endowment is engaged in analyses of problems before the U.N. and studies directed toward making the world organization more effective. (The construction in New York of an 11-story building for the Endowment, to face the new United Nations plaza, was planned for early 1951.) As part of its program of education it has sponsored lectures, conferences, institutes, and fellowships for study abroad. It works also with about 850 International Relations Clubs on college and university campuses throughout the world. Among its recent publications are studies on selected administrative problems of the United Nations, books on international problems and international law, and a *United Nations Studies* series. The pamphlet series, *International Conciliation*, begun in 1907, was taken over by the Endowment in 1924 and is published ten times in the year; each pamphlet deals with a particular question in international relations.

A trustee of the World Peace Foundation, since 1948 he has been a member of the editorial board of its magazine, *International Organization*. To this and other periodicals he has contributed articles on international topics; he has also lectured on the United Nations at the National War College. The historian is a member of the American Historical Association, the Academy of Political Science, the Society of American Historians, and the Council on Foreign Relations. His clubs are the Harvard, the American Alpine (in New York) and the Alpine in London. As a voter he is independent of party affiliation.

Brown-eyed and brown-haired Johnson is six feet two inches tall, weighs 185 pounds. On weekends he commutes from New York to his home in Williamstown, Massachusetts. His wife is the former Catherine D. W. Abbot; married December 31, 1930, the couple has two children, Anne S. and William R. A. Johnson has been described as a man of quiet voice and alert manner; he names mountain-climbing—"now mostly from an armchair"—and fishing as two of his recreations.

References

N Y Herald Tribune p15 My 5 '50
N Y Times p10 Ap 10 '47; p11 My 5 '50
Nation 165:373-6 O 11 '47
Who's Who in America, 1950-51
Who's Who in the East (1948)

JOLSON, AL May 26, 1886—Oct. 23, 1950
Actor and singer; first appearance in the stage in a mob scene in Zangwill's *Children of the Ghetto* (1899); toured in vaudeville and minstrel shows; in 1909 sang his first "mammy" song in blackface; starred in a succession of extravaganzas, among them *La Belle Paree* (1911), *Honeymoon Express* (1913), *Robinson Crusoe, Jr.* (1916), *Sinbad* (1918), *Bombo* (1921), *Big Boy* (1925); later in *Sonny Boy*, *The Singing Fool*, and *Wonderbar*, after his success in *The Jazz Singer*, the earliest talking picture; appeared in other films, *The Singing Fool*, *Say It With Songs*; his voice was heard in *The Jolson Story* and *Jolson Sings Again*, two pictures based on his life; became a film producer in 1944; star of his own radio program. See *Current Biography*, 1940.

Obituary

N Y Times p38 O 25 '50 por

KATZ, MILTON Nov. 29, 1907- United States Government official; lawyer

Address: b. c/o Economic Cooperation Administration, 800 Connecticut Ave., N.W., Washington, D.C.; h. 16 Channing St., Cambridge, Mass.

Milton Katz, a law professor on leave from Harvard University, in July 1950 succeeded W. Averell Harriman [46] as United States Special Representative in Europe for the Economic Cooperation Administration (popularly known as the Marshall Plan). He had previously seen service with various Government agencies, including the Reconstruction Finance Corporation, the National Recovery Administration, and the War Production Board. A member of the ECA European headquarters staff in Paris since 1948, he was made Deputy United States Special Representative in 1949.

The son of Morris and Clara (Schiffman) Katz, Milton Katz was born November 29, 1907, in Brooklyn, New York. For his college education he enrolled at Harvard University, where his initial interest was anthropology. An anthropological expedition for the school's Peabody Museum in 1927 and 1928, after his graduation with the B.A. degree, took him across central Africa, where he suffered an attack of malaria. Deciding on a change of profession, he returned to Harvard to study law, and there received the LL.B. degree; he was admitted to the New York bar in 1931.

The young lawyer's first employment was under United States Circuit Judge Julian W. Mack, for whom he was legal secretary for one year; the following year, 1932-33, he spent as attorney for the Reconstruction Finance Corporation. With the advent of the New Deal, Katz served, successively, with the NRA as assistant counsel from 1933 to 1935; as executive assistant to the chairman of the Securities and Exchange Commission from 1935 to 1938; and during 1938-39 with the Department of Justice, where he was special assistant to the Attorney General of the United States.

Katz returned to his alma mater in 1939 to be a lecturer on law, and was promoted to the rank of professor in 1940. Obtaining a leave of absence in 1941 to extend from that date to January 1946, he joined the legal staff of the War Production Board, where he served as a solicitor from 1941 to 1943. During 1942-43 he was United States executive officer of the Combined Production and Resources Board (United States and Great Britain), and during 1943-44 was with the Office of Strategic Services. From April 1944 to January 1946 he served in the United States Naval Reserve as lieutenant commander on active duty in the Mediterranean and European theaters of war. For his World War II record he was awarded the Legion of Merit and the Commendation Ribbon.

Again on leave of absence from Harvard Katz became general counsel in European headquarters of the Economic Cooperation Administration in 1948, and chairman of the Policy Board and Acting Director of the Program Division in 1949. He received the title of Deputy United States Special Representative in Europe in June 1949. As such Katz was assistant to ECA "roving" Ambassador W. Averell Harriman (Special Representative in Europe since the institution of the ECA in 1948), and frequently acted as the organization's spokesman. After two years of Marshall Plan payments, Katz stated that in his opinion they were "well worth it" in that they supported the United States foreign policy of maintaining peace without surrender to the Russians and raised living standards of people abroad. He added that he estimated the Marshall Plan's third year would cost each American taxpayer an average of about one hundred dollars.

In June 1950, when Harriman was named special assistant (to coordinate work of departments bearing on foreign affairs) to President Truman, Katz was nominated to succeed him. Unanimous Senate approval was given the nomination on June 26, and on July 6 he was sworn in at the Paris headquarters of the

Wide World Photos

MILTON KATZ

ECA as United States Special Representative in Europe. In this position, which carries the rank of ambassador extraordinary and plenipotentiary, Katz is direct representative of the ECA Administrator William C. Foster in Europe, and also the chief representative of the United States Government to the Organization for European Economic Cooperation (*United States Government Organization Manual 1950-51*). It is one of his functions to coordinate the activities of the chiefs of special missions in countries participating in ECA.

In one of his first statements to the press, the new ECA Ambassador gave assurance that the change in leadership did not forecast a change in the ECA policy of furnishing material and financial help to countries participating in the program, which is due to end in June 1952. The project places emphasis on individual and collective efforts of the countries concerned, which it aids by promotion of industrial and agricultural production, furthering of the restoration and maintenance of sound currencies, budgets, and finances, and by the stimulation and facilitation of international trade. As deputy Katz had been prominent in seven months of negotiations toward a plan for clearing current accounts among Marshall Plan countries. When the European Payments Union (which had been in operation since June 30, 1950) was formally signed by the eighteen member nations in the Marshall Plan on September 19, Katz described it as "a concrete major step forward to European unity and strength . . . an essential technical means of putting to common use the resources of all the countries of Western Europe through a freer flow of European trade." The union is designed to make it ultimately unnecessary for those countries to depend upon Marshall Plan aid.

Speaking of the implications of the Korean conflict, Katz stated in a press interview that United States action there had done much to strengthen morale in ECA countries, particularly those along the Russian border, pointing out that to them it represented assurance that America would stand with them if they would stand together. "The thing that mattered was that we acted positively and clearly," he said. In July he conferred with Lewis W. Douglas [47], United States Ambassador to Great Britain, and with David K. E. Bruce [49], Ambassador to France, on the economic implications of a rearming of Europe. Katz, who also succeeded Harriman as chairman of the Finance and Economic Committee of the North Atlantic Treaty Organization, attended a meeting of the Deputies' Council of the Treaty. Later, at a conference with French officials (the Premier, his Ministers of Finance and Defense, the French representative on the Deputies' Council, and the chief negotiator for France on the Schuman plan) he and Ambassador Bruce explained that in view of the world situation it was felt that greater emphasis must be given to defense in European recovery plans; it was suggested that North Atlantic nations would be expected to be prepared to do more for a common defense, while being strengthened to that end.

A contributor to law periodicals, Katz is the author of the book *Cases and Materials in Administrative Law* (1947). On July 2, 1933, he married Vivian Greenberg; they have three children, John, Robert, and Peter. Katz is a member of the Harvard Travelers Club of Boston, the Faculty Club of Cambridge, and the Harvard Club of New York City. It is told that he enjoys playing softball and football with his children and their friends, and social dancing.

References

N Y Herald Tribune p3 Jl 7 '50; II p1 Jl 9 '50 por; p7 Jl 14 '50
N Y Times p10 Ag 1 '50
Time 41:11 Mr 1 '43 por
Washington (D.C.) Post p8 Jl 7 '50
Who's Who in America, 1950-51
Who's Who in New York, 1947
Who's Who in the East (1948)
World Biography (1948)

KEATING, KENNETH B(ARNARD)
May 18, 1900- United States Representative from New York

Address: b. House Office Bldg., Washington 25, D.C.; Harris, Beach, Keating, Wilcox and Dale, 5 S. Fitzhugh St., Rochester 4, N.Y.; h. 3500 Elmwood Ave., Rochester 10, N.Y.

Kenneth B. Keating, Republican Congressman from New York's Fortieth District, was elected to the United States House of Representatives in 1946 and re-elected to the post in 1948. A lawyer, he became a member of a law firm of Rochester, New York, in the early 1920's. He served as a sergeant in the United States Army during World War I and during World War II for more than two years as executive assistant to the Deputy Supreme Commander of the Southeast Asia Command

Kenneth Barnard Keating was born in Lima, New York, on May 18, 1900; he is the only son (he has a sister) of Thomas Mosgrove and Louise (Barnard) Keating. Civic-minded Mrs. Keating had been a teacher. Upon his graduation in 1915 from the Genesee Wesleyan Seminary (in Lima), young Keating entered the University of Rochester (New York), which awarded him the B.A. degree in 1919. After teaching Latin and Greek at the East High School of Rochester for a year (1919-20), he became a student at the Harvard Law School. Granted the LL.B. degree by that institution in 1923, he began legal practice in the same year. He has practiced in Rochester since that date, and is a member of the firm of Harris, Beach, Keating, Wilcox and Dale.

Keating, who served as a sergeant with the United States Army in World War I, served again in the armed forces during World War II. Commissioned a major on April 15, 1942, he was promoted to the rank of lieutenant colonel on October 19 of the same year. A year and four months later he received the rank of colonel. His overseas service was largely in the China-Burma-India theater of operations, where he acted as executive assistant to Lieutenant General Raymond A. Wheeler, Deputy Supreme Commander of the Southeast Asia Command, from November 1943 to January 1946; he was made a brigadier general on January 24, 1948. Keating is the recipient of the American, European and Asiatic Theater Ribbons with three battle stars and the Legion of Merit with Oak Leaf Cluster, and was awarded the Order of the British Empire.

Keating's political career began with his election in November 1946 to the Eightieth Congress as Republican Representative of New York State's Fortieth District. The district, which comprises part of the city of Rochester and a number of towns in Monroe County, returned Keating to the House of Representatives in 1948. In the second term he is a member of the Committee on the Judiciary. As a member of the subcommittee on study of monopoly power, he participated in the 1949 hearings to determine whether existing antitrust laws were curbing monopoly and unfair trade practices, as a result of which plans were made to introduce specific legislation. His feeling on the Clayton Antitrust Act was: "Either we should repeal it entirely, or we should amend it to make it effective." The Republican Congressman was also a member, in 1949, of the subcommitee on civil rights and, with other committee members, held hearings on a proposed amendment to the Hatch Act to increase protection of civil rights. He introduced an anti-lynching bill to the committee, but the group failed to report such a bill during 1949.

Keating's voting record on foreign issues shows general support for foreign aid. In April 1947 he voted for the foreign relief bill and against the amendment to cut it, and in May that year for the Greek-Turkish aid bill. In May 1948 he gave his "Yea" to the Europe-China omnibus foreign assistance bill. He voted for the European Recovery Program,

KENNETH B. KEATING

and, following a tour of Europe in the fall of 1948, he reported on problems affecting the program. On the Mutual Assistance Defense Act of 1949, providing arms aid to North Atlantic Pact nations, Keating acted with the majority of Congress in favoring a reduced appropriation; the amended bill, however (which he supported), called for one and a third billion dollars. In January 1950 he voted against a bill to give continued economic aid to the South Korean Republic and in February of 1950, opposed the Korea-Formosa aid measure. Together with the majority of Congress in July 1950 he voted for the $1,222,500,000 arms aid bill which, aside from European and Near East arms aid, authorized $16,000,000 for South Korea and the Philippines and granted the President authority to spend up to $75,-000,000 in assisting anti-Communist nations in the Far East. Keating has indicated that he favors, as a corollary to the arms aid program, "a well formulated plan for the defense of Western Europe." On the subject of the 1950 Korean crisis, he declared: "We should have decided when the Republic of Korea was created by the United Nations what our future foreign policy toward it and the entire Asiatic powder keg would be, for the strategic difficulty of defending Korea was apparent from the beginning." Earlier in 1950, the Congressman had given his support to the $3,100,000,000 Foreign Assistance bill, which included $100,-000,000 for Korean aid. In July 1950 he voted against the Point Four bill.

In voting on domestic affairs, Keating has frequently supported the Republican drive for economy. In 1947 and 1948, he joined the majority of Congress in a vote which succeeded in passing the income tax reduction bill over President Truman's veto. Earlier in 1948 the Congressman had introduced a bill to increase personal income tax exemptions and reduce surtaxes, and in 1947 he had introduced another

KEATING, KENNETH B.—*Continued*

tax reduction bill aimed at easing the tax burden on persons with small incomes. He voted for the extension of selective service in 1948 and again in June 1950; in 1949, after the Appropriation Committee's statement that the Army expected to make no draft calls in the ensuing year, Keating, objecting to the committee's recommended $9,000,000 appropriation, proposed that the Selective Service System be reduced, supported by $4,500,000 for the ensuing fiscal year. According to the New York *Times*, "The House at that time was sitting in committee status, with many members absent, but the vote for Mr. Keating's suggestion was so overwhelming—82 to 9—that the leadership accepted it as being final." In 1950 Keating voted for an amendment which made a blanket $600,000,000 cut in the general appropriations bill and voted against appropriations for flood control and river and harbor projects.

Congressman Keating supported the Taft-Hartley bill in 1947, introduced an amendment thereto to equalize legal responsibilities of labor organizations and employers (1948). In 1947 he voted for the bill forbidding portal-to-portal suits. Keating supported the Fair Labor Standards Act amendment (1949) providing for a minimum wage of 75 cents an hour. He voted for the McConnell FEPC bill but against the Powell bill in February 1950. The Congressman has favored benefits for veterans and has introduced and voted for legislation designed to liberalize old age insurance benefits and extend social security coverage. On immigration questions, he favored admission of 202,000 displaced persons (1948), and advocated elimination of "discrimination against religious and racial groups," which he felt existed in the law. In 1949 he criticized the State Department for "closing the door" to the immigration of German nationals.

On other domestic issues Keating in 1947 supported voluntary 15 per cent rent increases and extension of control; in March 1949 voted for the Rent Control Bill, allowing States, cities, counties, to determine when controls should be lifted; later in the year he favored a compromise bill, containing a fifteen-month extension of controls; in 1950 he opposed extension of Federal rent control. He voted for the bill to extend the RFC for two years (1947), eliminating some of its functions and reducing its borrowing power from eighteen billion to two billion. He is on the record as favoring the Mundt-Nixon anti-Communist bill (1948) and the bill requiring Communists to register (1950); he supported the anti-inflation bill (1948), the anti-poll tax bill (1949), and the reorganization of Government departments.

A critic of the Brannan plan, he declared that President Truman's farm policy would lead to increased taxes and was on the same pattern "that contributed to bringing England to the brink of disaster"; in the voting on the Agricultural Act of 1949 he supported an amendment extending the existing (rigid) support as opposed to the flexible price support originally provided in the act. He voted for statehood for Hawaii (1950) but against it for Alaska, for the Middle Income Housing Bill

(1950), and the Defense Production Act (August 1950) giving the President sweeping authority to put the home front on a ready-for-war footing. The Congressman had declared in 1949, "The United States is getting closer to statism. . . .Never before in our history have such bold and far-reaching proposals been made for domination of the individual by the state as those proposed by the present occupant of the White House." All government subsidies, Keating maintains, are "badges of statism."

Representative Keating makes his home in Rochester, where he is a director of a bank. Among organizations to which he belongs are the American, Rochester, and New York State bar associations; the American Legion, Veterans of Foreign Wars, Reserve Officers' Association, YMCA, Delta Upsilon, and Phi Beta Kappa fraternities. A 33d Degree Mason (Shriner), he is also a member of the Moose, Eagles, Benevolent Protective Order of Elks, the Empire State Society, and the Sons of the American Revolution. He is associated with the Genesee Valley Country, Pundit and Harvard Clubs of Rochester, the Metropolitan Club (Washington), the Sojourner, the Rochester Chamber of Commerce, and the Lincoln's Inn Society. He is a member of the National Republican Club of New York; in religious affiliation he is Presbyterian. By his marriage on April 11, 1928, to Louise DuPuy, he has one daughter, Judith DuPuy. The Congressman is five feet nine inches in height, weighs 152 pounds, has gray hair and blue eyes.

References

Congressional Directory (1950)
Who's Who in America, 1950-51
Who's Who in New York, 1947

KEE, JOHN Aug. 22, 1874- United States Representative from West Virginia

Address: b. House Office Bldg., Washington, D.C.; h. Woodland Dr., Bluefield, W.Va.

John Kee, Democratic Representative from the Fifth Congressional District of West Virginia, became chairman of the House Foreign Affairs Committee in March 1949. He was first elected to Congress in 1932 and has been re-elected for eight successive terms. The Congressman has been a member of the Foreign Affairs Committee from his early days in the House of Representatives, where he has been a consistent supporter of Administration policies, first those of President Roosevelt and later those of President Truman. Prior to his election to Congress, Kee had served in the West Virginia State Legislature, from 1923 to 1927. A lawyer with a private practice, he has been a railroad and corporation counsel.

One of a family of five children, John Kee was born to Jasper Newton and Louisa (Campbell) Kee in Glenville, West Virginia, on August 22, 1874. His Irish grandfather came to that State about the middle of the nineteenth century, from Dublin. As a boy, John Kee developed a certain interest in botany—one summer he helped a professor to classify the wildflowers in one county of West Virginia. The exactness of the science, it has been pointed out, appealed to him, as law was to do later. He attended Glenville State Normal School from 1887 to 1890, and the University of West Virginia for the study of law in 18′,8-99.

In 1897 Kee had begun to practice law in his native town. Three years later (1900) he obtained a position with the South Penn Oil Company; and during 1902-10 he was counsel for the Virginian Railway Company, which engaged him to acquire land and rights of way for it in the vicinity of the West Virginia coal fields. Kee opened a law office in Bluefield in the Pocahontas coal region of West Virginia in 1910, an office he has maintained. During 1916-18 the lawyer went to Mexico to acquire lands for Standard Oil of New Jersey.

When asked in 1922 by the Democratic leaders of his district to run for the State Senate, the lawyer agreed with some reluctance. He gave his consent, stated the Washington *Post*, on condition that he would not be obliged to campaign vigorously in that Republican stronghold. However, opposition to his nomination in the primaries aroused his campaigning instinct with the result that he defeated his Republican opponent. After serving in the State Senate from 1923 to 1927, Kee ran for the United States House of Representatives in the Fifth District of West Virginia in 1928, but lost the election. In 1932 he won his seat, to which he has been re-elected every two years, thus serving eight terms as of 1950. The Congressman is proud of the fact that he won his seat in that district in the face of its record of having elected only two Democrats to the House in the preceding forty years, and that for only one term each.

Before becoming Foreign Affairs Committee chairman, Kee was best known for his sponsorship in 1946 of the Foreign Service Act, drafted in the State Department, which aimed at providing the United States with well-trained career diplomats. As a New Dealer under Roosevelt and a Fair Dealer under Truman, Kee regularly supported State Department policies, including extension of the reciprocal trade act (1943), extension of Lend-Lease, the Bretton Woods agreement, the British loan, and full Marshall Plan appropriations. He was a member of the Joint Congressional Committee on Foreign Economic Cooperation. Kee favored admission of a maximum number of displaced persons to the United States, and the "good neighbor policy" in relations with Latin America. On domestic issues he voted for price control, rent control, civil liberties, the labor and tax programs. The Fulbright resolution (1943) had his "aye" as did the Federal soldier vote bill (1944). He lined up with the Administration against the bill to curb strikes in war industries and to outlaw them in Government-operated plants (1943), and against the maintenance of a permanent Un-American Activities Committee (1945). He voted to sustain Presidential vetoes of the Commodity Credit bill (1943), the Smith-Connally bill (1943), and of a bill to prohibit food subsidies (1944).

Kee succeeded to the post of chairman of the House Foreign Affairs Committee in March 1949, under the seniority rule, upon the death

Wide World Photos

JOHN KEE

of the previous chairman, Sol Bloom '43. He had been serving on that committee since his appointment to it at his own request when he first took his seat in Congress, and had earned a reputation for "serious application, and for finding legal language which reconciles conflicting points of view." On assuming the chairmanship Kee stated that he would follow a bipartisan policy, as had his predecessor, commenting that "this nation's foreign policy is not a political issue." In an article on this occasion, James Reston in the New York *Times* pointed out that the importance of the committee is growing with the increase in expenditures entailed by postwar foreign policy; it is the duty of the committee to study proposed expenditures and advise the House with regard to appropriations. Reston reported that at the opening of the Eighty-first Congress the demand for positions on the House Foreign Affairs Committee was greater than that for posts on any other, in strong contrast to the attitude formerly prevailing. The committee itself, in a statement on its position in the last Congress said, "The responsibility for the purse as it relates to foreign policy cannot be separated from the root and substance of foreign policy."

After his elevation to the Foreign Affairs Committee chairmanship, Kee continued to support the Administration in the House. In August 1949 he introduced the revised foreign military aid bill to extend such aid to North Atlantic Pact members and certain other specified noncommunist countries; in this connection he backed the President's request for full appropriations, asking his committee "to forget half-way measures and do the job right." To implement President Truman's Point Four program, he sponsored the State Department bill proposing authorization of a $40 million appropriation, creation of a Foreign Economic Development Administration and technical as-

KEE, JOHN—*Continued*

sistance to underdeveloped areas with the initiative in administration left to the participating countries. (Republicans introduced a rival bill proposing closer American administration of such aid.) Early in 1950 the West Virginian gave the House an analysis of the situation with regard to recognition of Franco Spain, urging resumption of full diplomatic relations. On the question of development of the hydrogen bomb, Kee has said that he would favor its production if the Joint Chiefs of Staff considered it necessary to meet any anticipated aggression.

Representative Kee gave his support to the Administration stand extending economic aid to Korea and Formosa until June 30, 1950, while adhering strictly to a policy of no military aid and no political interference. When former President Hoover [43] and Senator Robert Taft [48] urged early in 1950 that the United States extend naval aid to help hold Formosa against the Chinese Communists, Kee gave it as his opinion that such an action would eventually involve the army also and "put us in the gravest danger of starting World War III." With the Far Eastern Economic Assistance bill under debate in the House, his committee heard State Department answers to questions on Far Eastern policy sought in a resolution of Republican Representative John Davis Lodge [48]. In what has been regarded as a move to aid passage of the bill, the replies were made public (with the exception of two classed permanently secret) only after the bill on economic aid had been passed, and Kee then moved tabling the resolution.

Kee is on the roster of the Elks, Moose, Odd Fellows, Knights of Pythias, and Kiwanis, and is an honorary member of the Veterans of Foreign Wars. His fraternity is Phi Sigma Kappa, and his church, the Episcopal. The Representative's wife, Maude Elizabeth (Frazier) Kee, acts as his secretary. There are two children, James and Frances, and two grand-daughters.

Kee has been described as dapper; his gray hair is parted in the middle with "great exactitude." A lawyer who is said to prefer desk work to the courtroom, Kee has been called "scholarly, quiet, precise . . . friendly and unruffled."

References

> Congressional Directory (1950)
> Who's Who in America, 1950-51
> Who's Who in the Nation's Capital, 1934-35

KEECH, RICHMOND B(OWLING) Nov. 28, 1896- Judge

Address: b. c/o United States District Court, Washington, D.C.; h. 2746 Woodley Place, N.W., Washington, D.C.

One of twelve justices assigned to the United States District Court for the District of Columbia, Justice Richmond B. Keech was appointed in 1946. Previously he had been an administrative assistant to President Truman, a member of the Public Utilities Commission,

and a corporation counsel for the District of Columbia. He entered private practice of law in 1922. In a notable decision Associate Justice Keech in March 1950 found the United Mine Workers not guilty of contempt of court after striking members had disobeyed the order issued by their union officials to return to the pits, in accordance with an injunction from his court.

Richmond Bowling Keech was born in Washington, D.C., on November 28, 1896, the son of Leigh R. and Anne L. (Contee) Keech. His father was a member of the District of Columbia police force. The future justice received his early education in the public schools of the nation's capital, attending Business High School from 1912 to 1916. While at that school he played football, gaining the name of "Bullet" Keech for his fullback playing.

In 1917 young Keech entered Georgetown University, where his studies were interrupted during the period of World War I by service in the transport service of the United States Navy in the U.S.S. *Matsonia*. At the time of his discharge he held the rank of chief petty officer. He received a certificate from Georgetown University and subsequently entered the university's Law School. From that institution he obtained his LL.B. in 1922, and that same year was admitted to the practice of law in the District Court and the Court of Appeals in the District of Columbia. Keech also in that year became associated with the law firm of Gregory and Todd. He continued his studies at the Georgetown University Law School and in 1923 was granted an LL.M degree. In that year he was admitted to practice before the Court of Claims, and two years later before the Supreme Court. In 1924 he joined the law firm of Joseph A. Burkhart and Henry I. Quinn.

The next year, in 1925, Keech received his first public appointment—as assistant corporation counsel for the District of Columbia. Five years later, in 1930, President Hoover named him people's counsel of the District. In that position he remained until 1934, when he was appointed, by President Roosevelt, a law member and vice-chairman of the Public Utilities Commission. In 1940 he resigned from the commission to become District corporation counsel. With the coming of President Truman to the White House he became an administrative assistant to the Chief Executive. This title he held until November 1946, the month he received the Presidential appointment as Associate Justice of the District Court of the United States for the District of Columbia.

The District Court of the United States for the District of Columbia, by virtue of the authority of the United States over District of Columbia, has the jurisdiction of a State court as well as the jurisdiction which in a State would be exercised by the United States District Court. Thus its province covers cases involving the Federal Government. Justice Keech was presiding over the District Court in March 1948 when it issued a subpoena to John L. Lewis, head of the United Mines Workers, to appear before a Federal fact-finding board inquiring into a strike of that month by the miners against the soft coal operators. He was also the judge in September of that same year when Otis and Company was granted a temporary injunction halting an investigation by the National Association of Security Dealers into the Kaiser-Frazer stock case.

In February 1950 Keech was again presiding over the District Court when two Federal requests to halt an eight-month dispute between the United Mine Workers and the soft coal operators were presented. On application of the National Labor Relations Board, Keech ruled that four of the U.M.W.'s non-wage demands (maintenance of a union shop, a welfare fund for the benefit of U.M.W. members only, a provision that the miners were to work only when "willing and able," and the union privilege of calling "memorial" work stoppages) were illegal under the provisions of the Taft-Hartley labor law. Keech's decision was called, editorially, in the New York *Herald Tribune* "important in legal history" since it clarified the application of the Taft-Hartley law and marked the third time that a court had found a union refusing to bargain in good faith. Following his ruling, Judge Keech issued on February 11 two injunctions: one, in response to a request from the NLRB, restraining the union from engaging in a strike or slowdown in support of the four illegal contract demands; the second, in response to a request of the Attorney General, restraining the union from continuing the strike for ten days, pending a hearing to determine whether the injunction should be continued for eighty days as allowed under the "national emergency" provisions of the Taft-Hartley law. (On March 3, Judge Keech found it proper to issue the eighty-day injunction.)

When the striking miners refused to obey two "back-to-work" orders issued by officers of the U.M.W., Keech, on February 21, at the request of the Justice Department issued another injunction and at the same time cited the U.M.W. for civil and criminal contempt of court. In the ensuing trial, the Judge declared that the question before the court was "whether or not there has been compliance with the orders of this court." Justice Keech found the prosecution unable to shake the union position that the attitude and conduct of the miners were self-determined and that the union had fully complied with the court's restraining order. On March 2, 1950, he pronounced the U.M.W. not guilty of contempt. The Department of Justice entered an appeal from the decison. (During the month of court action, the union and the operators had resumed negotiations and soon after the not-guilty verdict had been rendered, agreement was reached on a new contract.)

In handing down his decision, Judge Keech remarked that he could not "convict on conjecture." A *Christian Science Monitor* editorial pointed out, "The question before Judge Keech was not one of expediency, but of law, precedent, and fact," and the *World-Telegram and Sun* commented, "His duty was to consider the evidence put before him and to apply the law as he saw it, and we think he did that." One

Wide World Photos
RICHMOND B. KEECH

result of the justice's decision has been the calling into question of the efficacy of the Taft-Hartley law, which lacks definite statement of the relations between the officers and members of a national union.

Justice Keech has been described as "a square-jawed man with close cropped hair." He is said to have "a tremendous liking for people." He is a member of the Bar Association of the District of Columbia and has served as its vice-president. He is also a member of the National Institute of Municipal Law Officers, the Barristers, the American Legion, and the Rotarians. His clubs are the Potomac Hunt, the National Press, and the Metropolitan; and Phi Alpha Delta is his fraternity. Judge Keech is a member of the Board of Trade and a director of the D.C. chapter of the American Red Cross. Unmarried, he makes his home with his mother. He owns a small farm near Potomac, Maryland. For relaxation he rides to hounds.

References

Who's Who in America, 1948-49
Who's Who in Law, 1937
Who's Who in the Nation's Capital, 1938-39
World Biography (1948)

KEKKONEN, URHO K(ALEVA) (kĕk′ kō-nĕn ōōr′hô kàl′ĕv-à) Sept. 3, 1900- Premier of Finland

Address: b. Office of the Prime Minister, Helsinki, Finland

Urho K. Kekkonen, Agrarian party leader, became the Premier of Finland and Minister of the Interior in March 1950. He had held the portfolios of Minister of Justice and of the Interior in several previous Cabinets, and during 1948-50 was Speaker of the Parliament.

A. Pietine, Helsinki
URHO K. KEKKONEN

Early associating himself with the Agrarian party, he engaged in legal work in municipal and government offices during 1927-36. Since 1936 he has been a member of Finland's Parliament. Kekkonen is also known for his work in behalf of refugees during World War II.

Urho Kaleva Kekkonen was born September 3, 1900, in Pielavesi, Finland, the son of Juho and Emilia (Pylvänäinen) Kekkonen. At the age of nineteen he was graduated from the senior high school at Kajaani. Next studying at the University of Helsinki, he took the higher law examination in 1926 and was awarded the degree of Bachelor of Civil Law in 1928, the year he became an attorney. In 1936 Kekkonen received the D.C.L. degree.

The young lawyer began his association with farm groups in 1927, when he was appointed counselor in the Agrarian party. He also became jurist of the Federation of Rural Communities in 1927, serving through 1931. His appointment as administrative secretary in the Finnish Ministry of Agriculture took place in 1932; that post he held until 1936, in the meantime becoming increasingly prominent in the Agrarian movement. In 1934 he was made a deputy member and in 1937 a full member of the central governing committee of the Agrarian party, serving until 1944; from 1934 to 1946 he was on its executive committee. Kekkonen was elected to Parliament in 1936 and served as a presidential elector in 1937, 1940, and 1943. Appointed Minister of Justice in Kallio's Cabinet in 1936, he next was Minister of the Interior in Cajander's Cabinet during 1937-39.

During 1940-43 Kekkonen was chief of the bureau for displaced persons, which aided many war refugees. Soviet troops had invaded Finland in November 1939; after a peace settlement had been made with Russia in 1940, Finland, under pro-German President Risto Ryti [41], joined the Nazis in fighting the Russians. In 1944 Kekkonen was one of the group which forced President Ryti to resign, to be replaced by Mannerheim [40]. Kekkonen had also served as adviser in the Ministry of Finance during 1943. In November 1944, when Paasikivi [44] became Premier of Finland, he appointed Kekkonen Minister of Justice, reappointing him in March 1945 after the general elections. Meanwhile, on March 3, 1945, Finland formally declared war on Germany, and on August 7, 1945, it resumed normal diplomatic relations with Soviet Russia.

When Paasikivi was elected to the Presidency on March 4, 1946, to fill Mannerheim's unexpired term, Mauno Pekkala of the pro-Communist Popular Democrats was appointed Premier. Kekkonen held no portfolio in this Cabinet. The year following the war (in 1946) he became a member of the executive board of the Bank of Finland, a post he still holds. As leader of the Agrarians, Finland's strongest party, Kekkonen in 1948 was elected Speaker of the Parliament, succeeding Karl August Fagerholm [48], Social Democrat, who had been appointed Premier after the July general elections of 1948. According to C. L. Sulzberger (New York Times, January 17, 1950), Kekkonen worked "hand-in-hand" with the Communists in "bitter efforts to unseat the Cabinet of his great rival, Fagerholm." In 1948 Kekkonen visited Russia to sign the Soviet-Finnish pact of mutual aid and friendship.

In the Finnish presidential election of January 1950, Kekkonen as leader of the Agrarians, opposed Paasikivi, who had the support of the four moderate parties (Social Democrats, Conservatives, Liberals, and Swedish party), and Pekkala, leader of the Popular Democrats. A hard-working campaigner, Kekkonen made more than two hundred speeches in remote parts of Finland, directing his words mainly against Fagerholm's farm policy. An intense cold wave over northern Finland on election day was said to have worked against Kekkonen's chances for winning, and of the three hundred electoral votes, Kekkonen received 63 to Pekkala's 65 and Paasikivi's 172. The Agrarian party, which in 1948 elections had polled the second largest number of votes, fell to fourth place in 1950, the Social Democrats registering the largest vote, the Popular Democrats second, and the Conservatives third.

Kekkonen was re-elected Speaker of the Parliament on February 1, 1950, by a vote of 177 to 19. On March 1 Fagerholm's Social Democratic Cabinet resigned. When Paasikivi began his second term as President, Kekkonen, who was charged by the President to form a new Government, favored a coalition of his own party and Social Democrats, with members of the Swedish minority, Liberals, and Communists. When the Social Democrats refused to cooperate with the Communists, on March 17 Kekkonen formed a coalition Cabinet of center parties, including ten Agrarians, three Swedish party members and two Progressives. Although it commanded only 75 seats of the 200 in Parliament, it was expected to obtain full Conservative support (thus assuring it 108 votes) and some Communist support. In addition to being Premier, Kekkonen heads the Ministry of the Interior, which includes the office of chief of police.

On assuming the Premiership, Kekkonen declared that Finland's foreign policy would continue to be tempered by strict official adherence to the ten-year pact of friendship and military assistance it had signed with the Soviet Union. Kekkonen and four members of his Cabinet belong to the board of the Finland-Soviet Union Society, which works for better relations between the two countries. In April 1950, at a gathering marking the second anniversary of the pact, Kekkonen stated that Finland would fight "if necessary" against any aggressor who tried to attack the Soviet Union through Finland.

When locomotive engineers went on strike in Finland in May 1950, Kekkonen issued an order drafting the train crews for military service in order to keep trains running. The engineers ignored the order, and organized labor threatened a general strike, whereupon representatives of labor and management asked Kekkonen to call on Fagerholm to act as mediator. The Government canceled its order conscripting the engineers, the strike was called off, and the issue of a general wage increase was referred to Parliament. Kekkonen's Cabinet was said (reported the New York *Times*) to have lost prestige as a result of its handling of the situation.

Other pressing domestic problems faced Kekkonen's Government. Though it had agreed to give civil servants a wage increase and had brought the Trade Union Federation and the Employers Federation together to plan for pegging wages to the cost-of-living index, there was still considerable Communist opposition to the agreement and Communist pressure for "no compromise on union demands." Farmers sought corresponding increases in prices of their products, while Government efforts to increase taxes met with Conservative opposition. To these demands were added difficulties in balancing the budget and the threat of inflation.

On the international scene Kekkonen set about improving relations with the Soviet Union, a goal which had been given priority in the Cabinet's program. The Premier and most of his Ministers signed the Communist-supported peace petition (which was launched by the Partisans of Peace convening in Stockholm in March 1950), demanding the outlawing of atomic weapons in warfare and branding the nation which first uses atomic weapons in war as a war criminal. Kekkonen on several occasions expressed displeasure over the publication of material unfriendly to the Soviet Union.

Under Kekkonen's leadership trade negotiations were resumed with the Soviet Union. These had begun in November 1949 but had broken down during Fagerholm's Government. A new delegation succeeded in drawing up an agreement with Russia, which was signed by Kekkonen in Moscow on June 13, 1950. Described as the "biggest trade pact in Finland's history," the agreement called for a $350,000,000 trade pact betwen the two countries from 1951 through 1955, and $30,000,000 worth of trade for the remainder of 1950. From 1951 to 1955, Finland agreed to sell from 40 to 70 per cent of exported machines, ships, and industrial products to Russia, and to buy in return oil, grain, fertilizers, steel, automobiles, machinery, and optical instruments. Prices after the first year were to be adjusted to world market conditions. On his return to Helsinki, Kekkonen, who had talked with Stalin while in Moscow, declared, "No political subject was ever touched upon during my meetings with the Russians, nor were any political demands presented to us."

A sportsman himself, Kekkonen was chairman of the sports division of the Finnish Gymnastics and Sport Association during 1929-31, becoming chairman of the Finland League for 1931-32. Since 1932 he has been chairman of Finland's Sport Association, and he was chairman of the Olympic Committee from 1938 to 1946. Married to Sylvi Uino in 1928, Kekkonen is the father of two children. He is known for his wit.

References

International Who's Who, 1950
Who's Who in Central and East Europe, 1935-36
World Biography (1948)

KELLY, EDNA F(LANNERY) Aug. 20, 1906- United States Representative from New York

Address: b. House Office Bldg., Washington, D.C.; h. 1247 Carroll St., Brooklyn, N.Y.

The first Democratic Congresswoman to be sent to Washington from Greater New York, Edna F. Kelly was sworn in the House of Representatives on January 3, 1950. For seven years, from 1943 through 1949, Representative Kelly had been research director for the Democratic party in the New York State legislature.

Of Irish ancestry, Mrs. Kelly was born Edna Patricia Kathleen Flannery on August 20, 1906, in East Hampton, Long Island, New York. Her father was Patrick Joseph Flannery, a horticulturist, and her mother is Mary Ellen (McCarthy) Flannery. Edna Kelly is one of seven daughters (two of whom were adopted), the only one who did not become a school teacher. She attended East Hampton High School, and Hunter College in New York City. As a high school student one of her extracurricular activities, in addition to basketball and hockey, was debating; it was with her high school debating team that she first traveled to Washington. At Hunter College she majored in history and economics. There, too, she participated in swimming, basketball, and golf, was a member of the student council, and president of Kappa Delta sorority.

Edna Flannery graduated from college in June of 1928, and was married to Edward Leo Kelly, a young Brooklyn lawyer, in East Hampton in the following October. Her husband was the son of the late William E. Kelly, who had been postmaster of Brooklyn for many years. Edward Kelly maintained his own law office in that borough until January 1942, when Governor Lehman appointed him city court justice there. During that time he was the politically active member of the family—Mrs.

EDNA F. KELLY

Kelly was interested "behind the scenes." Kelly was head of the Madison Democratic Club of the Eighteenth Assembly District for several years, while Irwin Steingut, later Mrs. Kelly's political friend and mentor, was district leader. Mrs. Kelly's activities at that time centered about her home, into which two children, William Edward and Maura Patricia, had been born.

Life was radically changed for Mrs. Kelly on August 22, 1942, when her husband was killed in an automobile accident. Not long afterward the widow became active in politics "to carry on in the Kelly family tradition." Steingut, then minority leaders in the New York State Assembly and leader of the Eighteenth Assembly District, encouraged Mrs. Kelly in her political work. She "rejuvenated" the women's auxiliary of the Madison Club, became a member of the New York State Democratic Executive Committee, and coleader, with Steingut, of the Eighteenth Assembly District.

In 1943 Mrs. Kelly received the position of research director for the Democratic party in the New York State legislature. Having had that experience, she was not uneasy at the prospect of entering Congress: when nominated she said: "I've been analyzing all sides of bills in the New York State legislature and making reports on them for seven years. I never knew when I'd be called to a committee meeting to explain certain aspects of bills. It has been good training, seeing different sides of questions. All these years I have been studying what went on in Washington" (New York *World-Telegram*, July 20, 1949). Among the bills which interested Mrs. Kelly most while she was at Albany were those concerned with slum clearance, State aid to education, schools for spastic children, and appropriations for youth recreation.

Nomination of Mrs. Kelly for Representative from the Tenth District was made at King's

County Democratic headquarters on July 15, 1949. Questioned as to why she thought she had been chosen, Mrs. Kelly pointed to her years in Albany. "Perhaps, too," she added, "the leaders may have decided that it would be a sound thing for the Democratic party in Brooklyn to express its confidence in women by nominating one to run in an election that looked like a sure thing" (New York *Herald Tribune*, November 13, 1949). The Tenth Congressional District, which includes the Eighteenth, First, and Seventeenth Assembly Districts, has been heavily Democratic for years. Its population is largely Catholic and Jewish. In Congress she succeeded the recently deceased Andrew L. Somers, who was a member for twenty-five years.

Mrs. Kelly, who in a pre-campaign statement had declared her willingness to support the Truman program, campaigned at dinners, meetings, and street-corner rallies in her neighborhood. She promised to support the United Nations, the Marshall Plan, the Atlantic Pact, civil rights, Federal aid to education, the extension of social security, and the admission of 400,000 displaced persons. She also advocated slum clearance, more Federal low-cost housing, called for full aid to Israel, and declared herself opposed to the Taft-Hartley measure and other legislation unfavorable to labor. She opposed excise taxes (with those on cosmetics specifically in mind), and pledged herself to the establishment of child-care centers and the investigation of milk prices, all matters considered to be of particular interest to the woman voter.

In her victory Mrs. Kelly polled 48,769 votes against Republican George H. Fankuchen's 15,112 and Liberal Jules Cohen's 24,505. She followed four other women from New York State into the House of Representatives; she is the youngest of the nine women in the House, the fifth on the Democratic side of the aisle. In addition to the issues she brought forward in her campaign she stated she intended to press for better educational standards in backward areas through Federal aid. She is opposed to the Barden bill '⁴⁰', believing that private and parochial schools as well as public schools should receive aid; she does not favor the granting of Federal funds for salaries and textbooks in privately supported schools (New York *Herald Tribune*, November 13, 1949).

Mrs. Kelly would like to be regarded as representing men as well as women in Washington. But she feels that women need to be more interested in politics; as first steps she suggests they learn the names of their local assemblymen, the location of their district club. The new Representative believes that a Congresswoman should know "that woman at the other end of your own block, the one whose husband recently lost his job" (*Christian Science Monitor*, December 10, 1949). She plans to fly home every weekend to make herself available to her constituents, and to be with her children in their two-storied brick home in Brooklyn.

Community work has occupied much of Mrs. Kelly's attention. She has been active in Catholic charities, the Immaculate Conception Day

Nursery, and in campaigns for the blind, cancer research, infantile paralysis, and the Red Cross; she is a director of Brooklyn's Youth United. Described as a handsome woman. Mrs. Kelly is tall and slender, with deep-set brown eyes, and sleek dark hair which she arranges in a knot at the nape of her neck. She is five feet nine inches in height and weighs 127 pounds. A sports enthusiast, she golfs, skis, skates, and swims, likes to watch hockey, basketball, and Brooklyn Dodgers games.

References

Christian Sci Mon p13 D 10 '49
Cue 18:16 D 3 '49
N Y Democrat 4:1 Jan-Feb. 1950 por
N Y Herald Tribune II p7 N 13 '49 por
N Y Sun p8 N 9 '49 por
N Y Times p15 Jl 16 '49 por
N Y World-Telegram p 11 Jl 20 '49 por

KEM, JAMES P(RESTON) Apr. 2, 1890-
United States Senator from Missouri

Address: b. Senate Office Bldg., Washington 25, D.C.; c/o Kem, Gordon, and Gilmore, Federal Reserve Bank Bldg., Kansas City, Mo.; h. 5353 Sunset Dr., Kansas City, Mo.

The junior United States Senator from Missouri, Republican James P. Kem, was elected to the upper chamber of the United States Congress in the sweeping Republican victories of November 1946. He has since earned the reputation in the Senate of being an outspoken critic of most of the Truman Administration's foreign and domestic policies. An attorney by profession, he is a comparative newcomer to politics, having practiced law for many years in Kansas City. Kem, whose six-year term ends January 1953, in 1950 holds membership in the Senate Agricultural and Forestry Committee, the Senate Public Works Committee, and the Special Committee on Remodeling the Senate Chamber.

James Preston Kem was born in Macon, Missouri, on April 2, 1890, the son of James P. and Evelyn Lee (Smith) Kem. After graduating at the age of sixteen from Blees Military Academy in Macon, he entered the University of Missouri, where he was a member of Beta Theta Pi fraternity. He received his Bachelor of Arts degree in 1910, and continued his studies at the Harvard Law School.

Obtaining his Doctor of Laws degree in 1913, Kem was admitted to the Missouri bar and began his legal career as a junior lawyer in the office of Warner, Dean, McLeod, and Langworthy. During World War I he served as a first lieutenant in the infantry of the United States Army (1917-19). He was admitted to the Wyoming bar in 1920 and to the Texas bar in 1926. Since the latter date he has been engaged in the general practice of law in Kansas City. In 1930 he was acting as general counsel and a director of the White Eagle Refining Company. He is, in 1950, a senior partner in the Kansas City law firm of Kem, Gordon and Gilmore, which handles corporation, tax, oil and gas, real property, and probate law.

Kem first became prominent in Kansas City politics in 1944, when he was chairman of the Jackson County Republican Committee and a delegate to the Republican National Convention. Entering the Missouri primaries in August 1946, he defeated his four opponents for the Republican Senatorial nomination. The Democrats had renominated Frank P. Briggs, who had been appointed to Harry S. Truman's old Senate seat in January 1945, after the latter had been elected Vice-President. Kem campaigned on a platform opposing "New Deal bureaucracy" and the revived Pendergast machine. According to P. J. Phelan-Rand (in the New York *Sun*), he countered Democratic campaign charges of his close association with big oil interests by showing a record that put him in the role of an instigator of the lawsuit that revealed the Teapot Dome scandal. On November 5, 1946, he won the Senatorial contest from Briggs by 61,012 votes. His election put two Republicans (the senior Senator is Forrest C. Donnell [49]) into the Missouri Senatorial seats for the first time since Civil War reconstruction days.

"I think the first objective of our governmental policy should be to restore the solvency of America," Senator Kem told a New York Herald Tribune Forum in 1949. "It is time to stop coddling socialism, both at home and abroad." Such considerations have determined the course of his voting record. Most conspicuously, he has fought the Administration's foreign policies. In 1947 he opposed Greek-Turkish aid and submitted an amendment to cut general foreign relief from $350,000,000 to $200,000,000, which the Senate rejected by a 64-to-19 vote. Although later that year Kem voted for stopgap aid to Europe, he offered several amendments to the bill, one of which required that every individual abroad who received any of the authorized aid be sent a notice that the United States was the donor. These amendments were approved by the Senate. When President Truman first announced the four-year European Recovery Plan in December, Kem stated: "I shall be unable to follow the President further in this foreign venture." Since 1948 he has backed efforts to cut ERP funds, contending that the Marshall Plan threatened to undermine American economy and provided no real protection against communism. He took a firm stand against military aid to China in 1948, and offered a substitute measure to reduce the admission of displaced persons to 70,000 a year (the Senate finally accepted a figure of 202,000 for two years).

Kem's amendment to withhold Marshall Plan funds from any country which further nationalizes its basic industries stirred up controversy in both sessions of the Eighty-first Congress; it was voted down several times and finally rejected. During the Senate debate Kem spoke of the "strange paradox of the United States spending billions of dollars in an effort to stop Marxist communism, but at the same time . . . spending billions of dollars to subsidize Marxist socialism." He also assailed the Administration for allowing Britain to use Marshall Plan dollars for wheat purchases in Canada while there was a surplus of wheat in the United

JAMES P. KEM

States. One of the thirteen Senators who voted against ratification of the North Atlantic Pact in 1949, Kem also voiced his opposition to extending the Trade Agreements Act and sending military aid to Europe. In 1950 he attempted unsuccessfully to deny Marshall Plan aid to any European coutry which exported goods with a war potential to Russia or any of her satellites. On June 27, 1950, he interrupted the reading of President Truman's statement ordering military action in Korea to ask if the President had "arrogated to himself the authority of declaring war." In August he voted for a loan of $100,000,000 to Spain.

On the domestic front Senator Kem has consistently advocated more local self-government, a balanced budget, and the elimination of bureaucracy. Measures he supported during the Eightieth Congress included income tax reductions, the Taft-Hartley bill, the ban on portal-to-portal pay suits, and antitrust exemption for railroads. With regard to rent control extension, he upheld proposals for a 15 per cent increase optional with tenants, and local state options on further controls. In the fall of 1947 he served on a subcommittee which investigated prices for the Joint Committee on the Economic Report. Favoring the peacetime draft in 1948, he introduced an amendment which the Senate adopted to improve the army court martial system. He was one of the sponsors of a farm policy bill to provide the Secretary of Agriculture with a revolving fund for the purchase of agricultural commodities to be processed and sold in occupied areas overseas. On the other hand, he was the leading opponent of extending the wartime program of importing farm laborers, but his proposal to spread the cost of the program among the farmers was defeated in the Senate. Strongly opposed to Federal aid to education, he also voted against the Federal housing program,

which he described as an "experiment in socialism."

During the Eighty-first Congress, Kem was also appointed to a special subcommittee to study proposals for a Missouri Valley Authority (1949) and an agricultural subcommittee to consider a bill to ban imports of canned pork from Europe (1950). He cast votes in favor of the Dixie-G.O.P. compromise revision of the cloture rule; cutting all Federal expenditures from 5 to 10 per cent; and allowing larger cotton and peanut plantings while regulating price-supported potato crops. He recorded a "Nay" on reducing farm price supports; on the provision allowing the Secretary of Agriculture to appoint Commodity Credit Corporation directors; and on the Kerr bill to exempt independent natural gas producers from price regulations by the Federal Power Commission.

A delegate to the Republican National Convention in 1948, Kem helped to swing the Missouri votes in support of Governor Thomas E. Dewey [44] as the Presidential candidate. The legislator is a member of the American, Missouri, and Kansas City bar associations, the Lawyers Association of Kansas City (president, 1943), the Cass County (Missouri) Farm Bureau, and the Missouri Farmers Association, Inc. In Kansas City he belongs to the Farmers' Club (president, 1942), the William S. Bland Post No. 50 of the American Legion, the Ivanhoe Masonic Lodge, the University Club, and the Country Club. He is a member of St. Paul's Episcopal Church in that city. Since 1943 he has served as a director of St. Luke's Hospital in Kansas City and he is also vice-chairman of the board of trustees of the University of Kansas City.

The Missouri Senator met his wife, the former Mary Elizabeth Carroll, while he was stationed at Camp Zachary Taylor in Kentucky during World War I. They were married in Louisville on January 12, 1920, and have two daughters, Carroll (Mrs. Virginius Randolph Shackelford, Jr.) and Evelyn. He is tall, gray-haired, and round-faced. Calling himself a "retired golfer," Kem lists walking and riding as his favorite forms of exercise; he also enjoys vacationing at his 160-acre Missouri farm near Belton, where he raises Shorthorn cattle.

References

N Y Herald Tribune X p28 O 30 '49
por
N Y Sun p20 N 18 '46
Congressional Directory (1950)
Who's Who in America, 1950-51
Who's Who in Kansas City, 1930
Who's Who in the Midwest (1949)
World Biography (1948)

KENDALL, EDWARD C(ALVIN) Mar. 8, 1886- Chemist
Address: b. c/o Mayo Foundation, Rochester, Minn.; h. 627 8th Ave., S.W. Rochester, Minn.

Dr. Edward C. Kendall, professor of biochemistry at the University of Minnesota under the Mayo Foundation, together with his medical colleague, Dr. Philip S. Hench '50, and Dr. Tadeus Reichstein of Switzerland, was awarded the Nobel Prize in medicine in 1950. Their achievement was discoveries concerning the suprarenal cortex hormones, their structure and biological effects. Between 1930 and 1938 Kendall isolated six hormones of the adrenal cortex, one of which (cortisone) in 1949 was used with dramatic results by Dr. Hench in the treatment of rheumatoid arthritis. Since 1914 the scientist has had the posts of professor of physiological chemistry and head of the section of biochemistry at the Mayo Foundation.

The son of George Stanley and Eva Frances (Abbott) Kendall, Edward Calvin Kendall was born on March 8, 1886, in South Norwalk, Connecticut. A student at Columbia University, he there received the B.S. degree (1908), the M.S. (1909), and the Ph.D. in chemistry (1910). During 1909-10 young Kendall was a Goldschmidt Fellow. Joining Parke, Davis and Company (Detroit) as a research chemist, he remained with that drug manufacturer until 1911, when he became attached to St. Luke's Hospital in New York City. Three years later the Mayo Foundation appointed him professor of physiological chemistry and head of the section of biochemistry, positions he still holds.

In December of 1914 Kendall saw for the first time the crystals of thyroxine, the active principle of the thyroid gland. "This minute quantity of thyroid hormone," wrote Richard Parke in the New York *Times* (June 13, 1950) "had been isolated, after months of labor, from some tons of cattle thyroids." When in 1925, Columbia University awarded him the Chandler Medal, it cited his work on the thyroid hormone—"which has made up for deficiencies in glandular secretions in countless human beings and helped them to grow normally." Another achievement was his isolation of glutathione from yeast, carried out between 1926 and 1930. This resulted in its preparation in crystalline form and the determination of its structure.

Kendall now began his research on the chemical nature, physiological activity, and synthesis of hormones of the adrenal cortex. By 1938 he had isolated six hormones of the gland which he named Compounds A, B, C, D, E, and F. Five of these, isolated in 1937, include "E," which was to become famous under the name of cortisone. "In the years following," related W. L. Laurence (New York *Times,* April 22, 1949), Kendall "succeeded, after enormous travail, in identifying the chemical structure and composition of the various adrenal compounds, and in accomplishing a partial synthesis, using as his starting material a complex substance named desoxycholic acid. Prepared from the bile secreted by the gall bladder of beef cattle, it took twenty-nine steps to go from the bile substance to the partial synthesis of Compound E."

At about the same time, Professor Tadeus Reichstein of Switzerland, who shares in the 1950 Nobel Prize, working independently of Kendall isolated twenty-eight compounds from the adrenal cortex, among which was Compound E. The potentialities of the compound, however, had to wait on its synthetic prepara-

Wide World Photos
EDWARD C. KENDALL

tion, since it existed only in minute quantities. A medical colleague of Kendall's at the Mayo Foundation (the third of the group named to participate in the Nobel award) Dr. Philip S. Hench had numerous consultations with Kendall. From clinical observations they arrived at the theory that the compound might be effective in rheumatoid arthritis.

In 1941 the committee on medical research of the Office of Scientific Research and Development listed Compound E as "one of the three most important fields for wartime chemical investigation." Merck and Company, pharmaceutical house of Rahway, New Jersey, sent Dr. Lewis H. Sarett to work with Kendall on the completion of the synthesis of the compound, named cortisone, of which the chemical term is 17-hydroxy-11-dehydro-cortico-sterone. (It belongs to the group of chemicals known as steroids.) Though Kendall had completed thirty of the thirty-seven steps required for its synthesis, it was not until December 1946 that the first microscopic bits of the hormone were produced. Two more years elapsed before there was enough to use in experiments on human beings. Cortisone is the first hormone of the adrenal cortex that relieves symptoms of rheumatoid arthritis to be prepared by partial synthesis. About that time the University of California and Yale University biochemists succeeded in extracting ACTH (adreno-cortico-trophic hormone), a pituitary hormone governing the activity of the adrenal cortex. Armour and Company became the manufacturer of ACTH.

In September 1948 Hench and two associates began to use cortisone and, later, ACTH on rheumatoid arthritic patients, with dramatic results. But, while patients felt complete freedom from pain and of swelling in the joints, neither substance cured the condition. On the other hand, the hormones have also brought significant relief to patients suffering from

KENDALL, EDWARD C.—*Continued*

usually fatal skin diseases, several eye disorders, and asthma. Since the preparation of these substances from ox bile is costly, it is hoped that certain plants in time may be developed as a new source.

That Drs. Kendall, Hench, and Reichstein had been named by Sweden's Caroline Institute of Medicine as the recipients of the Nobel Prize in medicine was made known October 26, 1950. For the ceremony of bestowal Kendall went to Stockholm in December.

During World War II Kendall served as a civilian with the Office of Scientific Research and Development. In addition to the Nobel and Chandler prizes, he has received the Lasker Award from the American Public Health Association, the Page One award from the Newspaper Guild, the Passano Foundation award, the John Scott prize from the City of Philadelphia, the Squibb award, and the medal of honor of the Canadian Pharmaceutical Manufacturers' Association. He has received honorary Doctor of Science degrees from the University of Cincinnati and Yale University. Since 1908 the biochemist has contributed numerous articles to medical and other scientific periodicals; he is also the author of the work entitled *Thyroxine* (1929). Kendall is a member of the American Physiological Society, Association of American Physicians, American Chemical Society, American Society of Experimental Pathology, the Society of Biological Chemists (president, 1925), Association for the Study of the Glands of Internal Secretions (president, 1931), the Harvey Society, Sigma Xi, and Sigma Alpha Epsilon.

Married to Rebecca Kennedy on December 30, 1915, Kendall is the father of two children. His political party is the Republican, his church the Congregational. The tall, gray-haired scientist is described as having a genial personality.

References

N Y Times p1+ O 27 '50
Sat Eve Post 222:28+ Jl 23 '49
American Men of Science (1949)
Who's Who in America, 1950-51
World Biography (1948)

KENNEDY, JOHN F(ITZGERALD) May 29, 1917- United States Representative from Massachusetts

Address: b. House Office Bldg., Washington 25, D.C.; h. 1400 34th St., N.W., Washington, D.C.; 122 Bowdoin St., Boston, Mass.

John F. Kennedy, Democratic Congressman from Massachusetts' Eleventh District, was elected to the United States House of Representatives in 1946. He is one of the youngest men to be seated in the House. Other distinctions had come to him before his entry into politics. For four years during World War II he served as a Navy lieutenant; while a senior at Harvard University he was author of *Why England Slept*, published in 1940; after his discharge from the Navy in 1945 he became a special correspondent for International News Service; he was chosen by the United States

Junior Chamber of Commerce as "one of the ten outstanding young men of 1946."

John Fitzgerald Kennedy was born May 29, 1917, in Brookline, Massachusetts, and was reared there. On both sides of the family, he has had predecessors who attained political and financial prominence. His father, Joseph Patrick Kennedy, Sr. '40, former United States Ambassador to Great Britain (1937-40), is a wealthy business executive. His paternal grandfather, Patrick Kennedy, served in the Massachusetts State Senate; and his grandfather on his mother's side (she was born Rose Fitzgerald), John F. Fitzgerald, is a former United States Congressman and onetime Mayor of Boston. When John was six years old, it was an especial treat for him to tour the Boston political wards with his grandfather Fitzgerald, who was then a candidate for the United States Senate. At other times, while Fitzgerald was Mayor of Boston the boy became an "audience of one" in the Mayor's study while his grandfather rehearsed campaign speeches. John was the second eldest of nine children—four boys (one deceased) and five girls (one deceased)—born to the Kennedys. He attended the public elementary schools in Brookline, Riverdale School in New York, and the Choate Preparatory School, in Connecticut.

Kennedy entered Harvard College, where he participated in various sports. When he was a sophomore and his brother (Joseph) a senior, the two youths won the MacMillan Trophy in intercollegiate sailing against the ten top college teams in the annual competition held off Cape Cod. John was also a backstroke swimmer on the Harvard team and played football and golf. He received a serious back injury in scrimmage which was to be the reason for his rejection when he tried to enlist in the Army and which required him to go through five months strengthening exercises before he was declared physically fit and was accepted by the Navy.

For a time in 1938 Kennedy was secretary to his father, who was then the United States Ambassador to Great Britain. The young man had taken a six-month leave from Harvard. On the eve of World War II he made trips to Poland, Russia, Palestine, Greece, Lebanon, Egypt, and Germany. Returning to the United States in the fall of 1939, Kennedy resumed his studies at Harvard, and was graduated *cum laude* in 1940, with a major in economics. (He had also taken courses in that subject at the London School of Economics in 1935-36.) At Harvard the young man wrote a thesis which became the basis of his book, *Why England Slept* (1940), with a foreword by Henry R. Luce. Intended to draw a warning parallel between England's unpreparedness for war and the danger of war to the United States, the book drew laudatory reviews from the critics: "A book of such painstaking scholarship, such mature understanding and fair-mindedness, and of such penetrating and timely conclusions, that it is a notable textbook for our times" (New York *Times*); "a startlingly timely, strenuously objective, book" (*Time*); "it contains much wisdom for older men" (London *Times*). The young writer, whose style was called "quiet and unassuming" by the *Christian Science Monitor*, was also to do a series of articles on Ireland for the International News Service.

Kennedy enlisted in the Navy in September 1941, three months before the Japanese attack on Pearl Harbor. As a PT boat commander he served with the rank of lieutenant during 1941-45 in the southwest Pacific. While operating in the region of the Solomon Islands, Kennedy's ship was rammed and sunk. The naval lieutenant was credited with saving the lives of three of the crew, one of whom he towed for three miles—for "extremely heroic conduct" he was awarded the Navy and Marine Corps Medal. The disabilities incurred, for which he received the Purple Heart, confined him to a military hospital in Massachusetts for a lengthy period prior to his discharge from the armed services in March 1945. Occasional recurrences of malarial attacks still trouble him.

Upon his return to civilian life, Kennedy became for a time a special correspondent for International News Service. Among his assignments were the San Francisco U.N. conference, the 1945 British election, and the Potsdam Conference. In April 1946 he announced his candidacy for Democratic nominee for Massachusett's Eleventh District in that fall's Congressional elections. (The incumbent, Democrat Mayor James M. Curley of Boston, was not a candidate for re-election.) On June 20 he won in the Democratic primary over a field of nine candidates, two of them veteran campaigners. For his campaign he enlisted the aid of a youthful "amateur brain trust"—friends from Harvard and the Pacific, and of the political veteran, his grandfather. Kennedy delivered about six speeches a day and a total of 128 in five months. He spoke frequently about the prospect of a struggle between collectivism and capitalism; in them the young candidate urged his audience "to battle for the old ideas with the same enthusiasm that people have for new ideas."

In the November 1946 balloting the strongly Democratic Massachusetts Eleventh District (which is one of the poorest in the State, with a population largely of Irish and Italian descent) elected Kennedy to represent it in the Eightieth Congress. In January 1947, accordingly, the new Representative took his seat in Washington, to which his constituents returned him for the Eighty-first Congress.

The Massachusetts Congressman did not consistently align himself with his party when he cast his vote. The record shows his stand in the chief domestic issues as follows: against the Taft-Hartley bill, the FEPC bill (which he thought was not strong enough—he had supported the original bill in committee), the bill to give Congress access to files of certain Government agencies, reduction in taxes, the Republican anti-inflation bill, the admission of Hawaii to Statehood; he supported broadening of provisions for social security, the draft bill, the pension bill for veterans, the extension of

Harris & Ewing

JOHN F. KENNEDY

Federal rent control, the cut in the general appropriations bill, the anti-poll tax bill (1949), and admitting Alaska to Statehood (1950). In international issues he opposed the reduction by 50 per cent of European arms aid (1949), voting for the passage of economic and military aid to Europe, economic aid to South Korea and China, and the admittance of 202,000 displaced persons.

The University of Notre Dame in January 1950 conferred an honorary Doctor of Laws degree on Representative Kennedy. Of the Roman Catholic faith, he is a member of The Knights of Columbus. He owns an interest in Chicago's Merchandise Mart. Each of the Kennedy children was given a million-dollar trust fund by their father so as "to dedicate themselves and their talents to the public service as fully and ably as they can." The young Massachusetts Representative, who is described as "boyish, well-built, sandy-haired," is six feet tall and weighs 150 pounds. He belongs to the Veterans of Foreign Wars, Disabled American Veterans, and the American Legion. He was named one of the ten outstanding young men of 1946 by the United States Junior Chamber of Commerce. Sailing is listed as his preferred recreation.

References

Look 10:32 Je 11 '46 por
N Y Journal-American Mag p12 My 30 '48 por
N Y Sun p20 S 25 '46 por
N Y World-Telegram p4 Ag 19 '43 por
New Yorker 20:31+ Je 17 '44
Who's Who in America, 1950-51
Who's Who in New England (1949)
Who's Who in the East (1948)

KENNEDY, WILLIAM P(ARKER) Apr. 3, 1892- Labor union official
Address: b. c/o Brotherhood of Railroad Trainmen, Standard Bldg., Cleveland 13, Ohio; h. 2120 West Forest Dr., Minneapolis 19, Minn.

Shortly after the death of A. F. Whitney [46], for twenty-one years head of the Brotherhood of Railroad Trainmen, William P. Kennedy in July 1949 was chosen by the board of directors to serve as president. Upon the expiration

Trainman News

WILLIAM P. KENNEDY

of that term, at the October 1950 convention he was elected to a new four-year term. As president, in 1949 Kennedy led his union in its forty-four-day strike against the Missouri Pacific Railroad and in October reached an agreement with management to arbitrate unsettled union claims. A member of the union since 1910, Kennedy has served as chairman and president of local units and as a member of the board of trustees of the organization. In 1946 he was elected its general secretary and treasurer.

William Parker Kennedy was born April 3, 1892, in Huttonville, a small town in the Province of Ontario, Canada. His father, William James Kennedy, a descendant of immigrants from North Ireland, was a weaver in the local woolen mills. His mother, Margaret (Parker) Kennedy came from a family of English immigrants. There was another son and a daughter in the family. Until 1902 the Kennedys lived in Canada, then moved to Chicago, Illinois, where William completed his elementary education. Influenced by an uncle, a locomotive engineer on the Great Northern Railway, the young boy decided to earn his living on the railroads. At seventeen he was a "news butcher," selling papers and magazines on the Rock Island line, between Chicago and Des Moines. A few months later, in October 1909, he was

hired as a freight brakeman for the Dakota division of the Great Northern Railway, remaining with that road until 1911, when he became a switchman for the Canadian Pacific Railway (May-October 1911). In the beginning of 1912, again as switchman, he went to work for the Chicago, Milwaukee and St. Paul Railroad, with headquarters in Minneapolis. In the Minnesota city he established his permanent residence—he remained with the same railroad until 1935, when his work for the union assumed full-time proportions.

Kennedy's association with the Brotherhood of Railroad Trainmen began in 1910: a freight brakeman, he joined the Wheat Sheaf Lodge 463, in Grand Forks, North Dakota. After moving to Minneapolis he became a member (in 1913) of the Minnehaha Lodge 625 of that city and served the local body as president and as chairman. In January 1920 he was elected secretary of the general grievance committee for union members employed by the Chicago, Milwaukee, St. Paul and Pacific Railroad, and the next year was elected general chairman of that committee. He served in this capacity until June 1935. From 1917 to 1928 he had attended the regular conventions of the Brotherhood of Railroad Trainmen as a delegate from his local unit. In 1928 he was elected to the board of trustees, and served as secretary until 1935. In that year he was elected vice-president and placed in charge of the union's membership in the northwestern territory of the United States and in that part of Canada west of Fort William and Port Arthur. While vice-president he negotiated the electric lantern agreements and in 1938 was in charge of the committee in Washington, D.C., which fought against the wage reduction proposals. From 1944 to 1946 he was in charge of the super-promotion department of the union at Chicago, and at the 1946 convention was elected general secretary and treasurer. In July 1949, on the death of A. F. Whitney, Kennedy was chosen president of the union. In the 1946-49 years he had served as national reporting officer for the Railroad Retirement Board and as secretary of the board of trustees of the Home for Aged and Disabled Railroad Employees of America.

A union with a 1950 membership of 200,000 railway employees, the Brotherhood of Railroad Trainmen was organized in 1883 at Oneonta, New York, and adopted its present name in 1899. Its 1,072 local lodges are located in the United States, Alaska, and Canada. One of the four independent unions which represent operating employees on the nation's railways, the Brotherhood of Railroad Trainmen has jurisdiction over both "in-road service" employees and "in-yard service" groups, including conductors, dining-car stewards, baggagemen, brakemen, yardmasters, switchmen, and car retarder operators. The Brotherhood is concerned with the development of operating rules and working conditions, such as the rates of pay, maximum amounts of mileage worked, and numbers of employees necessary for operating under prescribed safety regulations. As situations demand, the union appears before emergency boards appointed by the President of the United States, and union grievances are referred to the first division of the National Railroad Adjustment Board, which was established under the Railway Labor Act of 1934. Kennedy has stated that almost since that year many grievance claims have accumulated before the board, a good number of them during World War II.

It is with the settlement of these claims that Kennedy, as head of one of the four unions affected, has been concerned since becoming president. One example was the case of the Missouri Pacific Ralroad, whose trainmen had filed 1,838 complaints; by 1948 all except 282 claims had been settled, and those the management wished to bring before a board of arbitration. The union, however, contended that "questions of the validity of things which have been standard in railroad-union contracts for years" should not be subject to arbitration. It was then agreed upon that some of the claims did involve the establishment of new precedents in the operating procedure, particularly those touching upon the increased use of Diesel locomotives and the consequent reduction in the size of the operating forces. (*Fortune* estimated that about 50,000 fewer men will be needed to maintain Diesel than steam locomotives.)

By December 1948 it had been agreed by the four railroad brotherhoods to strike against the Missouri Pacific Railroad over the unsettled union claims, amounting to approximately three million dollars. The strike was postponed, however, pending new negotiations; and again, in June 1949, to permit intervention by the National Railway Mediation Board. This attempt to settle the issues failed and, under the provisions of the Railway Labor Act, a special fact-finding panel was created. Both groups had suggested arbitration, but the unions refused. On September 9, 1949, 5,000 engineers, firemen, conductors, and trainmen of the Missouri Pacific Railroad went on strike, curtailing transportation in the Mid- and Southwest served by the railroad for more than a month. At the end of that time the opponents had retreated from their original positions and had accepted the settlement proposed by Governors of the ten States affected. Under the terms of the agreement, 63 of the cases are subject to arbitration, the remainder to be adjusted under normal union procedure.

The head of the trainmen's brotherhood in 1949 launched a program to include yardmen and other operating employees in the forty-hour week for forty-eight-hour pay schedule granted nonoperating employees of the nation's railroads. This request, as well as other changes in the operating rules, was brought before the representatives of the major railroads in September 1949. Kennedy has also announced his intention to work for stricter safety rules and regulations and to fight for the repeal of the Taft-Hartley Labor Act. He favors improved pensions for railroad workers, extension of the Social Security Act, a national health insurance program, adequate housing, better living standards for all, and a comprehensive program for national conservation of natural resources. When the B.R.T. convened in October 1950 Kennedy was elected to a new four-year term, by a 824-229 vote.

Kennedy is affiliated with the Farmer-Labor party in his home State; in the 1949 New York State election, he urged the election of the Democratic candidate, Herbert H. Lehman, to the United States Senate. Kennedy, who lists basketball, football, and hockey as his favorite sports, is five feet, eight inches tall, weighs 175 pounds, and has brown hair and brown eyes. He was married January 21, 1913, to Amy Hannah Berglund and has a daughter, Phyllis, and three sons, R. P., W. H., and D. C. Kennedy. He is a Mason and a member of the Lutheran Church.

KERR, ROBERT S(AMUEL) Sept. 11, 1896- United States Senator from Oklahoma
Address: b. Senate Office Bldg., Washington, D.C.; h. 327 Northwest 18th St., Oklahoma City, Okla.; 120 Elmwood Rd., Kenwood, Chevy Chase, Md.

President Truman's first veto of 1950, which has been called "one of the most difficult decisions he has had to make on a domestic issue," was that of the natural gas bill sponsored by Senator Robert S. Kerr, Democrat, of Oklahoma. Kerr is serving his first term in the Senate. His career has been called "archetypically American": born in a log cabin in Indian Territory, he became a "self-made" millionaire with extensive oil interests, and was elected the first Oklahoma-born Governor of that State.

Robert Samuel Kerr was born on September 11, 1896, near Ada, in that part of Oklahoma then called Indian Territory, the second of seven children of William Samuel and Margaret Eloda (Wright) Kerr. His parents, of Scotch-Irish and English descent, had come from Texas, where his father had worked as a sharecropper, to build a frontier homestead. (Their first house was a fourteen-foot log cabin.) The elder Kerr, a stanch Southern Democrat and a self-educated man, was successively a farmer, a rancher, a rural school teacher, a merchant, and a cotton buyer. He served one term as clerk of Pontotoc County after Oklahoma became a State in 1907. His ambition and his advice are said to have been important in his son's career—he "never doubted Bob would be Governor of the new State." Young Kerr was educated in the public school at Ada, attended the East Central Normal School (also in Ada) in 1909-11, went on to Oklahoma Baptist University at Shawnee for one year, and studied at East Central again from 1912 to 1915. After two years of teaching in rural schools, he was a student for one year at the University of Oklahoma at Norman He worked in the law office of B. Robert Elliott at Webb City, Missouri, until the spring of 1917, when the United States entered World War I.

Although he was under age, Kerr entered the first officers' training camp established at Fort Logan H. Roots near Little Rock, Arkansas. As a second lieutenant of field artillery he was sent overseas in August 1918, but the armistice was signed before he went into active combat. He remained in the Officers' Reserve

Wide World Photos

ROBERT S. KERR

Corps after returning to civilian life, and in 1921 joined the Oklahoma National Guard, holding the rank of captain of field artillery (1921-25) and of major (1925-29). He was active in forming a local American Legion post; in 1924 he was elected post commander, in 1925 he was a judge advocate, and in 1926 served as State commander.

Following his army service, Kerr and two friends entered the wholesale produce business in Ada, but lost their borrowed capital when the warehouse was destroyed by fire. He then turned to a law career, studying in the law office of J. F. McKeel. Passing the State bar examination in 1922, he practiced in Ada as a member of the firm of Kerr, Lambert and Conn.

In 1925 Kerr went to work for a brother-in-law who owned a small oil drilling business. The following year he bought out the business on a mortgage basis, borrowed working capital, and moved to Oklahoma City, where oil had just been discovered. According to Marquis W. Childs, writing in the *Saturday Evening Post*, Kerr's entrance into "big-time" oil production was a result of his being asked by a representative of the Phillips Petroleum Company "to take charge of a campaign to convince the voters of Oklahoma City that it was in their own best interest to approve drilling operations" inside the city. As a reward for his successful completion of this campaign, his drilling company was employed to drill Phillips Petroleum wells, with a share in the wells as part of the payment. Kerr formed a partnership with D. A. McGee, a Phillips employee, in 1936. Today, the Childs article said, "Kerr-McGee Oil Industries, Inc., [of which Kerr is president] with branches in Louisiana and Wyoming, is in every phase [of the oil business] except distribution." Kerr's personal fortune is estimated by Childs at about $10,000,000.

In the spring of 1942 Kerr realized his father's ambition by running for Governor of Oklahoma. Winning an easy victory over Gomer Smith in the primaries, Kerr was elected by a majority of only 16,000, and narrowly missed having a Republican majority in the lower house of the State legislature. However, he was successful in obtaining legislation which achieved most of his announced objectives: a sound fiscal program, retirement of the State debt, a businesslike administration, and curbing of the power of the Governor. His administration also emphasized soil conservation and agricultural and industrial development. In 1944 he convened a three-day "clinic" of 700 farmers and others to study new industrial crops which could be raised in the Southwest.

Kerr's chief aim, he declared, was to "humanize the Governor's office," and he is said (by one biographer, Otis Sullivant, Capitol reporter for the *Daily Oklahoman*), to have "won support for his program in quiet, congenial conferences" rather than by patronage and use of "the political club." The Oklahoma Governor's vigorous support of a fourth term for Franklin D. Roosevelt and his record as keynote speaker in several State Democratic conventions, were cited by the press as probable reasons for his choice to make the keynote speech at the Democratic National Convention of 1944. His speech, which according to the New York *Times* was based on the dual themes of all-out support for "Roosevelt, Commander in Chief," and "indictment of the Republicans and [their] ticket," brought Kerr into the national political limelight. His name was frequently mentioned in the press as a Vice-Presidential candidate, although Kerr denied having such aspirations. In the ensuing campaign he spoke throughout his own State and in nine other Southern and Midwestern States.

In his successful campaign for the Democratic nomination to the Senate in 1948, Kerr's opponent was again Gomer Smith. His election to the Senate, against what *Time* called "the best organized and best financed campaign in years" of Ross Rizley, former Representative, was by a majority of 170,000. On October 22, shortly before the election, Senator William Jenner, Republican of Indiana, chairman of the Senate Elections Investigation subcommittee, charged that Kerr had spent on his campaign $61,140 more than he reported, or $59,500 more than the Oklahoma law allows. After the election, the matter was referred to the Eighty-first Congress, and Kerr called the charges (as quoted by the New York *Times*) "utterly, totally, and, I believe, maliciously false." In July 1949 the Senate Rules Committee unanimously dismissed the charges.

Kerr's record in the Senate has been generally one of support of the Truman Administration. He has, however, adhered to a campaign promise that, when civil rights were involved, he would vote in accordance with the laws of Oklahoma, laws for strict racial segregation. In the first session of the Eighty-first Congress he voted for Federal aid to education, for a long-range housing bill, for rent control extension, for the extension of ECA; his vote was against cuts in appropriations to farm aid, labor, and rivers and harbors improvement. He testified before the Senate Appropriations Committee in favor of the Southwestern Power Administration appropriation. He opposed nonsegregation bills for schools and housing, and an antifilibuster bill. He opposed the bill designed to keep the basic principles of the Taft-Hartley law, favored the creation of a Department of Welfare and an amendment providing for a change in the method of electing the President and Vice-President. In the international sphere, he voted for the North Atlantic Treaty and for the arms aid bill. During the second session he favored the equal-rights-for-women amendment, voted for repeal of the Federal tax on margarine, and for the bill providing for middle-income housing. In the first session Kerr was assigned to the Committee on Interior and Insular Affairs and the Committee on Public Works; in the second session, to the Finance and Public Works committees.

One of the most controversial issues in Congress during that 1950 session was Kerr's own "natural gas bill," which "tore the usual party line-ups to ribbons." The bill, in the form of an amendment to the Natural Gas Act of 1938, would have exempted "independent" producers of natural gas (those who do not distribute gas themselves, but sell it to interstate pipeline companies) from the rate-fixing authority of the Federal Power Commission. One of the early issues was the failure of the Senate to confirm the President's reappointment of Leland Olds, an opponent of the bill, to the Federal Power Commission in 1949. In March 1950 the bill was passed by Congress by the narrow margins of 44 to 38 in the House, and 176 to 174 in the Senate. Kerr and the supporters of his bill contended that the bill would prevent the Government from treating natural gas as a public utility, and that competition among producers would keep prices and profits down. The bill's opponents declared that concentration of ownership among "independent" producers amounted to monopoly, and that removal of price control would result in a possible rise of from $300,000,000 to $500,000,000 a year in the cost of gas to consumers. Supporters of the bill included Sam Rayburn, Speaker of the House, and Senator Tom Connally of Texas. Truman's veto of the bill was called by Joseph C. Harsch in the *Christian Science Monitor* "probably the most difficult and painful action he felt impelled to make since he became president of the United States." Kerr told the American Petroleum Institute that "the veto has made the threat of Federal regulation of gas production more nearly a reality. . . .Producers will not be free to sell more gas for present consumers —nor any gas for future consumers."

The Oklahoma Senator has been a member of the Democratic National Committee since 1940. In 1945-46 he was a member of the executive committee of the National Governors' Conference, and was chairman of the Southern Governors' Conference. He served as a special justice in the Oklahoma Supreme Court in 1931, was on the Unofficial Pardon and Parole Board of his State (1935-38), and was president of the Oklahoma County Juvenile Council (1935-36). He held the position of president of the Kansas-Oklahoma division of the Mid-Continent Oil and Gas Association from 1936 until he resigned in 1941 to run for the Governorship. In 1946 he served on the Interstate Oil Compact Commission. He is on the board of directors of Republic Supply Company and is board chairman of the West Central Broadcasting Company; with his wife, he holds a 60 per cent interest in two radio stations, one in Oklahoma, another in Illinois. Active in such organizations as the YMCA and the Red Cross, Kerr is also a member of the Forty and Eight Club, the Last Man's club, and the Masonic order. In 1944 he served as president of the Oklahoma Baptist General Convention. He belongs to the Beacon Club of Oklahoma City, and to the Tulsa Club.

Kerr's first marriage was to Reba Shelton, on December 5, 1919. After her death in February 1924, he married Grayce Breene on December 26, 1925. Their four children are Robert Samuel, Jr., Breene Mitchell, Kay, and William Graycen. The whole family is extraordinarily tall: the Senator is six feet, three inches, his wife five feet ten and a half inches, and all their children except the youngest (as yet not full grown) are six feet or over. Mrs. Kerr, who studied singing before her marriage, takes an active part in her husband's political life. Kerr, who weighs about 245 pounds, has been called "a large and lively man . . . full of agility and bounce." An officer in the Baptist Sunday School when he was ten, he is now chairman of the Oklahoma Baptist Orphans Home Committee, and for twenty years he taught a large Sunday school class at the First Baptist Church of Oklahoma City. In his speeches biblical references are frequent. (Mrs. Kerr and the children attend the Christian Science Church.) Kerr is "personally and politically dry," and has campaigned to keep Oklahoma a dry State. He likes to "swap yarns" with anyone he meets. His chief recreation is fishing—he manages to spend part of every year at his fishing lodge on Pelican Lake in northern Minnesota. An aviation enthusiast, he flies in his own plane on many trips. He likes chess, bridge, cribbage, and poker. An observer once said of him: "He can talk the language of the farmer, the laborer, the banker, the business executive. He has a genuine enthusiasm for people, a friendliness that is real."

References

N Y World-Telegram and Sun p15 Ap 8 '50
Sat Eve Post 221:22 Ap 9 '49
Congressional Directory (1st ed., 1949)
Gunther, J. Inside USA (1947)
Salter, J. T. ed. Public Men In and Out of Office (1946)
Who's Who in America, 1950-51
World Biography (1948)

KERST, DONALD W(ILLIAM) Nov. 1,
1911- Physicist
Address: b. c/o Physics Research Laboratory,
University of Illinois, Urbana, Ill.; h. 507 S.
Willis Ave., Champaign, Ill.

The world's largest betatron, which accelerates the speed of electrons to such a degree that they split the meson from the atomic nucleus, was demonstrated for the first time on February 28, 1950, at the University of Illinois

DONALD W. KERST

by Dr. Donald Kerst, its inventor. The betatron, also known as a rheotron, has been perfected to its present power by Kerst, who presented his first model to the scientific world in 1940, his second in 1941. The second model has been manufactured commercially for use in industrial radiography and in electron therapy of cancer; the present model, with its power of 300,000,000 X-ray volts, will be used exclusively for nuclear research. Kerst has been a member of the physics faculty of the University of Illinois since 1938. He had been granted two leaves of absence, the first in 1940 for concentrated work on the development of the betatron at the laboratories of the General Electric Company at Schenectady, New York, and the second from 1943 to 1945 for work on the atomic bomb project at Los Alamos, New Mexico.

The son of Herman Samuel and Lillian (Wetz) Kerst, Donald William Kerst was born in Galena, Illinois, on November 1, 1911. The family moved to Wauwatosa, Wisconsin, where the youth attended the town's high school. It was at this time that he discovered his interest in science while assisting a neighbor in the construction of an amateur radio station. He completed his education at the University of Wisconsin, receiving his B.A. degree in 1934 and his Ph.D. in 1937. In 1938, after a year

of work on X-ray tube development with the General Electric X-ray Corporation, Kerst became an instructor in physics at the University of Illinois. He was made assistant professor in 1940, associate professor in 1942, and full professor in 1943.

Kerst's research into the nature of the atom began while he was still at work on his Ph. D. at the University of Wisconsin. He and two other physicists, Dr. R. G. Herb and D. B. Parkinson, conducted experiments in 1936 with the aid of an electrostatic generator newly developed at the university; it permitted them to hurl protons at a velocity of 15,000 miles a second. On December 27, 1941, *Science News Letter* announced that Kerst had achieved "a new instrument of research. . . .called by him the rheotron" and capable of accelerating electrons to a velocity approximating the velocity of light, or 186,000 miles a second. This prototype of today's betatron, constructed by Kerst at the University of Illinois in 1940, was described by *Time* as "a 2,300,000-volt table-top model" of the 20,000,000-volt machine which Kerst constructed in 1941 for the General Electric Company at its laboratories in Schenectady, New York. "The heart of the betatron," explained Kerst, "is a doughnut-shaped glass vacuum tube between the poles of a large electromagnet" (*Time*, December 29, 1941). The magnetically guided electrons given off from a hot filament inside the tube were constantly accelerated in their rotation by electrical impulses until they achieved the energy of 20,000,000 volts at which time they were either released from the tube as a beam of beta rays, source of the betatron's name, or were bombarded at a metal target to create X rays. Kerst shipped the 20,000,000-volt betatron to his laboratory in Illinois, and returned to the university for experiment with the completed machine while the General Electric Company commenced the construction of what was then considered a "giant 100,000,000-volt model" based on Kerst's design.

The physicist's 20,000,000-volt betatron, although perfected for general use in 1941, was not offered commercially until November 1946. It was then revealed that the United States Government had made wartime use of the machine on the Manhattan (atomic) Project and in arsenals. The New York *Times* (November 15, 1946), reported Kerst as saying that "virtually all fields of industry have an immediate or potential interest in the unit." The commercial betatron was a five-by-ten-foot machine housed behind three-foot thick reenforced concrete walls in a specially designed building. Kerst described the machine as a "dependable, foolproof and economical tool with the radiation ability to penetrate twenty inches of steel in twenty minutes and detect flaws of .002 inches." Picatinny Arsenal in New Jersey had used one of these units to detect those flaws in shells and bombs that might otherwise have caused premature explosions.

Kerst's work on the betatron during the war had again extended its application. Whereas previously it had been used only to produce high-voltage X rays (*Newsweek*, August 5, 1946), Kerst announced shortly after his return to the University of Illinois from Los Alamos that the betatron could now achieve a 22,000,-000-volt free-electron beam with which he and other physicists at the university hoped "to penetrate the core of the atom and study the nucleus in a way never before possible." In the meantime, *Science News Letter* in its issue of June 10, 1944, had already published the announcement by Prof. G. M. Almy, physicist of the University of Illinois, of "plans for the postwar construction of a 250,000,000-volt betatron, also called the rheotron, the most powerful X-ray and atom-smashing machine ever built, which will open wholly new fields to scientific research by bringing cosmic ray effects into the laboratory." In 1947, with this super-betatron already under construction at Urbana-Champaign, Illinois, Kerst is quoted in the *Christian Science Monitor*, (January 14, 1947) as follows: "As soon as the first betatron began to work, an obvious desire was to plan for the production of particles with energies which we have observed only in cosmic rays—in particular, the production of mesotrons, the heavy electrons which have been observed in cosmic rays." The mesotron, or more commonly, the meson, is the fourth basic particle of subatomic matter (in addition to the proton, the electron, and the neutron) whose existence was forecast in 1935 by the Japanese physicist, Hideki Yukawa [50], Nobel Prize winner.

"That most ephemeral and mysterious particle of matter, the meson" (*Life,* March 22, 1948) is believed to be the "binding force that holds nuclei together." Heretofore mesons have had to be studied by means of high altitude balloons equipped with special photographic apparatus to record their passage once they had been split from nuclei in the earth's atmosphere by the incoming cosmic rays. Kerst's new betatron, with the enormous energy that it will impart to the beam of electrons, is designed to bombard nuclei with such force that the meson will be released for convenient study.

The first public demonstration of the super-betatron, after fifteen months spent in its construction and assembly, took place in "Betatron Barn" at the University of Illinois on February 28, 1950. When asked by reporters about the meson and the "elusive secret of what holds the nucleus of the atom together," Kerst (according to *Life* magazine) replied: "To ask what we expect to find is like asking what one would expect to see if he were going to look around a corner beyond which he never before had peered. This machine will at least take us up to that corner." Only two days, however, after Kerst's machine was unveiled, it "fulfilled his hopes and produced torrents of mesons." Photographs of the trails of the released mesons were obtained, and *Life* conjectured that "by amassing this kind of data physicists may find out what the meson is and how it behaves."

In 1945, at a joint meeting of the National Academy of Sciences and the American Philosophical Society held at the University of Pennsylvania on November 17, recognition had been given to Kerst with the award of the Cyrus B. Comstock Prize. This honor, with $3,000, is awarded every five years by the National Academy of Sciences; it was presented to Kerst

for "his pioneer work in connection with the development of the betatron and the results which he has obtained with this new and powerful scientific tool." Frank B. Jewett of the National Academy, in making the award, announced that Kerst had been selected for the honor in 1943, but that "wartime secrecy in all work involving nuclear physics" had delayed the award until 1945. Kerst also received the John Scott Award in 1947. He holds, as well, an honorary doctorate in science from Wisconsin's Lawrence College (1942). Among the scientific periodicals for which he has written are *Review of Scientific Instruments, Radiology, Nature,* the *Physical Review,* the *Scientific Monthly,* and *American Scientist.*

Kerst is six feet two inches in height, weighs 155 pounds, has blue eyes and light-brown hair. Married on August 12, 1940, to Dorothy Birkett, he has two children, Marilyn Elizabeth and Stephen Marshall. The physicist, who is a Protestant, lists his favorite recreations as canoeing and skiing.

References

American Men of Science (1949)
Who's Who in America, 1950-51

KHAN, BEGUM LIAQUAT ALI Pakistan women's leader

Address: Kahkashan, Muzaffarnagar, Dominion of Pakistan

Often referred to as "the Mrs. Roosevelt of the East," Begum Liaquat Ali Khan, wife of Prime Minister Liaquat Ali Khan of Pakistan, made with her husband an official visit to the United States in May 1950, and gave lectures on the customs, problems, and future of her country. A professor of economics at a Delhi college before her marriage in 1933, she is a foremost leader in women's activities in Pakistan.

Almora, a hill resort in what was then the United Provinces of India, is the birthplace of Begum Liaquat Ali Khan, whose name, prior to marriage, was Raana Begum ("'Begum'", an official of the Pakistan Consulate in New York City has explained, "has become in my country the equivalent to the English 'Miss' or 'Mrs.'; while 'Khan,' once strictly a title, is now often used as part of a proper name, like the English surnames 'Knight' or 'Lord.'") She attended the Wellesley Girls' High School at Naini Tal and the Isabella Thoburn College in Lucknow, the latter an American-endowed and operated institution.

After receiving the B.A. degree in 1927 from Thoburn College Raana Begum entered Lucknow University, where she was the only girl student in her class, and in 1929 took first place in the examination for the M.A. degree in economics and sociology. Her thesis, "Women Labor in Agriculture in the United Provinces, India," was pronounced the best of the year and brought her what an official biographical release describes as "a very high honors grade and great praise from her professors." In 1929-30 she took the graduate teachers training course at the University of Calcutta, winning

BEGUM LIAQUAT ALI KHAN

first place in both theory and practice of teaching. After six months as an instructor in a high school for girls in Calcutta, she was appointed professor of economics at the Indraprastha Girls' College at Delhi. There she taught for a year and a half, until her marriage to Liaquat Ali Khan in April 1933.

In Moslem India (now Pakistan), Begum Liaquat Ali Khan has frequently explained to interviewers, it is usual for the mother to choose the daughter's husband, though no marriage takes place without the daughter's consent; and she believes that "there's a lot to be said" for arranged matches. She adds, however, that her own was a love match. "I heard Mr. Ali Khan give a speech in the assembly," she has said, "and that got me." The "assembly" was the United Province Legislative Council, to which the future Premier of Pakistan had been elected in 1926, and in which he became leader of the Democratic party.

In 1936, when Liaquat Ali Khan became honorary secretary of the All-India Moslem League and the "right-hand man" of the League's President, Quaid-i-Azam Mohammed Ali Jinnah '48, the Begum worked with her husband; she learned to typewrite so as to help him as well in his correspondence. Four years later (1942), Liaquat Ali Khan became a member of the Central Legislative Assembly and deputy leader of the Moslem League party. In October 1946 he was named first Finance Minister in the interim government of India formed after British Prime Minister Attlee's '47 promise, in the House of Commons on March 15 of that year, that India would be granted independence; and in December he was one of four Hindu and Moslem leaders who conferred with British officials in London and worked out the plan for the partitioning of the former Indian Empire into the independent nations of India and Pakistan.

Pakistan (with a population of about 76,000,000 and an area of over 357,000 square miles of territory in its two separated regions—one to the northwest and the other to the northeast of the Indian peninsula) became a self-governing nation on August 15, 1947. At the new capital, Karachi, Liaquat Ali Khan took oath as Prime Minister after Mohammed Ali Jinnah had been installed as Governor General. The birth of the new nation was accompanied by widespread violence, especially in the Punjab; and three days after independence the provincial capital, Lahore, was in ruins, with starvation and cholera rife. The new Premier hurried to the scene; and it was at this time that his wife stood forth as a leader of Pakistan's women.

"Being with my husband, I was in the thick of it when refugees by the hundred thousand started pouring in," she was later to tell reporters. "I appealed to women to come forward, as they have born in them the ability to do some sort of nursing." Thus the Pakistan Women's Voluntary Service was established; in addition to nursing, the volunteers instituted employment, marriage, and missing persons bureaus, refuges for the homeless women, and other services. The problem of overcoming the shortage of trained nurses at first presented "uphill work" to the Begum, as it "entailed a clash" with ancient customs and prejudices. Combating these obstacles, she worked for betterment in the living conditions, wages and social status of the nursing profession, and on subsequent visits to England was able to arrange for English nurses to go to Pakistan to give training, and also for English hospitals to accept Pakistan nurses for training. (The Premier, who is an Oxford graduate, is known as a firm believer in close, cordial relations with Great Britain.)

A second organization established by the Premier's wife is the Pakistan Women's National Guard, under military control, of which she is chief comptroller with the honorary rank of brigadier. "The women serve voluntarily and part time," stated an account in the *Christian Science Monitor*. "There is compulsory training in drill and nursing, and optional training in rifle drill. Advanced training includes shorthand, typing, ciphering, signals, ambulance driving and canteen work." Three battalions consisting of about 2,400 girls was the strength by 1949-50.

In March 1948 Begum Liaquat Ali Khan organized and became president of the Pakistan Cottage Industries Association, which has as its object "providing steady and fair employment and wages for millions of village and refugee men and women, and of finding a suitable market for their goods." In June 1949, the association opened a Pakistan Cottage Industries Emporium; the work had previously been housed in the Begum's residence. The project is financed by gifts, and is managed by voluntary workers. All profits go to charities.

In February 1949, the wife of the Prime Minister, believing that "an all-Pakistan organization . . . to coordinate the women's work and activities" was "long overdue," established the All-Pakistan Women's Association. This association of which Begum Liaquat Ali Khan is president, is open to all women of Pakistan regardless of creed, and has become affiliated with the International Alliance of Women. It also maintains contacts with the General Federation of Women's Clubs in the United States. In the summer of 1949, when *America's Town Meeting of the Air* made a round-the-world tour, Begum Liaquat Ali Khan arranged a panel broadcast at Karachi in which four representatives of the association participated. Another of her activities is as a member of the Karachi Educational Inquiry Committee set up "to deal with general educational problems and suggest future plans and requirements." Under the interim constitution, women over twenty-one years of age have the vote in Pakistan, provided they can pass a literacy test (over half the population is today illiterate).

During May 1950 the Pakistan Premier and his wife were the guests of the United States on a good-will tour, and visited Washington, New York, Chicago, Boston, San Francisco and other cities. In the course of the visit Begum Liaquat Ali Kahn lectured at Town Hall and Barnard College in New York City, at Hood College in Frederick, Maryland, at Stanford University, before the California World Affairs Council, and at numerous women's clubs. She was a guest on Mrs. Eleanor Roosevelt's television program. Told that she was called "the Mrs. Roosevelt of Pakistan," she appeared to enjoy the remark. "But I'm afraid I am not half as brilliant as she is," she commented.

"Dark, serene, and very bright," is a descriptive phrase applied by writer Elise Morrow to Begum Liaquat Ali Khan; Elizabeth Maguire called her "quick-witted and gracious." During her American visit she revealed herself as an enthusiastic shopper, taking particular delight in purchasing cowboy suits and equipment for her two young sons, Ashraf and Akbar. A lover of books, she is also "an accomplished player of the piano and guitar," has "a very pleasant alto singing voice" and a "keen and critical appreciation of classical Western music."

References

Christian Sci Mon p4 My 17 '49 por; p10 My 12 '50
Ind Woman 29:173 Je '50 por
N Y Times p11 My 5 '50 por
San Francisco Chronicle p2 My 21 '50 pors
Washington (D.C.) Post p2B My 5 '50

KING, WILLIAM LYON MACKENZIE Dec. 17, 1874—July 22, 1950 Canadian statesman; Deputy Minister of Labor 1900-08; first elected to Parliament 1908; Minister of Labor 1909-11; leader of the Liberal party 1919-48; Prime Minister 1921-25, 1926-30, 1935-48; promoted policy of closer relations with the United States and greater nationhood for Canada within the Commonwealth of Nations; scholar in the fields of economics and political science; author of *Industry and Humanity*. See *Current Biography*, 1940.

Obituary

N Y Times p1 Jl 23 '50

KINGSLEY, J(OHN) DONALD Feb. 25, 1908- United Nations official
Address: b. c/o International Refugee Organization, Geneva, Switzerland

J. Donald Kingsley is the Director-General of the International Refugee Organization, the specialized agency of the United Nations charged with the resettlement or repatriation of the many thousands who became "stateless"

Official United Nations Photo.
J. DONALD KINGSLEY

as a result of the war. The author of books and articles on public affairs, he was formerly an administrator in the United States Government and professor of government at Antioch College, in Ohio. He entered his U.N. post in July 1949.

The eldest of three sons, John Donald Kingsley was born February 25, 1908, in Cambridge, New York, where his father, John Henry Kingsley, was a high school principal. His mother was the former Carolyn Donaldson. The elder Kingsley subsequently went to Albany where from 1919 to 1938 he was an educator in the Albany public school system, the last five years as assistant superintendent. After attending Syracuse University young Kingsley received his B.A. degree in 1929. On a fellowship for the year 1929-33, he earned his M.A. degree at Syracuse's Maxwell School of Public Affairs in 1930, and his Ph.D. in 1933; he had worked as an employment research assistant and as an instructor at the university while pursuing graduate studies. During 1933 he was an instructor and in 1935 an assistant professor at Antioch College in Ohio; he returned to Syracuse to teach in the three summer sessions of 1935-36.

Public Personnel Administration (1936), was written by Kingsley in collaboration with William E. Mosher, director of the Syracuse School of Public Affairs. It is "a study of methods

KINGSLEY, J. DONALD—*Continued*

employed by public bodies, national, State and municipal, in their dealings with civil servants and other public employees . . . together with suggestions for improvement of the public service." The 1940 edition (revised) was described by the *Annals of the American Academy of Political and Social Science* as "a contemporary record of present personnel policies and methods which should prove of great value to anyone working in the public personnel field."

The book completed, Kingsley left for England to study at the University of London School of Economics from 1936 to 1938 as a postdoctoral fellow of the Social Science Research Council. When he returned to Antioch College in 1938 it was as professor of government; and during his subsequent years on the Antioch faculty he was also editor of the *Antioch Review* and from 1939 to 1940 assistant to the president. In 1942 appeared a second book, which he prepared with David W. Petegorsky: *Strategy for Democracy*, a symposium on a program for American postwar world reconstruction, written before Pearl Harbor, and based on papers presented at a June 1941 Antioch conference. The *Saturday Review of Literature* critic wrote: "Of all the books attempting to blue print the future of democracy this study by two youthful teachers . . . belongs among the most provocative and inclusive"; Reinhold Niebuhr's notice in *Nation* was that the book was the "first real attempt in America to state the goals of democracy in both domestic and foreign terms."

With America's involvement in World War II the professor was drawn into public service—in 1942-43 as the chief of the program division of the War Manpower Commission in Cleveland, in 1943-44 as assistant regional director, and in 1944 as deputy executive director of the Commission. The last post took him to Washington, where after a year he entered the Office of War Mobilization and Reconversion as director for manpower and veterans affairs (1945-46). His special interest in reconversion had been indicated in four articles he wrote for the *New Republic* in the spring and fall of 1944. The first two, under the heading "Hell-Bent for Chaos," took issue with the Baruch-Hancock Report on War and Postwar Adjustment Policies as marking "repudiation of the New Deal," and suggested that governmental purchases "used as a compensatory and stabilizing device" would provide "a flexible means of maintaining a given level of employment." The second two articles, dealing with "Veterans, Unions and Jobs," held that "plans are far advanced for a big-business drive to break the back of organized labor as soon as the war in Europe ends," and urged that steps be taken to close "the disastrous breach between labor and the veterans."

Shortly after the publication of these articles Kingsley's third book appeared, with the title *Representative Bureaucracy; an Interpretation of the British Civil Service* (1944). A reviewer for *Foreign Affairs* noted that "the author has departed from the usual politico-constitutional analysis and has emphasized social and class interests"; while Reinhard Bendix said in the *American Journal of Sociology* that the study demonstrated "the great analytical value of an examination of personnel policies for an understanding of governmental bureaucracy."

In Washington Kingsley worked under John R. Steelman [41], who was director of the Office of War Mobilization and Reconversion. When Steelman reorganized the Office in August 1946 he named Kingsley deputy for fiscal policy, employment and social security, explaining that the post was that of "coordinator and expediter of the Government's production and stabilization policies." The duties of the former professor of government also took him to the White House, as liaison officer for the President's Commission on Higher Education (1946-47), and as executive secretary of the President's Scientific Research Board (1947).

Kingsley came into the international scene in 1947 when he was appointed chief of sections of the International Labor Office in Geneva, and later headed the I.L.O. mission to Greece. He was in London with the first when his appointment as Assistant Administrator of the Federal Security Agency, under Federal Security Administrator Oscar R. Ewing [48], was made known. In that post, to which he came in late 1947, stated the *United Nations Bulletin*, he had a large part in directing the Federal programs "in the fields of public assistance, social insurance, employment services, public health, public education, and vocational rehabilitation."

On July 8, 1949, the news came from Geneva that forty-one-year-old Kingsley had been elected Director-General of the United Nations' International Refugee Organization by the IRO's fifteen-government General Council. The IRO, which has functioned since mid-1947, was organized for the purpose of re-establishing 1,500,000 refugees and displaced persons uprooted by the war—this to be accomplished through the maintenance of camps and assembly centers, repatriation of those who wished to return to their native countries, and resettlement of nonrepatriable displaced persons in new countries.

In a review of IRO's work ("The Final Humanitarian Challenge," *United Nations Bulletin*, January 1, 1950) Kingsley reported that 756,000 persons would have been repatriated or resettled in the course of the two and a half years it had operated (of these, 686,000 stateless individuals would have been transported to new homes). "Many nations," he wrote, "have responded generously to IRO appeals to liberalize their immigration restrictions, but the barriers are still high." One of the most difficult problems is to provide for the so-called "hard core" cases, the many thousand sick, blind, aged, and otherwise dependent persons, who must become the charge of public or private charity; another group comprises "the forgotten elite" of professions such as scientists, doctors, artists, educators, whom "the world still rejects . . . under the criteria established for mass migration schemes." The liquidation of IRO, originally scheduled to take place in mid-1950, is planned for September 30, 1951. Before this, in January 1951, the superseding office of United Nations High Commissioner for Refugees will have been established, as provided for by the

December 1949 action of the U.N. General Assembly.

Other writings of Kingsley's have appeared in such publications as *Public Administration* and *Public Personnel Review*; and during 1942 and 1943 he was a contributing editor of *Current History*. A member of the American Political Science Association, he also belongs to the American Society for Public Administration, and the British Institute of Public Administrators. Kingsley's family consists of his wife, the former Ruth Caplan (his second marriage took place in June 1946), and a daughter, Jennifer Ann, who is eight years old in 1950. The administrator paints for a hobby, sails and golfs for more active recreation.

References

N Y Times p4 Jl 9 '49
U N Bul 7:97 Jl 15 '49
American Men in Government (1949)
Directory of the American Political Science Association, 1948

KINTNER, ROBERT E(DMONDS) Sept. 12, 1909- Broadcasting company executive
Address: b. c/o American Broadcasting Company, 30 Rockefeller Plaza, New York 20; h. 17 E. 89th St., New York 28

Robert Kintner, president of the American Broadcasting Company, was a journalist before entering radio. After covering New York's financial district as a newspaper reporter, he gained recognition as a Washington columnist and author, in collaboration with Joseph Wright Alsop, Jr. With the latter he wrote *Men Around the President* (1939) and *American White Paper* (1940). Upon discharge from the Army (with the rank of lieutenant colonel), in 1944 Kintner joined ABC as a vice-president; his election to the presidency of that company became effective in 1950.

Robert Edmonds Kintner is a native Pennsylvanian, born in Stroudsburg, on September 12, 1909, the son of Albert H. and Lillian M. (Stofflet) Kintner. After graduation from the local high school, he entered Swarthmore College, from which he received the B.A. degree in 1931. Two years later he joined the staff of the New York *Herald Tribune* as a financial news reporter on Wall Street, later becoming a columnist for that paper and the North American Newspaper Alliance.

Kintner's reputation as a top-ranking news columnist was established between the years 1937 and 1941, when he joined forces with Joseph Wright Alsop, Jr., another young *Herald Tribune* newspaperman, in writing a nationally syndicated column in Washington, D.C. This column, called *The Capital Parade*, made use of "inside" information the young men were able to gather and appeared in ninety-five newspapers in the United States. The team wrote a number of articles, including "The Guffey: Biography of a Boss, New Style", "Battle of the Market Place", "Republican With a Bite", "Let Them Do the Talking," and "Never Leave Them Angry" for the *Saturday Evening Post*; and "Taft and Taft" and "Roosevelt Family Album" for *Life*.

Two best-selling books by Alsop and Kintner appeared in 1939 and 1940. The first, *Men Around the President*, was a study of the inner circle of Roosevelt's advisers. Reviewing it in the *New Republic*, Jonathan Mitchell commented on its quality of immediacy, remarking that the authors wrote about Washington "as if it were a police precinct." S. T. Williamson in the New York *Times* called it "a vibrant action story, brimful of incident, responsible gossip, and phrase-making as neat as surgical incisions." "The authors have mastered the difficult job of being fair without being stilted," he added.

American White Paper; the Story of American Diplomacy and the Second World War, Alsop and Kintner's second work, appeared in 1940, an inexpensive paper-bound book. Its authors, who were sympathetic to the Administration's course in shaping the country's foreign policy, described the actions of policy makers in Washington from the time of the Munich agreement through the dangerous period which followed the outbreak of war in Europe. Described by Harold Hinton, New York *Times* reviewer, as "a sort of literary newsreel" and by columnist Ralph Thompson, also of the *Times*, as "a journalistic stunt of the first order," the book was discussed at length by *Time*. It devoted the first half of its National Affairs Section on April 29, 1940, to the book, pointing out that the detailed intimate conferences and conversations between Roosevelt, Cordell Hull, Sumner Welles, and Adolf Augustus Berle, Jr., were "almost eye-witness in effect." George Soule, the reviewer for *New Republic*, questioned the use of "White Paper" in the title—he pointed out that the book contained no documents not previously made public.

The Kintner-Alsop partnership was dissolved in June 1941 when both members joined the armed services. Kintner joined the Army and Alsop was sworn into service as a Naval Intelligence officer. (Neither young man would have been called to serve under the draft regulations.) Kintner, who was stationed both overseas and in Washington with the War Department Bureau of Public Relations, received a medical discharge in 1944 after a plane crash; at that time he held the rank of lieutenant colonel. He received the Legion of Merit before returning to civilian life.

In Washington Kintner had known the then Under Secretary of Commerce, Edward J. Noble,[44] later to become owner and chairman of the American Broadcasting Company. Offered a post in radio by the latter in 1944, the journalist accepted it and joined ABC as a vice-president. After starting in public relations at ABC, Kintner transferred to radio news, before the end of the war. There he learned about what he has called "a basic difference" between radio news and printed news when he discovered that the listener's ear is "selective"—a news bulletin which contained the phrase "peace rumors" started a run of telephone calls to the radio station.

(Continued next page)

ROBERT E. KINTNER

In his sixth year at ABC Kintner was elected to the presidency, as of January 1, 1950, to succeed Mark Woods '46, the president since January 1942. At that date the company had emerged as a separate network after severing relations with NBC, where it had previously functioned as the Blue Network. For a year it was a Radio Corporation of America subsidiary, then was bought in 1943 by Noble for eight million dollars. To the three stations (WJZ in New York, WENR in Chicago, and KGO in San Francisco) owned and operated by ABC at the time of its purchase, the company had added two more by August 1, 1949: WXYZ in Detroit and KECA in Los Angeles; in addition it represented WMAL (owned by the *Evening Star*) in Washington, D.C. Affiliated stations numbered 270. (Data from *Radio Annual*, 1949, and *Information Please Almanac*, 1950.) The year 1949 saw ABC a newcomer on the New York Stock Exchange. In the previous year it had inaugurated television service over three owned and operated stations (in New York, Chicago, and Detroit) and had begun regular programs service to an Eastern and Midwestern TV network; ABC-owned-and-operated TV stations in Los Angeles and San Francisco were projected for 1949.

Among programs originating in ABC studios, which operate on a theory of "planned programming," aimed at large continuing audiences, are the commentaries of Drew Pearson, Walter Winchell, Elmer Davis; *The Greatest Story Ever Told; Carnegie Hall; Stop the Music; America's Town Meeting of the Air;* the Milton Berle, Groucho Marx, Bing Crosby shows; public service programs offered on behalf of both labor and management in equal "frozen" time segments. ABC was commended in a New York *Times* article by Jack Gould for its coverage of the U.N.

In March 1950 ABC made a $2,500,000 standby loan agreement with the New York Trust Company. The network that year resigned from the National Association of Broadcasters, stating it questioned the value of benefits derived by membership. Kintner, before the end of his first six months as president, was able to announce a record week in television in new programs purchased and network sales. A gross business of $4,000,000 was acquired by the sale of eight half-hour periods to nine sponsors. The company has concentrated on what Kintner calls "package" programs such as *The Screen Guild Players* and *Inner Sanctum* in the belief that television will lend itself to programs of this kind over a period of time better than to individual star performers. Kintner's refusal to drop a program featuring an artist accused of Communist sympathies without proof of the charges was praised in a Washington *Post* editorial, which called the ABC president's stand an "effective bit of old-fashioned Americanism."

By his marriage on March 9, 1940, to Jean Rodney, Kintner has two children, Susan and Michael. Mrs. Kintner was a theatrical producer before her marriage. The radio executive's fraternity is Phi Delta Theta.

References

   N Y Herald Tribune V p1 Jl 16 '50
   N Y Post p18 Ag 8 '44
   N Y Times p15 Ap 22 '40; p25 D 30 '49; III p3 Je 25 '50
   N Y World-Telegram p17 Ap 27 '40
   Nation 150:558 My 4 '40
   New Repub 104:857 Je 23 '41
   Newsweek 23:20 Mr 6 '44
   Time 35:13 Ap 29 '40; 37-67 Je 16 '41
   Variety 177:23 Ja 11 '50

   Business Executives of America (1950)
   Who's Who in America, 1950-51

KIRKPATRICK, SIR IVONE (AUGUSTINE) (ĭ-vōn') Feb. 3, 1897- British Government official

Address: b. Office of British High Commissioner, Bonn, Germany; h. 38 Ormonde Gate, London, S.W. 3; Celbridge, County Kildare, Republic of Ireland

The newly appointed British High Commissioner for Germany, Sir Ivone Kirkpatrick, succeeded Sir Brian Robertson '48 in that post on March 16, 1950. Kirkpatrick, whose career in the Foreign Office began in 1919, has a long acquaintance with German affairs, preceded by some years as an envoy in Rio de Janeiro and Rome. Sent to the British Embassy in Berlin in August 1933, the year the Nazis came into power, he remained there until 1938.

Ivone Augustine Kirkpatrick was born February 3, 1897, in Wellington, India. Of an Irish family, he is the elder son of Colonel Ivone Kirkpatrick, C.B.E; his mother, the Honorable Mary (Hardinge) Kirkpatrick was sometime maid of honor to Queen Victoria. Young Kirkpatrick attended Downside School, was admitted to Balliol College, Oxford. In World War I he served with the Royal Inniskilling Fusiliers, from 1914 to 1918. Seriously wounded at Gallipoli, he received mention in two dispatches; he was awarded the Belgian Croix de Guerre.

Passing an examination which granted him a Civil Service certificate as third secretary in the diplomatic service or Foreign Office, Kirkpatrick was appointed to the British Legation at Rio de Janeiro on July 15, 1919, shortly after leaving the military service. He was recalled to the Foreign Office on August 19, 1920, and four months later was promoted to the rank of second secretary. With the rank of first secretary (which he received October 13, 1928), he was sent to Rome on May 19, 1930. His next appointment was to the Holy See, in November 1932, where he acted as chargé d'affaires until the end of August 1933. (He received the Maltese cross of the papal Order of St. Gregory the Great.) In that year he was transferred to Berlin, to serve under two Ambassadors, Sir Eric Phipps and Sir Nevile Henderson. Remaining there until 1938, he was able to observe the Nazis from the time they came into power until the year before the outbreak of World War II. As chargé d'affaires he was present at the Godesberg and Munich conferences. Kirkpatrick returned to England in December 1938, and in the New Year's Honors of 1939 was named Companion of St. Michael and St. George. Attached to the Foreign Office's Central Department under Sir William Strang, he succeeded him as head of the department later in the year. His title was now acting counselor, a promotion which came to him September 11, 1939. During 1940 Kirkpatrick was assigned to the Ministry of Information (April 8), to the Home Office (August 25), again to the Foreign Office (December 8). In the same year he was director of foreign publicity at the Ministry of Information during several months. With Lord Simon he shared the responsibility of identifying Rudolf Hess [41] in the summer of 1941, when the Deputy Fuehrer made his surprise landing in Britain.

Another promotion came to Kirkpatrick on September 11, 1941, when he was made a counselor of the Foreign Office. Less than a month later, on October 9, he was assigned to the British Broadcasting Corporation, to become controller of European services and director of the "V" campaign of the political warfare department. He was in charge of all broadcast services to enemy and enemy-occupied countries and frequently participated in broadcasts.

Kirkpatrick attained the rank of ambassador on September 1, 1944, when he was appointed to the Control Commission for Germany (British Element) as civil deputy commissioner, after having served for about six months in the Foreign Office (from April to September) as director of the organization of the British Element in the Allied Control Commission for Germany. His duties as deputy commissioner consisted of preparing plans and recruiting civilians. When the headquarters moved to Germany in the summer of 1945, Kirkpatrick, who was then political adviser to Field Marshal Montgomery, left the organization, and Sir William Strang, now succeeded Kirkpatrick in the advisory post. Kirkpatrick remained in England to head the British publicity services, which

British Inf. Services
SIR IVONE KIRKPATRICK

were transferred after the war from the Ministry of Information to the Foreign Office. He was appointed an Assistant Under Secretary of State on August 1, 1945, to take charge of both the German and Western European departments at the Foreign Office, and also of the diplomatic notes about Berlin which preceded the Russian blockade and Allied airlift. He was promoted to Deputy Under Secretary of State in 1948, and again he succeeded Sir William Strang in February of 1949, this time as Permanent Under Secretary of State and head of the German section.

The appointment of Sir Ivone (he became Knight Commander of St. Michael and St. George on January 1, 1948) on March 16, 1950, as United Kingdom High Commissioner in Germany, followed upon several routine reassignments of other high officers. General Sir James Steele, Adjutant General of the British Army, was due to complete his duties at the War Office the summer of 1950, and General Sir John Crocker, who has been in command of the Middle East forces, was chosen to succeed him. General Sir Brian Robertson, British High Commissioner for Germany, was to take the place of General Crocker. This left the post of British High Commissioner in Germany to be filled.

According to the New York *Herald Tribune* (March 18, 1950), one of the principal reasons for Kirkpatrick's appointment was an anticipated dissolution of the Western Allied High Commission, and its replacement by other controls which "would grant West Germany virtual independence and sovereignty." However, the New York *Times* stated that, since Sir Ivone had been in charge of the German section of the Foreign Office, "no fundamental revision of British policy is expected as a result of the change." While Kirkpatrick was serving in

KIRKPATRICK, SIR IVONE—*Continued*
Berlin during 1933 to 1938, he became a friend of André François-Poncet [49], then French Ambassador, who now holds the position of High Commissioner of the French Zone of Germany. (Their American colleague is United States High Commissioner John J. McCloy [47].) From the Central Office of Information came the following comment on Sir Ivone: "He has a high reputation in the diplomatic world as a man of quick thought and prompt decisions, courage in assuming responsibility when necessary, and a dislike of unnecessary formality and red tape."

Kirkpatrick married Violet Caulfeild Cottell on January 10, 1929; their children are named Ivone Peter and Cecilia Sybil. For recreation the British official may turn to tennis, golf, or hunting. His club is the St. James's. It is told that as a soldier in World War I he kept a record of one of the campaigns, which he called "Gallipoli Diary." It makes "excellent reading" in the opinion of those who have had an opportunity to see it—the Foreign Office circular tells that Sir Ivone "is esteemed as a witty and brilliant conversationalist and raconteur."

References

N Y Herald Tribune p5 Mr 18 '50
N Y Times p2 Mr 17 '50 por
Burke's Peerage (1949)
Who's Who, 1949
World Biography (1948)

KNOX, RONALD (ARBUTHNOTT), MSGR. Feb. 17, 1888- English prelate of the Roman Catholic Church; author

Address: h. Manor House, Mells, Frome, Somersetshire, England

With publication in March 1950 of the second volume of his translation of the Old Testament, the Right Reverend Monsignor Ronald Knox brought to a conclusion the work of approximately a decade, in which he had, at the request of the English hierarchy of the Roman Catholic Church, prepared a new version "in timeless English" of the Vulgate, the Latin translation of the Bible made by St. Jerome in the fourth century, and adopted as the standard text of the Catholic Church. A well-known author in the fields of Christian apologetics and *belles lettres*, Msgr. Knox was converted to Catholicism while Anglican chaplain at Oxford; he later held the Catholic chaplaincy at the same university, resigning it in 1939 to devote himself to the task of translating the Bible.

Ronald Arbuthnott Knox was born February 17, 1888, to Edmund Arbuthnott and Ellen Penelope (French) Knox, in Kibworth Beauchamp (Leicestershire, England), where his father (to be Anglican Bishop of Manchester from 1903 to 1921) was Church of England rector at the time of the boy's birth. Both grandfathers had been Protestant divines. Ronald was the youngest of a family of six. (One of his three elder brothers, Edmund Valpy Knox, became editor of the English periodical, *Punch*, and a contributor to it under the pseudonym "Evoe.") At the age of four, when

his mother died, Ronald and an elder brother went to live for three years with his father's family in a country rectory. His childhood surroundings Knox was to describe in the autobiographical *A Spiritual Aeneid*, as characterized by that Christian piety which finds expression in devotion to Scripture, strict observance of Sunday, framed texts, and family prayers.

After a private school education (during which his training in the classics was such that he was writing Greek and Latin verses at the age of ten, as recounted by Hoehn in *Catholic Authors*), he won a scholarship to Eton College in 1900. There he came into contact with Tractarianism, the catholicizing or "ritualistic" movement within the Church of England, and joined its ranks. At the age of seventeen Ronald Knox vowed himself to celibacy, in order to "have power to attend to the Lord without impediment." He became editor of the Eton *College Chronicle*, and contributed to *Cornhill* and the *World*. In 1906 Knox proceeded to Balliol College, Oxford, on a scholarship, and there established a reputation as a wit and lively participant in the university debating society, of which he was elected president in 1909. At Oxford he won the Hertford (1907), Ireland and Craven (1908) scholarships, and the Gaisford (1908) and Chancellor's Latin Verse (1910) prizes. In 1910 he was graduated with a first in "Greats" (studies in the classics) and was elected a fellow of Trinity College, Oxford.

Following ordination in the Church of England, as deacon in 1911 and as priest in 1912, Knox was appointed chaplain of Trinity College. There he gave a series of lectures exposing contradictions in the theories of recognized authorities on the *Iliad*; a similar critical examination of the theories of various Biblical scholars revealed inconsistencies in that field also. Associated at the same time with a group of dons preparing a symposium of Anglican beliefs (published with the title *Foundations*), Knox found himself in disagreement with the liberal views of the group; he has indicated that "authority" has always played a large part in his belief. He expressed his reaction in *Absolute and a Bitofhell*, a satire in the style of Dryden's *Absalom and Achitophel*, and in *Some Loose Stones* (1913), a systematic criticism of the contents of *Foundations*. In *Reunion All Around* (1914) his ridicule of modernist views took the form of comic travesty. In 1917 Knox resigned the Anglican chaplaincy of Trinity to become a convert to Roman Catholicism. Two years later, upon completion of theological studies at St. Edmund's College, he was ordained a priest in the Catholic Church. (The previous year had seen the publication of *A Spiritual Aeneid*, in which he traced the course of his religious development.)

During the course of the next eight years Knox produced a number of books in a variety of literary forms, including *Memories of the Future* (1923), a satirical fantasy; a translation of *The Miracles of King Henry VI* (1923); an edition of Virgil's *Aeneid*, Books VII-IX (1924); and *Sanctions, A Frivolity* (1924). In 1926 he was appointed to the Catholic chaplaincy at Oxford, to remain in the post of spiritual director of the undergraduates there for thirteen years. (Under the title, *In Soft Garments*, his conferences as chaplain at Oxford were published in 1942.) In this period he became known for his books of Catholic apologetics, such as *The Belief of Catholics* (1927), *Anglican Cobwebs* (1928). He also became more widely known to the general non-academic public, largely as a result of his broadcasts and of his criticism of certain popular writers, for example, Wells, the Huxleys, and Mencken. In 1936 Father Knox was made a domestic prelate by the Pope, an honor bearing with it the title of Monsignor.

Three years later (1939) Msgr. Knox was requested by the Archbishops and Bishops of England and Wales to make a new translation in "timeless English" of the Vulgate—that is, the version of the Bible prepared by St Jerome in Latin (the popular tongue of the day) late in the fourth century, and approved by the Council of Trent in 1546 as the official Church version. A Catholic translation of it in English, the Douay version, appeared in 1610, and, with revisions made in 1750 by Bishop Challoner, has remained the standard Catholic text. (Previous to this task of translation, Knox had prepared *The Holy Bible: An Abridgement and Rearrangement* in 1936.)

For his work Msgr. Knox withdrew to the Chapel House at Aldenham Park, Lord Acton's estate at Bridgnorth in Shropshire. There, with the aid of a small advisory committee, and a library containing almost every known English version of the Bible and the standard commentaries, as well as the best Greek codices, the ecclesiastic completed his translation in approximately a decade. His version of the New Testament appeared in 1944, the first volume of the Old Testament (Genesis through Esther) in 1949, and the second and completing volume (Job to Machabees) in early 1950. (An edition of the Psalms in Latin and English was also published as a separate unit in 1947.) A consideration of the Knox translation in the *Saturday Review of Literature*, February 18, 1950, pointed out that the volumes, while bearing the licensing imprimatur, are an "independent piece of work," and quoted Msgr. Knox as saying: "Neither common sense nor canon law would justify its authorization for public use without further, more rigid, and more expert scrutiny." In 1949 a new Latin-English Daily Missal was issued, in which the Scriptural passages were in the Knox translation.

In his work Msgr. Knox relied on the direct impression of the Latin and aimed at rendering its meaning in an English that would not become dated; to that end he had constant recourse to the *Oxford English Dictionary*, refusing any expression which had not been current in the language for the last 300 years. This and other problems confronting him have been expounded by the prelate in *Trials of a Translator*, a collection of essays published in 1948.

The Knox version is in prose, employs paragraphs rather than verses, and is liberally supplied with footnotes which give alternative

MSGR. RONALD KNOX

readings from the Greek and Hebrew and explain the reasons governing the translator's renditions from the Vulgate. A passage from a familiar Psalm reads as follows in the new translation: "The Lord is my shepherd; how can I lack anything? He gives me a resting-place where there is pasture, and leads me out by cool waters, to make me live anew. As in honor pledged, by sure paths he leads me" (Psalm 22 in both the Douay and Knox versions).

As the several volumes of the Knox translation came from the press they were enthusiastically received by the Roman Catholic clergy. "The beginning of a fresh epoch in Catholic Bible translation . . . not a mere modernization, not a touching up of the Douay, but an entirely new text which modernizes the authentic message of the New Testament," wrote the Reverend James A. Kleist, S. J., in the *American Ecclesiastical Review*. Estimates in the lay press stressed "readability" and an increase in lucidity in the new translation, while expressing reservations as to the literary quality (in comparison with that of the Douay and King James versions). "It does not strike into the heart and set the harps of the mind singing," remarked Thomas Sugrue in the *Saturday Review of Literature* (February 18, 1950), after appraising its values: "As a translation . . . into modern English prose it is an excellent work. It reads easily; it clarifies the narrative as it rolls along; its style is smooth and breaks frequently into lyricism; there are phrases here and there of startling grandeur. . . .As a companion to either the Douay or King James translation it is a friend and helpmeet."

During the years of World War II, Msgr. Knox also prepared two books of instruction, *The Mass in Slow Motion* (1948) and *The Creed in Slow Motion* (1949), collections of sermons he gave to a convent of girls evacu-

KNOX, RONALD, MSGR.—*Continued*

ated to Bridgnorth. In them he took the Mass and the Creed part by part, explaining them and relating them to everyday life. *The Creed in Slow Motion* was declared by the *Catholic World* to be "as solid in substance and attractive in form as it is arresting in title." Mary Stack McNiff, reviewing it in *The Pilot*, pointed out that the articles of faith are presented "with a refreshing informality." Other activities undertaken by the Monsignor in the course of the war years included presidency of the committee for providing Catholic books for servicemen, and membership on the committee which in 1940 produced the new *Westminster Hymnal*.

Msgr. Knox's versatility in literature is evidenced by the variety of forms he has used: satire, serious apologetic, acrostic, scholarly commentary, essay, and the detective novel (he has written six of the last-named). A few of some twenty titles not already mentioned are: *Bread or Stone* (1915); *Meditations on the Psalms* (1919); *A Book of Acrostics* (1924); *The Mystery of the Kingdom* (1928); *Caliban in Grub Street* (1930); *Broadcast Minds* (1932); *The Body in the Silo* (1933); *Barchester Pilgrimage* (1934; a parody on Trollope's style); *Double-Cross Purposes* (1937; United States edition *Settled Out of Court*); *Let Dons Delight* (1939); *The Epistles and Gospels for Sundays and Holidays* (1945). Contemporary topics were treated in *Nazi and Nazarene* (1940) and *God and the Atom* (1945).

Msgr. Knox, whose hair is white, is lean in build. He has always been noted for his witty, agile mind. When cabled by the American publisher of his works that the sales in that country of *The Mass in Slow Motion* were good, Knox is related (*Newsweek*, November 15, 1948) to have enquired: "Are they Sauline or Davidic?" To this the publisher was able to answer—after recalling that Saul had slain his thousands, David his ten thousands—that the sales were Davidic. The English prelate smokes a pipe, finds relaxation in writing humorous verse, working anagrams, acrostics, and the *London Times* crossword puzzles. He is a member of the English Detection Club, and was coeditor of the *Best English Detective Stories of 1928*.

References

Newsweek 32:75-7 N 15 '48
The Sign p33-5 D '49
Time 52:69-71 N 15 '48
Hoehn, M. A ed. Catholic Authors, 1930-47
International Who's Who, 1950
Kunitz, S. J. and Haycraft, H. eds. Twentieth Century Authors (1942)
World Biography (1948)

KNOX, MRS. ROSE M(ARKWARD) Nov. 18, 1857—Sept. 27, 1950 President of the Charles B. Knox Gelatine Company, founded by her husband, from 1908 to 1947; financed research in industrial and nutritional uses of gelatine; honored for her executive ability, for her fair employment practices, and for her benefactions. See *Current Biography*, 1949.

Obituary

N Y Times p27 S 29 '50

KOHLER, FOY D(AVID) Feb. 15, 1908- United States Government official

Address: b. c/o United States Department of State, Washington, D.C.; International Broadcasting Division, 224 W. 57th St., New York

Foy D. Kohler, who directs *Voice of America*, the United States Department of State's radio project designed to give listeners abroad an understanding of life and events in the United States, assumed the position of chief of the Department's International Broadcasting Division in November 1949. (The broadcasting division is under the administration of the newly named Assistant Secretary of State for Public Affairs, Edward W. Barrett[47].) Kohler had spent eighteen years in the Department's Foreign Service, of which two years were spent in Russia as chargé d'affaires at the American Embassy in Moscow. For about five months in 1945-46 he had served as secretary general of the mission which observed the Greek elections, and before that he has been assigned to various United States Embassies in eastern European countries, including those in Bucharest, Belgrade, and in Cairo.

A native of the Middle West, Foy David Kohler was born February 15, 1908, in Oakwood, a small town in Ohio. His father, Leander David Kohler, was of Pennsylvania Dutch ancestry, and his mother, Myrtle (McClure) Kohler, was of Scotch-Irish extraction. There were also two girls in the family. Young Kohler, who attended Scott High School in Toledo, was graduated in 1924 and then began work as a bank teller in that city. In the same year he registered for courses at the University of Toledo, where until 1927 he continued to study while working in the bank. In 1928 he enrolled for full-time study at Ohio State University, at Columbus. Having decided to train for a diplomatic career, Kohler selected geography and economics for his major studies. This choice of a career had been inspired by Brand Whitlock, a former Mayor of Toledo and the Ambassador to Belgium during World War I. Although he did not know Whitlock personally, Kohler says he was impressed with the diplomat's record as a "real Midwestern liberal." For his scholastic achievements he won election to Phi Beta Kappa; and he held first place in his class of the College of Commerce and Administration upon being graduated with a B.S. degree in 1931. At the university Kohler had been elected president of the Student Senate, to membership in the Sphinx, the senior honorary society, to the fraternities of Delta Upsilon and Beta Gamma Sigma, and to the junior honorary society of the Bucket and Dipper. In the summers of 1928 and 1929 he served as assistant secretary of the university's alumni association, and during 1930 and 1931 he was business manager of the university paper.

Wide World Photos
FOY D. KOHLER

Kohler's career with the Foreign Service of the State Department began in December 1931, and several weeks after his appointment he was sent to Windsor, Canada, as vice-consul. There he remained for most of 1932, in November of that year returning to Washington to attend the Foreign Service School conducted by the Department of State. His next assignment took him, in March 1933, to Bucharest as vice-consul of the American Embassy there. Except for a brief appointment to the Belgrade Embassy, Kohler remained in Rumania for three years. As is customary after such a period of service, Kohler received a new assignment: he was transferred to Athens in 1936, to serve as third secretary of the American Embassy. At the end of 1938 he was given the position of vice-consul in Athens, a post that included as well the Dodecanese Islands of the Aegean. Two years later he returned to the United States, reporting to the State Department in the capital. In mid-1941 he was sent as third secretary and vice-consul to Cairo, Egypt, and later that year once more returned to Washington to handle Greek problems for the Department. In July 1944 he was named Assistant Chief of the Division of Near Eastern Affairs, in which capacity he was (in September 1944) an adviser to the United States delegation to the Second Session of the Council of UNRRA, held in Montreal. During the San Francisco Conference, which drew up the charter of the United Nations, Kohler served as political and liaison officer for the United States delegation.

Because of his knowledge of Near Eastern affairs, Kohler in November 1945 was chosen secretary general of the United States mission to Greece to observe the first postwar elections to be held in that country, a duty which kept him there until March 1946. In April 1946 he received his first appointment to Russia, as first secretary and counselor of the American Embassy; he arrived in Moscow in January 1947 to assume his position of minister counselor under Lieutenant General Walter Bedell Smith '44. When Smith left Russia in the fall of 1948, Kohler became chargé d'affaires, with the rank of minister. It was while Kohler was the principal United States official in Moscow that Anna Louise Strong '49, the American journalist, was arrested by Russian police on charges of espionage and subversive activities, and deported from Russia. The diplomat protested the arrest, but was denied the request to interview her. In July 1949 Kohler returned to the United States and that November assumed the post of Chief of the International Broadcasting Division of the State Department's Office of International Information.

The Office of International Information (according to the *United States Government Manual*) has the responsibility of disseminating abroad information about the United States, of promoting the freedom of information, and of encouraging and assisting private agencies in their international information activities. These objectives also guide the activities of the Division of International Broadcasting, which, under Kohler, is responsible for the extent and quality of the State Department's participation in the international dissemination of information through the medium of radio broadcasting. Chief objective of the division (one for which Congress in 1949 appropriated $11,500,000) is the *Voice of America*. Much of this 1949 appropriation is earmarked for use in developing a world-wide network powerful enough to combat Russian attempts to "jam" the State Department radio programs. Kohler is particularly anxious to avail himself of what he calls the "healthy skepticism" developed by the Russians under the Czars. In a New York *Times* interview he is quoted: "It's up to us to keep their [the Russians] skepticism alive, to keep persuading them that the United States doesn't want to attack them, doesn't covet their land, and extends a genuine welcome to them into the family of nations."

In Kohler's own words (as reported by Richard M. Barr in the Washington *Post*), the function of his division is "to further the policy of the United States by giving peoples abroad a true picture of the aims, policies, and institutions of the United States. . . .Our medium uses thirty-six transmitters, ranging from 10,000 to 200,000 watts in power. These transmitters beam broadcasts in twenty languages to Europe, Latin America, the Far East, and the Middle East. [In December 1949 broadcasts were inaugurated to Turkey and the Ukraine.] We shape our programs in three main categories: about 34 per cent are news, about 45 per cent editorial and commentary, and about 21 per cent music and entertainment." The United States also owns or leases relay stations. The potential audience is estimated at 295 million people. Barr continued: "Actual writing of news for broadcast is done by a staff of thirty editors and rewrite men, working in three shifts around the clock."

Kohler, who has brown hair and hazel eyes, weighs 150 pounds and is five feet, eight inches tall. He states that he has no political affilia-

KOHLER, FOY D.—*Continued*

tions, that he is a member of the Methodist Episcopal Church, and that for recreation he plays golf and badminton. On August 7, 1935, he married Phyllis Penn, who has accompanied him on his various foreign assignments. Kohler is a member of the American Foreign Service Association and of its journal's editorial board, and of the Middle East Institute.

References

> N Y Times p17 N 11 '49
> Biographic Register of the Department of State, 1949
> Who's Who in America, 1948-49

KOLAROV, VASSIL (PETROV) (kō-lä′rŏv vä-sĭl′) July 16, 1877—Jan. 23, 1950 Premier of Bulgaria; teacher; lawyer; one of the founders of the Bulgarian Communist party; Secretary General of the Communist International in 1922; a leader in the Bulgarian people's uprising in 1923; holder of posts in the Comintern while in exile in Russia from 1923 to 1945; Provisional President of the People's Republic of Bulgaria in 1945; later Vice-Premier and Minister of Foreign Affairs (1947); attended the Paris Peace Conference (1946) and the Warsaw conference of Foreign Ministers of the Soviet bloc (1948); named Premier in July 1949. See *Current Biography*, 1949.

Obituary

> N Y Times p8 Ja 24 '50

KRICK, IRVING P(ARKHURST) Dec. 20, 1906- Meteorologist

Address: b. 1276 E. Colorado St., Pasadena 1, Calif.; h. 3634 Shannon Rd., Los Angeles, Calif.

The president and chairman of the board of trustees of the American Institute of Aerological Research, a California organization for the analysis of weather, Irving P. Krick was a pioneer in long-range weather forecasting in the United States. He directed its introduction and development at the California Institute of Technology, where he was head of the meteorology department from 1938 to 1948. In World War II he served as a weather strategist with the United States armed forces. Krick is also head of a business enterprise which supplies specialized forecasts to a variety of industries and individuals.

Irving Parkhurst Krick, son of Harry I. and Mabel (Royal) Krick, was born in San Francisco, California, on December 20, 1906. When Irving was ten, his father died, and Mrs. Krick turned to music teaching to support the boy and his sister. Krick, who is a pianist of considerable talent (at thirteen and again at fifteen he gave Sunday afternoon concerts in the open-air Greek Theatre in near-by Berkeley), financed by his piano playing his studies at the University of California. There he majored in physics, to receive the B.A. in 1928. A tour of the United States and the

Far East by the university glee club, for which he was pianist, led to employment after his graduation as assistant manager of radio station KTAB in San Francisco—Krick's work included preparing programs and playing over the air.

For a time Krick was associated in stockbroking with an uncle, who was a banker. By the end of 1929 he was again employed in a musical capacity, in a small job with a publishing house. With ambitions for a concert career, he undertook further study in Denver with a concert pianist, then joined his teacher in establishing a Los Angeles music school which, however, did not prosper. Krick found employment with Western Air Express, and it was this work, he has said, that stimulated his interest in meteorology. In pursuit of his hobby of operating an amateur short-wave transmitter, his attention had been directed to the problems created by the weather as a result of the disturbances caused by "thunderstorm static" (Steve King has related in an article in the *American Magazine*, June 1950). Deciding to turn his knowledge of physics to the study of weather, Krick enrolled at the California Institute of Technology for refresher courses in the necessary mathematics.

In 1932, while working for his Master's degree, Krick joined the institute's staff as an instructor. In that year, too, he set up for Western Air Express the first modern airline weather forecasting service. In his work Krick applied a new method of weather forecasting which had been developed at the Geophysical Institute of Bergen, Norway—it based predictions on a study of air masses and weather fronts, rather than on moving areas of high and low pressure. This technique made possible the prediction of upper-air weather. The president of Western Air Express found Krick's experimental forecasts 96.1 per cent accurate. Krick was engaged as a technical adviser to a committee appointed by President Roosevelt in 1933 to investigate the United States Weather Bureau.

In 1933 Krick received his M.Sc. in meteorology and was promoted to assistant professor in that science at the California Institute of Technology's Daniel Guggenheim Laboratory of Aeronautics. He spent the year 1934 in Europe on a Rockefeller Foundation grant, surveying weather science in nine countries. That year he won his Ph.D. with a dissertation contending that foehn (descending) winds, not masses of warm dry desert air, were mainly responsible for California's mild winter climate. In 1935 Krick was made an associate professor and in 1938 appointed head of the department of meteorology. This post he continued to fill until 1948, with the status of full professor from 1942.

In the course of his European survey in 1934, Krick had observed German experiments in a long-range weather forecasting technique, and on his return introduced the system at the California institute. The method (according to the article on Krick in the June 1950 *American*) is based on the theory that weather runs in patterns governed by eruptions of the sun (sunspots), the recurrent patterns therefore originating in the high upper air. Forecasting, then, is a matter of tracing the pattern in effect. To this end, charts and graphs are made of prevailing conditions, with particular reference to flow of air currents; the resulting map is compared with daily records of the past, and when an analogous period is found, a forecast can be made. Among the correct predictions which drew attention to Krick's work was his forecast (unheeded) in the fall of 1936 of a January cold wave for California. At about that time, the California Junior Chamber of Commerce gave him its Distinguished Service Award for 1936, and the Chamber of Commerce of the United States listed him as one of the ten most outstanding men under thirty-five years of age.

According to an article in the *Saturday Evening Post*, "commercial demand led Caltech to divorce the Krick Industrial Weather Service from other activities." Overhead costs and a percentage of receipts went to the meteorology department (of which Krick remained head), while the rest was Professor Krick's own profit. The service grew: power companies and fuel businesses made use of it to learn when to expect peak demands, when repair crews should be mobilized before storms; sellers of warm-weather and cold-weather goods, large department stores, hotels, sports promoters found it could be of use to them. From the first, leading aircraft companies— Boeing, Lockheed, Vultee, North American, Douglas—engaged the meteorological consultant's services.

The new technique of weather prediction became of strategic importance in World War II. A class of selected meteorologists sent to learn long-range forecasting from him became the nucleus of the first Air Force Weather Research Center. Krick, who had been a member of ROTC at college, was a lieutenant in the Coast Artillery Corps of the United States Army Reserve from 1928 to 1936, and became a commissioned ensign in the Naval Reserve in 1938. In 1942, with the rank of major, he joined the Army Air Corps, to be weather director of the Weather Central Division, and unit commander of Long-Range Forecasting Unit A. He served as deputy director of Weather Services for the European Theater of Operations during 1944-45, and in 1945 became chief of the weather information section, United States Strategic Air Forces. An aspect of Krick's method that had particular wartime application was the fact that it made possible forecasting for given areas by an analysis of conditions in surrounding regions; consequent improvement in knowledge of weather behind enemy lines enabled Allied bombers to increase their raids from an average of five to thirteen a month. Krick's forecast, stated the *American*, was a vital factor in the choice of D-day. The meteorologist was demobilized with the rank of lieutenant colonel; he had been awarded the Legion of Merit, two Bronze Stars, and the Croix de Guerre (France). During 1945-46 he was a member of the Army Air Forces Scientific Advisory Group.

Wide World Photos

IRVING P. KRICK

In 1948 (the year in which he left the California Institute of Technology) Krick became president of the American Institute of Aerological Research, located in Pasadena. Composed of Krick and forty colleagues, the institute, a nonprofit organization, charts the air currents of the world on information supplied by teletype and radio, and studies the resulting maps of conditions in the light of records of past weather. Affiliated with the institute is Irving P. Krick & Associates, an enterprise which supplies information to organizations and individuals who subscribe for its services. It does not issue general weather reports, but analyses the state of future weather in terms of its clients' particular interests. Among subscribers are the United States Air Force; agriculturalists interested in learning the ideal dates for planting and harvesting; railroad companies which can thus prepare their equipment and maintenance crews for climatic contingencies and distribute extra equipment for hauling bumper crops. Also in 1948, Krick became chairman and managing director of International Meteorological Consultant Services, Ltd., of London, England, an enterprise extending his meteorological service to British clients.

Krick's organization, which in 1950 has more than 60,000,000 acres either under survey or operation, has undertaken rain-increasing projects in Arizona, Colorado, New Mexico, Idaho, and Washington. First using dry ice injected into the atmosphere from airplanes, Krick began in 1948 to develop the ground generator method of adapting the Vonnegut-Langmuir '50-Schaefer '48 method of cloud seeding with silver iodide particles. Ground generators, which force the particles skyward by means of powerful blowers, were found far more satisfactory than the early experiments conducted with airplanes. Instances of precipitation increase over

KRICK, IRVING P.—*Continued*

normal rainfall have been as high as 500 per cent, one case increasing the crop yield per acre from 10 to 20 bushels. There were also instances in which the increase was general in a region, both in the unseeded and seeded areas.

The California meteorologist has contributed to both technical and popular journals a number of articles on weather analysis and forecasting and its application to agriculture and industry. He has recently put on the market the Weather Guide, which he describes as "a weather forecasting instrument of high accuracy for the layman." Krick is a member of the American Meteorological Society, the American Association for the Advancement of Science, and the Institute of Aeronautical Sciences. As an undergraduate he became a member of Tau Kappa Epsilon, and as a graduate student was elected to Sigma Xi, science honor fraternity for scientific research. In politics Krick is a Republican, in religion a Protestant. On November 18, 1946, he married Marie Spiro, a British girl. He has a daughter, Marilynn, by a first marriage, to Jane Clark. The weather forecaster has blue eyes, a mustache, graying hair. His club is Scabbard and Blade. He still plays the piano and pipe organ; and a favorite sport is flying.

References

> Am Mag 124:92 Ag '37; 149:28 Je '50
> Coronet 26:53 Ag '49
> Read Digest 41:109 N '42
> Sat Eve Post 212:14 F 10 '40 por
> American Men of Science (1944)
> America's Young Men, 1938-39
> Who's Who in America, 1950-51
> Who's Who in Aviation, 1942-43
> Who's Who in the West (1949)

LAFOLLETTE, CHARLES M(ARION)

Feb. 27, 1898- Political leader

Address: b. c/o Americans for Democratic Action, 1740 K St., N.W., Washington, D.C.; h. 4000 Cathedral Ave., N.W., Washington, D.C.; Park Ave., Evansville, Ind.

By unanimous approval in June 1949, the national board of Americans for Democratic Action named as ADA national director Charles M. LaFollette, former United States Congressman and more recently Military Governor of Wuerttemberg-Baden, Germany. As Republican Representative from Indiana's Eighth District he expressed the political independence which led New Deal sympathizers to found the ADA, a supporter of liberals in both Democratic and Republican ranks.

Charles Marion LaFollette, the only child of Harry C. and Marian (Allis) LaFollette, was born February 27, 1898, in New Albany, Indiana. His great-grandfather on his mother's side was United States Representative William Heilman, who also was elected to Congress from Indiana's Eighth District (in 1878 and in 1880). He is a third cousin of Governor Philip La Follette and of Senator Robert La Follette [44]

of Wisconsin. When he was three years old his parents moved to Evansville (Indiana), where he has continued to live. After graduating from Central High School in 1916, LaFollette entered Wabash College. On April 8 of the following year, two days after the United States declared war on Germany, he enlisted in the First Indiana Cavalry, from which he was later transferred to the 151st Infantry. After serving four and a half months with the AEF he received his discharge in February 1919. The young man returned to Wabash College to choose a curriculum centered on the study of government. He remained at Wabash until 1920, when he enrolled at Vanderbilt University, in Nashville (Tennessee), to study law. The following year he left Vanderbilt, but continued reading law in attorneys' offices in Dayton (Ohio) and his home city of Evansville, until his admission to the Indiana bar in 1925. He started a practice in Evansville and still maintains his office there. In September 1943 he was admitted to the bar of the Supreme Court of the United States.

In the years that ensued, LaFollette made practical use of the knowledge he had acquired, in both government and law. From 1927 to 1929 he sat in the Indiana Legislature; from 1934 to 1942 he was general counsel of the Central Labor Union of the AFL; and he also handled a large volume of business for insurance companies. In 1942 the lawyer was elected Representative to the Congress of the United States from Indiana's Eighth District.

After taking the oath of office Congressman LaFollette indicated that he would follow the liberal and progressive wing of the Republican party rather than the conservative. In 1943 he joined his third cousin, Senator Robert La Follette, a Progressive from Wisconsin, in pleading for "a streamlined Congress that can meet modern needs" (New York *World-Telegram*, August 3, 1943). During the same term, Representative LaFollette (called by *PM* "one of the best insurance lawyers in Congress") attacked proposed legislation exempting insurance companies from antitrust laws as being worded in such a way as to prevent the Supreme Court from ruling on certain pending prosecutions, and labeled it an "unconscionable and immoral attempt to interfere with orderly judicial procedure" (*PM*, December 10, 1943). He charged that the immunity granted by such a bill would permit insurance companies to engage in monopolistic practices which would be burdensome both to the small policyholder and to the small independent businessman and which would eventually interfere with the development of the American democratic system of capitalism.

When the House Labor Committee in August 1944 postponed, until after the year's election, hearings on a bill to make the Fair Employment Practice Committee permanent, Representative LaFollette censured both Democrats and Republicans, stating that the issue of discrimination in the field of employment was one that should transcend party lines. A year later he drew up a full employment bill which went beyond the one then presented by the Administration to include a fair employment practice clause; it proposed legislation on freight rates, on the location and relocation of industry, and on urban and rural housing. He also suggested a means of testing the "relative merits of the so-called free enterprise system of production and that of workers' cooperatives or Government operation"; this test could be procured by setting aside two surplus war plants to produce consumer goods in conditions of fair competition, one to be operated by the Government, the other by a workers' cooperative (*Christian Science Monitor*, October 13, 1945).

In June 1944, the Republican Representative affirmed his independent position by demanding the resignation of Republican State chairman John Lauer and national committeeman Robert W. Lyons, charging them with making political capital of racial and religious intolerance. During the 1946 General Motors strike, LaFollette on the floor of the House defended Walter Reuther '49, vice-president of the United Automobile Workers Union and leader of the strike, as one of the country's most competent labor leaders and urged that the executive of the General Motors Corporation be summoned before the House Un-American Activities Committee.

In both the Seventy-eighth and Seventy-ninth Congresses LaFollette was prominent in the drive for civil rights legislation; he called the poll tax "un-American" and voted against the old Dies Committee and John E. Rankin's attempt to revive it. He also worked against efforts to return the United States to a policy of isolation in foreign relations. Other votes of his (in the Seventy-eighth Congress) were: against the antiracketeering bill which included labor unions; for extension of reciprocal trade agreements for two years; against bill providing prison sentences and fines for persons instigating strikes in Government-operated plants; against repealing the Administration's food subsidy program; for the compromise soldier vote bill; for Lend-Lease. Among his votes in the Seventy-ninth Congress were these: for $2,500 annual tax-free expense allowance for Congressmen (paired); for extension of OPA for a year; against tax bill (the only Republican); for full participation in the U.N; and it was in this Congress that he opposed the extension of the Dies Committee and favored the bill outlawing the poll tax.

Charles M. LaFollette in 1946 did not seek renomination for his seat in the House but was the candidate for nomination for United States Senator from Indiana, thereby challenging Senator Raymond E. Willis, an old-guard Republican. The New York *Herald Tribune* (January 5, 1946) reported that the candidate, calling himself a "radical," stated: "The Republican party is the vehicle presently available to the people if they will come in and make [it] the radical party in America. 'Radical' means 'fundamental': therefore, it means 'forthright,' and 'forthright' includes those intellectual and moral integrities which are essential to the maintenance of our Republic." Conducting a progressive policy campaign in which he attempted to force the issue between his propounded liberalism and the party's conservatism, he supported price control, many of the social programs then pending in Congress, opposed antilabor legislation and proposed Government

Harris & Ewing
CHARLES M. LAFOLLETTE

control of mines and railroads. However, an alignment of conservative Republicans defeated his bid for nomination, securing instead the choice of William E. Jenner, chairman of the State Republican Committee.

In January 1947, LaFollette was appointed Deputy Chief Counsel for the Nuremberg trials and as such prosecuted Nazi Ministry of Justice officials. In December of that year he was made Military Governor of Wuerttemberg-Baden. He resigned from this post in January 1949, he has said, because of his conviction that the United States policy was endangering the chance to develop a democratic Germany by alienating the support of workers and economically unfortunate groups.

Appointment as national director of Americans for Democratic Action came to LaFollette in June of 1949. The ADA is described as an independent national political organization of "non-Communist liberals" set up in 1947 by New Deal sympathizers to offset those leftist groups which maintain they represent New Deal ideas. The organization has a national office in Washington, D.C., and 120 chapters in some forty States; its chairman is Hubert H. Humphrey '49, United States Senator from Minnesota. LaFollette stated that he was accepting the ADA post as a political independent. Comment in the New York *Post* on the report of the proceedings of the ADA Full Employment Conference, held in July 1949, called it "as good a statement as can be found anywhere of economic thinking among independent progressives in the postwar period." In addressing this conference, at which enactment of the Brannan farm program and passage of the Economic Expansion Act of 1949 were urged, director LaFollette said that people "do not exist to sustain an economy" but that an economic system justifies itself in the manner it meets the rightful needs of the people. "By every test of the American ethic," he declared, "it is clear that those who own the means of

LAFOLLETTE, CHARLES M.—*Continued*
production and distribution hold it at the sufferance of the American people and subject to their power" (New York *Post*, September 4, 1949).

As ADA director, LaFollette commended a resolution by Senator Scott W. Lucas [47] to reform Senate investigating methods in order to protect people summoned for Senate investigation from unfair treatment. In a letter to the President stressing the importance of strengthening civil rights, LaFollette described an Army plan for improving the opportunities of Negroes in the Armed Forces as "sham" since it retained a "quota" system of enlistment and made no provision for reassignment of Negro soldiers qualified for special ratings (New York *Times*, October 3, 1949). In January 1950, the ADA director voiced disapproval of United States support of a predicted United Nations resolution freeing member nations to restore normal diplomatic relations with the Franco regime in Spain.

LaFollette belongs to the American Legion, the Veterans of Foreign Wars, Forty and Eight, is a Thirty-second Degree Mason, an Elk, an Eagle, and a member of Phi Delta Theta. He is a member of the Episcopal Church. On May 14, 1925, he married Frances Hartmetz. Two daughters were born to them, Marian Louise and Frances Ann, who is deceased. The ADA's director is five feet nine inches tall, weighs 175 pounds, has red hair and gray eyes.

References

N Y Sun p20 Ja 18 '46
PM p13 Ja 8 '46
Congressional Directory (2nd ed., 1945)
Who's Who in America, 1948-49

LANCHESTER, ELSA Oct. 28, 1902- Actress
Address: b. c/o Turnabout Theatre, 716 N. La Cienega Blvd., Los Angeles, Calif.; h. Pacific Palisades, Calif.; Palos Verdes, Calif.

The British-born actress Elsa Lanchester, who is Mrs. Charles Laughton [48], first became known to American motion picture audiences in 1933, in the part of Anne of Cleves, one of the monarch's wives in *The Private Life of Henry VIII*. In 1950 she named the role of Amelia Potts in *Come to the Stable* as the one she liked best. During the intervening years her many screen appearances have been regarded as among the most entertaining in filmdom. At the beginning of her career in England Miss Lanchester was a dancer and singer before she entered the theater. The stage still claims much of her time as the comedienne of Hollywood's Turnabout Theatre.

Elsa Lanchester sometimes calls herself a Cockney, though she was born beyond the sound of Bow Bells, in Lewisham, London, on October 28, 1902. Her parents, James and Edith (Lanchester) Sullivan, socialists, pacifists, and vegetarians, were of small means: the family of four lived, she tells in *Charles Laughton and I*, on the two pounds ten—about

$12 a week—her father earned as an accountant. They managed, however, to send Elsa's brother to a private progressive school for boys, and they sent her there, too, after the six-year-old had "failed in everything but tears" at the local school. During the seven "divinely happy" years the little redhead attended Mr. Kettle's school, she was not late once.

When she was about ten, Elsa Sullivan attended Raymond Duncan's free dancing classes in Chelsea, and was one of about twenty children from many countries who were given all-expense scholarships to Isadora Duncan's school of dancing in Paris. At first delighted, Elsa was soon disillusioned: she disliked the whole luxurious, artificial atmosphere (she tells in *Charles Laughton and I*). After three months, much to her relief, she was sent home because of the outbreak of World War I. Back in London, the eleven-year-old immediately started to teach classical dancing to neighborhood children. She also took to wearing homemade Grecian sandals and deliberately conspicuous hand-woven draperies.

From teaching at the Margaret Morris dancing school, young Miss Sullivan went on to become a full-fledged teacher of the dance. ("I always had an itch to organize everybody round me," she has said.) By the age of fifteen and a half, she had several private pupils, a paying class, and a free class in the heart of London. It was the last-named which took much of her attention; and as it grew into the Children's Theatre in 1918, the young teacher kept only enough paying pupils to pay her living expenses and to make up the deficits of the performances. These were Fielding's *Tom Thumb*, Andersen fairy tale adaptations, and Jane Austen's *Love and Friendship*, most performances being for charity. In 1921 the London County Council forbade the performances as violations of the child labor law.

After this, Miss Lanchester (she had now taken that name) and some friends opened the Cave of Harmony on the same premises, a new kind of night club. No liquor was served and the entertainment, a midnight show, was as likely to be a one-act play by Pirandello, Chekhov, Anatole France, Laurence Housman, as an original revue. It was largely a labor of love: the management realized only pocket money, and noted actors often gave their services gratis, after their own final curtains, for the sake of appearing in seldom-performed masterpieces. Subsequently the group moved to its own studio, where for two years Elsa Lanchester slept in a loft she had built. From dancing she went on to singing and taking part in skits; she claims two "firsts," that the Cave of Harmony was the first to revive Victorian songs, and that she originated the costume of top hat, ballet dress, and high heels later used by Marlene Dietrich. Like the others, Miss Lanchester continued at the Cave of Harmony while working at other commitments. Her first stage appearance was made in April 1922 as the Second Shop Girl in *Thirty Minutes in a Street*. Sir Nigel Playfair, who had several times appeared at the club, gave her the part of the Larva in *The Insect Play* and, after her success as that *enfant terrible*, cast her as Peggy in *The Way of the World* in early 1924, Sancho in *The Duenna* that October, and Sophie Binner in *Cobra* a year later.

In April 1926 came *Riverside Nights*, a hit revue in which Elsa Lanchester repeated her old Cave of Harmony successes, "tear-jerking" ballads and comic specialty numbers. After the show she drove to her night club engagements, for which she might change her costume in a cab. One cafe engagement came to a sudden end when a distinguished guest left in the middle of "Please Sell No More Drink to My Father," but another club soon engaged the singer. The most lucrative of Miss Lanchester's engagements were her appearances at private parties—but at these, she has said, she never knew whether she would be treated strictly as a hired entertainer or an honored guest.

Four roles later, in late 1927, Elsa Lanchester was cast opposite Charles Laughton, a rising young character actor, in Arnold Bennett's *Mr. Prohack*; they received equal salaries, but he had the title role and she the smaller part of his secretary, Mimi Winstock. As a lark, Laughton took the parts of a policeman and a wicked Rajah in two of the three short films which H. G. Wells wrote for her. (Miss Lanchester's official screen debut was in the silent British version of *The Constant Nymph*, which she followed with *Potiphar's Wife*). Laughton also acted with her in some skits at the Cave of Harmony, which closed a few months before their marriage in February 1929.

Having played parts in *The Outskirts* in 1929 and *Ten Nights in a Bar Room* in 1930, in January 1931 Miss Lanchester hid her red hair under long golden ringlets to play Little Lord Fauntleroy, a part which she did not satirize. That May she again had the role of a child, as Laughton's twelve-year-old daughter in the grim study of a murderer, *Payment Deferred*. This was a success which they repeated in New York that September. While her husband began his Hollywood career in 1932, Miss Lanchester found herself without engagements for the first time. When Laughton returned to England, the couple started work with Alexander Korda on a comedy about Henry VIII and Anne of Cleves. This grew into *The Private Life of Henry VIII*, which won her husband the 1933 Academy Award, and herself "paeans of praise, but few offers." Before the film was premièred, the Laughtons had entered upon a nine-month repertory season with the Old Vic-Sadler's Wells Company, during which Miss Lanchester played the part of the governess in *The Cherry Orchard*, Ariel in *The Tempest*, Wilde's Miss Prism (a part she disliked), several small roles in Shakespeare, and the "silly, giggling country girl," fifteen-year-old Miss Prue in Congreve's *Love for Love*.

According to Miss Lanchester, Metro-Goldwyn-Mayer, which had signed her to a contract on the strength of her performance as the unattractive Anne of Cleves, "never quite knew what to do with the redheaded Londoner" who arrived. After small character parts in *David Copperfield* and *Naughty*

Marietta in 1935, the studio lent her to Universal for *The Bride of Frankenstein*, in which she played both the gentle Mary Shelley and the woman monster. (In the latter part make-up application required three hours, and she could neither sit nor walk in her mummy-like bandages.) So different were the two characterizations that many in the audiences did not realize they were played by the same actress. Back in England the next year, Elsa Lanchester acted in *The Ghost Goes West*, and then in *Rembrandt* with Laughton and Gertrude Lawrence. Playing the sweet, simple kitchenmaid who becomes the painter's model and wife, she silenced the whispers that "Laughton got his wife into the picture" by a successful performance. She also wrote her own song, in forty-five minutes, picking out the tune on the piano with one finger.

Elsa Lanchester was Peter Pan in the traditional Christmas revival at London's Palladium in 1936, and then toured with it, giving two shows a day six days a week, despite a fractured rib. She considers herself fortunate to have been, in 1937, in the first picture produced by Laughton and Erich Pommer—the next two leading ladies were Vivien Leigh and Maureen O'Hara. The sanctimonious but determined missionary Martha Jones in *Vessel of Wrath* (*The Beachcomber*) has been considered her best screen part. After this success, she refused many comic spinster roles. Her book, *Charles Laughton and I* (1938) the reviewers found gay, witty, unassuming, artless. In 1941 she essayed the lead role of the murderous housemaid Emmy Beaudine in *They Walk Alone* on the New York stage. Many reviewers found her performance admirable, others thought she overacted, but all agreed that the play made impossible demands upon the leading actress.

In the summer of 1941, in Los Angeles, Elsa Lanchester came upon a site where three puppeteers were building a 160-seat theater with reversible seats (so the audience could turn about after seeing a puppet show, to face a stage for "live" presentations.) She expressed a wish to join the show. Accepting no salary, because the little theater could not pay a salary commensurate with her earning power, Miss Lanchester was to be a guest artist for two weeks. She has remained with the project ever since, appearing nightly except Monday for eleven months of the year. Four frequently freshened programs are rotated, with Miss Lanchester's first number always finding her tattered and frowzy, her second in a costume piece, and her third in "a sexy sort of number." "In some of them," said *Time*, "she rivals Bea Lillie at her best." Miss Lanchester's recompense for this work, besides what she calls "the chance to use every bit of creative energy I have," is copyright ownership of about fifty songs written for her by Forman Brown.

While working two hours a night at the Turnabout Theatre, Miss Lanchester has continued her daytime screen work. She was one of the lunatic sisters in *Ladies in Retirement* (1941), appeared in *Son of Fury* and *Tales of*

ELSA LANCHESTER

Manhattan in 1942, *Forever and a Day* in 1943, and was described as "wonderfully right" as the impoverished Yorkshire mother in *Lassie Come Home* (1943). Most of the Lanchester parts are what reviewers often call "delightful bits," and she "ably carried" *Passport to Adventure* (1944) as a London charwoman who makes her way to the Reichschancellory to assassinate Hitler. A bibulous cook in *The Spiral Staircase* (1946), a kittenish secretary in *The Razor's Edge* (1946), a maid in *The Secret Garden* (1949) she liked best her role as the bewildered, put-upon artist Amelia Potts in *Come to the Stable* (1949). Other Lanchester performances were in *Northwest Outpost* (1947) and *The Bishop's Wife* (1947), and she had the largest female role in *The Inspector General* (1949) as the mayor's wife who pursues Danny Kaye. Her first unsympathetic role in ten years, a blackmailer in *Mystery Street*, was assigned to her in 1950. Her comment on it was: "It's a detour in character I cheerfully admit I love." Miss Lanchester was scheduled to entertain in the Wedgwood Room of New York's Waldorf-Astoria Hotel in the fall of that year.

Of naturally striking appearance, Elsa Lanchester stands five feet four, has wavy, unruly dark red hair and large brown eyes. She has told that she and her husband both live their roles, which sometimes makes for confusion, and experience "mental anguish" while searching for a character. Miss Lanchester is fond of riding, backgammon, arranging flowers, making home movies, enjoys her husband's art collection. She says of herself, "I love elemental displays of any sort . . . thunderstorms, rough seas, volcanoes. . . .I don't really like pets . . . intense heat, new places, new people, and new food." Between pictures and on weekends, the Laughtons leave their large Hollywood home for a servantless three-room cottage, where they

tend bees and six kinds of fruit trees. On April 28, 1950, the British-born couple became American citizens.

References

Collier's 103:19 Mr 4 '39
N Y Herald Tribune VI p2 Mr 30 '41
International Motion Picture Almanac, 1949-50
Lanchester, E. Charles Laughton and I (1938)
Who's Who, 1949
Who's Who in the Theatre (1947)
World Biography (1948)

LANGLIE, ARTHUR B(ERNARD) July 25, 1900- Governor of Washington

Address: b. Legislative Building, State Capitol, Olympia, Wash.; h. Executive Mansion, Olympia, Wash.

The Governor of the State of Washington, Republican Arthur B. Langlie, is a lawyer who came to the Governorship after serving on the City Council and in the office of Mayor of Seattle. A champion of "business methods" in government, Langlie is in 1950 serving the second year of a second, but not consecutive, term as Governor: he had previously been in office from 1941 to 1945.

Arthur Bernard Langlie was born July 25, 1900, in Lanesboro, Minnesota, one of the three sons of Norwegian immigrants, Bjarne Alfred and Carrie (Dahl) Langlie. The family moved westward, so that Arthur was reared in Bremerton, Washington, where, as a boy, he helped in his father's grocery store. While attending Bremerton High School he participated in the extracurricular activities of debating, dramatics, and sports. After his graduation in 1919 he entered the University of Washington, in Seattle. As a student he earned his expenses by working in logging camps, sawmills, gas stations, and harvest fields. Meanwhile, he won distinction in athletics at the university, becoming captain of the baseball team (he toured Japan with the team in 1925) and captain of the tennis team. He was also a member of the Oval Club, the Fir Tree, Phi Alpha Delta, and Phi Kappa Sigma (as president for two years). Having been awarded the B.A. degree, followed by the Bachelor of Laws in 1926, Langlie was admitted to the Washington bar the same year. His choice of law as a career was determined, he has said, by influences at home (his mother in particular), at church, and among his other associations.

Young Langlie's first position was with the firm of Shank, Belt and Rode in Seattle. In 1935 he entered political life, the year after he joined one of a group of young men in Seattle who organized the New Order of Cincinnatus; this, according to Kate Archibald of the *Christian Science Monitor*, "was premised upon the theory that government should not be a matter of politics but of business—good business." Their efforts resulted in the election of three of their members to the City Council of Seattle; one of the three was the relatively unknown young attorney, Arthur Langlie. In 1936 the same group put forward Langlie for Mayor, but he was defeated. He remained in the City Council, however, until 1938, when he again ran for Mayor, this time successfully. He fulfilled his campaign promises to rehabilitate the "obsolete and bankrupt municipal streetcar system and to restore the city's impaired financial status" (reporter Archibald's words). Nominated in February 1940 for a second term by a landslide primary vote of 44,278, Langlie was again elected Mayor of Seattle.

In 1940 Mayor Langlie was "drafted" as a candidate for Governor by a group of citizens from eastern Washington. Running ahead of the Republican slate, Langlie defeated former Senator Clarence C. Dill by only 5,816 votes in the election, in which all other State offices went to Democrats. Supporters of Dill filed charges of fraud and irregularities in the vote; but the predominantly Democratic legislature, in a joint session, refused in a 97-to-45 vote to investigate the challenge. Thus Langlie was inaugurated to succeed the Democratic Governor Clarence D. Martin in January 1941 for a four-year term. In his inaugural address the new Governor outlined a policy of services to the people to be financed by savings made through applying business methods to government. He expressed approval of a $40-a-month pension plan for the aged and State aid to schools, and advocated increased aid for dependent and crippled children and a better State Workmen's Industrial Insurance law. (Washington had traditionally been among the States which lead in welfare legislation.) He also submitted proposals for streamlining the State Government, promising that such a reorganization would save the State $3,500,000 during the next two years, and urged the adoption of the merit system in the selection and promotion of State employees.

At the Mackinac Island meeting of Republican party leaders in September 1943, Langlie was one of eighteen Republican Governors (out of twenty-four) who "revolted" against the party leadership to force a recasting of the Republican platform to make it more specific. Langlie and Governor Warren of California revised the section on labor. In the Presidential race that followed two months later Langlie campaigned for Governor Thomas E. Dewey as a champion of the "enterprise system of business" and as a man who would halt the trend toward "bureaucratic government." At stake, Langlie said, was "the very foundation of our governmental structure," which was endangered by "the black shadow of socialism." Langlie's challenger for the Governorship in that election was Democratic Senator Mon C. Wallgren[48]. During the campaign, speculation centered on whether Republican Governor Langlie's popularity might help carry the State for Dewey, although Washington had given its vote to President Roosevelt previously. As discussed by columnist Marquis Childs (New York *Post*, October 18, 1944), Langlie's influence in the State was the result of his "sound administration" after "a succession of incompetents. While there has been nothing spectacular or showy about Langlie's administration, he has

Grady

ARTHUR B. LANGLIE

gained wide popularity." Langlie was defeated, however. In February 1945, called to active duty in the Naval Reserve with the rank of lieutenant, he served with the Atlantic Fleet and on the Hawaiian Sea Frontier.

Upon his discharge from service, in 1946 Langlie returned to his legal practice as a senior member of the firm of Langlie, Todd and Nickell. Two years later Langlie was again nominated to run against Wallgren, who sought a second term as Governor. Despite a national sweep by Democrats, from the Presidency to most of the Governorships, Langlie was elected, one of the two Republicans who won Governorships from Democrats. In the same election in the State of Washington the Democrat-sponsored Citizens Security Act was passed by a referendum. The act raised minimum old-age benefits to about sixty dollars a month, and secured free medical care to anyone on the State relief rolls as well as to those receiving old age benefits. Seven months after the law went into effect *United States News* reported (July 22, 1949) that free health care was taking about one-half the State's tax money. Governor Langlie's request for more taxes to meet the costs of the program was refused by the legislature.

The plan was widely discussed as an American experiment in socialized medicine. Those entitled to the free care, about 8 per cent of the State's population by February 1950, could choose their own physicians; the bills went to the State. By May 1950 petitioners were campaigning for signatures for changes in the bill in the November elections. While some asked for higher benefits for the aged, another group, supported by Governor Langlie, sought to tighten the legislation to end "abuses," and thus to save the State an estimated $25,000,000 to $40,000,000 biennially. Langlie described the law as going beyond the socialist system in

LANGLIE, ARTHUR B.—*Continued*

Great Britain—"And I'm not plugging for the British system."

At the Governors Conference at Colorado Springs in June 1949 Langlie joined a minority group of Governors who opposed Federal aid to education. Later Langlie also opposed the proposed Columbia Valley Authority for the Pacific Northwest as "a complete and unprecedented departure from the dual Federal-State form of government contemplated by the Constitution and treasured by the people." During discussions of the CVA in early 1950, Governor Langlie, according to the *Christian Science Monitor* (February 27, 1950) led the opposition to the plan (based on the organization of the Tennessee Valley Authority) on the ground that it would place the region's economy entirely in the hands of three commissioners, appointed by the President and not responsible to Congress or to the people of the region. In January 1950, too, Langlie was one of three Republican Governors who met with Republican party leaders to draft a policy statement for the 1950 Congressional elections.

The Governor of Washington is a member of the American Legion, the Veterans of Foreign Wars, the Sons of Norway, the Norwegian Commercial Club, and the Rotary Club; he belongs also to the Royal Arcanum, the Eagles, Moose, Kiwanis, and Lions. Three colleges have awarded him honorary Doctor of Laws degrees: Whitman College (1942), College of Puget Sound (1943), and Seattle Pacific College (1944). In recognition of his achievements he was given the decoration of the Royal Order of St. Olav by Norway in 1940. His article "Go West Again, Young Man!" predicting great expansion and opportunity in the Pacific Northwest after the end of World War II, appeared in *Liberty* for October 30, 1943. A Presbyterian in religion, Langlie once said, "Democracy can succeed in only one way, by a spiritual revival and the carrying on of Christian principles." Mrs. Langlie is the former Evelyn P. Baker, whom he married September 15, 1928; their children are Arthur Sheridan and Carrie Ellen. Of medium build, Langlie stands five feet eight inches, weighs 165 pounds; he has gray hair, blue eyes, and "a ready laugh." His recreations are fishing and golf.

References

Christian Sci Mon Mag p5 F 8 '41 por
America's Young Men, 1938-39
Who's Who in America, 1950-51
Who's Who in the West (1949)
World Biography (1948)

LANGMUIR, IRVING   Jan. 31, 1881-

Chemist; industrial scientist

Address: h. 1176 Stratford Rd., Schenectady, N.Y.

> NOTE: This biography supersedes the article which appeared in *Current Biography* in 1940.

"Few scientists have managed to combine pure and applied research as successfully as Dr. Irving Langmuir," John E. Pfeiffer of *Scientific American* has written. Chemist and physicist, Dr. Langmuir was for forty years associated with the General Electric Research Laboratory, first as assistant and then as associate director. His researches, largely in pure science, have resulted in the modern gas-filled light bulb, the high-vacuum radio tube, the atomic hydrogen welding torch, and numerous electronic devices. Of the more than sixty-five patents that have been issued to Langmuir, half are in the field of radio engineering. His even more important theoretical work in surface chemistry and the structure of matter brought him the 1932 Nobel Prize in chemistry. His most recent important research has been in meteorology—more specifically, meteorological engineering—which developed the principle of spraying dry ice and silver iodide into moisture-laden clouds to produce artificial rainfall.

Irving Langmuir was born in Brooklyn, New York, on January 31, 1881, one of the four sons of Charles and Sadie (Comings) Langmuir. His grandfather, a minister, had emigrated from Scotland to Canada, and later settled in Connecticut. A "self-made" businessman who was a clerk at the age of fourteen, Charles Langmuir had made and lost a fortune by his middle years. Irving Langmuir began school at a public elementary school in Brooklyn, but his education was proceeding more rapidly in the basement of the Langmuir home, where his elder brother Arthur (who was to become a chemist of note himself) had helped nine-year-old Irving build a workshop. "Until I was fourteen I always hated school and did poorly at it," Langmuir has written in *Phenomena, Atoms, and Molecules*. In 1892 the Langmuirs left for Europe, there to spend three years while the senior Langmuir's insurance interests in Paris needed his attention. Irving, now twelve, was sent to a boarding school in a suburb of Paris; again his brother aided him in setting up a small laboratory adjoining his room.

Since he was an American, Irving Langmuir was freed from what he has called "the absurdly rigorous discipline" of the French school, thus enabling him to spend time alone in the school laboratory, and, encouraged by one of his teachers, to learn logarithms and trigonometry, subjects not required in the school. On his thirteenth birthday his mother wrote to a friend: "Irving's brain is working like an engine all the time, and it is wonderful to hear him talk with Herbert [another brother] on scientific subjects. Herbert says he fairly has to shun electricity, for the child gets beside himself with enthusiasm, and shows such intelligence on the subject that it fairly scares him." With a brother, and later alone, Irving climbed Swiss mountains before he was in his teens. The mountain climbing became a lifelong hobby and eventually led to his work in meteorology.

At the school he next attended, Chestnut Hill Academy in Philadelphia (the story is told) fourteen-year-old Langmuir came upon a book on calculus and mastered it in six weeks. The same year he entered the Pratt Institute, in Brooklyn, and three years later the Columbia

School of Mines, from which he was graduated in 1903 with the degree in metallurgical engineering. Thereupon he left for Germany for graduate work in physical chemistry under Professor Walther Nernst (1920 Nobel Prize winner) at Göttingen University. In 1906 Langmuir was granted the Ph.D. degree; his dissertation was on the action of gases in cooling.

On his return to America, Langmuir became a chemistry instructor at the Stevens Institute of Technology, in Hoboken, New Jersey. The summer of 1909, after three years of teaching elementary chemistry, Langmuir decided that instead of climbing mountains he would work during his vacation. He took a summer position with the recently established (1901) General Electric Company Research Laboratory in Schenectady, New York, a new type of industrial laboratory that sought not the solution of known problems but rather "new fundamental knowledge" related to the company's work. Dr. W. R. Whitney, the director, told Langmuir to work at whatever interested him. This freedom, greater than any permitted in a university, was so interesting that the young scientist readily accepted when Dr. Whitney offered him a place in the laboratory. Langmuir was to remain at General Electric for more than forty years, becoming its assistant director in a year, and serving as its associate director from 1932 to January 1950.

Langmuir had chosen for that summer's work (in 1909) an investigation into gases obtained when tungsten filaments were heated in a high vacuum, and what happened when various other gases were introduced into vacuum light bulbs. This was related to a General Electric problem —the fact that tungsten filaments of electric light bulbs deteriorated rapidly. The company's lamp engineers were working on the theory that a better vacuum in the bulb would make a better lamp, but Langmuir's interest was "curiosity." He did not foresee that the results of his "purely theoretical" research in chemical reactions would be the basis of three new industries. In 1912 came his discovery that the filling of a lamp bulb with nitrogen or argon protected the tungsten wires from deterioration. The use of Langmuir's gas-filled incandescent lamp is estimated to have saved the American public $1,000,000 nightly in light bills.

In his work with the lamps and gases Langmuir had unexpectedly made the discovery that hydrogen at high temperatures was dissociated into atoms, then recombined, causing an enormous increase in heat conduction. This led to fifteen years of experiments with atomic hydrogen, which became the basis for Langmuir's (in 1927) of the atomic hydrogen welding torch, making it possible to weld metals that melt only at extremely high temperatures. A third industry grew out of the fact that his work on the lamp demanded the development of better vacuum pumps. His high vacuum mercury pump was the "most perfect vacuum pump in existence," stated Bernard Jaffe in *Crucibles* (1930). This work resulted in the high-vacuum transmitting tube, which is basic to modern radio broadcasting. Langmuir's study of the flow of electrons in high vacuums and in gases

made it possible for him to "set the electron to work" in a number of other electronic devices.

It was principally Langmuir's discoveries in surface chemistry that brought him the 1932 Nobel Prize in chemistry—the first American industrial chemist to win the award. These researches began with his study of the catalysis involved in the mechanism of reactions on solid surfaces. As he has explained, he soon found that "most of these phenomena depended upon the presence of a single layer of atoms." This turned his interest to work on surfaces of liquids, surface tension and monomolecular films on water and other liquids. His findings, thought at first to be of interest only as pure science, led to the development of "invisible" glass, and had applications in biology. For example, in 1941 Langmuir developed an instrument that made it possible to detect poisons and viruses that could not be seen under a microscope; the method involved coating glass slides with invisible films of one molecule in thickness and treating the films in a way that reflected characteristic colors for different viruses.

Langmuir's work during World War I on submarine detection devices (at the Naval Experimental Station in Nahant, Massachusetts) stimulated his interest in studies in the motion of water in rivers and lakes as influenced by wind on its surface. These studies proved useful to him in connection with his World War II work on smoke screens and aircraft icing. Together with Vincent J. Schaefer '48, a General Electric research chemist, Langmuir developed new techniques for producing large quantities of dense smoke for concealing military movements. His enthusiasm for mountain climbing and skiing, he has said, led him into his subsequent researches. In the winter of 1945-46 Langmuir and Schaefer studied the forming of ice on aircraft at a weather station in the midst of supercooled clouds on Mount Washington, New Hampshire. It was while engaged in this work that the two scientists began to think about artificial snow or rainmaking. They introduced a variety of substances into supercooled air, hoping to provide nuclei for the formation of ice crystals, and eventually tried seeding the air with dry ice and with vaporized silver iodide. The particles acted as nuclei for the condensation, forming snowflakes and setting off a chain reaction that resulted in violent thunder storms "when conditions were right." Langmuir and Schaefer conducted rain-making experiments in New Mexico in July 1949 as members of Project Cirrus, established in 1947 by the Army Signal Corps and the Office of Naval Research in consultation with the General Electric laboratory.

The scientist's experiments with Project Cirrus took him on trips to Puerto Rico, Central America, and New Mexico. When he retired as associate director of the General Electric Research Laboratory in January 1950 (which he continues to serve as consultant) he announced that he would continue his work on Project Cirrus. In a letter to Governor Thomas E. Dewey in March 1950 Langmuir explained that he must give up the post he had held since

Wide World Photos

IRVING LANGMUIR

September 1948 as a member of the board of trustees of the State University of New York in order to devote more time to that project, which he felt was the way he could best serve the national welfare.

Since 1909 Langmuir has published more than two hundred papers in about twenty-five technical journals in the United States and abroad. Twenty of the papers were reprinted as a volume entitled *Phenomena, Atoms, and Molecules; an Attempt to Interpret Phenomena in Terms of Mechanisms or Atomic and Molecular Interactions* (1950). Aside from the technical papers in the book, the author has expressed himself on a number of nonscientific subjects, such as the work of the House Un-American Activities Committee and the value of hobbies. One reviewer pointed out that the collection represented Langmuir's more important contributions; another, that "throughout, the writer advances his arguments in a thorough, logical manner, even on those subjects which are treated lightly." For the lay public he contributed the chapter "Atomic Arms Race and Its Alternatives" to the book *One World or None*; and "World Control of Atomic Energy" to *Symposium on Atomic Energy and Its Implications*. The titles of other nontechnical articles by Langmuir are "Science and Incentives in Russia", "Scientists of the U.S.S.R.", "Across Nation in an Hour?" and "Science, Common Sense and Decency."

Langmuir has received almost every honor a scientist can win, from the Nobel Prize for 1932 to fourteen honorary degrees (as of 1950) from universities in the United States, England, and Germany. In the 1950-51 *Who's Who in America* seventeen medals and prizes are listed as having been awarded to him: the first (in 1915) was a Nichols medal awarded to him by the New York section of the American Chemists Society, and in 1943 he was the recipient

of the Faraday Medal Award of the Electrical Engineers of Great Britain. He has also been named an honorary member of important scientific bodies in the United States, Europe, and South America. A fellow of the American Association for the Advancement of Science, he was president of that organization in 1941, an office he had held in the American Chemists Society in 1929. He lectured in London in 1938 and was the Hitchcock Foundation lecturer at the University of California in 1946.

The scientist married Marion Mersereau on April 27, 1912; their two children are Kenneth and Barbara. Langmuir, who is described as a "stocky man of middle height with plentiful white hair," finds pleasure in motor boating and flying; still fond of mountain climbing, he also likes to ski. Given also to scientific observation in leisure moments, he has noted the speed at which a deer fly travels and the behavior of ants when threatened by a rising stream. In speaking of the incentives for his lifetime of achievement he has said, "Whatever work I've done, I've done for the fun of it."

References

Coronet 26:78-82 Je '49
N Y Times p20 Ja 3 '50
N Y World-Telegram F 26 '40
Newsweek 17:59 Ja 13 '41 por
Sat Eve Post 220:24-5+ O 25 '47
Sci Am 157:131 S '37 por; 160:41 Ja '39
Time 56:52 Ag 28 '50 por
American Men of Science (1949)
Dunlap, O. E. Radio's 100 Men of Science (1944)
Gray, G. W. Advancing Front of Science (1937)
Hylander, C. J. American Scientists (1935)
Jaffe, B. Crucibles (1930)
Kendall, J. Young Chemists and Great Discoveries (1939)
Langmuir, I. Phenomena, Atoms, and Molecules (1950)
Who's Who in America, 1950-51
World Biography (1948)

LARKIN, OLIVER W(ATERMAN) Aug. 17, 1896- Educator; author

Address: b. c/o Smith College, Northampton, Mass.; h. 65 Bridge St., Northampton, Mass.

The Pulitzer Prize in history "for a distinguished book of the year [1949] on the history of the United States" went to Oliver W. Larkin, for his *Art and Life in America*. A survey of American art from its beginnings in the seventeenth century up to 1945, the book traces the development of painting, sculpture, architecture, and, to a lesser extent, the minor arts, as related to the general social and cultural background. It is the first time that a book devoted to the visual arts has won the Pulitzer Prize in history. Since 1931 Larkin has been a professor of art at Smith College, and in 1950 heads the art department of that school.

Born in Medford, Massachusetts, on August 17, 1896, Oliver Waterman Larkin is the son of Charles Ernest and Kate Mary (Waterman)

Larkin. He has two brothers and a sister. Both sides of the family are of New England descent, one branch dating back to the early colonial period in Massachusetts. His father, now living in West Newbury, Massachusetts, has been well known as an antique dealer and collector throughout the Merrimack Valley for fifty years. Young Larkin was reared first in Medford and later in Georgetown, Massachusetts, where he graduated with honors from the Perley Free School in 1914. At that time he was already interested in painting, drawing, and dramatics. He subsequently entered Harvard College, majored in French and Latin, and received his Bachelor of Arts degree in 1918. While an undergraduate at Harvard he won several scholarships and was elected to Phi Beta Kappa in his senior year. In 1918-19, in World War I, he served as a private in the Medical Corps of the 73d Infantry Regiment of the United States Army.

"My inclination to become a teacher of art was fostered by my father," Larkin has told, "and encouraged by Dr. Denman Ross and Professor Arthur Pope '47, who were my teachers in art courses at Harvard." In 1919 he obtained his Master of Arts degree from Harvard, to which he returned as an assistant in fine arts two years later. At this time, too, he directed plays and designed scenery for Lincoln House, a settlement house in Boston. At the age of twenty-eight (1924) he was made assistant professor of art at Smith College, in Northampton, Massachusetts. Promoted to associate professor in 1926, he became a full professor in 1931. For a time during 1925 and 1926, he also taught at Iowa State University; and in the summer of 1950 he lectured on American art at the Harvard Student Council's American Seminar Studies for European students in Salzburg, Austria.

Larkin has contributed numerous articles and book reviews to various periodicals, including *Theatre Arts, Magazine of Art, Saturday Review of Literature, College Art Journal, School and Society, Antiques, Stage,* and the *William and Mary Quarterly.* Among the topics on which he has written are "Alfred Stieglitz and 291", "The Thoughtful Laughter of Jules Romains", "Daumier, Bourgeois Playgoer", "Air Waves and Sight Lines", "Domesticating Modern Art," and "Charles Kean, Pedant-Showman." In an article entitled "The Critic and the Work of Art," contributed to a symposium conducted by the Artists League of America, Larkin outlined the three qualifications which he thought an art critic ought to possess: "First, he must develop superb responsiveness to the *sensations* which the work offers, and to those visual relationships which constitute its form; second, the critic must try to understand what the artist was trying to do, and know something about the materials, technically and materially speaking, with which the artist was doing it; third, we expect the critic to judge the work, not only in itself, but in relation to the whole work of the artist, sometimes to an entire art movement, or to the art of a period."

The writing of *Art and Life in America* was undertaken at the suggestion of his pub-

OLIVER W. LARKIN

lishers—Larkin had been giving a course in American art at Smith College for many years. In the author's foreword, he says: "Five years ago, when I sat down with a mass of notes at my elbow to write this book, I composed a prospectus of my undertaking. I wrote: 'This book would be an introductory survey of the history of architecture, sculpture, painting, and to some degree of the so-called "minor arts" in the United States. It would show how these arts have expressed American ways of living and how they have been related to the development of American ideas, particularly the idea of democracy.'" Dedicated to Larkin's father, wife, and son, this 547-page book was written to appeal to the general reader as well as to serve as a college text for students of American civilization and art. It is arranged chronologically in six "books," each covering a period with a character of its own: The Colonial Arts; Self-Conscious Republic; Democratic Vistas; Between Two Panics; Progressivism, Culture, and War; and New Horizons. Each "book," in turn, is divided into two or three parts, dealing with a particular phase of the period; each part is preceded by an introduction setting forth the cultural environment, while the chapters that follow treat the lives and works of the artists themselves. According to the publishers, Larkin rewrote the text at least three times, and assisted the book's designer, Stefan Salter, in making-up the pages of the volume, which contains more than 400 illustrations. Larkin's work was awarded the $500 Pulitzer Prize in history on May 1, 1950.

Art and Life in America was published in the fall of 1949. In the estimation of Alfred Frankenstein of the San Francisco *Chronicle,* it is "by far the finest general history of the visual arts in America that has yet been writ-

LARKIN, OLIVER W.—*Continued*

ten, and one that might well supersede all other general histories." According to Benjamin Rowland, Jr., of the *Nation*, the book "achieves a unity because it is a work of objective reporting rather than interpretation colored by personal bias." Lincoln Kirstein of *New Republic* found "the attempt to balance chronology and personal or regional styles against individual peak achievement . . . manfully undertaken," and went on to say that "until somebody else solves this all but impossible problem of organization, Professor Larkin's study is the best one to give Europeans or Americans unfamiliar with the grand aspects of our visual culture." In letters to the New York *Times*, Howard Mumford Jones wrote that it was "the first book in which the arts in America are made to fit into an understandable cultural and social framework in historical time," and Lloyd Goodrich claimed that it was "the most complete account of American painting since 1905, of American sculpture since 1903, and the first book since 1935 to cover American architecture and photography."

James Johnson Sweeney, writer on modern art, in a New York *Times* article expressed the opinion that Larkin had failed to supply a pattern for the reader which would enable him to grasp "the broad picture of the features of America's creative contribution." Oscar Handlin of *The Magazine of Art* thought Larkin did not account for the "melancholy meagerness of our achievement," since he limited his conception of life in the United States to the "dominant social groups."

On July 30, 1925, Larkin married Ruth Lily McIntire, of Dedham, Massachusetts. They have one son, Peter Sidney, who in 1950 is a stage designer and technician for the Wellesley College theater. Larkin himself has continued to maintain his interest in the theater by directing plays for the Northampton Players, a civic group, and by making puppets and producing several marionette shows. His wife has also been active in the production end of the theater. Known as "Pete" to his friends, Larkin is described as being "unassuming." He is five feet four inches tall and weighs 165 pounds; his hair and his eyes are brown. He is a member of the Teachers Union of Western Massachusetts and of the Descendants of the American Revolution. Politically he lists himself as "independent."

References

N Y Herald Tribune My 2 '50 por
N Y Times p22 My 2 '50 por
Who's Who in America, 1950-51
Who's Who in American Art, 1940-47

LARSEN, ROY E(DWARD) Apr. 20, 1899- Publishing executive
Address: b. c/o Time, Inc., 9 Rockefeller Center, New York 20; h. Greens Farms, Conn.

As president of Time, Inc., publishers of magazines *Time*, *Life*, *Fortune*, and *Architectural Forum*, and the producers of *The March of Time*, Roy E. Larsen heads what has frequently been called one of the most successful publishing enterprises of our time. Associated with Time, Inc., in various executive capacities since it was founded in 1922, he is generally considered to be second in command to Henry R. Luce [41], co-founder and editor in chief of all its publications. Larsen has also gained prominence as chairman of the National Citizens Commission for the Public Schools, a group which the New York *Times* described as "the first independent national association of laymen dedicated to the improvement of the public schools in this century."

Born in Boston, Massachusetts, on April 20, 1899, Roy Edward Larsen is the son of Robert and Stella (Belyea) Larsen. His father was a newspaperman. After graduating from Boston Latin School in 1917, young Larsen entered Harvard College, where he served on several freshman committees and was secretary-treasurer of his class during the junior and senior years. A member of the Dramatic Club, Pi Eta Society, Institute of 1770, Signet Society, Speakers' Club, Delta Kappa Epsilon, and the Phoenix Club, he was perhaps best known for his efforts in behalf of the *Harvard Advocate*, the college literary magazine. As the *Advocate*'s treasurer and business manager, he increased its circulation by effective canvassing, restored its finances to solvency, and helped to secure its own building. In 1921 he received his Bachelor of Arts degree and began working at the New York Trust Company.

"I met Henry Luce and Briton Hadden for the first time" (Larsen told Tex McCrary and Jinx Falkenburg in an interview) "on November 22, 1921, at the Harvard Club. I worked in a bank and I was ready to do anything to escape banking." Luce and Hadden, who had been classmates at Hotchkiss and Yale, were then working on plans to start a magazine which was to summarize and interpret the significant news of the week. They had heard of Larsen's success with the *Advocate* and were looking for a Harvard man to join their staff. Hadden and Luce wanted Larsen to work as advertising manager, a job he declined; later, however, he accepted the post of circulation manager at forty dollars a week. Thus, in 1922, Larsen became the first noneditorial employee of *Time*. By November of that year Luce and Hadden had succeeded in raising $86,000 to finance the project.

The first issue of *Time: The Weekly Newsmagazine*, dated March 3, 1923, went out to some 12,000 readers. In the beginning (writes Noel Busch in *Briton Hadden*) *Time* attracted little notice from the general public. Larsen sold it mainly to subscribers, rather than to newsstands, through a series of direct mail campaigns. Its circulation mounted steadily from 25,000 in 1923, to 200,000 in 1928, when the magazine showed its first substantial net profit of $125,000. In 1925 *Time*'s offices were moved to Cleveland, where they remained until 1927, when the editorial offices were returned to New York City; shortly afterward the printing and circulation offices were established in Chicago, to provide more rapid distribution to all parts of the United States. Larsen also served as circulation manager of *Tide*, an advertising magazine which Hadden launched in 1927, and which was sold later to another publisher.

Soon after Hadden's death in 1929, Luce deputized the business management of Time, Inc., to Larsen, who became vice-president and a director of the corporation. His next assignment was to obtain 30,000 subscribers for *Fortune*, a new magazine devoted to business and industry. Although the single copy price of *Fortune* was a dollar and it first appeared in February 1930, not long after the stock market crash, its circulation made rapid strides and before the depression was half over *Fortune* was showing a profit. Larsen also promoted *Architectural Forum*, the only property which Time, Inc., has purchased (in 1932) instead of developing from an original journalistic concept, and a less profitable venture; and *Letters*, a biweekly magazine presenting readers' letters and *Time*'s replies, "the only editorial project Time, Inc., really abandoned" (*Business Week*).

Larsen had a major role in organizing and developing *The March of Time*, an extension of *Time*'s journalistic principles to the radio and screen media, employing the technique of re-enactment to give a dramatic continuity to current events. The first *March of Time* broadcast took place on March 6, 1931, and the program was repeatedly voted the most popular dramatic one on the air. As president and treasurer of The March of Time, Inc., a separate company formed to produce the screen news feature, Larsen chose subjects, assisted in the editing and in the marketing of the thirteen two-reel issues of *The March of Time* issued in a year. First released in February 1935, *The March of Time* won a special "Oscar" two years later for "revolutionizing the newsreel."

In 1936 Larsen was reported to be earning a salary of $35,000 a year, in addition to his annual income of $120,000 from Time, Inc., stock, of which he is the second largest shareholder. That year saw the corporation launching its most ambitious venture, the weekly newspicture magazine, *Life*, which first appeared on November 23. Advertising rates for *Life* had been figured on the basis of a guaranteed weekly minimum of only 250,000 copies, and when its circulation rose to over a million in four months, bills for paper and ink alone consumed every cent of the magazine's revenue. Over $5,000,000 was spent by Time, Inc., to keep *Life* going until the advertising rates were adjusted to fit its enormous circulation. When the various Time, Inc., magazines were made autonomous in 1937, Larsen became the publisher of *Life*. It was he who decided the following year to print "stills" from the controversial film *The Birth of a Baby*. He submitted to arrest by selling a copy of *Life* in the Bronx, where the issue had been confiscated, in order to furnish a test case. At the ensuing trial he was acquitted of the charge of selling "indecent pictorial matter," the judges deciding that "the subject had been treated with delicacy."

By September 1939, when Larsen was made president, Time, Inc., had expanded into an organization with a staff of trained researchers, a world-wide network of news bureaus, several

ROY E. LARSEN

printing plants in the United States and abroad, paper mills, research laboratories, and real estate. The part he plays in all phases of the operation of Time, Inc.'s properties is seen as an expansion of his role in the company's affairs far beyond the usual corporate executive's preoccupation with balance sheets, sales, revenues, and employees relations. Of this *Business Week* said that he has "harnessed an idea factory . . . to dollars and cents." For 1949 the corporation reported its second largest year in its history (1948 was its best thus far). According to the annual report, gross sales revenues in 1949 were $128,270,000; gross income amounted to $10,327,000; and the earned net profit was $6,758,000. The report listed the average net paid circulation of domestic editions of the corporation's magazines as follows: *Life*, 5,324,000; *Time*, 1,560,000; *Fortune*, 248,- 000; and *Architectural Forum*, 62,000. (These figures are from New York *Times*.)

Larsen has served as chairman of the National Citizens Commission for the Public Schools since that independent group of twenty-eight prominent laymen was set up in May 1949. The primary purpose of the commission is to arouse a broad and active public interest in the public schools throughout the nation. Convinced that the most successful efforts to improve the schools are conducted at the community level, the organization works to assist and encourage the formation of local citizens' committees to help solve their own school problems. Among the most important problems in the estimation of the commission, are the lack of clarity in educational goals; the shortage of trained teachers; overcrowded classrooms; and the inequalities of educational opportunities for children in many parts of the United States. Acting as a clearing house, the commission gathers and disseminates information about what community groups are doing to improve

LARSEN, ROY E.—*Continued*

their schools. With financial support from the Carnegie Corporation and the Rockefeller-sponsored General Education Board, the commission's program calls for the expenditure of approximately $250,000 annually for the next six years. President Harry S. Truman has declared that the commission's goal "is one which should rank among the first objectives of every thoughtful community leader and every parent." In February 1950 Larsen received the first annual Tuition Plan, Inc., medal as "the person who has made the most significant contribution to education in the last year." (The selection was made by seven education editors.)

The publishing executive is a trustee of the New York Public Library and of the Committee for Economic Development. He has served as chairman of the campaign committee (1940-41), president (1942-49), and since 1950 as chairman of the board of the United Hospital Fund of Greater New York; during 1945-47 he was a director of the Blue Cross. Long active in Harvard affairs, he has served as a member of the board of overseers (1940-46); as a member of the board's visiting committee on university resources, the Graduate School of Business Administration (1942-46), the University Library, and the University Press (he was chairman of the latter two committees from 1940 to 1946). Elected president of the Harvard Alumni Association in 1950 for a one-year term, he is also a director of the Harvard Alumni *Bulletin,* permanent class treasurer of the class of 1921, and has been active in the affairs of the Harvard Club of New York. His other clubs include the Century, the River, and the University (New York). Honorary degrees were bestowed upon him by Marietta (Ohio) College in 1946, and by Bucknell University in 1950.

On June 20, 1927, Larsen married Margaret Zerbe of Cleveland; they have four children, Anne, Robert, Christopher, and Jonathan. He has been described as a "ruddy and dynamic" individual, "with an executive look, the spring of a sprinter in his gait, and a quiet voice." Among his favorite recreations are tennis and deep-sea fishing. Dwight MacDonald (in the *Nation*) wrote of him as "impersonal, realistic."

References

Adv & Sell 33:1 Ja '40
Busch, N. F. Briton Hadden (1949)
Who's Who in America, 1950-51

LARSSEN, PEDAR *See* Mallette, G. E.

LASKI, HAROLD (JOSEPH) June 30, 1893—Mar. 24, 1950 British political scientist of international influence; author of books, pamphlets and articles; university professor; lecturer in political science at London University since 1926, connected with the London School of Economics since 1920; influential in the development of the British Labor party,

member of its executive board from 1936 to 1947 (chairman 1945 and 1946). See *Current Biography*, 1941.

Obituary

N Y Times p13 Mr 25 '50 por

LATHAM, HAROLD S(TRONG) Feb. 14, 1887- Publishing executive; denominational president

Address: b. c/o The Macmillan Co., 60 5th Ave., New York 11; c/o The Universalist Church of America, 16 Beacon St., Boston, Mass.; h. 17 Pleasant Pl., Arlington, N.J.

Harold S. Latham, who is a vice-president of the publishing house of Macmillan Company, is the twice-chosen president of the Universalist Church of America, an office to which he was first elected in 1947. His association with the Macmillan firm began in 1909, immediately upon his graduation from college. An editor (as well as a writer), he later became one of the first publishing executives to make tours of the country in search of new authors, the most notable of whom is considered to have been Margaret Mitchell, author of *Gone With the Wind.* As president of the Universalist denomination, Latham presides at its general assemblies, at which about five hundred churches with a membership of eighty thousand were represented in 1949.

Descended on his mother's side from Elder John Strong, founder of Northampton, Massachusetts, Harold Strong Latham is one of the two sons of Charles Arthur and Minnie Alice (Strong) Latham. (His brother is William N. Latham of Asheville, North Carolina). He was born February 14, 1887, in Marlborough, Connecticut, where he passed part of his boyhood. He later lived in Ohio, then in New York; there he attended Erasmus Hall High School in Brooklyn, participated in amateur dramatics and the literary societies, and was graduated in 1905. "Abigail E. Leonard, teacher of English at Erasmus Hall," Latham has said, "had a great influence on my life and interested me initially in books and writing. This was strengthened enormously by my association in college with Professor Algernon Tassin of the English department. . . .Tassin taught creative writing, and was a great inspiration to me." The college was Columbia University, where Tassin's course was so long celebrated. Latham, who while at Columbia founded the undergraduate writing group known as the Scribblers (now defunct), received his B.A. in 1909.

It was as the result of an introduction from Professor Tassin that Latham joined the staff of the Macmillan Company, with which organization he has remained without interruption. He began his career one week after graduation, as assistant in the advertising department. "I worked in the advertising department for less than a year," he writes, "and was then transferred to the editorial department where, for several years, I did all sorts of editorial work." He also contributed many short stories and articles to magazines, and wrote a number of dramas for school or club amateur performance, such as *The Little Rebel* (1912), described as "a sane Fourth of July play," *The Perry Boys* (1913), a "social center historical play," and *The Making of Larry* (1914), for the Boy Scouts. These were followed, before and just after the end of World War I, by a series of three novels for teen-age boys: *Under Orders* (1918), *Marty Lends a Hand* (1919), and *Jimmy Quigg, Office Boy* (1920). Each was distinguished for what the New York *Times* commended as "simple, wholesome, natural and unconsciously democratic" qualities, and each combined an inspirational success story with a timely "spy" interest. In 1931 Latham was advanced to a vice-presidency in the Macmillan Company, when he assumed charge of the publishing end of the trade department.

In the latter capacity he brought such authors as Richard Llewellyn, Phyllis Bentley, Mary Ellen Chase, Rachel Field, Agnes Sligh Turnbull, Ernest Poole, and most conspicuously, the late Margaret Mitchell, to the Macmillan "list." It was Latham, who, while on a "scouting" trip through the South, acquired for Macmillan the fabulously successful *Gone With the Wind.* "I believe I was one of the first publishing executives to make tours of this country in search of new authors," he has said. He has made thirteen trips to England, France and Germany, looking for foreign writers and preserving contacts with those for whom the Macmillan house already publishes.

The Universalist Church of America, in the work of which the publishing executive has been actively engaged for many years, is (as of 1949) comprised of about five hundred self-governing congregations with a total membership of approximately eighty thousand. The denomination (which the New York *Herald Tribune* termed "one of the most liberal of all the Protestant churches") traces its origin to the landing of the Reverend John Murray, of England, in New Jersey. The first church was built in Massachusetts in 1780, and its denominational organization was begun in 1785. At its Winchester (New Hampshire) convention in 1803, the church adopted its essential principles, which, as expressed by President Latham on the occasion of the fifty-third biennial assembly in October 1949, are: "(1) the universal fatherhood of God; (2) the spiritual leadership of Jesus; (3) the Bible as containing a revelation from God; (4) just retribution for sin; (5) the final harmony of all souls with God" (New York *Herald Tribune*). Theological seminaries are maintained at Tufts College, in Medford, Massachusetts, and at St. Lawrence University, in Canton, New York; the national headquarters of the church is in Boston. Policy is formulated by a general assembly which meets biennially, and to which each member parish may send two lay delegates; it is carried out between assemblies by the trustees of the national board.

Before his membership in the latter body (from 1939 to 1947) Latham has for many years been the president of the East Orange-Glen Ridge parish in New Jersey. He has also served as president of the General Sunday School Association. His election as president of the Universalist Church for the term 1948-49 took place on September 13, 1947, at the fifty-second general assembly meeting on the campus of St. Lawrence University. (On that occasion the assembly adopted resolutions in opposition to compulsory military service, in favor of extension of public health services, and advocating formation of "a universalist commission on world order to promote support for the work of the United Nations.") At the fifty-third biennial assembly meeting in Rochester, New York, from October 13 to 19, 1949, Latham was re-elected president for the years 1950-51.

Volpe Studios

HAROLD S. LATHAM

Latham, who is unmarried, resides in Arlington, New Jersey, where he indulges his hobbies of amateur photography and gardening. Tall and broadly built—he stands an even six feet and weighs 225 pounds—he has brown eyes, and brown hair with touches of gray. His political affiliation is Republican. Clubs of which he is a member include the Players, the Columbia University, the Quill, and the Century Association of New York. His fraternity is the Phi Sigma Kappa.

References

International World Who's Who (1947)
Who's Who in America, 1948-49
Who's Who in New York, 1947
Who's Who in the East (1948)

LAUBACH, FRANK C(HARLES) Sept. 2, 1884- Missionary; educator

Address: b. c/o Committee on World Literacy and Christian Literature, Foreign Missions Conference of North America, 156 5th Ave., New York 10; c/o American Board of Foreign Missions, 14 Beacon St., Boston, Mass.; h. Benton, Pa.

(Continued next page)

FRANK C. LAUBACH

Dr. Frank C. Laubach, American missionary and educator, is the perfecter and sponsor of a method of teaching primitive and illiterate peoples to read by means of phonetic symbols and pictures. His career as a missionary began in the Philippines in 1915, where he developed a technique for teaching the Maranaw language, and set up folk schools that were to be the inspiration and model for teaching campaigns in many lands. Programs initiated by him, as special counselor and representative of the Committee on World Literacy and Christian Literature of the Foreign Missions Conference, are now being carried out by the governments of the Philippines, Korea, Siam, New Guinea, India, Egypt, Iran, Pakistan, and a number of the countries of Africa and Latin America.

Born in Benton, Pennsylvania, on September 2, 1884, Frank Charles Laubach is the son of John Brittain Laubach, a dentist, and Harriet (Derr) Laubach, a teacher. His parents had one other child, a daughter, who died in 1928. On his father's side he is descended from an Alsatian family which settled in Pennsylvania in 1738. After attending the schools in his native town Laubach studied at the State Normal School at Bloomsburg, Pennsylvania, from which he graduated in 1901. At the age of twenty he returned to school at Perkiomen Seminary, in Pennsylvania, before enrolling at Princeton, where he received his B.A. degree in 1909. Having majored in sociology, Laubach obtained a position as a social worker at the Spring Street Community House in New York City. Two years later he entered Union Theological Seminary and for the next three years took courses both there and at Columbia University. He received his M.A. degree in sociology from Columbia in 1911 and graduated from the seminary in 1913. Upon his ordination as a Congregational minister in 1914, he became secretary of the Charity Organization Society of New York. A year later, after completing his thesis, "Why There Are Vagrants," he received his Ph.D. degree in sociology from Columbia University.

The Congregational minister was assigned in 1915 to general mission work in the Philippines by the American Board of Foreign Missions; he sailed for Manila with his wife, Effa Seely Laubach, a nurse and teacher from Benton, whom he had married in 1912. The couple had become interested in the Mohammedan Moros of Lanao (on Mindanao Island) through missionary friends who were among the first American teachers to go to that area. However, being advised by American authorities that conditions among the fierce Moros were especially unfavorable to missionary endeavor at that time, the Laubachs went to Cagayan, on the island of Luzon. In 1922 they were transferred to Manila, where Laubach became dean of Union College, a position he filled until 1927.

In 1929 the missionary went to Lanao alone, leaving his wife and son, Robert, in Manila. He was able to establish friendly relations with the Moros through emphasis on similarities between Mohammedanism and Christianity. As a means to the end of teaching Christianity, he set out, after learning Maranaw, the Moro dialect, to teach the natives (95 per cent of whom were illiterate) to read. With the help of a Filipino educator, Donato Galia, he broke down into its basic phonetic sounds the language, which had never been printed. By developing charts presenting these sounds in a modified Roman alphabet accompanied by pictures, Laubach produced a method through which the illiterate adult of average intelligence could be taught to read and write his whole speaking vocabulary in a week's time. Reading matter for the new literates was provided in a newspaper, *Lanao Progress*, founded by Laubach and printed biweekly; it carried articles stressing resemblances between the Moslem and Christian faith, Moro epic poems, world news items, and discussions of local problems in such fields as law, sanitation, and agriculture. Because of a shortage of funds, the practice of "each one teach one" was evolved—every one who learned taught someone else. This approach has remained a working principle of the Laubach teaching method.

The reading classes in time developed into the Maranaw Folk Schools, with Laubach as director (1929-40). To help in the work of his schools he prepared the *English Maranaw Dictionary* (1937) and edited a volume of *Moro Folklore* (1939). The schools (which have been credited with teaching seventy per cent of the Moros to read) proved so successful that Laubach was asked by the National Christian Council to help prepare lessons in other Filipino dialects. By the time the missionary's 1935-36 furlough was due, he had received requests for information from Malaya, Singapore, Ceylon, India, Cairo, Palestine, Syria and Turkey. Thus he spent his furlough visiting those countries and helping local educators and missionaries to prepare literacy charts in the languages. In India he met Mohandas Gandhi, who was skeptical about teaching illiterates, believing India's economic problem more pressing. Four years later, however, Gandhi wrote, "I am converted, and now believe that literacy should be required for the franchise."

Before the end of this furlough, the World Literacy Committee (now incorporated into the Committee on World Literacy and Christian Literature of the Foreign Missions Conference of North America) had been formed in New York to make funds available to Laubach (then its special counselor and representative) to further his work. The group now represents forty-two missionary societies in the United States and collaborates with a British group representing about twelve societies. In addition to arranging Dr. Laubach's literacy tours and undertaking their implementation, the committee coordinates the efforts of literacy missionaries of various denominations; pools information on teaching illiterates; initiates the publication of charts, primers, and lessons, and the creation of reading material for new literates.

In 1936 Laubach returned to his post in the Philippines, from which he went in 1936-37 and in 1938-39 to India, where he held forty regional conferences to develop phonetic lessons in five major languages. Next he traveled to East Africa for a fifty-day tour at the invitation of the League of Nations. (In Africa he was also to go to Ethiopia, Liberia, Nigeria, and Northern Rhodesia.) The year 1941 found him in Mexico. When Pearl Harbor was attacked, Laubach was in the United States. Since World War II prevented his return to the Far East, he devoted the next years to covering the South and Central Americas, Mexico, and the West Indies in three tours between 1942 and 1946, preparing charts in Spanish, Portuguese, French, and various Indian dialects. He obtained notably successful results in Haiti, where 70,000 natives were taught to read and write simple English, reputedly the most difficult language to teach phonetically. In 1946 Laubach drafted recommendations for a world plan of fundamental education at the request of the United Nations Educational, Scientific and Cultural Organization (UNESCO). More recent tours, on some of which he has been accompanied by his son, have taken him to the Near East and Ethiopia (1947); West Central and South Africa (1948); and Asia and Australia (1949). Early in 1950 newspapers announced Laubach's fifth trip to Africa. In these surveys, many of which are made at the request of the governments, Laubach spends about two weeks in each language area; he assists local leaders to find key words for their languages and to prepare picture-word-syllable charts so that they can carry on the teaching after his departure.

"The curve of literacy, which has been nearly stationary in Asia and Africa and Russia for centuries, has turned upward recently, especially in the past twenty years. A hundred million more adults read today than twenty years ago," writes Laubach in his book, *The Silent Billion Speak* (1943). He points out the task of providing these new literates with good reading material that will keep "the training of the heart abreast with the training of the mind" (*Toward a Literate World*, published 1939). Along with education for depressed peoples he

believes material assistance to be necessary. To supply this he would like to see the church set up a central recruiting station for Christian technicians under proper legislative authority to carry out President Truman's "Point Four" (New York *Times*, January 7, 1950).

Dr. Laubach is the author of a number of books and of pamphlets on his missionary and pedagogical experiences. Among those on his teaching methods are: *India Shall Be Literate* (1940); *Streamlined English Lessons* (1945) prepared at the request of the British Government for use in Jamaica; *Teaching the World to Read* (1947). *The Silent Billion Speak* is an account of his literacy tours up to 1943; and for those who have recently learned to read, he has written *The Story of Jesus* (1946) and *Making Everybody's World Safe* (1947). His publications on religious subjects include *You Are My Friends* (1942) and *Prayer, the Mightiest Force in the World* (1946). Early books about the Philippines are, *People of the Philippines* (1924), *Seven Thousand Emeralds* (1929, a children's book), *Rizal, Man and Martyr* (1936, a study of a Philippine hero and poet). His articles have appeared in *Moslem World*, *Missionary Review*, and *International Review of Missions*.

Laubach is a member and missionary representative of the Union Congregational Church in Upper Montclair, New Jersey. During 1939-41 he was chairman of the board of trustees of the Presbyterian college, Silliman University, in Dumaguete, the Philippines. He is a Thirty-second Degree Mason, and has the title of Commander from the Haitian Government in recognition of his services there. A New York *Times* reporter has said that the "tall, enthusiastic missionary faintly resembles Gilbert Stuart's Washington." Another has described the "mild" educator as "lean and leathery."

References

Christian Sci Mon Mag p4+ F 5 '49
Read Digest p44 S '44
Time 41:79+ Je 28 '43
Hewitt, G. Nothing Can Stop It Now (1947)
Laubach, F. C. The Silent Billion Speak (1943); Teaching the World to Read (1948)
Leaders in Education (1948)
Who's Who in America, 1948-49
World Biography (1948)

LAUGHTON, MRS. CHARLES *See* Lanchester, E.

LAY, JAMES S(ELDEN) JR. Aug. 24, 1911- United States Government official
Address: c/o National Security Council, Executive Office Bldg., Washington 25, D.C.; h. 202 Forest Dr., Falls Church, Va.

Administration of the top security advisory body of the United States, the National Security Council, passed on December 21, 1949, from Sidney W. Souers[49] to his former assistant, James S. Lay, Jr. Lay's background

JAMES S. LAY, JR.

includes a period of business administration, four years of military service in intelligence work, and a postwar service in various Government intelligence agencies. He had been Souers' assistant since the establishment of the National Security Council in September 1947.

Born in Washington, D.C., on August 24, 1911, James Selden Lay, Jr., is the only child of James Selden and Lillian Lee (Lockhart) Lay. The Lay forebears had been pioneer settlers of Connecticut, and the Seldens were a Virginia family. For several generations the Lays has resided in the nation's capital. James Lay, Sr., served in the United States Navy during the Spanish-American War; for many years before his death he was employed in the Bureau of Internal Revenue. Young Lay attended the McKinley High School in Washington, from which he graduated in 1929. At the Virginia Military Institute he majored in electrical engineering. His extracurricular activities there included duties on the editorial staff of the school newspaper, work on the business staff of the yearbook, a cadet officership, and membership in various student clubs. Graduating second in his class in electrical engineering, he received a B.S. in June 1933. He then entered the Harvard Graduate School of Business Administration, from which, in 1935, he obtained a Master's degree in the field of public utilities.

For the next six years Lay was to work for various public utility companies, all of which were under the management of Stone & Webster Service Corporation. His first position was with the Virginia Electric & Power Company, at Richmond, where for seven months he was a commercial and industrial power sales engineer; in February 1936 he was promoted to assistant to the general sales manager. In March of 1937 he went to the New York City office of Stone & Webster, where for two years he held the post of assistant to

the vice-president in charge of sales. He joined the Hagerstown (Maryland) Gas Company as sales manager in April 1939.

Lay retained his membership in the Field Artillery Reserve after his graduation from V.M.I., and was promoted from second to first lieutenant in 1938. Called into active service before World War II in May 1941, he trained with the 353d Field Artillery Regiment at Camp Livingston, Louisiana, until August of that year, when he was assigned to the British Empire Branch of the Military Intelligence Service of the War Department, with headquarters in Washington. He was promoted to the rank of captain of field artillery in February 1942. In November he was made chief of the branch of the Military Intelligence with which he was serving.

After being commissioned a major (in December 1942), Lay went to London in July 1943 for temporary duty in the office of the United States military attaché. In December of that year, with the rank of lieutenant colonel, he returned to Washington and was assigned as secretary to the Joint Intelligence Committee of the Joint Chiefs of Staff. From June until October of 1945 he was representative of the assistant chief of staff, G-2, on the Joint Intelligence Staff of the Joint Chiefs of Staff. He was relieved of active duty in October 1945. Lay has said that his interest in foreign and military affairs, his present field, stems from this war experience.

Upon his discharge from the Army, Lay joined the State Department as management analyst for the special assistant in charge of research and intelligence. Two months later, when the National Intelligence Authority was established, he became its secretary, and after a year was appointed division chief of the Central Intelligence Group. In 1947 the National Intelligence Authority was superseded by the National Security Council, and Lay was named to the post of assistant executive secretary to the new body.

The National Security Council established by the National Security Act of 1947 was designed to further the integration of domestic, foreign and military policies relating to national security. Its top-level membership consists of the President of the United States, the Secretary of State, the Secretaries of Defense, the Army, the Navy, and the Air Force, the chairman of the National Security Resources Board, and such other members from a specified group as the President may from time to time appoint. By the terms of the establishing act, the duties of the NSC are "to assess and appraise the objectives, commitments, and risks of the United States in relation to our actual and potential military power", "to consider policies on matters of common interest to the departments and agencies of the Government concerned with the national security" and to advise the President thereon. The Council meets regularly at the White House twice a month, but may be summoned more often in times of crisis.

The actual day-to-day work of the Council is carried on by a staff under the direction of a civilian executive secretary appointed by the

President with the approval of the Senate. From the establishment of the Council, this important executive position had been held by Sidney W. Souers, who had previously been head of the Central Intelligence Group. Announcements of his resignation in December 1949 stated that he would continue to serve as a "consultant on top national security problems," on a per diem basis. Reporting on the appointment of Lay to the post, *Time* (January 2, 1950) commented that Lay had been "hand-picked" by Souers as his successor, and "carefully trained for the post through twenty-eight months as Souers' principal assistant." The *United States News* has called the new Executive Secretary "a young career man of the type to which Mr. Truman is turning increasingly . . . to fill big jobs." One of Lay's new duties is that of personally briefing the President daily in the light of intelligence information assembled by the security agency.

In an article in the *American Foreign Service Journal* (March 1948) on the work of the NSC, Lay emphasized that its function is purely that of an advisory body to the President, and that except for its direction of the Central Intelligence Agency it never determines policy. It insures, in Lay's words, that "all views on security matters are heard, and, if agreement cannot be reached, that the divergent opinions are presented to the President." In all disputed matters, final decision rests with the President, who must "reconcile, correlate, coordinate and integrate all of these diverse interests into national policies which will insure the security of the United States."

The security executive has retained membership in the Reserve Officers Association. In recognition of his war services, he was awarded the Legion of Merit (United States) and the Order of the British Empire in 1945. He is a member of the school board of Falls Church, Virginia, where he makes his home. His wife, the former Emily Graham Miller, continued her work as a psychiatric social worker for a time after their marriage on February 27, 1937. They have three daughters, Carolyn Miller, Patricia Lockhart, and Emily Graham. Lay's favorite recreations are reading and woodworking, and he enjoys the active sports of swimming, sailing, skiing, and golf. He is a Roman Catholic; he says he has no political affiliation. The Government executive, who is five feet eight inches tall and weighs 140 pounds, has green eyes and brown hair. He has been characterized as "self-effacing."

References

N Y Times p6 D 22 '49 por
U S News 27:36-7 D 30 '49 por
Washington (D.C.) Post p 1 D 22 '49 por
American Men in Government (1949)

LEE, MRS. JOHN G. July 4, 1906- Civic leader

Address: b. c/o League of Women Voters of the United States, 1026 17th St., N.W., Washington, D.C.; h. Box 61, Farmington, Conn.

Mrs. John G. Lee was elected to a two-year term as president of the League of Women Voters at the nineteenth biennial convention of the organization, held in Atlantic City, April 24-28, 1950. Called "a force with which lawmakers reckon" (*Annals of the American Academy of Political and Social Science*), the organization was formed in 1920 to promote effective and intelligent political participation on the part of newly enfranchised women. Mrs. Lee had for six years been president of the League of Women Voters in Connecticut, and had served on the board of the national body as director of the organization committee. She succeeded Anna Lord Strauss [45], who retired after three two-year terms in office.

Baptized Percy Maxim, Mrs. John G. Lee is the daughter of Hiram Percy and Josephine (Hamilton) Maxim, both now deceased. She was reared in Hartford, Connecticut, the town where she was born July 4, 1906. The girl attended Masters School, Dobbs Ferry, New York, from which she graduated in 1925. When asked how she has been able to accomplish all the activity of a long career both as a housewife and a civic leader, Mrs. Lee has replied that she is only following the precedent in her family and perhaps using some of the energy which she inherited. Her grandfather, Hiram Stephens Maxim, was inventor of the now famous Maxim gun, and was the founder of the firm of Maxim-Vickers, now Vickers, Ltd., of England. Mrs. Lee's father also became famous as an inventor with his contribution of a silencer for the Maxim gun; her brother, Hiram Hamilton Maxim, has succeeded to the presidency of the Maxim Silencer Company of Hartford, Connecticut.

Percy Maxim became Mrs. Lee in 1926, at the age of nineteen, when, instead of entering college, she married John G. Lee, an aeronautical engineer (at present assistant director of research for United Aircraft, Inc.). Four children were born to the couple, Hamilton Lee and John Maxim, and two daughters, Percy and Nancy. When their children became of school age, the Lees started the cooperative Junior School of West Hartford. The institution has grown to a school which accommodates 200 pupils from kindergarten to the sixth grade. The Lees maintained their connection with it for many years, he as president of the board, and she as secretary-treasurer and general manager. During World War II Mrs. Lee took into her home in Farmington (Connecticut) two children from Oxford, England (who lived with the Lees for five years), a family of three who had escaped from Danzig, and a young Hollander. Mrs. Lee was a member of the Connecticut War Council. She was hostess to four women from Japan who had come to the United States under the auspices of the United States Army to study the participation of women in government.

Mrs. Lee's early interest in the work of the National League of Women Voters can be traced to the influence of her mother, a prominent suffragist who helped set up the State organization of the league in Connecticut. Mrs. Lee joined the league in Farmington, and later became that local association's president. After

MRS. JOHN G. LEE

serving as chairman of the local economic committee, she was elected to the presidency of the State league, a post she filled for six years. Under Mrs. Lee's supervision, the Connecticut league grew rapidly, stated a biographical release, listing among achievements the publication of *Can You Nominate the President?* (1948) and of *Government Pattern—Connecticut Style* (1950). Mrs. Lee has also served on the national board of the league as director of the organization committee. In this capacity she traveled extensively in the fall of 1949, visiting every local league in Oklahoma, New Mexico, and Arizona, and again in January 1950, when she visited the leagues in California, Oregon, and Washington.

The formal organization of the League of Women Voters took place in Chicago in February 1920, at the victory convention of the National Woman's Suffrage Association. Such a league had been proposed the previous year at the woman's suffrage convention in St. Louis by Carrie Chapman Catt, who, aware that the Twentieth Amendment would soon be a fact, called for "a living memorial dedicated to the memory of our departed leaders and the sacrifices they made for our cause." From the first, the league was organized to function on all political levels, national, State, and local. It moved quickly into action, and numbers among its first victories the insertion of the phrase "equal compensation for equal work irrespective of sex" in the Civil Service Reclassification Act (1923). "Get-out-the-vote" campaigns during elections, general training in citizenship, and propaganda for a Federal amendment against child labor were among the other early objectives of the organization.

At its first convention, the league espoused the principle of political nonpartisanship, formulated in the phrase which has become tantamount to a league law, "We support principles, but never a candidate; we take stands on issues,

not on individuals." Consistent use of this tactic led to what has come to be regarded by the group as the classic joke about its members: "In Republican circles they are considered a 'bunch of Democrats,' in Democratic circles 'a bunch of Republicans,' while occasionally both groups have dubbed them 'a bunch of Socialists.'" In a *Reader's Digest* article of July 1940, the prime function of the league was called that of "digging up facts"; it prepares reports on candidates and issues, based on extensive research, personal interviews, and questionnaires. "I doubt whether any organization in America is so effective a force for good government," added the author of the *Reader's Digest* article.

The league's membership has increased 90 per cent between 1944 and 1950, to a total of 93,000. Approximately a thousand delegates from the 739 local organizations in thirty-six States attended the 1950 convention. The delegates, who meet biennially, approved a three-point program for the period 1950 to 1952 as proposed by the executive board. "The expansion of world trade and international economic development with maximum use of United Nations agencies; a continued analysis of the Federal budget in relation to a stable and expanding domestic economy; and reorganization measures to improve administrative efficiency in the development and use of natural resources." A proposal from the floor to include a fourth point on civil rights in the major program was rejected but the league passed a substitute resolution affirming its conviction that the "protection of the citizen in his constitutional rights is basic to our system of government."

At the closing session of the convention, on April 28, 1950, Mrs. Lee was elected by the league delegates at Atlantic City as their new national president, for a two-year term. At a preconvention meeting in February the nominating committee of the league had selected Mrs. Lee to head the new slate of officers, and her election at the convention was uncontested. The term of a league president is two years, but past presidents have been re-elected so often that Mrs. Lee is the fifth in line since the founding of the league. She succeeded Anna Lord Strauss of New York City, who served from 1944 to 1950. Of the new president one of the national league's first members said: "Mrs. Lee will bring you integrity, superior intelligence, a gift for administration." For the next two years Mrs. Lee will spend five days every two weeks at league headquarters in Washington. One of the organization's immediate aims, stated Mrs. Lee, is to develop a nucleus of women experts on Government financial policies.

A "youthful-looking" woman with blue eyes and black, curly hair, Mrs. Lee is five feet, five and one-half inches tall and weighs 130 pounds. She lists herself as a Republican and an Episcopalian. Mrs. Lee established the annual Hiram Percy Maxim Memorial Award for the outstanding amateur movie made anywhere in the world, and each year personally bestows this award under the auspices of the Amateur Cinema League. Her favorite outdoor recreations are horseback riding, and sailing off Mason's Island in Mystic, Connecticut, where the Lees have a summer cottage. The women's leader belongs to the Town and Country Club and the Garden Club of Hartford, Connecticut.

References

N Y Times p18 Ap 29 '50; p30 Jl 4 '50
Washington (D.C.) Post p5B F 7 '50

LEE, PERCY MAXIM *See* Lee, Mrs. J. G.

LEFFINGWELL, R(USSELL) C(OR-NELL) Sept. 10, 1878- Financier; lawyer

Address: b. c/o J. P. Morgan & Co., Inc., 23 Wall St., New York 5; h. Yellowcote Road, Oyster Bay, N.Y.

R. C. Leffingwell, chairman of the board of directors of J. P. Morgan & Company, Inc., from February 1948 to November 1950, entered the world of finance as partner of the Morgan firm in 1923. Leffingwell succeeded the late Thomas W. Lamont [40] as chairman. In April 1940, after the firm had been incorporated, Leffingwell became a director and vice-chairman of the executive committee. A comment in *Fortune* (October 1948) describes Leffingwell as standing for "the best traditional policies of the House of Morgan, which are confidence in America's future and belief in freer world trade." Before his association with the Morgan institution, Leffingwell spent eighteen years in law practice and three years as Assistant Secretary of the United States Treasury.

Russell Cornell Leffingwell was born September 10, 1878, in New York City. His parents, Charles Russell and Mary Elizabeth (Cornell) Leffingwell, are of English descent, their ancestors having left Essex in the early part of the seventeenth century. Leffingwell's father was in the iron business with the J. B. and J. M. Cornell Company, in New York. Young Leffingwell, an only son in a family of three children, spent his undergraduate years in Yonkers, New York, where he attended the Yonkers Military Academy, and in New York City at the Halsey School, from which he was graduated in 1895. Four years later he received his B.A. degree from Yale University. He then returned to New York to enter Columbia Law School, where he was to become editor in chief of the *Columbia Law Review* and to receive his LL.B. degree in 1902. An honorary M.A. degree was bestowed upon him by Yale University in 1919.

Starting his career as a law clerk in the office of Guthrie, Cravath & Henderson, he progressed to a partnership in the firms of Cravath, Henderson & de Gersdorff, and Cravath & Henderson between 1907 and 1917. In May 1917 he was summoned to Washington by Secretary of the Treasury McAdoo to work in the flotation of Liberty Loan Bonds. In the autumn of that year he was appointed Fiscal Assistant Secretary of the Treasury, which necessitated absence from his law practice until his resignation from the Treasury

Underwood & Underwood

R. C. LEFFINGWELL

post in 1920. Then he rejoined his former law associates, the firm name becoming Cravath, Henderson, Leffingwell & de Gersdorff.

Leffingwell severed his law partnership three years later to assume a new role as banking partner with the house of Morgan. Here he was plunged into postwar financing, during which the Morgan company floated forty-two separate issues for foreign governments, in all $2.2 billion, and arranged loans to the amount of $68 million for foreign corporations. Thomas W. Lamont, Leffingwell, and Whitney were among the company's senior partners during the years of the depression, New Deal, and World War II. Leffingwell approved President Roosevelt's action in going off the gold standard, saying in March of 1934 at a meeting of the Academy of Political Science: "When 'the horrible cycle of deflation began to revolve toward the abyss,' the only hope for humanity was to stop gold payments, to go off gold. . . . Cheap money opens the door to recovery." When he was made chairman of the executive committee in 1943, Leffingwell's associates, according to *Business Week* (February 21, 1948) "learned to look to him for the long view—with an especial interest in problems of monetary policy. In 1945, when others were talking postwar deflation, he stood against the popular position."

Leffingwell, who was named chairman of the board of the Morgan house in early 1948, assumed that post February 14, 1948. After serving for about two years and nine months, the financier resigned from the board chairmanship on November 1, 1950. He continued as a director of the firm, as a member of its executive committee, and as vice-chairman of the board.

From time to time Leffingwell voices his opinions through the printed word; as of 1950 twenty-two of his articles on various phases of finance had appeared in national publications.

LEFFINGWELL, R. C.—*Continued*

In *Fortune*, October 1948, he outlined some "do-and-don't" principles in "How to Control Inflation." He advocated no price fixing, no change in the gold standard, no increase in reserve requirements of Reserve Banks or commercial banks, and no further par pegging. "But," he said, "there should be still further reductions in tariffs, and reduction in subsidies and civil expenditure, and continued high taxes, and a surplus for debt reduction. The authorities should sail the narrow channel between. . . inflation and deflation, between cheap money and dear money." Thirty years before the appearance of the *Fortune* article, Leffingwell dealt with inflation in an article, "Treasury Methods of Financing the War in Reference to Inflation". (*Proceedings of the Academy of Political Science*, June 1920). Another 1920 article (in the *Saturday Evening Post*) had the title "The Soldier and His Bonus."

Later writings of Leffingwell's covered other financial problems growing out of two world wars. He wrote about "War Debts" for the *Yale Review* in 1922, and in 1948 he discussed "Treasury Methods in Two Wars," which appeared in *Proceedings of the Academy of Political Science*. Economic recovery, management of our economy, monetary problems, currency revaluation, the causes of depressions, and America's interest in European prosperity are other topics which he has analyzed for general and specialized journals. His book review entitled "Reserve Banks and the Future" appeared on the front page of the *Saturday Review of Literature* for September 27, 1930. In it he evaluated Paul M. Warburg's *The Federal Reserve System, Its Origin and Growth, Reflections and Recollections*, a two-volume treatise. The financier contributed a discussion of the devaluation of the British pound to *Foreign Affairs*, January 1950. Seeing that measure as only of temporary efficacy, Leffingwell considers that international prosperity can be maintained by allowing more men and goods to come into America and by Europeans earning money from shipping, banking, insurance and trading services in free and fair competition.

Leffingwell is a trustee and chairman of the board of the Carnegie Corporation of New York and is a director and chairman of the board of the Council on Foreign Relations, also in that city. In June 1943 he became a member of the War Finance Committee for New York State. He is an honorary vice-president of the Community Service Society of New York, an honorary trustee of the Yale Library Associates, and a fellow of the Royal Economic Society. Professional organizations in which he holds membership are the American Economic Association, the Association of the Bar of the City of New York, and the Alumni Council of the Yale Institute of International Studies. His social clubs are the Knickerbocker, Century, University, Pilgrims, Yale, Down Town, Piping Rock, and Seawanhaka-Corinthian Yacht, all in New York, and the Metropolitan and Chevy Chase in Washington. He married Lucy Hewitt on January 27, 1906;

they have one daughter, Lucy (Mrs. Edward Pulling). Leffingwell is six feet tall, weighs 175 pounds, has white hair and brown eyes. "To Wall Street," said *Business Week* (February 21, 1948), "he is a business intellectual, a man who gains his points by persuasive argument, not by table pounding."

References

Bsns W p6 F 21 '48
International Who's Who, 1949
Who's Who in America, 1948-49
Who's Who in Commerce & Industry (1948)
World Biography (1948)

LEHRBAS, LLOYD (ALLAN) (lĕr'bås) Oct. 15, 1898- United States Government official; journalist

Address: c/o Department of State, Washington, D.C.; h. 1815 17th St., N.W., Washington

NOTE: This biography supersedes the article which appeared in *Current Biography* in 1940.

Lloyd Lehrbas, who covered the Sino-Japanese War and World War II for the Associated Press, among other assignments in his twenty-five years as news reporter and editor, in 1948 was appointed news director of the State Department's Office of International Information. Perhaps best known of that office's activities is the broadcasting of the shortwave program *Voice of America*. In January 1950 he was named special assistant to the Under Secretary of State.

The son of Louis A. and Marjorie (Morris) Lehrbas, Lloyd Allan Lehrbas was born October 15, 1898, in Montpelier, Idaho. For his early education he attended schools in Montpelier and Boise, then spent a year (1915-16) at the University of Idaho at Moscow, meanwhile working as a correspondent for the Salt Lake City *Tribune*. He continued his studies in 1916-17 at the University of Wisconsin, taking courses in journalism, English, economics, philosophy, French, and German. When the United States entered World War I, he became a cadet in the air service at the age of nineteen. Before he could be sent overseas the Armistice was signed, at which time he held the rank of lieutenant.

Lehrbas' first position after his discharge from the army was as a reporter on the San Francisco *Chronicle*. Soon after he reached the West Coast, acting on an urge to travel, he obtained a civilian job on an army transport which took him to the Orient; he was able to see parts of China and Japan. Returning to the United States, he worked in Chicago successively as a reporter for the *American* and the *Tribune*, and as assistant city editor of the *Evening American*. In 1919 he returned to the Far East, where for nine months he was a writer and editor on the Manila *Bulletin*, and for five years (1920 to 1925) held the same positions on the *China Press*, in Shanghai.

The year 1925 saw Lehrbas back in the United States as a staff correspondent in Washington, D.C., for Hearst's International News

Service. During 1926-27 he was news editor for Underwood and Underwood, also in Washington. His next position took him to New York as the news editor for Fox Movietone News, during the three years 1927-30. There followed a period of free-lance reporting in the Orient and Europe.

In 1932 the journalist returned to Washington as staff correspondent for the Associated Press. He continued in the employ of the A.P. for nine years, writing on foreign affairs and traveling in China, France, Italy, Spain, Poland, Rumania, and Turkey as a war correspondent. The news agency assigned him to London to cover the Naval Conference in December 1935, brought him back to Washington the following month for the Republican and Democratic conventions, and in November 1936 sent him to Buenos Aires to cover the Inter-American Conference for Peace. Then, in early 1937 Lehrbas took ship for Shanghai.

The roving correspondent reported on the last stand of China's "Lost Battalion" in the Sino-Japanese War. From a pillbox to which he crawled on the edge of no-man's land he saw "Japanese and Chinese twenty yards away in hand-to-hand bayonet, machine gun and grenade fighting nearly every day for three weeks." A six-day airplane flight took him by stages from Shanghai to Warsaw, where, he wrote, the China scenes were repeated. He gave an eyewitness account of the first German air raid on Warsaw, of planes diving and bombs exploding along the Vistula River as he watched from a stairway window at his headquarters, telephone in hand, describing the scene for forty minutes to the A.P. bureau in Budapest. That episode (his description of it appeared in the Kansas City *Star* for January 1, 1940) brought him honorable mention for the 1939 Pulitzer Prize award for distinguished foreign correspondence. The raid was the first of seventeen days and nights of attack in Poland which the journalist covered. In an old German car he followed the retreating Polish Government, and when it surrendered, he continued to Bucharest. He arrived there just before the assassination of Rumanian Premier Calinescu and scored a world scoop for the A.P. by getting the story out before censorship barred the news.

Lehrbas' next foreign assignment, after an interim in Washington, took him to the Italian front, and thence to occupied France. In Vichy, capital of the Pétain-Laval Government, three months of "hard work and a dull daily routine," as he described it for *Editor & Publisher* (October 5, 1940), brought "unsatisfactory final results," largely because correspondents were handicapped by three censorships, French, German, and Italian. Leaving Vichy, Lehrbas traveled throughout unoccupied France to report on living conditions among the French. He returned by air to the United States in October 1940, assigned by the A.P. to cover the State Department.

In February 1942 the forty-four-year-old correspondent was commissioned a lieutenant colonel in the Army, and within a month he was en route to Australia, to join the staff of General Douglas MacArthur [45]. Lehrbas and

LLOYD LEHRBAS

MacArthur had become friends in 1933 when the newspaperman was working in Washington at the time the General was Chief of Staff. Lehrbas acted as one of MacArthur's two top press officers. In June 1942 he was appointed aide-de-camp to the General and in that capacity observed the major Pacific campaigns from Australia to the Philippines.

At the time of Lehrbas' discharge from the Army in 1946 he was a full colonel, with the Legion of Merit and Bronze Star decorations. Back in civilian journalism, in January 1946 he became executive editor of *World Report*, weekly news magazine on international affairs scheduled to make its first appearance that May. (The publisher was David Lawrence [43].) *World Report* reached a circulation of 125,000 before it merged, on January 7, 1948, with Lawrence's *United States News* (circulation 300,-000).

In May 1948 Lehrbas entered Government service—he was named director of the State Department's Office of International Information, succeeding William T. Stone. Functioning under the Assistant Secretary of State for Public Affairs, the office is charged with "responsibility for initiating, coordinating and executing the international information policies of the Department; disseminating abroad information about the United States through all appropriate media; promoting freedom of information; and encouraging and assisting private agencies in their international information activities" (from the Government *Manual*). The Division of International Broadcasting (headed by Charles Thayer [49]), which operates the shortwave program, *Voice of America*, is one of its three divisions; the others are the Division of International Motion Pictures, and the Division of International Press and Publications. Controversies about appropriations for the information office have been frequent in Congress (the State Department international information and

LEHRBAS, LLOYD—*Continued*
cultural program was made permanent and given legal authority by Congress in January 1948). In January 1950 the United States Advisory Commission on Information, headed by publisher Mark Ethridge '46, stated that budget cuts were crippling the nation's information program, pointing out that Congress had provided only $35,800,000 to run *Voice of America*, about half the needed amount.

Another State Department post came to Lehrbas in early 1950, when on January 28 it was announced that he had been appointed special assistant to Under Secretary of State James E. Webb '46. The Government *Manual* defines the duties of the Under Secretary as serving "as the Secretary's principal adviser and, in the absence of the Secretary, as Acting Secretary of State."

The unmarried Government official has a height of five feet eight and a half inches, a weight of 155 pounds. His facial characteristics are a firm jaw and high cheekbones. He is an Episcopalian and a member of the Masonic order. In Washington his clubs are the National Press, Army and Navy, and Overseas Writers. He was made a member of Sigma Delta Chi, the journalistic fraternity.

References

Ed & Pub O 5 '40
Kansas City (Mo.) Star Ja 1 '40
N Y Herald Tribune Ja 4 '42; My 27 '48; p36 Ja 29 '50
N Y Sun p7 O 8 '40
N Y Times p30 Ja 28 '50
Newsweek 19:68-9 Ap 6 '42
Who's Who in America, 1950-51

LEMKIN, RAPHAEL   June 24, 1901-
Professor; lawyer

Address: b. c/o School of Law, Yale University, New Haven, Conn.

A Polish-born lawyer, Raphael Lemkin, is responsible for the United Nations' outlawing of genocide, defined as "the purposeful destruction of nations, races or groups." Lemkin, who originated the term "genocide" for the theretofore unnamed crime, assisted in the framing of the agreement adopted by the U.N. Assembly on December 9, 1948. Once a public prosecutor in Warsaw, he entered the United States to join the faculty of Duke University in 1941. He became a special adviser in the War Department, and was on the American staff at the Nuremberg war guilt trials. Assisted by the Carnegie Endowment for International Peace, Professor Lemkin in 1944 issued *Axis Rule in Occupied Europe,* comprising texts of the laws and decrees effected by the Axis powers for the government of occupied areas, together with his analysis of them.

Raphael Lemkin was born to Jewish parents on June 24, 1901, in Eastern Poland, on a farm near Bezwodene, situated "in the corridor of events," he has said—the farm was three times destroyed by war. Until the age of fourteen, he, with his two brothers, received his education (mainly in the humanities) from tutors,

the family library, and his mother, "a brilliant intellectual. . . .Somehow, she saw to it we had a tendency to practice what we were learning," he has said. Before taking legal training, Lemkin studied philology at the universities of Lwow in Poland and Heidelberg in Germany (he speaks nine languages, reads fourteen). He has also pursued studies in France and Italy. Terming law "social engineering," Lemkin has stated that he went into that field because "law gives you an instrument to influence society by way of formulation."

After earning his doctorate, the lawyer entered the post of secretary for the Court of Appeals in Warsaw. He later became a public prosecutor in that city, and represented Poland at international conferences in many countries in the Western Hemisphere. Instances of mass murder that occurred in 1933 shocked him into focusing his attention on the crime. He began to write on the subject, drawing up a document to outlaw "acts of barbarism and vandalism," which he presented before the Legal Council of the League of Nations in Madrid. He urged that it be adopted as an instrument for the protection of minorities, a proposal the council refused to consider. Lemkin's efforts in this cause brought him into disfavor with the Polish Government, which was pursuing a policy of conciliation of Nazi Germany, and he eventually retired from his public post to private law practice.

In the 1939 German invasion of Poland, Lemkin was wounded in the left leg in guerrilla fighting outside Warsaw. In hiding, for six months he subsisted in the Polish forests before making his escape by way of Lithuania and the Baltic Sea to Sweden. There he taught at a university and began the work of compiling documents on Nazi rule in the occupied countries of Europe. After making his way to the United States via Russia, Japan, and Canada, the Polish lawyer in 1941 joined the law faculty of Duke University. Subsequently he was appointed to the United States Board of Economic Warfare, and later became a special adviser on foreign affairs to the War Department.

The compilation of documents on Axis rule Lemkin began in Sweden, was completed in Washington, in 1943. Under the title *Axis Rule in Occupied Europe* it was published in 1944 by the Carnegie Endowment for International Peace through the International Documents Service of Columbia University. Designed to provide "undeniable and objective evidence regarding the treatment of the subjugated peoples of Europe by the Axis powers," in the words of Professor Lemkin's foreword, the major part of the book consists of the texts of laws and decrees issued by the occupying forces and an examination of the organization set up in each region. Preceding chapters analyze "the purposes and applications of the measures as parts of a general scheme of conquest."

In this book the law professor applied the term "genocide," which he had compounded from the Greek *genos* (race) and the Latin *cide* (killing) to the policy of "destruction of a nation or of an ethnic group"; he further defined the concept as "a coordinated plan of different actions aiming at the destruction of essential foundations of the life of national groups, with the aim of annihilating the groups themselves." Commenting on the long history of wars of extermination as such, Lemkin elucidated the objectives of the modern version as "the disintegration of the political and social institutions of culture, language, national feelings, religion, and the economic existence of national groups, and the destruction of the personal security, liberty, health, dignity, and even the lives of the individuals belonging to such groups."

The book was well received by reviewers, who called it "vital reading", "an indispensable handbook" for scholars and for authorities responsible for dealing with the Germans. Praising Professor Lemkin's scholarly approach, Merle Fainsod, associate professor of government and deputy director of Harvard University's Civil Affairs Training School, wrote in the *Harvard Law Review*: "The Carnegie Endowment for International Peace has performed an important public service in publishing this volume at this time. . . .Those charged with the responsibility of disentangling the spider web of Axis legislation should profit enormously from studying Dr. Lemkin's discussion of the problems involved."

Material from *Axis Rule in Occupied Europe* was used in establishing a basis for the war trials program, and Lemkin was appointed an adviser to Supreme Court Justice Robert Jackson [40] at the Nuremberg trials. Since these trials handled cases of war guilt only and genocide in times of peace was unpunishable under them, Lemkin resolved to carry on the campaign begun in Poland in 1933 for its establishment as a crime under international law. To that end he attended the Paris peace conference in 1945, but was unable to persuade the delegates to adopt such a measure. The lawyer continued to write and speak on the subject, enlisting the support of public opinion, of nongovernmental bodies, writers and prominent humanitarians. Though termed by some a "dreamer" and "fanatic," he persuaded United Nations delegates to propose and support a resolution naming genocide a crime under internationl law; and in 1946 the U.N. General Assembly approved the resolution and directed the formulation of a treaty to that effect for the consideration of the U.N. Legal Committee. With two associates Lemkin drafted the document and submitted it. After fruitless deliberation by the committee, the draft was rewritten by the Economic and Social Council with Lemkin as adviser, and in December 1948, in Paris, the Assembly by a vote of 55 to 0 approved the treaty.

In an article entitled "U.N. Portrait" in the New York *Times*, Gertrude Samuels commented on the convention as adopted: "One of the two documents called 'durable' by the Assembly (the other is the Declaration of Human Rights), the genocide treaty is a triumph of one man's ideal over cynicism." By the terms of the treaty, genocide is established as a crime, punishable in an international penal tribunal; the crime is defined as the mass murder or per-

United Nations Official Photo.

RAPHAEL LEMKIN

secution of a group for reasons of race, religion or culture. (A form of the definition including "political groups" was modified to the ultimately accepted form to facilitate adoption.) To give the document the power of law twenty ratifications are necessary; the appending of twelve by April 9, 1950, is credited to the efforts of the Polish lawyer, who visited several European capitals in this connection immediately after the Assembly action. The treaty, which is binding only on countries that ratify it, provides for the punishment of responsible individuals, "whether they are constitutionally responsible rulers, public officials, private individuals." The new international pact became a part of international law on October 16, 1950, after the last of the necessary ratifications were deposited with U. N. Secretary General Lie. The international convention against genocide will become operative legally on January 14, 1951.

In 1948 Lemkin became a member of the faculty of Yale University to teach international law, including the first course ever given on United Nations law. Periodicals to which he has contributed include the *Nation,* the *American Scholar,* and the *American Journal of International Law*; with Malcolm McDermott he collaborated in the translation of the *Polish Penal Code of 1932* and the *Law of Minor Offenses,* published in 1950. Lemkin was among twenty-eight persons nominated for the 1950 Nobel Peace Prize early that year. Of a family numbering some forty in close relationship he is the sole survivor. He is tall, has blue eyes, uses glasses. His hobbies are landscape painting, checkers, fishing, and reading. Speaking of formative influences, he indicated that reading Tolstoy in his youth had affected him deeply: "Tolstoy taught me to live an idea," he commented. The unmarried professor has

LEMKIN, RAPHAEL—*Continued*

been described as "a gentle and kindly man who likes to talk history and philosophy by the hour."

References

N Y Herald Tribune II p5 Ap 9 '50 por
N Y Post Mag p49 Ja 10 '47 por; p43 Je 17 '48 por; p33 D 13 '48 por
N Y Times Mag VI p20 Mr 20 '49 por

LENROOT, KATHARINE F(REDRICA)
Mar. 8, 1891- United States Government official; social worker

Address: b. c/o Children's Bureau, Federal Security Agency, 4th St. & Independence Ave., S.W., Washington, D.C.; h. 4402 Volta Pl., N.W., Washington, D.C.

NOTE: This biography supersedes the article which appeared in *Current Biography* in 1940.

Associated with the Children's Bureau, which is now a division of the Federal Security Agency, for thirty-six years as of 1950, Katha-

Wide World Photos
KATHARINE F. LENROOT

rine F. Lenroot has been lauded for her "unceasing efforts to make more secure the lot of children and youth" (in the words of *Survey*). The purpose of the Bureau, of which she became Chief in 1934, is (in official language): "To investigate and report on all matters related to child life and to increase opportunity for the full development of all children by promoting their health and social welfare." She has served since 1947 as United States member of the United Nations International Children's Emergency Fund executive board. A past chairman of U.N.'s Temporary Social Committee, she is United States alternate representative to the Social Commission of the Economic and

Social Council of the United Nations. Miss Lenroot was executive secretary of the 1940 White House Conference on Children in a Democracy and in 1950 serves as secretary of the Midcentury White House Conference on Children and Youth, to be held in December 1950.

Katharine Fredrica Lenroot was born in Superior, Wisconsin, on March 8, 1891. Her mother was the former Clara Pamelia Clough. Her father, Irvine Luther Lenroot, whose parents came from Sweden to settle in St. Croix Falls, Wisconsin, was, successively, State legislator (1901-09), United States Representative and Senator (1909-27), and Judge of the United States Court of Customs and Patent Appeals. When she was ten years of age, Lenroot would take his daughter with him to the floor of the Wisconsin State Legislature. Later she accompanied him to Washington, where she spent a year during his term in Congress.

Miss Lenroot early developed an interest in social problems and welfare movements. Two years after her 1909 graduation from the Superior State Normal School, at 20 she appeared before a committee of the State legislature to speak in favor of a minimum wage law. At the same time, she was a junior at the University of Wisconsin, where she studied under sociologist and labor legislation authority Dr. John R. Commons. In 1912 she received her B.A. degree from Wisconsin, which was to award her an honorary LL.D. degree twenty-six years later (1938).

Following a civil service examination, Miss Lenroot in 1913 was appointed to her first position—as $1,200-a-year woman deputy of the Industrial Commission of Wisconsin. In this post she made cost-of-living investigations in Milwaukee preparatory to plans for the administration of the newly enacted minimum wage law, for which she had fought while a student at the University of Wisconsin. She resigned from the position in 1914 to become a special agent of the recently created United States Children's Bureau, where she served under her two predecessors in her present post, Julia Lathrop and Grace Abbott. At the close of the summer of 1915, during which she had attended the New York School of Social Work, Miss Lenroot was made assistant director of the Social Service Division of the Children's Bureau. In this capacity she made studies concerning provision for dependent children and methods of juvenile court administration. She held the post until 1921, when she became director of the Editorial Division. In November of the following year she was named Assistant Chief and twelve years later, in 1934, she was appointed by President Roosevelt to her present position as Chief of the Children's Bureau.

The Children's Bureau (states the *United States Government Organization Manual*) "makes studies in the fields of child development and services for children, compiles statistics relating to children, develops standards for the protection of and services to children, gives advisory service, and issues publications, both technical and popular." It administers grants: to State health agencies for extending and improving health services for mothers and children, to State crippled children's agencies, and State welfare agencies. (In August 1950 State grants were raised, for 1952, to $41,500,-000.) It "receives information and responds to requests for information and advice on services for children and youth from agencies in other countries." Among Miss Lenroot's other duties, she represents the United States on the executive board of the U.N. International Children's Emergency Fund, and she serves as secretary of the Midcentury White House Conference on Children and Youth, to be held in December 1950. In 1946 the Bureau was transferred from the Department of Labor to the Federal Security Agency, becoming a part of the Social Security Administration. Miss Lenroot heads a staff which (in 1949) numbered approximately three hundred.

In the capacity of Children's Bureau Chief, Miss Lenroot has frequently appeared before Senate and House committees on matters pertaining to child welfare. She testified on juvenile delinquence (1943), pressed for a proposed amendment to the Fair Labor Standards Act designed to increase protection for children under the act's child labor provisions (1945), spoke on Federal aid for maternal and child welfare (1946) and for the school health service bill (1947). Serving in 1937 and 1938 as a member of the Advisory Committee on Education appointed by President Roosevelt to review Federal relations to State and local conduct of education, Miss Lenroot in 1940 was also research secretary of the Delinquency Committee of Child Health and Protection and was executive secretary of the 1940 White House Conference on Children in a Democracy. She is vice-chairman of the Interdepartmental Committee on Children and Youth, which was formed in 1948 at the suggestion of President Truman.

Miss Lenroot has taken part in many international conferences on child welfare. She attended the first International Congress of Social Economy, held in Buenos Aires in 1924; and she has been active in Pan American Child Congresses, as chairman of the United States delegations to the meetings in Cuba (1927), Peru (1930), and Venezuela (1948), and as president of the 1942 meeting in Washington. (Miss Lenroot is fluent in Spanish.) She was United States representative on the League of Nation's Advisory Committee on Social Questions, was appointed adviser to United States government delegates to the October 1945 International Labor Organization Conference in Paris and also in 1945 attended a Montreal meeting on the preliminary draft of an International Youth Charter. Since 1946, when she became secretary of the United Nations Temporary Social Commission, she has been associated with the United Nations in several posts. Elected U.N. Temporary Social Committee chairman in 1947, she has served since then as United States member of the U.N.'s International Children's Emergency Fund executive board. Her work in the latter post has taken her to Europe several times. Miss Lenroot also serves as alternate United States representative

for 1950 to the Social Commission of the U.N. Economic and Social Council.

The Children's Bureau Chief is the author of pamphlets, articles, and books on child welfare. Reviewing the work of the Bureau for the New York *Times* (April 6, 1947), she listed general goals in child welfare: the expansion and strengthening of public and private social and child welfare programs, "adequate food and good medical care" for all families, and "good schools, ably taught" for all children. "This means," she said, "that a high level of employment at adequate wages must be maintained; that an extensive housing program must be pushed forward . . . that. . . teachers must receive adequate salaries and that good school facilities must be provided. . . .One further thing," she said, is necessary: "Children must be taught a fundamental respect for . . . all people, no matter what their race, their creed, or color." It is Miss Lenroot's belief, according to the Washington *Post* (July 13, 1950) that "as the first half of the twentieth century was notable for specialization" in child welfare, "the last half will be a period of integration."

"The name of Miss Lenroot and the cause of child welfare," said a New York *Times* editorial (April 26, 1950) "are almost synonymous in the United States." She has been praised for her "sensitive and skillful approach to the multitudinous problems that arise in administering a many-sided and complex program." *Survey* has described her as "a person whose regard for spiritual values . . . has been. . . demonstrated . . . in her professional and official relations in the cause of children." At the 125th anniversary convocation of the American Unitarian Association (held in May 1950), Miss Lenroot emphasized the place of religion in child training.

Awarded an honorary LL.D. degree by Tulane University and an honorary Doctor of Humane Letters degree by Russell Sage College (both in 1948), Miss Lenroot is the recipient of numerous other awards. Among them are: the 1940 *Parents' Magazine* Medal for Outstanding Service to Children; the 1942 Chicago University Rosenburger Medal; the 1947 Gold Medal of the National Institute of Social Sciences for distinguished services to humanity; the Congregational Church Council for Social Action Churchmanship Award in 1949, and the 1950 *Survey* Annual Award "for an imaginative and constructive contribution to social work." In May 1948, she was named woman of the month by the American Woman's Association. She is a member of Phi Beta Kappa, the American Association of University Women, American Association of Social Workers, of the National Conference of Social Work (president 1935), and of the board of directors of the Child Welfare League of America.

In her church membership Miss Lenroot is a Congregationalist. Genevieve Reynolds of the Washington *Post*, who called the Chief of the Children's Bureau "the nation's most vigilant foster mother," described her as "a white-haired lady with deep blue eyes, a round face, and an understanding smile."

(Continued next page)

LENROOT, KATHARINE F.—*Continued*

References

N Y Times p24 D 19 '42
Parents Mag 15:34 N '40 por
Survey 80:93-5+ Mr '44; 86:318-19 Je
'50
Washington (D.C.) Post p4B D 31 '49
American Women, 1939-40
Who's Who in America, 1950-51
Who's Who in the Nation's Capital, 1938-
39
World Biography (1948)

LESINSKI, JOHN Jan. 3, 1885—May 27,
1950 United States Democratic Representative
of Michigan's Sixteenth Congressional District
since 1933; chairman of the House Committee
on Education and Labor since 1949; vigorous
opponent of the Taft-Hartley act; engaged in
the building and real estate business in the
Detroit area; head of lumber companies in
Hamtramck and Dearborn; founder of a Hamtramck bank; leader in Polish-American organizations since World War I. See *Current
Biography*, 1949.

Obituary

N Y Times p44 My 28 '50 por

**L'ESPERANCE, ELISE (DEPEW
STRANG)** (lĕs'pēr-àns" ā-lĕz') Physician;
pathologist

Address: b. 2 E. 61st St., New York 21; h.
533 Pelham Manor Rd., Pelham Manor, N.Y.

Cancer prevention clinics which provided
the models for similar centers elsewhere in the
United States were established by Dr. Elise
L'Esperance, New York physician and pathologist. Under her direction, the first clinic for
the detection of cancer was established at the
New York Infirmary for Women and Children
(with which she was associated for a number
of years as pathologist and director of laboratories), to be succeeded in 1937 by the foundation of a second cancer prevention clinic at the
same hospital, and in 1940 by one at Memorial
Hospital. These were operating guides for
about seventeen similar clinics in the New York
area, and for others in large American cities.
For forty years Dr. L'Esperance has been a
member of the faculty of the Cornell University Medical School, of which in 1950 she became the first woman to hold a full professorship, in the field of preventive medicine.

The second of the two daughters of a Westchester (New York) County physician, Albert
Strang, and of his wife, Kate (Depew) Strang,
Elise Depew Strang was born in Yorktown,
New York. After attending St. Agnes Episcopal School in Albany, the sixteen-year-old girl,
deciding to follow her father's profession, in
1896 entered the Woman's Medical College of
the New York Infirmary for Women and Children (later to become affiliated with the Cornell
Medical College), from which she received her
degree in medicine in 1899. Her marriage to

David L'Esperance, a lawyer, took place while
she was a student.

Following her graduation from medical
school, Dr. L'Esperance interned during one
year at New York's Babies Hospital under
Dr. Holt (the author of the famous *Care and
Feeding of Children*), before entering the private practice of pediatrics in that city, in which
she continued until 1908. Her interest in tuberculosis research becoming stimulated about that
time, she became a member of the Tuberculosis
Research Commission of the research laboratory of New York City, then directed by Dr.
William H. Park. Through this work in bacteriology for the New York City Department
of Health, she was drawn increasingly into
pathological research. With the intention of
specializing in that field, she sought a position
as pathologist with Cornell's cancer specialist,
Dr. James Ewing, who had refused previously
to employ a woman as his assistant. In 1910,
however, he engaged Dr. L'Esperance, who remained associated with the Cornell University
Medical School thereafter. "It was only a
technician's job," she remarked once to Frederick Woltman of the New York *World-Telegram*, "but I knew I could pick up a tremendous amount of information from one of the
greatest pathologists in the world." For the
first two years she was assistant in pathology;
then, from 1912 to 1920, an instructor in the
department of pathology, in which she held the
rank of assistant professor between 1920 and
1932, the first woman to attain that rank on
that faculty. Subsequently she was to hold an
assistant professorship of the department of
preventive medicine at Cornell for six years.
Her promotion to a full professorship came in
April 1950.

After 1910, for twenty-six years Dr.
L'Esperance also held the posts of pathologist
and director of laboratories at the New York
Infirmary for Women and Children, except for
the academic year of 1014, when she spent six
months studying tumor pathology in Munich,
Germany, on a Mary Putnam Jacoby fellowship. The research she pursued there under
Professor Borst resulted in the publication of
an article, "Primary Atypical Malignant Hepa-
tomia," in the *Journal of Medical Research*.
Forced to return to the United States by the
outbreak of World War I, she reported the *Medical Woman's Journal*, she published the findings
of subsequent research undertaken at Cornell in
the Johns Hopkins *Bulletin*. For the years
1917-20 she was assistant pathologist at New
York Hospital, pathologist at Harlem Hospital,
pathologist at Manhattan Maternity Hospital,
and assistant pathologist at Memorial Hospital
for Cancer. Assuming the post of instructor
in surgical pathology of the second surgical
division of Bellevue Hospital in 1919, she continued as an associate of that hospital until her
resignation in 1932.

Because the death of their mother resulted
from cancer, Dr. L'Esperance and her sister,
May Strang, decided to devote an inheritance
from their uncle, Chauncey Depew (onetime
head of the New York Central), to the establishment in 1932 of the Kate Depew Strang

Tumor Clinic at the New York Infirmary for Women and Children. Of this and subsequent preventive clinics founded with their aid, the sisters told Margaret Follin Eicks of the New York *World-Telegram,* "We thought they made more sense than a stained-glass window." Believing that cancer could be halted if detected in time, Dr. L'Esperance in 1937 was instrumental in extending the work at New York Infirmary by the foundation of the Strang Cancer Prevention Clinic. Within three years she had organized a third clinic for women at Memorial Hospital, the Cancer Prevention Clinic, which was subsequently expanded to provide facilities for men (1944), and for children between the ages of one and fifteen. When the new building of the clinic was dedicated on November 12, 1947, it also provided equipment for the examination of boys and girls between fourteen and twenty-one. "People do not normally think of cancer as a children's disease," the New York *Herald Tribune* quoted Dr. L'Esperance as saying, "but it is not a rare children's disease." In examining individuals for traces of precancerous or cancerous conditions, Dr. L'Esperance reported that about 1 per cent of those examined revealed indications of cancer, while another 18 per cent showed precancerous conditions. The two clinics are staffed by eighty-four doctors, nurses, and technicians, who as of 1950 had examined more than 35,000 patients. Check-up examinations are given periodically. To the cancer detection programs Dr. L'Esperance in 1948 added an auxiliary service for the recognition of diabetes. According to *American Men of Science,* she has also worked in the fields of tuberculosis and Hodgkin's disease.

Among articles Dr. L'Esperance has contributed to medical journals are "Early Carcinoma of the Cervix," to the *American Journal of Obstetrics and Gynecology* (October 1924), "The Influence of the New York Infirmary on Women in Medicine," to the *Journal of the American Medical Women's Association* (1949) ; she has also written for the *Proceedings of the New York Pathology Society,* the *Archives of Internal Medicine,* and the *Journal of Immunology.* From 1936 to 1941 she was a member of the editorial board—and at one time a managing editor—of the *Medical Woman's Journal.* Honors have been bestowed upon Dr. L'Esperance by the American Woman's Association, which in 1946 gave her its Friendship Award for Eminent Achievement; by the Annual Women's International Exposition of Arts and Industries, which in 1947 honored her for research in cancer; by the New York City Cancer Committee, which a year later awarded her its Clement Cleveland Medal "for outstanding contribution to cancer control work;" and by the bestowal of the Elizabeth Blackwell Citation for 1950 for her achievements in pathology and cancer detection. President Truman in 1947 named Dr. L'Esperance a member of the American delegation to the fourth international cancer research conference, held in St. Louis that year.

President of the Women's Medical Society of New York State in 1935, Dr. L'Esperance

Wide World Photos
ELISE L'ESPERANCE

is also a member of the Westchester County, New York County, and New York State medical societies, and of the American Medical Association. Member of the American Medical Women's Association, she was its president during 1948. The doctor is a fellow of the New York Academy of Medicine. Other of her memberships are in the New York Pathological Society, the American Association of Pathology and Bacteriology, the American Association of Immunologists, the American Radium Society, the Harvey Society, the Association for Cancer Research, and the American Cancer Society. The American Radiologists Society has made her an honorary member.

Dr. L'Esperance has been described in *County Life* as a "tall, fast-moving, strongly built woman." Known for her unusual hats, which she may wear in her office, Dr. L'Esperance has ascribed this habit to her days in the X-ray laboratory; "There never was any place to hang the thing. So I kept it on. Got in the habit. Now I'd feel headless without it." Dr. L'Esperance and her sister make their home in suburban Westchester County. "It's nice to have your own horses and cats," they have said, "and see your own grass." For several years the doctor has entered her harness pony in the National Horse Show (at New York's Madison Square Garden), with herself driving.

References

County Life 1 :41 My '48
J Am Med Women's Assn 3 :310 Jl '48
Med Woman's J 50 :14 Ja '43 ; 56 :23 Mr '49
N Y World-Telegram p8 Ja 11 '47
Time 55 :178-9 Ap 3 '50 por
American Men of Science (1949)
Who's Who in America, 1950-51

LEVESON-GOWER, WILLIAM SPEN-CER *See* Granville, W. S. L.-G., 4th Earl

LEWIS, CLYDE A(UGUSTINE) June 20, 1913- Veterans organization official: lawyer

Address: b. c/o Feinberg & Jerry, Plattsburgh, N.Y.; h. 85 Margaret St., Plattsburgh, N.Y.

Clyde A. Lewis was unanimously elected commander in chief of the Veterans of Foreign Wars of the United States at the 1949 annual convention, for the 1949-50 term. An attorney of Plattsburgh, New York, he is the first

CLYDE A. LEWIS

World War II veteran to head that organization. Lewis had entered its national executive board in 1947 when he was chosen the junior vice-commander in chief; and in 1948 he was elevated to the post of senior vice-commander in chief.

One of the five children of J. D. Clyde and Loretta C. (Adelsberger) Lewis, Clyde Augustine Lewis was born June 20, 1913, in Hoquiam, Washington. One of his brothers, Jesse, was killed in action in the battle of the Java Sea; another brother, Joseph, served in the Naval Air Corps. His grandfather had settled in the State of Washington, where he pioneered in lumbering. The family is still in this field, his father conducting a lumber and shingle manufacturing business.

Lewis was reared in the State of his birth. After graduating in 1929 from the South Bend (Washington) High School, where he was active in debating and football, he went East to Indiana to attend the University of Notre Dame. There he received his Bachelor of Arts degree in 1934. While at Notre Dame, Lewis was football manager in his senior year. He has said that contacts with Knute Rockne influenced

him greatly. Having decided to study law, he entered the law school of Harvard University and received the degree of Bachelor of Laws from that institution in 1939. In 1940 he was admitted to the New York State bar; and in 1946 he became a member of the law firm of Feinberg and Jerry, Plattsburgh, New York.

Enlisting in the Army Air Forces in April 1942, Lewis subsequently was appointed an aviation cadet, and received his wings and commission at Moody Field, Georgia, in March 1943. He then underwent B-17 pilot training and, upon being made flight commander, joined the 401st Bomber Group. In October 1943 he was sent overseas, where he served twenty-one months with the Eighth Air Force, flying first as a squadron leader, then as group and wing air commander; he was, successively, flight commander, operations officer, and squadron commander. By V-E Day he had completed one tour of duty and eleven missions of a second, for which he had volunteered. Altogether he flew a total of more than three hundred combat hours before being discharged in September 1945 with one hundred and fifty-two points. He now holds a reserve commission as lieutenant colonel in the United States Air Forces.

In 1945 Lewis returned to the practice of law, holding also the post of veterans' counselor in the New York State Division of Veterans Affairs during 1945-47. He became active in the Veterans of Foreign Wars of the United States when he joined the Plattsburgh Post 125 immediately after his separation from service; in 1946 he was made vice-chairman of its national legislative committee.

The V.F.W., which was organized in 1899, at the close of the Spanish-American War, has a membership of approximately one and a half million—among veterans groups it is second in size to the American Legion. At the Miami (Florida) golden anniversary convention, held from August 21 to August 26, 1949, Lewis was unanimously chosen commander in chief. The V.F.W., in outlining its objectives, approved the following resolutions: to endorse the principle of military aid to member-nations of the North Atlantic Pact (terming that treaty "a means of curbing the spread of communism"); to ask Congress: (1) to outlaw the Communist party and remove Communist party members from Federal Government positions; (2) to establish in colleges and universities a department of Americanism to counteract "communistic teachings." The convention, however, rejected a resolution requiring all public school teachers to sign loyalty affidavits and one imposing an anti-Communist oath on V.F.W. members.

Upon assuming leadership of the V.F.W., for the term of August 1949-August 1950, Lewis said he hoped to achieve two principal objectives while he was the national commander. These are: to weld the four leading veterans organizations into a "united front," and to wage an "uncompromising fight against an antiveteran sentiment that is developing in this country today." In pledging himself to work against adverse legislation, he declared: "We need this greater force [a united front] to successfully fight a new and well-organized anti-veteran movement, which includes groups within our Government which would deny to the veteran his traditional preference in civil service employment" (New York *Times*, August 27, 1949). The new leader also affirmed the V.F.W.'s support of requests for a Government bonus for World War II veterans, better housing for them, and adequate national military preparedness; it would oppose any reduction in hospital facilities for ex-servicemen.

On various occasions Lewis expressed his confidence that the four major veterans groups will be able to cooperate in supporting common legislation. (As major groups he has listed the American Legion, of which he is a member; his own Veterans of Foreign Wars of the United States; the Disabled American veterans; and the American Veterans of World War II, known as Amvets.) "The need for unity among veterans," he stated in an interview, "was never greater than it is today. My ambition is for the four organizations to understand so well their mutual problems that any one can speak for the other three" (New York *Herald Tribune*, August 29, 1949). He stressed the point that in forming a common front on leading issues, none of the organizations would lose its identity, but that its power and prestige would be enhanced. On a radio program, "The Veteran Wants to Know," broadcast September 25, 1949, he and George Craig [50], commander of the American Legion, pledged their two organizations to teamwork; a number of parallel resolutions which the groups had adopted at their respective conventions a few weeks before were noted, and Americanism, national security, foreign relations and veterans' benefits were pointed out as major fields for cooperation.

While standing behind his organization's resolution to outlaw communism in the United States, Lewis has decried illegal acts by groups of veterans, such as occurred when rioting broke out at the time of Paul Robeson's concert in Peekskill, New York, in the summer of 1949. On the occasion of conferring the V.F.W.'s Citizenship Award on Judge Harold F. Medina [49] of New York for his handling of the Communist conspiracy trial, Commander Lewis observed: "Judge Medina leaned over backwards in allowing the democratic process of trial by jury to function." Lewis has also placed his group on record as opposing the draft and as advocating its replacement, for reasons of economy and efficiency, with "a realistic national security training program" (Washington *Post*, December 21, 1949). In January 1950 Lewis, in conjunction with the head of Amvets, Harold Russell [50], urged Congress to approve a bonus for veterans of World War II.

Decorations awarded to Lewis are the Distinguished Flying Cross with two Oak Leaf Clusters, the Air Medal with four Oak Leaf Clusters, the Croix de Guerre with Star, the Distinguished Unit Citation with Oak Leaf Cluster, the European-African-Middle-Eastern Campaign ribbon with six battle stars, and the American Theater ribbon. A Roman Catholic,

Clyde A. Lewis is a member of the Knights of Columbus. He is also a member of the Elks, the Rotary International, and the American, New York State and Clinton County (New York) bar associations. He is a Republican. On September 22, 1936, he married Helen M. Judge; they have two sons, Clyde A., Jr., and John E. Five feet, eleven inches in height, and weighing 190 pounds, Lewis has blue eyes and brown hair. Flying his own plane is his favorite recreation.

References

N Y Herald Tribune p5 Ag 29 '49
N Y Times p30 Ag 26 '49
Who's Who in the East (1948)

LEWIS, SIR WILLMOTT (HARSANT)

June 18, 1877—Jan. 4, 1950 Journalist; Washington (D.C.) correspondent for the London *Times* from 1920 to 1948; newspaperman in Far East (1899-1910) during Boxer Rebellion, Russo-Japanese War, Chinese Revolution; in the Philippine Islands (1911-17) as editor of Manila *Times*; in Paris on various assignments, including short period with the New York *Herald Tribune's* Paris edition; joined staff of the London *Times* in 1919; sent to Washington as its correspondent in 1920; retired from active duty in 1948; regarded as unofficial envoy of Britain; known for keen analysis and humor. See *Current Biography*, 1941.

Obituary

N Y Times p25 Ja 5 '50

LIAQUAT ALI KHAN, BEGUM *See* Khan, Begum Liaquat Ali

LITCHFIELD, P(AUL) W(EEKS) July 26, 1875- Industrialist

Address: b. c/o Goodyear Tire and Rubber Company, 1144 E. Market St., Akron, Ohio; h. 1010 Merriman Rd., Akron, Ohio

Chairman of the board of the Goodyear Tire and Rubber Company, P. W. Litchfield in 1950 observed his fiftieth year with that company. In the course of those five decades the company grew from a small plant into one of the world's largest rubber manufacturers. The executive is known for his contributions to the development of rubber and of automotive and aeronautical technology, and for the leading part he took in the program of synthetic rubber production during World War II.

The son of Charles Manfred and Julia Winter (Weeks) Litchfield, Paul Weeks Litchfield was born in Boston, Massachusetts, on July 26, 1875. He is a descendant of George Soule, one of the passengers on the *Mayflower*, and of Laurence Litchfield, who also settled in Massachusetts after leaving England in 1639. Some of the names of the Goodyear dirigibles—the "Pilgrim", "Puritan", "Mayflower"—are indicative of Litchfield's New England background. His mother came from a family of seafarers and shipbuilders, and it is said that his interest

P. W. LITCHFIELD

in transportation stemmed from the experiences during his boyhood vacations in Bath, Maine, where he used to visit the shipyards. In later life he conceived the idea that tires should be made to absorb road shocks, not to resist them—an idea which reportedly occurred to him from his recollection of having seen ships at a New England seaport held to the dock by flexible ropes instead of by steel cables. In Boston Litchfield attended the Hugh O'Brien Grammar School and the Boston English High School, graduating from the latter in 1892. He studied chemical engineering at the Massachusetts Institute of Technology, from which he was graduated in 1896 with a B.S. degree. In his last year at M.I.T. he investigated the possibilities of a number of industries, and was impressed with the prospects of the rubber industry, then in its infancy.

For a year after graduation, failing to find a position in the technical line in which he had trained, Litchfield worked as a surveyor for the Metropolitan Park Commission of Boston. His association with the rubber industry began in 1897, when he accepted a position at nine dollars a week in a bicycle tire factory in Reading, Massachusetts, operated by L. C. Chase and Company of Boston. After a period in which he familiarized himself with the processes of the manufacture of bicycle tires, he became assistant superintendent of a new plant opened by the Chase company at Chelsea. Released in January 1898, when a new superintendent bringing his own assistants was placed in charge of the factory, Litchfield found employment with the Bath Iron Works as draftsman on torpedo boat design. Later he was foreman in the molded goods and packing department of the New York Belting and Packing Company. In June 1899 he returned as superintendent to the Chase plant in Chelsea. The company had in the meantime been in a merger, and was then part of the International Auto-

mobile and Vehicle Tire Company. One of Litchfield's first assignments in the automobile tire line was designing tires for the new Fifth Avenue buses in New York City.

In July 1900 Litchfield joined the Goodyear Tire and Rubber Company as superintendent of production at a salary of $2,500 a year. The company, named after the developer of vulcanization, had been organized two years before by Frank A. Seiberling. In its small factory two miles east of Akron, Ohio, it manufactured bicycle and carriage tires. There Litchfield continued to experiment until he developed the "straight-side" tire, which was able to absorb road bumps; his design eventually became standard in the industry. Litchfield's career as a production executive has been described as being "marked by unusual foresight." In 1908, the year in which he became a member of Goodyear's board of directors, he established a research and development department. Among the numerous innovations originating in that department were: the first practical airplane tire in 1910, the first pneumatic truck tire in 1916, hydraulic disk brakes for airplanes in 1932, and during World War II, an improved fuel tank for military planes. The "Life-Guard" automobile tube, developed in 1935, brought the company the Franklin Institute Certificate of Merit in 1942 for contribution to motoring safety.

Litchfield was made vice-president of the Goodyear company in 1915. Additions to production facilities of the rapidly growing organization included a plant in New Toronto, Ontario (1917), a tire plant and textile mill at Los Angeles (1919), textile mills in Georgia, New England, and Canada, and tire plants at Wolverhampton, England, and Sydney, Australia. (Litchfield is in 1950 chairman of the boards of the Goodyear Tyre and Rubber Company, Ltd., of Great Britain and of Australia.) In 1916 the company began to acquire fabric mills and to produce long staple cotton on its experimental farms in Arizona, an agricultural project which now includes an apprentice farmer program developed by Litchfield to help young men interested in agriculture to become independent farmers. After World War I the Goodyear company faced a threat of bankruptcy, and the Seiberling brothers lost control of the company they had founded. Under the new administration of a banking group, however, Litchfield remained as vice-president and factory manager.

In 1926, the year in which Goodyear, on the basis of total sales, was called the world's largest rubber company, Litchfield was appointed president. He was re-elected president in 1930 and in the same year was also elected chairman of the board, a position which he retained while resigning from the presidency in 1940. He also remained president of the Goodyear Aircraft Corporation.

Over the years Goodyear has acquired mills, factories and cotton plantations in thirteen States. Its products, which it distributes through some 50,000 retail dealers and more than 400 company-owned stores include, in addition to tires and inner tubes, rubber heels and soles, rubber mechanical goods, molded goods,

Airfoam cushioning material, fire and garden hose, belting, packing, flooring. An advocate of foreign investment, Litchfield has traveled to many of the countries where the company has undertaken enterprises, purchasing rubber plantations and setting up also several types of establishments in Java, Sumatra, the Philippines, Mexico, various countries in South America, South Africa, and in Europe. The Goodyear executive has received decorations from Brazil, Peru, and Sweden for the contributions to the economic welfare and development of those countries made by the establishment of Goodyear enterprises there. (In 1950 a five-million-dollar tire plant in Luxembourg is nearing completion.)

An aeronautics department, formed at Goodyear in 1910 under Litchfield's direction, early began to specialize in lighter-than-air craft, producing military and observation balloons and some hundred airships for use in World War I. In 1924 Goodyear acquired Zeppelin patents, and in 1928 Litchfield, long an advocate of airships, signed a contract to build for the United States Navy two giant dirigibles. An airdock was constructed in Akron, and in 1931 the U.S.S. *Akron*, largest airship built up to that time, was launched, followed by the U.S.S. *Macon* in 1933. (Both dirigibles were destroyed in disasters, the Akron in 1933, the Macon in 1935.) Other craft produced by the Goodyear Zeppelin Corporation, which in 1939 became the Goodyear Aircraft Corporation, include the Goodyear "blimps," the stratosphere balloon which in 1935 set an altitude record, and 168 Navy patrol and training airships in World War II. In the latter period Goodyear Aircraft expanded from an enterprise employing 40 workers to one employing 37,000, and came to rank as one of the ten largest producers of airplane parts and fighter aircraft in the United States. Its war production included barrage balloons, rubber life boats, Corsairs (fighter planes), aircraft parts for other companies, K-type Navy airships, for use by anti-submarine patrols. (In 1950 Goodyear Aircraft is completing work on America's largest blimp, designated by the Navy as the ZPN.) In 1948 Litchfield received the United States Air Force award of the President's Certificate of Merit for Goodyear Aircraft Corporation's outstanding wartime services. An oak and bronze plaque was presented to him in 1950 by Capital Airlines in recognition of the corporation's contribution to aviation by the development of cross-wind landing wheels for aircraft.

During the war Goodyear, which had filed its first patent on synthetic rubber in 1927, also cooperated with other companies of the rubber industry in solving the problems of synthetic rubber production. Since the war Litchfield has continued his interest in questions of national importance relating to the stockpiling and price of rubber and the disposition of Government-owned synthetic plants. Attention was drawn to his opinions by *Business Week* (July 29, 1950) which stated: "During recent Congressional hearings on a new synthetic rubber bill, Litchfield stood alone among industry leaders in opposing further sale or lease of the Government's synthetic rubber plants at this time. He holds that further breaking up of the synthetic production package at this time would endanger national security."

Litchfield has stated that as a corporation grows its responsibilities to employees, stockholders, and customers also grows. During his association with Goodyear, he has been concerned with labor relations, and thirty-five years ago, jointly with Mrs. Litchfield, he financed a company welfare fund of $100,000. He gave his ideas on employee relations in his book *The Industrial Republic: Reflections of an Industrial Lieutenant* (1946) and in magazine articles, one of which was entitled "A Labor Relations Program." He is the author of two other books, *Why? Why Has America No Rigid Airships?* (1945) and *Autumn Leaves*, (1945) an expression of philosophical reflections. He has also written many other articles and pamphlets, among them "History's Lesson to the Motor Truck" (1916), "The Republic of Business" (1920), and "History's Lesson to Air Power" (1944).

The numerous awards that Litchfield has received include: the second "Spirit of St. Louis" medal (1932) conferred on him by the American Society of Mechanical Engineers for contributions to the advancement of airship design and construction; an honorary D.Sc. from the University of Akron (1946); a twenty-year Veteran Boy Scout pin and the Silver Beaver, Silver Antelope, and Silver Buffalo in 1936 (he was instrumental in creating Air Scouting and is a former member of the executive board of the Boy Scouts of America); Special Merit Award (1950) from Air Service Post 501, American Legion, in recognition of his forty years of contributions to aviation.

Formerly a member of the board of directors of the Massachusetts Institute of Technology, Litchfield has also been president of the alumni association of that institution and a director of Akron University. A former director of the United States Chamber of Commerce, he is a member of the Rubber Manufacturers Association (president 1928-29), of the Society of Automotive Engineers, of the National Association of Manufacturers, and of the National Aeronautical Association. Other organizations to which he belongs include the Arizona Club, Phoenix; Union Club, Cleveland; Wings Club and National Air Council, New York; Navy League, Washington; Portage Country Club, City Club, University Club, Akron; Automobile Old Timers, Inc.; the Masonic Order (33d Degree).

Litchfield and Mrs. Litchfield, the former Florence Brinton, who were married June 23, 1904, live at "The Anchorage," their home in Akron; they also own a ranch in Arizona. Their two daughters are Mrs. Howard L. Hyde, of Akron, and Mrs. A. Wallace Denny, of New Toronto, Ontario. Litchfield is a member of the Protestant Episcopal Church. He finds relaxation in playing the organ in his home, and enjoys flying and fishing.

(Continued next page)

LITCHFIELD, P. W.—*Continued*

References

Bsns W p22+ Jl 29 '50
N Y Times III p3 Ag 21 '49 por
Business Executives of America (1950)
Hunsaker, J. C. Foreword to "Autumn
    Leaves," by P. W. Litchfield (1945)
International Who's Who, 1950
National Cyclopædia of American Biog-
    raphy Current vol G, 1943-46
Who's Who in America, 1950-51
Who's Who in Commerce and Industry
    (1948)
Who's Who in the Midwest (1949)
World Biography (1948)

LOCKHART, EUGENE *See* Lockhart, G.

LOCKHART, GENE July 18, 1891- Actor
Address: h. Beverly Hills, Calif.; The Players,
16 Gramercy Pk., New York 3

Gene Lockhart, who in December 1949 was
given the part of Willy Loman in the New
York company of Arthur Miller's prize-winning
play, *Death of a Salesman*, has played a wide
range of roles in musical comedies, dramas,
radio, and motion pictures. He has directed,
produced, and written plays for stage and radio,
and is responsible for the score of one musical,
the lyrics and book of several others. Since
1933 he has played in some seventy motion
pictures, including *Algiers*, *Blackmail*, *Hangmen Also Die*, *Miracle on 34th Street*, and *The
Inspector General*.

Born Eugene Lockhart in London, Ontario,
Canada, on July 18, 1891, Gene Lockhart is
the son of John Coates and Ellen Mary (De-
laney) Lockhart. Among the ancestors of the
Scottish Lockharts is John Gibson Lockhart,
biographer of Sir Walter Scott. The boy received his education at St. Michael's School
and at De La Salle Institute in Toronto. In an
interview with Helen Ormsbee (New York
Herald Tribune, March 11, 1945), the actor
gave credit to his mother for encouraging
his career. Comparing her to the character of
"Mama" in *I Remember Mama*, he said, "She
had the same wonderful sense of her family
as a unit, and she was always looking for
opportunities for us."

John Lockhart had studied singing, and
shortly after his seven-year-old son had danced
a Highland fling in a concert given by the
48th Highlanders' regimental band (which later
became famous as the Canadian Kilties Band)
the father joined the band, billed as a Scottish
tenor. The Lockhart family accompanied the
band to England, where John Lockhart toured
with it while Gene studied at the Brompton
Oratory school in London.

When Lockhart reached manhood his mother
urged him to try for a part on Broadway.
After a season of playing under canvas on a
Chautauqua circuit, twenty-five-year-old Lockhart won a place in a New York play in September 1917; he played Gustave in Klaw and
Erlanger's musical, *The Riviera Girl*, which

closed its New York run after seventy-eight
performances. Between acting engagements,
which included roles in Gilbert and Sullivan
operas with a Boston light opera company
(1922), Lockhart wrote for the stage. His
first production, *The Pierrot Players*, a musical for which he wrote both book and music,
toured Canada in 1919 with Lockhart in the
cast. *Heigho-Ho* (1920) followed—a musical
fantasy with score by Deems Taylor, book
and lyrics by Lockhart. The production had
a short run (with Lockhart in the cast), but
the song introduced in it, "The World is
Waiting for the Sunrise," the words of which
are by Lockhart (the music by Ernest Seitz),
became a widely popular ballad.

For the *Bunk of 1926*, a musical revue, Lockhart composed the score, was co-author with
Percy Waxman of the sketches and lyrics,
and was one of the cast. The play was sold
later to another producer who introduced
objectionable burlesque material into the
revue over Lockhart's protests. (The new
version, which was banned by the district
attorney, closed after 104 performances.)
Lockhart has written several serious plays,
none of which reached production, and some
four hundred sketches which have been presented in vaudeville, revues, or on the radio.

Lockhart's first hit as a dramatic actor was
as Bud, a mountaineer moonshiner, a supporting
role in Lula Vollmer's *Sun Up*. This was an
American folk play, which was presented by
the Players, Inc., cast in a Greenwich Village little theater in 1923. Highly praised by
the press, the play, after moving to a larger
New York house, had a two-year run. In 1924,
during this engagement, Lockhart married
Kathleen Arthur, an English actress and musician, who had played in America in *Three
Faces East* and in *Irene*.

The Lockharts have carried on the tradition
of the family as a unit in the theater. After
1925-26, when Gene Lockhart appeared in two
New York plays, *The Handy Man* and *Sure
Fire*, the husband and wife toured the United
States (1927-31) in *Recital-Revue* programs.
During this time Lockhart also appeared in
a series of performances presented by The
Players, a theatrical club: as Gregoire in *The
Little Father of the Wilderness*, as Waitwell in
The Way of the World, and as Gumption Cute
in *Uncle Tom's Cabin* (1933), all in New
York theaters. In 1931 he played the part of
Faust in *Mephisto*. Gene and Mrs. Lockhart
went on tour in 1932 in Lockhart's own crea-
tion, *How's Your Code?*

The Lockharts' daughter, June (who was
born in 1925) was to make a sensational Broadway success in *For Love or Money* in 1947.
She had made her debut at the age of eight
as Mimsey in the Metropolitan Opera Company's production of *Peter Ibbetson*. Her first
film appearance was as Belinda Crachit in *A
Christmas Carol*, a motion picture in which
Gene and Kathleen Lockhart also played. In
1933 the Lockharts were featured in *Sunday
Nights at Nine*, a program presented at New
York's Barbizon-Plaza Hotel.

In addition to his acting, Lockhart has engaged in a number of related activities: the

writing of articles for theatrical magazines and of a weekly column for a Canadian publication, coaching members of New York's Junior League in dramatics, lecturing on dramatic technique at the Julliard School of Music, and directing a revival of *The Warrior's Husband*. In 1933 he portrayed Uncle Sid in the Theatre Guild's production of Eugene O'Neill's popular comedy, *Ah, Wilderness*, which starred George M. Cohan. The Canadian's success in this role, calling for "subtle character shading," won him a contract from RKO for *By Your Leave* (1934).

After proceeding to Hollywood, where he remained until 1945, Lockhart played in a variety of pictures. Among some seventy roles he has performed on the screen are Lushin in *Crime and Punishment*, Bob Crachit in *A Christmas Carol*, Stephen Douglas in *Abe Lincoln in Illinois*. In Walter Wanger's *Algiers* (1938), starring Charles Boyer and Hedy Lamarr, Lockhart as the scoundrel Regis drew laudatory reviews and awards from London's *Film Review* and the Pacific Coast critics for the best supporting role of the year, as well as nomination for an Academy Award. Between early picture engagements he in 1935 staged "Sumurun," a Persian pantomime, in the Hollywood bowl. His acting in *Blackmail* (1939) won him first place in the estimation of the London *Film Review* for the best performance by a character actor that year.

In August 1941 Lockhart was signed by Warner Brothers to his first long-term contract, which called for featured billing. Since then he has played in *One Foot in Heaven* (1941), *All That Money Can Buy* (1941), the picturization of Stephen Vincent Benét's *The Devil and Daniel Webster*. Then, during the war years, the actor was cast in traitor roles in *Hangmen Also Die* (1943), *Northern Pursuit* (1943), and *Action in Arabia* (1943). Other oustanding pictures of his career include *Mission to Moscow* (1943), *Going My Way* (1944), *The House on 92nd Street* (1945). The actor terminated his contract with Warners in 1943. In a recent interview he said, "The character actor has a better chance as a free lance. He can choose his roles and avoids being cast in unsuitable parts because he is on the salary roll of one company."

The Lockharts returned to Broadway in 1945 in the leading roles, the Reverend Homer Whatcoat and his wife, Martha, of the play, *Happily Ever After*. Critic Howard Barnes (New York *Herald Tribune*), likening the comedy to "a collapsed soufflé," credited the Lockharts with giving it "a recurring lift of sharp characterization and pungent pantomime." On the air, the Lockharts teamed in *The Nebbs*, a family comedy series, heard over Mutual network on Sundays during 1945. As a writing team they have done many sketches both for vaudeville and the radio. The actor continued his movie career, being seen in the pictures *Meet Me on Broadway* (1946), *Leave Her to Heaven* (1946; Mrs. Lockhart was also in the cast), *Miracle on 34th Street* (1947), *Joan of Arc* (1948), and *The Inspector General* (1949), among others.

GENE LOCKHART

The actor was engaged in December 1949 to follow Lee Cobb as Willy Loman, the leading character in *Death of a Salesman*. Richard Watts, Jr., (New York *Post*), who called the play one of the "most notable dramas of the nation's postwar theater," pronounced Lockhart's playing of the hapless drummer "more convincingly pathetic" than that of "his dynamic predecessor." "The summary impact of Lockhart's performance comes from the increasing energy he displays as the story rides to its end," wrote William Hawkins in the New York *World-Telegram*. The critical concensus was that Lockhart reached the "heights of sensitive acting" in this, one of the "most human," but physically exhausting roles of the American theater. The actor has said he finds it, as Lee Cobb before him did, a great strain on his health. He ends his engagement in May 1950, when he will return to Hollywood to fulfill commitments there.

The Lockharts have a home in Beverly Hills. A veteran member of The Players (founded by Edwin Booth), he assisted in establishing a Hollywood branch, whose "West Room" is a popular feature. Lockhart's other clubs are the Dutch Treat, Coffee House, and Writers, all of New York, Masquers of Hollywood. Lockhart, who has blue eyes, is said to be the most genial of talkers. He is a Roman Catholic. As a youth he excelled in sports— in 1909 he held the Canadian one-mile swimming championship, and from 1910 to 1913 he played on the Toronto Argonauts football team. Today his recreations are swimming and golf.

References

N Y Herald Tribune IV p1 Mr 11 '45
International Motion Picture Almanac, 1947-48
Who's Who in the Theatre (1947)
Winchester's Screen Encyclopedia (1948)

LONG, EARL K(EMP)   Aug. 26, 1895-
Governor of Louisiana
Address: b. Louisiana State Capitol, Baton
Rouge, La.; h. Governor's Mansion, Baton
Rouge, La.

In the election held April 20, 1948, Earl K.
Long, Democrat, was chosen Governor of
Louisiana for a four-year term ending in May
1952. He has been active in the politics of
his native State since 1928, when he was appointed attorney for inheritance tax collector

Wide World Photos
EARL K. LONG

for Orleans Parish by his brother, Huey P.
Long, then Governor. In 1931 he was defeated
for the office of Lieutenant Governor, but was
elected to that post in 1936, and, as the result
of the resignation of the elected Governor,
served as chief executive of the State from
June 1939 to May 1940. His successful return
to the Governorship in the 1948 elections, in
which he received the greatest vote ever polled
by one candidate, has been described as "one of
the most intriguing paradoxes of modern
politics."

Earl Kemp Long was born August 26, 1895,
in Winnfield, Louisiana, a poor, agricultural
section of the State. He was the younger son
of Huey Pierce and Caledonia (Tison) Long.
With his brother Huey, two years his senior,
he grew up in an environment of want and
of rebellion against the rich, aristocratic Louisi-
anians of the southern areas of the State,
particularly New Orleans. Though the father
eventually became prosperous through the sale
of land to a railroad company, he spoke often
of the need for "a revolution" that would lift
the blight of poverty and neglect from his
native region. This attitude of their father
made an indelible impression on the two boys,
who left home at an early age to go to work.
Earl was a clerk in a lumber company for two

years, and then, in 1914, became a traveling
salesman in shoe polish, stove polish, and
patent medicines. Following the course taken
by his brother, he became a special student at
Tulane and Loyola universities, in New
Orleans, where he studied law. In July 1926
he passed his examinations and was admitted
to practice in the State.

Earl Long received his first political office in
1928, shortly after his brother had become
Governor of Louisiana; he was appointed attorney for inheritance tax collector for the
Orleans Parish, the district in Louisiana of
which the city of New Orleans comprises the
principal part. This position Huey P. Long
had promised to abolish in order to use its
$15,000-a-year salary for additional hospital
facilities. However, in the legislative hearing
concerning the appointment, the Governor justified his action and Earl Long held the position
until 1932. During this period he was a supporter of his brother, being particularly helpful
in organizing sufficient votes to defeat the 1929
impeachment proceedings against the Governor.

Earl Long began to oppose his brother in
1931-32, when he ran for the office of Lieutenant Governor on an anti-Long ticket when
Huey (who had resigned the Governorship to
run for the United States Senate) refused to
support him. Defeated in that election (1932),
and removed from the post of attorney for
inheritance tax collector, Earl Long retired to
farm and raise stock in his native parish of
Winn. During 1932-34 he was assistant State
counsel for the Home Owners' Loan Corporation, and in 1937 was named consultant for the
Louisiana Public Service Commission. Still
bitter at his brother's refusal to back him in
the 1932 elections, Earl Long testified against
him at a Senate investigation held in 1933 on
charges of fraud in the Louisiana Senatorial
primary elections. Although their mutual accusations were strongly worded, most political
observers agree that a reconciliation was effected
before September 1935, when Huey P. Long
was assassinated.

In the 1936 elections, Richard W. Leche, a
member of the Long political organization was
elected Governor, and Earl K. Long Lieutenant
Governor on the same ticket. Many constitutional amendments were passed, particularly one
permitting a 1 per cent State sales tax to
support the social security program. In June
1939, however, gross mismanagement of public
funds by the President of the Louisiana State
University and by executives of other State
agencies, which came to be referred to as the
"Louisiana Scandals," were revealed. In the
course of the indictments, the Governor resigned,
and Long became chief executive for the
remainder of the term. Although many of the
political figures associated with the administration were found guilty and were sentenced to
terms in Federal and State penitentiaries, no
charges were brought against Earl Long. A
frequent comment of his on this period of his
career is: "I was the most investigated man in
Louisiana and nobody ever was able to prove
anything against me."

The "scandals" provided the main issue of
the January 1940 gubernatorial primary elec-

tions, with Long a candidate in opposition to several representatives of reform groups. Since the Republican Party in Louisiana is not considered a major opposition, it is the Democratic primary elections which in effect decide the voters' final choice. In his bid for the primary, Earl Long denounced the scandals as "a shame and a disgrace." The first primary was indecisive, but in the runoff, Long was defeated by Sam Houston Jones '40, leader of the reform group. His defeat marked the decline of the organization which had dominated Louisiana politics for twelve years: in subsequent elections other members of the regime were defeated, and the legislature of the reform party instituted constitutional amendments.

On the completion of his term in May 1940, Long again returned to his farm. Appearing in the political picture briefly in 1944, he was a candidate for Lieutenant Governor and was again defeated by the reform candidate. In 1947 he began to make preparations for the 1948 election by touring the States, as his brother had before him, in the back-country districts of Louisiana, and campaigning on the same issues and with the same methods as his brother. He invoked "the magic name of Brother Huey" (to quote from a report in the March 8, 1948, issue of *Time*) and promised a $50-a-month old age pension, a bonus to veterans, and improvement of the school system, highways, hospitals, and other public works. His nephew, Russell Long (later a United States Senator), son of the late Huey P. Long, assisted in the campaign, appearing on the same platform with the candidate to dispel any lingering doubt in the voters' minds as to the reconciliation between the two brothers.

Three candidates opposed Long in the January 1948 primary, with Jones, the man who had defeated him in the 1940 elections, the most significant opponent. Long polled 41.5 per cent of the votes, but he lacked a sufficient number for a clear majority. In the runoff election between Jones and Long, held the next month, Long received 422,766 votes, the greatest number ever polled by one candidate. He even carried the Parish of Orleans, a district which had never given its vote to his brother. Because of the one-party dominance, his election on April 20 followed as a matter of course. A New York *Times* editorial judged the swing from the reform party back to the Long organization to mean that the 1948 campaign could not be fought on the scandals of 1939, and that most of the State's residents did not believe Earl Long participated in the looting accomplished by men with whom he was elected to office in 1936. In March, a resolution in the United States House of Representatives to investigate Long's income tax returns was defeated. He became Governor on May 11, 1948, when the inaugural ceremony (in the stadium of the State University) and the festivities resembled the public occasions of Huey Long's days. In his address the new Governor stressed his intention of creating a condition in which every man would be "a king and every lady a queen, with no one wearing the crown."

At the regular May 1948 session, and later, at a special session in September, Governor Long asked the State Legislature for laws and constitutional amendments which would effectuate his campaign promises. Over protests from labor and business groups, his program was launched with but "token" opposition in the legislature. Tax laws increasing the State income by about $190,000 a day, or approximately 50 per cent above the former taxes, were passed to pay for a $60,000,000 bond issue for veterans' bonuses, $40,000,000 a year to increase old age benefits to $50 a month, a guaranteed minimum pay scale for teachers, and increased highway construction and hospital facilities. Both the gasoline tax and the tax on bottled beer were raised, and the retail sales tax was increased to 2 per cent. In addition, the legislature gave the new Governor the power to reorganize and reappoint boards in charge of State institutions and to supervise liquor sales. In the special September session, Long was successful in abolishing the six-year-old civil service system.

Governor Long, who in the spring of 1948 had declared himself opposed to a Fair Employment Practice Act but not to the national Democratic leadership, in September of that year called a special session of the State Legislature to consider allowing the name of President Truman to appear on the State ballot in the 1948 presidential election. Previously, the State Central Committee had ordered the States' Rights ticket of J. Strom Thurmond '48 to be substituted for the regular Democratic ticket of Truman and Barkley. A bill which bore the Governor's approval was passed to permit the inclusion of the name of President Truman on the ballot.

Earl Long, who resembles his brother in appearance, is said to have the same "shrewd insight" into the mind of the common man of Louisiana. On August 17, 1932, he married Blanche B. Revere. His New Orleans clubs are the Athletic and International House.

References

N Y Times Mag p14 N 7 '48 por
Time 52:16 Ag 30 '48 por
Washington (D.C.) Post p2 F 26 '48
Who's Who in America, 1950-51

LONGSTRETH, T(HOMAS) MORRIS
Feb. 17, 1886- Author
Address: h. Westtown, Pa.

Reprinted from the *Wilson Library Bulletin*, June 1950.

Longstreths now in America originally came from the north of England, and the name derives from Lang Streth, a valley running into Scotland. It seems an appropriate name for T. Morris Longstreth, writer of a series of regional travel books, who has also traversed the length and breadth of Canada (every province except Prince Edward Island) following the trail of the Royal Canadian Mounted Police. Of recent years Longstreth has also written biographies for young people, notably of Tad Lincoln and Daniel Chester French (*The Great Venture*, 1948).

(Continued next page)

LONGSTRETH, T. MORRIS—*Continued*

Thomas Morris Longstreth was born in Philadelphia on February 17, 1886, the son of Benjamin T. Longstreth, an iron merchant in that city, and Frances (Haldeman) Longstreth, who died when the boy was two. Benjamin Longstreth married again and had three sons. Writer Longstreth has said: "I enjoyed the adjacent large estate of my grandmother Longstreth, with farm, orchard, horses, and nearly thirty cousins." After kindergarten he attended Friends Select School until he was thirteen, when he went to Westtown Boarding School, "a country heaven, a square mile of orchard, farm, and lake in Chester County, Pennsylvania." Here he played tennis and football, skated, bobsledded, and went on solitary hikes. Graduating in 1904, he continued to Haverford College on a scholarship, going out there for track and tennis, and receiving his B.A. in 1908, with another solemn admonition from an instructor to beware of writing as a profession. (At Haverford he had written a description of the cane rush for the Philadelphia *Evening Bulletin,* and some personality sketches for the *Haverfordian.*)

Since Longstreth had in any case decided to study and compose music, he was not unduly perturbed by this advice. He taught at the Delancy School, Philadelphia, and the Montgomery School, Wynnewood. "Finally a gentleman whose boys I had tutored into St. Paul's offered to stake me to an education in Vienna (this was in 1912), but when I returned from Europe in order to make arrangements to go back there, I found my father fatally ill and I must earn money."

"I think the Germans, without meaning to, stimulated me out of my pleasure-loving existence (for I had had five trips to Europe as tutor) and into serious work. For in 1914, the outbreak of war, with much of the world taken on by Germans and Austrians, was somewhat like a sporting event, and stirred my blood. I was in London when it broke out and felt the impact. It made a profound difference to my feeling and thinking. Of course, I soon got over the sporting-event phase as my friends began to get killed in August 1914, but the stimulus remained. This is a unique and not very intelligent entrance into letters, but a true one."

Reading the Weather (1915), reissued in 1943 as *Knowing the Weather* ("not a book for the rank beginner," said Edward Tatnall Canby in the *Saturday Review of Literature* then), and *The Adirondacks* (1917) were Longstreth's first two books. A chapter in one of them resulted in an invitation from Melvil Dewey to be a guest at the Lake Placid Club for a year. Accepting, Longstreth remained for ten years, keeping weather records and writing. In quick succession came *The Catskills* (1918), *Mac of Placid* (1920), *The Laurentians* (1922), *The Lake Superior Country* (1923), *The Silent Five* (1924), and *Coin and Crossbones* (1925). The New York *Tribune* summed up the travel books as "[evoking] the spirit of the place he writes about with a rare combination of feeling

for the wilds and words" and "[adorning] the whole with many a humorous incident."

Leaving Placid for Canada, Longstreth next began his exciting authoritative stories and histories of the Mounted Police, one of which (*In Scarlet and Plain Clothes*) is one of three titles recommended by the corps itself for prospective recruits. *The Silent Force* (1927) "excellently accomplishes an extremely difficult purpose," wrote Bernard De Voto in the *Saturday Review.* "It does by significant details suggest the essence, and so compresses many volumes into one." *Sons of the Mounted Police* (1928), its successor, was a semifictional account for boys nearing college age based on authentic episodes and illustrated from photographs of life among the Police.

After writing *Sky Through Branches* (1930), lyrics of the outdoors and blank verse narratives which Granville Hicks in the New York *World* called unpretentious and uncommonly pleasant to read, and a mystery, *Murder at Belly Butte* (1931), Longstreth returned to the Mounties with *In Scarlet and Plain Clothes* (1933), one of his best.

Quebec, Montreal, Ottawa (1932) and *To Nova Scotia* (1935) were new travel accounts in Longstreth's familiar picturesque and anecdotal vein. He then settled down in Washington for five years; spent seven years at Concord, Massachusetts; and is now living close to his old Westtown school, which often figures in the familiar essays he has written once a month for the *Christian Science Monitor* during the last twenty years.

Book written during this period, chiefly for younger readers, include *At Mountain Prep* (1939), *Trial by Wilderness* (1940), *Trooper's Friend* (1940); *The Missouri Clipper, In Lightning or in Rain,* and *Jess,* all in 1941; and *Tad Lincoln, the President's Son* (1944). The Springfield *Republican*'s opinion was: "For all its slight fictionizing, this study may well be an important addition to any library of Lincolniana." The Thoreau brothers, John and Henry, are important figures in *Hide-Out* (1948), complimented by the *Horn Book* for its "real sense of the period." *The Great Venture* (1948) was called by Virginia Kirkus a "solid, sound book; well organized." *Mounty in a Jeep* (1949) was rather sharply criticized for slackness of style, although considered another exciting story. *Showdown* appeared in 1950.

In view of the fact that Longstreth does not consider himself photogenic, and thinks press photographs misleading anyway, no picture of him appears here. He is of medium height, with fair hair and blue-gray eyes. He is a member of the Society of Friends, a bachelor, and a Republican in politics ("for default of better"). Skiing and canoeing were his favorite sports, and he still enjoys music and the outdoors. Besides his nearly thirty books, he has written hundreds of magazine articles. His most widely quoted sentence is, "As youth goes, so goes the nation." And he has read *Huckleberry Finn* as often as *The Virginian* and the poems of Robert Frost—as well as *Hamlet* and "the great pieces in the Bible."

LORD, MILTON E(DWARD) June 12, 1898- Librarian; library association president
Address: b. c/o Boston Public Library, Boston 17, Mass.; h. Boxford, Mass.

Milton E. Lord was inaugurated as the 1949-50 president of the American Library Association at its Southwestern Regional Conference in November 1949. The director of the Boston Public Library since 1932, he is as well a participant in library groups, both national and international. The American Library Association, "the chief spokesman for the modern library movement in North America, and to considerable extent throughout the world" (from the A.L.A. *Handbook*), is an organization of nineteen thousand librarians, libraries, library trustees, and other friends of libraries.

The son of William Delbert and Eliza Anna (Bishop) Lord, Milton Edward Lord was born in Lynn, Massachusetts, on June 12, 1898. After the completion of his secondary education, he became in 1915 a freshman in the Harvard College class of 1919. He did not, however, receive his B.A. degree until 1921, his studies having been interrupted by World War I. At the end of his sophomore year he entered the Heavy Artillery School at Fort Monroe, Virginia, to train during 1918-19; upon his discharge he held the commission of second lieutenant in the Coast Artillery Officers' Reserve Corps, in which he remained until 1924.

Lord first became interested in library work in 1919, when he returned to Harvard to complete his college work and served as a part-time assistant in the library until 1925. During this period, from 1919 to 1923, he also acted as librarian of Harvard Union in Cambridge, and from 1921 to 1924 he devoted himself to graduate study. Following a year (1925-26) at the Ecole des Sciences Politiques in Paris, Lord spent four years in Italy as librarian of the American Academy in Rome (1926-30). In 1928 he was selected one of the members of the commission of five American librarians who assisted in the recataloging of the Vatican Library. He served as the United States delegate to the First International Library Congress held in Rome, Naples, Florence, and Venice in 1929. Returning to the United States in 1930, Lord assumed the post of professor and director of university libraries and of the library school at the State University of Iowa.

On February 1, 1932, Lord succeeded the late Charles F. D. Belden as director of the Boston Public Library, said to be the oldest free municipal library in the world supported by taxation. Founded in 1852 and opened to the public in 1854, the Boston library system today comprises the main library and thirty branches, a book stock of almost two million volumes, and an annual circulation record close to three million. The main library's building, erected in 1895, was designed by McKim, Mead, and White (the country's leading architects) and contains murals by Sargent, Abbey, Elliott, and De Chavannes, and sculpture by St. Gaudens, French, MacMonnies, and Pratt.

Lord soon effected a reorganization of the library, providing for the redistribution of its functions among the circulation division (pri-

Armand Studio
MILTON E. LORD

marily the branches), the reference division, and the division of business operations (as stated in the 1933 annual report of the Boston Public Library). This was necessary, Lord felt, because the institution is not only a large active public library in the usual sense, but is as well a scholarly reference and research institution possessing many of the characteristics of the university library. The director also recast the work of the library training class: in an enlarged program some two hundred members of his staff undertook courses designed for self-development and improved service to the public.

Milton E. Lord became a member of the American Library Association in 1930. As chairman of its international relations committee (1934-36), Lord attended the Second International Library Congress held at Madrid, Seville, and Barcelona during May 20-30, 1935. The chief topic raised for consideration (by the more than five hundred delegates representing more than thirty-four countries) was that of international library loans; this, Lord wrote, was a problem more pressing in Europe than in America. To the discussion of cooperation among libraries, Lord presented the report "Union Cataloging in the United States." Especially interested in the discussions of Spanish libraries and bibliography because of the valuable Ticknor collection of Spanish and Portuguese literature in his own library, Lord also offered the paper "Spanish Collections in American Libraries." He is now chairman of the American Committee on Arrangements for the Third International Library Congress to be held in the United States in 1950.

From 1935 to 1940 Lord gave his services to the A.L.A. Council. In 1937 he acted as chairman of the library administration committee. Three years later he joined the executive board of the body (1940-44). Lord became its rep-

LORD, MILTON E.—*Continued*

resentative on the Council of National Library Associations in the capacity of secretary-treasurer (1942-44) and later as its chairman (1944-45). In the field of international library activities, Lord has been a member of the A.L.A. international relations board since its creation in June 1942. In 1944 he became chairman of the A.L.A. joint committee on books for war-devastated libraries, and in 1946 he assumed the duties of chairman of the board of directors of the American Book Center for War Devastated Libraries, Inc. He has represented A.L.A. at the meetings of the International Library Committee in Geneva (1946) and in Oslo (1947). Since 1947 he has served as first vice-president of the International Federation of Library Associations.

As reorganization director of the American Library in Paris, Lord arrived there to begin his duties in January 1945, a few months after the liberation. In a statement issued after the termination of his post on March 31, he recommended that the library expand its functions by aiding the libraries of the United States in acquiring French publications on an exchange basis; and by becoming a center of cultural activities designed to interpret the United States to the French people through the use of exhibits, lectures, documentary films, and concerts. Since 1947 the director of the Boston Public Library has served as a member of the American advisory committee of the American Library in Paris, and as honorary trustee.

Seeking to improve library service in his own State, Lord has been chairman of the Conference on State Aid for Libraries in Massachusetts since 1947. This group has made "perhaps the most thoroughgoing and extensive study of Massachusetts public libraries yet undertaken," Lord stated in January 1949; the next steps in the plan are to educate trustees and librarians themselves and many organized groups on the need for State aid, to draft a legislative proposal, and finally to press for the passage of such legislation.

During his term as first vice-president and president-elect of the American Library Association for 1948-49, Lord succeeded Ralph A. Ulveling as the association's member of the United States National Commission for UNESCO, which held its first and second conferences in late March and early April of 1949 in Cleveland, Ohio. Lord also represented the American Library Association in the World Town Hall Seminar, composed of representatives of leading American organizations in the fields of business, labor, education, and civic activity. Sponsored by America's Town Meeting of the Air, the group participated in discussions with foreign leaders in fourteen national capitals during July and August 1949.

Milton E. Lord was installed November 23, 1949, as president of the American Library Association. In his inaugural address he discussed three points with which he would be concerned: action on the recommendations of the committee which had made a study of the activities and structure of A.L.A.; the strengthening of the organization's State and regional programs; the study of means of relating A.L.A. more closely with other library groups, and they with it (*A.L.A. Bulletin*, February 1950).

The library director is a member of other library organizations: the American Library Institute, the Association of College and Reference Libraries, the Association of Research Libraries, the Special Libraries Association, the Bibliographical Society of America, the Massachusetts Library Association, and the Massachusetts Historical Society. He is, too, a fellow of the American Academy of Arts and Sciences, trustee of Simmons College, and a member of the Old Cambridge Shakespeare Association and of the Harvard, Odd Volumes, Examiner, Thursday Evening, and Harvard Faculty clubs.

Lord was married to Rosamond Lane, daughter of William C. Lane, librarian of Harvard College, on September 8, 1928. Their children are Peter Palmer, Joan, Mary Wyman, Anne, and Sarah Peabody. In one of his replies for a report of the Harvard class of 1919 (as quoted in the *Bulletin of Bibliography*) Lord wrote that while his personal pleasure was centered in his family, he derives "much additional satisfaction from walking, mountain climbing, music, poetry, foreign languages, reading, travel."

References

Bul Bibliog 17:61-2 Ja-Ap '41
N Y Times p33 N 24 '49
Who's Who in America, 1948-49
Who's Who in Library Service (1943)

LOUGHLIN, DAME ANNE June 28, 1894-
Trade union official

Address: b. c/o National Union of Tailors and Garment Workers, 41 Portman Sq., London, England

Well to the front of the British labor movement stands Dame Anne Loughlin, who was one of two women on the British delegation sent to the Free World Labor Conference, held in London in December 1949. That conference resulted in the formation of the new International Confederation of Free Trade Unions, which was organized in opposition to the Communist-dominated World Federation of Trade Unions. The general secretary of the National Union of Tailors and Garment Workers, Dame Anne has been a member of the general council of England's powerful Trades Union Congress since 1929.

Eldest of the four daughters of a shoe-factory worker of Irish descent, Anne Loughlin was born June 28, 1894, in the Yorkshire city of Leeds, England's principal woolens-manufacturing center. Attendance at a public elementary school in Leeds came to an end when she was twelve; her mother had died, and it devolved upon the girl to cook, scour, and sew for her father and her younger sisters. When she was sixteen years old, her father also died, and, to support the family, she took a job as a machine worker in a local factory. The hourly wage was threepence. "We've come a long way since those days," she was to observe many years later, "when out of ten shillings weekly we had to pay a penny a week for hot water whether we used it or not, and were fined threepence for being fifteen minutes late and sixpence for half an hour's time off." Alerted to the needs for effective organization if better conditions were to be obtained, not long after she joined the National Union of Tailors and Garment Workers she found herself the leader of a strike of some two hundred girls. At the same time she discovered her own "great power to sway a crowd" with what has been described as her "natural oratory"; she also (stated Mary Bradley in a biographical sketch supplied by the British Information Services) "had the gift of being able to negotiate sensibly when the fiery speeches were done." In the meantime, she continued her formal education at night school, and in 1914 she became an organizer for her union, which necessitated traveling throughout the British Isles.

Miss Loughlin's work as an organizer entailed negotiation on hours and wages for women and children, and consultation on factory conditions and insurance. Accordingly, during the years of World War I she devoted considerable time to the study of legal problems and today (it is said) "can quote industrial law and the constitution of the trades unions [federation] with never a slip." She attracted the notice of the powerful parent Trades Union Congress—the British equivalent (founded in 1868) of the AFL or CIO. Thus, in the early summer of 1925 she was one of four women delegates named by the congress to attend the fourteenth conference of the Communists of the U.S.S.R. at Leningrad, and on return was one of the signatories to a report commenting favorably on working conditions in Russian factories.

Four years later, at the 1929 T.U.C. conference at Belfast, Miss Loughlin was a delegate for her union. In this capacity she achieved prominence by offering a resolution (which was adopted) calling for amendment of the Trade Boards Act "to ensure more efficient observance of minimum rates and hours." At the conclusion of the conference she was elevated to membership in the general council, the governing body of the T.U.C., to which she has been regularly re-elected. In June 1933 Miss Loughlin was for the first time named to a governmental investigating committee appointed by the Home Secretary "to review the existing law relating to the enforcement of fines imposed by Courts of Summary Jurisdiction in wife-maintenance orders" (imprisonment for nonpayment of alimony). At Weymouth T.U.C. conference in September 1934, she again attracted attention by her sponsorship of a resolution "to instruct the general council . . . to induce the Government to adopt a forty-hour working week without reduction of wages and earnings." Two months later (in November) she was elected chairman of the Women's Labor Party for the term 1934-35.

The title of Commander of the Order of the British Empire (O.B.E.) came to Miss Loughlin with the New Year's Honors List for 1935. At the Margate T.U.C. conference

DAME ANNE LOUGHLIN

in September of the same year she advocated "raising of the school-leaving age" to prevent "lowering of wage standards due to increasing employment of juveniles in the tailoring industry." Also, in 1935, she made her first visit to the United States, as a T.U.C. representative at the AFL convention in Atlantic City, where she spoke on the subject "Women Trade Unionists"; and later, at a reception by the International Ladies Garment Workers Union in New York, she predicted that the "American trade union movement would eventually join forces with socialism." In March 1937 she was named to a committee appointed by the House of Commons to "investigate the extent to which holidays with pay are given to employed workpeople, and the possibility of extending the provision of such holidays"; and on August 29, 1939, she was made an additional member of the National Food Council and of the Consumers' Committee for Great Britain, under the Agricultural Marketing Act of 1931. In her World War II service Miss Loughlin "concentrated her efforts on the use of women power and on the country's obligations to the mobile workers," especially girls, and was called in by the Ministry of Supply "to advise it on arranging billets and hostels for these girls."

Appearance of Anne Loughlin's name (on the King's Birthday Honors List for June 1943) as that of a Dame Commander of the Order of the British Empire (D.B.E.) followed her election in the previous September as chairman of the general council of the Trades Union Congress for the ensuing year. She was the second woman to be chosen for this office, thus becoming the first woman to preside over a T.U.C. conference, at Southport, Lancashire, beginning September 5, 1943. In May 1944 Dame Anne was again in America, to attend the International Labor Organization conference at Philadelphia as an adviser to the British

LOUGHLIN, DAME ANNE—*Continued*

delegation. (She had also participated in several earlier ILO assemblies in Geneva.) The Philadelphia conference endorsed the principle of equal compensation for equal work, and at its conclusion Dame Anne told the British delegation that "now that forty nations have said it is the job and not the sex that ought to determine the rate of pay, we will present this to our Government." A Royal Commission on Equal Pay held its first meeting in October, under the chairmanship of Lord Asquith; Dame Anne, who was one of four women members, was subsequently one of three to render a minority report. (The majority, though recommending equal pay in the civil service, did not extend the principle to industry.)

In the postwar period Dame Anne became concerned over the growth of Communist power within British unions and over the general trend of Soviet world policy. At the 1947 T.U.C. convention she told the assembly that her own union "was disappointed that Russia had not made common cause with us in efforts to unify the democratic countries of Europe"; and she was author of the resolution adopted endorsing the policy of Foreign Secretary Ernest Bevin '49. At the beginning of the following year she offered herself as a candidate for the general secretaryship of the National Union of Tailors and Garment Workers (which had attained a membership of about 100,000 women and 30,000 men). She was elected January 6, 1948, from a list of six candidates, polling nearly one half of the total votes cast. (The Communist-backed candidate ran third.) This distinction, as the first woman general secretary of a British union, was hailed by the London *Times* as "an important victory for the Right wing." A little less than two years later (November 28, 1949), when the Free World Labor Conference consisting of the delegates of 48,000,000 workers met in London to set up a democratic international labor organization in opposition to the Communist-dominated World Federation of Trade Unions, Dame Anne was one of two women on the British delegation of eight. (The other was Florence Hancock '48, 1948 chairman of the T.U.C.) The conference closed December 7 with the adoption of the constitution of the new International Confederation of Free Trade Unions, headquarters of which are in Brussels.

Little more than five feet in height, dark haired, with gray-brown eyes and a "crisp" North Country accent, Dame Anne Loughlin is said to bring "an air of brisk and businesslike efficiency" to her duties. She is practical in attire, preferring "stout tweed suits and strong shoes," makes her home in the Hertfordshire countryside, about twenty-five miles north of London, and drives a small car to and from her work. Week ends are apt to be occupied with speeches, conferences, or lectures on industrial law and union organization. In *Who's Who* she lists reading as her recreation: with trade unionism as her hobby, she has collected a personal library consisting largely of law books and government reports; but for lighter reading she may turn to a novel or detective story.

References

Christian Sci Mon p4 Mr 28 '44
Newsweek 22:67 S 20 '43
International Who's Who, 1949
Who's Who, 1949

LOVE, GEORGE H(UTCHINSON) Sept. 4, 1900- Coal producer; industry representative

Address: b. c/o Pittsburgh Consolidation Coal Company, Inc., Koppers Bldg., Pittsburgh, Pa.; h. 5920 Braeburn Pl., Pittsburgh, Pa.

George H. Love, president of the Pittsburgh Consolidation Coal Company, represented the Northern and Western coal operators in the 1949-50 negotiations with the United Mine Workers union whose members were out on strike. Love has been the head of Pittsburgh Consolidation, estimated to be the world's largest coal company, since 1945, when that organization was formed after a merger of three leading coal production companies; with one of them, the Consolidation Coal Company, he had been associated in an executive capacity for the two years previous to the merger.

George Hutchinson Love was born in Johnstown, Pennsylvania, on September 4, 1900. He is the son of Joseph K. and Sarah (Jennings) Love. From 1914 to 1918 Love received his secondary education at Phillips Exeter Academy (in New Hampshire), and in 1918 he entered Princeton University. Four years later, having received his B.S. degree, he enrolled in the Harvard Graduate School of Business Administration. Upon completion of his studies there in 1924, he entered the business world as an investment salesman. From 1926 dates his identification with the coal industry; for several years he was executive assistant to Frank Samuel Love (a relative), president of the Union Collieries Company. In 1933, on the death of the president, Love was appointed to fill the vacancy.

Leaving the Union Collieries Company in 1943, he joined the Consolidation Coal Company, Inc., to become its executive vice-president, chairman of the executive committee, and a member of the board of directors. In 1944 he became president. Two years after Love joined the firm, a merger of three leading coal companies was completed, an event *Business Week* described as a "major milestone in coal history." The three firms merged were the Consolidation Coal Company, the Pittsburgh Coal Company of Pennsylvania, and the Monongahela River Consolidated Coal and Coke Company. The transaction was consumated in November 1945, and the enlarged organization was given the name of the Pittsburgh Consolidation Coal Company. Love was made president and a member of the board of directors.

The coal company which Love directs is considered to be the world's largest commercial producer of bituminous coal. It has a total productive capacity of more than 30,000,000 tons annually; as of 1950 it holds approximately 1,750,000,000 tons of unmined coal in fields which include almost 20,000 acres of land in

West Virginia bought by the company in 1948. The Pittsburgh Consolidation Coal Company owns 100 per cent of the voting stock in more than twenty subsidiaries. It operates mines in Ohio, Kentucky, and West Virginia, owns steamships, barges, marine ways, and landings, and manages its own selling agencies for distribution of its coal to manufacturing plants, public utilities, and railroads. Reports on production and earnings of the firm since Love became president indicate that it has made profits of more than $40,000,000 in the three-year period 1946 through 1948. Net profit for the year 1948 was $21,316,340, a 50 per cent increase over the 1947 profit. (These figures are from *Business Week*.) Love instituted a program of modernization of mines and techniques and of installation of new machinery which has been mentioned by various commentators as a large factor in the company's success.

According to *Business Week*, Love has the goal of building coal "into a healthy industry, financially—to meet the nation's long range need for coal through 'long-sighted' management." It is estimated that there is enough unmined coal in the United States to supply the entire future needs of the country for 1,700 years. Increased use of machinery, which has resulted in 90 per cent of all coal mined being cut mechanically, has increased the accessibility of coal at a time when oil and gasoline are becoming serious competitors in the fuel and power markets. Management has therefore been investigating new uses for coal and has been particularly interested in coal gasification, a process for converting low-grade coal into so-called "water-gas" and then into synthetic oil and gas fuels. Up until January 1950 the Pittsburgh Consolidation Coal Company jointly with the Standard Oil Company had been operating a pilot plant for developing a commercially practical process for converting coal to synthetic gasoline; at that time the plant was closed because, Love declared, of the uncertain supply of coal due to labor difficulties.

The president of Pittsburgh Consolidation has held a prominent position in negotiations with labor. In 1943 he served as vice-president of the Western Pennsylvania Coal Operators Association. He was named chief of negotiations for Northern and Western operators, producers of more than two-thirds of the nation's supply of soft coal, in a contract controversy with the United Mine Workers, which lasted from July 1949 to March 1950. In the preliminary negotiations, Love offered to continue the existing contract through March 1951; however, this offer was rejected by the union. By September 1949 some 480,000 miners were out on a strike called "voluntary" and "unauthorized" by union officials, who attributed it to the suspension of payments from the union welfare fund following the refusal of some Southern operators to continue paying a 20-cents-a-ton royalty to the welfare and retirement fund of the U.M.W. Love declared that the nonpayment by a small section of the industry was not the cause of the suspension, but that the real reason was the "profligate spending by the union-controlled trustees who

Wide World Photos

GEORGE H. LOVE

have poured out the money collected over three years of boom production in about twelve months."

Negotiations broke down in October 1949. From then until intervention by the United States Government in February 1950, the mines were worked intermittently. Under the powers of the Taft-Hartley labor law, President Truman named a fact-finding board, which, after considering the arguments of Love and John L. Lewis, felt that "the parties concerned have been more concerned with gaining tactical advantages" than in reaching the issues for arbitration. A court injunction was issued in February ordering the workers back to the mines and preventing Lewis, in future negotiations with the operators, from pressing for four specific requests which the Federal Court held constituted "unfair labor practices." The union was instructed to send its members back to work, but orders to that effect issued by union officials were disregarded by the miners. After the union had been acquitted of a resultant civil contempt accusation (by Judge Richmond B. Keech [50]) and after President Truman had asked of Congress authority to seize the strike-bound mines, operators and labor agreed to a new contract, signed March 5, 1950.

Upon signing the new contract, Love, as spokesman for the Northern and Western operators, commented: "This two-and-a-half-year contract gives the industry its first real stability in the last decade. . . . This country is one of the very few where coal mining is still in private hands operating under a free enterprise system. It carried the country's enormous needs during the war and since without Government help or subsidy. It is a modern agressive industry. . . . I hope that from this contract will come such mutual understanding that we will do away with coal strikes in the future."

(Continued next page)

LOVE, GEORGE H.—*Continued*

Love is a director of the M. A. Hanna Company, the Mellon National Bank & Trust Company of Pittsburgh, and the St. Joseph Lead Company; in January 1950 he was elected to the board of directors of General Electric Company. He is a director of the American Mining Congress and the National Coal Association. In civic affairs he has served as director and on the board of trustees of the Pittsburgh Community Chest, and he is a trustee of the Magee Hospital of Pittsburgh. In 1929 he married Margaret McClintic; their children are Howard, Margaret, and Sara. The executive has been described as "energetic, genial, but forthright." He is "ruddy-faced" and stands six feet. Hunting is his chief outdoor pleasure—occasionally he goes duck shooting in Georgia.

References

Bsns W p6 Ap 2 '49 por
Business Executives of America (1950)
Who's Who in America, 1948-49
Who's Who in Commerce and Industry (1948)
World Biography (1948)

LOY, MYRNA Aug. 2, 1905- Motion picture actress; civic leader

Address: b. c/o Hollywood Committee for UNESCO, Hollywood, Calif.; c/o RKO Studios, 760 N. Gower St., Hollywood 38, Calif.

In the course of twenty-five years as a motion picture actress, Myrna Loy has been able to change her "type" twice. She broke a long succession of Oriental *femme fatale* roles in melodrama, and fourteen years later she refused to continue in the "perfect wife" parts with which she had been identified since her success in *The Thin Man,* the first of a comedy series. As a member of the United States National Commission for the United Nations Educational, Scientific and Cultural Organization (UNESCO), she attends the general conferences of UNESCO in an advisory capacity. A free-lance actress, she continues to appear in one or two pictures a year.

Myrna Loy, who was born August 2, 1905, is the daughter of David and Della Williams. Her birthplace is Raidersburg, near Helena, Montana. (The ranch which was her childhood home she now owns.) It is said that her father, a cattle rancher, had been attracted by the name of a railroad water stop—Myrna—the name he was to give his daughter. The desire of the little girl to be an actress dates from the age of six, when she was taken to see Maeterlinck's new fantasy, *The Blue Bird.* During Myrna's school years, the family moved to California for her mother's health, and there she attended grammar school and "plunged into school dramatics" at the Venice High School in Los Angeles. According to a *Collier's* article, a statue of Myrna Williams stands on the high school lawn, for the sculpture teacher chose her

to represent the spiritual in a group symbolizing mental, physical, and spiritual development.

After the death of her father in 1918, the young girl began to work as a dancing teacher. (The family then consisted of Mrs. Williams, Myrna, and a younger brother, David.) For a salary which was to rise to thirty dollars a week, she taught ballroom dancing to a class of thirty children in Culver City, within yards of the MGM studios. For weeks she spent her free time waiting in MGM's outer office. When she was finally admitted, it was for a screen test—of a dress; she was not even made up for the task. It has been told that the future star found work as a film cutter at the Horsley studio, and that she was once chosen by director Christy Cabanne for the role of the Madonna in *Ben Hur,* only to have the part go to Betty Bronson, while she herself played a "fallen woman." When she was chosen to dance the Spirit of the Arctic Circle in the stage prologue to *The Thief of Bagdad* at Grauman's Chinese Theatre, Miss Loy has related, "the plain old Welsh name Williams just didn't seem flossy enough. Someone suggested Loy [for its Oriental sound], and it seemed all right. I didn't intend to keep it very long. But then I signed a contract, and . . . I was stuck with it."

At the Grauman theater Myrna Loy was seen by Rudolph Valentino and his wife Natacha Rambova, who were looking for someone to play an Oriental siren in *What Price Beauty.* After her part in that 1925 production, Myrna Loy was in constant demand to play roles of a *femme fatale.* For seven or eight years the red-haired, tilt-nosed Myrna Loy was cast exclusively as Chinese, Japanese, Javanese, Malayan, Hindu sirens, with an occasional Polynesian or quadroon role, in the melodramas of the period. When talking pictures arrived she delivered her lines in pidgin English.

Miss Loy's first Occidental role was in *Renegades,* with Warner Baxter, around 1930. Not until 1932, however, did she receive a major role as a Caucasian: a small part in support of Jeannette MacDonald and Maurice Chevalier led to a leading role opposite Leslie Howard in *The Animal Kingdom,* Philip Barry's comedy. "When allowed to speak English and make sense, even as the heavy," commented the *Literary Digest,* "it suddenly was discovered that she possessed genuine ability of no mean order." David O. Selznick next cast Miss Loy in another comedy role, the leading part in *Topaze,* opposite John Barrymore. *Transatlantic* was the first picture in which Miss Loy played a dutiful wife. Other early sound pictures in which she appeared included *The Devil to Pay, Emma, The Wet Parade, New Morals for Old, The Barbarians, Vanity Fair, The Last of the Duanes, When Ladies Meet,* and *The Mask of Fu Manchu.* In November 1933 Myrna Loy signed her third MGM contract, providing for regular increases from her $1,000 weekly salary to $3,000 a week during the next seven years.

Although a leading lady, Miss Loy did not attain stardom until she appeared in *Penthouse,* in which she "revealed a delightful vein of comedy and refinement." This was followed by the lead opposite Max Baer in *The Prize-fighter and the Lady* and by *Manhattan Melo-drama*, in which she portrayed the lady in the triangle involving Clark Gable and William Powell. *The Thin Man*, one of the screen's comedy classics, was planned and produced in fourteen days as a low-budget "B" picture. When it was released in June 1934, critics and public joined in praising the charm and gaiety William Powell and Myrna Loy brought to the roles of the suave, bibulous detective and his sophisticated, adoring wife. The part of Nora Charles, calm, witty, never at a loss in difficult or dangerous situations, ready to quip with a safecracker, give a dinner party for murder suspects, or accompany her husband into a criminal's hideout, established Myrna Loy as "the perfect wife," a type which she has played in some thirty pictures. Five of these were profitable *Thin Man* sequels, in 1935, 1936, 1941, 1944, and 1947. Among other outstanding pictures starring Myrna Loy were *Wife versus Secretary* (with Jean Harlow and Clark Gable), *Petticoat Fever* (with Robert Mont-gomery), *Test Pilot*, *Too Hot to Handle*, and *Parnell* (opposite Clark Gable), and *The Rains Came* (opposite Tyrone Power). The year 1936 was particularly successful for the Powell-Loy team; it saw the release of *Libeled Lady*, the "sparkling" comedy in which Jean Harlow and Spencer Tracy were also starred, *The Great Ziegfeld*, in which Myrna played the young Billie Burke, and *After the Thin Man*. Re-portedly (*Newsweek*), MGM "made many times Miss Loy's weekly salary by renting her to other studios." In 1937 and 1938 the moving picture exhibitors voted her one of the ten stars who attracted most of the patronage.

During World War II Myrna Loy lived in New York and served as an assistant head of Red Cross welfare activities in that area; for a time she worked twelve hours nightly in a canteen, and for two years she had charge of the entertainment program for fifty service hospitals. In June 1942, following a divorce from movie producer Arthur Hornblow, Jr., she was married to New York advertising exec-utive John D. Hertz, Jr. After their divorce in 1944 Miss Loy returned to Hollywood to make *The Thin Man Goes Home*, her first pic-ture in two years. She disliked the role, partly because she felt that the frivolous Charleses had no place in the world today, but agreed to make one more *Thin Man* picture in exchange for release from her MGM contract. Since that time Miss Loy has played two real-life characters, Mrs. Hiram Maxim of *A Genius in the Family*, and Lillian M. Gilbreth, the effi-ciency engineer and mother of twelve children, in *Cheaper by the Dozen*. She was a ranch wife in *The Red Pony*, a young judge in *The Bachelor and the Bobby-Soxer*, and Mrs. Bland-ings in *Mr. Blandings Builds His Dream House*. In *The Best Years of Our Lives*, Miss Loy accepted the relatively small part of the banker's wife, mother of a grown daughter played by Teresa Wright—another perfect wife, but one, Miss Loy felt, whose problems were typical of "Mrs. 1946." For this she was awarded the Brussels World Film Festival prize for the best performance by an actress.

MYRNA LOY

Her latest movie is *If This Be Sin*, made in England from a screenplay by Gene Markey.

Miss Loy has stated that she comes from a "politically aware" family and has long had a social conscience. In 1947 she was one of a Hollywood group which, in protest against the manner in which actors were being questioned in Washington, formed the Committee of the First Amendment to work for the abolition of the House Committee on Un-American Ac-tivities. Her statement was: "Congress has the right to investigate . . . but we question the right of any official to abuse citizens in order to make headlines." A year earlier, Matthew Woll, vice-president of the American Federa-tion of Labor had charged Miss Loy with spon-soring a Communist-front organization; after she brought suit against Woll he retracted (New York *Post*).

Of her United Nations work, Miss Loy has said: "It began under the influence of "good friends whom I admired, Jan Masaryk, Mrs. Roosevelt, Ralph Bunche." (She never met President Roosevelt, who was one of her fans: several invitations to meet him were canceled because of wartime developments.) At the Pacific Regional Conference on the United Nations Educational, Scientific and Cul-tural Organization in the summer of 1948, Miss Loy gave her views as to the manner in which mass communications could best serve the in-ternational organization. (That March she had pledged herself to organize a Hollywood branch of the Association for the United Nations.) In Paris at the time of the UNESCO general conference in September 1949, the actress was asked to serve the United States delegation with the title of film adviser. Later the State Department's United States National Commis-sion for UNESCO requested her to organize a Hollywood Film Committee to act as liaison with the industry and to supply it with ideas for articles promoting international brother-

LOY, MYRNA—*Continued*

hood. "One little incident to battle international prejudice, dropped into the middle of an entertaining film . . . is worth all the documentaries ever made," she believes, because the documentary film must overcome some audience resistance. Miss Loy was invited to the Washington conference in April 1950 and was sent to the general conference in Florence, Italy, in May. A comment of the Washington *Post* was: "Miss Loy's work for UNESCO has made news wherever she has gone and has made friends for her wherever the news has gone." Her work has been made much easier, the film star has said, because fellow delegates felt they knew her from her screen performances; and she is glad that interviews with a screen personality can win extra publicity for the international organization.

On the studio set, and off, Myrna Loy is known for her poise and unpretentiousness. The "pert-nosed," freckled actress has blue-green eyes, is five feet six inches tall. Her third marriage, to screenwriter and producer Gene Markey, was terminated by divorce in August 1950. Recreations Miss Loy enjoys include gardening, horseback riding, clay modeling, collecting art and antiques, and "just relaxing"; in her reading she turns chiefly to history and biography.

References

　　Collier's 94:17 D 22 '34
　　Extra 1:3 Je '50
　　Lit Digest 118:11 Jl 28 '34
　　N Y Herald Tribune p15 Ag 25 '50
　　N Y Post p6 Je 10 '44
　　N Y Times V p5 Mr 21 '48
　　Newsweek 6:29 Ag 24 '35
　　Photoplay 21:32 Je '42
　　Pict R 38:25 Je '37
　　Woman's Home C 62:12 My '35
　　International Motion Picture Almanac, 1949-50
　　Who's Who in America, 1950-51
　　World Biography (1948)

MCAULIFFE, ANTHONY C(LEMENT)
July 2, 1898- United States Army officer
Address: b. Office of the Chief, Chemical Corps, Department of the Army, Washington 25, D.C.; h. 3600 Porter St., N.W., Washington 16, D.C.

The new chief of the Chemical Corps of the Department of the Army, National Military Establishment of the United States, Major General Anthony C. McAuliffe, was appointed to that post in September 1949, as the successor to Major General Alden H. Waitt [47]. Following World War II, in which he gained wide fame as the defender of Bastogne in the Battle of the Bulge, he was Army secretary of the Joint Research and Development Board (1946) and in December 1947 was designated deputy director for research and development of the Logistics Division of the General Staff. In the Bikini atom bomb tests he served as ground forces adviser to Vice-Admiral W. H. P. Blandy [48].

Anthony Clement McAuliffe was born July 2, 1898, in Washington, D.C., where his father was for many years head of the stenographic division of the Interstate Commerce Division. His parents, John Joseph and Alice Katherine (Gannon) McAuliffe, had four sons and two daughters. Both of Anthony's grandfathers had come to America from Ireland. The youth attended Eastern High School in his native city, where his membership in the cadet corps led to a desire to enter West Point. After a year at the University of West Virginia in 1916-17, McAuliffe succeeded in being admitted to the class of 1921 at the United States Military Academy. While his small stature prevented him from playing on the regular basketball and baseball teams, wrote Sidney Shalett (in the *Saturday Evening Post*), the cadet "shone in the annual battles royal between the 'runts' and the 'flankers'—giants of the class. He did lead the academy orchestra with his violin, doubling on banjo-mandolin." In his scholastic record McAuliffe stood twenty-ninth in his class of 277.

After graduation from West Point in November 1918, McAuliffe was commissioned a second lieutenant of Field Artillery ten days before the end of World War I. Therefore, instead of being put into active service according to plan, he and his classmates were kept at West Point for further training until the following June. In July 1919 he was sent to Europe for a tour of the battlefields of Belgium and France. Upon his return in September he was detailed, with the rank of first lieutenant, to Field Artillery School at Camp Zachary Taylor, Kentucky. After his graduation from that school in August 1920, he was assigned to the Sixteenth Field Artillery at Camp Lewis, Washington. In the course of the succeeding twenty years, McAuliffe had the usual peacetime career of a regular Army officer. Ordered to a different Army post approximately every two years, he made two tours of duty in Hawaii and was stationed at camps in California, Kansas, Maryland, and Oklahoma. During this period, too, he received an additional year of training at Fort Leavenworth Command and General Staff School in 1936-37. Since promotion is slow in time of peace, McAuliffe did not attain the rank of captain until May 1935.

In September 1939, just as World War II broke out in Europe, McAuliffe was ordered to Washington to enter the Army War College. Upon graduation in June 1940 he was assigned as a major to developing the jeep and the new weapons such as the armored car and bazooka. In two years on that assignment he was promoted, on September 15, 1941, to lieutenant colonel (temporary), and on February 1, 1942, to colonel (temporary).

In August 1942 McAuliffe (then holding the temporary rank of brigadier general) succeeded in getting himself sent to Camp Claiborne, Louisiana, as artillery commander of the 101st Airborne Division, which was among the early divisions dispatched to Europe to prepare for the invasion of France. In a full-dress rehearsal for D-Day (in England, April 1944) McAuliffe, reported the *Saturday Evening Post* writer, broke his back in a parachute jump, but by early June was well enough to jump when his division flew over Normandy on the night of June 5-6. When Brigadier General Don Pratt, deputy division commander, was killed that same night, McAuliffe was promoted on the field to the vacant post by his chief, Major General Maxwell Taylor "[46].

The new deputy division commander was given the task of seizing Carentan. In the airborne invasion of Holland, he was in charge of the glider echelon that entered that country on September 18, 1944. Here again McAuliffe commanded a special task force in the defense of the bridge and town of Vechel. McAuliffe was resting with his division at Reims in December when the Germans started their great counteroffensive in a desperate attempt to stop the Allied invasion. When the Nazi troops broke through the American lines in the Battle of the Bulge, McAuliffe, who was temporarily in command of the 101st Airborne Division during the absence of General Taylor in the United States, was ordered back to the front. He rushed his troops in any conveyance at hand to the defense of the strategic little town of Bastogne in the Ardennes forest. (Bastogne must be held because it was the center of a network of roads over which the advancing German armies must pass.) When the Americans were surrounded like "the hole in a doughnut," as a soldier put it, McAuliffe made his famous reply of "Nuts" to the German demand that he surrender. In the words of a New York *Herald Tribune* reporter, "His men [then] fought on with renewed spirit and finally helped break the last great enemy offensive of the war."

When General George Patton arrived in Bastogne as the Germans were driven back, he pinned the Distinguished Service Cross on McAuliffe. The hero of Bastogne was decorated as well by the Belgian Government, and in the town itself one of the principal city squares was named after him. The men of the 101st were the first of an entire division to be rewarded by the Presidential Citation, on March 15, 1945. McAuliffe was next promoted to the temporary rank of major general and given command of the 103d Infantry Division. With his division he broke through the Siegfried Line from Alsace in March 1945. Later he led that division in the race across Germany and Austria to capture Innsbruck and the Brenner Pass. In the Italian Alps he made the planned junction with the American Fifth Army from Italy.

At the end of the war in Europe, McAuliffe returned to the United States in June 1945 to await reassignment. In September he was placed in charge of the Airborne Center at Camp Mackall, North Carolina, and in December he assumed command at Fort Bragg, North Carolina. Early in 1946 he was appointed ground forces adviser to Vice-Admiral W. H. P. Blandy, commander of the Joint Army-Navy Task Force One, for Operation Crossroads, as the atomic bomb tests at Bikini were officially known. Upon his return to the United States in August 1946 he became Army secretary of the Joint Research and Development

U. S. Army

MAJ. GEN. ANTHONY C. MCAULIFFE

Board. In December of the following year he was made deputy director for research and development of the Army Logistics Division. After more than two years in Washington, McAuliffe in March 1949 was once again given active duty, when he went to Japan to assume command of the Twenty-fourth Infantry Division there.

While McAuliffe was still in Japan, President Truman on September 14, 1949, appointed him the successor to Major General Alden H. Waitt as chief of the Chemical Corps of the Department of the Army. At the same time the President announced the officer's permanent rank of major general. (Waitt's retirement came as the result of his being involved in the Senate "5-percenter" probe.) Editorial comment on the choice of an officer from outside the Chemical Corps staff pointed to his record with the Joint Research and Development Board, with the Army Logistics Division, and his knowledge of new weapons, particularly in bacteriological and atomic warfare.

McAuliffe believes the United States must be ready to defend itself against, or even use, bacteriological warfare. Since he feels that a single surprise attack with atomic bombs "may well be decisive," he maintains that the United States should stockpile atomic bombs and airplanes to carry them until it has a great enough advantage to insure peace. He is of the opinion that atomic bombs will not make useless the traditional methods of defense—Bikini demonstrated that soldiers in dugouts or tanks can continue fighting even after bombs explode near-by. In broad Army policy McAuliffe favors universal military training, because he thinks it "would make every American a part of our national defense and would safeguard against militarism that grows where security is intrusted to a professional group." About the need for unifying the Armed Forces: "Aggression of the future," he has said, "will

MCAULIFFE, ANTHONY C.—*Continued*

not be limited to the ground, sea or air. . . . Security cannot be departmentalized." In regard to scientists, a special Army board, headed by McAuliffe, expressed his opinion when it stated that it was wasteful of vital knowledge to put a scientist into a private's uniform.

McAuliffe is a member of the National Inventors Council. Other decorations he has been awarded by the United States are the Distinguished Service Medal, Silver Star, Legion of Merit, Bronze Star Medal and one Oak Leaf Cluster, and a second Presidential Citation. From foreign countries he has received the British Distinguished Service Order with Bar, the French Legion of Honor, the Croix de Guerre, and Fourragère; the Belgian Order of Leopold; and the Dutch Order of William of Orange and Order of the Netherlands Lion. He holds memberships in the Army and Navy Club, the American Legion, the Veterans of Foreign Wars, and the Military Order of World Wars. His religious faith is the Catholic.

In August 1920 McAuliffe married Helen Willet Whitman, "his girl" from high school days. They have two children, Patricia Ann and John Hilary. The General, who was known to his troops as "Old Crock"—he called himself that once in a "pep talk" to his men—is five feet eight inches tall, weighs 150 pounds; his eyes are blue and his hair is brown. A sports enthusiast, he is also judged "a keen chess player."

References

Sat Eve Post 218:20+ Je 29 '46 por
Who's Who in America, 1948-49

MCCAFFREY, JOHN L(AWRENCE)
Sept. 23, 1892- Industrialist; business executive
Address: b. c/o International Harvester Company, 180 N. Michigan Ave., Chicago 1, Ill.; h. 6138 N. Kenmore Ave., Chicago 40, Ill.

President of International Harvester Company, the largest agricultural implement manufacturing concern in the world, John L. McCaffrey has been associated with the firm since the age of fifteen. His election to the presidency in 1946 was preceded by years of experience in a succession of positions from salesman and sales manager to vice-president in charge of sales and second and first vice-president. He has been a member of the board of directors of the company since 1941.

John Lawrence McCaffrey, son of John F. and Ida (Smith) McCaffrey, was born September 23, 1892, in the small Ohio town of Fayetteville, where his father was a dealer for the McCormick Harvesting Machine Company (McCormick became the International Harvester Company in 1902); his grandfather, James McCaffrey, had emigrated to America from County Mayo, Ireland. The boy, who attended the public schools in his home town, is a graduate of its high school. With his father encouraging him to become a farm implement salesman, young McCaffrey spent much of his spare time tinkering with the machines in his father's store. During the summer of his fifteenth year he spent his school vacation as an employee of the International Harvester Company sales branch in Cincinnati, becoming familiar with machine parts as he kept them in order in the parts division; later he learned how to assemble binders.

In 1909 the Cincinnati sales branch hired seventeen-year-old McCaffrey as a "likely sales trainee." He was put to work in an apprenticeship, as a forty-dollars-a-month warehouse clerk. Advanced to the repairs department a year later, the youth was prepared by the following year to become a promotion man; and during 1911 he traveled a circuit of county fairs, where he was in charge of exhibits of I.H.C. equipment. In 1912 he became a salesman of Harvester high-wheeler trucks. The company soon advanced the young man to sales supervisor in charge of a group of dealers; his territory was in the Kentucky hills, which he traveled on horseback. *Pathfinder* (October 18, 1950) pointed to his experiences in that underdeveloped region as a foreshadow of I.H.C.'s 1950-51 investments in Argentina and Brazil. (For South America McCaffrey has formulated a program of plant construction, which includes the employment of agricultural and technical specialists and the training of South Americans in the use of farm machinery.)

Seven years after becoming a salesman McCaffrey in 1919 was made assistant manager of the Cincinnati branch. Four years later (1923) he became assistant sales manager of the Central District, and in 1925, manager. He also served as sales manager of the northwest district. In 1929 he came to know Fowler McCormick [47], grandson of International Harvester's founder, then acquiring sales training in Omaha, and who later became chairman of the board. McCaffrey was advanced to assistant manager of domestic sales at the main office in Chicago in 1930, was made director of domestic sales in 1933, and director of both domestic and Canadian sales in 1937.

In 1940 McCaffrey was elected vice-president in charge of all I.H.C. sales, and second vice-president and a director in 1941. Advancement to the office of first vice-president took place in March 1945, and on May 16, 1946, he was elected president of the International Harvester Company. Meanwhile, with the entry of the United States into World War II, production in various Harvester plants was chiefly for national defense. McCaffrey was made chairman of the company's postwar planning committee, and focused his attention on plans for future expansion, development of new products, and better manufacturing and distributing methods.

In the year following his election to the presidency of I.H.C. McCaffrey was able to announce to stockholders on May 8, 1947, that sales in the first half of the fiscal year exceeded even the wartime record, and that April of that year was the largest sales month in the history of the company. During the 1949 fiscal year, record earnings of $4.36 a share as against the previous high in 1948 of $3.92 were announced in McCaffrey's annual report in January 1950.

Another record was announced by McCaffrey in May 1950, when he told stockholders that sales in the second quarter of the 1950 fiscal year were the highest in the history of the I.H.C., totaling $258,983,000. However, Mc-Caffrey announced in August of that year that, although sales for the nine-month period ending July 31 totaled a record $722,860,000, net income fell to $3.19 a share, because of increases in costs; an increase in prices of the company's products was forecast.

As president of International Harvester, Mc-Caffrey has participated in the firm's public relations projects. In June 1947, he made a radio debut on the company's *Harvest of Stars* program over NBC network, introducing the new Farmall Cub tractor, a small, low-cost machine designed "to take the small farmer out from behind the plowhorse." McCaffrey pointed out the social and economic significance of the "Cub": "It is our answer to those who have been predicting the end of the small family-size farm in the United States." In 1950, International Harvester introduced "get-acquainted" luncheon meetings in communities where its plants are located; at them either McCaffrey or McCormick is present to answer questions about the company from citizens of the various communities. To such questions as "Why do company officials vote themselves tremendous pensions?" and "What about high salaries?" McCaffrey replied, "When I retire at 65, I will have been with the company almost fifty years. I am now contributing $6,000 a year of my own earnings toward a pension. When I retire I will get a pension of $21,000 a year"; and, "We could fire all the officers of the company today and I do not think the saving in money would be enough to pay the company's light bill for six months." At a national conference of public relations executives, McCaffrey, speaking on the subject "What Industry Expects from Public Relations," gave it as his opinion that techniques are not as important as " a sense of direction." Further: "I don't believe we [business] can go to the public with a story of unbroken success. . . .I believe . . . that it is better to have a red face once in a while and have people believe what we have to tell them, than to pretend we're perfect and have them discount everything we say."

At a Chicago World Trade Conference, held in February 1947, McCaffrey urged support of the United States foreign trade program through a high level of imports and pointed out the "futility" of making foreign loans while "erecting or continuing tariff barriers which prevent payment . . . in goods and services." The farm implements executive was one of a committee of American industrialists, appointed by the then chief of the Economic Cooperation Administration, Paul Hoffman, which went to Europe in 1948 to make a firsthand study of the functioning of the Marshall Plan. On his return McCaffrey told a New York *Times* correspondent in Chicago, "I don't see how we can rebuild the economy of the world. . . .If we continue to ship abroad $5,000,000,000 a year it looks to me as if we were shipping our seed away." At the convention of the National For-

Moffett Studio

JOHN L. MCCAFFREY

eign Trade Council in New York on November 9, 1948, McCaffrey stated that the charter for the International Trade Organization drawn up and signed in Havana in the spring of 1947, "attempts to set up a system which would lodge authority over international trade in a sort of superstate" and that it "goes far toward a planned economy for the world."

McCaffrey is a member of the board of directors of the Harris Trust and Savings Bank of Chicago, the Illinois Bell Telephone Company, the Atchison, Topeka and Santa Fe Railroad. The executive is the president of the Farm Equipment Institute, is active in the International Dairy Exposition and the Foundation for American Agriculture, and has served on the business advisory council and agricultural equipment advisory council of the United States Department of Commerce. In industrial associations, he is a member of the Council for Economic Development, has been a director at large of the National Association of Manufacturers, is a regional vice-president of that body, and was a member of the agricultural department committee of the Chamber of Commerce of the United States. Humanitarian and educational institutions to which he lends his support include the Goodwill Industries and the University of Chicago Cancer Research Foundation (he is on the board of trustees of the latter) ; and Loyola University and Notre Dame University (a Catholic, he is an associate member of the board of lay trustees of the latter). Holy Cross College presented the industrialist with the honorary degree of Doctor of Commercial Science in 1949. All in the Chicago area, his clubs are the Commercial, the Illinois Athletic, the Chicago, the Westmoreland Country, and the Skokie. He is a Republican voter.

McCaffrey married Florence Springmeier on October 8, 1914. Their two sons, Robert L. and James F., are employed by the International

MCCAFFREY, JOHN L.—*Continued*

Harvester Company. The executive, who is six feet one inch tall and weighs 200 pounds, has blue eyes and gray-brown hair. Fowler McCormick has described McCaffrey (in *Forbes*) as "a delightful person to meet, tall, large-framed, with a deep voice of fine timbre and an engaging twinkle of the eye. . . .He's dynamic in whatever he does and positive in his approach to every situation." McCaffrey likes to golf and fish, and enjoys the spectator sports of baseball and football.

References

Forbes Ja 1 '47
American Catholic Who's Who, 1950-51
Business Executives of America (1950)
Who's Who in America, 1950-51
Who's Who in Chicago and Illinois (1950)
Who's Who in Commerce and Industry (1948)
Who's Who in the Midwest (1949)
World Biography (1948)

MCCARTHY, JOSEPH R(AYMOND)
Nov. 14, 1909- United States Senator from Wisconsin

Address: b. Senate Office Bldg., Washington, D.C.; h. 127 N. Appleton St., Appleton, Wis.

Republican Senator Joseph R. McCarthy of Wisconsin was elected to the United States Senate in 1946 when he defeated Robert M. La Follette '44. His first elective office was circuit court judge, after which he saw service in World War II.

Born in Grand Chute, Wisconsin, on November 14, 1909, Joseph Raymond McCarthy is one of the seven children of Timothy Thomas and Bridget (Tierney) McCarthy. The father,

Wide World Photos
JOSEPH R. MCCARTHY

a farmer, was the son of Irish-German immigrants; the mother, of Irish extraction. Joseph attended the Underhill country school until sixteen, at the same time working on his father's farm. At the age of nineteen he went to Manawa to run a grocery. Encouraged by a friend, he resumed his education at the Little Wolf High School, and completed the four-year course in a year, on the honor list. To support himself while going to school he worked in a grocery store and was an usher in a theater in the evening. In 1939 he enrolled in Marquette University's school of engineering, but changed to the study of law in the following year; in 1935 he received the LL.B. degree and was admitted to the bar. He had earned his way through college by working in restaurants and a gas station.

McCarthy practiced law in Waupaca until 1936, when he entered the law office of M. G. Eberlein, a prominent lawyer in near-by Shawano. McCarthy's first effort to gain a public office, that of county attorney, was not successful. Later, the *Wisconsin State Journal* (July 16-20, 1946) related that in 1939, "there was a certain amount of dissatisfaction among attorneys of the Tenth District with the circuit judge," who had held the post for twenty-four years. Against the advice of friends and the objection of Eberlein, McCarthy decided to run for the judgeship, this time on the Republican ticket. After an intensive campaign, he was elected; at 29 he became the youngest circuit judge in the State's history.

In 1942, McCarthy (at thirty-three in the deferred class) enlisted in the wartime United States Marines. Commissioned a lieutenant, he trained before he was sent to the Pacific theater as a ground officer in the Marine Air Force Intelligence. By the time of his discharge about eighteen months later, McCarthy had been promoted to a captaincy, had taken part in seventeen missions, and had won several citations for "courageous devotion to duty." During his absence from Wisconsin, his friends put his name up for nomination to the United States Senate. In the subsequent contest he received 100,000 votes, running, however, second for the nomination. A few weeks after his discharge, in 1945, he was re-elected as circuit judge; and early in 1946, McCarthy, again against the advice of the "politically wise," decided to run against Senator Robert La Follette for United States Senator.

The La Follettes, father and son, had represented Wisconsin in the Senate for forty successive years, elected by the Progressive party, which the elder La Follette had founded. The New Deal had enacted much of the legislation that party had advocated, and in 1945, "young Bob read a funeral oration over his party" and announced he would seek nomination for the Senate in the forthcoming election on the Republican ticket. Jack Alexander, in a *Saturday Evening Post* article (August 9, 1947) stated that McCarthy, the "audacious" Senatorial aspirant, "sent sales letters to the several thousand members of the Republican Voluntary Committee. Although it was seeking a candidate who gave promise of defeating La Follette, the committee was "apathetic" to McCarthy. He nevertheless continued his campaigning and when the committee met in the spring of 1946, he received its endorsement. La Follette, underestimating his opponent, spent less than two weeks in primary campaigning, while McCarthy, again conducted "a tireless and ingenious campaign." On August 14, 1946, in an "upset" election, he won the Republican nomination and in November was chosen Wisconsin's United States Senator for the six-year term ending January 3, 1953.

When the Taft-Ellender-Wagner housing bill and a bill originating in the House failed of enactment, a new, substitute measure, introduced by McCarthy, became the Housing Act of 1948. Its main provisions were private loans for building low-cost apartment houses and homes and government research on low-cost housing; and it forbade discrimination on the part of beneficiaries against families with children. The public housing and slum clearance legislation of 1949, the Senator has pointed out, contains provisions he had previously demanded, among them, that public housing should be available to those who need it most, regardless of source of income.

On other key issues before the Eightieth and Eighty-first Congresses, McCarthy supported the Constitutional amendment to limit Presidential tenure, all the Taft amendments to the Senate's labor bill, including the rejected one limiting industry-wide bargaining, the passage of the second income tax reduction bill over the President's veto, the Greek-Turkish aid bill, the passage of the Taft-Hartley labor bill over the veto, the Temporary Draft Selective Service bill, the ERP authorization bill, the bill to outlaw portal-to-portal payment suits. He opposed universal military training, the Barkley amendment to the anti-inflation bill to grant the President stand-by rationing and price-wage control authority, and the Federal aid to education bill; and he also voted against the confirmation of David Lilienthal as chairman of the Atomic Energy Commission and of Leland Olds as head of the Federal Power Commission; and against Truman's proposal for the establishment of a Department of Welfare. He was a supporter of the Republican anti-inflation bill and of the North Atlantic Pact, and he signed a letter asking for early hearings on a bill for aid to Nationalist China.

Among the bills and amendments which Senator McCarthy introduced during the Eightieth Congress were: to provide Government assistance for special housing for paraplegic veterans, and an increase in FHA insurance for new housing. During the next Congress he supported the Foreign Military Assistance Act of 1949 and the Reciprocal Trade Agreements bill. To the latter he suggested an amendment (defeated) which called for the establishment of import quotas on furs if deemed necessary by the Tariff Commission to prevent injury to the domestic fur industry. Throughout the "five-percenter" inquiry on "influence selling," which was conducted during August 1949 by the sub-committee of the Senate Committee on Expenditures in the Executive Departments, McCarthy was one of the most persistent and sharpest questioners, demanding the dismissal of Truman's military aide, General Harry H. Vaughan as Coordinator of Veteran Affairs. As the ranking Republican member of that Senate committee, the Senator worked closely during 1949, with the Hoover Commission on Organization of the Executive Branch of the Government, drafting and introducing twelve bills based on the Commission's recommendations for government reorganization legislation.

Five feet eleven inches in height and weighing about 195 pounds, Joseph R. McCarthy has been described as "handsome in a dark, square-jawed way. . . . He has an agile mind, a retentive memory . . . and is warmhearted," said the *Saturday Evening Post* writer. He is a member of the Veterans of Foreign Wars, the American Legion, the Lions, Elks, and Eagles, and an honorary member of Boys Town. A Roman Catholic, he belongs to the Knights of Columbus.

References

Sat Eve Post 220:15 Ag 9 '47
Scholastic 49:13 S 23 '46
U S News 21:62 Ag 23 '46
Wisconsin State J Jl 16-20 '46

Congressional Directory (1st ed., 1949)
National Cyclopædia of American Biography Current vol G, 1943-46
Who's Who in America, 1948-49
World Biography (1948)

MCCLELLAN, JOHN L(ITTLE) Feb. 25, 1896- United States Senator from Arkansas
Address: b. Senate Office Bldg., Washington, D.C.; h. 2100 Massachusetts Ave., N.W., Washington, D.C.; Camden, Ark.

The United States senior Senator from Arkansas, John L. McClellan of Camden, was first elected to the upper house of the Federal legislature in November 1942, and was re-elected in November 1948 for a second term ending January 1955. He had previously served in the House of Representatives, from 1935 to 1939. Chairman of the Senate Committee on Expenditures in the Executive Departments and a member of the Appropriations Committee, he is known as a proponent of economy measures, an authority on flood control, and he is a stanch defender of the poll tax. At odds with the Truman Administration on the civil rights question, he prefers to be known as an independent Democrat.

John Little McClellan was born on a farm near the town of Sheridan in south-central Arkansas, on February 25, 1896. His parents, Isaac Scott and Belle (Suddeth) McClellan, were also native to that area. "My father became a country lawyer when I was twelve," the Senator has written, "and I studied law in his office for five years and was admitted to the bar when I was seventeen years old." This was in 1913, after he had attended Sheridan High School. He was in practice at Sheridan until August 1917, when he joined the Army for

Moss Photo.

JOHN L. MCCLELLAN

World War I service; commissioned a first lieutenant in the Signal Corps, he was demobilized in February 1919. Returning to Arkansas, he established himself at Malvern, the capital of Hot Spring County, where he served as city attorney from January 1920 to January 1926, when he became prosecuting attorney for the State's Seventh Judicial District for two terms, 1927-30. His record was of such character as to persuade the voters of the Sixth Congressional District of Arkansas (twelve counties in the southern central part of the State) to choose him as their representative in Washington in the election of November 1934.

Taking his seat in the Seventy-fourth Congress in January 1935, Representative McClellan was assigned to the committees for House Elections, Flood Control, Irrigation and Reclamation, and Roads. Re-elected in November 1936, he served in the Seventy-fifth Congress on the Flood Control, Public Lands, Patents and Roads committees. Examination of his voting record during the four years he was a member of the lower house at Washington reveals a general support of New Deal policy, except where it conflicted too sharply with Arkansas interests. Examples which might be cited include his "Yeas" for the soil conservation act and the Administration tax bill in 1936, extension of the Reciprocal Tariff Act and passage of the Wagner housing bill in 1937, and Naval Expansion in 1938. In 1937 McClellan opposed the Supreme Court retirement bill, the Gavagan anti-lynching bill, and the departmental reorganization bill. A speech he delivered against the clauses in the latter extending the principle of tenure of office to postmasters attracted considerable attention ("Camouflage" was his word for the proposal and he characterized the measure as a whole as "not a Civil Service bill" and one which would "not

obtain the results its sponsors claim for it.") Earlier (in March 1936), he had assailed the action of the Columbia Broadcasting System in scheduling an address by Earl Browder, the secretary of the Communist Party in the United States, as "nothing less than treason."

In the summer of 1938 the Arkansas Representative was one of three contestants for the Democratic nomination for United States Senator from his State. The incumbent, Mrs. Hattie Caraway[45], had the asset of what a New York Times writer summed up as "a direct showing of Roosevelt favor." McClellan countered that he had "served the President as well as Mrs. Caraway," the chief difference in their recent voting records having been in regard to the Government reorganization bill. He also charged before the Senate Campaign Expenditures Investigating Committee that "the Federal employees in the State" were "exerting improper influence for Senator Caraway." At the primary (August 10) the latter emerged the winner by a margin of about 8,000, though the third candidate, J. R. Venable, who polled only a scattering of votes, charged "irregularities and falsified returns" and said that he believed McClellan had been elected. McClellan, however, accepted defeat and moved to Camden, a town in the southern part of the State, where, as a member of the firm of Gaughan, McClellan and Gaughan, he practiced in the State and Federal courts. (He had been licensed to practice before the United States Supreme Court in 1935.) At the State primaries of July 1942, he was again a candidate for the nomination he had lost four years earlier. The strongest of several other contestants was State Attorney General Holt, who led McClellan by only a few hundred votes; a runoff on August 11 was therefore required, with McClellan winning by well over 50,000.

Democrat McClellan won in the November 1942 election with ease, and was sworn into the Senate at the beginning of January 1943. His assignments in the Seventy-eighth Congress were to the Banking and Currency, Expenditures in Executive Departments, Manufactures, and Post Offices and Post Roads committees. As spokesman for a predominantly agricultural area he voted for blanket deferment for farm labor in the World War II draft (March 1943) and continuance of the Farm Security Administration (June). In May he supported President Roosevelt when the strike-bound coal mines were taken over by the Government. When the Federal servicemen's voting bill was debated in 1943, Senators McClellan, Eastland, and McKellar offered a substitute bill limiting soldier absentee voting to those who had registered in their home States and paid poll taxes where required. He voted for the States' rights substitute bill in February 1944, and against the compromise eventually passed. In the same Congress he expressed himself in favor of an international police force (April) and supported the Fulbright resolution (October).

Early 1945 ballots cast by McClellan in the Seventy-ninth Congress (in which he served on the Commerce, Expenditures in Executive Departments, Manufactures, Naval Affairs, and

Post Offices and Post Roads committees) were for confirmation of Henry A. Wallace as Secretary of Commerce (after RFC was no longer in that Department), and against Aubrey Williams as head of the Rural Electrification Administration. As president of the National Rivers and Harbors Congress, he was a strong advocate of river resources development, but generally opposes "valley authorities." He favored ratification of the Bretton Woods Agreement, the United Nations Charter (July 1945), and American participation in the United Nations (December) (he had opposed authorization of UNRRA in the previous Congress). He voted against the loan to Great Britain in May 1946. McClellan took a leading part in the Southern filibuster against the fair employment practices bill during January 1946. He cast his "Yea" for the veterans emergency housing bill in April of the same year, though personally opposing Federal subsidies, and in the following month supported the Case strike control bill. Other 1946 votes cast by the Democratic Senator were for the extension of Lend Lease for a year, against the Wagner full employment bill.

Streamlining of the legislative branch of the Government under the Modernization Act of 1946 (which McClellan opposed) and the Republican victories in November combined to reduce the Arkansas Senator's committee assignments in the Eightieth Congress to two—Public Works and Expenditures in the Executive Departments, of which he became ranking minority member. McClellan was not long in championing what was described as "a tax break for the little fellow," and in April 1947 advocated raising income tax exemption to $750 for single persons and $1,500 for the heads of families. In May he sponsored an amendment (defeated by 51 to 29) to the Republican tax reduction bill which would have granted all married persons the right to split their incomes for tax purposes. This provision was made a part of the tax reduction bill which was passed later and became law. In the same month McClellan was among those voting in favor of the Taft-Hartley labor-management act. Also, in May 1947, McClellan was a center of attention as sponsor of a proposed amendment (eventually defeated) to the Truman $350,000,000 foreign relief bill, which would have barred American aid to "Russian-dominated" countries. In the summer of 1948, after the adoption by the Democratic National Convention of the civil rights plank in its platform, McClellan was one of the Southern Democrats who disapproved—he designates himself as an independent Democrat. That November he was re-elected to the Senate by an overwhelming majority, for the term expiring January 1955.

With the return of the Senate to Democratic control, McClellan became, in the Eighty-first Congress convening January 1949, a member of the important Appropriations Committee as well as of the Public Works Committee and chairman of the Expenditures in the Executive Departments Committee. In the latter capacity he was in a strategic position in regard to implementation of the recommendations of the Hoover Commission, of which he had been a member. Among the recommendations with which he disagreed was that of merging the Army's flood control powers and the Interior Department's reclamation and power projects in a single Public Works Administration. On general fiscal matters he was critical of waste, and in June 1949 obtained the signatures of sixty-one Senators to a petition to force a vote on an economy resolution directing the President to cut 5 to 10 per cent from the appropriation voted for the executive branch of the government for the ensuing fiscal year. In the following month he introduced an amendment to the new Marshall Plan appropriation bill directing that an estimated $1,800,000,000 of ECA funds be used to finance disposal of surplus farm products in Marshall Plan countries. The amendment was voted down (August). McClellan's 1949 voting record included support of local-State operation of rent controls, the aid to education bill, and the 65- as opposed to 75-cent minimum wage. He also supported (July) the North Atlantic Security Pact, but after touring Europe in the fall of the year as one of a group of Senators, returned to say that "at least $1,000,000,000 should be trimmed" from Marshall Plan funds. In February 1950, as chairman of the Expenditures in Executive Departments Committee he suggested the establishment of a joint House-Senate committee "adequately and capably staffed, to work all the year round and study the executive budget while it is being prepared." This idea, opposed by President Truman and his Budget Director, Frank Pace, Jr.,[50] was regarded as "eminently sensible" by the Republican and conservative press.

Among the Senator's other stands in 1949 were his vote against the long-range housing bill (April), approval of the use of injunctions and plant seizure in national emergency strikes (June), opposition to President Truman's plan for a Department of Welfare (August), and against the arms aid bill (September). In early 1950 he voted for the repeal of the tax on oleomargarine and for a resolution for a Constitutional amendment providing equal rights for women.

Senator McClellan is a member of the Arkansas State and American bar associations; he is a Rotarian and a Baptist. In 1913 he married Eula Hicks, by whom he had two children, Max Eldon (who died in the North African campaign in 1943) and Doris (Mrs. Dale Elliott). In November 1922 he married Lucille Smith, who is also deceased. She was the mother of John Little, Jr. (who died in an automobile accident after having served three years in the Navy in World War II), James Howard, and Mary Alice. The Senator and Mrs. Norma Myers Cheatham, whose daughter is Mrs. Fred Lefevers, Jr., were married on November 10, 1937. He is described by Time as "taciturn." His physical characteristics are a height of five feet nine inches, a weight of 160 pounds, brown eyes, and black hair.

(Continued next page)

MCCLELLAN, JOHN L.—*Continued*

References

N Y Sun p12 Jl 5 '45
Congressional Directory (1950)
International Who's Who, 1949
Who's Who in America, 1950-51
Who's Who in Law, 1937
Who's Who in the Nation's Capital, 1938-39
World Biography (1948)

MCCONNELL, JOSEPH H(OWARD)
May 13, 1906- Broadcasting company executive; lawyer

Address: b. c/o National Broadcasting Company, Inc., 30 Rockefeller Plaza, New York 20; h. Bronxville, N.Y.

As president of the National Broadcasting Company, Inc., Joseph H. McConnell has directed the plans for a reorganization and expansion of the company's radio and television networks, necessitated by the widespread growth of the television industry. He was elected to the network presidency by its board of directors,

NBC Photo.

JOSEPH H. MCCONNELL

acting upon the recommendation of Niles Trammell [40], its former president, who then became chairman of the board. Prior to his appointment as president in October 1949, McConnell held the position of executive vice-president of the Radio Corporation of America, parent company of the National Broadcasting Company, with which he had been associated since 1941 in legal and financial capacities.

Born in Chester, South Carolina, on May 13, 1906, Joseph Howard McConnell is the son of Joseph Moore and Eliza Howard (Riggs) McConnell. He was reared in Davidson, North Carolina, where he attended public school and Davidson College, of which his father was dean. At college he played varsity football for three years, was president of the senior class, and was a member of Kappa Alpha fraternity. After receiving the degree of Bachelor of Science (in chemistry) in 1927, McConnell taught chemistry at the Woodberry Forest (preparatory) School in Virginia, where he was football coach as well.

At that time McConnell decided upon law for his profession, and in 1928 entered the University of Virginia Law School, adding to his studies the jobs of coaching the freshman football team and scouting for the varsity team. In 1931 he was graduated with a Bachelor of Laws degree and was elected to membership in Phi Beta Kappa. After a year's association with a law firm in West Palm Beach, Florida, McConnell joined a law firm in Charlotte, North Carolina. In 1933 he was offered a position on the legal staff of the NRA in Washington, D.C., where he served under Donald Richberg [49]. He was director of one of the agency's three legal sections at the time NRA was dissolved in 1936.

The young lawyer's first association with the Radio Corporation of America began when he joined the law firm of Cotton, Franklin, Wright, and Gordon (in 1950 Cahill, Gordon, Zachry, and Reindel) in New York City. There specializing in legal phases of Government regulations of corporated enterprises, he had as major client the RCA Manufacturing Company, Inc. A post in its legal department (in Camden, New Jersey) was offered him in 1941. This he accepted and within a year became general counsel of that organization, known now as the RCA Victor Division. Three years later he was elected a vice-president and general attorney of the division, later (in April 1947) was named vice-president in charge of law and finance. In January 1949 McConnell was elevated to an executive post in the parent company when he was appointed RCA vice-president in charge of finance, a position he held until promoted to the executive vice-presidency in July of that year.

The advent of television was credited with being responsible for a "changing era" in the broadcasting industry, entailing changes in key executive positions. On October 7, 1949, Niles Trammell resigned the presidency of the National Broadcasting Company to become chairman of its board of directors, succeeding General David Sarnoff [40]. To fill the presidency the board of directors elected McConnell.

Early in McConnell's presidency of NBC the network was realigned as three major divisions, one for the radio network, one for the television network, and one for the six radio and five televison stations which the company owns and operates. The executive and administrative corps of the company was also enlarged by the addition of a number of executives from advertising agencies and allied industries to augment the advertising and programming activities of the broadcasting company. In a program of expansion of the television network, McConnell supervised the addition of new station affiliations and the acquisition of several additional studios, among them the Center Theatre, in New York's Rockefeller Center. With a seating capacity of over three thousand, the theater gives NBC possession of the largest television studio in the United States, having such facilities as a stage of 4,200 square feet and a revolving center section, a particular advantage in the rapid changes of scenery demanded by the medium.

As the result of an agreement signed by McConnell on January 23, 1950, NBC agreed to relinquish its exclusive rights (held for eighteen years) to use the top of the Empire State Building for radio and television transmission. The company gave up its rights in order to allow for the construction by the building owners of a steel mast to support the antennas of four television transmitters. The project was hailed by former mayor William O'Dwyer of New York City as an outstanding example of cooperation among the television interests of New York in striving to make that city the nation's television center.

In his first year in office the NBC president acted as spokesman for the television industry at a meeting with the National Collegiate Athletic Association, which was considering barring TV from its games. Comparing the situation to the early days of radio when the colleges banned football broadcasts, McConnell pointed out that in 1949 attendance at college football games (televised) had risen 4 per cent while that at professional games (not televised) had dropped 9 per cent. On behalf of the industry he offered to finance a survey of the effects of TV on sports box-office receipts.

Questioned as to the possible "life expectancy" of the radio medium in consideration of television's rapid expansion, McConnell stated in *Variety* on July 26, 1950, that radio can be expected to continue in popularity—"It has all the ingredients for continued strength as a service to the people and a basic advertising medium—universality of coverage, economy, flexibility, and an appeal which has made it a part of the daily lives of Americans." McConnell, on signing an agreement for the Radio Corporation of America to provide the financial backing for *Call Me Madam*, 1950 Broadway musical, in return for radio, television, and cast album recording rights, said: 'This is a historic marriage between radio and the theater.'

McConnell married on October 31, 1936, Elizabeth Bernard, of Jacksonville, South Carolina, whom he had known since childhood. They are the parents of three daughters, Elizabeth Howard, Mary Meade, and Catharine Riggs. McConnell, who is six feet tall and weighs 185 pounds, has gray eyes and black hair. He is a Democrat and a Presbyterian. He belongs to the North Carolina Society in New York City, to the University Club in that city and to the Rittenhouse Club in Philadelphia; his fraternity is Phi Delta Phi (legal). In addition to golf, at which he maintains a handicap of ten strokes, McConnell is a devotee of deep-sea fishing.

References

Christian Sci Mon p13 O 7 '49
Who's Who in America, 1950-51

MCGHEE, GEORGE C(REWS) Mar. 10, 1912-   United States Government official; geologist

Address: b. c/o Department of State, Washington 25, D.C.; h. 2406 Kalorama Rd., Washington 8, D.C.; "Farmer's Delight," Middleburg, Va.

In the planning and implementation of President Truman's Point Four program for providing technological and other aid to undeveloped areas of the world, George C. McGhee is Assistant Secretary of State for Near Eastern, South Asian and African Affairs. He was appointed to the post in the summer of 1949, after having served the State Department as Special Representative to the Near East on the Palestine Refugee Problem, and as Coordinator for Aid to Greece and Turkey. A trained geologist, McGhee, through successful prospecting for new oil fields in Louisiana and elsewhere, became a millionaire before reaching the age of thirty. He is a veteran of World War II.

Born March 10, 1912, in Waco, Texas, George Crews McGhee is the son of George Summers and Magnolia (Spruce) McGhee. (His sister is Beulah McGhee Dunlap.) "As a youngster," observed Roger Stuart, the New York *World-Telegram and Sun* staff writer, he "showed a marked enthusiasm for rock formations. It developed that he was good at physics, too, so he thought about being a geologist or geophysicist." Accordingly, after graduation from the Bryan Street High School in Dallas, in 1928, and one year at Southern Methodist University (also in Dallas), he transferred to the University of Oklahoma to take that institution's courses in geology and physics. To finance his expenses he worked for one year (1930-31) as a subsurface geologist for the Atlantic Refining Company at Dallas, and consequently did not acquire his B. S. from Oklahoma until 1933. At the university he won letters in cross-country track and in dramatics, and was elected to Phi Beta Kappa, Sigma Xi, Sigma Gamma Epsilon, Sigma Pi Sigma, and Sigma Alpha Epsilon. He was also a candidate, though unsuccessfully on first attempt, for a Rhodes scholarship.

After graduation McGhee entered the employ of the Continental Oil Company as a seismic computer at Ponca City, Oklahoma. He had, however, completed only about a year at this work when his second application for a Rhodes scholarship was accepted and he left (in 1934) to take up a three-year residence at Queen's College, Oxford. (His dean and tutor there was Oliver Franks, who later became Great Britain's Ambassador to the United States.) McGhee received his D. Phil. from Oxford in 1937, the title of his doctoral thesis (published 1938) being *The Mapping of the Subsurface Geological Formations of South-Eastern England with the Reflection Seismograph*. In his last year in England he also studied at the University of London.

"I decided to steer myself toward a career in public service while I was in college," McGhee (who is a Democrat) has been quoted as telling the *World-Telegram* writer, who added that McGhee "deliberately chose to engage in the

Harris & Ewing

GEORGE C. MCGHEE

oil business . . . simply because that seemed to offer the best way to get rich in a hurry—so he could afford to work for the government." Well before he had completed his residence at Oxford he had become the holder of a United States patent (granted May 14, 1935) for a new method of making dip determination of geological formations. It was partly because of the patent that in June 1937 he was made vice-president of the National Geophysical Company, geophysical contractors, in Dallas. A little more than a year later he married Cecilia Jeanne De Golyer, daughter of Everette Lee De Golyer of Dallas, a prominent oil producer and geological expert. Not long afterward, with the assistance of his father-in-law, McGhee organized a small prospecting group to seek and buy up new oil fields. The result was discoveries in the Lake Charles region of Louisiana and elsewhere, which made McGhee a millionaire before he was thirty years old. In January 1940 he left the National Geophysical Company to join his father-in-law as a partner in what became the Dallas firm of De Golyer, MacNaughton and McGhee, consulting geologists; and in 1941 he was elected a director of both the Pantepec Oil Company of Venezuela and the Great National Life Insurance Company of Dallas.

McGhee's ambition to serve his country in an administrative capacity was first realized in June 1941, when he was appointed senior liaison officer of the Stockpile and Import Shipping Branch of the War Production Board, at Washington, D.C. In January 1942 he was transferred (within the War Production Board) to the Combined Raw Materials Board as United States deputy executive secretary. After a year and a half he resigned to enlist (June 1943) in the United States Navy. Following four months' service as a seaman, he was commissioned a lieutenant (junior grade) and sent

to Colorado to become the Navy's liaison officer with the Army Twentieth Air Force's Twenty-first Bomber Command then being activated under Major General Curtis LeMay '44. Promoted to full lieutenant, McGhee served in the Marianas. For his war record McGhee has been awarded the Asiatic Ribbon with three battle stars, and the Legion of Merit, the latter for "developing and coordinating an air-sea operation which saved the lives of more than 600 airmen." He is now a lieutenant colonel in the Air Force Reserve.

Upon demobilization McGhee returned to Dallas, where he organized the Community Guidance Service, which in a period of two years was to assist some three thousand young men and women and to put out $25,000 in student loans. In January 1946, at the suggestion of his fellow Texan, Under Secretary of State William L. Clayton '44, he was appointed Special Assistant to the Deputy to the Assistant Secretary for Economic Affairs in the State Department at Washington; and in the following August he moved up to become Special Assistant to Clayton. (Also in 1946, McGhee served briefly as a director of the United States Commercial Company, and was named a director of the Institute of Inter-American Affairs, Education Division, which position he continues to occupy.)

McGhee's prominence in national and international affairs may be considered to date from June 1947, when he was named Coordinator for Aid to Greece and Turkey (and Special Assistant to the Under Secretary of State) by President Truman. By Act of Congress approved May 22 and authorizing $400,000,000 for aid to Greece and Turkey, the United States had taken over former British functions; and on June 26 the post of coordinator was created, the coordinator being directed to "take all necessary action relating to the administration in Washington . . . of funds under the Act." McGhee paid a three weeks' visit to Athens in October; on his return he said that the necessary economic program had been completed and he expressed hope for "quick results in restoring the country's agricultural-export economy." McGhee (who in 1947 was named by the Dallas Junior Chamber of Commerce as the city's "outstanding young man," and in the same year became a director of the Diplomatic Affairs Foundation and the Foreign Service Educational Foundation) continued as coordinator until March 1949, when (as Special Assistant to the Secretary of State) he was named Special Representative of the Secretary of State to the Near East on the Palestine Refugee Problem, with personal rank as Minister.

On May 27, 1949, President Truman completed what James Reston of the New York *Times* called "the top-level reorganization of the State Department" by appointing five new Assistant Secretaries of State. One of these was McGhee, who was named Assistant Secretary for Near Eastern, South Asian and African Affairs; his confirmation by the Senate was by unanimous vote. In his new post McGhee has answerable to him (stated Alfred A. Strelsin in the *United Nations World*) "fifty-three foreign service stations, of which fourteen are embassies." The regions involved have a total area of about fourteen and a half million square miles and a population of more than seven hundred million.

In view of President Truman's impending Point Four program for providing technological aid to industrially undeveloped areas, McGhee's post assumed strategic importance. In November and December of 1949 he made an extensive tour of the territory within his sphere, presided at Istanbul (beginning November 26) over a five-day conference of ranking United States diplomats from eleven countries, then proceeded to Iran, Pakistan, India, and Burma. Later (upon his return to the United States) he spoke in January 1950 on Point Four prospects and the ability of Asiatic nations to resist the wave of Communism: "American assistance cannot furnish the determination, it cannot furnish the will, it cannot furnish the loyalty of a people to its government. But if the will and the determination exist, and if the people are behind their government, then, and not always then, there is a very good chance." In regard to India and Pakistan, he was to issue a statement that the need in those countries "is equity capital, not loans"; while in India "the Government's policy tends toward nationalization of industry and has been a factor in drying up the sources of domestic equity capital that now exist" (in the words of the New York Times). Meanwhile the United States had with Great Britain, France, Belgium, and Portugal been discussing enterprises involving up to $3,000,000,000 for the development of Africa over a ten-year period. At the end of May a Big Three conference of Acheson, Bevin, and Schuman concluded with a resolve to permit "a certain level of armed forces" in the Near East (in Israel and the adjacent Arab states) as a bulwark against the Sovet Union, and with an agreement "establishing close collaboration between the colonial powers and the United States" as a matter of immediate interest to all Africa. This (said the *Christian Science Monitor*) was "interpreted as clearly giving the United States direct influence in all African affairs."

A member since July 1950 of the advisory council of the Department of Oriental Languages and Literatures at Princeton University, George C. McGhee is also a member (since 1949) of the international committee of the YMCA and of the board of trustees of the Thessalonica Agricultural and Industrial Institute (American Farm School) in Greece. Professional bodies to which he belongs include the American Association of Petroleum Geologists, the Society of Exploration Geophysicists, the American Institute of Mining and Metallurgical Engineers, and the British Institute of Petroleum. He is, too, a member of the American Political Science Association, the Foreign Policy Association, the Association of American Rhodes Scholars, the Council on Foreign Relations, the Academy of Political Science, the Middle East Institute, the American Society for Public Administration, and the Philosophical Society of Texas. The Texan has also been prominent in community affairs in

Dallas, as a member of the Civic Federation of that city, its Little Theater, the Dallas Symphony Society, the local Council of Social Agencies, and the YMCA Boys Work Committee.

McGhee is an American Legionnaire and an "Amvet." His clubs are the Dallas Petroleum Club, the Brookhollow Golf Club in that city; the Pioneer Club in Lake Charles, Louisiana, the Farmington Country in Virginia, the Gibson Island in Maryland, and the Metropolitan and National Press in Washington. He attends a Methodist church. His marriage to Miss De Golyer took place November 24, 1938; their four children are Marcia Spruce, George De Golyer, Dorothy Hart, and Michael Anthony. The McGhees maintain a home in Washington and have a property, "Farmer's Delight," near Middleburg, Virginia. Five feet eleven and a half inches tall, the Assistant Secretary of State weighs 195 pounds, and has blue-gray eyes and brown hair. Photography, tennis, travel, and art, are listed by him as recreations of choice, when he finds time for them. "I don't mind speechmaking," he told an interviewer, "and attending receptions is O.K. too. But I agree with my kids that it would be better if these affairs could be spaced out with occasional visits to a trout stream."

References

N Y World-Telegram and Sun p17 My 20 '50 por
This Week p21 My 16 '48 por
U N World 3:25-27 S '49 pors
U S News 28:32 My 5 '50
American Men in Government (1949)
Directory of American Political Science Association, 1948
International Who's Who, 1950
Who's Who in America, 1950-51

MCGRAW, CURTIS W(HITTLESEY)
Oct. 13, 1895- Publisher

Address: b. c/o McGraw-Hill Publishing Co., 330 W. 42nd St., New York 18; h. 130 Hodge Rd., Princeton, N.J.

On February 24, 1950, the McGraw-Hill Publishing Company, Inc., announced the election of Curtis W. McGraw as its board chairman and president. He is the third successive McGraw to hold those offices, having succeeded his brother, James H. McGraw, Jr., (now retired), who in turn assumed the presidency and chairmanship of the board in 1935 when James H. McGraw, Sr., founder of the company, resigned. The new head of McGraw-Hill has been with the firm throughout his business career, which began in November 1920, when he entered the employ of the McGraw-Hill Book Company, a subsidiary of the publishing organization.

Curtis Whittlesey McGraw was born in Madison, New Jersey, on October 13, 1895. His parents, James H. and Mildred (Whittlesey) McGraw, had four other children, a daughter, Catherine (now Mrs. John E. Osmun) and three sons, James H. Jr., Harold, and Donald, all of whom, like Curtis, eventuallly

CURTIS W. MCGRAW

assumed positions of importance in the Mc-Graw-Hill enterprises. McGraw's maternal grandfather, Curtis E. Whittlesey, was the first treasurer of McGraw-Hill. In 1915, Curtis McGraw graduated from the Lawrenceville (New Jersey) School, a preparatory school for Princeton University, and enrolled in the latter. Throughout his school years, McGraw maintained an interest in athletics. He was selected captain of Lawrenceville's basketball team, and later became captain of the Princeton football squad.

McGraw's final years at Princeton were interrupted by World War I. He was sent overseas upon his induction into the army in April 1917, as a captain in the 320th Infantry. After having taken part in three major offensives, including the Meuse-Argonne, he was wounded in June 1918, and was returned to the United States. There he remained in the army until July 1919, by which time he had achieved the rank of major. That fall he was back at Princeton, where he received the B.A. degree in 1920; after graduation he was assistant coach of the football teams of 1920, 1921, and 1922. In 1920 he joined the rapidly growing publishing firm of which his father was co-founder. (James McGraw, who retired from the board chairmanship in 1935, died in February 1948.)

The *Magazine of Wall Street* (January 6, 1945) described the McGraw-Hill Publishing Company, Inc., as "the country's leading publisher of business magazines, directories, catalogs, and books of scientific, technical and business character." The enterprise had its beginnings in 1889, when James H. McGraw, Sr., county schoolteacher in upstate New York, resigned to enter the field of technical publishing. After several years as an employee, he became an independent publisher in 1899 with his purchase of the *Street Railway Journal*, a publication at that time primarily concerned with horse-drawn cars. Recognizing the importance of

electricity for transportation, lighting, and industrial power, McGraw's journals on electrical subjects became the core of his expanding technical publishing projects. In 1888 John A. Hill, an engineer on the Denver and Rio Grande Railroad in Colorado, had become editor of his industry's journal, *The Locomotive*. From the production of these two journals, two independent publishing companies devoted to several technical periodicals developed, the McGraw and the Hill firms.

Within each of these publishing houses a technical book department developed as a natural outgrowth of specialized magazine publishing. These departments, however, were small in comparison with the magazine departments, and it was therefore to increase efficiency and reduce costs that the book divisions were consolidated on July 1, 1909, as the McGraw-Hill Book Company. In 1917, shortly after the death of John Hill, the magazine activities of the two companies were merged to form the McGraw-Hill Company, to be known later as the McGraw-Hill Publishing Company. (The McGraw-Hill Book Company functioned as a subsidiary.) Already in 1917, as publisher of ten technical and industrial magazines, the firm had become the world's largest organization in that field of publishing. By 1949 McGraw-Hill periodicals numbered thirty-four, and included such well-known titles as *Business Week, Aviation Week, Coal Age, Electrical World, Textile World, American Machinist, Engineering and Mining Journal,* and *Electronics.*

With the purchase of the A. W. Shaw Company in 1928 and of the Gregg Publishing Company in 1948, both of which were firms specializing in the publication of business books, McGraw-Hill has also become preeminent in this field. The company also entered the line of trade books in 1930, and established a division of the McGraw-Hill Book Company to publish books of general interest to the lay public, both fiction and nonfiction, under the imprint Whittlesey House. This imprint commemorates the name of the first treasurer of McGraw-Hill, Curtis E. Whittlesey.

In the fall of 1920, Curtis McGraw joined the McGraw-Hill Book Company, working at first in the shipping and production departments. From 1922 to 1927, he was assistant to the treasurer of this subsidiary, and from 1925 to 1927 he was secretary and assistant treasurer. In the latter year he was elected vice-president and treasurer as well as being made a director of the book company, and he subsequently became chairman of its board of directors.

In 1930 McGraw became a director of the parent organization, the McGraw-Hill Publishing Company, Inc. From 1943 to 1948 he served as vice-president and treasurer, and from 1948 to February 1950, as vice-chairman of the board. When his brother James H. McGraw retired from the presidency of the company, Curtis W. McGraw was elected to succeed him in that office and in the chairmanship of the board. His election was made known on February 24, 1950.

The publishing firm has an interest in the paper-manufacturing field: it has a 50 per cent ownership in a paper company, and is thus independent of outside sources of paper (*Barron's*, September 4, 1944). Because of Curtis McGraw's experience in both fields he was appointed by the Government as a member of the Book Publishing Advisory Paper Committee of the War Production Board, set up to deal with the national shortage of paper, the chief problem of publishers during World War II.

McGraw, who was elected president of the American Book Publishers Council in 1948, was returned for a second term of office extending through May 11, 1950. He is also a director of the council, having been re-elected to a three-year term at the meeting of the council in New York in 1949. At this same meeting, in a review of the problems of publishing in the United States, McGraw stated: "Authors, manufacturers, booksellers and librarians and even readers are not well enough acquainted with us as publishers, and I think we should work toward some program to intensify the opportunities for that acquaintanceship." McGraw has also been a director of the Book Publishers Association.

The publisher is a director of the Lawrence Portland Cement Company (New York) of the Joseph Woodwell Company (Pittsburgh), and of the First National Bank of Princeton. A resident of Princeton, he is president of the board of trustees of Princeton Hospital and treasurer of Princeton University Press. McGraw, who is a Republican, attends the Presbyterian church. He has blue eyes and brown hair. On May 7, 1921, he married Elizabeth Woodwell; their daughter, Elizabeth Murtland, is now Mrs. James L. Stoltzfus. His clubs include the University, Players, and Princeton in New York, and, for the playing of his favorite sport, the Pine Valley and Springdale golf clubs in Princeton.

References

Bsns W p20 Mr 11 '50
Who's Who in America, 1950-51
World Biography (1948)

MCGUIGAN, JAMES (CHARLES), CARDINAL (má-gwĭg'ăn) Nov. 26, 1894- Roman Catholic prelate

Address: h. Archbishop's House, York Mills, Ont., Canada; b. 200 Church Street, Toronto 2, Ont., Canada

His Eminence, James, Cardinal McGuigan is the Archbishop of the ecclesiastical province of Toronto, the largest English-speaking Roman Catholic archdiocese in Canada. He was assigned to Toronto in 1934, four years after being consecrated Archbishop of Regina at the age of thirty-six. In 1946, when he was named to the Sacred College of Cardinals, he was the first English-speaking Canadian prelate of that rank. Archbishop McGuigan has been the prime mover in a program of educational expansion in his archdiocese. With the spread of communism in Europe and Asia he has become increasingly outspoken in his pronouncements against it.

James Charles McGuigan was born in the town of Hunter River, in Canada's smallest province, Prince Edward Island, on November 26, 1894, the son of George Hugh and Anne (Monaghan) McGuigan. He has two brothers and three sisters. James McGuigan attended public school at Hunter River, Prince of Wales College (1908-11), and St. Dunstan's University (1912-14), all in his home province. After winning the Governor-General's medal with his B.A. degree at St. Dunstan's, he went to the Grand Seminary and Laval University (with which St. Dunstan's is affiliated) in Quebec City, where he received the theological doctorate (*summa cum laude*) in 1918. Returning to Prince Edward Island, he was ordained a priest on May 26, 1918, by Bishop O'Leary of Charlottetown. His academic record and his work for two years as a professor at St. Dunstan's (1918-20) recommended him to Bishop O'Leary, whom he accompanied as secretary when the latter was appointed Archbishop of Edmonton, Alberta, in 1920.

At Edmonton Father McGuigan became chancellor (1923-25) and vicar-general (1923-30) of the archdiocese. He was appointed rector of St. Joseph's Cathedral there in 1925. In 1927 he took a postgraduate course in canon law at the Catholic University of America, which earned him the degrees of Ph.D. and J.C.D. In 1927, too, he was made a prothonotary apostolic with the title of Monsignor, and appointed rector and president of the newly established St. Joseph's Seminary.

In January of 1930, in Edmonton, the ecclesiastic was consecrated Archbishop, after which he proceeded to Regina, the capital of the neighboring Province of Saskatchewan, where he took up the duties of that office. During this period, in which Saskatchewan suffered from the effects of the great depression and from the worst droughts in its history, Archbishop McGuigan attracted considerable attention in his efforts to ameliorate bad living conditions. With some of the churches closed and services held in homes to save fuel, he turned over his residence to the Franciscan Fathers and for some time made his home with them. In 1930 he organized the Catholic Federated Charities in Regina. The prelate's warnings against the doctrines of communism, sounded in pastoral letters, were said to have had "a steadying effect upon his flock." (A selection of the letters was published at Regina in 1935.) Archbishop McGuigan was the first to conduct a Eucharistic Congress in Western Canada. He also established in Saskatchewan a "religious vacation school movement" designed to bring a knowledge of Catholic doctrine to prairie children; it was reported that 7,000 children were reached by this movement in Regina in 1934.

Archbishop McGuigan in December 1934 was named fifth Archbishop of the ecclesiastical province of Toronto, succeeding the Most Reverend Neil McNeil. As the head of the chief See of English-speaking Catholicism in Canada, the Archbishop was enthroned in St. Michael's Cathedral, an event ceremoniously recognized by both civic and provincial governments.

(Continued next page)

Karsh

JAMES CARDINAL MCGUIGAN

In 1943 Archbishop McGuigan was elevated to the dignity of Assistant at the Pontifical Throne, and made a Papal Count; in December of 1945 he received a communication from Pope Pius informing him of his appointment to the Sacred College of Cardinals. He traveled to Rome in February 1946 to receive the traditional red hat of a Cardinal and to be publicly invested with the office on February 18.

Describing the significance of his becoming the first native-born English-speaking Canadian Cardinal, McGuigan commented: "It is evident that the Holy Father wished to recognize the English-speaking section of the country. . . .To be ranked among the Princes of the Church, to be exalted to the Senate of the Holy Father, to partake of the eminence of those who throughout the Christian centuries have kept the gates of the City of God—this is the meaning of the ineffable honor to which I have been raised." The new Cardinal received as his titular Roman See the Church of Santa Maria del Popolo, built in 1099 upon the site of Nero's tomb. As Cardinal, in 1947 he was named personal representative of the Pope (papal legate) to the five-day Marian Congress held in Ottawa's Cathedral of Our Lady of the Immaculate Conception, and later that year went to Rome to report on the congress.

Shortly after his appointment to Toronto, the Archbishop campaigned to expand the parochial school facilities of his archdiocese. Extending the financial appeal in this connection he said in June 1943: "We want Catholic secondary education which will be second to none and distinctive in every way. I cannot rest when I see our boys and girls thumbing their way past the glorious collegiates to their own high schools where the teaching is good but the buildings poor." A year later in a pastoral letter, he asserted: "There is no firmer bulwark against anarchy and revolution than the teaching of religion in our Christian schools."

The Catholic school expansion program has resulted in the completion of several new separate schools in the Toronto vicinity.

In commenting on Canada's social program (such as family allowances and old-age benefits), the churchman has said that the belief in personal liberty will help avoid "the rocks which might completely overturn our democratic system into a totalitarian one." In condemning the spread of social drinking, he has asked all Catholics to practice total abstinence during Lent; he viewed the legalization of Sunday commercial sport in Toronto with disfavor.

The call for progressive thought on social problems, as one dike against the "rising tide of communism," has been a recurrent theme in Cardinal McGuigan's talks and pastorals. He has praised the work of St. Francis Xavier University (Antigonish, Nova Scotia) in furthering cooperatives, and the zeal of Catholics who prepare themselves for labor union service. These are developments which he believes will "stem the advance of materialism and atheism." During the Spanish civil war he called for a new crusade against such trends in Europe. Since 1945 he has appealed for aid to Italy and other noncommunist lands of Europe. Calling for a "broad and tolerant" policy on immigration into Canada (April 1946), he told the Toronto Canadian Club that Canadians should be more concerned about "the Red armies quartered in Hungary, Austria, and in Germany, as well as the horrors committed under Tito in Yugoslavia and in martyred Poland." In August of 1949 the Cardinal announced that any Catholic who read, wrote for, or distributed the *Canadian Tribune* or other communist publications would be excluded from the blessings of the Church. The papal decree establishing this policy, he said, meant that "the sentence of excommunication is pronounced only in the case of apostates who profess the materialistic and anti-Christian doctrines of communism."

During World War II the Canadian ecclesiastic placed the weight of his influence behind the Canadian war effort. When, in the spring of 1942, the Government held a plebiscite to obtain release from its earlier promise not to introduce conscription, the Archbishop declared it to be the most solemn duty to release the Government in this respect. He argued that, while Roman Catholic spiritual leaders do not direct the people in their personal civic responsibility of voting, it is still true that even in democratic countries the authority of Government has its origin in God. In the crisis of 1942, he stated, the Government had a sacred claim upon the "respect, loyalty and confidence" of the people.

His Eminence Cardinal McGuigan is governor of St. Augustine's Seminary, director of St. Francis Xavier Seminary, chancellor of the Catholic Church Extension Society of Canada, and chancellor of the Pontifical Institute of Medieval Studies in Toronto. He has received honorary degrees (LL.D.) from the University of Toronto and from the Catholic University of America. The prelate has been described as a "pleasing speaker, a kind man with simple tastes, a good sense of humor and a hearty laugh." He has blue eyes and fair hair. His chosen forms of relaxation are reading and walking.

References

N Y Times p2 D 24 '45
Saturday Night Mr 23 '35 por
Toronto Globe D 25 '34
Toronto Star Mr 25 '35
Canadian Who's Who, 1948
International Who's Who, 1950
10 Eventful Years (1947)
Who's Who, 1950
Who's Who in America, 1950-51
Who's Who in Canada, 1947-48
World Biography (1948)

MACK, PAULINE BEERY Dec. 19, 1891-
Chemist; research institute director; educator
Address: b. Ellen H. Richards Institute, Pennsylvania State College, State College, Pa.; h. 245 E. Hamilton Ave., State College, Pa.

The recipient of the 1950 Francis P. Garvan Gold Medal, the American Chemical Society's highest chemistry award for women, is Pauline Beery Mack. The award was in recognition of her work in the calcium chemistry of bone density, which led to development of a microphotometric technique for bone density measurement. Dr. Mack, who has been associated with the teaching staff of Pennsylvania State College's School of Chemistry and Physics since 1919, is director of the Ellen H. Richards Institute for research which in 1940 was made a department of the college. She has directed the Pennsylvania mass studies in human nutrition and served during World War II as Pennsylvania State Director of Nutrition. Her research has included work in the fields of textiles and detergency, aspects of physical chemistry related to the problems of everyday living.

Pauline Beery Mack was born December 19, 1891, the only child of John and Dora (Woodford) Beery, who gave her the middle name Gracia. Her parents' forebears were chiefly English, with a Scottish strain on the maternal side and some Swiss blood on the paternal. She was born and reared in Norborne, Missouri, where her father owner a store. Her mother cooperated in the latter undertaking and also engaged in the real estate business.

Miss Beery was graduated in 1909 from Norborne High School, where her studies, the classical course of that time, included four years of Latin, three years of German, and four years of mathematics; her extracurricular activities were music and athletics. Turned from her original ambition to become an opera singer by her parents, who urged her to prepare for a career in Latin teaching, she entered Missouri State University to specialize in that subject. However, she recalls, "the lack of inspiration . . . of the Latin teacher and the marvelous course of lectures in freshman chemistry given by the late Dr. Herman Schlundt" caused her to change to a major in chemistry, with minors in the supporting fields of physiology, mathematics, and English. A member of Phi Beta

PAULINE BEERY MACK

Kappa, she received honors in chemistry and mathematics. She devoted extracurricular hours to basketball.

Following her graduation with the B.A. degree in 1913, Miss Beery was assistant principal and science teacher at the Norborne High School for two years. She was head of the Webb City (Missouri) High School's science department from 1915 to 1918 and of the Springfield (Missouri) High School's department of physical science in the following year. Meanwhile, having continued her studies during summer vacations at Columbia University, where physical chemistry was her major and physics and biological chemistry her minor fields of study, she was awarded the M.A. degree in 1919.

In the same year (1919), finding procurement of a university research and teaching position in physical chemistry difficult for a woman in her generation, she accepted a position at Pennsylvania State College, where she was engaged to teach freshman chemistry for home economics and liberal arts students, and household chemistry for sophomore students of home economics. On December 27, 1923, Miss Beery was married to a teaching associate, Dr. Warren Bryan Mack, head of the college's Department of Horticulture. She became Dr. Mack in 1932, when she received the Ph.D. degree from Pennsylvania State College, where she had made biological chemistry her major and physics her minor field of concentration.

During her first fifteen years on the teaching staff of the State College, Dr. Mack taught from thirty to thirty-five hours a week in lecture room, classroom, and laboratory and, declining tutorial fees, gave special help to students on an extracurricular activity basis. In 1919, although her official position was con-

MACK, PAULINE BEERY—*Continued*

fined to teaching, she began independent research projects in household chemistry (working on the application of chemistry to food, clothing, and housing) and gradually enlarged her research area to include fundamental chemistry as well.

Her research projects, which she conducted alone or with the help of graduate students and associates, were supported by funds raised personally from many sources. In the early 1920's she elicited the cooperation of Pennsylvania's Department of Welfare for work on textile durability testing methods by a graduate student working under her direction. The project led to the establishment in the early 1930's of a formal fellowship supported by Pennsylvania's Departments of Health, Public Instruction, Military Affairs and Welfare. In 1932 a fellowship supported by the Pennsylvania Association of Dyers and Cleaners resulted from informal studies for the association conducted under Dr. Mack's direction since 1927. It was followed shortly by a Pennsylvania Laundryowners Association fellowship and by a more recent detergency fellowship from the Diaper Service Institute. Among the fellowships from textile manufacturing and distributing groups also placed under Dr. Mack's direction is one supported by the American Viscose Corporation and two large rayon mills.

During her second fifteen years of association with Pennsylvania State College, Dr. Mack gradually turned over to associates all undergraduate work with the exception of her freshman and sophomore lectures. In 1935 she was able to begin a long-planned series of studies which became known as the Pennsylvania mass studies in human nutrition. The work, on which she received help from graduate students, her husband, and her mother during the first year, attracted the attention of Pennsylvania's Department of Health, and led to Dr. Mack's cooperation with that department in the direction of the studies. Called "the first comprehensive program in human nutrition research" and the only one with a fifteen-year continuous history, the studies have received annual financial support from the Pennsylvania State Legislature since 1936.

Under the Pennsylvania Department of Health and the State Council for Defense, Dr. Mack served during World War II as State Director of Nutrition. Meanwhile, the research studies she had inaugurated had expanded until, in 1940, under the name of the Ellen H. Richards Institute, they were made a department of Pennsylvania State College. Director of the institute since its founding, Dr. Mack heads a staff which in 1950 numbers 65.

The research chemist's chief scientific contribution and the one for which she received the 1950 Francis P. Garvan Gold Medal (the highest chemistry award for women awarded by the American Chemical Society) is in the calcium chemistry of bone mineralization. The result of the work which Dr. Mack began in this field in 1927 is development of a measuring technique (based on roentgenograms) to determine the mineral content of bones, thus providing a way to analyze the changing calcium content in the living human skeleton and making it possible to assess with accuracy the relation of an individual's skeletal calcium content to his needs for proper growth and functioning. Known as the Ellen H. Richards microphotometric technique, the method consists of the photoelectric tracing of X-ray films by means of microphotometers developed under Dr. Mack's direction. The research institute which she heads cooperates with the Children's Hospital of Philadelphia, the Naval Medical Research Institute, (Bethesda, Maryland), and twelve foreign and fourteen American universities in use of the technique.

Dr. Mack, whose Pennsylvania State College lectures have been attended by more than 12,000 undergraduate students, is author of *Chemistry Applied to Home and Community* and *Stuff— the Science of Materials in the Service of Man.* Of two recent works by Dr. Mack describing the microphotometric measuring technique developed under her direction, one has been accepted for separate publication, while the other is to be included in a University of Minnesota Press book. Founder of the *Chemistry Leaflet* (now *Chemistry*) in 1927, Dr. Mack edited the publication until 1944, now serves it as consulting editor. She has contributed numerous articles and research papers to scientific and medical journals, and to State, college, and trade publications.

In 1938 Dr. Mack was admitted to membership in the Faraday Society of England, one of the six women honored thus far in its history. In 1948, Dr. Mack became a member of Phi Beta Kappa, and she was recipient of the 1949 Distinguished Daughters of Pennsylvania Medal. National president from 1945 to 1948 of Iota Sigma Pi, chemistry honor society, she is a fellow of the American Institute of Chemists, the American Association for the Advancement of Science, the Society for Research in Child Development, and the American Public Health Association. Among her other memberships are numerous professional, academic, and fraternal societies; and she maintains membership in several Pennsylvania State educational, scientific, and charitable organizations. She is a Republican and an Episcopalian. The color of her eyes and hair is brown; her height is five feet five inches, her weight 155 pounds. She retains her interest in vocal music. As a hobby, she says, she assists the State police in some scientific testing related to the solution of crimes.

References

Chem & Eng N 28:1032 Mr 27 '50
Ind Woman 29:201 Jl '50
Pathfinder 53:39 S 11 '46

Who's Who in America, 1950-51

MCNICHOLAS, JOHN T(IMOTHY), ARCHBISHOP

Dec. 15, 1877—Apr. 22, 1950 Roman Catholic prelate in the United States, noted as spokesman for the Church on the use of public funds for parochial schools and the relation of church and state; organizer and first national director of the Holy Name

Society; consecrated Bishop of Duluth, 1918; Archbishop of Cincinnati since 1925; founded graduate school of science in Cincinnati (Institutum Divi Thomae) in 1935; in 1946 and 1948 elected chairman of the administrative board of the National Catholic Welfare Conference; a member of the committee which prepared the *Catechism of Christian Doctrine,* 1949; president-general of the National Catholic Education Association since 1946. See *Current Biography,* 1949.

Obituary

N Y Times p92 Ap 23 '50 por

MAGEE, ELIZABETH S(TEWART)

June 29, 1889- Social worker; labor organization official

Address: b. c/o National Consumers League, 348 Engineers' Bldg., Cleveland 14, Ohio; h. 2196 Ambleside Dr., Cleveland 6, Ohio

The National Consumers League, which in 1949 observed the fiftieth year of its founding, has been directed since 1943 by Elizabeth S. Magee. Credit for many industrial and labor reforms has been given to Miss Magee and her associates, who pioneered in the struggle for fair labor standards, including legislation on child labor, minimum wages, better working conditions for women and social security. A former teacher and YWCA secretary, Miss Magee became executive secretary of the Ohio Consumers League in 1925.

Elizabeth Stewart Magee was born June 29, 1889, in Des Moines, Iowa, one of the three children of William Archibald and Lizzie (Dysart) Magee. (Her sister became a librarian; her brother, James, now deceased, was for twenty years head of the economics department of New York University.) The parents were descended from Scottish and Irish forebears who, settling in Pennsylvania, fought in the American Revolution. Elizabeth attended grammar school in Des Moines, where her father was a YMCA secretary. At the West Des Moines High School, from which she graduated in 1907, she edited the school paper, *The Tatler.* In the fall of 1907 she enrolled at Oberlin (Ohio) College, there to major in the social sciences and to become active in the student YWCA, and the campus literary society (Aeolian). She graduated with a B.A. degree in 1911.

For the five years that followed, Miss Magee taught in the public schools of Altoona, Pennsylvania, in the elementary school and in the English department of the high school. She has said that this early experience in an industrial community stimulated her interest in labor problems. In 1917 she became a YWCA secretary, doing advisory work with student branches of that organization in four States, and having headquarters in Denver, Colorado. The following year she went to Detroit, Michigan, where for four years, as industrial secretary of the YWCA, she initiated and supervised an educational and recreational program among women industrial workers. She has been quoted as saying, "It was in Detroit that I first

Trout-Ware

ELIZABETH S. MAGEE

came into close contact with industrial workers. In those days we went right into the plants at the lunch hour and after work. . . .Now, every time I walk into the United Automobile Workers building in Detroit, I get the biggest thrill! It's such a contrast with the state of the unions after the first World War." From 1922 to 1924 Miss Magee was national industrial secretary of the YWCA, in the association's New York office; in addition to giving program assistance to the YWCA's industrial secretaries throughout the United States, she organized regional and national conferences of women industrial workers.

Interest in labor legislation aroused by her YWCA experience led Miss Magee to enroll at Columbia University for a year of graduate study in the field of economics. She received the M.A. degree in the spring of 1925 for a thesis entitled "Class Consciousness Among Women in Industry in the United States." That summer she directed the Summer School for Women Workers in Industry at the University of Wisconsin.

It was as the result of a suggestion by one of her Columbia professors that Miss Magee went to Cleveland in the fall of 1925 to work with the Consumers League of Ohio as its executive secretary. The first organization of this kind had been founded in New York in 1896 on the principal that consumers should realize their responsibility for conditions of employment and of their duty to purchase those things produced under satisfactory labor conditions. Similar groups were formed in Pennsylvania, Massachusetts, and Illinois. In 1899 these State bodies joined to organize the National Consumers League, with Mrs. Florence Kelley as its first executive secretary. There are, in 1950, eight State leagues (New York, New Jersey, Massachusetts, Rhode Island, Connecticut, Michigan, Ohio, and Kentucky) which

MAGEE, ELIZABETH S.—*Continued*

operate in a semiautonomous relationship with the national organization, each State group being free to initiate local projects outside the national program.

Using the slogan "Investigate, agitate, legislate," the founders of the league did pioneer work which has been largely credited with the establishment of the Children's Bureau and Women's Bureau of the United States Department of Labor, and with the passage of minimum wage and hour laws. In 1907 Louis D. Brandeis represented the league before the Supreme Court in a hearing on the first ten-hour working day law for women, enacted in Oregon. Miss Magee recently pointed out that the league had a major part in the enactment of the minimum wage law in Massachusetts in 1912, the first such legislation in the United States.

In 1931-32 Miss Magee interrupted her work with National Consumers League to serve for fifteen months as executive secretary of the Ohio Commission on Unemployment Insurance, to which she was appointed by the Governor to investigate the need for such a measure. In this capacity she directed the investigation, arranged public hearings on the question, and edited the two-volume report of the commission. The Cleveland *Union Leader* has stated that this report "was drawn on heavily when the Federal Social Security Act was debated and passed five years later in 1938." At the conclusion of the commission's work Miss Magee returned to the secretaryship of the Ohio Consumers League. In 1943 she became general secretary of the national organization, the year the headquarters of the league were moved to Cleveland from New York. (She has retained her post with the Ohio body.)

One of Miss Magee's first public activities as the N.C.L. general secretary was membership on the Government's Emergency Committee for Food Production, formed in April of 1943 when a farm lobby threatened the New Deal's farm security program. In the same year Miss Magee made public a letter signed by eighty women leaders throughout the country, which had been sent to all members of Congress. In its statement the league enumerated its objections to the Equal Rights Amendment: while believing in equal rights for women, the N.C.L. opposes "the so-called 'Equal Rights Amendment' . . . because it would imperil hardwon legislation enacted to safeguard women as homemakers and mothers. . . .Because, while risking these safeguards, it would not redress major inequalities persisting today. . . ." Miss Magee has been given a large measure of credit for the passage of the Fair Labor Standards Act, and is known for her work for such reforms as raising of the minimum wage, broader application of social security provisions, and the equal status bill setting labor standards for Government workers.

The fiftieth anniversary of the founding of the National Consumers League was observed on December 9, 1949. The New York *Times* editorial comment on the occasion: "We live in a happier country because of the work the League has done." Miss Magee was quoted as saying that in spite of its achievements "there is still a big job to be done." One of the areas of present concentration, she said, is the problems of migrant agricultural workers, who do not come under the jurisdiction of most existing State labor legislation.

Among the Government advisory posts held by Miss Magee have been membership on the Advisory Committee for the Protection of Young Workers of the United States, the Children's Bureau, the Consumers Advisory Committee to the Council of Economic Advisers, the National Commission on Children and Youth, and the executive committee of the Ohio Commission on Children and Youth. She has served as public member of several wage boards established under the Federal Fair Labor Standards Act. In 1947 she was chairman of a conference which set up the National Citizens' Committee on Migrant Labor. The league secretary is the author of several articles, including "The Role of Women's Legislation in Meeting Basic Problems of Working Conditions" in the bulletin *The American Woman— Her Changing Role*, published by the Women's Bureau of the Department of Labor. Other published articles are "Child Laborers' Gains and Losses Since the War" (1930) and "Impact of the War on Child Labor" (1944), both in the *Annals of the American Academy of Political and Social Science*; and the New York *Times* columns contain her letters to its editor. She is a member of the American Association of Social Workers, the National Conference of Social Work, and is on the board of the Cleveland Urban League. Her clubs are the Women's City Club of Cleveland and the Oberlin Women's Club of Cleveland.

The league executive has been described in the *Cleveland Union Leader* as "a comfortable-looking gray-haired lady who looks like that aunt of yours who bakes the best apple pie you've ever eaten." Her eyes are brown; she weighs 150 pounds and is five feet five inches tall. She lists her political affiliation as Democratic, and her church as the Presbyterian. For recreation she prefers travel, music, and cooking.

References

    Cleveland (Ohio) Plain Dealer p8A Mr 26 '50 por
    Cleveland (Ohio) Union Leader N 7 '47 por
    Who's Who in America, 1950-51

MAIER, WALTER A(RTHUR), REV. (mī'ēr) Oct. 4, 1893—Jan. 11, 1950 Lutheran clergyman; preacher on, and supervisor of, the *International Lutheran Hour* broadcast, inaugurated in 1935; a member of the faculty of Concordia Theological Seminary (St. Louis, Missouri) since 1922; editor (1922-45) of the *Walther League Messenger*; a fundamentalist and, in delivery, an old-time evangelist; theological scholar and author. See *Current Biography*, 1947.

Obituary

    N Y Times p3 Ja 12 '50

MALIN, PATRICK MURPHY (mä'lĭn)
May 8, 1903- Official of civil liberties organization
Address: b. c/o American Civil Liberties Union, 170 5th Ave., New York 10; h. 221 N. Princeton Ave., Swarthmore, Pa.

On February 1, 1950, Patrick Murphy Malin became director of the American Civil Liberties Union, the second leader the organization has had since its foundation in 1920. A national nonpartisan organization, it is dedicated to maintaining and promoting the tenets of the United States Bill of Rights. In the international sphere freedom of communication and an international Bill of Rights are its two main objectives. Before becoming director of the A.C.L.U., Malin was a member of the economics department of Swarthmore College for twenty years. During the World War II period, on leave from the college, he held for four years the office of vice-director of the Intergovernmental Committee on Refugees. In his new position he will devote himself particularly to the question of civil liberties on the domestic scene.

Patrick Murphy Malin was born to Hanson Atkins Malin, a banker, and the former Ida Elizabeth Murphy in Joplin, Missouri, on May 8, 1903; he has one brother, Quintin Campbell. English Quakers, the first American Malins came to Pennsylvania about 1680; and the Campbells, the other branch of Malin's paternal grandparents, were Scottish Presbyterians who settled in the same region toward the end of the eighteenth century. His maternal grandparents were also Pennsylvanians: the Workizers, German Lutherans, arrived there in 1700, and the Murphys, Irish Catholics, in 1847. Both branches of grandparents moved westward in the second half of the 1800's.

In 1920, at the age of seventeen, Patrick Murphy Malin was graduated from the Joplin High School. At the University of Pennsylvania he majored in finance and commerce at the Wharton School, receiving the B.S. degree in economics in 1924. Throughout his school days Malin was prominent in numerous extracurricular activities, including basketball, ROTC, dramatics, the editing of school publications, and debating. He was class president in his junior and senior years. In college he became a member of the national forensic fraternity Delta Sigma Rho, presided over the Beta Pi chapter of the national social fraternity Pi Kappa Alpha, the Wharton School chapter of the honorary scholastic fraternity Beta Gamma Sigma, the Friars Senior Society, the Christian Association, and was news editor of *The Daily Pennsylvanian*. He was class valedictorian at both his high school and his college graduations. Over this period he held several part-time jobs, as milk deliverer, bank messenger, clerk, stenographer, and district agent for the Curtis Publishing Company.

Malin has stated that in his youth he was much impressed by the speeches of Woodrow Wilson. That, together with the influence of his English teacher at the Joplin High School, inclined him toward consular and diplomatic work. However, after a brief consideration of the ministry, upon graduating from college in 1924, he became private secretary to Sherwood Eddy of the International YMCA, a position he held until 1929. It was part of his duties to give talks and write articles on religious and social questions. He also managed an annual summer tour of approximately one hundred Americans to Western and Central Europe and to the Soviet Union. Part-time postgraduate studies in New York, at the Union Theological Seminary and Teachers College of Columbia University were concurrent with these activities from 1925 to 1927.

Still working with Sherwood Eddy, Malin considered entering the field of social administration, while his father-in-law, Clement M. Biddle, advised him to go into the teaching profession. In deliberating as to a choice between the teaching of religion and economics, Malin discussed the question with Reinhold Niebuhr [*], professor of applied Christianity at Union Theological Seminary. Upon the clergyman's advice, Malin enrolled in the graduate faculty of political science at Columbia University, where he studied economics in 1929-30 and 1931-32.

In 1930 Malin was called to Swarthmore (Pennsylvania) College, where he became an instructor in the department of economics. He remained on the faculty of that college until he assumed the position of director of the American Civil Liberties Union. In the course of those years he advanced to assistant, associate and full professor in his department. "I am not a research scholar," Malin has said, "and I am as much interested in practical nonacademic activity as I am in teaching, and live in a time when the world is in catastrophe or constant crisis." The emphasis of his instruction was therefore put on teaching his subject *"with a sense* of the infinite and the urgent, because that is how every bit of life should be lived, that is how everything should be taught. Nothing is fully taught or learned without relating it to its total environment; we need not be ashamed of the gospel of wholeness, the integrity of life." (This quotation is from *Teaching Economics with a Sense of The Infinite and The Urgent*, published by the Edward W. Hazen Foundation.)

Another of Malin's articles, "The Refugee: a Problem for International Organization," appeared in *International Organization*, September 1947; he also edited, with Clair Wilcox [*] and Herbert F. Fraser, *America's Recovery Program* (1934). In this collection of lectures on important aspects of the New Deal, the editors declare in their joint introduction that they "are in sympathy with the major purposes of Administration policy and find themselves in accord with many of the measures which have been adopted for their realization." In a similar spirit Malin has described himself as an "independent Democrat" whose "faith in a democratic society is grounded on the religious belief that every man should have the chance to fulfill his life, and should be free to contribute to the common fund of ideas his own idea of fulfillment."

(Continued next page)

Ihrig & Thomas

PATRICK MURPHY MALIN

In 1925 Malin became a fellow of the National Council on Religion in Higher Education, on whose board he served from 1937 to 1943 and whose president he was from 1939 to 1943; in 1947 he again became a member of the board. He was vice-chairman of the American Friends Service Committee from 1936 to 1938, where his activity included work in relief administration for both the Loyalists and the Insurgents in the Spanish Civil War. Various duties on an administrative level resulted in his obtaining a leave of absence from Swarthmore College from 1940 to 1947. Until 1942 American director of the International Migration Service in New York (which worked in the interests of refugees in Europe and the West Indies), Malin moved to Washington in that year to serve first as price executive of the Chemicals and Drugs Branch of the OPA and then as deputy chief of the Division of Programs and Requirements, Office of Foreign Relief and Rehabilitation Operations, Department of State. From 1943 to 1947 Malin was vice-director for the Intergovernmental Committee on Refugees in London, visiting in that capacity French North Africa, Italy, Egypt, Palestine, and Turkey in 1944, Germany and Austria in 1945, and Brazil in 1946.

The American Civil Liberties Union, established as an independent organization in 1920, is a corporation organized under the laws of New York. Its active membership consists of a board of directors numbering thirty-five (which meets biweekly) and a national committee of seventy-five individuals in various parts of the country; in addition there are local committees and branches. The staff at the national office is headed by a director, assistant director and office counsel. Funds are derived solely from contributing members (of whom there are some 8,000) to support an an nual budget of about $70,000; special projects have been financed by bequests and gifts. The union works chiefly through the courts, where its attorneys volunteer their services in cases involving civil liberties issues. The body also presses for its principles with administrative and legislative officials. In its efforts to enlist public support, the organization promotes publications, research and campaigns, and in 1950 sponsors, jointly with three other American agencies, a series of weekly radio dramatized programs, *How Secure These Rights.*

Having been active in the American Civil Liberties Union since its early years, Malin was unanimously elected director of the body by its board of directors on February 1, 1950. The new director considers its functions, according to the New York *Times*, the "most vital sort of work that can be done in a free society." In his new position, in addition to working for the implementation of President Truman's civil rights plan, he will concern himself with the problem of Government control and the imperilment of civil rights resulting from fear of Communist infiltration. While Malin will attack, for the present, such issues as loyalty tests and minority rights, his predecessor Roger N. Baldwin [40], as international affairs chairman, will continue to handle the union's international efforts; in that field the organization is cooperating with other American agencies to work with the United Nations Commission on Human Rights for an international Bill of Rights.

The establishment of a $25,000 Roger N. Baldwin Civil Liberties Foundation to encourage study in the subject by both foreign and American students was announced at a dinner on February 22, 1950, celebrating the thirtieth anniversary of the establishment of the union and honoring its retiring director. A recapitulation of the society's achievements included many instances of legal assistance rendered, of court cases initiated and supported defending civil liberties, and of participation in campaigns in Congress to promote the rights of labor. The occasion drew forth editorials in the *Christian Science Monitor*, the New York *World-Telegram and Sun*, and the New York *Times*, the last-named commenting, "The A.C.L.U. has been a valiant defender of some American fundamentals at the ground level, where it counts."

Malin is a member of the American Economic Association, the American Association of University Professors, the Council on Foreign Relations, the Garrick Club of London. In June 1928 he married Caroline Cooper Biddle, who that year had received the B.A. degree from Swarthmore College. Three sons were born to the couple—Robert Abernethy, Clement Biddle, and Randall. Malin is a brown-haired, blue-eyed, five-foot-eleven man with a weight of 175 pounds. He plays tennis and participates in amateur dramatics, likes symphony music and the theater, and considers it recreation to speak on economic, political, and religious topics.

References

Christian Cent 67:35 Ja 11 '50
Christian Sci Mon p4 Mr 11 '50
N Y Herald Tribune p16 D 23 '49; p3
    F 2 '50
N Y Post p5 F 12 '50 por
N Y Times p23 D 23 '49; p4 D 30 '49

MALLETTE, GERTRUDE E(THEL)
(mȧ-lĕt') Dec. 4, 1887- Author

Address: b. c/o Doubleday & Company, Inc., 14 W. 49th St., New York 20

GERTRUDE E. MALLETTE

Reprinted from the *Wilson Library Bulletin*, April 1950.

Gertrude E. Mallette is one of those fortunate authors who has mastered the art of concentration. As a result she finds that she can write under any conditions, by night or by day, in shorthand, longhand with pen or pencil, by typewriter or dictaphone. It is no wonder she has turned out an immense volume of work that includes more than twenty full-length juveniles as well as innumerable short stories and articles. To keep pace with her output she uses two pseudonyms in addition to her own name. She is Gertrude E. Mallette on one publisher's list, Alan Gregg on another, and Pedar Larssen on a third.

Gertrude Ethel Mallette was born December 4, 1887, in Victoria, British Columbia, the daughter of Charles E and Mary (Johnson) Mallette. She attended Washington State University in Seattle, doing postgraduate work in journalism. During her college years she began her career as a free-lance writer, with interviews and feature articles for various state newspapers and for syndicates. She also made good use of her camera, selling some fifteen thousand picture postcards of local views as well as scenes of industrial and farm progress to newspapers. She was a reporter and later editor for a college magazine. As a member of Professor Merle Thorpe's short-story class she produced a privately printed book of children's stories.

After leaving the university in 1912 Miss Mallette divided her time between newspaper work and teaching. She traveled a great deal, working as a reporter in Alaska, and later spending some years in New York City. There she studied juvenile story writing at Columbia University under Dr. Mabel L. Robinson. Her first book, *For Keeps* (1936), was a Junior Literary Guild selection, as were several of those that followed it. *For Keeps* was the first of a long series of career books for older girls, published under the author's own name. The "Alan Gregg" titles, seven of them since 1940, are boys' mystery stories. *Landlubber* (1940) and *Offshore Gold* (1941) are adventure stories for boys, ascribed to "Pedar Larssen."

Here are comments on the more recent Mallette books. *Single Stones* (1940) seemed to *Library Journal* "a good vocational story but less effective than some others." Ellen Buell in the New York *Times* thought it lacked individual characterization, but adds, "Marcia's fight against time, distraction, and weariness, in the

cause of medicine, is told with a mounting tensity and a clarity of detail which claim and hold the attention as closely as the complicated plot of a mystery story." *Into the Wind* (1941) was found by *Horn Book* to "depict the discipline and devotion of the nurse's training without the sentimentality that frequently mars books on this subject." Sonja Wennerblad in *Library Journal* found the book lacking in humor, but added, "It will, no doubt, be read with pleasure by a good many of our girls, and is deserving of a place on our shelves." *Inside Out* (1942) dealt with an ambitious young art student. *Library Journal* called it a "good fast-moving story with an interesting vocational element." Mrs. Becker in *Books* said, "There is a trace of romance, the art study is authentic, and so is the Hudson."

Wenderley (1943) describes life in a defense-worker trailer camp. Phyllis Whitney in *Book Week* said, "This is a vocational novel in the better sense and no mere guidebook to a job. . . . Interesting and solidly good." *Mystery in Blue* (1945) was a combined career and mystery-spy story that impressed Mrs. Becker as "unusually competent." *Once is Forever* (1946) describes a girl's attempt to rehabilitate her war-wounded fiancé. *Saturday Review of Literature* called it "an interesting novel on a timely theme." *Priceless Moment* (1947) shows a girl photographer involved in a mystery; *Library Journal* recommended it. *Unexpected Summer* (1949) recounts a girl's attempt to earn her college expenses by journalism and candy-making. *Library Journal*: "The value of the story lies in showing the caution and experience needed in both careers and the heroine's modestly reasonable success. In spite of the addition of a mystery and a love affair, the story seems to move slowly and be solider reading than many of this type." Virginia Kirkus said, "There's plenty of level-headed busi-

MALLETTE, GERTRUDE E.—*Continued*
ness thinking procedure in the story, and some
very good writing."

Miss Mallette lives and writes now in a
cabin on a California hillside, surrounded by
the beauties of nature which she has always
loved. Her favorite recreation is taking long
walks, five or ten miles or more, accompanied
by her dogs. Here, she says, she has "stayed
put" for the first time in her life, but adds
cheerfully, "I am just about to take off!" She
does not need, however, to travel for story
ideas. Those come of themselves, more than
she can use. And if the typewriter breaks down,
a pencil will do just as well.

MALONE, GEORGE W(ILSON) Aug. 7,
1890- United States Senator from Nevada
Address: b. Senate Office Bldg., Washington,
D.C.; h. Reno, Nev.

The junior United States Senator from Nevada, George W. Malone, was elected in the
Republican victory of 1946. A civil engineer,
he has a wide knowledge of natural resources
of the West, particularly in the fields of water
supply and power, irrigation, and flood control.
Before being sent to Washington, he was for
eight years State Engineer of Nevada and at
various times served as consulting engineer to
State and Federal officials. In Congress he, has
become known as a leader of opposition to
Marshall Plan appropriations.

George Wilson Malone was born in Fredonia,
Kansas, on August 7, 1890. He is the son
of J. W. and Vienna (McPherson) Malone.
Reared in Kansas and Nevada, he entered the
University of Nevada in the class of 1917 to
study civil and electrical engineering. He had
not yet graduated when, in 1914, he obtained
work as a civil and hydraulic engineer. In 1916
he organized a firm of construction engineers,
King and Malone (today The Malone Engineers). At the university he won distinction
as an athlete, captaining the university football
and baseball teams. Later, in 1920, representing
the university, he won the amateur middleweight
boxing championship of the Pacific coast.

With America's entry into World War I in
1917, Malone enlisted as a private in the United
States Army. Advanced to sergeant in the
Field Artillery with the Fortieth Division of
the AEF and then to lieutenant, he served during 1918-19 in England and France as line officer and regimental intelligence officer. Upon
his discharge Malone re-entered the University
of Nevada for further engineering studies.

Malone's engineering firm was especially engaged (according to *Who's Who in Engineering*) in projects of industrial engineering, power, reclamation, flood control, public utilities,
city works, traffic, and valuation work for tax
and rate making. Such engineering work led
Malone into a variety of public positions that
drew on his knowledge of Nevada's natural
resources. For eight years, from 1927 until his
resignation in 1935, Malone was State Engineer.
During those years he served as a member of
the Public Service Commission in Nevada, as
secretary and member of the Colorado River

Commission, and as a member of the National
Committee on Conservation and Administration
of Public Domain. He was also on the State
Bond Commission, the State's Irrigation and
Range Committees, and on the State Planning
Board.

Malone resigned from his State post in 1935
to resume practice as a consulting engineer.
That year he was adviser to the Secretary of
the Interior on the construction of Boulder
Dam (later named the Hoover Dam). His
*Report on Resources and Use of Power in the
Boulder Dam Area* was published in 1935. He
was also consulting engineer in organization
and financing for the Central Valley Water
Project in Nevada, and worked on the Board of
Supervisors of Los Angeles County, Orange
County, and Newport Harbor, California, on
flood control, water storage, and harbor im-
provements. In Nevada he was active as a
member of the Colorado River Advisory Board
and as engineer member of the Colorado River
Commission.

A non-Government project in which Malone
was engaged during these years was the Industrial West Foundation, a nonprofit corporation he founded and of which he was managing
director. From offices in San Francisco and
Washington, D.C. the foundation provided business and industrial information on eleven Western states, Alaska, Hawaii, and the Philippines,
and published an industrial encyclopedia on these
areas, edited by Malone. (The foundation's
data was used in the preparation of a 100-foot-
square relief map of the area for the Golden
Gate International Exposition in 1939.)

World War II took the Western engineer to
Washington, D.C., where in 1942 and 1943 the
Senate several times called him in as a consultant. His posts included that of special consultant to the Senate Military Affairs Subcommittee, special consultant on strategic and critical minerals and materials, and consultant to
the Chandler Committee of the Senate on Examination of Military Establishments. In the
last-named post he made an inspection tour of
military bases and strategic and critical minerals and materials in the Aleutian Islands,
Alaska, and the South Seas. He was also expert consultant to the Secretary of War.

In 1946 the Nevada Republican nomination
for United States Senator went to Malone, and
in November the engineer defeated his Democratic opponent, Berkeley L. Bunker (who had
been Nevada's Representative in the House) to
become his State's junior Senator. (Senior
Senator is Patrick A. McCarran '⁴⁷, a Democrat.) Malone was said to have received not
only the Republican vote but the vote of the
"Carville Democrats," a group who were angered when the Democratic nomination had not
gone to the then Senator Edward P. Carville.
Malone took his seat in the Republican-controlled Eightieth Congress in January 1947.
His term ends January 3, 1953.

Almost immediately the Nevadan won attention in the Senate as one of four Republican
legislators to propose a bill providing for an
immediate and substantial increase in rent ceilings and the removal of all rent controls by
the end of the year. He later voted for exten-

sion of controls to April 1948, and again, in the Eighty-first Congress, voted for rent control extension. Other controversial domestic legislation in which Malone had a part included a bill (of his drafting) in March 1947, to abolish the Atomic Energy Commission; he was one of a group which proposed instead a board to be headed by Secretary of State George C. Marshall and to include the Secretaries of War and Navy, with the aim of removing the bomb from civilian control.

When the Taft-Hartley bill passed the Senate in May 1947 Malone was one of three Republicans to oppose it. The Nevadan's opposition, however, rested on a different basis from that of most of the bill's opponents—Malone opposed any national labor legislation. Two years later (June 1949) in a Senate discussion of labor legislation Malone suggested repealing both the Taft-Hartley Act and the Wagner Act, leaving labor problems to the States, with some regulation from a Federal mediation service. Malone's vote was "Nay" on other Republican bills designed to curb union activity, such as bills to outlaw union shops and curb industry-wide bargaining.

In December 1947, after a survey trip to Europe, the Nevada Republican acted as leader of a group of eight Senators who proposed (without success) to slash the Administration's stop-gap relief program for France, Italy, and Austria from $597,000,000 to $400,000,000. At the Western Governors Conference in Portland, Oregon, December 12, 1947, Senator Malone, who had voted against the Greek-Turkish Aid Bill, attacked the Marshall Plan as a "world-wide WPA." In March Malone led the group of Senators working to cut funds for the European Recovery Program. With other Republicans he charged that the United States was arming Russia for a third world war through shipments to countries trading behind the Iron Curtain; he later proposed an amendment to the Marshall Plan to block aid to countries having trade treaties with Russia.

In late 1948 Malone undertook a survey (for the Natural Resources Economic Committee of the Senate, of which he was chairman) of the availability to the United States of the natural resources of Asiatic and other Eastern countries. In November, after conferences in China with Generalissimo Chiang Kai-shek, United States Ambassador J. Leighton Stuart, and others, Malone said he believed the Communist advance in China could be stopped if the United States provided sufficient supervised military aid to the Nationalists. (When, in 1950 he predicted the departure of Dean Acheson as Secretary of State, he charged State Department officials with "building up the Communist victory in China . . . advancing the cause of the Soviets through the world.") In 1948 Malone visited the Philippines, southeast Asia, and India. In New Delhi in December he charged that Marshall Plan aid, in supporting colonial powers (he named France and the Netherlands) against freedom movements in Southeast Asia, was costing America the good will of Asiatic peoples. (Other committees on which the Senator from Nevada has sat

GEORGE W. MALONE

include Public Works, Special Senate War Investigating, and Interior and Insular Affairs; he also serves on the Senate Office Building Commission.)

When the Economic Cooperation Act came up for discussion in April 1949 Malone proposed an amendment: that the United States provide assistance on the basis of loans only, the loans to be "fully and adequately secured," except where it was necessary to supply food or medicine to relieve human suffering. Shortly thereafter he voted against the North Atlantic Pact. He also opposed the military unification bill on the ground that it did not give enough power to the Secretary of Defense. Meanwhile, a new fight was developing in which Malone was to take a leading part—the opposition of a minority of Senators to the Reciprocal Trade Program (September 1949). Malone maintained that free trade was "importing unemployment." On this basis he had argued some months earlier for the restoration of a tariff on copper. The Reciprocal Trade Agreements bill passed the Senate 62-19, after the defeat 63-17 of Malone's "flexible import fee" proposal, which would tax imports to make up the differential between the cost of labor in the United States and abroad.

Senator Malone came into newspaper headlines in February 1950 when he called for a Congressional investigation of the loyalty of Michael J. Lee, chief of the Far Eastern Division of the Commerce Department, whom he accused of delaying supply shipments to Nationalist China. In June Malone introduced a Senate bill to supplant the Federal Loyalty Review Board with another board, independent of the Executive. In September of that year he made an eleven-hour filibuster against a bill to bar interstate shipment of slot machines.

Comments on the Nevada Senator have ranged from high praise to classification among the Senate's "most expendable" by *Time* maga-

MALONE, GEORGE W.—*Continued*
zine. In his April 1, 1950, column M. S. Rukeyser (International News Service) listed Malone as one of fifteen men who were "making significant contributions to the survival of the American competitive system," and praised him for his "levelheadedness in avoiding the bandwagon of internationalism." *Time* (March 20, 1950) called this "isolationism."

The Senator has been at various times department commander and national vice-commander of the American Legion, president of the Nevada Council of the Boy Scouts of America, and chairman of the organization and extension committee of the Boy Scouts, chairman of the Nevada State Board of Registered Professional Engineers, chairman of the Western States Silver Commission, and vice-president of the National Reclamation Association. He continues to hold membership in the American Society of Civil Engineers and the American Institute of Mining and Metallurgical Engineers (he was commissioned a United States Mineral Surveyor in California and Nevada). He is a Mason (32d Degree and a Shriner). A member of the San Francisco and Washington, D.C., press clubs, Malone has contributed articles to technical journals (*Engineering News Record* and *Electrical World*) as well as more recently (August 1949) an article to the *American Magazine* entitled, "We Can Give Away Too Much." He belongs to the Army and Navy Club in the capital.

Mrs. Malone, a San Francisco realtor, is the former Ruth Moslander. The Malones were married March 20, 1921. Their one daughter, Molly Patricia, is the wife of Dr. Michael J. O'Connor of Tucson, Arizona. ("Molly" is also the Senator's nickname.) The black-haired, blue-eyed Nevadan lists his recreations as hunting, fishing, and golf.

References

N Y Sun p16 Ja 20 '47
Congressional Directory (1950)
Who's Who in America, 1950-51
Who's Who in Engineering, 1948
Who's Who in Nevada, 1949-50
Who's Who in United States Politics (1950)

MANNING, WILLIAM THOMAS, BISHOP May 12, 1866—Nov. 18, 1949
American Protestant Episcopal bishop; educated at Sewanee (Tennessee) Seminary and the University of the South; professor of dogmatic theology at the University of the South, 1893-95; rector of churches in California and Tennessee; became assistant rector, then rector (1908) of Trinity Church in New York; served as Army chaplain at Camp Upton (Long Island) in 1918; consecrated Protestant Episcopal Bishop of New York on May 11, 1921; retired December 31, 1946; direct and sympathetic in manner, of ascetic nature; dogmatic in theology, "high church" in service; frequently center of controversy on questions of theology and morality; prominent in raising of funds for building of the Cathedral of St. John the Divine in New York City and in supervising its construction. See *Current Biography*, 1940.

Obituary

N Y Times p1 N 19 '49

MARQUIS, FREDERICK JAMES, 1st BARON WOOLTON *See* Woolton, F. J. M., 1st Baron

MARRIOTT, ALICE (LEE) (măr'rĭ-ŏt)
Jan. 8, 1910- Author; ethnologist
Address: h. 814 N.W. 31st St., Oklahoma City 3, Okla.

Reprinted from the *Wilson Library Bulletin*, Feb. 1950.

Besides being author of five books, with a sixth novel in progress (as of 1950), and having many articles both learned and popular published in periodicals, Alice Lee Marriott is a research ethnologist, museum consultant, and librarian. Additional diversion is derived from hobbies, chief of which are cooking and traveling. When asked about sports, however, she says, "The only sport I can honestly list is walking the dog—under protest from both of us."

Alice Marriott was born January 8, 1910, in Wilmette, Illinois. Her father, Richard Goulding Marriott, came to this country from England as a boy and settled near Chicago. Her mother, Sydney Kenner Cunningham, of a pre-Revolutionary Southern family, had been born and reared in Ohio. Little Alice was seven when the family settled in Oklahoma City. It was there she received most of her education and the first college degree, granted *magna cum laude*, in 1930. In 1935 a B.A. degree in anthropology (the first to a woman) was conferred upon her at the University of Oklahoma. Honors include Sigma Xi, 1935; Phi Beta Kappa, 1945; State's Outstanding Woman of 1945. "They were hard up for women that year," she has remarked.

She has filled many professional positions, among which are cataloger for the Muskogee (Oklahoma) Public Library; graduate assistant in the Department of Anthropology at the University of Oklahoma; and specialist in Indian Arts and Crafts for the United States Department of the Interior. Fortunately lacking the heavy hand of the pedant that results so often from the accumulation of scientific background, she writes superbly of Indians, Spanish Americans, and Anglo-Americans. A critic remarked in the Houston *Post*, "Alice Marriott won't make you laugh out loud. But she will give you a continuous, lasting, warm risibility, a feeling of well-being bordering on happiness, an almost symphonic sense of rightness that is missing from too much present day experience."

Her first writing success occurred during junior year at Central High School in Oklahoma City: she won first prize in a short story contest. But she promptly forgot all about writing,

ALICE MARRIOTT

vidual must make his own contribution to the goodness of the whole."

Blue-eyed and red-haired, Miss Marriott is five feet, six inches tall and pleasantly proportioned. She is an Episcopalian and a Democrat. "I have had a finger in a number of civic pies that never quite got baked," she states candidly. She is an interesting paradox, an infinitely shy person with an enormously intuitive gift for understanding people. Although she seems never to be "the artist at work" when carrying on a conversation, no detail of personality escapes her. It is particularly the women of the human race who claim her attention, and whom she depicts in her books.

The favorite authors of this versatile writer may come as somewhat of a surprise to her readers. Jane Austen, Mark Twain, and Thomas Beer are tied for first place. They are the writers whom she reads time and again without growing tired or bored. But they would not accompany her to that legendary desert island, where most of us expect to be stranded with our ultimate choice in good reading. Only one volume will be Miss Marriott's companion when that great day comes, because in that finite boundary of two covers she has found everything she wants. Its author? William Shakespeare.

except for necessary term papers, until she started *The Ten Grandmothers,* which was published (1945) by the University of Oklahoma Press. Since then her short stories and articles have appeared in *Mademoiselle, Harper's, American Mercury,* and the *Southwest Review,* as well as in the *Journal of the Texas Geographic Society.* Her other published books are *Winter-Telling Stories* (1947), *Maria, the Potter of San Ildefonso* (1948), *Indians on Horseback* (1948), and *The Valley Below* (1949). *Maria* was the choice of the Natural History Book Club for July 1948.

In spite of such literary achievement, Miss Marriott steadfastly refuses to regard herself as a writer in the usual sense of the word. "I am a research ethnologist, and the writing of reports is necessary to the completion of a research job." American critics, however, have differed with her opinion. "I do not know how high Miss Marriott may rank as an anthropologist, but in the management of her material as an author she is a genius," wrote E. DeGolyer in the *Saturday Review of Literature.* W. C. Tyrrel commented in part, "The author, an experienced ethnologist who has lived with descendants of the original inhabitants of this area, writes about her subject with sympathetic understanding. Readers of this book cannot help but obtain insight into the character and story of these 'first Americans' as well as a vivid impression of the Plains Indians." Writing of *Maria* in the New York *Herald Tribune,* critic Erna Fergusson pointed out: "In this book Maria lives as a woman, a noble woman, calm and finely tempered in herself and firmly integrated as one of an integrated society. Her book is refreshing and healing for us to read, especially now when we see our own society so sadly shattered by the results of our own cleverness. It is healing to see how people can live unquestioningly, knowing that each indi-

MARSHALL, M(APLE) LEE June 17, 1884—Aug. 1, 1950 Chairman of the board of the Continental Baking Corporation since 1926; president of that company, 1933-42; during World War II served with the United States Army Services of Supply, on the War Production Board, with the War Food Administration (director of the Office of Distribution, 1944); executive director of the Famine Relief Collection Drive, 1946; national chairman of American Overseas Aid, 1947. See *Current Biography,* 1948.

Obituary

N Y Times p25 Ag 2 '50

MARSHALL, WALTER P(ETER) Nov. 20, 1901- Telegraph company executive

Address: b. c/o Western Union Telegraph Company, 60 Hudson St., New York 12; h. 373 N. Village Ave., Rockville Centre, N.Y.

Walter P. Marshall became the president of the Western Union Telegraph Company in December 1948, when he succeeded the late Joseph L. Egan. Marshall has been connected with the business aspect of telegraph communications since he left college in 1921. An official of the Postal Telegraph System for thirteen years, he was appointed assistant to the president of Western Union when the two companies merged in 1943.

Born in Brooklyn, New York, on November 20, 1901, Walter Peter Marshall is the son of Peter Walter and Bertha H. (Fredericks) Marshall. He graduated from Bushwick High School, of that city, in 1918. For his college education he attended Pratt Institute (1918-19), Columbia University (1919-20), and the Col-

WALTER P. MARSHALL

lege of the City of New York (1920-21). His major studies were engineering and accounting.

In an interview published in the New York *Herald Tribune* Marshall told that he entered the communications field by sheer accident when he applied for a position as accountant at the All America Cable and Radio Company, in New York. "I thought they manufactured wire cables," he said. "Instead, they *sent* cables by wire!" For the next six years he was an accountant with that company and the Mexican Telegraph Company. In 1928 he entered the employ of the International Telephone and Telegraph Corporation, with which he remained until 1930. In that year he began his long association with the Postal Telegraph System, then the only major competitor of Western Union. From 1930 to 1943 Marshall was comptroller of Postal Telegraph, in the course of the same years also serving as chief accountant for the Commercial Cable Company (1930-38) and as comptroller for the Mackay Radio and Telegraph Company (1933-38). On December 30, 1942, he was elected vice-president and a director of Postal Telegraph System, and on May 24, 1943 became executive vice-president of the company.

Postal Telegraph Cable Company and its subsidiaries (founded in 1886 by John W. Mackay) were operating at a deficit in the 1930's. Although the Senate Committee on Interstate Commerce had reported favorably on a petition for the union of Postal Telegraph and Western Union in 1939, it was not until March 1943 that Congress passed a bill authorizing the amalgamation. By that time Western Union was transmitting 80 per cent of the nation's telegraph business, and Postal Telegraph had operated in 1942 with a loss of more than $4,000,000. In October 1943 Postal Telegraph became the 540th company to be absorbed by Western Union.

In the process of the merger Walter Marshall became assistant to the president of West-

ern Union and was elected a director. In 1945 he was made treasurer of the company, and in 1946 was elected vice-president in charge of the contract department, in which capacity he renegotiated contracts between the telegraph company and various railway lines. As assistant to president Joseph L. Egan he represented the company at Federal Communication Commission hearings, and took a leading part in rate proceedings in 1946. From 1946 to 1948 he was chief adviser to Egan in formulating company policy. Upon Egan's death on December 6, 1948, Marshall was named acting president, and on December 21 was elected to the presidency.

The Western Union Company was incorporated in New York in 1851 (seven years after Morse sent the first telegram) under the name of the New York and Mississippi Valley Printing Telegraph Company, with a single telegraph line running from Buffalo to St. Louis. In 1856 the corporation bought out thirteen competing lines, and changed its name to the Western Union Telegraph Company. *Business Week* (November 19, 1949) has pointed out that in spite of the fact that the company has operated at a loss for the past few years, it has carried out a mechanization program since the war at a cost of $80,000,000. Except for a $10,000,000 loan by the Reconstruction Finance Corporation, of which $7,000,000 has been repaid, this program has been largely financed, under Marshall's direction, out of depreciation and amortization reserves. As treasurer, he handled the reacquisition of what in March 1950 amounted to $17,105,000's worth of outstanding Western Union bonds, effecting an interest saving of more than $800,000 a year.

In 1948 Marshall "conceived and negotiated" the sale of the Western Union Building on the lower west side of New York City for $12,500,000 in cash. Use of the building was retained by Western Union on a twenty-five-year lease with a series of renewal options amounting to one hundred years. The net rental for the building, according to a press release issued by the company, amounts to less than "interest charges on an equivalent amount of the company's own bonds, and the previous depreciation charges on the building." The company announced at the time of the sale that the proceeds were to be used for the mechanization program and for additional debt retirement.

Two features of the company's mechanization program, designed to increase the speed, efficiency, and economy of telegraph operation, are the replacement of wire channels by radio-beam channels, and the establishment of fifteen regional "switching centers." The radio-beam system, announced in 1945, on a beamed channel 150 kilocycles wide, enables 1,280 messages to be transmitted simultaneously. It was termed, by a laboratories executive, "one of the most significant developments in communications in modern times, climaxing more than twenty years of research." Marshall has announced that the fifteenth and final switching center will be established at Portland, Oregon, in 1950. This nation-wide system of centers eliminates many manual processes in re-transmission of messages.

As a result of a continued drop in revenue (amounting, according to *Business Week*, to 6 per cent in the first nine months of 1949 as compared with the same period in 1948), Marshall presented to the United States Congress in October 1949 what has been called the "Marshall Plan—of Communications." Pointing to what he termed "wasteful duplication" of service in the field of "record" communication (any means of communication which produces a message recorded on paper, such as teletype or telespring), he has proposed a "streamlined, world-wide telegraph and teletype system operated by his company." Denying that Western Union has a monopoly, Marshall is quoted by the New York *Times* as saying, "It competes with the subsidized and tax-free air mail, with long-distance telephone and telegraph services of telephone companies, and with the Government communications system."

In an exchange of letters with Senator Ernest W. McFarland, chairman of the communications subcommittee of the Senate Interstate and Foreign Commerce Committee, the Western Union head proposed that Congress adopt a policy which would permit unification with Western Union of the domestic record communications services of the American Telephone and Telegraph Company and independent companies, and of the international record communications services of RCA Communications, Inc., American Cable and Radio Corporation, and other United States companies operating in the international field. He also proposed that the problem of Government facilities competing with the private companies be solved. Writing of the need for adequate telegraph service "in an atomic era," Marshall assured Congress that the result of such action would be "a sound, solvent and aggressive record communication system both in the domestic and international field." The 1943 merger legislation stated Western Union must dispose of its international communications system, but other laws do not permit a merger of international carriers, and Marshall requested enabling legislation.

Another deterrent to Western Union's solvency, Marshall has declared, is the 25 per cent Government tax on telegrams, which in 1949 amounted to $36,514,236. He has been quoted as saying, "People pay a heavier tax to send a wire than they do to sit in a night club." *Business Week* quoted a Federal Communications Commission estimate that "if the tax were taken off both telegrams and toll calls, Western Union's net operating revenue would increase from $3,000,000 to $5,000,000 annually," an increase which would have kept the company out of the red in 1949. Marshall has urged repeal of this "discriminatory" tax.

The communications executive was elected chairman of the board of directors of The American District Telegraph Company in 1949. In addition to his directorship at Western Union and numerous subsidiaries of that company, he is a director of the American Express Company, United Paramount Theatres, Inc., and the Teleregister Corporation. He is a member of the Controllers Institute of America, the National Association of Cost Accountants, and the Newcomen Society of England. His clubs are the Arkwright and the Rockville Country Club, his political affiliation is Republican. He is a communicant of the Lutheran Church. Mrs. Marshall is the former Alice Barnes; married in 1930, they have two children, Peter Walter and Nancy Alice.

References

N Y Herald Tribune p27 Ja 18 '50 por
N Y Times p5 D 22 '48 por
Who's Who in America, 1950-51

MATTHEWS, BURNITA SHELTON
Dec. 28, 1894- Judge

Address: b. Investment Bldg., Washington, D.C.; h. 1915 Kalorama Rd., N.W., Washington, D.C.

Mrs. Burnita Shelton Matthews, one of America's foremost champions of equal rights for women, is the second woman to sit on the bench of a United States Court of general jurisdiction. (The first is Judge Florence Allen '41, of the Sixth Circuit Court of Appeals.) Mrs. Matthews was nominated by President Truman to one of the judgeships in the United States District Court for the District of Columbia in October 1949. She donned her judicial robes in November to preside under interim appointment until confirmed by the Senate. During more than twenty years of law practice in Washington, D.C., Mrs. Matthews helped to advance the cause of rights for women by drafting laws for sponsorship by the National Woman's Party. In that organization she has held the positions of legal research secretary and chairman of the lawyers council, and is a member of its national council.

Burnita Shelton Matthews was born in Burnell, Mississippi, on December 28, 1894, to Burnell and Lora Drew (Barlow) Shelton; she was the only girl in a family of five children. Early she showed an aptitude for oratory by winning several contests. When a noted Mississippi attorney once remarked to her father, "You ought to make a lawyer out of that little girl," her father's reply was "monumentally negative," according to Bill Brinkley, writing in the Washington *Post* of November 7, 1949. The possessor as well of a musical talent, in her teens she was sent to the Cincinnati Conservatory of Music to study piano and voice in preparation for teaching or concert work—her father thought she would be "happier doing what women did down there in Mississippi."

It has been related of Mrs. Matthews that she acquired a taste for the courtroom in her formative years. Her father, a tax collector, later became court clerk in the Mississippi town of Hazelhurst, to which the family had moved. She would often go to the courthouse, and when her father traveled on political campaigns she accompanied him. Accordingly, while the conservatory student pursued her musical education, at night she studied legal volumes, some of which she obtained from cousins who were lawyers. "Thinking to discourage this flighty 18-year-old girl," Brinkley wrote, "they

Wide World Photos
BURNITA SHELTON MATTHEWS

sent back their biggest, dustiest, and most technical law books." "Fascinated" by the tomes, she has said, she continued her unguided law reading for several years after leaving the conservatory, while she was teaching music in public schools in Texas, Georgia, and Mississippi.

After two years of teaching, Miss Shelton went to Washington, D.C. There, by working during the day at the Veterans Administration, she was able to support herself and to begin studying in evening classes at the National University Law School. Having become established in the capital, she wrote to her father of her intention, and he replied with an offer of assistance. Her law course completed, she received her LL.B. degree from the National University Law School in 1919, and her LL.M. in 1920, after which she began practicing law in Washington. She was admitted to the District bar in 1920 and to the bar of the Supreme Court in 1924. (She is also a member of the Mississippi bar.)

An enthusiastic feminist, the future judge became a member of the National Woman's Party: she took part in the fight for the passage of the suffrage amendment, picketing the White House along with other members of her sex; and on Sundays, she has related, she went to the organization's headquarters to seal envelopes. In the N.W.P. she has held the positions of legal research secretary and chairman of the lawyers council, and is a member of its national council. She took part in the National Woman's Party conferences preparing for the organization of the Inter-American Commission of Women in 1928. The lawyer also promoted the cause of women's rights on the committee of experts on women's work of the International Labor Office. The position of women before the law has been the subject of a number of monographs, pamphlets and maga-

zine articles by Mrs. Matthews. A compendium of laws from all States which were discriminatory toward women, regarded as an authority on the subject, was compiled by a research staff of attorneys under her leadership. On the basis of this study, she wrote an article entitled "Legal Discrimination Against Women Existing in the United States Today," which appeared in the *Congressional Digest* in March 1924. In it she discussed injustices in the law relating to guardianship of children, inheritance rights, public positions, jury duty, citizenship rights, burdens of illegitimate parenthood, married women's disabilities, and the restriction of women's property rights.

Mrs. Matthews was instrumental in getting on the statute books the 1927 law which gives women the right to serve on juries in the District of Columbia and she framed the 1935 statute revising the District of Columbia law on descent and distribution so as to eliminate preferences for the male line. She drafted similar inheritance bills enacted by the States of New York and Arkansas. Mrs. Matthews is author also of general laws: one passed in 1944 providing means whereby a District of Columbia property owner may free his real estate from an obsolete tax sale is of her framing.

President Truman nominated Mrs. Burnita Shelton Matthews to be a Federal district judge for the District of Columbia on October 17, 1949, and on November 9 Mrs. Matthews' investiture took place under interim appointment, pending confirmation in the permanent position by the Senate. The new judge attributed her appointment to "the fact that women throughout the country have wanted representation." Mrs. Matthews was the only woman endorsed for the post by the District Bar Association. To this support was added the backing of Mrs. India Edwards, head of the Women's Division of the Democratic National Committee. Mrs. Edwards wrote President Truman as follows: "If among the twenty-seven new judges there is not one woman included, then I think every law school should close its doors to women." Mrs. Edwards said the real credit belonged to united backing of more than twenty national and local women's groups, both Negro and white, and the support of several Administration Senators, spearheaded by Senator Estes Kefauver '49.

The new judge has long been an advocate of an equal rights amendment to the Constitution. In an article in the *Congressional Digest* of November 1930, entitled "The Next Step Toward Complete Independent Nationality for Women," she stated the case for amendment as a desirable method of establishing equal rights. Soon after her nomination to the judgeship she emphasized the point anew in a speech, saying, "An equal rights amendment to the Constitution would. . .secure equality of legal rights for women as far as they can be secured by law".

Judge Matthews is a member of the American Bar Association, the National Association of Women Lawyers (president, 1934-35), the Women's Bar Association of the District of Columbia (ex-president), Kappa Beta Pi, Women's City Club of Washington, D.C. (ex-president), and the Hazelhurst Business and

Professional Women's Club. At one time she served on the research committee of the Inter-American Commission of Women. She is a former member of the faculty of the Washington College of Law. Her lawyer husband, Percy A. Matthews, is with the office of the Judge Advocate. A colleague has described Judge Matthews as having "the judicial temperament, poise, a pleasing manner, yet firmness." In politics she is a Democrat, in religion a Methodist.

References

Equal Rights 35:49 N-D '49
Ind Woman 29:60 F '50
Washington (D.C.) Post p1 O 18 '49; p1B N 7 '49

Who's Who in America, 1950-51
Who's Who in the East (1948)

MATTHEWS, T(HOMAS) S(TANLEY)
Jan. 16, 1901- Editor; journalist
Address: b. c/o Time, Time & Life Bldg., Rockefeller Plaza, New York; h. 32 Edgehill St., Princeton, N.J.

T. S. Matthews, the managing editor of *Time* ("The Weekly Newsmagazine" is its subtitle) since 1943 and a member of its staff since 1929, became the editor of the weekly newsmagazine in December 1949. He succeeded Henry R. Luce [41], cofounder and principal stockholder, who retains the title of editor in chief of the several enterprises of Time Incorporated. Before joining *Time*, Matthews was on the editorial staff of *New Republic*.

Matthews is of English, Irish, and Welsh descent, a paternal ancestor having settled in America about 1660, a maternal ancestor about 1800. His father, the Right Rev. Paul Matthews, an Episcopalian clergyman now retired, was Bishop of New Jersey when he ended his active ministry in 1937; editor Matthews' mother was the former Elsie Procter. The second child and the only son in a family of six children, Thomas Stanley Matthews was born January 16, 1901, in Cincinnati, Ohio, where his father had been rector of St. Luke's Church since 1896; later (1904-13) the elder Matthews was dean of St. Paul's Cathedral in the same city. It was accordingly in Cincinnati and suburban Glendale that the boy received his early education; and during his eleventh and twelfth years he attended the Park Hill School, in Hampshire, England. In 1913, when his father became dean of the Episcopal cathedral at Faribault, Minnesota, and professor in the Seabury Divinity School, young Matthews returned to America to be enrolled in Shattuck School in the Minnesota town. Later he became a student at St. Paul's School, in New Hampshire, where his extracurricular activities included a minor editorship of the school paper and tennis playing.

Graduated from St. Paul's in 1918, Matthews enrolled at Princeton University (his family had moved to Princeton when his father was made Bishop of New Jersey) to major in English. He was a sergeant in the Student

Halsman

T. S. MATTHEWS

Army Training Corps in 1918. While at Princeton he became chairman of the *Nassau Literary Magazine* and contributed to the 1922 *Book of the Tuesday Evening Club*. After receiving the B.A. degree in 1922, Matthews took further studies in England, at New College, Oxford, and was granted the B.A. degree in 1924 (Honours School of English Language and Literature).

Matthews began his career in the magazine field the following year, when he became proofreader and make-up man for the weekly *New Republic*. Later he was a contributor to the columns of that periodical, one of his earliest pieces being "Good News for Sinners" (December 1936), a parody of the style of the Reverend Frank Buchman [40], founder of the Oxford Group movement. After 1927, when Matthews became an associate editor of *New Republic*, his name was regularly attached to book reviews and special articles; he also wrote unsigned editorials and editorial paragraphs. Some of his signed pieces were in a light or satiric vein (for example, a series of *Premature Obituaries* for such public figures as President Coolidge and Judge Webster Thayer, the latter of Sacco-Vanzetti trial fame), a skit on Mayor James J. Walker in the style of Archibald Marshall). In December 1927, he revealed in "Mass Meeting" (on college football rallies) an eye and ear for impressionistic reporting and in September 1929 his article "Gastonia on Trial" evoked admiration as a criticism of certain facets of American justice.

It was in 1929 that Matthews accepted the offer of books editorship of the newsmagazine *Time*, founded six years earlier by Henry R. Luce and the late Briton Hadden. Matthews remained the magazine's book critic for approximately eight years. By 1936 the weekly circulation of *Time* had risen to well over half a million copies. (The newsmagazine's pro-

MATTHEWS, T. S.—*Continued*

prietors had in the meantime added to their publishing enterprises the monthly *Fortune* in 1930, *Architectural Forum* in 1932, and the pictorial weekly *Life* in 1936.) In September 1937 Manfred Gottfried, appointed managing editor of *Time*, chose three new assistant managing editors, one of whom was Matthews. The latter was placed in charge of "back-of-the-book departments"—the book, theater, press, religion, and sports pages. These reviews and reports, in common with the magazine's longer articles, are unsigned.

The newsmagazine was meanwhile moving into the field of general reporting. Definitely committed to this field by the outbreak of World War II, it began to establish its exclusive news-gathering services (Time Incorporated today has its own bureaus in some thirty American and foreign cities, plus many part-time "stringers" elsewhere). Its greatly expanded scope (including a Latin-American edition inaugurated in 1941), losses of personnel to the armed forces, and other factors brought about a staff reorganization in March 1942. At that time Matthews was promoted to the post of executive editor. A further "reshuffle" followed in February 1, 1943, when Gottfried became co-editor with Henry Luce. Matthews succeeded Gottfried as managing editor and thus (in the words of *Newsweek*) was to "see the magazine through the newsiest period of its career." Among the notable innovations of his managership was the launching, in 1946, of *Time*'s Atlantic and Pacific overseas editions, printed abroad in English from air-expressed film.

Time observed its twenty-fifth year on March 3, 1948—its circulation was then upwards of one and one-half million. The anniversary issue (March 8) described in detail the evolution of a *Time* news story, from assignment through research, writing, styling and final editing. The articles are passed by senior departmental editors to the managing editor (Matthews' title at that time), who, "from the start of the work week has been reading papers, magazines, dispatches, trying to get the 'feel' of the week's news. . . .He has probably sent out forty or fifty notes to editors and writers." "Matthews," the account continued, "is the 'one man' through whose head all *Time* stories go before they are directed toward *Time*'s methodical 'one man' reader. Before he scribbles 'TSM' in the upper right-hand corner of the copy, Matthews has to understand the story, to believe it, and to admit grudgingly that its language is as clear, forceful, and readable as it can reasonably be made. His taste sets *Time*'s style, his interest and values have an important . . . influence on what *Time* says." By this time Gottfried had gone to Europe as chief of correspondents, and Matthews had become Luce's principal consultant on policy.

Early in 1949 Matthews was temporarily placed (in the words of *Newsweek*) "on the sidelines pondering, according to Luce's direction, ways and means of making *Time* not only a better magazine, but a better place to work." This assignment included a personnel research project and a tour of the newsmagazine's European offices. On December 21, 1949, it was announced that Luce, while retaining the title of editor in chief of *Time, Life* and *Fortune*, had relinquished the post of editor of *Time* to Matthews. "This marks a great step forward in the history of *Time*," Luce declared. "Henceforth *Time* will have a full-time editor instead of only my part-time services in that capacity." With his managing editor (former executive editor Roy Alexander), Matthews (in *Time*'s words) "stands responsible for whatever *Time* says." As was Editor Luce's province, "he watches the *Time* operation for opportunities to improve methods, and for signs that standards are not being met."

The journalist-editor is the author of two novels which made their appearance in the 1930's; *To the Gallows I Must Go* (1931), based on the Snyder-Gray murder case; *The Moon's No Fool* (1936), "a bold imaginative flight . . . a myth sermon" (*Time*), which the New York *Herald Tribune* critic saw as an attempt "to externalize in action and character the growth of the inner mind." In the year Matthews joined *New Republic*, he married Juliana Stevens Cuyler (May 16, 1925); four sons were born to them—Thomas Stanley, Jr., John Potter Cuyler, Paul Clement 2d, and William Alexander Procter. (Mrs. Matthews died in December 1949.) The editor, who is an Episcopalian, votes as an independent. Five feet eleven inches tall, he weighs 175 pounds; the color of his eyes is green, and his hair has become grizzled. For physical recreation he may play tennis or squash racquets. In New York his clubs are the Century Association, the River Club, the Coffee House; in Princeton, his place of residence, he is a member of Pretty Brook Tennis Club and Nassau Gun Club.

References

Newsweek 35:49 Ja 2 '50
Time 55:66+ Mar 8 '48 pors
America's Young Men, 1938-39
Who's Who in America, 1950-51
Who's Who in the East (1948)

MAYES, MRS. GILFORD (HAROLD)
May 16, 1898- Political leader

Address: b. c/o Republican National Committee. 1337 Connecticut Ave., Washington 6, D.C.; h. 807 McKinley Ave., Kellogg, Idaho

Mrs. Gilford Mayes became the assistant chairman of the Republican National Committee in January 1950. In this post, to which she was appointed by Chairman Guy George Gabrielson [49], she will attend regional conferences of precinct workers, particularly in the Republican pivotal States, to arouse their efforts toward making the 1950 Congressional elections a Republican victory. After twenty years of campaign work for the Republican party in city and State groups in Idaho, Mrs. Mayes was elected Republican National Committeewoman for that State in 1948. In this capacity she has served on various projects, among them the fifteen-member policy committee which drafted the sixteen-point statement of principles (supplementing the 1948 G.O.P. platform) for the 1950 election campaign.

Rose Gorr Mayes was born May 16, 1898, in Anaconda, Montana, to Frank B. and Maude (Sunderland) Gorr. The parents of Mrs. Gorr, a granddaughter of a Methodist minister in Missouri, left that State when their daughter was a child, to settle in Anaconda. Frank B. Gorr, described as "a grand old Pennsylvania Dutchman," migrated to Anaconda from Pennsylvania in 1895. There he maintained the baggage room for the Butte, Anaconda, and Pacific Railway, later becoming the railroad agent. Mrs. Mayes has one brother, Charles (an automobile dealer in Anaconda), and one sister Alice (Mrs. Don McKinley).

Rose Gorr attended Anaconda High School, where she went in for basketball and dramatics; she was graduated in 1917. Walter Todd Scott, then teaching at that school, recognized young Miss Gorr's flair for public speaking and coached her. In 1917 she won the school's extemporaneous speaking contest. From high school she went to the Anaconda Business College to study bookkeeping. In 1918 she became a billing clerk in the Anaconda Copper Mining Company's brick department— "I billed every brick in the tallest smelter stack in the United States," said Mrs. Mayes in an interview years later. In 1919 she became office manager for the Zellerbach Paper Company (Spokane, Washington), a position she held until the early 1920's, when she moved to Kellogg, Idaho, (her present home) to work as bookkeeper and office manager for the Smith & McIntosh Lumber Company. By that time she had become Mrs. Gilford Harold Mayes, her marriage having taken place on October 1, 1919. She ended her business career in 1928, before the birth of her son Hal. Mrs. Mayes's interest in politics is shared by her husband, who before his present position (he is assistant purchasing agent for a mining company) served a term in the Idaho State Legislature.

The Idaho housewife's first office within the Republican party was as committeewoman for Shoshone County. From that time, the early 1920's, she was active in precinct, district, and county work until 1942, when she was elected vice-chairman of the Idaho State Republican Committee. Active also in women's political groups, she organized the Idaho Federation of Women's Republican Clubs in 1943, was its president from that year until 1948. She served on the advisory board and executive committee of the National Federation of Women's Republican Clubs during the years 1944-48 and as its fourth vice-president after 1948. While holding the vice-chairmanship of the Idaho State Republican Committee, she was credited by Knox Manning, CBS radio commentator, with saving Idaho Republicans from defeat in the 1946 Congressional election. In a biographical piece Manning broadcast over a national hookup in 1950, he said, "Rose Mayes has prodded, cajoled, and sometimes insulted party workers to get results." Not sharing the confidence with which State committee members were accepting predictions for "an easy G.O.P. victory" in 1946, Mrs. Mayes sent out urgent

MRS. GILFORD MAYES

pleas to party workers to carry on a strenuous vote-getting campaign. In the 1948 Presidential election Mrs. Mayes, who in that year had been elected Republican National Committeewoman for Idaho, cautioned fellow Republicans "not to count their votes before they were cast, though victory on paper sounded a cinch." That year the Democrats swept her State. Chosen as an Idaho delegate to the 1944 Republican National Convention, Rose Mayes distinguished herself by being the only woman delegate to make a seconding speech for the nomination of Thomas E. Dewey as President. She acted also as a member of the convention platform committee and as chairman of the special Western conference on Pacific Coast problems.

The fifteen-member policy committee, on which Mrs. Mayes served during January 1950, adopted (with the approval of the Republican Senate and House committees) for the Republican party slogan, "Liberty vs. Socialism." The declaration of principles, approved unanimously, included a restatement of the 1948 platform principles and sixteen supplementary principles. The latter deal with greater government economy and efficiency; protection of liberty from big labor, from big business, and from big government; a foreign policy, "to repair damage" of Administration's Far Eastern policy, in which lack of coherence resulted in loss of China to Communist control, and a continued bipartisan cooperation, provided Democratic Administration will consult in advance with Republican leaders; a farm program; equal opportunity or civil rights; a national health program; a stand against subversive activities; a program for social security and pensions, war veterans, national defense, natural resources, and foreign trade; release by the Federal Government (to States) of certain taxable areas; the Hoover Commission report. It was while sitting with this Policy committee that the Idaho committeewoman was

MAYES, MRS. GILFORD—*Continued*

chosen on January 21, 1950, by Republican National Chairman Guy George Gabrielson for the assistant chairmanship, which had been vacant since the resignation of Mrs. Robert W. Macauley '49 the previous year.

Though the Idaho political leader had planned to come forward as a candidate for Congress, she accepted the post. In April 1950, on her return from her first precampaign tour of five Western States, Mrs. Mayes reported, "I found women voters everywhere worried about the cost of government and about the foreign situation." The old Guard of Republican party women, she said, were "in a campaign mood," but there were too many indifferent voters who needed to be awakened to their political responsibilities. On March 19, she had been quoted in the New York *Herald Tribune*: "I expect to travel constantly. . . .I intend to speak only facts—hard, cold facts—and I am confident that the sound common sense and judgment of American women will awaken and become active. against the genuine crisis that faces our country." She also remarked that elaborate social functions have no place in women's political groups: "They restrict attendance to women who can afford such luxuries."

Aside from her political activities, Mrs. Mayes lists memberships in the following organizations: American Legion Auxiliary, Order of the Eastern Star (past matron of the local chapter), Rainbow for Girls in Kellogg Assembly (mother adviser), Daughters of the Nile (Spokane, Washington). "During World War II," Mrs. Mayes reports, "I was a supervisor of bandage rolling and county bookkeeper for the Red Cross; and I've worked on every antituberculosis, Red Cross, and Youth Center drive ever held in Kellogg."

The Mayes live in a modest but comfortable home in Kellogg. Their son Hal in 1950 was a senior at the University of Idaho; Frank Gorr, their second son, is a sophomore at Northwestern University. Both boys work during summer vacations to finance their college expenses. Five feet four and one-half inches in height, the Republican leader weighs 130 pounds, has brown eyes and brown hair. She dresses simply, frequently wearing suits of black, gray, or green. A sports fan, she likes to watch basketball games. Her church is the Christian Science.

References

N Y Herald Tribune II p2 Mr 19 '50
Who's Who in America, 1950-51

MAYES, ROSE GORR *See* Mayes, Mrs. G. H.

MEILING, RICHARD L(EWIS) (mī'lĭng)

Dec. 21, 1908- United States Government official; physician

Address: b c/o Department of Defense, Washington 25, D.C.; h. 2205 E. Broad St., Columbus, Ohio

When the Office of Medical Services of the Department of Defense was organized in July 1949, Dr. Richard L. Meiling was appointed deputy director of the new service; on October 1, 1949 he became its director. Established as part of the program unifying the armed forces, the office's chief function is to coordinate the medical facilities of the Army, Navy, and Air Force to achieve their "maximum economic use." Meiling, a specialist in gynecology and obstetrics on the Ohio State University faculty, had been consultant for a year to the Surgeon General of the Army and the Surgeon General of the Air Force. In 1950 a brigadier general in the United States Air Force Reserve, he had served with the Air Force in World War II, and was responsible for organization of the air evacuation program of military patients from battlefields and overseas medical stations to hospitals in the United States

Richard Lewis Meiling was born December 21, 1908, in Springfield, Ohio, one of three sons of Lester Lewis and Matilda (Lobenherz) Meiling. His father, a diamond expert, owned a jewelry store in Springfield. The elder Meiling's father came from Norway, his mother stemmed from a Maryland family which had migrated to Ohio in 1827. Of German descent, Matilda Meiling taught that language in the Springfield public schools before her marriage; her father was the proprietor of a large bakery and dairy establishment.

Meiling attended Springfield High School, where he was manager of the football and basketball teams, and business manager of the school paper and yearbook. Following his graduation in 1926, he enrolled at Springfield's Wittenberg College as a premedical student. Here his extracurricular activities included intramural athletics, and he was a member of the Phi Kappa Psi fraternity. In his junior year he was circulation manager of the college yearbook. When he graduated in 1930 with a B.A. degree, he was selected to deliver the Class Gift Oration.

In 1932 Meiling went to Germany for his medical training, to the University of Erlangen (1932-34) and the University of Munich; the latter conferred the M.D. degree upon him in 1937. The subject of his thesis was "Vitamin C Content of the Wild Rose (crataegus oxyacantha) and its Use in the Daily Diet." He returned to the United States to serve his internship at Ohio State University Hospital in Columbus (1938), at University Hospital at Cleveland (1938-39), and at White Cross Hospital at Columbus (1939-40). His specialty was obstetrics and gynecology.

On October 7, 1940, Meiling entered the United States Army as a first lieutenant in the Medical Corps Reserve. After a short period as adjutant of the 52d Medical Battalion, Medical Supply Officer, First Army Corps, he went to the Army Air Force School of Aviation Medicine, from which he graduated in 1941. He now became Assistant Surgeon of the First Air Force and Eastern Defense Command. In 1942 he attended and graduated from the Command and General Staff School. "The combination of military medicine and staff work," he has said, "has been stimulated by a desire to work hand in hand with the military leaders and provide them with the best medical advice obtainable based on an intimate knowledge of their military staff problems."

In September 1942 Meiling was placed in charge of the "planning, organization and administration" of the new program of air evacuation of wounded from world-wide stations. During the next year 173,000 patients of the United States and Allied forces were evacuated from combat zones by air. Writing in *Plane Talk* (organ of the Consolidated Vultee Aircraft Corporation) in 1944, Meiling emphasized the benefits of this program: "Had the patients from Karachi [India] been returned by hospital or transport ship, it would have required a minimum of two and one-half months' travel. By air they were en route less than one week. Consider how this affects the patient's medical course and morale." In a speech made before the Aero Medical Association of the United States and reported in the *Journal of Aviation Medicine* (April 1944), Meiling discussed the special problems of air-borne patients, and concluded. "We, who tomorrow will practice medicine, must think in terms of global medicine and we who will specialize in aviation medicine must consider our patients, regardless of ailment or physical condition, from the standpoint of global air travel."

During 1943 and 1944 Meiling was stationed at AAF headquarters in Washington, D.C., where he served successively as chief of the plans division of the Office of the Air Surgeon, as air evacuation officer and special assistant to the Air Surgeon. In 1944 he served, in addition to his other duties, as Assistant Surgeon to the Twentieth Air Force. From late 1944 through 1945 he was chief of the morale division of the United States Strategic Bombing Survey (Europe). He was relieved from extended active duty on January 2, 1946, with the rank of colonel; in the United States Armed Forces Reserve he holds the active reserve status of brigadier general. In recognition of his war services he was awarded the Secretary of War Commendation Ribbon in 1942 and the Legion of Merit in 1945; he was a recipient of the ETO medal with two battle clusters.

Upon his return to civilian life Dr. Meiling joined the faculty of Western Reserve University at Cleveland, in the department of gynecology. In 1947 he returned to Ohio State University to be instructor in the department of pathology and assistant professor in the department of gynecology and obstetrics.

The American Medical Association in 1948 instituted a council on national emergency medicine "to make continuing studies of the multitude of problems related to the medical, health and sanitary services required by the civilian population, industry, agriculture, as well as the armed forces, in time of national emergency." As secretary of that council, Meiling met with Arthur M. Hill '48, chairman of the National Security Resources Board, to discuss medical problems involved in a "coordinated civilian, industrial and armed forces mobilization," and with the Secretaries of Defense, the Army, Navy and Air Force to discuss "immediate

U. S. Air Force Photo.
RICHARD L. MEILING

and future problems" of the medical services of the armed forces.

In 1949 a civilian advisory committee was appointed by the late Secretary of Defense James Forrestal to study the economy of the medical services of the armed forces following the unification program. A result of the work of this committee was the establishment of the Office of Medical Services in July 1949. Upon the resignation of the first director of the latter, Dr. Raymond Allen (president of the University of Washington), Meiling was appointed to the post on October 1, 1949.

Secretary of Defense Louis Johnson announced on February 1, 1950, that, upon Meiling's recommendation, eighteen military hospitals in the United States would be closed or changed in status, effecting an estimated economy of $25,000,000 a year. A House Armed Services Committee investigating the proposed economy program, on March 8, 1950, requested the Secretary of Defense to suspend the reduction order until after further Congressional study of objections which had been raised. The Veterans Administration's need for hospital facilities pending the completion of its own building program was mentioned, and a possible curtailment of the professional training program of the Army Medical Corps as a result of the cutback was envisaged. Both Meiling and his proposal were endorsed by civilian doctors, including ten members of the Armed Forces Medical Advisory Committee. Meiling's "ability and objectivity" were commended, and the need for reduction in military medical services were characterized as having been apparent for some time.

The medical executive has held such advisory posts as medical adviser to the Task Force on National Security Organization, membership on the Commission on the Organization of the Executive Branch of the Government (the

MEILING, RICHARD L.—*Continued*

Hoover Commission), and on the Armed Forces Medical Advisory Committee to the Secretary of Defense. He was adviser to the United States delegation to the Third World Health Assembly of the World Health Organization, in Switzerland in May 1950. He holds an honorary degree of D.Sc., conferred by Wittenberg College in 1950, and is an honorary fellow of the Airline Medical Examiners Association. A diplomate of the American Board of Obstetrics and Gynecology, a fellow of the American College of Surgeons, and a fellow of the Aero Medical Association, Meiling has written articles for medical periodicals, including *The Journal of the Indiana Medical Association, Surgery, Gynecology and Obstetrics*, and the *Ohio State Medical Journal*. Some of the medical societies in which he holds membership are the Central Association of Obstetricians and Gynecologists, the Royal Society of Medicine (London), the Association for Study of Internal Secretion, the American Medical Association, and the Columbus Surgical Society. He belongs to Alpha Kappa Kappa (medical fraternity), to the American Legion, the Reserve Officers Association, the Air Force Association, and the Air Reserve Officers Association. His clubs are the Army-Navy Club of Washington, and the Athletic Club of Columbus.

Meiling, who is five feet six and three-quarter inches tall and weighs 168 pounds, has auburn hair and blue eyes. He is affiliated with the Lutheran Church; he lists himself as a Republican. On June 21, 1940, he married Ann Elizabeth Lucas, a teacher. They have a son, George Robert Lucas. The doctor's recreations are horseback riding, skiing, sailing, and attending football games. He has two hobbies, collecting military historical documents and autobiographies of military leaders.

References

Directory of Medical Specialists (1949)
Who's Who in America, 1950-51
Who's Who in the Midwest (1949)

MENZIES, ROBERT G(ORDON) (měn′zēz) Dec. 20, 1894- Prime Minister of Australia

Address: b. Parliament House, Canberra, Australia; h. 10 Howard St., Kew, E. 4, Victoria, Australia

NOTE: This biography supersedes the article which appeared in *Current Biography* in 1941.

After an interim of eight years during which the Labor party controlled the Government of Australia, a coalition of the Liberal party, headed by the Right Honorable Robert G. Menzies, and of the Country party, won the majority in the Australian House of Representatives in December 1949. Menzies was chosen Prime Minister of the new Government, a position he had held from April 1939 until August 1941. A figure in Australian politics since 1928, Menzies has served in the Legislative Assembly

and Council of Victoria, represented the district of Kooyong in the Australian Federal Parliament since 1934, served as Attorney General and Privy Councilor, and has been leader of the United Australia party, and later, of the Liberal party. Unable to reconcile the Labor party to his Government during the time he was Prime Minister, he resigned his office in 1941, and in 1944, after establishing the Liberal party, became head of the opposition in the Australian Parliament. Menzies had a highly successful law practice before he entered the political field.

Robert Gordon Menzies is a native of Australia, having been born in the country town of Jeparit, in Victoria County, on December 20, 1894. His father, James Menzies, who was elected to the Legislative Assembly of Victoria, was a storekeeper at the time of his son's birth. When attacked by political opponents for the wealth he accumulated in his law practice, Robert Menzies replied: "I am the grandson of a working miner who could not get a job because he organized a union"; on another occasion: "I am a singularly plain Australian." He received his early education at local schools, where his scholastic record was high. At Ballarat School he headed the State's scholarships list and won four years of free tuition at Wesley College, Melbourne; there he again achieved high scholastic honors and another scholarship for his law study at Melbourne University. When he graduated he received the first class honors in law, in addition to other prizes and scholarships, including the Supreme Court Judges' Prize. He was editor of the *Melbourne University Magazine* and served as president of the University Students' Representative Council.

In 1918 Menzies was called to the Victoria County bar and High Court of Australia, and by 1921, when he had successfully pleaded for the State of Tasmania before the High Court on a constitutional issue of major importance, his reputation as a lawyer had become nationwide. In 1927 he became arbitrator on salaries and conditions of work among the metropolitan daily papers of the Australian Journalists Association. In 1929 he was selected to be a King's Counsel. The income from his law practice was large. "It is said that Menzies threw away a £10,000-a-year bar practice to enter politics," stated a party press release.

Menzies' political career began in 1928, when he founded and headed the Young Nationalists Organization and in the same year was elected to the Victoria Legislative Council from East Yarra. The next year he resigned from the council in order to be elected to the State Assembly, where he represented Nunawading from 1929 to 1934. During 1928-29 he was Honorary Minister in the McPherson Government; and during the last two years of his term in the State Assembly he was Attorney General for Victoria as well as Minister of Railways and Deputy Premier. Then, in 1934, as a member of the United Australia party, he was elected to represent Kooyong in the Federal Parliament. The next year the Government of Joseph A. Lyons, which was a coalition of the United Australia and the Country parties, chose Menzies Attorney General for Australia; and he was then made deputy leader of the United

Australia party. In 1937 he was made a Privy Councilor and until March 1939 continued as Attorney General. In the Cabinet from 1934 to 1939, he was Minister for Industry. During this period, Australia, which had just recovered from a severe depression, was debating a national insurance program which would provide for general sickness and disability benefits, as well as a contributory old-age pension. In October 1937 the United Australia and Country parties coalition Government was retained in power, one of its election pledges having been the enactment of the welfare program. When the Government decided to postpone that plan, Menzies in March 1939 resigned from the Cabinet in protest. A month later Prime Minister Lyons died, the coalition Government collapsed, the United Australia party was reorganized with Menzies as leader, and in April 1939 Menzies was chosen Prime Minister and formed a new Government.

Menzies remained Prime Minister until August 1941. During this period his Government was not regarded as very secure, because of disunion within his party and because of the growing strength of the Labor party. The Government, however, was returned to power in the 1940 elections, but with only a majority of one seat in the lower house and two seats in the Senate over the Labor opposition. As Prime Minister, it was Menzies who in September 1939 declared war on Germany. Thereafter, until his resignation in August 1941, Menzies initiated Australia's war program, which included the establishment of the Australian aircraft industry, the training of pilots, and the building of merchant and naval shipyards and dry docks; he formed an advisory war council of eight members, of whom four were from the opposition. From January to May 1941 he represented Australia at the London war conferences, visited the battlefronts where Australian troops were stationed, and came to the United States, where he addressed a nationwide radio audience on Australia's need for aid.

The Labor party criticized Menzies for his absences from Australia as well as his war program. While still in London Menzies answered the criticism by suggesting that a new Government be formed, in which the Labor party should hold half the Cabinet offices. This proposal was rejected. Again, in August 1941, Menzies suggested that the Labor party, jointly with the United Australia and Country parties, elect a leader for the national Government. The Labor Party, maintaining that Menzies was unable to provide a stable Government, asked him to resign, which he did on August 29, 1941. The new Government, under the leadership of A. W. Fadden of the Country party, with Menzies as Minister of Defense Co-ordination, was defeated five weeks later and the Labor party, with John Curtin [41] as its head, and supported by two independent members, formed a new Government. The Labor party was supported with a record majority in 1943 and survived as the head of the Australian government until the December 1949 elections. (In 1945, upon Curtin's death, Joseph B. Chifley [45] had become

Australian Official Photo.
ROBERT G. MENZIES

Prime Minister.) During the period, the alliance between the United Australia and the Country parties had dissolved and Menzies led in the formation of a new party, the Liberal, representing principally the professional and business groups in Australia. The Country party represented farmers and grazers.

During the period of the Labor party regime, Australia initiated a broad national welfare program and, at the end of World War II, introduced legislation for making permanent the main features of the wartime banking regulations, designating the management of the Commonwealth Bank as responsible to the Government in matters of broad policy. However, the Labor party's program to nationalize all private banks was declared unconstitutional. In 1946, when these questions were being contested, the Labor party was returned to power, but with a reduction in its former large majority. Menzies' party won three additional seats in the House of Representatives, increasing its members from 14 to 17 in a House of 75. By the time of the December 1949 election, the Liberal party held 33.11 per cent of the total electoral. As a result of the 1949 election, the Liberal-Country coalition has a majority of twenty-seven seats over the Labor party in Australia's House of Representatives; in the Senate, according to the New York Times, the count probably will be: "Labor, thirty-four; Liberal and Country parties, twenty-six." Menzies was thus chosen Prime Minister of the coalition Government, whereupon he named a new Cabinet, in which fourteen of the ministries are held by Liberals and five by Country party members.

In the 1949 campaign Menzies' coalition group, described by the Christian Science Monitor as "middle of the road," highlighted the importance of halting the advance of socialism,

MENZIES, ROBERT G.—*Continued*

increasing industrial production, and reducing taxes. The social welfare program of pensions, maternity benefits, and hospital insurance, however, was not a campaign issue. Menzies also campaigned on a program to illegalize the Communist party and to remove all members of that party from public office. He also promised to repeal the controversial bank nationalization act and to introduce a restricted form of compulsory military training. Though Menzies has asserted his belief in social services and in protecting the public from private monopoly, he believes that as many as possible of the controls instituted by the Labor Government should be removed. The New York *Times* quoted him as describing the 1949 election as a "deliverance from the dominance of an all-powerful state." Concerning the international situation, Menzies wrote in a *Times* magazine article (December 18, 1949) that the United Nations is the permanent solution in the search for peace, that the immediate safeguards are such regional defenses as the Atlantic Pact; he looks to the setting up of a similar Pacific plan. The Conservative party of Britain considered the Australian rejection of the Labor party a second indication of a turn that might occur in a 1950 general election in England. The first indication had come from New Zealand a few weeks earlier, when Sidney G. Holland [50] was named Prime Minister following a victory over the Labor party.

During the 1949 campaign, Menzies, who had the reputation for being austere and aloof when addressing the public, showed himself to be more willing to accept good-naturedly the heckling of political gatherings. He is recognized as a brilliant debater, often using wit or irony to gain a point. In appearance he is "formidable," being six feet tall and weighing 200 pounds. As a student he played football, and in 1950 enjoys walking, playing tennis, and watching cricket matches. He dislikes bridge, dancing, and golf. In 1920 he married Pattie Maie Leckie, daughter of the late Senator J. W. Leckie; he has two sons, Kenneth and Ian, and a daughter, Heather. The author of articles on law, he has also written several books: *The Rule of Law During the War* (1917), *Studies in the Australian Constitution* (1933), *To the People of Britain at War* (1941), and *The Forgotten People*. He is a member of the Australian and the Savage clubs of Melbourne. The honorary Doctor of Laws degree has been conferred upon him by Queens University (of Belfast), and by Bristol and Melbourne Universities. He is an Honorary Master of the Bench, Gray's Inn, London. His church is the Presbyterian.

References

N Y Times VII p7 Ap 6 '41 por
International Who's Who (1949)
Pan-Pacific Who's Who (1940)
Who's Who (1947)
Who's Who in Australia (1947)
World Biography (1948)

MERRICK, ELLIOTT (TUCKER) May 11, 1905- Author

Address: h. Route 1, Swannanoa, N.C.

Reprinted from the *Wilson Library Bulletin*, Jan. 1950.

Three present-day writers who have done most, perhaps, to make Vermont's way of life familiar to readers are Dorothy Canfield Fisher (born in Kansas), Anne Bosworth Greene (born in England), and Elliott Tucker Merrick, who was born May 11, 1905, in Montclair, New Jersey, the son of Elliott T. Merrick and Margaret (Day) Merrick. Merrick's second book, *From This Hill Look Down* (1934), received the accolade of approval from Mrs. Fisher when she wrote in *Books*: "He has become an insider. A real one. This authenticity can be felt all through this collection of Vermont stories and sketches."

Merrick's preparatory school was Phillips Exeter Academy, and he was graduated from Yale University with a B.A. degree in 1927. His first job was as cub reporter on the Passaic (New Jersey) *Daily News*, which he reached from Montclair in a ten-year-old model-T roadster bought from a brother-in-law for $2.50. "My first by-line story was an account of a gypsy wedding held at Passaic, attended by clans from New Mexico, Maine, Ohio, Florida, and Oregon. Most of them traveled in big old Cadillac touring cars. At the wedding they served chunks of broiled beef, and everybody wiped his hands on his hair. A girl did a dance with a rose in her teeth."

In 1928-29 Merrick worked at advertising and publishing in New York, quitting this job to join the Grenfell Mission in Labrador as a teacher—a move of great importance to his later personal and literary life. At the mission he met his wife, then Kate Irene Austen, an Australian-born nurse, whom he married in 1930. They have three children, Eliott T., Austen David, and Susan Elizabeth. For a time the couple lived in a lonely cove where the Goose Bay airport now stands. *True North* (1933), Merrick's first book, described in diary form their joint experiences.

Returning to New Jersey in 1931 in the depth of the depression, Merrick drove a truck in Newark for six months before moving to Vermont. For a little cash income, indispensable to most subsistence farmers in that state, he taught in a high school for a year, besides writing his books and the articles and stories published in *Scribner's*, *The New Yorker*, *Reader's Digest*, and *American Mercury*. *Ever the Winds Blow* (1936), a biographical novel about Henry Frain, a young man happily married and living on a Vermont farm, seemed to Lewis Gannett "not a very good novel but a singularly appealing book."

It was the depression of the 1930's that had sent the Merricks to Vermont, where they rented a farm on Lake Champlain. It was not for reasons of "escape," a fighting word to the author, who pithily inquires, "There are a few steam-heated reviewers who persistently call my tales of the modern frontier or rugged living 'escapist.' If it is 'escapism' to go from unreal-

ELLIOTT MERRICK

ity to reality, and from an unsuitable life to one that is rich and deeply natural, how would you characterize the apartment dweller who thinks everything above Seventy-Second Street a blank desert?" (An exception is Frederic Melcher, editor of *Publishers' Weekly*, who "has always thought highly of my work and given me much encouragement.") *Green Mountain Farm* (1948), Merrick's most recent nonescapist book, describes life on this farm and his present one at Craftsbury Common, bought for a thousand dollars. Hal Borland in the New York *Times* wrote, "It is the human warmth which makes [his] books so rich, that and the man's thinking. He likes people, and he found an assortment of deeply human people among his neighbors."

For three years, beginning in 1939, Merrick was an instructor in English at the University of Vermont in Burlington, and after the war he was (1945-46) associate professor of English at Black Mountain College in North Carolina. The war put him in the Office of War Information, where he did the research for and wrote a booklet concerning the achievements of the combined United Nations merchant marine, which was translated into several languages and distributed to occupied and neutral countries to combat German propaganda. In the course of his work he met various seafaring men, heard stories of lifeboat voyages, and shipped one voyage himself. The resultant novel was *Passing By* (1947), which the *Saturday Review of Literature* found full of true portraits, while the New York *Times* thought the conversations unlifelike.

Northern Nurse (1942), on the best-seller lists for a time, set forth the adventures of a mission nurse who had to be doctor, dentist, surgeon, dressmaker, bookkeeper, and church soloist besides. *Frost and Fire* (1939), described by the *Times* as a "strong and sober novel," is the story of Jim McKenzie, half-

Scot and half-Eskimo, and his life in Labrador as a trapper and trader.

Merrick is now editor of the Southeastern Forest Experiment Station, United States Department of Agriculture Forest Service, Asheville, and lives on Route 1, Swannanoa, North Carolina. His station has charge of Forest Service research in Florida, Georgia, Virginia, and the Carolinas. His likeness on the jacket of *Green Mountain Farm* is that of a typical young farmer, dark, lean, weather-beaten, and slightly quizzical. He is fond of sailing, tennis, and walking the hills, and has "probably worn out twenty pairs of shoes writing seven books."

MEYERSON, MRS. GOLDA May 3, 1898-
Israeli Cabinet member
Address: b. Ministry of Labor of Israel, Jerusalem

The first Minister of Labor and Social Security of the new state of Israel is Mrs. Golda Meyerson, who was appointed to that post in the spring of 1949. Mrs. Meyerson had come to Palestine from the United States in her early twenties, and in subsequent years became increasingly important in the Zionist movement and in the struggle for independence. Head of the political department of the Jewish Agency and Administrator of the Jewish section of Jerusalem, she was named Israel's first Minister to the Soviet Union in 1948. In October 1950, upon the formation of a new coalition Cabinet in Israel, Mrs. Meyerson received the same portfolio.

Born Golda Mabovitz in Kiev, the capital of the Ukraine, on May 3, 1898, Mrs. Golda Meyerson (sometimes spelled "Myerson") was 8 years old when the family went to Milwaukee, Wisconsin. There her father worked as a carpenter and her mother operated a small grocery store. The girl attended the local schools and later became a student at the Teachers Seminary in that city. After her graduation from the seminary she taught school and worked in public libraries in Milwaukee, Chicago, and New York. During World War I she did volunteer relief work.

Miss Mabovitz met her future husband while she was a student in Denver. Her marriage to Morris Meyerson, an ardent Zionist, drew her interest toward Jewish questions. After joining the American Labor Zionist Organization (Poale Zion) she became active in its Pioneer Women of America. In 1921, when Mrs. Meyerson was twenty-three, the Meyersons moved to Palestine to enter the new collective settlement of Merhavia (one of the earliest of its kind) as agricultural workers. During her three years' stay in the settlement Mrs. Meyerson studied Hebrew and Arabic, occupied herself with questions of grain production and poultry raising, and was instrumental in the establishment of community nurseries.

The contractors' cooperative Solel Boneh, founded by Histadrut, the general federation of Jewish labor, is today the largest public works and building contracting agency of Israel. In 1924 Mrs. Meyerson became treasurer of its branches in Jerusalem and Tel-Aviv.

Israel Office of Information
MRS. GOLDA MEYERSON

Since that appointment her career has been devoted to executive community positions. Elected to the Women's Labor Council in 1926, she also became a member of the executive of Histadrut. The latter organization she represented at six international labor conferences in England and the United States, beginning in 1928. Since 1929 she has also been a delegate to the Zionist World Congresses. At the International Socialist Congress in Zurich in 1947 she was the chief delegate for Palestine and demanded, against the opposition of the British delegation, a discussion of the Palestine problem by the congress.

The Histadrut appointed Mrs. Meyerson to other posts, among them the secretaryship of its executive board. When the air-transport company Aviron was founded by Histadrut, Mrs. Meyerson was made a director. In another organization of Histadrut, the Kupat Cholim (Sick Fund), Mrs. Meyerson served as chairman of the supervisory board. The Kupat Cholim was founded in 1912 by the Union of Agricultural Workers in Judea which later became part of the Histadrut; it is the oldest social insurance institution in Palestine. Other posts filled by Mrs. Meyerson were in the Zionist Actions Committee, the Jewish National Council, and the Palestine Government's War Economics Advisory Council.

The Jewish Agency is the official representative of the Jewish people in matters which concern the establishment of the Jewish National Home in Palestine. A labor party member in the executive of the Jewish Agency, Mrs. Meyerson became acting head of its political department in June 1946, when its chief, Moshe Shertok [48], later Israel's Foreign Minister, was interned together with other Zionist leaders. Later made its new head, she stated in her first interview in January 1947, according to the New York *Herald Tribune*, that "the Jews in

Palestine would be able to defend themselves without British help against an Arab uprising." Her spirit was revealed on one occasion when the British refused to let a refugee ship leave Italy for Palestine. She fasted 101 hours and persuaded eleven members of the Jewish Agency to do likewise until the British permitted the ship to sail. Throughout the struggle for the new state and after its establishment Mrs. Meyerson has asserted her belief in unlimited immigration. In the spring of 1948 she was made Administrator of the Jewish section of Jerusalem.

In January 1948 Mrs. Meyerson returned to the United States for the first time in ten years. It was believed, according to the New York *Times*, that the main purpose of her trip was to persuade the American authorities to lift the embargo on arms for Palestine. Mrs. Meyerson herself stated that her mission was "to mobilize American Jewry to give assistance —political, moral, financial"—to the Jews of Israel, and emphasized that the Jews in Palestine would fight to the very end. When the new state was proclaimed on May 14, 1948, Mrs. Meyerson was one of the signers of the Proclamation of Independence and became the only woman member of the Provisional Council of the new state. On May 19 she arrived again in the United States (the first official of the new state to visit that country) to participate in the fund-raising campaign of the United Jewish Appeal. Her purpose was "to enlist the support of both Jews and the American Government for a Jewish victory in the war, and to get financial aid for the permanent economic development of Palestine." In her appeal Mrs. Meyerson gave the assembly which she addressed in New York a vivid account of her country's struggle for full sovereignty. She advocated large-scale immigration to Israel and outlined an extensive resettlement program. A loan of $1,000,000 requested by her was authorized by the International Ladies' Garment Workers Union, AFL.

In June 1948 Mrs. Meyerson was named the first Israeli Minister to the Soviet Government, a post she held until April 1949. (She was the second woman envoy to be sent to Moscow, the first being India's Ambassador Mrs. Pandit [46].) During her stay in the U.S.S.R. Mrs. Meyerson succeeded in obtaining a building for the Israel legation and established trade relations between the two countries. In November 1948 she went to Paris (as Deputy Foreign Minister) to assist Foreign Minister Shertok in discussions before various United Nations committees on the United Nations plan for partitioning Palestine.

As a member of the Mapai, the Jewish Labor party of Israel (moderate socialist as opposed to the left-wing Mapam), Mrs. Meyerson was elected to the Constitutent Assembly (Knesset) in January 1949, in which election her party became the strongest by winning 46 of the 120 seats. When the first Government of Israel was formed in March, Mrs. Meyerson was appointed Minister of Labor and Social Security (which includes housing and public works). In this capacity she was called upon to deal with a "new type of class struggle." When clashes occurred between veteran laborers and newly hired immigrants, Mrs. Meyerson sought the solution in a law forbidding unorganized, below standard, labor. An accelerated program of public works was to absorb the unemployed.

In mid-October 1950 a Cabinet crisis developed when three Orthodox (Conservative) Cabinet members withdrew over an economic issue, and Premier Ben-Gurion resigned. After two weeks the crisis ended: Ben-Gurion retained the premiership and the four-party coalition Cabinet was formed in which Mrs. Meyerson was again named Minister of Labor and Social Security.

The first Israeli Cabinet member to arrive in the United States, Mrs. Meyerson toured twenty cities in June 1949 to mobilize the help of the American Jews to provide for the immediate needs of the young state. The housing of new immigrants was described by Mrs. Meyerson as the most urgent problem which could not be solved without outside assistance—160,000 housing units were needed to take care of the prewar population and the new immigrants. In addition, she expected 1,500,000 Jews from the Arab countries and Europe to settle in Israel within the next four or five years.

In February 1950 Mrs. Meyerson was awarded a bronze medallion by the Women's National Institute of the United States as the "outstanding woman of Israel." She was honored by the Women's International Exposition held in New York in November 1949, when five women (three Americans and Mrs. Meyerson and Mrs. Pandit) were awarded medallions for "outstanding achievement." The award was accepted for her by the president of the Pioneer Women of America in which Mrs. Meyerson has been active.

The Meyerson son is a cellist who played in the Palestine Symphony orchestra, and who studied in 1948 at the Juilliard School of Music in New York. A daughter was reported in 1948 to be a member of the settlement Revivim, the most isolated Jewish settlement in the Negev, then the scene of clashes between Jewish and Egyptian forces. Mrs. Meyerson has gray hair, which she arranges simply. She enjoys doing such housewifely tasks as cooking, baking, and laundering.

References

Ivriah Journal p2 S '48
Jewish Advocate 18:12 Je '49
N Y Herald Tribune II p5 F 9 '47; p5 Je 26 '48
N Y Post p75 Mr 10 '48 por
N Y Star p8 Je 26 '48
Palestine Affairs 2:32+ Mr '47
Palestine Post Ja 10 '47
Pioneer Woman p8+ Mr '47
Who's Who in the State of Israel, 1949
World Biography (1948)

MILLER, MERLE May 17, 1919- Author
Address: 277 Park Ave., New York 17

Reprinted from the *Wilson Library Bulletin,* April 1950.

Merle Miller, author of the novel *The Sure Thing* published late in 1949, was born in Montour, Iowa, on May 17, 1919, the son of Monte M. and Dora B. (Winders) Miller. He attended high school in Marshalltown, Iowa, where he engaged in such extracurricular activities as writing a column for the high school weekly, playing first violin in the orchestra, helping edit the yearbook, and acting in the senior class play. He attended the University of Iowa between 1935 and 1940, with an interim year, 1938-39, at the London School of Economics on a scholarship. Although not a pacifist, he didn't like the ROTC and because military training was required for a degree, he left before graduating. During his college days he won a freshman speech award, a debate award, several undergraduate writing awards, corrected English themes "honestly and unpopularly," was editor of the undergraduate daily, and wrote a daily column for it. He was also on the debating team. Since he likes writing and talking better than anything else in the world, his early education and avocations proved excellent training, but he comments: "There have been no writers in the family, ever. Some people think I haven't changed the situation."

In 1942 Miller joined the Air Corps and was attached to the staff of *Yank,* for which he worked in both hemispheres from its very beginning until he was released from the Army in September 1945. Since then, he has been associated with *Time* ("for five unhappy months"), engaged in Project X, and has worked as assistant editor of *Harper's* magazine for almost two years. Besides *The Sure Thing,* his published books are *That Winter, Island 69,* and a nonfiction book of collaboration, *We Dropped the A-Bomb.* His articles have appeared in such magazines as the *Saturday Review of Literature, Harper's, Mademoiselle, Survey,* and the *Nation. The Sure Thing* was reviewed with wide divergence of opinion.

His first appearance in print occurred at the age of twelve, when That Poem, called "The Bridge of Life," was published in the Marshalltown *Times-Republican.* "There was a very nice letter from the editor asking for more. I should hope! It was free, wasn't it?"

Miller is convinced that a writer's job is to write. He has frequently quoted Sinclair Lewis who once reluctantly consented to speak to a writing class at Columbia University. Mr. Lewis, never a tactful type, opened his lecture by saying, "I understand you all want to be writers." Half the class nodded happily, and the rest, most of them surely graduate students, recorded the sentence in their notebooks. "Then," inquired Lewis, "what in God's name are you doing here? Why aren't you home writing?" Although Miller is in process of creating a new novel ready for publication probably in the fall of 1951, he will not talk about it.

In Merle Miller's opinion, Scott Fitzgerald is the best American novelist of the twentieth century, with *The Great Gatsby* at the top of the list. However, he considers James Gould Cozzens almost as good, and in some ways even better, with *Guard of Honor* taking first place. "I was brought up on the Bunny Brown series,

MERLE MILLER

had entire sets of Horatio Alger and the Rover Boys. I never heard of Ernest Hemingway until I was at least sixteen and never even saw him at the 21 Restaurant." Other distinctions Miller claims that set him apart from most contemporary authors of his generation are these: "I never jerked sodas, never cut down a tree, never ran a six-hundred-acre farm, never went to jail, never spent summers on the Left Bank of the Seine (but spent one uniformed winter there), never hitchhiked from New York to San Francisco. I was unable to read and write knowing essays on the *Critique of Pure Reason* at the age of eight and a half and still can't at the age of thirty."

Although not pedagogically inclined, he decided in the fall and winter of 1949 to test his reactions to the academicians by teaching a course in creative writing at the New School, in New York. Admitting that the experience was enjoyable, he concluded nevertheless that the good students simply got better, as they would have anyway; that the ones without talent remained untalented to the end; and that a great many other writers were wise enough to stay at home and write.

Since writing serious novels does not make it possible for an author to eat regularly, feed a family, and pay the rent, Miller does permit himself some extracurricular activities, including speaking at book and author luncheons, autographing, and writing pieces about writing. He is also secretary of the Authors Guild, a member of the Writers Board for World Government, of the board of directors of the American Civil Liberties Union, and a member of Americans for Democratic Action. His fraternities are Pi Kappa Alpha, a social fraternity; Delta Sigma Chi, an honorary journalism fraternity; and Sigma Delta Rho, an honorary speech fraternity.

Five feet, ten inches tall, with brown eyes and brown hair, Miller weighs 167 pounds. He was married on February 14, 1948, to Eleanor Green, who is in the publishing business. They live in New York City. Besides talking and writing, Miller's favorite recreations are drinking beer, seeing bad movies, going to the theater, and traveling (especially in Europe but preferably not at the expense of the United States government).

MILSTEIN, NATHAN (mĭl′shtĭn) Dec. 31, 1904- Violinist
Address: b. c/o Paul Bechert, 525 E. 89th St., New York 28

The 1949-50 concert season marks the twentieth anniversary of the American debut of Russian-born violinist Nathan Milstein. The virtuoso had come to the United States at the age of twenty-five equipped with an "amazing technique of finger and bow" (Noel Straus), and has since matured "into one of the greatest musicians of our time" (Olin Downes). The violinist has played with most of the world's great musical organizations and conductors on his world-wide tours.

Nathan Milstein was born in Odessa, Russia, on December 31, 1904. His father was Myron Milstein. It was his mother (who was Maria Bluestein before her marriage) who was responsible for her son's eventual choice of his career. She wanted something that would keep her "wild young Nathan" out of the mischief into which he was constantly getting; and, on the advice of a neighbor who was using that method for her own son (as related in the article on Milstein by Howard Taubman in the New York *Times Magazine*) she had him begin studying the violin. Milstein's first teacher, according to Taubman, was a young man from the Odessa Conservatory of Music who spent more time considering the five-year-old boy's "true fiddler's hands" than teaching him how to play the instrument. His second teacher, and the mentor with whom he remained until he was old enough to enter the conservatory some six years later, was Peter Stoliarsky, a teacher of established reputation in Odessa.

At first Nathan had to be disciplined to practice, with his mother present at every session. But Stoliarsky had a remedy for this: he put the boy in a class with more advanced students, with the result that young Nathan responded by practicing in an attempt to keep abreast of them. Soon he was beginning to accumulate a repertoire and, not content with that, began the difficult and unorthodox feat of using piano scores when playing his instrument, if only for the challenge it offered. Looking back on those early days of his music study, he has said: "I started to play the violin not because I was drawn to it but because my mother made me. I was attracted to music, wanted to hear it, but I had to be forced to learn how to make it. It was only when I had progressed far enough to feel the music itself in my playing that I practiced willingly and eagerly." At the age of ten young Milstein was called upon to play the solo part in the Glazunoff

Violin Concerto, with the composer himself on the podium, when the scheduled soloist fell ill. The next day a critic predicted that Milstein would go far as a violinist.

When Nathan Milstein was eleven, the famous violinist Leopold Auer came to Odessa. Milstein played for him, and, impressed with what he heard, Auer invited the boy to become one of his pupils at the St. Petersburg Conservatory of Music. Permission for Milstein and his mother to go to that city was accordingly sought from the authorities and with some difficulty obtained, and in 1916 he became a pupil of Auer. Milstein told interviewer Taubman that he vividly remembers the circumstances of his introduction to the Auer circle. All of Auer's pupils were present at the event, for which the young violinist had chosen the technically exacting Ernst F-Sharp Minor Concerto. Much to everyone's surprise he played with assurance and authority amazing in one so young. Word of the prowess of the twelve-year-old got about, for a St. Petersburg newspaper reported that he had played so brilliantly that Auer had fainted. But the truth of the matter was, the violinist himself told Taubman, "if anybody had fainted, it would have been Milstein." During the next several years, which brought communism to Russia, Milstein remained at the St. Petersburg Conservatory under the tutelage of Auer. Later he was to spend some time with Auer's great contemporary, the Belgian violinist Eugène Ysaÿe, who, Milstein has said, had a profound influence on him.

Milstein's first public recitals were given in Odessa in 1919 (he was then fifteen years old), with his sister as his piano accompanist. The recitals were necessary to help offset the financial reverses his family had suffered in the Revolution of 1917. Meeting with success, he next played in Kiev, where he was equally successful. After one of the concerts in that city a young pianist came backstage to felicitate Milstein and to invite him to his home for an evening of music making. The pianist was Vladimir Horowitz '43; the two became close friends, and in the course of the next few years made occasional joint tours in Russia. Milstein remained in Russia until 1926. Then, succeeding in securing permission from the Soviet Government to go to Paris, he arrived in the French capital (where he had no connections) without funds or a violin. It was not long, however, before friends and an enterprising manager arranged for a recital. His debut has been described as "sensational," and extended tours of Europe followed immediately.

In the three years after his debut in Paris, before he came to the United States for the first time, Milstein gave performances throughout the Continent, in recitals and with the leading symphony orchestras. A tour of South America preceded his American debut, which was made in October 1929 with the Philadelphia Orchestra under Leopold Stokowski. Annual tours of the United States and Canada followed, and the virtuoso continued to tour Europe until the outbreak of World War II. He made several other tours of South and Central America, Mexico and Cuba, and Egypt

Paul Bechert

NATHAN MILSTEIN

and Palestine. Since 1947 Milstein has resumed his annual concert tours of the principal European music centers, where he has been greeted by full houses and hailed as "one of the greatest musical figures before the public today." The reception has been similar in the United States: with the New York Philharmonic Symphony Society of New York (one of the leading American orchestras with which he appeared as soloist) he performed forty-eight times in the twenty years since his American debut. The conductors with whom Milstein has shared the platform include Toscanini, Koussevitzky, Stokowski, Münch, Monteux, Bruno Walter, Stock, Reiner, Rodzinski, Furtwängler, Mengelberg, Muck, Klemperer, Ormandy, De Sabata.

Milstein received the commendation of American critics from the day of his debut with the Philadelphia Orchestra. In the 1930's it was generally his "superlative technical skill" or the "sheer beauty" of his violin tone which won him the praise. With the 1940's he began to be acclaimed as one of the select few who are profound interpreters as well as "dazzling" virtuosi. Then, for instance, Robert Bagar of the New York World-Telegram wrote on one occasion, "To listen to Nathan Milstein . . . is to listen to a musician versed in the manifold aspects of his art, to a poet with his feet in the solid earth while spiritually he can reach the clouds." Olin Downes of the New York Times, commenting on the Carnegie Hall recital which marked the violinist's twentieth year on the American concert platform said, "Certain performances of yesterday evening represented such a level of style, emotional communication and noble thinking that one looks back upon them as an experience that stands out in a retrospect of seasons." The artist's own comment on his musical maturity to Howard Taubman was, "Of course, I have grown. . . .You try to refresh and enrich what you do every

MILSTEIN, NATHAN—*Continued*

time you play. You must or you become an automaton. . . .My great gain, I suspect, is that I have learned to project what I had in my mind and heart. . . .What makes an artist? In the end it is temperament, personality, character that count most. Some musicians are not great technicians, but they give you a rich point of view . . . it is that rich point of view that matters most."

Milstein is also a composer. His works include violin arrangements of music for other instruments by Liszt, Chopin, and Moussorgski; cadenzas for the concertos of Beethoven, Brahms and Paganini; and a set of variations based on Paganini's Twenty-fourth Caprice and other themes, entitled *Paganiniana*, noted for its "violin pyrotechnics." Among the artist's best-known recordings (for Columbia) are Tchaikovsky's D-Major Violin Concerto, Bruch's G-Minor and Mendelssohn's E-Minor concertos, Lalo's *Symphonie Espagnole*, and sonatas by Mozart, Beethoven and Bach; since 1948 his recordings have been made for RCA-Victor, the earliest of which are the Glazunoff concerto and two works by Mozart.

The violinist, who became an American citizen in 1942, was married to Thérèse Kauffman in 1945. The Milsteins are the parents of a daughter, named Maria Bernadette. In appearance Milstein is of medium height; he has brown eyes and dark brown hair. He admits to superstitions; for instance, he attaches much importance to the objects that surround him at any particularly successful concert. Two objects he is never without are a watch given him as a recital fee in the days of the Russian Revolution and its gold chain, given to him by a friend just before his first concert in Vienna. To his Stradivarius (the instrument formerly known as the "ex-Goldmann") he has given the combined name of his daughter and wife, Maria-Thérèse. One of his hobbies is his collection of violin bows; another is painting—he often works on a water color as relaxation on the day of a concert. Other of his recreations are tennis and ping-pong, chess, and reading.

References

N Y Sun p28 Ja 20 '40
N Y Times Mag VI p20+ N 13 '49 por
Newsweek 19:56 Mr 2 '42 por; 34-74 D 19 '49 por
Time 41:70 F 22 '43 por
America's Young Men, 1938-39
Baker, T. ed. Biographical Dictionary of Musicians (1940)
Ewen, D. ed. Living Musicians (1940); Men and Women Who Make Music (1949)
Thompson, O. ed. International Cyclopedia of Music and Musicians (1949)
Saleski, G. Famous Musicians of Jewish Origin (1949)
Who's Who in America, 1948-49
Who's Who in American Jewry, 1938-39
Wier, A. E. ed. Macmillan Encyclopedia of Music and Musicians (1938)
World Biography (1948)

MOCH, JULES (SALVADOR) (môsh zhül säl"vä"dôr') Mar. 15, 1893- French Cabinet Minister

Address: b. c/o Ministry of National Defense, Paris; h. 137 Avenue Malakoff, Paris

In July 1950 Jules Moch was appointed the Minister of National Defense for France in the coalition Cabinet headed by René Pleven [60]. A leading Socialist, Moch served in the Popular Front government during the 1930's, was imprisoned by the Vichy regime, and escaped to join the Free French in 1943. After the Liberation, he was the only Minister to hold Cabinet posts continuously from 1945 to 1950. Designated Premier in the Cabinet crisis of October 1949, he failed to win the support of enough party groups to form a new Government. He is known as one of the most vigorous defenders of the "Third Force" in its struggle against the Communists on the left and General Charles de Gaulle's [40] Rally of the French People on the right.

Jules Salvador Moch was born in Paris on March 15, 1893, the son of Gaston and Alice (Pontremoli) Moch. His grandfather was a colonel in the Crimean and Franco-Prussian wars, his father an army captain. After attending the Lycée Janson-de-Sailly, young Moch entered the Ecole Polytechnique in 1912 to study marine engineering, and at the same time he studied for the law. During World War I he served as a second lieutenant in the engineering corps, was wounded, promoted to captain, and awarded the Croix de Guerre with four citations. During 1919-20 he directed the Service for Industrial and Agricultural Restitution in Germany and other former enemy countries. He worked for the next seven years as an engineer, managing various industrial enterprises in the Baltic countries and France.

After joining the Socialist party, Moch was elected to the Chamber of Deputies from Valence in 1928. Two years later he became a judge of the Court of Appeals, and in 1931 was appointed Minister without Portfolio. He was re-elected to the Assembly in 1932, but lost his seat in 1936. However, on June 5 of the latter year Premier Léon Blum [40] assigned him to the post of Secretary-General of the Presidency of the Council of Ministers in his Popular Front government. (Moch was referred to as "Cousin Jules" by opponents of the Popular Front because he was related to Blum.) Elected a deputy from Sète in 1937, he was promoted to Under Secretary of State of the Presidency of the Council that same year. Blum chose him as Minister of Public Works in his second Cabinet of March-April 1938. During this period Moch also served on the Public Works and Air Commission (1926-32), the Finance Commission (1936), and the Labor Commission (1937).

At the outbreak of World War II, Moch volunteered for active service in the Navy. He took part in the Narvik landings during the Norwegian campaign, for which he later received a captain's commission and the Croix de Guerre with a fifth citation. Returning to France, he was one of the eighty members of the National Assembly who voted against giving

Marshal Pétain [40] unlimited powers on July 10, 1940. The following September the Nazis arrested and interned him at Pellevoisin since he was both a Jew and a Socialist. He was released in March 1941, whereupon he immediately organized Resistance Group "1793," which soon fused with the Socialist Comité d'Action in the underground network. Hunted by the Germans, he was forced to flee the country, and in April 1943 he joined General de Gaulle in London, where he enlisted in the Free French naval forces and was appointed to the Army's General Staff. Subsequently he became a member of the Provisional Consultatives Assembly in Algiers (October 1943), served on military missions to the Levant (in 1943 and 1944), and was a delegate to the Brazzaville Conference on the French Colonial Territories (January 1944). Later in 1944 he participated in the Allied landings in Italy and the south of France.

After the liberation of his country Moch continued to serve in the Provisional Consultative Assembly and took part in the work of the Finance, Foreign Affairs, National Defense, Economic Affairs, and Moslem Affairs Commissions. In October 1945 he was elected to the Provisional Constituent Assembly from the Department of Hérault. President-Premier de Gaulle appointed him Minister of Public Works and Transport in his second Cabinet, which took office on November 21, 1945. Moch retained this portfolio in the three succeeding Cabinets (Félix Gouin [46], January-June 1946; Georges Bidault [45], June-November 1946; Léon Blum, December 1946-January 1947), devoting his efforts to rebuilding the nation's highways, ports, merchant marine, and commercial air fleet. Elected to the first National Assembly of the Fourth French Republic in November 1946, he was again assigned the Ministry of Public Works and Transport in the first Cabinet of the new republic, which was installed on January 22, 1947, with Paul Ramadier [47] as Premier. When the Communists were dropped from the Cabinet early in May he took over the portfolio of Minister of Reconstruction. In September he served on the French delegation to the United Nations General Assembly meeting at Lake Success, New York. After Ramadier reduced his Cabinet in October, Moch was named Minister of National Economy and Reconstruction. He introduced a vigorous campaign to hold down food prices, but the Cabinet fell on November 19 in the midst of a wave of strikes and mounting political unrest.

On November 24, 1947, Moch was given the portfolio of Minister of the Interior in the new Cabinet of Robert Schuman [48], a post he continued to hold during the three following governments (André Marie [48], July-August 1948; Schuman's second Cabinet, September 5-7, 1948; Henri Queuille [48], September 1948-October 1949). Declaring, "I will defend the Republican order against whatever side may threaten it," Moch emerged as "the strong man" of the 1947 strike wave. He authorized police and troops to fire on rioters if "serious and widespread violence" were used against them, or in defense of positions they could not otherwise

French Embassy Inf. Div.

JULES MOCH

hold. During the spring of 1948 he organized an army-police internal security control force, divided into eight superprecincts covering all France, and equipped with airplanes and radio-controlled mobile units. This Compagnie Républicaine de Sécurité was first employed against the sit-down strike at Clermont-Ferrand in June 1948 and later that year broke up clashes between the Communists and the followers of De Gaulle. Moch withdrew De Gaulle's government-supplied bodyguard, declaring that the Rally of the French People actually had 15,000 "private, motorized police, which is inadmissible in a democracy." The wave of strikes culminated in the nation-wide coal strike of October-November 1948, which had been called by the Communist-led General Confederation of Labor. Appearing before the National Assembly, Moch submitted documentary evidence, which proved, he claimed, that the mine strike had been ordered and financed by the Communist Information Bureau (Cominform), with the aim of wrecking French economy and disrupting the operation of the Marshall Plan.

The Queuille Cabinet fell early in October 1949, when the Socialists demanded an immediate bonus for low-paid workers. President Vincent Auriol [47] on October 8 entrusted Moch with an "information mandate" to find a wage-price formula that might form the basis of a new Government. Three days later he nominated Moch as Premier. On October 14 Moch was supported by a National Assembly vote of 311, just one vote above the required majority. His proposals called for an early return to collective bargaining and a single cost-of-living bonus of 2,000 francs ($8.50) for the lowest-paid workers. The Independent Republicans opposed this bonus as leading to inflation, while the Communists denounced him as "the assassin of the working class." After repeated attempts

MOCH, JULES—*Continued*

to reach an agreement on the assignment of Cabinet posts, Moch handed in his resignation on October 17. The crises was finally brought to an end on October 28, when Bidault won a vote of confidence on his coalition Cabinet, in which Moch was given the posts of Vice-Premier and Minister of the Interior.

Moch and four other Socialist Ministers resigned from Bidault's Cabinet on February 4, 1950, after a dispute on the cost-of-living bonus. According to the New York *Times* (February 5, 1950), the basic issue, however, was Socialist concern over the Rightist tendencies of the Government and misgivings lest their party lose the remainder of working-class support to the Communists. At the Socialist party congress the following May, when he was elected to the party's executive board, Moch stated that unless Europe could create a common authority and with it an expanding economy, the Soviet Union, without any war, would "take first Italy, then Germany, and finally France." On July 12 the Socialists rejoined the "Third Force" coalition, and Moch was named Minister of National Defense in the new Cabinet of Premier René Pleven. After conferring with British defense chiefs, he told the National Assembly: "The situation is serious but not desperate. It is such that France has a duty to make a powerful effort which may be rapidly increased if she does not wish to suffer the fate of Czechoslovakia or what has happened in Korea." He outlined a five-year plan to build 2,000 combat planes, but laid greatest stress on the need to quadruple France's internal defenses against fifth columnists and saboteurs.

Moch, together with Foreign Minister Schuman, conferred with Bevin and Shinwell of Britain and Acheson and Marshall of the United States in New York in September 1950 on all matters relating to the defense of Western Europe. Agreement was reached on the utilizing of German police and labor forces, the raising of the steel production in that country, and the ending of the state of war with Germany. One question was not completely resolved—the organizing and arming of German troops—because of France's traditional fear of a strong Germany.

France's Minister of Defense is the French Minister for the Council of Europe, in which he served as rapporteur for the General Affairs Committee. At the committee's new session held in Strasbourg in November 1950, Moch resigned as rapporteur on November 17, explaining his action "as an indication of his belief that recent conflicts between the French and British parliaments over the Council of Europe had reduced the Council's effectiveness as an agency for European unity" (in the words of the New York *Times*).

An officer of the Legion of Honor, Moch has been awarded the Grand Cross of the Luxembourg Crown Order and the Order of Cedar of the Lebanese Republic. His writings, which began to appear in the early 1920's, have been on reparations, socialism, finance and capitalism, the rail transportation system, on Jean Jaurès, Soviet Russia, and republican

Spain. France's Defense Minister has been described as a "tall, spare, benign, bespectacled extrovert" (*Newsweek*). He married, on January 24, 1917, Germaine Picard, one of the first women admitted to the French bar. During the Nazi occupation, she was forced to flee to Switzerland, and their elder son, André, was killed by the Gestapo. There remains a younger son, Raymond. Moch's heavy duties have forced him to give up most of his recreational sports; his one relaxation is flying his own plane, which he has named "L'Évasion." He is a heavy smoker, beginning each day with an American cigarette before breakfast. "At that hour," he has remarked, "I smoke in dollars."

References

Christian Sci Mon p2 S 30 '48
Free France 8:9-12 N-D '48
Newsweek 32:44 O 25 '48
Archives Internationales (1949)
Dictionnaire National des Contemporains (1936)
International Who's Who, 1950
World Biography (1948)

MOHAMMED RIZA PAHLEVI (mŏ-häm'măd rĭ-zä' pä'lä-vē) Oct. 26, 1919- Shah of Iran

Address: Teheran, Iran

The ruler of the ancient kingdom of Iran (Persia) is His Imperial Majesty Mohammed Riza Pahlevi, Shahinshah of Iran, and Commander in Chief of the Iranian Armed Forces. Since the year 1941, when his father abdicated the Peacock Throne in favor of the twenty-one-year-old Crown Prince, the Shah has followed a policy aimed at strengthening British and American interests in Iran in an effort to stem Russian infiltration. The first Eastern monarch to pay a visit of state to the United States, in November-December of 1949 on a tour of six weeks he sought increased American military aid for his country, as well as financial help for his seven-year-plan to improve the social and economic condition of his people. Iran is rich in oil resources, the fourth largest producer in the world.

Born October 26, 1919, in Teheran, Iran, Mohammed Riza Pahlevi is the eldest son of Riza Shah Pahlevi and his consort Tajomolouk Pahlevi. In the family there are eight other children, one of whom, Princess Ashraf Pahlevi, is his twin sister. The Shah's father, first of Iran's Pahlevi ruling family, was the son of a small landowner in Mazanderan Province. Rising to the rank of colonel in the Persian Cossack Brigade, the elder Pahlevi took control of the tottering government of Ahmed Shah on February 21, 1921. In quick succession he became War Minister, Prime Minister, and, in 1925 was chosen Shah by the National Assembly. Seeking to modernize medieval Persia, he instituted military and civic reform, even changing his country's name from Persia to Iran. (In October 1949 it was reported that the ancient name of Persia might be taken again.) Riza Shah Pahlevi, who amassed a fortune, ruled as dictator.

Mohammed Riza Pahlevi grew up in an "atmosphere of despotic splendor," in "awe and admiration of his domineering father" (*Time*'s words). The boy attended the Teheran Cadet School until 1930, then was sent to Le Rosey, a private school in Rolle, Switzerland, where he studied during 1931-36, becoming proficient in English and French. Well liked by his companions, the young Prince was chosen captain of the football team. He has been described at this time as a "friendly youth" who found outlet for his energy in athletics and in driving fast cars.

Riza Shah Pahlevi called his son home from Switzerland in 1936. After two years at the Officer Cadet Training Academy in Teheran, the Crown Prince attained officer's rank in the Iranian Army and commanded his own regiment. Under his father's guidance, he participated in affairs of state to gain experience in governmental administration. His marriage to Princess Fawzia, sister of King Farouk of Egypt, took place on March 15, 1939.

Iran, which is larger than the combined area of Germany, France, and Spain, is the world's fourth largest producer of oil. Because of that and its strategic geographical position, it is of much importance in the eyes of Russia, Great Britain, and, in recent years, United States. During World War II, Riza Shah Pahlevi permitted increased Axis activity in Iran. Needing a supply route to Russia, the Allies issued an ultimatum to the Shah to oust Axis nationals from the country. When he failed to comply, troops from Britain and Russia entered the country. After a sixteen-year rule, he was forced to abdicate his throne in favor of his son, who became Shahinshah on September 16, 1941.

Seeking to "dissociate himself from his heritage" (*Current History*), the young ruler ceded his father's wealth to the nation and proclaimed, on September 20, 1941, the end of absolutism, the granting of political power to the Cabinet and Majlis (Parliament), a general amnesty to political prisoners, and other reforms. His Government concluded a tripartite treaty of alliance with Great Britain and the Soviet Union on January 29, 1942, regularizing the presence of their troops in Iran. The Shah, who had entertained Wendell Willkie in September 1942, was host to President Roosevelt, Prime Minister Churchill and Marshal Stalin when they met at Teheran in December 1943 for the first of their wartime conferences. At that meeting, the Allied leaders promised to evacuate their troops and restore and preserve Iran's independence after the war. Iran declared war on Germany on September 9, 1943.

In the next few years Anglo-Russian cleavage developed in Iran. The Shah supported the British, seeking with them to interest the United States in Iran's oil and in the country's postwar development plans. In November 1945, a reportedly Soviet-inspired autonomous movement won political control of Azerbaijan, Iran's northwestern province bordering on Russia. Protecting their advantage, Russian troops remained there after the treaty evacuation date of March 2, 1946. When the Shah's Government protested to the United Nations, Russia

Wide World Photos
MOHAMMED RIZA PAHLEVI

withdrew her troops on May 6, after having gained a promise of oil concessions in northern Iran from Prime Minister Ahmad Ghavam. "Showing great personal courage," the Shah restored Iranian control in Azerbaijan before the parliamentary elections held in January 1947. The Majlis rejected the Soviet oil pact in October 1947, its action being ratified by the Shah the following month. A Soviet note of protest cost Ghavam the support of the Majlis, and the Shah appointed Dr. Ibrahim Hakimi Prime Minister in December 1947. The anti-Russian party took complete control in Iran on November 16, 1948, when the Shah appointed a new Prime Minister in Mohammed Maraghei Said, whose political reputation was gained by resisting wartime Russian demands for oil leases.

On February 4, 1949, following a student demonstration protesting the Anglo-Iranian Oil Company's concession to take oil out of Iran, the Shah was shot in an assassination attempt. As a consequence, the Iranian Government outlawed the Left-wing Tudeh political party. While recovering from his bullet wounds, the Shah issued a statement saying that the assassination attempt had reinforced his decision to sacrifice his life, if necessary, for his countrymen. "Our primary tasks today," he said, "are to secure our independence, guarantee justice and liberty, and raise our standards of living and literacy."

For several years the Shah had been working on plans that would raise the living standards of his 16,500,000 subjects, most of whom are illiterate and live at a low subsistence level. He had personally retained two training missions of American officers assigned to the Iranian Army and the gendarmerie. He had also called in a staff (organized by Clifford S. Strike [49]) of American engineering, irrigation, health, sanitation, industrial, financial, and administrative experts. They drew up a seven-year plan for

MOHAMMED RIZA PAHLEVI—*Cont.*

the development of the entire country, to be carried out at a cost of $650,000,000, and providing for development in the fields of agriculture, communications, ports, mines and industry, oil, posts and telegraphs, and social reforms. The last-named, to include broad housing and health projects, would be the costliest—more than one-fourth of the total. The Shah placed his brother, Prince Abdor Riza Pahlevi (Harvard '47) at the head of the supreme planning board for the program in September 1949, and began making arrangements to finance the program partly from Iran oil royalties, partly by expected loans from the World Bank, and partly by private loans. Meanwhile, a constituent assembly, held in May 1949, drafted major revisions of the Iranian Constitution, including provision for a balance of power between the three branches of the Government, and creation of a second chamber (a Senate) in the Majlis. The Majlis was also made responsible to the will of the people.

At the invitation of President Truman, the Shah of Iran paid a state visit to the United States in November 1949. Transported in the President's own plane, he arrived in Washington on November 16. The trip was described as a good-will tour to promote better understanding of Iran in the United States, and to enable the Shah to study American ways and methods which he might apply at home for the benefit of his people. He also sought support for his requests for increased military aid from the United States as well as economic aid to help carry out his seven-year plan for improving the living standards of his country. After attending various state receptions the Shah addressed the U.N. General Assembly, making a plea on behalf of small nations for permanent global peace. The Shah then traveled for three weeks in the United States, visiting industrial plants, air fields, power projects, as well as points of scenic interest. Earlier travels included a visit to Great Britain in July 1948, to attend the Olympic games, as the guest of the British royal family. On his way home by way of Paris and Rome, he was received by Pope Pius, who presented him with the Sovereign Order of the Golden Spur, and praised his treatment of Catholics in Iran.

As summarized and commented upon editorially by the New York *Times*, the visit of the Shah "came to a happy conclusion" in the joint statement issued by him and President Truman. That pledged "American support for World Bank loans to Iran, economic development through the Truman Point Four program, and military aid for the defense of Iran's independence." The Shah, stated the editorial, "made plain that Iran would meet American assistance with reciprocal action"—with a plan for social and economic progress, for which technical assistance would be welcomed and private investment encouraged.

Among the other decorations that have been presented to the Shah of Iran are: the Order of Pahlevi and the Order of the Crown (Iran); Order of Mohammed Ali the Great (Egypt); Order of Rafeddin (Iraq); Order of Leopold (Belgium); Order of White Lion (Czechoslovakia); Order of Legion of Honor (France); Order of St. Saviour (Greece); Order of the Cedar (Lebanon Republic); Order of the Almar Aali (Afghanistan); Order of the Bath (Great Britain); Order of the Ommegah (Syrian Republic); Order of the Propitious Cloud (China); Legion of Merit Award (United States, 1947); honorary doctorate of civil law (University of Michigan, 1949).

The Shah's marriage to Princess Fawzia was dissolved "by mutual accord" on November 19, 1948, after a separation since 1945. (Their daughter, Shahnaz, is being educated in Switzerland.) Three brothers of the Shah, the Princes Gholam, Abdor and Mahmoud, and one sister, Princess Fatmeh, came to the United States in 1944 for their advanced education. A fourth brother, fifteen-year-old Prince Hamid, flew to Paris from New York in June 1947 to escape attending school in the United States. The Shah's twin sister, Princess Ashraf, visited the United States in August 1947 to study social work programs; she is the president of the Imperial Foundation of Social Service.

Slender and of medium height, the Shah has jet black hair, a sharp prominent nose, brown eyes, a broad mouth, and an angular chin. A sportsman, he is accounted a skillful horseman, hunter, tennis player, skier, and boxer. He also enjoys driving automobiles and flying his own plane, a B-17. The Shah, who usually wears informal European clothes, asked American newsmen to describe him as "a 'working' monarch."

References

Collier's 119:21 Ap 5 '47
N Y Herald Tribune II p3 N 20 '49
N Y Sun p6 Mr 17 '45
N Y Times p1 F 5 '49
Pathfinder 56:9+ N 30 '49
Time 38:23 S 29 '41 por; 39:29 Ja 19 '42 por; 46:28 D 17 '45
Washington (D.C.) Post II p1 B N 13 '49 por

Britannica Book of the Year, 1949
10 Eventful Years (1947)
World Biography (1948)

MOLLET, GUY (mô"lĕ' gē) Dec. 31, 1905-
French political leader

Address: b. 12 Cité Malesherbes, Paris 9, France; h. 33 Place des Héros, Arras, Pas-de-Calais, France

Called the "Sword of Damocles" hanging over the French Government, Guy Mollet has been secretary general of the French Socialist party since September 1946, when he led a successful drive against the middle-of-the-road policies of Léon Blum [40]. Because it controls the balance of power, his party has been able to "make or break" French Cabinets, usually over issues of social reform and wage increases. In the Cabinet of René Pleven [50], installed in July 1950, Mollet became a vice-president of the Council of Ministers and was appointed to the post of representative on the Council of Europe. During 1949-50 Mollet has been active in the Council of Europe and has favored the Schuman plan for a coal-steel pool as a means of achieving an economically integrated Europe.

Guy Mollet was born in Flers, Orne, in Normandy on December 31, 1905, the son of Pierre and Marie (Lelievre) Mollet. While Guy was still a boy, his father, a weaver, died of wounds received during World War I. Continuing his studies as a ward of the State, the youth thought of a career in the merchant marine, but his interests turned him instead to English and literature. He studied at Le Havre and Lisieux, where he earned his B.A., Lic. Litt., and diploma in advanced studies. To perfect his English, the student spent some time in England, at Margate, Canterbury, and Oxford. At seventeen Mollet had obtained his first position as a master in a boarding school at Le Havre in 1923. Promoted to tutor, he later became professor of English and Latin at the lycée for boys in Arras. He organized their sports events and started a dramatic group in whose productions he sometimes took part.

The same year he began teaching, Mollet joined the Socialist party. Because of his activity in the party's publicity programs, he was dismissed from his teaching position in 1932, after he had conducted a political campaign against André Tardieu. Devoting full time to the party, Mollet became well known in syndicalist and socialist circles, and one of the outstanding men in local politics in Arras. He also, in 1932, became secretary of the Fédération de l'Enseignement (teachers' union) of the C.G.T. (Confédération Générale du Travail).

In World War II Mollet was mobilized as a medical aide in August 1939. Captured by the Germans in June 1940, he was held prisoner until February 1942, when he was repatriated. He then joined the clandestine Socialist Action Committee in Arras, becoming responsible in February 1943 for the second bureau of the O.C.M. (Organization Civile et Militaire) in the department of Pas-de-Calais. His a ;tivities, watched by the Gestapo, resulted in his arrest in December 1943. He managed to escape, however, and rejoined the movement for the liberation of the North of France. While in hiding Mollet wrote an English grammar for the use of French students of English. Mollet returned to Arras after its liberation in 1944. He was made secretary of the Committee of Liberation and in 1945 became, successively, mayor of Arras and president of the general council of Pas-de-Calais. He was also president of the Committee for Aid to Prisoners of War and was awarded a Resistance Medal.

In the first postwar elections, held October 21, 1945, Mollet was elected deputy from Pas-de-Calais to the Constituent Assembly. He succeeded André Philip [43] as president of the Constitution Commission of the Assembly on January 30, 1946, and presided over the work of this commission "with a conscientiousness and scrupulousness to which even his opponents paid homage" (*Presse Agence France*, December 16, 1946). On April 19, 1946, the Assembly voted to accept the new constitution (which provided for a strong legislature and a weak executive). In a referendum vote on May 5,

GUY MOLLET

however, the proposed constitution was rejected. In the new elections, held June 2, 1946, Mollet was re-elected as deputy from Pas-de-Calais.

The Socialist party, which had split in the constitutional referendum in May, suffered a loss of strength in the June elections, while the Communists and Popular Republicans (M.R.P.) gained. The middle-of-the-road policies of Léon Blum were blamed for these losses, whereupon an insurgent group led by Mollet in September 1946 chose a new board of directors at its congress, with Mollet replacing Daniel Mayer [49] as secretary general of S.F.I.O. (Section Française de l'Internationale Ouvrière, the official name of the party). Mollet was re-elected to the National Assembly in November 1946, but his party continued to lose votes. When an effort to form a coalition Government of Socialists and Communists failed, in December 1946 Léon Blum succeeded in establishing an all-Socialist Cabinet in which Mollet was named Minister of State. In Ramadier's [47] Coalition Cabinet, which followed, Mollet was not a Minister.

On May 9, 1947, Ramadier reorganized his Cabinet to exclude the Communists. (As of mid-1950 they have been excluded from all Cabinets.) In July the Socialist National Council approved Ramadier's action, and adopted a motion supporting Marshall [47] proposals for American aid to Europe. Mollet, who had formerly sought a compromise with the Communists, now opposed them. Though not so strong numerically as the Communists or the Popular Republicans, the Socialists were able to gain a strategic position in the French Government because they held the balance of power. Mollet sought to increase the numerical strength of the Socialists by holding Ramadier to stricter doctrinal policy. Lansing Warren, writing in the New York *Times* (August 18, 1947), ob-

MOLLET, GUY—*Continued*

served that Mollet's position did not "indicate any *rapprochement* with the Communists, but rather the beginning of a contest between the Socialists and the Communists for ascendancy with the French workers."

Ramadier's Cabinet fell in November 1947; he was succeeded by Schuman '48, a Popular Republican. During the eight months this Cabinet lasted, there was increasing dissatisfaction on the part of the Socialist Party with the way in which its eight Socialist Ministers in the "Third Force" Government were compromising with the Popular Republicans on such matters as wage and price stabilization. Socialist demands for reduction of the armed forces budget finally forced Schuman's resignation in July 1948.

The Cabinet of Henri Queuille '48, which lasted from September 1948 to October 1949, fell after a wage-price controversy was raised by the Socialists. Following two other short-lived Governments, Georges Bidault '45 on October 29 formed a Cabinet which included Socialist Ministers, but in January 1950 Mollet headed a party delegation to Bidault to inform him that the Socialists could not continue to participate in the Government unless a cost-of-living bonus were granted to workers. With the approval of the Socialist National Council, the Socialists withdrew from the Cabinet in February, but the party continued to give Bidault its qualified support until June 24, 1950, when he was defeated by a vote of confidence precipitated by the Socialists over their demands for civil service wage increases.

The defeat of Bidault's Cabinet in June coincided with the culmination of other events of international significance in which Mollet played an important role. As secretary of the General Affairs (Political) Committee of the European Consultative Assembly, Mollet consolidated suggestions for the federation of Europe and for giving the Council of Europe a measure of real political power. These proposals were considered by the General Affairs Committee at its meeting in Strasbourg in December 1949. Britain and the northwestern European countries urged that the existing Council of Europe be made more effective rather than changed radically in structure, while the southern countries tended to favor a greater degree of federation with real, though limited, legislative and executive functions. After the sessions, Mollet indicated that the delegates had generally agreed to let "practical politics" be their guide, which was interpreted as a victory for Britain.

In April 1950 the Socialist newspaper *Populaire* published an article by Mollet in which he spoke against expansion of the Atlantic Pact into an economic and political "Atlantic Community," favoring instead a united Europe playing "the indispensable role of mediators and conciliators between the great forces which are distrustful of each other and ready to become antagonists." At the 1950 annual congress of the Socialist party (at which he was re-elected secretary general on May 29), Mollet commented on the seriousness of the international situation, and urged the party to take a "middle policy" between the increased Communist agitation in France and the development of the De Gaullist forces into a "clearly neo-fascist" movement. The congress backed a resolution for admission of the Chinese Communist Government representatives to the United Nations, and urged the French Government to refer the civil warfare in French Indo-China to the U.N. Security Council for settlement.

The Socialist congress also declared itself in favor of the Schuman plan for pooling French and German coal and steel industries as well as those of other European countries, but said its approval was conditional on Great Britain's agreement to join in the plan. When the British Labor party opposed the coal-steel pool on the ground that it meant the yielding of sovereignty to a supranational European authority, Mollet sought to bridge the differences between British and Continental Socialists by suggesting that "for the present the Schuman plan be carried out by an intergovernmental committee." Following an International Socialist Conference in London on June 16-17, Mollet made these proposals to the British Socialists. Though the Labor Government did not bar Britain's entry into the pool, it won a confidence vote on June 27 on its decision to stay out until the plan had taken more definite shape.

While the coal-steel conference was in progress in Paris, Socialist opposition to the Bidault Cabinet ended in the defeat of that Government. The war in Korea (Mollet approved the U.N. military action) and the subsequent sending of aid by the United States and Britain sharpened the Government crisis in France to the point where Mollet agreed in June 1950 to give qualified Socialist support to a Cabinet formed by Henri Queuille. The participation of Socialist ministers in a Cabinet, however, was made conditional on adoption of a plan of social reform. On July 4 Queuille's newly formed Cabinet resigned over the pay-raise issue; Mollet then volunteered to seek Radical-Socialist and Popular Republican (MRP) support for a limited legislative program that would be in accord with Socialist demands. Though he was offered the nomination of premier-designate, Mollet declined the post but succeeded in re-uniting the "Third Force" Parliamentary majority under René Pleven, head of the Democratic and Socialist Union of the Resistance (U.D.S.R.). Pleven was installed as Premier on July 11. His Cabinet included members from Socialist (S.F.I.O.), M.R.P., Radical-Socialist, and U.D.S.R. parties. In it Mollet was appointed a vice-president of the Council of Ministers and named to the post of representative on the Council of Europe. The program agreed upon by Pleven included most of the points demanded by Mollet's party: salary adjustments for Government workers, increased pensions for war veterans, an increase in basic minimum wage for industrial employees, and interparty committees to study and revise electoral laws and the educational system.

Mollet is slender, of medium height, scholarly in appearance; he has blue eyes, sandy hair, a high forehead and wears horn-rimmed glasses. When his duties permit, he visits his family in Arras—his wife, an active Socialist party member whom he married in 1930, and their two daughters. For light reading he turns to detective stories, especially those by English writers.

References

La France et Monde Mr 23 '46 por
Inter Ja 20 '50
Newsweek 28:45 D 9 '46
Presse Agence France D 16 '46
Archives Internationales (1946)
World Biography (1948)

MONSARRAT, NICHOLAS (JOHN TURNEY) (mŏn'sär-rȧt") Mar. 22, 1910- Author

Address: b. c/o United Kingdom Information Office, London House, Johannesburg, U. of S. Afr.; h. 20 Kensington Pk. Rd., London, W. 11

Reprinted from the *Wilson Library Bulletin*, Dec. 1950.

"I have the most interesting job in Africa. I write as much as I can, make one speech a month, review books on the radio, and act as question master in discussion programs and a program called 'Twenty Questions.' I like work." It is fortunate that Nicholas Monsarrat does like work, for the activities he mentions are only a few of his duties as director of the United Kingdom Information Office in South Africa. The office, in Johannesburg, distributes films, photographs, pamphlets, and news releases, maintains a reference library, and answers an unending stream of questions. Yet with all this, Monsarrat finds time to write the books whose American publication is winning him an appreciative audience on this side of the Atlantic.

Nicholas John Turney Monsarrat was born March 22, 1910, in Liverpool, England, to Dr. Keith Waldegrave Monsarrat and Marguerite (Turney) Monsarrat. He had one brother and two sisters. The Monsarrat family, originally from Castres, near Toulouse in France, emigrated to Dublin early in the nineteenth century, and then to England about 1860.

Dr. Monsarrat was a distinguished surgeon. Young Nicholas, growing up in Liverpool, was sent to Winchester and then to Trinity College, Cambridge, where he took his honors law degree in 1931. Two years in a Nottingham solicitor's office convinced him that the law was not what he wanted for his life's work. With his typewriter and a half-finished novel he went to London to begin the career of a free-lance writer. His first three books, *Think of Tomorrow*, *At First Sight*, and *The Whipping Boy*, had a moderate success.

In these years before the war, besides publishing magazine stories and articles, Monsarrat saw his play, *The Visitors*, produced with Greer Garson as leading lady. Early in the war he joined the navy and served on convoy escort in the North Atlantic and on the east coast of England. He attained the rank of lieutenant commander, and commanded three escort vessels, a corvette and two frigates. He was mentioned in dispatches.

NICHOLAS MONSARRAT

His introduction to American readers came with the publication of an American edition of his fourth novel, *This Is the Schoolroom* (1940). F. H. Bullock in *Books* said, "Mr. Monsarrat writes with a notably lucid and flexible style, transferring to paper far more readily than most, the impulses, ideas, moods, experiences, sensations of an able young Englishman during four crucial years."

H. M. Corvette, East Coast Corvette, Corvette Comand, and *H.M. Frigate* were nonfiction, written during the writer's war service, and describing naval operations. The *New Republic*'s appraisal of *H. M. Corvette* is typical: "Having at present little opportunity for creative writing, Mr. Monsarrat has, fortunately, been able to expend his imaginative energy on his style, giving it a rich, rhythmical finish, with the feeling for great spaces and small details that has marked the best sea stories. The experience of patrolling, convoying merchantmen, and chasing subs has been related many times during this war, but never with the excellence of *H. M. Corvette*."

Leave Cancelled (1945) was a short novel detailing the twenty-four-hour honeymoon of a British officer and his young bride. Its frankness provoked violent reactions of both praise and censure. Jennings Rice in *Weekly Book Review* found it "utterly frank without sordidness, bitter-sweet without self-pity, tender without sentimentality." Hamilton Basso said in the *New Yorker*, "Needn't take up too much of our time. . . . I felt damned embarrassed and I got no enjoyment out of listening in."

Depends What You Mean by Love (1948), three volumes in one, contains *Heavy Rescue, Leave Cancelled*, and *H.M.S. Marlborough Will Enter Harbour*. James McBride wrote in the New York *Times*, "This talented young Englishman . . . displays an impressive ability on every page of this collection." James Hilton in the Herald Tribune *Weekly Book Review*:

MONSARRAT, NICHOLAS—*Continued*

"Mr. Monsarrat's three war stories are peculiarly English, not only in their technique of understatement but in their absence of rancor. . . . Contains fine work."

My Brother Denys (1949) is a memoir of the author's youth, shared with the brother who fell in World War II. Virginia Kirkus said of it, "There's casual charm characteristic of Monsarrat, some nostalgia, and a neatness of phrase which gives this a modest distinction." The new work in progress, not yet titled, is a long novel about the Battle of the Atlantic.

Nicholas Monsarrat, married and the father of a son, has lived in South Africa for four years. Besides his native England, he knows the European continent well, has lived for a year in Paris, and nine months in Boston and New York. He is a member of the British Labor Party, and "a great believer in the British Commonwealth as an alternative to other systems." He likes the United States, but feels New York is too distracting for creative work. London remains for him "the only town in the world."

MOON, BUCKLIN May 13, 1911- Author

Address: b. c/o Doubleday and Company, Inc.; 14 W. 49th St., New York 20; h. Route 1, Patterson, N.Y.

Reprinted from the *Wilson Library Bulletin*, Feb. 1950.

Bucklin Moon, who has received a Rosenwald Fellowship and the George Washington Carver Award for his book on Negro life in America, is not a Negro. Since a writer's bid for public favor is properly made on the basis of literary excellence and not racial origin, this fact is not stressed by Moon or his publishers.

BUCKLIN MOON

It is mentioned here only because librarians are so frequently asked the question.

Bucklin Moon was born in Eau Claire, Wisconsin, on May 13, 1911, the only son of Chester D. and Edith (Bucklin) Moon. The parents were both of New England stock, the mother's brother the president of the National Shawmut Bank, Boston, and the father in the lumber business. Bucklin Moon attended Shattuck Military Academy at Fairibault, Minnesota, graduating in 1929. He went on to Rollins College, Winter Park, Florida, majoring in English. Graduating with a B.A. degree in 1935, he was voted the most improved member of the senior class. He began writing short stories while at Rollins, where his many extracurricular activities included editorship of the literary magazine. Two of his stories won honorable mention in a *Story* magazine college contest, although they were not published.

In his graduation year Moon married Elizabeth Vogler. He came to New York and joined the staff of the *Review of Reviews* as "junior editor and ringmaster." He then tried a new magazine and a small literary agency, both of which were unsuccessful. He found a job with the Edward L. Bernays office, writing publicity on beer. In 1938 he sold his first short story to *Harper's* magazine. Deciding that he wanted to give more time to writing, Moon took his wife and small daughter to Orlando, Florida. He worked as bartender in a hotel there, spending his free hours from midnight to morning on his first novel. He finished the book a year and a half later in New York, where he was selling books in one of the Doubleday shops.

His first book, *The Darker Brother*, appeared in 1943. A. C. Spectorsky said in *Book Week*, "The book has a far more telling and lasting impact than a dozen tales of horror. Bucklin Moon knows Negro life inside out. He is right in his attitude and outlook and sympathies, not in a pedantic way and not in a mushy uplift way, but as an intelligent and knowledgeable man who sees wrong and hypocrisy and persecution . . . being visited on his fellow men." The *New Yorker* called it "a pitiful, unhappy story of white man's inhumanity to black, which, however, leaves unexplored the deeper issues involved."

Primer for White Folks (1945) was an anthology edited by Moon. The collection of historical documents, sketches, and short stories, all bearing on Negro-white relations, included such authors as Carey McWilliams, Lillian Smith, Richard Wright, W. E. B. DuBois, and Wendell Willkie. John Caswell Smith, Jr., said in *Atlantic*, "Mr. Moon has done an excellent and knowing job in selecting the material for this book."

High Cost of Prejudice (1947) was a factual study of the costs—in dollars and cents and cultural values—of America's intolerance of Negroes in the field of labor, in politics, in social life. Virginia Kirkus called it "a realistic down-to-earth analysis of the Negro problem . . . in succinct, challenging terms." Carey McWilliams wrote in the *Nation*, "The publication of this volume is further proof of how an understanding of the factors, involved in what we used to call 'the race problem' has increased since 1940. Merely to compare Mr. Moon's clear, calm-mannered, realistic analysis with some of the frightened myth-ridden analyses that appeared in the twenties gives proof of the progress that has been made."

Without Magnolias, Moon's second novel and fourth book, appeared in 1949. W. F. Weaver said in the New York *Times*: "Unlike many novels about the problems of Negroes in this country, *Without Magnolias* is a good story. In addition to an effective sympathy, Bucklin Moon has a good eye, a sharp ear, and an unobtrusively smooth narrative style. . . .One particularly interesting aspect of this book is that it never uses violence as a plot device." Ann Petry in the New York *Herald Tribune*: "This is Bucklin Moon's second novel and it deserves the prize it won, for he has painted an accurate, realistic picture of the delicate balance of race relations in the South, spicing it with small vulgarities and an occasional bitter joke."

Bucklin Moon is now associated editorially with the publishing house of Doubleday and Company. He lives with his wife and three children at Patterson, New York. He is hazel-eyed and brown-haired, over six feet in height. He calls himself a liberal in politics and disclaims any church affiliation. His favorite authors are Faulkner, Hemingway, and William March. His hobbies are Siamese cats and hot jazz, his favorite recreation chess.

MORGAN, THOMAS A(LFRED) Sept, 27, 1887- Industrialist

Address: b. c/o The Sperry Corporation, 30 Rockefeller Plaza, New York 20; h. 217 E. 62d St., New York 21

Thomas A. Morgan has been the chief executive of the Sperry Corporation since its organization in 1933; and in 1949 he became president as well as chairman of the board. Sperry's activities include the manufacture and development of precision instruments and controls for naval, military, electrical, and farm equipment. During World War II Morgan guided the Sperry Corporation in the production of more than one and a half billion dollars' worth of equipment for the armed forces. In July 1949 President Truman created the Advisory Committee on Management Improvement and named Morgan as its chairman.

Thomas Alfred Morgan was born near Henderson, in Vance County, North Carolina, on September 27, 1887, the eldest of six children —four sons and two daughters—of James T. and Virginia (Wilson) Morgan. Thomas had his share of chores to do on his father's farm— and also became one of the best coon and possum hunters in the county. He walked three miles to the Flint Hill public school, where he received good grades "without too much study." In 1905 he entered Littleton (North Carolina) High School. He also did spare-time work as a carpenter, telephone lineman, traveling salesman for a "family-portrait" firm, and power-plant worker. In 1908, young Mor-

Delar

THOMAS A. MORGAN

gan entered the United States Navy, where he received training as an apprentice electrician.

It was his service aboard the U.S.S. *Delaware* that determined Morgan's career. The Sperry Corporation is said to have been "founded" on the *Delaware*, which was commissioned as the first dreadnaught in 1910. One day in 1911 Elmer Sperry, American inventor, brought to the ship his gyrocompass, "a queer-looking machine that he announced was a new kind of compass—a compass which sought and held true north because of the earth's rotation." To help install the compass and keep it in adjustment was the duty of Morgan, who had become one of the ship's electricians. When the instrument proved imperfect in tests at sea, Morgan took it apart twice, found the defect, and put it into working condition. The result was "a great day" for Elmer Sperry, the Navy (which promptly ordered ten compasses), and Morgan.

At Sperry's invitation, Morgan joined the inventor's company after his four-year enlistment period ended in 1912. That was a year after the Sperry Gyroscope Company had been founded to develop and market the marine gyrostabilizer and similar inventions of Sperry's. Starting as a service engineer, Morgan installed new compasses ordered by the United States Navy and instructed the men in their use. Then followed four years as the company's representative abroad. "Morgan was one of the most ingenious salesmen ever turned loose in Europe," wrote Don Wharton in the *Saturday Evening Post*. "Speaking nothing but English with a Southern accent, he sold gyroscopes when neither salesman nor customer could understand a word the other was saying."

When Morgan (then sales manager) returned to the United States, Elmer Sperry put him in charge of the company's aeronautical instrument department. Under his direction (as

MORGAN, THOMAS A.—*Continued*

general manager) such devices as airplane bank-and-turn indicators, air-speed meters, compasses, and altimeter were developed. After the end of World War I Morgan became a salesman in China and Japan. In Tokyo at the time of the great earthquake in the year 1923, he was so resourceful in organizing relief that he was commended by the United States Secretary of State and decorated by the Japanese Government with the Order of the Rising Sun.

It was during the 1928 airplane boom that North American Aviation, Inc., purchased the Sperry Gyroscope Company for $4,000,000, and Morgan became the latter's president. He subsequently became president of Berliner and Joyce Aircraft, vice-president of Eastern Air Transport (formerly Pitcairn), vice-president of the Ford Instrument Company, president of North American itself in 1930, and a year later he was made president of the Curtiss-Wright Corporation. Morgan is said to have "put the latter firm on its feet." When the General Motors Corporation acquired a 29 per cent interest in North American Aviation in 1933, the Sperry Corporation was formed to "nurture the orphaned divisions," Sperry Gyroscope and Ford Instrument. Morgan became president of the company and chairman of the Sperry Gyroscope's board.

Morgan's first step as head of the Sperry Corporation was to eliminate certain subsidiary firms and acquire others. The company's "growth pattern," according to *Fortune*, was based on two new manufacturing interests. The first was designed to fill the needs of the United States armed forces and national defense generally. Morgan led the development of new and improved military devices, among them anti-aircraft fire-control mechanisms, sound locators, searchlights, better hydraulic gun controls, and gyroscopic applications of fire control. Sperry's other development trend was toward "peace insurance" through the manufacture, by its subsidiaries, of such products as hydraulic pumps and transmissions, and in Sperry Gyroscope's expansion in the civil aviation field. The gyroscope is the "backbone" of many important Sperry products.

Morgan served as president of the Sperry Corporation from 1933 to 1946, the year he was elected chairman of the board. He retained that post when he received the title of president again on February 16, 1949. During World War II Sperry manufactured about one and a half billion dollars' worth of equipment for the United States armed forces. One and one-half billion dollars represented production in Sperry plants, and material estimated at one-half billion dollars in cost was made by twenty-six prime contractors under royalty-free licenses from Sperry. Under Morgan's direction the corporation developed one hundred and forty new military and naval products. These developments were in the fields of aircraft and marine armament and navigation, including radar and bombsights; servo-mechanisms and hydraulic controls; anti-aircraft devices; microwave communication equipment, and engine-control instruments. The company earned

thirty-four Government awards, and the President's Certificate of Merit was presented to Morgan by Secretary Forrestal on March 22, 1948. The citation read (in part): "Through Mr. Morgan's exceptional foresight, ingenious organizing and business abilities and patriotic and earnest endeavors in the direction and operation of the Sperry Corporation, a substantial contribution was made to the success of the Allied Nations during World War II by that organization."

Early in 1949 Morgan announced his company's entry into the farm-equipment field. Although material for the United States national defense program is manufactured by the Sperry Gyroscope plant, its busiest division, at Lake Success, Long Island, the corporation has fourteen units elsewhere. These various plants, according to *Investor's Reader* (February 2, 1949), are "spotted" from California to North Carolina, "plus one in Britain." Sperry's corporate division and subsidiaries in 1950 are Sperry Gyroscope Company Division, the Wheeler Insulated Wire Company, the Wright Machinery Company, Vickers, Inc., New Holland Machine Company, Ford Instrument Company, E. G. Staude Division, New Holland Division and Sperry Gyroscope, Ltd.

In July 1949, President Truman appointed Thomas A. Morgan the chairman of the newly created Advisory Committee on Management Improvement. The purpose of the committee is to assist the President in reviewing progress and accomplishments in the better management expected under the Government reorganization plans sent to Congress by the Hoover Commission. At the first meeting of the committee, in October 1949, President Truman said that better management is essential to cut government costs, meet security requirements, expand the economy, and carry out foreign policy commitments. Much of Morgan's "non-Sperry" time is devoted to civic activities. He was a member of several New York State and national war agencies during World War II; in 1949 he was elected chairman of the New York City Cancer Committee, and in 1950 he is serving his third term as chairman of the board of the United Negro College Fund, which assists thirty-two leading Negro colleges and universities in the United States. Another assignment, in early 1950 by Mayor O'Dwyer of New York, was to a four-man fact-finding board to study the demands of the Board of Transportation employees for higher wages and improved working conditions.

The industrialist was awarded honorary D. Sc. degrees by Elon (North Carolina) College in 1939 and by Duke University in 1943; in the latter year he also received an honorary D. Eng. degree from the North Carolina State College of Agriculture and Engineering. Morgan is the board chairman and a director of Vickers, Inc.; New Holland Machine Company, and the Wheeler Insulated Wire Company, Inc. He holds directorships in the Sperry Gyroscope Company, Ltd., Bankers Trust Company, the Lehman Corporation, and the Shell Union Oil Corporation. A member of the board of trustees of the Atlantic Mutual Insurance Company, he holds similar posts in the Atlantic Mutual Indemnity Company, and the

National Safety Council. In addition, he is a member of the board of directors of the North Carolina Engineering Foundation, Inc., a member of the advisory council of the Department of Aeronautical Engineering, Princeton University, and a director of the American Arbitration Association.

The industrialist is on the membership rolls of the American Society of Mechanical Engineers, American Ordnance Association, the Chamber of Commerce of the State of New York, the Chamber of Commerce of the United States, the Council on Foreign Relations, the Institute of Aeronautical Sciences, the National Aeronautic Association, the National Air Council, the Navy League of the United States, the Newcomen Society of England, the New York Southern Society, the Pan-American Society of the United States, and the United States Naval Institute. He belongs to the Army and Navy Country Club, and the Metropolitan Club (in Washington, D.C.), the Economic Club, Madison Square Garden Club, Rockefeller Center Luncheon Club, University Club, and Wings Club (in New York City), and the Sleepy Hollow Country Club (in Scarborough, New York).

On December 23, 1941, Morgan married Celeste Walker Page; by former marriages he has two children, Thomas Alfred and Mary. The corporation executive is five feet nine inches tall, has gray hair and gray eyes, and weighs 180 pounds. He is a Democrat. An active sportsman, he enjoys riding, fishing, hunting and golf.

References

Fortune 21:52+ My '49 por
Investor's Reader F 2 '49 por
N Y Post Mag p21 My 28 '45 por
Sat Eve Post 215:22-3+ My 22 '43 pors
Who's Who in America, 1948-49
Who's Who in Commerce and Industry
   (1948)
Who's Who in Engineering, 1948

MOSHER, A(ARON ALEXANDER) R(OLAND) May 10, 1881- Labor union official

Address: b. c/o Canadian Brotherhood of Railway Employees and Other Transport Workers, 230 Laurier Ave. W., Ottawa, Ont., Canada; h. 722 Parkdale Ave., Ottawa, Ont., Canada

A. R. Mosher, president of the Canadian Congress of Labor, was first elected chief executive of that central body, which comprises both national and international unions, at the time of its formation in 1940. Long active in Canadian trade unions, he had played an important part in the founding of the All-Canadian Congress of Labor, out of which the C.C.L. grew. His first contact with union organization had come when he was instrumental in the establishment of the Canadian Brotherhood of Railway Employees in 1908, and was elected its president, a post in which he has continued to serve. As such he was prominent in the August 1950 national railway strike in Canada. During World War II he was a member of a number of Government labor boards.

A fifth-generation Canadian, Aaron Alexander Roland Mosher was born May 10, 1881, in Halifax County, Nova Scotia, to Samuel Isaiah and Mary Jane (Stevens) Mosher. His father, a farmer, was of Dutch descent. At the age of fifteen the son left public school to work, successively, as a farm laborer, in a gold mine, and as storekeeper for a Halifax coal merchant. In sympathy with the case of a fellow employee whom he considered to have been unfairly discharged, he left the coal yard in 1903 to work as freight handler in the Halifax sheds of the Government-owned Intercolonial Railway.

In 1907 Mosher led a group of freight handlers in a one-week strike for improved wages and working conditions. The effort was successful, and later in the same year an American organizer for a union known as the International Brotherhood of Railway Employees established a local unit covering the employees of the Halifax freight sheds and offices. Mosher, elected financial secretary and treasurer of the local, accompanied the organizer on a tour of other points on the Intercolonial, helping set up more locals. When it was discovered that the Canadian locals formed the larger part of the international union, they decided to withdraw and to found their own headquarters. At Moncton, New Brunswick, in October 1908, the Canadian Brotherhood of Railway Employees, comprising clerks, freight handlers, and station employees, was founded with Mosher as president. When the work of the union began to demand Mosher's full time he applied for, and, after some friction with the local management, received from the Federal Government leave of absence to conduct the business of the brotherhood; the leave was continued down to Mosher's retirement from the Government railways a few years ago.

Under Mosher's leadership the C.B.R.E. attempted organization of similar classes of employees in other Canadian railway lines, and by 1913 had added thirteen new divisions with a substantial membership. In 1916 the union was able to negotiate wage schedules with the Government-owned railways in the Maritime provinces and with several private lines in the West, thus establishing itself as a significant representative of the nonoperating trades. Express employees were successfully organized in 1917, a development in which Mosher had an important part. By 1918 the national scope of the union necessitated the moving of its headquarters to Ottawa.

In June 1949 the C.B.R.E. together with seventeen international railway craft unions (nonoperating trades) demanded new contracts with the two Canadian railways, the Canadian Pacific (privately owned) and the Canadian National (Government-owned). The demands included a 40-hour week with no loss in take-home pay, a seven-cent hourly wage increase and the union check-off. Recommendations made by conciliation boards, which held hearings intermittently until April 1950, proved unacceptable to the unions, and in August they voted to strike. Mosher refused an appeal from

Vincent Thomas

A. R. MOSHER

the Prime Minister to delay the strike, pointing to the lengthy preceding negotiations and the railway workers' good strike record. (Their only previous union-wide strike had been in 1912.) A Government-appointed mediator failed to obtain agreement, and on August 22 the strike commenced. It immediately stopped all rail transport, telegraph communication, and a considerable amount of hotel and steamship service across the country. (Many of Canada's leading hotels are owned and operated by the railway companies.) Approximately 124,000 workers went directly off the job and many others were idle during the nine-day strike. Mosher stated: "It is not principle we are fighting for. It is bread and butter and the opportunity to rest and relax and spend more time with our families."

On August 25, 1950, Prime Minister St. Laurent summoned Parliament to deal with the strike and national defense problems in view of the Korean situation. Parliament passed legislation empowering the Government to use compulsory arbitration after a thirty-day period upon those matters still at issue. A provisional four-cent hourly increase was granted, and the unions obeyed the Government order to return to work on August 30. The report of the Government arbitrator, Mr. Justice R. L. Kellock of the Supreme Court, was expected before the end of the year.

Mosher, an advocate of unity in Canadian labor organization, in 1917 led the C.B.R.E. into affiliation with the Canada Trades and Labor Congress. The latter, since its establishment in 1895, had been based upon AFL-affiliated craft unions. When, in 1920 one of these affiliates persuaded the Congress to revoke the C.B.R.E. charter, Mosher became convinced that the influence of "foreign-controlled" craft unions was deleterious to the position of Canadian labor. In 1927, to promote complete au-

tonomy in Canadian organization, he led in founding the All-Canadian Congress of Labor, and was elected president of the new body. The congress provided for affiliation of both local and national unions. Surviving a split in the Congress executive in 1936, Mosher was confirmed as president. By 1940 A.C.C.L. membership numbered 35,000.

In 1940 the A.C.C.L. decided to amalgamate with the Canadian branches of CIO unions which had been expelled from the Trades and Labor Congress in 1939. At the first convention of the new grouping, named the Canadian Congress of Labor, Mosher was elected president, an office which he has retained. The problem of independence in Canadian organization was solved by the CIO granting complete autonomy to its Canadian branches, and the constitution of the C.C.L. gave its executive larger powers over such matters as jurisdictional disputes than those enjoyed by the AFL or the T.L.C. The C.C.L. membership at the time of its formation was 60,000.

The C.C.L. undertook a program of organizing new unions, mostly on an industrial basis. It established a research department (1942) under a professional economist, a political action committee, a department of public relations, and a leadership educational plan. The congress in its 1943 convention declared that the Co-operative Commonwealth Federation party was "the political arm of labor" and recommended that affiliated and chartered unions affiliate with this social democratic party. The only sustained opposition to this policy has come from Communist-dominated unions. Three such unions have been expelled from the Congress at the direction of Mosher—the International Woodworkers of America, the International Union of Mine, Mill and Smelter Workers, and the United Electrical Workers. In each case the C.C.L. has supported competing unions in the field, and by 1950 its membership reached 350,000, having passed that of the older T.L.C. in 1944. At the 1950 tenth anniversary convention, held in Winnipeg, Mosher was re-elected president (his executive slate was also re-elected). He called for a revision of the Government's conciliation laws to provide for trained panels instead of *ad hoc* appointees. The convention formally expelled the United Electrical Workers because of Communist domination and granted Mosher and his executive full power for the future to expel (rather than to suspend) Communist unions.

The Canadian Congress of Labor president is an advocate of political action by labor. In the 1920's and 1930's he supported J. S. Woodsworth, first Socialist member of the Canadian Parliament. In 1935 he declared: "Our ultimate objective is the transformation of the economic system into one based on service instead of profit; one in which production and consumption will be correlated, and work, leisure, and products will be equitably shared among the workers." During the years of the depression he urged a planned economy and a national system of unemployment insurance. Claiming that the capitalist system had broken down, in 1938 he stated: "If the workers find they cannot induce any existing party to bring about such changes as will meet the needs of the people, they will undoubtedly be forced to establish a labor party on the basis of their economic organization."

During World War II Mosher was a member of the consultative National Wartime Labor Relations Board, of the National Advisory Committee on Selective Service, and of the Minister of Labor's Advisory Committee. In 1946 he was appointed to the Canada Labor Relations Board which administers Government labor policy in the fields under Federal jurisdiction; he has constantly pressed for a national labor code. Declaring in 1949 that the workers of Canada were in danger of losing earlier gains through the rising cost of living, Mosher called for reimposition of price controls and a constitutional amendment to permit nation-wide social security legislation. Mosher is the author of bulletins and articles on labor topics.

In 1946 Mosher received the C.B.E. (Commander of the Order of the British Empire) for his service in furthering the cooperation of labor in the war effort. The labor leader is enrolled in the Co-operative Commonwealth Federation party; his religious affiliation is with the United Church of Canada. He is a member of the Masonic Order and of the Canadian Club. In April 1903 he married Leila Ernest, who died in 1948; their four children are Leila Pearl, Alice Genevieve, Cyril McKay, and Llyod Arnold. The Congress president has been described as a "vigorous, burly, six-footer." Actually his height is five feet ten inches, and he weighs 210 pounds. He has blue eyes and gray hair. According to the *Canadian Unionist,* "one of the secrets of Mr. Mosher's success is his youthful spirit, and his amazing capacity to bear heavy responsibilities without any evidence of undue strain. Even when debates become heated at Congress conventions, Mr. Mosher manages to remain cool and even-tempered." Recreations he enjoys are bridge and salmon fishing.

References

Canadian Unionist S '50
Canadian Who's Who, 1948
Who's Who in Labor (1946)

MOWREY, CORMA (ALICE) Oct. 10, 1907- Education association official

Address: b. c/o National Education Association, 1201 16th St., N.W., Washington, D.C.; c/o West Virginia State Education Assn., 2012 Quarrier St., Charleston 1, W.Va.; h. Clarksburg, W.Va.

The unopposed candidate for the 1950-51 presidency of the National Education Association, Corma Mowrey, was elected to office on July 7, 1950, to succeed Dr. Andrew D. Holt '49. In other offices Miss Mowrey had served as executive committee member and as first vice-president of the organization during 1947-49 and 1949-50 respectively; and she has been active in the West Virginia Education Association, the West Virginia Classroom Teachers Association, and the Harrison County

(West Virginia) Education Association. At the time of her election as president of N.E.A. she had been a teacher in the West Virginia public' school system for twenty years.

Corma Alice Mowrey was born and reared in West Virginia, where her father was a merchant. The daughter of Lloyd and Ida Alice (Adams) Mowrey, she was born in Big Isaac on October 10, 1907, one of seven children. (She had three sisters and three brothers.) For her secondary schooling she attended the Washington Irving High School in Clarksburg, where her extracurricular activities included sports and work in speech and dramatics. Graduated from the school in 1926, she continued her studies at Salem (West Virginia) College, majoring in English; she was a member of the college's scholastic honor roll. While at Salem she held the position of assistant librarian, was cheer leader, and played tennis. She was graduated in 1931 with the degree of B.A. Later, specializing in American literature, she continued her advanced education at North Carolina's Duke University, from which she received the M.A. degree in education in 1942.

Miss Mowrey's career in teaching began with a position as sixth grade teacher at the Wolf Summit (West Virginia) Grade School which she filled from 1927 to 1930 while she was still a student at Salem College. From 1930 to 1941 she taught English and Latin at the Bristol High School, and from 1941 to 1948, at Victory High School, in Clarksburg, her subjects were English and mathematics. Aside from teaching, her duties included presiding an hour each day over the study hall, acting as chairman of the student assembly, chairman of the School Spirit Committee, home-room adviser to thirty-five students, coach for junior class plays, and chairman of the faculty social committee.

Said to feel that it is the duty of a good teacher to belong to professional groups, she has been active in several associations. She was vice-president during the year 1944-45 and president of the West Virginia Classroom Teachers Association in 1945-47. In 1945-46 she acted as president of the Harrison County (West Virginia) Education Association and was president of the West Virginia Education Association during 1947-48. From 1948 to 1950 she was on leave from her Clarksburg teaching position to serve as acting director of professional services for the West Virginia Education Association in Charleston.

At the Cleveland convention of the National Education Association in 1948 Miss Mowrey spoke on behalf of national improvement of teaching conditions. Stating that she taught five classes a day, a total of 176 students, she said (as reported in *Time*): "Under these circumstances, I can barely cover the subject matter of my courses, let alone give my students the individual attention they need." Her service in an official capacity with the National Education Association, which, according to the New York *Times* (July 9, 1950) "is generally considered . . . the most influential policy-making school group in the United States," began with 1947-49 membership on the association's executive committee, and continued when Miss Mowrey served as the organization's first vice-presi-

Buckingham

CORMA MOWREY

dent during 1949-50. She was elected without opposition as the 1950-51 president of N.E.A. on July 7, 1950, at the eighty-eighth annual conference in St. Louis. Declaring in her acceptance address that to offer every school child in America equal opportunity for public education is one of the greatest needs of the country, Miss Mowrey asserted the organization's intention to make "vigorous efforts" to see enacted Federal aid to education and to be "militant . . . in establishing higher standards of training and qualification" among teachers (*Christian Science Monitor*, July 8, 1950). She also stressed the need of offering greater economic security to teachers.

In her new post Miss Mowrey is president of an association which has grown from a membership of 154,000 in 1934 to a direct membership of 450,000 and an affiliated membership of more than 850,000 in 1950. At its 1950 conference the N.E.A. debated the desirability of creation of a national board of education and establishment of uniform school attendance laws in the various states. It urged Federal aid for public schools while opposing it for parochial schools. An amendment barring Communists from organization membership was adopted, as was a resolution that they be barred from teaching. The association decided to meet in future only in cities providing "a maximum degree of equality" for all races.

Miss Mowrey, who stressed the place that education can play in thwarting Communism and strengthening democracy, was among speakers at the fourth delegate assembly of the World Organization of the Teaching Profession held in Ottawa, Canada, in July 1950. She is the author of several articles published during 1949-50 in the *West Virginia School Journal*. The recipient of an honorary Pd.D. degree from Salem College in June 1950, Miss Mowrey has said that she takes great pride in her profession, that in teaching "there is a great service to be rendered to the young people of the nation."

A life member of N.E.A., the West Virginia Classroom Teachers Association and the West Virginia Education Association, the educator also lists among her organizational memberships the American Association of University Women, Kappa Delta Pi, and Delta Kappa Gamma, education society. During her years of teaching in Clarksburg Miss Mowrey taught Sunday school classes and aided Clarksburg's Red Cross and Community Chest drives. In her religious affiliation she is a Methodist, and in politics a Republican. She lists her favorite recreations as "swimming, fishing—all sports, particularly baseball and football."

Miss Mowrey, who has been called "tall and robust," is five feet eight inches in height, weighs 158 pounds, and has brown eyes and brown hair. Referring in 1948 to the salary she earned while she taught at the Clarksburg school ($276 a month, nine months a year) and to her heavy schedule there, she was quoted (*Time* July 19, 1948) as follows: "I guess you might say that I am overworked and underpaid. But I stay in teaching because I like it. There is a satisfaction to it that is missing from most jobs—even better paid ones. The realization that you are making an important contribution to the lives of individuals gives you the zest to go on."

References

Christian Sci Mon p1 Jl 8 '50
N Y Times p25 Jl 6 '48
Time 52:60 Jl 19 '48 por

MUIR, JAMES Banker

Address: b. c/o The Royal Bank of Canada, Montreal, Que., Canada; h. 3495 Holton Ave., Westmount, Que., Canada

The Royal Bank of Canada, one of the world's thirteen largest banking institutions, has as its president James Muir. An employee of the Bank of Scotland, Muir joined the staff of the Canadian bank in 1912, and has participated in its growth into an institution having over 725 branches in Canada, Cuba, Puerto Rico, Dominican Republic, Haiti, British West Indies, the Central and South Americas. During his years with the bank, Muir served in several of its branches in Western Canada, managing the Winnipeg branch from 1928 until 1932. His appointment as president took place in October 1949.

Born in Peebles, Scotland, James Muir gained a reputation at school as "the laddie who was aye guid at sums." He attended private schools, where he was better than average in athletics, participating in soccer, rugby, and amateur boxing. In the last-named, he learned a lesson which he was to apply to advantage in the business world: "It is unwise to relax before the bout is won." His ability in mathematics having led him to choose banking as his profession, in 1907, shortly after the end of his formal schooling, he applied and was admitted to the Commercial Bank of Scotland as an apprentice. In 1910, after a three-year apprenticeship, Muir joined the staff of the Chartered Bank of India, in London, where he gained knowledge of world finance. Preferring the Western Hemisphere, the young Scotsman refused an offer of a post in the Far East with the Indian banking house. An application he made at the London office of The Royal Bank of Canada was accepted, and in 1912 he was sent to its Moose Jaw, Saskatchewan, branch.

The Royal Bank of Canada was founded in 1864 under the name of Merchants Bank of Halifax to facilitate the purchases made by the United States in Canada during the Civil War. In less than a century the organization grew from a small-town bank into one of the thirteen largest banking institutions in the world. Strong from the beginning, it weathered the 1873 panic, during which many banks both in Canada and the United States failed. With the coming of the Spanish-American War the Halifax bank opened branches in Cuba; and by 1901, when the new name, the Royal Bank of Canada, was sanctioned by the Canadian Parliament, it was internationally known. In 1950 it had 670 branches across Canada and 62 in foreign countries; its assets were then in excess of $2,300,000,000.

After filling posts in several of the bank's smaller Western Canadian branches, Muir was promoted to the inspector's department in Winnipeg. This was followed by a move to the accounting department of the Grain Exchange Branch, in the same city. In 1917 he was advanced to a place in the bank's head office at Montreal. Promoted to inspector, he was posted to the supervisor's department in Winnipeg. His work between 1920 and 1923 as assistant to the Quebec supervisor attracted the attention of senior executives, and from then on he advanced rapidly. In 1925 Muir was named assistant supervisor of the Central and South American business, with headquarters in New York. In this capacity he visited the bank's branches in Cuba, Brazil, Uruguay, Argentina, and Peru, and made surveys of potential opportunities for branches in other countries of Latin America.

Three years later (1928) the banker was elevated to the position of manager of the Winnipeg branch. He filled this post until 1932, when he was again attached to the head office staff, this time as general inspector. In 1935 he was named assistant general manager, in 1945 general manager. After being appointed director in 1947 and vice-president in 1948, Muir on October 18, 1949, became president of Canada's largest chartered bank.

President Muir has pointed out that a banking institution performs many acts of public service: it gives banking counsel that is valuable to both small and big business enterprise and by aiding business in its routine way, the bank helps every person in the community. The bank, Muir has declared, renders a service through its broad outlook upon the affairs of the Dominion and of the world. Its interest in world affairs is indicated in its publication, *The Monthly Letter*, a two-page sheet the bank has been issuing for a number of years. Each issue is devoted exclusively to an editorial article on a subject of current interest, such as the world water situation, a subject during the recent period of water shortage.

Karsh

JAMES MUIR

Muir, at the bank's 1950 annual meeting, advocated an agreement to remove Britain's war-incurred debt to "wipe out the greatest single threat to the value of the pound." He also declared that stabilization of foreign exchange rates would necessitate the implementation of some such mechanism as the gold standard. He voiced a belief that it would be advisable to abandon the exchange parities established by the International Monetary Fund, and to allow the market to determine the rates of exchange. The fund agreement, however, he thought might be "useful after the free exchange market had done its work," when, at the end of a free market period, currencies should be stabilized at rates determined by the free market. Though deeming a return to the mechanism of the gold standard most desirable, he thought that in view of "the modern vogue for managed currencies" this would not be "politically acceptable." As a compromise, he suggested the use of stabilized loans.

Muir is quoted as saying, "Occasional bursts of energy and moments of brilliance," are not so effective as steady application of one's abilities. The habitual brief-case carrier he regards as a person who does not delegate his work to his assistants properly or who fails to organize his work systematically or who postpones decisions, "leaving the challenge until later." Muir himself is reported to have tremendous energy and great organizing ability. He is said to be a stickler for efficiency and a strict disciplinarian.

The banking executive is a life governor and chairman of the finance committee of Verdun Protestant Hospital, a governor of the Royal Edward Laurentian Hospital and of the Royal Victoria Hospital (Montreal). In 1948 he was chairman of the welfare campaign, which, for the first time in four years, reached its objective of $1,140,000. He is a member of

MUIR, JAMES—*Continued*

the board of honorary advisory directors of the Health League of Canada, president of the Canadian Association for Adult Education, and associate honorary treasurer of the Canadian Chamber of Commerce. On September 27, 1919, James Muir married Phyllis Marguerite Brayley of Montreal. The couple have one child, a daughter. Muir's clubs are the St. James, Mount Royal, Mount Bruno Golf, and Country (Montreal), Manitoba (Winnipeg), and the Mattawin Fishing.

References

Who's Who in Canada, 1945-46
World Biography (1948)

MURPHY, CHARLES S(PRINGS) Aug. 20, 1909- United States Government official
Address: b. Executive Office of the President, The White House, Washington 25, D.C.; h. 905 Columbia Blvd., Silver Spring, Md.

At his last news conference of 1949 President Truman announced the appointment of Charles S. Murphy as special counsel to the Chief Executive. On February 1, 1950, Murphy succeeded Clark M. Clifford[47] in that office, seen as one of the most important in the so-called "Little Cabinet." A graduate of Duke University Law School, Murphy spent thirteen years in the Office of the Legislative Counsel of the Senate before joining the White House staff as an administrative assistant in 1947.

Born in Wallace, North Carolina, on August 20, 1909, Charles Springs Murphy was one of three sons of William Faison and Kate (Westbrook) Murphy. (One of his brothers is now a farmer near Durham, North Carolina; the other, a physician, is president of the North Carolina Medical Society.) Charles Murphy graduated from the Wallace High School, then

Wide World Photos
CHARLES S. MURPHY

enrolled at Duke University, Durham, where he received the B.A. degree in 1931. In 1934 he was awarded the LL.B. degree by that university's law school. Having passed a Civil Service examination in 1928 for a Post Office position, he worked for eight months (1928-29) in the Post Office at Wilmington, North Carolina; the position, which paid $1,500 a year, included opening parcel post bags and sorting packages. During five of his years at Duke University (1929-34), he worked a full night shift in the Durham Post Office.

Admitted to the North Carolina bar upon receiving his law degree in 1934, Murphy went to Washington, D.C., "looking for a job." Through Justin Miller[47], former dean of Duke Law School and at that time with the Department of Justice, he heard of a vacancy in the office of the legislative counsel of the Senate, and after an interview secured appointment as assistant counsel on that staff. The chief function of this office is to draft bills in legal language and form before they are introduced into the Senate. Early in his Washington career, Murphy, a Democrat, was called upon to assist Truman, then a newly elected Senator. Thereafter Truman frequently asked for his assistance—Murphy, for example, aided in drafting the resolution for the forming of the Senate War Investigating Committee. It was as chairman of this committee that Truman first received national recognition as a political figure. Murphy was admitted to the Supreme Court bar in 1944, and to the District of Columbia bar in 1947.

Since January 1947 the lawyer has been one of the small group of administrative assistants to the President often referred to as the "Little Cabinet." The press has used the phrase "a passion for anonymity" when describing the traditional characteristic of this group comprised, in *Time*'s words, of "men the U.S. knows little about, who make it their business to know a lot about the U.S." Murphy's function in this post was, as in his preceding one, to draft bills, and to help analyze legislation sent to the President for his signature. Aiding also on the speeches for the Chief Executive, he is credited with playing "a leading part" in planning the strategy and speeches of Truman's 1948 campaign, in cooperation with Clifford. During the early part of the campaign he remained in Washington, sending material from the capital to writers aboard the Presidential train. In the "decisive last two weeks" of the campaign, he was aboard the train.

On February 1, 1950, more than one hundred Cabinet members, Congressmen, and other officials saw Murphy sworn in as special counsel to the President by Associate Supreme Court Justice Tom Clark[45]. His predecessor, Clark Clifford, had resigned from the $20,000-a-year post to engage in private law practice. *Time* Magazine quoted "a Truman intimate" as saying that Murphy "lacks Clifford's flair and imagination." In general, the appointment was received as an indication that there would be little or no change in policy. It has been said that Murphy has written more Presidential speeches than Clifford has during the past year; the New York *Times* credited him with "a high degree of acumen in the planning, timing and the expression of Mr. Truman's official actions." He is seen as important in formulating the Presidential policy on all major issues, including Truman's civil rights program. *Business Week* has noted that Murphy is "adept at putting on paper the simple words that are Truman's best stock in trade."

Among the "devotedly anonymous" administrative aides, Murphy is reported to be one of the most self-effacing. (One anecdote is that, in spite of his important role in the Government, he has been so little known that the White House Correspondents' Association neglected to remember to invite him to their 1949 annual dinner for the President.) The comment has been made that he ranks high in prestige among his colleagues for the "sheer orderliness of his legalistic mind." Among the duties of his new post are checking on the progress of the Administration program in Congress, and timing the introduction of new programs. He is also kept "pretty busy. . . answering Truman's questions."

A member of the North Carolina State Bar Association, Murphy belongs as well to the Order of the Coif (honorary legal fraternity), Pi Gamma Mu fraternity, and Delta Sigma Phi (national legal fraternity); he attends a Methodist church. While he was a law student, Murphy married Kate Chestney Graham on December 24, 1931. The family, in which there are three children (two daughters, Courtenay and Elizabeth; a son, Westbrook), lives in Silver Spring, a Washington suburb. The White House aide is an inch under six feet in height and weighs 185 pounds; the color of his eyes is blue, of his hair light-brown. In a New York *Herald Tribune* paragraph he is reported to have remarked that he has no special hobbies.

References

    N Y Herald Tribune p4 D 23 '49; p19 II D 25 '49
    N Y Times p1 D 23 '49
    Time 55:13 Ja 2 '50 por
    U S News 27:37 D 30 '49 por
    Washington (D.C.) Post p1 D 23 '49 por
    Who's Who in America, 1950-51

MURRAY, THOMAS E(DWARD) June 20, 1891- United States Government official; industrial executive; engineer

Address: b. c/o United States Atomic Energy Commission, 19th St. & Constitution Ave., N.W., Washington 25, D.C.; c/o Murray Manufacturing Corp., 1250 Atlantic Ave., Brooklyn 16, New York; h. 686 Park Ave., New York 21

Thomas E. Murray, industrial engineer, inventor, and corporation executive, was named in March 1950 to the United States Atomic Energy Commission to fill out the unexpired term of David E. Lilienthal '44, who had resigned in February of that year. Murray, whose name became familiar to New Yorkers between 1932 and 1940, when he was receiver for the bankrupt Interborough Rapid Transit lines, was again much in the public eye in

THOMAS E. MURRAY

1947-48, as one of three trustees named to administer the welfare fund of the United Mine Workers of America. His appointment to the unexpired Lilienthal term on the AEC was confirmed by the Senate on March 30. In June he was reconfirmed for a new two-year term ending in 1952.

The second of the eight children (four sons and four daughters) of Thomas Edward and Catherine (Bradley) Murray, Thomas Edward Murray, Jr., was born in Albany, New York, on June 20, 1891. His father, an electrical engineer and inventor, was associated with the late Anthony N. Brady in the development of the Albany Electric Light Company and, subsequently, of the New York Edison Company. The family moved to Brooklyn, and it was at Our Lady of Victory School young Murray began his education. After being graduated from the St. Francis Xavier High School in Manhattan, he proceeded to the Yale University Sheffield Scientific School, where he received his B.S. degree in mechanical engineering in 1911.

On leaving college Murray worked briefly for the New York Edison Company, then joined the Metropolitan Engineering Company and Thomas E. Murray, Inc., the Brooklyn businesses established by his father to develop, manufacture, and market inventions and patents (eventually exceeding one thousand in number) and to design and build electric power plants. (Today, the younger Murray personally holds some two hundred patents in the electrical and welding fields; among other patents he holds are those for the Murray copper radiator and for a water-cooled furnace wall for power plants.)

When the United States entered World War I the Government commissioned the Murray firms to apply a new electric welding process to the making of munitions, and to design ma-

MURRAY, THOMAS E.—*Continued*

chinery to produce and weld trench mortar shells, gas shells, and other equipment for the Trench Warfare Division. After the war the junior Murray became increasingly interested in problems of automobile manufacture, and evolved an improved type of rear axle housing. He became president of the Metropolitan Engineering Company and chairman of the board of Thomas E. Murray, Inc., after his father's death in July of 1929. The elder Murray left an estate estimated at about ten million dollars·

"Thomas E. Murray," stated Carl Levin of the New York *Herald Tribune* (March 23, 1950), "was known to millions of New York City's I. R. T. subway riders in the days before unification came in 1940, because every statement or note of cheer pasted in the cars was signed: 'Thomas E. Murray, Receiver.'" The Interborough Rapid Transit Company, which operated most of the elevated railway lines of the metropolis as well as the first subway and its extensions, went into bankruptcy in 1932. On August 26 of that year, Murray and former Judge Victor J. Dowling were named coreceivers. Murray, who shortly became the sole receiver, is credited with having brought about a substantial reduction in the operating deficit within two years, with tiding the transit system over labor crises, and, in general, with exhibiting conspicuous executive ability in the eight difficult years before the city took over and merged all subway and elevated lines.

In November 1938 Murray was elected to the board of trustees of the Bank of New York and the Fifth Avenue Bank; and during the next year (1939) organized the Murray Manufacturing Company of Brooklyn, makers of electrical switches and circuit breakers. Two years later (1941) his experience in labor-management relations led to his appointment as arbitrator of union demands on the Bell Aircraft Corporation and the New York City Omnibus and Fifth Avenue Coach Companies; Murray was successful in bringing about a settlement in both disputes.

During World War II the Murray plants were again turned to war production. Two of Murray's inventions, designs for mass production of 81-millimeter trench mortar shells and for a new 60-millimeter mortar shell, brought him in 1943 a citation for distinguished service and the written thanks of President Roosevelt. In May 1945 Murray was named by Edward J. Flynn[40], Bronx County leader and former chairman of the Democratic National Committee, as his personal first choice for the party's nomination for Mayor of the City of New York; but the nomination, and subsequent election, went to District Attorney William O'Dwyer[47].

In 1947 Murray was selected as the presiding trustee of a three-man board to administer the $15,000,000 health and welfare fund of the United Mine Workers of America. (The other members were John L. Lewis[42] for the U. M. W. A., and Captain N. H. Collisson representing the Federal Government, which had at that time taken over operation of the soft coal mines.) Unable to effect agreement between his colleagues (by which time Collisson had been replaced by Ezra Van Horn, representing mineowners) on the distribution of the fund benefits, Murray resigned in February 1948, criticizing the other board members for having "established themselves in fixed positions from which they would not consider retreat." For the next two years Murray was not prominent in public life. His business interests by that time included membership on the finance committee and on the board of directors of the Chrysler Corporation.

President Truman on March 22, 1950, nominated Murray to the five-man Atomic Energy Commission, to fill out the unexpired term of David E. Lilienthal, who had resigned about seven weeks earlier. One week later, March 29, the Congressional Joint Committee on Atomic Energy heard Murray discuss his qualifications, and a poll of its members revealed full approval of the President's choice. ("I think he is exactly the type of man we need at this time in this field," said Republican Senator John W. Bricker, Ohio, of the Democratic appointee.) Murray was confirmed by the Senate on March 31; his appointment was to replace Lilienthal as member but not as chairman. At the expiration of the Lilienthal term, Murray was reconfirmed, for a new two-year term ending in 1952. He resigned his bank trusteeships and his Chrysler directorship on confirmation to the commission, membership on which carries a salary of $15,000 a year.

Murray's wife is the former Marie Brady, of Brooklyn. Married January 4, 1917, they have four daughters and seven sons: Thomas E., Jr., Marie (Mrs. Basil Harris), James, Paul, D. Bradley, Joseph G., Anne, Jane, Peter, Frank, and Margot (D. Bradley and Joseph G. Murray are members of the Jesuit Order). Regarded as one of the leading Roman Catholic laymen in the United States, Murray was, while a resident of Brooklyn, the head of the Catholic Charities of that borough. He has been a member of the board of trustees of the National Foundation for Infantile Paralysis, which he helped to establish, and he is a trustee of Manhattanville College. Titles of honor conferred on him include those of Knight of St. Gregory, Knight of Malta, and Knight of the Holy Sepulchre, all of which are Papal titles. Honorary LL.D. degrees were given him by Marquette, Fordham, Georgetown, and St. John's universities. He is a fellow of the American Society of Mechanical Engineers and of the American Institute of Electrical Engineers; his clubs are the Shinnecock, Yale, Creek, and University.

References

N Y Herald Tribune p17 My 15 '45; p1+ Mr 23 '50 por; IIp3 Mr 26 '50 por
N Y Times p1+ Mr 23 '50 por
N Y World-Telegram p8 Mr 23 '50 por
Transit Journal 73:428+ D '34 por
American Catholic Who's Who, 1950-51
Who's Who in America, 1950-51

MYERSON, MRS. GOLDA *See* Meyerson, Mrs. G.

MYRDAL, MRS. ALVA (mür'däl) Jan. 31, 1902- United Nations official; sociologist
Address: c/o United Nations, New York

An internationally known Swedish sociologist, Mrs. Alva Myrdal, with her husband, economist Gunnar Myrdal [46], was prominent in the social and economic program adopted by her country in the 1930's. From 1936 to 1948 she directed the Training College for Nursery and Kindergarten Teachers, which she had helped found. After World War II she became active in the United Nations, and in February 1949 was named principal director of that organization's Department of Social Affairs. Her appointment as director of the Department of Social Sciences of UNESCO, to become effective early in 1951, was announced in September 1950.

Mrs. Alva Myrdal was born January 31, 1902, to Albert and Lowa (Larsson) Reimer in Uppsala, Sweden, where her father was a building contractor. Miss Reimer attended Stockholm University, working as a library assistant during her student days, and holding the Sökestraus scholarship for two years. In 1924 she was graduated wtih the B.A. degree, and became a study group leader in the adult education movement. This early work in the Workers' Educational Association Mrs. Myrdal has attributed to the influence of her father, who was a member of the Eskilstuna City Council, where he was chiefly concerned with social welfare. A member of the Swedish Labor party, he was active in the establishment of cooperatives. Another influence in her early years was that of Per Sundberg, leader of the Quakers in Sweden, who was her teacher in the primary grades.

On October 8, 1924, the year she graduated from university, Miss Reimer was married to Gunnar Myrdal, who was at that time practicing law in Stockholm, and who was to become internationally known as one of Sweden's outstanding economists. Sharing a deep concern in social and economic problems, the Myrdals together pursued studies in those fields during 1925-28 in London, Leipzig, and Stockholm. During 1929-30 they traveled in the United States on Rockefeller fellowships. Studies in Geneva followed in 1930-31. In 1932 the Myrdals returned to Sweden.

In the course of the 1930's the Myrdals established themselves as significant socioeconomic thinkers. Gunnar Myrdal was appointed to the chair of political economics and public finance at Stockholm University, in 1945 became secretary of commerce, and in 1947 was named secretary of the United Nations Economic Commission for Europe. Mrs. Myrdal continued her studies, specializing in philosophy, psychology, and education; during 1932-34 she was psychological assistant at Sweden's main prison. She received the M.A. degree from Uppsala University in 1934. That year also saw the publication of "Crisis in the Population

Official United Nations Photo.
MRS. ALVA MYRDAL

Problem," a study on which she and her husband had collaborated. The book aroused wide public interest and appeared in Danish and Norwegian editions the same year. It is credited with having a direct influence on the social policies of the Scandinavian countries during the 1930's; the Swedish Government undertook a program based on state responsibility for the care of children without regard to parents' economic means.

In this program housing was to have a central role. The Myrdals were called upon by the Government to advise on the direction of the program, Mrs. Myrdal serving in 1935 as expert to the Government Committee on Social Housing (she contributed to its report an appendix, "The Influence of Housing Conditions on Children"), and in 1935 as adviser to the Royal Population Commission, writing its report on "Day Care of Children". In *Nation and Family*, she described for the English-speaking world the Swedish experiment in "democratic family and population policy." *Survey* commented: "The mere outline of the contents of this exceptional book can give no adequate impression of its high quality in style, in factual adequacy, and in the objectivity of its analysis. It should be required reading in every course on the family." The growth of Mrs. Myrdal's international reputation as an expert in population problems led to her being consulted by the Royal Population Commission in London in 1945.

In 1936 Mrs. Myrdal was founder of the Training College for Nursery and Kindergarten Teachers, an undertaking of the Swedish Cooperative Housing Society. She became the institution's director, and remained with it in that capacity until 1948. In 1935 she had published "City Children" and in 1936 produced "Right Playthings." Since 1946 Mrs. Myrdal has been a member of the Royal Commission on

MYRDAL, MRS. ALVA—*Continued*

Educational Reform, and chairman of its section on curriculum and methods, and since the same year chairman of the Interim Commission of the World Council for Early Childhood Education. A member of the Government Committee on the Handicapped, 1944-47, she served as chairman of its section on vocational guidance and vocational training.

A member of the Social Democratic party of Sweden (also known abroad as the Labor party), Mrs. Myrdal in 1943 served on the committee charged with the postwar program of the Labor Party and Trade Union Federation. She was elected a member of the party's program commission for the period 1944-48. During 1936-38 the sociologist was one of four editors of *Morgonbris*, monthly magazine of Labor Party Women. She was organizer in 1946 of Round Table Discussions of the Co-operative Movement, and editor of its four publications. At the International Labor Organization Conference in Paris in 1945 Mrs. Myrdal was Swedish representative, and was, together with Katharine Lenroot [50] of the United States, rapporteur of the committee preparing the convention on young workers. Representing her country again at the 1947 ILO conference in Geneva, Mrs. Myrdal was a member of the committee on freedom of association.

Prominent in the movement for greater participation of women in the political and economic life of the community, Mrs. Myrdal during 1935-38 was chief secretary of the State Commission on Women's Work. For the year 1935-36 she was vice-chairman of the Stockholm Organization of Business and Professional Women. She was president of the Swedish Federation of B.P.W. for two terms, 1936-38 and 1940-42. From 1938 until 1947 the Swedish women's leader was a vice-president of the International Federation of B.P.W. Chairman during 1945-47 of the committee on economic and professional questions of the International Federation of University Women, she was responsible for preparing its report on the international aspect of married women's work.

Other national and civic organizations through which the sociologist contributed to the social program of Sweden include the Government Committee on Organization of Social Information Services (chairman since 1946); the Central Association for Social Work (vice-chairman 1944-47); the Board of the Stockholm School for Social Work, 1946-48. Since 1946 Mrs. Myrdal has been one of three members of the editorial board supervising the publication of an official handbook on social conditions and social legislation in Sweden. The Scientific Council for a Swedish Gallup Institute counted her a member from its formation in 1943 until 1948. As a representative for her country, Mrs. Myrdal was a member of the Government-appointed board for Swedish participation in the New York World's Fair in 1939, and was a member of the Swedish Institute's committee on international exhibitions during 1945-47.

Meanwhile, the Myrdals had gone again to the United States, being in residence there from September 1938 to April 1940 while Professor Myrdal, at the invitation of the Carnegie Corporation of New York directed research for a study of the American Negro. (The study resulted in the publication in 1944 of the book *An American Dilemma*.) While her husband was engaged in this work Alva Myrdal investigated social and educational problems in the United States, lectured, and wrote articles for several periodicals, including *Parents' Magazine* and *Independent Woman*. On their return to Sweden the Myrdals collaborated on a book describing American democratic forces in times of social change and international crisis, entitled "Contact with America" (1941).

Sweden, though a neutral in World War II, was beset by special social problems arising out of it, many of which centered on the influx of refugees. During 1945-46 Mrs. Myrdal was editor of *Via Suecia*, a multilingual weekly published to help refugees understand their new environment, and was vice-chairman from 1943 to 1947 of the Joint Committee of Swedish Civic Organizations for Cultural Relief in Europe, which was set up to deal with the rehabilitation of refugees. She was a member of the Swedish Government Committee for International Relief, a centralizing body.

In 1949 the Swedish sociologist was appointed to succeed Jan Stanczyk of Poland as Principal Director of the Department of Social Affairs of the United Nations. Mrs. Myrdal's position as a department director made her the highest ranking woman member of the Secretariat. Chief responsibility of her post, which she assumed in February 1949, is the coordination of U.N. projects in the social field, such as the work of the divisions serving the commissions on social activities, human rights, freedom of information, status of women, narcotic drugs, population. An indication of the director's viewpoint may be gathered from one of her remarks quoted in an article on her in *Survey*: "To the internationally minded men and women of the world social ills are as real and urgent as political and economic problems."

In an address given at the fifty-third annual meeting of the American Academy of Political and Social Science in 1949, on the topic "World Government: Why? When? How?" Mrs. Myrdal, acknowledging that social problems are primarily national problems, maintained that international action could be of value "as a mutual support in the endeavors within the different nations." It is her conviction that the Social Affairs Department's compilation of data on world social conditions can be effective in stimulating world-wide social improvements by process of emulation, and that its program of technical training and assistance will be of great influence (from the *Survey* article). As of the summer of 1950, the department had given more than 400 fellowships to persons from eighteen countries for training in countries other than their own, and had sent a number of technical consultants to help train local social leaders in countries requesting such help.

Announcement was made in September 1950 that early in 1951 Mrs. Myrdal would become director of the Department of Social Sciences of the United Nations Educational, Scientific, and Cultural Organization in Paris. The sociologist had previously been associated with UNESCO as her country's representative at the 1946 conference in Paris. She had also served as consultant on International Understanding through Schools to UNESCO's Social Science Department in 1947, and had written a pamphlet on population for the Mass Communication Division in 1948.

Alva Myrdal became a member of the board of the World Federation of United Nations Associations in 1948. She has participated in the work of two research committees of the Carnegie Endowment for International Peace, one on national cultural relations programs in international affairs (1948), and one on population problems and international tension (1948). Other books she has written in Swedish are: "Cross Section of Great Britain" (1942), "Postwar Planning" (1944), "Comments" (1944; a collection of articles on foreign affairs published in "Labor Daily" during 1943-44). Her contributions to newspapers, periodicals, books, and reports are numerous. A number of her Swedish books have appeared in other European languages.

In 1947 Mrs. Myrdal was awarded a Danish prize (of 5,000 crowns) for outstanding achievement in the field of education. She has refused Swedish and foreign decorations as a matter of principle. Her religious affiliation is with the Swedish Lutheran Church, in which, however, she is not active. The Myrdals have a son, Jan Gunnar, two daughters, Sissela and Kaj. The Swedish sociologist, who is five feet five inches tall, weighs 130 pounds, has blue eyes and fair hair, has been described as "vivacious" in manner. Her favorite forms of recreation are travel and walking tours.

References

Ind Woman 17:379 D '38; 28:165 Je '49
Survey 85:330 Je '49
Washington (D.C.) Post p8 N 6 '49
International Who's Who, 1950
Vem är Det, 1949
World Biography (1948)

MYRDAL, MRS. GUNNAR *See* Myrdal, Mrs. A.

NEELY, MATTHEW M(ANSFIELD)
Nov. 9, 1874- United States Senator from West Virginia
Address: b. Senate Office Bldg., Washington, D.C.; Home Savings Bank Bldg., Fairmont, W.Va.; h. 225 Watson Ave., Fairmont, W.Va.

When J. Howard McGrath '45 resigned from the Senate to become Attorney General of the United States in August 1949, Senator Matthew M. Neely of West Virginia succeeded him as chairman of the Senate District Committee, a position better known as the "unofficial mayor" of Washington, D.C. Neely has spent approximately twenty-six years in Congress, having served five terms in the House of Representatives, and in 1950 is serving his

fourth term in the Senate. The Democratic legislator began his career as a lawyer and was elected Mayor of Fairmont, West Virginia, and Governor of the State.

Matthew Mansfield Neely was born on a farm near Groves, West Virginia, the son of Alfred Neely, a doctor, and Mary (Morris) Neely. The date of his birth is November 9, 1874; he is of Scotch-Irish-Welsh descent. An ancestor was a cousin of Robert Burns, the Scottish poet; and a forebear of his father's was John Neely, who emigrated from County Tyrone, Ireland, to Ulster County, New York, and served in the Continental Army in the Revolutionary War. (Matthew Neely's two sisters, Mrs. Dagmar Keyser and Mrs. Delmonde Jones, live in Belington, West Virginia.) He attended the local rural school, and taught for four years before he entered Salem College. His education was interrupted by service in the Spanish-American War in 1898, when he was a private in the First Infantry of the West Virginia Volunteers (He remained a member of the West Virginia National Guard from 1899 to 1912, advancing to the rank of major before resigning.)

Returning to civilian life, Neely entered West Virginia University, from which he was graduated with a B.A. degree in 1901. In the course of his college years he won several intercollegiate oratorical contests, shared the Wills Prize for oratory, and received a gold medal for being the best drilled cadet in the university's military department. In 1902 he received the LL.B. degree from its law school, and was admitted to the Marion County bar. The following year he established a law practice in Fairmont, in partnership with Henry A. Lively.

Five years later (1908), in what the New York *Sun* labeled "a scrappy campaign," Neely was elected Mayor of Fairmont on a "Dry" platform, for a two-year term. For the next three (1911-13) years he was clerk of the House of Delegates of West Virginia. In 1913, in a special election to fill the unexpired term of Congressman John W. Davis, who had been appointed Solicitor General of the United States, Neely was sent to the United States House of Representatives, and was re-elected to three successive terms from the First District of West Virginia. He failed of re-election in 1921, but in 1922 was sent to the Senate for his first term. Defeated in the 1928 campaign, he was again returned to the Senate in 1931, and re-elected in 1936. In 1940, while still a member of the Senate, he campaigned successfully for the Governorship of West Virginia, whereupon he resigned his Senate seat on January 12, 1941, to take the State office. In 1942 the Governor was a candidate for the Senate, but was defeated by Chapman Revercomb, his Republican opponent. Two years later he was elected to his fifth term in the House of Representatives. The veteran legislator won the Democratic nomination to the Senate in 1948 over Rush D. Holt, whom Neely had supported in the '30's when Holt was known as "the boy Senator" from West Virginia, but with whom he had broken when Holt opposed the New Deal Administration.

Photo Crafters

MATTHEW M. NEELY

Defeating Revercomb in the election, Neely returned to the Senate on January 3, 1949.

Neely's political career has been characterized generally as liberal, pro-labor, and pro-Administration in Roosevelt's and Truman's terms. His campaign for Governor was based on a program calling for safeguards of the right to collective bargaining, greater benefits for the blind and needy aged, elimination of sales tax on basic foods, and better salaries for teachers. Most of this program was enacted into law by the State legislature, which also, in special session, passed the Governor's law providing voting machinery for the State's men and women in the armed forces. A more rebellious legislature during the latter half of Neely's administration defeated his State labor relations act. In April 1944 the Governor sent State police to take over law enforcement in the steel town of Weirton, after United Steel Workers' representatives had been arrested by local police for distributing strike leaflets.

Despite political differences, Neely and John L. Lewis [42] have had what Fred W. Perkins, Scripps-Howard staff writer, has called "a political Damon and Pythias relationship." The State CIO, AFL and United Mine Workers have supported Neely in his political contest, their influence being particularly strong in his campaign against Revercomb, who had supported the Taft-Hartley bill in the Senate. Neely, who has consistently opposed the bill, took part in Senate debate in June 1949, going "down the line" for the Administration labor bill, and opposing all amendments, which he declared were proposed "to appease" Taft-Hartley bill proponents.

Another issue on which Neely was in direct opposition to Revercomb in the last election was that of the Displaced Persons Act of 1948, sponsored by Revercomb in the Senate. Neely's substitute act, introduced in January 1949 and backed by Truman, would double the quota of displaced persons admitted to the country (raising the figure from 200,000 to 400,000) and would ease other restrictions on entry. It would eliminate what Neely regards as "overtly discriminatory" features of the Revercomb bill, which has been called anti-Catholic and anti-Jewish by its opponents. "As democracy preaches equality of opportunity," Neely has declared, "it must practice it by promptly substituting a fair, liberal, and humanitarian measure" for the present DP law. In June 1949 a group of 250 prominent citizens and business leaders, headed by Herbert H. Lehman [43], Harper Sibley and James A. Farley [44], made public an appeal for the passage of the McGrath-Neely bill.

In 1943 Neely campaigned in support of a fourth term for President Roosevelt. At a *Town Meeting of the Air* radio program held in Pittsburgh on April 29, at which "four speakers . . . nearly came to blows," Neely declared with characteristic oratory that he believed Roosevelt's Presidency to be as indispensable, under existing circumstances, "as a fire department is to a city that is wrapped in the flames of its own combustion and shrouded with the smoke of its own conflagration." Questioned before the 1948 election on his intentions of supporting "Democratic party control" in the Senate, especially in relation to the President's civil rights program, Neely replied, "No sort of political expediency could induce or tempt me to desert the humanitarian civil rights program." His candidacy was supported by Truman in a speech in Huntington, West Virginia. The *New Republic* (October 25, 1948) quoted the President as saying, "If you don't elect this fellow, you don't know which side your bread's buttered on, I'll tell you that." The Senator's loyalty to the Truman Administration has been consistent, although *Business Week* (January 29, 1949) has predicted that "if he fails to see eye to eye with the President on the labor issue" he may support labor's position.

A bill introduced into the House by Neely in 1946 would have allocated $100,000,000 to finance scientific cancer research "on a mass cooperative scale similar to that established in the manufacture of the atomic bomb." The bill was defeated by a few votes, in spite of a "dramatic and personalized campaign" by Neely; upon his election to the Senate in 1949 he introduced a similar proposal. Another recent measure with which his name is associated was a bill for more stringent mine-safety regulations and enforcement, supported by both John L. Lewis and James Boyd [49], director of the United States Bureau of Mines.

In August 1949 Neely became the "unofficial mayor" of Washington, D.C., as chairman of the Senate District Committee. The Senator's first action in this capacity was to call for a round-table discussion by representatives of Washington's groups and organizations to determine the needs and desires of the citizens of the District, which has no local Government. Representatives of some sixty bodies accepted the invitation, and a four-day forum resulted. "I'm hoping that some things will be found in an area of general agreement," Neely said, "about which we can do something without stirring up a fight." Among the suggestions made were home rule and representation in Congress, slum clearance, repeal of the local sales tax (Neely had said, when it passed in the Senate two months earlier, "I'd rather be caught stealing sheep than voting for the sales tax"), and educational improvements. The Washington *Post* commented editorially on the "enlightened attitude" of the new District Committee chairman and commended his "idea clinic," but advanced the opinion that enactment of a home-rule bill "is infinitely more important to the District than any plan to grease the wheels of the present creaking system."

As a first result of the round table Neely introduced into the Senate a bill which would establish a twenty-five-member independent District agency, known as the Commission on Human Rights for the District of Columbia. The purpose of the commission would be "to promote amicable relations among racial, religious, and cultural groups, and to endeavor to establish and maintain a meticulous observance of the Golden Rule in all matters pertaining to interracial relations in the District." A further result was increased pressure on the House by citizens' groups to pass the home-rule bill already passed by the Senate. On September 27, 1949, Neely introduced a constitutional amendment which would permit the citizens of the District ("shipwrecked on a voiceless, voteless island in the midst of the greatest ocean of democracy in the world") to elect Senators and Representatives to Congress.

The legislator has received three honorary degrees: an LL.D. from Waynesburg College of Pennsylvania in 1938, an LL.D. from his alma mater in 1941, and a Litt.D. from Salem College in 1942. He is a member of Phi Beta Kappa, Delta Chi, and Phi Sigma Kappa fraternities. A Thirty-second Degree Mason, he is also a past Grand Chancellor of the Knights of Pythias, a life member and past Exalted Ruler of the Elks, and a life member and past Supreme Governor of the Loyal Order of Moose. He also belongs to the Odd Fellows, the Eagles, the Sons of the American Revolution, and the United Spanish-American War Veterans. His religious faith is the Presbyterian.

On October 21, 1903, Neely married Alberta Claire Ramage, daughter of Benjamin Ramage, a Fairmont attorney. Their three children are Alfred R., John Champ, and Corinne (Neely) Pettit. The Senator, who is "silver-haired," tall, and lean, has a delivery described as "torrential" and makes use frequently of Biblical and classical quotations.

References

New Repub 119:15 O 25 '48 por
Washington (D.C.) Post p5B Ag 7 '49
Congressional Directory (1st ed., 1949)
National Cyclopædia of American Biography Current vol C (1930)
Who's Who in America, 1948-49

NEWCOMER, FRANCIS K(OSIER) Sept. 14, 1889- Governor of the Panama Canal Zone

Address: b. Administration Building, Balboa Heights, Canal Zone; h. 141 Heights Rd., Balboa Heights, Canal Zone

After serving for four years as engineer of maintenance of the Panama Canal, Brigadier General Francis K. Newcomer was appointed Governor of the Panama Canal Zone in May 1948 for the term of office ending in 1952. In the new Governor's tenure policy questions of

U. S. Army

BRIG. GEN. FRANCIS K.
NEWCOMER (RET.)

increasing the toll charges on privately owned vessels which use the canal's facilities and of converting the lake canal to a sea-level route have been under consideration. In October 1949 Newcomer resigned from active Army duty. He had been an officer in the engineering service of the United States Army since 1914 and served in World Wars I and II.

The son of Henry Clay and Rebecca (Kosier) Newcomer, Francis Kosier Newcomer was born in Byron, Illinois on September 14, 1889. In 1909 he received an appointment as a cadet to the United States Military Academy. At West Point for the usual four years, he received the B.S. degree upon graduation in June 1913 and was commissioned a second lieutenant in the Corps of Engineers. His initial army appointment was to the First Engineer Battalion in Washington (D.C.) Barracks. From there he entered the United States Engineer School in that city, from which he was graduated in 1916. That same year he was promoted to the rank of captain and was assigned consecutively to the Second and Fourth Engineer Corps, located in Vancouver, Washington, and Camp Greene, North Carolina, respectively. When the United States joined the Allies in World War I, Newcomer went to France, there to take part in the Aisne-Marne offensive

NEWCOMER, FRANCIS K.—*Continued*

and the Serre and Vesle defensives. From August 1918 to February 1919 he served as assistant commandant of the Army Engineer School at Langres, France, and later resumed duty with the Fourth Engineers. In the fall of 1919 he returned to the United States with the temporary rank of lieutenant colonel.

For the next five years, from 1919 to 1924, Newcomer was an associate professor of mathematics at the United States Military Academy. Then, in July 1924, he was appointed district engineer of the Southeastern Division at Charleston, South Carolina, where he was in charge of fortification and river and harbor works. The following year he was transferred to the Boston District, first as district engineer, and then as engineer of the First Corps Area. In 1928 he was assigned to Fort Belvoir, Virginia, as an instructor in the Engineer School there. Later that same year he was appointed assistant chief engineer for the Federal Power Commission, in Washington, in charge of administration of the engineering division. This agency, which, during the time of Newcomer's service, had the task of licensing hydroelectric projects on United States Government land and on navigable waters of the United States, became an independent commission by a 1930 Act of Congress. After its reorganization with civilian personnel, Newcomer was sent to Schofield Barracks, Hawaii, as commanding officer of the First Battalion of the Third Engineers.

Following two years in the Territory he returned to the United States, where he studied at the Command and General Staff School, Fort Leavenworth, Kansas; upon the completion of a two-year course there in 1935, he was assigned to the Office of the Chief of Engineers in the War Department, in the capital. There he was head of the Finance Division and later of the Finance and Contracts Section. According to the *United States Government Organization Manual*, this office has "responsibility for all Army construction, and in addition, is charged with the production and distribution of military maps, the development, procurement and storage of certain types of military equipment, and with the supervision of investigation and improvements for navigation, flood control, and power development on rivers and harbors." Newcomer remained with this office until September 1939.

Having advanced through the Army officer grades to that of permanent lieutenant colonel, Newcomer in 1939 entered the Army War College, Fort Humphreys, Washington, D.C., where officers received special training for wartime command and staff positions. He graduated from the college in June 1940 and was appointed assistant to the president of the Mississippi River Commission and to the division engineer of the Lower Mississippi Valley Division at Vicksburg, Mississippi. He remained here for a little over a year and then was assigned to duty with the Third Army at San Antonio, Texas, as engineer officer. Newcomer was promoted to the rank of temporary colonel in 1941 and permanent colonel in 1942. In December 1942 he began a two-year overseas assignment as theater engineer officer in the China-Burma-India Theater. There he remained until May 1944, when he became engineer of maintenance of the Panama Canal, then part of the Caribbean Defense Command. That same year he was appointed to the rank of brigadier general (temporary). Newcomer served as chief assistant to the then Governor of the Panama Canal Zone, Major General Joseph C. Mehaffey [48]; in May 1948 he was appointed by President Truman to succeed Mehaffey for a four-year term.

By Act of Congress, approved in August 1912, the Panama Canal is under the supervision of the Secretary of Defense, with a Governor (appointed by the President) in charge of the maintenance and operation of the canal and of the government of the Canal Zone. The latter is a Government reservation, a strip of territory five miles wide on either side of the canal, comprising approximately 552 square miles, with a population in 1949 of 47,077, exclusive of military personnel. Operation of all services for the population of the Zone, including maintenance of a health department, transportation facilities, and public utilities is under the Governor's direction. Newcomer is also (by virtue of his post) president of the Panama Railroad Company, a Government corporation which operates the one railroad on the isthmus and other public facilities, and which pays into the United States Treasury all dividends on the company's capital investments.

In February 1950 President Truman requested Congress to authorize reorganization of the Canal and Zone by merging the names and activities of the Panama Canal and the Panama Railroad Company into one Government corporation to be known as the Panama Canal Company, such company to have the right to establish, subject to Presidential approval, toll rates and to retain and utilize toll revenues. Congress was also asked to authorize appropriations to cover any losses of the proposed company resulting from changing economic conditions. The President's unifying plan follows in the main the recommendations of the Hoover Commission on Organization of the Executive Branch of the Government, by-passing, however, that body's suggestion that the canal be transferred from the jurisdiction of the Army to that of the Department of Commerce.

Establishment of satisfactory toll rates for commercial shipping using the canal's facilities has been a controversial issue since the end of World War II. Governor Newcomer in his 1949 report pointed to the profit of one-tenth of 1 per cent made on the canal's operation and asked that toll charges be raised in order to bring an annual return of 3 per cent on the Government's investment. Shipowners who use the canal, however, consider the waterway to be as much an instrument of American defense as a channel for private transportation. They maintain therefore that private corporations should not meet all the operating costs, pointing to the 14,398 Government vessels which during a four-year period ending in June 1949 used the canal without paying any charges. Governor Newcomer's proposals for increased toll charges have also been attacked by private shipping interests as being based on an accounting system that includes, in expenses to be paid by revenue from shipping tolls, expenses extraneous to the actual cost of handling vessels in transit. In Governor Newcomer's opinion, the canal is "an international public utility" that should be operated at a profit. As early as October 1948 he requested that an increase from 90 cents to $1 a ton on dry cargo and from 78 cents to 80 cents on ballast go into effect. The increases were postponed several times, pending investigations, but were expected to go into effect by April 1950.

While chief assistant to Governor Mehaffey, Newcomer supported recommendations that the canal be converted from a lake canal by lowering it to sea level, widening and deepening it, and eliminating locks. Newcomer's 1949 report reiterated a request for almost two and a half billion dollars to create a sea-level route with a minimum depth of 60 feet and a minimum width of 600 feet at a 40-foot depth. Should the project be authorized, it would be expected to require nearly ten years to complete, with a labor force of approximately 37,000. However, traffic movement during the period of construction would be interrupted for only one week according to estimates (reported in the *Christian Science Monitor*). Newcomer's recommendations are opposed by those who wish to combine the Pacific locks and raise most of the route to the present maximum of 85 feet above sea level. Newcomer defends the sea-level plan as practical, efficient, and justifiable as a calculated risk against atomic and other attack.

In October 1949 Governor Newcomer, after forty years of military service, resigned from active Army duty. In 1918 he had received the Distinguished Service Cross for action near Fismes, France; another World War I award he holds is the Victory, Army of Occupation. For his services in World War II he received the Legion of Merit in 1945 for service at the Panama Canal; the Chinese Order of Yun Whei, 1st Grade, for duty as Chief Engineer of the China-Burma-India Theater; and Asiatic and American Theater Medals. In 1914 he married Mary Brunot Roberts. The Newcomers have three children, Rebecca, Francis K., an officer in the United States Army, and Thomas Roberts. Newcomer is a member of the Society of American Military Engineers and belongs to the Army-Navy Country Club of Washington.

References

Official Army Register, 1949
Who's Who in America, 1948-49

NIJINSKY, WASLAW (nē-jǐn'skǐ väs'läf) Feb. 28, 1890—Apr. 8, 1950 World-famous Russian ballet dancer; made his Moscow debut in 1907; with the Russian Imperial Ballet 1908-11; soloist with Diaghilev's company of Russian Ballet at historic performance in Paris in 1909, which started a new era of the ballet in Europe; with that company until 1913 and again in 1916 in the United States; retired from ballet in 1917 because of mental illness; two of his most famous roles were in *Le Spectre de la Rose* and *Petrouchka*, created for him by Fokine; choreographer of four ballets of unorthodox tendencies; regarded as the finest male dancer in the history of ballet, noted for his leaps and *entrechats*. See *Current Biography*, 1940.

Obituary

N Y Times p84 Ap 9 '50 por

NORMAN, MONTAGU (COLLET, 1st) BARON Sept. 6, 1871—Feb. 4, 1950 Banker and financier; Governor of the Bank of England from 1920 to 1944; entered the banking firm of Brown, Shipley & Company in 1890; served some time in the associated firm of Brown Brothers & Company in New York City; became a director of Brown, Shipley & Company in 1900; elected to the board of the Bank of England in 1907; was made deputy governor of the Bank of England in 1915; in 1930 became a director of the Bank for International Settlements; favored retention of the gold standard; during the depression of the 1930's supported a policy of international currency stabilization. See *Current Biography*, 1940.

Obituary

N Y Times p85 F 5 '50 por

OAKES, GRANT W(ILSON) Apr. 8, 1905- Labor union official

Address: b. c/o Farm Equipment and Metal Workers Council, United Electrical, Radio and Machine Workers of America, 11 E. 51st St., New York 22; h. 12632 Harold Ave., Palos Heights, Ill.

In October 1949 Grant W. Oakes led the United Farm Equipment and Metal Workers of America (CIO) into the United Electrical, Radio, and Machine Workers of America, in opposition to a CIO directive to merge with Walter Reuther's '49 anti-Communist United Automobile, Aircraft, and Agricultural Implement Workers. As a result, the leftist F.E. and U.E. were expelled from the CIO. Oakes, who organized the first strong union in the farm equipment industry, was third-party candidate for the Governorship of Illinois on the Henry Wallace '47 ticket in 1948.

Born April 8, 1905, to railroad electrician Fred J. Oakes and Ellen (Lawson) Oakes, Grant Wilson Oakes is of English-Swedish stock. He attended grammar and high school in his native Westfield, New York, then spent seven years as an employee of the General Electric Company. During this period, according to his union's publicity office, "he secured an electrical engineering degree through industrial college." *Who's Who in Labor* gives his period of study as three years.

Moving to Chicago in 1928, young Oakes found employment with the International Harvester Company and rose to the position of a skilled experimental mechanic. In April 1936 the thirty-one-year-old mechanic helped to or-

GRANT W. OAKES

ganize the "first genuine union in the farm equipment industry," Tractor Local 101, at the International Harvester Tractor Works in Chicago. According to his office, Grant Oakes "was instrumental in wiping out long-standing company unionism policies, and Tractor Works was the first I.H. property where genuine unionism developed since the Haymarket disturbances of 1886, during which several McCormick Reaper workers were killed." A member of the CIO since its formation, Oakes became head of the grievance committee and secretary of the local union, in the days when union activity was beset with a high rate of occupational hazards.

Oakes's union was one of the locals which in 1938 withdrew from the CIO Steel Workers Organizing Committee to form the Farm Equipment Workers Organizing Committee, CIO. Elected as the first president of the new committee, Grant Oakes was re-elected at each of the union's biennial conventions that followed. On assuming the presidential office, he "came out of the shop" and has since given his working hours entirely to union activities. Those activities include competing with other unions (AFL, CIO, or independent) for recognition as the workers' bargaining agent, cooperating with these other unions for the success of joint strike actions, and coordinating the activity of widely scattered locals. His union first made headlines nationally in 1941, with a record 76-day strike against International Harvester, a wages, recognition, and grievance strike which began at the Rock Falls (Illinois) plant on January 25, at the Chicago works four days later, in Richmond (Indiana) on February 19, and at the Chicago McCormick works February 28, involved some 7,000 strikers, developed into "pitched battles," and was ended March 30 at the request of the National Defense Mediation Board. An eight-day strike in May against Allis-Chalmers, which held $5,000,000 worth of defense contracts, was ended similarly.

After that the CIO chartered the Farm Equipment Workers Committee in 1942 as a full-fledged international union named the United Farm Equipment and Metal Workers of America, with wide jurisdiction. Its overlapping with the much larger U.A.W. is indicated by the full name of the latter, the United Automobile, Aircraft, and Agricultural Implement Workers. As defense production increased, the problem of lack of raw material arose, and in late August 1941 Oakes asked Government officials to confer with him on preventing layoffs due to such scarcities. During World War II the Oakes union accepted the WLB maintenance-of-membership plan. "Oakes's leadership during the war against fascism," writes his publicity director, "resulted in record-breaking production in all F.E. plants, and not one wartime strike; union cited by Army, Navy, and Government heads." Figures given out by the union show that its membership reached 60,000 in this period.

After the war Oakes's union resumed action so militantly that in 1945 its locals were responsible for 102 work stoppages at International Harvester plants, while twenty-six other unions together accounted for 41 such stoppages. Union officials considered this proof that F.E. was the "pace-setter," while company president John L. McCaffrey charged that "many" of the officers were "irresponsible radicals who are more interested in disruption than in labor-management peace" (*Business Week*, November 1, 1947). The year 1946 was also active in this respect, beginning with a four-month International Harvester strike, which overlapped with the record-breaking seven-month strike against the Allis Chalmers Manufacturing Company and a three-month strike against J. I. Case Company. In this F.E. worked closely, not only with the U.A.W. and other locals, but with the National Farmers Union—the latter for the purpose of mobilizing farmer support and explaining "how small a part of the price of various farm implements is paid out in direct labor costs" (*Labor Fact Book*). In that year Oakes established something new in American unionism, a farm relations department, headed by a livestock farmer, Homer Ayres. A regular column by Ayres, *The Farmer's Angle*, was released to the Federated Press, a labor news service serving 250 newspapers. (The long strike won wage increases, one- and two-week paid vacations, and counting of seniority on a plant-wide rather than departmental basis.)

Usually termed "Left-wing," Oakes's union was described by *Newsweek* (June 2, 1947) as having "no appreciable opposition to its consistent pro-Communist line." In February 1948 its special convention voted 433 to 203 against compliance with the Taft '48-Hartley '47 Act; but when the F.E. lost its bargaining rights for 17,000 Caterpillar Tractor workers in Peoria (Illinois) because it was ineligible for a place on the NLRB ballot, Oakes's international executive board ordered a special referendum, as a result of which Oakes and eight others signed "distasteful" non-Communist affidavits (*New Republic*), and four officers resigned. A member of the CIO executive board, Oakes opposed the majority policy of supporting the Marshall

Plan and opposing Henry Wallace's third party movement, and was chosen Progressive party candidate for Governor of Illinois at the State convention. He did not campaign against Dwight Green '48 and Adlai Stevenson '49, however; his party was barred from the ballot.

Another source of friction between F.E. and the CIO was the jurisdictional overlapping with the U.A.W., which had a much larger membership in the farm equipment field. (F.E. claimed that its workers' contracts were better than those obtained for similar workers by U.A.W.) In 1947 F.E. offered to join U.A.W. as a separate department, at a time when Left-wing elements dominated the U.A.W. board; the 450 votes F.E. would have carried into the U.A.W. convention equalled nearly four times the margin by which Walter Reuther had defeated Left-wing R. J. Thomas in 1946. In May 1948, however, with Reuther firmly in control of the U.A.W., the predominantly anti-Communist CIO convention ordered Oakes's union to merge with U.A.W. within sixty days, an order that was defied. A year later, in an unprecedented step, the CIO leadership made plans to revoke F.E.'s charter. In October 1949, before the CIO convention, the F.E. entered Albert Fitzgerald's '48 United Electrical, Radio and Machine Workers, the third largest CIO affiliate and the largest member of its Left wing. Oakes and his staff now function as the Farm Equipment and Metal Workers Council of U.E.W. Upon the expulsion of the two merged unions from the CIO, the latter's new Right-wing International Union of Electrical, Radio and Machine Workers of America was founded in December 1949.

A member of the CIO-PAC formed in 1943 to campaign for President Roosevelt, Oakes called himself a Roosevelt Democrat until 1948, then joined Wallace's Progressive party "when he felt Truman was reversing constructive Rooseveltian trends." Outspoken in his opposition to racial and religious discrimination, the "rugged-faced, aggressive" unionist is a member of the Chicago Civil Liberties Committee. Grant Oakes and Hazel A. Bacon, married February 14, 1931, are the parents of Grant, Jr., Marilyn, and James; the family's religious faith is Protestant. The labor leader names hunting and fishing as his vacation recreations.

Reference

Who's Who in Labor (1946)

O'CONOR, HERBERT R(OMULUS)
Nov. 17, 1896- United States Senator from Maryland

Address: b. Senate Office Building, Washington 25, D.C.; h. 16 Charlcote Place, Baltimore 18, Md.

Herbert R. O'Conor, the Democratic United States Senator from Maryland, took his seat in Congress in 1947. He came to Washington after two terms as Governor of his State (1939-47), during which he effected a drastic program in cutting the State government expenses and in reducing taxes. In the Senate O'Conor has been concerned with "threats to security" from Communist agents, tightened

HERBERT R. O'CONOR

immigration laws against possible subversives, but more liberal admission of displaced persons, and economy in government. He has maintained a philosophy of "dual sovereignty," holding that social legislation is the province of States, and that increasing federalization of social programs is a threat to the American system of government.

One of a family of five sons and three daughters, Herbert Romulus O'Conor was born November 17, 1896, in Baltimore where his father was the manager of the famous old Rennert Hotel. His parents, the late James P. A. and Mary Ann (Galvin) O'Conor, both of Irish descent, were born in the United States; the boy's uncle was a well-known Baltimore ward leader. James O'Conor remained active in hotel management until his death in 1924, when he was managing director of the Hotel Bellevue-Stratford in Philadelphia. Young O'Conor attended Loyola College in his native city, where he was elected class president every year. After graduation in 1917 he saw service in World War I in the United States Naval Reserve. On his discharge, he returned to Baltimore to study law at the University of Maryland at night while working during the day as a newspaper reporter; in 1920 he received his LL.B. degree.

Admitted to the bar in 1919, he began practicing law in Baltimore. Two years later he was appointed to his first public office—Assistant State's Attorney for the city. This post he held until 1923, when he became, at twenty-seven, the youngest State's Attorney ever to be elected for Baltimore. In 1923, also, he was appointed People's Counsel of the Public Service Commission. Re-elected in 1926 and again in 1930 for four-year terms, he was Baltimore State's Attorney for eleven years. It was at this time that he organized and became the first president of the State's Attorneys Association of Maryland. In 1932 he served on the committee of criminal law and statistics of the

O'CONOR, HERBERT R.—*Continued*

American Prison Association (he is the author of a criminal law syllabus). Also, while State's Attorney he was chairman of the State Judicial Commission. In November 1934 O'Conor was elected Attorney General of Maryland on the Democratic ticket by a record-breaking majority. The new Attorney General was especially concerned with interstate compacts; he became chairman of the Maryland commission for such agreements, helping prepare legislation which was later adopted without change by the State legislature.

In 1938 the Attorney General was nominated for Maryland's Governor, and in the November election he defeated the Republican Governor Harry Nice. In his campaign he stated it would be necessary to raise taxes; but he promised to balance the budget with the increased tax revenue and to cut expenses through efficient administration to effect an eventual reduction in taxes. This he achieved: O. K. Armstrong wrote in the New York *Herald Tribune Magazine*, July 5, 1942, that Maryland was the only State with a balanced budget, large surplus, and falling taxes. (Its 1943 tax rates were the lowest since 1861.) His program, said Governor O'Conor was simple: he held a tight administrative checkrein upon expenditures; he established a pay-as-you-go budget system, with money for "essentials"; and he applied business methods to public administration, hiring experts on a merit system as opposed to a system of political patronage. Other aspects of the Governor's political philosophy were convictions that the right to work was as important as the right to strike and bargain collectively, and that the four primary social needs were law and order, public health, transportation, and education. In 1941 Governor O'Conor served as chairman of the Interstate Commission on the Potomac River Basin, an agency of the District of Columbia and the States situated in that river's area.

During his two four-year terms in the State House O'Conor, an active member of the annual Governors Conference, was a member of the executive committee of the conference in 1940, chairman of the committee on law enforcement and the administration of justice of the conference in 1941, and chairman of the conference in 1942 and 1943. He was also president in 1943 of the Council of State Governments (a continuing body with headquarters in Chicago) and one of nine Governors who met as the council's executive committee on postwar reconstruction. A defender of States' rights. at a regional conference of Middle Atlantic and New England States in New York City in April 1943, Governor O'Conor joined New York's Governor Thomas E. Dewey in asking for a return to the States as soon as possible of powers granted the Federal Government to prosecute the war. In an address before the June 1944 Governors Conference (reprinted in the December 1944 *Congressional Digest*), he scored legislation before Congress that would, he said, "completely federalize" State programs of social security and "regiment medical science"; the speech was considered an attack on the Wagner-Murray-Dingell social security bill then before Congress.

In June 1946, with the endorsement of the Political Action Committee of the Congress of Industrial Organizations, O'Conor won the Democratic nomination over the incumbent Senator, George L. Radcliffe, who was seeking a third term. In the November election his Republican opponent, Brigadier General D. John Markey, lost by little more than 2,000 votes. Because the defeated Republican demanded a recount, the new Senator's seat was in some doubt until the spring of 1948, when, after a recount, the Senate Rules committee (eight Republicans, five Democrats) unanimously declared O'Conor the victor.

In his first months in Congress (he went to Washington in January 1947) the Maryland Democrat came forward as a supporter of the Administration foreign policy, joining Republican Senator Arthur H. Vandenberg [48] in marshaling support for President Truman's Greek-Turkish aid plans. He voted for the European Recovery Program bill (second session, Eightieth Congress), and later for the extension of the program (the Economic Cooperation Act of the Eighty-first Congress). O'Conor opposed Administration policy on China and Spain, however, calling for a formal announcement by the State Department that it would never recognize the Communist regime in China, and also for the establishment of full diplomatic and economic relations with Spain "which wants to be our friend, and wants to be part of the Western Democratic family of anti-Communist nations" (Washington *Post*, January 17, 1950). He approved the ratification of the North Atlantic Pact in 1949.

O'Conor was also concerned with the problems of displaced persons (he visited DP camps and pressed for legislation to admit more DP's to the United States), and with the question of "unrestricted diplomatic immunity" for foreigners on United Nations business (he said the door of the United States was "wide open for Communist infiltration"). He voted for the appointment of David Lilienthal [44] as Atomic Energy Commission chairman, "with entire assurance" that America's rights and the world's hope for development of the new force would be in "the safest possible hands." In the spring of 1949 as chairman of a Senate judiciary subcommittee, O'Conor conducted hearings on pending bills to impose Federal controls on Communist activities.

On questions of labor and social legislation, the junior Senator from Maryland stood with the conservative Democrats and Republicans. His vote went to the Taft-Hartley labor bill (1947), to outlawing portal-to-portal suits, to striking out the public housing provision in the Federal housing bill; and he voted against Federal aid to education (he favored limiting school aid to less prosperous States). He voted for reduced income taxes, and for the Republican anti-inflation bill. Though rent control received his support, he voted against the long-range housing bill containing provisions for slum clearance and public housing. In that Congress he acted with other Southern Democrats to prevent civil rights legislation from coming to a vote. In March 1949 he was one of five Senators who proposed, in opposition to the Administration health insurance program, a bipartisan voluntary health insurance bill which would emphasize action by the State to help citizens unable to pay for insurance. He opposed the establishment of a Cabinet post for a department of welfare.

As a member of Senate subcommittees (a number of which he chaired) O'Conor watched Government spending—in November 1947 he asked for a thorough auditing for the fiscal year 1945 of some of the books of the Federal Housing Authority. In May 1949 he was co-sponsor of a bipartisan bill for a single consolidated appropriation that would base Government spending on Government income, and in August he supported immediate repeal of wartime excise taxes. While a member of the Senate Committee on Expenditures in the Executive Departments, Senator O'Conor called for increased salaries for high Government executives, pointing out that Federal officials were resigning to take positions with private industry because they could not afford to work for the Government. (An article on this thesis by the Senator, "We've Got to Pay More for Leadership," appeared in the January 1949 issue of the *American Magazine*.) O'Conor indicated in January 1950, that he would again be alert to means of cutting expenditures in the 1950 session of Congress. His voting record also includes: opposition to the confirmation of Leland Olds as head of the Federal Power Commission; approval of the extension of reciprocal trade agreements without restrictions to June 1951, and of the compromise farm bill. In 1950 he voted for the repeal of the margarine tax and for a proposed constitutional amendment to give women equal rights under the law. Two other Senate committees on which O'Conor has served are those for Interstate and Foreign, and Post Office and Civil Service.

The Senator is a member of the American, Maryland State and the Baltimore bar associations and was president of the National Association of Attorneys General in 1937. He belongs to the American Legion, Veterans of Foreign Wars, the Ancient Order of Hibernians, the Knights of Columbus (he is a Catholic), the Elks, the Baltimore Country and Athletic clubs, and the Wednesday Club. His fraternity is Phi Sigma Kappa. The honorary degree of Doctor of Laws has been conferred on him by the University of Maryland, Loyola College, Villanova College (Pennsylvania), Georgetown University (Washington, D.C.) and Washington College (Chestertown, Maryland). The Senator's wife is the former Mary Eugenia Byrnes, whom he married November 24, 1920. They have five children, Herbert Romulus, Jr., Eugene F., Mary Patricia, James P., and Robert A. Frequently described as handsome, Senator O'Conor has blue eyes and black hair that is graying; his height is five feet ten inches. Among his recreations are gardening, golf and swimming. He is said to be something of a gourmet.

References

N Y Herald Tribune Mag IX p7 Jl 5 '42
N Y Sun p25 Ja 28 '43
Congressional Directory, (1st ed., 1949)
National Cyclopædia of American Biography Current vol F, 1939-42
Who's Who in America, 1948-49

OLDENBROEK, JACOBUS H (ENDRIK) (ōl-děn-brōōk) Nov. 1897- International trade union official
Address: b. c/o International Confederation of Free Trade Unions, Brussels, Belgium

As general secretary of the democratic International Confederation of Free Trade Unions, Jacobus H. Oldenbroek directs the administration of that body. Elected without dissent at the constituent congress held in London in December 1949 to establish the organization, Oldenbroek had a background of trade unionism in the International Federation of Transport Workers; active in the leadership of that organization from 1921, he served as its general secretary after 1942. During 1939-49 Jacobus Oldenbroek worked in London, to which the secretariat of the International Federation of Transport Workers had been transferred at the outbreak of the war. His headquarters as general secretary of the International Confederation of Free Trade Unions is located in Brussels, Belgium.

Jacobus Hendrik Oldenbroek was born in Amsterdam, the Netherlands, in November 1897. His father, a cigarmaker and an active trade unionist, worked for a time in London and then in Hamburg. The boy grew up and received his elementary school education in those cities. Later he attended evening classes at a secondary commercial school. Possessed of natural linguistic ability, he became proficient in foreign languages—in English, German, French, and Swedish. When he reached fourteen he went to work as an office clerk in Amsterdam. His interest in the growth of the labor movement and his country's political problems began early. In 1915 he became a clerk in the office of the Netherlands Federation of Trade Unions. His work there, however, was soon interrupted by conscription for military service in World War I.

Oldenbroek returned in 1918 to the Netherlands Federation of Trade Unions, where he worked under the secretary of the organization, Edo Fimmen. In July 1919 Oldenbroek was appointed office manager of the International Association of Trade Unions. From this position he moved in November 1921 to a corresponding post with the International Federation of Transport Workers, where he eventually became manager of the division of navigation affairs. He often served as translator at various congresses and meetings. Appointed assistant general secretary of the International Federation of Transport Workers in 1938, Oldenbroek was again associated with Fimmen, who had become general secretary of that body. In 1939, when the headquarters of the organization was transferred to Great Britain, Oldenbroek went to London with Fimmen. Poor

JACOBUS H. OLDENBROEK

health forced the latter to leave in 1941, and Oldenbroek took over his chief's duties. Upon Fimmen's death in 1942 Oldenbroek was made acting general secretary. During World War II Oldenbroek's work was directed to improving conditions for transport workers and to increasing their role in the war effort of the Western Allies. He frequently spoke on broadcasts to workers in Nazi-dominated countries. As a member of the governing body of the International Labor Organization, he helped in the planning of international labor conferences; he also served on the I.L.O.'s Joint Maritime Commission.

At the first postwar congress of the International Federation of Transport Workers in 1946, Oldenbroek was elected general secretary, to which office he was re-elected at the congress of 1948; he has also been a member of the extraordinary council of advice, acting as chairman of its commission for social affairs. He has been president of the contact committee of employers' organizations of the Netherlands merchant marine, and a member of the bargaining committee for the regulation of labor conditions in that merchant marine. Other services of his have been on the advisory committee for labor affairs of the Netherlands Shipping and Trading Committee and on the committee of appeal for the settlement of controversies in the Netherlands merchant marine.

Strongly anticommunistic, Oldenbroek in September 1949 participated in a congress held in Havana by the Inter-American Confederation of Labor, which endorsed the formation of a new world labor organization to rival the pro-Soviet World Federation of Trade Unions. According to Omer Becu, president of the International Federation of Transport Workers, Oldenbroek had always opposed absorption of that body in the W.F.T.U. Plans for the organization of a rival body had been drawn up in the summer of 1949 by a commission under

the chairmanship of Paul Finet, head of the Belgian Federation of Labor.

In November-December 1949 delegates from fifty-three countries, representing eighty-seven national organizations whose membership totaled over forty-eight million workers, met at the London Free World Labor Conference to organize the new, non-Communist International Confederation of Free Trade Unions. (Pressure for establishing a new world union had come with Communist control of the W.F.T.U.) Participating unions included the AFL, CIO, United Mine Workers of America, British Trades Union Congress; the European Catholic unions, which were offered membership on the condition that within two years they adopt the principle of affiliation to one trade union international, were represented at the organizational meeting but abstained from voting. On December 7 the delegates unanimously chose Oldenbroek as permanent general secretary; Paul Finet was chosen as president and chairman of the executive board. "For the first time in an international labor movement," wrote David Lasser in the Washington *Post* (December 18, 1949), "the I.C.F.T.U. leadership comes mainly from the small nations. . . . Oldenbroek, who will administer the organization, built the International Transport Workers Federation into one of the most successful of the trade secretariats."

Asserting that "economic and political democracy are inseparable," the I.C.F.T.U.'s constitution pledges its members to fight against all forms of totalitarianism, and to work for a world of "economic security, social justice and political freedom." Its objectives are higher living standards everywhere; a guaranteed weekly and annual wage; the industrialization of backward areas, with freedom from imperialist exploitation; and organizational and financial aid to weak trade union movements, with probable priority for non-Communist unions in France, Italy, and Asia. (*Rad*, newspaper of the Central Trade Union Council of Yugoslavia, denounced the I.C.F.T.U. as a "strike-breaking" instrument of "imperialist agents" designed to destroy the unity of the international workers movement.) The organization will hold congresses at intervals of two years. It has a twenty-man executive board (Oldenbroek is a member) which gives geographical representation as follows: Africa, one member; Asia and Middle East, three; Australia and New Zealand, one; Great Britain, two; Europe, five; Latin America, two; North America, four; and the West Indies, one. The board will meet every six months.

The I.C.F.T.U. plans to work in close collaboration with the twenty International Trade Organization secretariats, and to seek recognition by the United Nations' Economic and Social Council, the Food and Agriculture Organization, the World Bank and similar bodies with a view to offsetting W.F.T.U. representations to them. (It was reported in the New York *Herald Tribune* of January 26, 1950, that an application, signed by Oldenbroek, asking top consultative status, status "A", for the I.C.F.T.U. had been submitted to the U.N. Economic and Social Council.)

At the time of his election as general secretary of the I.C.F.T.U., Oldenbroek warned that "time is running short for the implementing of a social and economic program." He called for the "wisdom of the East, the civilization of the West, and the dynamism of the New World" to unite in making the confederation a success. He has said further: "We are going to be efficient, in the American sense. That means when you want something, you go all out, and no rest until you've got it." In addition to his union work, Oldenbroek has had a part in political affairs. He was a member of the Dutch Socialist movement from its beginning, and has held posts in the Social-Democratic Labor party. He also served for a time as a member of the Municipal Council of Nieuwer-Amstel, one of the suburbs of Amsterdam.

The labor leader, who is short in stature, has been described as plump and pink-cheeked. He has the reputation of being a "crack administrator" as well as a "good-natured, soft-spoken labor diplomat." He is fond of music, especially of the opera.

Reference

Time 54:18 D 19 '49 por

OSCAR OF. THE WALDORF *See* Tschirky, O. M.

OSPINA PEREZ, MARIANO (ōs-pē'nä pä'räs mä-ryä'nō) Nov. 24, 1891- President of Colombia

Address: Palacia Presidencial, Bogotá, Colombia, S. A.

The President of Colombia, which has been called one of the most democratic of Latin American countries, is Mariano Ospina Pérez. Elected May 6, 1946, to succeed Alberto Lleras Camargo '47, Ospina Pérez is the first Conservative to be chief executive of that country since 1930; he is the third member of his family to head his country's Government. A mining engineer and professor, he was named principal Senator for his home department of Antioquía in 1923 and has been Minister of Public Works.

Mariano Ospina Pérez was born in Medellín, Colombia's second largest city, to Dr. Tulio Ospina and Anna Rosa Pérez on November 24, 1891. His grandfather, Mariano Ospina Rodriguez, and an uncle, General Pedro Nel Ospina had also headed Governments, in 1858-60 and 1922-26, respectively. The boy completed his elementary and secondary school educations at San José School and Colegio de San Ignacio, both in his native town, before entering the University of Antioquía, also in Medellín, where his father, a mining engineer, was a teacher and dean of the School of Mines. After receiving a B.S. degree he completed in 1911 the work of a graduate engineer at the university's School of Mines. As a student Ospina Pérez edited a Medellín newspaper. In 1912 he went to the United States, where he earned the M.S. from Louisiana State University. Before returning to Colombia he took courses in economics and industrial chemistry at the University of Wisconsin and pursued graduate studies at Catholic University, Liége, Belgium.

Ospina Pérez began public life as a member of the municipal council of Medellín; and he was later a deputy to the Assembly of the Department of Antioquía. Three times a representative to the national Congress, he was elected principal Senator for Antioquía in 1923. As Senator, he was concerned with a project related to the organization of the Crédito Agrario and the formation of the Banco Agrícola Hipotecario; and with the creation of Caja Agraria. In 1926 he was appointed Minister of Public Works; while he was in this post a National Council of Communication Routes was created and the national railways were reorganized. In 1946 the *Inter-American* called his record "that of a levelheaded and practical man."

On May 5, 1946, Ospina Pérez was elected Colombia's first Conservative president in sixteen years, polling fewer votes than his two Liberal opponents combined, but with 461,473 votes giving him 115,891 more than the 345,582 polled for rightist Liberal Gabriel Torbay, who split his party's vote with leftist Liberal Jorge Eliécer Gaitán (291,962). The election was described in the New York *Times* as "the most orderly in the country's history." After a pre-inaugural visit to North America as guest of the United States and Canada, during which he devoted much time to study of the United Nations, he took office on August 7, 1946. President Ospina Pérez opened a campaign to reduce the cost of living, to combat inflation, and to form a "national unity government." He divided Cabinet posts and department governorships equally between Conservatives and Liberals. The Congress he inherited was Liberal and remained so in the March 16, 1947, election. "Despite the minority position of the President," wrote a *Christian Science Monitor* reporter in April 1947, "the Government is regarded as highly stable."

This state of affairs deteriorated, however, as extremists in both parties increasingly refused to cooperate. Gaitán, Liberal of the left, became leader of his party and candidate for the 1950 presidential elections; and in his order to quit "all government positions that may impose political responsibility," the Liberal ministers withdrew from office (with the exception of Foreign Minister Domingo Esguerra) shortly before the Ninth International Conference of American States was to convene in Bogotá. Gaitán's move has been variously reported as the result of pique at not being invited to attend the conference and as a protest against alleged political violence. Thereupon, President Ospina Pérez on March 22, 1948, named an all-Conservative Cabinet, which included in its numbers Laureano Gómez, reputed to be a particular enemy of the Liberals. Disturbances took place, in which nearly one hundred Liberals were killed, while others fled the country.

The political situation in Colombia was tense but quiet when President Ospina Pérez opened the Inter-American Conference in Bogotá on March 30, 1948, with representatives of twenty-one nations in attendance. On April 9 Gaitán

MARIANO OSPINA PEREZ

was shot as he stood in front of his office; at his death rioting started and spread across Colombia; the Capitol Building in which the Conference was being held was destroyed, and the President's windows were stoned. "The mob showed where it was placing the blame— squarely on his Government," wrote Mac R. Johnson in the New York *Herald Tribune*. Rioting in Bogotá continued for six hours; Communists are reported to have been implicated. Gómez left the country, going first to Brazil, then to Spain. On April 10, despite Liberal demands for his resignation, President Ospina Pérez formed a new coalition Cabinet with one non-partisan, the Minister of War. He declared a state of siege in Colombia on April 12 in an effort to restore order. The Inter-American Conference was able to resume on April 14, and completed its work on April 29. In November 1948, Gaitán's house and library were created a national memorial.

The Liberals now endorsed the candidacy of Darío Echandía for the 1950 elections. Political violence flared anew in September 1949 when, over the veto of President Ospina Pérez, a Liberal-sponsored bill advanced the June 1950 presidential election to November 27, 1949. When Gómez returned from Spain in September and his candidacy was announced by the Conservatives, Liberals tried unsuccessfully to restore the original date. President Ospina Pérez then advanced a plan, reportedly blocked by Gómez, to end the political strife by setting up a bipartisan junta to rule with special powers until 1954. Meanwhile, rioting increased when Liberal Echandía accused Conservatives of turning the contest into a "bloody farce" and announced that his party would not recognize the November election. Again the President used his powers and, on November 9, 1949, declared a state of siege suspending constitutional rights, including sessions of State Legislatures,

and imposing a nine o'clock curfew and full censorship on press, radio, and cables. He also offset the Liberal majority in the Supreme Court by a decree that the Court's ruling on constitutional questions must be passed by a three-quarter majority vote. The national Congress was dissolved after a congressional commission informed Ospina Pérez it would "explore" means to impeach him. A declaration was made by a Liberal-sponsored secret session of Congress that "the Government has placed itself outside the Constitution" (New York *Times*, November 12, 1949). According to a New York *Herald Tribune* report, Dr. Eduardo Santos, Liberal Vice-President said, "If this is not dictatorship, I do not know what it can be." The Conservatives passed decrees requiring employers to give two pairs of shoes and two pairs of overalls a year to low-paid workers, setting a minimum daily wage and raising all salaries under $155 a month from 6 to 15 per cent, effective January 1, 1950. This legislation was regarded as a bid for labor support.

The Liberal party boycotted the November 27 elections and called for a general strike over that week end. Conservative Gómez, sole candidate for the presidency, received 956,315 votes while he remained in his heavily guarded house. The polls, closely guarded by troops, were reported as quiet. Echandía, however, in company with twenty-one Liberals had been fired on by military police on election eve, and three of his party, including his brother, had been killed. The President issued a statement regretting these events and announcing an investigation by authorities. On December 30, 1949, Ospina Pérez, using his state of siege powers, reformed his Council of State, increasing the number of councilors from seven to ten and eliminating the five-to-two Liberal majority by naming three Conservatives to the new posts.

The Conservative President said in December 1949 that he expects the state of siege to last at least two years. C. H. Calhoun of the New York *Times* reported both President Ospina Pérez and an anonymous former Liberal president as saying that the present unrest in Colombia is not political alone but involves human, social, and economic relations between the upper, middle and lower classes. The President's critics contend, according to the New York *Times*, that his government's "arbitrary decreeing of minimum wages and over-all increases in salary without regard to the ability of the employer to pay or to the production of the worker, is not the answer." When questioned concerning political prisoners, the President of Colombia said arrests had been made only for subversive actions against the Government.

A millionaire when he became chief executive of Colombia at the age of fifty-five, President Ospina Pérez comes of a family with important holdings at Medellín—smelters for precious metals, cotton mills, coffee plantations and cattle ranches. He has contributed occasional articles to Colombian and other publications. At the University of Antioquía he was named to replace his father as dean of the School of Mines and became professor of hydrology, geology and development of mines; he has been professor of mathematics at the School of Engineering and of political economy at the same university. He has taught also at the Universidad Nacional y Javeriana de Bogotá, and was on the Faculty of Law of Colegio Mayor de Nuestra Señora de Rosario. A member of his father's Bogotan engineering firm, he has been manager of the Antioquía Railway, director of the Compañía Colombiana de Tabaco, manager (1931) of the Federación de Cafeteros, and Colombian delegate to the Conferencia Cafetera in São Paulo, Brazil.

For his part in promoting hemisphere understanding, President Ospina Pérez was awarded the Pan American Society's highest honor, the "Gold Insignia," on June 19, 1946. "Pan American unity," he has said "is essential for our well-being, our very survival. Yours and ours. No nation can exclude itself from the family of nations anymore. That day's passed. What could Colombia's foreign policy be but that? It is truly one world—or else."

By his marriage to Bertha Hernandez in 1926 President Ospina Pérez has four sons— Mariano, Rodrigo, Fernando and Gonzalo—and a daughter. Three of his sons were reported to be students in the United States. The Colombian President's recreations are horseback riding and growing orchids.

References
    International World Who's Who (1949)
    Quien es Quien en Colombia (1948)
    Who's Who in America, 1948-49
    World Biography (1948)

OVERSTREET, HARRY A(LLEN) Oct. 25, 1875- Author
Address: b. c/o W. W. Norton & Company, 101 5th Ave., New York 3

Dr. Harry A. Overstreet, head of the Department of Philosophy at the College of the City of New York from 1911 to 1939, is perhaps best known to the public through his books on sociological topics. Published over the years since 1925, when his first book, *Influencing Human Behavior*, appeared, his works include *About Ourselves*, *The Enduring Quest*, and *Our Free Minds*. *The Mature Mind*, a study in the problems of adult education (a field of endeavor with which Overstreet has increasingly identified himself), published in the summer of 1949, had gone into its eighteenth large printing by the middle of the following year and was one of the leaders on the nonfiction best-seller lists.

San Francisco, California, was the boyhood home of Harry Allen Overstreet, who was born in that city on October 25, 1875. His father, William Franklin Overstreet, a native of Missouri and a veteran of the Civil War, was a compositor on the San Francisco *Bulletin*; his mother, Julia (Detje) Overstreet, was born in Germany, from which she had come to California as a young girl. Their circumstances were not affluent—during his boyhood the future educator helped to pay for his support by sweeping floors and delivering orders for neigh-

HARRY A. OVERSTREET

borhood storekeepers or by assisting his father in the *Bulletin*'s composing room. His social consciousness was meanwhile being developed by the sight of "drunks" being brought to the city jail (near his home) and by street-corner orators. For reading in boyhood and youth he delighted in the classics of history or adventure; later he was attracted to the writings of Herbert Spencer, Emerson, and Darwin and, most significantly (according to the *Town Crier*), by that milestone in the Christian Socialist movement, Mrs. Humphrey Ward's novel *Robert Elsmere*.

When Overstreet entered the University of California as a member of the class of 1898, it was with the intention of majoring in literature, and then going on to law school. During his freshman year, however, he came under the influence of Professor George Holmes Howison, first incumbent of the Mills Chair of Philosophy; and, partly because of his already pronounced "socialistic leanings and a wholehearted interest in the struggles of the laboring class" (*California Monthly*), partly at the prompting of Professor Howison, became convinced "that his education must be along philosophical lines." A biographical article in an issue of the *California Monthly* of the 1930's described the difficulties and distinctions that marked Overstreet's undergraduate days. The elder Overstreet was stricken with paralysis when his son was a sophomore, so that young Overstreet became the sole support of the family, working six hours a day in the recorder's office; thus he required five years to complete undergraduate requirements. When he received the B.A. degree in 1899, it was with election to the Phi Beta Kappa and Beta Theta Pi fraternities, winning of the Carnot medal, high recognition as an intercollegiate debater, and the award of the Mills Traveling Fellowship

OVERSTREET, HARRY A.—*Continued*
to the University of Oxford for the period 1899-1901. After summering in Europe as secretary to Professor Howison, he took up residence at Balliol College, where he pursued his philosophy studies. He received the B. S. from Oxford in 1901, offering "The Theory of Knowledge in Aristotle and Hegel" as his dissertation subject.

On returning to the United States Overstreet was appointed an instructor in philosophy at the University of California. During his ten years at Berkeley he wrote a number of monographs and other papers, among them *Principles of Truth Evaluation* (1904), "The American College Course" (in the *Education Review* for February 1904), and *The Dialectic of Plotinus* (1909). Early in 1911 he was promoted to an associate professorship, but later in the year accepted a full professorship as head of the Department of Philosophy at the College of the City of New York. During the early 1920's, having become concerned about industrial disputes, he decided to make a study of that subject and accordingly was granted a leave of absence from his academic duties for a year. To obtain firsthand knowledge he took several factory jobs, making rubber shoes in Connecticut, polishing lathes in a California machine shop, sewing sacks for the Hawaiian Sugar Company, as well as going on the road as a salesman. His experience convinced him that the conflict was "not between capital and labor but between the intelligent and the unintelligent," and that the true solution of the problem of industrial unrest lay "in education, not only of the young, but of everybody, from the cradle to the grave" (from the *Town Crier*). After his return to New York he taught every Sunday morning at the International Ladies' Garment Workers Union, was a frequent speaker at Labor Temple and the People's Institute, and conducted a regular course in adult education at the New School for Social Research.

Overstreet's first book-length work appeared in 1925. This was *Influencing Human Behavior*, described by A. J. Levine in *Nation* as a "brilliant exposition of behaviorist philosophy" and by the New York *Times* as "thoroughly practical throughout." It was followed in 1927 by *About Ourselves: Psychology for Normal People*. In this book Overstreet made extensive use of clinical cases dealing with the "flight from reality, the flight into disease." Both works have had many printings, the former having attained a twenty-sixth and the latter a twenty-fifth by 1950. Both were based on the author's work with what he characterizes as "a large group of business and professional men" who "suffered the onslaught" of his lectures at the New School and "contributed their own experiences and history."

Of Overstreet's teaching methods, Fred Hawkins, Jr., was later to write in the *Town Crier*: "His students use no books, working rather from mimeographed sheets. . . .His audiences are enthusiastic and attentive—especially when he illustrates some point by selecting two or three people to come up on the platform, represent the types the problem involves, and discuss it from various points of view." This

was in November 1933, after Overstreet's name had become further familiar through numerous magazine articles (in *New Republic*, *Century Magazine*, *Survey*, and elsewhere) ; and through two later books, *The Enduring Quest* (1931; a study of human problems and reactions toward their solutions in the light of the 'new physics') and *We Move in New Directions* (1933; lectures on the new social structure). His fifth book, *A Guide to Civilized Leisure* (ideas on how to make the most of the "new leisure"), appeared in 1934, and his sixth, *A Declaration of Interdependence* (an attempt to see current social problems in the larger setting of American history), in 1937. All were generally well received, with praise for Overstreet's liberal attitude and simple presentation of concepts; a few critics expressed reservations as to the academic rigor of the author's thinking. In 1938 the educator became a regular lecturer at, and a trustee of, The Town Hall, Inc., in New York City, and was active in the development of *America's Town Meeting of the Air* radio program as a medium for adult education. (*Town Meeting Comes to Town*, written in collaboration with his second wife, Bonaro Wilkinson Overstreet, appeared in the same year.)

In the following year (1939), at the age of fifty-six, Overstreet resigned his chair at the College of the City of New York, receiving at the same time the title of professor emeritus. It was his belief that he could more effectively promote the cause of adult education through his writing, independent lecturing, and affiliation with such organizations as the American Association for Adult Education (of which he served as president in 1940 and 1943, and is today a trustee and research associate), and Town Hall. (Overstreet has also served as trustee of the New School, Finch Junior College, and the Philosophical Association.) In 1939 his next book, *Let Me Think*, which dealt with the management of the mind, appeared. This volume was followed in 1940 by *Leaders for Adult Education* (in collaboration with Mrs. Overstreet; a consideration of desirable leadership qualities and a program), the appearance of which approximately coincided with the appointment of the Overstreets as directors of the Town Hall Leadership School, which was launched with a three-week course in May 1941.

The year 1941 saw the publication of another of Overstreet's books—*Our Free Minds*, of which *Book Review Digest* noted: "In our present situation the author sees two threats to our American way of life, the threat from without, and the threat from within. He chooses to consider in detail only the second, but this he reviews in all its varied aspects, from careless use of words, to social injustices, anti-Semitism and Red-baiting." The New York *Times* critic felt the volume's value lay in "its generous liberalism and stimulating vigor."

After his country became a belligerent in World War II Overstreet told those present at an "I Am an American" luncheon sponsored by the New York City Board of Education (at which he was the recipient of the Evening Adult Students Association award) that he was "saying good-by" to his "old self" and was embarking on a new phase of work "to help win the war and build a new world . . . decent to live in" (from the New York *Times*). After the war Overstreet lectured widely, giving extension courses at the University of Michigan and in Hawaii, and conducting forum discussions under the auspices of universities and large industrial concerns; he also devoted much study to, and wrote many articles on, an approach to the Negro question. Overstreet maintains that our "behavior toward people is chiefly determined by the images we have of them," and that white conceptions of the Negro as "congenitally inferior" have "wrought immeasurable harm."

These and other interests and activities were to delay completion and publication of the philosopher-educator's much-praised *The Mature Mind* until the summer of 1949. A Book-of-the-Month Club choice, this work attained an immediate and continuing popularity; by the middle of 1950 it had reached its eighteenth large printing and was still one of the first three titles on nonfiction best-seller lists. The book is summed up by *Library Journal* as containing "first a review of the 'psychological foundations' which now allow us to define maturity in men, then a discussion of the how and how-not of maturity, and finally of the forces that shape us," such as politics, economics, education, family life, and religion. To G. W. Johnson, who reviewed the volume for the New York *Times*, *The Mature Mind* seemed "the philosophy of Rabbi Ezra expanded" and "a charming and salubrious book which should be an excellent prophylactic against the pandemic hysteria" of the age. Sterling North in his syndicated book column lauded the author for "brilliant suggestions on how most of us can attain a greater degree of maturity"; while the neuropsychiatrist Richard M. Brickner, writing in the *Saturday Review of Literature*, was impressed by the chapters on economics and the author's "satisfactory linkage" of psychological themes with religion.

Professor Overstreet's first marriage, to Elsie L. Burr, took place on May 18, 1907. Three sons, Edmund William, Robert Howison, and Alan Burr, were born of the union. Bonaro Wilkinson, author and lecturer, became Mrs. Overstreet on August 23, 1932. The couple now make their winter home in a modern ranch house at Mt. Tamalpais, California, and usually spend their summers on a farm in Vermont. Tennis and swimming have been Overstreet's favorite forms of exercise. He has been described as "above medium height, with a low, soft voice and dark hair, now graying."

References

Book-of-the-Month Club N Midsummer '49 por
Sat R Lit 32:8 Ag 13 '49 por
Town Crier p11 N '33 por
International Who's Who, 1950
Kunitz, S. J. and Haycraft, H. eds. Twentieth Century Authors (1942)
Who's Who, 1950
Who's Who in America, 1950-51
Who's Who in American Education, 1947-48
Who's Who in New York, 1947
Who's Who in Philosophy (1942)
World Biography (1948)

PACE, FRANK, JR. July 5, 1912- United States Government official; lawyer
Address: b. Department of the Army, The Pentagon, Washington, D.C.; h. 5024 Macomb St., N.W., Washington, D.C.

Frank Pace, Jr., who served as Director of the United States Budget for nearly fifteen months, became Secretary of the Army in April 1950. Earlier he had served for two years as executive assistant to the Postmaster General, had seen four years of World War II duty as an Air Transport officer, and had held public offices in his home State of Arkansas. The Budget Bureau, created in 1921, was in 1939 placed under the direct authority of the Chief Executive.

The son of Frank and Flora (Layton) Pace, Frank Pace, Jr. was born July 5, 1912, in Little Rock, Arkansas. His father, who is a lawyer in that city, was formerly district attorney for the Fourteenth Judicial District of Arkansas. After attending the Little Rock High School, young Frank Pace completed his secondary education at the Hill School, Pottstown, Pennsylvania. He then entered Princeton University, where he was graduated with the Bachelor of Arts degree in 1933.

Three years later, having received the LL.B. degree from the Harvard University Law School, he became in 1936 an assistant district attorney in Arkansas' Twelfth Judicial District. Success in the handling of cases involving tax-delinquency problems led to his appointment, in 1938, as general counsel to the Arkansas State Department of Revenue, which position he retained through 1940. At the beginning of the ensuing year he joined his father's Little Rock law firm of Pace and Davis. He was, however, in private practice for little more than one year —after the Pearl Harbor attack he offered himself for duty in World War II. Commissioned a second lieutenant in the Army Air Corps early in 1942, Pace served for four years in the Air Transport Command.

After demobilization, in the rank of major, early in 1946 Pace was briefly attached to the United States Department of Justice in Washington, as a special assistant on tax matters to Attorney General Tom Clark [45]; in May of the same year he transferred to the postal service as executive assistant to Postmaster General Robert Hannegan [44]. In this capacity he headed (in 1946) the United States delegation to the Conference of Postal Experts called by the United Nations at Lake Success, New York, and in 1947 he was chief of the American delegation to the Twelfth Universal Postal Congress in Paris. Elected vice-president of the Universal Postal Union, he became the union's representative to the United Nations. These posts he retained until the first month of 1948, when President Truman announced his appoint-

Wide World Photos

FRANK PACE, JR.

ment as Assistant Director of the Bureau of the Budget.

"The Act of Congress approved June 10, 1921, providing a national budget system," states the *United States Government Organization Manual*, "places upon the President the duty of transmitting to the Congress the Annual Budget, together with his estimates of receipts, expenditures and other budgetary data. To aid the President in this duty, the same act created the Bureau of the Budget." For some eighteen years it functioned under the Treasury Department, then was transferred to the authority of the Executive Office, and now "under rules prescribed by the President . . . prepares for him an Annual Budget and such supplemental and deficiency estimates as he may from time to time recommend to the Congress." The Bureau is empowered (states the *Government Manual*) to "assemble, correlate, revise, reduce or increase the estimates of the several departments and establishments." It has five divisions: administrative management, estimates, fiscal analysis, legislative reference, and statistical standards.

This is the organization of which Pace became second-in-command on January 20, 1948, and of which one year later he was to be the chief. He is credited with key work in preparation of the $41,858,000,000 budget for the fiscal year of July 1949 to June 1950, which President Truman submitted to the Eighty-first Congress early in January 1949. At approximately the same time (January 7, 1949) the President named Pace to the position of Director of the Budget, in succession to James E. Webb,[46] who was simultaneously nominated to be Under Secretary of State.

The new Director of the Budget Bureau was thirty-six years old when sworn in on February 1, 1949; he is said to be the youngest man ever to occupy this position, which at the time commanded an annual salary of $10,000, but has since been increased. Despite the fact that the 1950 fiscal estimate was the highest in peacetime history, Pace was generally regarded as a believer in the principle of the "balanced budget," though at the same time sympathetic toward what *Newsweek* characterized as "most of President Truman's costly welfare measures" and also, later, toward the Brannan farm-price guarantee plan. In March 1949, Pace vigorously opposed the Rankin bill to provide all veterans of sixty-five and older with monthly pensions of ninety dollars, stating in a letter to Representative John Carroll of Colorado that the measure would "cost more than $125,000,000,000 in the next fifty years" and that it was "not possible to justify such a commitment now." Another official letter from Pace, emphasizing price declines in the United States, was used by the President in support of his suggestion (April 26) that European recovery (Marshall Plan) funds for the fiscal year 1950 be cut by $157,800,000 below the amount already authorized by Congress.

At the beginning of November 1949 Pace issued, by direction of the President, a special budgetary statement re-estimating Government revenues in the 1950 fiscal year at 38 billion dollars as against the 41 billion dollars announced in January, and an estimated expenditure of $43,500,000,000, an increase of something less than two billion over the January figure. In the middle of the month he stated in a memorandum to the Congressional Joint Subcommittee on the Economic Report that "for any given year it is impractical to count on achieving any specific goal, whether a balanced budget or a predetermined surplus or deficit." The New York *Times* commented editorially: "Budget Director Pace rejects both the annually balanced budget and the compensatory, or cyclical budget. . . .He thinks that so long as the tension between the United States and Russia exists, at least, this country might as well get used to the idea of continued deficit spending." After a conference with the President on December 9, Pace told reporters (in the words of the *Times*) that while "planned expenditures would not exceed $45,000,000,000," the previous year, while the deficit for the 1951 fiscal year budget without additional taxes."

During February 1949, when the Commission on the Executive Branch of the Government (Hoover Commission) rendered the first of its reports, the recommendation was made that there be adopted a "performance budget," which has been defined by the Commission, as one "based upon functions, activities, and projects which would focus attention upon the general character and relative importance of the work to be done or upon the service to be rendered."

President Truman informed Congress in June 1949 he had issued directives to work on a performance budget, which, a budget executive said, "the average taxpayer will better understand where his dollar is going and what he is getting for it." On August 3 Pace stated that such a system would be instituted. The budget for 1951 (July 1950-June 1951) was prepared accordingly, and when the 1,400-page document was transmitted to Congress on January 9, 1950, it was hailed for its clarity, if not for its controversial content. ("The form of the new budget in the adoption of the performance principle is the greatest step in the advance of this problem since 1920," declared former President Herbert Hoover.) A further clarification is a forty-page, chart-illustrated "midget budget" (*Federal Budget in Brief*, available at twenty cents from the Superintendent of Documents), designed for the information of the taxpayer. As the budget figures, an expenditure of $42,439,000,000 was estimated, as contrasted with $43,297,000,000 of the previous year, while the deficit for the 1951 budget was reckoned at $5,133,000,000, about $400,000,000 less than 1950.

In early April 1950 President Truman named Pace to the post of Secretary of the Army, to succeed Gordon Gray [49], who resigned to become president of the University of North Carolina. The Senate approved the nomination on April 19, and two days later Pace took the oath of office. As Secretary of the Army, states the *Government Manual*, "he is charged with the supervision of all estimates of appropriations for the expenses of the Department of the Army . . . of all purchases . . . of all expenditures. He is held responsible for the performance of the Army's mission in occupied areas and for the installations and facilities" in the United States and Territories "vital to national security; for the development of improved weapons and matériel; for the proper instruction of all military personnel; and for the discipline and morale of the Army."

A member of the Arkansas, District of Columbia and American bar associations (he has served on the last-named's committee on legal aspects of national defense), Pace was a member of the Joint Congressional Committee on Reduction of Nonessential Federal Expenditures, and is a reserve officer of the Air Force. He belongs to the National Press, and the University clubs in Washington. The Paces (Mrs. Pace is the former Margaret Janney) have two daughters. The Government official, who is about six feet tall, slender and athletic, was described in the New York *Times* on the occasion of his appointment, as "a congenial young man who consistently scores in the seventies in golf and was runner-up for the singles title" in the 1948 National Press Club tennis tournament.

References

Bsns W p6 Jl 2 '49 por
N Y Times p29 Ja 21 '48; p3 Ja 8 '49 por
Newsweek 34:16 Ag 15 '49 por
American Men in Government (1949)
International Who's Who, 1949
Who's Who in America, 1950-51

PACELLI, EUGENIO *See* Pius XII, Pope

PAGE, JOE Oct. 28, 1917- Baseball player
Address: b. c/o New York Yankees, Inc., 745 5th Ave., New York 22; h. 402 Ridge Ave., Springdale, Pa.

Joe Page, a "southpaw" relief pitcher for the New York Yankees, winners of the 1947 and 1949 World Series, was named to receive the first Babe Ruth [44] Memorial Award as the

JOE PAGE

outstanding player in the 1949 World Series. Page, who until 1947 had an uncertain major league career, in that year began to make his mark as a pitcher. On announcement of the award early in 1950, sports writer John Drebinger in the New York *Times* observed that Page was "regarded as one of the top relief hurlers of all time." The Yankees' winning of the World Series in 1947 and 1949 has been frequently credited to Page's playing in those seasons. Signing with the Yankees for 1950, the pitcher commented, "I think this is the first time a relief pitcher is getting paid like a starter."

Joseph Francis Page was named for his father, who was a coal miner in Cherry Valley, Pennsylvania, when Joseph, the first of seven children, was born October 28, 1917. His mother was the former Lorena Couch; both parents were of Irish ancestry. Later the family moved to Cheswick, Pennsylvania, the town in which the boy spent his adolescent years, and became known as a fine baseball player. With the encouragement of his father, himself a ball player, the youth planned a future in professional baseball. That was his goal during the years he attended Springdale (Pennsylvania) High School. However, when he graduated in 1934, he went to work in the coal mines, where he was employed steadily for two years, and then intermittently until 1943.

PAGE, JOE—*Continued*

Among the jobs he held were bratticer, electrician's helper, loader, stump man, and coupler. In the course of these early years, he played in one exhibition baseball game, for which he was paid fifty dollars.

In 1936 Page, at his father's urging, began to play semiprofessional baseball. This phase of his career was interrupted by an accident—he was run over by a truck, and spent eleven months in a hospital, barely escaping amputation of his left leg. (Until 1947 Page was to wear a protective shin guard.) In 1939 at the age of twenty-two, he returned to baseball, to try out on the Pittsburgh Pirates farm team in the Class D. Pennsylvania State Association, but he was let out before the season started and played semiprofessional only that season. The following year he was recommended to and engaged to play on the Butler, Pennsylvania, team in that State's League. Butler was a Class D team owned by the New York Yankees. Because of an appendectomy Page pitched only sixteen games in his first professional season. He won eleven of these for a percentage of .786. His earned-run average was 3.67. In a *Saturday Evening Post* article, "I was Baseball's Bad Boy," by Page with Joe Trimble, the Yankee pitcher said of his time with Butler, "Tom (Shakey) Kain was the manager . . . and he really taught me some things about pitching."

The next year, 1941, Page was moved up to the Augusta (Georgia) team in the Southern Atlantic League, playing Class B baseball. On August 7, he pitched a no-hitter against Savannah, winning the game 4 to 0. His average that year was twelve wins, twelve defeats in forty games for a percentage of .500, with 165 strikeouts; his earned-run average was 4.39. In 1942 (Page's old leg injury prevented him from serving in World War II) he made another advance—to the International League, where he became a pitcher for Newark, the New York Yankees farm team. During his first year on the New Jersey team he won seven games, lost six, played twenty for a percentage of .538; his earned-run average was 4.19. In 1943 Page again played with Newark after a suspension caused by his failure to report on schedule—he had gone home to convalesce after a hospital stay of ten days due to stomach ulcers, according to an article in the *Saturday Evening Post*. That year his percentage rose to .737, when he won fourteen, lost five of the twenty-eight games in which he played. His earned-run average was 3.05.

The left-handed pitcher in 1944 was brought to New York by the Yankees. There Page, starting well, was hailed as the rookie of the season when he won five of his first six games and was given a place on the American League All-Star Team. Page has related (in the *Saturday Evening Post*) that in a game with Cleveland he injured a shoulder, an injury he did not report. In August, having played in nineteen games, with five wins and seven losses, he was shipped back to Newark. There he slightly topped his .417 percentage for New York with a .444 percentage (he won four, lost five of the nine games he played) and

earned a place on the International League All-Star Team. His earned-run average in the American League had been 4.54; back in Newark it was 2.71.

Joe McCarthy [48], Yankee manager until early in 1946, brought Page back to the American League in 1945. According to Milton Gross in *Yankee Doodles*, Page did not get along well with McCarthy or with his teammates. His only "buddy" in those days, Gross says, was Joe DiMaggio [41], his roommate. In 1945 Page's percentage was .667 (he won six, lost three, and played in twenty games); his earned-run average was 2.82. The following year the percentage dropped to .529 (nine wins, eight losses, thirty-one games). During this period, Page has said, "I had won little more than a reputation as a playboy" (*Saturday Evening Post*).

"I was so deep in the doghouse," Page wrote of the opening days of the 1947 season, "it would have taken a bloodhound to find me. I was working under a special 'bad-boy' contract in which my pay varied with my behavior." Writers and players expressed the belief that Page was a capable pitcher who was indifferent or who lacked essential confidence. On May 26, 1947, came the turning point in Page's career. It was during a night game against the Boston Red Sox (defending champions that year) that Page was called into the game in the third inning with the score 3 to 1 in the Red Sox's favor, two men on bases, and no outs. Shortly after Page came to the mound an error put a player on first to load the bases. Page struck out the next two players and caused the third to bat out a fly, ending the innings. He allowed two hits during the rest of the game, but the Yankees won 9 to 3, and Page had laid the basis for a reputation as a great relief pitcher, a reputation he consolidated during the rest of the season. (It has been reported that Red Sox players later in the season said that was "the game that broke our backs.")

That season Page established a record by being the first New York American League pitcher to play in fifty-six games in one season (he later broke his own record). Of these games he was credited officially with fourteen wins to eight losses for a percentage of .636, and was also said to have saved thirteen additional games for the Yankees. His earned-run average of 2.49 was the fifth best in the league.

When the Yankees topped the league at the end of the 1947 season, Tom Meany told *PM* readers, "The American League pennant was won by the Yanks because of the great relief pitching of Page." The "clinching" seventh game of that year's World Series, Meany said, was won because of Page—"Page's contribution can't be overestimated. He was a gem of consistency and steadiness at a time when all around him Yankee pitchers were reeling and falling." Commented his teammates, "We wouldn't be here without him." Page also appeared in an All-Star game that season for one and one-third innings.

Page kept his place on the Yankee roster in 1948, but it was not a year of outstanding play for him. He pitched in fifty-five games, was credited with seven wins and eight losses for a .467 pecentage. His earned-run average was 4.25. In 1949 Page's name figured prominently in the sports pages, with the writers applauding him. He entered the eighth inning of the 1949 All-Star game to "save" the American League's winning score. The relief pitcher received much credit for the Yankees' winning the American League pennant and the World Series (he appeared in three games in the series, was credited with one win). Joe Williams of the New York *World-Telegram* commented, "What other team in baseball has a Joe Page? His presence alone moves the entire Yank staff up two or three points in class." Yankee manager Casey Stengel '49 is reported to have pointed to Page as the reason the team was able to survive the loss of Joe DiMaggio during half a season of play. Pitching in sixty games in 1949, Page won thirteen, lost eight; of the entire sixty games in which he appeared the Yankees won forty-two, lost seventeen and tied one.

Page was named to be the first recipient of the Babe Ruth Memorial Award, established in 1949, by the New York Chapter of the Baseball Writers Association of America as an annual award for World Series performance. The plaque will be presented to Page at Yankee Stadium at one of the early games of the 1950 season. His name was mentioned often as the Most Valuable Player for the American League Award; this, however went to Phil Rizzuto, Yankee short-stop. (A pitcher is seldom considered for this award because he plays in relatively few games.) In 1950 Page was thought to have become the highest paid pitcher in Yankee history. New York sports writer Joe Williams in the *World-Telegram and Sun* (February 2, 1950) pointed it out as a significant fact that "the physical conditions under which baseball is played today have changed so that the importance of relief pitching cannot be overestimated."

In the *Saturday Evening Post* article, Page gave former Yankee manager Bucky Harris '48 much of the credit for his success, mentioning Harris' patience in giving him many chances; he also cited DiMaggio's friendship and good counsel as decisive factors in his making good. To Larry MacPhail '46, president of the Yankees in 1945-47, he attributed the idea that he would make a relief pitcher—the southpaw had previously been regarded as a starter. (MacPhail was also the originator of the "bad-boy" contract of 1947.) "I'm a relief pitcher now, and proud of it," commented Page in the *Post* article. One of the things fitting him for the role of relief pitcher, Page said, is the fact that it is easy for him to warm up—"nine or ten tosses, and I'm ready to go."

Page married, on February 25, 1941, Catherine Aquina Carrigan. His religious faith is the Roman Catholic, his political party the Democratic. Hunting and fishing are among his diversions. Six feet three inches in height, he weighs 205 pounds; he has blue eyes and brown hair.

References

Sat Eve Post 220:28+ My 22 '48 por
Baseball Register (1949)
Gross, M. Yankee Doodles (1948)

PAGE, JOSEPH FRANCIS *See* Page, Joe

PAHLEVI, MOHAMMED RIZA. *See* Mohammed Riza Pahlevi

PANNELL, ANNE GARY Sept. 15, 1910-
College president
Address: b. c/o Sweet Briar College, Sweet Briar, Va.; h. Sweet Briar House, Sweet Briar, Va.

In May 1950 it was announced by the Sweet Briar College board of overseers that Anne Gary Pannell had been chosen as the fifth president of the liberal arts college for women in the Piedmont section of Virginia. She took over the new post on July 1, 1950, succeeding Martha B. Lucas '47, who had been president of Sweet Briar for four years. A scholar in the field of American history, Mrs. Pannell had previously served as assistant and associate professor of history at the University of Alabama, and for the academic year 1949-50 as academic dean of Goucher College.

Born in Durham, North Carolina, on September 15, 1910, Anne Gary Pannell is the only child of Alexander Henry and Anne Roche (Thomas) Gary, both natives of Virginia. She is of Scottish extraction, one branch of her family having come in 1645 to "Hotwaters," a plantation in Prince George County, Virginia. After living her early years in Petersburg, she was educated at the Scoville School in New York City, from which she graduated in 1927. She then entered Barnard College to major in history. There she was editor of *Mortarboard*, the annual publication of the junior class, and was elected president of the senior class. She received the Gerard Gold Medal in Colonial History and a summer scholarship at the Geneva School of International Studies in Switzerland. Obtaining the Bachelor of Arts degree with honors in 1931, she won the Phi Beta Kappa key and was awarded the Barnard College International Fellowship, then financed yearly by the student body, which entitled her to a year's graduate study at any accredited European university. She was chosen to receive this fellowship by undergraduate vote from a group of six selected by a nominating committee. Before sailing for Europe she spent the summer as an instructor in history at the Barnard Summer School.

In the fall of 1931 Miss Gary began her studies at St. Hugh's College, Oxford University. At the end of her 1931-32 year at the English university, she was elected to an Oxford research place at the Institute of Historical Research, London University. She spent another year and a half in research work at the Bibliothèque Nationale in Paris, the Archivo General de Indias in Seville, and in Germany,

Bradford Bachrach

ANNE GARY PANNELL

as well as at Quaker manuscript depositories in England and the United States. This period also included travels in Italy, Austria, Hungary, Yugoslavia, Bulgaria, Greece, and Turkey. Returning to the United States in 1934, Miss Gary served for two years as an instructor in history at Alabama College, the State college for women in Montevallo. In January 1936 she was awarded a Doctor of Philosophy degree at Oxford, having submitted as her dissertation *The Political and Economic Relations of English and American Quakers*, published the preceding year.

Mrs. Pannell (as Miss Gary had become by her marriage in 1936) was appointed an instructor in history at the University of Alabama in 1939. In 1946 she became an assistant professor, and directed the club study service and library extension. In 1947 she was associate professor and chairman of freshman history. She was appointed academic dean and professor of history at Goucher College (for women) in Baltimore, Maryland, in the spring of 1949.

Sweet Briar College, of which Dr. Pannell became president in July 1950, is a nonsectarian, privately controlled college of liberal arts and sciences for women. Chartered in 1901, Sweet Briar was opened five years later with thirty-six students and four college buildings; in 1949 there was a total of 454 students and about fifteen buildings. Nearly half the student body comes from the South or Southwest, although the enrollment includes students from other parts of the United States and from foreign countries. It confers the degree of Bachelor of Arts, and its academic standing is accredited by the Southern Association, the Association of American Universities, and the American Association of University Women. Educational developments at Sweet Briar include the honors plan of study, scholarship funds for foreign students, and the junior year abroad, either at the University of Paris or at St. Andrews University in Scotland, for a few selected students. It is the aim of the college to make "a general liberal education as rich and valuable as possible to the young women who are preparing to serve their generation."

Dr. Pannell has been an active member of the American Association of University Women since 1934. She has served as secretary, vice-president, and president (1942-43) of the Alabama State Division of the A.A.U.W., as well as international relations chairman of that division from 1945 to 1948, as social studies chairman, and as president of the Tuscaloosa branch. The Alabama division has named an international study grant in her honor. One of the most significant phases of the international work of the A.A.U.W. is its liaison with the university women of other countries through the International Federation of University Women. Mrs. Pannell delivered an address before the ninth, and first postwar, conference of the I.F.U.W., held at Toronto, Canada, in 1947, and spoke at the tenth I.F.U.W. conference (which had as its theme, "Human Rights—The Task Ahead"), at Zurich, Switzerland, in August 1950.

Since 1948 Mrs. Pannell has been a member of the national A.A.U.W. committee on international relations (which, in addition to its other activities, has been surveying the instruction given on the United Nations in American public schools), and in 1950 she represented that committee on the national A.A.U.W. committee on legislative program. To the spring 1950 issue of the A.A.U.W. *Journal*, Mrs. Pannell contributed an article entitled "Continue Building," which summarized the A.A.U.W.'s position on the various proposals and plans for attaining world order. Affirming the association's belief in the methods of international cooperation as exemplified in the United Nations, the college president criticized the tendency to rely on regional commitments, such as the North Atlantic Pact, rather than on the United Nations Charter: such a course she regarded as being dangerous to the achievement of international order and tending to divide the world into two opposing camps. "It is far better to start from the minimum of agreement which we now have and endeavor to improve it to the utmost," she declared, "than to try to substitute other forms of alliance. . . . Constitutions can be written but they cannot be put into force without the will. The United Nations, therefore, must be strengthened. As it grows in power and authority based upon the sincere desire of the peoples of the world for peace, security, and social and economic advancement, then and then only can lasting peace be achieved."

During World War II Mrs. Pannell was a Red Cross Gray Lady at Northington General Hospital. An Episcopalian, she served as educational secretary of the Protestant Episcopal Diocese of Alabama (1943-45) and chairman of college work for the women's auxiliary, Province of Sewanee, for the same church (1943-46).

Among the other associations to which the Sweet Briar president belongs are the Alabama, Southern, and American historical societies; the Alabama Congress of Parents and Teachers; the Alabama Education Association; and Phi Alpha Theta. She has contributed reviews to the *Journal of Politics* and to publications of the Society of Friends. On September 2, 1936, she was married to Henry Clifton Pannell, then associate professor of education at the University of Alabama. At the time of his death, ten years later, he was full professor of education at the University of Alabama, superintendent of city schools in Tuscaloosa, and newly elected Alabama State Superintendent of Education. Their two sons are Henry Gary and Clifton Wyndham. Mrs. Pannell, who is five feet four inches tall, weighs 117 pounds; her eyes are hazel and her hair is brown. In her political affiliation the Southern educator is a Democrat. She finds relaxation in gardening.

References

N Y Herald Tribune p12 My 9 '50 por
N Y Times p22 My 9 '50 por
Time 55:53 My 22 '50 por

MRS. JAMES B. PATTON

PATTON, MRS. JAMES B(LAINE) Feb. 5, 1889- Women's organization official

Address: b. c/o National Society Daughters of the American Revolution, 1776 D St., N.W., Washington, D.C.; h. 1676 Franklin Ave., Columbus, Ohio

Mrs. James B. Patton, of Columbus, Ohio, was installed as president general of the National Society of the Daughters of the American Revolution on April 21, 1950, in Washington, D.C., during the organization's fifty-ninth continental congress. First vice-president general since 1947, Mrs. Patton succeeded Mrs. Roscoe C. O'Byrne [48]. Mrs. Patton, who became a member of the D.A.R. in 1910, has held many posts of graduating importance.

Born Marguerite Courtright in Circleville, Ohio, on February 5, 1889, Mrs. Patton is the daughter of Judge Samuel Wilson and Jennie Rosalthea (Martin) Courtright. Her ancestors, several of whom were Huguenots, had left Holland for New Amsterdam in the seventeeth century, had moved to Ohio about 1800. Marguerite Courtright was reared in Circleville with her two sisters, and, on July 4, 1911, was married to James Blaine Patton, who was in the wholesale lumber business.

Mrs. Patton had become a member of the Daughters of the American Revolution in Ohio the year before her marriage. The society is composed of women descendants of ancestors, any of whom "with unfailing loyalty rendered material aid to the cause of independence as a recognized patriot, as a soldier or sailor, or as a civil officer in one of the several colonies or states" (*Encyclopedia Americana*). Its objects are to perpetuate the memory of the spirit of the men and women who achieved American independence, to foster knowledge, freedom, and patriotism, and to aid in securing for mankind the blessings of liberty.

The D.A.R. was organized in Washington, D.C. in October 1890. It has today 167,000 members, whose delegates meet in annual conference in Washington the third week of April. The society has preserved many historical relics, and owns a valuable historical and genealogical library at Constitution Hall, the D.A.R. headquarters. The society's publication is the *Daughters of the American Revolution Magazine*.

Mrs. Patton is a former member of the advisory board for the D.A.R. school at Tamassee, South Carolina. While residing in New Jersey, she became an associate member of the Orange Mountain chapter. She served five years as second and first vice-regent of her Columbus chapter; as regent she administered a chapter of more than five hundred members. Four of ten years on the Ohio State board were served as the D.A.R. State librarian. In that office Mrs. Patton procured a librarian for every chapter.

During the early years of World War II Mrs. Patton was State vice-regent and chairman of national defense. At the same time she was a member of the Franklin (Ohio) County council of defense, and was on the Columbus speakers' bureau for all bond drives. In addition she assisted in the work of the USO. Under Mrs. Patton's direction (reported a D.A.R. biography) Ohio D.A.R.'s purchased more than twelve million dollars' worth of bonds and stamps, contributed thousands of "Buddy Bags" to the armed forces, and gave generously to the D.A.R. war projects fund. For her activities, Mrs. Patton received a citation from the American Red Cross. During three war and postwar years, as State regent, Mrs. Patton continued to lead the Ohio group. She is today an honorary State regent. Mrs. Patton is also a past national vice-chairman of membership, and for

PATTON, MRS. JAMES B.—*Continued*

a number of years has been a promoter of the Children of the American Revolution.

In April 1947, the Ohio member was elected first vice-president general of the national body. At that time Mrs. Patton received the largest number of votes cast for any candidate for cabinet office. During her term, she edited the 1948 *D.A.R. Handbook.* Present at all meetings of the national board and the executive committee, she from time to time represented the president general. Mrs. Patton also assisted in the realization of the new $1,250,000 Washington headquarters building of the society, having since 1948 been a national vice-chairman of the building promotion committee. In March 1950, during the forty-ninth annual conference of the District of Columbia D.A.R., Mrs. Patton, then a candidate for president general, had voiced strong disapproval of world government (Washington *Post*, March 29, 1950).

The 1950 triennial election year saw one of the most spirited elections in D.A.R. history. In a campaign featuring rival receptions and rival contributions to the building fund, Mrs. James B. Patton ultimately defeated Mrs. Edwin Stanton Lammers of Texas by a vote of 1494 to 762. Taking office for her three-year term on April 21, 1950 (the day of her election), Mrs. Patton stressed the importance of the national defense committee of the society. She declared that it can become, in a community, "the nucleus of information concerning the various phases of our national security" (Washington *Post*, April 22, 1950).

During its fifty-ninth congress, the D.A.R. as a body called for the maintenance of United States defense forces sufficient to repel attack from any quarter, and for continued military research and development; it also reaffirmed opposition to world government. The organization opposed any change in the United Nations Charter that might destroy the sovereignty of the United States, or any international agreement that would permit interference in the country's domestic affairs. The D.A.R. delegates took the stand that socialism is a greater immediate menace than communism, and called for an immediate balancing of the national budget. Reasserting their belief in "free capitalism," they maintained that the teaching of social sciences should support free enterprise ideals. They declared their opposition to socialized medicine, and to the immigration of aliens over and above the regular quota system; the registration of Communists was proposed. The Un-American Activities Committee, Judge Harold Medina [49] (who presided at the Communists' trial), the Federal Bureau of Investigation, and J. Edgar Hoover [50] were commended. It urged that the findings of the Hoover Report be adopted insofar as practicable. The society asked President Truman and Congress to observe a "Bill of Rights Day" on December 15.

As president general, working to extend the aims of the Daughters of the American Revolution, Mrs. Patton will be making trips to the conferences of D.A.R. societies in every State. During the campaign her advocates pointed out that she is able to devote her full time to her duties, for the carrying out of which (stated the New York *Herald Tribune*) probably about "$50,000 of her own or her friends' money" will be expended during the three years of her term.

In the past the D.A.R. officer has given her time to community service, war work, and other projects. Organizations to which she belongs include Daughters of Founders and Patriots, the Huguenot Society, the Daughters of Colonial Wars, Daughters of American Colonists, Sons and Daughters of the Pilgrims, the United States Daughters of 1812, the National Society of Arts and Letters, the Ohio State Archaeological and Historical Society, the Franklin County Historical Association, and Washington Headquarters Association.

The supporters of her candidacy praised Mrs. Patton for her executive ability and qualities of personality. Mrs. Patton, who is a widow, is the mother of two sons, James Courtright and Robert Miller. She has blue eyes and brown and gray hair, weighs 128 pounds, and is five feet, five inches tall. A Republican and Presbyterian, Mrs. Patton was a Presbyterial treasurer for six years. Her hobby is genealogy.

PATTON, MARGUERITE COURT-RIGHT *See* Patton, Mrs. J. B.

PEARSON, C(HESTER) C(HARLES)

July 15, 1906- Aircraft company executive

Address: b. c/o The Glenn L. Martin Company, Baltimore 3, Md.; h. Darlington, Md.

Prominent among the personalities determining the course of the aircraft industry in the United States is C. C. Pearson, the president and general manager of the Glenn L. Martin Company of Baltimore. Pearson who came to the Maryland city as the result of a top-level reorganization of the Martin enterprise effected in the summer of 1949, had previously served the Douglas Aircraft Company in the capacities of aeronautical engineer and plant manager for over sixteen years, and the Curtiss-Wright Corporation in those of aircraft division general manager and vice-president, for two and a half years. He is known as a contributor to the development of many of America's military and civilian airplanes.

A native of Los Angeles County, California, the airplane manufacturing executive is one of the four children (three sons and a daughter) of Joseph Charles and Edith Ellen (Hall) Pearson. Born July 15, 1906, in El Monte, Chester Charles Pearson was brought up in the Los Angeles area, and was graduated from the Union High School of Covina in 1923. After taking a four-year liberal arts course (1923-27) at Whittier College, near the Southern California metropolis, he entered the Western College of Aeronautics at Los Angeles. He received that institution's aeronautical engineering degree in 1930.

In the same year he joined the landing gear section of the engineering department of the

Douglas Aircraft Company at Santa Monica, California, as an engineering draftsman. Through the greater part of the 1930's he served as a project engineer on what has been described as "a succession of important military aircraft," was made assistant to the chief engineer at the Santa Monica plant in 1939; in the year following he was placed in charge of master schedules at all seven plants of the Douglas company. Pearson was appointed general manager, in May 1942, of the new Douglas Oklahoma plant in Oklahoma City, where under his supervision more than five thousand multi-engine cargo planes were produced for the armed forces. He is a member of the Aircraft Industry Advisory Committee of the Munitions Board. After the war Pearson was appointed Eastern manager and assistant to the president of the Douglas company, positions which he occupied until the end of 1946, when he resigned to accept the post of general manager of the airplane division of the Curtiss-Wright Corporation.

With the peacetime prospect of conversion to the building of jet-propelled and other new-design commercial planes, the Curtiss-Wright Corporation, manufacturers of the famous wartime P-40 and C-46, had decided to concentrate its aircraft-building activity in a single plant at Columbus, Ohio. Here, under the president, Guy W. Vaughan '48, Pearson took over as general manager on January 1, 1947, assuming responsibility for what the *World Aviation Annual* for 1948 was to sum up as "a well-rounded experimental and development program . . . including the development of the CW-32, a 100,000-pound cargo transport and the XP-87, a four-jet all-weather fighter." (The XP-87 was said to be "the first fighter ever powered by four jet engines," while the CW-32 "Skytruck" would, it was asserted, be capable of delivering sixteen tons of freight from coast to coast at 300 miles per hour). While at Columbus, Pearson also supervised "extensive research and development work on guided missiles and pilotless aircraft." He was advanced to the vice-presidency of the Curtiss-Wright Company in New York City on June 1, 1948. A year later Pearson resigned.

Glenn L. Martin '43, pioneer in American aviation and head of the company which bears his name, had built up a record in the war as manufacturer of the Marylands, Marauders, Mariners, and Mars craft. Looking toward the postwar period he planned to develop a "modern twin-engine" airliner, the Martin 2-0-2. Early orders had been plentiful, but the expected postwar aviation boom was of short duration, and eventually Northwest Air Lines was the only domestic concern ordering the Martin 2-0-2, reported *Business Week*. A large Reconstruction Finance Corporation loan was floated to help the company over losses entailed in 1947.

According to a company statement, on July 15, 1949, Martin (at that time chairman of the board) brought Pearson to the presidency and general managership of the aircraft-manufacturing concern. The first six months of 1949 had shown a net income (before "special adjustments") which swept it

C. C. PEARSON

away) of $976,974 as against a net loss of $719,034 for the same period in 1948. Large Government contracts were held by the company, including "development of a big jet bomber, a high-powered fighter aircraft carrier, and supersonic guided missiles," stated the *Christian Science Monitor* at the time of Pearson's appointment. His appointment, said the Baltimore *Evening Sun*, was believed to have been the result of dissatisfaction with the financial condition of the firm.

At the end of July, a new one-million-dollar RFC loan was granted to the Martin company. In announcing this loan, Harvey L. Gunderson, an official of RFC, not only expressed the Corporation's confidence in the company's future, but pointed out that its financial difficulties had their inception in the fact that "Mr. Martin, gentleman that he is . . . took an inventory loss of from 12 to 16 million dollars" by refunding down payments on canceled 2-0-2 contracts.

The newest addition to the Martin commercial line is the Martin 4-0-4, a pressurized twin-engine transport specifically designed for the medium and short trip services operated by leading domestic air lines; the first of these are due off the production line in the spring of 1951. The company also holds contracts from the Government for the development of a three-jet ground support bomber for the Air Force, and two types of multi-engine patrol planes for the Navy; and it has several research and production projects under way in the fields of guided missiles and rockets.

In November 1949 Pearson accepted a directorship of the Baltimore National Bank. The aircraft manufacturing executive is a trustee of the National Security Industrial Association and a member of the Aircraft Manufacturers Council (East Coast). At Santa Barbara, California, on December 11, 1949, he was one of five new members elected to the board of gov-

PEARSON, C. C.—*Continued*

ernors of the Aircraft Industries Association of America. Professional bodies to which he belongs include the Institute of the Aeronautical Sciences and the Society of Automotive Engineers. He is a member of the Wings Club. For his services in this vital industry during World War II, Pearson was awarded the President's Certificate of Merit, receiving it from Secretary of the Air Force W. Stuart Symington on December 16, 1948.

Mrs. C. C. Pearson is the former Wanda May Stanley; the couple reside at Darlington, Maryland. Pearson, who attends the meetings of the Society of Friends, is a Republican. Five feet ten and a half inches tall, he weighs 210 pounds, has gray hair and gray eyes. He finds diversion in gardening and is an amateur radio operator.

References

Baltimore Ag '49 por; D '49 por
N Y Times p18 Jl 16 '49 por
U S Air Service p11 Ag '49 por

PEEL, ROY V(ICTOR) July 26, 1896- United States Government official

Address: b. c/o Bureau of the Census, Department of Commerce, Washington, D.C.

The seventeenth decennial census of the United States, taken in April 1950, was made under the over-all supervision of Dr. Roy V. Peel, for nearly fourteen years professor of government at Indiana University and a one-time chairman of the New York City Fusion party. He is author, co-author or editor of a number of books on politics, among them *The*

Wide World Photos

ROY V. PEEL

Political Clubs of New York City (1935), *Introduction to Politics* (1941), and *State Government Today.* His appointment as Director of the Bureau of the Census, a unit of the Department of Commerce, became effective early in March 1950.

Roy Victor Peel was born to Victor R. and Hannah (Anderson) Peel in Des Moines, Iowa, on July 26, 1896. Upon the completion of his secondary schooling he began his college education. That, however, was interrupted by World War I, during which he held a second lieutenant's commission in the Army Air Service (1918-19). He was able to complete the requirements for the B.A. degree at Augustana College, Rock Island, Illinois in 1920.

Peel was engaged until the summer of 1921 as an instructor at Trinity College, Round Rock, Texas, and in the ensuing academic year taught at a Minneapolis college. Then, a graduate student at the University of Chicago, he received the M.A. degree in 1923. In 1924-25 he was a history instructor at New York University, and in 1926-27 an instructor in government at the University of Rochester, New York. Acquiring his Ph.D. from the University of Chicago in 1927, he returned in the fall to New York University as an assistant professor of government.

During the five years that followed, Peel did extensive research on the subject of the role of political clubs in metropolitan municipal elections: in 1931, as co-author, with Thomas Claude Donnelly, of *The 1928 Campaign: An Analysis,* he attained stature as an authority on national political trends. This comparatively short book, lauded by the *American Political Science Review* as revealing "more of political science . . . than is contained in many a ponderous tome," was adjudged "fairly complete" by the *Annals of the American Academy.* A speech delivered by Peel, "The Displacement of States by Political Regions" at the Conference on Metropolitan Government on October 19, 1932, elicited discussion. Elimination of the system of forty-eight States in order to divide the nation into a number of economically unified regions was, he said, "the next step in man's quest for self-government." An article which he contributed to the New York *Times* of July 9, 1933, bore the caption "Our Makers of Laws: Their Traits Viewed." The year 1933 also saw the appearance of a work jointly by Peel and Donnelly, *The 1932 Campaign,* a companion volume to their study of the previous contest for the Presidency.

Named director of the division of research in public administration at New York University, Peel was on July 12, 1934, elected chairman of the city's Fusion party, a post he filled for three months—he was in September appointed professor at New York University. Shortly thereafter he was granted a leave of absence to conduct a survey of public administration in the Scandinavian countries for the Institute of Public Administration. He was able to complete the manuscript of his book *The Political Clubs of New York City* (published in 1935) before departing for Europe. There he spent nearly two years in field research in Sweden, Norway, and Denmark.

Among the results of his study was a paper, "Consumers' Cooperatives in the Scandinavian Countries," in the *Annals of the American Academy* for May 1937, and a bibliography, "Social Policies and Problems of Sweden."

Peel, who had returned to the United States in September 1936, became professor of government at Indiana University that fall. Continuing to contribute to the literature in his field, in 1938 he edited, and compiled the bibliography for, the symposium "Better City Government" in the *Annals of the American Academy*. Also, in 1938, appeared his *Plunkitt of Tammany Hall*, a study of the one-time sachem, George W. Plunkitt. In 1939 Peel became director of the university's Institute of Politics and of research for the Municipal League; and, in association with Dr. Joseph C. Roucek of Hofstra College, Long Island, New York, he embarked on the compilation of *Introduction to Politics*, completed and published in 1941. The *American Political Science Review* described this work as "a cooperative scholarship project wherein a number of collaborators joined their efforts with those of the editors" to "satisfy the demand for an appropriate introductory textbook in the field of political science." The *Annals of the American Academy* felt that the various chapters were "uneven in value and widely different in style and presentation."

From 1942 to 1946 the educator had a wartime leave of absence, while he was attached to the government in civilian capacities, notably as chief of the United States Information Service in Copenhagen in 1945. His *Roosevelt Talar*, in the meantime, had made its appearance in 1943. Returning to Indiana University, Peel in 1947 became a member of the city planning commission of Bloomington, and also worked on his next book, *State Government Today*, prepared in cooperation with the University of New Mexico and published in 1948.

The nomination of the political scientist as Director of the Census (relieving Dr. Philip C. Hauser of the University of Chicago who had been acting director since the retirement of the late James C. Capt in July 1949) was announced by President Truman on February 3, 1950. The appointment was unanimously confirmed by the Senate on March 2. The broad function of the Bureau of the Census is to serve as the major fact-finding and statistical service agency for the Government, to supply data as well to business. The decennial enumeration is only one of the many censuses it conducts. Under Peel's direction are several thousand permanent employees.

The April 1950 census is the seventeenth in the nation's history, the first having been made in 1790 in compliance with Article One of the Constitution of the United States, which calls for an enumeration of the country's population every tenth year, as a basis for apportionment of "representatives and direct taxation . . . among the several States." By 1810 the population census (states the *United States Government Organization Manual*) had been "broadened to include other subjects"; additional questions pertaining to agriculture, public health, migration, industry and so forth were added in 1840, 1850, and 1880; until by 1902 the scope of the decennial tally had grown to such extent that Congress established a permanent Bureau of the Census. In 1929 this Bureau was incorporated by Act of Congress into the Department of Commerce, authority to determine questions to be asked being delegated to the Bureau director, subject to approval of the Secretary of Commerce. (It was under this provision that in 1950 every fifth person was required to state his income.) The actual (door-to-door) enumerating is carried out by some 140,000 special census takers engaged for the April 1950 count, for which $86,000,000 was appropriated. An agricultural, a manufacturing and a business census, using a scientific "sampling" method, is taken every fifth year, and monthly surveys are made on current population and business trends.

Census Director Peel has made several public statements since he was installed in that post in March of 1950. Describing the 1950 enumeration as "the biggest single statistical undertaking in American history"—it is estimated that the population of the United States has reached 151,000,000—he termed the task "a democratic self-appraisal" which will be "as accurate and complete as public cooperation makes it possible to be. I therefore appeal to the public to give us wholehearted assistance." He reiterated the pledge that all information given to the census takers would be held in strictest confidence.

Professional and other organizations of which Census Director Peel is a member include the American Political Science Association, the American Society of Public Administration, the National Civil Service League, the National Association of Civic Secretaries, and Swedish Statsvetenskapliga Föreningen. Married August 18, 1927, to Esther Peterson, he has two children, Sonya Frances and Peter Robert. Peel is a Democrat in politics and attends the Lutheran Church.

References

> Who's Who in America, 1950-51
> Who's Who in the Midwest (1949)

PEKER, RECEP (pĕ'kâr rä'zhĕb) 1888— Apr. 2, 1950 Former Prime Minister of Turkey (July 1946-September 1947); early associate of Kemal Ataturk, founder of the Turkish Republic, and a member of the body that established the Turkish Constitution of 1923; became a member of the Nationalist Army's general staff in 1920; parliamentary secretary-general in the Grand National Assembly of 1923; elected representative in 1923 and became secretary-general of the Republican People's Party; Minister of the Interior (1924); Minister of National Defense (1925-27); Minister of Public Works (1928-31); Minister of the Interior (1942-43). See *Current Biography*, 1947.

Obituary

> N Y Times p23 Ap 3 '50 por

PEMBERTON, BROCK Dec. 14, 1885—
Mar. 11, 1950 Producer and director on
Broadway from 1920 to 1950; formerly re-
porter and drama critic with the New York
Evening Mail, New York *World* and New
York *Times*; produced such hits as *Miss Lulu
Bett,* winner of the Pulitzer Prize in 1920, and
Harvey, Pulitzer Prize winner in 1944; other
among his productions were *Enter Madame,
Six Characters in Search of an Author, Strictly
Dishonorable,* and *Kiss the Boys Goodbye*; one
of the founders of the USO camp shows; a
member of the board of directors of the
American Theatre Wing War Service; held
executive posts in the New York Theatre
League, the Stage Relief Fund and the Ameri-
can Theatre Council. See *Current Biography,*
1945.

Obituary

N Y Times p78 Mr 12 '50 por

PEREZ, MARIANO OSPINA. *See* Ospina Pérez, M.

PERKINS, GEORGE W(ALBRIDGE)
May 2, 1895- United States Government
official

Address: b. c/o Department of State, Washington 25, D.C.; 342 Madison Ave., New York 17;
h. Glynwood Farm, Cold Spring-on-Hudson,
New York; 6 E. 94th St., New York

In May 1949, upon the reorganization of the
United States Department of State, George W.
Perkins was one of five new Assistant Secre-
taries of State appointed by President Truman.
As Assistant Secretary of State for European
Affairs, Perkins is closely associated with the
development of the United States foreign policy toward Russia, the states behind the "Iron
Curtain," all of the Continent's other countries,
and Britain. Before joining the State Department, Perkins was an official of the Economic
Cooperation Administration and during World
War II he was an officer in the Chemical Warfare Service. He has been executive vice-
president, treasurer, and director of the chemical firm of Merck & Company, Inc.

George Walbridge Perkins was born May 2,
1895, at his family's home in Riverdale-on-
Hudson, New York. He is the son of George
Walbridge and Evelina (Ball) Perkins. His
father was for a number of years a partner in
the banking firm of J. P. Morgan and Company and also a director of the United States
Steel Corporation. An admirer of Theodore
Roosevelt, according to a correspondent for
the New York *World-Telegram,* the elder
Perkins became a "true convert to trust-bust-
ing." At the age of fifteen young Perkins became a student at the Hill School, Pottstown,
Pennsylvania. Completing his college preparatory studies in 1913, he entered Princeton University. There he was president of the senior
council, manager of the Princeton crew, and
president of the Philadelphia Society. Upon
receiving his Litt. B. from the university in
1917, he joined the United States Army as a

private, eventually becoming regimental supply
sergeant and then second lieutenant of the First
Division of the AEF. He remained overseas
in the Army of Occupation until 1919.

On his return to the United States, Perkins
was for one year term secretary of the Princeton Endowment Committee. In the fall of 1920
he entered Columbia University from which
he received the M.A. degree in 1921. Meanwhile, the elder Perkins had died and the son
was named executor of the estate—a service he
continues to perform in 1950. He left New
York in 1921 to go to Washington, D.C., as
executive secretary to the Postmaster General.
In 1922 he was named assistant treasurer of the
Republican State Committee of New York.
His more than twenty-year association with
Merck & Company began in 1927. Of that
firm he became executive vice-president, treasurer, and director. Founded in New York in
1908 and subsequently enlarged and incorporated under New Jersey law in 1934, Merck &
Company is engaged in the manufacture and
distribution of chemicals and drugs. It deals in
approximately 1,200 separate products, including
streptomycin, penicillin, synthetic vitamins, nar-
cotics, and quinine. In addition to operating a
subsidiary company in Canada, of which Perkins became a director in 1929, the corporation
owns plantations in Guatemala, Costa Rica, and
Java, and factories in Rahway and Linden,
New Jersey.

Perkins remained actively associated with the
chemical firm until 1942, when he was granted
a leave of absence in order to accept duty with
the Chemical Warfare Service of the United
States Army. He was first appointed a lieutenant colonel, later was promoted to the rank
of colonel, and saw service in the European
and Pacific theaters of war and in Washington. Three years later, in April 1945, Perkins
returned to his executive positions with the
Merck company, where he remained until June
1948. At that time he was appointed director
of the industry division of the Economic Cooperation Administration, in the office of the
special representative in Paris. He resigned
from Merck & Company in order to assume
responsibility for the approval of ECA funds
for use in rehabilitating and developing heavy
industry in European countries. During the
first fiscal years of ECA, orders were approved
for $2,287,800,000 in industrial commodi-
ties, $632,300,000 in machinery, $465,900,000 in
petrol and products, and $235,600,000 in coal
and related products. The industry division also
assisted the various countries in planning production of commodities for export, in an attempt to reduce the possibility of surpluses in
some goods and shortages in others. Production
plans for textiles, fertilizers, and aluminum
were particularly influenced by ECA discussions, Perkins told reporters.

A reorganization of the State Department,
carrying out the recommendations of the Commission on Organization of the Executive
Branch of the Government, was authorized by
Congress in May 1949, and at the end of that
month President Truman named five Assistant
Secretaries of State to administer the newly
created functions of the Department. Perkins

was appointed Assistant Secretary in charge of European affairs, one of the four regional divisions made by the State Department for purposes of administration. (The three other areas are Latin America, the Near East and Africa, and the Far East.) Perkins has the responsibility for formulating a comprehensive policy for America's relations with the nations of Europe, including the United Kingdom and the Scandinavian countries, as well as the U.S.S.R. and other countries behind the "Iron Curtain."

Soon after assuming office in August 1949, Perkins served as the United States representative to the international group engaged in the task of forming the council of twelve nations called for in the North Atlantic Treaty. The Assistant Secretary of State early in 1950 ordered the closing of the Hungarian consulates in Cleveland and New York in retaliation for the arrest and imprisonment of an American official of the International Telephone and Telegraph Company and for restrictions placed on the United States Legation in Budapest. He charged Czechoslovakia and Poland with being remiss in the search for three missing American citizens. At a luncheon with labor leaders Perkins indicated that the United States policy toward the Spanish government might be modified. He stated, however, that such modification would not necessarily carry with it approval of the Franco regime.

In October 1949 Perkins held consultations with United States diplomats serving in the countries under his administration, characterizing the meetings as the first application of a new technique in the "correlation of views." The first of the meetings was held in Paris with United States Ambassadors and State Department officials from the Western European nations; the second was held in London for the purpose of consulting with American diplomats from Russia, Poland, Czechoslovakia, Hungary, Rumania, and Bulgaria. At the close of another meeting held in Rome in March 1950, it was indicated that continuation of such discussions at intervals of a few months was a probability. (Berlin was suggested as the site for the next consultation.) It was emphasized that the conferences are informational in nature, policy remaining the function of Washington; the meetings give Perkins an opportunity to hear accounts of programs and activities in the various areas. "There are no isolated problems any more. If we are going to consider things that concern Europe, we know that now we've got to do it in relation to all the other countries," commented Perkins. (Regional conferences have also been held in the Middle East, South Africa, and Southeast Asia.)

Perkins was from 1935 to 1949 a director of the City Bank Farmers Trust Company and from 1935 to 1939 a trustee of Princeton University. From 1931 to 1942 he served as a director of the New York City YMCA, filling the post of treasurer also for eight of these years. One of his continuing interests has been the Palisades Interstate Park Commission, an organization of which his father had been president, and one of which Perkins has been a member since 1922; he was its president in

GEORGE W. PERKINS

1945. He has also served on the boards of several educational institutions, including Robert College of Constantinople (founded with American funds for the higher education of the natives of Turkey) and Hill School, his own prep school. From 1933 to 1942 he was president of the board of education of Central School District of Cold Spring-on-Hudson, New York. For his services during World War II he received the Legion of Merit.

The Assistant Secretary of State is a member of several New York clubs, including the Union League, the Down Town Association, and the Princeton Club. In Washington, D.C., his clubs are the Chevy Chase and the Metropolitan. He is a Republican in politics and a Presbyterian in religion. His first marriage, to Katharine Trowbridge, took place in 1917. Three years after her death, in 1921 he married Linn Merck. There are three children of this union—Penelope (Perkins) Wilson, George Walbridge, and Anne (Perkins) Cabot. Perkins is tall (six feet, two and one-half inches), has blue eyes and light-brown hair, and weighs 175 pounds.

References

Who's Who in America, 1950-51
Who's Who in the East (1948)

PETERSON, F(RANK) RAYMOND Nov. 13, 1895- Banker
Address: b. c/o First National Bank and Trust Co., Paterson, N.J.; h. 100 E. Palisade Ave., Englewood, N.J.

The president of the American Bankers Association for 1949-50 is F. Raymond Peterson who has been for many years head of the First National Bank and Trust Company of Paterson, New Jersey. He has seen long and varied service in the national banking organization, as

Fabian Bachrach

F. RAYMOND PETERSON

well as in State and local banking groups. For fourteen years Peterson was a national bank examiner in a number of Federal Reserve Districts.

Frank Raymond Peterson was born on November 13, 1895, to J. Walford and Adelaide C. (Schatz) Peterson in Farlington, Kansas, where his father had a mercantile and grain elevator business. Peterson was educated chiefly in Kansas, in the public schools of Girard, and at the Kansas State Normal School in Pittsburg. Later he took specialized training at Gem City Business College, Quincy, Illinois, and at New York University. While still in high school, the youth received his initiation into his life-work when he was employed for odd jobs after school and on week ends in the State Bank of Girard, of which his uncle was cashier. When the United States entered World War I Peterson enlisted in the Army. Instead of being posted overseas as he had hoped, he was assigned as a clerk to the Army's Finance Department, and spent the period from 1917 to 1919 in various camps in the United States paying off troops. He attained the rank of second lieutenant.

After the close of the war Peterson held, for a short time, a post as a State bank examiner in Kansas. Later, in 1919, when his father bought a large interest in the First State Bank in Cherokee, Kansas, he became the bank's cashier. There Peterson remained until, in 1922, the family sold their interest in the bank. He then entered the employ of the Federal Government as a national bank examiner in the Tenth Federal Reserve District. For the next fourteen years, with the exception of 1927-28 when he was vice-president and cashier of the Citizens National Bank, Okmulgee, Oklahoma, Peterson continued to serve, successively, as a national bank examiner in the Tenth, Eighth, Eleventh, and Second Federal Reserve Districts. With his superior he was moved to New York

in 1930, when the depression was affecting banks adversely—the examiners had seen the near panic in the Southwest during 1922-26. In 1936 Peterson returned to the commercial banking field upon being elected to the executive vice-presidency of the First National Bank of Paterson, New Jersey, directors of which were impressed with his insight into that bank's problems in his capacity of bank examiner. The following year he was made president, and in 1942 was given the title of chairman of the board as well. When the First National and Paterson National banks merged on June 1, 1946, to form a new institution, the First Paterson National Bank and Trust Company, Peterson became chairman and chief executive officer. On November 1, 1948, the Second National Bank of Paterson was also taken over, and he was elected chairman of the board of the First National Bank and Trust Company, as the new consolidation was named.

Soon after his appointment to the Paterson bank, Peterson began to take an active part in banking associations. In 1936 he was appointed a member of the executive committee of the Paterson Clearing House Association, and became its president for 1942-43. Two years after joining the New Jersey Bankers Association, he was made chairman of its legislative committee, a post which he held from 1938 to 1944. In 1944 he became its treasurer, and from that position he was in 1945 advanced to the vice-presidency, and in 1946 to the presidency. In the American Bankers Association Peterson was a member of the executive committee of its national bank division from 1939 to 1945. During 1941-43 he was chairman of the committee, and president of the division for 1943-44. His election to the vice-presidency of the A.B.A. in 1948 was automatically followed by election as president in November 1949 for the term ending in September 1950. (A.B.A., founded in 1875, observes its seventy-fifth anniversary in 1950, which is being marked by the issuance of a commemorative three-cent postage stamp.)

As president of the American Bankers Association, Peterson, it is expected, will continue the policies of his predecessor, Evans Woollen, Jr. [48]. In line with the general objectives of the association "to promote the general welfare and usefulness of banks," as he saw them, Woollen conducted a campaign to tighten the credit restrictions of banks in order to forestall any increase in Government control. Peterson was his supporter in this campaign, considered an important contributing factor in the curtailment of bank credit which characterized 1948-49. However, with the restriction of bank credit through the raising of interest rates and the imposition of greater security requirements on those seeking loans, pressure was brought to bear on Congress to open up other channels of credit. Consequently, Peterson anticipates an active campaign in Congress in 1950 against expansion of loans to business through the Reconstruction Finance Corporation and against direct loans by Government to veterans to build or buy homes. Such measures he regards as unfair competition by Government in the domain of banking. Also, in his opinion, such loans, while perhaps of benefit to the borrower, are unlikely to be of advantage "to the lender, and to the economy as a whole," which is considered to be a fundamental condition of sound credit.

Peterson also condemns extreme control by, and centralization of, banking functions in the Federal Government. He believes that "preservation of the dual banking system"—the system under which banks may be chartered by either State or Federal Government—is essential to the maintenance of the American economic system. Peterson therefore testified before a Congressional committee against a proposal by the Hoover Commission on Government Reorganization to consolidate into one three agencies of the Federal Government dealing with bank regulation, the Federal Deposit Insurance Corporation, the Comptroller of Currency, and the Federal Reserve System. Such concentration of Federal authority, Peterson said, "would be a long step . . . in the direction . . . of nationalized banking." His opinion of the results of such an eventuality were expressed at the Reno convention of the National Association of State Banks in the fall of 1949, when he declared: "One short cut to the socialist state is the centralization of banking authority. Control the administration of credit and you control almost all." The banker is nonetheless optimistic about the future of banking in the United States. "Never before in our history have the banks been in sounder position financially than they are today," he has remarked. Peterson's A.B.A. post entails addresses at bankers' meetings held throughout the United States.

Peterson has been active in Paterson's civic affairs. Among the groups with which he has been associated are the Paterson Industrial Commission and the Paterson Plant Management Commission. At one time he was also a member of the board of governors of the New York Chapter of the Robert Morris Associates and vice-president of the Money Marketeers, an association which grew out of the weekly forums he attends at New York University. His clubs are the Hamilton, Ridgewood and Arcola Country, Englewood, and Charter in New Jersey, and the Union League Club in New York City.

The marriage of Peterson and Grace C. Crouch, a newspaperwoman, took place December 31, 1919. Although his home is in the East, he is described as a "Kansan at heart." There he gained his "inherent distrust of alien 'isms' and controls," according to *Finance*; and he is "definitely allergic to flamboyant oratory and spectacular statements." One reporter has described the gray-haired banker as "a friendly, forthright man who smiles easily."

References

Banking 42:36+ N '49 por
Burroughs Clearing House 34:25+ N '49
Finance p39+ N 15 '49
Who's Who in America, 1950-51
Who's Who in Commerce and Industry (1948)

PHUMIPHON ADULDET *See* Rama IX, King of Thailand

PIAF, EDITH (pē-ăf' ā-dēt') Dec. 19, 1915-
Singer; actress
Address: c/o International Theatrical Corp., 1501 Broadway, New York 18

The French *chanteuse*, Edith Piaf, whose European success was followed by appearances in America beginning in 1947, has become widely admired in the latter country for her interpretation of the melancholy ballad. There her "seen" audience currently consists of the patrons of a New York restaurant; a wider public knows her through her recordings of original *chansons* and her television and motion picture appearances—her own composition, "La Vie en Rose," in particular has won widespread popularity. Richard Watts, Jr., of the New York *Post* wrote that she sings "with a dramatic power, a suggestion of greater inner fire, and a hint of unquenchable tragedy of heart."

Edith Piaf was was born Edith Giovanna Gassion on December 19, 1915, in Belleville, a working-class district of Paris. Her mother was an Italian cafe singer, her father a Norman circus acrobat. The circumstances of her early years are told by Miss Piaf herself. Abandoned by her mother, the infant, then two months old, was placed in the care of her maternal grandmother; and about two years later she was taken away by her paternal grandmother to live in Bernay, a village in Normandy. At the age of three the child suddenly became blind. This condition lasted for four years, until her grandmother took her on a pilgrimage to the shrine of Saint Teresa of Lisieux. It is to the intercession of that saint that she ascribes the restoration of her sight. "Miracle or not," she has said, "I am forever grateful."

The little girl now began to travel with her father on his circus tours. First he tried to train her in acrobatics; then, noticing her musical talent, he encouraged her to sing. (Except for desultory teaching by her father, she received no schooling.) Singing in the circus, market places, and cafes developed the girl's sense of independence, so that she was ready to start her own "fight for life" (Miss Piaf's phrase) at the age of fifteen. Leaving her father, she went to Paris. When her rounds of auditions and music publishers proved fruitless, she turned to singing in the streets of the metropolis. "I never begged," she has said. "If passers-by offered me pennies, I pretended not to see them, and my girl friend would take the money."

It was in this period that she was discovered by Louis Leplée, proprietor of Gerny's, a smart cabaret. In presenting her at his night club, Leplée insisted upon her wearing a costume similar to the worn sweater and skirt in which he had first seen her, and suggested that she change her last name to "Piaf," which is the Parisian slang for "sparrow." He also selected ten new songs, more suited to her than those she had been singing. Her first appearance at the night club was greeted with long applause from the listeners, among whom were Maurice Chevalier and Mistinguett. Chevalier encouraged her with his remark, "She has what it takes." Her engagement at Gerny's lasted six

EDITH PIAF

months, ending when Leplée was found murdered in a robbery, and Miss Piaf was detained for questioning. "When the police were unable to find any evidence that would involve me in the crime, they let me go," Miss Piaf recalls, "but they failed to mention to the press that I was absolutely in the clear." The tragedy deeply affected the *chanteuse*, who always refers to Leplée as her "second father."

Subsequently Miss Piaf received other engagements, but those, she has pointed out, capitalized on her notoriety at the time; and when that subsided, her services were no longer wanted. It was not until she met Raymond Asse, an author, who wrote songs for her—"He taught me what a song really is"—that wider recognition came. In 1935, at twenty, she made her adult debut at a large vaudeville theater in Paris and was acclaimed a "hit." Later, other authors and composers—Michel Emer, Henri Contet, and Marguerite Monnet—enlarged the Piaf repertoire with the haunting, "blues" type of songs. These she sang in the simple, throaty-voiced, undramatic style she had evolved in her street-singing days. By 1940 she was sufficiently well known to star in *Le Bel Indifférent*, a play written for her by Jean Cocteau and presented at the Bouffes-Parisiens. "All the critics said I was a better actress than a singer," she told Marie Torre of the New York *Journal-American*.

During World War II Mlle. Piaf was the "godmother" of French prisoners held in Germany, where she went to sing several times. According to the *Dictionnaire Biographique Français Contemporain*, she was instrumental in helping several prisoners to escape. "She gave refuge to Jewish friends," reported the New York *Herald Tribune*, "helping many to hide or escape." An anecdote from this period tells of her having had the "singular honor of snubbing Herr Goebbels by arriving two hours late, thus avoiding a command performance."

These facts were revealed after the war, when the singer was accused, and cleared, of collaborationist charges (New York *Times*).

Miss Piaf, who had already appeared in the film *Montmartre sur Seine,* in 1945 made another motion picture, *Etoile sans Lumière.* Upon its release in the United States in 1947, Cecelia Ager, *PM* critic, remarked: "The heartbreak she sings of—remembering, working up to a torrent of shattering grief from a quiet, standing start—is universal." In 1945, when Miss Piaf sang for an air force group in Paris, she met nine young Frenchmen who appeared on the same program as "Les Compagnons de la Chanson." After the war, for two years she and Les Compagnons traveled together through Europe on singing engagements. They were also cofeatured in 1947 in the motion picture *Neuf Garçons—Un Coeur.*

The American debut of the French *chanteuse* took place in October 1947, when she and Les Compagnons opened in a variety show at a New York theater. As had become her custom, she used no make-up and wore a simple black dress. Howard Barnes of the New York *Herald Tribune* found that "her voice itself is less important than the manner in which she blends and modulates it with subtle and evocative pantomime." To Richard Watts, Jr., of the New York *Post* she was "an exceptionally fine and distinguished performer of authentic style and forcefulness." Virgil Thomson, in a New York *Herald Tribune* column devoted to a study of her artistry, observed: "The vocalism is styled and powerful; her diction is clarity itself; her phrasing and gestures are of the simplest. . . .She is a great technician because her methods are of the simplest, in every way classical and direct. She is a great artist because she gives you a clear vision of the scene or subject she is depicting with a minimum injection of personality." Brooks Atkinson, of the New York *Times*, who called her "a genuine artist in a particular tradition," described her voice as "loud, with a metallic volume that would fill a street," and "off key consistently." "But the longer Mlle. Piaf sings of a poor factory girl living in a barren room," continued Atkinson, "or a married woman recalling the joy and anguish of her shattered life, or a sinner petitioning St. Peter for hospitality—the more respect you have for her sincerity."

Miss Piaf's return to the New York entertainment scene in January 1948 in a series of night club performances (at the Versailles) brought more plaudits, as did her subsequent appearances at the same place that year, in September. "Dynamic as she was last season," said Robert W. Dana of the New York *World-Telegram*, "she seems even better." Virginia Forbes of the New York *Sun* commented: "Whether she sings in French or in English . . . she has the double gift of inflection and pantomime that is universally understood. She appeared again at the Versailles for twenty weeks in the autumn of 1949 and returned in September 1950, when a "glamorized" coiffure and a new style of dress were remarked upon by the reviewers. At this time the *New Yorker* critic declared that she was "devastating everybody within range with one of the canniest and most beautifully executed routines in show business."

Aside from her night club engagements, Miss Piaf has also been seen by American audiences on television the fall of 1950. She sang her own song "La Vie en Rose," which had already become known in the United States as the song, "You're too Dangerous, Chérie." About that time, too, she made a thirty-minute film for television distribution. Recordings of her songs which are available on Columbia, Decca, Polydor, and Vox disks comprise about twenty titles, singly or in albums. Some of these songs are "La Vie en Rose", "M. St. Pierre", "Le Chant du Pirate", "Les Trois Cloches", "Amour du Mois de Mai", "L'Accordéoniste," and "Si Tu Partais."

Descriptions of the French *chanteuse* make frequent mention of her tousled, auburn hair, her "wan, peaked" face, her waif-like figure— under five feet in height and weighing some ninety pounds, in France she was nicknamed "La Môme," meaning "the Kid." In reality, said writer Virginia Forbes, "she looks much younger and prettier than her usual anguished picture."

References

N Y Herald Tribune II p5 O 17 '48; Xp9 O 30 '49
N Y Times II p3 O 26 '47
New Yorker 23:27 N 15 '47
Dictionnaire Biographique Français Contemporain (1950)
World Biography (1948)

PITZER, K(ENNETH) S(ANBORN) Jan. 6, 1914- United States Government official; chemist

Address: b. c/o Division of Research, Atomic Energy Commission, 1901 Constitution Ave., N.W., Washington, D.C.; University of California, Berkeley 4, Calif.; h. 6100 Nebraska Ave., Washington, D.C.; 12 Eagle Hill, Berkeley, Calif.

The division of research of the United States Atomic Energy Commission is directed by Dr. K. S. Pitzer, who entered that post in January 1949. In mid-April 1950 Pitzer received a John Simon Guggenheim Memorial Foundation award for work in chemical applications of quantum and statistical mechanics. In March of the same year at the 117th national meeting of the American Chemical Society in Houston, Texas, he had been presented with the Precision Scientific Company's $1,000 award in petroleum chemistry in recognition of his achievements in the field of thermodynamics. Upon his appointment to the AEC post he was granted leave of absence from the University of California, Berkeley, where he has held the rank of professor of chemistry since 1946.

The son of Russell Kelly Pitzer, a citrus farmer and businessman (formerly a lawyer) and of the former Flora Anna Sanborn, Kenneth Sanborn Pitzer was born in Pomona, California, on January 6, 1914. He attended Pomona High School, where his chief extracurricular activity was debating. *Time* re-

Wide World Photos

K. S. PITZER

counted an incident of his first session in plane geometry: the teacher drew a difficult problem on the blackboard and announced that its solution at the end of the course would win an "A" grade; five minutes later Pitzer had the correct answer. After graduation from high school in 1931, he enrolled in the California Institute of Technology in Pasadena, and four years afterward received his B.S. degree, with a major in chemistry. A prize scholarship student in his freshman, sophomore, and junior years, he belonged to the debating club and the Pi Kappa Delta, Sigma Xi, and Tau Beta Pi. During his college years, Pitzer has said, he was greatly influenced by the late A. A. Noyes, who was then head of the chemistry department.

For two years after receiving his degree Pitzer took graduate work in chemistry at the University of California, where the doctorate was conferred on him in 1937. A teaching assistant during his first year of graduate study, he became a Shell research fellow the next year. Appointment to the faculty of the university followed in 1937, when he was named an instructor in chemistry. In 1939 he was promoted to assistant professor, in 1942 to associate professor, and in 1946 to professor. During the period 1947-48 he served as assistant dean in the College of Letters and Science. A leave of absence in 1943-44 enabled him to act at that time as the technical director of the Maryland Research Laboratories, an institution which had been organized for war research under the Office of Scientific Research and Development.

In January 1949 Pitzer was granted a leave of absence to assume the post of director of the research division of the United States Atomic Energy Commission, in Washington,

PITZER, K. S.—*Continued*

D.C. His appointment to succeed Dr. James B. Fisk of Harvard, who had resigned the position in August 1948, was announced December 5 of that year. The Atomic Energy Commission had been created in 1946, when the Atomic Energy Act was passed by Congress, followed by passage of the McMahon bill which authorized the membership of the Commission, the representatives to be appointed by the President. In December 1946 it was announced that formal control of the Manhattan District of the United States Army Engineers, under whose direction the atom bomb project was developed, would henceforward be assumed by the newly created Commission. The five-member Commission, under which there are eight research laboratories, has as its function the development of atomic weapons as well as the utilization of atomic energy for power production, medical purposes, and similar peacetime applications. The coordination of research in these projects is now the responsibility of the California scientist. In pointing out that a chemist rather than a physicist heads that research, *Time* mentioned as two urgent tasks the extraction of uranium from low-grade ores and the chemical separation of radioactive by-products of the manufacture of plutonium. Dr. Pitzer was quoted as saying: "The problems holding up the Atomic Energy Commission are chiefly chemical ones. The problems of physics were handled first, and they are far better in hand than the problems of chemistry."

The scientist, who had originally intended to enter the field of physics or engineering, turned his attention during his college years toward chemistry. In the year of his graduation he contributed to a paper in the *Journal of the American Chemical Society* treating of argentic salts in acid solution. The field of chemical thermodynamics became his special interest, particularly the structure of molecules. He developed general methods for treating various molecules involving internal rotation. In later papers he extended the spectroscopic-statistical methods used for simple molecules to virtually all volatile substances. The combination of experimental measurements and theoretical calculations by means of methods developed largely by Pitzer himself is characteristic of his work. His discovery of the restricted rotation in ethane has had wide application and has stimulated much further research. The number of papers he has written, or on which he has collaborated in the course of his research (from 1935 to 1948) exceeds seventy; they have appeared in various scientific journals, chiefly the *Journal of the American Chemical Society, Journal of Chemical Physics,* and *Journal of Research of the National Bureau of Standards.*

Associate editor of the *Journal of Chemical Physics* from 1943 to 1945, Pitzer became associate editor of the *Journal of the American Chemical Society* in 1944. This society elected him a councilor in 1946 and in the following year made him a member of its standing committee on publications. Also in 1947, he became a member of the committee on physical chemistry of the National Research Council, and

associate director for Project 44 of the American Petroleum Institute. This project deals with the "collection, analysis and calculation of data on the properties of hydro-carbons." Particularly for his research in the thermodynamics of hydro-carbons Pitzer was awarded the Precision Scientific Company award in Petroleum Chemistry in March 1950; his work in this field has been of direct use to petroleum chemists and engineers in their efforts to improve the yield and quality of gasoline and other products.

Other honors the scientist has received are: the American Chemical Society Award in Pure Chemistry, in 1943, for his work in chemical thermodynamics; the Army and Navy Certificate, presented to him in 1948 for his work during World War II. He has been named in 1950 as one of the ten outstanding young men of the year by the United States Junior Chamber of Commerce and its national magazine, *Future.*

The research director is a member of the American Chemical Society, the American Physical Society, the American Association for the Advancement of Science and the National Academy of Sciences. On July 7, 1935, Pitzer married Jean Mosher; they have one daughter Ann, and two sons, Russell and John. The scientist is six feet two inches tall, weighs 180 pounds, and has blue eyes and brown hair. Hiking, boat-building and sailing are his favorite recreations. When he moved to Washington he brought with him a 28-foot ketch, the largest boat he has built thus far.

References

Chem & Eng N 27:273 Ja 31 '49 por; 28:1122 Ap 3 '50 por
Christian Sci Mon p6 S 10 '43 por
Time 53:32 Ja 3 '49 por
American Men of Science (1949)
Who's Who in America, 1950-51
Who's Who in the West (1949)
World Biography (1948)

PIUS XII, POPE Mar. 2, 1876- Supreme Pontiff of the Roman Catholic Church

Address: Vatican City

> NOTE: This biography supersedes the article which appeared in *Current Biography* in 1941.

In a papal letter, the bull entitled *Jubilaeum Maximum,* Pope Pius XII on June 26, 1949, proclaimed 1950 a Holy Year of Jubilee, which will cause millions of Roman Catholics to make pilgrimages to Rome to reaffirm their religious faith and to seek "a full indulgence for pardon of all the punishment due to sin" (as translated in *The National Catholic Almanac*). The focus of interest is the Pope, spiritual leader of the world's 423,000,000 Roman Catholics. Pius XII, who is hailed as the 260th successor to Peter, was elected Supreme Pontiff on March 2, 1939, on the eve of World War II, which called forth his pleas for peace. Of the fourteen encyclicals (communications of doctrine and admonition), which he issued in the years 1939-48, seven are concerned with the world situation.

Eugenio Maria Giuseppe Giovanni Pacelli was born March 2, 1876, in Rome, the second son of Filippo and Virginia (Graziosi) Pacelli. (There are also two daughters in the family, Elisabetta and Giuseppina.) His mother's family was of the nobility. The aristocratic Pacelli family had long been specialists in ecclesiastical law; the grandfather, Marcantonio Pacelli, had served as the Papal State's Under Secretary of the Interior from 1851 to 1870, and founded *L'Osservatore Romano*, which was to become the official newspaper of the Vatican. Filippo Pacelli was dean of the College of Consistorial Advocates (secular lawyers for the Papacy), and his elder brother, Francisco, was one of the lawyers who aided in drafting the Lateran Treaty by which Vatican City was established in 1929 by concordat between the Holy See and the Kingdom of Italy.

Eugenio Pacelli attended a primary school conducted by nuns, and the Visconti Grammar School, where, as head of his class, he won a national essay contest on the topic "Universal History" and began to distinguish himself as a linguist. Having decided at the age of seventeen to enter the priesthood, the student lived as a seminarian at Capranica College, at the same time attending classes at Gregorian University. Some years later, in 1895, he began his studies at the Pontifical University (Collegio Romano), from which he received a doctorate in theology in 1898. He was ordained a priest on April 2, 1899. Continuing his studies at Collegio Romano, he obtained the degree of Doctor of Civil and Canon Law (with highest honors) in 1902. His brilliant scholastic record attracted the attention of Msgr. Gasparri, the secretary of the Congregation of Extraordinary Ecclesiastical Affairs (the Congregation is one of twelve in the Roman Curia, the administrative offices through which the Pope governs the Church). After a short period as professor of law at the Roman Seminary, Pacelli entered Gasparri's department as a junior clerk; he later became principal copyist, then its Under Secretary. Twice he was invited to accept professorships in Catholic institutions, but each time was persuaded by Gasparri to remain at the Vatican. At the age of twenty-eight, in 1904, the future Pope was elevated to the rank of Monsignor, at the same time becoming a canon of St. Peter's. (The canons gather each day in the basilica of St. Peter's to sing the Divine Office. Msgr. Pacelli was consecrated as archbishop in the Sistine Chapel on May 13, 1917, of the titular See of Sardes.

The prelate was early marked for diplomatic services for his church. The first of his many trips abroad as papal emissary was in 1901, when he accompanied Archbishop Merry del Val to London at the time of the death of Queen Victoria. In 1908 he returned for the London Eucharistic Congress. On his third visit, for the coronation of King George V, he received the Coronation Medal; he is thus the only Pope in history with a British decoration. Pope Benedict XV, succeeding Pius X in 1914, promoted Gasparri to be his Secretary

Wide World Photos
POPE PIUS XII

of State, while Pacelli received the latter's position in the Congregation of Extraordinary Ecclesiastical Affairs. In the same year Pacelli became Under Secretary of State. Pope Benedict was highly pleased with Pacelli's work in arranging the exchange of prisoners in World War I, the moving of the wounded, the relaying of information about the missing, and also with the codification of Canon Law, which he completed in 1916. In May 1917, with a new title, Archbishop of Sardes, he was sent as Papal Nuncio to Munich, bearing a proposal of peace from the Pope to Kaiser Wilhelm. He remained in Bavaria through the war, until 1925, when the concordat between the Vatican and Bavaria was signed. The Archbishop was then transferred to Berlin as the Pope's representative to the Weimar Republic, where he concluded the concordat with Prussia in 1929, considered a difficult achievement because Prussia is predominantly Protestant.

Upon his return to Rome Archbishop Pacelli was elevated to the College of Cardinals on December 16, 1929. In February he succeeded, as Papal Secretary of State, aging Cardinal Gasparri, who had concluded the Lateran Treaty with Italy. In addition to the office of Secretary of State, the new Cardinal was appointed Archpriest of St. Peter's, thus becoming the Pope's principal assistant at all functions in the great basilica. He also succeeded Gasparri as Cardinal Chamberlain, who governs the Church during the interregnum between the death of one Pope and the election of his successor, and has as well the direction of the Papal household and Vatican properties.

Cardinal Pacelli first crossed the Atlantic in 1934, as Papal Legate to the Eucharistic Congress held in Buenos Aires, stopping in Spain on the homeward trip. Two years later he made an eight-thousand-mile tour of the United States in the fall of 1936: in the course of a

PIUS XII, POPE—*Continued*

month he visited the nineteen ecclesiastical provinces and most of the dioceses, and was seen by many thousand American Catholics when he went to their educational institutions. He is the first Pope, who (as Cardinal) has visited America. Upon returning to Europe, he was also to visit Paris (in 1937), to which a Pope had not gone in more than a hundred years; and in 1938 he made his last journey as the "world-traveling" prelate to Budapest as Cardinal-Legate to the Eucharistic Congress.

On February 10, 1939, Cardinal Pacelli, as Chamberlain, announced to his fellow Cardinals, "The Pope is truly dead." Three weeks later he himself was elected to the office whose spiritual titles include those of Vicar of Christ, Successor of St. Peter, Bishop of Rome, Primate of Italy, Patriarch of the West, Supreme Pontiff of the Universal Church, and the temporal title, Sovereign of the State of Vatican City. The one hundred and eight acres and approximately one thousand inhabitants of the Vatican compose the smallest independent state in the world. It has its own postal service, coins, radio, telephone and telegraph system, and railway. Thirty-six countries are represented at the Vatican by ambassadors, ministers, or personal envoys. (An example of the latter category is Myron Taylor, who went to Rome as the personal ambassador of President Franklin D. Roosevelt in 1940, and remained there at his own expense as the informal representative of the United States to the Vatican until February 1950.) Information on economic, social, and political (as well as religious) matters pours into the Vatican daily in reports from its forty-three Apostolic Nunciatori, twenty-three Apostolic delegations, 1,358 patriarchs, archbishops, and bishops, and thousands of priests, as well as by way of the hundreds of thousands of individuals whom the Pope receives in the course of a year at audiences. The greatest single organ of expression used by the pontiff is the Vatican radio, aside from the daily journal *L'Osservatore Romano*.

The voice of the Vatican during World War II often pleaded for peace and for the preservation of human rights. Mundane diplomacy, offers of mediation, and appeals to the military and political leaders were reinforced with orders for public Masses and crusades of prayer, and with speeches broadcast over the Vatican radio to the world calling for a just and generous peace. Early in the war the Pope proclaimed the five points of his Peace Plan, which he was to repeat many times: (1) freedom for all nations; (2) protection of minorities; (3) a new economic order based on free access to sources of raw materials; (4) disarmament and respect for treaties; (5) respect for religion. To be so pledged, and spiritual leader of millions of Catholics aligned on opposite sides of the struggle, placed the Pope in a position that gave rise to praise, criticism, and speculation.

Leaders on both sides of the conflict sought the enormous moral value of the approbation of the Church's head. The Pope received ambassadors from Hitler and Mussolini, and in March 1942 established diplomatic relations with Japan. However, in October of that year Camille M. Cianfarra, the New York *Times* Vatican correspondent, wrote: "Flagrant breaches of the Concordat with the Holy See by both dictators have convinced the Pope that the Church would have no place in a Nazi-dominated Europe." The Christmas Speech of 1942, condemning the conception of the state as an "absolute and supreme entity" and assailing racial discrimination, although at the same time emphasizing that the Church "does not intend to take sides," was looked upon as an attack on the totalitarian governments. Never disavowing the Church's opposition to communism, the Pope nevertheless refused, in spite of what Herbert L. Matthews (New York *Times*, June 30, 1941) called "heavy political pressure," to endorse the Axis attack on Russia as an "anti-bolshevist crusade." Cianfarra reported (October 4, 1942), that, according to officials and members of the diplomatic corps of the Vatican, "the Vatican considers the spread of communism in Europe as the consequence of a Russian victory less of a danger than the spread of the pagan doctrine of the Nazis."

The fall and winter of 1943-44 found the Pope virtually a prisoner of the Nazis within Vatican City's walls. Its radio was cut off, Nazi guards stood at all entrances, and access to St. Peter's was forbidden to all Italians. Curfew laws barred the customary broadcast of the Pontiff's Christmas Eve message to the world. It was not until Rome was liberated in June 1944 that comparative freedom of communication (subject to Allied military controls) was restored. On June 8, following the liberation, the Pope reiterated the neutrality of the Vatican.

Since end of the war the main object of the Church's condemnation has been communism. The New York *Times* (February 20, 1949) characterized this as "the most difficult period of the Roman Catholic Church since the Reformation"—in its struggle for survival in some countries of Europe and in China. The Pope's influence is believed to have been the decisive factor in the victory of the pro-Catholic Christian Democratic party over the Communist party in the 1948 elections in Italy. In July 1949 the Church threatened excommunication to Catholics who joined the Communist party. In January 1950 Pius called for the establishment of Catholic Action (anti-Communist) organizations in every parish in Italy. Pius' encyclicals have emphasized his attitude on international affairs and his interest. The titles of some of them are: "Function of State in Modern World" (1939), "To the Church in the United States" (1939), "Call for Intensified Aid to Youth in the World Crisis" (1946), "Peace and Social Disorders" (1947), "The Crisis in Palestine" (1948). He has reiterated statements of Pope Leo XIII's encyclical *Rerum Novarum*, on the rights and duties of labor. A supporter of the social reforms of Italy's Social Democratic party, he has urged better housing and food for the poor classes and the alleviation of unemployment.

The Holy Year was first instituted in 1300, by Pope Boniface VIII, who proclaimed that it was to be observed at the beginning of every century. After several changes in the intervals by later Popes, it is now (since 1450) celebrated every twenty-fifth year. When he struck the Holy Door of St. Peter's Basilica with a silver hammer on Christmas Eve of 1949, Pope Pius XII opened the twenty-fifth Holy Year; and he designated three cardinals to open the Holy Doors of the other three major basilicas in Rome—St. John Lateran, St. Paul (on the Ostian Way), and St. Mary Major. As summarized by *The National Catholic Almanac,* the purpose of the Holy Year is "to recall all Christians to the expiation of their faults and the correction of their lives; to aim at increasing virtue and sanctity as indispensable conditions for a better and happier order of things; and world peace." To obtain the Holy Year indulgences, the millions of Catholics who go to Rome will observe prescribed religious duties as well as visit the four basilicas to pray; for those who cannot make the pilgrimage, the Holy Year's benefits may be gained, under conditions laid down by their bishop, in the year following its close. Throughout 1950 beatifications and canonizations will take place.

Pope Pius XII is a somewhat frail-appearing man, but his tall, straight body and "elastic, youthful step" suggest "dynamic vitality." He is described as receiving people at the audiences with a simple manner of informal affability showing interest in their affairs. The Pontiff rises at 6:30, usually after only four or five hours of sleep. He eats lightly, including very little meat in his diet. His exercise consists of a short period in his private gymnasium upon arising, and a daily afternoon walk in the Vatican gardens· (he likes especially to walk in the rain), during which he frequently reads or studies. Summers (with the exception of the war years) are spent at Castel Gandolfo, about fifteen miles from Rome. Pope Pius is the first Pope to use the typewriter, telephone, and airplane. He shaves himself with an electric razor, and is said to enjoy very fast motor trips. His favorite recreation is listening to music, particularly to his large collection of Wagnerian recordings; *Etude* reported that he is a violinist of "more than ordinary merit." Possessed of a "prodigious memory," the Italian-speaking Pope reportedly learned German in less than six months and is also fluent in Latin, French, Polish, English, Spanish and Portuguese.

References

Cath World 149:108-10 Ap '39; 149:364-5 Je '39; 152:1-9 O '40; 152:491-3 Ja '41
Christian Cent 56:342-3 Mr 15 '39
Collier's 117:50 Ja 5 '46
Commonweal 29:677-9 Ap 14 '39
N Y Times p5 Ag 3 '40; p3 Ag 5 '40; p5 Ag 8 '40; p8 S 5 '40; IV p2 Mr 2 '41; p3 Mr 13 '41; p7 F 20 '49
Newsweek 13:32 F 20 '39 por; 13:25-6 Mr 13 '39 il pors; 16:28 Jl 8 '40; 33:72-4 Ap 4 '49
Time 33:30 F 20 '39 por; 33:36+ Mr 13 '39 por
Britannica Book of the Year, 1949
Chi è? (1948)
Dinneen, J. F. Pius XII, Pope of Peace (1939)
Encyclopædia Britannica (1947)
Farrow, J. Pageant of the Popes (1950)
Lenn, L. H. and Reardon, M. A. Pope Pius XII (1950)
National Catholic Almanac, 1950
Smit, J. O. Angelic Shepherd: the Life of Pope Pius XII (1950)
10 Eventful Years (1947)
Van Hoek, K. Pope Pius XII (1940)
Who's Who, 1949
Who's Who in America, 1948-49

PLASTIRAS, NICHOLAS (plá-stī′rás) 1883- Former Premier of Greece
Address: Athens, Greece

General Nicholas Plastiras, veteran revolutionist and antimonarchist leader over a period of nearly thirty years, became the Premier of Greece on April 15, 1950. A disciple of the late Eleutherios Venizelos and one of the heroes of the Greek-Turkish war of 1920-22, he had twice wielded power as a dictator. In September 1922, he forced the abdication of King Constantine after a *coup d'état*; and, again, in 1933, he held absolute power for a span of eighteen hours. Politically his present-day party, the National Progressive Union, stands to the left of center. Premier Plastiras was pledged to a program of reforms, economies, and an early end to Greece's Communist-Royalist civil strife. In August 1950 his Government fell as the result of opposition to his policy toward Greek Communists.

Karditza, a small town in Thessaly, is the birthplace of Nicholas Plastiras, who comes of peasant stock. Born 1883, two years after the province was incorporated into the modern kingdom of Greece, he has been a professional soldier since youth, having joined the army as a private. After passing through successive noncommissioned grades he was admitted to the officers training school, from which he was graduated in 1912 with a second lieutenant's commission. "He served in all Greece's wars from 1912 to 1922," stated a biographical sketch in the *Christian Science Monitor*, "fighting in Macedonia against the Turks, Germans and Bulgarians, in north Epirus against Albanian nationalists, in the Ukraine against Russian Bolsheviks," and was "repeatedly promoted for bravery on the battlefield."

A sympathizer with the democratic statesman Eleutherios Venizelos, who deposed the pro-German King Constantine in 1917 and brought Greece into World War I on the side of the Allies, Plastiras was in 1920 advanced to colonel and placed in command of the famous regiment of Evzones ("Greek kilted troops. . . picked recruits from the mountains"). He led them through the Greek expedition of 1920-22 to occupy the Turkish province of Anatolia,

NICHOLAS PLASTIRAS

as authorized by the Treaty of Sèvres. Known to his own troops as the "Black Cavalier" and to the Turks as "Black Pepper," Colonel Plastiras distinguished himself, when the Asia Minor venture collapsed in August 1922, by holding the tip of the Smyrna peninsula while twenty thousand hemmed-in troops were evacuated to transports.

Meanwhile (in December 1921) the republican Government of Venizelos had been overthrown and King Constantine had reassumed the crown. "The defeated Greek army, under the leadership of Colonels Plastiras and Gonatas," states the *Near East Year Book*, "returned to Greece on revolution bent." Through a *coup d'état* on September 2, 1922, the two colonels forced the abdication of Constantine in favor of his son, who became King George II [43], and organized a Revolutionary Committee with Plastiras as acting premier. This junta court-martialed the military leaders and ministers who had supported Constantine, and in November 1923 six of these were condemned to death, including Prince Andrew, father of the Duke of Edinburgh [47], husband of Princess Elizabeth of Britain. However (stated *Time*) "a British destroyer dashed up and rescued Andrew from Plastiras," and the ministry was forced to resign. Gonatas temporarily succeeded Plastiras, and the other executions were carried out, shortly after which Plastiras returned to the helm.

Elections for a Constituent Assembly were held, and on January 2, 1924, Plastiras turned over authority thereto and recommended the adoption of a republican form of government, expressing the belief that "monarchism is incompatible with the spirit of the times." Two days later he welcomed Venizelos back to Athens; and on March 24 King George renounced the crown and a republic was proclaimed.

The new Venizelos Government did not long survive. During the ensuing year it was overturned by the monarchist General Pangalos, and in October 1925 Plastiras, accused of plotting against the new regime, was deported. He took refuge in Yugoslavia, from which in February 1926 he attempted to return to Greece for a new *coup*, but was apprehended and interned at Belgrade. He made his escape to Albania, and toward the end of March was in Salonika, where he made an unsuccessful attempt at counterrevolution. On April 7 the Pangalos Government annulled a vote of the Constituent Assembly giving Plastiras the honorary rank of lieutenant general, and placed a price of 500,000 drachmas on his head. Plastiras, however, had already escaped to France. A little more than four months later (August 26) the Pangalos dictatorship was overturned, and Pangalos himself was imprisoned. The new Government of General George Kondylos, then a close friend of Plastiras, promptly announced that the latter was "free to return."

Venizelos again became Premier in 1928. During the next four years, under the idol of his young manhood, Plastiras (stated a biographical note issued by the Greek Information Service) "helped reorganize and streamline the Greek army and conducted the resettlement program of Greek inhabitants of Asia Minor." (The New York *Times* has commented editorially on "the kindliness of the man who cared so humanely for a million refugees, even adopting nine refugee orphans himself.") On March 6, 1933, nevertheless, an election resulted in an "upset" triumph for the Royalist opposition, headed by Constantin Tsaldaris [46]; and on the following day (March 7), after secret consultation with Venizelos, Plastiras seized power by force. His dictatorship lasted only eighteen hours, being overthrown by his former friend, General Kondylos. Venizelos and Plastiras both fled, the former to Paris (where he died in exile in 1936), the latter to Bulgaria and subsequently to Egypt. In 1935, after a plebiscite had restored King George II to the throne, Plastiras participated in a brief ill-starred republican uprising; his escape this time was to the Riviera, where he was later reported under treatment for tuberculosis. From 1936, when General John Metaxas [40] abolished the Greek parliament and set up a dictatorship, to Metaxas' death in 1941, Plastiras conducted his revolutionary campaign from Italy, France, Switzerland, and Yugoslavia (New York *Sun*). He has been described as being active in the resistance movement during German occupation of Greece.

Following the liberation of Greece by British troops and the return of the Government-in-exile to Athens (October 1944), the country became (according to *Information Please Almanac*) "a land of conflict with armed bands of Royalists and Communists terrorizing the nation." Finally, in December, King George again renounced the throne and the elderly Archbishop Damaskinos [45] was named regent. The Government of George Papandreou [44] resigned, and Plastiras, who had been rushed to Athens by a British warship, was called upon to form a Cabinet. This he did on January 2,

1945, assuming, in addition to the Premiership, the portfolios of War, Navy, Air, and Merchant Marine. His aim was to form a Government representative of all shades of opinion, and to this end he left several ministries vacant in the hope that leaders of the Communist EAM (National Liberation Front) could be induced to accept posts. A week later, however, he was refusing to admit Communists and was threatening the ELAS (military wing of EAM) with "annihilation." On January 11, the British occupation forces, under Lieutenant General Ronald M. Scobie [45], concluded a truce with the ELAS; but Plastiras declined to feel bound by its terms, and friction developed between him and the British. By the beginning of March "well informed sources" in London were saying that Plastiras had "outlived his usefulness." A month later Plastiras had resigned.

The General's successor, Admiral Petros Voulgaris, held office only briefly. An election in March 1946 resulted in a victory for the Populist (Royalist) party, and on April 18 Tsaldaris again became Premier. A new plebiscite was held on September 1, and King George regained the throne, which he continued to occupy until his death in April 1947, when he was succeeded by his brother, who became King Paul I [47]. A sequence of ministries (several of them short-lived) followed in which Plastiras was not included—those of Demetrios Maximos, Themistocles Sophoulis [47], Alexander Diomedes. In the meantime Plastiras was building up his own political following, the new Progressive Democratic Party (which usually worked in conjunction with the Liberal Party of Sophocles Venizelos, but differed from it in that it stood further to the left) and advocated the formation of a coalition Cabinet which would include the Communists. In elections held March 5, 1950, two months after Diomedes' resignation, Plastiras showed what was considered surprising strength. Though in a close contest the Populist (Royalist) Party topped the polls, the National Progressive Union (as the Progressive Democrats now called themselves) trailed by only 13,000 votes, and led the Liberals by about 7,000.

Tsaldaris was unable to form a Cabinet, and a Government organized by Sophocles Venizelos on March 23, 1950 (with Populist support) failed to survive, following a warning by United States Ambassador Henry F. Grady [47] that "economic and fiscal reforms by a Greek Government supported by the people might be the price of further Marshall Plan aid." Venizelos resigned on April 14, and the King (to whom Plastiras had always been *persona non grata* because of the events of 1922-24) was forced to call upon the National Progressive Union leader to form a Government. "I know the prospects are grim," Plastiras was quoted as saying after taking office on April 15, at the head of a coalition Cabinet representing all major parties except the Populists and the outlawed Communists. "We must economize. We must use American aid properly." Accordingly, in a policy speech to Parliament nine days later he announced that the army would be reduced from 146,000 to 80,000, and

he promised other retrenchments, including a reduction of consumer subsidies. He also announced a policy of gradually freeing all except "leading Communist and criminal elements" from detention camps, and proclaimed the intention of restoring diplomatic relations with Yugoslavia, which had been broken off in 1947. Three days later Marshal Tito [43] announced that his Government would "soon appoint" an envoy to Greece.

On August 17, 1950, when five Liberal members of Plastiras' Cabinet resigned, Sophocles Venizelos [50], the Liberal party leader, demanded Plastiras' resignation. It was reported that resentment had been mounting against Plastiras over his policy of amnesty for Communists convicted of treason. Plastiras' resignation followed on the next day, after which Venizelos formed a new all-Liberal Cabinet; this in turn was superseded by a coalition on September 13, with Venizelos continuing as Premier.

In 1922-23, when he first attained international note, Plastiras was described by an American correspondent as "a tall [six feet three inches], dark man full of nervous energy, with flashing dark eyes, who makes his subordinates fly when he touches a bell." His hair and his upturned mustache are now white, and an interviewer found him "gentle and democratic in manner."

References

Christian Sci Mon p6 Ap 17 '50 por
N Y Herald Tribune II p3 Mr 12 '50 por
N Y Sun p20 F 13 '41
Time 55:30 Mr 13 '50 por
International Who's Who, 1949
World Biography (1948)

PLEVEN, RENE (JEAN) (plĕ-väN rĕ-nā' zhäN) Apr. 15, 1901- French statesman
Address: c/o Ministry of National Defense, Paris, France; h. 16 rue de Mortignac, Paris, France

In October 1949 René Pleven was appointed France's Minister of National Defense. A stanch supporter of General Charles de Gaulle [49], Pleven rallied the colonies in French Equatorial Africa to the Free French cause during 1940-44. He was, successively, Minister of the Colonies, of Finance, and of National Economy and Finance in the Provisional Government of De Gaulle, resigning when the latter was no longer Prime Minister. Pleven was elected deputy from Côtes-du-Nord in 1945; two years later he became head of the Democratic and Socialist Union of the Resistance. Since his appointment as Minister of National Defense, Pleven has worked to obtain military aid from the United States for his country under the terms of the North Atlantic Pact. In this he has been strongly opposed by the Communists.

The son of Jules and Valerie (Synave) Pleven, René Jean Pleven comes of an old Breton family. His father attained the rank of colonel and was director of studies at the Ecole

French Embassy Inf. Div.
RENE PLEVEN

Militaire at Saint-Cyr. His grandfather took part in the 1848 revolution; another ancestor, Libéral Préauchat, was mayor of Morlaix and a renowned republican. René Pleven was born in Rennes, France, on April 15, 1901. Studying first at the academies in Rennes and Laval, he went to Paris, where he took his doctorate in law at the University of Paris and received a diploma at the Ecole des Sciences Politiques. At the University, Pleven was president of the Association of Catholic Students.

The young man's first employment was in the Ministry of Finance, where he earned twenty francs a day—"enough for one good meal," he observed later, "but hardly enough for two." Seeing no future there, Pleven went to Canada. In Quebec he was hired as a workingman by a telephone company, in which he rose to an executive position in two years. After 1931 he held a similar post in Great Britain.

With the outbreak of war, Pleven was called into service on September 3, 1939. Because of his knowledge of England and America, he was appointed assistant to the president of the Anglo-French Coordinating Committee. Soon afterward, as assistant head of the French Air Mission, he journeyed to the United States to suggest a plan for accelerating production of military aircraft. Returning to London in May 1940, he joined De Gaulle on June 19 to continue the fight of the Free French against the Nazis.

Pleven, together with General Leclerc '" and Lieutenant de Boislambert, flew from England to French Equatorial Africa on August 5, 1940. Working out of Chad, Pleven rallied colonial support for the mother country. One by one, Cameroun, Chad, Gabon, Middle Congo, and Ubangi-Shari voted to put themselves under De Gaulle; other colonies followed, and the Free French grew in strength. Appointed Secretary-General of French Equatorial Africa,

Pleven left Chad for Brazzaville where he took charge of civil administration of the colonies and mobilized colonial resources for the fight.

In January 1941 Pleven was recalled to London; and in September of that year he was appointed National Commissioner for Economy, Finance and the Colonies in the newly organized French National Committee. In Washington he negotiated with the United States Government the first agreement by which lend-lease aid was accorded the Free French. He also arranged with the British Government for the withdrawal of English troops from Madagascar. In October 1942 he was made Commissioner for Economy, Colonies, Merchant Marine, and Foreign Affairs. When the French Committee of National Liberation was formed in Algiers in June 1943, Pleven was reappointed Commissioner for the Colonies. In February 1944 he became president of the Commission for Modernization and Development of Colonial Territories. Its Brazzaville conference, at which plans for reform were made, was based on the concept that "the peoples of Africa (and all other colonial peoples) are no less entitled than others to claim not only the right to live, but also the right to greatness and to prosperity" (quoted from the wartime *Tricolore*). Pleven retained his post as Commissioner of Colonies for two months after the Provisional Government of France returned to Paris in August 1944.

In October 1944 the accidental death of Minister of Finance, Aimé Lepercq, brought about the appointment of Pleven to the office. A national liberation loan having just been launched, Pleven took command of the drive, bringing some measure of relief from inflation. He established the first budget of Free France, concluded a financial agreement with England, and strengthened the drive against fiscal evasion and illicit profits.

During 1945 Pleven clashed with Pierre Mendès-France, the Minister of National Economy, over the country's financial policies. Mendès-France favored a deflationist policy while Pleven favored expansion of production even if it involved some measure of inflation. With the resignation of Mendès-France in April, Pleven became Minister of National Economy and Finance and soon pushed through the Cabinet's approval of higher wages and an increase in the price of bread. As one of France's delegates to the San Francisco United Nations Conference on International Organization in April 1945, he stressed the importance of the Economic and Social Council in the new world organization.

Theoretically nonpolitical, De Gaulle's Provisional Government was attempting to establish an economy in accordance with the program announced by the National Resistance Council in March 1944. In pre-election speeches in July 1945, Pleven repeated De Gaulle's pledge that electrical power and banks would be nationalized before the year's end. He indicated that nationalization of other industries would follow, but declared, "We shall proceed step by step, taking the cue from successful private industry." Pleven was elected deputy from Côtes-du-Nord in Brittany in the October elections. De Gaulle, who remained at the head of a coalition Government of Popular Republicans, Communists and Socialists, named Pleven Minister of Finance on November 21 and appointed Marcel Paul, a Communist, the Minister of National Economy. On December 2, 1945, the National Assembly voted to nationalize the Bank of France. Later that month Pleven agreed to the devaluation of the franc, saying that the new level "could be defended only by common determination to increase production, to curb internal expenditure, and to do without luxury items so that these can be sold abroad to gain needed credit."

Serious rifts had been developing between De Gaulle and the Communists during the latter part of 1945, followed by a new crisis over the constitution and army credits in January 1946. The Socialists were aligned with the Communists against the Gaullists, and De Gaulle resigned. Pleven, who resigned at the same time, lost his seat in the Assembly in the elections on June 2, 1946, but regained it on November 10, 1946. He began to emerge as the leader of a political group in the National Assembly known as the Democratic and Socialist Union of the Resistance (U.D.S.R.), being elected president of its board of directors in May 1947. Meanwhile De Gaulle's newly created party, the Rally of the French People (R.P.F.) also began to take form, winning considerable support in the municipal elections of October 1947.

During 1947 and 1948 Pleven repeatedly urged the Socialists and the Popular Republicans to come to an understanding with the Gaullists so that they might join forces against the Communists, still the largest single party in France. Though Pleven's U.D.S.R. party was small, its block of votes controlled the balance of power in the Assembly. In the November 1948 elections, both De Gaulle's R.P.F. and Pleven's U.D.S.R. gained in strength, controlling a total of 135 seats as against a former 44. After the fall of the Queuille [48] Cabinet, which had lasted from September 1948 to October 1949, Georges Bidault [45], leader of the Popular Republicans, succeeded in forming a coalition Cabinet in which representation was given to the U.D.S.R., with Pleven named as Minister of National Defense. He assumed the office October 28, 1949.

René Pleven immediately set about strengthening the military establishment by means of a general reorganization plan. Speaking in support of bilateral accords with the United States, Pleven told the National Assembly in March 1950 that without such agreements France's army would have obsolete equipment. When the first arms shipment from the United States under North Atlantic Pact military agreements arrived in March and April 1950, the Defense Minister took steps to protect the unloading of the equipment at French ports because of the danger of Communist intervention. In April Pleven attended a meeting of the defense committee of the twelve-nation North Atlantic Treaty organization at The Hague, where a secret plan for the integrated defense of the West was approved. Because he is determined to build up France's air power, Pleven opposed

the unofficial recommendation of General Lucius D. Clay [45] that France and Germany concentrate on furnishing the infantry for Western European defense. He told the National Assembly in May 1950 that France's security "can be solved with our forces alone. But the security of the world is no longer bound up with the security of our country alone, and when the burden of defense is shared by many nations it becomes less heavy." Pleven's Government weathered several crises during the latter half of 1950, receiving votes of confidence in the National Assembly. On December 1, on the eve of his departure for London for a conference with Attlee on the world situation, he won a 347-184 vote of confidence which also met his demand for indorsement of his Defense Minister, Jules Moch [50], and new defense taxes.

Besides being president of U.D.S.R. Pleven is president of the Council General of Côtes-du-Nord, having been elected May 2, 1949. Since 1948 he has been a member of the Academy of Colonial Sciences, holding the seat left vacant by the death of General Leclerc. He is also president of the National Association for Indochina, an organization he helped to found in Algiers in 1944. He has been awarded the Croix de la Libération and is a Compagnon de l'Ordre de la Libération.

Tall, bespectacled René Pleven has been described as a man of intelligence, will, and decision, and as "one of the most forceful personalities of the Fourth Republic." He spends time regularly in Dinan and Saint-Brieuc, where he edits the newspaper Le Petit Bleu, and listens to the complaints and problems of his electorate. Pleven's marriage to Anne Bompard took place on July 30, 1924. They have two daughters, Françoise and Nicole (both married to officers), and six grandchildren. A good Breton, Pleven enjoys swimming, fishing, and sailing; and an admirer of modern painting, he names Matisse and Van Gogh as his favorite artists.

References

France Soir S 27 '45
Monde O 28 '49
International Who's Who, 1949
World Biography (1948)

POLITIS, ATHANASE G(EORGE) (pô-lē'tēs ä-tä-näz') Mar. 24, 1893- Greek Ambassador to the United States

Address: b. c/o Royal Greek Embassy, 2211 Massachusetts Ave., N.W., Washington, D.C.

A career diplomat, Athanase G. Politis, the Ambassador from Greece to the United States, has spent more than thirty years in his country's legations and embassies in Egypt, England, Japan, and Russia, in the Ministry of Foreign Affairs in Athens, and on special missions to European capitals. When Politis came to the United States in July 1950, he succeeded Vassili Dendramis [47]

Athanase George Politis was born on the island of Corfu, Greece, on March 24, 1893, the son of George Politis, a physician; his mother

ATHANASE G. POLITIS

was the former Argyri Ralli. His uncle, Niko-laos Politis, an internationally known jurist, who for many years was Greek minister to France and a professor in the University of Paris, urged young Politis to study law there. After receiving his M.A. degree, he left the University in 1914, at the beginning of World War I. His diplomatic career, begun in 1917 with his employ in the Ministry of Foreign Affairs, was interrupted temporarily by service in the Army, beginning early in 1918. But he was back in Paris by 1919 as a Greek delegate to the Paris Peace Conference. At the Austrian Commission on Reparations, held in Vienna in 1920, Politis served as secretary-general of the Greek Delegation. During the same year he completed his work for the LL.D. degree at the University of Paris.

Another period of military service occupied young Politis from March 1921 until early in 1922; then he returned to the Foreign Office in Athens, where he remained for two years. The next seven years, 1924 to 1931, were spent in Egypt, first as secretary of the Greek Consulate General in Alexandria until early in 1926, later as first secretary of the Greek Legation and chargé d'affaires in Cairo. Working from firsthand knowledge, the diplomat in the meantime was writing a history of the Greek colonies in modern Egypt, which was published in two volumes under the title *Hellenism and Modern Egypt* in Greek and French editions. Three smaller works also were produced during this period, all published in 1931 in Egypt: *Proposals Toward an Alliance Between Egypt and Greece in 1867* (in French); *The Turco-Egyptian Conflict of 1838-1841; the Last Years of the Reign of Mohamed Aly, Based on Greek Diplomatic Documents* (in French); and *Suggestions for the Organization of the Greeks in Egypt* (in Greek).

A special mission took Politis to scattered destinations—Abyssinia, Paris, London, Berlin, Copenhagen, Vienna, and Geneva during 1931 and 1932, after which he was recalled to Athens to the post of director in the Ministry of Foreign Affairs, which he held until sent to London in 1936 as counselor of the Greek Legation. The Royal Geographic Society of Egypt published another book written by Politis during his stay in Athens. This one-volume work, bearing the title *Relations Between Greece and Egypt during the Reign of Mohamed Aly 1833-1849*, was written in French and published in Rome in 1935.

Appointed Minister to Japan in 1939, Politis ended his three-year assignment in London, and proceeded to Tokyo; but with Japan's entrance into World War II, he left that country for Russia to represent Greece as her Ambassador in Moscow. While still serving in that capacity, he went to France in 1946 as a ranking member of the Greek delegation to his second Paris Peace Conference. When Soviet Ambassador, Konstantin Rodionov, was recalled from Greece in 1947, Politis left Russia to assume the duties of chief of the directorate of economic affairs in the Ministry of Foreign Affairs in Athens.

At a number of United Nations divisional conferences during the next few years Politis represented his country. As chief of the Greek delegation, he attended the International Trade Organization Conference in Havana, Cuba, late in 1947; and the second session of the ITO in Geneva, in 1948 (the charter of the ITO proposes to insure free trade and international high employment). Politis was again chief of the Greek delegation to the conference known as General Agreement on Tariffs and Trade, held in Annecy, France, in the spring of 1949, at which a series of tariff reductions was agreed upon by thirty-three nations.

A year later, on April 22, 1950, the appointment of the diplomat to the Embassy at Washington, D.C., was proposed by the Greek Cabinet, to succeed Vassili Dendramis, who was then approaching the age limit for foreign service. When Politis presented his credentials to President Truman on July 13, he stated that his countrymen looked on the United States "as the symbol of hope of freedom in the world." Earlier he had said, "All danger of Communist infiltration in Greece has now been eliminated, thanks to the tremendous aid given us by the American people."

The new Greek Ambassador, who has a command of English, French, German, Italian, Spanish, Russian, is a member of the International Rotary Club and of the Institute of Egypt. His honors in his own country include: Grand Officer of the Royal Greek Order of the Phoenix, Knight of the Royal Greek Order of the Savior, and Commander of the Order of the Holy Sepulchre. He is also recipient of several foreign distinctions, being an Officer of the French Legion of Honor, a Grand Officer of the Ethiopian Order of Menelik, Officer of the Chinese Order of the Golden Ray, and of the Royal Yugoslav Order of the White Eagle. According to the biographical release issued by the Greece Embassy, Politis married Lena Vassilieva, a Russian national in Moscow, was not permitted to take his wife out of that country, and is now divorced. In diplomatic circles the "personable" envoy is known as a good host.

References

International Who's Who, 1950
World Biography (1948)

POOLE, DEWITT C(LINTON) Oct. 28, 1885- Organization president
Address: b. c/o National Committee for a Free Europe, Inc., 350 5th Ave., New York 1; h. Princeton, N.J.

The National Committee for a Free Europe, Inc., was formed by a group of American citizens who seek to combat communist domination as seen in the countries of Eastern Europe. When the committee was organized in June 1949, DeWitt C. Poole was chosen president. He is experienced in international affairs, having been associated with Princeton University's School of Public and International Affairs for eighteen years, and having previously served in the United States consular and diplomatic corps; he was stationed in Russia at the time the Bolshevik Government was established. During World War II he was director of the Foreign Nationalities Branch of the Office of Strategic Services. One of the N.C.F.E.'s projects is Radio Free Europe, which on July 14, 1950, inaugurated a program of broadcasts to peoples behind the Iron Curtain, carrying talks by political exiles and other messages which the Government-operated *Voice of America* could not broadcast.

On both sides of his family DeWitt Clinton Poole, a tenth-generation American, is descended from colonial stock of English origin. The first Poole to come to America settled in Boston in the early part of the seventeenth century. Later generations lived in the Mohawk Valley and southern counties of New York. The first DeWitt Clinton Poole, the father of the present DeWitt Clinton, served in the Civil War and later became a Regular Army officer. His namesake, the youngest of three children of his marriage to Maria Woodward Pettes, was born October 28, 1885, in an army post in Vancouver, Washington. (His brother was Colonel John Hudson Poole, his sister, Louisa, is Mrs. Frank Bowen of Wisconsin.) When DeWitt was six years old the family moved to Fort Sam Houston (Texas), and a year later, after the retirement of his father from the Army, to Washington and then to Madison, Wisconsin. There the boy was graduated from high school in 1902.

Poole entered the University of Wisconsin, where he majored in history, worked on the college newspaper, became a member of Chi Psi, and in 1906 obtained his B.A. degree. Editorial work on the Moline (Illinois) *Dispatch* occupied him during 1906-9. In 1910, after advanced study at the George Washington University (in Washington, D.C.) leading to the M.Dip. degree, he entered government service, influenced by family tradition. President Theodore Roosevelt, then engaged in reorganizing

Brown's Studio
DEWITT C. POOLE

the consular service, gave him a post in that branch of the government on December 20, 1910. From 1911 to 1914 Poole was in Germany, as vice-consul in Berlin. Upon the outbreak of World War I he was transferred to Paris, to serve there in the same capacity until 1915. A period of service in Washington followed, with promotion to consul in July 1916. In July 1917 he was assigned to Moscow, where he was to witness the downfall of the Czar and the establishment of the Bolshevik Government.

While in Russia, Poole rose from special assistant to the American Ambassador (October 1918) to American chargé d'affaires (November 1918-June 1919). On February 4, 1919, he asked to be relieved of his duties in Russia because of his disapproval on moral grounds of the statement of policy toward Russia at the Paris Peace Conference. "Knowing as I do, possibly better than any other American," stated Poole in his communication to the Acting Secretary of State—contained in *Foreign Relations of the United States; Russia* (1919) —"the complete unmorality of the Bolshevik leaders . . . and the demoralization which their cynicism and cruelty work upon those whom they lead, I can not in honesty or self-respect do other than protest."

Poole left his duties in Russia to become chief of the Division of Russian Affairs in the State Department (October 1, 1919), and on November 23, 1921, was raised to the rank of consul general. During 1921-22 he was a member of the technical staff of the Conference on Limitation of Armament. His next assignment (October 1, 1923) was to Cape Town, South Africa, as consul general. He entered his last post in the United States foreign service in January 1926, when he went to the Embassy in Berlin, there to be counselor until 1930, the year he resigned.

Turning to the field of education, Poole served as chairman of the advisory board of

POOLE, DEWITT C.—*Continued*

the School of Public and International Affairs, Princeton University, from 1930 to 1948, and from 1933 to 1939 was a director of that board. In 1941 he was a member of the Institute for Advanced Study at Princeton, and during 1946-47 was a visiting lecturer on international politics at Harvard University. To these university posts was added in 1941 the directorship of the Foreign Nationalities Branch of the Office of Strategic Services, the emergency war agency which collected and analyzed such information required by the Joint Chiefs of Staff for military operations. After four years with OSS, Poole in 1945 became the special representative of the Secretary of State on a mission to Germany. On his return, in addressing a meeting of the Foreign Policy Association (January 1946) he proposed that Germany be divided permanently along the Elbe River, the western part becoming a federated state under French control and the eastern part joining a Central European federation. Stating that war was waged to establish peace, not to destroy nations, he pronounced the terms exacted from the Germans after World War I as "too severe," and those after World War II as "barbarous" (in a 1950 interview).

Since its formation in 1949 Poole has been president of the National Committee for a Free Europe, Inc. Membership in it is open to all citizens interested in its purposes: (1) to keep alive the hope of freedom in the countries of Eastern Europe dominated by Russia—Poland, Rumania, Yugoslavia, Czechoslovakia, Hungary, Albania, Bulgaria; (2) to preserve such exiled leaders of those satellite countries as have found asylum in the United States for the day of liberation; (3) to help rededicate Americans to their heritage of freedom. The organization has the approval of the Department of State, as expressed by Secretary Dean Acheson: "The State Department is very happy to see the formation of this group. It thinks that the purpose of the organization is excellent, and is glad to welcome its entrance into this field and give it its hearty endorsement."

Poole, in explaining the basic purpose of the group and its emphasis on work with political exiles, has said: "One of the first objects of the Communists, when they take over a country, is to eliminate the country's existing leaders in every walk of life. It is essential to maintain as many of those leaders as we can—against the day of the country's liberation. This must be done spiritually as well as physically. These men need work in the intellectual fields they know. The N.C.F.E. attempts to fill that need."

Radio Free Europe, a division of the committee, broadcasts a schedule of daily programs directed to some 80,000,000 people in the Soviet-dominated countries in their own languages. The programs of the network are planned to complement the State Department's *Voice of America*, and the programs of the British Broadcasting Corporation; being unofficial, *Radio Free Europe* can be more "hard-hitting" than broadcasts of Government-operated net-

works. Besides talks by exiles, the broadcasts, recorded in America, include satires and commentaries on the Communist system, and folk music forbidden by the Communists.

The Intellectual Cooperation division, in collaboration with the Library of Congress, has set up in Washington, D.C., a research center where exiles with scholarly training study new laws and decrees and economic developments. One of the main studies, known as the Danubian Inquiry, which is being made in cooperation with New York University and the Carnegie Endowment for International Peace, continues work begun under the auspices of the League of Nations. American Contacts is another division of the committee headed by Poole. It is charged with familiarizing the exiles with the ways of American democracy, and with introducing them and their work to the American public through lectures, informal talks, and pamphlets. In an attempt to "provide formal basis of cooperation and to stand as a symbol of hope to . . . Eastern Europeans enduring Communist oppression," (in the words of the committee's pamphlet) National Councils for each country are being formed, under the direction of the National Councils Division. To acquaint the American people with the work of the committee and to enlist their support, both moral and financial, a "Crusade for Freedom" was undertaken in the early fall of 1950. A "Freedom Scroll" for signature by citizens affirming their faith in democracy accompanied a "Freedom Bell" on a tour of the United States; installed in Berlin in October, the bell was sounded on October 24, United Nations Day, as a signal of hope for freedom to the countries behind the Iron Curtain.

Poole is the author of *Conduct of Foreign Relations Under Modern Democratic Conditions* (1924), a series of papers contributed to round table discussions at the Institute of Politics at Williams College. He is a member of the editorial board of *The Public Opinion Quarterly* and has written a number of articles for *Foreign Affairs* and other periodicals. In "The Balance of Power" (his article in *Life*, September 22, 1947), Poole declared that despite the "widespread support of the Marshall Plan the debate about United States foreign policy has not yet produced real agreement in its final answer." Advocating the maintenance of "a complex balance of power in the world" in which six or eight centers would be comparably powerful, he pointed out that the present situation in which Russia and the United States are incomparably stronger than any other countries in the world has resulted in a "dangerous and unstable situation."

Poole is a fellow of the American Geographical Society, a member of the Council on Foreign Relations, the Institute of Pacific Relations, Academie Diplomatique Internationale. He was awarded the LL.D. degree by the University of Delaware in 1934. His clubs are the Century (New York), Metropolitan (Washington), Nassau (Princeton). He has a stepson, Alan Cornell Poole, through his marriage to the widowed Mrs. Rachel Simmons Blanding on September 1, 1920. Five feet eight inches in height, Poole weighs 170 pounds, has blue-gray eyes, white hair, and a ruddy complexion.

References

Leaders in Education (1948)
Who's Who in Amerca, 1950-51
World Biography (1948)

POWER, TYRONE (tĭ-rōn') May 5, 1914-
Actor

Address: b. c/o Twentieth Century-Fox Pictures, Beverly Hills, Calif.; h. 407 N. Rockingham, Los Angeles 24, Calif.

Tyrone Power, Twentieth Century-Fox film star since 1936, entered motion pictures by way of the stage. He began his professional career at the age of seventeen, appearing in Chicago and New York productions. Among the thirty-odd films he has made (as of 1950) are *Alexander's Ragtime Band, Marie Antoinette, Rose of Washington Square, A Yank in the R.A.F., The Razor's Edge, Captain from Castile,* and *The Black Rose.* In 1950 he made a successful stage appearance in the lead role of the London production of *Mister Roberts.*

Tyrone Edmund Power comes from a family of theatrical traditions. His great-grandfather, the first Tyrone Power, was the leading Irish comedian at London's Drury Lane in the early part of the nineteenth century. His London-born grandson, also Tyrone Power and the father of the present Tyrone, was a member of Augustin Daly's company and leading man of Mrs. Fiske, Mrs. Leslie Carter, and Julia Marlowe. The third Tyrone Power was born of his marriage to Helen Emma Reaume of Indiana, who under the name of Patia Power played with her husband in Shakespearean productions; his birthplace is Cincinnati, Ohio, where his mother's family was living at the time of his birth, on May 5, 1914.

The future screen star's early years were spent in New York and Hollywood, where his parents were engaged in stage and screen work, including productions for the Famous Players and the Selig motion picture companies. From 1917 to 1923 he and his younger sister, Ann, lived with their mother in California, the climate of which was thought would benefit the boy's frail health. There he twice performed in San Gabriel Mission plays in which his mother had a leading role.

In 1923 the family moved to Cincinnati, where Mrs. Power taught voice and dramatic expression at the Schuster-Martin School of Drama. For his third-to-sixth-grade schooling Tyrone attended the Sisters of Mercy Academy, and later was enrolled at St. Xavier Academy. During 1928-29 he attended the Preparatory School of the University of Dayton, and from 1929 until his graduation (1931) the Purcell High School; both of the last-named schools were conducted by the Brothers of Mary. He took an active part in school dramatics, studied the speech arts under his mother, and earned some money by working as a drugstore clerk and an usher during vacations.

TYRONE POWER

After being coached by his father, young Power in 1931 had a short season in minor roles with a Shakespearean repertory company at the Chicago Civic Auditorium; Power senior was also a member of the cast. That year father and son proceeded to Hollywood, where the former had been engaged for a role in a film. After his father's death, which occurred in December of that year, Tyrone Power and his mother and sister took up residence in Santa Barbara and became associated with the Community Theatre. Unsuccessful in his attempts to enter motion pictures, Power two years later decided to try to get an engagement on the New York stage. En route to that city he stopped off at Chicago, where the Century of Progress Exposition was being held. He remained to play with the Circuit Theatre productions, did a few radio shows, and in 1934 was engaged to play the part of Freddie in a revival of *Romance,* in which Eugenie Leontovich was starred during an eight-week run at Chicago's Blackstone Theatre.

When *Romance* closed, Power went on to New York. There he was aided by family friends (Michael Strange, author and former wife of John Barrymore, and actress Helen Mencken) and was introduced to Guthrie McClintic, New York producer and husband of Katharine Cornell. This led to understudy roles in Miss Cornell's *Flowers of the Forest,* but no opportunity to appear in a part offered itself. A season of summer stock at West Falmouth (Massachusetts) was followed by the role of Benvolio with Miss Cornell in *Romeo and Juliet* (1935) and of De Poulengy in her *Saint Joan* (1936). His success was such that in the same year he signed a seven-year motion picture contract with Twentieth Century-Fox for leading roles.

Power, who made four pictures in his first year with Twentieth Century-Fox, scored his first screen success in the star role of *Lloyds*

POWER, TYRONE—*Continued*

of London (1936), a story of the famous British insurance house. Outstanding among some twenty films in which he played leading parts before World War II were *Cafe Metropole* (1937), *Alexander's Ragtime Band* (1938), *Rose of Washington Square* (1939). In *Blood and Sand* (1941), a Vicente Ibáñez story, Power essayed a role previously brought to the screen by Rudolph Valentino. *Time* found the American lacking in the spirit and authority of the part when compared with the Latin. *A Yank in the R.A.F.* (1941) won for Power from Howard Barnes of the New York *Herald Tribune* the tribute of playing with "genuine conviction" the role of a happy-go-lucky flier. In 1942 he made *This Above All, The Black Swan*, a Sabatini story of the Spanish Main, and *Crash Dive*.

In World War II Power served from August 24, 1942, to January 14, 1946, with the United States Marine Corps in which he enlisted as a private. He was given his basic training at Camp Elliot, San Diego, then qualified for Officer Candidate School, and upon graduation was commissioned a second lieutenant. After flight training in Corpus Christi, Texas, and in other training camps Lieutenant Power was sent overseas in February 1945 with the Marine Transport Command, Squadron 353. He was based at Kwajalein, Saipan, Okinawa, and Kyushu, and was among the first pilots to fly supplies to Iwo Jima when it was under constant artillery fire. He made flights also to Guam, Omura, Nogoya, and Tokyo, before returning to the United States in November 1945. When he received his discharge in 1946 he held the rank of first lieutenant.

While on terminal leave from the Marine Corps in December 1945, Power signed a new contract with Twentieth Century-Fox calling for starring parts in two films a year. In 1946 he played the role of Larry Darrell in the picturization of Somerset Maugham's best-seller novel, *The Razor's Edge*. With a cast including Gene Tierney, Anne Baxter, Herbert Marshall, and Clifton Webb, the picture made record runs. While its noted author pronounced the acting "perfect," critical opinion varied as to its merits. *Variety* considered that Power, in his characterization of a man whose peace of mind was disturbed by the killing in World War I, "was thoroughly believable as the youth who learns 'the path to salvation is as hard to travel as the sharp edge of a razor.'" The New York *Sun* critic Eileen Creelman gave as her opinion: "Larry, in spite of Tyrone Power's straightforward portrayal, comes through secondhand in *The Razor's Edge*, both in picture and book." In *Nightmare Alley* (1947), Power, as a "mind reader" in a carnival show "has a juicy role and sinks his teeth into it, performing with considerable versatility and persuasiveness," stated a New York *Times* reviewer. The actor made a good will tour of South America, where his pictures have also been popular, in 1946.

There followed a series of leading roles in historical romances shot on locations rather than on sets: *Captain from Castile* (1947), a Technicolor production of the Samuel Shellabarger novel about the Cortez conquest, was made in Mexico; the same author's *Prince of Foxes* (1949), a tale of the Italy of the Borgias, was filmed in Italy; *The Black Rose* (1950), adapted from Thomas Costain's best seller, is set in thirteenth century England and the Far East and was shot in England and Morocco. In general, critical opinion of these period pieces characterized them as lacking in vitality while abounding in performances in "the grand manner." Power's playing of the role of a young Spanish nobleman in *Captain from Castile* was described by a New York *Herald Tribune* critic as "acting of the elder Douglas Fairbanks school done to the queen's taste." In *Prince of Foxes* he was "handsome and agile as the scalawag turned hero," commented Eileen Creelman in the New York *Sun*. A number of critics felt that *The Black Rose* did not give full scope for Power's talent, although there was much in the picture and in his presence to "delight the eye." (According to the New York *World-Telegram*, the actor "has protested at times about getting so many roles based entirely on the appeal of his face and figure.")

Power was also starred in *Luck of the Irish* and *That Wonderful Urge* (comedies), and *Rawhide*, a western. In *American Guerrilla in the Philippines* (1950) Power was cast as a Navy officer turned guerrilla after the defeat at Bataan; criticizing the plot as episodic and undramatic, Bosley Crowther (New York *Times*) felt that Power played "with a solemn, lackluster attitude," as if he sensed "the basic emptiness." "Performances are good," was *Variety's* opinion. The actor's next picture was expected to be a new version of the 1933 hit, *Berkeley Square*, to be filmed in England under a new title.

In July 1950 Power returned to the stage for the first time in over nine years, to play the title role in the London production of the Broadway play, *Mister Roberts*. Harold Hobson, London critic for the *Christian Science Monitor*, called Power's performance of the officer on a United States Navy cargo ship stationed in the Pacific during World War II "beautifully quiet and well judged." "He gives the performance of his life as Mister Roberts, his quietness redeeming the character from goody-goodness," wrote John Barber from London to the *Herald Tribune*.

On April 23, 1939, Tyrone Power married Annabella, French movie star (whose full name is Suzanne Charpentier Murat), whom he met while playing opposite her in the film *Suez*. In 1940 they appeared together in the Screen Guild radio production of *Seventh Heaven*. The year 1941 saw them teamed in another revival, a summer stock production of *Liliom*, the stage hit by Ferenc Molnar. They were divorced in 1948. On January 27, 1949, Power married Linda Christian, film actress, in the ancient Santa Francesca Romana church in Rome. The daughter of a petroleum engineer from Holland, she has traveled extensively, and first met the actor in Mexico, when he was making *Captain from Castile*.

Power is a member of the Screen Actors Guild, Actors Equity Association, American Federation of Radio Artists. In 1937 and 1938 he received the Old Gold Popularity Award, and in 1946 won the International Sound Research Institute award for diction. He belongs to the Lambs, the Players in New York, and is a member of the Hollywood Athletic Club. His religious faith is the Catholic. The actor is six feet tall, weighs 175 pounds, and has brown hair and brown eyes. He swims, golfs, bowls, plays tennis, rides horseback; and he enjoys football as a spectator.

References

Look 18:29 S 3 '46
N Y Post Mag p5 D 29 '46; p12 Ja 23 '49
Photoplay 54:14 Ap '40; 28:33 My '46
International Motion Picture Almanac, 1950-51
Who's Who in America, 1950-51
Who's Who in the Theatre (1947)
World Biography (1948)

PRASAD, RAJENDRA (prá-säd' rä-jän' drá) Dec. 3, 1884- President of India

Address: Government House, New Delhi, India

The first President of India is Dr. Rajendra Prasad, a close friend and disciple of Mohandas K. Gandhi '42. Prasad's inauguration on January 26, 1950, twenty years after Gandhi's pledge of freedom was adopted by the Indian National Congress, marked the beginning of India's new status as a sovereign democratic republic. India's President, who was once a university professor, left his law practice in 1920 to join Gandhi's civil disobedience movement. During the next thirty years, during which he was frequently imprisoned for his nationalist activities, he founded several newspapers, directed earthquake relief work, and wrote books and articles about Gandhi and India. He has been president of the National Congress party three times, and presided over the National Assembly that drafted the new Indian constitution during 1946-49.

Rajendra Prasad was born December 3, 1884, in the district of Saran in the province of Bihar, India. His father, a high-caste Hindu, was a wealthy landowner. The youth was educated in law at Presidency College in Calcutta, receiving the degrees of Master of Arts and Master of Laws. A brilliant student, he continued his studies at Allahabad University, where he earned his doctorate in law. Between 1911 and 1920 Prasad practiced that profession. For two years, during 1914-16, he served as professor at the University Law College in Calcutta. He was one of the founding members of the Senate of Patna University, and was the founder as well of the *Patna Law Weekly*.

Prasad joined Gandhi in 1917 in the Mahatma's effort to improve the conditions of the peasants in the Champaran District by means of an Agrarian *Satyagraha*, a form of resistance movement based on nonviolence and noncooperation. In the years that followed, Prasad worked so closely with Gandhi that Jawaharlal Nehru observed in his autobiography: "Few others, if any, can be said to have imbibed more thoroughly the real message of Gandhi than Rajendra Prasad." In 1920 Prasad abandoned his law practice to devote his life to the cause of Indian independence. He became the leader of Gandhi's movement in Bihar, serving as secretary and president of the Bihar Provincial Congress Committee and president of the Bihar Provincial Conference in 1920 and again in 1929. When the Indian National Congress met at Gaya in Bihar in 1922, Prasad served as its general secretary.

Gandhi's attempts to come to terms with the British on constitutional reforms during the 1920's were unsuccessful; and when the Congress met in Lahore it voted on January 26, 1930, to begin its campaign for *Purna Swaraj* (complete independence). A civil disobedience movement was initiated, during which Prasad was imprisoned three times in the years 1930-32. In May 1934 civil disobedience ended, and the following month the Government of India lifted its ban on the Congress. When Gandhi resigned as president of the Congress in October 1934 (but retained control of the party direction), Prasad was elected president in his place. During 1935 the Congress grew in membership due largely to its opposition to the new India Act promulgated by Britain. Prasad served as secretary of the All-India Parliamentary Committee in 1936 and was a member of the working committee of the All-India Congress Committee. In the elections of 1937, the Congress carried eight out of eleven provinces. This victory resulted in a dispute within the Congress between Gandhi's moderate group and Nehru's group to the left. In 1939 Subhas Chandra Bose '44 was elected president of the Congress by a small margin, the first leader to be elected without Gandhi's approval. He resigned on April 29 over a disagreement with Gandhi, and on April 30 Prasad succeeded him as president.

When the Viceroy of India in September 1939 declared India a belligerent in World War II without consulting representatives of the Indian people, his action was condemned by the Congress. In July 1940, however, the Congress offered to cooperate with Britain if a national government were formed and a definite date set for independence. Failing to receive a satisfactory answer, the Congress decided on a course of "token civil disobedience" under which selected leaders were to brave arrest. In 1942 when Sir Stafford Cripps came to India to offer it a share in the conference of the British Empire and the United Nations, with independence to be given after the end of the war, major religious groups in India opposed the plan, because it called for immediate participation in the Empire's defense. In August 1942 Prasad and Nehru were arrested and imprisoned, together with other Indian leaders, under the Defense of India Rules. Prasad was not released until June 15, 1945.

The Labor party, which came into power in England after World War II, fulfilled the pledge to grant India full independence. Prasad was one of fourteen Indian leaders

RAJENDRA PRASAD

asked by Britain to form an interim government. On September 6, 1946, India's first All-Indian Executive Council took office in New Delhi, with Prasad as Minister of Food and Agriculture. On December 9 he was unanimously elected permanent president of the Indian Constituent Assembly called to draw up a "model Constitution which would satisfy the people of all groups, communities and religions of India." As had Gandhi, Prasad had pressed for Hindu-Moslem co-operation, opposing the partitioning of India into the Indian Republic and Pakistan. However, in April 1947, at the third session of the Constituent Assembly, Prasad stated that partition might be the only solution for India. On July 10, 1947, the British Parliament passed the Indian Independence Act, dividing the subcontinent into Pakistan and the Republic of India. When the Interim Government was reconstituted into two provisional governments to take over full control from Britain on August 15, 1947, Prasad retained his post as Minister of Food and Agriculture in the Indian Cabinet, until he was elected president of the Indian National Congress in November 1947.

For three years Prasad presided over the Constituent Assembly as it formulated a constitution for the new republic. The document finally adopted on November 26, 1949, provided for protection of "fundamental rights," including freedom of speech, of the press, and of assembly, and other basic civil rights. It also provided for the abolition of untouchability, the ancient caste system which for four thousand years had kept millions of people in that depressed class. Under the new constitution, the President of the Republic of India is elected for a five-year term by an electoral college composed of members of the provincial (state) legislatures and members of the Central (national) Parliament. The real political power

rests in the hands of the Prime Minister, with the President functioning as the formal head of state.

Dr. Rajendra Prasad was nominated for the presidency of India by Prime Minister Pandit Nehru, and was unanimously elected on January 24, 1950, a fact that was considered "significant of the continuing personal influence of Gandhi." His inauguration took place on January 26, 1950, in New Delhi, at Durbar Hall in Government House, the imposing sandstone mansion formerly occupied by the Viceroys of India. At the ceremony "India, that is Bharat" (its Sanskrit name) was proclaimed a republic. The occasion thus marked the emergence of the largest member of the British Commonwealth of Nations. India is a republic which disavows the sovereignty of the British King while remaining in equal association within the Commonwealth. Hindi is its official language.

In his inaugural speech Prasad said: "The objective of our republic is to secure justice liberty and equality to its citizens and to promote fraternity among the people who inhabit its vast territories and follow different religions speak various languages and observe their peculiar customs. . . . We want to live on terms of friendship with all other countries. Our program is to get rid of disease, poverty and ignorance."

Many problems confront President Prasad and the new Government of India. The partition of India brought with it frequent religious strife. In his opening address to the new Indian Parliament on January 31, 1950, Prasad renewed the offer of a "no war" pact with Pakistan. "I trust that the Pakistan Government will accept this offer . . . and thus help to reduce the unfortunate tension that has existed between these two countries." Prasad also called attention to India's "grave" economic situation and revealed the Government's intention of establishing a planning commission to provide for better use of resources.

Nehru once described Prasad as "the man who knows more about earthquake relief work than almost any other person in India. At the time of the earthquake in Bihar in 1934, Prasad served as president of the Bihar Central Relief Committee and of the Quetta Central Relief Committee in Karachi in 1935; he also organized the Congress Bihar Earthquake Relief Fund. After the assassination of Gandhi in 1948, Prasad was made head of the Gandhi National Memorial Fund. Prasad was one of the founders of the Patna English-language daily, *The Searchlight,* and of the Hindi-language weekly *Desh.* He has written numerous articles about Gandhi, including "Satyagraha in Champaran" (1929), "Mahatma at Champaran" (1940), and "Gandhi at Bihar." He is also the author of such economic treatises as "Economics of Khadi" (hand-spinning) and "A Constructive Program and its Problems" (1942). Other writings of particular importance by Prasad are "Pakistan" (1940), "India Divided" (1946), and "Demands of the Moslem League." His language dissertations include a work on Sanskrit. The Indian leader was twice president of the All-India Hindi Literary Conference which met in Cocanada in

1928 and in Nagpur in 1936. He is Rector of the *Bharatiya Itihas Parishad* (Indian Academy of History).

Prasad has been characterized by Nehru as "somewhat unsophisticated from the point of view of the modern world, but his outstanding ability, his perfect straightness, his energy and his devotion to the cause of Indian freedom are qualities which have made him loved not only in his own province but throughout India." In keeping with the simplicity in Gandhi's mode of living, Prasad eats only two meals a day of vegetables, soup, and bread, as he is seated on the floor in orthodox Hindu fashion. His daily routine includes rising at 3 A.M., practicing Yoga exercises, reading the *Ramayana*, and spinning cotton, a symbolic task of devout followers of Gandhi which was started in protest against importation of British finished goods. Prasad, it is said, did not look forward to living in the splendor of Government House, into which he moved with his wife, Rajbanshi, his sister, seventeen granddaughters, and two grandsons. As a hobby he has studied modern farming methods, which he encourages Indians to adopt.

References

N Y Herald Tribune II p3 Ja 29 '50 por; p11 Ja 11 '50
N Y Times p11 Ja 3 '50; p11 Ja 24 '50 por
Pathfinder 57:24 F 8 '50 por
Indian and Pakistan Year Book and Who's Who, 1948
International Who's Who, 1949
International World Who's Who (1949)
Who's Who in India, 1946-47

PRIEST, J(AMES) PERCY Apr. 1, 1900-
United States Representative from Tennessee
Address: b. House Office Bldg., Washington, D.C.; h. 4305 Elkins Ave., Nashville, Tenn.

At the beginning of his fourth consecutive term in the United States House of Representatives, when the Eighty-first Congress convened in January 1949, Democrat J. Percy Priest was chosen House majority whip. The Representative from Tennessee's Sixth District, who is not regarded as a "rubber-stamp" legislator—he has not supported the Roosevelt and Truman Administrations in all their measures—took his seat in Congress in 1941 after a fourteen-year career as a newspaperman. Priest is given credit for the enactment of the National Mental Health Act and has served on the House Committee on Interstate and Foreign Commerce. In 1946 the Congressman from Tennessee was chairman of the House Campaign Expenditures Committee, which made an investigation of violations of the Federal Corrupt Practices Act.

Born in the town of Carters Creek, Tennessee, on April 1, 1900, James Percy Priest is the son of George Madison and Harriet Axie (Hastings) Priest. He was reared in that State, where he attended elementary schools in Maury County and Central High School in Columbia. From the age of nineteen to twenty-one Priest

was a rural school teacher. Then, after a period (1921) at State Teachers College (in Murfreesboro) he became a teacher of English and history at Culleoka High School. While there (1921-26), he studied between terms at the University of Tennessee (1923) and at the George Peabody College for Teachers, in Nashville (1925-26). In 1926 he joined the editorial staff of the *Tennessean*, the newspaper published in Nashville, where he remained until 1940, when for the first time he entered politics as candidate for Congress.

After what Delos W. Lovelace in the New York *Sun* termed "a strictly amateur campaign," Priest, a Democrat, emerged as victor at the polls, defeating the regular Democratic organization candidate, who had opposed conscription. He took his seat in the Seventy-seventh Congress in January 1941 to represent Tennessee's Sixth District, or Davidson County, which includes Nashville, the State capital. Re-election followed in due course to the Seventy-eighth, Seventy-ninth, Eightieth and Eighty-first Congresses.

An analysis of Congressman Priest's voting record made by the *Congressional Quarterly* in 1945 showed that he had voted with the Roosevelt Administration on about 85 per cent of the measures, supporting the President in foreign policy; the selective service bill, fifty-dollar pay for servicemen (1941), the rescind salary limit (1943), the Federal vote for soldiers (1944), price control, and the Government reorganization bill. He was among the "Nays" on the Smith-Connally Act veto, on the override of the tax bill veto (1944), freezing of social security taxes, and on a permanent Un-American Activities Committee.

In 1946 Priest voted against abolishing OPA, against nondiscrimination (Amendment to HR 3370) on school lunch program (but supported Federal aid for the program), against the passage of the tidewater land bill over President Truman's veto, and shelving the atomic energy control bill. He was with the "Yeas" on draft extension, the passage of the Case labor bill over the President's veto, the passage of the first price control bill over the President's veto, full employment bill, housing subsidies, and the President's strike control bill. In the Eightieth Congress the Tennessean, in circumstances of a Republican majority in Congress, swung his allegiance closer to his party's line, though he voted for the passage of the Taft-Hartley labor bill over the President's veto. After becoming Democratic whip in January 1949, Priest supported all major measures of Truman's Fair Deal program with the exception of the anti-poll bill and the repeal of the Taft-Hartley labor law. He voted with the Administration on the mutual defense assistance legislation, the Korean aid act, the Marshall Plan extension, and the Point Four program.

One of the first bills framed by the Tennesseean proposed "mandatory civilian war service for draft-deferred men." In 1943 Priest authored one of several resolutions introduced in Congress for a Constitutional amendment on treaty power. The *Congressional Digest* (October 1943) quoted him as saying it was "a paradoxical procedure wherein a majority of both

Wide World Photos

J. PERCY PRIEST

Houses could begin a war but in which two-thirds of one body alone can officially end it. . . .If we can trust a body to declare war," argued Priest, "can we not with equal . . . wisdom . . . trust it to ratify a peace treaty?"

Guiding the National Mental Health Act through Congress in 1946, Priest shared credit with Senator Claude Pepper '41 for its passing. Called an epochal measure by *PM*'s Albert Deutsch, it provided for a nation-wide attack on the problem of mental diseases, which previously had been handled on a State or local level. The measure authorized appropriations for a National Mental Health Institute (under the administration of the United States Public Health Service) to serve as a coordinating center for research on mental diseases. Among other provisions were Federal grants-in-aid for psychiatric research in universities, hospitals, and other institutions, and to help finance the training of psychiatrists and other personnel needed to treat mental diseases.

A supporter of the Administration's program for Federal aid to education, Congressman Priest, a Baptist, in July 1949 coauthored with Representative John W. McCormack '43, a Catholic, a bill as a compromise to Representative Graham A. Barden's '49 bill providing Federal aid to States for schools, exclusive of parochial and private schools. It was hoped that the Priest-McCormack bill, which called for $35,000,000 a year from Federal funds to be spent on health aid to all schools, public, parochial, and private, would appease the opponents of the major program. The Washington *Post*, pointing out that it was not a substitute for the aid-to-education program, called it a "health bill," since it would be concerned with school lunches and children's health rather than contribute directly to school systems.

In 1946 Priest was chairman of the House Campaign Expenditures Committee investigat-

ing alleged violations of the Federal Corrupt Practices Act. (Among those questioned at public hearings in the investigations were labor and industry groups, the Communist party, the Ku Klux Klan.) The committee, whose investigation was praised by the New York *Herald Tribune* as "frank and energetic," reported "widespread violations," of the Act, which Priest said was "full of loopholes," and recommended it be either more vigorously enforced, or repealed. Under Priest's chairmanship this committee investigated also alleged violations of the election laws in 1946 during the Kansas City (Missouri) Democratic primary and in New York City's Eighteenth Congressional District. As chairman of a subcommittee of the House Interstate and Foreign Commerce Committee (to which he was appointed in 1943), Priest handled the bill which proposed the establishment of a National Science Foundation, an independent Government agency designed to make surveys of scientific needs, and through grants and fellowships, concentrate research projects in appropriate fields. Proposed first in 1946 (repeatedly urged upon Congress by President Truman), the bill, after many delays, was passed by both Houses in the spring of 1950 with security provisions inserted by the House to insure loyalty of all workers in the foundation. Expenditure in 1951 for its establishment in that year was set at $500,000, and a future budget of $15,000,000 per year was authorized.

In January 1949 the Congressman from Tennessee was designated House Democratic whip in the Eighty-first Congress. Assessing the temper of this Democrat-controlled Congress which yet failed to enact many of the measures of President Truman's Fair Deal program, Craig Thompson in a *Collier's* article (August 27, 1949) quoted Priest as saying: "This is the most independent-minded bunch of Representatives in my time. . . .Lots of them are war veterans . . . who can't be stampeded. . . .They work hard, study the bills, and make up their own minds." The House Democratic whip suggested in the summer of 1950 that, because of world developments, Secretary of State Acheson and Secretary of Defense Johnson resign in the interest of national unity, a feeling opposed by President Truman.

Representative Priest married Mildred Webster Noland on February 14, 1947. The Congressman is a Mason, a member of the Civitan Club (Nashville), and the National Press Club (Washington). In his own church (the Baptist) he has sung in the choir, and he taught a men's Bible class in the Methodist church.

References

Congressional Directory (1950)
Who's Who in America, 1950-51
World Biography (1948)

PRUDEN, EDWARD HUGHES, REV.
Aug. 30, 1903- Religious organization president; clergyman
Address: b. c/o First Baptist Church, 16th and O Sts., N.W., Washington 6, D.C.; h. 3029 Ordway St., N.W., Washington 8, D.C.

Pastor of the First Baptist Church of Washington, D.C. (which President Truman attends), the Rev. Dr. Edward Hughes Pruden was unanimously elected to the presidency of the American (formerly Northern) Baptist Convention, which met in Boston in May of 1950. The Northern Baptists voted during that session to change their name to American Baptists in the hope of a future union with the Southern Baptist Convention, which is composed of six million coreligionists. Himself a native of the South, Dr. Pruden is a graduate of the Southern Baptist Theological Seminary and a member of the Southern Baptists group.

Edward Hughes Pruden, born in Chase City, Virginia, on August 30, 1903, is the son of James Richard and Frances Woodfin (Hughes) Pruden. His father, a merchant, was one of the founders of the firm of Pruden and Hutcheson in the town. John E. Hughes, Edward's maternal grandfather, was mayor of Chase City; his maternal great-grandfather, also of Virginia, was Colonel John A. Clark, who fought in the Revolutionary War. His only brother was George B. Pruden, now deceased.

After graduation in 1921 from the Chase City High School, where he took part in dramatic productions and literary activities, Edward Hughes Pruden entered the University of Richmond. Pursuing his interest in writing and dramatics while at college, he became business manager of the school paper, the *Richmond Collegian*, president of the school's literary society, and a member of the intercollegiate debating team. After receiving his B.A. degree with a major in sociology in 1925, Pruden went to Louisville, Kentucky, to prepare for the ministry at the Southern Baptist Theological Seminary. Pruden has said that his parents, his own pastor, and his Richmond College pastor influenced him in selecting that career. Having received the Th. M. degree in 1928, he studied further at Yale Divinity School during 1929 and 1930, and in the following year in Scotland, at the University of Edinburgh. In 1931 he was presented with a Ph.D. degree by the latter institution after his completion of the thesis, "The Doctrine of Holy Scripture in John Calvin." He belongs to Theta Sigma, and the honorary degree of Doctor of Divinity was conferred on him by the University of Richmond in 1932.

A five-year pastorate at the First Baptist Church in Petersburg, Virginia, was followed by a year at the University of Shanghai, China, as guest professor of English. His wife, Mae (Talmage) Pruden, whom he had married on August 1, 1933, was also a guest professor at Shanghai University that year; a graduate of the Cincinnati Conservatory, Mrs. Pruden was a member of the music faculty. The Prudens returned to the United States in December 1936, when Dr. Pruden accepted the call to the pulpit of the First Baptist Church in Washington, D.C.

Under Dr. Pruden (as of 1950), according to a leaflet issued by the church, the congregation increased from 775 to more than 2,000, necessitating the holding of two morning services each Sunday and the acquisition of additional buildings and an adjoining building site. During his pastorate, too, the yearly budget grew from $17,000 to $200,000. The church has occupied its present site for sixty years, the fourth since its founding in 1802. The church leaflet mentions the emphasis on the evangelistic phase of its spiritual program, in which professions of faith are invited at the close of each service. Training programs prepare members for productive activity as well as participation in one of the church's three choirs. The story is told that Dr. Pruden had prepared a sermon, "A Time for Greatness," for a certain Sunday in October 1945 before he was informed that President Truman would attend that service. He decided not to revise the sermon, in which he discussed international affairs in relation to the United States.

At its five-day forty-third annual conference, held in Boston, Massachusetts, in May 1950, Pruden was elected president of the Northern Baptist Convention, a name changed to American Baptist Convention in hopeful anticipation of a union with the Southern Baptist Convention. In this connection it was pointed out that the new president has his roots in the South, which formed its own group in 1845 because of political differences with the North. (The Northern Baptist Convention which has two million members in thirty-six States, came into being in 1907.) A major difference between the two conventions, Pruden said, is the matter of cooperation with interdenominational Protestant agencies—notably the Federal Council of Churches and the World Council of Churches. Southern Baptists, stated Pruden in the Washington *Post*, are traditionally conservative in theology and assume many in the Protestant agencies are liberal. Among some thirty resolutions passed by the American Baptist Convention were: opposition to peacetime military training and favoring the granting of amnesty to conscientious objectors; support of Federal

Harris & Ewing
REV. EDWARD HUGHES PRUDEN

PRUDEN, EDWARD HUGHES, REV.
—Continued

legislation to prohibit inter-State passage of information and equipment used in gambling; for the enforcement of laws designed to curb the production and sale of intoxicating liquors; criticism of "character assassination" as practiced by those who have developed a "Communist hysteria," although the convention recognized the threat of that form of totalitarianism; granting of time to school children for religious education; favoring Federal aid to education when the principle of separation of Church and State is maintained; the end to racial discrimination in Washington; improved labor-management relations; "repudiation" of Catholic "claims to authoritarianism" in marriage, in connection with which Baptist pastors were to inform their young people of the latters' "civil and religious rights" when contemplating marriage with Catholics.

Dr. Pruden has served as president of the Washington Federation of Churches (1939-1940); as president of the District of Columbia Baptist Convention; and as chairman of the board of managers of the Chinese Community Church of Washington. He is a member of the board of managers of the American Baptist Foreign Mission Society, and is on the board of founders of the University of Shanghai and the University of Nanking. Known as a speaker and writer, Dr. Pruden has addressed such bodies as the National Christian Mission, sponsored by the Federal Council of the Churches of Christ in America; he has written articles for various religious journals, is Washington correspondent for *The Christian Century*, and writes Sunday School lessons for both the American and Southern Baptist Conventions. He also belongs to the latter group as well as to Interchurch, and lists himself as a political independent. Some of his undertakings are described by Mrs. Pruden, who with several other pastors' wives contributed to the book *I Married a Minister*, edited by G. M. E. Bader (1942). The Prudens have three children, Patrician Carol, James Richard, and Edward Hughes, Jr. With a height of five feet nine inches, the minister weighs 180 pounds, has light hair and blue eyes. His favorite forms of recreation are golf, bowling, and travel.

References

Newsweek 27:83 Mr 11 '46 por

Bader, G. M. E. ed. I Married a Minister (1942)

Who's Who in the Clergy, 1941-42

Who's Who in the East (1948)

PUCKETT, B(ENJAMIN) EARL Dec. 6, 1897- Chain department store executive
Address: b. c/o Allied Stores Corp., 1440 Broadway, New York 18; h. 1008 Shore Rd., Douglaston, N.Y.

B. Earl Puckett was in February 1950 elected board chairman (the chief executive officer) of the Allied Stores Corporation, one of the largest department store chains in the United States. He came to Allied in 1933 as president and, according to *Fortune*, increased in fourteen years the annual profits from $25,000 to $20,-000,000 through what has been called "a remarkable engineering job in policies, operations, procedures, finances, and general reputation." Beginning his career as a country school teacher, Puckett after taking correspondence school courses became a certified public accountant. At the age of thirty he entered the department store field.

The son of Theodore G. and Joanna (Churchwell) Puckett, Benjamin Earl Puckett was born December 6, 1897, in the hill country of Wayne County, Illinois, on a farm near Fairfield. At an early age he showed a special aptitude for arithmetic. He attended local schools for his elementary education, but because of the distance to the nearest high school, his secondary education was acquired by study at home. So well did he apply himself that he was able to obtain a teacher's certification after a few months' attendance at the Southern Illinois State Normal University and Eureka (Illinois) College. During 1916-18 he taught school (he was one of six members of the Puckett family to be so occupied at the time), first at the Hall School in Barnhill, later at the Mill Shoals school.

Puckett was earning $600 a year when, in 1918, he became a bank clerk at a salary of $1,800 with the First National Bank in Fairfield. At the time of World War I, Puckett, after being rejected for service with the Navy because of underweight, entered the Army. He was still in training when the war ended. Returning to the Fairfield bank, he remained there until 1920 when he joined Ernst and Ernst, a firm of public accountants in Indianapolis. Correspondence courses in law, accounting, and business administration prepared Puckett for a position as public accountant, and in 1922 to pass the State examination for certified public accountant.

Puckett found his niche in the business world when he joined the E. H. Scull Company, a management, counseling, and auditing concern, specializing in the retail field. After remaining two years with this firm doing research and accounting, in 1924 he became head of the controller's division of the Retail Research Association at an annual salary of $7,000. In 1927, Puckett (who tells that as a boy he read all Horatio Alger's books) entered the retail merchandising field. Joining the Frederick Loeser Department Store, the second largest in Brooklyn, New York, as treasurer at $18,000 a year, one year later he was named vice-president, and in 1931 president. (He resigned in 1933, when its owner installed a relative as president.) The *Fortune* article (March 1947) credited Puckett with applying "a good approximation of scientific methods to the bazaar business of buying, storing, displaying, selling of upwards of 100,000 different items under a single roof."

Paul Mazur of Lehman Corporation, investor in Hahn Department Stores, Inc., (as the Allied Stores Corporation was known before 1935) sponsored Puckett's connection with that concern in 1933. The chain's stock had dropped from $57 a share in 1929 to less than one dollar a share by 1932, and its net profits were around

$25,000 annually. Both Mazur and Puckett had faith in Hahn's theory of "selective application of chain store methods to traditional department store merchandising," (*Fortune*'s words) but believed that Hahn had failed to cultivate his theory properly. Puckett, who was unanimously elected as president of the corporation in late 1933, began decentralizing responsibility in the management of the different stores. Other changes included reducing the management of the store to "basic textbook form." One of its principles of over-all management is a "Model Merchandising Plan" which establishes that "the art-needlework department should have a gross margin of 41.4 per cent, selling salaries around 6.5 per cent and the allowance for stealing should not be over 1.2 per cent." Through this method Puckett was to raise from the ranks about thirty-five managing directors. In an interview with Mary Braggiotti (New York *Post*) Puckett said he runs his business as a schoolteacher. He liked teaching, but not finding it remunerative, he added, "I just found a better paying school."

In 1948 Allied Stores Corporation owned seventy-eight stores in various sections of the United States, ranging from a Parma (Idaho) junior department store with a business of $170,000 a year, to the Boston Jordan Marsh Company with sales of $60,000,000 annually. In his business travels Puckett has visited every town in the country with populations over 20,000. The chain-store ownership affects only the "behind-the-scenes" management of a store —outwardly the store retains its individuality, carrying on business in the tradition of its original owner. A new plan of merchandising was inaugurated by the Allied head in 1949 in Cleveland: he bought a block of specialty shops and managed them as one department store, using a "ghost" or unoccupied building in the street for administration headquarters. Fifty to 80 per cent of the merchandise is the same in all the Allied stores, the remaining 50 or 20 per cent "setting the tone of the store." As many as 25,000 low-priced dresses have been shipped weekly to the entire chain membership. Allied's sales multiplied fivefold during fourteen years under Puckett's leadership. In the year ending January 31, 1948, the sales volume was $392,000,000, an increase of 8.4 per cent over the previous year.

In 1944, as reported in the New York *Times*, Puckett's income of $215,420 placed him among the Treasury Department's list of the twenty-five executives with the largest incomes. In 1945 he took a salary cut (New York *Post*) and at the same time arranged for a substantial pension to begin upon his retirement. The bylaws of Allied were changed on February 14, 1950, to provide for the chairman of the board to become the chief executive officer, who shall, under the control of the board of directors, have the general management of its affairs. At the same meeting Puckett was made chairman of the board and received a five-year contract dating from February 1, 1950. Puckett

B. EARL PUCKETT

also has oil interests. Two years after oil was discovered in his native Wayne County, Illinois, he became a member of Robinson-Puckett, Inc., with oil rights in some 11,000 acres in Wayne and Clay counties. He is also executive of the Allied Purchasing Corporation and Wayne Petroleum Company, and a director of the Lehman Corporation and of the Commercial National Bank and Trust Company of New York.

Benjamin Earl Puckett married Agnes C. Wiedenhorn on September 12, 1923. They had met in 1922, when Miss Wiedenhorn was employed as a bookkeeper for the Aetna Mortgage Company in Indianapolis, to which Puckett was on assignment as a public accountant. The couple have one son, Bruce E. The elder Puckett is described as a heavy-set man—he is five feet nine and weighs 180 pounds—with thinning light brown hair and brown eyes. Admitting to physical laziness, he told Mary Braggiotti of the *Post* that his only sports are those that require little energy, riding, sailing, and fishing. Television, the radio, historical novels, and detective stories are his indoor diversions. He is a chain cigar smoker. For his support of nonsectarian charities he received the 1948 honor award (a silver plaque) from the National Jewish Hospital of Denver (he is a Protestant). His clubs are the New York Athletic, the Bankers, and Douglaston; his political views are independent.

References

Bsns W p64 Ag 20 '49
Fortune 35:122+ Mr '47 por
Business Executives of America (1950)
Who's Who in America, 1950-51
Who's Who in Commerce and Industry (1948)
World Biography (1948)

PUTNAM, CLAUDE ADAMS, May 26, 1890- Manufacturers organization official

Address: b. c/o National Association of Manufacturers, 14 W. 49th St., New York 20; c/o Markem Machine Company, Keene, N.H.; h. Keene, N.H.

At the fifty-fourth annual meeting of the National Association of Manufacturers, Claude Adams Putnam was elected president for the 1950 term. The president of a machine-manufacturing firm in Keene, New Hampshire, Put-

CLAUDE ADAMS PUTNAM

nam had been a director of the NAM since 1944 and during 1949 had served on the executive committee of the association. His choice as president was considered by *Time* a continuation of NAM's policy of choosing a small businessman to head the organization. Like many other manufacturing firms represented in the NAM which employ less than five hundred workers (Putnam says they constitute "probably more than 70 per cent of NAM members"), Putnam's company has about two hundred production employees. Although small in comparison with other manufacturing firms, it is the largest in its particular field.

Claude Adams Putnam was born May 26, 1890, in Exeter, New Hampshire. His parents, Fred Asahel and Maude Linscott (Adams) Putnam also were natives of that State. Young Putnam attended the public schools of Melrose, Massachusetts, and when he graduated from the local high school at the age of sixteen he got his first job, as an apprentice in a machine shop in Torrington, Connecticut. Next he moved to Newark, New Jersey, to complete his training, and in 1909 he went to Boston as a journeyman machinist.

Two years later (1911) his father founded the Markem Machine Company in Keene, when the son joined the firm. Shortly afterward he became a salesman and engineering consultant,

installing the company's equipment in industrial plants in Eastern United States and in England, Ireland, and the principal countries of the Continent during the years 1911-13. In the latter year he became sales technician in the machine erection field, when he covered the company's Eastern United States and Canadian territories until 1917. With the coming of World War I he was called into Government service in Washington. His appointment to the presidency of the Markem Machine Company occurred in 1919, and in 1940 he received the additional title of treasurer. This dual post he has also held since 1940 in the F. A. Putnam Manufacturing Company, suppliers of inks and other materials used by purchasers of the Markem machines.

Although its production employees have rarely exceeded two hundred, the Markem Machine Company, manufacturers of power-driven devices for marking and identifying industrial parts and products, is the largest firm in this field. During the history of the company no employee, according to Putnam, has ever been laid off and only a few workers in the decade 1940-50 have been discharged. There is no union at Markem: instead (according to an interview with Putnam reported in the *Christian Science Monitor*) there is an "unwritten agreement that no gripe—or significant accomplishment—goes unrecognized for twenty-four hours." The workers at the plant are referred to by the president as the "Markem Gang" and the plant's janitor as "the man in charge of cleanliness facilities." Putnam believes that employers and supervisors should take a personal interest in every employee, but considers "outside intervention" inevitable in industries where the personal touch cannot be retained. Discrimination because of race or nationality has not been an issue at the Markem plant. (To the hospital at Keene of which Putnam is a trustee, was appointed the Negro doctor whose story was dramatized in the film *Lost Boundaries*.)

Having served for six years on the thirty-five-member board of directors of the NAM and one term (1949) on the association's executive committee, Putnam was elected to the NAM presidency for 1950. (He succeeded W. F. Bennett '40.) Generally regarded as America's representative of big business, the NAM, which was founded in 1895, has a membership of approximately 15,000. Its program of asserting the interests of manufacturers and businessmen is carried out by four divisions—economic policy, industrial relations, economic relations, and public relations. Each year at a meeting which the NAM has named "Congress of American Industry," officers and directors are chosen, national issues involving the interests of businessmen are discussed, and a program of action is agreed upon. The 1949 congress was concerned with the lack of venture capital and investment funds resulting from rising taxes, Federal deficits, and Federal welfare programs. As a solution to what were described in the convention as "monopolistic labor practices," the members heard NAM speakers recommend a "code of conduct for both management and labor to assure adequate self-discipline in negotiations." In spite of the decline in capital outlays in 1949 and the shortage of venture capital, analysts of the NAM declared that the national economy was "strong and reassuring to an exceptional degree."

This optimistic attitude was echoed by Putnam at a press conference held when he became NAM's president. He declared that the faith he has in the future of the United States, in the "basic soundness of people," and in the "imperishable nature of the American way of life" had guided him in his business and would continue to do so during his presidency of NAM. Putnam does not believe that the NAM represents only big business, nor does he think that only one point of view is given an opportunity for expression. He recounts that during the period of his association with the NAM he has often disagreed with its policy and expects, as president, that he may have occasion to disagree again. In his opinion the primary domestic problem according to an interview reported in the New York *World-Telegram,* is "to end confusion in management-labor relations."

In 1947 Putnam was president of the New Hampshire Manufacturers Association, having been its director and vice-president. He has served on the Keene City Council of the board of aldermen, is a past president of the Keene Rotary Club, and is a past president of the New Hampshire branch of the Young Men's Christian Association. He is also a trustee of the Elliot Community Hospital and a former vestry member of the St. James Protestant Episcopal Church in his community. A former chairman of the New Hampshire Apprenticeship Training Council, Putnam in 1950 is senior industry member of the Federal Apprenticeship Training Council, a management-labor advisory group in the United States Department of Labor. In the Masonic lodge he is a Knight Templar, and Shriner.

The manufacturer was married June 26, 1913, to Louise Bidwell Taylor; their two children are David Frederic (in 1950 vice-president of the Markem company) and Elizabeth (the wife of a Markem executive). Putnam, who speaks with a "trace of upper New England twang in his voice," is tall, "genial" in manner, with a "ruddy skin" and "trim figure." He enjoys skiing, sailing, and fishing, and occasionally plays baseball with Markem employees on the company's recreation field.

References

Christian Sci Mon p4 D 10 '49
N Y World-Telegram p11 D 9 '49 por
Who's Who in New England (1949)

QUESADA, ELWOOD R(ICHARD)

(kŭh-sä′dá) Apr. 13, 1904- United States Air Force officer

Address: b. c/o Department of Defense, The Pentagon, Washington, D.C.; h. 2554 Massachusetts Ave., N.W., Washington, D.C.

The over-all command of the new atomic bomb tests at Eniwetok, was given to Lieutenant General Elwood R. Quesada of the Air Force. Known as "the pilots' general," Quesada served during World War II as commanding general of the Twelfth Fighter Command during the African and Italian campaigns and of the Ninth Tactical Air Command in France, Belgium, and Luxembourg following the Normandy invasion. Subsequent to the termination of hostilities he was assigned (1946) to leadership of the new Tactical Air Command and later (1948) to the reorganization of the Air Reserve. He has been a strong advocate of unification of the armed services.

Elwood Richard Quesada is of Spanish and Irish extraction. The son of the late Lope Lopez and Helen A. (McNamara) Quesada, he was born in Washington, D.C., on April 13, 1904. He attended the Technical High School in the nation's capital and Wyoming Seminary at Wilkes-Barre, Pennsylvania; and he has studied at both the University of Maryland and at Georgetown University in the city of his birth.

In 1924, when he was twenty, he enlisted as a private in the Army, but by September of the same year had entered the Air Service Primary Flying School where, as a flying cadet, he was one of only thirteen in a class of one hundred and fifty successfully to complete the pursuit course. Graduated September 13, 1925, he was commissioned a second lieutenant in the Air Reserve on the day following, and on January 23, 1927, after about sixteen months of inactive status, received his commission as second lieutenant (permanent) in what was then known as the Air Corps of the Regular Army.

"In the days when he went through flying school" (stated the official biographical sketch supplied by the Department of Defense) "students were required to attain proficiency in tearing down and assembling engines, which tended to make for mechanically minded pilots." Quesada's first duty, accordingly, was as an engineering officer at Bolling Field, Washington, from April 1927 to June 1928. It was during this duty that the news columns introduced young Lieutenant Quesada's name to the general public. Flying a Loning amphibian for General James Edmond Fechet, then Chief of the Air Corps, to the rescue of the crew of the German aircraft *Bremen* which had crashed in Labrador after making the first East-West transatlantic flight, Quesada was forced down in the Bay of Fundy. He waited until low tide, dug holes in the now exposed sand, rolled down the wheels, and was able to take off. Quesada was again in the news in January 1929. Detached from duty as General Fechet's flying aide, he was relief pilot under Major (later General) Carl A. Spaatz of the three-engine Fokker monoplane *Question Mark* which remained aloft over San Diego, California, for six and a quarter days, in the first successful attempt to refuel in the air for a protracted period. For this feat he, with the other crew members, was awarded the Distinguished Flying Cross.

Advancement in the services during time of peace is slow, so that it was not until November 1, 1932, that Quesada was promoted to first lieutenant (permanent). Meanwhile he had served (October 1930-April 1932) at Havana, Cuba, as assistant military attaché to United

LT. GEN. ELWOOD R. QUESADA

States Ambassador Harry Guggenheim. Returning to his former duty as engineering officer at Bolling Field he was named flying aide to F. Trubee Davison, the Assistant Secretary of War, and served as such until the summer of 1933, when he devoted four months accumulated leave to piloting Davison and the big-game hunter Martin Johnson over Africa on a mission to collect animals for the Museum of Natural History in New York. When air mail contracts were canceled in the winter of 1933-34, Quesada became chief pilot on the New York-Cleveland route; and on May 7, 1934, made a coast-to-coast flight in 49 minutes under the existing time record. Later he was successively assigned (as flying aide) to General Hugh Johnson, administrator of the National Recovery Act, and Secretary of War George H. Dern.

Quesada was promoted to captain (temporary) on April 20, 1935. Marked for further advancement, he took the full-year course at the Command and General Staff School, Fort Leavenworth, Kansas, in 1936-37, receiving the rank of captain (permanent) on January 23, 1937. From June 1937 to June 1938 he was flight commander of the First Bombardment Squadron at Mitchel Field, Long Island, New York; then spent a little over two years on detached service as technical adviser to the Argentine Air Force. When World War II was declared, Quesada was air observer in London, but from October 1940 until July 1941 he was again in Washington, as chief of the Foreign Liaison Section of the Intelligence Division of the office of the Chief of Air Corps (General H. H. Arnold). He was promoted to major (temporary) on December 30, 1940.

His country's entrance into World War II found Quesada in command of the Thirty-third Pursuit Group at Mitchel Field, duty which he had assumed in July 1941. Advanced to lieutenant colonel (temporary) on January 5,

1942, and to colonel (temporary) on March 1, he became in the month following, the commanding officer of the Philadelphia Region of the First Fighter Command. Promoted to brigadier general (temporary) on December 11, 1942, he returned to Mitchel Field to become commanding general of the First Air Defense Wing, which he took to Africa early in 1943. There he was placed in charge of the Twelfth Fighter Command and was also assigned as deputy commander of the Northwest African Coastal Air Force. Popular with his men (by whom he was nicknamed "Pete") and frequently referred to as "the pilots' general," he flew on numerous combat missions during the Tunisian, Sicilian and Italian campaigns, (he was the first American airman to land on Corsica) and qualified for the Purple Heart, before being transferred to England in October to take charge of the Ninth Fighter Command. (That command comprised two-engine fighter-bombers and fighters, such as the P-51, P-47 and P-38, used for short range bombing, reconnaissance, and escort work).

"He established advance headquarters of the Normandy beachhead on D-Day plus one," stated the Defense Department release, "and directed the planes of the Ninth Fighter Command as they furnished aerial cover and air support for the Allied invasion of the Continent." Promoted to major general (temporary) on April 28, 1944, before the invasion, and named commanding general of the Ninth Tactical Air Command (a component of the Ninth Air Force) after the beachheads had been secured, Quesada personally led a squadron of six P-47's on a dive bombing mission along the Cherbourg peninsula early in July. ("Man, it's good to get away from a desk for a change!" the forty-year-old pilot was quoted as saying.) Quesada's Ninth Tactical Air Command, working in conjunction and cooperation with the First Army, inflicted destruction on enemy troops and communications in the advance through northern France and Belgium, and in December 1944, during the comparatively few good flying days of the Battle of the Bulge, put on a nonstop dive bombing and strafing attack which was a major factor in the halting of the final major offensive of the Germans.

With the termination of the war in Europe Quesada returned to Washington to assume office as Assistant Chief of Air Staff for Intelligence, at Air Force headquarters (June 1945). In late February 1946, he was named commanding general of the Third Air Force, with headquarters at Tampa, Florida; and at the beginning of March, when the Air Force was reorganized into three new major commands—Strategic, Tactical, and Continental—became head of the Tactical Air Command. As such, he was described as having "overall charge of . . . fighters, fighter bombers, medium and light bombers and troop-carrier aircraft." Quesada was promoted to lieutenant general (temporary) on October 1, 1947, just before the commencement of war games conducted at Fort Benning, Georgia. (He became brigadier general (permanent) February 19, 1948, dating from December 12, 1942.) In maneuvers held at Eglin Field, Florida, a year later by the Tactical Air Command, the Navy and Marine Corps were participants. "The Air Force at long last recognizes that it cannot win a war alone," declared Quesada, and his formal report on the maneuvers (known as Operation Combine III) was later editorially praised by the New York *Times* as a "promising beginning" for unification of the national defense. In November 1948, after the National Defense Act had gone into effect, a further reorganization of the Air Force took place, and the Tactical Air Command was merged into a new Air Defense Command; whereupon Quesada was named Special Assistant to the Chief of Staff, United States Air Force (General Hoyt Vandenberg) and charged with building up the reserve components—at, it is said, the personal request of President Truman.

In August 1949, Quesada (stated the Defense Department biographical release) "was named by the Joint Chiefs of Staff to head a Special Planning Project" which, three months later (November) was disclosed to be the creation of Joint Task Force III of Army, Navy, Air Force and Atomic Energy Commission personnel to carry out new atom bomb tests at Eniwetok Atoll. It was revealed that command of this task force would go to Quesada, on a rotation basis among the services, previous Eniwetok tests having been commanded by a high-ranking officer of the Army or Navy.

Quesada has service ratings as senior pilot, combat observer, aircraft observer and technical observer. (He flew no fewer than eighty-six combat missions during World War II.) American decorations (other than those already mentioned) which he has received are the Distinguished Service Medal, the Legion of Merit, the Air Medal with two Silver Oak Leaf Clusters, the American Defense Ribbon, and the European-African-Mediterranean Theater Ribbon with seven battle participation stars. His foreign decorations include the French Legion of Honor and Croix de Guerre with Palm, the Croix de Guerre of Luxembourg, the Order of Adolphe of Nassau and the Polish Pilot's Badge. A Commander of the British Empire, he is also a Companion of the Order of the Bath. He is a member of the Racquet Club (Philadelphia), and the Columbia Country and University Clubs of Washington.

Elwood Quesada and Mrs. Kate Davis Pulitzer Putnam (granddaughter of Joseph Pulitzer of the New York *World* and widow of Captain Henry Ware Putnam) were married on October 12, 1946; in their family are one son, Thomas Ricardo, and two daughters. The officer has been described by Delos Lovelace of the New York *Sun* as "dark, short, bold."

References

N Y Herald Tribune II p3 D 24 '44 por; II p3 D 4 '49 por
N Y Sun p12 Jl 7 '44
Who's Who in America, 1950-51
World Biography (1948)

RAMA IX, King of Thailand (rä'mä) Dec. 5, 1927-

Address: Grand Palace, Bangkok, Thailand

Prince Bhumibol Adulyadej succeeded his elder brother, Ananda Mahidol, as King of Thailand on June 9, 1946, about six months before his twentieth birthday; but for a number of reasons, political and personal, his coronation was delayed until May 5, 1950. At that time, in accordance with the precedent of his dynasty, he assumed the name Rama IX.

Somdet Phra Chao Yu Hua Bhumibol Adulyadej is the ninth sovereign of the Chakri dynasty, established in 1782. His grandfather was Chulalongkorn (Rama V), the picturesque autocrat who was to become familiar to many readers and movie-goers through *Anna and the King of Siam* (the book by Margaret Landon) and its motion picture adaptation. Prajadhipok (Rama VII), the last absolute monarch of Thailand, was Bhumibol's uncle. The latter's half brother and heir, Prince Mahidol of Songkhla, married a Siamese commoner and studied to be a doctor. Mahidol and his wife, Princess Sangwalya Mahidol, lived in Europe and the United States for the completion of the former's medical training; and it was in Germany in 1925 that their second child and first son, the future King Ananda (Rama VIII), was born. Mahidol was a student at the Harvard Medical School when Bhumibol Adulyadej, the third and last of his children, was born in a Cambridge (Massachusetts) hospital on December 5, 1927. (His personal name, stated *Time*, is pronounced to approximate "poom-ee-pone a-doon-l-dade.")

While he completed his medical training, Mahidol (Bhumibol's father) and his family lived in Brookline, Massachusetts. When he received his M.D. degree from Harvard in 1928 he returned with his wife and children to Thailand, where he joined the staff of the Siriraj Hospital; he died suddenly a few months later. Prajadhipok, who was a ruler with absolute power, himself childless, sent his brother's children to Switzerland to be educated "for future important duties." Bhumibol was two years old at the time.

Thailand, "Land of the Free," (the ancient name was revived to replace the Malayan name Siam and adopted by the Government on July 20, 1948) is situated in Southeast Asia between Burma and Indo-China and extends into the Malay peninsula. It is a country of some 200,000 square miles in area and an estimated 18,000,000 population; Bangkok, its only large city, is the capital. In a predominantly agricultural economy the main products are rice and rubber; its sapphires, rubies, and teakwood and tin are famous, and elephants are more numerous there than in any other country. Buddhism is the state religion. In 1932 the People's party, in cooperation with the army and navy, effected a bloodless revolution to replace the absolute monarchy with a constitutional monarchy. The new constitution established a senate, equal franchise, and compulsory education. The State Council, consisting of the Premier and all Ministers, is named

RAMA IX, KING OF THAILAND

by the King and charged with the duty of conducting the government. Since 1942 an elected Assembly of People's Representatives has also participated in the government.

Prajadhipok, who agreed to the constitution of 1932, abdicated in 1935 in favor of his nephew, Ananda Mahidol, then ten years old. (Prajadhipok died in exile in England.) At Lausanne, Switzerland, the boy king, his mother, and his brother "marked their new position in life by moving out of a small apartment" (*Life*) into a fifteen-room villa overlooking the Lake of Geneva. Bhumibol was raised to the rank of His Royal Highness and was made an honorary officer (lieutenant) in the First Infantry Regiment of the Guards. That year (1935) Bhumibol left the Ecole Miremont in Lausanne for the Ecole Nouvelle de la Suisse Romande, a preparatory school. The brothers visited Thailand briefly in 1938-39.

During the greater part of World War II, Thailand was controlled by a pro-Japanese puppet government, so that Ananda and Bhumibol did not again see the land of their forefathers until late 1945, when the former (who had reached his majority on September 20) returned to Bangkok for his coronation. Before the ceremony could be performed, on June 9, 1946, Ananda was found dead in the palace from a gunshot wound. The question of accident or murder has never been solved. Bhumibol was named his brother's successor by act of Parliament. Two months later—after the legislature had appointed a two-man regency council to rule pending the eighteen-year-old monarch's coming of age—Bhumibol returned to Switzerland to complete his education.

Bhumibol, who received the degree of Bachelor of Letters from the Gymnase de Lausanne in 1945, had planned to become an architect. Following Ananda's death, however, he entered the University of Lausanne for the study of law. An absorbing interest was music, both classical (particularly Bach) and jazz: at Lausanne he would lead a seven-man amateur orchestra he had formed. It is said that their mutual interest in music led to Bhumibol's engagement to Mom Rachawong Srikit Kitiyakara, a distant cousin, the daughter of Thailand's Ambassador to London. They met in Paris when the Princess was fifteen; and later she was sent to school at Lausanne. Their engagement was announced August 12, 1949, on her seventeenth birthday.

When Bhumibol attained his majority on December 5, 1946, the Siamese government allocated several hundred thousand dollars for the ceremonial cremation of the remains of King Ananda, a necessary preliminary to the coronation of his successor, who was required by religious custom to light the funeral pyre. Unsettled conditions in 1947, following a *coup d'état* at Bangkok forced a postponement. In September 1948, court astrologers pronounced March 2, 1949, an auspicious date for the coronation; but in October Bhumibol was severely injured in an automobile accident near Lausanne. The sight of his right eye seemed threatened, and both cremation and coronation were postponed once more. The six days ending April 1, 1950, and May 5, 1950, were next found suitable for the cremation ceremonies and the coronation, respectively; and on March 24 the King and his entourage, including his fiancée, arrived in Bangkok. There he was greeted with an enthusiasm, to some extent interpreted as reflecting "the urge to re-embrace the certainty of an ancient institution" (New York *Times*, March 31, 1950) in a country which had undergone five constitutional and nineteen administrative changes in eighteen years, and which had large Chinese and Indo-Chinese minorities regarded as likely material for a Communist fifth column.

On April 28, 1950, the King and Princess Srikit were married in what has been described as "the shortest, simplest royal wedding ever held in the land of gilded elephants and white umbrellas" (New York *Times*), the ceremony being performed by His Majesty's aged grandmother, Queen Sawang Vadhana. The picturesque coronation ceremony duly took place on May 5, at which time Bhumibol mounted the octagonal throne, placed on his head the royal crown; then, after reading a command raising his bride to the status of Queen of Thailand, he led a procession to pay homage to the Emerald Buddha, symbol of the Thai faith, and in the presence of the Prince Patriarch proclaimed himself defender of the faith. Assuming the royal name of his line, Thailand's new king became Rama IX.

In his first address to the Thai Parliament, at the opening of a special session, Rama IX exhorted that body to do everything within its power to prevent the entry into Thailand of the Communist conflict in progress in near-by countries. Rama IX and his Queen were expected shortly to return to Switzerland for the completion of their university studies, a matter he would be back in Thailand, to assume his manifest popularity and the "Red peril" from Communist China, there were predictions that he would be back in Thailand, to assume his full sovereign's responsibilities, before that span of time should have elapsed.

In addition to playing several musical instruments, King Rama IX is a composer of popular songs and dance tunes; one of these, a beguine entitled "Blue Night" (lyric by Prince Chakraband, the royal chamberlain) was incorporated in the 1950 Broadway revue *Peep Show.* "Blue Night" was described as "haunting and oriental." All his profits from the songs are to go to Royal Thailand Charities, Bhumibol has decreed. Next to music, photography is the favorite hobby of Thailand's "shy, slender, bespectacled" monarch.

References

Life 28:121-2+ F 26 '50 pors
Time 55:28+ Ap 3 '50 pors
International Who's Who, 1950
10 Eventful Years (1947)
Who's Who in America, 1950-51
World Biography (1948)

RAZMARA, ALI (răz-mä"rä' à-lē') 1901-
Prime Minister of Iran

Address: Teheran, Iran

The Prime Minister of Iran, Ali Razmara, has been called one of the most powerful leaders his country has known since Riza Shah Pahlevi seized the Government in 1921 and formed the present dynasty. A soldier by training, Razmara took part in the Shah's ten-year campaign to bring the nomadic tribes into submission. He served as a professor at and later as director of the Military Cadet College in Teheran, and has written on military geography. In 1946 General Razmara was made Chief of Staff of the Imperial Iranian Army. His appointment as Prime Minister, in June 1950, was his first civil office in a country which is regarded as an area of potential trouble in the "cold war" between Soviet Russia and the Western democracies.

Ali Razmara was born in Teheran in 1901, the son of Amir Paudjeh Hadji Mohammad Razmara and Anwar ol Molouk. His father, who is described as a scholar, was an army officer. The boy was enrolled in the Ajhdassieh school and in the Alliance Française (both in Teheran), where he completed his elementary and secondary education. In 1918 he entered military school in Teheran. Upon his graduation two years later, he joined the Ghazagh Division of the Army, and in 1922 he became an adjutant in the Infantry Division of Pahlavi. In accordance with the Shah's plans for westernizing the Persian Army, Razmara was then sent to Europe, to train at St. Cyr, the military academy of France, following which he served in a tank division of the French Army. He remained in France three years.

ALI RAZMARA

Upon his return to Iran, Razmara served in the Shah's pacification of the tribes in the outlying provinces. He was made head of an army division in Kirmanshah in 1927 and in 1931 was appointed head of a division in Lauristan. In 1933 Razmara was recalled to Teheran to assist General Gendre, leader of a French military mission, at the Military Cadet College. At this time Razmara was named head of the geographical section of the General Staff of the Army and appointed professor at the college. In 1935 he was made director of studies at the college and in 1938 taught infantry tactics, preparing a textbook on that subject. During these years, he also wrote twenty volumes on Persian military geography, some of which have been translated into English and Russian. He was aided in this by his brother, who is the inventor of a method of topographic photography. In 1940 Razmara was made head of the First Army.

During World War II, Russian and British troops entered Iran, causing the abdication of pro-Nazi Riza Shah Pahlevi and the formation of a constitutional monarchy under his son, Mohammed Riza Pahlevi [50]. As a result of the occupation there was considerable disintegration and loss of morale in the Iranian Army. The Shah, who exercises supreme command, promoted Razmara to be general and chief of the general staff in 1943. In three months Razmara re-formed the first division and within two years had reorganized the entire command of Iran's 150,000-man army.

During 1945 a Soviet-supported movement for self-government gained strength in Azerbaijan, the northwestern province of Iran bordering on Russia. Razmara led the expedition which suppressed the movement and brought about the withdrawal of Russian troops in May 1946 under pressure by the United Nations. Russia, however, had gained a promise of oil concessions, a promise that was later rejected

RAZMARA, ALI—*Continued*

by the Majlis (Parliament). In the course of the contest for control of the Iranian Government between pro-Russian and anti-Russian interests, Russia complained about the presence of an American military mission that was aiding in the reorganization of Iran's 20,000-man national police force. In November 1948 the anti-Russian party gained complete control in Iran when Mohammed Maraghei Said was appointed Prime Minister. Widespread hunger and unrest during the next few years provided a fertile field for propaganda by the country's outlawed Tudeh (Communist) party. In an effort to raise living standards, the Shah called for a liberalized constitution and engaged Overseas Consultants, Inc., a group of American engineering firms, to draw up a seven-year plan for the development of Iran.

When Said resigned as Prime Minister in March 1950, he was succeeded by Ali Kahn Mansur, head of the commission for the seven-year plan. Mansur's government was widely criticized, however, for "inaction and indecision" (New York *Times*). He resigned June 26, and General Haj Ali Razmara was appointed in his place. Described by Albion Ross (of the *Times*) as "a trusted friend of the Shah" who had been "held in reserve as a last hope," Razmara's appointment was regarded as a bulwark against the threat of Soviet attack. Also feared was the instigation of civil war by the underground Tudeh party. "There can be no doubt," wrote Ross, "that if the situation requires it he [Razmara] is capable . . . of introducing dictatorial government to halt the disintegration of the Iranian state."

Ridding his Cabinet of "distrusted professional politicians" (the *Times*), Razmara reappointed only two of the Ministers who had served under Mansur. In announcing his program, the new Prime Minister declared that his Government would seek decentralization of power and the delegation of authority to provincial councils. It would also strive to improve living conditions, reduce the high cost of living, and make tax paying more popular by using that money for local improvements. His "pro-American" Cabinet won a vote of confidence in the Majlis on July 4 and in the Senate on July 10. The arrival at this time of Henry F. Grady [47] as United States Ambassador was looked upon as a sign that American aid would soon be forthcoming.

On July 14, 1950, Razmara announced that military supplies valued at $10,000,000 to $15,-000,000 were on their way from the United States to Iran; he made a plea for economic aid for his rehabilitation program, which he estimated would cost over $100,000,000 a year. He declared that such help was necessary if an economic and political crisis were to be averted during the coming winter. Pointing to Korea as "a frightening example," he is reported by Clyde Farnsworth (New York *World Telegram and Sun*) to have observed that "almost any amount of money within reason which would keep Iran from falling to Russia, would be a bargain for the United States."

Meanwhile, Razmara received complaints from Soviet Russia that surveys and exploratory oil operations near the Soviet border were creating an "abnormal" situation. Denying these charges, he arranged for Soviet-Iranian talks aimed at a trade agreement, repatriation of Iranian soldiers, and the return of eleven tons of gold remaining in the Soviet Union since the end of the war.

Razmara's program for decentralizing the Government did not win the support of the Majlis, which is composed largely of wealthy landowners and businessmen. In September, after the Majlis had recessed, the Prime Minister announced he would put through his program by constitutional authority. Accordingly, he cut bread prices 15 per cent in Teheran and lowered sugar prices slightly, but because of the war in Korea his efforts were counteracted by increases in the prices of other essential commodities. The good harvest of 1950 was said to be aiding Razmara in his resistance to communism.

The Prime Minister of Iran has received all the decorations of the Iranian Army and has been honored seven times for outstanding service. He and his wife, Jhamar Hedayat, have a daughter and four sons, the eldest of whom is studying in the United States. Razmara's hair is dark, graying slightly at the temples, and he has a small brown mustache. His eyes are blue, his wiry figure is above average in height. He has a reputation for "relentless honesty and hard discipline." Since becoming Prime Minister, he has dropped the title of General, preferring to be called "Mister."

References

Epoque Ja 5 '49
Monde Je 28 '50
Washington (D.C.) Post p2B Jl 2 '50
por

REDGRAVE, MICHAEL Mar. 20, 1908-
Actor; stage director

Address: Bedford House, Chiswick Mall, London W.4, England; c/o Universal-International, Universal City, Calif.

Michael Redgrave, known to Americans primarily as a motion picture performer, enjoys a considerable reputation in his native England as a stage actor and director. London theatergoers know him for his performances with the Old Vic Company, and his direction and acting in such plays as *Uncle Harry* and *Jacobowsky and the Colonel*; and New Yorkers saw him in *Macbeth* in 1948. Recently notable of his screen appearances have been the British-made *Fame Is The Spur* and the Hollywood-made *Mourning Becomes Electra* (1947). In the latter, the American National Board of Review of Motion Pictures called his performance the best characterization of the year.

Michael Scudamore Redgrave was born in Bristol, England, on March 20, 1908, into a theatrical family. His father, George Ellsworthy Redgrave, was an actor, known as Roy Redgrave; Michael's mother used her maiden name, Margaret Scudamore, on the stage. His grandfather, too, was an actor. The boy, however, had little thought of following in his parents' footsteps; rather, he thought of becoming a writer. After study at Clifton College, at Magdalene College (Cambridge), and in Germany and France, Redgrave received a Bachelor of Arts degree in 1930 from Cambridge, with honors in French, German, and English.

Appointment as modern language master at Cranleigh, a private school, followed. There he became interested in stage production and helped to put on school plays. He also took part as a "walk-on" in the Stratford-on-Avon Shakespeare Festival during his holidays. Having decided to enter theatrical production, Redgrave went to London, where he found (he told a *Theatre World* interviewer) that in order to become a producer, he must have acting experience. He was auditioned for the Old Vic Company, but before he was informed of his acceptance by that group, he had arranged an audition with William Armstrong of the Liverpool Repertory Theatre. With the latter company Redgrave made his professional stage debut, on August 30, 1934, as Roy Darwin in *Counsellor-at-Law.*

During his two years with the Liverpool Repertory, the actor appeared in *Libel, The Flowers of the Forest, Youth at the Helm, Boyd's Shop, Storm in a Teacup,* and *Twelfth Night.* In 1936 he refused an offer for a part in a play which, as it turned out, was short-lived, to appear with the Old Vic under Tyrone Guthrie's direction, giving as his first performance Ferdinand in *Love's Labour's Lost.* In his performances in *The Country Wife* and as Orlando in *As You Like It,* Redgrave attracted the notice of British critics. He remained with Old Vic for a year and had roles in *The Witch of Edmonton, Hamlet, The Bat, Henry V, A Ship Comes Home,* and *Three Set Out.*

Michael Redgrave's name became well known when he was appearing in John Gielgud's company (1938). After that season Redgrave, who likes to work in repertory, appeared in a number of plays, including *White Guard, Family Reunion, Beggar's Opera* (1940), *Thunder Rock* (1940), *The Duke in Darkness* (1942) which he directed, *A Month in the Country* (1943), and *Parisienne* (1943), which he also directed. In 1944 he directed (in collaboration with William Armstrong) and appeared in the British version of a New York play, *Uncle Harry.* Of it James Redfern wrote in the *Spectator:* "I have never seen this highly gifted actor to such advantage as in this truly consummate display of magnificent acting." The *New Statesman and Nation* critic: "All that acting, imagination (and hard work) can do to realize the characters is done. . . .How brilliantly he shuffles, coughs . . . on the edge of hysteria. One criticism: he slips over the edge too often."

In 1945 the actor directed and appeared in *Jacobowsky and the Colonel,* a play which had been successful in New York. "Mr. Michael Redgrave as the quixotic Colonel . . . dominates the play," commented the *New Statesman* critic.

MICHAEL REDGRAVE

"He enjoys his opportunity for a bravura performance and his enthusiasm is infectious. . . . Mr. Redgrave has done much excellent work on the production which, in this critic's eyes, is altogether superior to that . . . which ran for so many months in New York."

New York audiences in 1948 for the first time saw Michael Redgrave on the stage, in *Macbeth,* with a cast directed by Norris Houghton. The New York performance directly followed a London run. Previous to the Broadway production Redgrave had written for the New York *Times* (March 28, 1948) his and Houghton's conception of the play: "*Macbeth* is . . . 'pure theater' in the sense that we say of a composition that it is 'pure music' or 'pure painting'. . . .We are aiming in this *Macbeth* to reach back into a world of semibarbarism, to mirror accurately a primitive people." In both London and New York, critical opinion of Redgrave's interpretation of Macbeth was divided. Louis Kronenberger (*PM*) said, "The more Mr. Redgrave goes in for heavy villainy, the more he reveals himself essentially a lightweight. Now and again one glimpses a competent performer." Richard Watts, Jr., of the New York *Post* said "On the whole, its defect is a lack of tragic power and consistent eloquence." John Chapman (New York *Daily News*) thought the part was "managed subtly"; and Brooks Atkinson (New York *Times*): "Completely the master of the part, he develops Macbeth out of timorous ambition into the reckless violence of the climax."

In the meantime, the stage actor Redgrave had become also a motion picture actor with a contract that permitted him to spend half of each year working in each medium. Most of his films have been British-made, with American showings following their British premières. His first picture, in 1938, was *The Lady Vanishes,* Alfred Hitchcock's early famous sus-

REDGRAVE, MICHAEL—*Continued*

pense film. As on the stage, the screen roles he has played have ranged from comedy (*Jeannie, Kipps*) to drama (*Thunder Rock*) and melodrama (*Dead of Night*). In those roles Redgrave pleased the critics, and in 1942 was voted one of the first ten money-making stars in British production. Other of his British-made films are *Climbing High, The Stars Look Down, The Way to the Stars, The Years Between* and *The Man Within*. In 1947, with the release of *The Captive Heart* (in which he plays the part of a central figure in a prisoner-of-war camp) and of *Fame Is The Spur* (adapted from the Howard Spring novel of a working man who rises to a post in the British Cabinet), Redgrave was named one of the year's best actors. *Fame Is The Spur* was released in 1949 in the United States, where it received special comment, with "sensitive", "skillful", "intelligent," and "forceful" being widely applied to the actor's performance.

In 1947 Redgrave went to Hollywood to make *Mourning Becomes Electra*, a film version of the O'Neill drama. The English actor, in the opinion of Bosley Crowther (*Times*) and Howard Barnes (New York *Herald Tribune*), sustained an otherwise unsatisfactory picture; Barnes called Redgrave's performance "beautifully modulated and intensely moving." The National Board of Review of Motion Pictures voted his characterization the best of the year. While in Hollywood, Redgrave also made *The Secret Beyond The Door*.

In 1949 it was reported that Redgrave would, upon completion of *The Astonished Heart*, request a year's suspension of his movie contract wth J. Arthur Rank in order to play a full season with the Old Vic Company. Later in the year the actor was signed by the director of the Danish National Open Air Theatre to play Hamlet at the 1950 Elsinore Castle performance of the classic. (The presentation of *Hamlet* at Elsinore is an annual event.) Redgrave, who is also author of two plays (*The Seventh Man* and *Circus Boy*, both produced in Liverpool in 1935), believes that the theater can benefit from discerning criticism. In 1943, after the failure of *Blow Your Own Trumpet* (his direction) he appealed in the *New Statesman and Nation* "to the critics as a body to aid and not to hinder the renaissance in the theater which we sincerely desire and which cannot occur without new writers." He asked the critics not to write what they might consider "good copy" at the expense of good criticism.

In 1941-42 Redgrave was a seaman in the British Navy, from which he was discharged for medical reasons. His height of six feet three inches has earned him the title of "England's tallest trouper." He weighs 176 pounds. Blue eyes, brown hair, and an "occasional" mustache also are among his physical characteristics. Married since 1935 to Rachel Kempson, an actress who has appeared with him in several productions, Redgrave is the father of a son and two daughters. For recreation he turns to music, walking, squash, and swimming.

References

Theatre World 31 :34-5 Ja '39 por
Who's Who, 1949
Who's Who in the Theatre (1947)
Winchester's Screen Encyclopedia (1948)
World Biography (1948)

REED, CAROL Dec. 30, 1906- Motion picture producer and director
Address: h. 213 Kings Rd., Chelsea, London, S.W.3, England

One of England's foremost film directors, Carol Reed is best known in America for his postwar pictures *Odd Man Out, The Fallen Idol*, and *The Third Man*. Before World War II he directed the popular thriller *Night Train*. Serving with the British Army Film Unit during the war, he was the English director assigned to work on the joint Anglo-American documentary of the Western front, *The True Glory*. For *The Fallen Idol* Reed was awarded the New York Film Critics' scroll for the best direction of the year 1949. *The Third Man* won the Grand Prix at the annual international Cannes (France) Film Festival (1949) and the British Film Tribunal award.

Carol Reed was born December 30, 1906 in London, England. He was educated at what is reputed to be the oldest British public (private) school, King's School, Canterbury. On leaving school, he spent six months with his elder brother in America, then entered the acting profession in England. He made his stage debut at the age of eighteen in London, appearing as Constantine and Justin in *Heraclius*. After being given parts in minor productions, in 1927 he acted the role of a sleuth in *The Terror*, a play by Edgar Wallace, English writer of detective stories. Reed entered association with the author, acting in and directing his melodramas until Wallace's death in 1932. Plays produced by the Reed-Wallace association include *The Flying Squad*; *Persons Unknown*, 1929; *The Calendar*, 1929; *On the Spot*, 1930 (also produced by Reed in New York in 1930); *The Smoky Cell* and *Charles the Third*. In 1933 Reed directed *Poet's Secret* and the same year assisted in open-air productions of *Twelfth Night, As You Like It*, and *A Midsummer Night's Dream*.

Early in the 1930's the actor-director left the theater for the motion picture studio to be a dialogue director for Associated Talking Pictures. During 1933-34 he served as assistant director, working on some early Gracie Fields [41] pictures among others, and in 1935 attained the status of full director with the film *Midshipman Easy*. Among Reed-directed pictures which followed were: *Laburnum Grove*, 1936 (a comedy-mystery from the J. B. Priestley play); *Talk of the Devil* (1936; for which Reed wrote the original story); *Bank Holiday* (1937; called *Three on a Holiday* for its American showing); *A Girl Must Live* (1938). With these, the director won a reputation for producing authentic and lively pictures of the working classes. In 1939 appeared *The Stars Look Down*, which adapted to the screen the A. J. Cronin novel of the same name about life in a mining community. In commending the "brilliant restraint" of the direction, a New York *Times* review stated, "Reed has produced a study of English miners that has the breath of life in it."

Night Train, filmed in 1939, brought the director popular acclaim, showing to advantage the effects of his familiarity with the "thriller" genre. Written by the famous team of Launder and Gilliat, who had done the script for the screen play for Alfred Hitchcock's '41 *The Lady Vanishes, Night Train* was almost invariably compared to that chase classic, frequently in terms resembling the praise voiced by William Boehnel in the New York *World-Telegram* of December 30, 1940: "One of the best melodramas I have ever seen . . . so typically in the Hitchcock vein that you might take it for one of the portly director's best efforts." It was followed by *The Girl in the News*, (1940), *Kipps* (1940; from the H. G. Wells novel), and *The Young Mr. Pitt* (1941). The last-named presented the life of the famous English prime minister (played by Robert Donat) in a series of authenticated episodes which made extensive use of his actual speeches. A commentator in *Sight and Sound* (periodical publication of the British Film Institute) commended the historical truth of the treatment.

With the advent of World War II, the realistic bent in Reed's work came to the fore when he directed for the Ministry of Information *A Letter from Home*, a semi-factual presentation of wartime life in England. In 1941 the director joined the Army and with its film unit made the British War Office training picture, *The New Lot*. This army short, depicting the molding of a group of untrained, unenthusiastic civilians from several walks of life into front-line soldiers, was taken as the basis for a full-length commercial picture, *The Way Ahead*, filmed under the direction of Reed on loan from the Army. An account from London (where *The Way Ahead* was released on D-Day) to *Variety* attributed to Reed's direction "the underlying genuineness of the picture as a semi- documentary." An American reaction to a showing a year later commended the director's "eye for presenting the infantryman as a real person" (*Christian Science Monitor*, June 4, 1945).

The joint British-American documentary of the war on the Western front, *The True Glory*, (made at General Eisenhower's suggestion), was codirected by Reed and Garson Kanin '41 (*A Man to Remember* and *The Great Man Votes* were two of Kanin's pictures). From more than 10,000,000 feet of film, shot in actual combat by service cameramen, they produced a war picture "of overwhelming eloquence" in the words of Bosley Crowther. With "sharp, clear editing," (Otis L. Guernsey, Jr., New York *Herald Tribune*), emphasis was placed on the man in the ranks. The picture had a sound track recorded by actual combatants and an introduction spoken by General Eisenhower. Perhaps the highest tribute paid the movie appeared in Crowther's column: "Veterans of Europe seeing it say, 'This is how it was.'" It was chosen as the best film

CAROL REED

of the year (1945) by the National Board of Review of Motion Pictures (Reed's *The Way Ahead* was named by the board as among the top ten) and was reported to be one of the ten that grossed the largest receipts at box offices. The New York Film Critics awarded it one of two special scrolls for documentary pictures.

Director Reed credits his wartime directing experiences with contributing a greater sense of realism to his work, according to an article by Ezra Goodman in *Theatre Arts*. This quality in motion pictures, he believes, has a stronger appeal in England than in America The same source indicated that Reed regards the function of the director as the prime factor in a production, but considers it to be an interpretive rather than originative role. Of technique he has declared, "If there is any one rule I have, it is that I want my films to be true to life and to the characters they are portraying and let the technique suit itself to the material at hand." Reed named William Wyler (director of *Dead End, The Little Foxes*) as one of the directors he most admired, and pointed out that the art of the latter's technique lay in its inconspicuousness.

Reed has been called "a players' director," his considerate and efficient treatment of casts being particularly remarked. The tenet that cooperation is of foremost importance on the set and that no picture is a one-man job Reed claims to have learned from the Hollywood director J. Walter Ruben, whom he assisted in the making of a British version of *Java Head*. That not all the work of a picture takes place before the cameras is strikingly evidenced by the English director's procedure. He is said to spend four months preparing a script for filming (he rates the validity of the story high among the requirements for a good picture), six months shooting, and two months editing; in all these processes, Reed has pointed out,

REED, CAROL—*Continued*

an English director takes a more directly active part than his American counterpart, who can count on the resources of a more elaborate organization. This organization is one of the aspects of Hollywood for which the Englishman has expressed admiration. It is a part of Reed's approach to do a good deal of shooting on the actual locale of his pictures rather than on artificial sets. He also likes to make the early sequences of a film in the order in which they appear, to help the cast become oriented to the story. "I believe in the story itself, in sincerity and in transmitting a feeling about people," he has said.

The first Reed postwar film, *Odd Man Out* (1946, starring James Mason '47) was termed by *Cue* "a great and tragic drama" of a manhunt in Dublin's alleys. The picture received comparison with *The Informer*, directed by John Ford '41, but was judged by Bosley Crowther to have "neither the substance nor the clarity of Mr. Ford's classic film," a hunt for a philosophy contained in the manhunt being considered a confusing element which detracted from the pacing of the pursuit. With this picture, Reed became Britain's "most-talked-of picture director," according to a London dispatch to the New York *Times* by Paul P. Kennedy; the same article stated it was this film that "brought him to America's general attention." *The Fallen Idol*, (story by Graham Greene, English author), which appeared the next year, won Reed the New York Film Critics' scroll for the best direction of 1949, his handling of Bobby Henrey, inexperienced child actor, receiving general commendation. The outstanding feature of the "sleek and urbane thriller" in the opinion of Bosley Crowther was "the brilliance of Mr. Reed . . . now generally conceded to be the top director on the British film scene." British *Sight and Sound* said, "The film is agreeable and intelligent, and cleverly done, but not indeed a universal masterpiece."

Reed's next picture, *The Third Man*, a tale of a manhunt in Vienna (with screen play by Graham Greene), was praised for its "technical virtuosity." "In a few broad strokes of character and incident Reed has caught the atmosphere of Vienna of the postwar period," said Archer Winsten (in the New York *Post*). "Superbly acted," was *Cue*'s comment. The director was responsible for the use of a zither to provide the musical accompaniment widely remarked upon as the outstanding feature of the film, in which it was said to supply the role of "emotional commentator." At the 1949 Cannes film festival, the picture was accorded the Grand Prix. It also brought its director the British Film Tribunal award. Critical estimation on both sides of the Atlantic, paid tribute to it as a tour de force.

At a meeting held in 1946 to organize a British film academy, Reed was chosen to be one of a nine-man committee to plan its establishment. The producer-director is married to Penelope Dudley Ward. (His first wife was Diana Wynyard, who played in *Kipps*.) "Serious" is the adjective frequently applied to the

English director. Descriptions give him a tall, slim build, a long oval face, light-brown hair, blue-gray eyes, and a "sensitive mouth."

References

N Y Times p3 S 7 '41 por; II p6 Ap 6
  '47; II p5 N 30 '47 por
N Y Times Mag p18 Ja 15 '50 por
Theatre Arts 31:57 My '47
International Motion Picture Almanac,
  1947-48
Who's Who, 1949
Who's Who in the Theatre (1947)
Winchester's Screen Encyclopedia (1948)
World Biography (1948)

REESE, HAROLD (HENRY) July 23, 1919 Baseball player

Address: b. c/o Brooklyn National League Baseball Club, 215 Montague St., Brooklyn 2, N.Y.

"One of the finest shortstops of all time," in the opinion of John Lardner, is Harold ("Pee Wee") Reese, captain of the Dodgers, the National League Brooklyn team. Reese has been rated high as a shortstop since he began playing baseball professionally at the age of eighteen with the Louisville Colonels. He was not quite twenty-one when he entered a major league, as a Dodger, in 1940. In the course of ten years Reese played in a thousand games, made a thousand hits, and was acclaimed by the Brooklyn team as "the best-hitting shortstop in the National League." He was also to break his own and the former all-time Brooklyn fielding average.

Harold Henry Reese was born in Ekron, Kentucky, on July 23, 1919, of Dutch and Irish ancestry. *PM* reported that his father, a yard detective for the Louisville and Nashville Railroad, was an enthusiastic baseball player in his free time. While no baseball feat is recorded about his son, in 1932 thirteen-year-old Harold became the national marble champion of the United States. Because he used the "peewee" type of marble as his shooter, he earned the nickname of "Pee Wee." Although that is the origin of the name, he was an unusually short boy, according to Arthur Daley (New York *Times*). Daley wrote that that accounted for Reese not trying out for his high school baseball team until he was a senior. In that year, he did play as a second baseman in a few games. (The adult Reese is of medium height.)

When Reese was graduated from high school in Louisville, he went to work as a cable-splicer for the telephone company. He spent his spring and summer week ends playing on the baseball team of the New Covenant Presbyterian Church in his city. In 1937 his team led the church league and was rewarded by a trip to New York to see the Giants and the Yankees in the World Series. Some sources say that it was Reese's performance at the final game of the church league that won him a place on the Louisville Colonels in 1938, while others say he tried out for the team "on his own." In either case, he was on the 1938 line-up of the team as shortstop.

"Because of Harold (Pee Wee) Reese, a baseball team was bought and sold," wrote Al Hirshberg and Joe McKenney in the tenth series of *Famous Athletes of Today*. At the time Reese joined the Colonels, the team was trailing the American Association, a triple-A minor league. Reese's presence did not suddenly pull Louisville out of its slump (although he batted .277, fielded .939, and was "the smoothest operator in the short field that the American Association had seen in a long time"), and the team was offered for sale. Reese's performance was so outstanding, however, that Tom Yawkey, owner of the Boston Red Sox, bought a third interest in the team with the expectation of bringing Reese to New England in the future. In 1939 Reese improved his hitting, bringing his percentage up to .279 and his fielding to .943. He led the association in triples (18) and stolen bases (35). In 1940 he was bought by the Brooklyn Dodgers for some $40,000.

Reese was a much-hailed rookie when he entered the National League. The Brooklyn manager, Leo Durocher, who had been a shortstop, asserted, "He's the best lead-off hitter in the National League, and if there is a better one in the American League I never heard of him." New York *Sun*'s Edward T. Murphy wrote: "Durocher is one of the eight National League managers who acclaims Reese the prize among this year's rookies. Seven managers envy Leo because he has the brilliant youngster." Reese's first year was cut short on August 15, 1940, when he fractured his heel sliding into second base. In 84 games, he earned a batting average of .272 and fielded .960.

In 1941 right-handed Reese played in his first World Series. Only a moderately good hitter, in 20 times at bat during the series, Reese got 4 hits, and 3 errors. He also led the National League in errors with a total 47, his fielding average of .946 was the lowest in his major league career, and his batting, too, hit an all-time low of .229. The shortstop's putout record, however, was the highest in the league that year—346; and again, in 1942, he was the National League leader in putouts—337. In 1942 Reese was chosen for the All-Star team. In this he only came up to the plate once, did not get on base, but his one assist was good. For the season, Reese's record was: batting, .255, fielding .959. He led the league with 482 assists and in double plays.

During the war, from 1943 to 1945, Pee Wee Reese was in the Navy. Around the time he was discharged with the rank of chief petty officer, the Dodgers had decided to groom another baseball player, a shortstop, by sending him to their AAA International League subsidiary. The player was Jackie Robinson [47]. By the time Robinson was brought to the major leagues in 1946 Reese was bettering his prewar record in the short field; Robinson was assigned to second base and the two became an infield team. "There have been a few stronger second-base partnerships in the history of baseball, but only a few," John Lardner wrote in the New York *Times Magazine* in 1949. Besides their fielding coordination, Lardner pointed out that when one is on base, the other usually

Brooklyn National League
HAROLD REESE

drives him home; and when both are on base, they combine to keep the opposing team's infielders busy. According to Lardner the two are the highest-paid players on the Brooklyn team, Reese probably earning $25,000 annually, and Robinson $20,000.

In 1946 Reese made a Brooklyn record for shortstops by fielding .966 (he batted .284). Both his fielding and batting averages were exactly the same in 1947. In that year (when Reese made his second All-Star and World Series appearances) his series record was 5 runs and 7 hits. The 1947 records show that he walked to first base 104 times, tying for league lead. In 1948 Reese made his third All-Star appearance. His record for that year was .274 in batting and .962 in fielding.

Reese was the leading National League shortstop in 1949 with a fielding average of .977. He also led the league, with 132 runs, 155 games played, and 316 putouts; his batting average was .279. The tabulation for the 1949 World Series shows at bat, 19; runs, 2; hits, 6; batting average, .316; putouts, 5; 1 error; fielding average, .933. Of all National League shortstops, Reese received the most votes from the Baseball Writers of America in determining the 1949 Major League All-Star Team. He made another mid-season All-Star appearance for the National League, and ranked fifth in the voting for the National League's "Most Valuable Player." When, in 1950, Reese was elected captain of the Dodgers, he was in his tenth year, and by the middle of May had played in his thousandth major league game and made his thousandth hit.

Light-haired and brown-eyed, Reese is said to have a "puckish" and "youthful" appearance that belies his years. He is five feet, nine and a half inches tall, and weighs 178 pounds. Married to Dorothy Walton on March 29, 1942, Reese is the father of a daughter, Barbara Lee. Two other sports which keep him in trim

REESE, HAROLD—*Continued*

are golf and bowling. In a Columbia Broadcasting System Documentary Unit radio presentation, *Play Ball*, Reese's life, which began as "a typical American kid with the great dream of every American youngster . . . of playing ball in the big leagues," was used to tell the story of baseball.

References

N Y Times V p2 S 7 '47

Hirshberg, A. and McKenney, J. Famous American Athletes of Today (1947)

Waldman, F. Famous American Athletes of Today (1949)

Who's Who in the Major Leagues (1947)

REESE, PEE WEE *See* Reese, H. H.

RENNEBOHM, OSCAR (rĕn'nĕ-bōm) May 25, 1889- Governor of Wisconsin

Address: b. State Capitol, Madison, Wis.; h. 130 E. Gilman St., Madison, Wis.

Oscar Rennebohm is one of the twelve Republicans who were elected to governorships in the United States in November 1948. A pharmacist by vocation and the president of a chain of drugstores, the Wisconsin Governor had been in politics for only four years: he first sought office in 1944, when he ran for and was elected to the lieutenant-governorship of his State. Re-elected in 1946 he became Acting Governor on March 13, 1947, following the death of the late Walter S. Goodland. Rennebohm's term expires in January 1951.

One of the eight children (four sons and four daughters) of William Carl and Julia

OSCAR RENNEBOHM

(Brandt) Rennebohm, Oscar Rennebohm was born on a farm near Leeds in Columbia County, Wisconsin, on May 25, 1889. From the time he was ten, however, his boyhood was passed in Milwaukee; there he attended East Division High School and was a member of several of the school's athletic teams. Graduated in 1908, he then worked to pay his expenses through the University of Wisconsin, in three years, majoring in pharmacy and taking the Ph.G. degree in 1911.

On leaving college he became the manager of a drugstore in Madison, and a year later (1912) bought the first of what subsequently became a chain of thirteen pharmacies in or around Madison employing some five hundred persons. Another similar purchase was made before Rennebohm's rise in the business world was interrupted by service in the Navy during World War I (he volunteered as an able-bodied seaman and rose to the commission grade of ensign). After the war, between 1920 and 1928, Rennebohm acquired eleven additional pharmacies. The chain was incorporated in 1929 as Rennebohm Drug Stores, with the future Governor as president. Twenty years a member of the Wisconsin State Board of Pharmacy, Rennebohm has also served as president of the Wisconsin Pharmaceutical Association, vice-president of the American Pharmaceutical Association, and treasurer of the National Association of Retail Druggists, and has been a recipient of the *American Druggist* citation for outstanding community work. The son of a farmer, he retained an interest in agriculture, purchased a modern 175-acre dairy farm near Madison which he still operates, developed a herd of purebred Holstein cattle, and served as a director of the Dane County Holstein Breeders Association. He is an honorary member of Future Farmers of America.

At State primaries in the same year Rennebohm made his first bid for political office, the goal he sought (on the Republican ticket) being the lieutenant governorship. There were no fewer than six other contestants; the reason for that, it was suggested, was that the Republican gubernatorial candidate, the liberally inclined Acting Governor Walter S. Goodland was 82 years old, and the prospect of stepping up to the chief executive's chair was, accordingly, far from improbable.

Rennebohm's qualifications as a politically balanced running mate for Goodland were evident; as a successful businessman he enjoyed the confidence of the commercial groups, he could appeal to the agricultural voter, and his expressed views were satisfactorily "middle of the road" in a State which, until two years earlier, had been effectively dominated politically by the La Follettes. Rennebohm was victorious at the primaries and in the November election came into office in a Republican landslide which sent to Madison a State Senate of 22 Republicans, only 6 Democrats, 5 La Follette Progressives; and an Assembly of 75 Republicans, 19 Democrats, and 6 Progressives. (Goodland won over his Democrat opponent D. W. Hoan, former Socialist and Mayor of Milwaukee, by a plurality of 161,000.)

The Wisconsin legislature meets biennially in odd-numbered years; there is ordinarily only one session, though it can be reconvened by the chief executive for action on specifically named measures. In the 1945 session friction early developed between Governor Goodland and his party's economy-minded "regulars." The budget he submitted was the largest in Wisconsin's history, and he offered an ambitious school-building plan. As the 1946 primaries approached, Goodland was "denied" renomination by the Republican State convention. Meanwhile, at Portage on March 17, the La Follette Progressives had voted to rejoin the Republican party; they proposed backing Goodland, who declined their support. In consequence there was a three-cornered race in the primary (August 13), with Goodland coming out ahead, the former Progressive Ralph L. Immell second, and the "machine" candidate trailing badly. Rennebohm was renominated for lieutenant governor, and both Goodland and Rennebohm were re-elected by comfortable margins in November.

Governor Goodland passed away on March 12, 1947, about two months after resuming office; and on the following day Rennebohm was sworn in as Acting Governor. "His friends," stated *Newsweek,* "regarded him as a conservative; they expected him to steer a safe and cautious course while laying the groundwork for his campaign for an elective term next year. Two changes were, however, expected immediately: a reconciliation between the Governor's office and the potent State machine led by Thomas E. Coleman, and a more intimate and amiable relationship with the State legislature G.O.P. majority." On July 23, 1947 the Governor signed a bill outlawing strikes in public utilities companies, providing $250 fines or one year prison terms for strikers, and setting up a compulsory arbitration system. In extraofficial appearances, Rennebohm was critical of "Fair Deal" trends. At the 73d Annual Convention of the National Wholesale Druggists Association at Atlantic City, New Jersey, in October 1947, he told the gathering that "economic dreamers in Washington . . . weep crocodile tears over the plight of the small businessman while they surreptitiously try to stick a knife in his back." An "underground movement," he declared, sought repeal of the Miller-Tydings Enabling Act. On the other hand, Rennebohm was responsible for calling the State legislature into special session beginning July 19, 1948, to act on the veterans' housing problem. To make possible State aid to housing, a change in the part of the Wisconsin constitution relating to internal improvements was necessary, and a joint resolution calling for such a change was adopted.

Something less than two months later, in the primaries on September 2, 1948, the former La Follette Progressive, Ralph Immell, again sought the Republican gubernatorial nomination, but was defeated by Acting Governor Rennebohm. At the election on November 2, Rennebohm was victor over Carl Thompson, Democrat, by 126,000 votes although in the State presidential contest Truman outran Dewey by about 56,000 votes. This outcome, said the New York *Times* observer, was "a complete upset of pre-election anticipating." It could be

interpreted as a rebuff for "me too-ism," and the record of the 1949 State legislature was, accordingly, one that on the whole made Rennebohm look "radical" by contrast. In the pending matter of veterans' housing the Assembly adopted a system of loans to protect private enterprise instead of public housing grants advocated by the Governor; and it passed an act abolishing rent controls to which Rennebohm yielded only at the last moment. However, the legislature defeated a new income tax law sponsored by the Governor, which was regarded as favoring the higher-bracket groups. In October 1949 Rennebohm issued a warning to President Truman on the need to take action to prevent a national coal emergency. This warning was repeated in January 1950. Also, early in the new year, Rennebohm was one of three Republican Governors who helped to draft the party's new policy statement. In May, however, he announced that he would not run again for Governor, giving his physician's advice as the reason. Rennebohm's term expires in January 1951.

A man of considerable means by the time of the outbreak of World War II—in which he was active in Red Cross as well as Community Union work—Rennebohm was in a position by 1944 to establish five general scholarships for high school graduates at the University of Wisconsin. (These scholarships are for $500 each and an insurance fund of $50,000 has been established to perpetuate them. The fund is administered by the University of Wisconsin Foundation, of which Rennebohm is a director.)

Oscar Rennebohm and Mary Fowler, who were married September 8, 1920, have a daughter, Carol Ann. The white-haired, blue-eyed Governor of the Badger State is five feet ten inches tall and weighs 190 pounds. He is a Mason, Elk, Eagle, Moose, Kiwanian, Knight of Pythias, American Legionnaire, and a member of the Forty and Eight. A director of the First National Bank in Madison, he is also a trustee of Northland College, Ashland. In 1949 he received an honorary LL.D. degree from Carroll College, in Waukesha. His fraternity is the Sigma Phi Epsilon, and he attends the Luther Memorial Church in Madison.

References

N Y Times p17 Mr 14 '47 por
Newsweek 29:25 Mr 24 '47
Who's Who in America, 1950-51
Who's Who in the Midwest (1949)
World Biography (1948)

REYNAUD, PAUL (rä"nō') Oct. 15, 1878-
French statesman

Address: 5 Place du Palais Bourbon, Paris 7ᵉ,
France

> NOTE: This biography supersedes the article which appeared in *Current Biography* in 1940.

Paul Reynaud, Premier of France in 1940, who was imprisoned by the Vichy Government and by the Nazis during 1940-45, returned to the political scene in 1946, when he was elected a Deputy to the French Constituent Assembly,

French Embassy Inf. Div.
PAUL REYNAUD

and later in the year, to the National Assembly. He served briefly as Finance Minister in July-August 1948. Since then he has been active in the formation and expansion of the Consultative Assembly of the Council of Europe, and is chairman of the Economic Commission of the Assembly. During the 1930's, Reynaud served variously as Minister of Finance, of Justice, and of the Colonies in several Cabinets. He succeeded Daladier '40 as Premier of France on March 21, 1940. After opposing capitulation to the Nazis, Reynaud resigned the Premiership in June 1940 when Pétain '40 insisted on an armistice with Germany.

The birth date of Paul Reynaud is October 15, 1878, his birthplace the French Alpine village of Barcelonette. His grandfather, a French soldier who had fought under Maximilian in Mexico, established a substantial dry goods business in that country before returning to France. The fact that Reynaud's father was a Conseiller Général and his uncles Deputies or Senators is seen as having influenced his choice of career. After his family moved to Paris when Paul was a child, the boy spent many summers in the French Alps and in England. Upon graduation from the Lycée Louis le Grand, he studied law at the University of Paris, where he received his LL.D. degree. After a voyage around the world, Reynaud returned to Paris to take a course at the Ecole des Hautes Etudes Commerciales and then to set up practice as a corporation lawyer, being admitted to the bar in 1910. He later became first secretary of the Paris Bar Association.

Reynaud received the Croix de Guerre with two citations for his service in World War I. With General Janin's army and the Czechoslovaks, he made the retreat across Siberia after the Bolshevik revolution. Entering postwar politics, he was elected Deputy for the Basses-Alpes district in 1919. He was one of the

overruled minority who believed it was to France's interest to prevent a complete economic breakdown in Germany. In 1924 he was defeated as Deputy from Basses-Alpes, but was elected again in 1928, this time representing the sixth Paris district, which centers around the Stock Exchange. He represented this constituency until the fall of France in 1940.

Becoming one of the leaders of the conservative Democratic Alliance party, Reynaud in 1930 was appointed to his first ministerial post as Finance Minister in the Tardieu Cabinet (March 2-December 8, 1930). As Colonial Minister (January 27, 1931-February 20, 1932) under Laval '40, Reynaud visited Indo-China. In 1932 he became Minister of Justice and vice-president of the Council under Tardieu.

Reynaud was to establish a reputation as a dissenter from Government policies. Early in the depression he advocated the devaluation of the franc, and in 1934 he was one of a delegation of voters who went to the President's palace to ask him to dismiss the Daladier Government. He opposed Laval's pro-Italian policy in Ethiopia. Though no friend of Communism nor of the People's Front, he favored the Franco-Russian pact and the policy of "collective security," and fought appeasement of the Axis powers. Influenced by De Gaulle '49, he in March 1935 introduced a bill to form eleven mechanized divisions in the French Army, a proposal which was defeated by Daladier. That same year he published *Le problème militaire français*, in which he advocated that the French Army be modernized and organized for the offensive as well as the defensive. He was outspoken in his warnings to the parliament, in March 1935 and again in January 1937, that France would fall if she did not prepare for an offensive war. As Minister of Justice under Daladier, he was one of the four deputies who in September 1938 offered their resignations after Chamberlain's visit to Hitler at Berchtesgaden, but who were persuaded to reconsider and remain in the Cabinet. At about that time Reynaud broke with the Democratic Alliance, because of pro-Munich elements in the party, to take the position of a moderate conservative independent.

When Daladier formed a Cabinet in April 1938 he appointed Reynaud Minister of Justice. On November 1 Reynaud replaced Marchandeau as Minister of Finance. His decrees, announced November 12, were based on a policy of increased production and decreased consumption for the purpose of strengthening the military power of France as rapidly as possible. Proclaiming a "policy of sacrifice," Reynaud slashed expenses, increased taxes, controlled prices, profits, wages, exchange. A general strike, proclaimed November 30, was broken. Conservative opinion supported Reynaud's measures; gold, invested abroad since 1932, began to flow back to France; the new Minister of Finance was hailed as the savior of France's economy. On December 25, 1939, Reynaud and Sir John Simon '40, Britain's Chancellor of the Exchequer, signed an agreement binding France and Britain in a financial and economic union. The clause prolonging this partnership until six months after the peace,

Reynaud stated, "could be the point of departure of that long-awaited reorganization of Europe."

On March 20, 1940, Daladier resigned as Premier, having failed to receive a vote of confidence on his conduct of the war. Reynaud formed a new Cabinet within twenty-four hours, retaining Daladier as War Minister. "My Government has but a single aim—to conquer," Reynaud told the Assembly. He then asked for a meeting of the Franco-British Supreme War Council, which took place in London on March 28. There a treaty against a separate peace was concluded. Reynaud won Chamberlain's agreement to a revision of the policy pursued toward the Scandinavian neutrals and agreed with the British Prime Minister about the steps needed to close to Germany the "sheltered channel" of Norway. Praised as a man of "decision, energy, and imagination," Reynaud was compared to Georges ("The Tiger") Clemenceau who had led France in World War I. On April 19 he was given a unanimous vote of confidence in the Assembly.

During the weeks that followed, Reynaud opposed the retreat of the British troops from Norway and tried to persuade Belgium to abandon its neutrality program. In the face of successive defeats of the French-British forces in the German attack on the Low Countries, Reynaud tried to uphold morale with staunch declarations: "It is on the day when all seems lost that the world will see what France can do. . . .We are resolved to win at all sacrifices." On May 19, he reorganized his Cabinet, assuming the portfolio of the War Ministry and naming Daladier Foreign Minister. He replaced General Gamelin [40] with Weygand [40] as Commander in Chief of the French forces, and named Pétain [40], hero of the World War I Battle of Verdun, to the vice-presidency of the Council with the office of supreme technical adviser to the Cabinet. On June 5, after Reynaud had revealed to the British the extremely serious position of the French Army, De Gaulle was made a general and appointed Under Secretary of War.

On June 2 Reynaud, at the request of his Cabinet but against his own wishes, asked Winston Churchill [42] to relieve France of its agreement not to sign a separate armistice. The Government withdrew from Paris, which had been declared an open city, on June 10, moving to Cangey and then to Bordeaux. On June 11 a Supreme Council took place at Briare, bringing together Reynaud, Weygand, Churchill, Eden, and Major Attlee. On June 12, when Weygand, supported by Pétain, judged a demand for an armistice as necessary, Reynaud and his Council of Ministers rejected the suggestion, believing with De Gaulle that it was still possible to continue the war from abroad. Reynaud appealed to the United States for aid, and when Churchill proposed a union of Great Britain and France and their possessions, Reynaud alone voted for this and against the armistice. Pétain's opinion prevailed, however, and he formally announced the armistice, Reynaud having resigned as Premier on June 16, not being able to accept "a

policy contrary to the interests and the honor of France."

Reynaud, who had been seriously injured in an automobile accident in June 1940, was arrested by Pétain's order on September 6. He was placed under guard at the Château de Chazeron, later at Bourrassol, with Daladier and Gamelin. On October 19, 1940, the Vichy Government accused Reynaud of "misappropriation of public funds." A year later, on October 16, 1941, he was sentenced to imprisonment and was transferred to the fort of Portalet in the Pyrenees. A trial at Riom in February 1942, failing to prove Reynaud guilty, developed into a series of indictments against his regime. In defending himself, Reynaud showed his old fighting spirit and force. He had kept himself in good physical trim during his imprisonment by skipping rope in his cell, and had occupied himself with writing, studying languages, and reading.

In March 1943, Reynaud was sent by the Vichy Government to Germany, where he was imprisoned. He was released by Allied troops in May 1945, and flown back to Paris, where he appeared as a prosecution witness in the trial of Pétain. Taking the stand on July 23, 1945, Reynaud asserted that he had been determined to carry on the war from Africa, but that he was unable to withstand Pétain, who had opposed the plan. A collection of memoirs of June 1940, *La France a sauvé l'Europe*, written by Reynaud during his years of imprisonment, was published in 1947.

Resuming political activity, Reynaud was elected Deputy to the new Constituent Assembly from the Nord Department on June 2, 1946. When his election was contested by French Communists on the ground that he had paved the way for Marshal Pétain's Vichy Government, Reynaud defended himself "with masterly parliamentary tactics," in the words of *Newsweek*, and was accepted by the Assembly on July 5, 1946, by a vote of 298 to 132. "They [the Communists] did me a great service," Reynaud said. "In a few hours I achieved what would otherwise have taken a full year in speeches. . . .It is hard for a man to get back into political life when the people associate him with defeat." He was elected as an Independent Republican to the National Assembly on November 10, 1946.

Reynaud was appointed to his first postwar ministerial post on July 25, 1948, when he became Finance Minister in the Cabinet of Premier André Marie [48] on the basis of his economic recovery plan designed to put France on its feet by the time Marshall Plan aid expired in 1952. Reynaud's major goals were to eliminate the heavy budget deficit, restore confidence in the currency, revise the tax structure, reorganize both civil and military services, tighten control over the social security system, increase production and exports, and put the nationalized industries on a paying basis. The plan was passed by the Assembly in August 1948. A few weeks later, however, when the Socialists became dissatisfied with the amount of cost-of-living bonuses, the Cabinet of André Marie fell. In April 1949, Reynaud became

REYNAUD, PAUL—*Continued*

head of a coalition of Independent Republicans and Republican Peasants, who demanded less Government economic control.

Related to France's economic recovery were Reynaud's broader plans for an economic reorganization of Europe—a program he had advocated before the war. He served as a member of the committee which met in Paris in December 1948 and January 1949 to study the question of unifying Europe's economy. As a result of agreements reached on May 5, 1949, a Consultative Assembly was formed which met at Strasbourg during August-September 1949. It is one of the two bodies of the Council of Europe. As chairman of the Economic Commission of the Assembly, Reynaud visited the United States in March-April 1950, under the auspices of the American Committee for a United Europe. There he spoke on the purposes and importance of the Consultative Assembly in view of threatened Russian aggression, and urged the admission of West Germany to the Assembly. He also stressed the importance of active British participation—without it Germany's economic strength would dominate the union.

In the short-lived Government of Henri Queuille in early July 1950 Paul Reynaud was named to take charge of a newly created Ministry, as Minister of State for the Associated States and Far Eastern Affairs. According to the New York *Times*, his appointment indicated that France proposed to adopt a stronger policy in Indo-China.

An article by Reynaud, "The Unifying Force of Europe" in *Foreign Affairs* (January 1950), described the necessity and means of unifying Europe's economy. The French statesman has contributed to many periodicals, and is the author of a number of books, including *Waldeck-Rousseau*; *Les trois glorieuses*; *Jeunesse, quelle France veux-tu?*; *Courage de la France*; and *Finances de guerre*. He has given numerous lectures. In addition to the Croix de Guerre, he has the Legion of Honor and is a Knight of the Grand Cross of the Royal Victorian Order.

Reynaud was married to Christiane Mabire in 1949. By his first marriage, which was ended by divorce, he has one child, Colette. Reynaud has been described as "gentler and mellower" than in the old days when Clemenceau remarked, "This mosquito certainly can sting." Small, debonair, and an active sportsman, he still enjoys hunting, swimming, fencing, and boxing. He has made a hobby of maps and is known as a connoisseur of Chinese art and a devotee of European belles-lettres.

References

Newsweek 32:32-4 Ag 23 '48
Observer Ag 15 '48 por
This Week p7 Je 7 '40 por
Dictionnaire National des Contemporains (1936)
International Who's Who, 1949

International World Who's Who (1949)
Les Archives Internationales Doc. No. 591, D '47
10 Eventful Years (1947)
World Biography (1948)

RICHARDS, A(LFRED) N(EWTON)
Mar. 22, 1876- Pharmacologist

Address: b. c/o University of Pennsylvania Medical School, Philadelphia 4, Pa.; h. 737 Rugby Rd., Bryn Mawr, Pa.

Dr. A. N. Richards, emeritus professor of pharmacology of the University of Pennsylvania, and one of his country's outstanding pharmacologists, has gained international reputation by his contributions to his field of science. A graduate of Yale in the class of 1897, with a Ph.D. from Columbia and honorary degrees from colleges in the United States and abroad, Richards has taught successively at Columbia, Northwestern University, and the University of Pennsylvania since 1898. A major in chemical warfare service in World War I, the scientist was chairman of the Committee on Medical Research in World War II. For his achievements in this capacity (one of the best-known among them was making penicillin available for widespread use) he was awarded the Medal for Merit in 1946. From July 1947 to June 1950 Dr. Richards was president of the National Academy of Sciences.

Born in Stamford, New York, on March 22, 1876, Alfred Newton Richards is the third son of the Reverend Leonard E. Richards, the pastor of the First Presbyterian Church in that town for forty years. His mother, Mary Elizabeth (Burbank) Richards, was of English ancestry, the daughter of a Presbyterian minister. His paternal grandfather, the son of a German immigrant, was a farmer in Kentucky and Ohio. Leonard Richards, one of Alfred's brothers, became an Episcopalian clergyman, and the other, James, entered law.

Upon graduating in 1892 from the Stamford Seminary, Richards entered Yale as a chemistry major. For two of his college years he managed an eating club to earn his board. Work with Professor R. H. Chittenden in the Sheffield Scientific School laboratory, he has said, excited his deep interest in physiological chemistry and physiology, and helped to determine his choice of career. He graduated from Yale with honors, receiving his B.A. degree in 1897 and the M.A. degree in 1898. In the fall of the latter year he went to Columbia University as assistant in the department of physiological chemistry in the College of Physicians and Surgeons, where he was a tutor in 1902-04. During his first two years at Columbia he was working on a thesis entitled *Chemical Composition of Yellow Elastic Connective Tissue*; on the basis of this work he received a Ph.D. degree in 1901. Later, honorary doctorates were to be awarded to him: D.Sc. from the University of Pennsylvania (1925), Western Reserve (1931), Yale (1933), Harvard (1940), Columbia (1942), Williams (1943), and Princeton (1946); LL.D. from the University of Edinburgh (1935) and Johns Hopkins University

(1949); and M.D. from the University of Pennsylvania (1932) and the University of Louvain, Belgium (1949).

At Columbia University Richards was strongly influenced by Professors Philip Hanson Hiss (in bacteriology) and Christian A. Herter (in pharmacology and medical research). Under the latter he assisted in the reorganization of the department of pharmacology, and from 1904 to 1908 served as instructor in that department. In 1908 he went to the Northwestern University Medical School as professor of pharmacology, and in 1910 he joined the faculty of the University of Pennsylvania in the same capacity, in each case reorganizing the department. He remained at the University of Pennsylvania until 1946, when he retired with the title of professor emeritus. Appointed vice-president of the University of Pennsylvania in charge of medical affairs from 1939 to 1948, Richards has continued to serve the University as an associate trustee since 1948.

Richards' World War I service began in London, where in September 1917 he joined the staff of the British Medical Research Committee, working with H. H. Dale (now Sir Henry) at the National Institute for Medical Research. On July 15, 1918, he was commissioned a major in the Sanitary Corps of the American Expeditionary Force, and sent to United States General Headquarters at Chaumont, France. There, on a Chemical Warfare Service assignment, he organized a laboratory for the study of gas warfare problems. He received his honorable discharge in December 1918.

In World War II Richards was one of what the New York *Times* called "the 'Big Six' in America's scientific high command," as chairman of the Committee on Medical Research of the Office of Scientific Research and Development (from July 1941 to June 1947). Among the scientist's achievements in this office was his part in taking penicillin out of the stage of limited use in the research laboratory and, by securing for its production Government funds and the manufacturing facilities of several big pharmaceutical and chemical firms, making it available for widespread use in the armed forces. Of Richards' organization of research in the use of penicillin, sulfa and plasma, it was said that the results had changed or modified the whole practice of medicine within three years. Improved methods of blood transfusion, more efficient measures against infections diseases, more effective insecticides, and increased knowledge of the effects of high and rapid plane flights resulted from the work of Richards' agency.

In recognition of his record in World War II Richards in 1946 was awarded the Medal for Merit by President Truman. In 1945 he was one of six scientists heading Government-created war agencies honored in the eighth Annual American Design Award of $25,000 (donated by Lord and Taylor, New York department store); the award was presented to the National Academy of Sciences rather than to the individuals on request of the men honored, "in recognition of the collective achievements of American scientists in supplying the arsenal of

Wide World Photos
A. N. RICHARDS

democracy with the greatest war weapons the world has ever seen" (New York *Times*, April 20, 1945). The scientist's work with the Committee on Medical Research was also honored in 1946 with a Lasker Foundation Award of $1,000. That year, too, he received the Procter Award of the Philadelphia Drug Exchange and the William Guggenheim Honor Cup (awarded yearly to the individual who has brought distinction to the University of Pennsylvania). Great Britain made him an Honorary Commander of the Order of the British Empire in 1948.

Dr. Richards was elected to the presidency of the National Academy of Sciences, succeeding Dr. Frank B. Jewett '46 on July 1, 1947; for reasons of health he resigned the office in June of 1950, one year before the expiration of his term, and was succeeded by Dr. Detlev W. Bronk '49 of Johns Hopkins. Established in 1863 by an act of Congress, the academy is an organization of distinguished scientists (the membership in 1950 is 462, with 46 foreign associates) which may be called upon by any department of the Government to "investigate, examine, experiment and report upon any subject of science or art." One of the functions of the academy in the last few years has been choosing, through its subsidiary, the National Research Council, recipients for research fellowships awarded by the Atomic Energy Commission. In May 1949 Richards, on behalf of the National Academy of Sciences, protested proposed Federal Bureau of Investigation loyalty checks on all students recommended for these fellowships, declaring such procedure "would be a blow to the principles of freedom of thought on which this country was founded." In December 1949 the AEC reduced its program of fellowships, restricting them to workers in fields requiring access to secret data, and the academy agreed to authorize the National Re-

RICHARDS, A. N.—*Continued*
search Council to continue administration of
the program until June 30, 1951. Dr. Richards,
in a letter advising the general manager of
the AEC of the academy's decision, emphasized
that it was the belief of the council of the
National Academy that FBI investigation (of
AEC fellows not having access to restricted
data) was unnecessary from the standpoint of
the national security and unwise from the point
of view of the advance of science in the United
States.

The pharmacologist has contributed a number of articles to professional journals on two
subjects in which he has specialized: the physiology of kidney function, and the action of
histamine in relation to capillary contractility
and shock. He helped to found (in 1905) the
Journal of Biological Chemistry and was ,suc-
cessively, assistant editor, associate editor, and
managing editor of the publication until 1914.
In 1926 he gave the Herter lectures at New
York University and Bellevue Hospital Medical
College, and gave the Beaumont lectures at
Detroit in 1929 and the Croonian lecture before
the Royal Society (London) in 1938. In 1948-
49 he was a member of the Medical Committee
of the Hoover commission for reorganization
of the executive branch of the Government.
He was a trustee of the Rockefeller Foundation
in 1937-41.

Honors the scientist has received in addition
to academic degrees and wartime awards include the William Wood Gerhard gold medal
given by the Pathological Society of Philadelphia (1932), the Kober Medal of the Association of American Physicians (1933), the Keyes
Medal from the American Association of
Genito-Urinary Surgeons (1933), the John
Scott Medal (1934), the New York Academy
of Medicine's Medal (1936), and the Philadelphia Bok Award (1937). A fellow of the
American Academy of Arts and Sciences, the
American Association for the Advancement of
Science, and honorary fellow of the College
of Physicians of Philadelphia, he holds mem-
bership in the American Urological Society, the
Association of American Physicians, American
Physiological Society (secretary, 1910-12),
American Philosophical Society (vice-president,
1944-47), American Society of Biological Chem-
ists, American Pharmacological Society, Society
of Experimental Biology and Medicine, Physi-
ological Society of Philadelphia, the Interurban
Clinical Club, the scholastic honor society Phi
Beta Kappa, the medical honor society Alpha
Omega Alpha, and the scientific honor society
Sigma Xi. The scientist has also been elected
to foreign membership in British associations—
the Royal Society, the British Physiological
Society, the Royal Society of Medicine, the
British Medical Association, the Royal Society
of Edinburgh; to the Royal Academy of Science (Denmark), and the Medical Association
of Vienna.

Richards has served on the board of directors
of Merck and Company, chemical manufacturers, since October 1948. His clubs are the
Rittenhouse (Philadelphia), Cosmos (Washington), St. Davids Golf (Philadelphia), and the
Century Association (New York). He married,

on December 26, 1908, Lillian Louise Woody.
They have one son, Alfred Newton, Jr. The
scientist, who has gray hair and brown eyes, is
five feet nine and one half inches tall, and
weighs 151 pounds. He is a Republican, and
was affiliated with the Presbyterian Church.
He turns to golf and fishing for recreation.

References

American Men of Science (1949)
International Who's Who, 1949
Who's Who in America, 1950-51
World Biography (1948)

RICHARDSON, SIR RALPH (rǎf) Dec.
19, 1902- Actor
Address: h. Bedegar's Lea, Kenwood Close,
Hampstead, London, N.W.3

Well received by motion picture audiences on
both sides of the Atlantic, Sir Ralph Richardson is a British actor who has made his mark
on both stage and screen. Among his outstanding postwar film roles have been Count Karenin
in *Anna Karenina*, the butler in *The Fallen
Idol*, the father in *The Heiress*. Much of his
stage career has been in association with London's Old Vic repertory company, of which he
was a director during 1945-49, and with which
he visited New York in the spring of 1946.
Stage creations in which he has scored particular successes are the Falstaff of *Henry IV,
Parts I and II*, and the title role in *Peer Gynt*.
In December 1949 he was voted the best film
actor of the year by the British National Board
of Review of Motion Pictures.

Born at Cheltenham, England, December 19,
1902, Ralph David Richardson is the third son
of Arthur Richardson, art master at Cheltenham College, and Lydia (Russell) Richardson.
He was educated at the Xaverian college,
Brighton, and privately, afterwards studying art
and doing some scene painting at the Little
Theatre, Brighton. An article in the London
News Chronicle stated he had read "all Shakespeare at fourteen." In 1921 he first "walked
on" as a gendarme in *Les Misérables*; in December 1921 he had his first speaking part, that
of Lorenzo in *The Merchant of Venice*, at the
Little Theatre, Brighton. The years up to 1925
were occupied by touring in England and Ireland with a Shakespeare repertory company.

"As a boy," Richardson once told *Picturegoer*, "I planned to stay an actor until I was
twenty-five, by which time I hoped to have
earned enough money to be a doctor." Evidently that ambition was abandoned, for in
1925 he joined Sir Barry Jackson at the Birmingham Repertory Theatre; and in November
1926 Jackson brought him to appear in London,
at the Haymarket Theatre, as Arthur Varwell,
in Eden Phillpotts' *Yellow Sands*. He had a
season at the Court Theatre in 1928, playing in
Back to Methuselah, and performing the part
of Gurth when Laurence Olivier [46] had his
London debut in *Harold*; the two actors were
to become firm friends. Among Richardson's
other roles that year was that of Tranio in a
modern-dress presentation of *The Taming of
the Shrew*. In 1929 Richardson made a South

African tour, and in 1930, after playing Gilbert Nash in *Silver Wings* and Roderigo in *Othello*, he had his first association with the Old Vic, classical repertory company, portraying Prince Hal in *Henry IV, Part I.* Subsequent roles included Sir Harry Beagle in *The Jealous Wife*, Caliban in *The Tempest* and Enobarbus in *Antony and Cleopatra.*

During 1930-32 the Old Vic company and Sadler's Wells Theatre claimed Richardson's services, except for two intervals, August 1931 and August 1932, when he appeared at the Malvern Festivals of those years. With the two London companies he was seen in *Twelfth Night* (Sir Toby Belch), *Arms and the Man* (Bluntschli), *Much Ado About Nothing, King Lear, The Taming of the Shrew* (Petruchio), *A Midsummer Night's Dream* (Bottom) *Henry V* (title role), *Julius Caesar* (Brutus), *Abraham Lincoln* (General Grant), *Othello* (Iago), *Hamlet* (the Ghost and the First Gravedigger). His Malvern roles included Nicholas in *A Woman Killed With Kindness*, Courtall in *She Would if She Could*, Merrygreek in *Ralph Roister Doister*, Face in *The Alchemist*, Sergeant Fielding in *Too True to be Good.*

In the remaining years of the decade, Richardson appeared in many important roles. A listing includes the title role in Somerset Maugham's *Sheppey* (1933); Captain Hook in *Peter Pan* (1933); the leads in *Eden End* (1934), *Cornelius* (1935), and *Johnson Over Jordan* (1939), three plays by J. B. Priestley written for Richardson; Emile Delbar in *Promise* (1936); the title role in *The Amazing Dr. Clitterhouse* (1936; ran for over a year). Again with the Old Vic, he played the Moor in *Othello* (1938). The year 1935 found the British actor on tour in America, playing Mercutio in *Romeo and Juliet*, with Katharine Cornell; his New York debut was made in it that year. Back in London the following year, in conjunction with Laurence Olivier he made his first venture in producing, *Bees on the Boat Deck*, in which he also acted.

Meanwhile, in 1933 Richardson had begun to appear in motion pictures, making his debut in *The Ghoul*, with Boris Karloff, and acting in three other films that year. In 1936 he signed a long contract with Sir Alexander Korda [46], of London Film Productions, and played in *The Shape of Things to Come, The Man Who Could Work Miracles, Bulldog Drummond.* By January 1938 the *Observer*, praising his work in the films *South Riding* and *The Divorce of Lady X*, could speak of "the steadily increasing hold that Mr. Richardson has on his public." Miss C. A. Lejeune (*Observer*'s critic) said: "He is not an intuitive or inspirational actor. Everything is built up from a groundwork of solid labor. . . .Two minutes on the stage or screen is as important to him as two hours. He is a hard-working technician who uses face, voice and body to convey a meaning. . . .I believe one can fairly call Ralph Richardson great." Other films in which he acted prior to World War II were *The Citadel, Q Planes, The Four Feathers*, and *The Lion Has Wings.*

A few weeks after the outbreak of World War II, Richardson, an amateur flier, joined the Royal Naval Volunteer Reserve, and was

SIR RALPH RICHARDSON

attached to the Fleet Air Arm as a sublieutenant. Serving as an instructor, he attained the rank of lieutenant commander in 1941. He came unscathed through a forced landing in 1939, and was hospitalized for a short time in October 1940 after a motorcycle accident. Terms of leave were arranged for him to play in Paul Soskin's Norway war film, *A Day Will Dawn* (December 1941), and to fly with Eric Linklater and Vincent Korda to Gibraltar to explore the possibilities of making a film there for the Ministry of Information (November 1943); he appeared in two other pictures of wartime date, *The Silver Fleet* and *The Volunteer.* In May 1944, he and Olivier were released from the Fleet Air Arm to be on a panel of three directors to resuscitate the Old Vic company (bombed out in 1940) at the New Theatre. (His term as a director expired in 1949; it was decided to have the company revert at that time to its former mode of direction under a single administrator rather than a panel of directors.)

In September 1944, Richardson played the title role in *Peer Gynt*, and was credited by W. A. Darlington, of the *Daily Telegraph*, with having shown "all the qualities needed for the role—the odd blend of simplicity and cunning, the bombast, the poetry." He was also seen in *Arms and the Man, Uncle Vanya*, and *Richard III.* On tour in Germany and France, he played at the Comédie Française in Paris. The 1945-46 season saw him in a *Henry IV* performance as what *Picture Post* called "a new and *natural* Falstaff: a credible creature at last, with some dignity in obesity." That year he also portrayed Tiresias in *Oedipus Rex*, and Lord Burleigh in *The Critic.* When the Old Vic company visited New York for six weeks in the spring of 1946, Richardson was seen in those roles, and in that of Uncle Vanya in the Chekhov play. New York critics particularly admired his interpretation of Falstaff: *Variety* called it "a performance always fascinating, and certainly unequaled in our days";

RICHARDSON, SIR RALPH—*Continued*

Howard Barnes of the *Herald Tribune* wrote: "In the hands of Richardson, Falstaff becomes a particularly wonderful rascal. The great actor misses no inflection of the part. . . . Richardson alone is worth seeing the Old Vic company for." His Uncle Vanya was less successful in the reviewers' opinions. As Lord Burleigh in *The Critic* he "contributed one of the most amusing moments of the Sheridan play," commented Herrick Brown in the *Sun*. He won a second to Olivier's first in the *Variety* poll for the best actor of 1946.

Back in London in the fall of 1946 Richardson played in Priestley's *An Inspector Calls* and *The King Stag*. The following year his performance of the title role in *Cyrano de Bergerac* was followed by a revival of Ben Jonson's *The Alchemist* and Shakespeare's *Richard II*, which he produced and in which he acted John of Gaunt. *Royal Circle*, which he produced in 1948 and in which he played lead, opposite his wife, Meriel Forbes, had but moderate success. Dame Lilian Braithwaite, who had an important role in it, told the magazine *Illustrated* that, as a producer, Richardson was "meticulous but not fussy." Another actor, John Salew, said: "I've never before known a play produced without any display of temperament." In 1949 Richardson was seen in a stage version of *The Heiress*, and in 1950 appeared in R. C. Sherriff's *Home at Seven* from March to November, when he left the cast to act in the film *An Outcast of the Islands.*

The British actor's screen performances had meanwhile been garnering him laurels at home and in the United States. Praising his portrayal of a leader of the Dutch underground movement in *The Silver Fleet*, Bosley Crowther (New York *Times*) called him "one of the finest and most suggestive performers in British films." *School For Secrets* (1946) was followed by *Anna Karenina* (1947), in which he played Count Karenin with "superb skill and feeling," wrote Howard Barnes in the New York *Herald Tribune*. "One of the greatest performances of his fine career," commented the *Herald Tribune* critic about his characterization of the butler (idolized by the little boy) in *The Fallen Idol*, prize-winning picture in 1948. In the latter year Richardson went to Hollywood to play the father in *The Heiress*, screen adaptation of the Henry James novel, *Washington Square*. Of this, Eileen Creelman (New York *Sun*) said, "Richardson makes his American debut in a strong role, played to the hilt." On December 18, 1949, Richardson was named the best film actor of the year by the National Board of Review of Motion Pictures for *The Heiress* and *The Fallen Idol*. (In 1948 he was nominated to a Government commission investigating the distribution and exhibition side of the film industry.)

Commenting on his profession, Richardson in 1947 told *Picturegoer* that he felt every actor ought to work in the live theater to learn to act and test audience reactions. "If you do something wrong in the theater," he said, "you know it instantly. The audience starts coughing! The art of acting consists in keeping people from coughing." Of screen work he has said: "It is a wonderful medium, and I love it, but I find that I cannot increase my talent by working in pictures, any more than a painter can do so by increasing the size of his brush." Director William Wyler, in an interview reported in the New York *World-Telegram*, pointed out that in Richardson's acting his hands play an importnt part—"a cane, a glass, anything at all, punctuates his speech."

In recognition of his services to the British theater, the actor was knighted in 1947. The same year he received from King Haakon of Norway the Medal of St. Olav, in tribute to his performance in *Peer Gynt*. Richardson has been twice married. His first wife, Muriel Hewitt, whom he married in 1924, died in 1942. In 1944 he married the actress, Meriel Forbes, who is a niece of Sir Johnston Forbes-Robertson, the famous actor. They have a son, Charles David (familiarly known as "Smallie").

Richardson, who is six feet tall, weighs 166 pounds, has brown hair and gray eyes, has been described as having "a humorous nose . . . and a voice, rich, gruff, that is unmistakable" (*News Chronicle*). The same paper said: "Nothing off stage to mark him as an actor. Likes crawling under a motor car, being a mechanic, tinkering." Golf, fishing, squash rackets, and drawing are among his recreations. His clubs are the Green Room, Savile, Queen's (tennis), and the Athenæum.

References

Illustrated (London) p18-19 Ap 24 '48 pors
News Chronicle (London) My 27 '32 pors
Observer (London) Mr 19 '39
Picture Post p22-23 O 20 '45 pors
Picturegoer p6-7 Ja 18 '47 pors
Playbill Je 27 '46 por
Burke's Peerage (1949)
International Motion Picture Almanac, 1947-48
Who's Who, 1950
Who's Who in the Theatre (1947)
Winchester's Screen Encyclopedia (1948)
World Biography (1948)

RIDDELL, R(OBERT) GERALD (rĭd-dĕl') May 4, 1908- United Nations delegate

Address: b. c/o Department of External Affairs, Ottawa, Ont., Canada

In June 1950 it was announced that in the fall of that year R. Gerald Riddell would replace General A. G. L. McNaughton [42] as Canada's permanent representative to the United Nations. Riddell, who in 1949 had held the position of assistant to Lester B. Pearson [47], Secretary of State for External Affairs, has been one of Canada's representatives at the United Nations since 1946. Formerly a professor of history at the University of Toronto, Riddell had entered the Department of External Affairs in the course of World War II, where he became, in 1946, head of a newly created departmental division charged with the administration of his country's relationship to the

United Nations Organization and to various postwar international conferences.

Robert Gerald Riddell was born in Edmonton, Alberta, (a city on the Canadian prairie) on May 4, 1908, to the Reverend John Henry Riddell and Florence May (Armstrong) Riddell. His father was principal of Alberta College which, as a leading Methodist, he had helped to found. In 1917 the family moved to Winnipeg (Manitoba), where Dr. Riddell became principal of Wesley College, affiliated with the University of Manitoba. "Gerry" attended Kelvin High School in that city, and in 1930 received an honors degree in arts from the university. During summer employment he gained a local reputation as an actor on a Chautauqua circuit. With the intention of pursuing an academic career he proceeded to postgraduate study at the University of Toronto, where he received the M.A. degree and an Imperial Order of the Daughters of the Empire scholarship to Oxford in 1931. At the English university he distinguished himself as a modern history student in New College, from which he obtained the B.A. degree in 1933. In 1934 he was made Beit Senior Scholar in colonial history at Oxford and subsequently was granted the B.Litt. and M.A. degrees. In the course of his years at Oxford, the Canadian student made several holiday walking and bicycle tours on the Continent.

Riddell returned to Canada in 1934 and was appointed senior tutor in residence at Victoria College of the University of Toronto. At the same time he obtained a lectureship in history in the university. As a professor, Riddell lectured in English history and the history of nineteenth century Europe. He took an active interest in student and professional organizations, being editor of the annual report of the Canadian Historical Association from 1940 to 1942, and frequently addressing student groups. In historical research he showed a special interest in land settlement policies, both imperial and Canadian, and in the general subject of Canadian government. During this period he wrote three articles for the *Canadian Historical Review*: "Study in the Land Policy of the Colonial Office, 1763-1855" (December 1937); "Egerton Ryerson's Views on the Government of Upper Canada in 1836" (December 1938); "Cycle in the Development of the Canadian West" (September 1940); and one in the Toronto weekly, *Saturday Night* (July 20, 1940), "Seventy Years of Canada's West."

In June of 1941 Riddell in an address to the Lions International Convention at Toronto expressed approbation of a policy of collective security. The following year 1942 brought a request from the Department of External Affairs, expanding because of wartime demands, that he enter the field of diplomacy, and he obtained a leave of absence from the university for this purpose.

After three years spent on affairs of the department in Canada's Parliament Buildings in Ottawa, as special assistant to the under secretary, Riddell found himself in 1946 at the head of a new division in External Affairs: the First Political Division, a section established to deal with Canada's participation in the United

R. GERALD RIDDELL

Nation's Organization and the various postwar international conferences. (The department was later known as the United Nations Division.) Early in 1949, shortly after L. B. Pearson rose from under secretary to cabinet rank as Secretary of State for External Affairs, Riddell was appointed to a new position as Pearson's special assistant. One of the chief tasks of his new post was the preparation of technical and political material on external problems for the Minister's use in the House of Commons.

Between 1946 and 1949 Riddell was active in Canada's United Nations affairs. In 1946 he had been named a member of the Canadian delegation to the fourth meeting of the Council of the United Nations Relief and Rehabilitation Administration, and alternate representative on the special commitee on refugees and displaced persons of the United Nations Economic and Social Council, which met in London. Later the same year he became an adviser to the Canadian delegation to the second and third sessions of ECOSOC in New York. At the fourth session of ECOSOC in 1942 he was designated an alternate delegate and an adviser to the delegation to the special U.N. Assembly meeting on Palestine in April and May. In September 1947 Riddell became principal adviser to the Canadian delegation to the U.N. General Assembly in New York (second session) and in 1948 was principal adviser and alternate delegate to the third session of the Assembly in Paris. In January of that year he had been Canadian delegate to the agenda committee of ECOSOC. While thus working at the legislative and committee level of U.N. he was also able to observe the problems of the Security Council in 1948 as one of General A. G. L. McNaughton's alternates on that body in New York and Paris.

In a speech delivered to the "Little Assembly" in March of 1949, Riddell indicated that Canada did not favor immediate amendment of

RIDDELL, R. GERALD—*Continued*

the U.N. Charter to eliminate the veto, but supported the view that the nations should seek to modify its use within the existing machinery. Emphasizing both the pragmatic approach toward U.N. and Canada's developing position as a "middle power," he went on to say that Canada thought it illogical that the five great powers were given voting privileges while all other members were left as an "undifferentiated mass." This theme he developed further in speeches both in the United States and Canada. In January of 1949 he warned an audience at St. Thomas, Ontario, that the general public had expected too much of U.N. and stated, "We must start thinking of the United Nations in a different fashion." At Mount Holyoke College in June of 1949 Riddell stressed further his argument for "commensurate recognition," stating that the resources placed at the disposal of U.N. by secondary powers well might tip the balance in resolving a threat of war. Canadians, he asserted, wanted a part in drawing up peace plans commensurate to their role in war; this was not desired in order to satisfy national honor but on pragmatic grounds —because if the peace were a bad one Canada would suffer in proportion to her size and resources.

On June 8, 1950, Riddell's appointment as head of the permanent Canadian delegation to the United Nations in New York was announced. There, according to the Toronto *Globe and Mail*, he will not only supervise Canada's U.N. activities, but also be in a key spot as a sort of special ambassador among the representatives of many nations. In this post Riddell succeeds General A. G. L. McNaughton, who has been appointed Canadian member on the International Joint Commission, a position which he holds in addition to that of Canadian member of the Permanent Joint Defense Board (United States-Canada). Riddell assumed his new duties on August 15, 1950.

The Canadian official has been described as "alert and vigorous, an easy and talented conversationalist." In 1936 Riddell married Katherine Page Dobson of St. Thomas, Ontario; they have a son and a daughter. Skiing in the Gatineau hills near Ottawa has been one of his favorite sports.

References

Montreal Standard Mr 26 '49
Ottawa Journal p1 Je 8 '50 por
Toronto Globe and Mail Je 8 '50; Je 22 '50
Toronto Star Ap 26 '50; p2 Je 8 '50 por
Winnipeg Free Press p14 Ap 27 '50 por
World Biography (1948)

RINGLING, ROBERT E(DWARD) Aug. 16, 1897—Jan. 2, 1950 Circus executive; sang baritone roles in opera (1922-39); one-time president of the former Ringling Trust and Savings Bank (Sarasota, Florida); director and senior vice-president of the Ringling Brothers and Barnum and Bailey Combined Shows, Inc. (1937); elected president of the circus 1943 and 1945; chairman of the board since 1947. See *Current Biography*, 1945.

Obituary

N Y Times p25 Ja 3 '50

RIZZUTO, PHIL(IP FRANCIS) Sept. 25, 1918- Baseball player
Address: b. c/o New York Yankees, Inc., 745 5th Ave., New York 17

"Rizzuto is baseball's best shortstop," Milton Gross wrote of Phil Rizzuto in 1949, after the Yankee player had completed a season during which he was acclaimed by sportswriters and fellow players. That year a runner-up in the vote for the American League Most Valuable Player award, he received the honor in 1950, when he was also named as the shortstop on the All-Star Baseball Team.

Philip Francis Rizzuto was named for his father, a dock worker on New York City's waterfront. Both Philip, Sr., and his wife, Mary, had come from the same town in Italy; they did not meet, however, until they both were living in Brooklyn. There the junior Philip, one of five children, was born on September 25, 1918. When the boy was twelve, the family moved to Glendale, Long Island. He attended Richmond Hill High School, where he was quarterback on the football team and captain of the baseball team. At the time of his graduation in 1937, he was offered, according to a *Saturday Evening Post* article, two athletic scholarships—one to Columbia University and the other to Fordham University. The boy preferred, however, to make baseball his career. He first tried out for the Brooklyn Dodgers. Hit by a wild pitch, he was told he would not have another chance because the Dodgers' manager thought the five-foot-six candidate was too small. (The manager of the Brooklyn team at that time was Casey Stengel '49, who was later to take over the New York Yankees and direct Rizzuto through one of his best seasons.)

Rejected by the Dodgers (and, according to some reports by the New York Giants, too), the right-handed player turned to the New York Yankees. His tryout proved successful and he was sent to Virginia to play shortstop on the Bassetts, a Class-D Yankee farm team in the Bi-State League. In the sixty-seven games he played with the Bassetts, Rizzuto hit .310 and fielded .933. As a result he moved on to the Norfolk team of the Piedmont League in 1938. From that time through his early years in the major leagues he was teamed with Gerald Priddy at second base; the two showed a fine record as an infield team. (Rizzuto also occasionally played third base for Norfolk.) Rizzuto's batting of .336 and fielding .938 earned him an advancement into the American Association, a top minor league, on the Kansas City team (Priddy, too, went to Kansas City). "It was at KC that Rizzuto opened the eyes of the Yankee moguls," said a *PM* writer. In 1939 he hit .316 and fielded .944, and in 1940 he was named (by *The Sporting News*) Number One Minor League Player of the Year, with a batting average of .347 and a fielding record of .949. He stole the most bases in the American Association in 1940.

When Rizzuto and Priddy were bought by the Yankees in 1941, *Cue* wrote: "The Heavenly Twins . . . are expected this season to save the New York Yankees from a fate worse than death: third place in the league." Both men opened the season in the American League team as regular players on the team and both were benched later in the season for poor playing. During the course of 1941, however, Rizzuto did play in 133 games, batted .307, and fielded .957. Though a "rookie," he led the American League by participating in the most double plays. His freshman year in the majors was also his introduction to World Series playing: he made two hits, twelve putouts, and one error in five series games. As Rizzuto's fielding improved, his batting dropped: 1942 was the first year he did not hit above .300—his batting was .284—but his fielding reached the highest he had achieved until then—.962. In his second World Series appearance (1942) he made one home run and eight hits for an average of .381 in five games; he fielded .967, making fifteen putouts and one error. He made a new major-league record by participating in five double plays in one game (August 14, 1942), and tied the major league record with five putouts in one game. He led the league in double plays and in putouts (324).

Service in the United States Navy kept Rizzuto out of professional baseball for the next three years, during World War II. After a year as a seaman in Norfolk, Rizzuto went to New Guinea. He contracted malaria, however, and was assigned to manage a Navy league team. In September 1944 he joined Bill Dickey's Navy All-Stars for the world series between the Army and the Navy; on the victorious Navy team Rizzuto played third base. He then returned to New Guinea, saw action in the Philippines, and was discharged in October 1945 as a chief specialist.

In 1946 Phil Rizzuto was again wearing the New York Yankee uniform. In the following three years he held his own on the team, batting .257 and fielding .961 in 1946; .273 and .969 in 1947; and .252 and .973 in 1948. He made his third World Series appearance in 1947, during which he fielded 1.000 with a hitting record of .308. The year 1949 is considered Rizzuto's best season: he led American League shortstops by fielding .971; as a batter he hit .275. Credited with the ability to make plays at which other shortstops failed, he was called "the key man in the infield." In the 837 major league games he played in the years 1941-1949, his totals were: at bat 3,166, runs 450, hits 872, batting average .275, fielding average .966. His World's Series record for 1941, 1942, 1947, and 1949 totaled: at bat 83, runs 7, hits 21, batting average .253, fielding average .982. As of June 30, 1950, the Yankee shortstop's record for the season was: at bat 276, hits 89, percentage .322.

For the year 1949 Rizzuto was chosen runner-up in the "Most Valuable Player in the American League" award of the Association of Base-

New York Yankees

PHIL RIZZUTO

ball Writers of America, a fact which caused controversy among sportswriters; some felt that Rizzuto should have been chosen the most valuable player. The New York chapter of the association gave him the Sid Mercer Memorial Plaque as the player of the year; and the Newark Athletic Club declared him the New Jersey athlete of the year. Arthur Daley wrote in the New York *Times* of the sportswriters' award to the shortstop: "They . . . realized that Stengel, the magician, never would have been able to pluck his last couple of rabbits out of the hat with such grandiloquent flourishes if it had not been for the extraordinarily efficient play of the impish Rizzuto. They saw little Phil save game after game with impossible performances." Milton Gross told New York *Post* readers: "I wish there was some way Phil's daily miracles in the field could have been recorded this season. Every day, not just now and then." Tim Cohane (in *Look*) began a series of quotations that praised Rizzuto by saying, "The raves for Phil Rizzuto, the little New York Yankee shortstop, suggest a Hollywood supercolossal."

When the Baseball Writers Association made its 1950 selection of the "Most Valuable Player in the American League," Rizzuto was given that honor when he received sixteen of the twenty-three first-place votes, in all, 284 points. The next month (November) the player was an "overwhelming favorite" in the Associated Press poll for the 1950 All-Star Baseball Team. One of three Yankees chosen, the shortstop was named on most (360) of the ballots.

Rizzuto is most often called "The Scooter," but his height and his youthful appearance are responsible for such nicknames as "The Kid" and "That Little Monkey." The five-foot-six-inch player weighs 160 pounds, has brown hair and brown eyes. Married on June 23, 1943, to Cora Anne Esselborn, he is the father of Patricia, Cynthia, and Penelope. During the winter Rizzuto, reported *Look*, works in a New-

RIZZUTO, PHIL—*Continued*

ark clothing store. An enthusiastic movie-goer, he also enjoys using his motion picture camera; another diversion is hunting. Milton Gross wrote that the Yankee shortstop is "a story-teller of immense Munchausen proportions."

References

Look 14:80 My 9 '50 pors
PM p24 Ja 12 '41 pors
Time 37:44 Ap 14 '41
Baseball Register (1950)

ROBERTSON, D(AVID) B(ROWN)
May 13, 1876- Labor leader

Address: b. c/o Brotherhood of Locomotive Firemen and Enginemen, Keith Bldg., Cleveland, Ohio; h. 3115 Scarborough Rd., Cleveland, Ohio

In 1922 D. B. Robertson was elected president of the Brotherhood of Locomotive Firemen and Enginemen, the second largest of the "Big Five" operating railway unions. An engine wiper when he was nineteen years old, Robertson, who in 1950 became seventy-four, has been a union official since 1905. In 1931 and 1932 he served as chairman of the Railway Labor

Wide World Photos
D. B. ROBERTSON

Executives Association. An eleven-year-old dispute between the union and the railroads over the number of firemen to be used on Diesel engines became a sharp issue in the spring of 1950.

David Brown Robertson was born in Austintown, Ohio, on May 13, 1876, the son of Robert and Jane (Brown) Robertson. He left the local public school when he was twelve years old to go to work, but continued his education some years later by taking correspondence school courses. His first employer was the

Andrews Brothers Nut and Bolt Works of Youngstown, Ohio, and subsequently he worked in a brick plant and machine shop. At the age of nineteen (1895) he got his first job on a railroad when he was hired by the Pennsylvania Railroad as an engine wiper. After three years he went to work for the Erie Railroad; there he remained until 1913 as (successively) hostler, fireman, and engineer. Eight years earlier (1905) Robertson had been elected general chairman of the Brotherhood of Locomotive Firemen and Enginemen, Erie System.

Organized on December 1, 1873, at Port Jervis, New York, by eleven firemen of the Erie Railroad, the union was originally called the Brotherhood of Locomotive Firemen. In 1913 Robertson became vice-president of the national union and at the twenty-ninth national convention, held in Houston, Texas, in June 1922, he was elected its international president. (His predecessor, William S. Carter, had held the office since 1909.) Robertson's most recent re-election was in 1947, when the B. of L. F. & E. national convention suspended a stipulation in the union's constitution setting an age limit of seventy years for office holders. Robertson, who was then seventy-one, was re-elected for a four-year term to lead the union, whose membership had passed 120,000.

Soon after the passage of the Railway Labor Act in 1926, a group of the AFL railroad unions, three of the "Big Five" independent railroad brotherhoods, and a few maritime unions, (twenty-one groups in all) merged to form the Railway Labor Executives Association, for the purpose of "cooperative action and to obtain and develop constant interpretations and utilization of all the privileges of the Act." In 1931, as chairman of this body, Robertson was called to testify before a Senate subcommittee on the advisability of establishing an economic planning council in the Federal government. Declaring that the great mass of the working people of the United States are "practically voiceless" in shaping the industrial policy of the country, the labor leader said, "Such a council . . . could accomplish, in my opinion, just the same thing for the Nation that an organization in a single industry accomplishes for that industry."

In February 1932, again as chairman of the association, Robertson presided over negotiations between the member unions and the railroads in which the unions voluntarily accepted a wage cut of 10 per cent for one year in order (in Robertson's words) "to do all within their power" to ease the depression. At the time of the negotiations on the union leader's competence to "discuss and argue" with the railroad operators "such intricate financial matters as railroad costs, rates and capitalization," the New York *Times* pointed out that the 56-year-old labor leader had already experienced more than a quarter of a century in "a hard, rough-and-ready, but acutely delicate school of negotiation."

In September 1932 Robertson resigned as chairman of the Railway Labor Executives Association in order to devote more time to his own union. In December of that year, writing in the magazine published by the B. of L.

F. & E., he declared that "conditions accepted by labor during the depression as its contribution toward national recovery cannot be permitted to become permanent."

Although the railway brotherhoods are craft organizations, there is overlapping of jurisdiction, particularly in the case of Robertson's union and the Brotherhood of Locomotive Engineers. This has resulted in two divergent trends: strong rivalry between the two unions and attempts to amalgamate them. Calling the maintenance of two such brotherhoods "irrational and illogical," Robertson has frequently pressed for such a merger. Successive conventions of the union have approved the move, but it has not reached fruition. The most recent action was taken in March 1949, when an agreement to merge the two bodies was signed by a joint committee and referred to a membership referendum

Dissatisfaction with the Railway Labor Act, which had served for years as a model instrument for effective labor relations, was first expressed by both labor and management during World War II years. Beginning with 1943, when President Roosevelt by-passed the act by offering to serve as sole arbiter in a wage dispute (an offer which Robertson and the heads of two others of the five brotherhoods rejected), the established machinery of the act has been in question. A strike set for December 30, 1943, by the five brotherhoods was called off. In late 1944 efforts by the National Mediation Board failed to settle a dispute between the firemen and enginemen's union and the Seaboard Air Line Railway, and a strike was averted only when President Roosevelt named an emergency mediation board. In the following January the army took control of the Bingham and Garfield Railroad to end a 12-hour strike by the union, and in August the Office of Defense Transportation took over the Illinois Central Railroad to prevent a threatened strike by that union. A nation-wide strike by three of the five brotherhoods in 1948 was averted when the Government seized the roads; arbitration achieved an agreement only after eleven months. Late in 1948 Robertson announced a strike vote against the Southern Pacific; again an emergency board appointed by President Truman effected a compromise.

Robertson was quoted by the New York World-Telegram in December 1949 as declaring that the Railway Labor Act had broken down "largely as a result of the appointment, to the adjustment board, of lawyers, economists and professors who have received more and more cases that could be settled on a local level." What gains have been made by railroad labor in recent years, he added, have been won at too great a cost to the unions. He blamed the threat of Federal seizure of the roads for the fact that the unions had had to accept "inadequate awards with which they completely disagree."

As early as 1931 Robertson, speaking before a Senate committee, criticized the railroads for failure "to care for rail workers displaced by technological improvements in railway operations." In the case of the locomotive firemen, he charged that the increased use of Diesel power has added to unemployment while it effected economies for the railroads. A proposal of the Brotherhood of Locomotive Firemen and Enginemen that an extra fireman be used on each Diesel-powered locomotive was rejected on September 19, 1949, by a fact-finding board appointed by President Truman. As a result, Robertson stated on April 19, 1950, that his union would strike against four railroads on April 26. After a postponement on May 10 the strike began, when 18,000 firemen did not report for work on four of the nation's key railroad systems. The strike ended May 16 on terms described as satisfactory to both sides—on the main issue arbitration was agreed upon.

In 1927 the Brotherhood of Locomotive Firemen and Enginemen published a book, *Feeding the Iron Hog*, with a foreword written by Robertson. His contributions to the union's magazine have been described as "sound and serious," by a *Liberty* writer (January 5, 1946), who considers Robertson the "intellectual among the brotherhood heads." A New York *Sun* columnist spoke of him as a "Grade-A diplomat," yet "pretty two-fisted" in labor disputes. He married, on September 8, 1907, Edna M. Hayes; their two children are Robert Hayes and Jane Elizabeth. The labor leader is a member of the United Presbyterian Church, and is a Mason.

References

N Y Sun p14 Ja 3 '44
N Y Times IX p2 F 7 '32
Who's Who in America, 1950-51

ROBINSON, BILL May 25, 1878—Nov. 25, 1949 American tap dancer, known as "Bojangles"; appeared in vaudeville; night club entertainer and musical comedy performer in New York (1906-30); made motion pictures (1930-39), notably *Little Colonel*, *Littlest Rebel* (both with Shirley Temple), *In Old Kentucky*; returned to Broadway in 1939; famous for the variety of his steps and as the originator of the stair tap routine; known for his wit and for his contributions to charitable organizations. See *Current Biography*, 1941.

Obituary

N Y Times p1 N 26 '49

ROBINSON, EDWARD G. Dec. 12, 1893- Actor

Address: b. c/o Berg and Allenberg, Hollywood, Calif.; h. 910 Rexford Dr., Beverly Hills, Calif.

Edward G. Robinson has played more than forty roles in motion pictures, achieving international fame in 1931 for his interpretation of the title role in *Little Caesar*, the gangster picture which established the significance of that genre. For his portrayal of Papa Gino Monetti in *House of Strangers* he was named as the best character actor of the 1948-49 season at

EDWARD G. ROBINSON

the Cannes (France) Film Festival. Prior to his film career, Robinson had reached stardom on the Broadway stage, where he was associated with ten Theatre Guild productions including *The Adding Machine* and *Peer Gynt*. The actor is known as a collector of modern paintings and rare books.

Edward G. Robinson began life under the name of Emanuel Goldenberg on December 12, 1893, in Bucharest, Rumania, one of six sons born to Morris and Sarah (Guttman) Goldenberg. Emanuel was ten years old when he came to the United States with his parents. His father, a building contractor in Rumania, settled in New York City and became a merchant. The boy attended New York public schools and graduated from Townsend Harris Hall High School in 1910. He then became a student at the College of the City of New York and at Columbia University. Attracted to the theater, he gave up his idea of studying law, and in 1912 entered the American Academy of Dramatic Arts, where he studied until 1913. His admiration of Robinson, a character in the play *The Passerby*, led him to adopt that name for his professional career; Emanuel was changed to Edward, Goldenberg became the "G" in his present name.

His stage debut was made as Sato in *Paid in Full* in 1913, but after a number of small roles his career was interrupted by service in the United States Navy during World War I. In 1919 he acted the part of Steve in *First is Last*. Several roles in minor productions followed before he was engaged by the Theatre Guild to play Louis in *Banco* (1922). Reviewing Robinson's Broadway career in 1933, R. Dana Skinner, *Commonweal's* critic, wrote that the actor had "dynamic instinct for creating character and illusion and dominating make-believe." Of his performance as "the effeminate emperor" in the Guild's production of Shaw's *Androcles and the Lion* (1925), Skinner said

that "as usual" Robinson "had rounded out every detail of the characterization." Further praise was given him for his interpretations of the epileptic brother in *The Brothers Karamazov* (1927) and of General Diaz in *Juarez and Maximilian* (1926).

The first role in which Robinson starred was Nick Scarsi in *The Racket* (1927), a gangster of the type of Al Capone. The actor's handling of the part, pronounced "a masterly creation of character" by *Theatre Magazine*, brought offers from Hollywood. These he refused because of the unsatisfactory results of a previous film role which he had played opposite Dick Barthelmess in the screen adaptation of Joseph Hergesheimer's novel, *The Bright Shawl* (1923). However, after his next play, *The Kibitzer* (1929), of which he was coauthor as well as star, he did go to Hollywood. There he made several motion pictures including *The Night Ride, They Knew What They Wanted*, and *Little Caesar*. Refusing a long-term contract, he returned to Broadway to star in *Mr. Samuel* (1930). The failure of this stage production and the release and unanimous acclaim of *Little Caesar* in 1931, led Robinson to decide to devote all his time to the films.

In his first Hollywood pictures Robinson played a series of hard-boiled characters, outstanding among which were the title character in *The Last Gangster* (1937), the gambler in *Smart Money* (1932), and the cynical city editor in *Five Star Final* (1932). His first sympathetic role was that of the scientist in *Dr. Ehrlich's Magic Bullet* (1940). Thereafter the parts he was assigned portrayed a greater variety of characters. Foremost among these was the role of the insurance claims adjuster on the trail of murderers in *Double Indemnity* (1944). Archer Winsten (New York *Post*) declared that Robinson had "never been better," and Alton Cook (New York *World-Telegram*) gave Robinson credit for "an elaborately detailed study of a grim sleuth." In the same year (1944), the actor played a college professor in *The Woman in the Window*. This "humdinger of a mystery" with Joan Bennett and Raymond Massey as costars, was, in the opinion of Irene Thirer (New York *Post*), a Robinson triumph, in which he played most effectively "the gamut from easy good nature to emotional frenzy." He was less fortunate in the reviews of *Mr. Winkle Goes to War* (1944), a Columbia picture. Cast as a mousy, henpecked, middle-aged draftee who is tormented for his blunders by his fellow soldiers, he was neither "meekly amusing nor properly courageous," said Howard Barnes (New York *Herald Tribune*). In his playing of the sympathetic father to actress Margaret O'Brien in *Our Vines Have Tender Grapes* (1945), a story of Scandinavian-descended farmers living in Wisconsin, Robinson was pronounced "stolid and lovable" (New York *Times*), but both the role and the picture did not evoke the usual enthusiastic notices.

Robinson, who has been a free-lance actor since he terminated his contract with Warner Brothers in the early 1940's, in 1946 formed a new motion picture company, the Film Guild Corporation, with producer Sol Lesser. However, shortly after the release of its first film, *The Red House* (1947), in which Robinson played the lead, the company ceased production and Robinson continued free-lance acting. In 1948, after playing prominent roles in the films, *Scarlet Street* (1946), *Night Has a Thousand Eyes* (1948), and *Key Largo* (1948) Robinson won praise for his portrayal of the father and businessman who shipped out defective war material in the screen adaptation of Arthur Miller's play hit, *All My Sons*. "A superior job of showing the shades of personality in a little tough guy who has a softer side," wrote the New York *Times* critic; "remarkably sincere and moving," was the comment from *PM*'s Cecelia Ager. The year 1949 saw Robinson honored by the Cannes Film Festival for his work in *House of Strangers*, a Twentieth Century-Fox picture with Susan Hayward and Richard Conte among the leading players. Wanda Hale of the *Daily News* (New York) said that in her estimation his portrayal of the "lusty, domineering Papa Monetti," head of a banking house in New York's Little Italy, surpassed all other roles of his twenty-year film career. In the fall of 1949 the star went to Europe to play the father role in *My Daughter Joy*, to be made under the direction of Gregory Ratoff.

The actor, who has also played frequently in radio dramas, was presented with a scroll by the *Motion Picture Daily* and the *Motion Picture Herald* for being "the most effective film personality on the radio." He has been heard in *Cavalcade of America, Watchtower for Tomorrow*, and *Big Town*. In the last-named, a weekly serial, he was featured during 1941 in its starring role, Steve Wilson, crusading newspaper editor. The American Legion of California awarded him a citation of honor for his outstanding contribution to Americanism through his patriotic appeals on this program. He was also honored by the National Safety Council for his aid in the cause of safe driving through these *Big Town* dramas.

During World War II Edward G. Robinson donated $100,000 to the United Service Organizations' campaign for army and navy recreation facilities, and spent three weeks in France entertaining the armed forces on a USO tour. While in Europe, he made broadcasts of Allied propaganda in seven languages to peoples of Europe, and, at the invitation of the British Ministry of Information, acted the part of an American flying instructor in a full-length documentary film (*Journey Together*) produced for the British Government. In 1942 he spoke the English commentary for a Russian documentary film, *Moscow Strikes Back*. He contributed his services as a narrator to *We Will Never Die* (1943), a mass memorial to the Jews who lost their lives during the Nazi regime, and again to the *Red Cross at War* (1943), a panorama staged by the Red Cross. *Too Long, America*, a radio program about racial intolerance, featured Robinson as narrator (1944).

A *Saturday Evening Post* article (July 1, 1944) devoted to Robinson as art collector relates how the actor bought his first picture for two dollars in 1913 at an auction sale. To-

day his pictures, considered to form one of America's finest private collections, include Corot's *L'Italienne*, Grant Wood's *Daughters of the Revolution*, Renoir's *Apres le Bain*, as well as copies of paintings of Cezanne, Van Gogh, and other moderns. Regarding his ownership of these works as giving him an obligation to the public, Robinson turned the site of the badminton court of his Beverly Hills Tudor-style home into an art gallery (designed by the Chicago Art Institute) which is open to the public. Mrs. Robinson is not only an equally enthusiastic collector, but in January 1948 held her first "one-man" show of oils at the New York Bignou Gallery. She is the former Gladys Lloyd, actress, the daughter of a sculptor of Philadelphia Quaker stock. The Robinsons met while she was playing a leading part in *Lady Be Good*, a play which starred Fred and Adele Astaire. They were married on January 21, 1927. Their family consists of two children, a daughter of Mrs. Robinson by a former marriage, and their son Emanuel.

In commenting on a report issued by the California State Senate Commission on Un-American Activities listing Robinson, as well as some hundred other film celebrities, as having followed or appeased some of the Communist party line programs, Robinson emphatically denied any such affiliation: "These accusations . . . emanate from sick and diseased minds." The actor is five feet seven inches tall, weighs 158 pounds, has brown eyes and black hair. He is a chain cigar smoker, likes to wear old clothes, dislikes physical exercise; his clubs are the Lambs (New York) and the Masquers (Hollywood). Valuing his wife's opinion, he will not play in a film until she has read the script. Among his recreations he counts music and travel; he is credited with speaking eight languages, among them Spanish, French, Yiddish, and Rumanian.

References

    Collier's 89:21+ Ja 2 '32; 104-18 S 2 '39
    Commonweal 18:190 Je 16 '33
    N Y Post Mag p7 F 2 '46
    Sat Eve Post 217:26+ Jl 1 '44
    Script p28 F 24 '40

    International Motion Picture Almanac, 1949-50
    Who's Who in America, 1948-49
    Who's Who in the Theatre (1947)
    World Biography (1948)

ROBINSON, HENRY MORTON Sept. 7, 1898- Author
Address: h. Woodstock, N.Y.

Author of one of 1950's best-selling novels, *The Cardinal*, Henry Morton Robinson has served literature as teacher, editor, critic, essayist, poet, historian, biographer, and novelist. Other works of his which brought him note were *The Skeleton Key to Finnegans Wake* and *The Great Snow*.

Born in Boston, Massachusetts, on September 7, 1898, Henry Morton Robinson is the eldest of the eleven children of Henry Morton Robinson (a moderately successful businessman) and

Halsman

HENRY MORTON ROBINSON

Ellen (Flynn) Robinson. The family, in which there were seven sons and four daughters, moved to Malden, a suburb of Boston, where Henry graduated from the town's high school in 1917. The student had been the editor of the school paper. Having finished high school a few months after the United States was drawn into World War I, young Robinson enlisted in the Navy, there to serve for twenty-two months on submarine chasers and rifle ranges. That he retains "an unextinguishable enthusiasm for boats and small arms" from those experiences is told in a biographical booklet issued by Robinson's publisher.

Enrolling at Columbia University in 1919, Robinson became an active participant in the literary and dramatic life of the college. His contributions to the campus daily, *Spectator*, included so many "neat" examples of French verse form that he was given the life-long nickname of "Rondo." He became editor of *Varsity*, the campus literary magazine, a member of Boar's Head, John Erskine's undergraduate poetry society, and president of Philolexian, the debating society. In a college production of *As You Like It* he played the part of Touchstone. Upon receiving the B.A. degree in 1923 he was awarded the Phi Beta Kappa key and the Moncrieff Proudfit Fellowship in Letters for 1923-24. Remaining at Columbia, he earned the M.A. degree in 1924; for his thesis on the poetry of Alan Seeger he was given the James S. O'Neal Poetry Prize. At John Erskine's invitation Robinson then taught English at Columbia for three years.

Robinson's first book, *Children of Morningside*, a novel in verse, was published in his senior year at college. During 1925-27 he edited *Contemporary Verse* in addition to contributing to several literary monthlies, among

them *Century, Bookman,* and *North American Review.* In 1927 he resigned from Columbia to launch on a free-lance writing career. A methodical and prolific worker, he wrote hundreds of stories, articles, poems for national magazines. His second book was *Buck Fever* (1929), containing lyric poems and two long narrative poems, which Conrad Aiken called "very good entertainment." *Stout Cortez,* subtitled *A Biography of the Spanish Conquest,* appeared two years later, and was accorded as diverse appraisals as "overwritten popular biography" (*Outlook*) and "a brilliant biographical study" (Boston *Transcript*).

In 1935 the writer joined the editorial staff of *Reader's Digest,* beginning as associate editor, becoming a senior editor in 1942, then a "roving editor." (He resigned from *Reader's Digest* in 1945.) Meanwhile he continued to write books in several fields: *Science Versus Crime* (1935) was called "a fascinating combination of *True Detective* and the *Scientific American*"; a third volume of poetry, *Second Wisdom,* appeared in 1937; and *Private Virtue, Public Good,* a defense of private enterprise, was published in 1938. The book which Robinson is said to consider his best nonfiction work is *Fantastic Interim,* which came from the press in 1943. An "outspoken" record of American "manners, morals, and business" during the twenties and thirties, its author's "epithetical vigor" was compared with Mencken's by Clifton Fadiman (in the *New Yorker*).

Shortly after the publication of James Joyce's *Finnegans Wake* in 1939, Robinson and Joseph Campbell, a professor at Sarah Lawrence College, embarked on a study of that work, which culminated in the 1944 publication of *A Skeleton Key to Finnegans Wake.* Favorably received by critics, this attempt to simplify the reading of Joyce's work was judged "meaty, brilliant, assertive, overwritten" (by Max Lerner, in the New York *Times*) and "indispensable" in that it brings Joyce into "vivid life, full of energy, brilliance, passion" (by Edmund Wilson, in the *New Yorker*).

Robinson's first novel, *The Perfect Round* (1945), a fantasy of the struggle between good and evil, was on the whole favorably received, approval coming from the critics for *Commonweal* and *Saturday Review of Literature.* Two years later Robinson's second novel, *The Great Snow,* appeared. Critics found much to commend in this allegory-chronicle of "manners and morals of people living under stress." "A mature and estimable novel," was the opinion of the *Nation's* reviewer, while the critic for the *Saturday Review of Literature* felt it was "quiet, firm, deliberate, and controlled." The *New Yorker* writer thought Robinson's treatment had "wit as well as a most human understanding."

The Cardinal, the best-selling novel of mid-1950 by Robinson (who is a Roman Catholic), traces twenty-five years in the life of an American Catholic priest from the beginning of World War I. It met with a rather mixed reception at the hands of the critics. While the *Atlantic* reviewer thought its militancy might be disconcerting to non-Catholic readers, he considered the book "a performance of remark-able virtuosity" from the standpoint of crafts-manship. The *Library Journal* recommended it highly; and the critic for the San Francisco *Chronicle* wrote that Robinson "brings [to it] the resources of a seasoned writer's sympathy and ability." The critics' columns in two Catho-lic periodicals summarized the book as "a grade-B rapid movement novel" (*Catholic World*), "an oversized version of one of those tract-in-dialogue pamphlets" (*Commonweal*). The Chicago *Sunday Tribune*'s reviewer felt that *The Cardinal* "deserves and will surely re-ceive wide popular attention," a correct pre-diction—the book reached the top of the best-sellers list, where, as of early July 1950 it still remained.

Publications in which Robinson's work has appeared, in addition to the *Reader's Digest*, are the *Saturday Review of Literature*, the *New Yorker*, the *Rotarian*, and the *Literary Digest*. A member of Phi Beta Kappa, scho-lastic honor society, the writer was chosen Phi Beta Kappa poet at the Columbia com-mencement ceremonies in 1931; he also belongs to Phi Kappa Psi fraternity. He is a member of the American-Irish Historical Society, of the Poetry Society of America, and he is a trustee of the Woodstock (New York) Public Library. Clubs to which he belongs are the Columbia University, the Century, the New York Athletic, and the Nantucket Yacht. He designates himself as a Democrat. Married on October 18, 1926, to Gertrude Ludwig, Robin-son has three children, Ellen, Hannele, and Anthony. A man of medium height (five feet seven and a half inches), he has a weight of 175 pounds; the color of his eyes is brown; and of his hair, black. His chief diversion is to cruise in his 31-foot cabin cruiser—"I take it anywhere a boat of that size can go," he says. Other interests are falconry and chess. Described in his publisher's brochure as re-flecting many-sidedness in his appearance, at various times he might be taken "for a country squire, a trial lawyer, a character actor, or an aesthete at large."

References

Sat R Lit 30:23 Ap 12 '47
Who's Who in America, 1950-51

ROOSEVELT, FRANKLIN D(ELANO), JR. Aug. 17, 1914- United States Repre-sentative from New York

Address: b. c/o House Office Bldg., Wash-ington, D.C.; 598 Madison Ave., New York 22; h. 305 West End Ave., New York 23

The election of New York's Franklin D. Roosevelt, Jr., to the United States House of Representatives in May 1949 was greeted by *Collier's* as "another step in the gradual decline of boss-ruled political machines throughout the United States." In his own words, the success-ful Liberal party candidate (who is a Democrat-Liberal) saw his victory over a Tammany Democrat as "proof that we are experiencing a revolution in American politics"; he predicts an end to "the monopoly on big-city party or-

ganizations formerly held by irresponsible club house loafers." The first of the four sons of President Roosevelt to hold an elective political office, Roosevelt (before serving during the war in the United States Navy) was a member of a Wall Street law firm. In April 1949, after several years of law practice and of activity on behalf of war veterans, he announced his can-didacy for the unexpired term of the late Sol Bloom[43], representing New York's Twentieth Congressional District. In a "record outpouring of voters for a special election" he received 50.9 per cent of the votes cast.

Franklin Delano Roosevelt, Jr., was born August 17, 1914; his birthplace is Campobello Island, New Brunswick, Canada, the summer home of his parents, Franklin Delano and Anna Eleanor (Roosevelt) Roosevelt. In the year of his birth, his father, who was to become the thirty-second President of the United States, was serving as Assistant Secretary of the Navy. His mother, in 1949 a permanent member of the United States Delegation to the United Nations, had not yet entered national affairs. In the Roosevelt family at the time of his birth there were three other children—his sister Anna and his two brothers, James and Elliott; another brother, John, was born later. Franklin, Jr., received his early education from private tutors, and according to his mother showed himself to be "an impressionable child . . . easily touched, easily hurt, generous and improvident" (Wesley Price, in the *Saturday Evening Post*). When he was twelve years old he entered Groton School, a tradition in the Roosevelt family and, according to an article by Arthur M. Schles-inger, Jr., in *Life*, the only firm requirement made by the Roosevelts of their sons. There he played football, rowed with the crew, and he excelled in debate. In 1933, when he was gradu-ated, he won a prize for combining scholarship and athletics "to the highest degree." That sum-mer he traveled in Europe, where the Roosevelt name caused correspondents and cameramen to report his doings in detail.

In the fall of 1933 Roosevelt entered Harvard University. There, too, his father's position made him the subject of newspaper accounts, some of them unfavorable, highlighting as they did any "playboy" stories. He majored in so-ciology and history and distinguished himself as a member of the Harvard rowing crew. Grad-uated from Harvard with a B.A. degree in 1937, in the fall of that year he moved to Charlottes-ville, Virginia, to study law at the State uni-versity. While there he was visited frequently by his father and mother. According to the *Saturday Evening Post* article, it was the Pres-ident who suggested to him that a few years in a law firm would be good preparation for a political career, and it was from his father, too, that young Roosevelt learned the lesson of "not worrying." He recalls that his father "always did the best he could, and slept soundly at night. He never worried. Neither do I."

In June 1940 Franklin Roosevelt received the LL.B. degree from the University of Virginia. During the late summer and the fall of that year he assisted in his father's campaign for re-election, appearing on the platform with the President and helping to coordinate the youth

FRANKLIN D. ROOSEVELT, JR.

work of the Democratic National Committee. He also initiated the activities of the various Roosevelt College Clubs. Later in 1940 he worked as a junior clerk in a Wall Street law firm and passed his New York State bar examination. From January to March 1941 he was a member of the law firm of Wright, Gordon, Zachary, Parlin, and Cahill.

Although the United States was not yet at war, Roosevelt left law practice in March 1941 to accept duty in the United States Navy. While at Harvard he had had four years' training in the Reserve Officers' Training Corps; he had been a member of the Naval Reserve since 1938, with the rank of ensign. He was placed in charge of a gun crew on the U.S.S. *Mayrant*, a destroyer patrolling the Atlantic, which later participated in the North African invasion and the landing in Sicily. After three years of service on the *Mayrant*, where he was called "Big Pancho" by the crew, he was transferred to the Pacific, where he was in command of a destroyer escort, the U.S.S. *Ulvert M. Moore*. He remained on active duty until the fall of 1945; returned to the United States for a short period of duty at the Naval War College in Newport, Rhode Island; and was discharged October 1945. In his service period he had been promoted to the rank of lieutenant commander and had received a number of awards and campaign ribbons, including the Purple Heart and a Silver Star for "conspicuous gallantry and intrepidity" during the attack at Palermo, and a Legion of Merit for his command of a destroyer when it tracked down a Japanese submarine.

In November 1945 Roosevelt joined the law firm of Poletti, Diamond, Rabin, Freidin, and Mackay, an organization handling all types of law cases except the criminal. Here he felt he could get a "good grounding in law." A year later he became a partner in the firm, with which he continues to be associated in 1950—

he says he believes in having a "bread-and-butter job so that he can afford as a politician to do what he thinks is right even though it may be unpopular" (in the words of the New York *Herald Tribune*).

When Roosevelt returned to civilian life he was, according to the Schlesinger article, "oddly sobered." He accepted the chairmanship of the housing activities of the American Veterans Committee. His first act in this connection was to participate in arranging for six hundred veterans to occupy Bronx apartments formerly occupied by Waves. At that time he also wrote an article for the *Nation* (November 1945) describing the housing shortage faced by returning servicemen. Throughout 1945, 1946, and much of 1947 Roosevelt took the lead in demanding housing for veterans. He petitioned Mayor La Guardia, Governor Dewey, and members of Congress for special legislation to provide emergency prefabricated houses, for continuation of rent control, and for the enactment of the Wagner-Ellender-Taft national housing bill. (In 1946 he served on the Committee of One Thousand to defend price and rent control.)

More closely related to politics was his association with the Americans for Democratic Action, a nonpartisan organization formed in January 1947 at a conference of one hundred and fifty prominent New Dealers. A campaign to recruit members from among non-Communist liberals has resulted in 1949 in the establishment of a hundred and twenty local chapters of the ADA in some thirty states and a total membership of 35,000. At the March 1947 meeting Roosevelt was elected national vice-chairman. Its program at that time called for fair employment practices, extension of the TVA principle to other areas, Federal aid to education, a housing law and rent control, opposition to increased military influence in the atomic energy program, and extension of social security. In the 1948 Presidential campaign Roosevelt supported Truman, continued his affiliation with the Democratic party, and spoke against the third-party candidacy of Henry A. Wallace.

Although there were rumors that Franklin Roosevelt had been offered several posts in Federal departments, Roosevelt accepted one, a year's service as vice-chairman of the President's Civil Rights Committee. In January 1949 he accepted an appointment to the New York City Mayor's Committee on Unity, a group designated by Mayor La Guardia to create better racial and religious understanding in the city.

As early as 1946 Roosevelt had been suggested as a candidate to the New York State Senate, and in 1948 he was offered the Democratic nomination for Congressman. It was not until March 1949, however, that he decided to run for a political office. This was occasioned by the death of Representative Sol Bloom and the calling of a special election in New York's Twentieth Congressional District to fill the vacancy.

In his own account of the election, "How We Won," in *Collier's* (August 6, 1949) Roosevelt described the district he represented as a "cross section of America," where nearly a half million people live in "homes that range from slums through average apartments to luxury dwellings." In a traditionally Democratic district he classifies himself as a Democrat-Liberal. Although one of the Democratic Club leaders suggested that Roosevelt be nominated for the Democratic party ticket, he failed to receive the Tammany Hall support. As a result he was a candidate on the Liberal party's ticket as well as the choice of the independent Four Freedoms party, which Roosevelt and his supporters had decided to place on the ballot as an additional incentive to voters. The issues on which he campaigned were public housing, civil rights, President Truman's Fair Deal, and a strengthened Israel. While it is not required of Congressional candidates in New York State that they be residents of the district they wish to represent, Roosevelt in April took up residence in the Twentieth District and began an intensive speaking program of one month. He was assisted by volunteer workers from the ADA, the Democrats for Roosevelt, the Fair Deal Democrats, several unions, and various foreign-born groups. In the final balloting, Roosevelt received 41,146 votes, as against the 24,352 cast for his nearest competitor, the Tammany Hall candidate.

Soon after arriving in Washington, Roosevelt introduced a bill to give direct Federal loans to families wishing to construct cooperative housing. He has voted for the foreign arms aid bill, the minimum wage bill, the national housing bill, and the anti-poll tax legislation. In October and November of 1949 he was active in the New York Senatorial election, campaigning for Herbert H. Lehman, and he supported the reelection of Mayor O'Dwyer of New York. Another public appearance Roosevelt made before his own election was at the New York *Herald Tribune* Forum (October 1949), at which his speech was entitled "How and Why the Democrats Will Win in 1950."

The New York Representative is a trustee and member of the executive committee of the Franklin D. Roosevelt Memorial Foundation, a member of the American Bar Association, and a trustee of Long Island University. In December 1949 he was named chairman of a newly created National Christian Committee to aid the United Jewish Appeal's 1950 fund campaign. He is a Mason and an adherent of the Episcopalian faith. In May 1949 he was divorced from his first wife, the former Ethel du Pont, whom he had married in June 1937, and by whom he had two sons, Franklin Delano 3d and Christopher du Pont. In August 1949 he married Suzanne Perrin, a former member of the Marine Corps Women's Reserve. Standing six feet, four inches in height, Roosevelt weighs about 200 pounds; the color of his eyes is gray-blue. His speech is reminiscent of his father's, as is his manner. *Life* has said that he "astounds people by his sudden reminders of F.D.R. . . . by his quick charm, the easy assurance, the politician's flair, the alert and flexible response to people." His mind has been described as "quick and well-organized." Among the sports he enjoys are sailing, horseback riding, and golf; and his reading is chiefly history and biography.

References

Life 22:112-+ Ap 7 '47
Sat Eve Post 222:30+ S 24 '49
Congressional Directory (1950)
Who's Who in the East (1948)
World Biography (1948)

ROOSEVELT, JAMES Dec. 23, 1907- Businessman; political figure

Address: b. 714 S. Hill St., Los Angeles 14, Calif.; h. 623 N. Bedford Dr., Beverly Hills, Calif.

The eldest son of President Franklin D. Roosevelt [42], James Roosevelt, who in November 1949 announced his candidacy for Governor of California in the 1950 elections, has been in the public eye from youth. While in his twenties he was Massachusetts campaign manager for his father and national secretary of the Young Democrats; at thirty a successful insurance broker, he became Government coordinator of the independent and emergency Federal agencies. His subsequent career has included motion picture production, radio commentaries, and active service with the United States Marines in World War II. He has been chairman of the California State Democratic Central Committee and a member of the Democratic National Committee. In the November 1950 election Roosevelt was defeated by the incumbent Governor, Earl Warren [44].

James Roosevelt, the second child of Franklin Delano and Anna Eleanor (Roosevelt) Roosevelt [48], was born in New York City on December 23, 1907. His first memories are of Albany, where his father was State Senator in 1911-12. In Washington, while Franklin Roosevelt was Assistant Secretary of the Navy in the Wilson Administration, James attended the Potomac School, and the National Cathedral School. At twelve, following family custom, he entered Groton, where, in his father's words, he "did very well . . . in athletics and leadership, rather poorly in studies—lower half of the form—but passed all his college board examinations, two with honors." In the summer of 1924, the sixteen-year-old youth was a page at the Democratic National Convention where his father made the "Happy Warrior" speech nominating Al Smith [44] for the Presidency.

In 1926, after a summer as a laborer in a Canadian paper mill, young Roosevelt entered Harvard. There he rowed on the junior varsity crew and was a member of Fly, Hasty Pudding, the Institute of 1770, and the literary Signet Society. He is permanent treasurer of the class of 1930, but his own graduation was delayed six months because of failure to pass German. Upon graduating, he entered Boston University Law School.

A married man (he was married in June 1930 to Betsey Cushing, second daughter of the brain specialist Dr. Harvey Cushing), Roosevelt decided to become self-supporting; he obtained a position selling insurance, having become interested in the field when his father was vice-president of a Maryland insurance company. He thought, too, that this type of work would help him overcome shyness which threatened to stand in the way of a hoped-for

JAMES ROOSEVELT

political career. He began on September 1, 1930, with part-time work at $25 a week for Victor de Gerard, a Boston insurance man. For two months, while a student at law school, Roosevelt also attended the Maryland Casualty School in Boston. A 1931 reorganization of his firm made him vice-president at a high salary for three months; another reorganization put him on commissions only. "Just as soon as it appeared that his father was likely to become President," De Gerard has said, "big men and big interests began to swarm down on us, begging us to insure them." This fact, and Roosevelt's frequently mentioned energy, hard work, and charm, brought him an income in five figures as an insurance broker. A partner in, and president of, the Boston firm of Roosevelt and Sargent, Inc., from March 1935, he was associated with five other insurance-selling companies.

James Roosevelt's political debut was made in 1928, when the Harvard junior and three classmates stumped Massachusetts for Smith. Roosevelt campaigned for the State ticket in 1930, and in 1932 he and Boston's Mayor, Michael J. Curley, tried unsuccessfully to swing the Bay State delegation to his father. Chosen as his father's campaign manager for Massachusetts, Roosevelt made about two hundred campaign speeches, and after the election he reportedly suggested to Postmaster General Farley [44] the names of deserving Democrats for possible Federal appointments. His reputed position as "czar of Massachusetts patronage" (phrase from *Time*) aroused resentment, which did not subside until he left on a trip abroad. James Roosevelt was a delegate to the 1933 Constitutional Convention which repealed Prohibition. The President's suggestion that he might make James his secretary in 1935 was dropped after evoking unfavorable reaction.

From May to November 1935 Roosevelt was president of the National Grain Yeast Corporation of Belleville, New Jersey, which planned to manufacture industrial alcohol. In the 1936 election year, as national secretary of the Young Democrats, he predicted the revival of NRA, a statement regarded as ammunition for the Republicans. After the election, the President took the young man to the Inter-American Conference at Buenos Aires as his aide, with the rank of lieutenant colonel, Marine Corps Reserve, on active duty. Later the son resigned this rank, after public criticism. He remained on the White House staff.

In January 1937 young Roosevelt resigned as president of Roosevelt and Sargent to become a $10,000-a-year administrative assistant to the President. That July he succeeded the deceased Louis Howe as the President's press secretary, and in October his father announced that his son would act as a clearing house and co-ordinator of twenty-three independent and emergency Federal agencies. *Time* dubbed him the "Modern Mercury," reporting that he received as many as 150 telephone calls on a typical day. Pearson and Allen remarked in *Redbook,* "He is doing a first-rate piece of work, and quietly," while *Look* recalled in 1945, "Jimmy did this job without any remarkable success but also without any remarkable failures." "His sole public venture into politics," wrote the *New Republic,* "the endorsement of Mr. Claude Pepper [40] in the Florida primaries, turned out to be a faultless political coup."

From July 1938 until the end of that year's Congressional campaign, the size and source of James Roosevelt's income was a matter of public conjecture. In a *Saturday Evening Post* article (July 2, 1938) Alva Johnston listed large insurance policies of different types which had been sold by Roosevelt in competition with specialists of long experience. "No matter how ethical he may have been" in his sales methods, wrote Drew Pearson and Robert S. Allen, "the general public gave him no benefit of the doubt." Roosevelt's detailed answer, published in *Collier's* of August 20 and 27, 1938, included photostatic copies of his income tax returns from 1932 through 1937, showing that in the five years his earnings had totaled some $170,000—1 to 20 per cent of the rumored amounts. After his statements were broadcast over NBC, *Christian Century,* which had criticized him editorially, remarked: "The total effect of James Roosevelt's statements, both in print and on the air, is to make one believe every word he says. . . .A man who could turn a bad impression into a good one so skillfully must be a whale of a good salesman, of insurance or anything else."

Resigning in November 1938 from his White House post, throughout the next year James Roosevelt served as vice-president of Samuel Goldwyn Productions, Inc., which, after six months, raised his salary from $25,000 to $30,000. *Time's* comment was: "Under another name Mr. Roosevelt might well make more money. . . .Representative on the board of United Artists and liaison with the New York sales and distributing organization . . . he easily earned a year's salary [just] by his successful European promotion trip for *Wuthering Heights."* In 1940 Roosevelt was president of the Goldwyn Studio Corporation, after which he became president and treasurer of his own company, Globe Productions—his movies include *Pastor Hall* and *Pot O' Gold.*

Recalled to active service as a Marine captain in November 1940, Roosevelt was sent as an official military observer to the Middle and Far East. In August 1941 he became military adviser and liaison man to Coordinator of Information William J. Donovan [41]. After Pearl Harbor, the "hopelessly 4-F" reserve officer, afflicted with gastric ulcers, "used his father's prestige shamelessly to get into the shooting," related *Look.* He served as executive officer (second in command) of Carlson's [43] Raiders, the 2d Marine Raider Battalion of hand-picked volunteers, and won the Navy Cross in the famous August 1942 raid on Makin Atoll, Gilbert Islands, when he "personally saved three men from drowning in the heavy surf." The Makin occupation in November 1943 brought him the Silver Star for gallantry in action. He had been promoted to major in May 1942, and in June 1943 to lieutenant colonel. "Jimmy did a magnificent job during the period he served with me and later when he commanded his own Raider battalion" (the Fourth, which he organized and trained in early 1943), Colonel Carlson said. His twenty-six months of combat duty included the battles of Guadalcanal, Tarawa, and the second Battle of Midway. Colonel Roosevelt, who had stood at his father's side at four inaugurations, arrived too late for the President's funeral after a sixty-hour flight from Manila. (He is one of three executor-trustees of the more than $1,000,000 estate.)

Released to an inactive status in the marines for medical reasons in August 1945, Roosevelt settled in Beverly Hills, and soon became active in Los Angeles Democratic politics. In January 1946 he accepted a $25,000-a-year position with Jo Davidson's [45] Independent Citizens Committee of the Arts, Sciences, and Professions; in June he re-entered Roosevelt and Sargent as executive vice-president, establishing a West Coast office, and he is said also to have resumed the film business. Roosevelt, who had made weekly broadcasts during the summer of 1933, now became a sponsored news commentator; on July 8, 1946, he broadcast the first of the five-a-week, fifteen-minute programs which he wrote himself, and which were spotted by transcription over forty-one stations across the country. Said *Variety:* "Roosevelt's delivery is good, much like his father's, with a lower pitch and a slower tempo."

The businessman-commentator severed connections with I.C.C.A.S.P. when he was elected, in late July, chairman of the State Democratic Central Committee. "He maneuvered himself into the State chairmanship at a time when the Democrats here were split in all directions," wrote Roscoe Drummond from Los Angeles in the *Christian Science Monitor,* "and even the Republicans wryly agree that he has done an herculean organizational job." Roosevelt's chairmanship survived the Republican sweep of the 1946 elections, and much party dissension. He was a critic of the Truman [45] Doctrine and a leader in the "Draft-Eisenhower [48]" (for Presidential candidate) movement. After the 1948 Democratic National Convention, the General having refused nomination, Roosevelt yielded the State chairmanship, but retained the Democratic National Committee membership in which he had succeeded Edwin W. Pauley [45], a Truman supporter.

In November 1949 James Roosevelt announced that he would seek nomination as Democratic candidate for Governor of the State of California in 1950. Roosevelt emphasized his civil rights record, stating, "I recently reaffirmed that position by again voting not to seat the States' Rights Democrats on the National Committee." His platform he summed up as "Bring the Fair Deal to California." He expressed a belief in "practical politics" as the best mode of prosecuting social reforms. In a State-wide speaking campaign, Roosevelt has charged the Administration of Governor Earl Warren (native son who is running for a third four-year term) with failure to plan adequately for problems raised by the extraordinary increase in California's population. (Also running for Democratic nomination is a "free-lance" Democrat, Welburn Mayock of Los Angeles.) Under the State's cross-filing system (which Roosevelt is on record as disapproving) gubernatorial candidates must compete in both the Republican and Democratic primaries, to be held June 6, 1950. In the gubernatorial election that November, Roosevelt failed to win the governorship, which was captured again by Republican Earl Warren in an approximate 2-to-1 victory.

James Roosevelt is a Mason, an Elk, a Moose, a member of both the American Legion and the AVC, and of numerous clubs and organizations in Boston, New York, Washington, and Hollywood. He has written a number of magazine articles on political questions. Sara Delano and Kate are the children of his marriage to Betsey Cushing, which was terminated by divorce in 1940. In April 1941 Roosevelt married Romelle Theresa Schneider, a nurse who had taken care of him at the Mayo Clinic in 1938. Their children, Anna Eleanor, James, and Michael Anthony, were baptized in the mother's Roman Catholic faith; Roosevelt himself is an Episcopalian. Commentators have remarked that President Roosevelt's rangy, six-foot-four, prematurely bald, eldest son has inherited "his father's charm, his father's boundless energy, and his father's speech and oratorical style." He seeks recreation in yachting.

References

Collier's 102:9 Ag 20; 102:11-14 Ag 27 '38

Lit Digest 123:9 Ap 10 '37

Look 7:32 S 21 '43; 9:44 O 30 '45

Newsweek 2:16 S 23 '33; 5:18 Mr 9 '35

Read Digest 31:73 N '37

Sat Eve Post 211:8 Jl 2 '38

Time 31:14 F 28 '38

America's Young Men, 1938-39
(Continued next page)

ROOSEVELT, JAMES—*Continued*

Perling, J. J. Presidents' Sons; the Prestige of Name in a Democracy (1947)
Who's Who in America, 1950-51
Who's Who in Commerce and Industry (1948)
Who's Who in the West (1949)
World Biography (1948)

ROSSEN, ROBERT Mar. 16, 1908- Motion picture writer, director, producer
Address: b. c/o Columbia Pictures Corp., 1438 N. Gower St., Hollywood 28, Calif.

The screenwriter-producer-director whose *All the King's Men* won the Academy Award for 1949, Robert Rossen, has said of his career: "I haven't made a picture that some one didn't protest. . . .If a picture is strong enough, it's bound to offend someone." He considers two such films to be *They Won't Forget,* for which he wrote the play, and *Body and Soul,* which he directed. *A Walk in the Sun*—the screen version was his work—was judged the best of Hollywood's war stories.

Robert Rossen, grandson of a rabbi, was born in New York City on March 16, 1908, and grew up in a poor East Side district. As a boy be began to box for the same reason the other boys of the congested neighborhood did; it was a sport which required little space and could be carried on indoors. Urged to become a fighter by friends who "chipped in" to pay his training expenses, he fought a few professional bouts only to decide against continuing in the ring. The youth, whose uncle was a Hebrew-language poet, had been drawn to writing since he first learned to use a pencil. By the time he entered New York University, creative writing was his principal interest.

At college Rossen became interested in the theater as a medium of expression. Soon he was writing, directing, acting, and helping to stage plays for the Washington Square Players, the group which was to grow into the Theatre Guild. When Rossen was twenty-one he directed his first play, Richard Maibaum's *The Tree,* an artistic success but a financial failure. Then came the depression, during which Rossen barely made a living at acting, stage managing, directing, working in summer stock; he directed some of the first anti-Fascist plays in the early 1930's. Rossen has since told of meeting an old friend, a producer, and of accounting for the long period of unemployment by using the old Broadway excuse, "I've been writing a play." Under his friend's questioning, Rossen outlined a story which led the producer to offer him an advance against royalties. "I had no idea then of writing anything, just thought the money would keep me going a while," Rossen said to a New York *Sun* writer but after thinking it over he told his friend the truth. Rossen then was given a larger advance, and he "sat down and wrote the play." Produced in 1935, Rossen's *The Body Beautiful* was a failure, but it led to Hollywood offers, and in 1939 Rossen arrived in Hollywood under contract to Mervyn LeRoy, then

at Warner Brothers. During the next seven years Rossen collaborated on and wrote many stories and screenplays for that studio, among the most memorable being James Cagney's *The Roaring Twenties. They Won't Forget,* the antilynching drama which was not shown in the South, came from his pen. In the year 1941 the screenwriter collaborated with Jerry Wald and Richard Macaulay on the screenplay of *Out of the Fog,* starring John Garfield and Ida Lupino—a motion picture of which the New York *Herald Tribune* critic wrote, "It follows the original Irwin Shaw play, *The Gentle People,* rather faithfully, but it has succeeded in converting a disappointing stage work into a vastly entertaining . . . stirring and exciting film . . . a work of genuine distinction."

In 1941, too, Rossen was the sole author of screenplays of Jack London's *Sea Wolf* (starring Edward G. Robinson) and *Blues in the Night* (in which Richard Whorf and Van Heflin played). Other scripts of his include *A Child Is Born* and *Dust Be My Destiny;* and in 1943 he adapted a novel by William Woods about the Norwegian underground for the film *Edge of Darkness.* His was the adaptation of Harry Brown's *A Walk in the Sun* (1946). Director Lewis Milestone, who had made *All Quiet on the Western Front* twenty-five years earlier, had had four versions of the *Walk* script prepared in four and a half weeks, before Rossen was assigned the task. Of the result Howard Barnes wrote: "Robert Rossen has converted the Harry Brown novel to screen coinage with something of an alchemist's skill." Screen Writers' Guild president Emmet Lavery gave his opinion: "That he [Rossen] was able to . . . fashion a screenplay for the peculiar needs of the motion picture camera . . . and still so faithfully preserve the essence of Mr. Brown's book, is as great a tribute as possible to . . . consummate professional and technical skill."

After seven years with Warner Brothers, Rossen returned to New York for a year "to sit and think about which medium he really wanted to work in, stage or screen" (in the words of the New York *Times* Hollywood correspondent). Having decided that the screen offered a greater scope than the stage proscenium, he returned to Hollywood in 1946. His last pictures in the single function of writer were two melodramas, *The Strange Love of Martha Ivers* and *Desert Fury.* After reading the first twenty pages of Rossen's script for *Johnny O'Clock,* a story of murder among gamblers, Dick Powell [48] said, "I'll make it, but only if the man who wrote the script directs the picture." Rossen thus directed *Johnny O'Clock,* which *Variety* termed, "a smart whodunit, with attention to scripting, casting, and camera-work lifting it above the average. . . . Brief bits are etched in as carefully as large parts." It was the opinion of another .critic that Rossen would not solely restrict his talents in the future to writing.

The picture which made Rossen's reputation as a director, the only one thus far for which he did not write his own script, was the prizefight exposé, *Body And Soul.* Much was made of the fact that the writer (Abraham

Polonsky), director Rossen, and the star (John Garfield) all came, as did the hero, from the East Side, and that Rossen, Garfield, and the prominent supporting player Canada Lee were all ex-fighters. Reviewers called this late 1947 release "terrific . . . top rank as social commentary and action thriller . . . throat-catching . . . overpowering illusion of truth," and praised the cameraman, the director, and the entire cast, especially Garfield, Lee, and newcomer Lilli Palmer.

Because the producers of *Body and Soul* had no previous production experience, they and Rossen learned together, and in 1949 Rossen became a producer himself. His first effort was *The Undercover Man* for Columbia, based on an article by Frank J. Wilson, the former Secret Service chief. A story of the trapping of criminals by agents of the United States Department of the Treasury, it was made in a semidocumentary style, which resulted in a convincing film with forceful acting and realistic settings. Here again Rossen was seen as excelling in attention to detail.

In 1949 Rossen became writer-director-producer of the screen version of Robert Penn Warren's Pulitzer Prize novel of a demagogue, *All the King's Men*. *Look* reported that Rossen made ten drafts "in his perfectionist attempt to preserve the realism and integrity of the original story"; while Broderick Crawford [50] and others said that Rossen wrote no dialogue in advance but made the actors study the book, take their long speeches from it and shorter ones from lines he often jotted down on the set. Rossen cast little-known actors in the leads and shot most of the film in three northern California towns, using local people as supporting players and extras. Often he shot a scene on the first take, when the players thought they were rehearsing. In bad weather which usually disrupts outdoor shooting schedules, Rossen adapted the script to conditions. Many of his scenes were "written" in the cutting room, where he combined different shots to get the effect he sought. The result was a drama which won some thirty awards, including Academy "Oscars" for the film, for players Broderick Crawford and Mercedes McCambridge. Awards to Rossen included the *Look* Achievement Award for the best screen writing of 1949, the Screen Directors' Guild prize for the year's best directing, and top honors in his three categories—writing, direction and production—from the Foreign Language Press Film Critics' Circle, which also voted this the best of the year's foreign and domestic films.

Shortly after completion of *All the King's Men* in August 1949, the writer-director-producer began work on his version of Tom Lea's best-selling novel, *The Brave Bulls*—he and Lea together selected actors, locations, and the animals in Mexico. Censorship regulations by the Mexican Government and the American Humane Association—the former aimed at presenting an approved picture of the country, the latter at preventing the filming of real or apparent cruelty to animals—complicated filming of the bullfight story, a problem Rossen met by combining telescopic shots of actual *corridas* with newsreel footage, and using closeups

ROBERT ROSSEN

of players' reactions to suggest the action. To heighten the effect of realism, Rossen is eliminating background music.

Stocky, square-faced Robert Rossen is described as quiet, modest, and unassuming, preferring to spend his leisure in a "close circle of his friends." He and Mrs. Rossen (who formerly was employed in a large New York publishing house) have three children, Carol, Steven, and Ellen. During World War II Rossen was chairman of the Hollywood Writers Mobilization, which in October 1943 held a three-day Writers in Wartime congress, co-sponsored by the University of California, greeted by President Roosevelt and Wendell Willkie. Something of Rossen's personal philosophy may be gathered from his remark, "Real life is ugly. But we can't make good pictures till we're ready to tell about it."

References

N Y Sun p15 Ap 15 '47
International Motion Picture Almanac, 1949-50

RUSSELL, HAROLD (JOHN) Jan. 14, 1914- Veterans organization official
Address: b. c/o Amvets National Headquarters, 724 9th St., N.W., Washington, D.C.; h. Watertown, Mass.

The AMVETS (American Veterans of World War II) at its convention in September 1949 elected as its national commander Harold Russell, the handless veteran who in 1946 won recognition in the motion picture *The Best Years of Our Lives*. Manager of a chain grocery store in Cambridge, Massachusetts, before the war, Russell has since become known as a speaker on the topics of interracial understanding and the physically handicapped, as well as on the various program of AMVETS. Rus-

Harris & Ewing

HAROLD RUSSELL

sell was re-elected national commander for another year on September 10, 1950.

Harold John Russell was born in North Sydney, Nova Scotia, on January 14, 1914. After his father, the manager of the local telegraph office, died when Harold was six years old, the family (in which there were two other boys) moved to Cambridge, Massachusetts, where Mrs. Russell became a nurse. Harold Russell attended the Merrill and Harvard grammar schools in that city, then entered Rindge Technical High School. He says he was "bitten by the airplane bug" after Lindbergh's transatlantic flight, and entered that school in the hope of obtaining a scholarship to Massachusetts Institute of Technology. As it was, he tells, "I was terrible at math and science, and I had no ability with my hands." He was graduated from Rindge in June 1933.

From the time he was ten years old, young Russell had added to the family income by working after school hours—he was errand boy, car washer, newsboy, and delivery boy for a local chain provision store. After leaving high school he obtained a part-time job in the store as counter man at fifteen dollars a week, learned meat cutting, and eventually became the store's manager. During summer months he worked as counselor in a YMCA boys' camp.

Immediately after the attack on Pearl Harbor, Russell enlisted in the army (he had been rejected by the navy and the marines), was inducted on February 2, 1942, at Fort Devens, Massachusetts, and was sent to Camp Croft in South Carolina for infantry training. He volunteered for paratroop training, after which he attended a demolition school, and became an instructor. For nearly two years he taught at the parachute school in Fort Benning, Georgia, with the rank of sergeant, making fifty-one parachute jumps during that time.

The accident that deprived Russell of his hands occurred at Camp Mackall, North Carolina, where he was instructing a demolition squad of the 515th Parachute Infantry Regiment of the Thirteenth Airborne Division. On June 6, 1944, a defective fuse on a charge of explosive which he was handling caused an explosion which shattered his hands and wounded him in the chest and stomach. The following day his hands were amputated three inches above the wrist. In his autobiography, Victory in My Hands (1949), written with Victor Rosen, Russell has described the complete despair of his first weeks at Walter Reed Hospital in Washington, D.C., and the difficulties of learning to manipulate the prosthetic devices designed to take the place of hands.

A motion picture, Meet McGonigle, which was used in rehabilitation work, showing a handless veteran of World War I going through the normal routine of daily living with the help of his "hooks," was one of the first factors in Russell's recovery. (McGonigle himself spent some time with the amputees at the hospital demonstrating that "any handicapped person could . . . take a normal place in society if he really wanted to.") As Russell was nearing the end of his convalescence, in September 1944 he was asked to take the leading part in a Signal Corps film, patterned after Meet McGonigle. Produced by Julian Blaustein, with the narration by Alfred Drake, Diary of a Sergeant was filmed at Walter Reed Hospital, in Long Island, and in Boston. The picture was widely used as a morale builder in the rehabilitation of amputees. "It did wonderful things for my ego," Russell has said.

On January 3, 1945, Russell was discharged from the Army. He returned to Cambridge and enrolled at the Boston University School of Business Administration, planning to prepare for a career in advertising. To supplement his total disability pension he directed, three nights each week, the boys' athletic program at the Cambridge YMCA. During the eighth war loan drive he spoke throughout New England in connection with showings of Diary of a Sergeant.

In January 1946 Russell obtained leave of absence from Boston University in order to go to Hollywood to play the role of Homer Parrish in The Best Years of Our Lives, the film based on MacKinlay Kantor's No Greater Glory. Russell spent the first few weeks in the film capital in attempting to lose his Boston accent (he was to play the part of a Middle-Westerner) and to reduce his weight. Robert Sherwood, who wrote the screen adaptation, talked with Russell about himself and his background and used much of this material in building the characterization of the sailor in the film. William Wyler, the director, said of Russell's performance: "He isn't an actor, of course, and he has no acting technique, but he gives the finest performance I have ever seen on the screen." The director declared that he concentrated on guiding Russell's thinking more than his acting." "I call his performance a 'thought' performance," he said, "because you know instinctively what he is feeling just by the expression on his face or the way he tilts his head or covers his hooks."

The picture drew superlative adjectives from the critics. Eight "Oscars," the annual awards of the Academy of Motion Picture Arts and Sciences, were given to the picture and to those connected with it. Harold Russell received two of these awards: one for "the best supporting performance by an actor in 1946" and a special award "for bringing aid and comfort to disabled veterans through the medium of motion pictures"; and he received *Look*'s award for the "best dramatic performance of 1946." The opinion of the New York *Times* was: "Russell rose to a superb opportunity. He revealed, as none but a crippled veteran could have done, the spiritual agonies and possible triumphs of the mutilated. He illuminated Sherwood's poignant story with his own courage. . . .Finally, he turned out to be a gifted actor."

Six weeks after the release of the picture, Russell's contract with Goldwyn for personal appearances in connection with it was allowed to lapse through an error. On the advice of his manager, Russell accepted another tour of appearances in theaters at $1,750 a week. At this time, the veteran has pointed out in his book, he was becoming concerned with the problem of race relations, and he therefore adopted the practice of closing his "act" with a plea for democracy, unity, and better racial understanding. After one week, Russell decided that he was not giving his audience their money's worth of entertainment, and accepted an offer to work with the Anti-Defamation League of B'nai B'rith. As its representative Russell visited forty-six States during 1948-49, speaking before high school and college groups. "I figure maybe if enough of us talk to enough people," he said, "they'll stop hurting democracy. Discrimination is like amputating America's hands." (In November 1947 B'nai B'rith gave him its humanitarian service award.)

In 1947 Harold Russell had joined the American Veterans of World War II, the only organization of that war's veterans to receive a Congressional charter. The AMVETS (its popular name), which was formally constituted in December 1944, today has three major aims, as presented in one of its pamphlets: "To promote peace, to preserve America's way of life, and to help veterans help themselves." The programs it supports are "more and cheaper housing, more and better social security, proper aid to veterans, international peace, economic stability." It seeks revision of the U.N. charter to achieve the elimination of the veto power, to establish international control and inspection of armaments, and also an international court and police to enforce its decisions. It approves the Marshall Plan and presses for adequate national defense. Through its National Youth Opportunity Committee, of which Russell was national chairman in 1948, it provides guidance for "fledgling citizens"; its National Service Department handles legitimate claims of disabled veterans; its National Peace and Preparedness Committee is concerned with international questions.

At the organization's convention at Des Moines, Iowa, on September 5, 1949, Russell was elected national commander. Other actions taken at the convention were: rejection of a proposed merger with the American Veterans Committee; recommendation of a Federal bonus of up to $4,500 for veterans of World War II; proposal of a Pacific military pact; approval of a plan for registration of Communists; opposition to compulsory health insurance; and support for Federal aid to education. The AMVETS commander discussed several of these issues as one of a five-member panel at the October 1949 New York *Herald Tribune* Forum. He also addressed an audience of handicapped people at the opening of National Employ the Physically Handicapped Week. As national commander he announced the presentation of a carillon by his organization to the amphitheater of Arlington National Cemetery.

At the 1950 convention of the AMVETS Russell was re-elected national commander by acclamation after the other candidates had withdrawn. Before that event the convention approved the lifting of the constitutional bar against second terms for national commanders, an amendment applying only to Russell. Earlier that year Russell was named one of the "Nation's Ten Outstanding Young Men of 1949" by the United States Junior Chamber of Commerce.

On February 27, 1946, in California, Russell married Rita (nee Russell), a childhood sweetheart, also from Massachusetts. With their two children, Jerry (Mrs. Russell's son by an earlier marriage) and Adele Rita, they live in Watertown, Massachusetts. In an interview with Russell for *PM* (April 14, 1946), Mary Morris described him as "chunky, of medium height, with brown hair" and as having "an infectious smile, a right-guy personality."

References

Life 21:74 D 16 '46 por
N Y Herald Tribune V p5 D 9 '46
N Y Post Mag p41 N 26 '46 por
PM Mag p7 Ap 14 '46 por
International Motion Picture Almanac, 1947-48
Russell, H. J. Victory in My Hands (1949)

SAARINEN, ELIEL (sä'rĭ-nĕn ē'lyĕl) Aug. 20, 1873—July 1, 1950 Finnish-born architect and city planner; won international acclaim with design for the Helsinki railroad station; his unexecuted plan of tower for Chicago *Tribune* building of great influence in modern architecture; won international prizes for city plans for Estonia, Latvia, and Australia; head of architectural department of Cranbrook Foundation near Detroit, Michigan, since 1925; other of his plans were for the Christian Church in Columbus, Indiana, and Kleinhans Music Hall in Buffalo, New York; author of *The City*. See *Current Biography*, 1942.

Obituary

N Y Times p15 Jl 3 '50

SADAK, NECMEDDIN (säd-äk nĕj-mĕd-dĭn) 1890- Former Foreign Minister of Turkey
Address: Ankara, Turkey

One of the men who have shaped the policy of Turkey since 1939 is Necmeddin Sadak, who became the Foreign Minister of his country in September 1947. A former professor of social sciences at the University of Istanbul, Sadak entered politics in 1929 as a member of the National Assembly. He is also noted as a journalist, having been editor in chief of the newspaper *Aksam* for more than thirty years. The foreign policy pursued by Sadak has been aimed at obtaining Turkey's inclusion in the Atlantic Pact or another regional pact linked to it; he has sought and been granted aid for his country under the Marshall Plan; and has resisted Soviet pressure for a share of the control of

Wide World Photos
NECMEDDIN SADAK

the Dardanelles. In the general elections held in April 1950, which brought Celâl Bayar's [50] Democratic party into power, the resultant Cabinet change eliminated twelve Ministers, of whom Sadak was one.

Necmeddin Sadak was born in Istanbul, Turkey, in 1890, the son of Chehabeddin Sadak Bey, a circuit judge, and his wife Arifé. Educated at the *lycée* of Galata Saray in Istanbul, Necmeddin prepared himself for a teaching career. He was granted a state fellowship to continue his studies in France, where he majored in political and social sciences at the University of Lyons; he received his diploma in 1914.

Returning to Turkey that year, the young man was appointed to the Department of Education and later became, successively, an assistant professor and professor of social sciences at the University of Istanbul. In 1917, when he was twenty-seven years old, Sadak founded a daily newspaper in Istanbul called *Aksam*. Delos W. Lovelace, writing for the New York

Sun (February 24, 1944), reported that that event marked the beginning of Sadak's public career in that the newspaper voiced his "ardent support of the nationalist cause" during the occupation of Turkey by Britain, Italy and France following World War I. Though the paper was "roughly censored," Sadak managed to continue its publication through the occupation; in 1950 he is still its editor in chief.

In 1929 Sadak resigned his professorship at the University of Istanbul when he was elected to the National Assembly by Sivas, as a candidate of the Republican People's party. He was appointed his country's delegate in the Disarmament Conference which opened in Geneva in 1932, and participated in 1936 as the Turkish delegate in the Conference on the Convention on the Straits held at Montreux. From 1936 to 1939 he served as permanent Turkish delegate to the League of Nations.

When World War II began, Sadak became a "roving envoy" for his country, visiting France, Germany, England, and India. Turkey, which had remained neutral since the outbreak of the war, declared war on Germany and Japan on February 23, 1945, but took no active part in the conflict. After the Soviet-Turkish non-aggression pact was abrogated in March 1945, the U.S.S.R. began to exert pressure on Turkey for a share in the control of the Dardanelles. In 1947 the United States agreed to advance $100,000,000 to Turkey to be used for the armed forces or for economic projects related to Turkish defense.

On September 9, 1947, an interim Government was formed in Turkey to serve until the National Assembly reconvened in November. Hasan Saka, who had been Foreign Minister, became Prime Minister of Turkey, and Necmeddin Sadak was appointed Foreign Minister. When, in June 1948, the Turkish Cabinet was again reorganized to admit more young "progressives" of the governing Republican People's party, Sadak was reappointed to his post. Peter Schmid, writing in *Fortnightly* (August 1949), stated that Sadak was one of the leaders of the progressive group within his party, a group which included Vice-Premier Nihat Erim and President of State Ismet Inönü [41]. According to *Information Please Almanac* (1949), centralization is the basic policy of the Government of the Republican People's party.

Foreign Minister Sadak conferred with British Foreign Minister Ernest Bevin in March 1948 to reaffirm the Anglo-Turkish military alliance; in April he went to Athens, to pave the way for closer economic cooperation between Turkey and Greece. In an interview with C. L. Sulzberger of the New York *Times* in June 1948, Sadak declared that Soviet Russia was again exerting pressure for revision of the Montreux Convention on control of the Dardanelles, and that Turkey wanted a formal alliance with the United States. In July Sadak signed the ERP accord under which Turkey received fifty million dollars of ERP funds allocated until July 1, 1949. Of the amount Turkey received, nineteen and a half million was for agriculture and thirty and a half million for industry. Joseph G. Harrison, writing in the *Christian Science Monitor* (April 2,

1949), reported that the effects of the Truman Doctrine and the Marshall Plan were encouraging in Turkey; that due to American equipment and advice, the Turkish armed forces were appreciably stronger, internal tension had declined, and democratic tendencies had been strengthened.

The Turkish Cabinet underwent another reorganization in January 1949, when Hasan Saka resigned under criticism from his own Republican People's party because of the high living costs. He was replaced on January 16 by Shemsettin Gunaltay, who reappointed Sadak as Foreign Minister. On February 17, 1949, after a conference in London, Sadak proposed in Paris that the North Atlantic Pact be supplemented by a Mediterranean area defense agreement, a view also supported by Greek Minister Tsaldaris '46, who reported accord among West European leaders for an eventual pact. Though Turkey and Greece were included in the proposed arms aid plans of the United States, the omission of Turkey from the North Atlantic Pact resulted in alarmed public opinion in that country.

In April 1949 Sadak left Turkey for the United States to head his country's delegation to the General Assembly of the United Nations, and also to explore the possibilities of obtaining additional military and economic aid. Turkey had asked $94,200,000 from the ECA for 1949-50, but ECA had recommended that it be granted $30,000,000. After conferring with Secretary of State Acheson and President Truman, Sadak held a press conference in which he stated that "Turkey considers the Atlantic Pact insufficient in some aspects for the maintenance of peace on the Continent of Europe. She believes and wishes that Turkish security should also be guaranteed by another regional pact which would be linked to the Atlantic Pact."

"Turkey Faces the Soviets," an article by the Turkish statesman in the April 1949, issue of *Foreign Affairs Quarterly*, reviewed Turkish foreign policy since 1919. It pointed out that Russian policy toward Turkey on the control of the Dardanelles has remained essentially the same since the time of the czars. Sadak stated that when Turkey refused to accede to Russian demands for the Dardanelles after World War II, the United States became interested in helping Turkey by means of the Truman Doctrine and Marshall Plan military aid. Sadak's journey to Washington in April 1949 was regarded as having strengthened already friendly ties between Turkey and the United States, although Turkey was not invited to join the Atlantic Pact group and the United States expressed disinterest at that time in joining any Mediterranean defense pact. In August 1949, the Committee of Ministers of the Council of Europe met at Strasbourg, France, for the first time, and invited Turkey to become a member. Sadak, as his country's Foreign Minister, represented Turkey at the meetings.

In the general elections held May 14, 1950, the Democratic party, which is headed by Celâl Bayar, won 408 seats in the national legislature, out of a total of 487. Bayar became president; and in the new Cabinet Sadak (one of the twelve who were not named to it) was replaced by Fuad Koprulu.

Necmeddin Sadak is the author of a number of works on social sciences and education—his textbook on sociology is used in Turkish schools. He has also written articles and editorials for *Aksam* as well as for other publications. When the Turkish statesman visited the United States in 1949 he was accompanied by his second wife, whom he had married in the early 1940's. (His first marriage took place in 1914.) One writer has described the thin-faced, mustached Sadak as having "a patient and reflective air."

References

N Y Sun p22 F 25 '44
U N Bul 6:440 My 1 '49 por
Who's Who in Central and East-Europe, 1935-36
World Biography (1948)

SAMPSON, MRS. EDITH S. Oct. 13, 1901- United States delegate to the United Nations; lawyer

Address: b. c/o United States Delegation to the General Assembly of the United Nations, 2 Park Ave., New York 16; 3518 S. State St., Chicago, Ill.; h. 310 E. 38th St., Chicago, Ill.

Mrs. Edith S. Sampson of Chicago, Illinois, in August 1950 was named alternate United States delegate to the fifth General Assembly of the United Nations. For eighteen years Mrs. Sampson, a Negro lawyer, had served as a probation officer and referee on the Juvenile Court of Chicago. Chairman of the executive committee of the National Council of Negro Women, she came to international attention in 1949 as a member of the World Town Hall of the Air lecture panel which toured the world.

Born to Louis Spurlock and Elizabeth A. (McGruder) Spurlock on October 13, 1901, Edith S. Sampson spent her early years in Pittsburgh, Pennsylvania, her birthplace. Her grade school studies were interrupted by the financial necessity of her going to work. Later able to resume her schooling, she did so and graduated from Pittsburgh's Peabody High School.

Through the good offices of her Sunday school teacher, Miss Spurlock was brought to the attention of Associated Charities; that organization employed her and later was responsible for arranging for her admission as a student to the New York School of Social Work. There she made the highest grade in a required course in criminology, a circumstance which led the professor, George W. Kirchwey of the Columbia University School of Law, to remark: "You are in the wrong field. You have the earmarks of a lawyer."

It was not until the young woman was a resident of Chicago and had met Dean Kirchwey again that she acted upon his advice. Then she matriculated as a night student at the John Marshall Law School, where she studied from 1922 to 1925. As the highest ranking student among ninety-five in the course on jurisprudence, she received special commendation from

Official United Nations Photo.
MRS. EDITH S. SAMPSON

Dean Edward T. Lee. This experience made her overconfident, reported Max Gilstrap of the *Christian Science Monitor*, so that, after receiving her Bachelor of Laws degree in 1925, she failed to pass the Illinois State bar examination. "That was the best thing that could have happened to me," Mrs. Sampson was later to observe—she began to work toward her Master of Laws degree at the Graduate Law School of Loyola University. When the advanced law degree was bestowed upon her in 1927, she was the first woman to have been the recipient of the LL.M. from that institution. She was admitted to the practice of law in Illinois that year.

In the meantime, during her law student years in Chicago, Miss Spurlock was employed at the Young Women's Christian Association and the Illinois Children's Home and Aid Society. In 1925 began her eighteen years of association with the Juvenile Court of Cook County, Illinois, when she was appointed a probation officer and later a referee. Concurrently, from 1924 until 1942 she maintained her own law office on Chicago's South Side, specializing in criminal law and domestic relations. In the year (1934) she was admitted to practice before the Supreme Court of the United States, the attorney was married to lawyer Joseph E. Clayton on November 5, with whom she continues her law practice. (By her first marriage, she became Mrs. Sampson, the name she uses in professional and public life.)

As chairman of the executive committee of the National Council of Negro Women, which encourages outstanding Negro women to become leaders in their communities, Mrs. Sampson in 1949 was invited to be one of the twenty-six American civic, cultural, labor, and welfare leaders to participate in the World Town Hall of the Air lecture tour. On it she participated in public debates on current political questions,

and met leading political figures in the foreign countries visited. Her "skill in the art of human relations" (in the words of the *Christian Science Monitor*) made her an outstanding member of the panel; when the organization was made permanent as the World Town Hall Seminar, the other members elected Mrs. Sampson its president.

"Mrs. Sampson had made the world tour at her own expense," reported Walter White in the New York *Herald Tribune*, "because she felt strongly that an American Negro woman should be there to tell the truth about the Negro's status as answer to the anti-American propaganda of the Moscow radio." An Indian heckler's comments on racial tensions in the United States were silenced when Mrs. Sampson, admitting that American democracy did not function perfectly yet, remarked: "I would rather be a Negro in America than a citizen in any other land." Her mention, in a speech to the League of Pakistan Women, of her efforts to raise the five thousand dollars for the expenses of the trip led to the collection of a like amount in the audience. This was offered to the American speaker by the Begum Liaquat Ali Khan '50, wife of the Premier of Pakistan; Mrs. Sampson accepted it and then gave a gift of the amount to the League for use in its social work.

Mrs. Sampson, a member of the executive board of the United Nations Association of Chicago, frequently was present at United Nations meetings at Lake Success as an observer for the National Council of Negro Women. In August 1950 she was nominated by President Truman to serve as an alternate United States delegate to the fifth regular session of the General Assembly of the United Nations, the first member of her race to be an official United States representative to that organization. (Dr. Ralph J. Bunche '48, the American Negro prominently associated with the United Nations, is a member of the Secretariat, being director of the Department of Trusteeship.) With Mrs. Eleanor Roosevelt, Mrs. Sampson is assigned to Committee Three—the Social, Humanitarian, and Cultural Committee. To suggestions that her appointment had been made as a refutation of Soviet propaganda, Mrs. Sampson replied, "I would be glad to refute such propaganda. There are pitfalls for our race in this country, of course, but they are not as bad as the Kremlin would like to picture them." She made her first appearance before Committee Three on September 28, 1950, in an appeal for the continuation of United Nations advisory work in the social welfare field. Several days previously she had been assigned to deal with the complaint that the Soviet Union had not carried out complete repatriation of prisoners of war. One of the lawyer's comments on her new post was: "I was used to defending one man; now it's all people."

At the Herald Tribune Forum in October 1950 Mrs. Sampson gave an address, "World Security Begins at Home." Speaking of the necessity of safeguarding the fundamental freedoms desired by all people—those of education, financial independence, speech, free association, justice, and religion—Mrs. Sampson urged the carrying out of the objectives of the United Nations charter. Emphasizing the importance of action along such lines on the home front, she suggested that individuals could contribute in several ways: "Act to strengthen America. . . . Fight against inflation. . . .Fight hoarding. . . . Increase production. The airplane, the radio, films, and the free press, including our own organization publications, are modern instruments for building a people's front against aggression and for world development. Let's use them with all the energy and imagination we can muster."

Bar associations to which Mrs. Sampson belongs are the Chicago and the National; she is also a life member of the National Association of Women Lawyers. In 1950 she is chairman of the committee on international relations of the National Council of Negro Women. Another of her memberships is in the League of Women Voters. The Claytons, who live in Chicago, have helped to rear her sister's two children. A description of the U.N. official at home mentioned the jelly that she had been making, and her paintings by young Negro artists. Interior decorating and canasta are among her pastimes.

References

Christian Sci Mon p12 S 19 '50
Look 13:13 N 22 '49
N Y Herald Tribune p1 Ag 19 '50; II S 3 '50
N Y Times p8 Ag 19 '50
Scholastic 57:16 S 27 '50
Time 56:14 Ag 28 '50
Who's Who in Colored America, 1950

Michael Tenzer

ALI SASTROAMIDJOJO

SASTROAMIDJOJO, ALI (săs-trō-ä-mē-jō-yō) May 21, 1903- Indonesian Ambassador to the United States
Address: b. c/o Embassy of the Republic of Indonesia, Washington, D.C.; h. Shoreham Hotel, Washington, D.C.

On January 23, 1950, Ali Sastroamidjojo was appointed by Soekarno '47, President of the Republic of the United States of Indonesia, as the first Ambassador to the United States from the world's youngest republic. Since his youth Sastroamidjojo had been closely associated with the Indonesian nationalist movement. A leading figure in the Indonesian Republican Government, he served for two years as its Minister of Education and Culture. He also played a prominent role in the extended negotiations with the Dutch, which culminated in December 1949 with the transfer of sovereignty to the United States of Indonesia, and in a treaty called the Indonesian-Netherlands Union, which provided for equal sovereign status of both countries. In August 1950 President Soekarno proclaimed that the new name of the country would be "Republic of Indonesia," abolishing the federated "United States of Indonesia."

Ali Sastroamidjojo was born in Grabag-Merbabu, Central Java, on May 21, 1903. His father held the title "Raden," a mark of nobility. After beginning his education at the Sekolah Desa (village school) in Grabag, the boy continued his studies at the elementary school in near-by Magelang. He subsequently attended the high school at Jakarta (then Batavia) from 1918 to 1923, and completed his education in the Netherlands, receiving his Doctor of Laws degree from the University of Leyden in 1927.

While a student in Holland, Sastroamidjojo was active in the Perhimpunan Indonesia (Indonesian Association), an organization dedicated to Indonesian independence. In September 1927 four members of this group, including Sastroamidjojo and Mohammed Hatta '49 (later to be the first Premier of the United States of Indonesia), were arrested and imprisoned for six months on a charge of instigating rebellion against the Dutch Government. After a sensational trial at The Hague, they were discharged. This *cause célèbre* gave rise to much excitement in Indonesia, heartening the nationalist cause. Sastroamidjojo returned to Java in 1928 and established a law practice in Jogjakarta.

Upon his return to Java, Sastroamidjojo became a member of the executive of the P.N.I. (Partai Nasional Indonesia—Indonesian Nationalist Party), founded by Soekarno with the aim of overthrowing Dutch rule by passive resistance and noncooperation. The young nationalist joined the editorial staff of the party organ, *Suluh Indonesia Muda* ("Torch of Young Indonesia"). He also helped edit the weekly *Djanget* ("Link"); contributed to the daily *Sedio Utomo* ("High Aim"); and taught at a Taman Siswo school. The latter were independently operated schools with a curricular emphasis on Indonesian culture and tradition in protest against the Dutch colonial educational system. Sastroamidjojo went to Surakarta in 1929, where he continued his law practice, and contributed articles to the weekly *Timbul* ("Awakening") and the newspaper

SASTROAMIDJOJO, ALI—*Continued*

Darmokondo ("The Monitor"). Later he moved to Surabaja and Madiun in East Java.

The Dutch Colonial Government tried to suppress the P.N.I., imprisoning Soekarno in 1929, dissolving the party in 1931, and outlawing its successor Partindo, of which the released Soekarno had become leader. Sastroamidjojo and other members of Partindo (of which Sastroamidjojo was an executive member) regrouped themselves in 1937 into a new party, Gerindo (Indonesian Movement). Under the leadership of Amir Sjarifuddin, the new organization advocated political, economic, and social democracy in an independent Indonesia, and adopted as its strategy cooperation with the Dutch, through representative councils in autonomous areas as well as in the central representative body. By such new tactics the Gerindo aimed at practicing parliamentary opposition to Dutch colonial policy. In 1939 a new national front, the Federation of Indonesian Parties (G.A.P.I.) was formed; but there was little time for consolidation before the Dutch East Indies fell to the Japanese invaders in March 1942.

During the Japanese occupation nationalist aspirations continued to grow, and on August 17, 1945 (three days after the Japanese surrender) Indonesian independence was proclaimed and the Republic was set up at Batavia (now Djakarta). To his first Cabinet Soekarno appointed Sastroamidjojo Deputy Minister of Information, to serve under Sjarifuddin. Later Sastroamidjojo was made secretary-general of the State Defense Council at Jogjakarta. In the spring of 1947 he was sent on his first important diplomatic mission as a member of the Republican delegation to the Inter-Asian Relations Conference at New Delhi, India. According to Virginia Thompson and Richard Adloff (writing in *Far Eastern Survey*), the delegation "lost no opportunity to invite negotiations for trade and political relations with other Asian countries."

Sastroamidjojo was prominent in the reestablished P.N.I., a group of nationalists, which held the balance of power between Left and Right in the Central National Indonesian Committee (K.N.I.P.), the provisional parliament. In June 1947 Premier Sutan Sjahrir resigned under pressure from K.N.I.P., and on July 3, he was succeeded by Sjarifuddin, who appointed Sastroamidjojo Minister of Education and Culture in the new Cabinet. In this post Sastroamidjojo assumed direction of the Republic's program to achieve total literacy (in a population of some 70,000,000 only 7 per cent could read or write) in a national, Oriental system of free education, with Indonesian as the medium of instruction.

Following a fresh outbreak of warfare between the Dutch and the Indonesian Republic, the United Nations Security Council intervened, appointing a three-man Committee of Good Offices to facilitate mediation. In the subsequent negotiations, Sastroamidjojo served as deputy chairman of the Indonesian delegation which, under Premier Sjarifuddin, agreed to the Renville Truce Agreement, signed on

January 17, 1948. This agreement provided for the establishment of a United States of Indonesia within the year, and for plebiscites to determine whether people in the Dutch-held areas wished to join the Republic or to enter the United States of Indonesia as separate states. The Right-wing bloc in the K.N.I.P. accused the administration of having yielded to Dutch demands in the Renville Agreement, and on January 23, Sjarifuddin resigned as Premier. Mohammed Hatta [49] formed a new Cabinet on January 31, 1948, retaining Sastroamidjojo in the post of Minister of Education and Culture. Simultaneously it was announced that the Republican delegation would continue negotiations with the Dutch, Mohammed Rum being the new chairman and Sastroamidjojo continuing as deputy chairman. When, in February 1948, the U.N. Security Council discussed the Dutch-Indonesian dispute, Sastroamidjojo was the spokesman for his country.

The next month Sastroamidjojo appeared before the U.N. Security Council, which met at Lake Success to discuss the Indonesian problem. There he charged that the Dutch were setting up puppet states in West Java, East Java, and Madura in an attempt to side-step fair plebiscites. Arguing that this was in direct violation of the Renville Agreement, the Indonesian spokesman asked that the Security Council guarantee free plebiscites in the disputed areas.

During the months following his return to Indonesia in April 1948, Sastroamidjojo was deputy chairman of the Republican delegation for negotiations with the Dutch to implement the truce and frame a final political settlement. After several months of deadlock, the discussions were broken off completely. On December 19 the Dutch, resorting to "police action," in a surprise attack on Jogjakarta captured President Soekarno, Premier Hatta, and seven Cabinet ministers including Sastroamidjojo, and interned them on the island of Bangka, off Sumatra. The Security Council eventually brought about a series of preliminary conferences between the two sides in the spring of 1949. The Indonesian delegation was led by Mohammed Rum, with Sastroamidjojo, who by then had been released, as deputy chairman. These discussions led to the Rum-Van Royen statements (Van Royen was head of the Dutch delegation), by which the Dutch agreed to release all political prisoners and restore the Republican Government to its capital, and the Indonesians agreed to participate in a round-table conference to settle the Indonesian question. Shortly after the return of the Republican Administration to Jogjakarta in July, Sastroamidjojo resigned his Cabinet post so that he would be free to attend the proposed conference.

Representing the P.N.I., together with its chairman, Sastroamidjojo was sent to The Hague as a member of the Republican delegation headed by Hatta. On November 2, 1949, the Dutch, the Republicans, and the Federalists agreed to create an Indonesian state with complete independence from the Netherlands Kingdom. The Republic of the

United States of Indonesia was to comprise the Republic of Indonesia and fifteen other Indonesian states (several of which have since merged with the Republic). Besides, the Indonesians agreed to enter into a treaty with the Dutch, called the Indonesian-Netherlands Union, in which both parties have equal status as sovereign countries. Formal transfer of sovereignty took place on December 27, 1949.

Sastroamidjojo's appointment as the first Ambassador of the Republic of the United States of Indonesia to the United States of America (which had recognized the former on December 28, 1949) was made on January 23, 1950. Upon his arrival in the United States, Ambassador Sastroamidjojo said he believed that financial assistance from the United States would make possible Indonesian economic recovery within four or five years. Making his first public address in Washington a week after presenting his credentials to President Truman on February 20, the Indonesian Ambassador declared that "by championing the ineluctable and impending social revolutions of the countries of South Asia, the United States stands its strongest chance of keeping them in the right paths." On another occasion, without specifically mentioning President Truman's Point Four Program to assist underdeveloped areas throughout the world, he referred to the help Indonesia needs in the task of reconstruction: "This is fundamentally a social rather than an industrial reform which must begin with education and technological assistance from all countries of the world which have the advantage of experience." After August 15, 1950, Sastroamidjojo represented the "Republic of Indonesia" in Washington, the new name proclaimed by President Soekarno to supersede the "Republic of the United States of Indonesia."

Ali Sastroamidjojo has written on nationalism and the rights of Indonesian women. His articles in English include "A Survey of the Indonesian Nationalist Movement" (*Indonesian Life*, March-April 1947) and "The Status of the Republic of Indonesia in International Law" (with Robert Delson, *Columbia Law Review*, March 1949). Like the majority of Indonesians, Sastroamidjojo professes the Moslem faith. His wife, the former Titi Roelia whom he married in 1922, takes an active part in the Indonesian women's movement. They have two boys, Kemal Mahisa and Karna Radjasa, and two girls, Sawitri and Gayatri. Five feet nine inches tall, the Ambassador weighs one hundred and seventy pounds; his eyes are brown, his hair is black, and he wears a Vandyke beard. He lists his recreations as tennis and violin music.

References

N Y Times p16 F 21 '50 por; p8 Mr 31 '50

Washington (D.C.) Post p9S F 26 '50 por; p7B Mr 1 '50

Thompson, V. M. & Adloff, R. The Left Wing in Southeast Asia (1950)

SAUNDERS, CARL M(AXON) Oct. 26, 1890- Editor

Address: b. c/o Jackson Citizen Patriot, 211 S. Jackson St., Jackson, Mich.; h. 312 S. Thompson St., Jackson, Mich.

Winner of the 1949 Pulitzer Prize for editorial writing, Carl M. Saunders is editor of the Jackson (Michigan) *Citizen Patriot*. The prize-winning editorial, published in that paper (Independent) February 20, 1949, led Congress to dedicate Memorial Day as a day of prayer for peace; and a prayer which he wrote was used in the official service at Arlington National Cemetery on Memorial Day of 1949.

Carl Maxon Saunders was born October 26, 1890, in Grand Rapids, Michigan. Fred Saunders, his father, was a hotel operator who later became local manager of the Bell Telephone Company; he also held two public offices, as city alderman and city assessor. Carl's mother (of German descent) was the former Fanny Fransisci Sommer. Of the five Saunders children, three were boys. As a student at Grand Rapids Central High School, Carl Saunders participated in track, basketball, and football (later he played professional football for a brief period). He also served as sports editor on the school paper. Upon his graduation in 1909, young Saunders entered newspaper work.

Beginning as a reporter on the Grand Rapids *News*, Saunders became its sports editor in 1910. The next year he joined the reportorial staff of the Kalamazoo (Michigan) *Telegraph Press*, of which he subsequently became managing editor. In 1912 he went to the Detroit *Free Press* as copy editor, and was sports writer for that newspaper until 1915, when he returned to his home town. There for nineteen years (until 1934) he was reporter, then editorial writer, and, finally, editor, of the Grand Rapids *Herald*. On the *Herald* he was assistant to Arthur S. Vandenberg [48] (later United States Senator from Michigan), who was the editor of that newspaper from 1906 to 1928.

In 1934 Saunders was appointed editor of the Jackson *Citizen Patriot*, one of the eight Michigan papers published by Booth Newspapers, Inc. (Saunders has said that he was influenced in editorial standards by the late George G. Booth of Detroit.) In his editorial of February 20, 1949, which won the Pulitzer Prize, Saunders urged that Memorial Day be devoted to peace because it is dedicated to those who died in war. The editor observed that the United States is "generally classified" as a Christian nation, yet, as a nation, seems "utterly unaware of God or His place in the making of history." He asked why, since as individuals many Americans pray, America should not pray as a nation in a time of dire need of help and guidance, an appeal in which all faiths should join. Referring to the threat of war, he declared, "The first defense against disaster should be prayer, the first appeal for peace should be made to the Omnipotent Master of the universe."

(Continued next page)

CARL M. SAUNDERS

Saunders' editorial brought unanimous action from both houses of Congress. The prayer which he wrote was used in Memorial Day services at Arlington National Cemetery, after receiving official status in a proclamation by President Truman. It read, in part:

We ask that governments may rule in Thy wisdom.
We ask that intolerance, bigotry, and greed As between nations and men and races May be overcome by the force of Thy will.

Announcement of the winners of the 1949 Pulitzer Prizes was made in New York on May 1, 1950, by President Dwight D. Eisenhower of Columbia University. Upon hearing the announcement, the Michigan editor telephoned to Washington to apprise Senator Vandenberg, his old friend and editorial colleague, of the honor.

Editor Saunders has also gained considerable note for instituting a new device in editorial campaigns—the use of coupons printed in newspapers. During 1949 readers of the *Citizen Patriot* signed 18,000 coupons urging Michigan Congressmen and President Truman to support the Hoover plan for reorganization of the Federal Government. The campaign was taken up by more than fifty daily newspapers throughout the United States. In further support of the Hoover plan Saunders has initiated a series of front-page paragraphs pointing out examples of waste in Federal Government. In this practice he has been followed by more than forty newspapers.

Under the pseudonym of Max Sandy, Saunders has written a number of magazine articles and pamphlets on the subject of conservation. Correspondence sent from Europe by Saunders during the last days of World War II and immediately afterward was published by a group of Michigan newspapers. He is also the author of a booklet on Grand Rapids in which are described its history, industries, and institutions, written at the time he was editor of the *Herald.*

Carl M. Saunders is a member of the American Society of Newspaper Editors, the National Press Club, and the professional fraternity, Sigma Delta Chi. A past director of the Associated Press Managing Editors' Association, he is also a past vice-president of the Michigan Press Association and a past president of the University of Michigan Press Club. From 1941 to 1945 the editor was president of the Jackson War Chest and the Jackson Service Men's Center. He is president of the Jackson Foundation, a founder and former vice-president of the Greater Jackson Association, past director of the Jackson County Conservation Club and of the Michigan Conservation Council, a present director of the East Michigan Tourist Association, an honorary member of the Grand Rapids Advertising Club, and a onetime president of Rotary Club of Jackson. His clubs are the Jackson Country, the Silver Lake Country, and the Tippycanoe; he is a former president of the Town Club.

Saunders and his wife, Grace (Strong) Saunders, whom he married July 5, 1914, have two daughters, Dorothy Saunders and Leila (Saunders) Tuttle. The gray-haired editor, who has blue eyes, stands five feet ten and a half inches and weighs 190 pounds. He is a Republican and a Mason. Reared as a Congregationalist, he is now a member of the Episcopal Church. His hobbies are fishing, hunting, and gardening.

References

N Y Times p22 My 2 '50
Who's Who in America, 1950-51

SAWYER, EDDIE Sept. 10, 1910- Baseball club manager
Address: b. c/o Phila. National League Baseball Club, Packard Bldg., 15 & Chestnut Sts., Philadelphia 2, Pa.; h. Aberdeen Rd., St. Davids, Pa.

Two years after he became manager of the Philadelphia Phillies, in 1950 Eddie Sawyer led that National League baseball club to its first pennant since 1915; the World Series, which they lost to the New York Yankees, was the lowest-scoring series ever played. Of Sawyer, who is credited with building an unseasoned team of unusual youth into a group of professional players, Arthur Daley wrote in the New York *Times* (September 5, 1950), "No one can deny that Sawyer has turned in the best managerial job of the campaign." Prior to his association with the Phillies, Eddie Sawyer had been in the minor leagues, as a player (1934-38) and player-manager (1939-43) in the "farm system" of the New York Yankees. He was named "Manager of the Year" in November 1950.

Of Scottish ancestry, Edwin Milby Sawyer was born in Westerly, Rhode Island, on September 10, 1910, son of Robert George and Isabelle (Milby) Sawyer. Reared in the Rhode

Island town, he later attended New York's Ithaca College, where he was an honor student, a member of Phi Beta Kappa, and one of the school's outstanding baseball players. (He also played football.) He received the B. S. degree from Ithaca in 1935, and later he was granted the M. S. degree by Cornell University.

Sawyer was engaged from 1937 to 1943 as instructor in the science department of Ithaca College, where he taught biology, zoology, and physiology. He also coached football, and from 1939 to 1943 was assistant director of athletics. According to Professor Laurence H. Hill, head of Ithaca's science department, Sawyer's "ability to impart knowledge was unusual. He had a phenomenal memory and was a great detailist." During his six years on the Ithaca faculty Sawyer alternated teaching with baseball playing, from spring to fall taking part in minor league games. He resigned his teaching post in 1943 to devote his full time to baseball.

Sawyer's professional baseball career had begun a year before his graduation from Ithaca College, when, following a 1933 stint as outfielder for the Malone (New York) team in a league of summer resort towns, he was hired by the New York Yankees as outfielder for their (1934) Norfolk (Virginia) Piedmont League club. This marked the beginning of Sawyer's nine-year association with the Yankee's farm system. In 1935 he was called for spring training with the Yankees but spent the remainder of the year, first with the Yankee's Binghamton team and then with its Norfolk team. He was returned to Binghamton in 1936, spent the first portion of 1937 playing for Oakland (Pacific Coast League) club, and went back to Binghamton for the remainder of the 1937 season and all of 1938. Sawyer's outstanding performance as a player came in 1939 when, as outfielder for the Yankee's Amsterdam (Canadian-American League) club, he had a batting average of .369 and led the league in total bases, doubles, runs batted in and batting and tied for the lead in base hits.

The year 1939 also marked the first of Sawyer's five years as player-manager. Continuing on the diamond as an outfielder, as manager he led the Amsterdam team to first place in its league in 1939 and to third place in the following year. In 1941 Sawyer became manager of the Norfolk team which, under his direction, finished in fourth place. Later, as manager of the Binghamton club, he led that team to third and sixth place in 1942 and 1943 respectively. The year 1943 was his last as a player. During the years in which he played outfielder, Sawyer's fielding average varied between a low of .954 in 1938 and a high of 1.000 in 1935 and 1942; his lowest batting average was .267 (1942) and his highest .369 (1939). Sawyer is right-handed.

In 1943 Sawyer was engaged as manager in the farm organization of the Philadelphia Phillies, at a salary which allowed him to leave academic life for baseball. Sawyer's first assignment for the National League club was

Phila. Nat. League Club

EDDIE SAWYER

as 1944-47 manager of the Utica (Eastern League) team which, under his direction, finished in third place in 1944, finished first (but lost the play-offs) in 1945, and slipped to seventh place in 1946. In the following year the team climbed to first place and won the play-offs to grasp the Eastern League championship. Sawyer's second National League assignment, as 1948 manager of Toronto, the Phillies' top farm club (International League), came at the end of nine years of minor league managing, in which Sawyer's teams had won three pennants and two play-off championships and finished in second division only twice.

On July 26, 1948, Sawyer, who, according to Phillies owner Robert R. M. Carpenter, Jr., was promoted to the position "because of the outstanding work" he had done for the Phillies' farm system in the four and a half years just previous, became manager of the Philadelphia club. With the appointment of Sawyer as manager, wrote Arthur Daley in the New York Times Magazine (September 17, 1950), "the Phillies started an upward surge which hasn't stopped since." In 1949, Sawyer's first full season with the Phillies, the club won a three-cornered race with the Boston Braves and the New York Giants for third place. According to Harry Robert in the Washington Post, Sawyer also "scared the daylights out of the pennant-winning Dodgers, whipping them next to the last day and sending them into extra innings the final day of the season before they managed to squeak through. It was the most impressive showing the cellar-dwelling Phils had made since 1917, when they finished second under . . . manager Pat Moran." Before the beginning of Sawyer's management in 1949, the Phillies between 1918 and 1948 had finished last sixteen times, next to last eight times, sixth four times, fifth twice; they had finished in the first division (fourth place) once.

(Continued next page)

SAWYER, EDDIE—*Continued*

The Philadelphia Phillies, long nicknamed the "Phutile Phillies" by sportswriters because of the poor showing they had made, were purchased in 1943 by Robert Carpenter. On the advice of manager Herb Pennock, Carpenter initiated a program of buying players and ruled that, instead of trying to build up the club's standing by spending big money for baseball veterans, the club would launch a program of building from the bottom up. The Phillies. who by 1948 had a fifteen-club $2,500,000 farm organization, have been called "the youngest club in big league baseball," (*Life*, March 27, 1950). In appointing Sawyer manager, Carpenter commented: "He knows how to get along with kids."

Sawyer, whom the *Sporting News* (September 27, 1950) described as "a master at developing the full possibilities of a young ball player" in 1950 led the Phillies, now called the "Whiz Kids," to the National League pennant in a four-cornered fight in which the Brooklyn Dodgers, the Boston Braves, and the St. Louis Cardinals were the other principal contenders for the championship. Despite a number of mid-season injuries to players and the drafting (for military service) of one of the team's top winning pitchers, the Phillies reached first place "because," said the *Sporting News*, "they have the best balanced team in the league, the best pitching staff in depth as well as in individual excellence, and the best defense." In the 1950 season, with games won and lost as follows, the Phillies won the season's series with the Boston Braves (13-9), the St. Louis Cardinals (12-10), the Cincinnati Reds (18-4), the Chicago Cubs (13-9), and the Pittsburgh Pirates (14-8); split the season's series with the Brooklyn Dodgers (11-11); and lost to the New York Giants (10-12). In the 1950 World Series, they lost in four straight games (1-0; 2-1; 3-2; 5-2) to the New York Yankees.

Sawyer is said to be "one of the few big league managers to have come up through the farm system" more by managing than by playing (*Sporting News*). "Sawyer," stated *Time* (May 29, 1950), "is no bench manager, works on the third-base coaching line ('It gives the boys confidence'), works hard in his office ('I'm always available') and on the field ('I never humiliate a boy')." In November 1950 Sawyer was honored as "Manager of the Year."

The National League manager married (July 8, 1935) shortly after his graduation from Ithaca College, Pauline Beatrice Bassett of Mount Morris, New York, who had also been a student at Ithaca. They have two daughters, Dale and Dyann. A tall man (six feet) with blue eyes and graying brown hair, Sawyer weighs 210 pounds. He has been described as a "soft-spoken, scholarly, fatherly chap" with a "broad amiable face." For relaxation he plays golf and attends hockey games.

References

N Y Times p10 Jl 17 '48
Newsweek 34:64-5 Jl 18 '49
Sporting N p3 Sep 27 '50
Washington (D.C.) Post p13 Mar 6 '50; p13 Mar 7; p7 Mar 8; p6B Mar 10; p11 Mar 11

SAWYER, EDWIN M(ILBY) *See* Sawyer, Eddie

SCHRICKER, HENRY F(REDERICK)

Aug. 30, 1883- Governor of Indiana

Address: b. State Capitol Bldg., Indianapolis, Ind.; 4343 N. Meridian St., Indianapolis, Ind.

The Governor of Indiana, for the term 1949-52, is a Democrat, Henry F. Schricker, who held that same office during 1941-44. He is the only man in Indiana's history to have held its Governorship twice. With a political career in the State Senate, Lieutenant Governorship, and other State offices, Schricker is considered by *Time* to be the "most popular Democrat in the State," and has a record of successes at the polls in otherwise Republican victories. In business he has been associated with the Farmers Bank and Trust Company of Knox (Indiana) and the Fletcher Trust Company of Indianapolis.

Henry Frederick Schricker was born in the town of North Judson, in Starke County, Indiana, on August 30, 1883. His parents, Christopher Schricker and the former Magdalena Meyer, were both natives of Bavaria, Germany. The senior Schricker, after emigrating to the United States, settled in North Judson in the late 1860's, where he was employed by a railroad, a flour mill, and engaged in farming. In 1893 he opened a general store there, which he continued to operate until the time of his death in 1928. (These and other facts come from the Citizens Historical Association of Indianapolis.) From 1889 to 1898 Henry Schricker attended North Judson's public schools, and completed one year of high school; and during 1900-01 he was a student at the South Bend (Indiana) Business College.

The youth's first employment was in his father's store. A biographical sketch in the Indianapolis *Star* (June 13, 1948) indicated that Schricker thought of entering Valparaiso (Indiana) University to study law, but gave up the project in 1905 to become deputy county clerk of the circuit court; the next year he was a candidate for the post of county clerk, but was defeated. After reading law and working in the law office of Adrian L. Courtright, Schricker was admitted to the bar in January 1907, and engaged in practice at Knox (Indiana) until 1908, when he became cashier of the State Bank in Hamlet, a community near Knox. Purchasing the *Starke County Democrat*, a weekly newspaper with offices in Knox, he in September 1908 became editor; he continued to edit and publish that journal for eleven years. While in that position he became associated with the Farmers Bank and Trust Company of Knox, first as a member of the board of directors, an elective post, and then as cashier in 1919, at which date he sold the

Starke County Democrat. He remained with the bank until 1937. For nine years Schricker was a member of the Knox Board of education, and served as secretary of the Knox Building Loan and Savings Association for sixteen years.

Schricker resumed his political career in 1932, when he ran as Democratic candidate for State Senator and won the election. After serving through the sessions of his four-year term, in 1936 he was elected Lieutenant Governor of the State, in which capacity he presided over the upper house. During his four years in this post, Schricker was also commissioner of agriculture, a member of the board of the Department of State, chairman of the Indiana Milk Control Board, a member of the George Rogers Clark Memorial Commission, of the New Harmony Memorial Commission, of the State Board of Education, and of the Commission on Interstate Cooperation. As Lieutenant Governor, Schricker, much in demand as a speaker for meetings and dinners, traveled widely in the Hoosier State.

In 1940 Henry Schricker was elected Governor of Indiana. His victory won him considerable attention since he was the only Democrat to be elected Governor in the Midwest in the year that Wendell Willkie amassed a large number of votes for the Republican party; all other elective offices in Indiana were at that time swept by big Republican majorities.

In the summer of 1943 Governor Schricker's name came to the fore at the Democratic National Convention. Considered the leading politician in Indiana, the man "who has made Hoosier Democrats forget...Paul V. McNutt" (*PM*'s words), Schricker was being strongly supported as the candidate for the Vice-Presidential nomination in what the New York *Herald Tribune* called "a considerable boom." It was Schricker himself who ended this movement, stating that he did not believe he was the man for the office—it might mean succession to the Presidency in a period which would demand that the President be "a profound student of both governmental affairs and international relations." A New York *Herald Tribune* article at the time described Governor Schricker as a "conservative Democrat" who "has been loyal to the President on major issues and in party affairs, but has not pulled any punches criticizing red tape and bureaucracy in Washington and fumbling administration of the food situation and other home front problems."

Schricker, who under the Indiana State Constitution, was ineligible to succeed himself as Governor, ran for the office of United States Senator in 1944. Although he headed Democratic polling in his State, he was defeated by Homer E. Capehart [47], Republican. The former Governor returned to banking, becoming vice-president of the Fletcher Trust Company in Indianapolis, a post which he retained until January 1949.

When the Democratic State Convention met in 1948 Schricker was "virtually drafted" to run for the Governorship a second time. After a campaign in which the white hat Schricker customarily wears figured as a symbol of clean government, the Democratic candidate (char-

HENRY F. SCHRICKER

acterized by W. H. Lawrence in the New York *Times* as "a man who encourages voters to cross party lines") was victorious at the polls, being supported in almost every large industrial center in Indiana. (Voting on other State offices again favored the Republicans.) Assuming office in January 1949, Schricker became the first man to hold the position of Governor of Indiana twice. His term of office expires in January 1953.

Calling himself "a middle-of-the-roader," Governor Schricker has said that his "patron saint of politics" was Thomas Jefferson. The record (according to the Indianapolis *Times*) shows him to be a Right-wing Democrat: he favors the pay-as-you-go principle (he has kept his State's budget balanced); regarding a social security program as a necessity, he has stated that he believes that both employer and employee should contribute to the workers' fund; he has expressed approval of the Compulsory Arbitration Utilities Law because "it prevents crippling strikes in key plants," but has deplored its cost; he has spoken in favor of a voluntary version of the Fair Employment Practice Committee.

Schricker is a member of the Kiwanis Club. He was once a captain in the Indiana State Guard (1915-16), and chief of the Knox volunteer fire department. His religious faith is the Lutheran. In 1914, on October 21, Schricker married Maude L. Brown, and is the father of three children—Margaret Ruth (Mrs. L. C. Robbins), Henry Frederick, and George W. A former Scoutmaster, he still wears the Scout pin in his lapel. Governor Schricker is five feet nine inches tall, weighs 150 pounds, has blue eyes; his hair is white. Described in Indianapolis newspapers as "intense, serious, and confident" in manner, he has a reputation as a good extemporaneous speaker. Fond of music, he plays the piano, and used to play the church organ in North Judson. Among his hobbies is

SCHRICKER, HENRY F.—*Continued*

stamp collecting, and he enjoys fishing. In his State he is sometimes called "Hank" and "Old Hickory."

References

Indianapolis (Ind.) Star p13 Je 13 '48
Indianapolis (Ind.) Times p2 Jl 2 '50
International Who's Who, 1950
Who's Who in America, 1950-51
World Biography (1948)

SCHUCK, ARTHUR A(LOYS) June 20, 1895- Boy Scouts executive

Address: b. c/o Boy Scouts of America, 2 Park Ave., New York 16; h. 100 Lake Rd., Short Hills, N.J.

When Arthur A. Schuck became Chief Scout Executive of the Boy Scouts of America on September 1, 1948, he had been active

ARTHUR A. SCHUCK

in that organization for more than thirty-five years, both as a volunteer and professional leader. He had also been co-author of a book and of pamphlets and articles on organizing and financing of social service groups. The chief administrative officer of the more than 2,500,000 boys and adult leaders who constitute the Boy Scouts movement today was cited by Tulsa (Oklahoma) University when that institution awarded him an honorary degree of Doctor of Humanities in 1949 as "youth leader, world citizen and organizer, inspirer of youth and challenger of age." The year previous he had received an honorary doctorate of laws from Missouri Valley College.

Born to Berthold and Frances (Hartung) Schuck on June 20, 1895, in Brooklyn, New York, Arthur Aloys Schuck attended the

public schools of his native city. In 1913, while living in Newark, New Jersey, Schuck became interested in Boy Scouts work and volunteered as a Scoutmaster.

Scouting, then three years old in America, had been organized in South Africa in the early 1900's by a young British army officer, General Robert Baden-Powell, as a means of training young city-bred soldiers in outdoor skills. It was soon developed among boys in England. An American publisher, impressed by the Boy Scouts while visiting Britain, transmitted his interest to other Americans with the result that on February 8, 1910, the Boy Scouts of America was incorporated with representatives of thirty-four national youth groups present at the ceremony. In the ensuing years, boys flocked to join the Scouts—to pledge a "Daily Good Turn," to take the oath to honor God and country, and to learn Scoutcraft.

Young Schuck continued his volunteer work with the Boy Scouts, as district commissioner, Scout commissioner, troop committeeman, member of a local Scout council, and a member of its executive board. In 1917 he decided, he told a *New Yorker* reporter, to make Scouting his profession. Success as Scout executive of the Lancaster (Pennsylvania) council, his first assignment (1917-18) and of the Chester County (in the same State) organization (1919) brought him appointment as regional Scout executive (1919-21) in Pennsylvania, Delaware, Maryland, Virginia, and the District of Columbia, with complete responsibility for organization and supervision of Scouting. After two years (1921-22) in a similar capacity in Reading, Pennsylvania, the young executive was assigned to the national headquarters in New York City (1922-31) as assistant national field director, to serve as director and consultant and specialist in finance and organization.

In 1926 Schuck was co-author (with Arthur W. Procter) of the book *The Financing of Social Work.* (Procter was formerly budget adviser to City of Pittsburgh and staff member of the President's Commission on Economy and Efficiency.) In the foreword, Mortimer L. Schiff, philanthropist and banker, expressed his "commendation of the very thorough piece of work" done by the authors—"I know of none better equipped than they to write authoritatively on this important subject." Based on experience gained in this period, Schuck addressed many social service bodies and "character building" organizations, and wrote numerous pamphlets and articles on the subject of organizing and financing social service groups.

The year 1929 saw Schuck's first participation in world Scouting when he accompanied 1,300 American Boy Scouts and leaders to Birkenhead, England, for the Third International Scout Jamboree. Ten years later he attended a Rover Moot, an international discussion group of young men (of eighteen years and older), in Scotland. In August 1949 he flew to Norway, where three international meetings—Scout leaders, Scout commissioners and a Rover Moot—were being held. He was made director of the division of operations of the national council when the "divisional plan" was inaugurated in 1931. At the First National Jamboree of the Boy Scouts held in Washington, D.C., in 1937, he was executive director of the 27,232 Scouts and leaders who attended. Appointed in May 1944 to the post of Scout Executive of the Los Angeles (California) area council, he was to see during his four-year tenure an oustanding increase in Scout membership and in financial support of Scouting.

At a regular meeting of the national council's executive board held May 19, 1948, before the thirty-eighth annual meeting of the Boy Scouts of America, the former Scoutmaster was unanimously elected to replace Dr. Elbert K. Fretwell, who had been chief Scout executive since 1943 and who was to become Chief Scout. Shortly after taking office, "Chief" Schuck announced the launching of a two-year plan to increase membership by several hundred thousand under the slogan, "Strengthen the Arm of Liberty." By January 1, 1950, an all-time high enrollment of 2,579,515 boys and adult leaders had been reached, an increase of 300,000 over the previous year.

To further this campaign, one project of Schuck's is execution of the organization's plan to have eight-foot replicas of the Statue of Liberty erected in each of the 4,000 Scout districts in the United States as a "lasting symbol of liberty and as a challenge to all citizens to preserve and enrich American democracy." With the Boy Scouts of the Philippines scheduled to receive the first replica to be given to an independent country, Schuck presented an inscribed miniature of the statue on March 8, 1950, to Carlos P. Romulo, a former Boy Scout himself. The Scout leader will participate in the celebration of the fortieth year of Scouting in America, of which the high point will be the Second National Jamboree at Valley Forge, Pennsylvania, June 30 to July 6, with an expected attendance of 40,000 boys and leaders. On February 8, when area dinners and public demonstrations of Scout skills marked the anniversary date of incorporation, Schuck accompanied the Scouts who presented their service report to President Truman.

Missouri Valley College (Marshall, Missouri) awarded the Chief Scout Executive an honorary LL.D. (Doctor of Laws) in 1948 and the following year elected him a trustee of the college. The University of Tulsa (Oklahoma) also recognized his service to the youth of America by conferring upon him an honorary L.H.D. (Doctor of Humanities) in May 1949. In 1940 the Boy Scouts of the Philippines awarded Schuck the Silver Carabao for distinguished service to boyhood. A past president of the Lions Club of New York City, Schuck lists other of his group activities, in the New York Rotary Club, the Masonic Order, and the American Legion. He is a member of the editorial board of the *Youth Leaders' Digest* and an advisory editor of *Parents' Magazine*.

Arthur Schuck and Olive L. Muller were married on February 12, 1918; they have two children, Mrs. S. Dwight (Virginia Florence) Curtis and the Rev. Arthur Alfred Schuck, a Methodist minister and former Eagle Scout. The Chief Scout Executive lists his height as five feet nine inches, his weight as 160 pounds; his eyes are blue and his hair is blond.

References

New Yorker 24:22 O 2 '48
Who's Who in America, 1950-51

SCOTT, SIR HAROLD (RICHARD)

Dec. 24, 1887- Commissioner of Police of the Metropolis, London

Address: b. New Scotland Yard, London, S.W.1; h. Campions, Ewhurst Green, Cranleigh, Surrey, England.

The appointment of Sir Harold Scott as Commissioner of Police of the Metropolis, London, England, in 1945, broke a long tradition of giving the post to a retired distinguished high-ranking officer from one of the armed services. On the staff of the Home Office since 1911, Scott had been chairman of the Prison Commissioners, 1932-39. He was administrative chief of London's Air Raid Precautions plan through the blitz of 1940-41, and Secretary to the Ministry of Aircraft Production from 1943 until his appointment to Scotland Yard, as the Metropolitan Police force at headquarters is popularly known.

Harold Richard Scott was born on December 24, 1887, youngest son of Richard and Hannah (Hopcraft) Scott, of Banbury, Oxfordshire. He was educated at Sexey's School, Bruton, and at Jesus College, Cambridge, of which he was a Scholar; he also attended the universities of Grenoble and Marburg. After graduation in 1911 he chose the home civil service as a career, and entered the Home Office in the administrative grade (the highest of three divisions, mainly staffed by university men with good degrees).

In 1916 Scott was temporarily transferred to the Foreign Trade Department. Two years later he was again moved, this time to the Ministry of Labor, where he acted as secretary to the Labor Resettlement Committee (1918-19), a body charged with rehabilitating ex-servicemen. In 1919 he returned to the Home Office, to be promoted regularly through the ranks of assistant principal and principal, until in 1932 he became one of the nine assistant secretaries in the Home Department.

In the same year Scott was appointed chairman of the Prison Commissioners for England and Wales. This body, which is not under the control of the police, has the task of regulating the routine, discipline, and general conditions in His Majesty's prisons. Scott occupied the chairmanship for seven years. "The routine of this post," stated the London *Observer*, "was occasionally broken by official visits, first to study the prisons of Belgium, then to Nazi Germany, where he felt that he learned nothing that could be of use in a civilized community." He published reports on these tours: *German*

SIR HAROLD SCOTT

Prisons (1934) and *Belgian Prisons and Re-formatory Institutions* (1936). Nine years later, when he became Commissioner of Police, he was credited by the London *Daily Express* with scathing remarks on English prisons: "The prisons of today are a disgrace, and there is only one thing to do about them—dynamite them." During his term of office he was prime mover in the establishment of a model prison camp at Wakefield, Yorkshire.

Scott was transferred from his duties with the Prison Commissioners for the years of World War II. On February 14, 1939, the Lord Privy Seal's department announced that he had been appointed London's Air Raid Precautions chief, to coordinate the organization of A.R.P. services in London. "Mr. Scott," said the announcement, "will be in a position to indicate approval of local authorities' general schemes of air raid precautions—e.g., the employment of staff and the provision or adaptation of buildings—without reference to headquarters." His title was Chief Administrative Officer, London Civil Defence Region. Throughout the "big blitz," from September 7, 1940, to May 10, 1941, the complicated structure of London's A.R.P. worked well. In the words of *Front Line, 1940-41*, the official account: "The A.R.P. services proved to be soundly conceived. In this respect the British, who have been said to begin each war in a state of some preparation for the one before it, had succeeded in correctly appreciating the fundamentals of a form of warfare never before practiced, and in making provision against it." On April 9, 1942, Scott, who during 1940-42 was Deputy Secretary of the Ministry of Home Security was appointed Secretary. In October 1943, when, in the words of the *Observer*,

"it suddenly became necessary to find a first-class administrator for the Ministry of Aircraft Production," Scott was made Permanent Secretary of that Ministry, and continued in that post until 1945. His war service brought Scott (who had been made a Companion of the Bath in 1933) two knighthoods: the K.B.E. (Knight of the British Empire) in 1942, and the K.C.B. (Knight Commander of the Bath) in 1944.

Sir Harold Scott's appointment as Commissioner of Police of the Metropolis was announced by the Home Office, under whose jurisdiction the force falls, on April 20, 1945, and took effect from June 1. The Metropolitan Police is the largest of 133 forces covering England and Wales. It is maintained by the Home Secretary, and its jurisdiction comprises an area of 700 square miles, with a population of 8,500,000 people, stretching about fifteen miles in every direction from Charing Cross, virtual center of London. (Excepted from its operation is the small and wealthy business center, east of Temple Bar, known as the City of London, which has its own force, maintained by the Court of Common Council of the City.) The Commissioner, whose authority derives directly from the Home Secretary, works with five assistant commissioners. His office is at New Scotland Yard on the Thames Embankment, which is also a national headquarters whose services may be called in by chief constables anywhere in the country to assist in the detection of major crimes. It houses the Criminal Investigation Department (also well known to American readers of English detective fiction), the forensic laboratories, files on criminals, fingerprint library, etc. (The name "Scotland Yard" was acquired by the force before it moved from its former location on a street of that name.)

Stanley Bishop, writing in *Illustrated* in May 1946, said: "It had been regarded by many Governments that the Commissioner of Police of the Metropolis must be a high-ranking officer from one of the fighting services. When Air Marshal Sid Philip Game retired . . . all manner of police reforms were in contemplation. To carry them through . . . a man of supreme administrative ability was wanted, not just a good fighting man whose active service days were ending. So Herbert Morrison nominated Sir Harold Scott."

One of Scott's first administrative moves was a campaign to encourage public cooperation with the police in the prevention of crime and the apprehension of criminals. There is an arrangement whereby the dialing of 999 on a telephone puts the caller in instant touch with an operational room at Scotland Yard, where officers, constantly informed by radio of the position of patrol cars, at once notify the car nearest to the incident. With Scott's promotion of the use of the 999 service (according to the *Observer*) "from 37,661 calls in 1945 the total has risen now (April 1950) to over 80,000 a year." The new Commissioner also improved the Scotland Yard press service, paying tribute to the help of newspapers in making known precautionary measures against crime. He has encouraged the voluntary work of many London policemen in helping to run boys' clubs. Also, in line with his policy of keeping the public well informed about police work, he gave the full assistance of the Yard in 1949 to the production of the police film, *The Blue Lamp.* One of Scott's biggest problems has been recruitment. The Metropolitan Police establishment, normally composed of 19,766 men, by the end of 1949 had a roll of 15,512 so that a force between 4,000 and 5,000 short had to cope with a crime ratio far above that of 1938.

"The Commissioner," wrote Stanley Bishop in *Illustrated,* "has won the loyalty of all ranks under him. First he is essentially a kindly, courteous human person. . . .His decisions are quick; his mind flexible and imaginative. New ideas and innovations, if for the improvement of the police force, gain his support, and he fights them through." The *Observer* commented on "an expression of humorous equanimity shining through his spectacles." According to the *Daily Express,* "Scott does his thinking without masses of papers—his desk is as neat as if he had just sat there doodling. . . . He has the habit of making the most damning and shrewd criticisms in a voice that would soothe a baby."

Scott was elected a governor of his old school in 1936, and on March 31, 1950, Jesus College, Cambridge, elected him honorary fellow. His club is the Oxford and Cambridge. Sir Harold is a commander of the Legion of Honor of France, grand officer of the Order of Orange-Nassau of the Netherlands, and Papal Knight of the Grace of the Order of St. John of Jerusalem.

On June 30, 1916, he married Ethel Mary, daughter of James Golledge. They have two daughters, Daphne Mary and Ynys Diana, and a son, Michael. The elder daughter is a doctor, the younger was for two and a half years with the Control Commission in Germany; the son was an officer in the Royal Engineers. Scott, who used to be fond of gardening when he lived in the country, found diversion, when obliged to live in London during and after the war, in "poking around" London's docks. He now lives in Surrey. Tennis is one of his favorite pastimes.

References

Daily Express (London) My 2 '47 por
Illustrated (London) p5-11 My 4 '46 pors
Observer (London) Ap 28 '50
Times (London) F 15 '39; Ap 21 '45; D 21 '45
Burke's Peerage (1949)
Kelly's Handbook to the Title, Landed, and Official Classes, 1949
Who's Who, 1950
World Biography (1948)

SENANAYAKE, DON STEPHEN (sĕn-ăn-ī'ă-kĕ) Oct. 20, 1884- Prime Minister of Ceylon

Address: The Temple Trees, Colombo 3, Ceylon.

The first Prime Minister of Ceylon, the Right Honorable Don Stephen Senanayake, has been participating in the government of his country since 1922, when he was elected to the Legislative Council. He has been one of Ceylon's most prominent figures during the period in which the country was attaining the self-governing status within the British Commonwealth of Nations, granted her on February 4, 1948. Minister of Agriculture and Lands from 1931 to 1947, he also served as vice-chairman of the Board of Ministers and leader of the Council of State from 1942 to 1947. In January 1950 Prime Minister Senanayake was host in Colombo, capital of the island, to a conference of the Commonwealth Foreign Ministers.

Don Stephen Senanayake was born October 20, 1884, the son of a Ceylon landowner. His parents were Mudaliyar Don Spater and Elizabeth Catherine Senanayake. (The name "Don" is a survival of the days when the Portuguese has possession of the island.) There he attended St. Thomas' College; his sports were cricket and football, boxing and wrestling. After a brief period of clerking in the Surveyor-General's office, Senanayake turned to rubber and coconut planting on his father's estate. An outdoor, vigorous man, he earned by his jungle-clearing activities the nickname of "Kelay [Jungle] John." He became a student of the literature of planting, and his theoretical and practical ability brought him material success.

The island of Ceylon, situated off the southeast tip of India, has seen western rule since the sixteenth century, under the Portuguese (who occupied it in 1505), the Dutch (who took control of it in 1658), and the British (into whose hands it came in 1796). The population of the 25,332 square miles of the island is mixed in race and religion. In an estimated total of 6,657,300 inhabitants, there are some 4,620,500 Singhalese (Low Country and Kandyan) of which 4,302,700 are of the Buddhist faith; 733,700 Ceylon Tamils and 780,600 Indian Tamils, of which 1,312,700 are of the Hindu persuasion; 373,500 Ceylon Moors and 35,600 Indian Moors; 5,400 Europeans; 41,900 Burghers and Eurasians; 22,500 Malays and 43,500 other (figures from the *Statistical Abstract of Ceylon,* 1949).

In 1833 Ceylon had been constituted a British crown colony. Her modern political constitutional development began with the formation of a reformed Legislative Council in 1912, and a reformed constitution came into being in 1920. In 1931 the proposals of the investigating Donoughmore Commission were embodied in a new constitution which granted universal adult suffrage. Under it the government was vested in the State Council of 61 members, the majority elected territorially, but a certain number nominated by the Governor. The Council was divided into seven executive committees, the chairmen of which together with chief secretary, financial secretary, and the legal secretary formed a Board of Ministers responsible for government and for framing the budget.

(Continued next page)

British Inf. Services
DON STEPHEN SENANAYAKE

One of Don Senanayake's earliest ventures into the field of public life came about in 1913, when he engaged in a campaign for local option in the matter of the liquor trade, a project which met with a large measure of success, and resulted in a decrease in drunkenness in the island. In 1915 he spent forty days in prison for his opposition to British measures under martial law.

It was in 1922 that Senanayake entered the Legislative Council of the crown colony as member for the Negombo District, which he continued to represent until 1931. In the early 1920's he had founded the Ceylonese cooperative movement, which was to become the major distributive agency for foodstuffs in the island. From 1927 to 1931 he was a member of Ceylon's Executive Council.

After the implementation of the Donoughmore Constitution in 1931, Senanayake rose to the status of an important political figure. In that year he was elected to the State Council and appointed Minister of Agriculture and Lands—a post he was to occupy for fifteen years. Within two years he had effected passage of the Land Development Ordinance, a law which greatly improved conditions for the peasants and agricultural workers. Lack of water has been a big problem in a certain area of Ceylon; to alleviate this situation Senanayake instituted irrigation projects. Pedigreed cattle were imported from Australia in an effort to raise the standard of stock breeding in the island, and a program of sending selected students to India for veterinary training was initiated.

Ceylon's Minister of Agriculture won for himself the reputation of always being ready to combat measures which seemed to him repressive and unjust. With the onset of World War II he made a speech in the Council of State against the Government's internal security plan in which he stigmatized the measure as "diabolical," charging that it empowered the military authorities to keep order without any effective civil control. He also complained that of 207 justices of the peace 180 were Europeans.

In 1942 Senanayake became vice-chairman of the Board of Ministers and leader of the Council of State, while retaining the post of Minister of Agriculture and Lands, at a time when, with the entry of Japan into the war, Ceylon was regarded as the "back-line fortress" against the invasion of India. The advance of the Japanese forces cut off four-fifths of the island's supply of rice, the staple of the country's diet, which came from Burma and Siam. Seeking alternative sources of food supplies, Senanayake arranged for imports of wheat first from Egypt and Brazil, later from Argentina, the United States, and Canada.

During his tenure of the Ministry of Agriculture, Senanayake introduced the policy of more production of rice, legumes, sugar, and dairy produce, and encouraged scientists to work on ecological, entomological, and botanical research. These programs were not carried out without opposition, because of the expense involved. In 1946 a meeting of the Young Bhikkus' (Buddhist priests) party accused Senanayake of wasteful expenditures on agriculture and of exporting rice needed by the Ceylonese, which charges he refuted.

Ceylon in 1946 reached the "threshold of dominion status" under a new constitution drafted for her that year by a commission presided over by Lord Soulbury, Governor of the island. The Council of State was replaced by a two-chamber Parliament having power to legislate in all domestic matters; protection of the rights of racial and religious minorities, foreign affairs, defense and currency were reserved to the power of the Governor until on February 4, 1948, Ceylon was granted full Dominion status.

In the new Dominion, the United National party holds power by the choice of the electorate. Senanayake, president of the party, became the country's first Prime Minister, and is as well Minister of Defense and External Affairs. Much of the credit for the smoothness of Ceylon's transition from colonial to dominion status has been attributed to Senanayake, who is said to have a gift for compromise. Lord Soulbury (framer of the 1946 constitution) in praising Senanayake's "judgment, patience, tolerance," said: "He is a Singhalese, who as leader of the Council has never thought of himself as a Singhalese representative. He has gained the trust of all the communities in the island to a degree unprecedented in its history, and in guiding the fortunes of his country to. . .full and complete self-government. . .no one has played a more important or noble part than he."

In January 1950 Ceylon's Prime Minister was appointed a member of the Commonwealth Privy Council, and in February of that year his capital was the site of a conference of Commonwealth Foreign Ministers, at which he presided. At the conference Senanayake expressed the opinion that the fundamental problem in Asia was economic rather than political.

Under Senanayake, Ceylon has embarked on two big tasks—one politico-legal, the other economic. In 1949 a judicial inquiry was made into corruption in the public service. The Prime Minister has launched a project designed to develop, by hydro-electric power, a region which was once fruitful but has been overrun by jungle for a thousand years; excavations have been begun for the foundations of a large multi-purpose dam in the Eastern Province.

Senanayake is the author of a book entitled *Agriculture and Patriotism*, published in 1935, in which he details Ceylon's needs as he sees them, and his hopes for their fulfillment. In 1946 he refused a British knighthood. He is a director of the school at which he received his education, St. Thomas' College. In 1909 he married Emily Maud Dunuwille; they have two sons. A six-foot man of robust appearance, the Ceylonese statesman is described as having "a determined but benevolent expression." He is an adherent of Buddhism. It is told of him that he once gave a demonstration of his ability to speak the elephant language when a pachyderm in a zoo in Britain obeyed his commands.

References

Observer (London) Ja 8 '50
International Who's Who, 1949
Lanka's Man of Destiny: D. S. Senanayake (1946)
Who's Who, 1950

SENDER, TONI Nov. 29, 1888- Labor union consultant to the U.N.

Address: b. c/o American Federation of Labor, U.N. Consultants, 20 W. 40th St., New York 11; h. 309 W. 71st St., New York 23

Consultant of the American Federation of Labor to the Economic and Social Council of the United Nations, Toni Sender is a veteran social-democrat of German origin. A political worker and journalist in Germany and a Social Democrat member of the Reichstag for fourteen years, Miss Sender in 1934 left her native land, and in 1936 arrived in the United States. During World War II she was employed by the United States Office of Strategic Services; after the war she served as a senior economist with UNRRA. As an AFL consultant she has twice been responsible for placing before the U.N. Council a proposal for an investigation of forced labor conditions.

Daughter of Moritz Sender, department store owner, and the former Marie Dreyfuss, Toni Sender was born November 29, 1888, in Biebrich on the Rhine, now part of the city of Wiesbaden. Her mother was a native of Switzerland, and her father had lived in France for many years before settling in Germany. After being graduated from the girls' school in her home town (she tells in *The Autobiography of a German Rebel*, her memoirs published in 1939), she entered a commercial high school in near-by Frankfort on the Main at the age of thirteen. The two-year course completed, she secured a position with a Frankfort real estate firm, where she was put in charge of the mortgage department after some time. During these years she took courses in the humanities and studied economics at the University of Berlin.

The writings of Theodor Barth (1849-1909), a liberal who edited a weekly in Berlin, first aroused Miss Sender's interest in questions of democracy. Attending meetings of various political parties, she was attracted to the labor movement. Her activity in a newly founded office workers' union led to the study of socialism and subsequently to membership in the Social Democratic party. When strong family opposition to her socialist leanings convinced her that she could find complete freedom only outside the German border, she accepted a position with the Paris agency of a Frankfort metal company.

In Paris from the autumn of 1910 until the summer of 1914, Miss Sender became active in the French socialist party. Shortly after joining the fourteenth district unit of the party she became the district's vice-chairman and was made a permanent delegate to the Federal Council of the Socialist Federation of the Seine. During this period she participated in the meetings of the German Socialist Reading Club and was instrumental in the founding of a socialist women's group. The party elected her a delegate to its national convention preparatory to the International Socialist Congress held in Vienna in the late summer of 1914. Jean Jaurès, the editor of the party's newspaper *L'Humanité*, deeply influenced her views during these years, as did Alexandre Bracke, who represented the fourteenth district in the Chamber of Deputies.

The outbreak of World War I forced Miss Sender to return to Germany. After a short period of work in a military hospital, the Frankfort metal firm for which she had worked in Paris asked her to organize and direct a new department engaged in the production of war goods; this position she held for the duration of the war. Dissatisfied with the voting of war credits by the Social Democrats in the Reichstag, she joined the opposition faction within her party and began to collaborate with Robert Dissman, one of the leaders of the provincial Social Democratic organization in Frankfort. Her first major task was the organization of a local branch of the National Federation of Proletarian Freethinkers. In this group antiwar activity centered until Easter of 1917, when the opposition group among the Social Democrats founded their own party, the Independent Social Democratic party.

In the spring of 1915 Miss Sender attended the first international antiwar conference in Bern and replaced Dissmann as leader of the opposition in southwestern Germany when the latter was organized. Expelled by her party together with most of the leading members of the opposition early in 1917, she was one of the founders of the new party. When Germany collapsed in November 1918 upon her defeat in World War I, Miss Sender was elected to

United Nations Official Photo.
TONI SENDER

the executive of the Workers' Council in Frankfort and was made its secretary. As a member of the Frankfort City Council for four years she directed her efforts particularly to the coordination of all welfare institutions and to modernizing and liberalizing the city school system.

When the Independent Social Democrats founded *Volksrecht* ("People's Rights"), a newspaper serving southwest Germany, Miss Sender became its political editor in April 1919. (In 1920 she wrote a pamphlet against communism.) Elected to the first postwar Reichstag in June 1920, she remained a member of that body for fourteen years and served on its committee on foreign affairs. The seizure of power by the Nazis ended her Reichstag career. In 1922 she, together with the majority of her party, rejoined the Social Democratic party. For thirteen years she edited the shop councils' magazine for the metal trade (founded by the metal workers union) and later was also the managing editor of the Social Democratic magazine *Frauenwelt* ("Women's World"). She filled both editorial posts until 1933. During these years she attended many international conferences, for the metal workers as well as for her party. When she returned to Paris in 1923 for the first time after the war, she was made an honorary member of the French Socialist party.

Upon the Nazi assumption of power in 1934, Miss Sender fled to Czechoslovakia, then to Belgium, where she joined the editorial department of the *Volksgazet* ("People's Gazette"), the daily of the Flemish Socialists published in Antwerp. Her frequent travels had taken Miss Sender to the United States as early as 1926, and after several visits and lecture tours she made the decision in 1936 to settle permanently in that country.

In the United States Miss Sender took graduate courses at the New School for Social Research in New York City and at the American University in Washington. She has been a lecturer, American correspondent for European papers, and has taught anti-Fascist refugees under the auspices of the Labor Education Service. During World War II Miss Sender worked in the Office of Strategic Services for more than two years, after which for three years she served as a senior economist with UNRRA.

After the American Federation of Labor secured consultative status to the Economic and Social Council of the United Nations in 1946, Miss Sender became one of the consultants. The AFL is one of the nine international organizations which belong to the first category of the nongovernmental organizations having consultative status. Because of this rating it has the right to submit proposals to the Council, enter written statements for circulation as U.N. documents, send observers to all public meetings of the Council, and voice opinions at meetings of the Council and commissions.

As AFL consultant to the Council, Miss Sender over a period of years has stressed the question of slave labor. When in 1947 a committee was in the process of drafting an international bill of rights, she suggested the specific prohibition of compulsory labor. She was responsible for a demand that the U.N. investigate alleged slave labor practices in Russia and other East European countries; the proposed investigation, while at first approved by the Council, was not carried as a resolution. Miss Sender renewed the question in February 1950 when she accused the Soviet Union of basing its economy on the manpower of millions of workers who were held in camps and forced to labor in construction, mining, uranium extraction, and other vital fields; in support of the charges she submitted photostatic copies of documents qualified as "strictly secret." Miss Sender emphasized that the corrective camps for criminals, the existence of which is admitted by the Russians, held as prisoners people who do not endorse the Soviet regime. The establishment of a fact-finding commission by the International Labor Organization in cooperation with the Council was suggested by Miss Sender. The Council deferred action on the proposal until its February 1951 session because of the boycott of the Council by Soviet delegates.

Another proposal brought forward by Miss Sender during the February 1950 meeting of the Council suggested setting up a permanent body of experts, similar to the OEEC, which would continuously survey the state of economic development and fight against unemployment in the Western world. Before the United Nations Subcommission on the Prevention of Discrimination and the Protection of Minorities she reiterated in January 1950 her organization's repeated request for the right of individuals and groups to petition United Nation bodies in the field of human rights. Commenting on the suggestion of the British delegate (made in February 1950) that the privilege of placing topics on the agenda of the Council held by the nine nongovernmental organizations should be rescinded because of its alleged abuse for "propaganda" purposes by the WFTU, Miss Sender contended that such a move would penalize all the organizations for "sins committed by one." In December 1949 she presented to the Council an AFL memorandum asking guarantees that labor would not be exploited in a new industrial revolution, and seeking the establishment of a forty-hour week for workers in all parts of the world as an immediate goal, while looking to a future policy of a thirty-hour week.

Miss Sender, who is unmarried, has a brother (a dentist in New York) and two married sisters. Of Jewish parentage, she classifies herself as a dissident. She is a member of the New York Town Hall Club. Five feet two inches tall, she weighs 115 pounds, and has brown hair and brown eyes. She finds her chief recreation in music.

References

PM p19 F 4 '41 por
Time 53:29 F 28 '49
International Who's Who, 1942
Reichstags-Handbuch IV Wahlperiode (1928)
Sender, T. The Autobiography of a German Rebel (1939)
Yearbook of the United Nations, 1947-48

SENN, MILTON J(OHN) E(DWARD)
Mar. 23, 1902- Physician; psychiatrist
Address: b. c/o Child Study Center, Yale University, 14 Davenport Ave., New Haven, Conn.; h. 972 Prospect St., Hamden, Conn.

A physician who has specialized in pediatrics and psychiatry for more than twenty years, Dr. Milton J. E. Senn was appointed in 1948 to the directorship of the Child Study Center of Yale University; he is also Sterling professor of pediatrics and psychiatry at that university. Before assuming his position at Yale, Senn had been a professor at the Cornell University Medical College and an attending pediatrician at New York Hospital. From 1937 to 1939 he was a Commonwealth Fund fellow in psychiatry, practicing at the Westchester Division of New York Hospital and in the Philadelphia Child Guidance Clinic. In April 1950 he was elected president of the American Psychosomatic Society.

Milton John Edward Senn was born in Milwaukee, Wisconsin, on March 23, 1902, the only son of John and Louise Barbara (Rosenkranz) Senn. His father, a business executive, is of Swiss descent; his mother is of Danish extraction. Growing up in the city of Milwaukee, the future physician attended the North Division High School. After graduation he enrolled at the University of Wisconsin and there received his premedical education, being granted his B.S. degree in 1925. He then entered the medical school of the university, and two years later, in 1927, received the M.D. degree. For his scholastic achievements he was named a member of Alpha Omega Alpha, honorary medical

society. Dr. Senn's interest in pediatrics and psychiatry arose from his observation of children who were, as he has written, "in emotional difficulty and needed help which was not available."

After serving his internship at Columbia Hospital in Milwaukee, the young doctor was granted a fellowship in 1928 by Washington University, in St. Louis. At the same time he became an assistant attending pediatrician to the St. Louis Children's Hospital. He remained with these institutions until 1933, during the last three years of this period serving as an instructor in pediatrics at Washington University. In 1933 he accepted the position of associate in pediatrics at the Cornell University Medical College in New York City. Four years later, in 1937, the Commonwealth Fund granted him a two-year fellowship in psychiatry, under which his studies involved work at the Westchester Division of New York Hospital and at the Philadelphia Child Guidance Clinic. According to an article in the *Encyclopedia of the Social Sciences*, the Commonwealth Fund in 1921 inaugurated the first well-organized effort in the United States to promote better study and treatment of juvenile behavior problems by establishing child guidance clinics. By 1927 there were nearly five hundred such clinics in cities throughout the country. The Philadelphia Clinic, where the pediatrician carried on his work, was one of these guidance units.

In 1939 Senn became assistant professor of pediatrics in psychiatry at Cornell University Medical College, and the next year was appointed associate professor. In 1948 he was promoted to the rank of full professor. In conjunction with his teaching activities, Senn served from 1947 to 1949 as attending pediatrician to the Children's Clinic of New York Hospital.

In 1948 the pediatrician and psychiatrist assumed the directorship of the Child Study Center of Yale University, and the post of Sterling professor of pediatrics and psychiatry at the university. The Child Study Center first became known as the Child Development Clinic, at which Dr. Arnold Gesell [40] initiated studies in the behavior of infants and children by means of photographic records. The center which Senn directs comprises a guidance nursery and film library, and its clinical resources supply research and teaching media for students from professional disciplines concerned with the growth and development, behavior and personality of the human organism. It provides an outpatient service for the care of individuals from birth to adolescence, for the guidance of parents, teachers, and others, through the integrated endeavors of staff workers drawn from the fields of medicine, public health, educational psychology, sociology, and psychosomatics.

In the course of his career, Senn has written numerous articles for pediatric, psychiatric, and public health journals. In 1927 he was co-author of "Studies in Exhaustion Due to Lack of Sleep" and in 1932 of "Studies in the Metabolism of Sodium Lactate." Of a more popular nature was his book *All About Feeding*

SENN, MILTON J. E.—*Continued*

Children, written in collaboration with P. K. Newill and published in 1944. The volume is intended as a guide to the proper foods for children from birth to the age of twelve, it includes recipes, formulas, special diets, and menus. Reviewers found the book to be both "comprehensive" and "easy to follow." In 1946 Senn extended his activities in the field of popular information by accepting the position of consultant to the child department of the *Woman's Home Companion.* In this capacity he guides the editors in the choice of articles in his field and answers questions asked by readers. He also contributes articles to the magazine on such topics as inducing sound sleep in children and the correction of physical abnormalities in infants. To the May 1947 issue of *Parents' Magazine* he contributed an article on the necessity of parents' understanding the phases of their children's development, pointing out that the pediatrician often plays the role of teacher, "explaining the behavior of infants and children and of parents, too." Among the professional bodies he has addressed is the American Orthopsychiatric Association—in a paper before it in February 1950 he emphasized the necessity for educating doctors and nurses to an awareness of the influence of emotions on the child's behavior.

In 1946 Senn was chosen to present the Rachford Memorial Lectures on pediatrics and psychiatry, later printed in the *Journal of Pediatrics.* He is a member of the training committee of the National Institute of Mental Health in the United States Public Health Service, and chairman of the board of trustees of the Connecticut Child Study and Treatment Home. In 1948 he was presented with an honorary Master of Arts degree by Yale University. He is a member of a number of scientific organizations, including the American Psychiatric Association, American Pediatric Society, Harvey Society, American Society for Research in Psychosomatic Problems, and New York Academy of Medicine. In April 1950 Senn was elected president of the American Psychosomatic Society. He belongs to the Faculty Club of Yale. Dr. Senn, who has brown eyes and brown hair, is over six feet tall and weighs 180 pounds. On September 8, 1932, he married Blanche Corelyn Forsyth, a registered nurse; the Senns have one daughter, Corelyn Forsyth. He lists his recreational interests as gardening, bird watching, and folklore.

References

> Directory of Medical Specialists (1949)
> Who's Who Among Physicians and Surgeons, 1938
> Who's Who in the East (1948)

SEYFERTH, O(TTO) A(DOLPH) (sī′fĕrth) Sept. 1, 1891- Industrialist; business group president

Address: b. c/o Chamber of Commerce of the United States, Washington, D.C.; c/o West Michigan Steel Foundry Co., Muskegon, Mich.; h. 1523 Forest Park Rd., Muskegon, Mich.

When O. A. Seyferth was elected president of the Chamber of Commerce of the United States on May 3, 1950, he became the first man with a labor union background to head that business group. A one-time American Federation of Labor union organizer, he is known for the successful labor-management relations existing in the companies which he controls. He is president of the West Michigan Steel Foundry Company in Muskegon and holds interests in a number of other Midwestern enterprises.

Otto Adolph Seyferth was born in Grand Rapids, Michigan, on September 1, 1891, to Charles Frederic and Caroline Johanna (Goetz) Seyferth. With his two brothers and two sisters, young Seyferth was "usefully employed at an early age," he writes. "We . . . carried papers, shoveled snow, delivered groceries, made a garden, mowed lawns, and did odd jobs." Seyferth received his elementary education at the Grand Rapids German Parochial School, but at the age of thirteen he left school to begin a term as machinist apprentice in June 1904. For 60 hours a week he received four dollars. When he had completed three years of his four-year apprenticeship, the youth, believing that stone masonry offered a good future, began another 60-hour week apprenticeship as stone carver. Soon after that apprenticeship was completed, he was earning 65 cents an hour.

Meanwhile, on August 15, 1912, Seyferth had married Alma Amanda Sundell, with whom he had grown up in Grand Rapids. Then nearing his twenty-first birthday, he saved money with which to purchase a home on a long-term installment plan land contract. Not long afterward, when he became unemployed, the Seyferths were in danger of losing their home. He was then fortunate in getting work as a machinist.

The experience had had its effect on Seyferth, who, in his article entitled "Make Way for Tomorrow" (*Nation's Business,* November 1946) recalled that it left him shaken at the realization that business recession could come at any time. It led to the conviction that the average man must be safeguarded against fluctuations of the economic cycle which threatens his security, in sickness, business depressions, and old age. To ensure his own security Seyferth joined a labor union when he returned to work as a machinist. He became active as a labor union organizer, then president of the Grand Rapids A. F. of L. local, and later president of the trades and labor council for his community.

During this time Seyferth, having enrolled in a correspondence course, was studying banking, economics, foremanship training, and accounting. He was employed during World War I as a timekeeper for the Linderman Steel and Machinery Company of Muskegon, Michigan, which manufactured gun mounts for the American army. By 1919, when he had become production manager of the company, he was earning $450 a month. There his work brought him in contact with banking houses, an interest which took him to New York, to a $100-a-month position with Bonbright and Company, an investment house. During his year with Bonbright he was able to study business financing.

In 1920 Seyferth left New York for independent work as a reorganizer of industrial firms. His career during the ensuing years included two years with the Toledo (Ohio) Bridge and Crane Company, of which he was vice-president and general manager. This was followed by four years as president of the Fairmont (West Virginia) Mining Machinery Corporation. Upon his return to Muskegon in 1929, Seyferth purchased a half interest in the West Michigan Foundry Company, the company with which he remains. By 1932, when he was named president and director of the company, he had also become sole owner of the firm except for a small block of public-held stock. The firm now employs 500 men, has a production of 1,000 tons a month, and is considered an example of successful labor-management relations.

In the meantime, the industrialist had established other connections in the machinery manufacturing field, with the Austin Machinery Corporation, of which he became president in 1924, with the Austin Trailer Equipment Company, of which he became president in 1934. These two companies are also in Muskegon. Seyferth's interests include directorship in Muskegon Piston Ring Company and American-Michigan Pipe Line Company, in Muskegon; the Michigan Associated Telephone Company in Muskegon and Lafayette, Indiana; the Michigan Consolidated Gas Company, the Michigan Mutual Liability Company, and the Associated General Fire Insurance Company, all in Detroit; the Eagle-Ottawa Leather Company, in Grand Haven; and the Michigan Bumper Corporation, in Grand Rapids. He was a trustee, from 1938 to 1940, of Reo Motors, Inc., a Lansing firm which he had reorganized. He is also a director of the Hackley-Union National Bank in Muskegon.

Seyferth's association with the Chamber of Commerce of the United States, one of the country's largest associations of businessmen, is of long standing. He had also joined local chambers wherever he had lived for any length of time, from 1940 to 1942 serving as president of the Muskegon Chamber of Commerce. Elected a member of the board of directors of the Chamber of Commerce of the United States in 1940, he has served as chairman of the chamber's committee on labor relations. When Seyferth was elected president of the national chamber on May 3, 1950, it marked the first time in the thirty-eight years of the body's history that a man with a labor union background had been selected to lead the group, which has a membership of 1,300,000. The Washington *Post* commented (May 10, 1950): "Mr. Seyferth's . . . counsel should prove extremely helpful to businessmen whose value to their companies will be enhanced by a better understanding of labor's needs and organizational problems." Seyferth succeeded Herman W. Steinkraus '49 in the one-year term.

The 1950 convention of the Chamber of Commerce of the United States reaffirmed the concern felt by businessmen over the international situation, mounting Federal spending,

Chase Studios

O. A. SEYFERTH

the budget, and tax problems. Public demand for reductions in Government expenditures was called "of crucial importance" in a convention declaration, which stated that economic stability was threatened by "excessive demands upon the financial resources of citizens to support broadening undertakings of the Government, especially moves in the direction of state paternalism."

During World War II the Midwestern executive was a member of the War Production Board and of the War Manpower Commission; and in 1945 he also served on the President's Labor-Management Conference. He is a past chairman of the Michigan Economic Development Committee. Active in educational and civic affairs, he is a trustee of Ripon (Wisconsin) College, a past director of the American Cancer Society and the Michigan Cancer Society, a director of Muskegon's Community Fund (since 1946) and of the West Shore Symphony of Muskegon. His clubs are Muskegon's Century Club and the Union League Club of Chicago; his political affiliation is Republican, and he attends the Episcopal Church. The Seyferths have three children, Donald Frederic, James Roger, and Thomas Herbert. The businessman, who has blue eyes and graying hair, weighs 165 pounds and stands five feet ten inches. He names his one hobby as his Michigan farm. According to the New York *Telegram and Sun*, Seyferth is not the "booster" type, but quiet to the "point of shyness."

References

N Y Times p19 My 4 '50 por
Nation's Bsns 34:39 N '46

Business Executives of America (1950)
Who's Who in America, 1950-51
Who's Who in Commerce and Industry (1948)
Who's Who in the Midwest (1949)
World Biography (1948)

SHAW, (GEORGE) BERNARD July 26, 1856—Nov. 2, 1950 Irish-born playwright, wit, and critic; author of Fabian tracts and books on socialism, including *The Intelligent Woman's Guide to Socialism and Capitalism*; established his reputation with sympathetic criticism of paintings of Whistler and of the impressionist school, of the music of Wagner, and of the drama of ideas; among his plays are *Candida, The Devil's Disciple, Caesar and Cleopatra, Man and Superman, Major Barbara, Pygmalion, Back to Methuselah, Saint Joan,* several of which have been presented in motion pictures; awarded the Nobel prize for literature in 1925. See *Current Biography,* 1944.

Obituary

N Y Times p1 N 2 '50

SHEARER, MOIRA (moi'rá) Jan. 17, 1926- Ballerina

Address: b. c/o Sadler's Wells Ballet, Royal Opera House, Covent Garden, London, England

Familiar to American motion picture audiences as the star of the film *The Red Shoes,* Moira Shearer made her United States debut as ballerina with the Sadler's Wells Ballet in the fall of 1949, when that company toured the principal cities of Eastern United States and Canada. Alternating in principal roles with the prima ballerina, Margot Fonteyn '49, Miss Shearer was acclaimed by the critics for her "wonderful skill and precision." The young dancer has been with the Sadler's Wells ballet since she joined the training school at the age of fourteen. By 1946 she had become proficient enough to interpret the taxing role of Aurora in *The Sleeping Beauty.* She was chosen by J. Arthur Rank '45 to dance the leading role in *The Red Shoes,* which had its American première in the fall of 1948.

MOIRA SHEARER

The dancer's full name is Moira Shearer King. She was born January 17, 1926, the daughter of Mr. and Mrs. Harold King of Kensington, England. Miss Shearer's birthplace is Dunfermline, Fifeshire, Scotland. When still very young she was taken to the town of Ndola in Northern Rhodesia, where her father was a civil engineer for a number of years. When she was six, her mother, an enthusiast of the dance, enrolled her in a Saturday morning dancing class. By the time she was eight she was a familiar figure in Ndola: "A skinny moppet with a turned-up nose and a mass of unruly carrot-coloured curls, hurrying . . . to her ballet class," is the description supplied by a British writer. In 1936 the family returned to England. There she was trained in the rigorous Russian school of ballet technique—one of her teachers would tap with his cane the legs of lagging pupils. She later came under the tutelage of Madame Nicholas Legat, and in 1940 entered the ballet school established by Ninette de Valois '49 in connection with the Sadler's Wells Ballet. The latter trained dancers for professional careers, with the possibility of becoming members of the Government-sponsored dance company. After a year in Miss de Valois' school, Miss Shearer made her debut with the International Ballet, a group experimenting in the use of dramatic material, such as *Twelfth Night* and *Everyman.*

In 1942 Miss Shearer, who was sixteen at the time, became a member of the Sadler's Wells Ballet. Bombs were falling on London during the performance in which she made her first appearance with the company. "Our theater was near a big air raid shelter," she has recalled. "When we started we felt that the people were waiting for something to fall on all of us. After a while we made them forget the raids a bit." Since that year Miss Shearer has remained with the Sadler's Wells, in time rising to important roles. By 1946 she was proficient enough to dance a leading role in *Les Sylphides,* and at the end of that season to be one of the three ballerinas to alternate as Aurora in *The Sleeping Beauty.* According to A. H. Franks, the dance critic, she demonstrated at these performances a possession of "all the qualities that combine to make a truly great dancer."

In 1947, under the sponsorship of J. Arthur Rank, it was decided to make a motion picture of ballet life inspired by Hans Christian Andersen's fairy tale of the bewitched red shoes that impelled the wearer to dance until she died; this is depicted as a full-length ballet within the story sequence of the Technicolor film. As told by Monk Gibbon in the book *The Red Shoes Ballet,* the choice of Miss Shearer to portray both the heroine of the moving picture as well as the ballerina of the fifteen-minute ballet was "inevitable." At first reluctant to appear before the camera, Miss Shearer finally agreed, influenced in part by the encouragement given her by Miss de Valois to accept the part. The film had its New York première in October 1948 and since that time has continued to be shown to capacity audiences at the same theater. The critics agreed on Miss Shearer's charm and beauty in the role, the New York *Star* deciding that the "loveliest" sequences in the spectacle were those in which the leading lady appears—"a delicate, red-haired sprite full of modesty and grace, whose dancing is light flame and spirit." Walter Terry, dance critic of the New York *Herald Tribune,* was the one critic who felt that the dancer, in "dance technique, style, and kinetic sensitiveness cannot bewitch one into actually believing that she is the potential genius which the plot calls upon her to be." Gibbon, however, finds her dancing in the film full of "grace, lightness and, above all, strength," as well as an "extraordinarily delicate accuracy of technique." (The choreography of *The Red Shoes* is by Robert Helpmann, who dances a leading part.)

Since her *Red Shoes* appearance, the English ballerina, who has said she does not consider herself mature enough as an actress, resisted suggestions that she dance in other screen presentations. "I am not ready to find satisfaction in the cinema," she told a *World-Telegram* interviewer, "because there I would not know how to strive for perfection. Perfection is what we strive for constantly in the ballet." She returned to the Sadler's Wells company, and in 1948 appeared in the new creation, *Cinderella.* London critics admired her work, the reviewer for the London *Star* declaring that she "at once captivates the audience by a tender little dance with her broom in the kitchen." The London *Daily Express* described her as "enchanting. . .incapable of an ungraceful movement."

In October 1949 Miss Shearer was a member of the Sadler's Wells Ballet which made its first American appearance at the Metropolitan Opera House, and thereafter toured Eastern United States and Canada. Alternating with Miss Fonteyn in the principal roles, she was well received by American audiences. Terry of the New York *Herald Tribune* found her performance of Aurora in *The Sleeping Beauty* "regal, mature rather than girlish. . .always wholly gracious in manner." Martin of the New York *Times* thought her "as sweet as a peach, dainty as the traditional fairy tale princess, and with a fillip of Irish perkiness." He judged that she had given "an extremely youthful performance in spirit, but danced with wonderful skill and precision." Miss Shearer's performance in *Cinderella* won from the New York *Herald Tribune* critic: "A completely winning characterization of fantasy's immortal heroine, and [she] augmented this enactment with a dance performance which was clean of line, precise in detail, and sharp of movement." Another interpretation in which Miss Shearer won praise was as one of the six dancers in "the quiet classicism" of *Symphonic Variations;* and of her dancing in *A Wedding Bouquet, Musical America* wrote that she displayed "a deliberate ineptness that revealed a superb gift for dance humor."

Miss Shearer has blue eyes, "flame-colored hair, and extraordinarily alabaster skin flecked with faint freckles." She has a height of five feet, five and one-half inches, weighs 108 pounds; her waist measurement is twenty-two inches. In the course of her career she has sprained an ankle, torn ligaments, and once fell through the trapdoor on the stage, but considers herself fortunate in that she has not had a serious injury. In June 1949 her engagement was announced to Ludovic Henry Kennedy, a former Lieutenant in the Royal Navy, now a college librarian, writer, and lecturer. (They were married early in 1950.) When she dances in *Swan Lake* the ballerina wears a buckle, once the possession of Pavlova, in her headdress.

References

N Y Herald Tribune V p1 O 30 '49

Franks, A. H. Approach to the Ballet (1948)

Gibbon, M. The Red Shoes Ballet (1948)

SHEELER, CHARLES July 16, 1883- Painter

Address: c/o Downtown Gallery, 32 E. 51st St., New York 22; h. Dow's Lane, Irvington-on-Hudson, N.Y.

The introduction of industrial forms into American painting is frequently attributed to Charles Sheeler, a painter who has specialized in the meticulous presentation of factories, dams, machinery, and other forms of power in his oils and temperas. Engaged in making photographic studies for some years, Sheeler photographs have been the subject of a Museum of Modern Arts "thoughtfully selected, seldom accorded" one-man show.

Born on July 16, 1883, Charles Sheeler is the son of Charles R. and Mary A. (Cunningham) Sheeler, Americans of Irish and Welsh descent, who at that time were residents of Philadelphia, Pennsylvania. During his childhood his interest in painting was encouraged by his family. Upon the advice of a director of an art school whom the young man consulted, with the resultant counsel to prepare himself to earn a livelihood from painting, Sheeler entered Philadelphia's School of Industrial Art, for a course in applied design. Constance Rourke, in her biography of the painter, records that his instructor, Henry Diegendesch, allowed Sheeler the use of his studio on Saturday mornings, as well as giving him lessons in the technique of etching.

Sheeler spent the years from 1900 to 1903 at the School of Industrial Art before enrolling at the Pennsylvania Academy of Fine Arts for another three years' study, under William M. Chase. Identified as one of Chase's favorite pupils, although he abjured the use of the flamboyant, slashing brushstroke taught by Chase, Sheeler visited Europe several times with his teacher and fellow students. In 1904, after sailing alone on a cattle boat to join the rest of the class in London, Sheeler visited England and Holland, and in the following year, Spain. In 1909 he returned to England and also spent some time in Italy and France. It was in the latter country that he was introduced to a new concept in painting, which required several years of intensive study before it became integrated into his own painting.

Establishing himself in Philadelphia, Charles Sheeler passed most of his time in that city,

Musya S. Sheeler. Courtesy Art News.
CHARLES SHEELER

going for week ends to paint at his rented farmhouse in Bucks County. To the New York Armory Show of 1913, the much-discussed initial presentation of modern paintings to the American eye, Sheeler contributed six of his paintings. He demonstrated in *White Chrysanthemums, Landscape with Farmhouse, White Tulips,* and *Mandarin*—the paintings particularly noted by the critics—his current preoccupation with cubism. Other of his paintings were shown at the Montross Gallery in New York in 1915, 1916, 1917, the years which immediately preceded his change of residence from Philadelphia to New York. The painter continued, however, to devote his week ends to painting in Bucks County, until 1923 or 1924.

Parallel with his painting, after 1912 or so, Sheeler applied himself to developing technical skill and esthetic presentation in photography. At first he accepted commissions to photograph houses for Philadelphia architects. His first one-man show of photographs was at the Modern Gallery in New York in 1918, the year he undertook the photography of African Negro masks. With Paul Strand, Sheeler in 1920 collaborated on the motion picture, *Mannahatta,* into which were injected elements of the cubist principles developed by the artist in his paintings. The year 1920 also found Sheeler an associate of the De Zayas Gallery in New York, where an exhibition of his paintings and his photographs was held. Chinese jades, porcelains, paintings in well-known collections, the Assyrian bas-reliefs at the Metropolitan Museum were to be among the future subjects for his camera. Some time after 1923 when De Zayas closed his gallery, Sheeler joined Edward Steichen [42] in creating fashion photographs for *Vogue.*

In 1927 Sheeler was commissioned by Henry Ford to make a series of photographs of the Ford plants at River Rouge, where six weeks

of preliminary planning and study of photo angles preceded the actual taking of the thirty-two pictures in the group. Of these unretouched photographs, subjected by the artist only to cropping, Samuel M. Kootz wrote in *Creative Art* (April 1931) : "The soundness, the essential dignity of these photos come from his highly developd sense of precision. The graphic elements are moulded by a sharp perception of measure, a rare understanding and realization of the basic truth of the original forms." Following a showing of the River Rouge series, Sheeler was invited to do similar work in the Soviet Union, an offer which he declined. A year or two later he photographed a number of studies of the Cathedral at Chartres. Sheeler has expressed a preference for working in the United States : "It seems to be a persistent necessity for me to feel a sense of derivation from the country in which I live and work." A one-man show of his photographs was held at the Art Center in New York in 1926; he also exhibited at the International Film and Photography Exhibition, held in Stuttgart, Germany, in 1929.

Under the influence of his motion picture work with Paul Strand, Sheeler in the early 1920's began painting a series of city "scapes," which indicate his first use of reversed perspective, a discovery he ascribes to Oriental painting. From this experimentation in the abstract, he drew such studies as *Yachts,* described by the painter as "polyphonic forms." The paintings he did during this period—among them, *Suspended Forms* (1922), *Geraniums, Pots, Spaces* (1923), *Half Nelson* (1921), *Demarcation of Forms* (1922)—were discussed by Forbes Watson in a 1923 issue of *The Arts.* "What he evidently looks at," wrote the critic of these and Sheeler's barn drawings, "and strives, successfully, I believe, to put down, is the structural character—the relation of its planes, the inherent qualities of its materials, the meaning of its forms."

One-man shows of his subsequent works were held in New York at the Daniel Gallery (1922), the Whitney Studio (1924), and the Downtown Gallery (1931). Along with the work of Louis Lozowick, Sheeler's paintings were displayed at Neumann's Print Room in New York in 1926, and with that of Charles Burchfield, at the Society of Arts and Crafts in Detroit in 1935. His show at the Downtown Gallery in 1931 led the *Art News* critic to comment that "his work continues to gain in strength and pictorial impressiveness with the years." Sheeler himself had already remarked upon a transition in his work, dating from *Upper Deck* of 1929, when he began to plan a painting entirely beforehand, rather than constructing it as the work progressed. Of *Americana,* Ernest Brace, in a critique of the artist's work written for *Creative Art* in 1932, observed that "his subject matter is always American." The same critic saw no presence of photographic qualities in Sheeler's painting, defining the emotional quality of a Sheeler study as "mathematical."

The Upstairs, contributed by Sheeler in 1938 to the Cincinnati Museum's Forty-fifth Annual Exhibition of American Art, was cited by *Art News* as "one of the most arresting items" in the show. "The chaste, geometric surfaces of factory architecture" were the chief elements of the canvas, *River Rouge Plant*, which the artist showed in the 1938 Labor in Art Exhibition at the Baltimore Museum. When *Clapboards*, acclaimed as one of the most popular paintings at the Pennsylvania Academy Annual and at the Corcoran Biennial, was given in 1939 by a group of admirers to the Pennsylvania Academy, *Art Digest* recalled that Sheeler "is credited with being the first American artist to spotlight the importance of industrial forms in art." Upon the opening of a large retrospective showing of Sheeler's work at New York's Museum of Modern Art in 1939, James W. Lane of *Art News* said: "One will be surprised to find in the oils a brilliance of color one had not associated with the cold palette of Sheeler: orange, pink, ochre, yellow, and brown." Lane was less enthusiastic about the more plastic paintings, *Lhasa* and *Flower Form.*

Commissioned to do a series of industrial paintings for *Fortune*, Sheeler completed a group of six, of which one, *Rolling Power*, was purchased for the Smith College Museum. "Documentary in the finest sense of the word," wrote the *Art News* reviewer of this study of locomotive wheels and pistons, "which conveys far more than any abstract picture the feeling of our mechanical age." *Parnassus* felt that the painting expressed "the mechanical because it is mechanically executed." *Water* in 1945 brought five hundred dollars and the Harris Prize Medal at the Fifty-sixth Annual American Exhibition at the Art Institute of Chicago.

The painter's first one-man show in six years opened at the Downtown Gallery in 1946, with seventeen oils and temperas, including *Water*, *Coal*, and *Shaker Barns* among the works displayed. Jo Gibbs of *Art Digest* summarized it: "Sheeler has stuck with his classic precision and solid architectural forms, developing and perfecting a technique so perfect as to be unnoticeable as such. . . .Each painting will reward careful study of the subtle complexities of color, light, and shade, and the unobtrusive perfection of ratio and proportion in composition, for their seeming simplicity is a delusion." The New York *World-Telegram* critic found that his "forms approach abstraction without ever losing their identity," while Edward Alden Jewell of the New York *Times* felt that the "curt repudiation of effects that connote the anemic tinted photograph, [are] refreshing." An *Art News* reviewer discerned that Sheeler was painting "increasingly flatly in oil as thin as gouache."

Sheeler's subsequent show, held three years later (1949) at the Downtown Gallery, inspired *Art Digest*'s Judith Kay Reed to comment upon his changes in style and color. "*Amoskeag Mills No. 2* . . . utilizes multiple perspective," she wrote, "to produce a painting that cloaks a familiar American scene with a dramatic Italianate aura." Dorothy Adlow of the *Christian Science Monitor* identified him as "the classicist of a technological generation, establishing a fine balance between form and content, using one to enforce the other." *Art News* considered *Industrial Forms* "the brilliant solution of a problem in abstract de-

sign . . . the newly liberated colors combine in superb harmonies." Other newspaper critics applied the adjectives "handsome" and "stunning" to the paintings exhibited.

Paintings by Charles Sheeler are in the permanent collections of the following institutions: the Boston Museum, the Worcester Museum, the Fogg Museum (in Massachusetts), the Cleveland Museum of Art, the Columbus Gallery of Fine Arts, the University of Nebraska, the Springfield Museum, the Newark Museum, the Metropolitan Museum of Art, the Whitney Museum, the Gallery of Living Art, the Santa Barbara Museum, the California Palace of the Legion of Honor, and the Phillips Memorial Gallery (Washington, D.C.). He supplied the photographs for the book, *The Great King of Assyria* (1945). To *The Arts*, he has contributed the articles, "Recent Photographs by Alfred Stieglitz" and "Notes on an Exhibition of Greek Art."

In October 1946 Charles Sheeler was artist in residence at Phillips Academy in Andover, Massachusetts, and in May 1948, at Manchester, New Hampshire. He is a member of Artist's Equity. The painter has been married twice, in 1923 to Katharine Shaffer, and in 1939, to Musya Sokolova. He has lived at Ridgefield, Connecticut, and in South Salem, New York, and in 1950 is a resident of Irvington, New York. Shaker furniture is a feature of the artist's houses.

References

Amour de l'Art 15:467 O '34
Museum of Modern Art: Sheeler (1939)
Rourke, C. Charles Sheeler: Artist in the American Tradition (1938)
Who's Who in America, 1950-51
Who's Who in American Art (1940-47)
World Biography (1948)

SMEDLEY, AGNES 1894—May 6, 1950 Author, journalist, lecturer, known for her eyewitness newspaper and magazine articles and books on China; correspondent in the far East, 1928-1941; publicist and field worker for the Chinese Red Cross Medical Corps, 1938-41; author of: *Daughter of Earth* (semiautobiographical, 1929), *Chinese Destinies* (1933), *China's Red Army Marches* (1934), *China Fights Back* (1938), *Battle Hymn of China* (1943). See *Current Biography*, 1944.

Obituary

N Y Times p29 My 9 '50 por

SMITH, AUSTIN E(DWARD) Nov. 25, 1912- Physician; editor

Address: b. c/o American Medical Association, 535 N. Dearborn St., Chicago, Ill.; 6200 N. Kenmore Ave., Chicago, Ill.

Assistant editor of the weekly *Journal of the American Medical Association* since February 1949, Dr. Austin E. Smith was appointed editor on December 6, 1949. He succeeded Dr. Morris Fishbein[40], "vigorous spokesman" for the American Medical Association, who, after

Blackstone Studios, Inc.
AUSTIN E. SMITH

guiding both the *Journal* and *Hygeia* for twenty-five years, announced his resignation on December 2, 1949, some months after his writing and speaking activities had been restricted to scientific subjects by the association's board of trustees. Smith had previously filled the posts of director of the division of therapy and research and secretary of the council on pharmacy and chemistry of the A.M.A. He has been at the A.M.A. headquarters staff since 1940.

Austin Edward Smith was born November 25, 1912, in Belleville, Ontario, Canada, the only child of Wilfred and Keitha (Crouter) Smith. His forebears had been Canadian for several generations; his father was of partly English descent, and his mother Dutch, her ancestors having settled in New York and Pennsylvania. Young Smith enrolled at the Queen's University Faculty of Medicine at Kingston, Ontario, and graduated in 1938 with the degrees of M.D. and C.M. Postgraduate work at the same institution brought him, in 1940, his M.Sc. in Medicine; there for two years (1938-40) he had been an instructor in the department of pharmacology. At college he was a member of the rifle team. (For some years he was in the active militia of Canada, later in the reserve.)

After completing his graduate studies, Smith interned at the Yonkers (New York) General Hospital, in 1939. His next move, in the year following, was to Chicago, where he joined the staff of the American Medical Association. During 1940-41 he was medical consultant for the council on pharmacy and chemistry, in 1941-42 he was acting secretary for the same council, and he served as secretary from 1942 until 1949. (In the meantime, he had become a citizen of the United States, in 1943.) Appointment as director of the division of therapy and research came to him in 1946. This division

tests and passes judgment on new drugs, foods, and medical apparatus. Smith has thus become known as an expert on drug selection and standardization. As the director of the division, he had charge of its work of evaluating new drugs offered to the public for the treatment of various disorders. The warnings issued by the A.M.A. in 1949 against the indiscriminate use of so-called "anti-cold" tablets, classified as anti-histaminics, were based on data supplied by this division.

The American Medical Association, which was organized in 1847, states in its constitution: "The objects of this association are to promote the science and art of medicine and the betterment of public health." In 1880 the association decided to publish a journal to record the transactions of the organization. Of the 40,000 physicians approached, 2,100 pledged to "sustain the *Journal*." Today the A.M.A. represents 142,000 doctors and the *Journal*—now the medical journal with the largest subscription list in the world—has a circulation of 136,000 copies weekly (13,000 of these go abroad) and brings the association over $1,000,000 annually.

The first issue of the *Journal* appeared on July 14, 1883, with Dr. N. S. Davis as its editor. It contained a complete record of that year's annual meeting of the association. The modern *Journal*, a weekly, totals in a year more than 3,800 pages of reading matter. "A recent issue," said the New York *Herald Tribune*, "carried seventy-five pages of scientific reports, comments and professional news and seventy pages of advertising." The periodical covers the whole field of general medicine. Its varied contents include original articles, clinical notes, descriptions of new instruments, therapeutic discussions, editorials, current comment, association news, medical news items from various States and foreign countries, letters from foreign centers by special correspondents, reports from the A.M.A. councils and bureaus, queries and minor notes, news on medical education and registration, book reviews, medico-legal discussions, society proceedings, and abstracts from current medical literature (including foreign bulletins). The "Bulletin" of the A.M.A., comprising about eight pages, is an integral part of the *Journal*, with the title "Organization Section." It is devoted to the economic, business, organizational, and social aspects of medicine. (These facts are from a brochure published by the association.)

At the December 1949 meeting of the A.M.A., announcement was made by the board of trustees of Dr. Smith's appointment to the editorship of the *Journal*. He had been assistant to the editor, Dr. Morris Fishbein, since June 1949. This was the first meeting of the A.M.A. in twenty-five years which Fishbein did not attend. He had become a member of the editorial staff of the *Journal* in 1913 as assistant to the editor, and in 1924 he had been appointed editor. In June 1949 the trustees put restrictions on the scope of his activities, and in December of that year he announced his resignation, declaring he found it "impossible . . . to continue under the circumstances." The new editor "is the opposite of Dr. Fishbein, in many ways; he is soft-spoken and reserved," commented *Newsweek*, "but he is not expected to swerve too far from the former editor's anti-socialized medicine views." His aim, reported the New York *Herald Tribune*, is to "maintain the *Journal's* position as the leading scientific medical journal."

As editor of the *Journal*, Smith will read approximately 5,000 manuscripts a year. He also serves as editor in chief of the books and pamphlets issued by the association for the profession; a number of the pamphlets are designed for layman reading. (One of the association's publications, best known to the layman—*Hygeia*—changed its name on March 1, 1950, to *Today's Health*. Dr. W. W. Bauer is now editor of that publication.)

The new editor of the A.M.A. weekly is the author of several books: *The Technic of Medication* (1948), *The Drugs You Use* (1948); is co-editor (with A. D. Herrick) of *Drug Research and Development*; was editor from 1942 to 1949 of these publications of A.M.A.'s council on pharmacy and chemistry: its *Annual Reports, New and Nonofficial Remedies, Useful Drugs, Epitome of the United States Pharmacopoeia and the National Formulary*. A former member of the staff of the University of Illinois College of Medicine, Smith is a lecturer at the University of Chicago in the department of pharmacology.

Smith is a fellow of the American Medical Association, the American Public Health Association, and the American Association for the Advancement of Science. Among the other scientific organizations to which he belongs are the Illinois Medical Society, the Society of Experimental Biology and Medicine, American Society of Pharmacology and Experimental Therapeutics, Canadian Physiological Society, American Human Serum Association, National Society of Medical Research, World Medical Association. He serves on the revision committee of the *United States Pharmacopoeia* and its subcommittees: subcommittee on biological assays, endocrine products advisory board, subcommittee on scope, amino acids advisory committee, subcommittee on nomenclature (chairman); in the American Pharmaceutical Association, he is on the committee on professional relations, and is technical consultant for the scientific edition, *Journal of the American Pharmaceutical Association*. He is science editor of the *American Druggist*.

The medical editor has a son, Craig Lance, by his marriage to Ruth Fischer in April 1940. He lists his church as Protestant. His fraternity is Alpha Kappa Kappa, of which he is an honorary member. A spectator at football, hockey, and wrestling matches, he also finds recreation in golf and boating.

References

American Men of Science (1944)
Who Knows—And What (1949)
Who's Who in Chicago and Illinois (1945)

SMITH, DAVID T(ILLERSON) Oct. 1, 1898- Physician; organization president

Address: b. c/o National Tuberculosis Assn., 1790 Broadway, New York 19; Duke University School of Medicine, Durham, N.C.; h. Hope Valley, Durham, N.C.

The National Tuberculosis Association is being headed during 1950-51 by Dr. David T. Smith, who has been professor at the school of medicine of Duke University since 1930. His academic career has been combined with research and practical application in his chosen fields of pathology and bacteriology. A graduate of Furman University, he trained for the medical profession at Johns Hopkins University, and was first associated with the Rockefeller Institute and the New York State Hospital for Tuberculosis.

Born in Anderson County, South Carolina, on October 1, 1898, David Tillerson Smith is one of the five children (four sons and one daughter) of William Whitaker and Florence Ellen (Sullivan) Smith. The family, which settled in upper South Carolina before the Civil War, has been engaged in farming down to the present generation—David's first twelve years were spent on the farm. He attended school in nearby Greenville, and developed, he has said, into an "amateur naturalist" between grammar school and high school. At the Greenville high school, from which he graduated in 1914, his chief extracurricular interests were debating and studies of insects, animals and birds. He entered Furman University (in the same town) to specialize in the social and natural science studies, and to become president of the undergraduate literary society and the winner of medals for debating and oratory. After receiving the B.A. degree in June 1918, from October to December of that year (during World War I) he was in the Student Army Training Corps of the United States Army.

Of his decision to enter the field of medicine, Smith has said, "I think my interests in insects, animals, and birds stimulated my interest in the organic structure and function of man." Proceeding to Baltimore, Maryland, he enrolled at the medical school of Johns Hopkins University, which awarded him the M.D. degree in 1922. Then followed a year (1922-23) as intern in pediatrics at that institution's hospital. While he was a medical student he published two research studies.

In 1923 Smith worked in New York with the Rockefeller Institute, as assistant in pathology and bacteriology. The next year he joined the staff of the New York State Hospital for Tuberculosis at Ray Brook, where he carried on his work as bacteriologist and pathologist, and directed the work of the hospital's research laboratory. During the six years the physician was at Ray Brook he also lectured at the nearby Trudeau Post Graduate School for Tuberculosis.

In 1930 Dr. Smith accepted an offer from Duke University, at Durham, North Carolina, the faculty on which he has remained as professor of bacteriology and associate professor of medicine. As a teacher he has summarized his philosophy: "I believe that enthusiasm for

Little

DAVID T. SMITH

an education is contagious, that students should be led and not driven, and that students who cannot be stimulated should be dropped from the university."

Smith has continued to carry on clinical and laboratory research. The annals of the American Academy of Political and Social Science noted in 1943 that he had been "working continuously since 1930 on pellagra and other vitamin deficiencies," and that prior to 1930 he had made a study of vitamin-C deficiency in intestinal tuberculosis. In 1948 a series of his lectures on fungus diseases of the lungs was published in book form. Speaking before the American College of Physicians at the 1949 annual meeting, Smith described his discovery that the fungus disease, blastomycosis, can "mimic" both cancer of the lungs and tuberculosis, and urged new methods of diagnosis based upon this knowledge.

The doctor's active association with the National Tuberculosis Association dates from 1942-43, when he was president of the North Carolina Tuberculosis and Health Association, an affiliate of the N.T.A. He has been a member of the board of directors of the national organization since 1944, and was elected its president in 1950. Organized in 1904, when pulmonary tuberculosis in the United States ranks highest as the cause of death, the association now has 3,000 State and local bodies affiliated with its continuing nation-wide war against the disease. Its work, which is supported by the annual sale of Christmas Seals, falls under four headings: education, case-finding, rehabilitation, and medical research. Figures issued by the association's public relations department indicate that the tuberculosis death rate in the United States has been cut 85 per cent since 1904 and that the disease has been lowered from first to seventh place as a cause of death. Smith has stated, however, that sus-

ceptibility to the disease rather than its death rate should be used as a measure of the tuberculosis problem. Deploring the fact that the amount spent on research by the N.T.A. is "infinitesimally small" compared with the amounts spent on certain other diseases, he has nevertheless declared himself to be optimistic that current research projects being financed by the association will uncover means of detecting persons particularly susceptible to tuberculosis. Today tuberculosis kills 45,000 Americans in a year, causing more deaths in the fifteen-to-thirty-five age group than any other disease.

The physician's World War II service was as consultant to the Secretary of War as a member of the Army Epidemiological Board and of the Commission on Epidemiological Survey from 1942 to 1945. In addition to *Fungus Diseases of the Lungs* (published in 1948), he is the author of *Oral Spirochetes and Related Organisms in Fuso-spirochetal Disease* (1932), co-author of *Manual of Clinical Mycology*, and senior author of Zinsser's revised *Textbook of Bacteriology* (1948), on the diagnosis, specific therapy, and prevention of infectious diseases. He has contributed chapters to five medical textbooks, and has published more than one hundred articles, based on his original research, in medical and scientific journals. In 1949 Furman University awarded him an honorary D. Litt. degree.

Memberships are held by Dr. Smith in the American Anatomical Association, the American Association of Thoracic Surgery, the American Association of Bacteriology and Pathology, the American Society of Clinical Investigation, the American Trudeau Society, the Southern Sanatorium Association, the Association of American Physicians, the American Medical Association, the American Society of Bacteriology, the Society for Experimental Biology and Medicine, the American Clinical and Climatological Association, the Tri-State Medical Society, the North Carolina Medical Society, and the Durham-Orange County Medical Society (of which he was president in 1940). He has been elected to Sigma Xi, honorary scientific society, and belongs to the Octopus Research Club and the Sociological Club.

On September 12, 1923, the physician married Susan Gower, a chemistry teacher. Mrs. Smith continued her career, after her marriage, as a research worker in nutrition. The Smiths have a daughter, Rosalind Gower. The blue-eyed, gray-haired physician is five feet ten inches tall and weighs 175 pounds. He is a Democrat, and a member of the Society of Friends. Among his leisure-time activities he lists gardening and fishing.

References

American Men of Science (1949)
International Who's Who in World Medicine, 1947
Who's Important in Medicine, 1945
Who's Who Among Physicians and Surgeons, 1938
Who's Who in America, 1950-51

SMUTS, JAN CHRISTIAAN (smŭts yän krĭs'tē-ăn) May 24, 1870—Sept. 11, 1950 Union of South Africa statesman; guerrilla general in the Boer War; credited with great influence in the creation of the Union of South Africa; held various Cabinet posts 1907-15; general, then field marshal in the British Army, World War I; member of British War Cabinet under Lloyd George; cofounder of League of Nations; Prime Minister of the Union of South Africa 1919-24 and 1939-48; one of drafters of preamble to U.N. Charter; supporter of British-Boer cooperation and promoter of British Empire solidarity; author of *Holism and Evolution*. See *Current Biography*, 1941.

Obituary

N Y Times p1+ S 12 '50

SOMMERFELD, A(RNOLD JOHANNES WILHELM) Dec. 5, 1868- Physicist

Address: b. c/o University of Munich, Munich, Germany; h. Dunantstr. 6, Munich, Germany

The recipient of the 1948 Oersted medal, presented annually by the American Association of Physics Teachers to an outstanding teacher in the field, Arnold Sommerfeld, who has been called "the teacher of atom physics in Germany," now resides as professor emeritus in Munich. During his long career as a university professor he taught future atomic physicists who are outstanding in various countries today. His book *Atombau und Spektrallinien* (*Atomic Structure and Spectral Lines*) is internationally recognized as the standard work in its field. Professor Sommerfeld is known for his contributions to the development of the quantum theory, the Bohr atomic theory, the quantum theory of spectral lines, and the theory of metallic electrons.

The son of Franz Sommerfeld, a physician, and Cäcilie (Mathias) Sommerfeld, Arnold Johannes Wilhelm Sommerfeld was born in Königsberg, East Prussia, on December 5, 1868. In his native city he attended the Altstädtisches Gymnasium, from which he was graduated in 1886. He received his Ph.D. five years later from Königsberg University. His studies there centered around mathematics. A principal teacher of his, to whom he dedicated his Ph.D. dissertation on the arbitrary functions in mathematical physics, was Ferdinand Lindemann; another was Franz Neumann, the first to teach theoretical physics at a German university.

After his graduation Sommerfeld became an assistant in mineralogy and in 1895 he was made instructor at Göttingen University, the German center for research in mathematics and physics. Here he came in close contact with the mathematician Felix Klein (known for his researches in geometry and the theory of functions) who strengthened Sommerfeld's interest in applied mathematics. Klein and Sommerfeld wrote *Theorie des Kreisels* ("Theory of the Gyroscope"), which was published in four parts from 1897 to 1910.

A. SOMMERFELD

In 1897 Sommerfeld became professor of mathematics at the Mining Academy in Clausthal in the Harz mountains, and three years later professor of mechanics at the Institute of Technology in Aachen. During these years he investigated a number of problems in applied physics, among them the hydrodynamical theory of lubrication. A lecture in Kassel in 1903, on "Problems of Modern Technical Mechanics," in which he directed attention away from the analytical mechanics of the classical school toward a more general concept of theoretical physico-mechanics, showed the direction of the scientist's thinking.

In 1906 Sommerfeld accepted the chair of theoretical physics at Munich University, succeeding Ludwig Boltzmann, known for his work on the kinetic theory of gases and radiation from dark bodies. The man who brought about Sommerfeld's appointment, was Roentgen, the discoverer of the X ray, and during his first Munich years Sommerfeld concentrated on the investigation of the wave character of X rays. These studies led physicist Von Laue to the discovery of the interference of X rays in crystals, and to a method of measuring the wave lengths of X rays by means of the resultant diffraction, for which he was awarded the Nobel Prize for physics in 1914.

Sommerfeld's institute at the university became the training center for atomic physicists who came from many countries. In the work carried forward there, significant contributions were made to the development of the quantum theory, the Bohr atomic theory, the quantum theory of spectral lines, and the theory of metallic electrons. In a lecture to a group of natural scientists in Karlsruhe in 1911, Sommerfeld formulated the view, in opposition to current thought on the subject, that Planck's quantum theory should be regarded as fundamental, and the properties of the atom might be deduced therefrom—a suggestion to which

SOMMERFELD, A.—*Continued*

Niels Bohr [45] has acknowledged his debt in the working out of his atomic theory in 1913.

In 1915 Sommerfeld considerably advanced the original Bohr atomic theory by adducing elliptical courses for the electrons. In the further development of the theory he was the first to originate general methods for obtaining the quanta for processes of an atomic nature. The method enabled him, in 1916, to establish a formula for the structure of spectral lines and a general quantum theory of spectral lines. Applying the principles of the quantum theory to the structure of metals, Sommerfeld in 1927 developed a theory of metallic electrons.

Professor Sommerfeld's students have paid tribute to his success in integrating in his over-all presentation of theoretical physics the latest achievements in the field and the unsolved problems which needed further investigation. The core of his teaching was a three-year course on theoretical physics, about which he has humorously remarked, "I used to organize my lectures in such a way that they were too easy for advanced students and too difficult for beginners." This course was supplemented by special lectures: between 1908 and 1910 he lectured on the theory of relativity; after 1912 on Bohr's theory of atomic structure; and after 1926 on wave mechanics. "My first lectures on this theory," Sommerfeld reports, "were heard by Linus Pauling [49], [the American physicist and chemist] who learned as much from them as I did myself."

The field of atomic structure Sommerfeld treated in a book *Atombau und Spektrallinien* (1919) which became a classic in its field and reached its fifth edition in 1931. (It has been translated into French, Russian, and English, the latter with the title of *Atomic Structure and Spectral Lines*, 1923). In 1929 Sommerfeld published *Wellenmechanischer Ergänzungsband* (in English under the title *Wave-Mechanics* the following year). Sommerfeld's course on theoretical physics was published in six volumes from 1943 to 1948 under the title *Vorlesungen über theoretische Physik* (an American translation is in progress). Other of the physicist's writings which have been translated into English are: *Three Lectures on Atomic Physics* (1926); *Lectures on Wave Mechanics* (1930); "Partial Differential Equations in Physics" in *Pure and Applied Mathematics* (1949).

Until his retirement in 1940, Sommerfeld continued to teach at the University of Munich. He went to the United States three times as a visiting professor: in 1922-23 he was Carl Schurz professor at the University of Wisconsin, the year 1928 professor at the California Institute of Technology, and in 1931 at the University of Michigan. The physicist is a member of many scientific societies, among them the academies of Berlin, Calcutta, Göttingen, Madrid, Munich, Rome, Vienna, and also the Royal Society of London, the National Academy of Sciences in Washington and the American Academy of Arts and Sciences in Boston. He was awarded the Planck medal

(so named in honor of the German physicist, originator of the quantum theory) in 1931, the Lorentz medal (named for the Dutch physicist, known for work basic to the theory of relativity) in 1939, and the Oersted medal (named in tribute to the Danish physicist who instituted the study of electromagnetism) in 1948.

The Oersted award, which is given annually by the American Association of Physics Teachers for notable contributions to the teaching of physics, was received for Sommerfeld by Edward U. Condon [46], the director of the National Bureau of Standards, at one time a student under the recipient. Other former students of Sommerfeld's are I. I. Rabi [48] (Nobel Prize winner), Hans Bethe [50], Wolfgang Pauli [46], and other eminent scientists. On two occasions Sommerfeld's pupils have expressed their debt to him: for his sixtieth birthday in 1928 Peter Debye edited a *Festschrift* entitled, *Probleme der modernen Physik*, and fifteen years later Werner Heissenberg edited a similar volume *Kosmische Strahlung*, 1943 (American edition *Cosmic Radiation*, 1946).

In December 1897 Sommerfeld married Johanna Höpfner; three children, two sons and a daughter, were born to them. Sommerfeld is of the Protestant faith. Politically he designates himself as a national liberal. His eyes are brown, his hair white; and he is about five feet four inches tall. He often made ski trips with his advanced students. Among his former diversions were mountain climbing and listening to music.

References

Am J of Physics 17:5 p312-316 por
N Y Times p7 Ja 29 '49
Naturwissenschaftliche Rundschau 1948:
    5 p232
Brockhaus 15th ed. v17
International Who's Who, 1949
Schweizer Lexikon v. 6
Sommerfeld, A. Die Willkürlichen
    Functionen in der Mathematischen
    Physik (1891); Vorlesungen über
    theoretische Physik. v. 3 (1948)

SORENSEN, VIRGINIA Feb. 17, 1912-
Author

Address: Route #1, Box 2A, Auburn, Ala.

Reprinted from the *Wilson
Library Bulletin*, Jan. 1950.

A century and less ago America was deeply agitated over "the Mormon menace." All those fears and the persecution they generated seem ridiculous now, when the Church of Jesus Christ of Latter Day Saints has taken its place among our respected religious sects. Virginia Sorensen is a Mormon, by birth and by conviction. Through her books she has done as much as any living author to bring those early days into proper perspective.

Virginia Sorensen was born February 17, 1912, in Provo, Utah, to Claud E. and Helen (Blackett) Eggertsen. Her ancestry is mostly Danish. Both great-grandfathers followed Brigham Young to Utah on the great covered wagon trek of 1846. Young Virginia grew up in Utah, first at Provo, then at Manti and American Fork, and finally at Springville, where her father is now station agent for the Denver and Rio Grande railroad. The six children, three boys and three girls, climbed mountains, went trout fishing, and visited the near-by sheep ranches, absorbing a colorful background which the observant young author-to-be stowed away in memory for future use.

After graduation from American Fork High School in 1929, Virginia Eggertsen returned to Provo to enter Brigham Young University, receiving her B.S. degree there in 1934. Her interest in writing, roused by the publication of a childhood poem in a church magazine, strengthened during her college days. She was awarded numerous prizes for poems and short stories. Later her work began appearing in the Salt Lake City *Tribune*, New Mexico *Quarterly Review*, Chicago *Tribune*, *Saturday Review of Literature*, and other periodicals.

Her first novel, *A Little Lower than the Angels*, was published in 1942. Its scene is the Mormon settlement at Nauvoo, Illinois, in the early period that includes the death of Joseph Smith and Brigham Young's accession to leadership. Milton Rugoff wrote of it in *Books*, "A novel of distinction. . . .Fusion of vivid imagery and a poetic impression, sudden insight and swift turns make the narrative continuously stimulating." Clifton Fadiman in the *New Yorker*: "I have read a number of Mormon novels, but none that more convincingly explores the minds of Mormon women confronted with the tragic, comic, and grotesque problems of plural marriage."

On This Star (1946) received mixed reviews. Vardis Fisher found fault with it in the New York *Times*, although he conceded that Mrs. Sorensen is "sensitive and intuitive; she knows her women." *Library Journal* said, "Virginia Sorensen writes authentically of the Mormon religion and customs, and her prose style is excellent. Heartily recommended for mature readers." It was after the publication of this novel that Mrs. Sorensen received a Guggenheim Fellowship in the field of fiction.

With *The Neighbors* (1947) Mrs. Sorensen departed from the Mormon background to tell a story of sheep ranching in present-day Colorado. James Hilton in the *Herald Tribune Weekly Book Review*: "*The Neighbors* is thoughtfully written, always with a satisfying knowledge of its background and a sure eye for detail." The *Chicago Sun Book Week* called it "a sensitive well-written and eminently readable book which adds appreciably to Mrs. Sorensen's considerable stature as a novelist."

The Evening and the Morning (1948) returns to the Mormon Utah scene. Virginia Kirkus said, "The story is valuable perhaps primarily as a study of a way of life written by someone who has been on the inside, and specifically of what that inheritance of traditional mores can mean to a woman's growth." Dale Morgan ends a long and enthusiastic review in the *Saturday Review of Literature* with, "This is a major novel that with all its technical brilliance is honest, simple, and direct, and distinguished for

VIRGINIA SORENSEN

its understanding, its justness, its intelligence, and its feeling."

Mrs. Sorensen, a petite, attractive young woman with brown hair and green eyes, is the wife of a college professor, Dr. Frederick Chester Sorensen. The couple, married in 1933, have two children. They have lived in a number of college towns, and are now in Auburn, Alabama. The entire family is devoted to bicycling, often making day-long excursions into the country. Mrs. Sorensen is now at work on a novel of Mexico, where she studied on her Guggenheim Fellowship. She says regretfully that her writing and her family keep her too busy for civic work, but in this she does herself less than justice. To aid and inspire the young hopefuls who will be our future writers is surely a civic cause, and it is one on which Mrs. Sorensen labors untiringly. She is gratefully remembered at Denver University, Utah Agricultural College and now at Alabama Polytechnic for her classes in creative writing. In addition she has been generous with informal talks before women's clubs and writers' groups. Quoting Henry James, she likes to tell literary aspirants that a writer must be creatively alive, a person "on whom nothing is lost." No better description could be found for Virginia Sorensen herself.

SPARKMAN, JOHN J(ACKSON) Dec. 20, 1899- United States Senator from Alabama

Address: b. Senate Office Bldg., Washington, D.C.; h. Huntsville, Ala.

Alabama's junior United States Senator, John Sparkman of Huntsville, was elected to the upper chamber at Washington in November 1946, to fill out the unexpired term of the deceased Senator John H. Bankhead '48; and he was re-elected in November 1948, for the full term ending January 1955. Sparkman had

Wide World Photos

JOHN J. SPARKMAN

Training Corps and after his graduation in 1921 received a reserve commission of second lieutenant in the Coast Artillery. (As a reserve officer he took part in special maneuvers at Plattsburg, New York, in 1939. In 1950 he held the rank of lieutenant colonel.)

On obtaining his B.A. in 1921, Sparkman sought newspaper work. Because the post-war recession was on, there were few openings; he accordingly returned to Tuscaloosa, where he studied law, and in 1923 received the LL.B. degree. In the same year he was appointed student secretary of the YMCA, a salaried position which, combined with teaching, enabled him to remain at the university to take the Master of Arts degree in 1924. In 1925 he qualified for admission to the Alabama bar, and began the practice of his profession. Establishing himself at Huntsville, the seat of Madison County, he divided the next two to three years between part-time legal practice and an instructorship at Huntsville College. In 1929 he became United States Commissioner, which post he held for about a year until he formed a law partnership with Douglass Taylor and Schuyler Richardson.

When United States Representative A. H. Carmichael of the Eighth Alabama District decided not to seek re-election in 1936, Sparkman was one of five candidates for nomination as his successor. Three of the contestants were eliminated by the regular Democratic primary; however, neither of the survivors, Sparkman or Robert Simpson (later a justice of the Alabama Supreme Court) had a clear majority of the ballots cast, and a run-off contest followed, from which Sparkman emerged the victor. This was the only strenuous campaign in which Sparkman was called upon to engage until he ran for the Senate in 1946; in the intervening biennial Democratic primaries he was unchallenged, while in this and subsequent elections Republican opposition was negligible.

Taking his seat in the Seventy-fifth Congress early in 1937, Sparkman was named to the Accounts, Civil Service, Immigration and Naturalization, and Roads committees; he made his maiden speech on behalf of a farm tenant agricultural bill. Within a year, however, the Congressman had resigned from all committees except the House Military Affairs Committee, to which he had been appointed in succession to his fellow Alabaman, Representative Lister Hill [43], who had moved to the upper chamber to succeed Senator Hugo Black [41], when the latter became a justice of the Supreme Court. As legislation affecting waterways was referred to the Military Affairs Committee, Sparkman was placed in a key position in regard to a matter of vital concern to the area he represented. Making the TVA "his major interest of the period," he authored and saw through the House by a margin of six votes the Sparkman bill to dam the Tennessee River in Kentucky, and sponsored in the House the Norris bill to authorize the TVA to buy power company properties in the region in which it operated.

Representative Sparkman was a supporter of President Roosevelt's policies, voting for enlargement of the Air Forces (1940), Lend-Lease (1941) and the Selective Service Act

earlier served in the House of Representatives for five successive terms as Congressman from his State's Eighth District. In his final year in the House of Representatives (1946), Sparkman was the chief Democratic whip. However, he split with the Truman Administration on the civil rights issue, and urged the nomination by the Democratic party in the 1948 Presidential campaign of someone other than President Harry Truman. In 1950 he was the author of proposed legislation to provide housing for "middle-income" groups.

Seventh of the eleven children of Whitten Joseph and Julia Mitchell (Kent) Sparkman, John Jackson Sparkman was born near the Tennessee Valley town of Hartselle, in northern Alabama, on December 20, 1899. (Both his father, a tenant farmer, and his mother were natives of Morgan County, in which Hartselle is located.) The boy attended the "one-room, one-teacher" Mount Tabor School near his birthplace, and received his secondary schooling at Morgan County High School, at Hartselle. With money secured by a bank loan on a cotton crop he raised in the summer of his senior year, the youth proceeded to Tuscaloosa to enroll at the University of Alabama. "I found a job soon after I landed in Tuscaloosa, at $4.20 a week," Sparkman was later to tell Marguerite Johnston of the Birmingham (Alabama) *News-Age-Herald*. "Later they raised me to $5.25. The third year the university gave me a teaching fellowship to teach history and political science, and the fourth year, I edited the *Crimson and White*" (the university newspaper). The following year Sparkman was elected president of the student body

Sparkman was below induction age when the United States entered World War I. He enlisted on October 7, 1918, and was honorably discharged on the following December 12. He then joined the university's Reserve Officers'

(1941). He authored the legislation (approved 1943) for the commissioning of women physicians and surgeons in the Army and Navy. (Later, in 1943 and again in 1945, he proposed parallel legislation for women dentists.) On labor issues, the Congressman's record was considered liberal. A speech by Sparkman early in 1944 advocating a fourth term for President Roosevelt attracted attention. He departed from the usual Southern stand by supporting the Administration's soldier vote bill. He was a member of the Committee Investigating National Defense Migration (1941-42).

In 1941 Drew Pearson and Robert Allen recorded in their column that Sparkman was "rated by House leaders as one of the ablest young members." The Congressman organized in 1943 the so-called "Tuesday Night" group of young Democrats pledged to support the Roosevelt policies (with a membership of approximately fifty). In the Seventy-ninth Congress, when Representative Robert Ramspeck of Georgia announced his intention of resigning from Congress in November 1945, Sparkman succeeded him as House Democratic whip. Notable in his record as whip was his delivery of a majority vote for the British Loan (1946).

Upon the death in June 1946 of the senior United States Senator from Alabama, John H. Bankhead, Sparkman, who had been renominated for his House seat in the regular Alabama primaries, became one of five candidates to complete Bankhead's unexpired term. In a special primary held July 30, 1946, Sparkman, with the backing of the CIO Political Action Committee, won a clear majority over all his four rivals. Later in the summer Sparkman was appointed chairman of the Democratic National Committee's speakers bureau for the 1946 campaign. From the voting on November 4, 1946, Sparkman emerged with the distinction of being simultaneously elected to both the House and the Senate—for reasons peculiar to Alabama election law he had not withdrawn his candidacy for the former. As soon as his election to the Senate had been certified, Sparkman resigned from the House of Representatives for both the Seventy-ninth and Eightieth Congresses and immediately became a member of the Senate.

Senator Sparkman in the Eightieth Congress was assigned to the Banking and Currency, and District of Columbia committees, and to the Joint Committee on the Economic Report. In the second session he became a member also of the Joint Committee on Housing. His voting record reveals support of: the appointment of David E. Lilienthal [44] as head of the Atomic Energy Commission; Greek-Turkish aid; ratification of the Italian peace treaty; and repeal of Federal taxes on oleomargarine; the Federal aid to education bill; continuance of Selective Service; extension of the Reciprocal Trade Agreements Act; the Vandenberg Foreign Policy Resolution. He supported the Taft-Hartley Act on its original passage through the Senate, though he later voted against overriding the President's veto; both in the Banking Committee and on the Senate floor he fought for extension of Federal rent controls and opposed the 15 per cent "voluntary" rent increase authorized by the act as finally amended. The Alabama Senator's relations with the Executive were impaired after President Truman announced his civil rights objectives; on March 19, 1948, Sparkman went on record as advocating General Dwight D. Eisenhower [48] as Democratic candidate in the approaching Presidential election. On July 30, after the Democratic National Convention had inserted the civil rights plank into the party platform, Sparkman announced his support of the Thurmond [48]-Wright [48] States' rights ("Dixiecrat") Presidential ticket. He himself was re-elected to the Senate (November 2, 1948) for the full term ending January 3, 1955.

When the Eighty-first Congress convened in January 1949, Sparkman was named to the Public Works Committee as well as to the Banking and Currency committee; Burnet Maybank [49] of South Carolina became chairman of the latter, with Sparkman as chairman of the subcommittee on housing (Sparkman continued as a member of the Joint Committee on the Economic Report and joined the Senate Office Building Commission.) Except on matters of civil rights—he was sympathetic toward the 1949 filibuster and voted for the Dixiecrat-Republican cloture rule on March 17—he has supported the Administration on most domestic and foreign policies, opposing all limitations to the Marshall Plan, casting his "aye" for both the North Atlantic Security Pact and the Foreign Military Aid Bill (July 21 and September 22, 1949), and standing in the front rank of fighters for the Federal aid to education bill and for the extension of rent controls.

As chairman of the subcommittee on housing, Sparkman developed and sponsored, during the summer of 1949, an "omnibus" housing bill which included provision for one billion dollars of direct Government loans to the building and purchase of homes for the "modest income" group. (The scope of this phase was not specified, but "modest income" was subsequently defined by Sparkman as possibly between $2,000 and $5,000 per annum). The Senator made a trip to Europe in November, to study Continental, especially Swedish, public housing financing methods. A revised version of the bill (which the New York Times had called "economically irresponsible") was introduced in both houses in early 1950; the opening debates indicated a close vote might be expected. That year the Senator was one of several sponsors of a proposed constitutional amendment to revise the method of electing Presidents and Vice-Presidents. He spoke before a Senate Foreign Relations subcommittee in favor of a plan for a world police force to be set up under the United Nations and advocated that the U.N. be entrusted with solution of the problem of control of the hydrogen bomb. In 1950 the Senator was appointed a member of the United States delegation to the U.N.

Sparkman is a trustee of Athens College (Alabama), of American University (Washington); is an American Legionnaire (past post commander), a member and former president (1935-39) of the Huntsville Chamber of Commerce, a Kiwanian (ex-district governor for

SPARKMAN, JOHN J.—*Continued*

Alabama), a Mason and a Woodman of the World. His fraternities are the Phi Beta Kappa, Pi Kappa Alpha and Phi Alpha Delta). He regularly conducts Bible class for adults at the Hamline Methodist Episcopal Church in Washington. Mrs. Sparkman is the former Ivo Hall of Albertsville, Alabama, also a graduate of the State University. They were married on June 2, 1923, while Sparkman was taking studies for his M.A. degree. They have one child, Julia Ann, now Mrs. Tazewell T. Shepard, Jr. The Senator from Alabama is six feet, one inch in height, weighs about 200 pounds, and keeps in good physical trim by playing tennis or paddleball. His hobbies are stamp collecting and gardening. Gray-eyed, with graying curly hair, a ruddy complexion, and a hearty manner, he "talks in a slow, pleasant voice."

References

Birmingham (Ala.) News-Age-Herald p6D Mr 10 '46 por
N Y Post p11 S 16 '46 por
N Y Sun p30 D 12 '45
U S News 21:64+ O 4 '46 por
America's Young Men, 1938-39
Congressional Directory (1950)
International World Who's Who (1949)
Who's Who in America, 1948-49
Who's Who in the Nation's Capital, 1938-39
World Biography (1948)

SPENDER, PERCY C(LAUDE) Oct. 5, 1897- Australian Government official

Address: b. Parliament House, Canberra, Australia; h. 11 Wellington St., Woollahra, Sydney, Australia

The Minister of External Affairs of Australia, the Honorable Percy C. Spender, is the chief author of the plan for mutual aid in Southeast Asia approved by the conference of British Commonwealth Foreign Ministers held in Colombo, Ceylon, in January 1950. The plan, hailed as an "entirely new Commonwealth concept," proposes material aid to the Commonwealth territories in Asia and to the non-Commonwealth countries, Burma, Indo-China, Thailand, and Indonesia, if they wish to be included. Spender, who assumed the office of Foreign Minister in December 1949, was first elected to the Australian House of Representatives in 1937. He held successively the portfolios of Federal Treasurer and Army Minister in the first years of World War II. On the fall of the Liberal party from power in 1941, he became an opposition member in the Advisory War Council, a post he held until 1945.

Born on October 5, 1897, in Sydney, Australia, to Frank Henry and Mary Hanson (Murray) Spender, Percy Claude Spender was reared in Sydney, there attending the city's Fort Street High School. Later he enrolled for night courses at Sydney University; during the day he was a clerk in Sydney Town Hall. In 1915, after winning first place among New South Wales participants in a public service examination, he was appointed to a clerkship in the Commonwealth Petty Sessions Office at Newtown, near Sydney. In 1918, when he was twenty-one years old, Spender enlisted in the Australian Imperial Forces of World War I. The date for his B.A. examinations having been advanced in view of his enlistment, he obtained the degree before departing for war service.

After the end of the war he returned to his studies at the university and in 1923 received an LL.B. degree with first-class honors, winning the University medal. Other scholastic honors awarded him in the course of his university years were the Morven K. Nolan Memorial Prize in political science, the Pitt-Cobett Prize for international law, the George and Matilda Harris Scholarship in law, and the Wigram Allen Prize and Scholarship. Meanwhile Spender transferred from the Commonwealth Petty Sessions office to a post in the Department of Justice, then to the Crown Solicitor's office of New South Wales. He was called to the bar in 1925; the young lawyer made company law his specialty. Ten years later (1935) Spender was appointed a King's Counsel.

In November 1937 Spender was elected to the Commonwealth of Australia's House of Representatives. Since he ran as an independent candidate for the Warringah district of New South Wales, which never before had elected a candidate not endorsed by a political party, his election "created a political sensation." One year after taking his seat in the House, Spender joined the United Australian Party. From April to November 1939 he served as assistant to the Commonwealth Treasurer, during 1939-40 as Acting Treasurer, and in 1949 was given full ministerial status and named Treasurer. In the same year he became vice-president of the Executive Council. Among problems facing him as the Commonwealth's Treasurer during the early years of World War II were the dangers of inflation and the conducting of the country's first war loan drive. He was chairman of the Australian Loan Council (1939-40), and the National Debt Commission (1940). Prime Minister Robert Gordon Menzies '50 appointed Spender in 1940 a member of the War Cabinet as Minister of the Army In this capacity Spender made an inspection tour of Australian troops, which took him to the Middle East during the Libyan campaign.

After the fall of the Menzies Government in 1941, Spender, who had been re-elected to the House of Representatives, continued to serve on the Advisory War Council, as an opposition member, until 1945. The Australian made a private tour of the United States and England in January 1945. In an interview with American press representatives, he expressed disappointment over the fact that proper credit was not being given in press releases to the Australian fighting forces. In England he addressed both houses of Parliament on "Australia in the War and after the War."

On December 10, 1949, a coalition of the Liberal and Country parties won a Parliamentary election, receiving seventy-three as against Labor's forty-eight of the 121 seats. Menzies, replacing Laborite Joseph B. Chifley [45] as Prime Minister, named Spender as Minister of External Affairs and External Territories. One of Spender's first acts was to reopen negotiations with the United States on a treaty of commercial friendship. The announcement of this move was made in a press interview given by Spender at the time of his departure for Ceylon, where he was to attend a meeting of British Commonwealth Foreign Ministers. Pointing out that in the last ten years the center of gravity in world affairs had shifted from the Atlantic to the Pacific, Spender stated, "It is in Asia and the Pacific that Australia should make its primary efforts in the field of foreign relations." With regard to aid for Asia from Australia and the United States, the Australian statesman said: "These are the two countries which can, in cooperation, make the greatest contribution to the stability and democratic development of the countries of southeast Asia."

The Foreign Minister on his way to the Commonwealth conference paid what he termed a "friendly relations" visit to Indonesia. (This state is one of the countries, not in the Commonwealth, later mentioned as possible future beneficiaries of the Commonwealth mutual aid plan to be evolved at Colombo.) Australia had not only recognized the United States of Indonesia as early as December 1949, but from the beginning of the dispute with the Dutch had supported the republican cause. When queried on the immigration question, Spender announced the traditional "White Australia" policy would be continued, but "in a more liberal-minded and humanitarian way." This policy, which bars Asian nationals from settling in Australia, said a New York *Times* correspondent, "has aroused widespread opposition, particularly in Southeast Asia, because of deportations of Indonesians and Malays."

The meeting of the Commonwealth Foreign Ministers held January 9-14, 1950, in Colombo, Ceylon, was called by Robert Trumbull in a special article to the New York *Times* "a striking illustration of the new concept of the Commonwealth." The Cabinet-ranking delegates to the conference represented Britain, Canada, New Zealand, South Africa, India, Pakistan, Ceylon, and Australia. The first decisions known to have been reached in the conference (which was closed to the press) were the acceptance in principle of recognition of the Bao Dai [49] regime in Indo-China and recommendation of financial assistance to Burma. It was generally agreed by the delegates (who were not empowered to make commitments for their Governments) to recommend contributions, tentatively estimated to total £7,500,000, from each country's sterling balance. These were regarded as measures to combat the spread of communism from China to Southeast Asia. On the question of the Communist regime in China, Spender said that he felt that Britain, India, Pakistan, and Ceylon might have delayed their recognition of Red China until all the Foreign Ministers had had opportunity to amplify previous consultations.

Australian Official Photo.
PERCY C. SPENDER

From a memorandum submitted by Spender on January 13, and later amalgamated with separate programs proposed by the Ceylon and New Zealand delegates, emerged a plan for aid to underdeveloped Commonwealth countries of Asia, with possible extension to other territories in the area. Spender emphasized the "Communist challenge to the democracies of the world" which "could best be met on the economic front through a long-term policy." Behind the Australian proposal is said to lie dissatisfaction with the methods of the International Bank for Reconstruction and Development. The plan endorsed calls for major Commonwealth countries to form a permanent consultative committee to arrange to give South and Southeast Asian countries technical advice, farm machinery and other needed capital equipment and sterling credits when necessary. It would be administered by a working commission with headquarters in Canberra, Australia, to which representatives of needy countries would present analyses of their requirements. The program will be recommended to the Colombo delegates' home Governments, and a further Commonwealth conference will be called by Australia, probably within four months of the Colombo meeting, at which delegates will express their Governments' views.

In the first statement in Australia's Parliament of the new Liberal Government's foreign policy, Spender on March 9, 1950, referred to a treaty of friendship, commerce and navigation and a convention on taxation, which he had previously announced in the press to be under discussion between Australia and the United States. He expressed the hope that his country might build up with the United States a relationship similar to that existing within the British Commonwealth. (Of this offer, a New York *Times* editorial said: "It makes so much sense and gives such great promise that it deserves a warm welcome.") Envisaging the

SPENDER, PERCY C.—*Continued*

possibility of a defensive military pact among countries vitally interested in stability in Asia and the Pacific, the Australian Minister expressed his Government's interest as well in positive aspects possible in such a pact—"the promotion of democratic political institutions, higher living standards and increased cultural and commercial ties."

Spender during 1942-45 was on the active list of the Australian Military Forces, having part-time special duties. He is now on the Reserve of Officers with the honorary rank of lieutenant colonel. In Parliament he has served on the committees of Broadcasting and of Privileges. Spender is the author of two books: *Company Law and Practice* (1939), regarded as a standard work in that field in Australia, and *Australia's Foreign Policy, the Next Phase* (1944). He was a fellow of Sydney University during 1939-44, and a member of that university's Senate; in the formation of a graduate association he took an active part. He is vice-president of the Council of the Royal Empire Society, a member of the advisory committee of Toc H (the Talbot House society), and a former director of the New South Wales Boy Scouts Association. He is a member of the Overseas League. Spender is a director of the Goodyear Tire & Rubber Company (Australian) Ltd., and of Airzone, Ltd. His clubs are the University, Elanora Country Golf, New South Wales Golf, Royal Prince Albert Yacht, Palm Beach Surf, (Sydney), Athenæum of Melbourne.

In 1925 Percy Claude Spender married Jean Maud Henderson. The couple has two sons, Peter and John. Mrs. Spender is the author of three "thrillers," *The Charge is Murder, Death Comes in the Night*, and *Murder by Moonlight*. The Spenders' recreations are golf, tennis, and swimming. The Australian statesman has been described as "short, fair, dapper." In debate he is said to be "forceful and, on occasion, truculent."

References

International Who's Who, 1949
Who's Who, 1949
Who's Who in Australia, 1947
World Biography (1948)

SPROUL, ALLAN Mar. 9, 1896- Bank official

Address: b. c/o Federal Reserve Bank of New York, 33 Liberty St., New York 5; h. 7 Dunham Rd., Scarsdale, N.Y.

The President of the Federal Reserve Bank of New York, Allan Sproul has been an employee or executive of the Federal Reserve System since his graduation from college, in 1919. He spent ten years with the Federal Reserve Bank in San Francisco before being transferred to the New York institution, where in 1941 he was named to the highest office in the largest bank in the system.

Allan Sproul, son of Robert and Sarah Elizabeth (Moore) Sproul, was born March 9, 1896, in San Francisco, California. His father, a native of Scotland, emigrated to California in the 1880's and found employment there as freight auditor for the Southern Pacific Railroad Company. His mother, of English and Welsh ancestry, was born in New York. His only brother, Robert Gordon Sproul [45], is president of the University of California.

As a youth Sproul carried newspapers, and worked in other jobs while attending high school in Berkeley. There he was the president of the student body and editor of the weekly paper and the 1914 class yearbook. At the University of California, where he majored in agriculture, he won the Alpha Zeta agricultural honor society award; was a member of Winged Helmet (junior honor society), of the Golden Bear (senior honor society), and of Alpha Delta Phi. He also worked on the *Daily Californian* and at other jobs. Interrupting his college course to join the United States Army Air Forces in 1918, he served as pilot with the rank of second lieutenant. He graduated from the university in 1919 with the B.S. degree.

Sproul has remarked that he then had a "general desire to engage in a career with public service aspects." Chance employment at the Federal Reserve Bank of San Francisco in 1920 and association there with John Perrin, chairman of the board of directors and Federal Reserve agent, led him to study economics in general and central banking in particular. Starting as head of the division of analysis and research, Sproul advanced in four years to secretary of the San Francisco institution and assistant Federal Reserve agent. After ten years he was transferred to the country's largest bank in terms of assets—the Federal Reserve Bank of New York, where his title was assistant deputy governor and secretary from 1930 to 1934. In the latter year, he was made assistant to the governor and retained the title of secretary. Two promotions occurred during 1936; first he was made deputy governor (a title changed to vice-president that year) and then first vice-president.

Sproul became president of the Federal Reserve Bank of New York on January 1, 1941, having been elected on December 19, 1940, by the directors of the bank who acted with approval of the board of governors of the Federal Reserve System. He was to hold the position until March 1 of that year, filling out the term of George L. Harrison, who had resigned. On March 1, 1941, he was elected president for a five-year term, and was reappointed for a second five-year term in February 1946.

The Federal Reserve Bank of New York is the largest of the twelve Federal Reserve Banks comprised in the Federal Reserve System. That was set up by the Federal Reserve Act in 1913 for the purpose of furnishing an elastic currency, affording means of rediscounting commercial paper, and establishing effective supervision over banking in the United States. The Federal Reserve Banks, which are banks of issue and rediscount serving districts not coterminous with State boundaries, are supervised by the Board of Governors of the Federal

Reserve System. They deal directly with banks, rarely with the public. (Other components of the System are the Federal Open Market Committee, of which Sproul is vice-chairman, the Federal Advisory Council, and member banks; members banks are all national banks, and others which may join voluntarily if requirements are met.) Situated in the principal money market of the United States, the Reserve Bank of which Sproul is president carried on between a quarter and a third of the system's operations as of 1943 (*Encyclopædia Britannica*), including the handling of all foreign accounts and a large part of all direct operations on the money market. Accounts for the central banks of governments of sixty foreign countries were held by the Federal Reserve Bank of New York at the end of 1945. It has a branch in Buffalo.

As head of the bank which in 1950 had total assets of about $8,000,000,000 for foreign and certain international accounts, Sproul has often been prominent in controversies on financial problems and policies. He has frequently testified at Congressional hearings. Appearing before the Senate Banking Committee's 1945 inquiry into the probable results of the proposed Bretton Woods agreement to set up an international currency, banking, and trade plan, Sproul advocated revising the plan to the extent of adopting only the proposed $9,100,000,000 international bank with expanded short-term lending authority and a "modest increase" in capital. The banker suggested before the joint House-Senate Economic Committee on May 12, 1948, that Congress should consider broad revisions of the Federal Reserve System. He disapproved a plan for raising reserve requirements through a secondary reserve, favoring "a more fruitful, long-term approach." Congress, he said, might consider charging the Open Market Committee with credit power, which had always been exercised solely by the Board of Governors, as well as with control of discount rates, reserve requirements, and margins.

In January 1950 Elliott V. Bell, chairman of the executive committee of McGraw-Hill Publishing Company and former New York State Superintendent of Banks, criticized the Federal Reserve System as "trying to whittle away the dual banking system," contending that the Federal Reserve's desire to control non-member banks was "unnecessary, unwarranted and unwise." To this Sproul replied: "If we are all agreed that it is necessary to have a central banking system . . . every commercial bank should be subject to the national reserve requirements." However, he added that in his estimation all banks need not necessarily become members of the Federal Reserve System. According to John Elliott, writing in the New York *Herald Tribune* on January 29, 1950, Bell was "expressing an ingrained American distrust of a highly centralized banking system." The Federal Reserve System was described by the journalist as a "sort of compromise that was acceptable alike to those who wanted and those who feared a central banking system," and one that eliminated inelasticity and lack

Underwood & Underwood
ALLAN SPROUL

of cooperation, which had been two defects in the monetary system.

Sproul has opposed any return to the gold standard, maintaining that such a move would be a backward step. In a discussion of the question of increasing the price of gold, at the convention of the American Bankers Association in 1949, the New York banker declared that the integrity of the national currency is not dependent on its convertability into gold but on the productive power of the economy and the competent management of fiscal and monetary affairs. Gold is useful chiefly as a medium for balancing international accounts and as a guide in disciplining international trade and finance, Sproul said. He also pointed to the fact that the Soviet Union, Switzerland, and the United Kingdom would profit most as holders of gold in a price rise, and that the Soviet Union, South Africa, and Canada would benefit most as its producers.

As to methods of curbing inflation, Sproul has spoken in favor of credit management as a means which can prevent currency owners "in sudden and unpredictable droves" from demanding their gold, thus embarrassing the banking system and halting industry. After the outbreak of war in Korea, when controls on mortgage and consumer credit were renewed and changes in reserve requirements were used to control inflation, Sproul warned that in case of emergency "runaway" inflation, reserve requirements as high as 100 per cent against new deposits could be initiated temporarily. In the latter part of August all the Federal Reserve Banks raised their discount rates, which put pressure on bankers to raise their interest rates on commercial loans. In addition, the Open Market Committee lowered the price at which it would support certain classes of Government securities, which, in effect, raised the interest rate. Sproul supported this action,

SPROUL, ALLAN—Continued
saying that the United States could not afford
to keep money cheap "if the counterpart of that
action is inflation, rising prices, and a steady
deterioration in the purchasing power of the
dollar."

Serving the Federal Government in two administrative posts, Sproul has been chairman
of the Advisory Committee on Fiscal and Monetary Problems of the Economic Cooperation
Administration since April 1950, and chairman
of the War Finance Committee for the Second
Federal Reserve District in 1942-43. While he
headed the latter committee in 1943 the New
York District topped its quota in the Second
War Loan Drive, reaching almost double the
figure named as the original goal. In December 1946 Sproul declined the offer of the presidency of the World Bank.

The degree of LL.D. was awarded to Sproul
by New York University in 1947; the inscrip-
tion on Sproul's scroll read, in part: "A banker
of exceptional talents, a resolute exponent of
financial conservatism, a private citizen sur-
charged with the keenest sense of public responsibility." Among his clubs are the Century
(New York) and Bohemian, in San Francisco.
Standing six feet, he weighs 200 pounds; he has
blue eyes and light hair. Sproul met Marion
Meredith Bogle, who was to become his wife,
while she was a college student. Married April
2, 1921, they have three children, Allan, Jr.,
Gordon John, and David Saffell. Sproul says
he is a Republican "with independent leanings,"
that his upbringing was Presbyterian. Tennis
was his favorite sport "until the court became
too large—then intermittent golf"; he also enjoys stream fishing, hiking, and reading.

References

N Y Herald Tribune p1+ D 21 '46
N Y Times p39 D 20 '40
International Who's Who, 1950
Who's Who in America, 1950-51
Who's Who in Commerce and Industry
(1948)
Who's Who in New York, 1947
World Biography (1948)

STEINBERG, MILTON, RABBI   Nov.
25, 1903—Mar. 20, 1950 Rabbi of the Park
Avenue Synagogue since 1933; taught classi-
cal languages at College of the City of New
York (1924-25); instructor in Jewish history
and religion at Jewish Theological Seminary
(1926-28); rabbi of Temple Beth El Zedeck,
Indianapolis (1928-33); lecturer; author of
The Making of the Modern Jew (1934), As a
Driven Leaf (a philosophical novel, 1940), A
Partisan Guide to the Jewish Problem (1945),
Basic Judaism (1947); on editorial board of
Reconstructionist. See Current Biography, 1940.

Obituary

N Y Times p29 Mr 21 '50

STEINHARDT, LAURENCE
A(DOLPH) Oct. 6, 1892—Mar. 28, 1950
United States diplomat; Ambassador to Canada since August 1948; previously served as
envoy to Sweden (1933-37), Peru (1937-39),
Russia (1939-41), Turkey (1942-45), Czechoslovakia (1945-48); employed as an accountant
briefly, later trained for the law; member of
Guggenheimer, Untermyer and Marshall during the years 1920-33; active in President
Roosevelt's preconvention campaign in 1932;
author of articles and books on medical jurisprudence, trade unions, economics, and finance.
See Current Biography, 1941.

Obituary

N Y Times p1+ Mr 29 '50

STEVENS, EDMUND (WILLIAM) July
22, 1910-   Journalist
Address: b. c/o Christian Science Monitor,
1 Norway St., Boston 15, Mass.; Christian Science Monitor, Via della Mercede 54, Rome,
Italy; h. Via del Casaletto 116, Rome, Italy.

For his series of forty-four articles, "This is
Russia—Uncensored," published in the Christian Science Monitor in the fall of 1949, Edmund Stevens in 1950 was awarded the Pulitzer
Prize for distinguished reporting on international affairs. His knowledge of Russia is the
result of having lived there for ten years. As
a war correspondent for the Monitor he covered many historic events, his assignments
again taking him to Moscow. Since November
1949 he has been chief of that paper's Mediterranean bureau. Stevens, who is the author
of Russia Is No Riddle (1945), has also appeared on the lecture platform.

Edmund William Stevens was born July 22,
1910, in Denver, Colorado, where his father,
Dr. Edmund William Stevens, an eye specialist,
began his practice upon graduating from medical school. The doctor was a native of Canada,
to which a Stevens forebear, loyal to the British cause, fled at the time of the American
Revolution. Florence (Ballance) Stevens, the
journalist's mother, was reared in Illinois, her
grandfather having settled in the Midwest in
1836. Dr. Stevens died two months after his
son's birth, and in 1913 Mrs. Stevens took him
to Italy, where they lived during 1913-1919 in
Rome, Florence, Bologna, and Milan. There
Mrs. Stevens worked with the American Red
Cross. The boy acquired his first foreign language—he was also to learn Russian, French,
and German. Upon their return to the United
States they lived in Peoria (Illinois) and New
York. Edmund attended the South Kent (Connecticut) School and the Dwight School in
New York.

At the age of seventeen Stevens entered
Columbia University, to major in the social
sciences; he contributed to The Spectator
(undergraduate daily) and became a Delta Phi
member. In 1930 he interrupted his college
studies for a year's stay on the Continent,
visiting Italy, France, and Germany. Returning to Columbia, he entered the class of 1932.
Subsequently he had a year of postgraduate

work in government and international law. Stevens, who says he had no journalistic aspirations at college, names as influences in his choice of his career Rexford G. Tugwell (under whom he studied economics), other New Dealers, and Lincoln Steffens' autobiography.

In the spring of 1934 Stevens went to Moscow to study Russian. His stay there was prolonged by his marriage on March 14, 1935, to a Russian girl, Nina Andreyevna. A New York *Post* "close-up" (April 12, 1946) of Mrs. Stevens, written after her graduation from Wellesley College in 1946, related that they had met in 1934 while both were attending Moscow University. (She had taught school, promoted recreations, and had been the only woman on the managerial staff of five on a collective farm in the Middle Urals.) Mrs. Stevens is quoted as saying that she consented to leave Russia because "I believed I would make a better American than Edmund a Russian." While Stevens was trying to obtain his wife's exit visa, he held a number of positions in Moscow. Until November 1937 he worked in a Moscow publishing house as a translator, when he became employed at the American-Russian Chamber of Commerce. At about this time he began writing for the British press (Manchester *Guardian,* London *Daily Herald,* and the *Observer*), and in the summer of 1938 he substituted for the Reuters Moscow correspondent. That fall he became the Moscow representative of the Cunard-White Star line.

In June 1939 the Supreme Soviet granted Mrs. Stevens' request to renounce her citizenship. With Vladimir, a son born in 1936, the Stevens went to the United States. At the end of that July, Stevens returned to Europe alone, planning to wind up his affairs in Moscow, but was unable to obtain a re-entry visa. He was in Stockholm when the Russians invaded Finland. Proceeding to Riga, Latvia, he filed his first story as a war correspondent—published in the *Christian Science Monitor,* it was the beginning of his association with that newspaper.

After the end of the Soviet-Finnish winter war, Stevens left for Oslo, arriving there on April 3, 1940. There he again found himself on the spot of a surprise invasion. He, Leland Stowe, and Warren Irvin, the only American newsmen in Oslo at the time, "scooped" the story of the Nazi attack on Norway. The last war correspondent to leave Norway before its surrender, Stevens had filed stories to the *Monitor* on the operations of the Quislings and German airborne troops. Returning to Stockholm, the journalist reported on the situation in Sweden until June, when the Communists granted him a transit visa to Rumania. He arrived at Bucharest one week before the Russians moved into Bessarabia. During the summer and fall of 1940 he covered the campaigns which brought Rumania and Bulgaria under the Nazis. "When Mussolini invaded Greece," Stevens has stated, "I drove to Athens with Leland Stowe and Russell Hill of the New York *Herald Tribune* and accompanied the Greek Army into Southern Albania." During this campaign Stevens had to pass his sto-

EDMUND STEVENS

ries to the *Monitor*'s Boston office through five censorships. In January 1941, he tells, he was in Bucharest "to cover the massacre of the Nazi Iron Guard by General Antonescu"; he interviewed General Dentz, the Vichy High Commissioner for Syria and Lebanon, while en route to Egypt, where he received instruction to interview Haile Selassie, who was then making his way into Ethiopia. At Khartoum the war correspondent joined a convoy of trucks, part of irregular British forces accompanying Selassie. This expedition won Stevens a world "scoop" on the retaking of Ethiopia. After two months' stay in that country, during which he interviewed the African chief, Stevens returned to the United States in May 1941.

The journalist worked in the *Christian Science Monitor*'s home office in Boston until February 1942, when he went to North Africa to cover the desert campaign of the Allies against the Nazi forces of General Rommel. He accompanied the British troops from El Alamein to Tripoli under General Montgomery and witnessed the recapture of Libya and of Tunis. In recognition of his work done under the hazards of war, the British War Office in 1945 awarded Stevens the African Star. He holds also the United States War Department's decoration for "outstanding and conspicuous service with the armed forces under difficult and hazardous combat conditions."

In August 1942, Stevens, as an adviser to General Russell Maxwell [42], accompanied Winston Churchill [42] and W. Averell Harriman [46] to the Moscow conference; one month later he flew with Wendell Willkie [40] to Baghdad on his Mid-East tour before returning to Africa. In November 1943 Stevens went to Russia, where he saw and reported the siege of Leningrad, Smolensk, the three campaigns of Kharkov, the Karelian Isthmus, and Minsk. Between re-

STEVENS, EDMUND—*Continued*

ports of campaigns the *Monitor* correspondent filed accounts of his stay with the Polish army and of a brief visit to United States air forces stationed on the Russian steppes. In July 1944 he returned to the United States for the publication of a book on Russia.

Russia Is No Riddle appeared in March 1945. Five weeks later the book had reached a third edition, and had been serialized in American, Canadian, and Australian newspapers; it was published in six other languages. The *Book-of-the-Month Club News* said of it: "The story jumps from swift accounts of big and little happenings . . . to eloquent expositions of the several facets of Russian policy." In it the author suggested that amicable relations between Russia and America could be maintained if each were tolerant and indulged in a "measure of give and take." During 1944 Stevens on a lecture tour of the United States drew "capacity audiences."

The journalist, who was again in Russia as the *Christian Science Monitor* correspondent January 1946-August 1949, at the same time dispatched regular news reports to the American Broadcasting Company. (He was one of three American newsmen affected by the Soviet abolition of broadcasting privileges in November 1946.) One of the events he reported in this period was the 1947 Foreign Ministers Conference in Moscow. When Stevens left Russia, the *Christian Science Monitor* editor, Erwin D. Canham,[45] stated, "It was no longer journalistically valuable or personally wise or safe for him to stay." (Mrs. Stevens and their children had been with the correspondent.)

In May 1950 it was announced that Stevens had been awarded the Pulitzer Prize for his series of forty-four articles, "This is Russia—Uncensored," written in Berlin and Rome immediately after his departure from the Soviet capital. They were published in the *Christian Science Monitor* during October and November 1949; and in the May 15, 1950 issue of *Life* highlights of the series were given. The articles, based on the correspondent's long residence in Moscow, a study of Russian history, and wide-range contacts among Russian people and officialdom, told of "the rising tide of suspicion and mistrust which surround all foreigners in Moscow . . . of the police surveillance which smothered his family's affairs and movements, and even of the maid who began to rifle his papers" (from the *Monitor* editorial introducing the series). They reported disaffection among the Jews and Balts, but pointed out: "The Soviet Union is a going concern." In them Stevens emphasized his conviction that the world's future depends on understanding and friendship between the United States and Russia, and urged that no opportunity be missed "to proffer the hand of friendship to the Russian people over the head of the Soviet government." Announcement that the articles would be published in book form was made in June 1950.

Articles by Stevens have appeared in the *New Republic, Life,* and the *Saturday Evening Post*. In November 1949, when the correspondent was made chief of the *Monitor*'s Mediterranean bureau, his family took up residence in Rome. Besides the son, Vladimir, there is a daughter, Anastasia, born in the United States. In his church affiliation Stevens is Protestant. He has fair hair and blue eyes, stands six feet one inch, and weighs 175 pounds. For outdoor recreation he swims and skiis.

References

Christian Sci Mon p6 N 20 '46; p6 My 2 '50
Life 28:125 My 15 '50
N Y Post Mag p49 Ap 12 '46

STIEBELING, HAZEL K(ATHERINE) stē′bling) Mar. 20, 1896- United States Government official

Address: b. c/o Bureau of Human Nutrition and Home Economics, Department of Agriculture, Washington 25, D.C.; h. Westchester Apartments, Washington 16, D.C.; Latty, Ohio

Dr. Hazel K. Stiebeling, Chief of the Bureau of Human Nutrition and Home Economics of the United States Department of Agriculture since 1944, "first made history in the nutritive field with her diet plans, based at different levels of cost," according to the New York *Herald Tribune* (January 27, 1945). She was appointed head of BHNHE after serving as its assistant chief in charge of research from 1942 to 1944. Her association with the Department of Agriculture dates from 1930, when she joined its staff as a food economist. The dietitian, who was a delegate to a meeting of the International Society of Agricultural Economists in Scotland in 1936 and to a League of Nations meeting the following year, in 1945 represented the United States at the U.N.'s Food and Agriculture Organization conferences.

Born March 20, 1896, at Haskins, Ohio, to Adam and Elizabeth (Brand) Stiebeling, Hazel Katherine Stiebeling grew up on a farm near Latty, Ohio. She attended the neighboring rural school until she was sent to live with her grandparents at Findlay, Ohio. There she took her eighth grade work preparatory to entering Central High School in that town; her favorite subjects at that time were languages and science. When domestic science was introduced into the high school curriculum, her mother urged her to take that subject. The result was that, after her graduation in 1913, she enrolled at Skidmore College (at Saratoga Springs, New York) for the two-year course in the domestic arts. While spending the summer of 1915 at the family farm, she heard of a vacancy in the domestic science department of the Findlay High School. Her application for the position accepted, she taught there for three years. She continued studying during free hours at a local college.

For further study Miss Stiebeling attended Teachers College, Columbia University, from which she was graduated with the B.S. degree, with a major in food and nutrition in 1919. She also worked as assistant in physiological chemistry at Columbia and, between 1919 and 1923, was head of the Department of Home Economics at Kansas State Teachers College in Emporia. The next year (1924) she received her M.A. degree in nutrition from Teachers College. She remained in New York as assistant to Dr. Mary Swartz Rose of Columbia's nutrition department while fulfilling the requirements for a doctorate. She also worked as research assistant in chemistry in the graduate school at Columbia between 1926 and 1930 as assistant to Dr. Henry C. Sherman [49] in the food and nutrition laboratory. Miss Stiebeling was awarded the Ph.D. degree in chemistry in 1928.

A book on the chemistry of food and nutrition by Dr. Sherman had first interested Miss Stiebeling in the research possibilities of home economics when she was a student at Skidmore College. At his urging she took a Civil Service examination that would qualify her for Government service. While working for her doctorate, Miss Stiebeling had studied the importance of Vitamin D in the baby's diet even when calcium and phosphorus are abundant. She found, through experiments on white rats, that there were quantitative relationships between Vitamin D intake and calcium deposition in the body. These scientific contributions brought a number of employment opportunities, among which, in 1930, was the Department of Agriculture's offer of a position as senior food economist in the Bureau of Home Economics. This appealed to her because the post entailed directing food economic studies, developing sample survey methods for determining and analyzing diets of population groups, and developing diet plans at various costs. When a food crisis developed in the South that summer, the recently appointed food economist was assigned to plan (with the Red Cross and the Public Health and Extension Services) for the provision of inexpensive but nutritive foods for the needy. During World War II, with its attendant food rationing, Dr. Stiebeling planned food budgets for people of different income levels. The information was dispensed to the public through various channels—in free bulletins and pamphlets issued by the Department of Agriculture, and in popular magazines. Alone or in collaboration with other experts, she wrote on such subjects as the iron content of vegetables and fruits, diets at various levels of nutritive content and cost, and food budgets for nutrition and production programs. She also wrote about diets peculiar to certain sections of the country.

Dr. Stiebeling became a contributor to the *Woman's Home Companion* in 1937. Typical of her articles was one entitled "Can Your Menus Pass This Test?", which appeared in 1939. A market list for one week showed the foods and quantities of each sufficient for a low-cost but adequate diet for a family of moderately active parents and two children. Emily Yost (in *American Women of Science*) paid special tribute to the food economist for the readable quality of her writings for the general public.

When Miss Stiebeling became Assistant Chief of the Bureau of Human Nutrition and

U.S. Bureau of Human Nutrition
& Home Economics

HAZEL K. STIEBELING

Home Economics of the United States Department of Agriculture in 1942, the Bureau's home economics research program was put in her hands. Two years later, after promotion to Chief in 1944, as successor to Dr. Sherman, she became director of food, nutrition, textiles, clothing, housing, household equipment, and family economics research for the Bureau; she also began taking part in national and international food and nutrition conferences. She has been a member of: Standing Advisory Committee on Nutrition of the Food and Agricultural Organization of the United Nations since 1946; of the United States Delegation to the United Nations Food and Agricultural Organization for four years (1945-46, 1948-49); of the United States Delegation to the Inter-American Conference on Agriculture in 1942 and 1945; and of the Food and Nutrition Board of the National Research Council since 1942. The Seventh Annual Borden Award was bestowed upon her in 1943 "for significant contribution to knowledge of food habits of the population of the United States" by direction of the American Home Economics Association. An honorary LL. D. degree from Skidmore College was presented Dr. Stiebeling in 1943, and an honorary D. Sc. from Iowa State College in 1947. She belongs to the American Institute of Nutrition, American Chemical Society, American Statistical Association, American Home Economics Association, American Association of University Women; she is a member of Sigmi Xi and of Omicron Nu. Her church is the Lutheran.

The nutritionist, who is five feet seven inches tall and of slender build, "wears clothes with tailored lines but a definitely feminine touch," according to Frances Lide in her column "Capital Silhouette" in the Washington *Sunday Star*. The color of her eyes and hair is brown.

STIEBELING, HAZEL K.—*Continued*

Music, travel, and outdoor life, especially hiking, golf, and study of wild flowers and of trees, are Dr. Stiebeling's diversions.

References

> N Y Herald Tribune p11 Ja 27 '45
> Washington (D.C.) Sunday Star Jl 28 '46
> Woman's Home C 66:54 O '39
> American Men of Science (1949)
> Borden Award Directory, 1937-43
> Who's Who in America, 1950-51
> Yost, E. American Women of Science (1943)

STIKKER, DIRK U(IPKO) (stĭk'ẽr dĭrk ŭp'kō) Feb. 5, 1897- Foreign Minister of the Netherlands

Address: b. Ministry of Foreign Affairs, The Hague; h. 2 Plein 1813, The Hague

Dirk U. Stikker, who became the Foreign Minister of the Netherlands in August 1948, has been concerned with such major issues as Indonesia's independence, the Benelux agreement, and the North Atlantic Pact. As political conciliator of the Organization for European Economic Cooperation, to which he was elected January 31, 1950, he will seek to bridge the economic and financial gaps between the Marshall Plan countries. Stikker was the head of the Netherlands delegation to the United Na-

Anefo

DIRK U. STIKKER

tions in 1949. A former businessman—in the banking and brewery fields—he became prominent in labor-management relations during and after World War II. He founded the Freedom party in 1946, the year he was elected to the States-General; and in 1948 he was cofounder of the People's Party for Freedom and Democracy.

Born in Holland on February 5, 1897, at Winschoten in the Province of Groningen, Dirk Uipko Stikker is the son of Uipko Obbo and Ida (Meursing) Stikker. After completing his pre-university education, he studied law at the University of Groningen. He received his LL.D. degree in 1922.

The young man began his career as an employee of the Groningen Bank, following which he worked for the Twentsche Bank in Amsterdam. His first executive position was that of manager of the Lissensche Bank Vereniging at Lisse. When this was taken over by the Twentsche Bank, he was appointed manager of its western section and transferred to the branch at Leyden, where he remained four years. Subsequently he managed the Haarlem branch for some months. In mid-1935 he became managing director of the Heineken Lagerbeer Brewery Company, one of the large breweries of the Netherlands. There his province was the foreign interests of the corporation, which called for much travel in Europe, Asia, and the United States. Stikker remained in that directorship until 1948.

After the outbreak of World War II Stikker began to devote himself to social problems. During the Nazi occupation of the Netherlands he organized cooperation between unions of workers and employers. Then, soon after the liberation his intermediary offices resulted in the establishment, in 1945, of the Labor Foundation (Stichting van den Arbeid), which has as its objective the promotion of cooperative programs between employers' associations and trade unions. Stikker has been chairman of the foundation since its formation. He attended the ILO Conference in Montreal in 1946 as the Netherlands' delegate. Stikker is also president of the Central Social Association of Employers and of the Labor Board. Because of his work in worker-employer relations, he was appointed a member of the National Advisory Committee of the Provisional Parliament which was set up as a "stop-gap" government in May 1945 after the liberation.

Stikker had not hitherto identified himself with any political party. In March 1946, in agreement with a group which did not endorse the existing party programs, he took the initiative in forming the Freedom party, drawing up a manifesto for it. Although several Young Liberals joined him in this action, his plan was at first opposed by the Liberal State party. However, when it won adherents from among the progressive Liberals and support of the political centrum and a large number of Liberal Democrats and Christian Historicals, an agreement was made with the political leaders of the Liberal State party, who promised to support the Freedom party in the election campaign. Stikker became president of the new party. In the May 1946 elections he was chosen a Freedom party member of the First Chamber (Senate) of the States-General. In the parliament he participated in debates on social and labor questions, on financial issues, and on matters relating to the colonial empire of the Netherlands.

In 1947 Dr. P. J. Oud, Mayor of Rotterdam, dissociated himself from the Labor party; and as a result of negotiations between Stikker and Oud, the People's Party for Freedom and Democracy was formed on January 24, 1948, in a merging of the Freedom party and of Oud partisans, who were for the most part former Liberal-Democrats. Stikker was elected president and Oud vice-president of this new political party.

Stikker was appointed by his Government to the Netherlands delegation at the Round Table Conference on the political status of the Netherlands West Indies, and was subsequently invited to act in a similar capacity at the Round Table Conference with the spokesmen for Indonesia. In June 1948 he attended the Conference with the Indonesian representatives at Bandung, which made the first preparations for the new structure of the United States of Indonesia.

In July 1948 the Netherlands' Cabinet was reorganized in order to command the two-thirds majority in the new States-General required for a revision of the Constitution to deal with the proposed Netherlands-Indonesian Union. A coalition was formed under the premiership of Willem Drees [49] of the Labor party, whose Cabinet included, in addition to Catholic People's and Labor party members, representatives of the Christian Historical Union and the People's Party for Freedom and Democracy. Stikker was appointed to the one seat available for his party, being sworn in as Minister of Foreign Affairs on August 7, 1948.

The new Foreign Minister was immediately faced with the problems brought forward by Indonesian independence. The Republic of Indonesia had been proclaimed in 1945 while the Japanese occupied the Dutch East Indies. After the Japanese capitulation, Mohammed Hatta [49] and his Indonesian Republican forces resisted Dutch efforts to regain control of the country on a colonial basis. The Netherlands Government took "police action" against the Indonesian Republicans in July 1947, at the same time declaring its intention of establishing a United States of Indonesia and giving the colony its independence. For nearly a year, negotiations and mediations had been carried on between the Netherlands and Indonesia by the United Nations Good Offices Committee. When Stikker became Foreign Minister, the Governments of both the United States and Great Britain informed him of their wishes for an agreement, pointing out that the conflict was impeding Marshall Plan progress in Europe and in Indonesia. After studying the situation in Java and conferring with his Government at The Hague, Stikker went to Java in late 1948 to confer with Hatta, when partially satisfactory conversations were held. By the end of the year, however, warfare had broken out again.

By May 1949 the United Nations effected an agreement between the Dutch and the Indonesian Republic to hold a Round Table Conference at The Hague. In June Stikker announced that the Netherlands Government was strengthening its commitments to grant complete sovereignty to Indonesia and to halt inroads of communism there. During August, September, and October the conference worked

out an agreement under which the Dutch exchanged their legal control over the islands for Indonesian pledges that Dutch economic and cultural interests would be protected. Near the close of the year, on December 27, 1949, Queen Juliana [44] transferred sovereignty over Indonesia to its seventy-five million inhabitants. Meanwhile, it was reported that plans for resumption of Marshall plan aid and military aid were being discussed by Stikker in Paris.

The Foreign Minister of the Netherlands represented his country in discussions with Great Britain, France, Belgium, and Luxembourg concerning the North Atlantic Pact. The treaty formulated, he went to Washington to sign it on April 4, 1949; and he participated in the first meeting of the North Atlantic Council there in September. In the matter of the Benelux agreement, the three countries moved toward the "pre-union" phase of their plan for economic union, as preparation for the time when there would be completely free trade and mutual convertibility of currencies. In these conferences Stikker opposed Belgian demands that, under full union, trade debts be settled in gold, winning agreement from Belgian Foreign Minister van Zeeland to accept sterling or French francs in lieu of gold.

Stikker was also concerned with the question of annexing border strips of German territory as set forth in the Paris protocol of March 26, 1949, an issue on which feeling in Holland was divided. Stikker spoke in favor of annexation before the First Chamber of the States-General and, reported the New York *Times*, forced the decision with "a declaration that the Cabinet would resign unless the protocol was ratified." The vote was 25 to 17 in favor of the annexation.

The Dutch statesman, who was a member of the Netherlands Commission on the United Nations Food and Agriculture Organization, was the head of his country's delegation to the U. N.'s Fourth Assembly, in 1949. After his return to Europe he attended the two-day meeting of the Organization for European Economic Cooperation (the European Marshall Plan Council) on January 31, and February 1, 1950. The member nations agreed on "the general outlines" of a new system of payments in an effort to liberalize intra-European trade. By unanimous vote of the eighteen delegations Dr. Stikker was chosen "political conciliator" of the OEEC, Paul-Henri Spaak [45] of Belgium having been opposed for the post by the British. While Stikker's exact duties were not defined, "the general idea," stated the New York *Herald Tribune*, "is that he will maintain constant contact with OEEC member governments in the intervals between council meetings, and will perhaps serve when necessary as a type of diplomatic representative for the entire group." Paul G. Hoffman [46], ECA Administrator looked upon the post as an important aid in fulfilling the OEEC objectives—the two principal goals sought by the United States are trade liberalization and the freeing of payments from the bilateral system now in existence.

Stikker's other interests have included chairmanship of the board of the Amsterdam daily

STIKKER, DIRK U.—*Continued*

newspaper, *Algemeen Handelsblad,* and membership on the board of directors of the Netherlands Bank and the Netherlands Trading Society. He has been decorated with the Order of the Netherlands Lion. Married on May 2, 1922, to Catharina Paulina van der Scheer, he has two sons. He has been described as "optimistic, jovial, obliging."

References

U N Bul 7:766 D 15 '49 por
International Who's Who, 1949
Wie is Dat? 1948
World Biography (1948)

STIMSON, HENRY L(EWIS) Sept. 21, 1867—Oct. 20, 1950 Lawyer and statesman; United States Secretary of War, 1911-13; served as a colonel in the United States Army in France during World War I; Governor General of the Philippines, 1927-29; Secretary of State, 1929-33; Secretary of War, 1940-45. See *Current Biography,* 1940.

Obituary

N Y Times p1 O 21 '50

STOOPNAGLE, COLONEL Oct. 4, 1897 —May 29, 1950 Radio comedian whose real name was Frederick Chase Taylor; entered radio work as a sideline to brokerage; joined the staff of the Buffalo Broadcasting Corporation in 1929; in comedy team, "Colonel Stoopnagle and Budd," with Budd Hulick was heard over national networks from 1930 to 1937; famous for nonsense words and inventions; author of a number of magazine articles and humorous books. See *Current Biography, 1947.*

Obituary

N Y Times p17 My 30 '50 por

STREIT, CLARENCE K(IRSHMAN) (strit) Jan. 21, 1896- Editor; author
Address: b. c/o Federal Union, Inc., 700 9th St., N.W., Washington 1, D.C.; h. 2853 Ontario Rd., Washington 9, D.C.

> NOTE: This biography supersedes the article which appeared in *Current Biography* in 1940.

Debate and discussion of the North Atlantic Treaty in the winter of 1949-50, by lawmakers and the general public, directed attention again to the name, personality, and ideas of Clarence K. Streit. His book *Union Now,* published in America and England in 1939 and in a new edition in 1949, presented the first considered and detailed outline for a federal union of Atlantic democracies. It is the outgrowth of the author's ten years' service as League of Nations correspondent for the New York *Times.* Since 1946 Streit has been the editor of *Freedom and Union,* a monthly magazine devoted to furthering "individual freedom and federal union."

One of a family of three boys and two girls, Clarence Kirshman Streit was born January 21, 1896, in California, Missouri. His father, Louis Leland Streit, was a farm machinery salesman; his mother, the late Emma (Kirshman) Streit, has been described as an idealist, whose faith in the motto "*I can't* never did do anything" was passed on to her children. When Clarence was fifteen the family moved to Missoula, Montana, where the boy founded the high school paper. By this time he had shown an ability in argument. Later, at Montana State University, Streit edited the undergraduate journal, *The Kaimin* (meaning "message" in Salish Indian) and developed a skeptical questioning attitude toward war which caused him to withhold (April 4, 1917) his signature to a telegram to President Wilson in which students pledged themselves to "stand behind him in whatever he undertakes." Nevertheless Streit in June 1917 was one of the first in the student body to volunteer for service in World War I.

With a background of experience amassed during summers spent between 1912 and 1916 in the Rocky Mountains and Alaska as a transitman in the United States Public Lands Surveys, Streit was sent to France with the Eighth (later Eighteenth) Railway Engineers as a private; in June 1918 he was promoted to sergeant and transferred to the Intelligence Service. Attached in December to the Archives Division of the United States Delegation to the Paris Peace Conference, he was one of those assigned to guard President Wilson on his return to Paris from Washington in the following spring.

Streit was demobilized in June 1919. Receiving his Bachelor of Arts degree from Montana State University in the same summer, he was named Montana's Rhodes Scholar to the University of Oxford for the period beginning with the fall of 1920. Prior to taking up residence at Oxford, however, he studied at the Sorbonne in Paris, worked in the Paris bureau of the Philadelphia *Public Ledger,* and saw the publication (1920) of his first book, *Where Iron Is, There Is the Fatherland.* There too he met his future wife, Jeanne Defrance. Their marriage on September 26, 1921, invalidated his Rhodes Scholarship and brought Streit's student years to an end. (Streit was subsequently to receive a number of honorary degrees, notably an LL.D. from his alma mater in 1939, the D. Litt. from Oberlin in 1940 and Hobart in 1941, and an LL.D. from Colby, also in 1941.)

During the eighteen years from 1921 to 1939, Streit was a practicing newspaperman. After rejoining the *Public Ledger,* he was assigned to cover the Greek-Turkish war in 1921; became the Philadelphia paper's Rome correspondent in the same year (he reported Mussolini's advent to power); the Constantinople correspondent in 1922; and returned to its Paris bureau in 1924. In the following year he joined the staff of the New York *Times* and was detailed to cover the Carthage excavations and the Riff war (in Morocco). Two years (1925-27) as Vienna correspondent were followed by a year in New York, after which Streit was sent to Geneva (1929) as League of Nations correspondent. This post he was to fill continuously for the next ten years, except for a brief assignment to the Washington bureau in 1930. In 1932 Streit was elected president of the International Association of Journalists Accredited to the League.

At this period Streit began to analyze causes and effects of the upsurge of totalitarianism and reached the conclusion that, while democratic nations controlled two-thirds of the world's trade and the bulk of its natural resources, the totalitarian powers were able to "push them around" almost at will, largely because of the mistrusts begotten by "unbridled nationalism." The outcome was his plan for a federal union of fifteen "Atlantic democracies," organized much along the lines established by the Constitution of the United States. Member nations (like the States of the Union) would continue to control their internal affairs, with foreign policy, defense, and supreme sovereignty delegated to a federal government chosen by popular ballot. Common citizenship and currency would be established, and trade barriers within the union would be abolished. Streit worked for five years (1933-38) on the perfecting of his plan, rewriting four separate times the manuscript of a book, *Union Now*, presenting it in detail. The book was first published in 1938, in a limited edition of three hundred copies. It was printed in France at the author's expense, for gratuitous distribution to educators and others.

The private edition of *Union Now* came out at the most crucial time in the Czechoslovakia crisis, and its timeliness induced an American and a British publisher to bring out trade editions in March 1939. Critics generally hailed the basic idea of the book, but questioned its practicability. "The vision is a great one," wrote the historian James Truslow Adams in the New York *Times* on the one hand; while on the other the magazine *Foreign Affairs* observed that "we cannot ignore the fact that present day tendencies are decidedly in the opposite direction from internationalism and free trade." A *Town Hall of the Air* radio discussion in New York City did much to focus attention on the Streit plan; and in April 1939, support came from editor Russell Davenport of *Fortune*. In June of that year a condensation appeared in the *Reader's Digest*.

Streit resigned from the New York *Times* staff and returned to the United States for a country-wide lecture tour on behalf of his proposed union, meanwhile organizing (July) a "holding company for his crusade" under the name of Federal Union, Incorporated. By the end of 1939, American sales of *Union Now* reached 10,000 copies, and in the following March an abridged version was published. *Union Now* was honored by *Current History* as "the outstanding book of the year." French and Swedish translations of *Union Now* (the world sale of which was eventually to reach some 300,000 copies) had already appeared.

After the fall of France in 1940, Streit proposed, in a full-page advertisement in the New York *Times*, a provisional union of the English-speaking democracies; and in the following year his new book, *Union Now With Britain*,

CLARENCE K. STREIT

was published. As had its predecessor, it evoked a mixed response. The American historian Allan Nevins, reviewing for the English weekly *Spectator*, declared it "one of the most impressive pieces of political pamphleteering published in our time"; while C. Hartley Grattan in the New York *Times*, commented chiefly on the "religio-moralistic tone" pervading the book and the "resolute dodging of the multitudinous problems involved." By 1943, when Federal Union, Incorporated, held its third annual convention at Peoria, Illinois, membership had risen to approximately 10,000.

As compared with the organization of the United Nations, chartered in 1945, Streit's plan stresses the efficiency of "unions" as opposed to "leagues"; it limits membership to democracies; and postulates delegation of supreme authority as a basic condition. (Streit is particularly critical of the veto power provided in the Security Council of the U.N.) Since the close of World War II, Streit's project of an Atlantic Union (in which the nucleus of union is provided by the seven original Atlantic Pact signatories) has attracted much influential support, notably from former Supreme Court Justice Owen J. Roberts [41], who resigned his judicial post to give a large part of his time to furthering the cause and is president of the Atlantic Union Committee, a group formed to promote the plan.

In 1946 a magazine, *Freedom and Union* (published eleven times a year), was established as an organ for the presentation of Streit's ideas and ideals. Its announced policy is "to educate the public, in the United States and abroad, in the principles of individual freedom and federal union." *Freedom and Union*, of which Streit is editor, Herbert Agar [44] associate editor, Helen B. Hamer managing editor, and Mrs. Streit European editor, is issued from Washington, D.C.; its 1949 circu-

STREIT, CLARENCE K.—*Continued*

lation amounted to some 9,000. Contributors include Owen Roberts, William L. Clayton '44, John Foster Dulles '44, and the atomic scientist Harold Urey '41.

Early in 1949 a postwar edition of *Union Now* was published; it includes five new chapters covering events since 1939 in which Streit comments on and analyzes the record of the United Nations and the claims of other federative projects such as that of Ely Culbertson '40, and of the United World Federalists led by Cord Meyer, Jr. '48. The new edition carries an introduction by the United States Senator from Tennessee, Estes Kefauver '49. It was largely at Kefauver's instance that Streit and several of his associates and supporters were called before the Thomas subcommittee of the Senate Foreign Affairs Committee in February 1950 to testify in hearings on the North Atlantic Treaty. "I am for Atlantic Union because it bases our hope of peace on something more powerful than . . . the hydrogen bomb," stated Streit. Kefauver also introduced into the Senate a resolution calling on the United States to invite Britain, France, Canada, the Netherlands, Belgium, and Luxembourg to "explore how far their peoples" would be prepared to pursue the road to federal union.

Clarence K. Streit, whose only income (stated *Time* in March 1950) is his salary as editor of *Freedom and Union*, lives "at the top of five flights of stairs in a crumbling Victorian pile" in the Mount Pleasant section of Washington. The Streits have one son, Travan Pierre Defrance, and two daughters, Jeanne Emma Defrance and Colette Helen Defrance (Mrs. Thomas N. Schroth). Streit is a member of the Academy of Political Science and of Phi Beta Kappa, Sigma Delta Chi, and Sigma Chi fraternities. He has a tall, thin figure, his eyes are a bright blue; his manner is described as quiet, unpretentious. In his free hours he likes to write verse: his *Hafiz—The Tongue of the Hidden*, an adaptation of the *Rubáiyát*, appeared in 1928. He is an admirer of Lincoln, Washington, Beethoven, Michelangelo, and the poet Walt Whitman. Among his outdoor recreations are skiing and fishing.

References

Time 35:89 F 17 '40 por; 55:22+ Mar 27 '50 pors
America's Young Men, 1936-37
International Who's Who, 1949
Streit, C. K. Union Now (new ed., 1949)
Who Knows—And What (1949)
Who's Who, 1949
Who's Who in America, 1950-51
Who's Who in the East (1948)
World Biography (1948)

SUITS, C(HAUNCEY) G(UY) Mar. 12, 1905- Research director; physicist

Address: b. Research Laboratory, General Electric Company, The Knolls, Schenectady, N.Y.; h. 1317 Regent St., Schenectady 9, N.Y.

Vice-president in charge of research at the General Electric Laboratory since 1945, C. G. Suits is also on the administrative bodies of two Government atomic energy projects. During World War II he was a member of one division and chief of another division of the National Defense Research Committee. Holder of more than sixty patents and author of some fifty articles, his chief contributions to science have been in the field of electronics.

Chauncey Guy Suits was born March 12, 1905, in Oshkosh, Wisconsin, the son of Chauncey Gibbs and Otillia M. (Berger) Suits. He was reared in Medford, Wisconsin, where his father was a pharmacist, a profession which two other sons in the family were to follow. The boy's early interest in pharmacy developed into a love of research, and at thirteen he had "a well-equipped experimental laboratory financed from earnings as a soda-jerker." A clarinetist, he paid for his studies at the University of Wisconsin in part from earnings as a musician: engagements in theater, dance, and concert bands and orchestras, and teaching as many as thirty-five pupils a week as clarinet instructor at the near-by Wisconsin School of Music, "made up financially for the untimely death of his father." The physics and mathematics student worked also for the university broadcasting station, played in the school orchestra and worked in the college bank throughout his four school years. He was chosen for four honor societies, Phi Beta Kappa, Sigma Xi (for original scientific research), Phi Mu Alpha (music) and Phi Sigma Phi (physics).

Upon his graduation in 1927 with the B.A. degree, Suits was awarded an Institute of International Education fellowship to the Technische Hochschule in Zurich, Switzerland, where he earned his science doctorate in two years. His interest in skiing, sharpened by Swiss surroundings, led him to a new method of strengthening the edges of skis which he patented. In 1929-30 the scientist was back in Madison, Wisconsin, as a physics consultant to the United States Forest Products Laboratory, and a graduate student at the university. His work there led to a patent, released for public use, on an electrical method of measuring the moisture content of wood.

In 1930 Suits moved to Schenectady to begin work as a research physicist, assisting Dr. Albert W. Hull in the General Electric Laboratory, which has been accounted one of the most diversified. "It has scientists working on nuclear physics, metallurgy, chemistry, optics, mechanical problems, and many others. . . .Its staff can work on basic problems, aware that no matter what they may uncover, the chances are that it will find some application in the organization" (*The Bridge of Eta Kappa Nu*, July 1946). Ten years yater, Suits was made assistant to the director of the laboratory.

Much of the physicist's work has been devoted to the study of nonlinear circuits, vacuum-tube methods of harmonic analysis, high-temperature and high-pressure arcs (about 1,000 times normal air pressure); also, application of measurement of such arc temperature and the theory of this discharge to the understanding of switching, lighting and welding arcs, and to the development of more effective circuit breakers for the protection of power lines. The honorary engineering fraternity, Eta Kappa Nu, named Suits the outstanding young electrical engineer of 1937 for developing a method of measuring arc temperatures by photographing, through luminescent glass, sound waves passing through an arc. An early hobby of photography and the resultant study of the resolving power of lenses, contributed to the solution of many problems in his work with arcs. The hottest temperature known to man, 18,000 degrees Fahrenheit, twice the temperature of the sun's surface, was produced by Suits in his experiments, in a double-walled steel cylinder, in an arc under 2700 atmospheres pressure. In April 1940 he lectured before the American Physical Society on a method of cooling a 10,000-degree flame to zero instantly.

The scientist was a member of the National Defense Research Committee of the Office of Scientific Research and Development, Microwave Section, in 1940. In October 1942 a new division (Division 15) of the committee was set up at the GE laboratory, with Suits at its head, to work out countermeasures to enemy radar and radio and to enemy countermeasures. Suits's work on this program included a study trip to wartime England in November-December 1942, and a 30,000-mile tour of the Pacific theater of war in May-June 1944. A thousand or more scientists and engineers, working in Division 15, spent more than $31,000,000 and saved uncounted Allied planes and flyers by the techniques they developed for offsetting the German radar system. (For example, it was discovered that aluminum foil dropped as "chaff" in thousands of tons over Germany would serve as an electronic smoke screen for Allied bombers.) Items of lasting significance developed under the Suits program included new tubes, originally devised for radar jammers, which provide higher power than ever before available at comparably short wave lengths. In addition to heading Division 15, Suits was a member of Division 14 (also secret) of the National Defense Research Committee.

Named vice-president of General Electric, in charge of research, in January 1945, Suits was, at thirty-nine, the youngest vice-president GE had had. A new $8,000,000 research laboratory was to be constructed under his direction, to have a greatly enlarged staff, with as many as 800 scientists in addition to technicians. According to *Fortune* Suits engaged more scientists in two years than GE had taken on in the previous twenty. "The biggest challenge for Dr. Suits," wrote a *Science Illustrated* contributor, "is sitting at the desk just vacated by Dr. William D. Coolidge '7.'" In 1946 Suits was named a member of the Nucleonics Committee directing the work of the newly formed General Electric Nucleonics Project; that year, too, his responsibilities were enlarged to include administering the Atomic Energy Commission's $350,000,000 Hanford plutonium works at Richland, Washington; and several months later the War Department announced plans for a $20,000,000, 4,500-acre Knolls Atomic Power Laboratory adjoining the site of the new GE laboratory, also to be under Dr. Suits's

C. G. SUITS

general supervision. This was to be the first atomic energy pile for the purpose of creating industrial power. Suits announced in September 1948, "We believe that a reactor can be developed which will . . . 'breed' more fissionable material than it uses." In 1949 the director was appointed to the Naval Ordnance Laboratory Advisory Board .

The scientist's patents, of which there were over sixty by 1949, include some on railway block signal improvements, circuits for sequence flashing electric signs, radio circuits, beacons, submarine signals, theater light dimmers, and photoelectric relays. As of mid-1948, a bibliography of his contributions in technical periodicals listed fifty articles, of which thirty dealt with arcs alone; among the titles are: "Measurement of Some Arc Characteristics at 1000 Atmospheres Pressure," *Journal of Applied Physics* (1939) ; "High-Temperature Gas Measurement in Arcs" in *Temperature, Its Measurement and Control in Science and Industry*, a symposium issued by the American Institute of Physics (1941) ; "Peacetime Uses of Atomic Energy," *Electrical Engineering* (1946) ; "Peacetime Atomic Energy," *Science News Letter* (1946). "Heed that Hunch" (condensed in *Reader's Digest*, February 1946) is an admonition to nurture the creative spark in children, who may be budding scientists.

Honors which have come to Dr. Suits include election to the National Academy of Sciences, honorary doctorates in science from Union and Hamilton colleges, the Presidential Medal for Merit (1948), and the ribbon of the King's Medal (British) in 1948. The physicist is a member of the Sigma Pi fraternity, of the American Physical Society, the Directors of Industrial Research, the American Society of Naval Engineers (civil member), and a fellow of the American Institute of Electrical Engineers. His political party is the Republican,

SUITS, C. G.—*Continued*

his church the Dutch Reformed. He is a trustee of the Schenectady County Public Library.

Married on October 28, 1931, to Laura E. Struckmeyer, a former fellow student at Wisconsin, he has two sons, James Carr and David Guy. The blue-eyed, sandy-haired scientist stands five feet eight and one half inches, weighs 158 pounds. An enthusiastic skier, Suits was a founder of the Schenectady Wintersports Club, was active in obtaining snow trains, and takes a special interest in GE's work on artificially induced snowfalls. He is also a member of the Mohawk Club and of the Mohawk Golf Club. His love of sports extends to swimming and sailing; other of his recreations are music and photography. *Fortune* of February 1947 attributed Suits's progress "in part to his policy of handling physicists as if they were temperamental artists, but even more to a personality that blends the energetic enthusiasm of a Boy Scout with the shrewd judgment of a mortgage broker."

References

> Bridge of Eta Kappa Nu 42:2 Jl '46
> Brooklyn (N.Y.) Eagle N 18 '40
> Fortune 35:134+ F '47
> N Y Post Mag p33 Je 13 '45
> Pop Sci 139:96 D '41
> Science Illus 2:6 F '47
> American Men of Science (1949)
> International Who's Who, 1949
> International World Who's Who (1949)
> Who's Who in America, 1948-49
> Who's Who in Commerce and Industry (1948)
> Who's Who in New York, 1947
> World Biography (1948)

SWANSON, GLORIA Mar. 27, 189? Motion picture actress

Address: b. c/o Paramount Pictures, Inc., 1501 Broadway, New York 18; Hollywood, Calif.

In her sixty-third film, *Sunset Boulevard*, Gloria Swanson in 1950 recaptured her position as a top star in motion pictures. Beginning her career in 1913 as an "extra," she rose within six months to main roles in Mack Sennett slapstick comedies. By 1917 she had progressed to dramatic pictures. Under the direction of Cecil B. De Mille '42 (1918-21) and while under contract to Paramount (1921-26), she became the film's leading box-office attraction. Possessing a piquant beauty which lent itself to elaborate costuming, she was seen in a long succession of "glamour" roles. In 1926 she formed her own company, producing, among her motion pictures, *Sadie Thompson*. After 1932 she appeared in only two pictures, and in two stage productions, and in 1948 she had her own television program, *The Gloria Swanson Hour*.

Gloria Swanson was born Josephine May, daughter of Joseph and Adelaide (Klanowski) Swenson. Her birthplace is Chicago, Illinois; her birthday is March 27. Sources differ as to the year of her birth, in 1950 some stating that she is fifty-one years old, others that she is a

year older. Joseph Swenson, a civilian official attached to the transport service of the United States Army, was stationed during his daughter's childhood in Key West (Florida), Texas, and Puerto Rico. As a schoolgirl the future actress appeared in school plays and looked forward to being a singer. Her formal education ended with her first year at high school when, at the age of fourteen, while visiting an aunt in Chicago, she was given the part of an extra in the Essanay productions, *Elvira Farina* and *The Meal Ticket*, made in their Chicago studio. Six months later, changing her name to Gloria Swanson, she went to California, where she played opposite Bobby Vernon in leading roles in Keystone pictures. This company, famous for its slapstick comedies, cast the actress in such pictures as *The Nick of Time Baby*, *Teddy at the Throttle*. Miss Swanson, who said that she was not one of Mack Sennett's "bathing beauties" but did appear in surf scenes in his comedies, was next seen in *The Pullman Bride*, a Sennett picture.

Miss Swanson's wish to leave slapstick comedy was soon realized. Under contract to Triangle, she played dramatic roles in *Everywoman's Husband* and *Her Decision*, both in 1918. Upon the expiration of her Triangle contract, in 1918 Miss Swanson joined Cecil B. De Mille, whose studio was noted for the grand-scale ornate settings of his productions. For his new star he had elaborate costumes designed, one of the most memorable being a gown made of ermine tails and a hat patterned after a Chinese pagoda.

In the six pictures she made under De Mille's direction, among which were *Don't Change Your Husband*, *Why Change Your Wife?*, and *Male and Female*, Gloria Swanson became one of the biggest box-office names in films, the idol of millions. The Philadelphia *Bulletin* review of her performance of Lady Mary in *Male and Female*, the screen's first adaptation of James Barrie's play, *The Admirable Crichton*, wrote: "Miss Swanson not only conveys perfectly the hauteur and splendor of Lady Mary, but is at all times an 'eyeful.'" The roles she appeared in during her first years as a Paramount star were one continuation of glamorous types. *Zaza* (1923), the picturization of a David Belasco light comedy stage hit, she considers her first real characterization. This led to more noteworthy roles—in *The Humming Bird* (1924) and *Manhandled* (1924)—and in 1924 she went to France to play the title role of *Madame Sans Gene*, Napoleon's washerwoman. The picture, made under the direction of Louis Perret with an otherwise all-French cast, was acclaimed by critics. She received a public ovation on her arrival in Hollywood and at the première of that film.

While in France she had married the Marquis de la Falaise de la Coudray (her third husband), becoming the first cinema star to marry a title. Among other "firsts" claimed for Miss Swanson are these: She was the first famous picture actress to have a child, to adopt a baby, to become a grandmother, to make a picture in France and a talking picture in England. The drawing power of her name, then at its height, prompted Paramount to offer her $18,000 a week with a new long-term contract.

Miss Swanson decided, however, to form her own producing company, which, with the backing of others (one of whom was Joseph P. Kennedy), became the Gloria Swanson Productions for pictures to be released through United Artists. *The Loves of Sonya* (1927) was followed by the sensational hit (grossing over a million dollars) of *Sadie Thompson*, the first screen version of *Rain*. Under the direction of Eric von Stroheim, Miss Swanson then began the production of *Queen Kelly*. After $800,000 had been spent on the picture, it was abandoned. Except for a brief glimpse of it in *Sunset Boulevard*, the film has not been seen by the public. After being coached by Laura Hope Crews, Miss Swanson made *The Trespasser* (1929), the first picture to record her speaking and singing voice. Before dissolving her own company in 1932, she was seen and heard in *What a Widow!* (1930), *Indiscreet* (1931), *Tonight or Never* (1931), and *Perfect Understanding*; the last-named was made in England in 1933.

Music in the Air (1934), a Fox adaptation of the Oscar Hammerstein 2d and Jerome Kern musical, was Miss Swanson's next vehicle. "A pleasing voice," wrote the New York *Times* of her singing, "gracious comedienne" of her acting. Then, after an absence of six years, Miss Swanson played opposite Adolphe Menjou in the RKO film, *Father Takes a Wife* (1941). "Still slim and glamorous," wrote Wanda Hale (New York *Daily News*), "Miss Swanson is captivating and competent in her role." *Reflected Glory* (1942), Miss Swanson's first vehicle in the legitimate theater, died before it reached Broadway. A season on the road, playing to what *Variety* called "good grosses" in a former Broadway hit, *Let Us Be Gay*, occupied the star in 1943. In 1945 she made her Broadway bow in *A Goose for the Gander*, after opening in Cambridge, Massachusetts. The play, which received mixed reviews, closed in Chicago after a total of forty-eight performances.

Sunset Boulevard, which received its first public showing in August 1950, was given a tremendous fanfare before its release. The reaction of those who saw previews was enthusiastic, both as to the picture and to Miss Swanson, who plays the tragic role of a faded film star attempting to regain past glories. (Miss Swanson herself made a promotional tour of some thirty cities in the spring and early summer, where she was greeted by admiring crowds.) When the motion picture was released, critics' opinions were equally laudatory: the writing and direction of the story were called "masterly," while superlatives were uniformly used to describe Miss Swanson's acting. The critic (Richard Griffith) for the *Saturday Review of Literature*, who entitled his column "Inhabited by Humans," wrote: "The signature of the artist is all over her performance, and its caliber is marked by her consistent refusal to play for sympathy."

The first Hollywood celebrity to have her own television show, Miss Swanson in 1948 produced and played in *The Gloria Swanson Hour*, an informal guest show, with a setting

GLORIA SWANSON

designed after the living room of her Fifth Avenue apartment. The "chitchat" program included news of the latest in clothes, food and other subjects of interest to a feminine audience. The actress had also become a business woman. In the 1940's she formed Multiprises, Inc., for the purpose of testing inventions and promoting the manufacture of promising ones. Although this concern was closed in 1949, she still owns an interest in a cutting tool patent as well as a plastic button factory and a travel agency. Despite these interests and her many years as a top-salaried film star, Miss Swanson has not always been wealthy, having fluctuated from what a *New Yorker* article describes as "Arabian Nights opulence, to gorgeous insolvency." The article related one of a number of incidents of her life which exemplify her lack of money sense. None of her five marriages (which were terminated by divorce) was a "money" marriage. In 1916 she married Wallace Beery, who, like herself at the time, was playing in short comedy films. Her second husband was Herbert K. Somborn, the father of her daughter Gloria, now Mrs. Robert Anderson and the mother of three children. Her marriage to the marquis was dissolved in 1930. Miss Swanson's fourth marriage was to Michael Farmer, the Irish sportsman. Michelle, their daughter, is interested in a theatrical career. In 1945 Miss Swanson was married to William N. Davey, investment broker; they were divorced three years later. The actress' third child is a son, Joseph (now an electronics engineer), whom she adopted when he was an infant.

A *Saturday Evening Post* article by Stanley Frank described at length how Miss Swanson arranged for the escape of four young industrial engineers from Nazi-controlled Austria before the war. The actress has concerned herself with other public affairs—she cam-

SWANSON, GLORIA—*Continued*

paigned for Wendell Willkie and she has urged Senators to increase Federal funds to be used in combatting heart disease. A project for the immediate future is a book in which Miss Swanson will tell women past forty how to be attractive. Described as retaining much of her beauty, Miss Swanson is petite in stature: her height is about five feet, her weight, 112 pounds. She has brown hair and deep blue eyes. Vivacious and energetic, her face has "warmth and meaning," wrote the *New Yorker.* At times she is the subject of her own humorous remarks: near the end of her "advance agent" tour for *Sunset Boulevard,* her comment on herself in the limelight was, "I'm pretty much fed up with me."

References

Collier's 83:28 Je 8 '29
Ladies Home J 58:29 N '41
Liberty 26:28 D '49
N Y Times II p5 My 22 '49
New Yorker p24 Ja 18 '30; 16:21-2 Mr 30 '40
Newsweek 35:82-3 Je 26 '50
Photoplay Jl '20; My '26; Ja '32
Red Book Je '20
Sat Eve Post 223:30 Jl 22 '50: 223-36 Jl 29 '50
Time p28 D 10 '34; 38:84 S 29 '41
Vanity Fair My '26; D '26; Ap '34
International Motion Picture Almanac, 1948-49

SWIFT, HAROLD H(IGGINS) Jan. 24, 1885- Meat packer

Address: b. c/o Swift & Company, Union Stock Yards, Chicago 9, Ill.; h. Blackstone Hotel, Chicago 5, Ill.

Swift & Company, the largest of the "Big Four" meat packers, has as chairman of its board of directors Harold H. Swift, youngest son of the founder of the firm. He entered that company in 1908. Active in philanthropic projects, he is a member of the Rockefeller General Education Board and of the executive committee of the Chicago Community Trust, and is a trustee of the Rockefeller Foundation. He was chairman of the United States Treasury War Finance Committee of Illinois during 1941-44 and a member of the President's Commission on Higher Education (1946-48).

Born in Chicago, Illinois, on January 24, 1885, Harold Higgins Swift is the youngest son in a family of eleven children. The parents, Gustavus Franklin and Ann Maria (Higgins) Swift, were descendants of English ancestors who came to America on the *Mayflower.* Among the members of the American Swift family were Doctor Thomas Swift, who settled in Dorchester, Massachusetts, in 1630, and General Joseph A. Swift, who was one of the first graduates of West Point (1802), and who served in the War of 1812. Harold Swift attended the Graham Grammar School and the Hyde Park High School in Chicago. He was president of his high school senior class when

HAROLD H. SWIFT

he was graduated in 1903 (the year his father died). Entering the University of Chicago, he majored in economics and English; he was president of the senior class and a member of the Delta Kappa Epsilon fraternity. Upon his graduation in 1907 he received the Ph.B. degree. One year later he joined the firm his father had founded.

Swift & Company was incorporated in 1885, with a capital stock of $300,000; one year later this was increased to $3,000,000 and in 1891 to $5,000,000. Its founder, Gustavus Franklin Swift, was a Massachusetts farmer's son, who with a capital of $25 had opened a butcher shop in 1855, in a small town in his home State. By 1873, he was the owner of a chain of butcher stores in the Cape Cod district. He conceived the idea of shipping dressed beef from Chicago to the Eastern markets during the winter season, and in 1875 moved to Chicago to put his plan into effect. He developed the refrigerator car for shipping dressed meats. In 1887, the firm, which had dealt in beef exclusively, added other meat products. The founder also pioneered in the use of by-products from the abattoir (such as the making of fertilizer from blood and tankage); this led to the saying that Swift utilized the whole pig except its squeal. To finance the search for improved methods and products, the company maintains a large fund, from which research projects in several different universities draw support. Among additions to the firm's products are new types of prepared meats, margarine, strained and diced meats for babies, an insecticide, plant foods, and soap.

When Harold Swift joined the company he was first trained in the buying and processing of livestock and the distributing of the finished products. He studied these processes in the various livestock departments, the plant operating, and the sales departments. Eventually he was made supervisor of a branch house. Having succeeded in that post, he was promoted to an executive office in car-route sales and in the produce department. When the latter became the dairy and poultry department, he was placed at its head. At the same time he supervised the buying of cattle, sheep, calves, and lambs. The only period in which he was absent from employment with the company during forty-odd years was during World War I. (In 1917, he served with the American Red Cross Mission to Russia with the rank of major. Before the end of the war he joined the United States Army and was assigned to the Personnel Division with the rank of captain.)

On March 20, 1918, Swift was made a vice-president of Swift & Company and a member of its board of directors. His duties were those of supervising industrial relations and directing the dairy and poultry department. Later, relieved of some of these responsibilities, he gave more time to matters of general policy. In 1937 he became vice-chairman, and on October 5, 1948, after the death of his elder brother, Charles H. Swift, succeeded to the chairmanship of the board of directors. "Stability of earnings," stated the *Magazine of Wall Street*, "rather than spectacular gains (as shown by other meat-packing concerns) is one of the company's features." Net income of the firm for the fiscal year ending October 29, 1949, was $25,826,129. Early in 1949 criminal antitrust indictments brought in 1941 against Swift and the other members of the "Big Four"—Armour, Wilson, Cudahy—were dismissed at the request of the Justice Department because the latter was filing civil suits based on the same charges.

Harold H. Swift has been lauded for his "distinguished public service" in *Look* magazine's *Look Applauds* (September 13, 1949). In 1914 he became a trustee of the University of Chicago; from 1922 to 1949, he acted as chairman of the board of trustees. He has been a member of the General Education Board (a Rockefeller-endowed body which supports educational and research agencies) since 1930, and of the Rockefeller Foundation since 1931. During World War II he was a member of the Treasury's War Finance Committee from December 1941 to April 1944. From 1946 to 1948 he served on the President's Commission on Higher Education. He is a director of the Harris Trust and Savings Bank of Chicago and a director of the Sunday Evening Club in that city.

In New York his clubs are the University and the Century; in Chicago, the Commercial, Union League, Chicago Literary, City, Quadrangle, Casino, Chicago, and University. He has been awarded honorary LL.D. degrees by Brown University (1933) and by the University of Chicago (1949). Unmarried, Swift maintains an apartment in Chicago's Blackstone Hotel. He is five feet, ten and three-quarter inches in height, weighs 180 pounds, and has graying brown hair and gray eyes.

References
International Who's Who, 1949
Who's Who in America, 1948-49
Who's Who in Chicago and Illinois (1945)
Who's Who in Commerce and Industry (1948)
World Biography (1948)

SYRAN, ARTHUR GEORGE (sĭ'rĕn) June 17, 1904- United States Government official
Address: b. c/o Economic Cooperation Administration, 800 Connecticut Ave., N.W., Washington 25, D.C.; h. 3913 Huntington St., N.W., Washington 15, D.C.

In the Economic Cooperation Administration, the official responsible for enforcement of the Marshall Plan regulations covering shipment of American cargoes to participant foreign countries is the Director of the Transportation Division. Arthur George Syran, who occupies this position, had been chief of ocean traffic for the Army Transportation Corps during World War II, and prior to that was well known as an admiralty lawyer. He assumed his ECA duties on June 21, 1948, after spending about seven months in Japan as an adviser to General Douglas MacArthur on shipping problems.

The only child of George Syran, an import-export broker, and Mary (Calangis) Syran, Arthur George Syran was born June 17, 1904, in Washington, D.C. He was reared in New York City. Far short of acceptance age for service in World War I, young Syran enlisted as a private in the United States Army Reserve in 1922, the year before his graduation from New York's DeWitt Clinton High School; and he was commissioned a second lieutenant in the Reserve in October 1925, or about eight months before receiving the LL.B. degree from Fordham University on June 15, 1926. As a law student Syran collaborated on the writing of the New York City Board of Education textbook on community civics, *Our Government*, and in 1926 was awarded the Alfred C. Bosson Medal for cooperation in government.

On leaving Fordham, Syran joined the staff of the Wall Street firm of Blackwell Brothers as a law clerk, at the same time taking postgraduate work at Columbia University (1927). Upon his admission to the New York State bar in the year following, he opened his own law office. "He specialized in trial and appellate practice in the State and Federal courts," stated a biographical release issued by the Economic Cooperation Administration, "particularly in the field of admiralty, and gained considerable experience in steamship operations." He was at the peak of his legal career when the Pearl Harbor attack brought his country abruptly into World War II.

Syran, with an uninterrupted record of sixteen years as a Reserve officer, went on active duty on February 4, 1941, was promoted through successive grades to colonel (Novem-

SYRAN, ARTHUR GEORGE—*Continued*

ber 1944) and saw, except for a few weeks, five years of war service. In view of his special professional experience, he was assigned to the Transportation Corps, serving on the staffs of Major Generals Charles P. Gross [46] and John M. Franklin [49]. "He was chief of ocean traffic," stated the ECA release, "and served on special planning committees of the Joint Military Transportation Committee of the Joint Chiefs of Staff. During the war he directed the cargo shipments on the Army's transports and the traffic movement of cargo on all WSA (War Shipping Administration) vessels allocated to the Army to all theaters of operations, including the redeployment program, preparatory for the invasion of Japan." Syran was decorated with the Legion of Merit, the citation calling attention to his "direction in the cargo traffic movement for the Normandy invasion." His active military duty terminated on January 14, 1946, but he remains a member of the Officers' Reserve Corps.

Five days afer his discharge, Syran became a civilian official of the United States Government, being appointed special deputy to the War Shipping Administrator, at Washington. He served as such from January 19 until the following August, when he was transferred to the United States Maritime Commission as special assistant to the chairman. Meanwhile, his "record as an Army transport expediter in the war" had (stated the New York *Times*) "attracted the attention of private shipping interests." The result was that in August 1947 he resigned from Government service to accept the position of executive assistant to the president of the National Federation of American Shipping. As representative of the federation, he headed, beginning November 14 of the same year, a group of shipping executives assigned to advise General Douglas MacArthur in Tokyo on the setting up of a program of Japanese maritime rehabilitation. Syran, who remained in the Far East until June of the year following, had the title of Chief of the Water Transportation Division at occupation headquarters.

When the Economic Cooperation Administration was set up by authority of the Act of Congress approved April 3, 1948, with Paul G. Hoffman [46] as the Administrator, the task of drafting preliminary plans and rules for transportation of cargoes to Marshall Plan countries was assigned to and carried out by Granville Conway, president of the Cosmopolitan Shipping Company. Conway was the former War Shipping Administrator whom Syran had served as special deputy in 1946. The Cosmopolitan executive had accepted the ECA assignment on a temporary basis, and it was presumably on his recommendation that in June 1948 the Government requested Syran's immediate return from Japan to take over as Director of the ECA Transportation Division. The appointment announced on the eighteenth of the month was (reported the New York *Times*) welcomed by "shipping men in New York . . . as a hopeful indication that cargoes

under the world aid plan would begin moving" through their harbor. (Most of the bulk cargo then on the way was proceeding through Gulf Coast ports.)

Syran, who assumed his new post on June 21, on July 8 warned the shipping missions of sixteen Marshall Plan countries that, while the European Recovery Act stipulated that cargoes should be transported in American and foreign bottoms on a roughly 50-50 basis of allotment, "the rate for American-flag ships should be a reasonable rate permitting a reasonable opportunity for profit to American operators and assurance of the existence of an American fleet in the market." As "the cost of operating a United States-flag vessel is considerably higher than foreign-flag vessels" this would mean a higher rate of payment to American owners. Though making it clear that too rigid observance of the 50-50 rule would not be insisted upon, Syran nevertheless warned (July 29) that "the law would be administered in a good, tough, practical and realistic manner." Some weeks later (September 11) he was able to estimate that United States and foreign ships would share about three and a half billion dollars' worth of tonnage in the first year of the Marshall Plan.

During the ensuing winter Administrator Paul Hoffman, who had been from the first doubtful of the practical effect of the 50-50 proviso, announced that it would be abandoned "to save recovery dollars." The United States Congress, however, again made the ratio mandatory in the new European Recovery Act. As a consequence the ECA charged (October 3, 1949) that seven European countries had failed to comply with the 50-50 rule and announced that it would refuse to foot the bill for certain ocean freight costs estimated at between ten and twelve million dollars. Addressing the Foreign Commerce Club of New York City on January 17, 1950, Syran asserted that the success of the Marshall Plan had "exceeded all expectations" and warned that should it be eventually permitted to fail, it would mean "the disappearance of America's No. 1 export market." Forty per cent of the dollar value of the nation's foreign trade, he pointed out to that group, had passed through New York in 1947 and 1948, and the 1949 percentage was "considerably" larger.

The ECA Transportation Division Director is a member of the New York County Lawyers and American Bar associations. His service organizations are the American Legion and the Army Transportation Corps Association, while his social clubs are the Propeller (New York) and the University (Washington). A Democrat in politics and an Episcopalian in creed, he is now a resident in the national capital. Mrs. Syran is the former Evangeline Vanech. The Syrans were married November 1, 1929, and have two children, John Alexander and Virginia Ellen. The official finds relaxation in swimming and photography.

References

American Men in Government (1949)
International Who's Who, 1949

TARCHIANI, ALBERTO (tär-kē-ä'nē äl-bĕr'tō) Nov. 1, 1885- Ambassador from Italy to the United States
Address: b. Italian Embassy, 1601 Fuller St., N.W., Washington 9, D.C.; h. 2700 16th St., N.W., Washington 9, D.C.

The first Ambassador to be sent to the United States by Italy after the downfall of Mussolini is Alberto Tarchiani, who was appointed his country's envoy to Washington in early 1945. As one of Italy's most influential journalists in the fight against Mussolini, Tarchiani was forced into exile in 1925, when the dictator destroyed freedom of the press. During his eighteen years of exile, the Ambassador has said, he continued to campaign strongly against Fascism "as a theory and as a regime, fighting for a free democratic Italy as it is now on the way to being organized and established." During World War II he aided in the organization of the Italian underground and effected the rescue of several Italian liberals who were political prisoners. In 1940 he came to the United States from France, at the time of the Nazi invasion; and three years later he returned to his homeland to participate in the establishment of the new Government being formed there. Before his appointment as Ambassador, he was Minister of Public Works and for a brief period was in charge of national reconstruction.

Alberto Tarchiani was born November 1, 1885, in Rome. His parents, Carlo and Ginevra (de Sanctis) Tarchiani, were ardent disciples of Mazzini, the Italian republican patriot of the nineteenth century. In the fifteenth century Alberto Tarchiani's ancestors were bourgeois merchants of Florence; in later centuries they were of the medical, legal, engineering, and other professions. After completing his studies at the universities of Rome, Genoa, and Florence, young Tarchiani became active in the Italian liberal movement. He began his journalistic career in 1903 as a reporter, later becoming a correspondent for several Italian newspapers. In 1907 he made his first trip to the United States, sending back articles to his papers on the American system of popular government. Subsequently he became editor of *Il Nuovo Giornale* of Florence and of *La Tribuna* of Rome. In 1915, when Italy entered World War I on the side of the Allies, Tarchiani, again in America, returned home to enlist as a volunteer. He saw action in the Italian campaign against Germany and Austria in 1916-18, and was made chief of the News Bureau of War Propaganda in Rome in 1918.

The following year Tarchiani became a member of the staff of *Il Corriere della Sera*, Milan's militant liberal daily. Advancing to the posts of coeditor and editor in chief, he became a spokesman for Italian democrats in their struggle against Fascism. Even after Mussolini seized power, Tarchiani continued his attacks. According to George Creel (*Collier's*, July 28, 1945), it was "to silence Tarchiani more than any other" that Mussolini in 1925 ended freedom of the press. Tarchiani consequently left his position on the newspaper and went into voluntary exile. From Paris he continued to publish articles against Fascism. Learning in 1929 that several of his friends were political prisoners on the island of Lipari, Tarchiani carried through a daring rescue of Carlo Rosselli, Emilio Lussu, and Fausto Nitti. He himself was imprisoned in the French prison of La Santé on complaint of Mussolini, but was released after a few weeks. He then joined with Rosselli and others to form the Giustizia e Libertà (Justice and Liberty) movement, Italian underground organization. Purchasing a plane, he and his compatriots flew over Italian cities from German and Swiss bases to drop anti-Fascist leaflets. For this exploit Tarchiani was imprisoned first by the Germans and then by the Swiss, but managed to win acquittal after pleading his own case. He was also detained in England, but was again released, convincing the judge that he was not "a dangerous alien." Tarchiani was sought by assassins sent to France by Mussolini, and his friend Carlo Rosselli was murdered.

When the Germans invaded France in 1940, Tarchiani, still marked for death, escaped to the United States. In New York he joined with Max Ascoli and others to found the Mazzini Society of Italian-Americans opposed to Fascism. He served as national secretary of the society and as editor of its newspaper. For the next three years he spoke and wrote against Mussolini, contributing articles to French, Belgian, Swiss, British, and American periodicals. (Some of his writings appeared in publications of the Carnegie Foundation for International Peace.) He also kept in touch with other prominent Italian anti-Fascists, including Alcide de Gasperi '46, Count Carlo Sforza '42, and Count Niccolo Carandini, who later became Italian Ambassador to London.

Tarchiani returned to Italy in 1943, landing with the first wave of American troops at Salerno in September, and remaining near the front line in the fighting at Anzio. Once again he engineered a daring rescue, the removal of the aged philosopher Benedetto Croce '44 and his family from imprisonment on Capri to the Allied headquarters. In October Tarchiani's articles in the Naples newspaper *Italia Libera* criticized the Allied attitude toward Italy. Later he joined the Action (democratic-radical, anticommunist) party in Naples, and took office in the second Cabinet of Pietro Badoglio '40 as Minister of Public Works. When Ivanoe Bonomi '44 succeeded Badoglio in June 1944, Tarchiani was placed in charge of national reconstruction.

Six months later, on January 18, 1945, the Italian Government announced the appointment of Alberto Tarchiani as its Ambassador to the United States. His appointment was at first opposed by certain Italian-Americans who claimed he had been ejected from the Mazzini Society in 1943 and had been employed by the British Government. These charges were denied by Tarchiani and refuted in a resolution adopted by the Mazzini Society. Arriving in the United States in February, the new Ambassador occupied the Italian Embassy that had been vacated by the last Ambassador from Mussolini's Government. President Roosevelt accepted Tarchiani's letters of credence on March 8, 1945.

ALBERTO TARCHIANI

Announcing that he would seek modification of the Italian armistice terms and acceptance of Italy as a full member of the United Nations, Tarchiani also appealed for American aid in rebuilding Italy, which was suffering from food shortages and inflation. He warned the United States that Italy's internal politics would incline toward the Anglo-American or Soviet ideologies "according to the intelligent and timely interest that occidental or oriental Allies take in Italian rehabilitation or future development." In December 1945 Tarchiani exchanged notes with Secretary of State James F. Byrnes, to effect the re-establishment of normal commercial relations between Italy and the United States.

When the Big Four Powers and the Paris Peace Conference decided to establish Trieste as a free city, Tarchiani made informal protest for his Government to Dean Acheson on July 9, 1946. He pleaded that a plebiscite be held to determine whether Trieste should be given to Italy or Yugoslavia. Together with the Italian Ambassadors from England, Russia, and France, Tarchiani presented Italy's case on the Trieste question before the General Assembly and the Security Council of the United Nations in November 1946.

On March 27, 1947, Tarchiani signed the articles of agreement on behalf of his country to make Italy the forty-second nation to join the International Bank and Monetary Fund, and the first former enemy country to be accepted. Two months later, on May 19, 1947, he presented Italy's formal application for membership in the United Nations. (As of January 1950 her entry is still blocked by veto.) With the approaching end of UNRRA shipments to Europe, Tarchiani returned to Italy in April, 1947, to discuss the question of a United States loan with Premier Alcide de Gasperi, Christian Democrat, who had formed a coalition Cabinet

on December 10, 1945. The Ambassador informed his Government that a practical plan showing how a loan would put Italy on the road to lasting recovery was essential to receiving that aid. On June 17 Tarchiani stated Italy was "ready to collaborate" in the Marshall Plan for an over-all long-range plan of European rehabilitation. In September, and again in October of 1947, the Ambassador made urgent pleas for speedy financial help to buy American food and fuel for Italy to meet its critical needs during 1947-48, and to check the spread of communism.

Though the peace treaty with Italy had been signed in 1947 and Allied troops had departed, the Republic (voted into existence in 1946) was being troubled by Communist riots and strikes. In the April 1948 elections the Communists were defeated, and De Gasperi formed a coalition Cabinet from which Communists and Left-wing Socialists were excluded. On a visit to Rome in May 1948, Tarchiani informed his countrymen that they could expect no increase in Italy's quota in ERP aid. He also told them of the American attitude on Italy's demands for peace treaty revisions, on the end of the scrapping of her warships, on control of her pre-Duce African colonies, and on her claims to Trieste. On his return to the United States, Tarchiani reported that Communist strength in his country was decreasing.

Tarchiani signed the program of the International Refugee Organization for Italy on March 24, 1949. On April 4 he and Foreign Minister Count Carlo Sforza signed the Atlantic Pact, and asked for military aid in terms of arms and money. Tarchiani presented Italy's case on the disposition of its former African colonies before the Political and Security Committee of the U.N. General Assembly in November 1949. The Committee voted for independence for Libya by 1952, for further study of the problem of Eritrea, and approved Italy as a ten-year trustee of Somaliland with independence promised thereafter.

In the course of his long career as journalist Alberto Tarchiani wrote thousands of articles and pamphlets; and he is the author of two books, his account of Anzio and the journal of De Gasperi in his visit to America. By his first marriage (in the United States) Tarchiani has two children, Lucio and Ginevra, who are American citizens. His second marriage, to Teresa Locchi, took place in August 1921; they have twin daughters, named Dora and Letizia. The Ambassador, who is six feet tall, weighs 175 pounds; his eyes are brown and his hair is gray. He has no time for hobbies, finds pleasure in long walks.

References

Collier's 116:30 Jl 28 '45 por
N Y Herald Tribune p11 Ja 18 '45; p3 Ja 19 '45; II p3 Mr 18 '45 por
N Y Sun p26 Mr 21 '45
N Y Times p8 Ja 19 '45 por
Time 45:16 Mr 5 '45 por
Chi è (1948)
International Who's Who, 1949
Who's Who in America, 1948-49
World Biography (1948)

TAYLOR, F(REDERICK) CHASE *See*
Stoopnagle, Colonel

TELKES, MARIA (DE) (tĕl′kĕs) Dec. 12,
1900- Physical chemist
Address: b. c/o Massachusetts Institute of
Technology, Cambridge 39, Mass; h. 29 Buckingham St., Cambridge 42, Mass.

One of the first to investigate the application of solar heating to architectural usages
is Dr. Maria Telkes of the Massachusetts
Institute of Technology. As a member of the
solar energy conversion project at the institute,
she designed the system of chemical storage of
solar energy used in the experimental house
at Dover, Massachusetts. Previously Dr. Telkes
had been a biophysicist at the Cleveland Clinic
Foundation and a research engineer at the
Westinghouse Research Laboratories.

The daughter of Aladar and Maria (Laban)
de Telkes, Maria de Telkes was born December
12, 1900, in Budapest, Hungary's capital.
She attended convent school. During her winter
leisure hours she might go ice-skating, or sled-
ding on the Budapest hills, and in the summer
there was swimming at St. Margaret's Island
in the Danube. Retaining her childhood interest
in, and aptitude for, science, at high school
she became acquainted with the theories for
utilizing solar energy, chiefly reported *Independent Woman*, through a book called "Future
Sources of Power." This stimulated her to
read all the available literature, both scientific
and poetic, on the sun, in the French, English,
German, and Hungarian languages. At .Buda-
pest University she was awarded a number
of prizes. Her Bachelor of Arts degree was
obtained in Budapest in 1920, four years prior
to her receiving her doctorate in philosophy.
For her doctorate, she had pursued studies in
physical chemistry. Physics was the subject
she taught in a Budapest school during the
academic year of 1923-24.

In 1925 Miss Telkes left Hungary to visit
an uncle (the Hungarian consul in Cleveland)
in the United States, where the following year
she was invited to join the staff of the Cleveland (Ohio) Clinic Foundation. Filling the
capacity of a biophysicist at the foundation, she
continued her research there until 1937. One
series of experiments, done in collaboration
with the late Dr. George Crile (with whom
she also worked on the book, *Phenomena of
Life*), resulted in the invention of a photoelectric mechanism capable of recording the
emanations of energy sent out by the human
brain. From 1937 to 1939 she was employed
as a research engineer in the research department of the Westinghouse Electrical and Manufacturing Company, at the laboratories in East
Pittsburgh, Pennsylvania. Miss Telkes became
an American citizen in 1937.

With the entrance of the United States into
World War II, Dr. Telkes was one of the
scientists called upon by the Government to
serve as a civilian adviser to the Office of
Scientific Research and Development. Revert-
ing to her early interest in solar energy, she

Harris & Ewing
MARIA TELKES

worked out a distilling system for installation
in life rafts, by which solar heat was the chief
means of converting sea water to drinking use.
In 1948, when she was once again called upon
to aid a Federal Government research program,
she blueprinted an amplification of the same
idea for use in alleviating the fresh water
shortage in the Virgin Islands, so that water
from the surrounding seas could be desalted
and employed as a supplement to the inadequate
fresh water reserves. In 1945 Miss Telkes was
awarded the Certificate of Merit by the OSRD.

After 1939 Dr. Telkes devoted herself chiefly
to studies of the use of solar energy, as a
research associate on the solar energy conversion project at the Massachusetts Institute of
Technology. (This project was made possible
by a 1937 bequest in the will of Doctor Godfrey Lowell Cabot for the investigation of the
practical applications of solar energy.) With
the encouragement of Miss Amelia Peabody, a
Boston sculptor who agreed to supply funds
necessary for the construction of a solar-heated
house on the grounds of her estate in Dover,
Massachusetts, Dr. Telkes planned the system
to be integrated into the house designed by
architect Eleanor Raymond. Data on the re-
currence and absence of sunshine in the Boston
area was supplied by Irving F. Hand, of the
near-by Blue Hill Observatory, who assured
that six days without sun was the usual maximum in that region.

One of the first descriptions of her heating
plan was given by Dr. Telkes before the American Association for the Advancement of Science in September 1948. (Other discussions,
as well as blueprints, have appeared in *Illustrated London News, Heating and Ventilation*,
and *Domestic Engineering*.) By this method,
in the actually constructed house, solar heat
collected by the 720 square feet of glass (painted black for better absorbency) passes into
the first of several air spaces behind the
windows. It is then caught by a metal sheet

TELKES, MARIA—*Continued*

which in turn distributes it into another air space, from which it is blown by a circulatory system into storage bins placed between the walls on the first floor. These bins, containing sodium sulphate decahydrate, a chemical compound that crystallizes and retains the heat, are the distinctive feature of Dr. Telkes' solar heating plant. By these it differs from the water circulated solar heating system employed in an M.I.T. experimental house, and from the crushed rock used in a University of Denver house. An easily obtainable, inexpensive chemical, the sodium compound was adjudged capable in preliminary estimates of storing 37 per cent of the sun's energy; in actual usage, this turned out to be 40 per cent. A further advantage, often cited in discussions of the possibility of solar heating replacing coal and other fuels, is that the chemical compound iself lasts indefinitely and needs no replacement. For the five-room house at Dover, three storage bins with a capacity of about one thousand gallons of chemicals, were found to be sufficient.

Miss Telkes, who occupied the house for several months before it was turned over to tenants, was able to report in March 1949 that the system had operated satisfactorily over two and a half winter months. That its comfort was sustained in hot weather was the testimony of the subsequent tenants, who reported that the house was kept at a steady 70-degree temperature during the summer by withdrawal of hot air from the house by the same circulating system used to distribute it in the winter. Records kept by them, and by the instruments placed in each of the rooms, revealed that the house was adequately heated in its second (1949-50) winter solely by the sun, at no cost whatsoever for supplementary fuel. Since the house at Dover had cost several thousand dollars more to construct than the $20,000 originally called for in the estimates, Dr. Telkes in June 1950 made plans for the construction of a $10,000 solar house, to be built, for comparison, beside a conventionally heated house. Dr. Telkes was one of the speakers at the New York Herald Tribune Forum in March 1949; and at the M.I.T. forum, "Space Heating with Solar Energy," held in August 1950. There she stressed that "every sun-heated house must be designed independently. No one house could be successfully set down in another locality where climate, surroundings, and family demands would be different." Miss Telkes, who has written several articles on solar house heating, contributed "Efficiency of Thermoelectric Generators" to the *Journal of Applied Physics.*

Of the future uses of solar heating, Dr. Telkes once remarked to W. Clifford Harvey of the *Christian Science Monitor*: "I envisage the day when solar heat-collecting shelters, like power stations, will be built apart from the house. One such solar heating building could develop enough heat from the sun for pumping into an entire community of homes." According to the New York *Herald Tribune*, she is also concerned with "the study of thermo-electricity, the process of converting solar radiation into electrical energy." Aside from the subject of solar heating, she has written articles on thermoelectric generators and distillers, and electrical conductivity of solids and electrolytes. The M.I.T. research associate is a member of the American Chemical Society, the Electrochemistry Society, Sigma Xi, and the Business and Professional Women's Club. The blue-eyed, blond-haired scientist has a height of five feet seven inches. She is fond of music.

References

Ind Woman 28:368 D '49
N Y Herald Tribune p28 Mr 7 '49
American Men of Science (1949)

THOMAS, ALBERT (LANGSTON) Apr. 12, 1898- United States Representative from Texas

Address: b. House Office Bldg., Washington 25, D.C.; h. Houston, Tex.

Democrat Albert Thomas was elected to the Seventy-fifth United States Congress by the Eighth Texas District, which has subsequently returned him to Washington every two years since 1939. In his seventh term (in 1949), after he became fifth in rank among the Democratic members of the House Appropriations Committee, he was a leader in efforts to effect economies in Government expenses, in May of 1950 joining a Republican colleague in authoring an amendment to cut more than half a billion dollars from the Federal budget.

The son of James and Lonnie (Langston) Thomas, Albert Langston Thomas was born April 12, 1898, near the historic Texas town of Nacogdoches, not far from the Louisiana border. He is a graduate of the Nacogdoches public high school, and of Rice Institute, in Houston, where he took his B.A. degree with the class of 1920. This followed his service with the United States Army as a second lieutenant in World War I. Six years later (1926) he completed the law course at the University of Texas, and the year after he received the LL.B. degree he was admitted to the bar of his State.

The young lawyer had been practicing in Nacogdoches County only a short time, when, in the fall of 1927, he was elected county attorney. Re-elected in 1929, he resigned during his second term to accept, in April 1930, appointment to the office of Assistant United States Attorney for the Southern District of Texas. Transferring his residence to the city of Houston, he filled this position for a little under six and a half years. On August 22, 1936, he was the victor, by 15,819 votes to 13,110, over the Mayor of Houston, Oscar Holcombe, in a "run-off" primary for the Democratic nomination for United States Representative from the Eighth Texas District. (The district comprises Harris County, in which Houston is located.) Election in November in this Democratic stronghold was a matter of course; and Thomas has been regularly re-elected biennially ever since.

Shortly after the Seventy-fifth Congress convened in January 1937, the new Representative from Texas was assigned to the House Committees on Irrigation and Reclamation, Labor, and Pensions, and remained a member thereof until January 1941. (He became chairman of the Elections No. 3 Committee in 1939.) Thomas' first year in the Federal legislature was marked by a generally loyal New Deal voting record—he supported, for instance, extension of the Reciprocal Tariffs Act, the President's Supreme Court Retirement Bill, the Roosevelt Departmental Reorganization Plan, and the Wagner Housing Bill. He opposed the peacetime munitions embargo, investigation of sit-down strikes, and the Gavagan antilynching bill. He was successful in securing Federal benefits for his home area, the extent of which funds was proudly stressed by Thomas himself in a document entitled "My First Year," printed in the appendix to the *Congressional Record* as an extension of remarks on December 31, 1937. Also, during 1937, Thomas served on a Joint Congressional Committee to consider the Black-Connery Wages and Hours Bill, and moved that the wage-fixing clauses be stricken out.

During the second and third sessions of the Seventy-fifth Congress (1938) the Texan was recorded in favor of the Administration's $5,380,000,000 tax bill and the Naval Expansion Bill (both in March) and of $212,000,000 for farm parity payments (June); while in the Seventy-sixth Congress he called "Yea" on the Hatch [44] "pernicious political activities" bill (July 1939), 17 per cent expansion of the Navy (March 1940) and the Conscription Act (September 1940); and "Nay" on elimination of the Guam Naval Base (February 1939), investigation of the Labor Relations Board (July 1939), and proposed drastic amendments ot the Wagner Labor Relations Act (June 1940).

The influence of Representative Thomas on national affairs was increased in the Seventy-seventh Congress, when on January 27, 1941, he was elected to the powerful forty-three-man House Appropriations Committee, of which Clarence Cannon [49] of Missouri was (and except during the Republican-controlled Eightieth Congress has continuously remained) the chairman. Prior to Pearl Harbor, the Houston Congressman supported, in roll calls of the House, such measures or propositions as the Lend-Lease Act (February 1941), repeal of the ban on arming merchant ships and on the entrance of American vessels into combat zones and belligerent ports (October and November 1941); while subsequent to his country's declaration of war he was recorded in favor of authorization of the WAAC (March 1942), increase of base pay for servicemen (October 1942), the Fulbright Resolution (September 1943) and, in January 1944, both the authorization of UNRRA and the Administration's soldier vote bill. He supported the Hobbs antiracketeering bill (April 1943) and opposed overriding President Roosevelt's veto of the Smith-Connally antistrike bill (June 1943). In May 1944 Thomas was successful in conjunction with his fellow Texan, Representative Joseph Mansfield, in persuading the Navy to

Wide World Photos

ALBERT THOMAS

grant permission to Spanish vessels to load cotton at the port of Houston; while in December of that year, during an acting chairmanship of the House Military Affairs Committee, he favored a Congressional inquiry into alleged extensive thefts of gasoline and food along American supply lines in the European Theater of Operations.

Early in the Seventy-ninth Congress (January 1945) Representative Thomas cast his vote against making permanent the Committee on Un-American Activities. He continued his objection against more stringent strike control when he opposed the Republican Case [46] bill but supported the Administration when he approved the legislation requested by Truman to bar strikes against the Government, an action that followed the 48-hour railroad strike. On May 23, 1946, in a House debate on a naval appropriations bill, Thomas was a member of a subcommittee which heard testimony from high officers. In debate (a year later, in the Eightieth Congress) on a new Naval appropriations bill, he offered (though unsuccessfully) two amendments which would have added $126,171,000 for Navy pay and subsistence and $54,500,000 for Naval aviation. In pointing out the reduction in the enlisted strength which he stated could be expected with the smaller appropriation, Thomas said he feared the House was gambling with national security in troubled times. Another 1946 vote of Thomas' was in favor of compromise price control legislation.

In addition to the vote on the appropriations for the Navy in the Republican-controlled Eightieth Congress, Thomas favored aid to Greece and Turkey (May 1947). He voted against the Taft-Hartley labor measure, but did not approve the Administration's $37,500,000,000 budget (February), and he favored limiting foreign relief to $200,000,000 (April). His vote is recorded against the bill which

THOMAS, ALBERT—*Continued*

sought to limit the Presidential tenure of office to two terms (February) and against the voluntary price curb bill (December). He supported the banning of portal-to-portal pay suits (February) and the bill to prohibit collection of the poll tax (July). On the G.O.P. tax reduction bill he cast his "Yea" vote. In the second session (1948) the Texas Democrat opposed the bill to give Congress access to secret files of Government agencies (May) as well as the Republican anti-inflation bill (August). His supporting votes were recorded for the admission of 202,000 displaced persons and for the draft bill (both in June).

When control of Congress returned to the Democrats in January 1949 (the Eighty-first Congress), Thomas became the fifth-ranking member of his party on the Appropriations Committee. As such he was named to important subcommittee chairmanships, and became identified with several economy proposals, the chief of which was his May 1950 declaration that he would seek to cut $750,000,000 from the $29,000,000,000 Omnibus Appropriations bill, the Federal budget for the year 1950-51. He introduced an amendment providing for a cut of $500,000,000 which Representative John Taber [48] of New York moved to raise to $600,000,000 (the proposal was adopted by the House on May 10 by a vote of 274 to 112). In the first session of the Eighty-first Congress he had voted against local option on rent controls; and on foreign aid measures had favored the April 1949 bill, had voted against the reduction of 50 per cent in the European arms fund (August) and the next month voted to help friendly nations in rearming, for which a $1,134,010,000 appropriation was passed. In June he voted against the provision for public housing in the housing bill.

Representative Thomas' record on measures brought before the second session of the Eighty-first Congress (in 1950) shows opposition to the FEPC (February), a Department of Welfare with Cabinet status (July), extension of rent control (June), and present granting of statehood to Hawaii and Alaska (March); support of the $3,102,000,000 appropriation for foreign economic aid (March), of the Point Four bill (July), appointment of General Marshall as Secretary of Defense, and the compromise subversive control bill (both in September).

The "dark, good-looking" Representative of the Eighth Texas District (as Delos Lovelace has described him) has been married since October 21, 1922, to the former Lera Millard, of Nacogdoches. Congressman and Mrs. Thomas have two daughters. In his religious affiliation the legislator is a Methodist.

References

> N Y Sun p14 D 28 '44
> Congressional Directory (1950)
> Who's Who in America, 1950-51
> Who's Who in the Nation's Capital, 1938-39
> World Biography (1948)

THOMAS, CHARLES ALLEN   Feb. 15, 1900-   Research chemist

Address: b. c/o Monsanto Chemical Co., 1700 S. 2d St., St. Louis 4, Mo.; h. 609 S. Warson Rd., St. Louis 24, Mo.

Charles Allen Thomas, executive vice-president of the Monsanto Chemical Company of St. Louis, Missouri, assumed the chairmanship of the board of directors of the American Chemical Society on January 1, 1950. During World War II Thomas was detailed to the Manhattan Project on the construction of the atomic bomb, his assignment being the supervision of the final purification and metallurgy of plutonium at the various installations of this project throughout the country. Early in 1946 he was one of the five co-authors of the Acheson-Lilienthal report on atomic energy control prepared for the Secretary of State's Committee on Atomic Energy, and in June of the same year he was appointed one of the scientific advisers to Bernard Baruch, United States representative on the United Nations Atomic Energy Commission. At the close of 1950 Thomas became chairman of the Scientific Manpower Advisory Committee of the National Security Resources Board. Thomas' work as a peacetime industrial chemist began in 1923, when, concurrent with advanced study at the Massachusetts Institute of Technology, he joined the General Motors Research Corporation and participated in the studies leading to the discovery of tetraethyl lead as an antiknock agent in motor fuels.

The only child of Charles Allen and Frances (Carrick) Thomas, Charles Allen Thomas was born February 15, 1900, on a farm in Scott County, Kentucky. The elder Thomas, a minister in the Christian Church, had come to the United States from Melbourne, Australia, in 1890; he died while his son was still an infant. Young Charles was reared by his mother on the farm and sent to school in near-by Lexington. At the age of ten the boy began to experiment with chemicals, purchasing apparatus with money his mother gave him and using as his laboratory a shed on the farm.

Thomas continued his education in Lexington at the Morton High School from which he graduated in 1916, and at Transylvania College. His enrollment at Transylvania was determined to a large extent by the fact that, as a boy, he had spent much time in the chemical laboratory of the college; there the professor's friendship influenced his choice of chemistry as his major subject. Possessed of a good tenor voice, Thomas was a soloist in the college glee club and Lexington churches. He also sang professionally; that, with working on a construction gang during the summer, helped him defray the college expenses not covered by the scholarship he had been granted. After receiving a B.A. degree from Transylvania College in 1920, he went on to Massachusetts Institute of Technology to receive an M.S. degree in chemistry in 1924, again making his expenses by singing professionally.

Thomas joined the General Motors Research Corporation as a research chemist in 1923. This was the period of his association with the late Thomas Midgley, Jr., C. F. Kettering [40] and Carroll A. Hochwalt (now a Monsanto vice-president) in the development of anti-knock agents for motor fuel. Thomas knew that bromine, useful for this purpose but not plentiful, was present in sea water. Collecting samples himself, he developed a method for extracting bromine which led to the establishment of large-scale extraction plants by the Ethyl Gasoline Corporation and the Dow Chemical Company. Anti-knock, or ethyl, gasoline became generally available.

In 1926 the Thomas and Hochwalt Laboratories was established in Dayton, Ohio, to provide chemical consultation service to industrial enterprises. For General Motors, their first client, the laboratory conducted research in synthetic rubber, achieving fifteen years before Pearl Harbor a laboratory product comparable, according to *Chemical and Engineering News* (January 5, 1948), with modern synthetics. This same source reported that during those years, Thomas' interests ranged "from smoked salt, for the curing of hams and bacon, to processes for the production of aliphatic chemicals from hydrocarbon bases."

In April 1936 Monsanto Chemical Company's president, Edgar Queeny, who "bought talent along with companies. . . , absorbed Dayton's Thomas and Hochwalt Laboratories mainly to snare Charles Allen Thomas and Carroll A. Hochwalt" (*Time* Magazine, May 10, 1948). The Dayton laboratories became the Central Research Department of Monsanto, and Thomas was named director. Successively thereafter Thomas became a member of the board of directors (1942), vice-president (April 1945), technical director, and a member of the executive committee (September 1945), executive vice-president (May 1947), and finally, in October of 1949, chairman of the executive committee of the Monsanto Chemical Company (formed in 1901 and named after the Spanish-Portuguese wife of its founder, Edgar's father, John Francis Queeny).

In 1940 Thomas began his contributions to wartime research, when he supplied the British with a synthetic resin to be used for the sabotage of their gasoline supplies in the event the Germans were able to invade Britain. In 1942 Thomas was asked to supervise the development of rocket fuels by the National Defense Research Committee, advancing shortly thereafter to become deputy chief of Division 8 of that committee. Also, in 1942, he was contributing his services to the Baruch Synthetic Rubber Committee. In 1943 General Leslie R. Groves [45] and James B. Conant [41] asked Thomas to assist in the Manhattan District atomic bomb project, placing him in charge of the final purification and metallurgy of plutonium, the new, ninety-fourth element essential to the construction of the atomic bomb. On July 1, 1945, when the Monsanto Chemical Company contracted with the Government to operate the Clinton Laboratories at Oak Ridge, Tennessee, for the production of radioactive isotopes, Thomas was appointed director of the project. Later, on January 1, 1948, with the signing of a new contract with the Government for the operation of an Atomic Energy

CHARLES ALLEN THOMAS

Commission plant at Miamisburg, Ohio, Thomas was placed in supervision.

In the meantime, Thomas' experience with the wartime development of fissionable materials had led to his selection in 1946 as one of the five men who drew up the report for the Secretary of State on the international control of atomic energy. (His colleagues were David E. Lilienthal [44], Harry A. Winne, Dr. J. Robert Oppenheimer [45], and Chester I. Barnard [45].)

For his work on the atomic bomb project, Thomas received, from Secretary of War Robert P. Patterson in March 1946, the Medal of Merit, highest award made by the United States to civilians. On June 1, 1947, the New York *Times* announced that Thomas had been awarded the 1947 Industrial Research Institute Medal "for leadership in the development of the American industrial research system"; a few months later he was awarded the 1948 gold medal of the American Institute of Chemists "for his work in development of atomic energy, his leadership in research, especially in synthetic resins, and his administrative ability and encouragement of basic research" (New York *Times*, January 11, 1948).

From 1930 to 1932, Thomas was chairman of the American Chemical Society's Dayton Section, and since 1942 he has been a member of the board of editors for the monographs of the society. In 1942 he was elected to the national board of the society, served as president during 1948, and in December 1949, was elected to the chairmanship of the board and to a four-year term as director at large. During his presidency of the society he emphasized the dangers in the overspecialization of scientific thinking—he proposed that "scientists, like members of some religions, be given time off to read, relax and think on matters far removed from their own specialties" (St. Louis *Post Dispatch*, February 22, 1948). At the

THOMAS, CHARLES ALLEN—*Cont.*

Mid-Century Convocation at the Massachusetts Institute of Technology, April 1949, he dealt again with the problem of specialization in twentieth century education, stressing the social implications of scientific progress.

Thomas was appointed Chairman of the Scientific Manpower Advisory Committee in December 1950 by W. Stuart Symington, Chairman of the National Security Resources Board. The purpose of the committee is to evaluate proposals for making the most effective use of qualified scientists in the defense program. As chairman of the board of directors of the American Chemical Society, Thomas in September 1950 had been one of the signers of a resolution urging President Truman to act promptly to prevent a waste of scientific manpower.

Thomas received the honorary degree of D.Sc. in chemistry from Transylvania College in 1933 and from Washington University (St. Louis) in 1947. He was elected to membership in the National Academy of Sciences in 1948 and is an honorary member of the American Institute of Chemists. He is also a member of the Electrochemical Society, the Institute of Chemical Engineers, the Kappa Alpha fraternity, the American Sigma Xi (science research society), Alpha Chi Sigma (chemistry fraternity), the Faraday Society, the Franklin Institute, and the National Citizens' Commission for the Public Schools. He is a fellow of the American Association for the Advancement of Science and the Chemical Society of London; a curator of Transylvania College and a member of the board of Barnard Free Skin and Cancer Hospital of St. Louis and the Central Institute for the Deaf, and a director of the board of governors of the National Farm Chemurgic Council. His clubs include the Cosmo (Washington), and the Chemists' and Links of New York City. Transylvania College, Antioch College, and the John and Olga Queeny Educational Foundation list Thomas as a trustee. He is also a director of the St. Louis Union Trust Company and the Southwestern Bell Telephone Company. In addition to numerous scientific papers he has written for technical journals, Thomas is the author of *Anhydrous Aluminum Chloride in Organic Chemistry*, and is the holder of over a hundred patents in the chemical and chemical engineering field. Thomas' church is the Disciples of Christ, his political affiliation is Republican.

Charles Allen Thomas and Margaret Stoddard Talbott were married on September 25, 1926. They have four children, Charles Allen 3d, Margaret Talbott, Frances Carrick and Katherine Tudor. Mrs. Thomas, who was a member of the All-American skeet team, joins her husband on quail and duck hunting trips. Fishing and tennis are other favored recreations of his. He is five feet, ten and one-half inches tall, weighs 165 pounds, and has blue eyes and red hair. He still enjoys singing with a group gathered about the family piano and enlivens meetings of Monsanto executives by demonstrations of chemical phenomena. He is proud of a trick which he helped devise for Blackstone, in which the magician walked away from his own shadow, a feat done with the aid of a fluorescent zinc sulfide screen.

References

Chem & Eng N 26:39 Ja 5 '48 por
St. Louis (Mo.) Post Dispatch F 22 '48 por
American Men of Science (1949)
Who's Who in America, 1948-49
Who's Who in Commerce and Industry (1948)
World Biography (1948)

THOMPSON, MARY WOLFE Dec. 7, 1886- Author

Address: Hohokus, N.J.

Reprinted from the *Wilson Library Bulletin*, Oct. 1950.

Too many "career books" for girls have shown a rose-strewn pathway, glamorous, thrilling, leading effortlessly to quick and certain success. The career books of Mary Wolfe Thompson are different. She knows that success in any worth-while work is neither quick nor easy. With invincible honesty she includes the obstacles, the setbacks, the mistakes that crop up in real life. It is the successful overcoming of these difficulties that gives depth and dimension to her stories. The fictional plot and characters provide plenty of gaiety and excitement, but girl readers have come to know that the job itself, as Mrs. Thompson pictures it, is *real*.

Mary Wolfe Thompson, daughter of Dr. Theodore F. Wolfe and Gertrude (Franklin) Wolfe, was born December 7, 1886, in Winsted, Connecticut. She comes, she says, "of good plain old stock, German, English, and Scotch; families who have been in this country since colonial days." She grew up in New Jersey, graduated from the New Jersey State Normal School at Trenton in 1905. After a few years of teaching and keeping house for her father, she married Charles D. Thompson, an electrical engineer, in 1915. Increased leisure revived a childhood desire to become a writer. In 1920 she enrolled in a short story class at Columbia University. "I would never have gone ahead with writing," she says, "but for the encouragement the instructors, Helen Hull and Mabel Robinson, gave me." Her first adult short stories were published in *Midland* magazine, several of them being starred in O'Brien collections.

In 1923 Mrs. Thompson published her first book for children, *Farmtown Tales*. Then came *Shoemaker's Shoes* (1924), *My Grandpa's Farm* (1929), and *Cherry Farm* (1932). Two Indian books for boys, *The Circle of the Braves* (1931) and *Moccasins on the Trail* (1935), were published under the pseudonym "Wolfe Thompson." *Miss Fanny's Bomb* (1937) was a one-act play. *Shiver, the Scaredest Dog in Town* (1938) was the last book for young children.

In the same year she produced her first career story for older girls, *Highways Past Her Door*.

MARY WOLFE THOMPSON

The New York *Times* said of it, "Girls will find it informative and interesting, and they may profit by the pluck by which Judy made a success of running a roadside stand." Next came *Blue Horizon* (1940), the story of a girl interior decorator. F. B. Sloan in *Christian Science Monitor* said, "The author writes convincingly about Janet's work. Here is the happy combination of a good story fused with the genuine career interest, a touch of mystery, and a romance, for good measure." The Springfield *Republican* called it "another appealing story especially designed for teen-age girl readers, with an underlying trend of helpfulness for persons confronted with the problem of living amid modern surroundings." *Blueberry Muffin* (1942) impressed *Wisconsin Library Bulletin* as "a well told story." May Lamberton Becker in *Books* said, "Special knack is needed for writing stories whose chief interest is in some way of making a living; this used with first hand information and a gift for writing, here produces so good a book on running a tearoom that chances are no one who opens it will skip a word."

Pattern for Penelope (1943) deals with the operation of a veterinary hospital. Ellen Buell said in the New York *Times*, "A touch of romance adds to the intrinsic interest which the story holds for all girls who love dogs, and Penelope's relation to her parents in a situation which is unfortunately all too common today is handled realistically and with understanding." *Crossroads for Penelope* (1945) carries the heroine of the preceding book on to her work for Dogs for Defense. Virginia Kirkus called it "timely, and of interest to teen-age and up." May Lamberton Becker said, "Good story in itself, this tells much about the technique of a hospital for animals and the varied encoun-ters with human beings that a veterinarian's work always involves. . . .Add to this an honest young love story and you have a book easy for the teens to read without stopping."

Hillhaven (1949) deals with occupational therapy. Phyllis Whitney in the New York *Times*: "The book's main purpose is to present an inside picture of a relatively new profession which is helping thousands of people to return to a useful place in life." E. R. Sickels in *Saturday Review of Literature*: "Teen-age girls have learned to expect convincing, well-told stories from Mary Wolfe Thompson. They will not be disappointed in this last book." These three most recent books are included in the current (1950) list of basic books for high schools, compiled by a joint committee of the American Library Association, the National Council of Teachers of English, and the National Education Association.

Mrs. Thompson, red-haired and blue-eyed, lives with her husband on a farm near Hohokus, New Jersey. To her deep disappointment, they have no children. She loves the country, and has fitted herself for country life by courses in fruit growing and market gardening at the New Jersey State Agricultural Station at New Brunswick. Next to gardening, she lists hand weaving as a favorite occupation. Her favorite book is Willa Cather's *Shadow on the Rock*. In the fall of 1950 she is engaged upon a new novel for teen-age girls.

THORPE, JAMES FRANCIS *See* Thorpe, Jim

THORPE, JIM May 28, 1888- Athlete

Address: h. 5162 Melrose Ave., Hollywood, Calif.

In 1950 Jim Thorpe was chosen in an Associated Press poll of sports writers and broadcasters as the greatest athlete of the first half of the twentieth century as well as the greatest football player. A famous gridiron star of Carlisle Indian School in 1911-12, he was twice named to Walter Camp's All-America team, and unofficial winner of both the pentathlon and the decathlon in the Stockholm Olympic Games of 1912. Subsequently Thorpe played major league baseball for the New York Giants, and other National League teams, and became active in the organization of professional football in the United States. His life story is the subject of a forthcoming film, *Jim Thorpe, All-American*.

Jim Thorpe's father, Hiram Thorpe, was half Indian (of the Sac-Fox tribe) and half Irish; his mother, Charlotte View Thorpe, who was a granddaughter of the famous Chippewa chief Black Hawk, was one-quarter of French extraction. One of twin boys, James Francis Thorpe (whose tribal name is Bright Path) was born May 28, 1888, near Prague in the Indian Territory, now part of the State of Oklahoma. (His twin, Charles, died in his ninth year; Jim has one older brother, two sisters and a younger brother surviving). The

JIM THORPE

future "greatest male athlete" of 1900-50 was reared on a 160-acre farm, which (stated Al Stump in a biographical article in *Sport* for December 1949) the elder Thorpe had acquired in the Oklahoma land rush. Jim was able to ride at three years old, could swim almost as early, and shot his first deer at ten. An education begun at the Sac-Fox reservation school was continued at the Haskell Institute at Lawrence, Kansas, and concluded at the Government-operated Carlisle Indian School at Carlisle, Pennsylvania.

Jim Thorpe entered Carlisle (a co-educational institution conducted on the half-study, half-earning principle) in 1904, expecting to learn the electrician's trade. Finding that the necessary course was not offered, he joined the tailoring school, and for two years played guard on the tailors' football eleven. It was not until 1907 that he attracted the special interest of Glenn L. ("Pop") Warner, then Carlisle's athletic coach. The story goes that Thorpe, watching track candidates in the high jump, became impatient with their showing and, rushing forward, cleared the high bar, although hampered by boots and heavy clothing. Warner, looking on, saw in the feat the promise of a future "great," and promptly put him on the "varsity" football squad, although it was his major intention to develop Thorpe as a track star. "During virtually the entire season," stated an article in the Washington *Post*, "Thorpe sat on the bench, but in 1908, when the Indians' regular halfback was injured, the Oklahoman got into the fray. In the very first encounter he sped 65 and 85 yards for touchdowns that brought the tiny school an upset triumph over mighty Pennsylvania. By season's end he was the most talked-about athlete in Pennsylvania." The following summer, when the athlete went south to do farm work in accordance with the Carlisle system, he joined the Carolina League and played professional baseball for Winston-Salem,

Fayetteville, Rocky Mount and other teams in the 1909 and 1910 seasons. ("I did not play for the money there was in it," he was later to explain, "but because I liked to play ball.")

Thorpe did not return to Carlisle (where for his two remaining academic years he majored in business administration) until 1911, when Warner held out the promise of developing him as an Olympics contestant. It was in the 1911 football season that Thorpe amassed the record which won him Warner's praise as "the greatest football player of all time," even though the coach was forced to take strict measures in disciplining Thorpe. The high spots of this season included Carlisle's victory over hitherto unbeaten Harvard, in which Thorpe scored four field goals and ran 70 yards for a touchdown; and the game with Army at West Point, wherein Thorpe accounted for 22 of Carlisle's 27 points to Army's 6, and ran 97 yards for a touchdown. These and other exploits scarcely less striking won him a place as halfback on Walter Camp's honorary All-America team. Thorpe also participated in all other sports offered by Carlisle, including basketball, hockey, boxing, and tennis, and in intercollegiate track meets. At one time or another in his career he has held championships in running, jumping, swimming, shooting, skating, baseball, tennis, hockey, lacrosse, shot putting, and pole vaulting.

Thorpe's feats in the 1912 Olympic Games at Stockholm, Sweden, were to provide the climax and the turning point of his meteoric athletic career. He won both the pentathlon and the decathlon, a feat not accomplished before nor since. (The pentathlon, a five-event contest, consists of the running broad jump, javelin throw, 200-meter flat race, discus throw, and 1500-meter flat race; the ten-event decathlon comprises the 100-meter dash, running broad jump, shot put, running high jump, 400-meter flat race, discus throw, 110-meter high hurdles, pole vault, javelin throw and 1500-meter race.) In the pentathlon Thorpe made four out of five first places; in the decathlon he scored 8,412 out of a possible 10,000 points, topping all previous records. (Details of his record appear in Menke's *New Encyclopedia of Sports*, as supplied by Helms Athletic Foundation.) His trophies included a chalice in the shape of a viking ship, the presentation of which was made by King Gustav of Sweden, who addressed him as the "greatest athlete in the world."

Back at Carlisle, Thorpe enjoyed another notable season on the gridiron, scoring 25 touchdowns and 198 points, and was named to Camps's All-America team for the second successive year. In January 1913, following a report that he had played professional baseball in the Carolina League prior to the Olympic Games Thorpe was called upon by the Amateur Athletic Union (which certifies the amateur status of American Olympics contestants) for a statement. Thorpe made no denial but did offer an explanation. "On the same teams I played with were several college men . . . who were regarded as amateurs at home," he wrote to the A.A.U. "I was simply an Indian schoolboy, not wise to the ways of the world." The A.A.U. decided Thorpe was not an amateur athlete, and at the end of January 1913, his name and accomplishments were expunged from the Olympics records, his trophies ordered returned, and two other contestants declared the winners of the pentathlon and decathlon.

On leaving Carlisle in the spring of 1913 Thorpe joined the New York Giants, to which he was to remain under contract for the next three years, first as the regular right fielder, and later as a utility man. "From the very beginning," stated a sportswriter in the New York *Times*, "he ran like a deer in the outfield, fielded well, but was absolutely helpless before the curved pitching of the big league stars." By 1915 he had been assigned to the Giants International League "farm" at Jersey City; and in the following year he was traded to the Cincinnati Reds, the Giants' manager John McGraw giving Thorpe's alleged inability to hit curves as the explanation. ("Jim's batter average while with the majors was .320," states Mrs. Patricia Thorpe.) Cincinnati eventually passed Thorpe on to the Boston Braves, who in turn sent him to the Akron, Ohio, team of the American Association. Thorpe's career as a professional baseball player ended in 1919 in the Eastern League, where he batted .364. In 1920 Thorpe helped to organize the American Professional Football Association (name changed to National Football League in 1922) at Canton, Ohio, and was elected its president. For several years he was the spectacular attraction of the Canton Bulldogs, whose record for 1922 and 1923 showed no games lost and three games tied. In 1925-26 he played for the New York Football Giants, and the St. Petersburg (Florida) team.

In May 1929, at Springfield, Missouri, Thorpe announced his retirement from professional football, and not long afterward applied to the A.A.U. for reinstatement as an amateur. His request was not granted, and shortly thereafter he went to Hollywood, where he sold the motion picture rights to his life story to Metro-Goldwyn-Mayer, which was contemplating production of a film to be entitled *Red Son of Carlisle*. The film was not made, and according to the New York *Times*, by March 1931 he was working at the excavation for the new Los Angeles County Hospital. When the 1932 Olympics were held in Los Angeles, Thorpe collaborated with T. F. Collison on a book, *Jim Thorpe's History of the Olympics*, a review of the contests, classical and modern. The following year (1933) found the former athlete playing occasional bit parts in Western films; three years later (1936) he was given what Edith Gwynn in her Hollywood letter has called "a good role with Errol Flynn" in *The Green Light* (1937).

By the end of 1937 Thorpe was back in Oklahoma, where he became active in Indian affairs, leading a movement to get the Sac-Fox tribe to rescind its adoption of a new constitution which, in Thorpe's judgment, surrendered too large a measure of tribal home rule

to the Federal government. ("Jim has spent thousands of dollars trying to help the Indians," writes Mrs. Thorpe.) In the winter of 1940 Thorpe embarked, under the management of the W. Colston Leigh bureau, on a country-wide lecture tour: his four subjects were a review of the current sports season, his "own story of his amazing career," an "inspirational talk on the significance of sports in modern life," and a survey of American Indian culture and traditions, given in costume. In March 1943 the Oklahoma legislature adopted a resolution, introduced by two Indian members, that the Amateur Athletic Union be petitioned to reinstate Thorpe's Olympic records; but the Union's attitude remained unchanged. Another Indian member urged that Thorpe be appointed director of athletics at one of the State colleges.

Past the age for acceptance by the Army or Navy in World War II, Thorpe joined the merchant marine in June 1945, and had sailed on an ammunition ship before hostilities ceased. After the war he returned to California. In the late 1949 summer Warner Brothers, who who had acquired the motion picture rights to Thorpe's life, announced the forthcoming production of *Jim Thorpe, All-American*, in which Burt Lancaster will be cast as the athlete. Thorpe, who was an employee of the Los Angeles Sports Club at the time, received what Al Stump has called a "lump sum payment" and engagement as technical adviser for the film, on which "shooting" began in August 1950.

Of even greater immediate effect in restoring Thorpe's name and feats to the news columns were the two polls conducted by the Associated Press among 393 sports writers and broadcasters for their opinions, first, as to the identity of the greatest football player, and secondly, as to the greatest male athlete, of the first half of the twentieth century. In the football poll, results of which were announced in January 1950, Thorpe led Harold ("Red") Grange by 170 votes to 138; in the "greatest male athlete" poll (in February), in which fifty-six luminaries from all the sports received votes, 252 writers chose Jim Thorpe. A "runaway" victor, he received 875 points to 539 for Babe Ruth, 246 for Jack Dempsey, and 148 for Ty Cobb. (Babe Didrikson Zaharias [47] was chosen the greatest female athlete.)

When Jim Thorpe first played football for Carlisle his height was given as five feet eleven and a half inches, and his weight as 185 pounds. In Olympics competition his height was six feet two inches and his weight still 185. Today he stands at six feet and one-half inch and weighs about 193 pounds. He has hazel eyes and dark brown hair; he is a Catholic in faith, and a Democrat in the voting booth. Thorpe has married three times. His first wife, the former Iva Miller, whom he married in 1913, was the mother of his three daughters, Gale, Charlotte, and Frances, and his first son, James Francis, Jr., deceased. His second marriage (in 1926) was to Freeda Kirkpatrick, who bore him four sons, Phillip, William, Rich-

THORPE, JIM—*Continued*

ard, and John. On June 2, 1945, Thorpe married Patricia Gladys Askew of Louisville, Kentucky, who is engaged in public relations work and now handles Thorpe's business affairs.

References

Am Mercury 57:210-15 Ag '43
Collier's 84:16-17 O 5; 84:40 O 12; 84: 30 O 26 '29 pors; 110-42+ N 14 '42 por
N Y Times p31 Ja 25 '50
Outlook 157:436 Mr 25 '31 por
Read Digest 43:7-10 Ag '43 por
Sport 7:49-58 D '49 pors
Johnston, C. H. L. Famous American Athletes of Today (1930)

TOPE, JOHN (K.) Apr. 14, 1912- Political organization official; businessman

Address: b. c/o Young Republican National Federation, 1337 Connecticut Ave., Washington 6, D.C.; c/o Republic Steel Corp., Fisher Bldg., Detroit 2, Mich.; h. 16779 Shaftsbury Rd., Detroit 19, Mich.

John K. Tope, the chairman of the Young Republican National Federation, was elected to that post at the federation's Salt Lake City convention in June 1949. A sales executive with the Republic Steel Corporation in Detroit, after the war Tope came to the front in the Young Republican Club as an organizer of new groups in Wayne County. In 1948 he became regional vice-chairman. During World War II he served as ordnance officer with the Navy.

The son of Jackson R. and Lettie E. (Brooks) Tope, John K. Tope was born in Delroy, Ohio, on April 14, 1912. (He has one brother and one sister.) Both the Tope and Brooks families, of Scotch-Irish ancestry, had been farmers for several generations in Ohio's

JOHN TOPE

Carroll County. John Tope was to live until the age of twenty-four on a farm to which his father had taken his family when the son was a boy. He has said that life on a farm, as well as his membership in the National Grange and Farmers Bureau, gave him an understanding of the problems of the American farmer.

While attending Minerva High School, from which he was graduated in 1929, the youth participated in football, debating, dramatics, and glee club events, joined the 4-H and Hi-Y clubs. Entering Maryville (Tennessee) College, he majored in economics and political science, continued his interest in dramatics, was captain of wrestling teams and played football. He added to his funds by working for the YMCA as a physical education instructor. In 1933, with a B.A. degree from Maryville, Tope returned to Ohio to work as a mill hand in the Canton mills of the Republic Steel Corporation.

In the course of three years at the mills Tope rose to an inspector. In 1936 he took postgraduate studies at the Ohio State University in business administration; and for the first time took a part in the Republican party activities as one of the workers at the Ohio headquarters of the party during the 1936 Presidential campaign. From 1937 to 1939 he was a student in the Republic Steel Corporation's sales training program in Cleveland. In 1939 Republic sent him to their Washington office, where, as the company's Washington representative, he did "contact work" with the United States Government during the rearmament period. A member of the United States Naval Reserve, Tope enlisted in the Navy in 1941 and was appointed an ordnance officer: in 1941-42 he served as assistant inspector of materials at the Washington Navy Yard; and during 1943-44 he was an aviation ordnance officer aboard the United States aircraft carrier *Essex* in the campaigns of the Gilbert and Marshall Islands, and in the raids on Truk, Guam, and Saipan. In 1944 the Navy returned Tope, who had risen to the rank of a commander, to Washington, where until his discharge in 1945 he served in the Aviation Ordnance Maintenance Division of the Bureau of Ordnance. He was awarded the Presidential Unit Citation and five battle campaign stars.

After the war, in 1946 Tope returned to the Republic Steel Corporation, in the Detroit office of which (in 1950) he is employed as a sales executive. In that city he continued to work in the ranks of the Young Republican Club. By 1948 he had been elected a precinct delegate (committeeman) to the convention of Michigan's Seventeenth Congressional District. His success in organizing the Young Republican groups in the district (the only Republican district in Wayne County) was recognized. At the 1948 convention of the Michigan branch of the Young Republican National Federation he was elected to the office of regional vice-chairman and appointed cochairman of the State organization and education committee.

The Young Republican National Federation is an independent group within the Republican party. Its chief purpose is to stimulate the younger Republicans (a recent ruling reduced the age limit from forty to thirty-six) and to provide "a sifting ground for ideas and a training ground for leaders." Resolutions passed by the federation are not necessarily adopted by the Republican party. It is composed of forty-seven State organizations, with branches as well in Puerto Rico and the District of Columbia. Within the State organizations are the local Young Republican clubs; in 1949 there were 2,400 of these, 400 college clubs, and 75 teen-age clubs. The Salt Lake City convention of June 1949 was the third postwar biennial meeting of the federation.

The succession of John Tope to Ralph E. Becker '48 as chairman of the Young Republican National Federation followed a three-day heated campaign fight, in which the closest contestant to Tope was Laughlin E. Waters of California. According to the New York morning papers of June 26, 1949, there was much talk of hostility toward Hugh Scott '48, chairman of the Republican National Committee (succeeded by Guy Gabrielson '49), who was charged with seeking to determine the outcome, a charge he denied. With the withdrawal of Frank McGlinn of Pennsylvania, Tope came forward as a "dark horse" to win substantial support from Eastern and Midwestern States. After a second ballot, which gave Tope 228 votes, Waters 202, and Joseph Bartlett of West Virginia 9, the election of Tope was made unanimous on the motion of his two competitors.

Eastern newspaper commentators generally regarded Tope's victory as a defeat for the "Old Guard" of the Republican National Committee. Tope, an "independent" within the party, after his election declared he was backing no candidate for future Presidential nomination. The Republican party, he said, needed aggressive leadership and less "me-tooism." The main planks of the platform adopted at the convention are as follows. Civil rights: defeat of the poll tax, enactment of antilynching and fair employment practices legislation. Foreign policy: support of the United Nations, of the European Recovery Program, immediate enactment of the Atlantic Pact; setting American tariff barriers "at a level which will enable other nations to market goods within our borders" so long as the farmer and industry are protected. Social security: extension of compulsory social security benefits to groups not now covered, but recommending that Congress should seek means of financing benefits through "private insurance." Health and hospitalization insurance: they should remain in "private hands," with the Government stepping in "only to equalize the coverage of these plans in areas with inadequate insurance developments." In a January 1950 statement, the leader of the young Republicans listed their grievances against the Truman Administration: "flirtation with socialism, living on borrowed money, punitive [taxation] which hampers growth of new business, [encouraging] labor bosses to paralyze the country with class warfare, colossal blunder" in its policy in China.

An active layman within the Methodist Church, Tope is also interested in the affairs of the YMCA. The steel sales executive is a member of the American Society for Metals, the American Ordnance Association, and the Naval Reserve Ordnance Engineering Society. In November 1939 he married Ruth C. Welsh (from Illinois), a Government stenographer; their daughters are named Suellyn, Judith, and Carolyn. Tope, who is stockily built (five feet six inches, 170 pounds), has blue eyes and light hair.

TRIGG, RALPH S(TOVALL) Mar. 2, 1908- United States Government official
Address: b. c/o Commodity Credit Corporation, United States Department of Agriculture, Washington 25, D.C.; h. 406 Cloverway, Alexandria, Va.

Under the Secretary of Agriculture, Charles F. Brannan '48, the official chiefly responsible for implementation of the Government's price support program for farm commodities is the Agriculture Department's Administrator of Production and Marketing, who is also president of the Commodity Credit Corporation. He is Ralph S. Trigg of New Mexico, who came to the joint post in 1948. Trigg was designated in September 1950 by the Department of Agriculture to direct emergency food controls should necessity for them arise.

One of the four children (three sons and a daughter) of Hayde and Blanche (Scripture) Trigg, Ralph Stovall Trigg was born March 2, 1908, in Dallas, Texas. His father was a cattle rancher, his mother's family was in the oil business. Ralph Trigg, who passed nearly all of his childhood and youth in New Mexico, is a 1926 graduate of the high school at Fort Sumner. His Bachelor of Science degree was conferred in June 1934 by the University of New Mexico, where he majored in economics. During his years at college he was a member of the football team, the basketball manager, a member of the student and interfraternity council, of the Khatali (honorary organization) and the Sigma Chi fraternity (for which he was house manager and treasurer); he was senior class president. To help meet his expenses he worked at night as the bookkeeper for a store in Albuquerque.

Upon being graduated in 1934 Trigg, finding there were no openings in business administration, the field in which he had prepared himself to work, became an employee of the New Mexico Transient Service. After a few months as a social worker and assistant camp manager with that organization, he joined the New Mexico Emergency Relief Administration as State auditor in 1935. In 1936 he was appointed assistant director of Unemployment Compensation in New Mexico, and four years later (1940) he became chairman and executive director of the New Mexico Merit System Commission. In these positions, stated an article in the *American Butter Review*, he built up a reputation for conspicuous executive ability.

Trigg's first appointment outside New Mexico came in 1941, when he joined the Public Administration Service as a field consultant in Indiana and Illinois. This lasted only about a year—in June 1942 he was commissioned a lieu-

RALPH S. TRIGG

tenant in the United States Navy. For the greater part of three and a half years of World War II he was engaged in administrative work in the Bureau of Ordnance. He rose to the rank of lieutenant commander and is now a reserve officer.

In January 1946 Trigg was appointed assistant to the United States Secretary of Agriculture, Clinton P. Anderson '45, at Washington, D.C. Six months later Trigg was named deputy administrator of the Agriculture Department's Production and Marketing Administration. The PMA had been created by executive memorandum on the previous August 18. "Its primary purpose," states the *United States Government Organization Manual*, "is to bring into one organization what are sometimes referred to as the 'action' programs of the Department. Its activities cover production planning, production adjustment, conservation aids, price support, foreign supply, surplus disposal, marketing agreements, marketing research, service and regulation, and school lunch." The personnel and facilities of PMA are "used extensively" by the Commodity Credit Corporation (the Government's purchasing agency for commodities at home and abroad), which had been organized in 1933 as an affiliate of the Reconstruction Finance Corporation, and was transferred to the Agriculture Department on July 1, 1939. The administrator of PMA is, accordingly, the *ex officio* president of the CCC and a member of its board of directors, and the deputy administrator is vice-president. Trigg became vice-president of the CCC in February 1947.

Announcement was made on April 15, 1948, that Jesse B. Gilmer, the PMA administrator and CCC president, had resigned, and that Ralph Trigg would be his successor. Before Trigg became its president, an important change in the status of the Commodity Credit Corpor-

ation was brought about. An act establishing the CCC "as an agency and instrumentality of the United States under a permanent Federal charter" was passed by the Republican Eightieth Congress on June 29, 1948, and became effective two days afterward. That Congress stipulated that at least two of the board must be farmers, a stipulation removed by the Democratic Eighty-first Congress in its first session. Truman named new board members on October 28, 1949, all of whom were Agriculture officials, with Trigg, serving since October 7, 1948, on interim appointment, as president.

The CCC, capitalized at $100,000,000, was given authority to borrow up to $4,750,000,000 for use in carrying out its program; this amount was increased to $6,750,000,000 in June 1950. Functions of the organization include the price support program; the purchasing abroad of commodities to meet both domestic and foreign requirements; the exchange of surplus agricultural commodities, acquired by the body, for strategic and critical materials produced abroad; the export at competitive world prices of any commodity or product not in domestic short supply; the storage of grain and farm products; the making of loans for construction and expansion of farm storage; the extending of loans to the Secretary of Agriculture to be applied to furtherance of soil conservation.

The CCC's price support program has proven controversial. Price support, mandatory for certain specified commodities and permissive for others, was set at 90 per cent of parity through 1950, 80 to 90 per cent for 1951-52, and 75 to 90 per cent thereafter. Under existing law, the CCC may not dispose of its stores at a price below support level plus 5 per cent plus carrying charges; CCC surpluses, when released, may not be purchased with United States Government funds. A report issued by Trigg toward the end of 1949 reported $2,680,000,000 invested for supports as of August 31; *Time* (December 19, 1949) stated the CCC had tied up the money "in mountains of produce it could not get off its hands." During the first half of 1950 numerous suggestions, in addition to the controversial Brannan Plan, were made of ways in which to remedy the situation. In January Trigg announced that for a period of six weeks the CCC would offer large quantities of eleven surplus commodities at practically "give-away" prices to buyers not using Government funds for disposal only outside the domestic market. A plan to barter surplus cotton and wheat for needed foreign products was proposed, but proved a failure. President Truman in his message to Congress on July 19 proposed that the CCC be permitted to release its holdings at the support price, but the provision was eliminated from the control bill passed. In August Trigg reported that the corporation's loss on its price support operations had been $249,230,000 for the fiscal year 1949-50 as against $254,000,000 in 1948-49, the loss being largely on potatoes, eggs, peanuts, and wheat. Among criticisms of the CCC administration was a New York *Times* editorial comment to the effect that the corporation had tended to "ride up with the market" instead of releasing its holdings as soon as prices reached a level at which it could legally do so.

The importance of the food supply in the United States was being stressed in the fall of 1950, particularly in relation to the Korean war and the demands of the defense program. In summarizing Trigg's task, *Look* stated: "He must feed the American Army at home and abroad, hold enough on hand in stockpiles to meet emergencies—and insure a meal for Mr. Average Citizen."

The clean-shaven president of the Commodity Credit Corporation has blue eyes and brown hair, stands half an inch under six feet, and weighs 190 pounds. As a registered Democrat he maintains his legal residence in New Mexico. He is an Episcopalian and is a Thirty-second Degree Mason (Blue Lodge, Scottish Rite, Shrine). Mrs. Trigg is the former Billie McCarley, who was a secretary before their marriage on December 28, 1940. The Triggs have two children, Ralph S., Jr. and Nancy Lee. Golf, hunting, and fishing are listed as Trigg's favorite outdoor diversions; and books, photography, and woodworking as other of his interests.

References

Am Butter R 10:44 My '48 por
American Men in Government (1949)
International World Who's Who (1949)
Who's Who in America, 1950-51

MARGARET TRUMAN

TRUMAN, (MARY) MARGARET Feb. 17, 1924- Daughter of the President of the United States; singer

Address: b. c/o James A. Davidson Management, Inc., 113 West 57th St., New York 19; h. Blair House, Washington 25, D.C.; Independence, Mo.

As the only daughter of the President of the United States, Margaret Truman has found herself sharing the limelight which centers on the Chief Executive. The first White House daughter to embark on a serious artistic career, the coloratura soprano has sung to enthusiastic audiences in concert halls since making her debut on a radio program in 1947. While critical estimate of her voice does not give it highest rating, the warmth and poise of her stage presence have been commended.

Mary Margaret Truman was born to County Judge Harry S. Truman '45 and Bess (Wallace) Truman '47 on February 17, 1924, in Independence, Missouri. Her birthplace and childhood home is a large Victorian-type house (built in 1860 by her maternal great-grandfather, a flour miller of considerable regional prominence) and presided over by her grandmother, Mrs. David W. Wallace. The only child in a large and close-knit family, Margaret was accustomed from birth to a warm family life.

In 1934, when Margaret was ten, her father was elected to the United States Senate. From that time until 1941, the family spent the first half of each year in Washington and the second half of the year in Independence. In Washington Margaret attended Gunston Hall, a private school for girls, where, she tells, her status

changed from that of "outsider" to one of the elect when her classmates discovered that she could sing F above high C. She made good grades both there and at the Independence secondary schools, won the prize for Spanish in her third and fourth years at Gunston Hall, and the cup for English in her last year there. At the commencement exercises in 1942 Senator Truman made the address and she sang. For her college education, Miss Truman enrolled in George Washington University, where she earned "A" grades in her major subjects, history and international relations. Upon her graduation in 1946, she was presented with her diploma by her father.

Apart from the greater demands made on her in the social sphere, Margaret Truman's life did not alter radically when her father became Vice-President in 1945. When he succeeded to the Presidency, one mark of the change was that Miss Truman was required to be guarded by Secret Service men. She was called upon to meet kings and presidents, to launch ships and planes, and to deny rumored engagements to men who might escort her to social events. On moving into the White House, Margaret Truman selected the Lincoln Bedroom and the Little Lincoln Bedroom for her rooms, the first-named for her study; her suite also included a small kitchen for preparing evening snacks.

The only daughter in the First Family has attended Washington functions "with becoming frequency and grace" (in the words of the New York *Times Magazine*), and compliments on her modesty and social sense are general. Her "simple dignity and unaffected attitude"— she resembles her mother in that—have been credited with countering initial criticism of the plainness of the Truman home life. As she grew into her new status, Miss Truman gradually increased the smartness of her clothes and toilette. Since her graduation from uni-

TRUMAN, MARGARET—*Continued*

versity she has accepted increasing responsibilities as the daughter of the President. In 1948 Miss Truman, together with her mother, accompanied the Chief Executive on his nationwide campaign tour, joining him in every "whistle stop" appearance except a few very early mornings. Upon occasion Margaret Truman has acted in her mother's place as hostess at White House functions.

"It seems to me that I grew up surrounded by music or talk of it," Margaret Truman has said (as told to Stanley Frank in the article "Why Shouldn't I Sing" in the *Saturday Evening Post*). "My most vivid recollections are concerned with it." Her grandmother Wallace had studied voice and piano at the Cincinnati Conservatory of Music, Mrs. Truman is an enthusiastic concert-goer, and her father's love of music and performances at the keyboard are well known. By the time Margaret was eight, her father had taught her to play simple pieces on Grandmother Truman's old upright piano, and that Christmas she was given a baby grand piano, to her disappointment—she had wanted an electric train. Her musical training began with piano lessons from Mrs. Joseph C. Story, organist of her church, who had given Mrs. Truman lessons also in that instrument years earlier. The young girl sang in the choir of Trinity Episcopal Church in her home town —when she was the soloist, her father, a Baptist, attended the Episcopal service—but at that time her heart was set on becoming a concert pianist. Urged to train her voice, however, by the choirmistress and by an old friend of the family, Mrs. Thomas J. Strickler, Miss Truman began taking weekly singing lessons from the latter, who, before her marriage, had been an opera and concert singer and an assistant to Galli-Curci's teacher. Once she had started her singing lessons, Miss Truman recalls, the voice seemed to her "a more delicate, satisfying instrument of expression than the piano."

In the winter of 1944, while she was a college sophomore, Miss Truman went to New York under the name of Margaret Wallace (her father had become nationally known as head of the Senate Committee to Investigate the National Defense Program). There she auditioned for vocal coach Estelle Liebling, whose verdict on her voice (as told in the *Saturday Evening Post* article) was: "A lovely soprano. You definitely should put time and work into it." From that time, Miss Truman, who for four years had been devoting her summers largely to vocal training, working on interpretation with Mrs. Strickler, set herself a schedule calling for at least two hours' practice a day. When her father became President, Margaret Truman was prepared to lay aside her plans for a concert career. She knew that almost any special activity on the part of a member of a Presidential family might be used to criticize the President, and that such a person would be accused of trading on the White House prestige. Nevertheless, her father encouraged her to go on with her planned career.

After her graduation from college Miss Truman sang for Lawrence Tibbett. She has described the relief in his voice as he told her,

"Thank God you've got it! You need more work, but you've got the natural ability and you can make the grade." After a period of intensive work with Mrs. Strickler, in early March 1947 Margaret sang for her teacher's old friend Karl Krueger, then conductor of the Detroit Symphony. He listened for an hour and forty minutes, then arranged to have the twenty-three-year-old coloratura make her debut four days later as soloist on his regular weekly broadcast. Postponed a week because of an attack of laryngitis suffered by the soprano, the debut took place on March 16, 1947.

"It seemed impossible," said *Newsweek*, "that any young debutante had ever faced a harder task" than this soprano; the studio audience consisted of music critics, and an estimated radio audience of fifteen million persons listened to her, giving the program a Hooper rating of 18.0, nine times its previous rating and about twice that of her father's recent aid-to-Greece-and-Turkey speech. Critical reaction ranged from "a good choir-average voice" (*Time*) to a comparison with "Mme. Galli-Curci in her prime" (Glenn Dillard Gunn, Washington *Times-Herald*). The New York *Times* remarked editorially on the impression of "warmth and sweetness . . . simplicity, sensitiveness, and sincerity." "Most [of the opinions] fell in between—agreeing on her good impression, but counseling further training," was *Newsweek*'s summary.

Miss Truman's first appearance on the concert stage took place in August 1947 when she sang with the ninety-piece Hollywood Bowl Symphony, conducted by Eugene Ormandy, before fifteen thousand ticket-holders, the second largest audience of the season. After a program of operatic arias, *Lieder*, and light classics, the singer was brought back for seven curtain calls. Again she was praised for her poise and stage presence, but better training recommended. Among the thirty-some cities in which she appeared in the course of three months were Pittsburgh (her first full-length program) and Oklahoma City, where she was called upon to make twenty-one curtain calls.

In 1949 Miss Truman acquired a new manager, who managed a number of stars. Terms of their agreement included that he was not to offer her to bookers, but to wait for specific requests; that no undignified offers were to be accepted; that there must be no advance in admission prices. Although higher offers were received, her fee was set "in the middle range, at $1,500 for a concert and $3,000 for a broadcast" (*Saturday Evening Post*). For vocal coaching and accompaniment Miss Truman chose Coenraad V. Bos, who had coached the only other President's daughter to make a concert debut (Margaret Wilson, in 1915) and who was the accompanist of St. Louis-born Helen Traubel, whom Miss Truman admired particularly. In February 1949 Miss Traubel "adopted" her fellow-Missourian as her only pupil, and subsequently directed her training. Only 30 of 200 engagements proffered her, and two broadcasts, were accepted for the 1949-50 season, Miss Truman has reported. One of the broadcasts was her first Carnegie Hall appearance (before an invited audience). A few days earlier, Miss Truman signed a long-term exclusive contract to make RCA-Victor Red Seal Records. The singer has been a member of the American Guild of Musical Artists, AFL, since 1947. Late in 1950 it was announced that Sidney Dietch of Danbury, Connecticut, would take the place of Miss Traubel and of Coenraad Bos as musical supervisor and coach to Miss Truman, but that Bos would continue to be her accompanist.

Many who have seen Margaret Truman say that the camera does not do her justice. Her best features are said to be her complexion, her large blue-green eyes, ash-blond hair, and dimples that do not show in photographs; she is five feet five inches in height. She "loves" shoes, dislikes wearing hats, cooking (although she does her share of it in the "hidden" New York apartment she shares with her mother's personal secretary), and exercise (but a cousin reports she does well at tennis, badminton, and swimming). A nonsmoker, she avoids smoke-laden air because of possible injury to her voice; nor does she drink liquor. Possessed of a "sunny, self-sufficient disposition" (in the words of her agents' release), she is "emotionally resistant . . . very stable." Newspaper accounts described her as an excellent dancer and "full of life at parties." She is like her parents (to whom she is very close) in enjoying visits to Independence, where their home has become the summer White House.

References

Look 13:41 O 25 '49
N Y Times Mag p15 S 8 '46
Redbook Ap '48
Sat Eve Post 219:20 N 30 '46; 222:24
Ap 22 '50

TSCHIRKY, OSCAR (MICHEL) (chĭr' kē) Sept. 28, 1866—Nov. 6, 1950 Maître d'hôtel; waiter at the Hoffman House in New York City, then with Delmonico's; later became dining-room steward, and manager of dining rooms and catering services; headwaiter at the Waldorf when it opened in 1893 and after it became the Waldorf-Astoria; became maître d'hôtel at the new Waldorf-Astoria upon its opening in 1931, and in 1943 named executive; originated the Waldorf salad. See *Current Biography,* 1947.

Obituary

N Y Times p29 N 8 '50

TWEED, HARRISON Oct. 18, 1885- Lawyer; legal aid association official

Address: b. Milbank Tweed, Hope & Hadley, 15 Broad St., New York 5; h. 10 Gracie Sq., New York 28

The National Legal Aid Association, in conference in Boston in October 1949, elected as its president Harrison Tweed, New York lawyer, who has long been associated with the work of providing legal aid without charge to those unable to pay lawyers' fees. Earlier, Tweed had been president of the New York

Legal Aid Society for nine years, is now serving on that society's board of directors. He has been president of the American Law Institute since 1947.

Harrison Tweed was born in New York City on October 18, 1885. His father was Charles Harrison Tweed, for many years general counsel for the Central Pacific, Chesapeake and Ohio, and associated railway corporations. His mother, Helen Minerva (Evarts) Tweed, was the daughter of William Maxwell Evarts, who was Attorney General of the United States in 1868-69, United States Secretary of State (1877-81), and a member of the United States Senate (1885-91). Harrison Tweed attended St. Mark's School at Southborough, Massachusetts; upon graduating in 1903 he entered Harvard. In college he played on baseball and football squads and became a member of the Porcellian and Hasty Pudding Clubs. He received his B.A. in 1907, and in 1910 was awarded an LL.B., *cum laude*, by Harvard Law School. During his last two years there he had edited the *Harvard Law Review.*

Having passed his bar examination, the young lawyer began his career in 1910 as an associate of the firm of Byrne and Cutcheon in New York. By 1916 he had become a member of the firm (then named Byrne, Cutcheon and Taylor). In World War I Tweed entered the army as a private in August 1918, and was at the field artillery officers' training school in Camp Zachary Taylor, in Kentucky, at the time of his discharge in December. In 1921 he became a partner in the law firm of Murray, Prentice and Aldrich; he is now a member of Milbank, Tweed, Hope and Hadley.

An article in the *Legal Aid Review* (July 1945) termed Tweed the "hero of a reverse Horatio Alger Story," fighting "the battle . . . of leaving the rarified plateau of privilege." In spite of his financial and social background, the article stated, "he assumed responsibility and equipped himself with the tools of hard work and there was a social conscience about which he could do nothing, even if he had chosen to." In a speech, "The Bar and the Public," broadcast on August 17, 1940, Tweed expressed his philosophy of the function of law: "It is the duty of lawyers to see to it that the law consists not only of rights and obligations, but of the sort of rights and obligations which will make the world a place in which people may live together in safety and happiness."

Work with the Legal Aid Society of New York has been one of Tweed's activities for many years. The purpose of the organization, as stated in its constitution, is "to render legal aid gratuitously, if necessary, to all who may appear worthy thereof, and who are unable to procure assistance elsewhere, and to promote measures for their protection." Tweed was president of the society from 1936 to 1945, and in 1950 is a member of the board of directors. At the close of his presidency, in 1945, the *Legal Aid Review* spoke of his "guidance and a response which have made the last few years of the Legal Aid Society truly significant." On October 15, 1949, Tweed was elected president of the newly organized National Legal

HARRISON TWEED

Aid Association. Speaking before the annual convention of the organization (formerly named the National Association of Legal Aid Organizations since its founding in 1923) he pointed out that there are nearly fifty cities with populations of over 100,000 which are without well-organized legal aid for persons unable to pay attorneys' fees, and he urged the expansion of the association's program on a national scale.

Tweed resigned as head of the Legal Aid Society in 1945 in order to become president (a position he held for three years) of the Association of the Bar of the City of New York, whose first president in 1870 had been his grandfather, William M. Evarts. From 1946 to 1948 he was chairman of the standing committee on legal aid work of the American Bar Association. His long association with the American Law Institute includes seven years (1930-37) as adviser on the institute's publication *Official Restatement of the Law of Trusts*, and membership on the executive committee of the council of the institute; in 1947 he was elected president, a position he still holds in 1950. The American Law Institute (founded 1923), to which about a thousand leading members of the legal profession and judges belong, conducts comprehensive research programs in the field of law; among its publications are *Code of Criminal Procedure*, restatements of the law of contracts, agency, torts, trusts.

The lawyer is a member of the American, New York State, County, and City bar associations, and of the New York Law Institute. An article by Tweed, "Death and Taxes are Certain, But What of Domicile?" was published in the *Harvard Law Review*; and in collaboration with William Parsons he wrote *Lifetime and Testamentary Estate Planning*, published by the American Law Institute.

Harrison Tweed has shown "keen interest in educational and sociological affairs," reported the New York *Times*. For several summers during the 1930's he conducted summer educational camps for boys at his Montauk, Long Island, home. He has been since 1947 chairman of the board of trustees of Sarah Lawrence College, is a trustee of the Twentieth Century Fund, and a director of the Visiting Nurse Service of New York. Harvard alumni activities have also claimed Tweed's time. He has been a member of the visiting committee for the Harvard Law School, on the board of managers of the New York Harvard Club, and on the committee to nominate the overseers of Harvard. He has been vice-president of the Harvard Alumni Association, and in April 1948 was elected to a one-year term as president of that body. His clubs are the Harvard, Century, Down Town (New York), and the Porcellian (Cambridge).

By his first marriage, in 1914, to Eleanor Roelker, Tweed has two daughters, Eleanor (Mrs. John Stockman) and Katharine Winthrop (Mrs. Archibald B. Roosevelt, Jr.). After a divorce in 1928, he married Blanche Oelrichs Barrymore, who had formerly been the wife of John Barrymore, and who is known, as a poet and diseuse, by the name of Michael Strange; the marriage was terminated by divorce in 1942. In November of 1942 he married Barbara Banning; they have a daughter, Sandra Barbette. Tweed is a tall man (six feet in height) and weighs 180 pounds; he has gray eyes and brown hair.

Tweed, a yachtsman, names fishing as a favorite sport. He is called a "Sunday painter"; in 1946, at his suggestion the New York Bar Association held an exhibition of painting and sculpture by its members, in which Tweed exhibited three oils, one entitled *Montauk From the Air, Fortune*, in a piece on the American bar (May 1949 issue) called Tweed "the *beau sabreur* of the bar," and "one of the breezier adornments of his generally glum profession."

References

N Y Times p14 Ap 26 '48

Who's Who in America, 1948-49
Who's Who in New York, 1947
Who's Who in the East (1948)
World Biography (1948)

VALENTINE, ALAN (CHESTER) Feb. 23, 1901- United States Government official; educator
Address: b. c/o Economic Stabilization Agency, Washington 25, D.C.

For approximately fifteen years (November 1935 to June 1950) the president of the University of Rochester (New York), Alan Valentine was named by President Truman to fill the newly created post of Administrator of the Economic Stabilization Agency. As such, he is empowered, under the Defense Production Act of 1950 to impose price and wage ceilings. Prior to this appointment Valentine had served the Government for a year (1948-49) as Chief of the Netherlands Mission of the Economic Cooperation Administration. He was sworn in as ESA Administrator on October 17, 1950.

Born in Glen Cove, Long Island, New York, on February 23, 1901, Alan Chester Valentine is the son of the late Charles Post and Annie (Laurie) Valentine, and is of English, Scottish, and Dutch extraction. His father, a bank cashier, was a member of the Society of Friends. He sent his son for schooling to the Friends Academy at Locust Valley, Long Island, where the boy took part in baseball, basketball and other sports. On graduation in 1917 young Alan entered Swarthmore (Pennsylvania) College to major in economics and political science. He won Swarthmore's highest scholastic honor (the Ivy award), and was elected to Phi Beta Kappa as well as to the Phi Kappa Psi, Delta Sigma Rho, and Pi Delta Epsilon fraternities. While at Swarthmore he attended, in the summer of 1918, the Officer Training Camp at Plattsburg. He also became editor of the college paper and of the yearbook of his class, was elected president of the student council, played lacrosse, and was for three years a varsity football linesman, winning honorable mention to one of the Walter Camp All-America teams.

After receiving his B.A. degree in 1921 Valentine went to the University of Pennsylvania, where he taught in the Wharton School of Business and Finance; then, having acquired his M.A. degree from Pennsylvania in 1922, he proceeded to Balliol College, Oxford, England, on a Rhodes scholarship. During his three years as an Oxonian, Valentine played college or university lacrosse, tennis, and Rugby football, and in 1924 coached and played on the American Rugby team which won the championship at that year's Olympic games in Paris. He took the B.A. degree at Oxford with honors in 1925. (He also had taken some graduate work at Columbia University.)

In the three years which followed, Valentine was attached to the Oxford University Press, first in England and then in the United States. His essays, *The English Novel* and *Biography*, written for "Oxford Reading Courses," were published in 1927, as was a revised edition of *Oxford of Today; a Manual for Prospective Rhodes Scholars*, originally prepared by Laurence A. Crosby and Frank Aydelotte. In 1928 he received the M.A. degree from Oxford. During the greater part of four ensuing years at Swarthmore as assistant professor of English and dean of men, he served also as assistant American secretary to the Rhodes scholarship trustees. (He was editor of *The American Oxonian* from 1930 to 1935). In 1932 he was called to Yale University as a professor of history, arts and letters; chairman of the board of admissions; and master of Pierson College, of which he was made associate fellow in 1936.

In January 1935, after eighteen months of search for an educator who would combine the attributes of "youth, sound academic background, administrative ability, personality, and a sympathetic interest in the professional schools," Alan Valentine was chosen president of Rochester University, in western New York. That university, established in 1850 as a small liberal arts college, had, during the 1920's and early 1930's, acquired university status; and it had become the fifth richest educational institution in the United States, with an endowment of $53,000,000 derived largely from benefactions or bequests by George Eastman of the Eastman Kodak Company. The famous Eastman School of Music had opened in 1921 and the School of Medicine and Dentistry in 1925, while a new campus and building for men were occupied in 1930.

Harris & Ewing

ALAN VALENTINE

In his inaugural address as president of the University of Rochester on November 15, 1935, Valentine defined it as the prime obligation of a university to see that its graduates "think of college in terms of intellectual maturity received there." He assailed the "sophomoric distortion" which overaccentuated football at many American colleges: "When the clamor of sports journalists and locker room critics affects its policies, a university has sold its birthright." In the ensuing fifteen years at Rochester he maintained a policy of high qualitative standards and limited enrollment, as well as the honor system.

Under Valentine (after Pearl Harbor) the University of Rochester played a notable role in the war effort. In July 1943 it started a Navy V-12 college training program, was one of twenty-five colleges and universities to which a Naval Reserve Officers' Training Corps was assigned in May 1945, and was, in addition, a center of medical atomic research under the Manhattan Engineer District.

A custodian of the College Entrance Examination Board for twelve years beginning 1936, and a member of the college advisory council of the University of the State of New York for ten years after 1937, Valentine served on the executive committee of the New York Association of Colleges and Universities from 1939 to 1943. He also became a frequent speaker before academic and other groups (a collection of fifteen of his addresses was published in 1941 under the title *Dusty Answers*).

(Continued next page)

VALENTINE, ALAN—*Continued*

"Most university presidents," wrote Saul Pett in the Washington *Post*, "discreetly avoid political questions. Valentine didn't. Many times in the 1930's he publicly questioned Roosevelt policies—especially the abortive Supreme Court packing plan and government spending." In the 1940 presidential campaign he became executive director of the National Committee of Democrats for Willkie. (In 1949 he was to be cochairman of the Independent Citizens Committee for the election of John Foster Dulles to the Senate.) He testified before a Congressional committee in opposition to Lend-Lease for Britain in 1941. He opposed the form, not the principle; and later in the year initiated the conferring by the University of Rochester of an honorary LL.D. degree *in absentia* on Winston Churchill in recognition of the British Premier's "distinction as an historian" and "as the leader of a great democracy."

A trustee since 1945 of the Carnegie Foundation for the Advancement of Teaching, Valentine became in 1946 a trustee of the Associated Colleges of Upper New York, a member of the Council on Foreign Relations, and (July 1946) a trustee of the Committee for Economic Development. In the latter capacity he worked with Paul Hoffman[46], future administrator of the Marshall Plan, who, two years later, recommended Valentine's appointment as Chief of the Netherlands Mission of the Economic Cooperation Administration. On leave of absence from Rochester for one year beginning July 1, 1948, Valentine ended on July 15, 1949, a service at The Hague which brought him decorations in the form of the Silver Coin of Limburg (a silver medal of the Netherlands Society of Commerce and Industry) and the decoration of Grand Officer of the Order of Orange-Nassau. Valentine, in commenting later on his support of the Marshall Plan and his earlier criticism of the Four Freedoms principle of the Atlantic Charter, has said (as reported by Pett in the Washington *Post*): "I still think we might bankrupt ourselves trying to give the whole world the Four Freedoms. But the Marshall Plan doesn't attempt that. We can afford five billion dollars for aid abroad, but not 500 billion dollars . . . to make the Four Freedoms really world-wide."

Valentine in November 1949 submitted his resignation as president of the University of Rochester, to become effective June 30, 1950. A little more than three months later (October 7, 1950) his appointment as Administrator of the newly established Economic Stabilization Agency was announced by President Truman. The function of the post, created by executive order under authority of the Defense Production Act of 1950, is "to plan and develop both short- and long-range price and wage stabilization policies and measures, and to create the necessary organization for their administration; to establish price ceilings and stabilize wages and salaries where necessary." Under

Valentine will be a Director of Price Administration and a nine-man Wage Stabilization Board, of which Cyrus S. Ching[48] was appointed chairman.

In a press interview the new administrator said he did not feel that acceptance of this assignment was inconsistent with his disapproval of controls under the New Deal—"This is a time of great emergency," he declared. "After the emergency passes I hope· that planned economy passes." Editorial comment on the President's choice was on the whole cordial, remarking on Valentine's force and ability as an administrator." Valentine was sworn into office on October 17, 1950.

The University of Syracuse, Amherst College, and Union University conferred the honorary LL.D. degree on Valentine in the summer of 1935. Similar degrees were awarded him by Rutgers in 1936, Swarthmore in 1937, Denison in 1940, Lake Forest in 1942, Allegheny in 1943, and Colgate in 1944; Hobart College made Valentine a Doctor of Humane Letters in 1936 and Alfred University conferred on him the Litt.D. degree in the year following. From 1933 to 1943 he was a trustee of Smith College. While in Rochester, Valentine took an active part in civic affairs, including the Community Chest and the Civic Music Association, of which he became a director in 1936. Named a member of the academic council of the Rochester Museum Association in 1938, the educator further served as a trustee of the local chamber of commerce and a council member of the United States Associates of the International Chamber of Commerce, a member of the Rochester YMCA advisory council and (appointed 1939) of the advisory board of the Child Education Foundation of New York. He was elected to the board of directors of the Freeport Sulphur Company in 1939, the Buffalo, Rochester and Pittsburgh Railway in 1940, the Security Trust Company of Rochester in 1942 and the Bausch and Lomb Optical Company in 1944. (Valentine ended his associations with all businesses operated for profit on assuming his government post.) He has contributed many articles to both the educational and the general periodical press. Among his clubs are the Genesee Valley (Rochester); University, Century Association (New York); University (Washington). He is a member of the Newcomen Society of England.

Valentine has been a Republican for some years: in religious affiliation he is a Quaker. He gives his height as six feet and one-half inch, his weight as 178 pounds. The color of his eyes is green, and his brown hair is graying. Mrs. Valentine is the former Lucia Garrison Norton of New York City, a granddaughter of William Lloyd Garrison and a student-architect before her marriage. Married on March 15, 1928, they have one son, Garrison Norton, and two daughters, Anne Laurie and Sarah McKim. "Valentine is tall, lean, ruddy and handsome," wrote Pett of the ESA Administrator. "His tennis game is still fast. He spends the summer in Maine, chopping trees, sailing, gardening."

References

Bsns W p26 O 14 '50 por
N Y Herald Tribune II p1 O 15 '50 por
N Y Times p1 O 8 '50 por
N Y World-Telegram p15 O 21 '50 por
Newsweek 5:33 Ja 12 '35
Sch and Soc 41:89-90 Ja 19 '35
Time 56:21 O 23 '50
U S News 29:38-9 O 20 '50 por
Washington (D.C.) Post Bp3 O 22 '50
  por

America's Young Men (1934)
Author's and Writer's Who's Who (1948-
  49)
Leaders in Education (1948)
Who's Who in America, 1950-51
Who's Who in the East (1948)
World Biography (1948)

Wide World Photos
REV. HENRY P. VAN DUSEN

**VAN DUSEN, HENRY P(ITNEY),
REV.** Dec. 11, 1897-   Clergyman; educator

Address: b. c/o Union Theological Seminary,
3041 Broadway, New York 27; h. 80 Claremont
Ave., New York 27

The tenth president of Union Theological
Seminary, the interdenominational training
school for ministers in New York City, is the
Reverend Dr. Henry P. Van Dusen. A graduate of the Seminary and a member of its staff
since 1926, prior to assuming the office of
president in 1945 he had served as Roosevelt
professor of systematic theology there. He is
also president of Auburn Theological Seminary,
which is closely associated with Union. A
leader in the ecumenical movement, Dr. Van
Dusen has participated in various world church
conferences and been active in missionary affairs. *Life* called him "one of the outstanding
younger leaders in the Protestant churches in
the United States."

Born in Chestnut Hill, Philadelphia, on December 11, 1897, Henry Pitney Van Dusen is
the son of George Richstein and Katharine
James (Pitney) Van Dusen. His father was
a lawyer; his maternal grandfather, Henry C.
Pitney, held the post of Vice-Chancellor of
New Jersey from 1889 to 1907. After preparing
at the William Penn Charter School in Philadelphia, young Van Dusen entered Princeton
University. As an undergraduate there, he was
active as chairman of the 1919 *Bric-à-Brac*,
Polity Club, Philadelphian Society, and the undergraduate council; captain of the university
debating team; Ivy orator; and a member of
the senior council, Whig Hall, the debating,
Nassau Herald, dining halls, and Episcopal
committees. In 1918 he went to the Plattsburg
(New York) Training Camp to become a second lieutenant in the infantry of the United
States Army of World War I. Elected to Phi
Beta Kappa, he received his Bachelor of Arts
degree from Princeton in 1919, and was voted
by his class the "best all-round man outside
athletics." He continued his studies at the
University of Edinburgh and New College
(Edinburgh) during 1921-22, and at Union

Theological Seminary from 1922 to 1924, when
he obtained his Bachelor of Divinity degree.

From 1924 to 1926 Dr. Van Dusen worked
with the Student Division of the Young Men's
Christian Association, in New York City as
associate executive secretary in 1927-28, and
served as a member of the Bowery board of
managers. He was appointed an instructor in
systematic theology and philosophy of religion
at Union Theological Seminary in 1926, promoted to assistant professor two years later,
and in 1931 became an associate professor. He
returned to the University of Edinburgh to
complete graduate work for his degree of
Doctor of Philosophy, which he received in
1932. Meanwhile, in January 1932, he was
appointed the third person to hold the office of
dean of students at Union Theological Seminary, the duties of which he assumed the following September, after his return from Scotland, and which he retained until 1939. He was
inaugurated as Roosevelt professor of systematic theology at the seminary in May 1936.

It was announced on May 17, 1944, that Dr.
Van Dusen had been elected to succeed Dr.
Henry Sloane Coffin[44] as president of the
faculty of Union Theological Seminary. Dr.
Coffin reached the retirement age of sixty-eight
in January 1945, and Dr. Van Dusen took over
his new duties on July 1 of that year. He was
officially installed on November 15, 1945, in
ceremonies held at Riverside Church. In his
inaugural address he declared that theological
seminaries react to all the tensions of the
world, and he emphasized the strain between
"the reality of the true Church and the actual-
ity of our churches." He pointed out that students enter the seminaries "ardent to bear the
gospel undiluted to Church and society," but
the "insistent demand of the market, of the
churches," was to   " 'send us no revolution-
aries, no questioners of the accepted conven-

VAN DUSEN, HENRY P. REV.—*Cont.*

tions, no disturbers of our comfortable complacencies.'" In 1945 Dr. Van Dusen also succeeded Dr. Coffin as president of the faculty of Auburn Theological Seminary, which has been collaborating with Union since 1939 in the training of theological students, and as president of the Union Settlement Association, a settlement house on New York's upper East Side which stands in close, though unofficial, relationship with Union Seminary.

The seminary which Dr. Van Dusen heads is a coeducational, interdenominational institution for the training of ministers, founded in 1836 by the New School Presbyterians, who had in view a service of wider boundaries than those of the Presbyterian Church alone. Except for the years between 1870 and 1892, the seminary has been independent of ecclesiastical control by the General Assembly of the Presbyterian Church, and since 1905 assent to the Westminster Standards by the faculty has been replaced by a new form of declaration which secures the Christian character of the institution in comprehensive terms. Instruction is given not only in the doctrine and polity of the Presbyterian Church, but also in those of other leading Protestant churches. In 1950 the board of directors and faculty included representatives of Baptist, Congregational, Evangelical and Reformed, Lutheran, Methodist, Presbyterian, and Protestant Episcopal churches. During the academic year of 1949-50 Union's enrollment totaled 614, and in May 1950 degrees were conferred upon 188 students, the largest graduating class in its history. In the fall of that year seventy Protestant denominations and Eastern Orthodox communions were represented among the students admitted to the seminary. Two Buddhists were also enrolled among the thirty-one students from sixteen foreign countries.

Dr. Van Dusen has been prominent in the ecumenical movement since 1937, when proposals for the creation of a World Council of Churches were made by both the Life and Work Movement, which held its world conference at Oxford (to which Dr. Van Dusen was a delegate), and the Faith and Order Movement, which met at Edinburgh. The following year he attended the Madras (India) World Conference, sponsored by the International Missionary Council, another ecumenical organization. During the formative period of the projected World Council of Churches, whose establishment was delayed by World War II, he served as chairman of its study commission (a post he still holds in 1950) and as a member of its provisional and executive committees. In 1948 the first General Assembly of the World Council of Churches gathered in Amsterdam to set up a permanent organization embracing within its membership 154 independent national churches in forty-four countries, including almost all the major Protestant groups and several of the Eastern Orthodox faith. Since that time, Dr. Van Dusen has attended the annual meetings of the World Council's Central Committee—in 1949 at Chichester, England, in 1950 at Toronto. "I foresee, within this century," he has written in the New York *Herald Trib-*

une (December 4, 1949), "the merging of most of the largest of the present 250 separate Protestant communions into six to eight major church bodies, and these so linked together that they will be virtually unified in much of their Christian work and influence."

Dr. Van Dusen's first book, *In Quest of Life's Meaning: Hints Toward a Christian Philosophy of Life for Students*, was published in 1926. This was followed in 1933 by *The Plain Man Seeks for God*, which the *Crozer Quarterly* called "a thought-provoking and clear presentation of the theistic problem." Its sequel, *God in These Times*, appeared in 1935. The results of Dr. Van Dusen's survey of missionary activity in the Far East in 1938 were summed up in *For the Healing of the Nations: Impressions of Christianity Around the World* (1940). That same year also saw the publication of *Methodism's World Mission: the Report of a Non-Methodist* and *Reality and Religion*. In *What Is the Church Doing?* (1943), according to the *Christian Century*, Dr. Van Dusen's main purpose was "to show that the church is still the most powerful institution in the world so far as concerns the rallying of the spirit of man to meet the most threatening and testing emergencies." His next book, *They Found the Church There* (1945), consisted of excerpts from diaries and letters of American fighting men to illustrate the influence of Christian missionaries on the natives of the Pacific Islands. Two years later appeared *World Christianity*, about which H. F. Reissig wrote in *The Churchman*: "Here, in outline, is pretty much the whole picture of what's keeping the churches apart and also the intermediate, as well as the ultimate, goals towards which ecumenical leadership is moving." In addition, Dr. Van Dusen has edited and contributed to a number of volumes on religious subjects, served as a member of the editorial board of *Religion in Life* and *Christendom*, and written many articles for various periodicals. In 1950 he was listed on the editorial boards of *The Presbyterian Tribune, Christianity and Crisis*, and *The Ecumenical Review*.

In 1946 Dr. Van Dusen was elected president of the United Board for Christian Colleges in China, and visited that country in the summer to confer with Chinese and American leaders. He holds membership in the American Theological Society; Council on Foreign Relations; American Association of Theological Schools (president, 1942-44); the Board of Foreign Missions of the Presbyterian Church; the YMCA (National Council and National Board, 1936-48 and chairman of the Student Department Committee, 1940-46); Federal Council of Churches of Christ in America (Department of Research and Education; Commission on Evangelism, Religion, and Health); and the Joint Committee on Religious Liberty of the Federal Council and the Foreign Missions Conference. He is also a fellow of the National Council on Religion in Higher Education, a director of United Service to China, and a trustee of Princeton University, Pennsylvania State College, Smith College, Rockefeller Foundation, General Education Board, The Little School,

Westminster Foundation, Ginling College (in Nanking, China), Nanking Theological Seminary, and Yenching University (in Peiping). His clubs include the Century and Princeton.

The theological school president has been awarded an honorary Doctor of Sacred Theology degree by New York University (1945), and Doctor of Divinity degrees from Amherst College and Edinburgh University (1946) and Oberlin College and Yale University (1947). On June 19, 1931, in Inveresk, Scotland, he married Elizabeth Coghill Bartholomew, daughter of the late J. G. Bartholomew, cartographer to the King. They have three sons: John George, Henry Hugh, and Derek Bartholomew. *Time* described Dr. Van Dusen as "tall, able, and energetic." He enjoys sailing—he spends his summers in Maine.

References

N Y Times p24 My 18 '44 por
Time 43:62 My 29 '44

Leaders in Education (1948)
Who's Who in America, 1950-51
Who's Who in New York, 1947
Who's Who in the East (1948)
World Biography (1948)

VAN ZANDT, JAMES E(DWARD) Dec. 18, 1898- United States Representative from Pennsylvania

Address: c/o House Office Bldg., Washington 25, D.C.; h. 1017 18th Ave., Altoona, Pa.

Congressman James E. Van Zandt, Republican, was first elected to represent the Twenty-second District of Pennsylvania in the House of Representatives in 1938. A veteran of World Wars I and II, and a former national commander of the Veterans of Foreign Wars, the Congressman has sponsored legislation dealing with veterans affairs, and has served on the World War I Veterans' Legislation Committee and the Armed Services Committee during his Congressional tenure.

James Edward Van Zandt was born in Altoona, Blair County, Pennsylvania, on December 18, 1898. His parents, James Theodore and Katherine (Smith) Van Zandt, were descendants of pioneers who settled in that county. James attended the Altoona public schools through high school, when he entered the Pennsylvania Railroad Apprentice School at Altoona. In 1916 he began work as a molder apprentice in the railroad's shops. When the United States entered World War I in 1917, Van Zandt enlisted in the Navy and spent two years in active overseas duty as a naval signalman; at the time of his discharge he was a chief quartermaster. At the end of the war he returned to Altoona and to his employment with the Pennsylvania Railroad, working, successively, as chainman (1919), clerk (1920), special representative (1930), and district passenger agent (1934-38).

Van Zandt, who in 1919 enlisted in the United States Naval Reserve and eventually reached the rank of captain in that service, has long been a member of several veterans organiza-tions. Active in the Veterans of Foreign Wars of the United States, he was elected commander of the Pennsylvania department in 1928 and 1929, and later to a seat on the national council of that organization. For three subsequent years of 1934, 1935, and 1936 he was elected National Commander in Chief of the V.F.W. In his last year in that office he led a delegation of veterans on a good-will tour of the Orient. For the years 1936, 1937, and 1938 he was chairman of the V.F.W.'s national legislative committee.

On November 8, 1938, with strong support from veterans, Van Zandt was elected to the Seventy-sixth Congress by a vote of 61,327 against the 45,692 votes received by the Democratic incumbent, Don Gingery. He served for two terms and a portion of the third consecutive term in the House of Representatives. In the second term (1941) he was recalled to active duty in the U.S.N.R. Commissioned a lieutenant, senior grade, in May, in the fall of that year he visited all United States naval bases in the Pacific, and on December 8 (the day after Pearl Harbor) was transferred to convoy duty in the North Atlantic, sailing between the United States, England, Iceland, and Russia. On September 24, 1943, in his third term, he resigned from his seat in the House to continue his naval service for the remainder of World War II. He was assigned to the Pacific Area, where he remained until January 25, 1946. During this time he was officially commended for his successful command of an LST group which landed Army, Navy, and Marine combat units and serviced them at some 20 beachheads. "In recognition of his courage, leadership, skill, and navigation and gunnery prowess," states the *Congressional Directory*, he was promoted to be a lieutenant commander, a commander (before his return from the Pacific), and subsequently to a captaincy.

Upon his return to the United States early in 1946, Van Zandt was assigned to duty on the Navy Board Formulating Post-War Policy on Promotion and Retirement of Officers. During March of that year he was given an assignment on the Civil Relations Division of the Office of the Secretary of the Navy. That fall he was again a successful candidate for Congress, being returned to the Eightieth Congress and re-elected to the Eighty-first in 1948.

As a legislator, Van Zandt has been primarily concerned with matters dealing with the armed forces of the United States. In addition to membership on the Patents Committee (Seventy-sixth Congress), the Immigration and Naturalization Committee (Seventy-seventh) and the Merchant Marine and Fisheries Committee (Seventy-eighth), he was a member of the World War I Veterans' Legislation Committee during his first three Congressional terms. Since his re-entry into the House, he has been a member of the Armed Services Committee and of the Joint Committee on Atomic Energy.

One of the first bills the Pennsylvania Republican introduced upon taking his seat in the House was an amendment to the WPA legislation (defeated), which would have given

JAMES E. VAN ZANDT

preferential employment to veterans of World War I. In 1940 he supported Representative Rankin's veterans pension bill, and voted against a conscription bill. During the early years of World War II Van Zandt opposed the lend-lease bill but after its passage, voted for a seven-billion-dollar appropriation to implement it; endorsed an American Legion permanent draft plan; opposed a proposed cut in WPA funds.

In the course of the first (1947) session of the Eightieth Congress Van Zandt's voting record shows he voted for: the outlawing of portal-to-portal pay suits, the income tax reduction bill, the Taft-Hartley bill, the foreign relief bill, the the repeal of poll taxes in elections to Federal office, and for the voluntary price curb bill; he voted against the loan to Greece and Turkey. In the second session (1948) he voted in favor of: the income tax reduction bill, aid to Europe and China, giving Congress access to the files of certain Government agencies, the Mundt-Nixon Communist control bill, and the Republican anti-inflation bill; he voted against the bill to admit 202,000 displaced persons, and led the opposition against the bill permitting women to become members of the regular armed forces. While he had previously opposed universal military training, in 1948 he voted for the selective service bill.

During the first session (1949) of the Eighty-first Congress, the Pennsylvania Congressman cast his vote in favor of local option in rent control and for a fifteen-month extension of controls, for the passage of the Marshall Plan authorization bill of April, for the pension bill liberalizing requirements and granting a $72-a-month pension to all veterans upon reaching the age of sixty-five, again for the abolition of the poll tax, for a 50 per cent cut in the European

arms fund; against the one-and-a-third-billion-dollar appropriation intended to aid friendly nations rearm. His 1950 record showed him favoring a FEPC, rent control extension and local option for six months, the registration of Communists, the foreign assistance bill (April) giving economic aid to Europe and Korea in the year 1951, a blanket cut of $600,000,000 in the Government appropriation bill, and for the admission of Hawaii as a State. He was against: granting statehood to Alaska, the Point Four program, the plan to set up a department of health, education, and security, and a bill which would prohibit the Federal Government from regulating certain independent natural gas producers.

In recognition of his services in the two wars, Van Zandt has received World War I and II Victory Medals, the Legion of Merit (Combat) Medal, Transport Clasp, American Defense Service Medal, Fleet Clasp, American Area Campaign Medal, European-African-Middle Eastern Area Campaign Medal, Philippine Liberation Ribbon, Bronze Star (Combat), and the Naval Reserve Medal and Star for thirty years honorable service. In 1941, at the time when he was recalled to active duty with the Naval Reserve, he announced that he had returned to the Japanese Ambassador a medal which he had received in 1936 from the Imperial Reservists Association of Japan.

The Congressman is a member of the Masonic Order, of the Mystic Shrine, the Royal Order of Jesters, the Grange, the Elks, the Eagles, the Patriotic Order of Sons of America. In addition to his membership in the V.F.W., he belongs to American Legion, the Military Order of World Wars, the Amvets, and is an honorary member of the United Spanish War Veterans. He is a member of the Blair County Historical Society and the Blair County Game, Fish and Forestry Association. The legislator has been married twice: to Frances Schoen of Brooklyn, New York, in 1921; and to Esther Laura Meisenhoelder of South Dakota, on September 21, 1947. His church is the Lutheran.

References

Congressional Directory (1950)
Who's Who in America, 1950-51
World Biography (1948)

VAN ZEELAND PAUL *See* Zeeland, P van

VENIZELOS, SOPHOCLES (vâ″nyē-zâ′lôs sŏf′ō-klēz) Nov. 17, 1894- Premier of Greece

Address: Athens, Greece

Sophocles Venizelos, Premier of Greece, has held that post during most of 1950 by virtue of a series of coalition Cabinets he has been able to form, including members of his Liberal party, and of Center and Rightist groups. Son of the founder of Greece's Liberal party, Venizelos became active in the party on the death of his father in 1936, and assumed leadership of it in 1949. He held a Cabinet post in the Greek Government-in-exile in Cairo, and has been prominent on the political scene in his homeland since its liberation from the Nazis in 1945.

The second son of a statesman "whose personality remains stamped upon Greek political life," Sophocles Venizelos was born November 17, 1894, to Eleutherios and Mary Venizelos. His father, an antimonarchist who brought Greece into World War I on the side of the Allies, was founder of the republic of 1924, and of the Liberal party in Greece. After being educated at the Greek Military Academy, young Venizelos served with his country's armed forces in World War I and in the Asia Minor campaign of 1919-20.

Upon his return to civilian life, Sophocles Venizelos was elected Deputy for Canea, a department on the island of Crete, in 1920, but he did not at that time play a very active part in political life. Two years later he was appointed military attaché and spent the period 1922-31 at the Greek Legation in Paris. In 1936 (the year his father, then an exile in Paris, died) Venizelos became a member of the executive committee of the Liberal party. He lived abroad during the totalitarian regime of General Metaxas (1936-41), for a while in France, and then in the United States from 1940 to 1943.

In the latter year Venizelos went to Egypt, where the Greek Government-in-exile was functioning. Himself an antimonarchist, he nevertheless joined its predominantly Populist (Royalist) ranks as Minister of Marine. When it was felt that the Populist Premier might not prove acceptable for negotiations with Greek resistance force leaders (largely Communist), Venizelos was named Premier in April 1944. Commented the New York *Times*: "Clearly Venizelos derives a good measure of his prestige from being the son of his illustrious father." Venizelos' Cabinet was shortly replaced by one headed by George Papandreou. From May to September of that year Venizelos was vice-president of the council and Minister without Portfolio, serving on a Government of National Unity, which included representatives of Communist-controlled EAM (National Liberation Front).

In the period of general political instability marked by frequent changes of Cabinet, which followed World War II in Greece, Venizelos has filled ministerial posts in a number of coalition Cabinets. Elected Deputy for Serrai in the 1946 general election, he was deputy leader of the Liberal party (which won 48 of the 354 seats) headed by Themistocles Sophoulis '47. Later breaking with Sophoulis, Venizelos became head of the Venizelist Liberal party. In a coalition Government he was Vice-President and Minister of Military Coordination during January and February 1947. In the latter month he exchanged his portfolio for that of Marine, Mercantile Mariné and National Economy. His resignation in August, precipitating the fall of the Cabinet, was followed by a move on his part to restore his group to the

Wide World Photos
SOPHOCLES VENIZELOS

Liberal party. The coalition Cabinet formed under Liberal Sophoulis on September 7, 1947, and reshuffled in May and November 1948, and January 1949, owed some of its instability to Venizelos' efforts, wielding the threat of Liberal dissidence, to have it replaced by a supra-party Government. In the new Cabinet formed by Sophoulis on January 20, 1949, Venizelos was given a post as Minister without Portfolio; he became Deputy Premier (sharing the post with a Populist Minister) in the coalition Cabinet of Liberal Alexander Diomedes, which was formed on the death of Sophoulis in June 1949. At that date Venizelos became leader of the Liberal party.

In the course of the postwar years, Venizelos has held a number of important non-Ministerial posts: in 1946 he headed a Greek economic mission on a visit to the United States; in 1947 he was chief of the newly formed Central Commission for Turco-Greek Cooperation, and again that year visited the United States in connection with that country's aid program to Greece; in 1949 he was appointed to the War Council.

The Liberal party made a gain in the elections held March 5, 1950, winning 55 seats, and although this was less than the number won by the Populists, the leader of the latter was unable to form a Cabinet upon being asked, and Venizelos was invited to do so. On March 23 he was sworn in as Premier of a Liberal regime. Counting on the support of the Populist party, Venizelos formed a Cabinet with but one non-Liberal member, the head of the Conservative National Rehabilitation party. This was contrary to a pre-election agreement with left-of-center leader General Nicholas Plastiras '50 according to which the latter would have headed a three-party Center group. Veni-

VENIZELOS, SOPHOCLES—*Continued*

zelos said considerations of a national character had compelled him to act otherwise. The Venizelos Cabinet of March 23 was the first of four Cabinets the Liberal leader was to form in the course of the year (March 23, August 21, September 13, and November 3) in attempts to achieve a combination of ministers with a wide enough base to ensure effective support. Venizelos' two-party Government (of Liberal and Democratic Socialist Ministers), which was sworn in on November 3, received a strong vote of confidence in the Chamber of Deputies two weeks later. In regard to the Populist party, which had had a representation in the September Cabinet, the Premier said later in November that it would not be included in the Government until it re-established order in its own ranks.

The chronic lack of stability in government was one of the greatest problems facing Venizelos. It led to a criticism by the United States Ambassador to Greece, Henry F. Gray'" suggesting that the country eliminate special privilege, Government inefficiency, excessive subsidies, high interest rates, and overcentralization of power; and that it establish an adequate social program and effective collection of taxes. On April 3, 1950, the United States Aid Mission in Athens suspended new power and industrial development projects, claiming that Venizelos had failed to organize a sufficiently stable and efficient Government to ensure Greece's paying her share of the undertakings. A cut by $67,200,000 in economic aid to Greece was announced for the next fiscal year, but hope was held out that the cut might not be so great if the Greek Government could reduce its budget and build up its tax revenues. In October Venizelos announced that his Government agreed to the terms of an ECA demand for reforms which stressed the same points as Ambassador Grady.

The Venizelos Cabinet made known in August 1950 its intention to effect clemency measures dealing with civil war participants. In the field of international affairs, Premier Venizelos has worked for cooperation with the Western democracies. The Premier announced October 3 that he was attempting to form a Mediterranean defense bloc which could cooperate with the Atlantic Pact countries; he has been invited to consult with the latter. A member of the United Nations, Greece on September 2 pledged herself to send an organized ground force to participate in the Korean fighting.

Sophocles and Kathleen Venizelos—married December 20, 1920—have one child, a daughter. The Greek Premier, who finds recreation in cards, was at one time a bridge champion.

References

N Y Times p9 Ap 4 '44
International Who's Who, 1950
World Biography (1948)

VIDELA, GABRIEL GONZALEZ *See* González Videla, G.

VOORHEES, DONALD July 26, 1903- Conductor; musical director

Address: b. c/o National Broadcasting Co., 30 Rockefeller Plaza, New York 20

The Monday evening *Telephone Hour* of orchestral music (and soloists) offered its five hundredth weekly concert over the National Broadcasting Company network on November 21, 1949, to a radio audience estimated at between eight and nine million persons. On that occasion, as well as at the first concert on April 24, 1940, the conductor and musical director was Donald Voorhees.

Born in Guthville, near Allentown, Pennsylvania, on July 26, 1903, Donald Voorhees comes of pioneer American stock dating back to the seventeenth century. His musical talent is said to have been evident from the age of five, when he began to take lessons on the violin; under teachers at Allentown and Harrisburg piano study began in his eighth year; and organ about three years later. While still at grammar school he became a pupil of the late Dr. J. Fred Wolle, founder and conductor of the Bethlehem (Pennsylvania) Bach Choir. At eleven young Voorhees was organist of the family church in Allentown; at twelve the pianist in the house orchestra of the local Lyric Theatre; and at fifteen the conductor of that orchestra as well as the organizer and leader of his own dance ensemble. In those days the Lyric Theatre was considered a "try-out" spot for Broadway. (The customary sequence would be final rehearsals and a Saturday night "break in" at Allentown, followed by a brief run in Philadelphia, and then Broadway). Thus the young conductor developed (in the words of a National Broadcasting Company biographical release) "a craftsmanship in music which proved of inestimable value a few years later with radio's necessity for split-second timing." It also brought the talents of young Voorhees to the attention of managers and others in the musical comedy and revue field.

After his graduation from the Allentown High School, Voorhees debated with himself as to whether he would "continue his studies with Dr. Wolle and make a modest living by giving music lessons, or strike out into something more profitable." One night the youth received a call from William Baker, Broadway orchestrator, who asked him to come at once to New York to conduct the opening of a musical revue, *Broadway Brevities of 1920*, starring Eddie Cantor and the late Bert Williams. Two nights later (September 29, 1920) seventeen-year-old Voorhees was in the pit of the Winter Garden for the New York première. A similar assignment with the second edition of George White's *Scandals* followed in 1921, and during the subsequent year Voorhees conducted the scores of the revue *Spice of 1922* (in July) and an early George Gershwin musical comedy, *Virginia*, in December. Five successful editions (1923-27) of Earl Carroll's *Vanities* followed, while other conducting assignments handled by

Voorhees at this period in his career included the Joe Cook show *Rain or Shine*, and *The Right Girl*, one of Victor Herbert's last scores.

Voorhees first explored the new territory of radio in 1925, when he conducted from the stage of the Earl Carroll Theatre in New York a series of experimental Saturday night concerts of light music which were broadcast. Their popularity soon led to commercial sponsorship, beginning with the old Atwater Kent hour. When the new Columbia Broadcasting System was launched in 1927, Voorhees became joint WABC house conductor with Howard Barlow [40], a post which he held for a little over a year, after which he became a free-lance music director. Since 1927 radio broadcasting has held exclusive call on Voorhees' time, except for a period between 1937 and 1940, when he conducted the Broadway musicals *Between the Devil* and *Swingin' the Dream* and was the musical director of *American Jubilee*, the patriotic spectacle given at the New York World's Fair.

In the interpretation of classical, semi-classical, popular, and incidental or background music, Voorhees was during his first fifteen years in radio the orchestral conductor for such entertainments as the Maxwell House *Show Boat*, the *General Motors Hour*, the Ed Wynn *Fire Chief* show, concert series featuring artists (Albert Spalding, Lawrence Tibbett, etc.). In connection with the Du Pont historical-dramatic feature *Cavalcade of America*, it has been noted that he "would pore over hundreds of pages of material for the right musical 'bridge.'" ("You must never use familiar music," he has asserted in comment on this type of program. "That might distract attention from the drama. . . . Often I can't find anything to fit, and I compose it myself." During the ten years beginning 1940, Voorhees has also at various times conducted the Ford summer concerts and regular winter series, the CBS *Family Hour* and *March of Time*, as well as the *Telephone Hour* and *Cavalcade of America*.

The conductor's association with the Bell *Telephone Hour* dates from its first Monday evening broadcast on April 24, 1940, over the NBC network. (Voorhees himself composed the *Bell Waltz*, the signature theme for the program.) For the first two years the program featured week-to-week soloists; but following the engagement of Wallace Magill, the present producer, a change in policy was initiated with the result that the now familiar "Great Artists" series was instituted on April 27, 1942. The regular procedure in making up programs, stated *Musical America*, is that "the guest artist submits a suggested list of numbers with possible alternatives, and Mr. Voorhees completes the program." The first soloist in the "Great Artists" series, the violinist Jascha Heifetz, has since played nearly forty return engagements on the Bell *Telephone Hour*; others heard during that inaugural season included John Charles Thomas, Lily Pons, Oscar Levant, and Marian Anderson. Among other singers and instrumentalists heard with Voorhees' orchestra have been Gladys Swarthout, Ezio Pinza, Fritz Kreisler, Gregor Piatigorsky, Jennie Tourel, Maggie Teyte, and Jussi

Yvonne Le Roux
DONALD VOORHEES

Bjoerling, Ferruccio Tagliavini was the soloist on the occasion of the five-hundredth broadcast on November 21, 1949.

Donald Voorhees has been voted radio's most popular concert and program conductor in the first and subsequent annual reader polls conducted by *Musical America*. In 1949 the *Telephone Hour* received the Peabody award, "the highest recognition given a radio series." *Etude* once called Voorhees "a musician's musician." In an editorial note in the January 1945 issue introducing an interview with Voorhees on the subject "How to Rehearse," it was pointed out that the *Telephone Hour* conductor is "noted for remarkable gift of tempo, austere artistic integrity, practical knowledge of each instrument, wide repertory of scores." He has "no patience with affectation or display" and "avoids stylized or over-orchestrated arrangements." Much of the conductor's success, it is said, may be attributed to his handling of the personnel of his fifty-seven-piece orchestra, of which thirty-six instrumentalists who participated in the first concert in 1940 remained with the ensemble in 1949. One full rehearsal with soloist is held before each concert. Voorhees likes to conduct with a lead pencil instead of a baton (he prefers the lighter "feel").

The conductor of the *Telephone Hour* was awarded an honorary Doctor of Music degree by Bates College, of Lewiston, Maine, on May 23, 1943, for his "contribution to American music." He is six feet tall, weighs between 185 and 190 pounds, has dark blue eyes and graying black hair. "He lives in a New York apartment on Park Avenue with his wife and son," stated a 1949 biographical release. "A married daughter by a previous marriage lives in upstate New York. A dog lover, Mr. Voorhees was well known as a breeder of Scotch terriers and was in demand as a judge at dog shows,

VOORHEES, DONALD—*Continued*
but recently has confined his hobby to one family pet."

References

Etude 63:7-8 Ja '45 pors
Musical Am 64:10 O '44
N Y Times II p7 Mr 11 '45
Newsweek 34:48 N 28 '49 por
Who's Who in Music, 1950

VORYS, JOHN M(ARTIN) (vôr'ĭs) June
16, 1896- United States Representative from
Ohio

Address: b. House Office Bldg., Washington,
D.C.; c/o Vorys, Sater, Seymour and Pease,
52 E. Gay St., Columbia, Ohio; h. 361 E. Broad
St., Columbus, Ohio

A senior and important member of the powerful House Foreign Affairs Committee is
Representative John M. Vorys, Republican, of
the Twelfth Ohio District. One of the first
naval aircraft pilots in World War I, Vorys
was a prominent Columbus lawyer and former
member of the Ohio House and Senate before

Wide World Photos
JOHN M. VORYS

being elected to Congress in 1938. An isolationist, before America's entrance into World
War II, today (in the words of the Arthur
Krock of the New York *Times*) he is "a sincere convert to internationalism, but with a
strong reservation as to self-help." Krock has
called him "one of the ablest members of the
House."

John Martin Vorys, the second of the four
sons of Arthur Isaiah and Jeanny (McNeill)
Vorys, was born June 16, 1896, in Lancaster,
Ohio. His father, a lawyer, had served as city
solicitor of that upper Hocking Valley industrial center; later, he was for seven years the

State Superintendent of Insurance, and still
later a Republican National Committeeman. The
future Congressman began his education in the
public schools of Lancaster; but when the elder
Vorys joined the law firm of Sater, Seymour
and Pease, the family moved to Columbus, and
it was from the East High School in Ohio's
capital city that the youth was graduated in
1914. He then entered Yale University, there
joining the unit of the Naval Reserve Flying Corps, which was to see action in World
War I. Vorys, listed as Naval Aviator Number
73, served overseas as a fighter pilot, and was
demobilized as a lieutenant, senior grade.

He returned to Yale to take his B.A. degree
as of 1918, then taught for a year (1919-20) in
the College of Yale at Changsha, China. In
1921-22 he was an assistant secretary of the
American delegation to the Conference on Limitation of Armaments and Pacific and Far East
Affairs at Washington, D.C. Deciding to enter
law, he studied for that profession at Ohio
State University, where he acquired the Doctor
of Jurisprudence degree in 1923. On admission
to the Ohio bar in the same year, he joined
his father's law firm, now Vorys, Sater, Seymour and Pease, and became a candidate for
the Ohio General Assembly. Elected, the Republican served one term (1923-24) as a
representative from Franklin County (of which
the city of Columbus is a part), then in 1925-26
sat in the Ohio Senate for the State's Tenth
District. The author of an article on State
supervision of aviation, he subsequently served
(1929-30) as Ohio's first Director of Aeronautics. Except for this, his professional activities
were confined to private practice from 1926
until the summer of 1938 when he campaigned
for election to the United States Congress as
Representative of his State's Twelfth (Franklin County) District.

The November 1938 election in Ohio was
(according to the New York *Times*) notable for
a "tidal wave of anti-New Deal and anti-CIO
sentiment" and resulted in the victory (over
Democratic incumbents) of John W. Bricker
for Governor and Robert A. Taft for Senator,
and the sending of ten new Republican Representatives to Washington. One of these was
Vorys, who was assigned, after the Seventy-
sixth Congress convened, (January 3, 1939)
to the Foreign Affairs Committee, of which he
has since been a member. He attracted attention in April 1939, when, as a member of the
committee, he stated that "the thing that
shocked" him about President Roosevelt's just-
uttered Pan-American Day plea to "sister nations to break the bonds of the ideas that con-
strain them to perpetual warfare" was "an
implication that the United States would help."
Vorys was strongly anti-Roosevelt and, in face
of the lowering war clouds, at that time firmly
isolationist. In that Congress he opposed farm
parity payments, called "Nay" on an additional
one hundred million dollars for work relief,
urged an investigation of the Labor Relations
Board and drastic amendments to the Wagner
Act, favored abandonment of the Guam naval
base and the mandatory arms embargo amendment to the Neutrality Act, and, on September
7, 1940, voted against conscription. On April

16, 1940, he made a noteworthy speech in support of the Logan-Walter bill to make the decisions and rulings of administration agencies subject to review by the courts.

Vorys' "freshman" record in Congress was manifestly in line with the views of the majority of his constituents; and in November 1940 he was not only re-elected without difficulty, but was in a position to return 25 per cent of his campaign funds to the donors. (He was subsequently re-elected biennially in the years 1942-48.) The voting record of the Ohio Representative in the first session of the new Congress resembled that of the preceding. He opposed passage of the lend-lease bill (March 1941), extension of conscription and repeal of the ban on army merchant ships (October) and price controls (November), and in Massachusetts and Virginia he made a number of speeches urging a "peace offensive" by the United States. (Clarence K. Streit, internationalist, who had debated with Vorys, declared himself "impressed from the start" by the Ohioan's "exceptionally thoughtful and studious attitude.")

Following the Japanese attack on Pearl Harbor Vorys devoted himself to the war effort. Rejected by the Navy on the ground that he would be more useful as a legislator, he joined the Civil Air Patrol and piloted an observation plane up and down the Florida coast in 1942. While in the House he supported increasing the base pay of servicemen, authorization of the WAAC, and the drafting of young men under twenty. A conspicuous shift from former views was reflected in his support (1943) of the Fulbright Resolution in favor of a world assembly; and in January 1944 he voted for the activation of UNRRA, though he was the author of an amendment to transfer supervision of expenditures from the President to the State Department. At the same time his views on domestic matters was seen in his votes against including farm labor in the parity formula (1942) and in favor of cutting the OPA appropriation (1943), passage of the Smith antistrike bill (1943), and terminating executive relief agencies (1944.) He also voted, during the war period, to make the Dies Un-American Activities Committee permanent, and in December 1944, was the sponsor of a bill to prohibit commercial exploitation of the Red Cross name and emblem.

During the first quarter of 1945 (in the first session of the Seventy-ninth Congress) when lend-lease came up for extension, Vorys was able to persuade the House to pass an amendment limiting the use of funds to war purposes and specifying that they should not be used for "postwar relief, rehabilitation, or reconstruction." In the second session of that Congress (1946) he was recorded in favor of the Case strike-control bill, he sponsored an UNRRA rider specifying a free press in assisted countries, and voted against the British loan and continuation of OPA. The Republican-controlled Eightieth Congress (1947-48) found him casting his approving votes for a two-term limit to the Presidency, the banning of portal-to-portal pay suits, the Taft-Hartley law, the tidelands oil bill, and the Wolcott housing bill. In January 1947 he sponsored a resolution to authorize American participation in the United Nations International Refugee Organization. This resolution was approved in May, the month of the Greek-Turkish aid bill, for which Vorys voted. When in June 1948 a bill approving admission of 200,000 displaced persons was before the house, Vorys introduced an amendment to the effect that the United States should withhold any commitment until other U. N. members "have accepted for resettlement their fair share" of such persons. This amendment was defeated by only four votes.

In the early months (1949) of the Eighty-first Congress Vorys strongly opposed the farm bloc's rider to the Marshall Plan bill which would have forced the ERP to ship surplus basic farm products to Europe, calling it a "gigantic pork barrel"; and when the bill, unhampered by the rider, came to a vote (April 12) he was recorded in support, though he favored a 10 per cent reduction in the appropriation. In June he was one of those critical of the Truman $1,450,000,000 arms program as too costly and as giving too great power to the Chief Executive. "The President is asking too much, too soon," he stated, adding that "we ought also to get a policy statement on China." In September he assailed the Truman Point Four program as "just another give-away plan." Three months later (January 1950) he moved to send back to committee the Administration bill to provide sixty million dollars in economic aid to Korea. When the measure eventually came to a vote, however, he was paired in its favor. During March the House Foreign Affairs Committee adopted by a nonpartisan 10-to-7 vote a proposal by Vorys to cut one billion dollars from the new ERP authorization and to give Europe surplus American agricultural commodities, which was criticized editorially by the New York *Times* and the *Herald Tribune*. In the latter part of July, observing that "the tragic events of the last few weeks in Korea have demonstrated that . . . the burden of meeting aggression falls directly upon us," Vorys voted in favor of the $1,222,-500,000 authorization for future military aid to free nations.

The Republican Congressman in 1947 was named to the board of regents of the Smithsonian Institution. A Methodist in church affiliation, Vorys is a director of the Columbus YMCA. He is a member of the Columbus Bar Association (president in 1938) and of the Ohio Bar Association; his fraternities are the Phi Beta Kappa, Psi Upsilon, Phi Delta Phi, Delta Sigma Rho, Pi Sigma Alpha, and the Order of the Coif, while his clubs are the Rocky Fort Hunt (Columbus) and the Country (Gahanna, Ohio). Lois West of Lucknow, India, became Mrs. Vorys on February 5, 1927; they have one son, Martin West, and two daughters, Jeanny Esther and Mary. In 1945 Delos Lovelace of the New York *Sun* described Vorys as "seeming settled . . . in an orderly political career. He looks settled. His clothes are conservative, his weight under control, his eyes placid behind spectacles, his dark hair trim above a square, quiet face."

(Continued next page)

VORYS, JOHN M.—*Continued*

References

Life 24:30-1 Je 14 '48 pors
N Y Sun p16 Mar 13 '45
Time 43:17-18 Ap 24 '44
Congressional Directory (1950)
Who's Who in America, 1950-51
Who's Who in Law (1937)
Who's Who in the Midwest (1949)
World Biography (1948)

WALKER, WALTON H(ARRIS) Dec. 3, 1899—Dec. 23, 1950 United States Army Officer

Bulletin: Lieut. Gen. Walton H. Walker died on December 23, 1950.

From September 1950 issue:

The United Nations ground forces, which are aiding South Korea in its struggle with Communist North Korea, are led by Lieutenant General Walton H. Walker, the Commanding General of the United States Eighth Army. Known for mobility in armored attack and for successful coordination of infantry and armor, the Texas-born general had commanded the Twentieth Corps of Patton's Third Army in the drive through France and Germany in World War II; he is known, too, for constantly visiting the firing line. Walker was assigned to his command in Korea on July 12, 1950, after serving nearly two years as commander of the Eighth Army in occupied Japan.

Walton Harris Walker was born December 3, 1889, in Belton, a small town in Texas, the son of Sam S. Walker, a drygoods merchant, and May Lydia (Harris) Walker; he is the grandson of Confederate Army officers. After attending the Wedemyer Military Academy in Belton, he was a student for a year at the Virginia Military Institute, which he left in 1908 to enter the United States Military Academy, at West Point. Upon his graduation from West Point in 1912, the newly commissioned second lieutenant was assigned to the Nineteenth Infantry at Fort Sheridan, Illinois.

An Army order next took young Walker to Fort Sill, Oklahoma, to serve there until April 1914, when his regiment was moved to Galveston, Texas. For the following seven months he was a member of the Vera Cruz expedition, after which he returned to Galveston for another seven months; then followed five months again at Fort Sill. The beginning of 1916 saw Walker back in his native State, where he was to remain until April 1918: at Del Rio, on border patrol duty, when he was promoted to be first lieutenant on July 1, 1916; at Fort Sam Houston, Camp Stanley, and Fort Brown. At the latter Captain Walker (he had been promoted May 15, 1917, the month after the United States entered World War I) organized the Second Battalion of the 57th Infantry "under unusual circumstances of being the only officer in the battalion," stated a biography issued by the Department of the Army. He was next ordered to organize a company of the Thirteenth Machine Gun Battalion, with which he went to France in April 1918.

As a major (temporary, June 7, 1918) of that unit Walker saw action at St. Mihiel and in the Meuse-Argonne, was twice cited for gallantry under fire, was awarded the Silver Star with Oak Leaf Cluster. He was promoted to the rank of lieutenant colonel (temporary) on May 6, 1919. After the end of the war, the officer served with the Army of Occupation in Germany, until his return to the United States in July 1919, to be assigned as instructor at the Infantry School at Fort Benning, Georgia. By this time he held three other decorations, that of Mexican Interior, Victory Medal with five stars, and Army of Occupation.

In the course of the twenty-two peacetime years from 1920 through 1941, Walker's ranks were as follows: he reverted to his prewar rank of captain (February 12, 1920), was promoted to be major (July 1, 1920), the rank he held for fifteen years until August 1, 1935, when he became lieutenant colonel. As the United States began its defense program after the outbreak of World War II in Europe, Walker received two promotions (temporary) within five months, as colonel on February 15, 1941, as brigadier general on July 10, 1941.

During the first three years of the 1920's he attended the Field Artillery School at Fort Benning (in 1920), was assigned to the Fort Benning Infantry School as chief of the machine gun and infantry weapons section, and in 1923 graduated from the advanced course. For the remaining years of the 1920's Major Walker was detailed as a tactical officer at West Point (for two years, until August 1925); as a student at the Command and General Staff School, Fort Leavenworth, Kansas, from which he graduated in June 1926; as instructor at Fort Monroe (Virginia) Coast Artillery School.

In 1930 the Major was ordered to Tientsin, China, where from October of that year to March 1933 he was with the Fifteenth Infantry Regiment on International Railroad Patrol. Then, back in the United States, he was assigned to duty in Maryland, first at Fort Meade, next at the Headquarters of the Third Corps Area, in Baltimore. Shortly after becoming a lieutenant colonel he attended the Army War College in Washington, and upon graduating in June 1936 he was assigned to the post of executive officer of the Fifteenth Infantry Brigade at Vancouver Barracks, Washington. In August 1937 he reported back to Washington for three years' duty in the War Department, with the War Plans Division of the General Staff, of which division he became executive officer in December 1940. As colonel (temporary), Walker in April 1941 was assigned to Camp Polk, Louisiana, as commanding officer of the 36th Infantry; and in July of that year, as brigadier general (temporary) he was given command of the Third Armored Brigade at the same camp.

The Army officer's change in command came a few months after the United States entered World War II: he assumed command of the Third Armored Division in January 1942, a month before he was advanced to major general (temporary) on February 16, 1942. In August of that year he became Commanding General of the Fourth Armored Corps, Camp

Young, California, and in October was assigned to organize and command the Desert Training Center, at which armored forces destined for fighting in Africa were trained under rigorous field conditions. "His idea," a colleague of his said later (as reported in *Time*), "was to make training so damned hard that combat would seem easy." Walker's last detail before going overseas began in April 1943, when he proceeded to Camp Campbell, Kentucky, with his corps.

Walker's command was redesignated the Twentieth Corps in October 1943, under which name it became famous as the "Ghost Corps" of General George S. Patton's Third Army in a swift nine-month drive from the Normandy beachhead (where it began 48 days after D-Day) across France and Germany and into Austria. The Twentieth Corps reduced Metz and forty-three intercommunicating fortresses and forced a crossing of the Moselle River in November 1944. In February 1945 it penetrated the Siegfried Line at Thorn and crossed the Saar to take Trier. It turned the Siegfried Line between the Moselle and the Rhine, and after crossing the Rhine it swung north to capture Kassel. Walker's corps liberated the Nazi-tortured prisoners in the Buchenwald camp, reached the outskirts of Chemnitz and drove south across the Danube to Austria. There, on April 27, 1945, General Patton presented to him the three stars of a lieutenant general (temporary) which Patton himself had received from General Eisenhower. Before this, in June 1944, Walker had been promoted to the permanent rank of brigadier general. The tank expert's successful coordination of infantry and armor was commended by the War Department, and his tactics praised by Prime Minister Churchill in the House of Commons. For extraordinary heroism near Melun, Walker received the Distinguished Service Cross; and for gallantry in action in June 1944, he was awarded a second Oak Leaf Cluster to the Silver Star he won in World War I.

In June 1945 Walker returned to Texas to command the Eighth Servce Command, with headquarters in Dallas. A year later (June 1946) he was given command of the Fifth Army Area, comprising twelve Midwestern and Mountain States, with headquarters in Chicago. It was as a major general (permanent), to which rank he was promoted on August 1, 1947, that Walker took over on September 24, 1948, as Commanding General of the Far East Command's Eighth Army. To the trainer of "green troops" it became apparent that a tough combat-training course for the Eighth Army should be begun: most of the men were young, without combat experience and "softened" by the light occupation duties. At the ceremonies in observation of the sixth anniversary of the Eighth Army's activation, General Walker on June 10, 1950, spoke on the necessity of maintaining "a degree of combat readiness" to meet any threat. "The Eighth Army's relation to preparedness is a very real, a very grave responsibility," he said.

A month after that event Eighth Army troops were fighting in South Korea, with Lieutenant General Walker taking command of the ground

U. S. Army

LIEUT. GEN. WALTON H. WALKER

forces on July 12, 1950, under the over-all command of his superior in Japan, General Douglas MacArthur. The war had begun June 25, when Communist North Koreans crossed the 38th parallel to invade South Korea (the Republic of Korea). In the course of the next few days United States air and naval forces had been ordered to aid the South Koreans and the United Nations invoked military sanctions against the Communists. American troops went into action on July 5, and two days after Walker had taken command the United Nations flag was raised over his headquarters.

Outnumbered and outgunned, the South Koreans and their American allies were forced to fall back southward and eastward. By the end of July they had withdrawn toward the Naktong River, into a beachhead with Pusan, the deep-harbor supply line port to the south, and Pohang, 65 miles northward, a shallower port with an airfield. It was then that the General, who maintained his reputation as a battle front commander as he appeared at many points along the semicircular line, issued his "stand-or-die" order to his troops, stressing that a successful withdrawal (a "Dunkirk") could not be made from Pusan. Throughout August the battle line shifted with Communist thrusts at weak points and with counterattacks by the United Nations forces in which Walker's mastery of mobility was demonstrated. Those forces now had been strengthened by experienced troops from the United States and aided by heavy air attacks by Americans and Australians on enemy troops, tanks, and strategic communications and bases. Pusan, said Walker, had been saved "by a miracle." By the end of August the 120-mile perimeter of the 4,000-square-mile beachhead was being defended on the north by Koreans, by Americans on the west and south, while American and British naval craft shelled shore targets and main-

WALKER, WALTON H.—*Continued*

tained a blockade of the peninsula. While Taegu, the advance U.N. supply line northwest of Pusan, and Pohang were still in the Allies' hands, Walker said that the Reds still retained the initiative, that there was "plenty of fighting and plenty of disappointment ahead," but that his forces were ready for "any eventuality."

In addition to the five awards and decorations mentioned before, General Walker has received fourteen others: the Distinguished Service Medal, Legion of Merit, Bronze Star, American Defense, American Theater, European Theater of Operations with six stars; from France he received the Legion of Honor, Croix de Guerre with Palm and Bronze Star, the Medals of Metz and Verdun; Luxembourg honored him with the Grand Ducal Order of the Oak Leaf of the Crown and the Croix de Guerre; and Russia awarded him the Order of the War for the Fatherland and the Medal of Russian Guards Army. The General is, as well, an honorary citizen of the cities he liberated—Metz, Thionville, Chartres, Verdun, Ste.-Symphorien, and the City of Luxembourg.

Walker and Caroline Victoria Emerson of Baltimore were married March 18, 1924. Their son, Sam Sims, a 1946 graduate of West Point, in 1950 is a first lieutenant with the 82d Airborne Division. *Time* reported that the General, who is a short, heavy-set man, is not interested in golf or polo, preferring hunting and fishing for diversion. For film entertainment he enjoys comedies and westerns. "He does not smoke," continued the description, "but takes an occasional drink." His "strong" language, it is reported, is infrequent and mild. He is a Mason (32d Degree, Knight Templar, and Shriner).

References

N Y Herald Tribune II p1 Jl 16 '50
Time 56:18 Jl 31 '50
U S News 29:38 Ag 4 '50
Who's Who in America, 1950-51

WALTARI, MIKA (TOIMI) (väl'tä-rĭ mĭ-kȧ toi-mĭ) Sept. 19, 1908- Author
Address: Tunturikatu 13, Helsinki, Finland

Mika Waltari's novel, *The Egyptian*, met with such popular success in the United States when its English translation appeared in August 1949 that it held a top position in the list of fiction best sellers into 1950. This well-authenticated and at the same time highly dramatic and colorful re-creation of an ancient era had already had a million-copy sale in Europe in the five years after its publication in 1945. It is the first of its author's many works to be made available in English.

The son of the Reverend Toimi Armes and Olga Maria (Johansson) Waltari, Mika Toimi Waltari was born in Helsinki, Finland, on September 19, 1908; his forebears, traced back to the early seventeenth century, had tilled the soil until his grandfather, losing his farm, went to the capital city and became a bricklayer. Waltari's imaginative and narrative gifts were early evident: while still at high school in the city of his birth, reported *Book-of-the-Month Club News*, he was "known as a poet, and had also tossed off two mystery novels, one of which, later produced by the writer as a joke, won first prize in the Scandinavian detective story competition" some fourteen years later.

Graduated from secondary school in 1926, Waltari entered Helsinki University as a theological student, but was not to follow in the footsteps of his pastor-schoolmaster father. Finding himself in what has been described as "almost revolutionary disagreement with his background," he changed to the philosophy course. In 1927 he went to Paris, where, freed from bourgeois constraint, he joined a group of young literary radicals who called themselves "The Torch Bearers" and wrote his first published novel, *Suuri illusioni* ("The Grand Illusion"—not related to the motion picture of the same name). This work, issued in Finland in 1928, was an immediate popular success and was soon translated into Swedish, Norwegian, and Estonian.

The author returned to Helsinki University to complete requirements for the Master of Arts degree, which he received in 1929; two years of wandering through Europe and the Middle East followed. In 1931 Waltari married and went to work in Finland for his publisher, Werner Söderström, as a translator and publicity man. Two years later (1933) another widely read Waltari novel, the title of which may be rendered as "The Orange Seed," appeared; an exposure of the author's "own generation, its wildness, its seeking, its unformulated desires, its disappointments," it won the National Literary Prize of Finland the following year.

During five years as a publisher's assistant, Waltari penned numerous poems, fairy stories, novels, and dramatic works, many of which, he himself admits, were not of first literary quality. At the same time, however, he was becoming increasingly engrossed in Finnish history and was already doing research for what has been called his "first great masterpiece," the three-volume historical novel *Vieras mies tuli taloon* ("From Father to Son"). This work appeared in 1937, one year after its author had been appointed editor of Finland's principal illustrated weekly, *Suomen Kuvalehti*; translated into fourteen languages, and later filmed, it brought its author the National Literary Prize. Meanwhile, on the lookout for a suitable new historical theme "with significance applicable to modern times," Waltari had been attracted to the figure of the Egyptian Pharaoh Akhnaton, prophet of "a single just God . . . to replace the corrupted gods of the entrenched political priests." The ruler was made the central figure of a drama, *Akhnaton*, written in 1937 and performed at the National Theatre in Helsinki in 1938. *Akhnaton* is but one of Waltari's fifteen works for the stage, most of them of the "strong and dramatic" character, and two of which have brought their author the Finnish Literary Society's dramatic prize.

When the Russo-Finnish war broke out in late 1939, Waltari resigned his editorship of *Suomen Kuvalehti*, volunteered for service.

and was assigned to the State Information Bureau. Outstanding among his wartime novels are: *Kaarina Maununtytär* ("Karen, Daughter of Magnus"), an historical romance which appeared in 1942 and was translated into Swedish, Danish, German, and French; and the now famous *Sinuhe, egyptiläinen*, published in Finland in 1945, and in the United States in August 1949 as *The Egyptian*.

With the appearance of Naomi Walford's translation of *The Egyptian* in America, Waltari's name became familiar to a transatlantic public. This work (abbreviated by about one third in its translation), on which the author had been doing intermittent research ever since he first became interested in the times and circle of Akhnaton, has been described as "a story of Egypt, its religious, political and everyday life, a thousand years before Christ," the chief character and narrator being "Sinuhe, the physician . . . whose fate it is to live amongst the lowly and the high born, to travel to far lands—Syria and Crete—to be the friend of Pharaohs and to end his days in exile." According to the 1947 *Finland Year Book*, its author's countrymen viewed it not only as "a historical novel in luxurious Renaissance style," but also as a covert "description of our own unhappy time, marked by deep disillusion," with parallels to World War II. The book, which was praised by Egyptologists for the authenticity of its background, was an instant success, and is said to have sold about a million copies in editions in eight European languages; its successor, *Mikael Karvajalka* (1948), an historical novel with a sixteenth century European setting, had already been published in Finland before *The Egyptian* reached bookstores in the United States in the late summer of 1949.

When *The Egyptian* was chosen by the Book-of-the-Month Club for its September choice, the board of that organization advised members not to select a substitute title—"to read this book is to become lost in a new world." In the book reviewing columns *The Egyptian* received a somewhat "mixed press." Gladys Schmitt wrote in the New York *Times* that "many of the incidents are sensational and unbelievable, and at best the characters are types"; while the *Library Journal* felt that the book was "detailed to the point of surfeit." Edmund Fuller, on the other hand, declared in the *Saturday Review of Literature* that "we see, feel, smell, and taste Waltari's Egypt"; and the *Christian Science Monitor* found that the book "displays unusual fluidity of treatment and largeness of concept." Thomas Sugrue predicted in the New York *Herald Tribune* that American readers would enjoy *The Egyptian*, since "it contains the ingredients which they relish—war, women, intrigue, romance, wassail, horror, and lavish scenes of violence, indulgence, suffering and death." The novel headed the American fiction best-seller lists almost immediately and maintained first place into 1950 in the *Times* compilation of best sellers.

Waltari has been a member of the board of directors of the Finnish Writers' Association since 1930, was its vice-president from 1938

MIKA WALTARI

to 1942, and is executive secretary of the P.E.N. Club of Finland and secretary of the preliminary general committee for the Congress of Scandinavian Authors. The Finnish writer's wife is the former Marjatta Luukkonen, daughter of an army officer; they have a daughter, who is sixteen in 1950. "Constantly studying and writing, he has little time for social affairs," stated the *Book-of-the-Month Club News*. "He has a special interest in modern art; in his house are many paintings by young Finnish artists."

References

Book-of-the-Month Club N p6-7 S '49 por
Sat R Lit 32:10 Ag 20 '49 por
Author's and Writer's Who's Who (1948-49)
Vem och Vad (1948)
World Biography (1948)

WARD, BARBARA (MARY) May 23, 1914- Editor; journalist
Address: b. c/o The Economist, 22 Ryder St., St. James, London, S.W.1, England; h. 208 Cranmer Ct., London, S.W.3, England

Barbara Ward, who was cited as "one of the most widely read and most influential persons in the entire Western world," when she received an honorary LL.D. degree from Smith College, Northampton, Massachusetts, in October 1949, has been the foreign editor of the British weekly *Economist* since 1940. A governor of the British Broadcasting Corporation since 1946, and a former member of its celebrated *Brain Trust* discussion panel, Miss Ward is known to Americans as a lecturer not only on economic topics but on the role of Catholicism in the modern world. She is also the author of the book *The West at Bay* (1948), in which she

BARBARA WARD

advocates formation of a Western European economic union. The *Economist,* founded by James Wilson in 1843, and controlled since 1928 by a syndicate including Brendan Bracken '41, is regarded as ranking with the financial pages of the *Times* of London and *Manchester Guardian* in authority on subjects within its sphere.

The eldest daughter of Walter and Teresa Mary (Burge) Ward, Barbara Mary Ward was born May 23, 1914, in York, England, but was brought up in the Suffolk seaside town of Felixstowe, near Ipswich, where her father practiced as a solicitor. He is said to "incline" toward the Quaker creed; his wife, however, is a devout Roman Catholic; and their children were brought up in the mother's faith. Barbara Ward accordingly received her early education at the neighboring Convent of Jesus and Mary. At the age of fourteen, she has told, she wrote a two-hundred-thousand-word novel "about two wonderful countesses of seventeenth century France." ("I have a horrible facility with words," she comments.) At fifteen she was sent to Paris for two years of study at the Lycée Molière and at the Sorbonne, and at seventeen to Germany for a year at a college in Jugenheim. In 1932, when she was eighteen, she entered Somerville College, Oxford, as an exhibitioner, and three years later took a "first" in "Modern Greats," the equivalent to a *summa cum laude* Bachelor's degree in politics, philosophy and economics.

Gifted with a "pleasant soprano voice," Miss Ward at first looked forward to a musical career, and at Somerville was a member of the operatic society and of a madrigals group, as well as secretary of the dramatic society; she was also considered a good fencer and rider. When the time came to leave Oxford, however, she decided to make music her recreation rather than her vocation, and accepted a postgraduate Vernon Harcourt scholarship which enabled her

for the next three years to spend most of her summers abroad, studying conditions in several countries, among them Italy and Austria, while giving university extension lectures during the winters to workers' groups. In 1938 appeared her first book, a brief study of the colonial question entitled *The International Share-Out,* which attracted the attention of Geoffrey Crowther, editor of the *Economist.* He invited her to contribute articles on foreign affairs to that periodical; and in 1939 she joined the regular staff of the weekly. Miss Ward supplied the chapter on Yugoslavia in the anthology entitled *Hitler's Route to Baghdad,* published in 1939, the year she visited Turkey, where her brother was an engineer. A result of this trip was her book *Turkey* (1941), which was praised by the *Manchester Guardian* as giving "a real insight into what the social changes of the last twenty years have meant"; later the *New Yorker* was to find it "marred by . . . a rather idealized view of Kemal Ataturk."

Appointed foreign editor of the *Economist* in 1940, Miss Ward became in the same year an enthusiastic crusader for the Sword of the Spirit movement initiated by the late Cardinal J. H. Hinsley, the aim of which she has defined as "to remind English Catholics of the fifth precept of Pope Pius' encyclical which inveighed against the division of the world into have and have-not nations." Further objectives include "abolition of extreme inequality in wealth, equal education for all children, safeguarding the family as a social unit and providing man with a sense of divine vocation." Miss Ward was honorary secretary of the movement from 1940 to 1943, the full tenure permissible. A co-author of the book *A Christian Basis for the Post-War World* (1941), she also contributed numerous articles on this liberal Catholic activity to such periodicals as the *Dublin Review, Blackfriars,* and *America,* and was a lecturer on its behalf, as well as on economic and labor topics. Her writings on various aspects in those fields have also appeared in *Atlantic Monthly, Harper's Magazine, Foreign Affairs,* and the New York *Times Magazine.*

Attached to the British Ministry of Information during World War II, Miss Ward made her first visit to the United States in late 1942, to lecture—her topics were "The Sword of the Spirit", "Democracy and Christianity in Britain," and kindred themes; and in the following year visited Sweden. Toward the end of 1943 she joined the staff of the British Broadcasting Corporation; she was heard on *Brain Trust,* a discussion feature resembling both the *American Forum of the Air* and *Information, Please.* A British newspaper poll in 1944 rated her "second in popularity among the nation's public speakers." Early in 1945 she toured the Belgian bases of the Second Tactical Air Force, organizing discussion groups; and later in the year, as a member of the Labor party, she campaigned against the Churchill Government. Miss Ward, whose socialism is described as "mitigated" by her "strong Catholicism," is, she declares, "a believer in planned economy with more thought for the content of policy, for its purpose and therefore for priorities, than for structure."

Barbara Ward's appointment, in September 1946 as a governor (the youngest) of BBC entailed her withdrawal from broadcasting, although she still appears on the lecture platform. During a considerable part of 1947 Miss Ward was again in the United States, studying trends of American opinion and making numerous addresses, notably on *America's Town Meeting of the Air* on March 13, when she debated the question "What Should Be Our Role in Greece and Turkey?" and at the New York *Herald Tribune* Forum on October 22, when her speech was "Catholicism in World Order." Her book, *The West at Bay*, published in America in September 1948, pleading for the establishment of "a unified free-trade area from Scandinavia to the Pyrenees, from the Elbe to Donegal" as the basis of a bulwark against Communist ideological as well as material expansion, was hailed by Orville Prescott in the New York *Times* as "informed, intelligent and enlightening," and by Lewis Gannett in the *Herald Tribune* as "important and impressive."

In October and November 1949, Miss Ward again visited the United States, primarily to receive an honorary LL.D. from Smith College; in her acceptance address at Northampton, Massachusetts, on October 30, she pressed for "American investment in world stability on an heroic scale" instead of "homeopathetic doses of fifteen million dollars." When she addressed the New York State Chamber of Commerce some days later, Miss Ward predicted that at least ten years would elapse before the recently devalued pound sterling would become freely convertible into dollars; and she "chided" the British government for failure to carry the Cripps austerity program "far enough." Taxation in Britain, she maintained, had reached levels which were disincentives. (She and Clare Boothe Luce are the only women who have addressed that chamber of commerce in almost two centuries.) Again a participant in the *Herald Tribune* Forum, she spoke on the subject "Partnership for Survival" at the 1949 gathering. Miss Ward was a member of the council of the Royal Institute of International Affairs in 1943-44, and was appointed a governor of Sadler's Wells-Old Vic trust in 1945.

Pictured in *Newsweek* as "a sprightly brown-eyed woman with short brown hair" and by Wambly Bald in the New York *Post* as "radiant and unaffected as a schoolgirl at a picnic," the foreign editor of the *Economist*, who is of medium height, dresses simply, wears little jewelry, does not play cards or smoke, and drinks only "a very occasional glass of wine." "She writes fast," states the author of a profile in the London *News Review*, "drafting articles in pencil, because she cannot type or dictate. She has a host of friends, mostly politicians, diplomats, scientists and intellectuals. Strongly allergic to bores and purely social functions, she likes good food, riding, music, and Jane Austen." Her London home is a "tiny flat" in Chelsea; weekends she usually spends with her parents in Suffolk, where she may bicycle or work in the garden. In mid-

November 1950 Miss Ward was married to Commander Robert G. A. Jackson of Australia, formerly an Assistant Secretary General of the United Nations.

References

N Y Herald Tribune X p26 O 26 '47
    por; X p59 O 30 '49 por
N Y Post Mag p27 My 26 '47 por
N Y World-Telegram Ap 26 '48 por
News R (London) O 21 '48
Newsweek 25:59 Ap 7 '47 por
Author's and Writer's Who's Who
    (1948-49)
Hoehn, M. A. ed. Catholic Authors,
    1930-47
International Who's Who, 1949
Who's Who, 1949
World Biography (1948)

WARNER, J(OHN) C(HRISTIAN) May 28, 1897- College president; chemist
Address: c/o Carnegie Institute of Technology, Schenley Park, Pittsburgh 13, Pa.; h. 650 Morewood Ave., Pittsburgh 13, Pa.

Upon the retirement of Dr. Robert E. Doherty [49] on July 1, 1950, from the presidency of the Carnegie Institute of Technology, Dr. J. C. Warner succeeded him in that office. A member of the faculty since 1926, head of the chemistry department since 1938, dean of graduate studies since 1945, assistant director since 1947 of the College of Engineering and Science, and vice-president during 1949-50, Warner, the fourth president of the institute, is the first to be appointed from the staff. During a two-year wartime leave, while assigned to the Manhattan Project, he was engaged in directing and coordinating research on the purification of plutonium, a vital contribution to the development of the atomic bomb. Educator, scientist, administrator, and author in the field of chemistry, he in 1945 was given the Pittsburgh Award for his services by the Pittsburgh section of the American Chemical Society, one of many professional organizations he has served as an officer.

John Christian Warner was born on a farm near Goshen, Indiana, on May 28, 1897, to Elias and Addie (Plank) Warner, the second of their four sons. On his father's side he is a descendant of a German who left that country in 1847 and with many of his countrymen settled in the Indiana farming district. His mother's family were pioneers of English, French Huguenot, and Pennsylvania Dutch colonial stock.

After his graduation from Goshen High School in 1915, John Warner, influenced by his mother (who had been a country schoolteacher) and drawn by his own love of science, entered Indiana University. He received the B.A. degree in 1919; then, specializing in physical chemistry, received the M.A. and Ph.D. degrees in 1919 and 1923, respectively. His extracurricular activities were varied: he won letters in wrestling and football, became a member of Phi Kappa Phi, Tau Beta Pi, Delta Upsilon, Alpha Chi Sigma, Sigma Xi, and Phi Beta

J. C. WARNER

Kappa. In the course of his student years he was employed as a chemist with the Barrett Company in Philadelphia (1918), with the Cosden Company in Tulsa, Oklahoma (1919-21), and as an instructor at Indiana University (1921-24). After he received his doctorate, he was a research chemist at the Wayne Chemicals Corporation, at Fort Wayne, Indiana, during 1925-26. Some years later (1933) he took post-doctorate work at the University of Michigan.

Warner joined the faculty of Carnegie Institute of Technology in 1926, as an instructor in chemistry. In the twenty-four years preceding his elevation to its presidency, he was successively, assistant professor of chemistry (1928-33), associate professor of theoretical chemistry (1933-36), associate professor of metallurgy (1936-38), and since 1938 professor of chemistry and head of the department of chemistry. In addition to these titles, in 1945, when the institute expanded its graduate program, Dr. Warner was appointed dean of graduate studies in the College of Engineering and Science, and in 1947 the assistant director of that college. On June 9, 1949, he was named vice-president and president-elect; on July 1, 1950, he took office, and on October 27 he was officially inaugurated. As president of Carnegie Institute of Technology, which was established and endowed by Andrew Carnegie in 1900, Warner will carry on the "Carnegie Plan" of professional education, which was initiated by Dr. Doherty. Warner had contributed to the development of the program.

Warner, as one of America's distinguished scientists, in 1943 was selected to direct and coordinate research on the purification of plutonium. This highly confidential work (with the wartime Manhattan Project) on the development of the atomic bomb was carried on in the laboratories of several universities and at Los Alamos, New Mexico. Later, he assisted in the operation of the Clinton Laboratories at Oak Ridge, Tennessee. His work as research chemist is summarized in *American Men of Science* as "kinetics of reactions in solutions; vapor-liquid equilibrium and heats of mixing in nonelectrolytic solutions; acid-base properties of mixed solvents; kinetics and equilibrium in gas carbonization of austenite; and equilibrium and rates in corrosion of metals."

The chemist is a member of the physical science advisory committee to the Brookhaven National Laboratory and a consultant to the Argonne National Laboratory. He is a founding member of the Pennsylvania Chemical Society; served as vice-president (1939-40) and president (1940-41) of the Pittsburgh Chemists Club; was chairman of the Pittsburgh section of the Electrochemical Society in 1937 and in 1949 became vice-president and a member of the board of directors of that society. Dr. Warner was a counselor during 1937-40 and in 1948 became a director at large of the American Chemical Society; in 1941 he was chairman of that society's Pittsburgh section (the largest section), which in 1945 honored him with its Pittsburgh Award for his work in chemistry. He is a member also of the American Institute of Mining and Metallurgical Engineers, American Society for Engineering Education, and a fellow of the New York Academy of Science. His clubs are the Duquesne and University (Pittsburgh) and the Cosmos (Washington).

The author of some fifty scientific and technical papers in the fields of physical chemistry and electrochemistry, Dr. Warner is also co-author of textbooks which have gone into several editions—*General Chemistry* and *Experimental General Chemistry*; he contributed to *General Chemistry Problems*, a laboratory work-book. In 1942 he served as editor on the rewriting (done by members of Carnegie's chemistry staff) of Leighou's *Chemistry of Engineering Materials*.

On June 17, 1925, John Christian Warner married Louise Hamer, who had been a student in a qualitative analysis class which Warner taught at Indiana University in his post-graduate days. Before her marriage Mrs. Warner was a high school teacher. In the Warner family there are two sons, William Hamer and Thomas Payton. During summer months the Warners like to swim and fish at a lakeside resort. Both Dr. and Mrs. Warner are enthusiastic golf players. His indoor pastimes are listening to music and reading in nonscientific fields, one of which is economics, his minor subject at college. The color of his hair and eyes is brown; he is five feet five inches in height, weighs 190 pounds. He is often seen smoking a plain, medium-stem pipe.

References

American Men of Science (1949)
Who's Who in America, 1950-51
Who's Who in American Education, 1947-48
World Biography (1948)

WARREN, SHIELDS Feb. 26, 1898-
Pathologist

Address: b. c/o Atomic Energy Commission, Division of Biology and Medicine, 1901 Constitution Ave., Washington 25, D.C.; h. 301 Otis St., West Newton 65, Mass.

Dr. Shields Warren, professor of pathology at Harvard Medical School, was appointed the director of the Division of Biology and Medicine of the United States Atomic Energy Commission in 1947. Under his supervision is carried out the research in the treatment of malignant diseases with radioactive materials, notably at Oak Ridge National Laboratory. Warren was chief of the medical team of the United States Navy's technical mission to Japan in 1945 and an officer of the Naval Medical Section at the Bikini tests in 1946.

Born in Cambridge, Massachusetts, on February 26, 1898, Shields Warren is the son of William Marshall and Sara Bainbridge (Shields) Warren. Reared in near-by Brookline, Shields attended the town's high school. He obtained his B.A. degree in 1918 from Boston University and his M.D. in 1923 from Harvard Medical School, where he was a member of Phi Beta Kappa.

From 1923 to 1925 he filled his first appointment, as first assistant in pathology in the laboratory of Boston City Hospital. In 1925 he joined the faculty of the Harvard Medical School, where he was, successively, instructor in pathology (1925-36), assistant professor in pathology (1936-48), and since 1948 a full professor. In addition he has been pathologist at the New England Deaconess Hospital since 1927; and has served in a similar capacity at the New England Baptist Hospital, the Huntington Memorial Hospital, and the Pondville State Hospital. He is, too, consulting pathologist at the House of the Good Samaritan and the Channing Home and was director of the State Tumor Diagnosis Service for Massachusetts. *American Men of Science* lists his fields as pathology of endocrine diseases, pathologic aspects of tumors, and biologic effect of ionizing radiation.

Pathologist Warren joined the United States Naval Reserve in 1943 with the rank of captain. He served also as an expert consultant to the Surgeon General on the scientific advisory board of the Army Institute of Pathology. In March 1946 *Time* stated that Warren ("the crack pathologist of the United States Naval Technical Mission to Japan") had confirmed that far more of the atom-bomb casualties at Hiroshima and Nagasaki came from the explosion's X-ray-like radiations than from the bomb itself. The pathologist attributed the second biggest cause of fatalities to flash burns from the blinding "atom light"—as bright "as though you had stepped up the intensity of the sun."

In 1947 when Congress appropriated $5,000,000 for cancer research to be carried on by the Atomic Energy Commission, an advisory committee of physicians chose Warren as director of the newly created Division of Biology and Medicine because of his extensive research work in malignant diseases. Since Warren's

Alfred Brown

SHIELDS WARREN

association with the Atomic Energy Commission, much has been learned about the handling of fissionable material in the treatment of diseases with radio isotopes. In August 1949 he ranked radioactive iodine first in usefulness, cobalt second, and phosphorous third. He added that radioactive arsenic for the treatment of bone cancer "looked promising." Cobalt, he ventured to say, might well supersede radium. Although the cost of cobalt varies from "one five-hundredth to one one-thousandth of that of radium," its "brief half life" precludes its shipment for use and makes it necessary for patients to travel to the clinic. The atomic laboratory at Oak Ridge (Tennessee), in addition to making cobalt, is developing new types of isotopes used in cancer treatment. These, boron, oxygen, flourine, and aluminum, like cobalt, have a "brief half life" and cannot be transported. The first group of selected patients was brought to the center for treatment with "perishable" atomic materials in the spring of 1950.

"A unique step in itself," was the opening of public hearings on March 17, 1950, on information given to the Joint Congressional Committee on Atomic Energy on the country's civil defense program against atomic attack. William S. White of the New York *Times* (March 18, 1950) reported that Warren, as director of the Division of Biology and Medicine, told the committee that "there was no ground for fears that an atomic blast would cause widespread sterility or other debilities." He pointed out that the birth rate in Hiroshima and Nagasaki had not fallen and there was "no unusual rate of abnormality among children born since then." "Great emphasis," he said, was being placed on the usefulness of antibiotics such as penicillin and streptomycin to "eliminate so far as possible secondary effects produced by overwhelming infections." The

WARREN, SHIELDS—*Continued*

public hearing revealed also that Warren's division had developed a new radiation meter costing only $10 or $15 (when produced commercially) in contrast with the $200 cost of a Geiger counter.

Dr. Warren is the author of *Medical Science for Everyday Use* (1927), *The Pathology of Diabetes Mellitus* (1930, 1938), *Introduction to Neuropathology* (with Dr. Samuel P. Hicks), *A Handbook for the Diagnosis of Cancer of the Uterus* (with Dr. Olive Gates, 1947, 1948, 1950), and of numerous articles contributed to the medical press. In 1949 Warren was awarded the honorary doctorate of science by Boston University and in April 1950 the annual citation of the Massachusetts Division of the American Cancer Society. He is a member and former vice-president of the American Association for the Advancement of Science, an ex-president of the American Society for Experimental Pathology; a member of the American Association for Cancer Research, (president, 1942-46), and a member of the American Association of Pathologists and Bacteriologists, (president in 1948). A member of the American Medical Association, he also belongs to the American Society of Clinical Pathologists and the Society of Experimental Biology and Medicine. He served on the Scientific Advisory Board of the National Cancer Institute during 1946-49, has been chairman of the subcommittee on oncology of the National Research Council since 1948, and a member of its atomic casualty commission, and is a trustee of Boston University.

The doctor's clubs are the Cosmos, Harvard, and Waquoit Yacht. His church is the Methodist. On August 11, 1923 he married Alice Springfield. They and their two children, Alice Emilie and Patricia, live in West Newton. Dr. Warren is described as having a scholarly appearance and as speaking "calmly and dryly."

References

American Men of Science (1949)
Who's Who in America, 1950-51
Who's Who in New England (1949)

WASON, ROBERT R(OSS) (wä'sŭn) May 1, 1888—July 7, 1950 American industrial executive; began as a laborer; for several years vice-president of the Proctor and Collier advertising agency in Cincinnati; president of Manning, Maxwell and Moore, Inc., New York engineering firm, since 1931; active member of the National Association of Manufacturers and its president for 1946; credited with innovations in merchandising methods and sales techniques. See *Current Biography*, 1946.

Obituary

N Y Times p13 Jl 8 '50

WATKINS, ARTHUR V(IVIAN) Dec. 18, 1886- United States Senator from Utah *Address*: b. Senate Office Bldg., Washington, D.C.; h. 1433 N. Inglewood St., Arlington, Va.; Orem, Utah

Utah's junior United States Senator, Arthur V. Watkins, a Republican, was elected to the Senate for his first term in 1946. His activities in politics prior to his election had included membership on the platform committee of the Republican National Convention in 1944. A lawyer by profession, Watkins practiced in h s home, where he was Judge for the Fourth Judicial District from 1928 to 1933. From 1919 to 1932 he was manager of commercial orchards and a turkey farm in the northern part of the State.

Arthur Vivian Watkins was born December 18, 1886, in Midway, Utah, where he lived during most of his childhood. One of six children (three boys and three girls), he is the son of Arthur and Emily A. (Gerber) Watkins. His father (of English descent) and his mother (of Swiss descent) were children of Mormon pioneers who had come from Europe to settle in Utah. There Arthur Watkins, the father, became a rancher and carpenter until his retirement, at which time he moved to Los Angeles, where he now lives. Watkins has commented of his childhood in the small community, located in the Wasatch mountains, that his "first associations were with the rugged pioneer life of the time, Indians, saw mills, logging, hunting and fishing; with the toil of homesteading."

The boy's early education was obtained in his home State at Uintah High School, in Vernal, and at Brigham Young High School, in Provo. Upon his graduation in 1904, Watkins attended Brigham Young University to study political science. While there, he was a member of the State champion basketball team. In 1907 he went to New York City, where he was a missionary for the Latter Day Saints Church until 1909. He enrolled at New York University and Columbia University for postgraduate work, and received the LL.B. degree from the latter in 1912.

That year Watkins was admitted to the bar in the State of Utah, and set up his law practice. In 1914 he became editor of the Vernal *Express*. Soon after assuming the editorship, he became assistant county attorney of Salt Lake County, a post he filled until 1915. From 1919 until 1932 Watkins was manager of commercial orchards and a turkey farm in Lehi and Orem communities, northern Utah. During this period Watkins took an increasingly active interest in politics, and in 1928 he was elected to the post of Judge for the Fourth Judicial District in Utah; he remained in this office until 1933. The lawyer also served as Commissioner of the Utah State Bar.

As chairman of a committee to organize water users in central Utah, Watkins in 1934 helped establish the Provo River Water Users Association, sponsoring agent for the Provo River Reclamation Project. Since that time he has acted as general counsel for the association. The year after becoming a judge, Watkins had been appointed to the office of president of Sharon Stake, Latter Day Saints Church (Mormon) at Orem; this position, the function of which is the spiritual supervision of seven parishes (wards), he continued to fill until 1946.

Watkins won the Republican nomination for Congress in 1936, but was defeated in the final election by a narrow margin. He was not again a candidate for public office until he ran in the Senatorial election in 1946 for the term of 1947-52. This contest he won. His election to the Senate marked a victory for the Republican party, as he succeeded New Dealer Abe Murdock. In 1944 Watkins had been a member of the platform committee of the Republican National Convention.

The Republican Senator from Utah took his seat in January 1947, in the second session of the Seventy-ninth Congress. His record there has shown support of the large majority of planks in the Republican party platform and also support of its leaders. At the first session of the Eightieth Congress Watkins was assigned to the Public Lands and Public Works committees, and the Joint Committee of the Economic Report. In the second session he again sat on the Public Works Committee and was a member of the Interior and Insular Affairs Committee, on both of which he continued to serve throughout the Eighty-first Congress, as on the Joint Committee of the Economic Report. Subcommittees on which Watkins has served include the Indian Affairs (chairman), the Irrigation and Reclamation, and the Public Roads.

A stormy protest marked the early stages of Watkins' Senatorial service, when he opposed President Truman's appointment of former Senator Murdock to the National Labor Relations Board. As Murdock's successor in the Senate, he voiced his opposition to the appointment in a statement that his objection was "impersonal and nonpolitical" and was based solely on Murdock's "prolabor record and associations which made him unfit to administer the Taft-Hartley Law." The simultaneous appointments of Murdock and J. Copeland Gray were confirmed by a majority vote of the Senate, overriding Watkins' protest.

Another issue on which Watkins took a stand in 1947 was rent control. With Senators Williams (Delaware) and Wherry (Nebraska) he sponsored a bill which would end OPA operations by April 30 of that year, leaving it optional for each State to enforce rent control. Later when rent control bills reached the floor of the Senate for a vote, Watkins voted against a twelve-month extension of the bill as opposed to an extension of eight months, and he voted for a 15 per cent rent increase, optional with tenants. When the rent control issue again came before the Senate in 1949, the Utah Senator resumed his stand in voting for the measure that provided for State option on rent controls.

Senator Watkins urged that reservations be set on the provisos of the North Atlantic Treaty, contending that as it stood the pact deprived Congress of the right to decide whether or not it would declare war in the event of an attack on an ally. Though not a member of the Senate Foreign Relations Committee, Watkins was permitted by Chairman Tom Connally '49

Wide World Photos
ARTHUR V. WATKINS

to interrogate the witnesses called by the committee to discuss the Atlantic Pact. During the course of the hearings, Watkins, accused of presenting his own views rather than eliciting those of the witnesses, quit the sessions, charging that Connally had not permitted him to question the witnesses adequately. When the Foreign Relations Committee gave unanimous endorsement to the pact, Watkins called for a publication of the bill sixty days before signing and full debate. However, he was overruled, and the pact reached the Senate in less than two weeks. At that time Senators Watkins, Taft, and Wherry took firm stands against it, proposing three reservations, all of which were defeated. The reservations would have: denied any pledge to give military supplies, including the atom bomb, to other nations; renounced any obligation to use United States armed forces without the approval of Congress; declared that Congress assumed no obligation to declare war if another Atlantic Pact country was attacked. Final ratification of the treaty without reservations was made by a vote of 82 to 13, with Watkins voting against it.

In 1949 Watkins voted in favor of Federal aid to education; an antisegregation amendment to the housing bill; a cut in Labor-Federal Security Funds of 5 per cent; and a proposal to cut the European Recovery Program by 10 per cent. He opposed establishing a Department of Welfare; the arms aid bill; confirmation of Leland S. Olds to the Federal Power Commission; an amendment for mandatory price support at 90 per cent of partity on basic farm crops (he voted for the compromise farm bill). Early in January 1950 Senator Watkins joined Senator Wherry in expressing opposition to continued support of bipartisan foreign policy. When several Republican Senators urged caution in the Korean crisis, the Utah Senator questioned the policy of giving mili-

WATKINS, ARTHUR V.—*Continued*

tary aid to countries threatened by attacks from Communists; he believed it showed a false reliance on arms. Watkins is one of the fifteen members on the Senatorial committee on the formulation of Republican party policy headed by Senator Taft.

Watkins married Andrea Rich on June 18, 1913. Their children are Nedra (Mrs. Thomas W. Reese), Arthur Rich, Venna May (Mrs. Carl Swalberg), Jeanene, and Nina Ilean. (Two other children are deceased.) The Senator stands five feet ten inches, weighs 175 pounds, has brown eyes and a shock of gray hair. Two recreations of the legislator are softball and fishing; and he belongs to the Rotary and Lions clubs.

References

Congressional Directory (1950)
Who's Who in America, 1950-51
Who's Who in the West (1949)

WATSON, THOMAS J(OHN) Feb. 17, 1874- Industrialist

Address: c/o International Business Machines Corp., 590 Madison Ave., New York 22; Endicott, N.Y.; h. 4 E. 75th St., New York 21; New Canaan, Conn.

NOTE: This biography supersedes the article which appeared in *Current Biography* in 1940.

Thomas J. Watson, chairman of the board of the International Business Machines Corporation, began his career at the age of seventeen as a bookkeeper in a small-town store. After fifteen years' association with the National Cash Register Company, in 1913 he joined, as president, the Computing-Tabulating-Recording Company, which became the International Business Machines Corporation, the world's foremost manufacturers of complex mechanical devices used for commercial records. Watson is known for his activity in the cause of world peace and for his patronage of art, education, and other aspects of public welfare.

Born in Campbell, New York, on February 17, 1874, Thomas John Watson is the son of Thomas and Jane (White) Watson. The elder Watson, a lumber dealer, urged his son to study law after the latter's graduation from the Addison (New York) Academy. Young Watson, however, eager to begin "paying his own way," took a year's course at the Elmira (New York) School of Commerce. Then, employed in a store at Painted Post, New York, which sold pianos, sewing machines, and organs, he replaced its haphazard bookkeeping methods with the ledger system. At the age of nineteen he entered the business machine field as a sales agent for a cash register company.

A few years later, in 1898, Watson entered upon a fifteen-year association with the National Cash Register Company as a member of the staff of its Buffalo sales office. With that firm he progressed to be sales manager of the Rochester branch, special representative, and eventually general sales manager. His contact with John Henry Patterson, president of the company, impressed upon him the philosophy of the "company spirit," of which Patterson has been called the "original apostle." One anecdote of Watson's early days at National Cash Register (as related in the *Saturday Evening Post,* May 24, 1941) tells how he was "fortified with certain tried and true homilies" when discouraged at initial lack of success in selling. To this incident is attributed the future IBM chief's faith in maxims as a means of stimulating employees. Today IBM's factory and office walls carry many framed exhortations such as "Aim High", "Sell and Serve," and "Think." Watson's employment at National Cash Register ended in 1913 as the result of a disagreement with the firm's president over an antitrust law issue.

Upon leaving National Cash Register thirty-nine-year-old Watson became president of the Computing-Tabulating-Recording Company, which in 1924 changed its name to International Business Machines Corporation. It had been formed in 1911 as a holding company controlling four business-machines manufacturers: the Bundy Manufacturing Company and the International Time Recording Company (both makers of time clocks), the Computing Scale Company of America, and the Tabulating Machine Company. One of Watson's first steps as president was to obtain loans large enough to finance expansion. The increase in the company's gross sales from two million in 1914 to more than thirty-three and a quarter million in 1949 has been largely attributed to the president's "ingenuity in creating new markets, perfecting of educational-sales technique, and stubborn strength for hard work" (*Saturday Evening Post*). The personnel in the same period increased from 235 to 12,000.

Wide World Photos

THOMAS J. WATSON

A basic IBM unit consists of three machines —the key punch, the card sorter, and the tabulator. Other products of the company include cost-recording and accounting machines, electrically operated typewriters, timing and alarm devices, an electric Chinese language typewriter which types 5,400 characters horizontally or vertically, and a calculator which performs computations in higher mathematics. About 1,400 patents (as of 1941) gave IBM a virtual world monopoly in its field. The main IBM factory is at Endicott, New York, where the corporation also maintains an engineering laboratory for research leading to improvements in its machines or services. Other plants are located at Washington, D.C., and at Rochester, New York.

Watson, who has been called "Salesman Number 1," stresses the importance of preparing a sales staff for maximum effectiveness. There is a training school for both mechanics and salesmen at Endicott, where the latter learn how to install, operate, and repair the IBM products, as a necessary step in learning how to sell them. Watson worked out the details of the three basic steps in the selling technique taught at Endicott—the approach, the demonstration, and the closing. The keynote of the IBM salesman's argument is that the company sells not machines, but service. The executive, who has begun to delegate much of the direct management of the business to the vice-president and general manager, has made a practice of frequent visits to Endicott; he addresses the "graduating classes" of the sales school and participates in the company's Endicott Civic Forum.

IBM is said to be a striking example of "one-man rule in business" (*Saturday Evening Post*). In 1934 the *Forbes* magazine cup for "the best job of modernization in American industry," was awarded to Watson's company. Laurence Bell, in an article in a 1948 issue of *Forbes,* declared that Watson had created "the nearest to ideal working conditions in the company." Starting at $1.25 an hour for qualified labor, average earnings of employees are approximately $3,500 annually. Piece work was abolished in the late 1930's. Welfare benefits include sick insurance, paying full salary for a maximum of six months; life insurance, increasing during first five years to $15,000, and thereafter to a maximum of $25,000; retirement pay, increasing to a maximum of $200 a month. The company maintains (at Endicott) a country club for all employees. Since 1927 IBM schools have trained thousands of machinists, customer-service men, and salesmen. Every salesman achieving 100 per cent of his quota becomes a member of the IBM "One Hundred Per Cent Club."

The company, which sells its products in seventy-nine countries, increased its foreign sales between 1938 and 1948 about 340 per cent. In September 1949 a single "wholly-owned subsidiary" company was formed of IBM international branches—IBM World Trade Corporation—and Watson was named chairman of its board. At the same time he became chairman of the board of directors of the parent company. His position in the top bracket of salaries in the United States is the result of the contract he made in 1913 when he joined the company. It calls for a specified percentage of net profits after the payment of a stated dividend on outstanding stock, in addition to salary. (The contract's terms in 1938 gave Watson 5 per cent of net profits, after payment of the dividend, and a salary of $100,000.) It has been estimated that, except during the years of World War II (when he refused to take his percentage of profits) the IBM president has averaged an annual income of $453,000 (figures from *Saturday Evening Post* and *Forbes*). He also serves on the boards of directors of a number of banks and insurance and real estate companies.

"World Peace through World Trade," is an IBM slogan coined by Watson. In 1939 as honorary president (he had been president in 1937) of the International Chamber of Commerce, chairman of its committee for economic reconstruction, chairman of the Inter-American Commercial Arbitration Commission, and as trustee of Carnegie Endowment for International Peace, he proposed that the Axis countries, Great Britain, France, and the United States "collaborate with their respective businessmen in a study of economic and financial conditions with respect to all countries sharing alike in world resources" as a means of preventing wars. The Captain Robert Dollar Memorial Award for 1940 was presented to Watson for his contribution to the advancement of American foreign trade, and that year he was cited during Court of Peace ceremonies at the New York World's Fair "for his important contributions to the laying of a solid foundation" for future world peace. The IBM chairman is a member of the American Friendship Committee, the Foreign Policy Association, Council on Foreign Relations, and a director of the American Association of the United Nations. In 1950 he was given the American Arbitration Association award.

Among Watson's numerous other interests (the listing of which fills almost two columns in *Who's Who in America*) is his patronage of art. Long a collector of art, he has a special interest in the work of American artists. In 1939, believing that "mutual benefit would result if the interest of business in art and of artists in business should be increased," he exhibited at the New York World's Fair and in the Golden Gate Exposition two sets of paintings by artists from seventy-nine foreign countries, which had been bought by IBM. President Roosevelt appointed Watson national director of the 1941 Art Week to encourage American painters. That year the IBM exhibit of foreign paintings at the New York World's Fair was replaced with a collection by American artists, which later was exhibited throughout the United States and in South America.

The industrialist's interests, as shown by his membership in a great many associations, also extends to the medical field, in which he encourages the development of the "eye bank" and research in arthritis; to religious education, in Sunday school and Bible class movements,

WATSON, THOMAS J.—*Continued*

Protestant welfare measures, the Salvation Army, and Christian-Jewish cooperation; to education, in the United Negro College fund, support of the Merchant Marine Library Association, aid in financing the development of the Massachusetts Institute of Technology, and serving as trustee of a number of universities and colleges; to young people's groups such as the YMCA, YWCA, the Boy and Girl Scouts.

For "meritorious service during World War II" the IBM chairman was given the United States Medal of Merit. Numerous decorations have been bestowed upon him by other countries—Great Britain, France, Italy, the Scandinavian countries, Finland, the Netherlands, Belgium, Greece, Luxembourg, Cambodia, and the Latin American countries. In 1940 Watson returned the Merit Cross of the German Eagle to Hitler, stating that the policies of the Nazi regime were contrary to the causes for which he (Watson) worked, and for which he had received the decoration.

Thomas J. Watson married Jeannette M. Kittredge on April 17, 1913. Their four children are Thomas John, Arthur Kittredge, Jane (Mrs. John Irwin 3d), and Helen Mary (Mrs. Walker G. Buckner). The two sons, who served in World War II, are now employed with IBM. The Watsons maintain a New York residence, and an estate at New Canaan, Connecticut. Among the clubs to which the industrialist belongs are the Explorers, Lotos, Metropolitan, River, the New York Yacht, and a number of country clubs in New York and Connecticut. His church is the Presbyterian. The tall, white-haired executive, who does not smoke or drink, is known for the conservatism of his dress and the dignity of his manner.

References

> Christian Sci Mon p15 My 24 '40 por
> Forbes p18 My 15 '48
> Fortune 21:36 Ja '40
> Newsweek 10:5 N 22 '37; 15:41 Je 17 '40
> Sat Eve Post p10 My 24 '41; p22 My 31 '41
> Time 27:73 Ap 20 '36; 35:57 Je 17 '40
> Business Executives of America (1950)
> Who's Who in America, 1950-51
> Who's Who in Commerce and Industry (1948)
> Who's Who in New York, 1947
> World Biography (1948)

WAVELL, ARCHIBALD (PERCIVAL), 1ST EARL   May 5, 1883—May 24, 1950

British field marshal; entered Black Watch Regiment in 1901; served in the South African War; on the Indian frontier; in World War I on the Western Front, 1914-16; as military attaché with the Russian Army in the Caucasus in 1916-17; with Egyptian Expeditionary Force 1917-20; commander of brigade, then of division, Aldershot, 1930-37; became general in 1940, field marshal in 1943; commander in chief of British troops in the Middle East, 1939-41; victor at Sidi Barrani, December 1940; defeated by General Rommel, 1941; assigned to supreme command of Allied forces in the Southwest Pacific in 1942; Viceroy and Governor General of India, 1943-47; made an earl in 1947; military writer of note: *The Palestine Campaigns* (1928), *Allenby: a Study in Greatness* (1940), *Generals and Generalship* (1941), *Allenby in Egypt* (1943); edited an anthology of verse, *Other Men's Flowers* (1944). See *Current Biography*, 1941.

Obituary

> N Y Times p29 My 25 '50 por

WEBB, MAURICE   Sept. 26, 1904- British Cabinet member

Address: b. c/o Ministry of Food, Dean Bradley House, Horseferry Rd., London, S. W. 1; h. Pinner, Middlesex, England

The Minister of Food in the Cabinet of Great Britain, Maurice Webb, is responsible for the formulation and regulation of the country's food-rationing plan. Until shortly after the general election of February 23, 1950, the Ministry of Food was headed by John Strachey.[46] Webb, whose appointment to the office was announced on February 28, had been prominent as a political journalist and radio commentator for more than fifteen years. He first sat as Labor member for the Central Bradford (Yorkshire) constituency in July 1945, and from 1946 to 1949 was chairman of the Parliamentary Labor party, the group of Laborites within Parliament. As the secretary (which he became in December 1949) he has been described as having "helped to plan Labor policy" in preparation for the 1950 general election campaign.

Maurice Webb, son of George and Annie Webb, was born in Lancaster, England, on September 26, 1904, and was educated at the local Christ Church School. He joined the Labor party as a youth and became a ward secretary a week afterward in his home town of Lancaster. Early in 1927 he moved to Skipton, Yorkshire, where he began full-time work for the Labor movement at the age of twenty-two, being appointed Labor agent there.

Two years later young Webb was summoned to London to become the first propaganda officer of the Labor party (he was to write numerous political pamphlets) and in 1931 he became a British Broadcasting Corporation commentator on labor and politics. The following year, at the request of the late Arthur Henderson (prominent British Labor leader), he took over the direction of a nation-wide drive to found a Labor League of Youth. Within five months he had succeeded in establishing 140 branches. In 1935 Webb joined the staff of his party's principal organ, the *Daily Herald*, as liaison officer between that newspaper and Labor party headquarters, and later became political correspondent, serving as such until 1944. During this span of nine years he was a member of the executive of the National Union of Journalists and member of the committee of the Parliamentary Press Gallery. He has held every office in the Parliamentary Lobby Journalists organization.

For reasons both of health and his value on the home front, Webb saw no military service in World War II. In April 1942 a speech he delivered at the annual conference of the National Union of Journalists, defending the part played by Home Secretary Herbert Morrison[40] in suppressing the London Communist newspaper *The Daily Worker*, made a deep impression and helped to cement an enduring personal as well as political association. During 1943 a sixty-four-page illustrated booklet, *Britain's Industrial Front*, describing the civilian war effort, which Webb wrote for the Government, was widely circulated. In the following year he joined the staff of the *Sunday Express* as a political commentator. He also did considerable home and overseas broadcasting, and was the first speaker, not a Member of Parliament, to give the *Week in Westminster* talk for the BBC.

In January 1945, Webb was chosen as prospective Labor candidate for the Central Bradford (Yorkshire) constituency; and in the July election was victorious in a three-cornered contest polling a majority of nearly 9,000 votes. In October of that year he was elected vice-chairman of the Parliamentary Labor party. The following February 15 he made a notable speech in the House of Commons on the matter of food supplies and world shortages. (At this time he was absent from Parliament for about three months because of complications arising from a knee injury sustained two years earlier, as a result of which he suffered the amputation of a leg.) A speech delivered on October 29, 1946, on behalf of the appointment of a Royal Commission of Inquiry into the "finance, control, management and ownership of British newspapers," was considered most effective. It was followed on November 5 by his election to the chairmanship of the Parliamentary Labor party, to which post he was re-elected in 1947 and again in 1948. During the course of the 1945-50 term of office of the Labor Government, Webb sat on a number of Select Committees.

During 1948 Webb, "concerned with the burden on families in lower income groups of the rising cost of living," made a survey of his Bradford constituency, and found "signs of incipient industrial unrest." In a Commons speech on December 17, he warned that "an upsurge of wage demands" might overturn his party's whole economic policy, and called on the Government "to restrict consumption by controls instead of prices." The Bradford Member of Parliament in September 1949 attended in Canada an unofficial Commonwealth Relations Conference, and at it proposed the setting up of some "permanent clearing house for Commonwealth economic ideas." Before returning to England he lectured in the United States.

In December 1949 Webb was made secretary of the Parliamentary Labor group, and thereupon began the task of planning and policy making for the general election, the imminence of which became inevitable early in the ensuing

MAURICE WEBB

year. A highlight of the brief three-week campaign preceding the polling on February 23, 1950, was a speech by Webb against Churchill, the Conservative leader.

Webb won his own contest in Central Bradford without much difficulty; but the Attlee Government was returned to power by the country at large only by "one of the slimmest margins in British Parliamentary history"—a majority of six in the House of Commons. The heavy Labor losses were attributed in part to hostility of women voters toward the rationing and commodity control program in general and Food Minister John Strachey in particular. In a reorganization of the Cabinet on February 28, Strachey was transferred to the War Office. Webb, with a reputation for being "much more diplomatic," was named as his successor. His appointment to a Cabinet post (which the New York *Times* called "the most uncomfortable seat of all") carries with it membership in the Privy Council and the title of Right Honorable.

The Ministry of Food, responsible for the formulation and administration of the country's food rationing policy, was formed in 1939 (by an Order in Council under wartime emergency powers) from the food department of the Board of Trade. In November 1945 it was announced that the Government had decided to make the Ministry a permanent Department of State, an announcement which was implemented by a Minister of the Crown Act in 1946. The Ministry comprises, in addition to its secretariat, three departments—establishment, services, and supply—and seventeen divisional food offices; it has under its direction four food and purchasing missions abroad, in Canada, Argentina, Southeast Asia, and Spain.

In his first press conference (March 17, 1950) after assuming office, Webb, announcing that he would talk about "food" and not "calories," hinted at an early though not a "dramatic" revision of the rationing system, with a view to

WEBB, MAURICE—*Continued*

bringing "greater variety to the people's tables." Five days later the Ministry weathered an attempt by the Opposition to cut its appropriations (the vote in Commons was 288 to 240), and by the middle of April increases in the butter and margarine rations were announced. Meanwhile, talks were held in London with James Dillon, Irish Minister of Agriculture, to explore the possibility of Ireland's supplying Great Britain with more dairy produce, and in Buenos Aires with Argentine officials on a renewal of the beef-purchasing contract. "We are going to try to show the Argentine Government that we are not going to be blackmailed any longer," stated Webb in Commons after Argentina had asked a 40 per cent increase in meat prices.

In April 1950 the Food Minister announced that, while the points rationing system for canned goods and table delicacies (introduced in 1941 in addition to the regular rationing of basic foods) would be continued, it would be modified, with the articles remaining on points being primarily those having a high sugar content. Price controls on fish had been removed a week earlier; early in May it was announced that the five-shilling ceiling on restaurant meals was removed—a step taken at the outset of the tourist season in view of Britain's need of dollars, Webb stated. In the House of Commons Webb endorsed a buyers' strike of housewives occasioned by the high price of vegetables, stating that buyer resistance was the only means of reducing prices; at the same time he referred to the Labor party's "long-term policy for the reorganization of fruit and vegetable marketing."

Mrs. Webb is the former Mabel Hughes of Lancaster. The Webbs, married in 1931, have one son; for many years they have made their home in Pinner, a residential suburb on the northwest fringe of Greater London. The Food Minister, who lists as his favorite recreation "watching cricket matches," is a member of the Press and Savage clubs in London.

> *References*
>
> Author's and Writer's Who's Who (1948-49)
> Who's Who, 1949

WEBSTER, MARGARET Mar. 15, 1905-
Theatrical producer; director; actress
Address: b. c/o Actors' Equity Association, 45 W. 47th St., New York 19

> NOTE: This biography supersedes the article which appeared in *Current Biography* in 1940.

Director and producer of Shakespeare's plays, Margaret Webster has made them "extraordinarily good entertainment" by sharpening and pruning them, and staging them as swift-paced, exciting dramas. Her revival of Shakespeare, first undertaken in the United States in 1937 (to which she had come from England), earned for her, in the consensus of a number of critics, the reputation of "America's foremost Shakespearean director." In the spring of 1950 the Margaret Webster Shakespeare Company completed its second annual tour of schools and colleges.

Margaret Webster comes from a distinguished English theatrical family. Her great-grandfather, Benjamin N. Webster, was a leading London actor-manager of the nineteenth century; her father, Ben Webster, won renown as a Shakespearean actor; and her mother, Dame May Whitty '45, was a popular actress of both stage and screen. Because May Whitty had accompanied her husband to America, where he was filling an engagement on Broadway at the time, Margaret Webster was born in New York City on March 15, 1905. This makes her a native American, although she is considered a subject of the King of England when she happens to be in Britain. (She writes herself down as a United States citizen and has voted in that country several times.) At the age of three, about the time that her mother first began reading Shakespeare to her, she was taken back to England and did not return to the United States for twenty-nine years.

"My parents objected to a stage career with the usual insincerity of theatrical parents," Miss Webster once said, but it was her mother who gave her the first taste of the stage by allowing her to watch from the wings and to "walk on" in mob scenes. When she was eight years old, she recited the prologue in a Nativity play being directed by the famous Ellen Terry. Her education was obtained spasmodically—through private tutors and at the Burlington School in London. In July 1917 she made her first official stage appearance as Youth in *Women's Tribute* for a war charity. From 1918 to 1923 she attended Queen Anne's School in Caversham. She contemplated going to Oxford, but changed her mind and studied for the stage at the Etlinger Dramatic School in London. It was at this time that she first met Maurice Evans, who was then a clerk in a music publishing house. They acted together in an amateur production of Bernard Shaw's *Major Barbara*.

Miss Webster received her first professional engagement in 1924, when she appeared in the chorus of Euripides' *The Trojan Women*, in a special performance featuring Sybil Thorndike. The next year she made her Shakespearean debut as the Gentlewoman in John Barrymore's London presentation of *Hamlet*, an appearance remarkable for the fact that immediately after her entrance the lights went out for three minutes. Subsequently she acted in several productions with Dame Sybil, toured with the Macdona Players in Shaw repertory, played stock with J. B. Fagan's Oxford Company, and in 1928 joined Sir Philip Ben Greet's Players. This latter group toured the provinces, putting on Shakespeare under all sorts of conditions, usually in the open air. "You had to learn to play Lady Macbeth up and down a fire escape," Miss Webster writes in *Shakespeare Without Tears*, "and convince an audience of irreverent children that you were really sleepwalking at the same time."

During the 1929-30 season Miss Webster was a member of the Old Vic Company, appearing in secondary roles in the Shakespearean repertory. In 1931 she played on the professional stage with Maurice Evans for the first time, in a touring company of *After All*, and acted with John Gielgud in *Musical Chairs*. The following season (1932-33) she was Lady Macbeth at the Old Vic, and the Countess of Derby in Gielgud's production of *Richard of Bordeaux*. It was during this period that she first took to directing plays between acting engagements. Her first real assignment as a director was drilling eight hundred women in an outdoor presentation of *Henry VIII*. Later came opportunities to direct small stock companies, Sunday evening performances for various membership societies, and eventually for productions in the West End, where, in the meantime, during 1934-36 she acted in fourteen plays, among them *Queen of Scots*, *Viceroy Sarah*, *Parnell*, and *Girl Unknown*, which she adapted from a play by Ferenc Molnár. During 1935-36 she directed *Return to Yesterday*, *Heads I Win*, *Lovers' Meeting*, *Three Set Out*, and *No Longer Mourn*; and in 1937 *Lady from the Sea* and *Old Music*.

The year 1937 marked the turning point in Margaret Webster's career. It was then that Maurice Evans invited her to stage his New York production of *Richard II*, which had not been seen on Broadway since 1878. Her work met with unanimous critical approval, and the play ran for 171 performances, establishing an all-time record for this drama anywhere. In 1938 Evans and Miss Webster duplicated their success with the first full-length version of *Hamlet* ever to be presented in New York. Their third successful collaboration was *Henry IV, Part I*, in 1939, with Evans playing Falstaff. Later that year Miss Webster staged condensed versions of four of Shakespeare's comedies for the Globe Theatre at the New York World's Fair. After spending six months in Hollywood acquainting herself with film-making under contract to Paramount, she let her option lapse and returned to New York in the fall of 1940 to direct Helen Hayes and Evans in the Theatre Guild production of *Twelfth Night*. She followed this with *Macbeth* (1941), starring Evans and Judith Anderson (whom Miss Webster replaced as Lady Macbeth on several occasions). Some critics felt less enthusiastic about these latter two productions, but they acclaimed the Theatre Guild presentation of Paul Robeson in *Othello* (1943), which she directed, besides appearing in the part of Emilia. Running for 296 performances, it established the American record for a Shakespearean play. Her most daring attempt to stage Shakespeare was *The Tempest* (1945), in which she cast the ballerina Vera Zorina as Ariel, and the Negro ex-boxer Canada Lee as Caliban. Each of these seven revivals flourished at the box office, and Miss Webster was hailed, in the words of George Jean Nathan, as "the best director of the plays of Shakespeare that we have."

Meanwhile, Miss Webster did not confine all of her directorial and acting talents to Shakespeare. She made her American acting debut

Bender

MARGARET WEBSTER

on March 28, 1938, as Masha in the Theatre Guild production of Chekhov's *The Sea Gull*, starring Alfred Lunt and Lynn Fontanne. Brooks Atkinson, of the New York *Times*, wrote that she was "the only member of the cast who plays with perception of the evanescent life that is hovering under and around the written skeleton of the drama." *Young Mr. Disraeli* (1937), in which she directed her father, was not successful, but two years later her direction and performance as Mary of Magdala in *Family Portrait* won much praise. Eager to promote the cause of noncommercial artistic ventures, she directed her mother and played the role of Andromache in *The Trojan Women*, the first production of the Experimental Theater in 1941. Two contemporary plays on war themes, *Flare Path* (1942) and *Counterattack* (1943) were her next directorial assignments. In 1944 she emerged for the first time as the theatrical producer, as well as the director of Chekhov's *The Cherry Orchard*; when the star, Eva Le Gallienne '42, was forced by illness to withdraw from the cast, she succeeded her in the role of Madame Ranevsky. During the 1945-46 season she directed her mother and Miss Le Gallienne in *Thérèse* and staged the sketches for the revue *Three to Make Ready*.

It had long been Miss Webster's ambition to found a permanent repertory theater in the United States. In the fall of 1945 she joined Cheryl Crawford '45 and Miss Le Gallienne in forming the American Repertory Theatre, Inc., the aim of which was to keep the great dramatic classics of the past on the stage and to offer new plays of merit. By selling stock in units of $500 each to some 300 investors, they succeeded in raising the $300,000 necessary to finance the project, of which Miss Webster was

WEBSTER, MARGARET—*Continued*

secretary-treasurer. A permanent acting company of thirty-eight, headed by Miss Le Gallienne, Walter Hampden, Victor Jory, and Ernest Truex, was then assembled. The enterprise was launched in November 1946 with three plays: *Henry VIII,* Barrie's *What Every Woman Knows* (both directed by Miss Webster) and Ibsen's *John Gabriel Borkman* (in which she played Mrs. Borkman), all of which were warmly received by the critics. More popular was her staging of Shaw's *Androcles and the Lion,* later added to the repertory in a double bill with O'Casey's *Pound on Demand.*

High operating costs soon forced the three managing directors to abandon the weekly rotation of plays under the repertory system in favor of offering a single play in a regular run; and fund-raising efforts were made by a committee of well-known actors. A revival of *Yellow Jack* and a successful run of *Alice in Wonderland* failed to recoup the company's initial investment. (In that play Miss Webster played the Red Queen, giving, said Howard Barnes, "solid support" to Miss Le Gallienne, the White Queen.) After a tour of *Alice* and a limited engagement of Miss Le Gallienne in Ibsen's *Ghosts* and *Hedda Gabler* (staged and supervised by Miss Webster) during the 1947-48 season, the American Repertory Theatre was dissolved with a considerable financial loss.

Refusing to abandon the repertory principle, Miss Webster undertook her most unusual Shakespearean venture in 1948. She sent out questionnaires to 500 universities, colleges, and cultural centers, asking if they would subscribe to a traveling repertory company of Broadway caliber. The response was so enthusiastic that she obtained an initial capitalization of $42,000 and set up the Margaret Webster Shakespeare Company, which was booked with a guaranteed weekly minimum. *Hamlet* and *Macbeth* were the two plays chosen for the 1948-49 season. The troupe traveled as a self-contained unit with its own truck for scenery, a station wagon to carry the technical crew of three, and a chartered bus for the twenty-two actors. Giving an average of five to six performances a week for twenty-nine weeks, it played in college auditoriums, high school gymnasiums, and public halls to large audiences, many of whose members had never before seen a Shakespeare performance on the stage. During the first season the company played 116 times in 36 states and three Canadian provinces; it followed a similar itinerary in 1949-50, offering *Julius Caesar* and *The Taming of the Shrew.* The group spent the summer of 1950 at the Woodstock (New York) Theatre, playing summer stock and preparing a wider repertory for its third touring season. As stage manager of *Don Carlo,* she prepared a new production of that opera, which was the opening presentation of the 1950-51 Metropolitan Opera season.

A Shakespearean scholar, Miss Webster has made lecture tours and is the author of *Shakespeare Without Tears* (1942), which includes chapters on general principles of Shakespeare production, notes on Elizabethan stages and actors, and comments on the problems of individual plays. Mark Van Doren called it "One of the best books written about Shakespeare in this century"; other critics commended the author for her scholarship and readable and quotable style. Elected one of the ten outstanding women of the year in 1946 by the Women's National Press Club, in the 1940's she received honorary degrees: from Lawrence College, Russell Sage College, and Rutgers University the Litt.D.; from Smith College the L.H.D. She is a council member of Actors' Equity Association and a board member of the American National Theatre and Academy. Blue-eyed and brown-haired, she has been described as a "tall, slender, attractive" woman with a hearty laugh. She does not care about clothes, and dislikes parties. Gardening, swimming, horseback riding, and writing articles are her recreations. Her dream is to live in the country, raise cabbages, study Russian, and walk the dog; but, she adds, "I also have to eat. Hence Shakespeare."

References

Arts & Dec 51:22-3 N '39 por
Collier's 104:11+ Jl 8 '39 por
Ind Woman 18:65 Mr '39
N Y Times Mag p16+ Ja 30 '44
New Yorker 20:32+ My 20 '44; 20:51 Ag 5 '44
St. Louis (Mo.) Post-Dispatch F 20 '40 por
American Women, 1939-40
Who's Who, 1950
Who's Who in America, 1950-51
Who's Who in the Theatre (1947)

WEBSTER, WILLIAM Dec. 6, 1900- United States Government official; utilities executive

Address: b. c/o Research and Development Board, Department of Defense, Washington, D.C.; c/o New England Electric System, 441 Stuart St., Boston 16, Mass.; h. 5 Upland Rd., Wellesley, Mass.

William Webster, chairman of the Research and Development Board in the United States Department of Defense, holds a position which has been described as the "Government's top scientific job" (New York *Times*). His duty as chairman of the RDB is to work with the Military Liaison Committee, the Atomic Energy Commission, and the Departments of the Army, Navy and Air Force in developing an integrated, well-balanced military program and national defense policy. This means testing and evaluating new techniques and new weapons, including the hydrogen bomb. When President Truman asked him to take the post, Webster was granted a leave of absence from his position as executive vice-president of the New England Electric System of Boston. Webster, who is a Naval Academy graduate, has been with the New England public utilities company since he left the Navy in 1928, after having served in the capacity of a naval constructor since 1922. His Government administrative experience has included service as consultant to the Joint Research and Development Board, chairman of the Military Liaison Committee to the Atomic Energy Commission, and chairman of the AEC's New England Council.

A son of Richard Henry and Harriet Archer (Williams) Webster, William Webster was born December 6, 1900, in Bel Air, Maryland, not far from Baltimore. His forebears had come from the British Isles, Germany, and Sweden, to settle in northeastern Maryland, and in Delaware and Pennsylvania before 1700. Young Webster attended St. James School in Hagerstown, Maryland, and, upon completing his high school studies there in 1916, entered the United States Naval Academy. After receiving his commission in 1920 he attended the Naval Academy's Post Graduate School in 1922, and subsequently, in 1924, received the B.S. and M.S. degrees from the Massachusetts Institute of Technology. As a lieutenant (junior grade) he submitted an article, "The Cruiser," in the Navy's Prize Essay Contest for 1926. While the article (in which he analyzed the requirements of the cruiser and its place in national defense) did not win a prize, it was ordered published in *United States Naval Institute Proceedings* in April 1926. Webster resigned from the Navy in 1928.

A long affiliation with the New England Electric System and its subsidiaries began when Webster became assistant to the general manager of the New England Power Association of Boston in 1928. He held the office of assistant to the president of the association from 1933 to 1935; assistant district manager of the Narragansett Electric Company in Providence, a subsidiary, from 1935 to 1942; and thereafter was vice-president of the New England Electric System; president of the Narragansett Electric Company and United Electric Railways; and executive vice-president of the New England Electric System.

While continuing to be a utilities executive, Webster worked in a number of administrative and advisory positions for the Government. From 1942 to 1945 he was management consultant in the Office of Price Administration; with the National Defense Research Committee from 1943 to 1946 he served as assistant chief of transmission. He was consultant to the Joint Research and Development Board (predecessor of the Research Development Board), created by charter in 1946 to coordinate research and development activities of common interest to the War and Navy Departments. As first chairman of the Military Liaison Committee to the Atomic Energy Commission he headed an organization "responsible for providing liaison between the National Military Establishment and the AEC on the military applications of atomic energy and for serving as the primary staff agency of the Secretary of Defense in atomic energy matters" (in the words of the *United States Government Organization Manual*). At one time he held the post of chairman of the AEC's New England Council.

Nomination of Webster to the post of chairman of the Research and Development Board was announced February 8, 1950. This board was created in 1947 by a National Security Act transferring to it all records and personnel of

WILLIAM WEBSTER

the Joint Research and Development Board which had been created in 1946. According to the *Government Manual*, the duty of the board, under the direction of the Secretary of Defense, is "to prepare a complete and integrated program of research and development for military purposes; to advise with regard to trends in scientific research relating to national security and the measures necessary to assure increasing progress; to recommend measures of coordination of research and development among the military departments, and allocation among them of responsibilities for specific programs of joint interest; to formulate policy for the National Military Establishment in connection with research and development matters involving agencies outside the Establishment . . . and to advise the Joint Chiefs of Staff therewith." The chairman of the board is assisted in the performance of his duties by an executive secretary, a programs division, a planning division, and various research and development committees. (On August 10, 1949, the National Military Establishment was transformed into an executive Department of Defense, a measure designed to strengthen armed forces unification.)

Secretary of Defense Louis Johnson [49] in recommending Webster's appointment to the post, emphasized the importance of the board, stating that the security of the country depended on having defense "planned in terms of significant new technological advances." Since the end of World War II, military expenditures on research and development have averaged more than $500,000,000 a year; it is the responsibility of the board to eliminate duplication of research among the three defense services in the interests of economy and efficiency. The establishment of the Weapons Systems Evaluation Group in the Department

WEBSTER, WILLIAM—*Continued*
of Defense was a recommendation of the Research and Development Board.

Commenting on Webster's nomination, *Time* pointed out that the executive was "more an administrator than scientist . . . an old hand at controlling the explosive combination of scientists in Government." The New York *Times* reported that he is "known at the Department of Defense as a capable administrator with considerable experience in the Defense Department and with the Atomic Energy Commission." As chairman, Webster succeeded Dr. Karl T. Compton [41], former president of the Massachusetts Institute of Technology, who resigned November 1949 (Dr. Vannevar Bush [47] had been chairman the preceding year). Webster's nomination is unique in that he is not primarily a scientist as were his predecessors. An appointment, supplementary to his main office, was made by President Truman on March 18, 1950, when the Chief Executive signed a commission naming Webster a member of the National Advisory Committee for Aeronautics.

Webster is a member of the United States Naval Academy Graduates Association. He is a vice-president of the American Institute for Counseling and Personnel Research; a trustee of Bates College (since 1946) and of Moses Brown School (since 1941), he is also a member of the Advisory Committee of the Woodrow Wilson School of Public and International Affairs, Princeton, New Jersey. His fraternity is Delta Psi, and his clubs are the Union and the University clubs of Boston, Wellesley Country Club, Agawam Hunt Club of Providence, the Turks Head Club, and the Providence Art Club. He is a director of Edison Electric Institute and of the American Transit Association. In religion he is an Episcopalian. Webster, who is six feet tall, weighs 180 pounds, has brown hair and hazel eyes. He married Eleanore Blodgett on April 21, 1924; the Websters have one son, Richard Henry. Badminton, bridge, and astronomy are named as the administrator's favorite forms of recreation.

References

N Y Herald Tribune p7 F 9 '50 por
N Y Times p24 F 9 '50
Time 55:53 F 20 '50
Who's Who in America, 1950-51
Who's Who in Commerce and Industry (1948)
Who's Who in Engineering, 1948
Who's Who in New England (1949)

WECTER, DIXON Jan. 12, 1906—June 24, 1950; American historian and educator; instructor, then professor of English at universities of Denver and Colorado, 1933-38; joined faculty of the University of California in 1939, and since 1949 occupied the Margaret Byrne chair of history there; among his books on American history are *The Saga of American Society, When Johnny Comes Marching Home,* and *The Age of the Great Depression*; literary editor of the Mark Twain estate since 1946,

and author of several books on Twain. See *Current Biography, 1944.*

Obituary

N Y Times p27 Je 26 '50

WEILL, KURT (wîl) Mar. 2, 1900—Apr. 3, 1950 Composer; studied in Berlin with Humperdinck and Busoni; director of the Lüdenscheid (Westphalia) Opera House in 1920; composed in Germany prior to 1933, in the United States since 1935; has written symphonic music, opera, songs, popular hits, for the theater, radio, and films; among his best known works are *Die Dreigroschenoper (The Three Penny Opera;* 1928), *Johnny Johnson* (1936), *Knickerbocker Holiday* (1938), *Lady in the Dark, One Touch of Venus, Lost in the Stars* (1949). See *Current Biography,* 1941.

Obituary

N Y Times p29 Ap 4 '50 por

WELLMAN, WILLIAM A(UGUSTUS) Feb. 29, 1896- Motion picture director; author
Address: c/o Metro-Goldwyn-Mayer Corp., Hollywood, Calif.; h. 410 N. Barrington, Brentwood Highlands, West Los Angeles, Calif.

The director of *Battleground,* considered by the critic of the New York *Times* to be "the best of the World War II pictures that have yet been made in Hollywood," is William A. Wellman, who has worked in the film capital since 1919. During his three decades in that industry, Wellman has directed more than sixty feature-length films, gaining a reputation for "documentary realism" in his treatment of such themes as war and aviation, for pioneering in the use of Technicolor, for his "instinct for casting" which has led him sometimes to choose comparative "unknowns" for major roles, and for the speed with which he usually shoots a scene, often finishing pictures four or five days ahead of schedule. He is also the author of several screen plays, including *A Star is Born,* for which he and the co-author won the 1936 writing award from the Academy of Motion Picture Arts and Sciences.

A New Englander of Irish-English parentage, the film director was born William Augustus Wellman on February 29, 1896. His parents, Arthur Gouverneur and Cecilia Guiness (McCarthy) Wellman were residents of Brookline, Massachusetts, at the time of Wellman's birth. He attended a public elementary school in Brookline, and was graduated from the high school in Newton, a neighboring community. When World War I broke out young Wellman joined the Norton-Harjes Ambulance Corps being formed in New York City for service in France. This was in April 1917. In June, after arriving in France, he entered the Foreign Legion of the French Army. Later, the United States having become a combatant, Wellman joined the Lafayette Flying Corps (Escadrille No. 87) as a pilot of a pursuit plane. He was shot down in battle and invalided home with an injured back. After his recovery he was assigned in December 1917 as a first lieutenant to the United States Aviation Service at Rockwell Field, California. For his war record he was awarded the Croix de Guerre (France), with four gold palm leaves, and five United States citations.

Wellman returned to Boston to work in the wool business. In 1919, given an opportunity to go to Hollywood as an actor, he signed to play a juvenile lead in *The Knickerbocker Buckaroo*, starring Douglas Fairbanks. After this one film appearance Wellman made his decision to remain in the motion picture industry, with the intention of becoming a director. He began with the Goldwyn Studio as a messenger, and shortly attained the rank of assistant director. By 1923 he had moved to the Fox Studios, where, as a full-fledged director, he made his first film, *The Man Who Won*. Also in that year he directed *Second Hand Love* and *Big Dan*. In 1926 he was engaged by the Paramount Lasky Corporation, for which in 1927 he directed his most notable picture up to that time, *Wings*. It was a narrative of pilots in World War I, the first of a series of aviation films which Wellman was to direct; because of its realistic shots of airplane warfare, it was considered a landmark in motion picture history. He remained with Paramount until the end of 1929, directing several other pictures for that company and being chosen one of the ten best directors in the 1928-29 Film Daily Annual Poll.

In 1930 Wellman joined Warner Brothers-First National Productions, from which, three years later, he went to Twentieth Century Pictures. Thereafter he signed contracts with leading studios, including one for a year in 1935 with Metro-Goldwyn-Mayer, one for a year with Selznick International Pictures, and one for five years with Paramount Pictures. He directed for Twentieth Century-Fox Productions in 1941 and again in 1944; in 1945 he directed several movies for Metro-Goldwyn-Mayer and United Artists; and in 1946 was both producer and director of *The Gallant Journey*, a Columbia release. During 1947 he directed for RKO and the next year for Twentieth Century-Fox. In 1949 he returned to Metro-Goldwyn-Mayer to direct *Battleground*. The success of this film led to a contract with MGM for one picture annually for three years. The first of these, to be shown in 1950, is "You're Only Young Twice," a cinema version of the stories by Owen Johnson on prep school life.

Wings was the first of a number of Wellman films in which he made use of his knowledge of aviation and his technique of "documentary realism." In 1932 he completed *The Conquerors*; in it the hero re-enacted scenes from the director's own experience with the Lafayette Flying Corps. Two years later Wellman wrote and directed *Men With Wings*, which traced the development of powered flight from the time of the Wright brothers. *Gallant Journey* (1946), which he produced and directed, presented the story of John Montgomery, who in the 1880's successfully launched and landed a heavier-than-air plane (a glider) a decade before the motor-propelled flight of the Wright brothers.

Films dealing with social issues have also been one of Wellman's specialties. *Public Enemy* (1931), which portrayed the life of two gangsters, was his first movie of this type. Some critics considered this the best gangster picture ever made. In 1933 Wellman was recognized for his direction of *Wild Boys of the Road*. Depicting in it the problem of homeless boys Wellman used a cast of virtual unknowns, none of whom was over twenty years of age. *The Last Gangster*, made in 1937, which he wrote as well as directed, also dealt in a realistic manner with the life of a criminal. An earlier film, *The President Vanishes* (1934), on the subject of a crisis in the national government, was considered a social film by some critics, who saw in it an implication that the President of the United States should be given dictatorial powers. Another view of the picture was taken by the New York *Sun* when it suggested that it was really just a startling movie, combining "all the excitement of a war, a kidnapping, and a hotbed of political intrigue."

Other Wellman-directed films based on historical fact or a social issue were *The Oxbow Incident*, distributed in 1943, and *Buffalo Bill*, released in 1944. The former is a story of a lynching which took place in a Western community in the 1890's. The *New Republic* reviewer found the film a decided change from the Hollywood tradition, since producer, director, and actors seemed to be "unhampered by the thought of the box office." The critic called it "an example of perfection in movie techniques of camera work and acting . . . the camera pace is slow, monosyllabic and stolid . . . its violence is blunt and dreadful . . . its details beautiful to watch." *Buffalo Bill*, a cinema version of the life of William F. Cody, the Indian scout, while not considered to be a contribution to historical knowledge of the life and times of Cody, was described by the New York *Times* reviewer as a "spectacular Western . . . directed in a magnificently exaggerated style."

Two of Wellman's most successful pictures were neither historical nor sociological. *A Star is Born* and *Nothing Sacred*, both released in 1937, were the first Technicolor films directed by Wellman and had the distinction of being the first pictures to remain three weeks at the Radio City Music Hall in New York. The *Time* reviewer of *A Star is Born*, which the director co-authored, described it as a "brilliant, honest, and unfailingly exciting picture which, in the welter of verbiage about Hollywood . . . stands as the last work and the best." The critic for the *New Republic* commended the "edge, clarity, old knowledge, feeling" with which the main part of the film was written, and noted that the direction was "firm through comedy and pathos." Wellman received an Academy Award as a writer on the picture. An article in the February 1950 issue of *Films in Review* (a periodical published by the National Board of Review of Motion Pictures) estimated that the director's "vigorous style matured with *A Star Is Born* and the two excellent comedies, *Nothing Sacred* and *Roxie Hart*."

(Continued next page)

Metro-Goldwyn-Mayer
WILLIAM A. WELLMAN

This Man's Navy, completed by Wellman early in 1945, was a narrative of one branch of the Armed Services, the blimp patrols. *Variety* stated that "good direction . . . and some excellent shots of Navy blimps . . . add much to the film." Later that same year *The Story of G.I. Joe*, for which Wellman chose his soldier cast from among unknown actors, was acclaimed for its "documentary realism." The New York *Herald Tribune* reported: "William A. Wellman has staged it almost in the manner of a documentary. He has skipped heroics for facts. He has built the continuity to the recurrent refrain that an infantryman lives miserably and dies miserably." In 1949, *Battleground*, the third of Wellman-directed World War II pictures was released. It tells the story of one group of soldiers in the Battle of the Bulge. Wellman's "enormous economy and insight" in directing the film, his ability to capture "both the tragic and funny aspects of a desperate conflict," and his success in "making all the action—and reaction—plausible" were noted by the critics of the New York *Herald Tribune* and the New York *Times*. The reviewer for the New York *Post* wrote, "It is a well produced picture of a great battle," adding the reservation that it was not a "great picture." In March 1950 *Look* magazine presented its Achievement Award as the director of the year (1949) to Wellman "for his authentic direction of *Battleground*."

Wellman is said to be "as sentimental as he is rough and ready" (New York *Times*). The nickname of "Wild Bill" conveys some idea of how he is said to handle actors, trying to arouse film players to fury and indignation by caustic comments, telling stories and joking with the technical staff. His aim, according to a piece on him in the New York *World-Telegram*, is to keep players and production crew fresh and enthusiastic. He also tries to maintain spon-

taneity by reducing retakes of scenes to a minimum, but he has been known to shoot an unsatisfactory sequence twelve times. The director, known for the speed with which he completes the filming of a script, commented on the feat of shooting *The Next Voice You Hear*, which was released in 1950, in fourteen days, that it involved "no mystery," paying tribute to his camera man and picked crew. He added: "You can't shoot every picture this fast. You can't do it if you have to use stars. They'll hold you up every time. . . .There was no silly make-up, and we didn't have hairdressers running around on the set."

The director is the author of a book, *Go, Get 'Em*, published in 1918. By his marriage to Dorothy Coonan in 1933 he has six children, Patricia, William Augustus 3d, Kathleen, Timothy, Celia, and Michael. (By a first marriage he has a daughter, Gloria.) Wellman is listed as a Republican and an Episcopalian. In stature he is lean and wiry.

References

N Y Post Mr 11 '38
N Y World-Telegram S 18 '37
International Motion Picture Almanac, 1948-49
1949 Film Daily Yearbook
Who's Who in America, 1950-51
Who's Who in the West (1949)

WHITE, CHARLES M(CELROY) June 13, 1891- Industrialist
Address: b. c/o Republic Steel Corp., Republic Bldg., Cleveland, O.; h. 16670 S. Park Blvd., Shaker Heights, Cleveland, O.

America's third largest steel-producing enterprise—it is exceeded in output only by the United States Steel and Bethlehem Steel companies—is Republic Steel Corporation, with headquarters at Cleveland, Ohio. Its president is Charles M. White, who was elected in May 1945. Attached to the twenty-year-old corporation since its formation, White was for several years its vice-president in charge of operations. He has been described by *Fortune* as "one of the smartest production men in the business" and "steel's most militant and articulate spokesman."

The son of Charles Franklin and Estella Virginia (Jarboe) White, Charles McElroy White was born in Oakland, in the western part of Maryland, on June 13, 1891. He passed most of his boyhood at nearby Hutton, where his father engaged in the lumber and sawmill business. By the time he was twelve, young "Charley" White began to work in the lumber camps of Maryland and adjacent West Virginia, starting as the driver of a team of mules. Later he also worked on railroad construction jobs and in tanneries. While not a high school graduate, he was able to qualify for admission to the University of Maryland at Baltimore, where he majored in mechanical engineering and was president of the class of 1913.

After taking his B.S. degree, White was for two years (1913-15) a millwright helper with the American Bridge Company. In 1915, with the Jones and Laughlin Steel Corporation of Pittsburgh, he became superintendent of a sintering plant; after one year he was made assistant superintendent of the blast furnace at the Eliza Works, Pittsburgh, Pennsylvania. During the years 1914-17 White also took courses at the Carnegie Institute of Technology. Classified in 1917 as a master mechanic, he was transferred in 1919 to the South Side works to become assistant to the general superintendant.

White was selected in 1920 for the task of operating the company's Monongahela Connecting Railroad. (The Jones and Laughlin company owned a number of railroads which, because of the antitrust laws, were "operated as separate institutions.") White was appointed general superintendent of the separately operated lines (the Montana, Connecticut and Aliquippa and Southern) and remained in this post until 1927. In that year he was named assistant superintendent of the Aliquippa (Pennsylvia) works. Subsequently for a few months (1929) he held the position of general superintendent, a post formerly filled by Tom M. Girdler [44], who was later to be the first chairman of Republic Steel Corporation, and with whom White had been associated for some time.

In 1929 Girdler had left Jones and Laughlin to become chairman of Republic Steel Corporation, then being formed to control a number of companies (including the Republic Iron & Steel Company). White followed Girdler to Republic, and on May 4, 1930, was appointed assistant vice-president in charge of operations, with headquarters at Youngstown (Ohio). The corporation, launched a short while after the stock market crash of the previous September, had a difficult initial period, losing some thirty million dollars during 1930-34. Girdler's stand against unionization resulted in several strikes at the company's plants in Youngstown, Massilon, and Canton. In this connection an anecdote was told in *Fortune* about White, who "loves a fight." Stated *Fortune*: "During the Canton strike . . . he went over to quell matters and while walking around the plant was heckled by a labor leader, who dared him to come over and fight. White dared, and the Canton sheriff, a strike sympathizer with a sense of humor, issued a warrant for White's arrest on a charge of assault and battery. Every steel company needs at least one hard-boiled driver of men, and for Republic, White is it." In his autobiography, *Boot Straps*, Girdler was to write: "Charley White's been taller and stronger than any one in any room full of men or any mob I ever saw him in."

In 1935 (the year in which Republic began to show profits) White became vice-president in charge of operations. In addition to building up a reputation as "one of the smartest production men in the industry," White had become known as an authority on air and hydraulic pressure, and had contributed papers on this subject to various technical journals. In May 1937, he read a paper, "Technological Advances in the Steel Industry," at the annual meeting of the American Iron and Steel Institute, for which he was awarded the institute's medal. During July 1938 White made a number of ap-

Wide World Photos

CHARLES M. WHITE

pearances as a witness before the Senate Civil Liberties Committee (then investigating Republic's record on collective bargaining), defending the corporation's employee representation plan (which the National Labor Relations Board had ordered disestablished as "company dominated") and testifying that both he, personally, and Republic Steel were "opposed to labor espionage if it is directed against unions."

"One great conviction White carried away from the thirties," stated *Fortune*, "was that steel entered the depression a technological laggard." He was resolved that Republic should be "armed" against "new blows from any quarter"; and by 1939, largely at his insistence, Republic had become the largest electric furnace operator in the industry. On April 12 of that year, he was elected a director of the corporation. In the following August he announced that Republic was "going to maintain this lead" with the addition (at the Canton works) of two "mammoth" new electric furnaces and other improvements. By the end of World War II the company could boast what has been described as "a mastery of alloy metallurgy second to none" (*Fortune*).

White succeeded R. J. Wysor as president of the Republic Steel Corporation on May 9, 1945. Participating in a program on "What Causes Strikes?" at a meeting of the National Industrial Conference Board, Republic's president declared that he believed a strong union and a strong company could settle any problem by discussion if allowed to do so without Government intervention. Expressing his view that labor should be made to take equal responsibility with management, White in a speech in 1947 stated: "I am not one of those who contend that unions are necessarily a menace to the country. . . .But I am against the way most unions are operated today." He went on to urge

WHITE, CHARLES M.—*Continued*

a revision of the Wagner Act, advocating a number of the restraints subsequently embodied in the Taft-Hartley law.

Republic's technological advances continued. On October 1, 1947, in an address ("Blast Furnace Blowing Engines, Past, Present and Future") delivered at a dinner of the Newcomen Society, White was able to point out that at two of Republic's plants a new blast furnace practice had been "developed and put into operation" with the result that "we have increased tonnage . . . as much as 20 per cent above normal." He further stated that "looking into the future, it is not too much to envision a blast furnace blown by a jet engine." In 1948 White drove what *Time* described as "a shrewd bargain" for his company, which was one of the principals in a dispute over the lease of a $28,000,000 blast furnace plant built by the Government during the war and operated by Republic until its classification as surplus. From the dispute Republic emerged as temporary operator of a plant on which the Kaiser-Frazer automobile manufacturing company held the lease—according to *Time*, Kaiser would lose a dime on every ton of iron made by Republic.

White defended the $5-a-ton increase in the price of steel in 1948 as providing compensation for past wage increases: "I firmly believe that steel prices are not high enough to assure the industry of firm financial experience in the months to come." A year later (August 19, 1949), when called before a Presidential fact-finding board seeking to avert a country-wide steel strike, White said: "There are worse things than a strike." Further: "I think that labor has got to be just as big as industry in seeing that the right results are reached. If labor is not big enough, then we have got to fight this thing out. That is the way I look at bargaining. If they think we are wrong, they strike us, see? That is the way this thing should work." In April 1950, in testimony before a House of Representatives subcommittee investigating monopolistic trends, he told the body it was "tampering with bigness, the thing that made this country great." Amplifying the statement, he asserted: "Our way of life is really our high standard of living . . . developed from the fact that we are a mass producing country. Mass production is big business. Big business is actually the assembly point of the products of hundreds of small businesses."

President and a director of Republic's subsidiary Truscon Steel Company, White holds the same offices in the Union Drawn Steel Company, Ltd., the Republic Collieries Company, and the Susquehanna Ore Company; he is a director of the Fretz-Moon Tube Company and of the James Manufacturing Company, a trustee of the National Industrial Conference Board and a member of the executive committee of the American Iron and Steel Institute. His clubs are the Union, Pepper Pike Golf, and Country in Cleveland; the Duquesne in Pittsburgh; the Cloud and Metropolitan in New York City; and the Everglades at Palm Beach, Florida. His fraternity is the Sigma Nu. "Lean, hard-bitten, tall, graying" are adjectives

applied by *Time* to Charles M. White, who is six feet four inches tall and weighs about 195 pounds. Mrs. White is the former Helen Gordon Bradley; the Whites were married on September 4, 1918, and have one daughter, Jean Bradley, now Mrs. George F. Thomas 2d. The industrialist is an Episcopalian.

References

Fortune 12:30 D '35 por; 40:10-11 S '49 por
Girdler, T. M. and Sparkes, B. Boot Straps (1943)
Who's Who in America, 1950-51
Who's Who in Commerce and Industry (1948)
Who's Who in the Midwest (1949)
World Biography (1948)

WHITE, FRANK (KIGGINS) Sept. 24, 1899- Broadcasting company executive

Address: b. c/o Mutual Broadcasting System, 1440 Broadway, New York 18; h. 8 Oxford Rd., Larchmont, N.Y.

Frank White succeeded Edgar Kobak [47] as president and director of the Mutual Broadcasting System, Inc., on May 1, 1949. Joining Mutual after a twelve-year association with the Columbia Broadcasting System, Inc., he brought to his new post a record of long experience in radio and an "outstanding reputation" in labor-management relations.

One of the two sons of William W. and Mary A. (Kiggins) White, Frank Kiggins White was born in Washington, D.C., on September 24, 1899. His ancestors were early settlers in the United States, his father's family having come from England to Massachusetts about 1700, later moving to Virginia; his mother's family journeyed from Ireland to settle in Tennessee in the early 1800's. Reared in near-by Rockville, Maryland, and in his native city, Frank White was graduated in 1916 from the capital's Central High School, where he participated in extracurricular activities as captain in the high school cadets and member and onetime president of the debating society. At George Washington University he became a member of Sigma Nu fraternity. After two years of study, he left college in 1918 to join the Naval Air Force as student flight officer. Although he had earlier planned to study law, after leaving the Navy he became interested in accounting.

In 1921 the future radio executive began his business career as an accountant in the accounting firm of Lybrand, Ross Brothers and Montgomery, New York City, a position which he held for three years. *Advertising Age* quotes Frank White as saying: "An accountant who is lucky gets sent out on a variety of assignments and learns a lot about how a business functions. If he is unlucky, he just checks figures for the rest of his life." One of the lucky men, he moved on to another field in 1924, as assistant to the president of the Union News Company, and from 1929 to 1935 holding the post of treasurer of the Literary Guild of America. In 1935 he was treasurer

two daughters, Barbara (Mrs. Raisbeck) and Margaret. For relaxation, Professor Wiener writes detective stories, which are submitted to publishers under the pseudonym "W. Norbert." Five feet six inches tall, with brown eyes, "graying hair, gray mustache, and gray chinbeard," Wiener is described by an interviewer as "full of nervous energy."

References

Sci Am 151:115 S '34
Time 32:28 S 19 '38

American Men of Science (1949)
Who's Who in America, 1948-49

WILKINS, ROY Aug. 30, 1901- Negro organization administrator

Address: b. c/o National Association for the Advancement of Colored People, 20 W. 40th St., New York 18; h. 409 Edgecombe Ave., New York

In June 1950 Roy Wilkins became administrator of the National Association for the Advancement of Colored People, after having been acting secretary for the preceding year. He was assistant secretary from 1931 into 1949 and editor of its official magazine, *The Crisis*, since 1934. Wilkins was at one time managing editor of the Kansas City *Call*.

Roy Wilkins was born in St. Louis, Missouri, on August 30, 1901. When he was four years old, his mother died, and the boy went to live with an uncle. He spent his childhood in St. Paul, Minnesota, where he received his elementary and secondary education. While in high school he was editor of the school paper. He enrolled in the University of Minnesota; for three years there he was night editor of the school's *Minnesota Daily*. At the same time he edited the St. Paul *Appeal*, a Negro weekly.

In 1923, when he was graduated from the University of Minnesota, Wilkins who at one time had thought he might become an engineer, went to work as managing editor for the Kansas City (Missouri) *Call*, also a Negro weekly. To Chester A. Franklin, the *Call*'s editor, Wilkins attributes much influence on his life. "He's still one of the finest newspapermen and most intelligent crusaders I know," Wilkins told an interviewer in 1949.

In St. Paul and in Kansas City, Wilkins was active with the National Association for the Advancement of Colored People, serving as secretary for the local chapters in each community. In 1931 he left the *Call* to become assistant secretary of the association, serving under Walter F. White '42, the executive secretary. This association was founded in 1909, by persons of both Negro and white races, to champion full economic, civil, legal, and political rights for the Negro. It investigates lynchings and violations of civil rights, encourages Negroes to exercise their political power, maintains a speakers' bureau, and assembles information on Negro participation in, or benefit from, expenditures of public tax money. A secretariat consisting of a staff and a field staff under the direction of a full-time executive secretary is locted in national head-

Morgan Smith

ROY WILKINS

quarters in New York City. Affiliates of the association are the numerous cooperating local branches, whose membership (Negro and white) was estimated at 500,000 in 1949. In prosecuting its ends, the NAACP has adopted many modes of operation: it has made itself an interested party in court cases involving Negroes and has initiated court cases when it has discovered instances of interference with civil rights; it carries on a public relations program and legislative activities; it helps individual Negroes further their education and obtain employment.

After joining the secretariat of NAACP Wilkins in 1932 undertook a field trip with George S. Schuyler, Negro editor. In investigating charges of discriminatory and unjust treatment of Negro workers on a flood-control project in Mississippi, the two association workers secured jobs as day laborers there. They discovered that Negroes on the project were underpaid and overworked; on the basis of their report the NAACP was able to bring Congressional action to improve the situation, obtaining a substantial increase in the wages of the Negro workers.

In 1934 Wilkins succeeded W. E. B. Du Bois '40 as editor of *The Crisis*, the official organ of the NAACP. He continued to serve as assistant secretary of the association, and to travel on its behalf speaking before clubs, forums, college groups, associations, and conventions on various aspects of race relations. His writings appeared in various pamphlets as well as in *The Crisis*. In 1943 he was sent by the NAACP to Philadelphia to represent Negro interests in a strike of transit workers prompted by the promoting of eight Negroes to jobs as motormen in the transit system. After six days the strike ended, with the white workers returning to work and the Negroes keeping their jobs; the September 1944 issue of *The*

WILKINS, ROY—*Continued*

Crisis set forth the details. At the time of the San Francisco conference for the formation of the United Nations in April 1945, Wilkins, together with White and DuBois, served as consultant to the American delegations.

One of the problems Wilkins has concerned himself with in articles for *The Crisis* is that of discrimination in the armed forces. In 1945, alarmed by specific incidents of anti-Negro stand in the Army and Navy, he wrote, "It looks as though someone is trying very hard with the mighty machinery of the powerful military regulations in wartime to manufacture a record of the Negro as a soldier so as to smother his progress toward the full and complete citizenship he is striving to achieve."

Wilkins contributed a chapter to the book *What The Negro Wants*, a symposium by fourteen prominent Negroes; his contribution was later reprinted as a pamphlet, *The Negro Wants Full Equality*, published in 1946 by the Committee of One Hundred (a group dedicated to improving race relations). In it he pointed out that "black America" had heard leading statesmen, radio stations, newspapers condemn the dictators, racial and religious bigotry, force, and brutality and had thought that this condemnation certainly must extend to discrimination against the Negro in the United States. Negroes, he said, "ask for complete equality in the body politic. They could not, in self respect, ask less. If it has seemed in the past that certain segments of the Negro population and certain leaders have demanded less, closer study will show that the goal has always been complete equality."

In June 1949, when Walter White was granted a year's leave of absence from his duties as NAACP executive secretary (the board refused to accept his resignation), Roy Wilkins was named acting secretary. In fulfilling the duties of chief administrator, Wilkins has been active in promoting public support for the early passage of the proposed Fair Employment Practices bill. (He is also chairman of the executive committee of the National Council for a permanent FEPC.) In a letter to the New York *Times* (May 17, 1950), he declared: "The establishment of equality of job opportunity would give tangible proof to our foes abroad that America is truly a democratic country in practice as well as in profession." Reviewing the achievements of 1949 at the forty-first annual meeting of the NAACP, the acting secretary pointed out that FEPC legislation had been enacted in Rhode Island, Oregon, Washington, and New Mexico; that civil rights laws in New Jersey had been strengthened. He cited advances made in the abolition of segregation in the army, public housing, and schools in several States.

Wilkins has met with opposition from Communist sympathizers within the NAACP. To urge support of President Truman's civil rights program, the NAACP initiated a National Emergency Civil Rights Mobilization to convene in Washington in January 1950, with Wilkins as general chairman. The mobilization received support from fifty-eight civic, religious, and labor organizations, but refused the aid of the reputedly left-wing Civil Rights Congress. In explaining the reason for the exclusion of this group, Wilkins asserted: "We of the NAACP remember that during the war, when Negro Americans were fighting for jobs on the home front and fighting for decent treatment in the armed services, we could get no help from organizations on the extreme Left. . . .As soon as Russia was attacked by Germany, they dropped the Negro question. . . . During the war years the disciples of the extreme Left sounded very much like the worst of the Negro-hating Southerners. American Negroes, and especially the NAACP, cannot forget this."

In May 1950 the board of directors of NAACP adopted for the body a new plan of organization, by which the directors assume greater control. The plan separates the internal operations of the association from its program in relation to outside agencies. The latter activity is to be under the direction of the executive secretary. The management of the national office, including complete supervision of the budget, is to be the responsibility of a newly created official, the administrator of internal affairs; this "second ranking executive" is to be responsible directly to the board of directors rather than to the executive secretary. At the meeting of the board, White was confirmed in the post of executive secretary, (which he was to resume in June 1950) and Wilkins was appointed administrator of internal affairs, both with terms of office effective to January 1951, "the normal period of appointments."

Roy Wilkins and Minnie Badeau were married in 1929. Formerly a golf player, the tall NAACP official has only one real sports interest now—he watches baseball. An avid reader, he finds mystery stories relaxing.

References

Crisis 56:213 Jl '49
N Y Post p35 Je 14 '49 por
N Y Sun Je 14 '49 por

WILLIAMS, EDWIN G(ANTT) Nov. 13, 1902- United States Government official; physiologist; radiologist

Address: b. c/o United States Public Health Service, Washington 25, D.C.; h. 4909 Battery Lane, Bethesda, Md.

In December 1949 the Federal Security Agency announced the establishment of the Radiological Health Branch of the United States Public Health Service, of which Dr. Edwin G. Williams is chief. The branch was formed for the purpose of controlling radiation hazards, which are mounting because of the rapid increase in the use of radioisotopes and radiation-producing machines. A senior surgeon with the Public Health Service, engaged in research on radiation protection and radiobiology since 1945, Dr. Williams has said that one of the chief objectives of any widespread educational program against atomic hazards "should be the dissemination of information to create respect for rather than fear of atomic energy." Since joining the USPHS in 1929 as an assistant surgeon, he has carried out several tours of duty in the United States and abroad and conducted ten years of research in drug addiction. Williams is the author of numerous articles on the medical aspects of atomic energy and drug addiction.

Edwin Gantt Williams, born on November 13, 1902, in Monticello, Florida, is the son of John Franklin and Mary Lizzie (Bearden) Williams. Both his parents came from large families: the father, a physician, had eleven brothers and sisters, most of whom are physicians, educators, or missionaries; the mother, a teacher, had twelve brothers and sisters, five of whom are teachers, the others ministers, merchants, or farmers. Of the five children of John Williams, Edwin is a physician, two sons and a daughter are educators, and another son is a forester. Reared in Florida, Edwin attended the local schools of Monticello and in 1919 was graduated from high school. In 1924 he obtained a B.S. degree from Emory University (Atlanta, Georgia) and in 1926 his M.D. from that university's School of Medicine. During his college days he belonged to the rifle team and was a member of the Phi Beta Pi medical fraternity.

After graduation young Williams was an instructor in physiology at Emory until 1929, when he was commissioned an assistant surgeon in the United States Public Health Service. Assigned to hospital and immigration duty, he then served in the Marine Hospitals in Baltimore and Detroit. From 1931 to 1933 he had a tour of immigration and foreign quarantine duty in Germany, the British Isles, and Poland. On a special assignment to the Liverpool School of Tropical Medicine, Williams earned diplomas in tropical medicine (1932) and tropical hygiene (1933). This was followed by a tour of duty in Italy in 1934. In 1941 he was appointed surgeon, and in 1944 senior surgeon with the United States Public Health Service.

During the period 1935-45 Dr. Williams was engaged in research in the physiological aspects of drug addiction at the USPHS hospital in Lexington, Kentucky. A number of articles by the health officer on findings made during the project have appeared in medical journals. These include "General Outline of Research on the Nature of Drug Addiction in Man" (*Hospital News*, December 1936); "Blood Concentration in Morphine Addiction" (*Journal of Pharmacology and Experimental Therapeutics*, November 1939), dealing with the relation of morphine addiction to changes in blood concentration; "A Cycle of Morphine Addiction" (*Public Health Reports*, January 1946), discussing biochemical, physiological, and psychological findings in relation to morphine addiction; "Studies on Marihuana and Pyrahexyl Compound" (*Public Health Reports*, July 19, 1946), a report of physiological, pharmacological, and psychological aspects of marihuana and a related synthetic compound.

The public health specialist has been engaged in work in the field of radiology since 1945. At the National Institutes of Health (the research division of the USPHS, composed of six institutes) he undertook research in, and supervised, protection from radiation; research and field work in radiobiology also came within the scope of his work there. A member of the radiological safety staff for "Operation Crossroads" at Bikini in 1946, Williams was one of those who, clad in protective clothing, boarded the radioactive ships with Geiger counters to investigate the effects of the historic atom bomb tests. His work was rewarded by a citation for "meritorious conduct in performance of outstanding service" from Vice-Admiral W. H. P. Blandy.

In an address ("Public Health Aspects of Atomic Energy") before the Michigan Public Health Conference in December 1948 (when he was senior surgeon of the radiological branch of the USPHS), Williams outlined the protective measures to be taken against atomic radiation, which he believed would be increasingly used in: clinical radiology for diagnostics and therapeutics; industries involving radioactive luminous compounds; research to determine radiation effects and isotopic tracings; atomic energy for power when it reaches the point of actual utilization—"maybe thirty years away"; military applications. A program to educate the general public as to measures against possible harmful effects of the various rays had become a necessity, Dr. Williams pointed out, stressing the desirability of creating "respect for, rather than fear of, atomic energy." He added that the USPHS was giving its officers progressive training in aspects of radiological health and "considering plans for the dissemination of information relative to practical protective measures to be taken by Federal, State and local health departments." The danger of atomic accidents (in research or industry) and atomic disasters, he said, were problems "differing only in magnitude and complexity."

At the 1949 convention of the Oklahoma State Medical Association, Williams, speaking of the benefits of the atomic age to the medical profession, said it assured a greater amount of radioactive substances for treatment and research uses because of the increasing cheapness of production of such materials. The Atomic Energy Commission, he stated, is providing radioactive substances to more than two hundred hospitals, clinics, and other institutions engaged in research and treatment of cancer. He urged that the public be encouraged to approach atomic age problems "from a standpoint of intelligence" rather than of emotion—"It should not be frightening just because everyone does not understand the principle of atomic power. We don't all understand the principles of electricity, either."

Formal announcement of the formation of a Radiological Health Branch of the Public Health Service under the direction of Dr. Edwin G. Williams was made by the Federal Security Agency on December 22, 1949. The branch was formed to plan control of radiation hazards resulting from the use of radioisotopes and radiation-producing machines in hospitals and experimental laboratories, to establish a training program in radiological health for Public Health Service officers and

WILLIAMS, EDWIN G.—*Continued*

other technologists, and to serve as a source of information for State and local health agencies. "We want to plan ahead so that, if twenty years from now atomic power comes into general use, no harm will come to the user or his neighbors," stated a USPHS spokesman.

In the field of radiation protection Williams is author of "Radiant Energy Hazards," published in an annual of the American Public Health Association in 1948. Approximately twelve articles by the medical director have appeared in medical and public health journals during the years from 1936 to 1949; they dealt with a variety of research projects, including several on work in drug addiction in addition to those previously mentioned. The Public Health Service official is a member of the American Association for the Advancement of Science, American Medical Association, American Public Health Association, Association of Military Surgeons of the United States, American Society for Pharmacology and Experimental Therapeutics, and National Committee of Radiation Protection.

A resident of Bethesda, Maryland, Williams belongs to the community's Citizens Association; his church is the Methodist. He has blue eyes, brown hair, stands five feet seven inches and weighs 165 pounds. Edwin Gantt Williams married Walter Harnesberger Dallas, a teacher, on March 1, 1929. The couple has four children, Edwin Gantt, Kate Weaver, Mary Bearden, and Stephen Harnesberger. Williams, whose recreations are hunting, fishing, and sailing, has been described as "a quiet, almost bashful man," who when speaking on such abstruse phenomena as X and gamma rays "is practical and down to earth."

References

American Men of Science (1949)
Who Knows—and What (1949)
Who's Important in Medicine, 1945
Who's Who in Kentucky (1945)
Who's Who in the East (1948)

WILSON, CHARLES E(RWIN) July 18, 1890- Industrialist; electrical engineer

Address: c/o General Motors Corp., Detroit 2, Mich.; h. "Longmeadow," Bloomfield Hills, Mich.

> NOTE: This biography supersedes the article which appeared in *Current Biography* in 1941.

Charles E. Wilson, president of General Motors Corporation, took over that office immediately before G.M.'s conversion to war production for World War II, during which it produced twelve billion dollars' worth of armaments. Since then its sales, payroll, and profits have reached new and continually increasing high figures for American industry.

Born in Minerva, Ohio, on July 18, 1890, Charles Erwin Wilson is one of the sons of Thomas Erwin Wilson, principal of the Minerva school, and of Rosalind (Unkefer) Wilson

(a descendant of pioneers), who had taught there before her marriage. A younger brother, Robert, who also became a corporation president, was mayor of Corpus Christi, Texas, at the time of his death in 1947. From his parents, Wilson has said, he learned to value education, to enjoy work for its own sake, and "to make a little extra effort to get along with people." According to *Time*, Wilson's childhood heroes were the two locomotive engineers whose homes adjoined his; they told him many stories of railroading, and took him for rides in their locomotive cabs. From the time he first saw an electric light, however, the youth wanted to become an electrical engineer.

Wilson attended public school in Mineral City, Ohio, and was graduated from the Bellevue (Pennsylvania) High School. In 1909, having completed a four-year electrical engineering course in three years at near-by Carnegie Institute of Technology in Pittsburgh, the eighteen-year-old engineer joined the staff of the Westinghouse Electric and Manufacturing Company as a student apprentice. His starting salary was eighteen cents an hour. Much of Wilson's later success he attributes to the training he received as student assistant to the company's chief engineer, B. G. Lamme. In 1912, when Wilson was twenty-one, he designed the first automobile starters made by Westinghouse; his salary then (on which he married) was $80 a month. Four years later, he was put in charge of all the company's automobile electrical equipment engineering. This work brought Wilson into contact with automobile manufacturers. Attracted to the automobile business, which he considers "dramatic," Wilson learned much about volume production and the importance of costs.

During World War I, Charles E. Wilson was in charge of designing and developing Westinghouse radio generators and dynamotors (special electric motor generators) for the Army and Navy. Subsequently, in April 1919, he joined the General Motors Corporation as chief engineer and sales manager of the automobile division of the Remy Electric Company, a Detroit subsidiary; later he was transferred to Anderson, Indiana. As chief engineer, Wilson initiated a redesigning program which, according to General Motors, "materially helped in putting the Remy Electric Company's operations on a sound financial basis." In December 1921 the engineer was made factory manager, and in February 1925, general manager. A year later, when the Dayton Engineering Laboratories Corporation was merged with Remy into the Delco Remy Corporation, Wilson was made president and general manager. His payroll then numbered about 12,000 employees. During the next two years Delco-Remy developed Lovejoy shock absorbers, motors for industrial refrigeration and washing machines, automobile lamps, and Delco batteries. While there Wilson established an employee suggestion plan which is still in operation; during World War II he put this into operation in all G.M. plants, and as of 1949 the various G.M. divisions were paying about a million dollars a year in rewards for usable suggestions.

In December 1928 Wilson was advanced to vice-president of the parent corporation and transferred to Detroit. For the next few years he devoted himself to developing G.M.'s parts and accessories business and to expanding its holdings; he arranged for the purchase of stock in the Bendix and North American aircraft companies, and for the acquisition of the Winton, Northeast, Allison, Sunlight, and Packard electric companies. (Part of G.M., in turn, is owned by Du Pont.) He was named to the board of directors in 1934. On May 1, 1939, Wilson was made executive vice-president, a position in which he had "executive relations" with all of the G.M. operating divisions: Chevrolet, Pontiac, Buick, Oldsmobile, Cadillac, Frigidaire, G.M. trucks, locomotives and Diesel engines, Delco household appliances, AC spark plugs, Hyatt bearings, Allison aircraft engines, and two dozen others. His particular interests lay in labor relations and the business planning of production, rather than in sales or finance.

On June 6, 1940, G.M.'s president William S. Knudsen having taken a leave of absence to direct industrial production for the Government's national defense program, Charles Erwin Wilson was named acting president of the corporation, and in January 1941, when Knudsen resigned from the presidency, Wilson succeeded him in that office. (Vice-president Charles Wilson of General Electric Company became president of that corporation about this time, a fact which added to the confusion of their similar prename initials. G.M.'s Wilson and G.E.'s Wilson may receive each other's mail and are asked by reporters and Congressmen to explain each other's statements.) When Wilson became the G.M. president the corporation had 201,000 employees at work in 102 plants valued at $850,000,000, used 250,000 tons of steel a month, and made, he has said, considerably more than 10 per cent profit from sales of its manufactured products. During World War II Wilson's payroll rose to 465,000; the average annual production was $3,359,212,255; manufacturing profits after taxes averaged 4.1 per cent, and returns from investments brought this up to 5 per cent. By mid-1945, G.M.'s working capital had risen from a prewar $434,173,000 to about $950,000,000. Wilson's income for that year was $459,041; for 1949, it was $586,100 in salary, bonus, and stock, making him the highest-paid corporation executive in the country (his Federal income tax was about $430,350). At the time of the 1950 annual meeting, the president's personal stock holdings in General Motors totaled 18,742 shares. (These figures are from Collier's, Business Week, New York Times, and New Yorker.)

About the time that Wilson became president, G.M. launched a program of intensive emergency training of new workers in forty of its plants (this was distinct from its long-range program of apprentice training). The first large-scale production of steel propellers for high-powered planes in the United States was begun by G.M. in 1941. That October Wilson announced the signing of the first employer-union agreement in the automotive industry protecting the seniority of workers displaced by the curtailment of nondefense production, and

Wide World Photos

CHARLES E. WILSON

giving first chance at defense jobs to them and to qualified workers in local nondefense plants who could be "spared or loaned" by their employers. A month after Pearl Harbor, Wilson was named to a ten-man labor-management committee with authority from OPM to work out the conversion of automobile plants to war production. Wilson's thought was that the industry should use up its $200,000,000 inventory by building 250,000 new cars; war production goals, he declared, could be met "in the same old way we used to run the auto business." Opposing the much-publicized Reuther plan for quick conversion of automobile factories to aircraft plants under joint labor-management supervision, Wilson accepted Reuther's invitation to a debate in March 1942 and held him "to a draw."

The industrialist, who served as an adviser to military and governmental bodies, including Congressional committees, on use of national resources and manpower, supervised the production of about a fourth of the tanks, armored cars, and airplane engines built in the United States, almost a half of the machine guns and carbines, two-thirds of the trucks of two and a half tons or more, as well as thousands of carrier aircraft, three-fourths of all the Diesel horsepower used by the Navy, and other items down to the smallest ball bearings.

Wilson's postwar reconversion plans were delayed by a strike which began after the war, in late 1945. In 1947 he offered the Senate Labor Committee a ten-point "program for industrial peace," in the course of which he compared the closed shop to compulsory membership in the Nazi party and said that he would sooner give up his job than sign a closed-shop labor contract. "When it gets around to that they can make a farmer out of me," was his remark. In his economic thinking, Wilson has gone on record as stating, "The profit and

WILSON, CHARLES E.—*Continued*

loss mechanism that . . . scales the rewards in proportion to ability and efficiency . . . is simple, automatic, and just."

According to *Business Week*, it was in 1947 that Wilson conceived the idea of G.M.'s "trailblazing" cost-of-living wage formula, and he helped write the contract incorporating it which was signed in May 1948. Faced with a shortage of steel for 1949, in 1948 the corporation president visited steelmakers in Pittsburgh, Cleveland, and New York and obtained promises of extra steel; in return, reported *Time*, he promised to move some Fisher Body operations to Pittsburgh, thus providing the steel mills with a permanent local market. Late in 1948 he was sent to Germany by ECA. The next year, while G.M. cars were leading the field in sales and future orders, two days after the Chrysler Corporation had raised its prices by about 7 per cent, G.M. announced $10 to $40 reductions in the prices of its passenger cars and Chevrolet trucks, reductions made possible by decreased materials and labor costs. "Detroiters recognize the characteristic flair of president Charles E. Wilson in the brilliant timing of the move," commented *Business Week*. Wilson has expressed himself in favor of the pension plan for hourly, as well as salaried employees. The industrialist said, "It is important that the nation's workmen should spend for what they need or feel they should have, and still have reasonable security." (The 1950 pension plan, it is estimated, will cost the company $67,227,000.) Meanwhile, G.M. sales, payroll, taxes, and profits rose to new peaks. In 1949, the profits set a national record, which it surpassed in 1950, when sales in the second quarter totaled 1,012,874 units, net sales for that three-month period $1,963,641,243, net working capital stood at $1,688,090,890, and net profit, $272,-889,624 (figures from New York *Times*).

Charles E. Wilson is a tall, slightly stooped, slow-talking man, with a mass of white hair. To his wife, Pennsylvania-born Jessie Ann Curtis (whom he married April 11, 1912) he is "Erwin," to his friends, "C. E." The Wilsons have three sons and three daughters, all married—Thomas Erwin, Jessie Lucille, Jean Curtis, Edward Everett, Rosemary, and Charles Erwin. One of his sons looks after the Michigan farm on which he breeds a large herd of Ayrshire cattle and keeps a stable of blooded horses. A good swimmer, a fair golfer, an occasional hunter and fisherman, Wilson gave up skating after breaking a hip on the ice, gave up riding to hounds after a fall from a balky hunter. He drives his own custom-made Cadillac "like a preoccupied Barney Oldfield." Wilson is a member of the Society of Automotive Engineers, and lists himself as a Republican and an Episcopalian. His professional association is the Society of Automotive Engineers, his clubs are the Detroit, Bloomfield Golf, Bloomfield Open Hunt.

References

Bsns W p28 O 13 '45
N Y Times Mag p25 F 17 '46
Newsweek 17:41 Ja 20 '41; 26:70 D 10 '45
PM p11 O 23 '45
Time 53:74 Ja 24 '49
Forbes, B. C., ed. America's Fifty Foremost Business Leaders (1948)
International Who's Who, 1950
National Cyclopædia of American Biography Current vol G (1943-46)
Who's Who in America, 1950-51
Who's Who in Commerce and Industry (1948)
Who's Who in Engineering, 1948
World Biography (1948)

WOLFE, HUGH C(AMPBELL) Dec. 18, 1905- Physicist; educator

Address: b. c/o Cooper Union School of Engineering, Cooper Sq., New York 3; h. 30 Lawrence Parkway, Tenafly, N.J.

Dr. Hugh C. Wolfe, prominent among American physicists and authorities on atomic energy, is the chairman of the Federation of American Scientists, a group interested primarily in the social aspects of nuclear energy development. Together with the Association of New York Scientists (since the beginning of 1950 a chapter of the Federation of American Scientists), of which Wolfe is also chairman, it has pressed for civilian control of atomic energy. A technical aide in the Office of Scientific Research and Development during the latter part of World War II, Wolfe was for fifteen years associated with the physics department of the College of the City of New York, before becoming head of that department at Cooper Union in the same city.

"I hope I am a good American," Dr. Wolfe has said, "in spite of the fact that I know of no immigrant ancestors more recent than a French Huguenot great-grandmother, who came here as a child from the Isle of Man." Through another great-grandmother, on his father's side, Dr. Wolfe is a descendant of Hugh Robarts, who came to New England in 1643 and whose son, Hugh, was one of the founders of Newark, New Jersey. The first American ancestor with the name of Wolfe came to these shores from Germany early in the eighteenth century. Hugh Wolfe's paternal grandfather was a Presbyterian minister who headed a young ladies' seminary in Montclair, New Jersey; his son, the scientist's father, was professor of Latin and Greek at Park College, Parkville, Missouri, from 1889 to 1931. It was, accordingly, in Parkville that Hugh Campbell Wolfe was born on December 18, 1905, the youngest of the five sons of Arthur Lester and Gertrude Remington (Snow) Wolfe; Mrs. Wolfe is also of old American ancestry that traces several lines to the middle of the seventeenth century. (He has four older brothers—now a minister, a missionary doctor, a university professor, and a high school teacher.) Hugh Wolfe was reared in Parkville. He was graduated from Park College Academy in 1922, then entered Park College itself, to major in physics; there he participated in forensics and dramatics.

Of persons and circumstances which influenced him in his choice of a lifework, Dr. Wolfe has written: "My physics professor was

Dr. Ray L. Edwards, now of Miami University, Oxford, Ohio, who received the Oersted Medal of the American Association of Physics Teachers a couple of years ago because of his exceptional success in inspiring his students to go on to graduate school and a career in physics. This was about the only subject in which I really felt that I had to work hard in order to do well." Wolfe was the valedictorian of his class when he received the Bachelor of Arts degree in 1926, and duly proceeded to the University of Michigan. In that university he was a graduate assistant in the physics department (1926-27) and a part-time laboratory and recitation instructor (1927-29) while working for the M.S. and Ph.D., which he received in 1927 and 1929, respectively.

After taking his doctorate (the title of his dissertation was *On the Principle of Microscopic Reversibility in the Kinetic Theory*) Wolfe did two years of research (1929-31) at the California Institute of Technology, in Pasadena, and at the University of California, as a National Research Fellow; and in 1931-32 he did further research, first at the University of Utrecht, Holland, as a fellow of the Lorentz Foundation, and later at Cornell University as a Heckscher research assistant. One year as an instructor in physics at Ohio State University preceded his appointment in 1934 to the staff of the College of the City of New York, in a similar capacity. Wolfe was advanced to an assistant professorship in physics in 1942, and to an associate professorship in early 1949. In September that year he was appointed professor of physics and head of the physics department at the Cooper Union School of Engineering, also in New York. He is the author of scientific articles in the *Physical Review* and the *American Journal of Physics*. The reference work *American Men of Science* (1944) lists among his fields of work theoretical physics, kinetic theory, and the theories of complex spectra, scattering, and x-ray satellites.

In 1944-46 Wolfe was on leave of absence from the New York college in order to serve as technical aide in the wartime Office of Scientific Research and Development. In recognition of his contributions to the war effort he was accorded the Navy Ordnance Development Award in December 1945 and the Certificate of Appreciation of the War and Navy Departments in June 1947. Since 1945 he has lectured to "all kinds of groups on atomic energy and related domestic and international problems" (the quoted words are Dr. Wolfe's). An early and convinced proponent of civilian atomic control, he told a CIO Communications Association convention in April 1946, that such control was the only effective means of providing "a framework within which we can work with other nations." In February 1947, speaking in the capacity of executive secretary of the Association of New York Scientists (an organization with a membership of 850 in the metropolitan area) he strongly urged the confirmation of David A. Lilienthal as head of the Atomic Energy Commission "because it will mean sound peacetime development of atomic energy in this country and because it will ad-

HUGH C. WOLFE

vance the cause of international cooperation to prevent war, which is the only real hope of security."

A fellow of the American Physical Society, by 1949 he had become chairman both of the Association of New York Scientists and of the Federation of American Scientists; and in the latter capacity he issued (May 28), with two fellow members, a statement on the subject of the Atomic Energy Commission fellowship security procedures to the effect that "Communists are no more dangerous to national security in nonsecret Government research than in private employment" (New York *Times'* words). This was at the time of Senator Bourke B. Hickenlooper's [47] accusation of "incredible mismanagement" against AEC chairman Lilienthal and of the revelation that a small quantity of uranium-235 was missing from the Argonne laboratory. The American Federation of Scientists chairman considered that there had been "altogether too much unwarranted hysteria" about the missing uranium, pointing out that the "strategic value" of the vanished one-seventh ounce was "negligible," and that Russian scientists could easily produce this quantity of uranium-235 by their own efforts (New York *Post*). In a letter to the New York *Times* of January 8, 1950, Wolfe voiced the endorsement of the Federation of American Scientists for a proposed cut in the AEC fellowship program, eliminating aid to men engaged in nonmilitary, nonsecret research. He objected to the security clearance procedures which Congress imposed upon all fellows whether engaged in secret work or not, claiming such precaution was inappropriate and contrary to public interest in the latter case. He said that the resultant handicap to scientific researchers should be removed by the passing of the National Science Foundation bill (already passed by the Senate

WOLFE, HUGH C.—*Continued*

and approved by the appropriate House committee) providing for Federal support of basic science; he emphasized the proviso that the bill should be restricted to aiding nonsecret research only.

Commenting as an individual on the hydrogen bomb, Wolfe pointed out that its control was implicit in the U.N. plan for control of the atom bomb, since, to the best of current knowledge, only by setting off one of the latter can an H-bomb be detonated. On February 5, 1950, the chairman of the Federation of American Scientists announced that body's proposal to the President that there be formed a new "nonpartisan commission," composed of men with breadth of vision, a small fraction of them being physical scientists. They would study problems of atomic control in relation to broad political and economic issues as a more realistic approach than that of treating the problem as an isolated issue. Stating that "not enough is officially disclosed," the scientists recommended that the proposals of such a commission should be reported to the people and be discussed by them before being made the basis of official governmental policy.

Hugh Campbell Wolfe and Mae Ithmer Coffman, a library science graduate of the University of Michigan, were married September 3, 1929. They have four children—Arthur, Elizabeth, James, and Helen—and reside in Tenafly, New Jersey, where both belong to the Parent-Teachers Association and the Mr. and Mrs. Club, and Dr. Wolfe is an elder of the Presbyterian Church. The scientist, who is a Republican in State politics, may vote Democratic in national elections. Greek letter societies to which he belongs are Pi Kappa Delta, Gamma Alpha, and Sigma Xi. He finds recreation in tennis playing (preferably doubles), camping out, and mountain hiking. He also enjoys "puttering around" his garden and doing carpentry jobs about his home; he is an "incorrigible reader" of novels, but cares little for the theater or motion pictures. He seldom drinks, and is a nonsmoker. Five feet eight and a half inches in height and weighing about 170 pounds, Wolfe has blue eyes and brown hair. "His speech," writes Wambly Bald in the New York *Post*, is "sharp and clipped, his laughter a bit sardonic."

References

N Y Post Mag p31 Jl 8 '49 por

American Men of Science (1949)

WOOLTON, FREDERICK JAMES MARQUIS, 1ST BARON Aug. 24, 1883-
British political party chairman; business executive

Address: b. c/o Conservative and Unionist Central Office, Abbey House, 2-8 Victoria St., London, S. W. 1; c/o Lewis's, Ltd., Ranelagh St., Liverpool; h. 68 Brook St., London, W.1

> NOTE: This biography supersedes the article which appeared in *Current Biography* in 1940.

Lord Woolton, Privy Councilor and chairman of the British Conservative party, entered politics in the course of World War II when, raised to the peerage as 1st Baron Woolton in 1939, he became a member of the House of Lords and shortly was appointed Minister of Food in the Coalition Government of the war period. Later he was Minister of Reconstruction in the same Government. Since 1936 chairman and senior managing director of Lewis's, Ltd., a Liverpool department store, Woolton had served on a number of Government committees and commissions in the years between World War I (when he was controller of civilian boots) and World War II, and had been named director-general of equipment and stores at the Ministry of Supply in 1939. His nomination to the chairmanship of the Conservative party came in 1946.

Frederick James Marquis was born in Manchester, England, on August 24, 1883, the only child of Thomas Robert Marquis and the former Margaret Ormerod. From Manchester Grammar School he proceeded to the University of Manchester, from which he was graduated in 1906 with the degree of B.Sc. While at college (as he revealed in an interview for *Who Runs Britain?* a "Contact Book") he joined the Fabian Society, the group devoted to the gradual interpenetration of British life with socialist ideas. After a period as a successful journalist, in 1908 he moved to Liverpool, to become warden jointly of the University Settlement and the David Lewis Club, organizations for practical social work among the poor, complementing the theoretical work of the University School of Social Science. In 1910 he was awarded a research fellowship in economics, he received the M.A. degree in 1912. His researches won him a fellowship of the Royal Statistical Society (of which he later became president).

With the advent of World War I Marquis made seven attempts to enlist, but was rejected each time on medical grounds. He was employed by the War Office in the raw materials section, and from there moved to the Leather Control Board as its secretary and controller of civilian boots. In the course of time he came to the conclusion that many of the controls were harmful and unnecessary. "I resigned," he told William Richmond, "because I thought that what I was doing was not in the best interests of the country." At the same time he withdrew from the Fabian Society. From 1918 to 1920 he undertook the reorganization of the Boot Manufacturers' Federation at its request, holding the position of secretary of the federation.

In 1920 Marquis was asked to join the directorate of Lewis's, Ltd., Liverpool department store, with branches in Manchester and Birmingham, at that time an all-Jewish family concern—its chairman, Alderman L. Cohen, said to Marquis, "It is the first time I have asked anyone who is not of my faith and of my family to join my board." For two years he was in charge of labor relations. Under him the policy was adopted of recruiting staff from University of Liverpool students; the Shop Assistants' Charter was devised, and agreements made with the trade unions and the Ministry of Labor to improve working conditions; he established a noncontributory pension scheme for women at the age of fifty-five and men at sixty. From staff control he went to direction of merchandising, and on the death of Rex D. Cohen in 1928, was appointed, with Harold Cohen, joint managing director. The company expanded, acquiring premises in Glasgow, Leeds, Leicester, and Hanley. Marquis' business interests widened: he became chairman of Bon Marché (Liverpool), Ltd. (another big general store), chairman of S. Reece and Sons, Ltd., owner of restaurants in Liverpool; and director of Martins Bank, the Royal Insurance Company, the Liverpool, London and Globe Insurance Company, Sofina (a large European utility and transport company), the Westpool Investment Trust, Ltd., the Birmingham Small Arms Company, the Birmingham Railway Carriage and Wagon Company, Ltd., and the London, Midland and Scottish Railway Company. Since August 1936 he has been chairman and senior managing director of Lewis's Investment Trust, Ltd., and its subsidiary and associated companies.

Concurrently Marquis served on several Government committees and commissions: he was a member of the Overseas Trade Development Council (1930-33), the Advisory Council of the Board of Trade (1930-34), the Advisory Council to the Post Office (1933-35). He was president of the Incorporated Association of Retail Distributors from 1930 to 1933 and chairman in 1934. During 1935-36 he was a member of the Home Office departmental committee concerned with the reorganization of fire brigades. In 1937-38 he was a member of the Cadman Committee on Civil Aviation, and in 1938 of the Lord Privy Seal's Committee to inquire into the need for deep shelters against air raids. The Hambledon Committee on the Teaching of Industrial Art counted him among its members. During April-September 1939 he was adviser to the Secretary of State for War.

In 1939 Britain had, for the first time in days of peace, a conscript army, and Marquis was called in to mobilize the clothing industry for the provision of new uniforms. His title was director-general of equipment and stores at the Ministry of Supply. In July 1939 he was raised to the peerage as Baron Woolton (the name of the title, created that year, comes from the outlying district of Liverpool where he had his home) and took his seat in the House of Lords as an independent. Nine months later he was named Minister of Food, (April 1940). The same month he was sworn into the Privy Council and given a seat in the War Cabinet.

With the enemy's submarine warfare and the heavy bombing that marked the period September 1940-June 1941, Lord Woolton, as Minister of Food, assembled provisions from all available sources and stockpiled them in widely scattered places from which fleets of trucks replaced bombed-out stocks. It has been credited to his organization that the British public, though on very short rations, escaped actual privation. His Ministry introduced the system of "British Restaurants" (often located in schools), where sustaining, hot, cheap meals could be procured; experimented with com-

British Inf. Services
LORD WOOLTON

munal kitchens for apartment blocks; inveighed against waste; publicized tasty ways of dealing with dull food (like the famous Woolton Pie). He became known for his informal press conferences, at which he "smoked, strolled about, used reporters' Christian names", and for his ability as a broadcaster: "he had the knack of talking with them [the housewives], not at them," Quentin Reynolds pointed out in an article in *Collier's* magazine.

From November 1943 to May 1945 Lord Woolton was Minister of the newly created Ministry of Reconstruction. There he was in charge of organizing the housing scheme and planning for the future of demobilized men. His recommendations were set out in a White Paper in 1944. In the so-called "caretaker Government," which held brief office from May to July 1945, he was Lord President of the Council.

When the return of Labor by a big majority in the general election of July 1945 put the Coalition Government out of office, Woolton wrote to Winston Churchill signifying his adherence to the Conservative party. "I understand," Woolton has said, "that he was very touched by someone wanting to join him in defeat. Later he asked me to be chairman of the party, and I thought it my duty to accept" (from *Who Runs Britain?*). Thus in 1946, after Woolton had been out of politics and had resumed his business interests, he became Chairman of the Conservative and Unionist Party Organization, as the Conservative party is formally named.

Under Lord Woolton's chairmanship the Conservative party undertook reorganization. It raised a campaign fund of £1,000,000, brought party membership up to 2,000,000, and Young Conservative groups to nearly 2,000, overhauled the publicity organization and the status of agents (trained, licensed and paid political experts employed by party associations), and made

WOOLTON, FREDERICK JAMES MARQUIS, 1ST BARON—*Continued*

it possible for Conservatives of small means to stand for Parliament. The party organization made itself felt in municipal elections with appreciable success, an unorthodox procedure, for until recent times individuals have counted for more than party labels in British municipal politics. The party scored a near-victory in the general election of February 1950, in which the Conservative popular vote was 43.4 per cent, the Labor 46.4 per cent. The Conservatives won 296 seats in Parliament, an increase of 83 over the 1945 results; the Laborites won 315 seats, a decrease of 78; a total of 308 seats are held by all the opposition parties.

Shortly before that election the party, during Woolton's chairmanship, issued a pamphlet on policy, entitled *The Right Road For Britain.* In it the party reaffirms its faith in a form of society based upon the value of the individua', the efficacy of personal energy and endeavor, the ownership of property, and the undesirability of a centralization of power. Stating the economic policy of the Conservative party to be production at competitive prices for world markets, the pamphlet declared that the country should aim at lower costs and freedom of action for producers and of choice for consumers, within the limits of basic public interest. Among items of policy are: a reduction in direct taxation and in the purchase tax on necessities; review of the income tax; reopening of the commodity markets within the limits of foreign exchange control; a progressive reduction of controls on the allocation of raw materials; abandoning of direction of labor and removal of the restrictions on freedom to enter retail trade; support of the trade union movement with the reservations that contributions to political funds should be entirely voluntary, and compulsory unionism should not be applied to contracts of employment with public bodies; recognition of small individual traders and manufacturers and of the professions; a pledge not to engage in state trading in competition with free enterprise; a promise to undertake no further nationalization, specifically not that of iron and steel, to restore free enterprise where practicable, and to reform those industries irrevocably nationalized by a system of decentralization of administration; opposition to nationalization of the land; maintenance of the new socal services, with some modifications in the details of their administration; the proposal of a reformed House of Lords with appropriate powers, to which heredity alone would not constitute sufficient qualification for admission.

In the international sphere the Conservative program provides for the promotion of the unity of the British Empire and Commonwealth as one of its basic objects. It favors a system of imperial priorities and preferential tariffs, of free migration within the Empire and Commonwealth and a policy looking to development of the colonies with a view to eventual self-government. In foreign policy it enunciates as a prime objective the establishment of a United Europe, including the ultimate union of Eastern and Western Germany under democratic conditions. It stresses the desirability of close association between the British Commonwealth and the United States in economic, cultural and defense spheres. Near and Far East policy, it advocates, should work for speedy stabilization in Greece and the Near East, and cooperation with nationalism in Asiatic countries as a foil to its exploitation by Communists. The Conservative stand is also presented in "Lord Woolton, the Man Behind Churchill," in *United Nations World,* February 1950.)

Many of Woolton's activities in the interests of social and cultural welfare centered in the City of Liverpool. He remained honorary secretary of the Liverpool University Settlement and chairman of the David Lewis Club, served on the University Council, acted as the University's deputy treasurer from 1931 to 1936 and as its treasurer thereafter. He was also a Justice of the Peace and chairman of the Liverpool Medical Research Council; in the same city a children's dental clinic and a prenatal clinic were two of his projects. He became a governor of Manchester Grammar School and of the Royal College of Art, and Chancellor of Manchester University (1944). He is a trustee of the National Central Library. Since 1943 he has been chairman of the executive committee of the British Red Cross, since 1944 vice-president of the National Institution for the Blind, and since 1945 president of the Central Council for Health Education.

Lord Woolton is a knight of the Order of St. John of Jerusalem (1935), and a Commander of the French Legion of Honor; in 1942 he was made a Companion of Honor. He is honorary colonel of the 113 Assault Engineer Regiment, Royal Engineers (Territorial Army), Deputy Lieutenant of Lancaster; and he has been named an honorary Freeman of Liverpool, and an honorary Freeman and member of the Court of Salters Company. The honorary LL.D. degree was bestowed on him by Manchester University in 1943 and by Liverpool University in 1944; Hamilton College (United States) and McGill University (Canada) presented him with honorary degrees in the spring of 1950, when he visited America. A selection of his speeches was published in 1945, under the title *The Adventures of Reconstruction.*

A Unitarian, he is on the council of Ullet Road Unitarian Church in Liverpool. In 1912 he married Maud Smith, of Manchester. His son and heir, the Honorable Roger David Marquis, is a Flying Officer in the Royal Air Force; the Wooltons also have a daughter, Margaret Judith, who is married to Major J. H. Sandeman Allen, of the Royal Artillery. Woolton's clubs are the Athenaeum, Carlton, Brooks's, and Beefsteak, and the University of Liverpool.

References

Collier's 106:16+ N 9 '40 por
Great Britain and the East p20 Ja 17 '42 por
Manchester Guardian p13 Ap 6 '40; p12 Ap 9 '40
New Statesm & Nation 26:395 D 18 '43
Observer (London) Ag 13 '42 por

Burke's Peerage (1949)
International Who's Who, 1949
10 Eventful Years (1947)
Who Runs Britain? (Contact Book No. 16 S '49 por)
Who's Who, 1950
Who's Who in America, 1950-51
World Biography (1948)

WRIGHT, LOUIS B(OOKER) Mar. 1, 1899- Historian; library director
Address: b. c/o Folger Shakespeare Library, 201 E. Capitol St., S.E., Washington 3, D.C.; h. 2915 Foxhall Road, N.W., Washington 16, D.C.

Louis B. Wright is the director of the Folger Shakespeare Library, in Washington, D.C., which is dedicated to the advancement of literary and historical scholarship. Prior to assuming this post in 1948, he had served for sixteen years as a member of the permanent research group of the Henry E. Huntington Library in California. As historian he has specialized in the fields of the English Renaissance and American civilization of the colonial period. In August 1950 he was appointed chairman of the advisory board of the John Simon Guggenheim Memorial Foundation, which assists the development of scholars and artists by aiding them to carry on research and artistic creation.

Born in Greenwood County, South Carolina, on March 1, 1899, Louis Booker Wright is the son of Thomas Fleming and Lena (Booker) Wright. His father was a school teacher. After attending the Greenwood public schools, young Wright entered Wofford College, at Spartanburg. In the year 1918 (in World War I) he served for six months in the United States Army, being stationed at the Plattsburg (New York) Training Camp, and was an infantry instructor, with the rank of sergeant, in the Students' Army Training Corps, at Wofford. That year he also began his journalistic career as a reporter on the Greenwood *Index-Journal*. "Next to my father," he has remarked (in the Columbia, South Carolina, *State Magazine*, September 3, 1950), "the man who taught me the most in Greenwood was Harry L. Watson, a wise and brilliant editor. Before I was out of Wofford, he gave me a job on his newspaper. . . . There I learned the principles of writing under the watchful eye of a model of accuracy." Elected to Phi Beta Kappa, he received his Bachelor of Arts degree from Wofford in 1920; this was followed by three years as city editor of the *Index-Journal*.

In 1924 Wright obtained his Master of Arts degree from the University of North Carolina and began teaching there as a fellow in English. Two years later he was awarded his Doctor of Philosophy degree from the same institution and won the Smith Prize for research in language and literature. He then served, successively, as instructor (1926-27), assistant professor (1929-30), and associate professor (1930-32) of English at the University of North Carolina. Given leave of absence from

the university in 1927, he worked as Johnston research scholar at Johns Hopkins University, and the next year received a Guggenheim Fellowship to study "the reflection of contemporary ideas in English drama before 1642." This grant enabled him to continue his research in England and on the Continent; it was renewed for the summer of 1930. In the winter of that same year he was visiting professor at Emory University, Atlanta, Georgia.

During 1931-32 Wright was one of the ten visiting scholars at the Henry E. Huntington Library and Art Gallery, at San Marino, California, where he engaged in research on the development of middle-class culture in England during the sixteenth and seventeenth centuries. He joined the permanent research group of the library in the latter year as research professor in charge of the field of English literature and as an editorial supervisor of the library's extensive publishing program. Established in 1919, the Huntington Library in 1927 initiated a policy of developing its collection from a repository of literary treasures into an active institute of historical research, primarily in the field of Anglo-American civilization, in which its source materials were especially strong. A permanent research staff was gradually gathered together, and a system of grants and fellowships set up to bring established and promising young scholars to the library, both from the United States and abroad, for a year of research in various fields of English and American civilization. Between 1932 and 1948 Wright had an important part in developing and administering this research program. He served as chairman of the committee on fellowships, as a member of the executive committee, and as editor of the *Huntington Library Quarterly* (1946-48). In the meanwhile carrying on his own research, he also assisted in building up the library's reference collection and in developing congenial working conditions so that scholars could use the library with the maximum of efficiency.

Throughout this period Wright also lectured and taught at various educational institutions in the Midwest and on the Pacific Coast. He served as an associate member of the faculty at the California Institute of Technology (1932-48); visiting professor of bibliography and research methods on the graduate faculty of the University of California at Los Angeles (1934-48); and visiting professor of American civilization at Pomona College (1941-48). In the summer of 1935 he was visiting professor of English at the University of Michigan; during the spring of 1942 he delivered the annual Walker-Ames lectures in English literature and history at the University of Washington; and the summer of 1946 found him as visiting professor at the University of Minnesota.

On July 1, 1948, Wright assumed his duties as director of the Folger Shakespeare Library in Washington, D.C. When his appointment was announced the previous November by the trustees of Amherst College, who administer the library's endowments, plans to broaden and extend the library's research program were also made public. Dedicated in 1932, the li-

LOUIS B. WRIGHT

brary was founded by the late Henry Clay Folger primarily as a collection relating to Shakespeare and his age—it contains the world's largest collection of Shakespeareana. Since that time the library's holdings have been increased until, in Wright's words, it "ranks among the three or four top libraries of the world in rare books valuable for the study of the history of English civilization in the sixteenth and seventeenth centuries," the period when England was establishing colonies in America and laying the foundations of American society. The *Christian Science Monitor* (July 17, 1948) further quoted Wright as saying: "The new policies of the library will serve to bring a wider variety of scholars to the institution and give greater opportunities for the exchange of information between historians and literary students." The ultimate goal of the library is to procure in some form every significant English book published from the invention of printing to the end of the seventeenth century.

Under Wright's directorship the Folger has been purchasing reference books as aids to scholars whose research is in the field of rare books. An advisory council has been organized, composed of a group of the most active scholars and bibliophiles in the United States and England. The Folger research group holds monthly conferences for scholars interested in Renaissance research. Fellowship funds have been used for short-term grants-in-aid to stimulate research and give as many scholars as possible an opportunity to investigate the extent of the library's source materials.

A member of the advisory board of the John Simon Guggenheim Foundation since 1942, Wright was appointed chairman of this board on August 5, 1950, following the retirement of Dr. Frank Aydelotte '41, who held the post since the establishment of the foundation in 1925. During this period the foundation has appointed 2,317 fellows. The fellowships are available

to assist research in any field of knowledge and creative work in any of the fine arts. As chairman, Wright will preside over the foundation's committees of selection for fellowships, which are granted annually to citizens and permanent residents of the United States, Canada, and Latin America.

Wright's principal books comprise six titles (as of 1950). The first, *Middle-Class Culture in Elizabethan English* (1935), was followed in 1936 by *Puritans in the South Seas*, written with Mary Isabel Fry. Another volume was *The First Gentlemen of Virginia: Intellectual Qualities of the Early Colonial Ruling Class* (1940). According to A. B. Shepperson, in the *New England Quarterly*, the book, "while written *con amore*, does not present a misleading idealization, but rather an amply documented reconstruction of its subject." Two years later appeared *Religion and Empire: The Alliance between Piety and Commerce in English Expansion, 1558-1625*, which B. I. Bell, in *Commonweal*, regarded as a "painstaking study of the sermons of the period." After the publication of *The First Americans in North Africa* (in collaboration with Julia MacLeod, 1945), Wright wrote *The Atlantic Frontier: Colonial American Civilization, 1607-1763* (1947). Perry Miller, in the New York *Times*, found the story of this latter book "readable, told with dispatch, pertinent quotations from the sources, and a refreshing disregard of pedantry." Wright is also the author of some fifty or sixty articles for various periodicals, and he has edited the letters, diaries, and papers of several prominent eighteenth century Virginians. He has been assistant editor of *Studies in Philology* (1930-31), and associate editor of the *William and Mary Quarterly* (1944-45), the *Pacific Spectator* (1947-48), and the *Journal of the History of Ideas* (since 1940).

The historian-library director has memberships in the Modern Language Association, American Historical Association, American Antiquarian Society, American Philosophical Society, American Academy of Arts and Sciences, the Grolier Club, and other professional organizations. Vice-chairman of the Pacific Coast Committee for the Humanities from 1946 to 1948, he is, in 1950, a member of the advisory board of the Institute of Early American History and Culture, Williamsburg, Virginia. Honorary Doctor of Letters degrees were bestowed upon him by Wofford College (1941), Mills College (1947), Princeton University (1948), Amherst College (1948), and Occidental College (1949), and he was awarded Doctor of Humanities degrees by Northwestern University (1948) and the University of North Carolina (1950). His clubs are Tudor and Stuart (Johns Hopkins), Athenaeum (Pasadena), and Cosmos (Washington). He lists his political affiliation as Democratic. On June 10, 1925, he married Frances Marion Black; they have one son, Louis Christopher. Five feet, five inches tall, Wright weighs 125 pounds, has brown eyes and brown hair. He names fly-fishing as his favorite form of relaxation.

References

Christian Sci Mon Jl 17 '48
State Mag (Columbia, S.C.) p10 S 3 '50
Directory of American Scholars, 1942
Who's Who in America, 1950-51

WRIGHT, RUSSEL Apr. 3, 1905- Industrial designer
Address: h. 221 E. 48th St., New York 17

NOTE: This biography supersedes the article which appeared in *Current Biography* in 1940.

Russel Wright has gained the reputation of being among the most influential of the industrial designers who are seeking to give a distinctly modern American character to the arts and crafts of the country. The aim of Wright's work is to combine functional efficiency with ease and with integrity of design. Regarding his work in home furnishing he has said, "I have always upheld the trend to informality. . . . To facilitate the way of ease and informality of living by design, in the postwar world is my 'cause.'"

A native of Ohio, Russel Wright was born in Lebanon on April 3, 1905, the son of Willard and Harriet (Morris) Wright. He is descended from early American pioneers, two of whom, Whipple and Morris, were signers of the Declaration of Independence. His paternal grandmother, one of the founders of Lebanon College, sought to impart to him some of her energetic spirit and will power, an influence for which Wright is grateful. As a boy he was so much interested in modeling and painting that he worked after school hours at an ammunition factory in order to pay for classes at the Cincinnati Academy of Arts. Here he studied painting under Frank Duveneck.

After finishing high school, Wright went to New York to enroll at the Art Students League, where he studied modeling with Leo Lentelli and painting with Kenneth Hayes Miller. In 1921 as a climax to his year at the Art Students League, he won the first and second prizes donated by Tiffany in a competition for a war memorial plaque. Of his years of studying art, Russel Wright wrote in *Design* of March 1941: "I was very religious as an art student and my work was mixed up with my religion. . . . I studied both painting and sculpture. My work had average merit. But I did not turn from the fine arts for the sake of making more money, and my esthetical conscience is just as energetic as it used to be. Designing articles which could be sold for use to every man seemed a more important service in my time."

When Wright did turn from the fine arts, he was not to venture into industrial arts immediately, but rather to enter Princeton University. Not only was Princeton a tradition in the Wright family, but the study of law was also, his father having been a county judge in Ohio. At Princeton, however, he became interested in the theater; and in addition to being general director of the Intime Playhouse, he designed sets and costumes for the productions

RUSSEL WRIGHT

of the Triangle Club. He continued this sort of work at the artists' colony at Woodstock, New York, where he designed the backgrounds and costumes for the "Maverick" festival, an annual Woodstock event. In 1925 he worked on the sets and costumes of the *Grand Street Follies*, a New York production. By this time Norman Bel Geddes '40, who had become acquainted with his work, offered him an opportunity, which he accepted. That took him to France, to assist with the Paris production of *Jeanne d'Arc*.

After his return to New York, Wright worked as a stage manager with Lee Simonson, George Cukor, and Rouben Mamoulian. During this time he was stage manager for the Theatre Guild, the Neighborhood Playhouse, the Group Theatre and for various other New York and out-of-town productions. He set up a workshop in which he produced stage properties, and from which soon came specially made furniture and decorative accessories for New York's department stores and decorators. Beginning with these comparatively modest undertakings in industrial design, he became an artist whose "ideas about home furnishings, from sofas to salt shakers, have helped to change the whole American mode of living" (*Pathfinder*, August 23, 1950).

One characteristic of Wright's work has been his innovations in employing commonplace materials in untraditional functions. In his emphasis upon the informal he was one of the pioneer designers who used spun aluminum for table accessories, wood for salad bowls and trays in the dining room, copper for decorative pieces, bamboo, rattan and rubber for lamps. In 1933 he designed an armchair with a carved wood frame, a fur-covered seat and a leather-covered swivel back, the only chair of American design chosen a few years later by the Museum

WRIGHT, RUSSEL—*Continued*

of Modern Art for its international exhibition of modern chairs.

In an undertaking described in *American Magazine of Art* as "the first successful effort to unite modern design with popular price levels and established production methods," Russel Wright was one of the first designers to use a bleached maple finish for modern furniture. He was soon exhibiting furniture notable for plasticity, flowing curves, form-fitting shapes, and for serviceability and ease, qualities which eventually became identifiably his own. He has designed a bedroom of day-long use with built-in furniture for functional ease in such activities as sewing, writing, reading, listening to music. Beds and other furniture pieces, as well as storage cabinets, are built and located so that they become a part of the room.

The work of Wright's that has perhaps received the greatest amount of attention from the public has been his "American Modern Dinnerware," a set of dishes which he produced about 1938. Since then Wright has designed and produced another set of tableware in fine china (1946), of which he said, "China lovers are going to be scandalized at the use of the material." Wright's tableware is made to be stacked compactly, requiring less space than conventional dishes in the closet; the simplicity of shape is intended to facilitate speed in washing and drying; the depressed grips and the rounded and raised rims are designed to reduce breakage. As Wright explains, "All the enforced cooking and dishwashing I did during the war made me want to do something practical for the housewife. . . .I have no sympathy with the idea of keeping traditional design alive" (*Time*, July 29, 1946). In 1946 it was reported that nearly fourteen million pieces of Wright's dinnerware had been sold since 1939, at the rate of $1,500,000 annually since 1943.

Edgar Kaufmann, Jr., in the *American Magazine of Art* (April 1948), wrote that "Wright passed through the major design metamorphoses of the past twenty years. Beginning with fantasy native to the theater and a romanticism related to Lachaise, he quickly adopted the discipline of pure geometry and surfaces typical of industry." Kaufmann finds much that is praiseworthy in the "strict style" of Wright's design, and observes that Wright's popular successes, by which he is often judged, do not reveal the entire scope of his work. An adverse criticism of Wright's dinnerware came from Manny Faber in *New Republic* (November 20, 1944), who found the design and colors hard and cold.

The range of Wright's art in industry includes as well glassware, furniture, radios, wallpaper, rugs, drapery and upholstery fabrics, lamps, flatware and designs of rooms and displays. Early examples of his work were the Focal Food Exhibit at the New York World's Fair in 1939 and his design of a showroom and displays for the International Handkerchief Company. Productions of his designs have been exhibited in both American and European museums, among them the Metropolitan Museum of Art and the Museum of Modern Art in New York, the Everyday Art Gallery in Minneapolis' Walker Art Center, the Philadelphia Art Alliance, and in many department stores. Pictures of his designs have appeared in numerous magazines devoted to design in industry and home furnishings.

In the early 1940's Russel Wright originated the "American Way" merchandising project, a cooperative undertaking of sixty-five designers, artists, craftsmen, and manufacturers in ten different home furnishings classifications. The group held an exhibition in August 1940 in Chicago's Merchandise Mart. The author of several magazine articles expressing his views on industrial design in America and art education in *Interiors* and *Design*, Wright (with Mrs. Wright) has also written a book entitled *Guide to Easier Living*, for publication in November of 1950. It is described as offering "a thoroughly practical plan for equipping and running a home without drudgery."

Typical of Wright's achievement in ease, utility, and design is his home in New York City, with its terraced garden, winding outdoor staircase, and the S-shaped glass enclosure that he uses for a workshop. His wife, the former Mary Einstein, is also a designer. According to an article in *House Beautiful* (May 1945), Wright is "a restless, exploratory, stubborn designer," who "likes to take long walks through the woods, wears overalls easily, reads little, and has a preference for exotic foods, especially Oriental dishes. He prefers a phonograph to a concert because people get in the way of the music."

References

Am Home 11:60-2 Ja '34 por
Am Mag of Art 41:144+ Ap '48
Arch Forum 67:283-5 O '37 por
Arts & Dec 42:26-9 F '35
Dec Digest p44-48+ Ap '35 por
Home & F 44 (House B 75):30-3 Ap '34
House B 87:78-9 My '45
Interiors p56+ D '44
Pathfinder 57:42+ Ag 23 '50 por
Pict R 37:55 O '35
Who's Who in American Art, 1940-41
Who's Who in the East (1948)

WRONG, (HUMPHREY) HUME Sept. 10, 1894- Ambassador from Canada to the United States

Address: c/o Embassy of Canada, 2825 Rock Creek Dr., Washington, D.C.

Hume Wrong, Ambassador from Canada to the United States since 1946, was previously connected with the Canadian representation in Washington from 1927 (when a Legation was established there) until 1937, and again saw service in the United States capital in 1941-42. He has been Canada's representative at various international assemblies, including the League of Nations, the San Francisco United Nations Conference of 1945 and the first session of the U.N. General Assembly in 1946.

Born in Toronto, Ontario, on September 10, 1894, Humphrey Hume Wrong is the son of George McKinnon and Sophia Hume (Blake) Wrong. His father was a noted scholar, an authority on French Canadian history and Canadian-American relations; his mother was the daughter of Edward Blake, for some years the leader of the Liberal party, and later Chancellor of the University of Toronto. Hume Wrong was educated at Upper Canada College (Toronto), Ridley College (St. Catherine's, Ontario), the University of Toronto, and Balliol College, Oxford.

Upon receiving the B.A. degree from Toronto in 1915 Wrong volunteered for the Canadian Army but was rejected because of a boyhood injury to one eye. Then he went to England and joined the Fourth battalion of the Oxford and Bucks Light Infantry, with which he served as a lieutenant in 1915 and 1916. Wounded in the battle of the Somme, he was invalided back to Canada, and there served as an administrative officer in the Canadian section of the Royal Flying Corps. At the time of his demobilization in 1919 he held the rank of captain. That year he took up the Sir Joseph Flavelle Scholarship, which had been deferred in 1915, and proceeded to Oxford, where he began the studies which are contained in his book, *The Government of the West Indies* (1923); from the English university he received the B.Litt. and M.A. degrees. He returned to Canada in 1921, to lecture in the history department of the University of Toronto. There his research resulted in the publication of *Sir Alexander MacKenzie, Explorer and Fur Trader* (1927).

When the Honorable Vincent Massey was selecting his staff for the opening of a Canadian legation at Washington in 1927 (the first separate Canadian representation there, apart from that implied in the British Embassy), he chose Wrong as first secretary. At that time the latter had risen to the rank of assistant professor of history at the University of Toronto. The young diplomat who served continuously in Washington until 1937, was made counselor to the Legation when Massey left Washington in 1930, and was in charge for a year; he was again chargé d'affaires in 1935-36. In October 1937 Wrong was named Canadian advisory officer at the League of Nations. At Geneva he sat on the governing board of the International Labor Office, and represented his country at three meetings of the League Assembly. Shortly after the outbreak of World War II he was sent to Canada House in London to help develop the plans for economic coordination between Canada and Britain. He was in London during the establishment of Canadian Military Headquarters, the arrival of the first Canadian contingents, and the bombing of the city.

Wrong returned to Washington in 1941 as senior counselor at the Canadian Legation. A year later he was appointed Assistant Under Secretary of State for External Affairs. At Ottawa he was in charge of the department's political divisions, handling relations with the British Commonwealth and Europe. Promoted to Associate Under Secretary in 1944, his area

Wide World Photos
HUME WRONG

of supervision was extended to include all of the department's political divisions. He attended the Commonwealth talks in London early in 1945, and was Senior Adviser and Canadian Alternate Delegate at the U.N. Conference on International Organization in San Francisco in April 1945. At the final meeting of the League of Nations Assembly in Geneva, and at the first meeting of the U.N. General Assembly in London, Wrong was Canada's representative.

In mid-September 1946 Wrong was named Ambassador Extraordinary and Plenipotentiary to the United States. In Washington he has been an advocate of full-scale aid to Europe, revising of the United Nations Charter, the North Atlantic Pact, and close economic-military integration of Canada and the United States. "If close integration of the economies," he said in New York in January 1948, "was good in war—good for both countries and good for our allies—why should we not with profit continue the same principle . . . indefinitely?" The Canadian Ambassador has been outspoken on the subject of his country's contribution to postwar recovery, pointing out that she was carrying on a "Marshall Plan of her own," which during 1946 and 1947 extended two billion dollars in credits to the United Kingdom and Europe. This, he noted, was a greater contribution in relation to population and national income than that made by the United States.

Wrong has been a consistent advocate of measures of collective security; in respect to the United Nations he has expressed the Canadian view that a modification of the charter is necessary. "The Canadian Government," he stated in 1948, "has never liked the veto. At San Francisco and before, their view was made known; they accepted it with reluctance as the necessary price of agreement." He suggested that an early "stop-gap" agreement between the

WRONG, HUME—*Continued*

great powers, limiting the fields in which the veto could be employed, would be a salutary development. In July 1948 Prime Minister St. Laurent [48] sent Lester Pearson [47] (then Under Secretary of State for External Affairs) to join Wrong in Washington for the talks which preceded the drafting of the Atlantic Pact. James Reston in the New York *Times* (July 8, 1948) commented that the two men were contributing "common sense and informality" to the discussions, and that the presence of Canadian representatives might influence the United States into full backing of western defense. In May of the following year Wrong was the first Ambassador to be able to present his country's certification of the Atlantic Pact to Dean Acheson. After the outbreak of war in Korea Wrong, announcing (July 1950) that the Canadian Government would send three destroyers to Korea, emphasized the importance, in his view, of underlining the U.N. character of all the forces under General MacArthur's command.

The Canadian Ambassador has been given credit for facilitating the negotiation of such international agreements as the Niagara River Power Treaty, signed by Acheson and Wrong in February 1950, and the Canada Military Assistance Pact, which regulates the purchase of arms in either country by its neighbor. The Niagara Treaty, regarded by the Canadian Government as a preliminary to a treaty designed to develop the St. Lawrence River's power and navigational facilities, has made possible a four-year generator construction program and replaces several older agreements dating from 1909.

On December 22, 1922, Wrong married Joyce Hutton, daughter of Maurice Hutton, principal of University College, Toronto. The Wrongs have one son, Dennis, and one daughter, June, both married. *Time* magazine has described the diplomat as tall, slim, and "lofty-browed." His recreations include reading, bridge, golf, and bird-watching. Wrong belongs to the Rideau Club (Ottawa) and the Metropolitan and Chevy Chase in Washington.

References

Liberty (Canadian ed.) S 14 '46
Montreal Star Ap 19 '41
Saturday Night Mr 14 '50
Time 48:40 S 16 '46 por
Toronto Globe and Mail O 12 '39
Toronto Star F 16 '27
Toronto Telegram O 2 '37
Canadian Who's Who, 1948
Who's Who, 1950
Who's Who in America, 1950-51
Who's Who in Canada, 1947-48
World Biography (1948)

YOUNG, ROBERT   Feb. 22, 1907-   Motion picture actor

Address: b. c/o National Broadcasting Co., Sunset Blvd. & Vine St., Los Angeles, Calif.; h. Beverly Hills, Calif.

Robert Young, who has been playing leading parts in motion pictures since 1931, entered the radio field a few years later. It was in connection with his broadcast program *Father Knows Best* that the Good Drivers Club movement, a safe-driving campaign among teen-age drivers, was launched in early 1950. Schooled in acting at the Pasadena Community Playhouse, Young has played in a wide variety of motion pictures (one of his first roles was that of son to Helen Hayes in *The Sin of Madelon Claudet*), including *Strange Interlude, Crossfire, Claudia,* and *Joe Smith, American.* Young, who is also interested in the production aspect of motion pictures, with a partner has formed an independent producing company, Cavalier Productions.

Born in Chicago, Illinois, on February 22, 1907, Robert Young (whose middle name is George) is one of the five children of Thomas E. Young, an Irish-American building contractor. The Young family moved west to Seattle and then to Los Angeles while Robert was still a boy. An elder brother, Joseph, who became a screen comedian, helped to support Robert while the latter attended Lincoln High School; the student, however, had "the usual paper-route and other adolescent jobs." He took part in high school dramatics and, after his graduation, studied and acted at night for four years at the Pasadena Community Playhouse. During this period he was able to support himself by working as a drugstore clerk, haberdashery salesman, reporter, collector for a building and loan company, and bank clerk.

Young played over forty parts as a member of the Pasadena Community Players, among them the roles of Marco Polo in *Marco Millions* and of Mellersh Wilkins in *Enchanted April.* In 1931 he traveled for four months with a touring stock company presenting a play called *The Ship.* It was during this tour that Young was seen by a talent scout of Metro-Goldwyn-Mayer and given a screen test which resulted in a five-year contract with that company.

For his first film the young actor, loaned to the Fox studio, appeared as a featured player in *The Black Camel,* which was made in Honolulu. This was followed by leading roles in *The Guilty Generation, The Sin of Madelon Claudet* (with Helen Hayes), *The Wet Parade,* and *Strange Interlude,* all for MGM. In the course of the next four years he appeared in twenty-four pictures, playing serious roles in most of them. In 1935 *Photoplay,* in reporting that he had been cast in his first comedy part in *Vagabond Lady,* stated that he had "never intended being a serious, dramatic actor." The same article described Young as having "a kind of sparkle that he must continuously repress before the cameras when playing a serious role." In England in 1936, Young played opposite Jessie Matthews in *It's Love Again,* and also made *Secret Agent.* After his return to the United States, a few of the many succeeding pictures in which he appeared, playing both serious and comedy parts, were *The Bride Wore Red, Three Com-*

rades, Bridal Suite, Northwest Passage, Western Union, and *The Trial of Mary Dugan.*

In 1942 Young appeared in three of the year's most notable pictures. In the title role in *H. M. Pulham, Esq.,* the screen adaptation of John Marquand's best-selling novel, Young's interpretation of "the inhibited, frustrated, baffled Boston gentleman," was called "a first-rate job" by *Time. Journey for Margaret,* in which Young played an American reporter who befriends two British children during the blitz, was ranked as one of the ten best films of the year by Bosley Crowther of the New York *Times,* while one of the "runners-up" on his list was *Joe Smith, American,* an unpretentious picture in which a mechanic in a defense factory defends secrets of a bomb-sight from enemy agents. *Newsweek* observed that "the acting—particularly Robert Young in the title role—is unaffected and credible."

Claudia, based on Rose Franken's popular magazine stories, novel, and play of the same name, in which Young appeared as the husband, was termed "a motion picture comedy triumph" of 1943. The New York *Sun* reviewer wrote: "Mr. Young has never had a part which approached this one. He handles the dramatic moments as skillfully as the lighter ones." A sequel, *Claudia and David,* released in 1946, was generally received by the critics as "anticlimactic" and a "feeble continuation" of the original. (Dorothy Mc-Guire was Claudia in both films.) Among other MGM films in which Young played were *Slightly Dangerous, Sweet Rosie O'Grady, Cairo,* and *The Canterville Ghost.*

In 1945 Young ended his long association with MGM. Deciding to free-lance, he signed a five-year contract to do one picture a year for RKO, for whom he had already made *Lady Luck.* A 1946 release, for Paramount, was *The Searching Wind.* For one of his first films at RKO he was again teamed with Dorothy McGuire, in *The Enchanted Cottage,* based on a play by Pinero and brought up to date to show the problems of a disfigured veteran of World War II. This was followed by *Those Endearing Young Charms,* adapted from a play by Edward Chodorov, and *They Won't Believe Me,* an "imaginative murder tale." *Crossfire,* released in 1947, was, in Young's own words, "a powerful indictment against anti-Semitism and other isms," based on the novel *The Brick Foxhole* by Richard Brooks. In an interview for the New York *Post* Young gave credit for the success of the film to Dore Schary[48], "the fellow who was responsible for *Joe Smith, American*—up to now the best picture I've ever made." As the harassed husband and father in the popular *Sitting Pretty* (in which Clifton Webb was the baby sitter), Young was considered by the New York *World-Telegram* critic as "one of our most likeable experts in sly gaiety."

In 1947 Young formed a partnership with Eugene Rodney to produce motion pictures under the independent company name of Cavalier Productions. Their first picture was

ROBERT YOUNG

the result of Young's purchase of a magazine story which he intended to resell to a studio as a vehicle for himself. Instead, Young and Rodney produced the picture, *Relentless,* a Western in Technicolor, which was released through Columbia. Young told Irene Thirer of the *Post* that producing had been a good experience for him. "I'm getting away from those juveniles," he said, "and the time may come when I want to permanently walk out on the camera and confine my knowledge of film business to what goes on behind the scenes."

The actor's radio career has run parallel with his motion picture work since his debut in a guest "spot" on NBC on August 6, 1936. Two years later he was master of ceremonies on the *Good News of 1938* program on the same station. He was heard as the star of Zane Grey's *Western Union* on the *Kate Smith Hour* over CBS in 1941, and co-starred with Joan Bennett and Ralph Bellamy in *Mr. and Mrs. Smith* on the *Screen Guild Players* program in 1942. In 1944 he joined the *Maxwell House Coffee Time* program on NBC as "straight man" to Frank Morgan's comedy. Two of his radio appearances relating to the war effort were on a bond-selling program, *It's Happening To Me,* written by Arch Oboler, and on a series designed "to promote better understanding of the peoples of the United Nations," written by Norman Corwin and Ranald Macdougall.

In August 1949 a new program was launched on NBC with the title *Father Knows Best.* Written by Ed James, the program runs for half an hour on Thursday nights. It tells the story of "an average family in an average American town," the family consisting of Father and Mother Anderson and their three

YOUNG, ROBERT—*Continued*

children. John Crosby, radio columnist for the New York *Herald Tribune*, wrote: "Robert Young, who plays father, is a far more expert comedian than I had realized. He is required by Mr. James to put his foot in his mouth at least once in every script, and he does so with as much poise as possible under the circumstances." *Variety*, reviewing the initial program of the series, called it a "honey of a package," adding, "It's real without being maudlin, and the comedy stems from hilarious situations and unforced punchy lines. . . . Robert Young as 'Father' was a neat casting trick."

Tied in with the radio program since January 5, 1950, has been the safe-driving campaign, with which Young is identified. Proposed by the Inter-Industry Highway Safety Committee, the campaign interested Young, according to the Washington *Post*, partly because his father was killed about ten years ago when an accident involving two teen-age drivers threw him from his horse. As a result of Young's safety discussions on his weekly program (the *Post* reported on March 12, 1950) one and a half million Robert Young Good Drivers Club cards had been distributed. In addition, more than two and a half million agreements have been signed by young people and their fathers, according to which, in return for their sons' and daughters' promise to abide by the "eight tenets of safe driving," the father promises occasional use of the family car. Young recently completed a tour of several Eastern cities in the United States, where he spoke before both groups of teen-agers and civic and safety organizations, under the auspices of the National Safety Council. For his guidance of young people, Young was one of five honored (from various entertainment fields) by the National Father's Day Committee in May 1950 as a "Father of the Year."

The actor's plans for the future include further productions by his own company. Two pictures have been tentatively announced for future production, *Storm Within a Heart* and *Twelve Against the Underworld*. Young and Rodney are reported to have discussed plans for a motion picture based on the *Father Knows Best* radio script, whose Hooper rating rose from 5 to 12.3 in eight months. Young has been quoted as saying he will not appear on television—"at least not until a sponsor will pay as much as a motion picture producer." After making *And Baby Makes Three* for Columbia, and *Bride for Sale* and *Here Lies Love* for RKO, he withdrew from the lead in *The Story of a Divorce* at the latter studio.

Young has been called "dependable" and "conservative" in his private as well as his professional life. In 1933 he married Elizabeth Louise Henderson, with whom he had gone to high school. Their four daughters are Carol Anne, Barbara Queen, Elizabeth Louise, and Kathleen Joy. In 1939, when the Youngs bought "Sleepy Hollow Ranch" in San Fernando Valley, the actor said, "Sooner or later everything I've ever wanted has come

to me. I've been so lucky since the first day I started in pictures." The family has a home in Beverly Hills; and Young recently purchased a 160-acre ranch near Carmel, where he plans to develop a walnut grove. He flies his own plane, is a television and motion picture fan. Six feet tall, he weighs 170 pounds; the color of his hair and eyes is brown. Young has been described as a "gay, carefree, active person."

References

Movie Classic 3:52 O '32
N Y Post Mag p12 Ja 31 '48 por
Photoplay 43:40 My '33
International Motion Picture Almanac, 1947-48
Winchester's   Screen   Encyclopedia (1948)

YOUNGER, KENNETH (GILMOUR)
Dec. 15, 1908- British Government official
Address: b. c/o Foreign Office, Whitehall, London, S.W.1; h. 3 Clareville Grove, South Kensington, London, S.W.7, England

The Minister of State in the British Labor Government, the Honorable Kenneth Younger has been a member of Parliament since 1945, having been re-elected in the general election of 1950. In his first year in the House he was Parliamentary private secretary to the then Minister of State, and later became Parliamentary Under Secretary of State at the Home Office. A lawyer by training, he has served on a number of his party's legal and judicial committees, and has been a British delegate to the United Nations.

Kenneth Gilmour Younger was born December 15, 1908, the second son of the second Viscount Younger of Leckie, D.S.O., proprietor of a well-known Edinburgh brewery. His grandfather, the first viscount, carried out a reorganization of the Conservative party, served as its chairman from 1916 to 1923, and subsequently as its treasurer until his death in 1929. Kenneth Younger started his education at the ancient college of Winchester; from there he proceeded to New College, Oxford, to read "Modern Greats," i.e., philosophy, politics, and economics. While at the university he joined the Fabian Society (a group devoted to the gradual spread of socialistic ideas) and the Oxford University Labor party.

After graduation Younger read law at the Inner Temple, London, and was called to the bar in 1932. He practiced as a barrister for some years, then joined the staff of the War Office. Just before the outbreak of World War II, in 1939 he joined the Intelligence Corps. Serving abroad through the war, he rose to the rank of major. In North Africa he distinguished himself by his part in an expedition which released 6,000 Allied prisoners from a concentration camp on the edge of the Sahara. After the invasion of Europe he served successively on the staffs of Field Marshal Montgomery[42] and of General Sir Miles Dempsey[44], commander in chief of the British Second Army. Here his fluency in the French language stood him in good stead; he also has a knowledge of German and Russian, the latter of which he began to study toward the end of the war.

In 1945 Younger went into politics. At the July general election he ran as the Labor candidate for Grimsby (one of Britain's foremost fishing ports), and defeated Sir Walter Womersley, a former Minister of Pensions. In accord with Attlee's apparent policy of quick promotion for young men of promise, Younger was made Parliamentary private secretary to P. J. Noel-Baker '46, then Minister of State, in his first year in the House. He took an active interest in UNRRA during its last two years, and in 1946 succeeded Sir Frederick Leith-Ross '42 in the chairmanship of the European committee of its Council to remain in this position until UNRRA was discontinued.

Younger has attended the meetings of the United Nations General Assembly, having been appointed British alternate delegate in December 1945. In the following month he was named one of the British delegates to help choose a permanent home for U.N.; his choice veered, with the changes of British policy, between Westchester, Philadelphia, and finally Manhattan, and he argued strongly against the selection of San Francisco. In the autumn of 1946 he attended the second part of the first session of the Assembly. Speaking on the subject of U.N. finances, in November 1946 he suggested that the United States could and should pay half the ordinary U.N. costs, because more than 80 per cent of the budget was an "invisible import" to the American economy, representing international money spent in that country for salaries and services. In September 1947 Younger advised the administrative and budgetary committee of the General Assembly to cut the 1948 budget of $39,403,792 to $30,-000,000. Among sundry economies he proposed were reductions in funds for the Department of Public Information (propaganda is no substitute for U.N. action, he said), in the number of secretariat staff receiving $10,000 a year or more, and in the amount spent on international conferences, traveling, and printing. A review by Younger of the accomplishments of the first session of the U.N. Assembly appeared in the *Spectator* (December 27, 1946); he has also contributed to it and other British periodicals on international questions and Labor party affairs. In August of 1950 it was announced that Younger would accompany Ernest Bevin '49 as one of the British delegation to the U.N. that fall.

Younger was a member of the Parliamentary Labor party's committees on fisheries, on legal and judicial matters, civil aviation, and external affairs. In October 1946, when Noel-Baker moved to the Air Ministry, Younger went with him as Parliamentary private secretary. The following year, in a minor reshuffle, he became Parliamentary Under Secretary of State at the Home Office, under Chuter Ede '46. He took part in the work on the Criminal Justice Act and the Children Act of 1948, the second reading of which he moved.

At the general election of February 23, 1950, Younger was again returned for Grimsby, with

Wide World Photos
KENNETH YOUNGER

a majority of 6,412 over the Conservative candidate, J. Hall. On March 1 of that year the Ministerial list transferred Hector McNeil '46 to the Scottish Office and named Younger to succeed him as Minister of State. This Ministry, of postwar creation, functions as an auxiliary to the Foreign Office. Its head, though not of Cabinet rank, is next in rank to the Foreign Secretary in the administration of Britain's relations with other countries and acts as deputy for the Foreign Secretary. Upon the illness of Ernest Bevin in 1950, it devolved on Younger as his deputy to make public the Government's decisions on questions in international affairs; he bears no direct responsibility for such decisions, however. On April 27 he announced the Government's sanction of the annexation of the Arab parts of Palestine by the Hashemite Kingdom of Jordan, and at the same time Britain's *de jure* diplomatic recognition of the State of Israel. Other matters in which he has deputized for Bevin include exchanges with the French Ambassador about the Schuman proposals for a European coal-steel pool, and the British position on the invasion of South Korea by North Korea.

Younger is a member of the Royal Institute of International Affairs. In 1934 he married Elizabeth Kirsteen Stewart, and is the father of two daughters, Susannah and Lucy. Both husband and wife are interested in the arts. The British M.P. is a short, slight man, with wavy, sandy hair and freckles. He has been described as cool and competent, rapid in apprehension, and a "tremendous" worker. He finds recreation in walking, skiing, and photography.

References

Daily Mirror (London) Je 10 '50
News Chronicle (London) Je 2 '50
Who's Who, 1950

YUKAWA, HIDEKI (yōo-kä-wä hē-dě-kē)
Jan. 23, 1907-   Physicist
Address: b. c/o Columbia University, Dept. of
Physics, New York 27

On November 3, 1949, the Royal Swedish
Academy of Science announced that the 1949
Nobel prize for physics had been awarded to
Dr. Hideki Yukawa, Japanese physicist who in
1950 is at Columbia University on leave from
his teaching post at Kyoto University of Japan.
Yukawa first came to the attention of the world
of physics in 1935 when, after a year of in-

Columbia Univ.—Warman
HIDEKI YUKAWA

vestigation, he published a series of equations
forecasting the existence of a fourth basic
particle of subatomic matter, the meson (in
addition to the proton, the electron, and the
neutron). During World War II Yukawa
taught as a professor of theoretical physics at
Kyoto University. In October 1948, Dr. J.
Robert Oppenheimer [45], director of the Institute
for Advanced Studies at Princeton, New Jersey, invited Yukawa to the United States for
a period of work with the group of nuclear
physicists at the institute. For the academic
year 1949-50, Yukawa is visiting professor of
physics at Columbia University. That post will
become permanent on July 1, 1951, according
to an announcement made in December 1950.

Hideki Yukawa was born in Tokyo, Japan,
on January 23, 1907. He is the son of Takuji
Ogawa, who was professor of geology at Kyoto
University, and Koyuki Ogawa. In the family
there are three other sons, who became university professors, and two daughters, who are
married to men in the same profession. Reared
in Kyoto, Hideki Yukawa graduated from the
city's Third High School, after which he entered Kyoto University in 1926, to major in
physics. From its faculty of science he received the degree of Master of Science in 1929.

Yukawa commenced his teaching career in
1932 as a lecturer at Kyoto University. His
next post, to which he went in 1933, was at
Osaka University, where he was named assistant
professor in 1936 and was awarded the degree
of Doctor of Science in 1938. In 1939 he returned to Kyoto University with the title of
professor. That year he made a trip around
the world, lecturing on theoretical physics before many scientific groups. Upon his return
to his university, he also served concurrently as
professor at the University of Tokyo, a post
from which he later resigned. He remained as
professor of physics at Kyoto throughout the
war.

The Japanese physicist names Professor K.
Tamaki of Kyoto University and Dr. Y. Ni-
shina of the Tokyo Institute for Scientific Research as two of the major influences in his
selection of theoretical physics as the field of
his investigations. He adds that this selection
was also influenced by his inability "to master
the art of making simple glass laboratory equipment"—he describes himself as "a not very
practical man." As early as 1933 Yukawa had
postulated the existence on the border line between matter and energy of a subatomic particle
larger than an electron and smaller than a
proton. He tells that it was during a sleepless
night in September 1934 that he saw the necessary relationship of that particle to the structure
of the atom. After a year of research he was
prepared in 1935 to announce to a scientific
society in Japan, that a hitherto unknown type
of particle was responsible for the special
properties of the forces which hold the atomic
nucleus together. As stated by the public information office of Columbia University, Yukawa had "deduced the existence of this particle
by a brilliant piece of mathematical reasoning
founded on the principles of the quantum mechanics in analogy with the theory of the emission and absorption of light quanta."

This forecast of a new particle of matter
instantly achieved world fame for the lecturer
at Osaka University, and, with the subsequent
verification of the particle's existence by British,
French, and American physicists, it was suggested that it be called "yukon" in honor of its
discoverer. In consideration, however, of the
confusion that would arise from this name with
that of the North American river and territory,
physicists have decided upon "meson" or, less
commonly, "mesotron," as the name of the new
atomic particle. Although Yukawa's famous
equations that result in the postulation of the
meson were worked out on the basis of the
structure of the atomic nucleus, the meson is
now primarily associated with cosmic rays.
This is due to the discovery of Dr. Carl Anderson (California Institute of Technology) of
the presence of the meson in photographic records of cosmic rays as the first experimental
proof of Yukawa's theory a few months after it
had been propounded. According to *Newsweek*
(May 23, 1949), "the huge plastic balloons that
have been mistaken for flying saucers" are
among the several types of balloons sent up to
sound the upper atmosphere for the presence
of mesons in cosmic rays. In the laboratory
the atomic collisions in cyclotrons and synchro-

trons make it possible to observe the meson. In such collisions, the meson is disengaged from the nucleus and, in the extremely brief time that it can maintain an independent existence, it is photographed.

In January 1949, Professor I. I. Rabi [48], Columbia University's Nobel prize physicist, returned to the United States from a visit to Japan with the information that the Japanese physicists Hideki Yukawa of Kyoto and Sinitiro Tomonaga of Tokyo, apart from occidental science during the war, had continued their advance in theoretical investigation parallel to those of western physicists. In the meantime the Institute for Advanced Study at Princeton, New Jersey, at the instance of its director, Dr. J. Robert Oppenheimer, had invited Yukawa to join the group of nuclear physicists working there; and the United States State Department, in collaboration with the American occupation authorities in Japan, in 1948 effected Yukawa's visit to the United States. Yukawa worked with the Oppenheimer group for about a year. In July 1949 Columbia University, with the cooperation of the Rockefeller Foundation, appointed Yukawa visiting professor of physics for the 1949-50 academic year. Upon Yukawa's departure from Princeton, Dr. Oppenheimer said: "Dr. Yukawa's anticipation of the meson is one of the few really fructifying ideas in the last decades. . . . He was deeply loved by all his colleagues in his year here, both as a scientist and a man." In December 1950 it was announced that the Japanese scientist had been named professor of physics at Columbia University, the appointment to become effective July 1, 1951.

The departments of physics and chemistry at Columbia University, having pioneered in research on the atomic bomb, were able to provide Professor Yukawa with extensive facilities for the continuation of his work. These facilities include the new synchro-cyclotron, which is expected to be put into operation in 1950, said Professor John R. Dunning [48]. This machine, the largest of its kind ever constructed, is designed for further penetration into the structure of the atom. Although Yukawa expects the synchro-cyclotron to confirm his theoretical investigations, he told the New York *Times* (November 4, 1949) that he hoped for "a more impressive" result that would reveal facts and evidence differing from his theories. Speaking before four hundred leading physicists of the American Physical Society, gathered for their annual meeting at Columbia University on January 28, 1949, Yukawa had already suggested that the development of a fifth dimension, which would have to do with "absolute mass," might pave the way for "clearing up the enigma of the meson."

According to the official citation of the Royal Swedish Academy of Science on November 3, 1949, the Japanese physicist was given the Nobel prize "for his prediction of the existence of the meson (an elusive mass, heavier than the electron, which theoretically glues the atomic nucleus together), based upon his theory of nuclear forces." As guest of honor at a luncheon given by the members of the Japanese colony in New York City, Yukawa said, "There

are no national boundaries in the field of science and we should all work together to bring out the truth—one truth." The presentation of the award took place in Stockholm on December 10, when William F. Giauque [50] was similarly honored for his achievement in chemistry; the subject of Yukawa's Nobel lecture, delivered two days later, was "The Meson Theory and Its Developments." Upon his return to the United States, the physicist announced that he would contribute part of the $30,000 prize toward a new Institute of Theoretical Physics at Kyoto.

Yukawa is the author of numerous writings (articles and books) on his specialties. His own country has recognized his achievements in awarding him the Imperial prize of the Imperial Academy (1940) and the Order of Decoration (1943); he holds membership in the Chemical Research Institute of Kyoto University, the Japan Academy; and is a foreign associate in the National Academy of Sciences (United States).

Newsweek describes Yukawa as "slightly built"—his height as five feet, seven inches, and his weight is 130 pounds; he has brown eyes and black hair. With Sumiko Yukawa, whom he married in April 1932, and their two sons, Harumi and Takaaki, he lives in New York, in the Columbia University neighborhood. Yukawa (who played baseball in college) lists as his favorite recreation the reading of philosophy, history and literature, and the writing of short poems in Japanese. He is a member of a committee which will sponsor the loan of a collection of Japanese paintings for exhibition in the museums of the United States.

References

N Y Herald Tribune p1 N 4 '49 por
N Y Post p2 N 3 '49 por
N Y Times p1 N 4 '49 por
Newsweek 33:52 My 23 '49 por; 34:61 N 14 '49 por

ZEELAND, PAUL VAN (zā'länt) Nov. 11, 1893- Foreign Minister of Belgium

Address: b. Ministry of Foreign Affairs, Brussels, Belgium; h. La Maison Flamande, 7 Avenue Charles-Albert, Boitsfort, Brussels; Château de la Houssière, par Braine-le-Comte, Belgium

The Minister of Foreign Affairs of Belgium since August 1949, Paul van Zeeland is also president of the Organization for European Economic Cooperation (the European Marshall Plan Council). Widely known as an economist and financial expert, he has proposed a number of plans for the reduction of international trade barriers. He is a leading member of the Catholic Christian Socialist Party in Belgium and a supporter of exiled King Leopold III [44]. Van Zeeland, Prime Minister of his country in 1935, is credited with saving it from impending financial disaster at that time.

Paul van Zeeland was born in Soignies, Belgium, the son of a prosperous merchant, on November 11, 1893. He studied law at the University of Louvain, obtaining the Ph.B.

PAUL VAN ZEELAND

degree in 1914. Soon after the outbreak of World War I he entered the army; and within a few months he had won the Croix de Guerre and found himself behind the barbed wire of a German prison camp, where he remained until the Armistice.

In 1920 he won a graduate scholarship to Princeton University. There he studied economics under Professor Edwin Walter Kemmerer [41], noted "currency doctor." Van Zeeland wrote his M.A. thesis on the United States Federal Reserve System. His study of the banking reforms of 1913-21 in the United States was published in 1922. Van Zeeland practiced law briefly after his Princeton studies, and in 1926 joined the staff of the National Bank of Belgium. Here he held the posts of secretary, director, and vice-governor. The banker, who has since written numerous articles in political and economic reviews, wrote in this early period on the establishment of a national fund for scientific research, and on the five-year plan; in 1933 *View of Europe* was published. He was a delegate to economic conferences at London (1922), Baden-Baden (1929), London, Berlin, and Paris (1930), Geneva (1930-31), Stresa (1932), and Paris (1932-33).

Van Zeeland made the transition from state banking to politics when he became Minister without Portfolio in the Cabinet of Count Charles de Broqueville in 1934. His special task was to deflate Belgium's dangerously inflated currency. Van Zeeland resigned in November when Parliament refused to accept his reforms, and the De Broqueville Cabinet fell. In March 1935 King Leopold summoned the banker-economist to head a coalition Cabinet of the country, which was in severe financial straits. Van Zeeland issued an immediate decree devaluating the belga by 28 per cent, a measure which effected a relief in the currency crisis.

In foreign policy, Prime Minister van Zeeland became the spokesman for the so-called "Oslo group," a bloc of European neutrals comprising the Scandinavian nations, Finland, the Netherlands, Luxembourg, and Belgium; in early 1937 Belgium repudiated her French and British military commitments. Under Van Zeeland the country pursued a policy of better relations with the Netherlands. In June 1937 Van Zeeland visited the United States as a spokesman for European democracy to confer with President Roosevelt. The economist remained at the head of the Belgian Government for two years. During this time he won for himself the reputation of being "perhaps the most efficient, the least confused, and the most surefooted of the statesmen who dealt with the depression" (in Walter Lippmann's words). His financial reforms were accepted, agriculture began to prosper, unemployment declined. The Flemish nationalists and the Rexists, a group with avowed Fascist leanings, combined to oppose measures of the Van Zeeland Cabinet. This opposition was brought to an end when Van Zeeland defeated the Rexist leader, Léon Degrelle, at the polls on April 11, 1937, by a vote of 275,840 to 69,242. However, Van Zeeland resigned from office in the fall of 1937 when Rexist deputies accused him of irregularities in the affairs of the National Bank. (A special Parliamentary session cleared him of the charges.)

Van Zeeland undertook a survey of the international economic situation in April 1937 for Premiers Baldwin of Great Britain and Blum [40] of France. During the next eight months he conferred with statesmen and economists in Europe and the United States. The resultant 24-page *Report to the Governments of the United Kingdom and France on the Possibility of Obtaining a General Reduction of the Obstacles to International Trade* (1938) urged "a pact of economic collaboration" open to all. In *Economics or Politics* (1939), a lecture delivered at Cambridge in October 1938, the ex-Premier made an "eloquent plea" for immediate action by the democratic powers on his *Report*.

As a private citizen, Van Zeeland made a lecture tour of the United States in 1938. He was professor of international economic science at Louvain University from 1938 to 1940 (a position he has resumed since the end of World War II). In 1939 he became president of the Coordinating Foundation for Refugees, an international organization with offices in New York City. Van Zeeland gave up this relief activity to join the army of King Leopold in its brief struggle after the invasion of his homeland in May 1940.

In 1941 Van Zeeland became chairman of Belgium's Commission for the Study of Postwar Problems, a body engaged in long-range planning for economic expansion, social security, and education. The exiled Belgian (who bought a home in Lebanon, New Jersey, in March 1941) lectured and attended conferences in the United States and abroad in connection with his post. In 1942 he became dean of the Faculty of Political Sciences in the Ecole Libre des Hautes Etudes, which was established that year under the sponsorship of the New School of Social Research of New York, where classes were held. The faculty of the school was composed of sixty exiled French and Belgian scholars. Van Zeeland contributed a chapter entitled "Belgium in the Postwar World" to *Belgium* (1945; edited by Johannes Albertus Goris), one of the volumes in the United Nations series on its member nations.

The former Premier was appointed High 'Commissioner for the Repatriation of Deported and Exiled Belgians, with the rank of Ambassador at large, in October 1944. In August 1945 he announced that 90 per cent of Belgium's nationals had been repatriated and that 700,000 displaced persons had passed through Belgium. For this repatriation work Van Zeeland received the United States Medal of Freedom award in June 1946. During visits to the United States in this period he promoted the activities of the newly organized Belgo-American Association, of which he was chairman.

The diplomat-economist accepted the invitation of Premier Ismail Sidky Pasha to confer with the Egyptian Government as a neutral expert in April 1946. (He had been called to Egypt on the same basis in 1930.) In 1947 Van Zeeland devoted himself to the organization of a private international committee known as the Independent League for European Cooperation. The league would "study the problem of collaboration both from the cultural and the economic point of view," Van Zeeland stated; it would attempt to interpret the aims of the United Nations and also to serve as a sounding board for world public opinion. In September 1947 Van Zeeland was named the Belgian representative to the United Nations' mediation committee on the Dutch-Indonesian dispute.

In August Van Zeeland became Minister of Foreign Affairs in the cabinet of Gaston Eyskens '49, who succeeded Paul-Henri Spaak '45. With the fall of Eyskens' Government in the spring of 1950 over the question of King Leopold's return to the throne, Van Zeeland as Premier-designate undertook to form a Cabinet which would bring the King back from exile. He was unsuccessful in this attempt because he could not get support from the Liberals. In the Cabinet formed in June under Premier Jean Duvieusart, Van Zeeland was named Minister of Foreign Affairs and Minister of Foreign Trade. After the abdication of Leopold in the summer of 1950 and the subsequent resignation of Duvieusart, Van Zeeland again made an unsuccessful effort to form a Government. He remained Minister of Foreign Affairs in the Cabinet of Premier Joseph Pholien, which was formed in August.

Belgium's Foreign Minister is president of the Committee of Ministers of the Council of Europe (organized January 28, 1949, as a step toward the creation of a federated Europe); he attended the meeting of the consultative body of the Council, called the European Consultative Assembly, held in Strasbourg in August 1949. In September Van Zeeland represented Belgium at the first session of the North Atlantic Council, composed of the Foreign Ministers of the signatory nations of the North Atlantic Pact. The following month he participated in the conference of the Cabinet Ministers of Benelux countries, participants in the plan for the economic union of Belgium, the Netherlands, and Luxembourg.

In August 1949, Van Zeeland succeeded Paul-Henri Spaak as president of the Organization for European Economic Cooperation (the European Marshall Plan Council). This body, composed of delegates of the eighteen Marshall Aid countries, in trying to forward the implementation of Marshall aid seeks the liberalization of trade and the freeing of payments from the bilateral system. At a meeting of the executive council, held in Paris on January 31 and February 1, 1950, the members agreed on the "general theory" of a new system of payments, details of the system to be worked out after further negotiations, and import quota cuts to come into force conjointly with the projected payments clearing plan. The council appointed Dirk U. Stikker '50, Foreign Minister of the Netherlands, as its "political conciliator." Commenting on the slow progress being made by the council, Van Zeeland emphasized "the difficulties of reconciling the views of eighteen delegations."

The Belgian Foreign Minister has been awarded numerous decorations (some twenty are listed in the 1949 *Who's Who*) from his own and foreign countries—Norway, Sweden, Greece, Finland, Luxembourg, Italy, the Netherlands, Rumania, Poland, and Egypt. During his Premiership he served as President of the Assembly of the League of Nations in a 1936 session. He holds honorary LL.D. degrees from Princeton (1937) and Brown universities, an honorary D.C.L. from Wesleyan (1941), and doctorates in law and political and diplomatic sciences from Louvain University. In 1926 Van Zeeland married Renée, the daughter of General Baron Dossin de St. Georges; they have two sons and two daughters.

References

Time 29 :17-18 Je 14 '37
International Who's Who, 1949
Who's Who, 1949
World Biography (1948)

ZUKOR, ADOLPH (zōō'kôr) Jan. 7, 1873- Motion picture executive
Address: b. c/o Paramount Pictures Corporation, Paramount Bldg., New York 18

Adolph Zukor, chairman of the board of Paramount Pictures Corporation, has been associated with the motion picture industry since 1903, when he opened a penny arcade and later, a chain of nickelodeons. He is now the executive who directs activities of the various producing and distributing companies which, beginning as the Famous Players Film Company, are known in 1950 as the Paramount Pictures Corporation. As a distributor he had the distinction of introducing Sarah Bernhardt to American motion picture audiences; and as a producer, he introduced such stars as Mary Pickford and Douglas Fairbanks. Fourteen of the films he has produced during the last half decade are among the "Great Hundred" selected

ADOLPH ZUKOR

by the editors of the *International Motion Picture Almanac*. In addition to producing films, Zukor, through the building of theaters in key cities in the United States and Canada and through mergers and partnerships with owners of other motion picture houses, has held a leading position in the film distribution industry.

A native of Hungary, where he was born in the city of Ricse, on January 7, 1873, Adolph Zukor is the son of Jacob and Hannah (Lieberman) Zukor. He received his elementary education in Hungary, from which he emigrated in 1888, going to New York City. There he lived with a married couple who had come from his home town several years before. It is related that when the youth arrived in America he had with him twenty-five dollars sewed in the lining of his clothing. Zukor soon found a job, as a sweeper in a furrier's shop, earning two dollars a week. In the evening he attended high school, to study the English language and American business methods.

Four years after his arrival in the United States he succeeded in establishing his own fur business in both Chicago and New York. In the course of this time he invented and patented a fur clasp. According to an article in the New York *Herald Tribune*, it was on one of his trips to New York, while he was still in the fur business, that Zukor saw a movie for the first time—a 30-second one in a penny arcade. Realizing the possibilities of these first primitive films, Zukor in 1903 joined Marcus Loew in founding a chain of penny arcades, known as the Loew Enterprises, with Zukor the treasurer of the firm. Each arcade was equipped with Edison phonographs.

In 1905 Zukor, no longer in the penny arcade business, joined William A. Brady in operating Hale's Tours, a chain of "theaters," in which the audience sat in a room built and equipped to resemble a railroad coach and watched the picture thrown on the screen at the front end of the car. With the supply of two-reel films increasing, Zukor next opened several five-cent "stores shows," later known as nickelodeons, in New York's Union Square and in Coney Island. He showed *The Great Train Robbery*, the first "plot" movie. In 1912 he formed, with others, the Engadine Corporation, which distributed the early multiple-reel feature film produced in Europe. The picture was *Queen Elizabeth*, a four-reeler with Sarah Bernhardt as the star, which was shown throughout the United States. This venture developed into a partnership with Daniel Frohman and the organization of the Famous Players Film Company for the production of multiple-reel features. Mary Pickford, Douglas Fairbanks, and Minnie Maddern Fiske were among his first stars; and *The Prisoner of Zenda*, the *Count of Monte Cristo*, and *Tess of the D'Urbervilles* were among his first pictures.

In 1914 the Paramount Pictures Corporation was formed by W. W. Hodkinson to distribute the products of Zukor's firm as well as those of the studios of the Jesse L. Lasky Feature Play Company. The latter firm in 1916 merged with Zukor's studio to form the Famous Players-Lasky Corporation and a year later, twelve other producing companies were merged with the parent firm. At the same time various film distribution organizations, including the Artcraft Pictures Corporation and the Paramount Pictures Corporation, were purchased by the Zukor firm to form a nation-wide distribution system. According to the history published in the *International Motion Picture Almanac*, Zukor took the most active part in these negotiations and remained "dominant" throughout the series of mergers. In 1919 the Famous Players-Lasky Corporation purchased 135 theaters in Southern States; the next year, fifty New England theaters were added to the chain; in 1926, in the Middle West, seventy theaters in Michigan were acquired, and fifty in Illinois. Somewhat later, the chain reached out to the West. In 1927 the name was changed to Paramount Famous Lasky Corporation and three years later, it became Paramount Publix Corporation. The firm was adjudicated bankrupt in 1933 and reorganized in 1935 as Paramount Pictures, Inc. Zukor was named chairman of the board of directors of the new firm.

It was during this period of expansion that Zukor, as the head of the far-reaching enterprise, was named by James W. Gerard, New York lawyer and financier, one of the sixty-four men who "ruled" America. The list caused considerable public discussion at the time because it did not contain the names of the President of the United States, or of several other political leaders.

By 1940 the activities of the Zukor firm had become world-wide, with the Paramount Theatre, built in 1926, on Times Square in New York City, the "showcase" for Paramount's Class-A pictures. In 1939 the company had been the first motion picture concern to form a television subsidiary.

In 1940 the Federal Government began an antitrust suit against the eight major film companies, including Paramount. *Variety* reported that Zukor was a frequent witness at the proceedings, where he defended Paramount's decision to build and operate its own theaters in order to offset competitive methods of the First National Circuit. Other Paramount executives stressed the number of independent producers in Hollywood, as well as the free competition for rights to stories and plays, and for acting talent. As a result of the suit, Paramount received a Government consent decree to reorganize its holdings so that its production activities would be separate from distribution. The reorganization was completed December 30, 1949, with the formation of Paramount Pictures Corporation for the production of films and United Paramount Theatres, Inc., for ownership and management of a chain of theaters. Each corporation was granted 3,263,-276 shares of common stock outstanding. Zukor was elected chairman of the board of Paramount Pictures Corporation. Both companies maintain an interest in the field of television, with Paramount Pictures Corporation owning station KTLA in Los Angeles and 29 per cent of the interest in Allen B. DuMont[46], Inc. (These figures are from the Paramount publicity office.)

Of the "Great Hundred" films made since the invention of the motion picture in 1893, chosen by the editors of the *International Motion Picture Almanac*, Zukor's organizations have produced fourteen. These include such early pictures as *The Sheik* (made in 1921); *The Covered Wagon* (1924); *King of Kings* (1927); and such later films as *Going My Way*, the 1944 Academy Award winner, *The Lost Weekend*, which also won the award, and *Unconquered*, released in 1947. *Samson and Delilah* was the major production of Paramount in 1949.

Zukor was married on January 10, 1897, to Lottie Kaufman of Chicago. There are two children from the marriage—Eugene J. Zukor, who has been associated with Paramount Pictures since 1916, and a daughter, Mildred, the wife of Arthur Loew. Zukor has four grandsons and a granddaughter. The executive was one of the founders in 1921 of the Motion Picture Producers and Distributors of America, Inc., which established regulations and production codes for the industry. During World War II Zukor was a member of the coordinating committee of the War Activities Committee of Hollywood. In 1947 he was honored by the Motion Picture Pioneers for his contributions to the film industry. He is a Mason, and a member of the Lambs and City Athletic clubs of New York City, and of the Congressional Country Club of Washington, D.C.

References

N Y Herald Tribune p19 N 23 '49
Variety 138:6 Ap 10 '40

International Motion Picture Almanac, 1947-48
Who's Who in America, 1948-49
Who's Who in American Jewry, 1938-39
World Biography (1948)

BIOGRAPHICAL REFERENCES CONSULTED

The publication dates listed are those of volumes in CURRENT BIOGRAPHY's reference collection.

American Catholic Who's Who, 1950-51
American Medical Directory, 1942
American Men in Government (1949)
American Men of Science (1949)
American Women, 1939-40
America's Young Men, 1938-39
ASCAP Biographical Dictionary of Composers, Authors, and Publishers (1948)
Author's and Writer's Who's Who (1948-49)

Baker, T. ed. Biographical Dictionary of Musicians (1940)
Baseball Register (1950)
Biographical Directory of the American Congress, 1774-1949
Blue Book of American Aviation (942)
British Film Annual, 1949
Burke's Peerage (1949)
Business Executives of America (1950)

Canadian Who's Who, 1948
Catholic Who's Who, 1941
Chemical Who's Who, 1937
Chi è? (1948)
Congressional Directory (1950)

Dictionnaire Biographique des Artistes Contemporains, 1910-30
Dictionnaire Biographique Français Contemporain (1950)
Dictionnaire de Biographie Française (1933-)
Dictionnaire National des Contemporains (1936)
Directory of American Scholars, 1942
Directory of Medical Specialists (1949)
Directory of Medical Women, 1949
Directory of the American Political Science Association, 1948

Ewen, D. ed. Composers of Today (1936); Living Musicians (1940); Men and Women Who Make Music (1949)

Grove, G. Dictionary of Music and Musicians (1927-28); Suppl vol (1940)

Hvem er Hvem? (1948)

Indian and Pakistan Year Book and Who's Who, 1948
International Motion Picture Almanac, 1950-51

International Press Who's Who; New Zealand, 1938
International Who's Who, 1950
International Who's Who in World Medicine, 1947
International World Who's Who (1949)

Japan Who's Who, 1950

Kelly's Handbook to the Titled, Landed, and Official Classes, 1949
Kraks Blaa Bog (1949)
Kunitz, S. J. and Haycraft, H. eds. Junior Book of Authors (1934); Twentieth Century Authors (1942)

Leaders in Education (1948)

National Cyclopædia of American Biography Current Volumes A-G (1926-46)
Near and Middle East Who's Who, 1945-46
Nobel Prize Winners (1938)

Prominent Personalities in American Methodism (1945)

Quem é Alguém (1947)

Religious Leaders of America, 1941-42

Salter, J. T. ed. Public Men in and Out of Office (1946)
Slavonic Encyclopaedia (1949)
South African Who's Who, 1949

Thompson, O. ed. International Cyclopedia of Music and Musicians (1949)

Universal Jewish Encyclopedia (1948)

Variety Radio Directory, 1940-41
Vem är Det, 1949
Vem och Vad, 1948

Webster's Biographical Dictionary (1943)
Wer ist Wer? (1948)
Wer ist's? (1935)
Who is Who in Music, 1941
Who Knows—and What (1949)
Who's Important in Medicine, 1945
Who's Who, 1950
Who's Who in Alaska, 1947
Who's Who in America, 1950-51
Who's Who in American Art, 1940-47
Who's Who in American Education, 1947-48

Who's Who in American Jewry, 1938-39
Who's Who in Australia, 1947
Who's Who in Aviation, 1942-43
Who's Who in Canada, 1949-50
Who's Who in Central and East-Europe, 1935-36
Who's Who in Chicago and Illinois (1950)
Who's Who in China (1936)
Who's Who in Colored America, 1950
Who's Who in Commerce and Industry (1948)
Who's Who in Engineering, 1948
Who's Who in Government, 1932-33
Who's Who in India, 1946-47
Who's Who in Japan, 1940-4:
Who's Who in Labor (1946)
Who's Who in Latin America (1940-47)
Who's Who in Law, 1937
Who's Who in Library Service (1943)
Who's Who in Music, 1950
Who's Who in New England (1949)
Who's Who in New York, 1947
Who's Who in New Zealand (1941)
Who's Who in Railroading, 1946
Who's Who in the Clergy, 1941-42
Who's Who in the East (1948)
Who's Who in the Major Leagues (1947)
Who's Who in the Midwest (1949)
Who's Who in the Nation's Capital, 1938-39
Who's Who in the State of Israel, 1949
Who's Who in the Theatre (1947)
Who's Who in the West (1949)
Who's Who in Transportation and Communication, 1942-43
Who's Who in United States Politics (1950)
Who's Who of the Allied Governments, 1943
Wie is Dat? 1948
Wier, A. E. ed. Macmillan Encyclopedia of Music and Musicians (1938)
Winchester's Screen Encyclopedia (1948)
Women of Achievement (1940)
World Biography (1948)

Yearbook of the United Nations, 1946-47; 1947-48
Yost, E. American Women of Science (1943)

PERIODICALS AND NEWSPAPERS CONSULTED

A. L. A. Bul—American Library Association Bulletin $1.50; free to members. American Library Assn, 50 E Huron St, Chicago 11

Adult Ed J—Adult Education Journal $2. American Association for Adult Education, 167 Public Square, Cleveland 14
Formerly Journal of Adult Education

Adv Age—Advertising Age $2. Advertising Publications, Inc, 100 E Ohio St, Chicago 11

Adv & Sell—Advertising and Selling $4. Moore-Robbins Pub Co, Inc, 9 E 38th St, New York 16

Am Artist—American Artist $4. Watson-Guptill Publications, Inc, 345 Hudson St, New York 14
Formerly Art Instruction

Am Assn Univ Women J—Journal of the American Association of University Women $1. American Assn of University Women, 1634 I St, N W, Washington 6, D.C.

Am Collector—American Collector $4. Collectors Pub Co, Inc, 19 W 44th St, New York 18

Am Federationist—American Federationist $2. American Federation of Labor, 901 Massachusetts Ave, Washington 1, D.C.

Am Hist R—American Historical Review $5; free to members of the American Historical Assn. Macmillan Co, 60 Fifth Ave, New York 11

Am Home—American Home $2.50. American Home Magazine Corp, Forest Hills, New York

Am Mag—American Magazine $3. Crowell-Collier Pub Co, Springfield, Ohio

Am Mercury—American Mercury $4. American Mercury, Inc, 570 Lexington Ave, New York 22

Am Phot—American Photography $2.50. American Photographic Pub Co, 421 Fifth Ave S, Minneapolis 15, Minn.

Am Pol Sci R—American Political Science Review $6.60; free to members of the American Political Science Assn, University Hall, Ohio State University, Columbus, Ohio

Am Scand R—American Scandinavian Review $3; free to members. American Scandinavian Foundation, 116 E 64th St, New York 21

Am Scholar—American Scholar $3. United Chapter of Phi Beta Kappa, 415 First Ave, New York 10

Am Sociol R—American Sociological Review $5. American Sociological Society, 427 W 117 St, New York 27

America—America $6. America Press, 70 E 45th St, New York 17

Américas—Américas $3. Pan American Union, 17th St and Constitution Ave, NW, Washington 6, D.C.

Ann Am Acad—Annals of the American Academy of Political and Social Science $5; free to members. 3817 Spruce St, Philadelphia 4

Apollo—Apollo, the Magazine of the Arts for Connoisseurs and Collectors 42s. 10 Vigo St, Regent St, London, W 1. ($6. 18 E 48th St, New York 17)

Arch Forum—Architectural Forum $12; $5.50 to firms and governments. Time, Inc, 540 N Michigan Ave, Chicago 11

Arch Rec—Architectural Record $4.50. F. W. Dodge Corp, 119 W 40th St, New York 18

Art Bul—Art Bulletin $10. College Art Assn, Inc, 625 Madison Ave, New York 22

Art Digest—Art Digest $4. Art Digest, Inc, 116 E 59th St, New York 22

Art N—Art News $9. Art Foundation, Inc, 136 E 57th St, New York 22

Arts & Arch—Arts and Architecture $5. John D. Entenza, 3305 Wilshire Blvd, Los Angeles 5

Arts & Dec—Arts and Decoration (discontinued)

Asia—Asia and the Americas.
Merged with United Nations World, February 1947

Asiatic R—Asiatic Review £1. East and West. Ltd. 3 Victoria St, London. SW 1

Atlan—Atlantic Monthly $6. Atlantic Monthly Co, 8 Arlington St, Boston 16

Automotive Ind—Automotive Industries $2. Chilton Co, 56th & Chestnut Sts, Philadelphia 39
Formerly Automotive and Aviation Industries

Aviation W—Aviation Week $6. McGraw-Hill Pub, Co, Inc, 330 W 42d St, New York 18

Banking—Banking $4. American Bankers Assn, 12 E 36th St, New York 16

Bet Hom & Gard—Better Homes & Gardens $2.50. Meredith Pub Co, 1714 Locust St, Des Moines 3, Iowa

Book-of-the-Month Club N—Book-of-the-Month Club News Free to members. Book-of-the-Month Club, Inc, 385 Madison Ave, New York 17

Books Abroad—Books Abroad $3. University of Oklahoma Press, Norman, Okla.

Bronx Home News. See N Y Post

Bsns W—Business Week $6. McGraw-Hill Pub Co, Inc, 330 W 42d St, New York 18

Bul Bibliog—Bulletin of Bibliography and Dramatic Index $3. F. W. Faxon Co, 83 Francis St, Boston 15

Bul Museum Modern Art. See New York City. Museum of Modern Art Bul

Bul Pan Am Union. See Américas

Calif Arts & Arch—California Arts & Architecture. See Arts and Architecture

Canad Forum—Canadian Forum $2. Canadian Forum, Ltd, 16 Huntley St, Toronto 5

Canad Hist R—Canadian Historical Review $3. University of Toronto Press, Toronto 5

Cath Lib World—Catholic Library World $5; free to members. Catholic Library Assn, P.O. Box 25, New York

Cath N—Catholic News $3. C. H. Ridder, 22 N William St, New York 7

Cath School J—Catholic School Journal $3. Bruce Pub Co, 400 N Broadway, Milwaukee 1, Wis.

Cath World—Catholic World $4. Paulist Press, 401 W 59th St, New York 19

Chem & Eng N—Chemical and Engineering News $6. American Chemical Society, 1155 16th St, N W, Washington 6, D.C.

Christian Cent—Christian Century $6. Christian Century Press, 407 S Dearborn St, Chicago 5

Christian Sci Mon—Christian Science Monitor (Atlantic edition) $14, including the Magazine. Christian Science Pub Soc, 1 Norway St, Boston 15

Christian Sci Mon Mag—Christian Science Monitor Weekly Magazine Section. Christian Science Pub Soc, 1 Norway St, Boston 15

Civil Eng—Civil Engineering $5. American Society of Civil Engineers, 33 W 39th St, New York 18

Col Engl—College English $4. University of Chicago Press, 5750 Ellis Ave, Chicago 37

Collier's—Collier's $5. Crowell-Collier Pub Co, Springfield, Ohio

Commonweal—Commonweal $7. Commonweal Pub Co, Inc, 386 Fourth Ave, New York 16

Cong Digest—Congressional Digest $6. Congressional Digest Corp, 1631 K St, N W, Washington 6, D.C.

Connoisseur—Connoisseur 43s. Connoisseur, Ltd, 28 & 30 Grosvenor Gardens, London, SW 1 ($7.50. Connoisseur and International Studio, 572 Madison Ave. New York 22)

Contemp—Contemporary Review $9.50. British Periodicals Ltd, 46-47 Chancery Lane, London, WC 2

Coronet—Coronet $3. Esquire, Inc, 65 E South Water St, Chicago 1

Cosmopolitan—Cosmopolitan $3.50. Hearst Magazines, Inc, 57th St & Eighth Ave, New York 19

Cue—Cue (Manhattan edition) $4.50. Cue Publishing Co, Inc, 6 E 39th St, New York 16

Cur Hist ns—Current History $4. Events Pub Co, Inc, 108-10 Walnut St, Philadelphia 6

Cur Opinion—Current Opinion (discontinued)

Dance—Dance Magazine $3.75. Rudor Pub Co, 503 W 33d St, New York 1

Design—Design $4. Design Pub Co, 337 S High St, Columbus 15, Ohio

Dublin R—Dublin Review 15s. Burns Oates & Washbourne, Ltd. 28 Ashley Pl, London, SW 1 ($4 International News Co, 131 Varick St, New York 13)

Ed & Pub—Editor and Publisher $5. Charles T. Stuart, 1475 Broadway, New York 18

Educ—Education $4. Palmer Co, 370 Atlantic Ave, Boston 10

El Engl—Elementry English $3.50. National Council of Teachers of English, 211 W 68th St, Chicago 21
    Formerly Elementary English Review

Engl J—English Journal $4. University of Chicago Press, 5750 Ellis Ave, Chicago 37

Esquire—Esquire $6. Esquire, Inc, 65 E South Water St, Chicago 1

Etude—Etude $3. Theodore Presser Co, Bryn Mawr, Pa.

Facts on File—Facts on File $45. Person's Index, Facts on File, Inc, 516 Fifth Ave, New York 9

Far Eastern S—Far Eastern Survey $6. 1 E 54th St, New York 22

Finance—Finance $5. Finance Pub Corp, 20 N Wacker Dr, Chicago 6

Flying—Flying $3. Ziff-Davis Pub Co, 185 N Wabash Ave, Chicago 1

For Affairs—Foreign Affairs $6. Council on Foreign Relations, Inc, 58 E 68th St, New York 21

For Policy Rep—Foreign Policy Reports $5. (to libraries subscription includes Foreign Policy Bulletins and 6 headline books); $4. to F, P. A. members. Foreign Policy Assn, Inc, 22 E 38th St, New York 16

Forbes—Forbes $4. B. C. Forbes & Sons Pub Co, Inc, 120 Fifth Ave, New York 11

Fortnightly—Fortnightly $6.50. Fortnightly Review, 4, 5, & 6 Soho Sq, London, W 1

Fortune—Fortune $12.50. Time, Inc, 540 N Michigan Ave, Chicago 11

Forum—Forum $4. Events Pub Co, Inc, 108-10 Walnut St, Philadelphia 6
    Forum combined with Current History from May 30, 1940, to August 31, 1945; resumed publication as an independent magazine in September of 1945.

Free World—Free World.
    Merged with United Nations World.

Good H—Good Housekeeping $3.50. Hearst Magazines, Inc, 57th St & Eighth Ave, New York 19

Harper—Harper's Magazine $5. Harper & Bros, 49 E 33d St, New York 16

Harper's Bazaar—Harper's Bazaar $5. Hearst Magazines, Inc. 572 Madison Ave, New York 22

Holiday—Holiday $5. Curtis Pub Co, Independence Square, Philadelphia 5

Home & F See House B

Horn Bk—Horn Book $3. Horn Book, Inc, 248 Boylston St, Boston 16

House & Gard—House and Garden $5. Condé Nast Publications, Inc, Boston Post Road, Greenwich, Conn.

House B—House Beautiful $5. Hearst Magazines, Inc, 572 Madison Ave, New York 22

Illus Lond N—Illustrated London News £5 1s. 1 New Oxford St, London, WC 1 (American edition $16. British edition $18. International News Co, 131 Varick St, New York 13)

Ind Woman—Independent Woman $1.50. National Federation of Business and Professional Women's Clubs, Inc, 1819 Broadway, New York 23

Inland Ptr—Inland Printer $4. The Inland Printer, 309 W Jackson Blvd, Chicago 6

Inter-American—Inter-American.
    Merged with United Nations World, February 1947.

J Am Med Assn—Journal of the American Medical Association $8. Am Med Assn, 535 N Dearborn St, Chicago 10

J Home Econ—Journal of Home Economics $5. American Home Economics Assn, Victor Bldg, Washington 1, D.C.

J Negro Hist—Journal of Negro History $4. Association for the Study of Negro Life and History, 1538 Ninth St, N W, Washington 1, D.C.

Knickerbocker—The Knickerbocker $3. The Netherlands Pub Co, 50 Rockefeller Plaza, New York 20

Ladies' Home J—Ladies' Home Journal $3. Curtis Pub Co, Independence Sq, Philadelphia 5

Liberty—Liberty $2.25. Liberty Magazine, Inc. 37 W 57th St, New York 19

Library J—Library Journal $6. R. R. Bowker Co, 62 W 45th St, New York 19

Life—Life $6. Time, Inc, 540 N Michigan Ave, Chicago 11

Life & Letters To-day—Life and Letters To-day 20s. 430 Strand, London WC 2 ($5. International News Co, 131 Varick St, New York 13)

Lit Digest—Literary Digest (discontinued)

Lon Studio. See Studio

Look—Look $3.50. Cowles Magazines, Inc, 511 Fifth Ave, New York 17

Mademoiselle—Mademoiselle $3.50. Street & Smith Publications, Inc, 122 E 42d St, New York 17

Mag Art—Magazine of Art $6; free to members. American Federation of Arts, 1262 N Hampshire Ave, N W, Washington 6, D.C.

Mag of Wall Street—Magazine of Wall Street $12.50. Ticker Pub Co, 90 Broad St, New York 4

Mo Labor R—Monthly Labor Review $4.50. Supt. of Documents, Washington 25, D.C.

Motion Pict—Motion Picture $1.20. Fawcett Publications, Inc, 67 W 44th St, New York 18

Mus Am—Musical America $4. Musical America Corp. 113 W 57th St, New York 19

Mus Courier—Musical Courier $3. Music Periodicals Corp, 119 W 57th St, New York 19

Mus Q—Musical Quarterly $4. G. Schirmer, Inc, 3 E 43d St, New York 17

Musician—Musician $3. Fellowship Concerts Service, Inc, 545 5th Ave, New York 17

N Y Herald Tribune—New York Herald Tribune $22, including Sunday edition. New York Tribune, Inc, 230 W 41st St, New York 18

N Y Post—New York Post $16.50, including Sunday edition. New York Post, Inc, 75 West St, New York 6
    Bronx Home News consolidated with N Y Post February 16, 1948

N Y Star—New York Star (discontinued January 28, 1949)

N Y State Ed—New York State Education $2. New York State Teachers Assn, 152 Washington Ave, Albany 6

N Y Sun. See N Y World-Telegram

N Y Times—New York Times $19.50, including Sunday edition. New York Times Co, 229 W 43d St, New York 18

N Y Times Book R—New York Times Book Review $3. New York Times Co, 229 W 43d St, New York 18

N Y Times Index—New York Times Index $35. New York Times Co, 229 W 43d St, New York 18

N Y Times Mag—New York Times Magazine $7.50. (Complete Sunday edition; not sold separately) New York Times Co, 229 W 43d St, New York 18

N Y World-Telegram—New York World-Telegram and Sun $15. N Y World-Telegram Corp, 125 Barclay St, New York 15
N Y Sun consolidated with N Y World-Telegram January 5, 1950

Nat Ed Assn J—Journal of the National Education Association $5. free to members. National Education Assn, 1201 16th St, N W, Washington 6, D.C.

Nat Geog Mag—National Geographic Magazine $5. National Geographic Soc, 1146 16th St, N W, Washington 6, D.C.

Nat R—National Review 36s. Rolls House, 2 Bream's Bldgs, Chancery Lane, London, EC 4 ($8.50 International News Co, 131 Varick St, New York 13)

Nation—The Nation $7. The Nation Associates, Inc, 20 Vesey St, New York 7

Nation's Bsns—Nation's Business $15 (3 years). Chamber of Commerce of the United States, 1615 H St, N W, Washington 6, D.C.

Natur Hist—Natural History $5. American Museum of Natural History, 79th St and Central Park West, New York 24

Nature—Nature £4 10s; single numbers 1s 6d. Macmillan & Co, Ltd, St Martin's St, London, WC 2 ($22.50; single numbers 50c. Macmillan Co, 60 Fifth Ave, New York 11)

Nature Mag—Nature Magazine $4. American Nature Assn, 1214 16th St, N W, Washington 6, D.C.

New Eng Q—New England Quarterly $4. New England Quarterly, Hubbard Hall, Bowdoin College, Brunswick, Me.

New Repub—New Republic $6.30. Editorial Publications, Inc, 1416 F St, NW, Washington, D.C.

New Statesm & Nation—New Statesman and Nation—Week-end Review 32s 6d. 10 Great Turnstile, London, WC 1 ($7 International News Co, 131 Varick St, New York 13)

New York City. Museum of Modern Art Bul—Bulletin of the Museum of Modern Art 15c to 25c a copy; free to members. Museum of Modern Art, 11 W 53d St, New York 19

New Yorker—New Yorker $7. F-R Pub Corp, 25 W 43d St, New York 18

Newsweek—Newsweek $6.50. Weekly Publications, Inc, Newsweek Bldg, 152 W 42d St, New York 18

19th Cent—Nineteenth Century and After $8.75. Constable & Co, Ltd, 10 Orange St, London, WC 2

Opera N—Opera News $4; free to members. Metropolitan Opera Guild, Inc, 654 Madison Ave, New York 21

Outlook—Outlook (discontinued)

Parents Mag—Parents' Magazine $3. Parents' Institute, Inc, 52 Vanderbilt Ave, New York 17

Parnassus—Parnassus (discontinued)

Pathfinder—Pathfinder $2. Farm Journal, Inc, Washington Square, Philadelphia 5

Photoplay—Photoplay $3.60 (two years) Macfadden Publications, Inc, 205 E 42d St, New York 17
Combined with Movie Mirror

PM—PM (changed to N Y Star, June 23, 1948)

Poetry—Poetry $5. 232 E Erie St, Chicago 11

Pol Sci Q—Political Science Quarterly $6; free to members. Academy of Political Science, Columbia University, New York 27

Pop Mech—Popular Mechanics Magazine $3.50. Popular Mechanics Co, 200 E Ontario St, Chicago 11

Pop Sci—Popular Science Monthly $3. Popular Science Pub Co, Inc, 353 Fourth Ave, New York 10

Progres Educ—Progressive Education $4.25. American Education Fellowship, 34 E Main St, Champaign, Ill.

Pub W—Publishers' Weekly $6. R. R. Bowker Co, 62 W 45th St, New York 19

Q R—Quarterly Review 31s 4d. J. Murray, 50 Albemarle St, London, W 1. ($6.50 International News Co, 131 Varick St, New York 13)

Queen's Q—Queen's Quarterly $3. Queen's University, Kingston, Canada

R of Rs—Review of Reviews (discontinued)

Read Digest—Reader's Digest $3. Reader's Digest Assn, Inc, Pleasantville, N.Y.

Reader's Scope—Reader's Scope $3. L. S. Gleason, Pub, 114 E 32d St, New York 16

Ref Shelf—Reference Shelf $7 per volume of six bound numbers, published irregularly. H. W. Wilson Co, 950-972 University Ave, New York 52

Rotarian—Rotarian $2. Rotary International, 35 E Wacker Dr, Chicago 1

Roy Inst Brit Arch J—Journal of the Royal Institute of British Architects £2 postpaid. The Institute, 66 Portland Pl, London, W 1

Sales Management—Sales Management $6. Sales Management, Inc, 386 Fourth Ave, New York 16

Sat Eve Post—Saturday Evening Post $6. Curtis Pub Co, Independence Sq, Philadelphia 5

Sat R Lit—Saturday Review of Literature $6. Saturday Review Associates, Inc, 25 W 45th St, New York 19

Sch & Soc—School and Society $7; free to members of the Society for the Advancement of Education, Inc, 15 Amsterdam Ave, New York 23

Sch Arts—School Arts $4. School Arts, Printers Bldg, 44 Portland St, Worcester 8, Mass.

Sch R—School Review $4.50. University of Chicago Press, 5750 Ellis Ave, Chicago 37

Scholastic—Senior Scholastic (High School Teacher edition) $2 (teacher ed. only); school group rate (two or more subscriptions to one address) $1.20 for special eds. $1.50 for combined ed. Scholastic Corp, 7 E 12th St, New York 3

Sci Am—Scientific American $5. Scientific American, Inc, 24 W 40th St, New York 18

Sci Mo—Scientific Monthly $7.50. American Assn for the Advancement of Science, 1515 Massachusetts Ave, N W, Washington 5, D.C.

Sci N L—Science News Letter $5.50. Science Service, Inc, 1719 N St, N W, Washington 6, D.C.

Science ns—Science (news series) $7.50. American Assn for the Advancement of Science, 1515 Massachusetts Ave, NW, Washington 5, D.C.

Scrib Mag—Scribner's Magazine (discontinued)

Sign—The Sign $3. Passionist Missions, Inc, Union City, N.J.

So Atlan Q—South Atlantic Quarterly $3. Duke University Press, Durham, N.C.

Spec—Spectator 30s. 99 Gower St, London, WC 1 ($7 International News Co, 131 Varick St, New York 13)

Sport—Sport $3. Macfadden Publications, Inc, 205 E 42nd St, New York 17

Sporting N—Sporting News $8. Sporting News Pub Co, 2012-18 Washington Ave, St. Louis, Mo.

Stage—Stage (discontinued)

Stage Pict—Stage Pictorial (discontinued)

Studio—Studio $6. Studio Publication, Inc, 381 Fourth Ave, New York 16 (30s; The Studio, Ltd, 66 Chandos Pl, London, WC 2)

Sunset Mag—Sunset Magazine $2. Lane Pub Co, 576 Sacramento St, San Francisco 11

Survey—Survey $5. Survey Associates, Inc, 112 E 19th St, New York 3

Survey Graphic. See Survey

Survey Midmonthly. See Survey

Theatre Arts—Theatre Arts $5. Theatre Arts, Inc, 130 W 56th St, New York 19

This Week—This Week Magazine. Distributed each Sunday with different newspapers. United Newspapers Magazine Corp, 420 Lexington Ave, New York 17. In New York included in Sunday edition of New York Herald Tribune.

Time—Time $6. Time, Inc, 540 N Michigan Ave, Chicago 11

Town and Country—Town and Country $7.50. Hearst Magazines, Inc, 572 Madison Ave, New York 22

Travel—Travel $4.50. Travel Mag, Inc, 115 W 45th St, New York 19

U N Bul—United Nations Bulletin $4.50. International Documents Service, Columbia University Press, 2960 Broadway, New York 27

U N World—United Nations World $4. U N World, Inc, 319 E 44th St, New York 17

U S Bur Labor. See Mo Labor R

U S Bur Labor Bul—United States Bureau of Labor Statistics. Bulletins. Free to libraries. Bureau of Labor Statistics, Washington, D.C. Purchase orders, Supt. of Documents. Washington 25, D.C.

U S News—United States News & World Report $5. United States News Pub Corp, 24th & N Sts, NW, Washington 7, D.C.

U S Office Educ Bul—United States Office of Education. Bulletins. Free to libraries. Office of Education, Washington, D.C. Purchase orders, Supt. of Documents, Washington 25, D.C.

Va Q R—Virginia Quarterly Review $3. University of Virginia, 1 West Range, Charlottesville, Va.

Variety—Variety $10. Variety, Inc, 154 W 46th St, New York 19

Vital Speeches—Vital Speeches of the Day $5. City News Pub Co, 33 W 42d St, New York 18

Vogue—Vogue (Incorporating Vanity Fair) $7.50. Condé Nast Publications, Inc, Greenwich, Conn.

Washington (D.C.) Post—Washington Post $10.80. P. L. Graham, Pub, 1337 E St, N W, Washington 4, D.C.

Wilson Lib Bul—Wilson Library Bulletin $2. H. W. Wilson Co, 950-972 University Ave, New York 52

Woman's Home C—Woman's Home Companion $2.50. Crowell-Collier Pub Co, Springfield, Ohio

World Rep—World Report. See U S News

World's Work—World's Work (discontinued)

Writer—The Writer $3. The Writer, Inc, 8 Arlington St, Boston 16

Yale R—Yale Review $3.50. 143 Elm St, New Haven 7, Conn.

NECROLOGY—1950

This is a list of biographees' obituaries for the year. Deaths which occurred in late 1950 are recorded in the January 1951 issue of CURRENT BIOGRAPHY; references to those obituaries are included in this list.

Arnold, Henry H(arley) (biog 1942)

Blum, Leon (biog 1940)
Booth, Evangeline (Cory) (biog 1941)
Bowman, Isaiah (biog 1945)
Buck, Frank (biog 1943)

Caraway, Hattie W(yatt) (biog 1945) See Jan 51

Damrosch, Walter (Johannes) (biog 1944) See Jan 51
De Luca, Giuseppe (biog 1947)
De Sylva, Buddy (biog 1943)
De Sylva, George Gard See De Sylva, B. (biog 1943)
Dickinson, Robert L(atou) (biog 1950) See Jan 51
Doherty, Robert E(rnest) (biog 1949)
Drew, Charles R(ichard) (biog 1944)
Dykstra, Clarence A(ddison) (biog 1941)

Embree, Edwin R(ogers) (biog 1948)

Fraser, Peter (biog 1942) See Jan 51

Goshorn, Clarence B(aker) (biog 1950) See Jan 51
Goss, Albert S. (biog 1945)
Gustaf V, King of Sweden (biog 1942)

Hopkins, Arthur (Melancthon) (biog 1947)

Houston, Charles H(amilton) (biog 1948)
Huston, Walter (biog 1949)
Jolson, Al (biog 1940)

King, William Lyon Mackenzie (biog 1940)
Knox, Mrs. Charles Briggs See Knox, Mrs. R. M. (biog 1949)
Knox, Mrs. Rose M(arkward) (biog 1949)
Kolarov, Vassil (Petrov) (biog 1949)

Laski, Harold (Joseph) (biog 1941)
Lesinski, John (biog 1949)
Lewis, Sir Willmott (Harsant) (biog 1941)

McNicholas, John T(imothy), Archbishop (biog 1949)
Maier, Walter A(rthur), Rev. (biog 1947)
Marshall, M(aple) Lee (biog 1948)

Nijinsky, Waslaw (biog 1940)
Norman, Montagu (Co'let, 1st Baron) (biog 1940)

Oscar of the Waldorf See Tschirky, O. M. (biog 1947)

Patel, Vallabhbhai (Jhaverbhai) (biog 1948) See Jan 51

Peker, Recep (biog 1947)
Pemberton, Brock (biog 1945)

Renner, Karl (biog 1945) See Jan 51
Ringling, Robert E(dward) (biog 1945)
Ross, Charles (Griffith) (biog 1945) See Jan 51

Saarinen, Eliel (biog 1942)
Shaw, (George) Bernard (biog 1944)
Smedley, Agnes (biog 1944)
Smuts, Jan Christiaan (biog 1941)
Stanley, Oliver (Frederick George) (biog 1943) See Jan 51
Steinberg, Milton, Rabbi (biog 1940)
Steinhardt, Laurence A(dolph) (biog 1941)
Stimson, Henry L(ewis) (biog 1940)
Stoopnagle, Colonel (biog 1947)

Taylor, F(rederick) Chase See Stoopnagle, Colonel (biog 1947)
Tschirky, Oscar (Michel) (biog 1947)

Walker, Walton H(arris) (biog 1950) See Jan 51
Wason, Robert R(oss) (biog 1946)
Wavell, Archibald (Percival), 1st Earl (biog 1941)
Wecter, Dixon (biog 1944)
Weill, Kurt (biog 1941)

CLASSIFICATION BY PROFESSION—1950

Agriculture

Beardsley, William S(hane)
Fisher, Walter C.
Fred, E(dwin) B(roun)
Goss, Albert S. obit
McCaffrey, John L(awrence)
Rennebohm, Oscar
Senanayake, Don Stephen
Trigg, Ralph S(tovall)
Watkins, Arthur V(ivian)

Architecture

Higgins, Daniel Paul
Saarinen, Eliel obit
Telkes, Maria (de)

Art

Berryman, James Thomas
Hopper, Edward
Larkin, Oliver W(aterman)
Sheeler, Charles
Wright, Russel

Aviation

Arnold, Henry H(arley) obit
Douglas, Donald W(ills)
Janas, Sigmund
Lewis, Clyde A(ugustine)
Litchfield, P(aul) W(eeks)
Morgan, Thomas A(lfred)
Pearson, C(hester) C(harles)
Quesada, Elwood R(ichard)

Business

Appley, Lawrence A(sa)
Baruch, Bernard M(annes)
Beardsley, William S(hane)
Black, Eugene R(obert)
Boylan, Robert P(eter)
Brown, David M.
Buck, Frank obit
Butler, Hugh (Alfred)
Chadwick, Florence (May)
Cranston, Alan (MacGregor)
Cuneo, John F.
Douglas, Arthur F(iske)
Enckell, Carl J(ohan) A(lexis)
Erhard, Ludwig
Folsom, Marion B(ayard)
Fuller, Alfred C(arl)
Giannini, L(awrence) M(ario)
Gimbel, Bernard F(eustman)
Goshorn, Clarence B(aker)
Griffith, Clark (Calvin)
Gurney, (John) Chan(dler)
Holland, Sidney G(eorge)

Janas, Sigmund
Johnson, Holgar J(oseph)
Kerr, Robert S(amuel)
Larsen, Roy E(dward)
Lay, James S(elden), Jr.
Leffingwell, R(ussell) C(ornell)
Lesinski, John obit
Marshall, Walter P(eter)
Muir, James
Ospina Pérez, Mariano
Peterson, F(rank) Raymond
Puckett, B(enjamin) Earl
Putnam, Claude Adams
Rennebohm, Oscar
Ringling, Robert E(dward)
    obit
Roosevelt, James
Schricker, Henry F(rederick)
Seyferth, O(tto) A(dolph)
Sproul, Allan
Swanson, Gloria
Tope, John (K.)
Tschirky, Oscar (Michel)
    obit
Watson, Thomas J(ohn)
Woolton, Frederick James
    Marquis, 1st Baron

Dance

Helpmann, Robert
Nijinsky, Waslaw obit
Robinson, Bill obit
Shearer, Moira

Diplomacy

Anderson, Mrs. (Helen)
    Eugenie (Moore)
Chauvel, Jean (Michel Henri)
Cochran, H(orace) Merle
Enckell, Carl J(ohan)
    A(lexis)
Entezam, Nasrollah
Fernandes, L(uis) Esteves
Garreau, Roger
Hearne, John J(oseph)
Hillenkoetter, Roscoe H(enry)
Kohler, Foy D(avid)
Politis, Athanase G(eorge)
Poole, DeWitt C(linton)
Sastroamidjojo, Ali
Steinhardt, Laurence A(dolph)
    obit
Tarchiani, Alberto
Wrong, (Humphrey) Hume

Education

Anderson, (Hobson) Dewey
Basdevant, Jules
Baumgartner, Leona

Beck, Mildred Buchwalder
Bemis, Samuel Flagg
Berggrav, Eivind (Josef),
    Bishop
Bethe, Hans A(lbrecht)
Bevis, Howard L(andis)
Blough, Roy
Bowman, Isaiah obit
Bryan, Ernest Rowlett
Cordier, Andrew W(ellington)
Dean, Gordon (Evans)
Denny, George V(ernon), Jr.
Dickinson, Robert L(atou)
Doherty, Robert E(rnest) obit
Douglas, William O(rville)
Drew, Charles R(ichard) obit
Dykstra, Clarence A(ddison)
    obit
Eisendrath, Maurice N(athan),
    Rabbi
Embree, Edwin R(ogers) obit
Fred, E(dwin) B(roun)
Giauque, William F(rancis)
Glennan, T(homas) Keith
Goldman, Mrs. Olive Reming-
    ton
Grace, Alonzo G(askell)
Graham, Clarence R(eginald)
Graham, Harry Chrysostom,
    Rev.
Griswold, A(lfred) Whitney
Guthrie, A(lfred) B(ertram),
    Jr.
Haworth, Leland J(ohn)
Hench, Philip S(howalter)
Herring, (Edward) Pendleton
Hill, Harry W(ilbur)
Hirschfelder, Joseph O(ak-
    land)
Hoskins, Lewis M(aloney)
Houston, Charles H(amilton)
    obit
Johnson, Joseph E(srey)
Katz, Milton
Kendall, Edward C(alvin)
Kerst, Donald W(illiam)
Khan, Begum Liaquat Ali
Kingsley, J(ohn) Donald
Krick, Irving P(arkhurst)
Larkin, Oliver W(aterman)
Larsen, Roy E(dward)
Laski, Harold (Joseph) obit
Laubach, Frank C(harles)
Lemkin, Raphael
Lenroot, Katharine F(redrica)
L'Esperance, Elise (Depew
    Strang)
Lord, Milton E(dward)
Mack, Pauline Beery
McNicholas, John T(imothy),
    Archbishop, obit
Maier, Walter A(rthur), Rev.
    obit
Malin, Patrick Murphy
Marriott, Alice (Lee) (WLB)

Mowrey, Corma (Alice)
Myrdal, Mrs. Alva
Ospina Pérez, Mariano
Overstreet, Harry A(llen)
Pannell, Anne Gary
Peel, Roy V(ictor)
Pitzer, K(enneth) S(anborn)
Poole, DeWitt C(linton)
Richards, A(lfred) N(ewton)
Riddell, R(obert) Gerald
Saarinen, Eliel obit
Sawyer, Eddie
Schuck, Arthur A(loys)
Senn, Milton J(ohn) E(dward)
Sommerfeld, A(rnold Johannes Wilhelm)
Stiebeling, Hazel K(atherine)
Valentine, Alan (Chester)
Van Dusen, Henry P(itney), Rev.
Warner, J(ohn) C(hristian)
Wecter, Dixon obit
Wiener, Norbert
Wolfe, Hugh C(ampbell)
Wright, Louis B(ooker)
Yukawa, Hideki

Engineering

Butler, Hugh (Alfred)
Cooke, Morris Llewellyn
Doherty, Robert E(rnest) obit
Douglas, Donald W(ills)
Foster, William C(hapman)
Glennan, T(homas) Keith
Guy, Raymond F(rederick)
Haslett, Dame Caroline
Jewett, Frank B(aldwin) obit
Litchfield, P(aul) W(eeks)
Malone, George W(ilson)
Moch, Jules (Salvador)
Morgan, Thomas A(lfred)
Murray, Thomas E(dward)
Newcomer, Francis K(osier)
Pearson, C(hester) C(harles)
Suits, C(hauncey) G(uy)
Webster, William
White, Charles M(cElroy)
Wilson, Charles E(rwin)

Finance

Baruch, Bernard M(annes)
Bayar, (Mahmut) Celál
Black, Eugene R(obert)
Boylan, Robert P(eter)
Buttenwieser, Benjamin J(oseph)
Erhard, Ludwig
Folsom, Marion B(ayard)
Giannini, L(awrence) M(ario)
Gordon, Donald
Muir, James
Norman, Montagu (Collet Norman, 1st) Baron obit
Pace, Frank, Jr.
Peterson, F(rank) Raymond
Sproul, Allan
Stikker, Dirk U(ipko)

Government— Foreign

Basdevant, Jules
Baudouin, Prince Royal of Belgium
Bayar, (Mahmut) Celál
Bebler, Ales
Bech, Joseph
Bernardino, Minerva
Bernhard, Prince of the Netherlands
Blum, Léon obit
Carmona, Antonio Oscar de Fragoso
Chauvel, Jean (Michel Henri)
Davies, Clement (Edward)
Duvieusart, Jean
Enckell, Carl J(ohn) A(lexis)
Entezam, Nasrollah
Erhard, Ludwig
Fernandes, L(uis) Esteves
Foot, Michael
Gaitskell, Hugh (Todd Naylor)
Garreau, Roger
Gómez, Laureano
González Videla, Gabriel
Gordon, Donald
Granville, William Spencer Leveson-Gower, 4th Earl
Grotewohl, Otto
Gustaf V, King of Sweden obit
Gustaf VI, King of Sweden
Haslett, Dame Caroline
Hearne, John J(oseph)
Hoffman, Johannes
Holland, Sidney G(eorge)
Hoxha, Enver
Kekkonen, Urho K(aleva)
King, William Lyon Mackenzie obit
Kirkpatrick, Sir Ivone (Augustine)
Kolarov, Vassil (Petrov) obit
Menzies, Robert G(ordon)
Meyerson, Mrs. Golda
Moch, Jules (Salvador)
Mohammed Riza Pahlevi
Mollet, Guy
Ospina Pérez, Mariano
Peker, Recep obit
Plastiras, Nicholas
Pleven, René (Jean)
Politis, Athanase G(eorge)
Prasad, Rajendra
Rama IX, King of Thailand
Razmara, Ali
Reynaud, Paul
Riddell, R(obert) Gerald
Sadak, Necmeddin
Sastroamidjojo, Ali
Scott, Sir Harold (Richard)
Senanayake, Don Stephen
Smuts, Jan Christiaan obit
Spender, Percy C(laude)
Stikker, Dirk U(ipko)
Tarchiani, Alberto
Venizelos, Sophocles
Webb, Maurice

Woolton, Frederick James Marquis, 1st Baron
Wrong, (Humphrey) Hume
Younger, Kenneth (Gilmour)
Zeeland, Paul van

Government— United States

Andersen, Mrs. (Helen) Eugenie (Moore)
Appley, Lawrence A(sa)
Baruch, Bernard M(annes)
Battle, John S(tewart)
Baumgartner, Leona
Beardsley, William S(hane)
Bergson, Herbert A(ugustus)
Blough, Roy
Bowman, Isaiah obit
Bowron, Fletcher
Bryan, Ernest Rowlett
Butler, Hugh (Alfred)
Buttenwieser, Benjamin J(oseph)
Cochran, H(orace) Merle
Cooke, Morris Llewellyn
Cooper, John Sherman
Cordier, Andrew W(ellington)
Dean, Gordon (Evans)
De Castro, Morris F(idanque)
Douglas, William O(rville)
Dworshak, Henry C(larence)
Dykstra, Clarence A(ddison) obit
Foster, William C(hapman)
Glennan, T(homas) Keith
Goldman, Mrs. Olive Remington
Goss, Albert S. obit
Green, Theodore Francis
Gurney, (John) Chan(dler)
Hand, Learned
Herring, (Edward) Pendleton
Hickerson, John D(ewey)
Hill, Harry W(ilbur)
Hillenkoetter, Roscoe H(enry)
Hoey, Jane M(argueretta)
Holland, Spessard L(indsey)
Holtz, Jackson J(acob)
Hoover, J(ohn) Edgar
Hughes, Sarah T(ilghman)
Jackson, Robert H(oughwout)
Katz, Milton
Keating, Kenneth B(arnard)
Kee, John
Kelly, Edna F(lannery)
Kem, James P(reston)
Kennedy, John F(itzgerald)
Kerr, Robert S(amuel)
Kingsley, J(ohn) Donald
Kohler, Foy D(avid)
LaFollette, Charles M(arion)
Langlie, Arthur B(ernard)
Lay, James S(elden), Jr.
Lehrbas, Lloyd (Allan)
Lenroot, Katharine F(redrica)
Lesinski, John obit
Long, Earl K(emp)
McAuliffe, Anthony C(lement)
McCarthy, Joseph R(aymond)

McClellan, John L(ittle)
McGhee, George C(rews)
Malone, George W(ilson)
Marshall, M(aple) Lee obit
Matthews, Burnita Shelton
Meiling, Richard L(ewis)
Murphy, Charles S(prings)
Murray, Thomas E(dward)
Neely, Matthew M(ansfield)
Newcomer, Francis K(osier)
O'Conor, Herbert R(omulus)
Pace, Frank, Jr.
Peel, Roy V(ictor)
Perkins, George W(albridge)
Pitzer, K(enneth) S(anborn)
Priest, J(ames) Percy
Quesada, Elwood R(ichard)
Rennebohm, Oscar
Richards, A(lfred) N(ewton)
Roosevelt, Franklin D(elano), Jr.
Sampson, Mrs. Edith S.
Schricker, Henry F(rederick)
Sparkman, John J(ackson)
Steinhardt, Laurence A(dolph) obit
Stiebeling, Hazel K(atherine)
Stimson, Henry L(ewis) obit
Thomas, Albert (Langston)
Trigg, Ralph S(tovall)
Valentine, Alan (Chester)
Van Zandt, James E(dward)
Vorys, John M(artin)
Warren, Shields
Watkins, Arthur V(ivian)
Webster, William
Williams, Edwin G(antt)

Industry

Appley, Lawrence A(sa)
Baruch, Bernard M(annes)
Cuneo, John F.
Douglas, Donald W(ills)
Folsom, Marion B(ayard)
Foster, William C(hapman)
Franklin, Walter S(imonds)
Fuller, Alfred C(arl)
Gordon, Donald
Igleheart, Austin S(mith)
Knox, Mrs. Rose M(arkward) obit
Langmuir, Irving
Litchfield, P(aul) W(eeks)
Love, George H(utchinson)
McCaffrey, John L(awrence)
McGhee, George C(rews)
Marshall, M(aple) Lee obit
Morgan, Thomas A(lfred)
Murray, Thomas E(dward)
Pearson, C(hester) C(harles)
Perkins, George W(albridge)
Puckett, B(enjamin) Earl
Putnam, Claude Adams
Seyferth, O(tto) A(dolph)
Stikker, Dirk U(ipko)
Suits, C(hauncey) G(uy)
Swift, Harold H(iggins)
Thomas, Charles Allen
Tope, John (K.)

Wason, Robert R(oss) obit
Watson, Thomas J(ohn)
White, Charles M(cElroy)
White, Frank (Kiggins)
Wilson, Charles E(rwin)
Wright, Russel

International Relations

Anderson, Mrs. (Helen) Eu-genie (Moore)
Basdevant, Jules
Bebler, Ales
Bech, Joseph
Berggrav, Eivind (Josef), Bishop
Bernardino, Minerva
Bernhard, Prince of the Nether-lands
Black, Eugene R(obert)
Bowman, Isaiah obit
Buttenwieser, Benjamin J(oseph)
Chauvel, Jean (Michel Henri)
Cochran, H(orace) Merle
Cooper, John Sherman
Cordier, Andrew W(ellington)
Cranston, Alan (MacGregor)
Entezam, Nasrollah
Fernandes, L(uis) Esteves
Foster, William C(hapman)
Garreau, Roger
Goldman, Mrs. Olive Reming-ton
González Videla, Gabriel
Grace, Alonzo G(askell)
Granville, William Spencer Leveson-Gower, 4th Earl
Gustaf V, King of Sweden obit
Gustaf VI, King of Sweden
Halprin, Mrs. Samuel W.
Hearne, John J(oseph)
Hickerson, John D(ewey)
Holland, Sidney G(eorge)
Hoxha, Enver
Jackson, Robert H(oughwout)
Johnson, Joseph E(srey)
Katz, Milton
Kee, John
Kekkonen, Urho K(aleva)
King, William Lyon Mackenzie obit
Kingsley, J(ohn) Donald
Kirkpatrick, Sir Ivone (Augus-tine)
Kohler, Foy D(avid)
Kolarov, Vassil (Petrov) obit
LaFollette, Charles M(arion)
Lehrbas, Lloyd (Allan)
Lemkin, Raphael
Loughlin, Dame Anne
Loy, Myrna
McGhee, George C(rews)
Meyerson, Mrs. Golda
Mohammed Riza Pahlevi
Myrdal, Mrs. Alva
Perkins, George W(albridge)
Pius XII, Pope
Plastiras, Nicholas
Pleven, René (Jean)

Politis, Athanase G(eorge)
Poole, DeWitt C(linton)
Reynaud, Paul
Riddell, R(obert) Gerald
Sadak, Necmeddin
Sampson, Mrs. Edith S.
Sastroamidjojo, Ali
Sender, Toni
Smuts, Jan Christiaan obit
Spender, Percy C(laude)
Steinhardt, Laurence A(dolph) obit
Stikker, Dirk U(ipko)
Stimson, Henry L(ewis) obit
Streit, Clarence K(irshman)
Tarchiani, Alberto
Venizelos, Sophocles
Vorys, John M(artin)
Wrong, (Humphrey) Hume
Younger, Kenneth (Gilmour)
Zeeland, Paul van

Journalism

Barnett, M(arvin) Robert
Berryman, James Thomas
Blum, Léon obit
Breen, Joseph I(gnatius)
Bryan, Ernest Rowlett
Cooke, Morris Llewellyn
Cranston, Alan (MacGregor)
Dworshak, Henry C(larence)
Forbes, B(ertie) C(harles)
Guthman, Edwin O(tto)
Guthrie, A(lfred) B(ertram), Jr.
Hoffman, Johannes
Kennedy, John F(itzgerald)
Kintner, Robert E(dmonds)
Lehrbas, Lloyd (Allan)
Lewis, Sir Willmott (Harsant) obit
Matthews, T(homas) S(tanley)
Priest, J(ames) Percy
Saunders, Carl M(axon)
Schricker, Henry F(rederick)
Sender, Toni
Smedley, Agnes obit
Stevens, Edmund (William)
Streit, Clarence K(irshman)
Tarchiani, Alberto
Ward, Barbara (Mary)
Webb, Maurice
Wilkins, Roy

Labor

Bridges, Harry (Renton)
Foot, Michael
Houston, Charles H(amilton) obit
Hughes, R(oy) O(rlo)
Kennedy, William P(arker)
Lenroot, Katharine F(redrica)
Loughlin, Dame Anne
Love, George H(utchinson)
Magee, Elizabeth S(tewart)
Meyerson, Mrs. Golda
Mosher, A(aron Alexander) R(oland)

Myrdal, Mrs. Alva
Oakes, Grant W(ilson)
Oldenbroek, Jacobus H(endrik)
Robertson, D(avid) B(rown)
Sender, Toni
Webb, Maurice

Law

Basdevant, Jules
Battle, John S(tewart)
Bergson, Herbert A(ugustus)
Bevis, Howard L(andis)
Blum, Léon obit
Bowron, Fletcher
Cooper, John Sherman
Craig, George N(orth)
Davies, Clement (Edward)
Dean, Gordon (Evans)
Douglas, Arthur F(iske)
Douglas, William O(rville)
Duvieusart, Jean
Fernandes, L(uis) Esteves
Gonzáles Videla, Gabriel
Green, Theodore Francis
Hand, Learned
Hearne, John J(oseph)
Holland, Spessard L(indsey)
Holtz, Jackson J(acob)
Hoover, J(ohn) Edgar
Houston, Charles H(amilton)
  obit
Hughes, Sarah T(ilghman)
Jackson, Robert H(oughwout)
Katz, Milton
Keating, Kenneth B(arnard)
Kee, John
Keech, Richmond B(owling)
Kekkonen, Urho K(aleva)
Kem, James P(reston)
Kerr, Robert S(amuel)
Kolarov, Vassil (Petrov) obit
LaFollette, Charles M(arion)
Langlie, Arthur B(ernard)
Leffingwell, R(ussell) C(ornell)
Lemkin, Raphael
Lewis, Clyde A(ugustine)
Long, Earl K(emp)
McCarthy, Joseph R(aymond)
McClellan, John L(ittle)
McConnell, Joseph H(oward)
Matthews, Burnita Shelton
Menzies, Robert G(ordon)
Murphy, Charles S(prings)
Neely, Matthew M(ansfield)
O'Conor, Herbert R(omulus)
Pace, Frank, Jr.
Pleven, René (Jean)
Politis, Athanase G(eorge)
Prasad, Rajendra
Reynaud, Paul
Roosevelt, Franklin D(elano),
  Jr.
Sampson, Mrs. Edith S.
Sastroamidjojo, Ali
Sparkman, John J(ackson)
Spender, Percy C(laude)
Steinhardt, Laurence A(dolph)
  obit

Stikker, Dirk U(ipko)
Stimson, Henry L(ewis) obit
Syran, Arthur George
Thomas, Albert (Langston)
Tweed, Harrison
Vorys, John M(artin)
Watkins, Arthur V(ivian)
Younger, Kenneth (Gilmour)

Literature

Blum, Léon obit
Bonner, Mary Graham (WLB)
Brooks, Gwendolyn
Caudill, Rebecca (WLB)
Cavanna, Betty (WLB)
Chute, (Beatrice) Joy (WLB)
Chute, Marchette (Gaylord)
  (WLB)
Cooper, Louise Field (WLB)
Feikema, Feike (Frederick)
  (WLB)
Frost, Frances Mary (WLB)
Gaither, Frances (WLB)
Guthrie, A(lfred) B(ertram),
  Jr.
Haig-Brown, Roderick (Lang-
  mere) (WLB)
Knox, Ronald (Arbuthnott),
  Msgr.
Longstreth, T(homas) Morris
  (WLB)
Mallette, Gertrude E(thel)
  (WLB)
Marriott, Alice (Lee) (WLB)
Merrick, Elliott (Tucker) (WLB)
Miller, Merle (WLB)
Monsarrat, Nicholas (John
  Turney) (WLB)
Moon, Bucklin (WLB)
Robinson, Henry Morton
Shaw, (George) Bernard obit
Sorensen, Virginia (WLB)
Thompson, Mary Wolfe (WLB)
Waltari, Mika (Toimi)
Wavell, Archibald (Percival),
  1st Earl obit
Wecter, Dixon obit
White, Nelia Gardner (WLB)
Wright, Louis B(ooker)

Medicine

Baumgartner, Leona
Dickinson, Robert L(atou)
Drew, Charles R(ichard) obit
Furey, Warren W(illiam)
Hench, Philip S(howalter)
Henderson, E(lmer) L(ee)
L'Esperance, Elise (Depew
  Strang)
Meiling, Richard L(ewis)
Richards, A(lfred) N(ewton)
Senn, Milton J(ohn) E(dward)
Smith, Austin E(dward)
Smith, David T(illerson)
Warren, Shields
Williams, Edwin G(antt)

Military

Arnold, Henry H(arley) obit
Brown, David M.
Carmona, Antonio Oscar de
  Fragoso
Cates, Clifton B(ledsoe)
Craig, George N(orth)
Gruenther, Alfred M(aximilian)
Holtz, Jackson J(acob)
Krick, Irving P(arkhurst)
Lewis, Clyde A(ugustine)
McAuliffe, Anthony C(lement)
Meiling, Richard L(ewis)
Newcomer, Francis K(osier)
Peker, Recep obit
Plastiras, Nicholas
Quesada, Elwood R(ichard)
Razmara, Ali
Russell, Harold (John)
Smuts, Jan Christiaan obit
Stimson, Henry L(ewis) obit
Venizelos, Sophocles
Walker, Walton H(arris)
Wavell, Archibald (Percival),
  1st Earl obit

Motion Pictures

Boyd, Bill
Breen, Joseph I(gnatius)
Buck, Frank obit
Crawford, Broderick
Depinet, Ned E(verett)
De Sylva, Buddy obit
Glennan, T(homas) Keith
Guinness, Alec
Helpmann, Robert
Huston, Walter obit
Hutton, Betty
Jolson, Al obit
Lanchester, Elsa
Lockhart, Gene
Loy, Myrna
Piaf, Edith
Power, Tyrone
Redgrave, Michael
Reed, Carol
Richardson, Sir Ralph
Robinson, Bill obit
Robinson, Edward G.
Rossen, Robert
Russell, Harold (John)
Shaw, (George) Bernard obit
Shearer, Moira
Swanson, Gloria
Wellman, William A(ugustus)
Young, Robert
Zukor, Adolph

Music

Anderson, Marian
Biggs, E(dward George) Power
Bing, Rudolf
Casals, Pablo
Curzon, Clifford
De Luca, Giuseppe obit
De Sylva, Buddy obit

Green, Martyn
Harbach, Otto A(bels)
Hutton, Betty
Milstein, Nathan
Piaf, Edith
Rama, IX, King of Thailand
Ringling, Robert E(dward) obit
Truman, (Mary) Margaret
Voorhees, Donald
Weill, Kurt obit

Naval

Cates, Clifton B(ledsoe)
Granville, William Spencer
    Leveson-Gower, 4th Earl
Hill, Harry W(ilbur)
Hillenkoetter, Roscoe H(enry)

Politics

Anderson, (Hobson) Dewey
Battle, John S(tewart)
Bayar, (Mahmut) Celál
Bech, Joseph
Blum, Léon obit
Bowron, Fletcher
Bridges, Harry (Renton)
Butler, Hugh (Alfred)
Carmona, Antonio Oscar de
    Fragoso
Cooper, John Sherman
Davies, Clement (Edward)
Duvieusart, Jean
Dworshak, Henry C(larence)
Erhard, Ludwig
Foot, Michael
Gaitskell, Hugh (Todd Naylor)
Gómez, Laureano
Gonzáles Videla, Gabriel
Green, Theodore Francis
Grotewohl, Otto
Gurney, (John) Chan(dler)
Holland, Sidney G(eorge)
Holland, Spessard L(indsey)
Holtz, Jackson J(acob)
Hoxha, Enver
Hughes, Sarah T(ilghman)
Keating, Kenneth B(arnard)
Kee, John
Kekkonen, Urho K(aleva)
Kem, James P(reston)
Kennedy, John F(itzgerald)
Kerr, Robert S(amuel)
King, William Lyon Mackenzie
    obit
Kolarov, Vassil (Petrov) obit
LaFollette, Charles M(arion)
Langlie, Arthur B(ernard)
Laski, Harold (Joseph) obit
Lee, Mrs. John G.
Lesinski, John obit
Long, Earl K(emp)
McCarthy, Joseph R(aymond)
McClellan, John L(ittle)
Malone, George W(ilson)
Mayes, Mrs. Gilford (Harold)
Menzies, Robert G(ordon)
Meyerson, Mrs. Golda

Moch, Jules (Salvador)
Mollet, Guy
Murphy, Charles S(prings)
Neely, Matthew M(ansfield)
O'Conor, Herbert R(omulus)
Ospina Pérez, Mariano
Peker, Recep obit
Plastiras, Nicholas
Pleven, René (Jean)
Prasad, Rajendra
Priest, J(ames) Percy
Razmara, Ali
Rennebohm, Oscar
Reynaud, Paul
Roosevelt, Franklin D(elano),
    Jr.
Roosevelt, James
Sadak, Necmeddin
Sastroamidjojo, Ali
Schricker, Henry F(rederick)
Senanayake, Don Stephen
Sender, Toni
Smuts, Jan Christiaan obit
Sparkman, John J(ackson)
Spender, Percy C(laude)
Stikker, Dirk U(ipko)
Tarchiani, Alberto
Thomas, Albert (Langston)
Tope, John (K.)
Van Zandt, James E(dward)
Venizelos, Sophocles
Vorys, John M(artin)
Watkins, Arthur V(ivian)
Webb, Maurice
Woolton, Frederick James
    Marquis, 1st Baron
Younger, Kenneth (Gilmour)

Publishing

Cuneo, John F.
Dworshak, Henry C(larence)
Forbes, B(ertie) C(harles)
Gómez, Laureano
Graham, Harry Chrysostom,
    Rev.
Larsen, Roy E(dward)
Latham, Harold S(trong)
McGraw, Curtis W(hittlesey)
Matthews, T(homas) S(tanley)
Saunders, Carl M(axon)
Smith, Austin E(dward)
Streit, Clarence K(irshman)

Radio

Allen, Mel
Biggs, E(dward George) Power
Boyd, Bill
Brokenshire, Norman (Ernest)
Curzon, Clifford
Denny, George V(ernon), Jr.
Depinet, Ned E(verett)
Gambling, John B(radley)
Goldmark, Peter C(arl)
Guy, Raymond F(rederick)
Huston, Walter obit
Jolson, Al obit
Kintner, Robert E(dmonds)

Lockhart, Gene
McConnell, Joseph H(oward)
Maier, Walter A(rthur), Rev.
    obit
Robinson, Edward G.
Stoopnagle, Colonel obit
Voorhees, Donald
White, Frank (Kiggins)
Young, Robert

Religion

Allan, John J(ames)
Berggrav, Eivind (Josef),
    Bishop
Booth, Evangeline (Cory) obit
Bryan, Ernest Rowlett
Eisendrath, Maurice N(athan),
    Rabbi
Evans, Hugh Ivan, Rev.
Graham, Harry Chrysostom,
    Rev.
Halprin, Mrs. Samuel W.
Hoskins, Lewis M(aloney)
Knox, Ronald (Arbuthnott),
    Msgr.
Latham, Harold S(trong)
Laubach, Frank C(harles)
McGuigan, James (Charles),
    Cardinal
McNicholas, John T(imothy),
    Archbishop obit
Maier, Walter A(rthur), Rev.
    obit
Manning, William Thomas,
    Bishop obit
Pius XII, Pope
Pruden, Edward Hughes, Rev.
Steinberg, Milton, Rabbi obit
Van Dusen, Henry P(itney),
    Rev.
Ward, Barbara (Mary)

Science

Baumgartner, Leona
Bethe, Hans A(lbrecht)
Bowman, Isaiah obit
Drew, Charles R(ichard) obit
Fred, E(dwin) B(roun)
Furey, Warren W(illiam)
Giauque, William F(rancis)
Haworth, Leland J(ohn)
Hirschfelder, Joseph O(ak-
    land)
Howell, Wallace E(gbert)
Jewett, Frank B(aldwin) obit
Kendall, Edward C(alvin)
Kerst, Donald W(illiam)
Krick, Irving P(arkhurst)
Langmuir, Irving
L'Esperance, Elise (Depew
    Strang)
McGhee, George C(rews)
Mack, Pauline Beery
Marriott, Alice (Lee) (WLB)
Pitzer, K(enneth) S(anborn)
Richards, A(lfred) N(ewton)
Smith, Austin E(dward)

Smith, David T(illerson)
Sommerfeld, A(rnold Johannes Wilhelm)
Stiebeling, Hazel K(atherine)
Suits, C(hauncey) G(uy)
Telkes, Maria (de)
Thomas, Charles Allen
Warner, J(ohn) C(hristian)
Warren, Shields
Wiener, Norbert
Williams, Edwin G(antt)
Wolfe, Hugh C(ampbell)
Yukawa, Hideki

Social Science

Anderson, (Hobson) Dewey
Appley, Lawrence A(sa)
Bayar, (Mahmut) Celál
Beck, Mildred Buchwalder
Bemis, Samuel Flagg
Blough, Roy
Bryan, Ernest Rowlett
Cooke, Morris Llewellyn
Cordier, Andrew W(ellington)
Denny, George V(ernon), Jr.
Dickinson, Robert L(atou)
Dykstra, Clarence A(ddison) obit
Embree, Edwin R(ogers) obit
Erhard, Ludwig
Folsom, Marion B(ayard)
Gaitskell, Hugh (Todd Naylor)
Goldman, Mrs. Olive Remington
Grace, Alonzo G(askell)
Griswold, A(lfred) W(hitney)
Haslett, Dame Caroline
Herring, (Edward) Pendleton
Hoey, Jane M(argueretta)
Hoover, J(ohn) Edgar
Johnson, Joseph E(srey)
King, William Lyon Mackenzie obit
Kingsley, J(ohn) Donald
Laski, Harold (Joseph) obit
Lenroot, Katharine F(redrica)
Malin, Patrick Murphy
Myrdal, Mrs. Alva
Overstreet, Harry A(llen)
Pannell, Anne Gary
Patton, Mrs. James B(laine)
Peel, Roy V(ictor)
Sadak, Necmeddin
Senn, Milton J(ohn) E(dward)
Shaw, (George) Bernard obit
Streit, Clarence K(irshman)
Trigg, Ralph S(tovall)
Ward, Barbara (Mary)
Wecter, Dixon obit
Woolton, Frederick James Marquis, 1st Baron
Wright, Louis B(ooker)
Zeeland, Paul van

Social Service

Allan, John J(ames)
Anderson, (Hobson) Dewey

Barnett, M(arvin) Robert
Baruch, Bernard M(annes)
Baumgartner, Leona
Beck, Mildred Buchwalder
Blalock, Mrs. Richard W(atts)
Booth, Evangeline (Cory) obit
Brown, David M.
Eisendrath, Maurice N(athan), Rabbi
Evans, Hugh Ivan, Rev.
Fisher, Walter C.
Graham, Harry Chrysostom, Rev.
Halprin, Mrs. Samuel W.
Higgins, Daniel Paul
Hoey, Jane M(argueretta)
Hoskins, Lewis M(aloney)
Houghton, Mrs. Hiram Cole
Houston, Charles H(amilton) obit
Khan, Begum Liaquat Ali
Kingsley, J(ohn) Donald
Knox, Mrs. Rose M(arkward) obit
Laubach, Frank C(harles)
Lee, Mrs. John G.
Lenroot, Katharine F(redrica)
L'Esperance, Elise (Depew Strang)
McGuigan, James (Charles), Cardinal
Magee, Elizabeth S(tewart)
Malin, Patrick Murphy
Marshall, M(aple) Lee obit
Mayes, Mrs. Gilford (Harold)
Meyerson, Mrs. Golda
Pius XII, Pope
Prasad, Rajendra
Russell, Harold (John)
Schuck, Arthur A(loys)
Smith, David T(illerson)
Tweed, Harrison
Van Dusen, Henry P(itney), Rev.
Watson, Thomas J(ohn)
Wilkins, Roy

Sports

Allen, Mel
Bell, Bert
Chadwick, Florence (May)
Durocher, Leo (Ernest)
Griffith, Clark (Calvin)
Page, Joe
Reese, Harold (Henry)
Rizzuto, Phil(ip Francis)
Sawyer, Eddie
Thorpe, Jim

Technology

Doherty, Robert E(rnest) obit
Douglas, Donald W(ills)
Glennan, T(homas) Keith
Goldmark, Peter C(arl)
Guy, Raymond F(rederick)

Haworth, Leland J(ohn)
Hirschfelder, Joseph O(akland)
Hoover, J(ohn) Edgar
Howell, Wallace E(gbert)
Jewett, Frank B(aldwin) obit
Kerst, Donald W(illiam)
Krick, Irving P(arkhurst)
Langmuir, Irving
Litchfield, P(aul) W(eeks)
McAuliffe, Anthony C(lement)
McGraw, Curtis W(hittlesey)
Morgan, Thomas A(lfred)
Ospina Pérez, Mariano
Putnam, Claude Adams
Suits, C(hauncey) G(uy)
Warner, J(ohn) C(hristian)
Watson, Thomas J(ohn)
Webster, William

Television

Allen, Mel
Boyd, Bill
Depinet, Ned E(verett)
Gambling, John B(radley)
Goldmark, Peter C(arl)
Guy, Raymond F(rederick)
Kintner, Robert E(dmonds)
McConnell, Joseph H(oward)
Piaf, Edith
Swanson, Gloria
Zukor, Adolph

Theater

Bing, Rudolf
Crawford, Broderick
De Sylva, Buddy obit
Goldman, Mrs. Olive Remington
Green, Martyn
Guinness, Alec
Harbach, Otto A(bels)
Helpmann, Robert
Hopkins, Arthur (Melancthon) obit
Huston, Walter obit
Jolson, Al obit
Lanchester, Elsa
Lockhart, Gene
Milstein, Nathan
Pemberton, Brock obit
Piaf, Edith
Power, Tyrone
Redgrave, Michael
Reed, Carol
Richardson, Sir Ralph
Robinson, Bill obit
Robinson, Edward G.
Rossen, Robert
Shaw, (George) Bernard obit
Swanson, Gloria
Waltari, Mika (Toimi)
Webster, Margaret
Weill, Kurt obit

CUMULATED INDEX—1940 - 1950

This is an eleven-year cumulation of all names which have appeared in CURRENT BIOGRAPHY from 1940 through 1950. The dates after names indicate monthly issues and/or Yearbooks in which biographies and obituaries are contained.

Beginning with the 1946 Yearbook, the twenty authors' biographies presented in the WILSON LIBRARY BULLETIN during the calendar year have been reprinted in CURRENT BIOGRAPHY Yearbooks; they are indicated in this index by the abbreviations "WLB," which is followed by the Yearbook date.

Please note that three of the 1940 references are not to monthly issues of CURRENT BIOG-RAPHY: "Jan-Feb" refers to the combined number which covered the first two months of that year; and since the June and December numbers were not published in monthly form, "Jan-Jun" refers to June material contained in that six-month cumulation, and "Yrbk 40" refers to December material contained in that Yearbook.

Aalto, (Hugo) Alvar (Henrik) Apr 48

Abbott, Anthony See Oursler, F. Oct 42

Abbott, Berenice Jul 42

Abbott, Bud, and Costello, Lou Oct 41

Abbott, Douglas (Charles) Jun 49

Abbott, Edith Sep 41

Abbott, Edwin Milton obit Jan 41

Abbott, George Apr 40

Abbott, Robert Sengstacke obit Mar 40

Abdullah, Achmed obit Jun 45

Abdullah, Seif-ul-Islam, Prince See Seif-ul-Islam Abdullah, Prince Dec 47

Abdullah ibn Hussein, King of Trans-Jordan Jun 48

Abend, Hallett (Edward) Sep 42

Abercrombie, Sir (Leslie) Patrick Apr 46

Aberhart, William C. obit Jul 43

Abetz, Otto Feb 41

Abul Kalam Azad, Maulana Jul 42

Ace, Goodman and Ace, Jane May 48

Ace, Jane See Ace, G. and Ace, J. May 48

Acheson, Albert R(obert) obit Apr 41

Acheson, Dean (Gooderham) Mar 41 Feb 49

Ackerman, Carl W(illiam) Oct 45

Acland, Sir Richard (Thomas Dyke) Aug 44

Adair, Frank E(arl) May 46

Adamic, Louis Yrbk 40

Adamowski, Timothée obit May 43

Adams, Alva B(lanchard) obit Jan 42

Adams, Franklin P(ierce) Jul 41

Adams, Herbert obit Jun 45

Adams, James Truslow biog Nov 41 obit Jul 49

Adams, Joseph H(enry) obit Apr 41

Adams, Joseph Quincy obit Dec 46

Adams, Randolph G(reenfield) Aug 43

Adams, Roger Jun 47

Adams, Thomas obit Apr 40

Addams, Clifford Isaac obit Jan 43

Addington, Sarah obit Yrbk 40

Addis Ababa, Pietro Badoglio, Duca d' Oct 40

Additon, Henrietta Silvis Sep 40

Ade, George obit Jul 44

Adenauer, Konrad Jul 49

Adkins, Charles obit May 41

Adler, Cyrus obit May 40

Adler, Guido obit May 41

Adler, Harry Clay obit Apr 40

Adler, Julius Ochs Jun 48

Adler, Larry Feb 44

Adler, Mortimer Jerome Apr 40

Adrian, (Gilbert) Feb 41

Aga Khan, The (Aga Sultan Sir Mahomed Shah) May 46

Agar, Herbert (Sebastian) Mar 44

Agar, William (Macdonough) May 49

Aguirre Cerda, Pedro biog Jan 41 obit Yrbk 41

Ahmed II, Sidi, Bey of Tunis obit Aug 42

Aiken, George D(avid) Jun 47

Aiken, Howard (Hathaway) Mar 47

Ainsworth, William Newman, Bishop obit Aug 42

Aitken, William Maxwell, 1st Baron Beaverbrook See Beaverbrook, W. M. A., 1st Baron Jul 40

Aked, Charles F(rederic), Rev. obit Oct 41

Alain, (Daniel A.) Sep 41

Alajálov, Constantin Jan 42

Albanese, Licia Mar 46

Albee, Fred H(oudlette) biog May 43 obit Apr 45

Alberto (Da Motta E Silva), Alvaro Mar 47

Albright, Ivan Le Lorraine Feb 44

Alcayaga, Lucila Godoy See Mistral, G. Feb 46

Aldrich, Chester Holmes obit Feb 41

Aldrich, Richard S(teere) obit Feb 42

Aldrich, Winthrop Williams Oct 40

Aldridge, James Mar 43

Alegría, Ciro Dec 41

Alekhine, Alexander obit May 46

Alemán, Miguel Sep 46

Alexander, Albert Victor Yrbk 40

Alexander, Franz Aug 42

Alexander, Sir Harold R(upert) L(eofric) G(eorge) Oct 42

Alexander, Harry Held obit Feb 41

Alexander, Ruth Mar 43

Alfonso XIII, Former King of Spain obit Apr 41

Alger, Ellice M(urdoch) obit Apr 45

Allan, John J(ames) Jan 50

Allee, Marjorie (Hill) obit Jun 45

Allee, Mrs. Warder Clyde See Allee, M. H. obit Jun 45

Allen, Betsy See Cavanna, B. (WLB) Yrbk 50

Allen, Edgar obit Mar 43

Allen, Florence (Ellinwood) Feb 41

Allen, Frank A(lbert, Jr.) Mar 45

Allen, Fred Feb 41

Allen, George E(dward) Mar 46

Allen, George V(enable) Nov 48

Allen, Gracie Jul 40

Allen, Jay (Cooke, Jr.) Oct 41

Allen, Joel Nott obit Mar 40

Allen, Larry Jul 42

Allen, Leo E(lwood) Jun 48

Allen, Marion obit Feb 42

Allen, Mel Oct 50

Cravath, Paul Drennan obit Aug 40

Craven, Frank obit Oct 45

Craven, Thomas Apr 44

Crawford, Broderick Apr 50

Crawford, Cheryl Dec 45

Crawford, Frederick C(oolidge) Feb 43

Crawford, Joan Jan 46

Crawford, Morris Barker obit Yrbk 40

Crawford, Phyllis Nov 40

Crawshaw, William Henry obit Aug 40

Cream, Arnold Raymond See Walcott, J. Jun 49

Creeft, José de See De Creeft, J. Dec 42

Creel, George (Edward) Jun 44

Cregar, Laird obit Jan 45

Crerar, H(enry) D(uncan) G(raham) Nov 44

Cresswell, Robert obit Nov 43

Cret, Paul P(hilippe) biog Nov 42 obit Nov 45

Crewe, Robert Offley Ashburton Crewe-Milnes, 1st Marquis of obit Jul 45

Crews, Laura Hope obit Jan 43

Crider, John H(enshaw) Jun 49

Crile, George (Washington) obit Feb 43

Cripps, Charles Alfred, 1st Baron Parmoor See Parmoor, C. A. C., 1st Baron obit Aug 41

Cripps, Sir (Richard) Stafford Jul 40 Apr 48

Crisler, Fritz See Crisler, H. O. Feb 48

Crisler, Herbert Orin Feb 48

Crispin, Edmund (WLB) Yrbk 49

Crist, William E(arl) Nov 45

Croce, Benedetto Jan 44

Crompton, Rookes Evelyn Bell obit Mar 40

Cromwell, James H. R. Mar 40

Cronin, A(rchibald) J(oseph) Jul 42

Crosby, Bing Sep 41

Crosley, Powel, Jr. Jun 47

Cross, Milton John Jan-Feb 40

Cross, Ronald H(ibbert), 1st Baronet Jun 41

Crossley, Archibald M(addock) Dec 41

Crossman, R(ichard) H(oward) S(tafford) May 47

Crouse, Russel Jun 41

Crow, Carl biog Oct 41 obit Jul 45

Crowell, T(homas) Irving obit Mar 42

Crowley, John J., Father obit Apr 40

Crowley, Leo T(homas) Jun 43

Crownfield, Gertrude obit Jul 45

Crum, Bartley C(avanaugh) May 47

Crumit, Frank obit Oct 43

Cruz, Hernán Santa See Santa Cruz, H. Dec 49

Cruze, James obit Sep 42

Cruzen, Richard H(arold) Mar 47

Csáky, István, Count See Csáky, S., Count obit Mar 41

Csáky, Stephen, Count obit Mar 41

Cubberley, Ellwood P(atterson) obit Nov 41

Cudahy, John C(larence) obit Oct 43

Cugat, Xavier May 42

Cukor, George Apr 43

Culbertson, Ely May 40

Culkin, Francis D. obit Sept 43

Cullen, Countee obit Mar 46

Cullen, Glenn Ernest obit May 40

Cullen, Thomas H. obit Apr 44

Cullis, Winifred C(lara) Nov 43

Culver, Essae Martha Sep 40

Cuneo, John F. Jun 50

Cunningham, Sir Alan (Gordon) Jun 46

Cunningham, Sir Andrew Browne May 41

Cunningham, Sir Graham Sep 49

Cunningham, William Francis obit Jan 41

Curie, Eve Mar 40

Curie, Irène See Joliot-Curie, I. Apr 40

Curran, Charles C(ourtney) obit Jan 43

Curran, Joseph E(dwin) Apr 45

Curren, Pearl Gildersleeve obit Jun 41

Currie, Lauchlin (Bernard) May 41

Curry, John Steuart biog Apr 41 obit Oct 46

Curtin, John biog Jul 41 obit Aug 45

Curtis, Ann Jun 45

Curtis, George Vaughan obit Oct 43

Curtis, Heber D(oust) obit Mar 42

Curzon, Clifford May 50

Cushing, Charles C(yprian) S(trong) obit Apr 41

Cushing, Tom See Cushing, C. C. S. obit Apr 41

Cuthbert, Margaret (Ross) May 47

Czettel, Ladislas biog Mar 41 obit Apr 49

Dabney, Virginius Sep 48

Daché, Lilly Jul 41

Dafoe, Allan (Roy) obit Jul 43

Dafoe, John Wesley obit Feb 44

Daladier, Edouard Apr 40

Dale, Benjamin J(ames) obit Sep 43

Dali, Salvador Sep 40

Dallas, C(harles) Donald Apr 49

Dallin, Cyrus Edwin obit Jan 45

Dalmia, (Seth) Ramkrishna Dec 48

Dalton, Charles obit Aug 42

Dalton, Hugh Aug 45

Daluege, Kurt obit Dec 46

Daly, John (Charles, Jr.) May 48

Daly, Maureen (Patricia) Jan 46

Daly, Thomas A., Father obit Mar 41

Dam, (Carl Peter) Henrik Sep 49

Damaskinos, Archbishop biog Nov 45 obit Jul 49

Damerel, Donna obit Apr 41

Damon, Lindsay Todd obit Jan-Jun 40

Damon, Ralph S(hepard) Jul 49

Damrosch, Walter (Johannes) Mar 44

Dandurand, Raoul obit Apr 42

Dandy, Walter E(dward) obit May 46

Danforth, William obit Jun 41

Daniell, (Francis) Raymond Mar 44

Daniels, Arthur Hill obit Apr 40

Daniels, Charles N. obit Mar 43

Daniels, Jonathan (Worth) Apr 42

Daniels, Josephus biog Oct 44 obit Feb 48

Dannay, Frederic See Queen, E. Jul 40

Danner, Louise Rutledge obit Nov 43

Dantchenko, Vladimir (Ivanovich), Nemirovich-. obit Jun 43

Danvin, Mme. Charles See Radziwill, C., Princess obit Jul 41

Dardel, Nils von obit Jul 43

Darden, Colgate W(hitehead), Jr. Sep 48

Dargan, E(dwin) Preston obit Feb 41

Darlan, Jean (Louis Xavier François) biog Mar 41 obit Feb 43

Darling, Jay Norwood Jul 42

Darré, R(ichard) Walther (Oskar) Nov 41

D'Arsonval, Jacques Arsène See Arsonval, J. A. d' obit Feb 41

Dart, Justin W(hitlock) Nov 46

Darwell, Jane Jun 41

Darwin, Leonard obit May 43

Dashiell, Willard obit Jun 43

Dashwood, Mrs. Edmée Elizabeth Monica (de la Pasture) See Delafield, E. M. obit Jan 44

Daudet, Léon obit Aug 42

Daugherty, Carroll R(oop) Oct 49

Daugherty, Harry M(icajah) obit Dec 41

Daugherty, James Henry Jul 40

D'Aulaire, Ingri, and D'Aulaire, Edgar Parin See Aulaire, I. d' and Aulaire, E. P. d' Aug 40

Elliott, William Thompson, Rev. obit Aug 40

Ellis, Carleton obit Mar 41

Elliston, Herbert (Berridge) Jun 49

Ellsberg, Edward Nov 42

Elman, Mischa Oct 45

Elson, Arthur obit Mar 40

Eltinge, Julian obit Apr 41

Elvehjem, C(onrad) A(rnold) May 48

Ely, Richard Theodore obit Nov 43

Elzy, Ruby obit Aug 43

Embree, Edwin R(ogers) biog Dec 48 obit Mar 50

Emeny, Brooks Nov 47

Emerson, Victor Lee obit Jul 41

Emery, DeWitt (McKinley) Oct 46

Emmerson, Louis Lincoln obit Mar 41

Emmet, William L(eRoy) obit Nov 41

Emmons, Delos C(arleton) Mar 42

Enckell, Carl J(ohan) A(lexis) Apr 50

Engel, Carl obit Jun 44

Engel, Kurt obit Mar 42

Engle, Paul (Hamilton) Jun 42

Englebright, Harry L(ane) obit Jul 43

Engleman, James Ozro obit Nov 43

Enright, Elizabeth (WLB) Yrbk 47

Ensor, James, Baron obit Feb 43

Enters, Angna Jan-Feb 40

Entezam, Nasrollah Dec 50

Epstein, Abraham obit Jun 42

Epstein, Eliahu Dec 48

Epstein, Jacob Jul 45

Ercoli, Ercole See Togliatti, P. Nov 47

Erhard, Ludwig Jan 50

Erickson, John Edward obit Jun 46

Erlander, Tage Oct 47

Erlanger, Mitchell Louis obit Oct 40

Ernst, Max Dec 42

Ernst, Morris Leopold Aug 40

Erskine G(raves) B(lanchard) Jul 46

Ertegun, Mehmet Munir obit Jan 45

Esch, John J(acob) obit Jun 41

Estes, Eleanor (WLB) Yrbk 46

Estes, Harlow Mar 41

Estes, Mrs. Rice See Estes, E. (WLB) Yrbk 46

Estigarribia, José Félix biog Mar 40 obit Oct 40

Ethridge, Mark (Foster) Jan 46

Ettl, John obit Feb 41

Eurich, Alvin C(hristian) Jun 49

Evans, Alice C(atherine) Oct 43

Evans, Anne obit Feb 4!

Evans, Sir Arthur (John) obit Sep 41

Evans, Sir Edward R(atcliffe) G(arth) R(ussell) May 41

Evans, Hugh Ivan, Rev. Nov 50

Evans, Luther H(arris) Aug 45

Evans, Maurice May 40

Evatt, Herbert V(ere) May 42

Evergood, Philip (Howard Francis Dixon) Oct 44

Eves, Reginald Grenville biog Sep 40 obit Aug 41

Ewing, James obit Jul 43

Ewing, Oscar R(oss) Jul 48

Exner, Max J(oseph) obit Nov 43

Eyde, Samuel obit Aug 40

Eyre, Mrs Dean Atherton See Eyre, K. W. (WLB) Yrbk 49

Eyre, Katherine Wigmore (WLB) Yrbk 49

Eyskens, Gaston Nov 49

Fackenthal, Frank D(iehl) Feb 49

Fadiman, Clifton May 41

Fagerholm, Karl August Oct 48

Fagnani, Charles P(rospero), Rev. obit Mar 41

Fahy, Charles Jan 42

Fairbanks, Douglas obit Jan-Feb 40

Fairbanks, Douglas (Elton), Jr. Nov 41

Fairchild, Benjamin Lewis obit Dec 46

Fairchild, Henry Pratt Dec 42

Fairfax, Beatrice biog Aug 44 obit Jan 46

Fairless, Benjamin F(ranklin) Jun 42

Faisal Ibn Abdul-Aziz al Saud, Prince Jan 48

Falk, Maurice obit Apr 46

Falkner, Roland Post obit Jan 41

Fall, Albert B(acon) obit Jan 45

Falla, Manuel de obit Dec 46

Faricy, William T(homas) Jun 48

Farish, William S(tamps) obit Jan 43

Farley, James A(loysius) Sep 44

Farley, Walter (Lorimer) (WLB) Yrbk 49

Farnsworth, Arthur obit Oct 43

Farny, George W(imbor) obit Oct 41

Farouk I, King of Egypt Oct 42

Farrell, James T(homas) Sep 42

Farrington, Joseph R(ider) May 48

Fast, Howard (Melvin) Apr 43

Fauley, Wilbur F(inley) obit Feb 43

Faurot, Joseph A. obit Jan 43

Faust, Frederick obit Jul 44

Faversham, William obit May 40

Fawcett, Edward obit Nov 42

Fay, Frank Aug 45

Fedorova, Nina Nov 40

Feikema, Feike (Frederick) (WLB) Yrbk 50

Feller, A(braham) H(oward) Nov 46

Feller, Bob Aug 41

Fellows, George Emory obit Mar 42

Fenimore-Cooper, Susan de Lancey obit Mar 40

Ferguson, Mrs. C(harles) Vaughan Jan 47

Ferguson, Elsie Feb 44

Ferguson, Garland S(evier) Jul 49

Ferguson, (George) Howard obit Apr 46

Ferguson, Homer May 43

Ferguson, James Edward obit Nov 44

Fermi, Enrico Oct 45

Fernandes, L(uis) Esteves Oct 50

Fernández Concheso, Aurelio See Concheso, A. F. May 42

Ferrer, José, and Hagen, Uta May 44

Ferrero, Gine L(ombroso) obit May 44

Ferrero, Guglielmo obit Sep 42

Ferris, Harry Burr obit Yrbk 40

Ferris, Scott obit Jul 45

Ferriss, Hugh Jul 45

Festing, Francis W(ogan) Feb 45

Feuermann, Emanuel obit Jul 42

Few, William Preston obit Yrbk 40

Fiedler, Arthur Sep 45

Field, Sir Frederick Laurence obit Dec 45

Field, Marshall, III Apr 41

Field, Rachel Lyman obit May 42

Fielding, Mantle obit May 41

Fields, Gracie Apr 41

Fields, Lew obit Sep 41

Fields, Stanley obit Jun 41

Fiene, Ernest Aug 41

Figgis, D(udley) W(eld) Nov 48

Figl, Leopold Apr 48

Filov, Bogdan Dimitrov See Philoff, B. D. Apr 41

Finch, Flora obit Jan-Feb 40

Finger, Charles Joseph obit Mar 41

Finkelstein, Louis, Rabbi Nov 40

Finletter, Thomas K(night) Jan 48

Finley, John Huston obit Mar 40

Finn, William Joseph, Father Jul 40

Firestone, Harvey S(amuel), Jr. Jul 44

Fischer, Hans obit May 45

Fischer, Israel Frederick obit Apr 40

Fischer, Louis May 40

Fish, Bert obit Sep 43

Fish, Hamilton Jan 41

Graham, Harry Chrysostom, Rev. Apr 50
Graham, Horace F(rench) obit Jan 42
Graham, Martha Feb 44
Graham, Philip L(eslie) Feb 48
Graham, Shirley Oct 46
Graham, Wallace H(arry) Feb 47
Grand, Sarah obit Jul 43
Grandi, Dino, Conte Jul 43
Grandjany, Marcel (Georges Lucien) May 43
Grandma Moses See Moses, A. M. R. Jan 49
Granger, Lester B(lackwell) Apr 46
Granger, Walter obit Oct 41
Grant, Cary Sep 41
Grant, Elihu obit Dec 42
Grant, Ethel Watts Mumford See Mumford, E. W. obit Jan-Jun 40
Grant, Heber J. obit Jun 45
Grant, Robert obit Jul 40
Grantley, John Richard Brinsley Norton, 5th Baron obit Sep 43
Granville, William Spencer Leveson-Gower, 4th Earl Sep 50
Graser, Earle W. obit Jun 41
Grau San Martin, Ramón Oct 44
Grauer, Ben(nett Franklin) Feb 41
Graves, Bibb obit May 42
Graves, Frederick Rogers, Bishop obit Jul 40
Graves, William Sidney obit Mar 40
Gray, Carl R(aymond), Jr. Mar 48
Gray, Elizabeth Janet Sep 43
Gray, George (Edward), Kruger- See Kruger-Gray, G. E. obit Jun 43
Gray, Gordon Sep 49
Grayson, David See Baker, R. S. biog Jan-Jun 40 obit Sep 46
Graziani, Rodolfo Apr 41
Green, Adolph See Comden, B. and Green, A. Mar 45
Green, Dwight H(erbert) Apr 48
Green, Florence Topping obit Jun 45
Green, Mrs. Howard See Green, F. T. obit Jun 45
Green, Julian Jan-Feb 40
Green, Martyn Jun 50
Green, Theodore Francis Feb 50
Green, William Mar 42
Greenberg, Hank Jun 47
Greenbie, Sydney Sep 41
Greene, Frank Russell obit Jan-Feb 40
Greenewalt, C(rawford) H(allock) Jan 49
Greenfield, Abraham Lincoln obit Sep 41
Greenough, Carroll obit Oct 41

Greenstreet, Sydney (Hughes) May 43
Greenway, Walter Burton, Rev. obit Feb 41
Greenwood, Allen obit Dec 42
Greenwood, Arthur Oct 40
Gregg, Alan See Mallette, G. E. (WLB) Yrbk 50
Gregory, Edmund B(ristol) Sep 45
Gregory, Menas S(arkis) obit Jan 42
Grenfell, Sir Wilfred Thomason obit Yrbk 40
Gresley, Sir (Herbert) Nigel obit May 41
Grew, Joseph Clark Feb 41
Grey, Clifford obit Nov 41
Gribble, Harry Wagstaff (Graham-) Sep 45
Grieff, Joseph Nicholas, Mgr. obit Aug 41
Griffin, Bernard (William), Cardinal Oct 46
Griffis, Stanton Oct 44
Griffith, Clark (Calvin) Jun 50
Griffith, Ernest S(tacey) Oct 47
Griffith, J(ohn) P(rice) Crozer obit Sep 41
Griffith, Paul H(oward) Jan 47
Grigg, Sir James Apr 42
Grigg, Sir Percy James See Grigg, Sir J. Apr 42
Grimes, W(illiam) H(enry) Jun 47
Grimshaw, Robert obit Jun 41
Griswold, A(lfred) Whitney Apr 50
Griswold, Augustus H. obit Mar 40
Griswold, Dwight P(almer) Dec 47
Griswold, Oscar W(oolverton) Sep 43
Grizodubova, Valentina (Stepanovna) Dec 41
Groenman, Frans Eyso Henricus obit Aug 43
Grofé, Ferde Jul 40
Gromyko, Andrei A. Oct 43
Groninger, Homer M. Aug 45
Groof, Adriaan M(artin) de obit Mar 42
Gropius, Walter (Adolf Georg) Nov 41
Gropper, William Mar 40
Gros, Edmund L(ouis) obit Dec 42
Gross, Chaim Nov 41
Gross, Charles P(hilip) Mar 46
Grosvenor, Gilbert (Hovey) Dec 46
Grosvenor, Graham Bethune obit Dec 43
Grosz, George Apr 42
Grotewohl, Otto Jul 50
Groth, John (August) Feb 43
Groves, Ernest R(utherford) biog Jun 43 obit Oct 46

Groves, Gladys Hoagland See Groves, E. R. and Groves, G. H. biog Jun 43
Groves, Leslie R(ichard) Aug 45
Gruber, Frank Nov 41
Gruber, Karl Feb 47
Gruber, L(evi) Franklin, Rev. obit Feb 42
Gruenberg, Sidonie Matsner May 40
Gruening, Ernest (Henry) Dec 46
Gruenther, Alfred M(aximilian) Dec 50
Grumman, Leroy R(andle) Aug 45
Gruppe, Charles Paul obit Nov 40
Guardia, Rafael Ángel Calderón See Calderón Guardia, R. Á. Jun 42
Guardia, Ricardo Adolfo de la See De La Guardia, R. A. May 42
Gubelman, Minei Izrailevich See Yaroslavsky, E. obit Jan 44
Guedalla, Philip obit Feb 45
Guérard, Albert J(oseph) (WLB) Yrbk 46
Guerrero, José Gustavo Jan 47
Guertner, Franz obit Mar 41
Guest, Edgar A(lbert) Sep 41
Guffey, Joseph F. Mar 44
Guggenheim, Mrs. Daniel obit Jul 44
Guggenheim, Florence (Shloss) See Guggenheim, Mrs. D. obit Jul 44
Guillaumat, Marie Louis Adolphe obit Jul 40
Guiñazú, Enrique Ruiz. See Ruiz Guiñazú, E. Apr 42
Guinness, Alec Oct 50
Guinness, Arthur (Rundell) Jun 48
Guinness, Walter Edward, 1st Baron Moyne See Moyne, W. E. G., 1st Baron obit Dec 44
Guise, Jean Pierre Clément Marie, Duc de obit Oct 40
Guiterman, Arthur obit Mar 43
Gulick, Luther (Halsey) Jun 45
Gullion, Allen W(yant) biog Feb 43 obit Jul 46
Gunn, Selskar Michael obit Sep 44
Gunter, Julius Caldeen obit Yrbk 40
Gunther, Franklin Mott obit Feb 42
Gunther, John Nov 41
Gurney, (John) Chan(dler) Oct 50
Gustaf V, King of Sweden biog Sep 42 obit Dec 50
Gustaf VI, King of Sweden Dec 50
Guthman, Edwin O(tto) Jun 50
Guthrie, A(lfred) B(ertram), Jr. Jul 50

Lambert, Sylvester Maxwell biog
Oct 41 obit Feb 47
Lamberton, Robert Eneas obit
Oct 41
Lamond, Felix obit Apr 40
Lamont, Corliss Jun 46
Lamont, Thomas William biog
Oct 40 obit Feb 48
Lanchester, Elsa May 50
Land, Emory S(cott) Sep 41
Landes, Bertha K(night) obit Jan
44
Landis, James M(cCauley) Mar
42
Landis, Kenesaw Mountain biog
May 44 obit Jan 45
Landon, Alf(red Mossman) Feb
44
Landon, Margaret (Dorothea
Mortenson) Feb 45
Landowska, Wanda Nov 45
Landsteiner, Karl obit Aug 43
Lane, Sir Arbuthnot obit Mar
43
Lane, Arthur Bliss Apr 48
Lane, Gertrude B(attles) obit
Nov 41
Lane, Keith Westmacott See
West, K. (WLB) Yrbk 47
Lane, Sir William Arbuthnot See
Lane, Sir A. obit Mar 43
Lane, William Preston, Jr. Jun
49
Lang, Cosmo Gordon, 1st Baron
Lang of Lambeth See Lang of
Lambeth, C. G. L., 1st Baron
biog Aug 41 obit Jan 46
Lang, Fritz Jun 43
Lang of Lambeth, Cosmo Gordon
Lang, 1st Baron biog Aug 41
obit Jan 46
Langdon, Harry obit Feb 45
Lange, Halvard M(anthey) Nov
47
Lange, Oscar (Richard) Apr 46
Langley, Adria Locke Aug 45
Langlie, Arthur B(ernard) Oct
50
Langmuir, Arthur Comings obit
Jul 41
Langmuir, Irving Mar 40 Oct 50
Langner, Lawrence, and Helburn,
Theresa Sep 44
Lanman, Charles Rockwell obit
Apr 41
Lannung, (Lars) Hermod
(Skræntskov Larsen) Dec 49
Lansbury, George obit Jan-Jun
40
Lanvin, Jeanne obit Sep 46
Lapham, Roger D(earborn) Jul
48
Lapointe, Ernest obit Jan 42
Largo Caballero, Francisco obit
May 46
Larkin, Oliver W(aterman) Jul 50
La Rocque, François de obit
Jun 46
La Roe, Wilbur, Jr. Mar 48
Larsen, Roy E(dward) Sep 50

Larssen, Pedar See Mallette,
G. E. (WLB) Yrbk 50
Lasker, Emanuel obit Mar 41
Laski, Harold (Joseph) biog Sep
41 obit Apr 50
Lasky, Jesse L(ouis) Apr 47
Lasser, J(acob) K(ay) May 46
Lasswell, Harold D(wight) Jul 47
Latham, Harold S(trong) Jan 50
Latouche, John Treville Jan-Jun
40
Lattes, C(esare) M(ansueto)
G(iulio) May 49
Lattimore, Owen Dec 45
Lattre de Tassigny, Jean (Joseph
Marie Gabriel) de Jan 45
Laubach, Frank C(harles) Feb 50
Läuger, Paul, and Müller, Paul
(Herman) Oct 45
Laughlin, Clara Elizabeth obit
Apr 41
Laughlin, Irwin (Boyle) obit Jun
41
Laughton, Charles Nov 48
Laughton, Mrs. Charles See Lan-
chester, E. May 50
Laugier, Henri Jul 48
Laurence, William L(eonard) Oct
45
Laurent, Robert Jul 42
Lauri, Lorenzo, Cardinal obit
Dec 41
Lausche, Frank J(ohn) Apr 46
Lauterbach, Jacob Zallel obit
Jun 42
Laval, Pierre biog Sep 40 obit
Nov 45
Laverty, Maura (WLB) Yrbk 47
Lavery, Emmet (Godfrey) Jul 47
Lavery, Sir John obit Mar 41
Law, Richard K(idston) Feb 44
Lawes, Lewis E(dward) biog
Oct 41 obit May 47
Lawford, Ernest obit Feb 41
Lawrence, Charles Edward obit
Apr 40
Lawrence, David Dec 43
Lawrence, Ernest Orlando Jan-
Feb 40
Lawrence, Sir Geoffrey Jan 46
Lawrence, Gertrude Aug 40
Lawrence, Hilda (WLB) Yrbk 47
Lawrence, Marjorie Apr 40
Lawrence, William, Bishop obit
Jan 42
Lawson, Mary obit Jul 41
Lawson, Robert Oct 41
Lawson, Ted (W.) Dec 43
Lawther, Sir William Dec 49
Laxness, Halldór (Kiljan) Oct 46
Lay, James S(elden), Jr. Mar 50
Laycock, Craven obit May 40
Laycock, R(obert) E(dward) May
44
Layton, Sir Geoffrey Feb 42
Lazareff, Pierre May 42
Lazzeri, Tony obit Sep 46
Lea, Clarence F(rederick) Nov
46
Lea, Luke obit Jan 46

Leach, Ruth M(arian) Mar 48
Leacock, Stephen (Butler) obit
May 44
Leahy, Frank (William) Dec 41
Leahy, William D(aniel) Jan 41
Leao Velloso, P(edro) biog Sep
46 obit Mar 47
Lear, Ben Jul 42
Leary, Herbert F(airfax) Aug 42
Leary, John Joseph, Jr. obit Feb
44
Leathers, Frederick James, 1st
Baron Jun 41
Leblanc, Georgette obit Dec
41
Leblanc, Maurice obit Jan 42
Lecky, Prescott obit Jul 41
Leclerc, Jacques-Philippe biog
Oct 44 obit Dec 47
Le Corbusier Apr 47
Lecuona, Ernesto May 44
Ledochowski, Vladimir, Rev. obit
Jan 43
Lee, Auriol obit Sep 41
Lee, Blair obit Feb 45
Lee, Canada Dec 44
Lee, Clark (Gould) Dec 43
Lee, Dorothy McCullough Jan 49
Lee, Gypsy Rose Dec 43
Lee, Jennie May 46
Lee, John Clarence, Rev. obit
Nov 40
Lee, John Clifford Hodges Jul
44
Lee, Mrs. John G. Jul 50
Lee, J(oseph) Bracken May 49
Lee, Manfred B. See Queen, E.
Jul 40
Lee, Percy Maxim See Lee, Mrs.
J. G. Jul 50
Lee, Mrs. William Scott See
Lee, D. M. Jan 49
Lee, Willis A(ugustus, Jr.) obit
Sep 45
Lee Bum Suk Jan 49
Leech, Margaret (Kernochan)
Jul 42
Leech, Paul Nicholas obit Mar
41
Leese, Sir Oliver (William Har-
greaves) Dec 44
Lefaucheux, Marie-Hélène Oct
47
Leffingwell, R(ussell) C(ornell)
Mar 50
Le Gallienne, Eva Oct 42
Léger, Fernand Jan 43
Lehman, Herbert H(enry) Jan
43
Lehmann, George obit Dec 41
Lehmann, Lotte May 41
Lehmann-Haupt, Hellmut E(mil)
Apr 42
Lehrbas, Lloyd (Allan) Jan-Jun
40 Apr 50
Leigh, Douglas May 40
Leigh, Robert D(evore) Jun 47
Leigh, Vivien Jul 46
Leigh, W(illiam) Colston Jan 42

Long, Tania   May 46
Longman, Sir Hubert Harry   obit Apr 40
Longstreth, T(homas) Morris (WLB) Yrbk 50
Longworth, Alice Lee   See Longworth, A. R.   Jun 43
Longworth, Alice Roosevelt   Jun 43
Loomis, Orland S.   obit Jan 43
Loosli, E(rnest) Fritz   Jan 42
López, Alfonso   Sep 42
Lopez, Encarnación   See Argentinita   biog Jun 42 obit Oct 45
Loram, Charles Templeman   obit Sep 40
Lord, F(rederick) T(aylor)   obit Jan 42
Lord, Milton E(dward)   Feb 50
Lorentz, Pare   Apr 40
Loring, Jules   See MacKaye, D. L., and MacKaye, J. J. G. (WLB) Yrbk 49
Losch, Tilly   Jul 44
Losovsky, Solomon Abramovich   See Lozovsky, S. A.   Nov 41
Lothar, Ernst (WLB) Yrbk 47
Lothian, Philip Henry Kerr, 11th Marquis of   obit Yrbk 40
Loudon, Alexander   Jul 42
Loughlin, Dame Anne   Feb 50
Louis, Joe   Oct 40
Louise Caroline Alberta, Duchess of Argyll, Princess   obit Jan-Feb 40
Love, George H(utchinson)   Mar 50
Loveman, Amy   Jun 43
Lovett, Robert A(bercrombie)   Aug 42
Lovett, Robert Morss   Aug 43
Low, David   Jan-Feb 40
Lowden, Frank O(rren)   obit May 43
Lowdermilk, W(alter) C(lay)   Feb 49
Lowell, A(bbott) Lawrence   obit Feb 43
Lowell, Robert (Traill Spence, Jr.)   Jul 47
Lownsbery, Eloise (WLB) Yrbk 47
Lowry, Edward G(eorge)   obit Sep 43
Loy, Myrna   Oct 50
Lozovsky, S(olomon) A(bramovich)   Nov 41
Lozowick, Louis   Apr 42
Lubin, Isador   Oct 41
Luca, Giuseppe De   See De Luca, G.   Mar 47
Lucas, Martha B.   May 47
Lucas, Scott W(ike)   Dec 47 See correction p26 Dec 48 issue
Luce, Clare Boothe   See Boothe, C.   Nov 42
Luce, Henry R(obinson)   Jul 41
Luce, Robert   obit May 46
Lucioni, Luigi   Oct 43

Luckman, Charles   Oct 47
Luckstone, Isidore   obit May 41
Luhan, Mabel Dodge   Jan-Feb 40
Luhring, Oscar Raymond   obit Oct 44
Lujack, John   See Lujack, Johnny   Dec 47
Lujack, Johnny   Dec 47
Lukas, Paul   Feb 42
Lumpkin, Alva M(oore)   obit Sep 41
Lund, Wendell L(uther)   Sep 42
Lundeen, Ernest   obit Oct 40
Lunn, Katharine Fowler   See Fowler-Billings, K.   Jan-Feb 40
Lunt, Alfred, and Fontanne, Lynn   Jun 41
Lupescu, Magda   Oct 40
Lupino, Ida   Sep 43
Lupino, Stanley   obit Aug 42
Luquiens, Frederick Bliss   obit May 40
Lurçat, Jean   Sep 48
Lusk, Mrs. Georgia L(ee)   Oct 47
Lutes, Della Thompson   obit Sep 42
Lutyens, Sir Edwin L(andseer)   biog Jun 42 obit Feb 44
Lutz, Frank E(ugene)   obit Jan 44
Lydenberg, Harry Miller   Sep 41
Lynch, J(ohn), Joseph, Rev.   Oct 46
Lynch, William J(oseph)   obit Aug 41
Lyndon, Edward   obit Yrbk 40
Lyons, Eugene   Jan 44
Lyttelton, Oliver   Sep 41

McAdie, Alexander George   obit Dec 43
McAdoo, William Gibbs   obit Mar 41
McAfee, Mildred H(elen)   Sep 42
MacAlarney, Robert E(mmet)   obit Jan 46
MacArthur, Douglas   Oct 41 May 48
Macartney, William Napier   obit Aug 40
Macauley, Jane Hamilton   See Macauley, Mrs. R. W.   Sep 49
Macauley, Mrs. Robert W(right)   Sep 49
McAuliffe, Anthony C(lement)   Feb 50
MacBride, Ernest William   obit Jan 41
McBride, Katherine E(lizabeth)   Feb 42
McBride, Mary Margaret   Apr 41
MacBride, Seán   Jun 49
McCabe, Thomas Bayard   Sep 48
McCaffrey, John L(awrence)   Nov 50
McCain, John S(idney)   biog Oct 43 obit Oct 45
MacCallum, William George   obit Mar 44

McCarey, (Thomas) Leo   Jul 46
McCarl, John Raymond   obit Sep 40
McCarran, Patrick A(nthony)   Jul 47
McCarrens, John S.   obit Sep 43
McCarthy, Clem   Oct 41
McCarthy, Frank   Sep 45
McCarthy, Joe   May 48
McCarthy, Joseph R(aymond)   Jan 50
McCarthy, Joseph Vincent   See McCarthy, J.   May 48
McCarthy, Leighton (Goldie)   Oct 42
McClellan, John L(ittle)   Apr 50
McClintic, Guthrie   May 43
McCloskey, John Robert   See McCloskey, R.   Sep 42
McCloskey, Robert   Sep 42
McCloy, John J(ay)   Apr 47
McConnell, Joseph H(oward)   Nov 50
McCormack, Arthur Thomas   obit Sep 43
McCormack, John   obit Oct 45
McCormack, John W.   Jun 43
McCormick, Anne O'Hare   Mar 40
MacCormick, Austin H.   May 40
McCormick, Fowler   Jun 47
McCormick, Jay (William)   Apr 43
McCormick, Robert R(utherford)   Aug 42
McCormick, William Patrick Glyn, Rev.   obit Yrbk 40
McCoy, Frank R(oss)   Nov 45
McCracken, Harold (WLB) Yrbk 49
MacCracken, Henry Noble   Sep 40
McCracken, Joan   Jun 45
McCracken, Robert James, Rev.   Jul 49
McCreery, Sir Richard L(oudon)   May 45
McCue, Mrs. George S.   See De la Torre-Bueno, L. (WLB) Yrbk 49
McCullers, Carson   Sep 40
McCune, Charles Andrew   obit Yrbk 40
McCune, George S(hannon), Rev.   obit Feb 42
McCurdy, William Albert, Rev.   obit Feb 42
McDaniel, Hattie   Sep 40
McDiarmid, E(rrett) W(eir)   Dec 48
MacDonald, Betty   Feb 46
MacDonald, Cordelia Howard   obit Oct 41
MacDonald, Duncan Black, Rev.   obit Oct 43
McDonald, Eugene F., Jr.   Oct 49
MacDonald, Sir George   obit Sep 40
McDonald, James G(rover)   Apr 49
MacDonald, Pirie   obit Jun 42

Mankin, Helen Douglas Apr 46
Manly, John Matthews obit May 40
Mann, Erika Yrbk 40
Mann, Klaus biog Yrbk 40 obit Jul 49
Mann, Mrs. Marty Jun 49
Mann, Thomas May 42
Mann, Tom obit May 41
Mannerheim, Carl Gustaf Emil, Baron von Apr 40
Manning, Marie See Fairfax, B. Aug 44
Manning, William Thomas, Bishop biog Apr 40 obit Jan 50
Mannstein, Fritz Erich von See Manstein, F. E. von Oct 42
Mansbridge, Albert Jun 42
Manship, Paul May 40
Manson, John T(homas) obit Apr 44
Manstein, Fritz Erich von Oct 42
Mantle, (Robert) Burns biog Nov 44 obit Mar 48
Manuilsky, Dmitri Z(akharovich) Dec 48
Mao Tse-tung Feb 43
Mapes, Victor obit Jan 44
Marble, Alice Nov 40
Marburg, Theodore obit Apr 46
Marcantonio, Vito Feb 49
March, Charles Hoyt obit Sep 45
March, Fredric, and Eldridge, Florence Mar 43
Marchal, Léon Sep 43
Marcial-Dorado, Carolina obit Sep 41
Marcus, (Harold) Stanley Jun 49
Mardikian, George M(agar) Nov 47
Marett, Robert R(anulph) obit Apr 43
Marge See Damerel, D. obit Apr 41
Margesson, David Feb 41
Margoliouth, David Samuel obit Apr 40
Margueritte, Victor obit May 42
Maria Theresa, Archduchess of Austria obit Apr 44
Marie, André Sep 48
Marin, John Jul 49
Marín, Luis Muñoz- See Muñoz-Marín, L. Oct 42
Marion, George obit Jan 46
Maritain, Jacques May 42
Marius, Emilie Alexander obit Apr 40
Marjolin, Robert (Ernest) Dec 48
Mark, Louis obit May 42
Markham, Beryl Nov 42
Markham, Edwin obit Mar 40
Markova, Alicia Sep 43
Marquand, J(ohn) P(hillips) Apr 42
Marquardt, Alexandria obit Jun 43
Marquis, Albert Nelson obit Feb 44

Marquis, Frederick James, 1st Baron Woolton See Woolton, F. J. M., 1st Baron Oct 40
Marriott, Alice (Lee) (WLB) Yrbk 50
Marriott, Sir John (Arthur Ransome) obit Jul 45
Marsh, Reginald Sep 41
Marshall, C(harles) Herbert, Jr. Oct 49
Marshall, George C(atlett) Oct 40 Mar 47
Marshall, M(aple) Lee biog Sep 48 obit Oct 50
Marshall, Peter, Rev. biog Apr 48 obit Feb 49
Marshall, Rosamond Van der Zee Aug 42
Marshall, Tully obit Apr 43
Marshall, Verne Feb 41
Marshall, Walter P(eter) Apr 50
Martel, Giffard Le Quesne Jul 43
Martin, Charles H(enry) obit Nov 46
Martin, Collier Ford obit May 41
Martin, Edgar Stanley, Jr. obit Sep 40
Martin, Edward Oct 45
Martin, Frank L(ee) obit Sep 41
Martin, George Brown obit Dec 45
Martin, Glenn L(uther) Feb 43
Martin, Harry (Leland, Jr.) Jun 48
Martin, Helen See Rood, H. M. obit Mar 43
Martin, Jackie Apr 43
Martin, Joseph W(illiam), Jr. Oct 40 May 48
Martin, Lillien J(ane) biog Apr 42 obit My 43
Martin, Mary Jan 44
Martin, Percy Alvin obit Apr 42
Martín Artajo, Alberto Nov 49
Martinelli, Giovanni Jan 45
Martínez, Maximiliano Hernández See Hernández Martínez, M. Jun 42
Martinů, Bohuslav Nov 44
Martland, Harrison Stanford Nov 40
Marvin, Charles F(rederick) obit Jul 43
Marvin, Cloyd H(eck) Dec 49
Marvin, Dwight Edwards, Rev. obit Mar 40
Marvin, Harry obit Jan-Feb 40
Marx, Arthur See Marx, H. May 48
Marx, Chico; Marx, Groucho; and Marx, Harpo May 48
Marx, Groucho See Marx, C.; Marx, G.; and Marx, H. May 48
Marx, Harpo See Marx, C.; Marx, G.; and Marx, M. May 48
Marx, Julius See Marx, G. May 48

Marx, Leonard See Marx, C. May 48
Mary Joseph Butler, Mother obit Jan-Jun 40
Masaryk, Jan (Garrigue) biog May 44 obit Apr 48
Mascagni, Pietro obit Sep 45
Masliansky, Zvei Hirsch, Rev. obit Mar 43
Mason, James May 47
Mason, Joseph Warren Teets obit Jul 41
Mason, Lowell B(lake) Jun 49
Massee, W(illiam) Wellington obit Oct 42
Massey, Raymond Feb 46
Massine, Léonide Apr 40
Matheson, Samuel Pritchard, Archbishop obit Jul 42
Mathews, Shailer, Rev. obit Dec 41
Matisse, Henri May 43
Matsui, Keishiro, Baron obit Jul 46
Matsuoka, Yôsuke biog Mar 41 obit Jul 46
Matthews, Burnita Shelton Apr 50
Matthews, Francis P(atrick) Sep 49
Matthews, H(arrison) Freeman Mar 45
Matthews, Herbert L(ionel) Nov 43
Matthews, J(oseph) B(rown) May 43
Matthews, T(homas) S(tanley) Apr 50
Mauldin, Bill May 45
Mauldin, William Henry See Mauldin, B. May 45
Maurier, Daphne du See Du Maurier, D. May 40
Maverick, Maury Mar 44
Maw, Herbert B(rown) Oct 48
Max, Adolphe obit Jan-Feb 40
Maximos, Demetrios Mar 48
Maxon, Lou R(ussell) Aug 43
Maxton, James obit Sep 46
Maxtone Graham, Joyce Jan 41
Maxwell, Elsa Mar 43
Maxwell, Russell L(amonte) Nov 42
Maxwell, William (Keepers, Jr.) (WLB) Yrbk 49
May, Andrew Jackson Apr 41
May, Charles H(enry) obit Jan 44
May, Geraldine P(ratt) Feb 49
May, Henry John obit Jan-Feb 40
Maybank, Burnet R(hett) Apr 49
Mayer, Daniel Nov 49
Mayer, Louis B(urt) Jun 43
Mayer, René May 48
Mayes, Mrs. Gilford (Harold) May 50
Mayes, Rose Gorr See Mayes, Mrs. G. H. May 50
Maynard, John A(lbert) F(onsegrive), Rev. Oct 43

Moisseiff, Leon S(olomon) obit Oct 43

Moley, Raymond (Charles) Jul 45

Molina, Rafael L(éonidas) Trujillo See Trujillo Molina, R. L. Jul 41

Mollet, Guy Sep 50

Mollison, Amy See Johnson, A. obit Feb 41

Molloy, Daniel M(urrah) obit Mar 44

Molloy, Robert (William) (WLB) Yrbk 48

Molotov, Viacheslav Mikhailovich Jan-Feb 40

Molyneux, Edward H. Jun 42

Momsen, C(harles) B(owers) Jul 46

Monaghan, Francis Joseph, Bishop obit Jan 43

Monaghan, Frank Nov 43

Mondriaan, Piet(er Cornelis) obit Mar 44

Monnet, Jean Sep 47

Monroe, Anne S(hannon) obit Dec 42

Monroe, Lucy Aug 42

Monroe, Vaughn (Wilton) Jul 42

Monsarrat, Nicholas (John Turney) (WLB) Yrbk 50

Monsky, Henry biog Nov 41 obit Jun 47

Montague, James J(ackson) obit Feb 42

Montessori, Maria Nov 40

Monteux, Pierre Apr 46

Montgomery, Sir Bernard Law Dec 42

Montgomery, James Shera, Rev. Apr 48

Montgomery, L(ucy) M(aud) obit Jun 42

Montgomery, Robert Jan 48

Montgomery, Robert Bruce See Crispin, E. (WLB) Yrbk 49

Moody, Joseph E(ugene) Dec 48

Moon, Bucklin (WLB) Yrbk 50

Mooney, Edward, Cardinal Apr 46

Mooney, Thomas J. obit Apr 42

Mooney, Tom See Mooney, Thomas, J. obit Apr 42

Moore, Bryant E(dward) Feb 49

Moore, Douglas (Stuart) Nov 47

Moore, Edward Caldwell, Rev. obit May 43

Moore, Grace biog Apr 44 obit Mar 47

Moore, Sir Henry R(uthven) Sep 43

Moore, Raymond obit Mar 40

Moore, R(obert) Walton obit Apr 41

Moore, Robert Webber obit Jan 43

Moore, T. Albert, Rev. obit Apr 40

Moore-Brabazon, J(ohn) C(uthbert) T(heodore) May 41

Moorland, Jesse Edward, Rev. obit Jan-Jun 40

Mora, Francis Luis obit Jul 40

Moran, Léon obit Oct 41

Mordkin, Mikhail obit Sep 44

More, Adelyne See Ogden C. K. Jan 44

Moreell, Ben Jun 46

Morehead, John H. obit Jul 42

Morehouse, Daniel Walter obit Mar 41

Morehouse, Ward Jan-Feb 40

Morell, Parker obit Apr 43

Morgan, Anne (Tracy) Jan 46

Morgan, Sir Frederick (Edgworth) Feb 46

Morgan, Henry Mar 47

Morgan, J(ohn) Pierpont obit Apr 43

Morgan, Joy Elmer Jan 46

Morgan, Thomas A(lfred) Mar 50

Morgan, Thomas Hunt obit Feb 46

Morgenstierne, Wilhelm (Thorleif) Munthe May 49

Morgenthau, Henry, Jr. Sep 40

Morini, Erica Apr 46

Moríñigo, Higinio Jun 42

Morón, Alonzo G(raseano) Oct 49

Morris, Dave Hennen obit Jun 44

Morris, Roland Sletor obit Jan 46

Morrison, Adrienne obit Jan 41

Morrison, deLesseps S(tory) Nov 49

Morrison, Henry Clinton obit May 45

Morrison, Herbert Stanley Jul 40

Morrow, Mrs. Dwight Whitney See Morrow, E. C. Apr 43

Morrow, Elizabeth Cutter Apr 43

Morrow, Honoré Willsie obit May 40

Morse, David A(bner) Mar 49

Morse, John Lovett obit May 40

Morse, Philip M(cCord) Jun 48

Morse, Wayne L(yman) Apr 42

Morton, Henry Holdich obit Jul 40

Morton, Sir James obit Oct 43

Morton, James F(erdinand) obit Dec 41

Morton, James Madison, Jr. obit Aug 40

Mosca, Gaetano obit Jan 42

Moscicki, Ignace obit Nov 46

Moscovitch, Maurice obit Aug 40

Moses, Anna Mary Robertson Jan 49

Moses, George Higgins obit Feb 45

Moses, Grandma See Moses, A. M. R. Jan 49

Moses, Harry M(organ) Oct 49

Moses, John obit Apr 45

Moses, Robert Nov 40

Mosher, A(aron Alexander) R(oland) Dec 50

Mosher, Gouverneur Frank, Bishop obit Sep 41

Mosher, Ira Feb 45

Mosley, Sir Oswald Ernald Jul 40

Mostel, Zero Apr 43

Motherwell, Hiram obit Jan 46

Moton, Robert Russa obit Jul 40

Mott, Frank Luther Oct 41

Mott, James W(heaton) obit Dec 45

Mott, John R(aleigh) Jan 47

Mott, Lewis F(reeman) obit Jan 42

Motta, Giuseppe obit Jan-Feb 40

Moulton, F(orest) R(ay) Jan 46

Moulton, Harold G(lenn) Nov 44

Mountbatten, Louis (Francis Albert Victor Nicholas), Lord Jun 42

Mountbatten, Philip See Edinburgh, Philip, 3d Duke of Oct 47

Mountbatten of Burma, Louis Mountbatten, 1st Viscount See Mountbatten, L. F. A. V. N., Lord Jun 42

Moutet, Marius Jul 47

Mowat, Robert B(almain) obit Nov 41

Mowinckel, Johan Ludwig obit Nov 43

Mowrer, Edgar Ansel Oct 41

Mowrer, Lilian Thomson May 40

Mowrey, Corma (Alice) Nov 50

Moyne, Walter Edward Guinness, 1st Baron obit Dec 44

Muck, Karl obit Mar 40

Muir, James May 50

Muir, Ramsay obit Jun 41

Muller, H(ermann) J(oseph) Feb 47

Müller, Paul (Herman) See Läuger, P. and Müller, P. H. Oct 45

Mumford, Ethel Watts obit Jan-Jun 40

Mumford, Lewis Nov 40

Münch, Charles Dec 47

Munch, Edvard biog Yrbk 40 obit Mar 44

Mundt, Karl E(arl) Jul 48

Mundy, Talbot Chetwynd obit Sep 40

Muni, Paul Jan 44

Munk, Kaj obit Feb 44

Munn, Frank May 44

Muñoz-Marín, Luis Oct 42

Munsel, Patrice Mar 45

Murdock, George J(ohn) obit Sep 42

Murdock, Victor obit Aug 45

Murphy, Charles S(prings) Apr 50

Murphy, Frank biog Jul 40 obit Sep 49

Murphy, Franklin W(illiam) obit Jan 41

Pugmire, Ernest I(vison) Apr 45
Pumarejo, Alfonso López See López, A. Sep 42
Pusey, William Allen obit Oct 40
Putnam, Claude Adams Feb 50
Putnam, James William obit Mar 40
Putnam, Thomas M(ilton) obit Nov 42
Pyle, Ernest Taylor See Pyle, E. biog Apr 41 obit May 45
Pyle, Ernie biog Apr 41 obit May 45

Queen, Ellery Jul 40
Quesada, Elwood R(ichard) Apr 50
Queuille, Henri Oct 48
Quezon, Manuel L(uis) biog Aug 41 obit Sep 44
Quidde, Ludwig obit Apr 41
Quill, Michael J(oseph) Aug 41
Quiller-Couch, Sir Arthur Thomas obit Jul 44
Quimby, Edith H(inkley) Jul 49
Quimby, Mrs. Shirley L. See Quimby, E. H. Jul 49
Quinn, Daniel Joseph, Father obit Mar 40
Quintanilla, Luis Nov 40
Quintero, Joaquín Alvarez See Alvarez Quintero, J. obit Aug 44
Quirino, Elpidio Sep 48
Quisling, Vidkun (Abraham Laur-itz) biog Nov 40 obit Yrbk 46
Quo Tai-chi May 46

Rabi, I(sidor) I(saac) Apr 48
Rachmaninoff, Sergei V(assilie-vitch) obit May 43
Radford, Arthur W(illiam) Nov 49
Radziwill, Catherine, Princess obit Jul 41
Raeder, Erich Apr 41
Ragland, Rags obit Oct 46
Ragon, Heartsill obit Nov 40
Raimu, Jules obit Nov 46
Rainey, Homer P(rice) Nov 46
Rains, Claude Nov 49
Rajagopalachari, Chakravarti Jul 42
Rákosi, Mátyás Mar 49
Rama IX, King of Thailand Jul 50
Rama Rau, Santha Aug 45
Ramadier, Paul Jun 47
Raman, Sir (Chandrasekhara) Venkata Nov 48
Rameau, Jean obit Apr 42
Ramey, Howard K. obit May 43
Ramírez, Pedro P(ablo) Aug 43
Ramm, Fredrik obit Jan 44
Ramsay, Sir Bertram (Home) biog Mar 44 obit Feb 45

Rand, Ellen (Emmet) obit Feb 42
Rand, James Henry, Sr. obit Nov 44
Randolph, Asa Philip May 40
Randolph, Woodruff May 48
Rank, Joseph obit Jan 44
Rank, J(oseph) Arthur Nov 45
Rankin, John E(lliott) Feb 44
Ranson, S(tephen) Walter obit Oct 42
Rapp, William J(ourdan) obit Oct 42
Rasmussen, Gustav Dec 47
Rathbone, Eleanor biog Jun 43 obit Feb 46
Rathbone, Josephine Adams obit Jul 41
Ratoff, Gregory Aug 43
Rattner, Abraham Mar 48
Rau, Sir Benegal Rama Feb 49
Rau, Santha Rama See Rama Rau, S. Aug 45
Rauschning, Hermann May 41
Rautenberg, Robert obit Mar 40
Raver, Paul J(erome) Sep 41
Rawlings, Sir (Henry) Bernard (Hughes) Aug 45
Rawlings, Marjorie Kinnan Jul 42
Ray, Charles obit Jan 44
Ray, (Jackson Harvelle) Ran-dolph, Rev. Apr 45
Ray, Ted obit Oct 43
Rayburn, Sam(uel Taliaferro) Oct 40 Mar 49
Razmara, Ali Oct 50
Rea, Gardner May 46
Reading, Stella (Charnaud Is-aacs), Marchioness of Apr 48
Reagan, Ronald Dec 49
Reavis, Smith Freeman obit Mar 40
Reber, Samuel Sep 49
Reckord, Milton A(tchison) Mar 45
Redgrave, Michael Feb 50
Redway, Jacques Wardlaw obit Jan 43
Reece, B(razilla) Carroll May 46
Reed, Carol Mar 50
Reed, Edward Bliss obit Mar 40
Reed, Herbert Calhoun obit Sep 40
Reed, James, Sr. obit Sep 41
Reed, James A. obit Oct 44
Reed, John Howard obit Mar 40
Reed, Philip D(unham) Jan 49
Reed, Stanley F(orman) Feb 42
Reese, Harold (Henry) Jun 50
Reese, Pee Wee See Reese, H. H. Jun 50
Reeve, Sidney A(rmor) obit Aug 41
Reeves, Jesse S(iddal) obit Aug 42
Reich, Nathaniel Julius obit Nov 43

Reichelderfer, F(rancis) W(il-ton) May 49
Reichenau, Walter von obit Mar 42
Reid, Frank R., Sr. obit Mar 45
Reid, Helen Rogers Feb 41
Reid, Ira De A(ugustine) Jul 46
Reid, Mont R(ogers) obit Jun 43
Reid, Mrs. Ogden Mills See Reid, H. R. Feb 41
Reiner, Fritz Apr 41
Reinhardt, Aurelia Henry biog May 41 obit Feb 48
Reinhardt, Max obit Dec 43
Reisner, Christian Fichthorne, Rev. obit Sep 40
Reisner, George Andrew obit Jul 42
Reith, John Charles Walsham, 1st Baron Nov 40
Relander, Lauri Kristian obit Apr 42
Renault, Louis obit Dec 44
Rennebohm, Oscar Jul 50
Renner, Karl Sept 45
Rentzel, Del(os Wilson) Oct 48
Resnick, Louis obit May 41
Resor, Stanley (Burnet) Jul 49
Reston, James B(arrett) Mar 43
Reuter, Ernst Oct 49
Reuter, Gabriele obit Jan 42
Reuther, Walter (Philip) Apr 41 Nov 49
Reventlow, Ernst, Graf zu obit Jan 44
Reves, Emery Jul 46
Revueltas, Silvestro obit Yrbk 40
Reybold, Eugene Jun 45
Reynaud, Paul Apr 40 May 50
Reynolds, Helen Wilkinson obit Feb 43
Reynolds, James A. obit May 40
Reynolds, Quentin (James) Mar 41
Reynolds, Robert Rice Oct 40
Rhee, Syngman Sep 47
Rhine, J(oseph) B(anks) Jan 49
Rhoades, Cornelia Harsen obit Jan 41
Rhodes, Edgar Nelson obit May 42
Rhodes, James A(llan) Mar 49
Rhys, Ernest obit Jan 46
Riasanovsky, Antonina See Fedor-ova, N. Nov 40
Ribbentrop, Joachim von biog May 41 obit Nov 46
Rice, Alice Caldwell Hegan obit Apr 42
Rice, Elmer (L.) Apr 43
Rice, Grantland Sep 41
Rice, Gregory Dec 41
Rice, Paul North Nov 47
Rich, Louise Dickinson May 43
Richard, Louis obit Sep 40
Richards, A(lfred) N(ewton) Sep 50

Richards, C(harles) R(uss) obit Jan 41

Richards, John G(ardiner) obit Dec 41

Richards, Laura E(lizabeth) obit Mar 43

Richards, Vincent Jul 47

Richardson, Henrietta See Richardson, H. H. obit May 46

Richardson, Henry Handel obit May 46

Richardson, Norval obit Yrbk 40

Richardson, Sir Ralph Nov 50

Richardson, Seth (Whitley) Feb 48

Richberg, Donald R(andall) Dec 49

Richman, Charles J. obit Jan 41

Richmond, Charles Alexander, Rev. obit Sep 40

Richter, George Martin obit Jul 42

Rickenbacker, Edward Nov 40

Ricketts, Louis Davidson obit Mar 40

Rickey, Branch (Wesley) Oct 45

Rickey, James W(alter) obit Jun 43

Riddell, R(obert) Gerald Sep 50

Ridge, Lola obit Jul 41

Ridgway, M(atthew) B(unker) Jul 47

Riefler, Winfield W(illiam) May 48

Riesman, David obit Jul 40

Rieve, Emil Jul 46

Rifkind, Simon H(irsch) May 46

Riggio, Vincent Jul 49

Riggs, Austen Fox obit Mar 40

Riggs, Bobby See Riggs, R. L. Sep 49

Riggs, Robert Larimore Sep 49

Riggs, T(homas) L(awrason), Rev. obit Jun 43

Rigling, Alfred obit Jan 41

Ring, Barbara T(aylor) obit Nov 41

Ringling, Robert E(dward) biog May 45 obit Feb 50

Río, Carlos Alberto Arroyo del See Arroyo del Río, C. A. Jun 42

Rios, Juan Antonio biog Apr 42 obit Jul 46

Ripley, Joseph obit Nov 40

Ripley, Robert L(eRoy) biog Jul 45 obit Jul 49

Ripley, William Z(ebina) obit Oct 41

Rittenhouse, Constance Morgan See Rittenhouse, Mrs. P. L. Mar 48

Rittenhouse, Mrs. Paul (Lockwood) Mar 48

Rivera, Diego Jul 48

Rivero (y Alonso), José Ignacio obit May 44

Rives, Amélie. See Troubetzkoy, A. R. obit Jul 45

Riza Shah Pahlavi obit Sep 44

Rizzuto, Phil(ip Francis) Jul 50

Robb, Hunter obit Jan-Jun 40

Robbins, Jerome May 47

Robert, Georges (Achille Marie-Joseph) Jun 43

Roberts, Albert H. obit Jul 46

Roberts, Sir Charles G(eorge) D(ouglas) obit Jan 44

Roberts, Elizabeth Madox obit May 41

Roberts, Florence obit Jul 40

Roberts, George Lucas obit Apr 41

Roberts, Kate L(ouise) obit Oct 41

Roberts, Owen J(osephus) Oct 41

Robertson, A. Willis Dec 49

Robertson, Ben, Jr. Nov 42

Robertson, Sir Brian (Hubert) Sep 48

Robertson, Constance (WLB) Yrbk 46

Robertson, D(avid) B(rown) May 50

Robertson, Mrs. Miles E. See Robertson, C. (WLB) Yrbk 46

Robeson, Eslanda (Cardoza) Goode Sep 45

Robeson, Mrs. Paul See Robeson, E.C.G. Sep 45

Robeson, Paul (Bustill) Mar 41

Robey, Ralph W(est) May 41

Robins, Edward obit Jul 43

Robins, Margaret Dreier obit Apr 45

Robins, Mrs. Raymond See Robins, M. D. obit Apr 45

Robinson, Bill biog Feb 41 obit Jan 50

Robinson, Boardman Dec 41

Robinson, Edward G. Jan 50

Robinson, Frederick B(ertrand) obit Dec 41

Robinson, Henry Morton Jul 50

Robinson, Holton D. obit Jun 45

Robinson, Jack Roosevelt See Robinson, Jackie Feb 47

Robinson, Jackie Feb 47

Robinson, Samuel M(urray) Feb 42

Robinson, William Heath obit Nov 44

Robson, May obit Dec 42

Roca, Julio A. obit Nov 42

Roche, Josephine (Aspinwall) Aug 41

Rockefeller, John D(avison), Jr. Jul 41

Rockefeller, Nelson (Aldrich) Mar 41

Rockley, Alice-Margaret Amherst, Baroness obit Nov 41

Rockwell, Norman Jun 45

Rodgers, Richard, and Hart, Lorenz May 40

Rodriquez, Nicolas obit Sep 40

Rodzinski, Artur Aug 40

Roelofs, Henrietta obit Mar 42

Rogers, Bruce Dec 46

Rogers, Edith Nourse Apr 42

Rogers, Ginger Apr 41

Rogers, Mark Homer obit Nov 41

Rogers, Norman McLeod obit Jul 40

Rogers, Robert Emmons obit Jul 41

Rogers, Roy Mar 48

Rogge, O(etje) John Feb 48

Rohde, Ruth Bryan Owen See Owen, R. B. Dec 44

Rokossovsky, Konstantin Jan 44

Rolland, Romain obit Dec 43

Rollins, Carl Purington Sep 48

Romano, Emanuel Mar 40

Romberg, Sigmund Mar 45

Rome, Harold J(acob) Apr 42

Rommel, Erwin biog Aug 42 obit Dec 44

Romulo, Carlos P(ena) Mar 43

Ronne, Finn Feb 48

Rood, Helen Martin obit Mar 43

Rooks, Lowell W(ard) Apr 47

Rooney, Mickey Feb 42

Roosevelt, (Anna) Eleanor Nov 40 Jan 49

Roosevelt, Elliott Dec 46

Roosevelt, Franklin D(elano) biog Mar 42 obit Apr 45

Roosevelt, Franklin D(elano), Jr. Jan 50

Roosevelt, Mrs. Franklin Delano See Roosevelt, A. E. Nov 40 Jan 49

Roosevelt, James Apr 50

Roosevelt, Kermit obit Jul 43

Roosevelt, Sara Delano obit Oct 41

Roosevelt, Theodore, Jr. obit Sep 44

Root, Oren, Jr. Aug 40

Root, Waverley (Lewis) May 43

Roper, Daniel C(alhoun) obit May 43

Roper, Elmo (Burns, Jr.) Jan 45

Rosanoff, Aaron J(oshua) obit Feb 43

Rosé, Arnold Josef obit Oct 46

Rose, Billy Aug 40

Rose, Mary D. Swartz obit Mar 41

Rose, Maurice obit May 45

Rosenbach, A(braham) S(imon) W(olf) May 46

Rosenberg, Alfred biog Oct 41 obit Nov 46

Rosenberg, Anna M(arie) Jan 43

Rosenberg, Arthur obit Mar 43

Rosenberg, William Samuel See Rose, B. Aug 40

Rosenfeld, Henry Nov 48

Rosenfeld, Kurt Nov 43

Rosenfeld, Paul obit Sep 46

Rosenman, Dorothy Reuben See Rosenman, Mrs. S. I. Apr 47

Rosenman, Samuel I(rving) Aug 42

Sarojini, Nayadu See Naidu, S. biog May 43 obit Mar 49

Saroyan, William Jul 40

Sarton, George (Alfred Léon) Jul 42

Sartre, Jean-Paul Mar 47

Sastroamidjojo, Ali Jun 50

Sauckel, Fritz obit Nov 46

Sauer, Emil von obit Jun 42

Sauer, George (Henry) Nov 48

Saunders, Carl M(axon) Jun 50

Saunders, Hilary A(idan) St. George Jun 43

Saunders, John Monk obit Apr 40

Savage, Augusta (Christine) Jan 41

Savage, John Lucian Apr 43

Savage, Michael Joseph obit Apr 40

Savery, Constance (Winifred) (WLB) Yrbk 48

Sawyer, Charles Jul 48

Sawyer, Eddie Nov 50

Sawyer, Edwin Milby See Sawyer, Eddie Nov 50

Saxon, Lyle obit May 46

Saxton, Alexander (Plaisted) Nov 43

Sayao, Bidu Feb 42

Sayles, R(obert) W(ilcox) obit Dec 42

Sayre, Francis Bowes Jan-Feb 40

Sayre, Morris Jan 48

Sayre, Mrs. Raymond May 49

Sayre, Ruth Buxton See Sayre, Mrs. R. May 49

Schacht, Al(exander) May 46

Schacht, Hjalmar (Horace Greeley) Oct 44

Schaefer, Vincent J(oseph) Jan 48

Schain, Josephine Jul 45

Schary, Dore May 48

Schechter, A(bel) A(lan) May 41

Scheele, Leonard A(ndrew) May 48

Scheiberling, Edward N(icholas) Dec 44

Schelling, Ernest Henry obit Jan-Feb 40

Schemm, Mrs. Ferdinand Ripley See Walker, M. (WLB) Yrbk 47

Scherer, Paul (Ehrman), Rev. May 41

Schereschewsky, Joseph Williams obit Sep 40

Scherman, Harry Sep 43

Schertzinger, Victor obit Dec 41

Schiaparelli, Elsa Jan-Feb 40

Schick, Béla Jul 44

Schilder, Paul Ferdinand obit Jan 41

Schillinger, Joseph obit May 43

Schiotz, Aksel Mar 49

Schiötz, Aksel Hauch See Schiotz, A. Mar 49

Schlauch, Margaret Dec 42

Schlee, Mrs. George Matthias See Valentina Dec 46

Schleich, Michel, Rev. obit Jun 45

Schlesinger, Arthur M(eier), Jr. Oct 46

Schlesinger, Frank obit Aug 43

Schlink, Frederick John Mar 41

Schlosser, Alex L. obit Mar 43

Schmelkes, Franz C(arl) obit Feb 43

Schmidt, Fritz obit Aug 43

Schmitt, Bernadotte E(verly) Dec 42

Schmitt, Gladys (Leonore) Mar 43

Schnabel, Artur Jul 42

Schneider, Eugene obit Jan 43

Schneider, Hannes Mar 41

Schneiderman, Rose Feb 46

Schoen-René, Anna Eugéne obit Jan 43

Schoenberg, Arnold Apr 42

Schoeneman, George J(eremiah) Nov 47

Schoff, Hannah Kent obit Feb 41

Schofield, Frank H(erman) obit Apr 42

Schönberg, Arnold See Schoenberg, A. Apr 42

Schoonmaker, Edwin Davies obit Jan-Jun 40

Schorr, Friedrich Jul 42

Schram, Emil Oct 41

Schratt, Katharina obit May 40

Schreiber, Georges May 43

Schrembs, Archbishop Joseph obit Dec 45

Schricker, Henry F(rederick) Sep 50

Schroeder, Frederick R(udolph), Jr. Oct 49

Schroeder, R(udolph) W(illiam) Jul 41

Schroeder, Ted See Schroeder, F. R., Jr. Oct 49

Schuchert, Charles obit Jan 43

Schuck, Arthur A(loys) Apr 50

Schulberg, Budd (Wilson) Jun 41

Schuller, Mary Craig McGeachy See McGeachy, M.A.C. Apr 44

Schulte, Karl Joseph, Cardinal obit May 41

Schulthess, Edmund obit Jun 44

Schultz, Sigrid (Lillian) Apr 44

Schulz, Leo obit Oct 44

Schumacher, Kurt Feb 48

Schuman, Robert Jan 48

Schuman, William (Howard) Jun 42

Schurman, Jacob G(ould) obit Oct 42

Schuster, Max Lincoln See Simon, R. L. and Schuster, M. L. Jul 41

Schweitzer, Albert Jan 48

Schwellenbach, Lewis B(axter) biog Jun 45 obit Jul 48

Schwidetzky, Oscar (Otto Rudolf) Dec 43

Scobie, Ronald M(acKenzie) Feb 45

Scott, Arthur Carroll obit Yrbk 40

Scott, Barbara Ann Jul 48

Scott, C(yril) Kay- See Wellman, F. C. Feb 44

Scott, Sir Harold (Richard) Dec 50

Scott, Hazel (Dorothy) Aug 43

Scott, Henry L(awrence) Jun 49

Scott, Hugh (Doggett) Sep 48

Scott, James B(rown) obit Aug 43

Scott, John R. K. obit Feb 46

Scott, K(ate) Frances Nov 48

Scott, Raymond Jul 41

Scott, Robert L(ee), Jr. Oct 43

Scott, Tom Nov 46

Scrugham, James Graves obit Jul 45

Scudder, Janet obit Jul 40

Seaborg, Glenn T(heodore) Jul 48

Seabrook, William B(euhler) biog Nov 40 obit Oct 45

Seabury, David Sep 41

Seagrave, Gordon S(tifler) Nov 43

Searing, Annie E(liza) P(idgeon) obit Jun 42

Sears, William Joseph, Sr. obit May 44

Seger, George N. obit Oct 40

Seghers, Anna Dec 42

Segovia, Andrés May 48

Seibert, Florence B(arbara) Nov 42

Seibold, Louis obit Jun 45

Seid, Ruth See Sinclair, J. Mar 46

Seif-ul-Islam Abdullah, Prince Dec 47

Seitz, George B. obit Aug 44

Selassie, Haile, I See Haile Selassie I, Emperor of Ethiopia Apr 41

Seldes, George Feb 41

Self, Sir Henry (Albert) Oct 42

Selfridge, H(arry) Gordon biog Mar 41 obit Jun 47

Sélincourt, Ernest de See De Sélincourt, E. obit Jul 43

Sell, Hildegarde Loretta See Hildegarde Nov 44

Selwyn, Edgar obit Apr 44

Selznick, David O(liver) Jun 41

Selznick, Myron obit May 44

Semon, Waldo Lonsbury Yrbk 40

Senanayake, Don Stephen Apr 50

Senarens, Luis Philip obit Jan-Feb 40

Sender, Toni May 50

Sengstacke, John H(erman Henry) Nov 49

Senn, Milton J(ohn) E(dward) Jun 50

Woolf, Virginia obit May 41
Woollcott, Alexander biog Jun 41 obit Mar 43
Woollen, Evans, Jr. Dec 48
Woolley, Edgar Montillion See Woolley, Monty Jul 40
Woolley, Mary E(mma) biog Mar 42 obit Nov 47
Woolley, Monty Jul 40
Woolton, Frederick James Marquis, 1st Baron Oct 40 Oct 50
Worcester, J(oseph) R(uggles) obit Jun 43
Worden, Edward Chauncey obit Nov 40
Work, Hubert obit Feb 43
Worsley, Frank Arthur obit Mar 43
Wray, John Griffith obit May 40
Wren, Percival C(hristopher) obit Jan 42
Wright, Berlin H(art) obit Jan 41
Wright, Mrs. Donald McCloud See Meadowcroft, E. La M. (WLB) Yrbk 49
Wright, Fielding L(ewis) Sep 48
Wright, Frank Lloyd Jan 41
Wright, Harold Bell obit Jul 44
Wright, Huntley obit Sep 41
Wright, Louis B(ooker) Nov 50
Wright, Orville biog Oct 46 obit Mar 48
Wright, Quincy Oct 43
Wright, Richard Mar 40
Wright, (Sir Robert Alderson Wright), Lord Jul 45
Wright, Russel Sep 40 Dec 50
Wright, Teresa May 43
Wright, Theodore P(aul) Nov 45
Wrinch, Dorothy (M.) Jul 47
Wrong, (Humphrey) Hume Oct 50
Wurster, William Wilson Nov 46
Wu Yi-fang Aug 45
Wyatt, John Whitlow Nov 41
Wyatt, Wilson W(atkins) Mar 46
Wyeth, N(ewell) C(onvers) obit Nov 45
Wylie, Max Jan-Feb 40
Wyman, Jane Mar 49
Wynkoop, Asa obit Dec 42
Wynn, Ed Jan 45

Yamamoto, Isoroko biog Feb 42 obit Jul 43
Yancey, Lewis Q. Alonzo obit Jan-Jun 40
Yaroslavsky, Emelyan obit Jan 44
Yarrow, William obit Jun 41
Yates, Elizabeth (WLB) Yrbk 48
Yates, Herbert J(ohn) Jul 49
Ybarra, Thomas Russell Jan-Jun 40
Yeats-Brown, Francis obit Feb 45
Yellin, Samuel obit Nov 40
Yen, Y(ang-) C(h'u) James Jul 46
Yerby, Frank (Garvin) Sep 46
Yergan, Max Sep 48
Yim, Louise Oct 47
Ying-chin, Ho See Ho Ying-chin Oct 42
Yoder, Albert Henry obit Nov 40
Yon, Pietro A(lessandro) obit Jan 44
Yonai, Mitsumasa biog Jan-Feb 40 obit Jun 48
Yorke, Oswald obit Mar 43
Yoshida, Shigeru Sep 46
Yost, Fielding Harris obit Oct 46
Youmans, Vincent biog Apr 44 obit May 46
Young, Art(hur Henry) biog Jan-Feb 40 obit Feb 44
Young, Charles Jac obit Apr 40
Young, Hugh (Hampton) obit Sep 45
Young, Karl obit Jan 44
Young, Loretta Mar 48
Young, Owen D. Aug 45
Young, Robert Jul 50
Young, Robert See Payne, P. S. R. (WLB) Yrbk 47
Young, Robert R(alph) Apr 47
Young, Rose (Emmet) obit Sep 41
Youngdahl, Luther W(allace) Mar 48
Younger, Kenneth (Gilmour) Sep 50
Younghusband, Sir Francis (Edward) obit Sep 42
Yukawa, Hideki Jan 50
Yust, Walter Apr 43

Yu-t'ang Lin. See Lin Yu-t'ang May 40
Zacharias, Ellis M(ark) Mar 49
Zafrullah Khan, Choudri Sir Mohammad Dec 47
Zaharias, Babe Didrikson Apr 47
Zaharias, Mrs. George See Zaharias, B. D. Apr 47
Zaharias, Mildred Didrikson See Zaharias, B. D. Apr 47
Zander, Arnold S(cheuer) Oct 47
Zandonai, Riccardo obit Aug 44
Zanuck, Darryl F(rancis) Aug 41
Zeeland, Paul van Mar 50
Zeeman, Pieter obit Dec 43
Zeidler, Carl Frederick biog Jul 40 obit Feb 43
Zellerbach, J(ames) D(avid) Dec 48
Zemlinsky, Alexander von obit May 42
Zenos, Andrew C(onstantinides) obit Mar 42
Zevin, B(enjamin) D(avid) Sep 43
Zhabotinskii, Vladimir Evgen'evich See Jabotinsky, V. E. obit Sep 40
Zhukov, Georgi K(onstantinovitch) Feb 42
Ziemer, Gregor (Athalwin) Apr 42
Ziff, William B(ernard) Oct 46
Zilboorg, Gregory Sep 41
Zimbalist, Efrem Mar 49
Zimmer, Henry (Robert) obit May 43
Zimmerman, Alfred F. M. obit Jul 40
Zinsser, Hans obit Oct 40
Zog I, King of the Albanians Aug 44
Zook, George F(rederick) Feb 46
Zorach, William Feb 43
Zorina, Vera Jan 41
Zukor, Adolph Mar 50
Zuloaga, Ignacio obit Dec 45
Zu Reventlow, Ernst, Graf See Reventlow, E., Graf zu obit Jan 44
Zweig, Stefan obit Apr 42
Zworykin, Vladimir K(osma) Dec 49